The World Today Series®
Stryker-Post Publications, Harpers Ferry, WV • USA

Nordic, Central, and Southeastern Europe

Wayne C. Thompson

2010

I0th edition
Next Edition: August 2011

Graphic Materials Acknowledgments

For their generosity in providing certain visual material for use in this book,
special thanks to the following:

European Community Information Services
Delegation of the European Commission, Washington
North Atlantic Treaty Organization
German Information Services, New York
German National Tourist Office, New York
Press and Information Office, Bonn and Berlin
The Royal Norwegian Embassy

The Royal Danish Embassy
The Embassy of Sweden
The Embassy of Finland
The Embassy of Austria
The Embassy of Iceland
The Embassy of Greece

First appearing as *Western Europe 1982,* this annually revised
book is published by

Stryker–Post Publications
P.O. Drawer 1200
Harpers Ferry, WV 25425
Telephones: 1–800–995–1400 (U.S.A. or Canada)
Other: 1–304–535–2593
Fax: 1–304–535–6513
www.strykerpost.com
VISA–MASTERCARD–AMERICAN EXPRESS

International Standard Book Number: 978-1-935264-14-9
International Standard Serial Number: 0084-2338

Library of Congress Catalog Card Number: 83-643780

Cover design by nvision graphic design

Cartographer: William L. Nelson

Typography by Barton Matheson Willse & Worthington
Baltimore, MD 21244

Printed in the United States of America by United Book Press, Inc.
Baltimore, MD 21207

The World Today Series has thousands of subscribers across
the U.S. and Canada. A sample list of users who annually
rely on this most up-to-date material includes:

Public library systems
Universities and colleges
High schools
Federal and state agencies
All branches of the armed forces & war colleges
National Geographic Society
National Democratic Institute
Agricultural Education Foundation
ExxonMobile Corporation
Chevron Corporation
CNN

Photographs used to illustrate *The World Today Series*
come from many sources, a great number from friends
who travel worldwide. If you have taken any which you
believe would enhance the visual impact and attractive-
ness of our books, do let us hear from you.

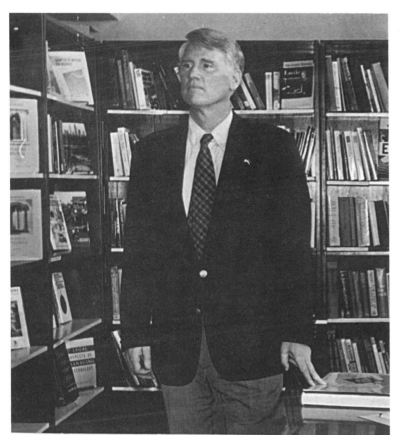

Author in front of book collection he organized and donated to the library of the Tallinn Technical University, Estonia, 1995

Wayne C. Thompson . . .

Professor Thompson teaches Politics at Washington and Lee University. Professor Emeritus of Political Science, Virginia Military Institute, Lexington, Virginia. Ohio State University (B.A. in Government); Claremont Graduate School (M.A. and Ph.D., with distinction). He did further graduate study at the universities of Göttingen, Paris/Sorbonne and Freiburg im Breisgau, where he has since been a guest professor. He has studied and researched many years in Germany as a Woodrow Wilson, Fulbright, *Deutscher Akademischer Austauschdienst*, Earhart and Alexander von Humboldt Fellow. He has served as scholar-in-residence at the Bundestag and as a Fulbright professor in Estonia. During the 1999–2000 academic year, he was a visiting professor at the Air War College in Montgomery, Alabama. In the spring semester of 2001 he had a second Fulbright professorship at the College of Europe in Bruges, Belgium, and continued to teach at that graduate institution in Bruges and Warsaw for seven years. In the fall semester 2003 he was a visiting professor at the American University of Bulgaria in Blagoevgrad. He is the author of *In the Eye of the Storm: Kurt Riezler and the Crises of Modern Germany* (Iowa City, University of Iowa Press, 1980), *The Political Odyssey of Herbert Wehner* (Boulder, CO: Westview Press, 1993), *Historical Dictionary of Germany* (Metuchen, NJ: Scarecrow, 1994), coauthored *Redefining Transatlantic Security Relations: The Challenge of Change* (Manchester University Press, 2004), and two other books in The World Today Series. He also co-edited *Perspectives on Strategic Defense and Space: National Programs and International Cooperation, and Margaret Thatcher: Prime Minister Indomitable* (Boulder, CO: Westview, 1987, 1989, 1994). He has written many articles on European politics, philosophy and history which have appeared in such periodicals as *The American Political Science Review, Western Political Quarterly, East European Quarterly, Journal of Politics, Central European History, The American Review of Canadian Studies, German Studies Review, Das Parlament, Current History, The Yearbook on International Communist Affairs, The History Teacher, Armed Forces and Society, Freedom at Issue, Communist and Post-Communist Studies, Europe-Asia Studies* and *Contemporary French Civilization*. He is currently editor in chief of Stryker-Post Publications.

Frankfurter Rundschau

UNABHÄNGIGE TAGESZEITUNG

Montag, 3. Mai 2004 | D-Ausgabe · · · www.fr-aktuell.de · · · D 2972 | Jahrgang 60 | Nr. 102/19 | Preis: 1,30 Euro

Frankfurter Rundschau
60266 Frankfurt am Main
Anzeigenannahme:
Telefon 0800/202 01 00, Fax 069/131 00 30
Abo-Leserservice:
Telefon 0800/866 68 66, Fax 069/21 99-32 64
Leserservice Redaktion:
Telefon 069/21 99-34 48
Internet: www.fr-aktuell.de

Belgien €1,70 - Frankreich €1,70 - Niederlande €1,70 Spanien €1,70
Italien €1,70 - Österreich €1,70 - Luxemburg €1,70 - Luxemburg CHF 3.00

1 0 0 1 9

Europa
ist wieder
vereint

Europäische Union nimmt
75 Millionen neue Bürger auf

Weitere Berichte zur EU-Erweiterung
Politik · Seite 3
Kommentar · Seite 3
Schwerpunkt · Seite 5

BILD: JENS WOLF/DPA

Klausur

Zuwanderungsgesetz vor dem Scheitern

BERLIN · 2. MAI · VGO · Das Zuwanderungsgesetz steht vor dem Aus. Nachdem die Kompromissverhandlungen am Wochenende ergebnislos abgebrochen worden waren, werden die Grünen voraussichtlich noch in dieser Woche den Ausstieg aus Verhandlungen beschließen.

Die 20 Unterhändler von Regierung und Opposition hatten ihre Verhandlungsklausur am Samstagabend abgebrochen, ohne einen neuen Gesprächstermin zu vereinbaren. Bei der 17-stündigen Verhandlungen der Arbeitsgruppe des Vermittlungsausschusses hatte es vor allem über die umstrittenen Sicherheitsfragen keine Annäherung gegeben. Regierung und Opposition wollen für ein mögliches nächstes Treffen schriftliche Vorschläge erarbeiten. Sie wollen dabei jedoch auch prüfen, ob weitere Gespräche sinnvoll sind. Der Verhandlungsführer der Grünen, Volker Beck, kündigte bereits an: „Ich kann meiner Partei nicht raten, diesen Weg weiterzugehen." Eine Entscheidung über das Ende der Verhandlungen könnte am Samstag auf dem Länderrat, dem zweithöchsten Parteigremium der Grünen, fallen.
Thema des Tages, Kommentar S. 3

„Nun ist es vollbracht"

EU-Spitzenpolitiker und Neu-Mitglieder feiern die historische Erweiterung des Bündnisses

Hunderttausende Menschen haben am Samstag die größte Erweiterung in der Geschichte der Europäischen Union gefeiert. EU-Spitzenpolitiker würdigten die Aufnahme von zehn neuen Mitgliedern in das Bündnis als „Wiedervereinigung" des Kontinents.

FRANKFURT A. M. · 2. MAI · DPA/AP/RTR/RECK/ME · Der amtierende EU-Ratspräsident und irische Ministerpräsident Bertie Ahern, EU-Kommissionspräsident Romano Prodi und EU-Parlamentspräsident Pat Cox bezeichneten die geschichtliche Bedeutung der EU-Erweiterung von zuvor gut 380 Millionen auf 455 Millionen Menschen.

Bei den offiziellen Erweiterungsfeiern in Dublin, zu der die Staats- und Regierungschefs aller 25 EU-Mitgliedstaaten angereist waren, unterstrichen die drei Spitzenpolitiker die Notwendigkeit, den Verfassungsentwurf wie vereinbart noch in diesem Sommer zu verabschieden. Ahern will noch in dieser Wo-

che eine Rundreise durch Europas Hauptstädte beginnen, um in Detailverhandlungen Kompromisslinien abzustecken. Weiterhin umstritten ist die Frage, welches Gewicht die Bevölkerungsstärke einzelner Mitgliedsstaaten bei Mehrheitsentscheidungen erhalten soll.

Am Rande der Feiern ging die irische Polizei mit Wasserwerfern gegen etwa 2000 Globalisierungskritiker vor, die versucht hatten, auf das Festgelände in Dublin vorzudringen. Es kam zu Handgemengen, 28 Demonstranten wurden festgenommen.

Den EU-Beitritt seines Landes sieht Tschechiens früherer Präsident Vaclav Havel als gute Gelegenheit für seine Landsleute, selbstbewusste Europäer zu werden. Sie seien einem Bündnis beigetreten, das nicht durch Kriege entstanden sei, sondern auf dem freien Willen europäischer Länder beruhe.

Ungarns Ministerpräsident Peter Medgyessy verkündete, sein Land sei „immer an den Toren Europas" gewesen, durch die EU-Erweiterung nun aber „innerhalb der Tore". In Litauens Hauptstadt

Vilnius sagte Präsident Arturas Paulauskas: „Wir haben viele Jahre gebraucht, um diese Reise zurückzulegen, Nun ist es vollbracht."

Einen Tag zuvor hatte der Kanzler in einer Regierungserklärung die „historische Mission" der europäischen Einigung herausgestellt, mit der sich jetzt ein Traum vieler Generationen erfüllt habe. Bundeskanzler Gerhard Schröder (SPD) würdigte die Erweiterung als Beitrag zum Frieden in Europa. „Die Spaltung des Kontinents und die Trennung seiner Bürger ist endgültig überwunden", sagte Schröder am Samstag bei einer Kundgebung am Dreiländereck in Zittau. Schröder feierte dort mit seinen Amtskollegen Leszek Miller aus

Polen und Vladimir Spidla aus Tschechien.

Einen Tag zuvor hatte der Kanzler in einer Regierungserklärung die „historische Mission" der europäischen Einigung herausgestellt, mit der sich jetzt ein Traum vieler Generationen erfüllt habe. Deutschland werde davon auch wirtschaftlich „am meisten profitieren". Gleichzeitig warnte er vor einem „einseitigen Steuerwettbewerb zu Lasten der Nettozahler" in der EU. Auch bei den Unternehmenssteuern müsse es EU-weit einen „Korridor" geben, den einzelne Staaten nicht verlassen dürften, um den Nachbarn Firmen abzuwerben.

Schröder sagte erstmals, dass bei notfalls auf eine formelle „verstärkte Zusammenarbeit" einiger EU-Staaten gesetzt werden müsse, falls eine Einstimmigkeit nicht zu erreichen sei. Im Unterschied zum Kanzler sprach sich CDU-Chefin Angela Merkel klar für weitere soziale Einschnitte aus. Wenn Deutschland nicht „in hohem Maß zum Verlierer" der Erweiterung werden wolle, müsse es sich „den Gesetzmäßigkeiten stellen".

> **DIE EUROPÄISCHE UNION**
>
> **1951** gründen Deutschland, Frankreich, Italien und die Benelux-Staaten die Europäische Gemeinschaft für Kohle und Stahl (EGKS),
> **1957** die Europäische Wirtschaftsgemeinschaft (EWG).
> **1973** stoßen Dänemark, Irland und Großbritannien zur EG,
> **1981** Griechenland,
> **1986** Spanien und Portugal,
> **1995** folgen Österreich, Finnland und Schweden. ap

Finanzpolitik

Koalition rückt von hartem Sparkurs ab

BERLIN · 2. MAI · ME · In Berlin mehren sich die Signale, dass die rot-grüne Koalition von ihrem harten Sparkurs abrückt und die zu erwartenden neuen Haushaltslöcher nicht mehr durch zusätzliche Einsparungen stopfen will. Außenminister Joschka Fischer (Grüne) und der SPD-Finanzpolitiker Joachim Poß unterstützen am Wochenende in Interviews den neuen Kurs von Bundeskanzler Gerhard Schröder (SPD), mit dem auch ein erneutes Verfehlen des EU-Stabilitätskriteriums 2005 in Kauf genommen wird.

Fischer sagte, „für einen begrenzten Zeitraum" müsse die Konjunkturerholung Priorität haben. Schröder hatte zuvor im Kabinett angekündigt, die Regierung wolle auf keinen Fall durch weitere Sparbeschlüsse die Konjunktur gefährden.

Der stellvertretende CDU-Chef Jürgen Rüttgers forderte den Rücktritt von Finanzminister Hans Eichel (SPD). In Regierungskreisen hieß es, Eichel werde einstweilen im Amt bleiben, er müsse allerdings seine Einsparforderungen zurückschrauben. Zuletzt hatte Verteidigungsminister Peter Struck (SPD) gegen Eichels Sparvorgaben protestiert.
Bericht Seite 4

TAG DER ARBEIT

Gewerkschaften gehen auf Konfrontation zu Rot-Grün

Die Stimmung zwischen Gewerkschaften und den Regierenden in Berlin ist schlecht. Am „Tag der Arbeit" musste sich Rot-Grün scharfe Angriffe gefallen lassen.

VON ULRIKE FÜSSEL
(FRANKFURT A. M.)

Mit markigen Worten haben führende Gewerkschafter bei den traditionellen Mai-Kundgebungen ihrer Organisationen ein deutliches Bild von der Kluft zwischen den Reformplänen der Regierung und gewerkschaftlichen Positionen gezeichnet. So warf der Vorsitzende des Deutschen Gewerkschafts-

da 2010 ist zum Synonym für die Zwei-Drittel-Gesellschaft geworden. Ganz offensichtlich wird ein Drittel unserer Bevölkerung einfach abgeschrieben." Die Gewerkschaften würden nicht nachlassen in ihrem Kampf um wirkliche Sozialreformen. Sie verwehrten sich einer „sozialen Abwärtsspirale mit niedrigeren Löhnen, längeren Arbeitszeiten oder Arbeitsbedingungen und Arbeitsrechten aus dem

le Spitzengewerkschafter nutzten die Stunde aber zu harscher Kritik an der Regierung. So warf der Vorsitzende der Gewerkschaft Bergbau-Chemie-Energie, Hubertus Schmoldt, der Koalition mangelnde soziale Ausgewogenheit vor. Mit Veränderungen, die nicht bis zu Ende gedacht seien, zerstöre die rot-grüne Koalition Vertrauen, sagte Schmoldt in Marl. So seien die neuen Regeln für die Zumutbarkeit von Arbeit hinzunehmen, wonach Arbeitslose künftig eine Stelle mit nahezu jedem Preis annehmen müssten. „Wir erwarten, dass die Bundesregierung gegen die zunehmende Verarmung

te ihr Vorsitzender Jürgen Peters in Mannheim an. Peters sagte, eine andere und bessere Politik sei unverzichtbar und machbar. Die Unterschriftensammlung solle den Druck für Korrekturen in der Wirtschafts- und Sozialpolitik erhöhen. Die Forderung nach einer höheren Wochenarbeitszeit nannte Peters angesichts der hohen Arbeitslosigkeit „Irrsinn".

Ähnlich deutlich waren auch die Akzente, die der Vorsitzende der IG Bauen-Agrar-Umwelt, Klaus Wiesehügel, in Mülheim (Ruhr) setzte. Wiesehügel wandte sich gegen die zunehmende Verarmung

di, blockte in Leipzig Forderungen ab, der Niedriglohnsektor müsse ausgeweitet werden. Die Menschen bräuchten mehr, nicht weniger Geld, sagte Bsirske.

Nach Angaben der Veranstalter folgten bundesweit rund 500 000 Menschen dem gewerkschaftlichen Aufruf zu Kundgebungen.

Vor dem 1. Mai hatte der neue Vorsitzende der SPD, Franz Müntefering, in einem Schreiben an Betriebsräte anlässlich der EU-Erweiterung um Verständnis geworben. Im erweiterten Europa werde die SPD weiter dafür einstehen, dass die Interessen der arbeitenden

---

DIE ECKE

Studienführer

LONDON · 2. MAI · DPA · Ungewöhnliche Konkurrenz hat Prinz William, der Sohn des britischen Thronfolgers, an der schottischen St.-Andrews-Universität erhalten. Der älteste Sohn von Prinz Charles und Prinzessin Di wird im Studium ständig von seinem Leibwächter Bill Noon begleitet. In den Vorlesungen und Seminaren sei Noon stets dabei, schreibt die britische Zeitung News of the World. Der Sicherheitsexperte nehme regen Anteil an den Studien. „Er meldet sich und beantwortet Fragen wie jeder andere Student auch", zitiert das Blatt einen Kommilitonen.

William war schon in der Schule

Europe is United Again!

CONTENTS

A new generation of Europeans—graduation day at the College of Europe, Warsaw

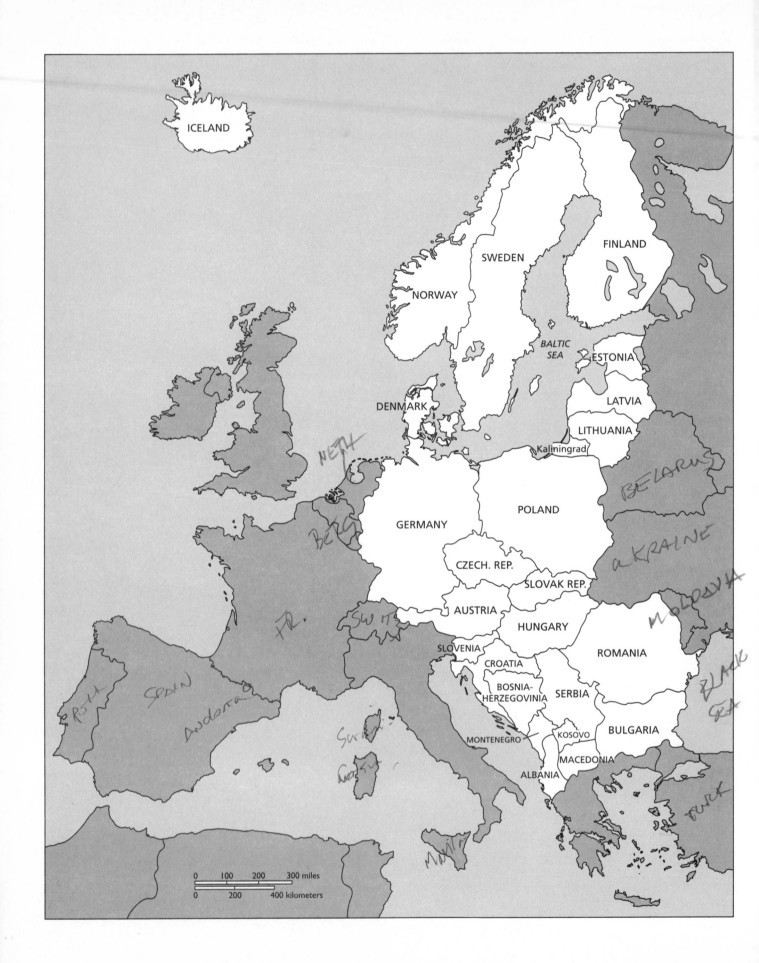

CENTRAL AND EASTERN EUROPE

. . . in 1877

. . . in 1914

CENTRAL EUROPE

The Danube River at Budapest, Hungary.

ACKNOWLEDGEMENTS

I am grateful to the Fulbright Commission, a farsighted educational exchange organization that since the Second World War has successfully sought to bring Americans and the other peoples of the world together in order to strengthen peace and to nurture the spirit of intellectual discovery. A Fulbright Teaching Fellowship to Estonia in 1995–6 enabled me to experience the challenges of transition in former communist states. This fellowship also made it possible for me to travel widely in the Nordic world, Russia, the Baltic States, and Poland. A 1998 Fulbright summer seminar in Germany, Poland and the Czech Republic on the subject of "Germany and the East" gave me the opportunity to discuss this region's history, problems and prospects with academics, journalists and policy makers in those three countries. A second Fulbright professorship in 2001 at the College of Europe in Bruges and Warsaw and my continuing affiliation there as a professor of politics provide me with intellectual stimulation through teaching top graduate students from all over Europe. I thank my students from both campuses of the College of Europe who carefully and critically read my chapters on their countries in this book and offered suggestions for improvement. They are: Andras Baneth (Hungary), Angel Bandjov (Bulgaria), Romina Besi (Slovenia), Simon Bojsen-Møller (Denmark), Alban Bokshi (Kosovo), Gustaf Brusewitz (Sweden), Ivane Chkhikvdze (Georgia), Andrea Cierna (Slovakia), Elena Cogalniceanu (Moldova), Andrei Covali (Moldova), Desara Dizdari (Albania), Gjergji Filipi (Albania), Casiana Irina Fometescu (Romania), Remigiusz Gawlik (Poland), Pavle Golicin (Serbia), Tobias Gräs Skovbjerg (Denmark), Aljaz Groselj (Slovenia), Taru Haapaniemi (Finland), Franziska Hirsch (Germany), Doru Iulian Hobjila (Romania), Rikard Jozwiak (Sweden), Piotr Kaczynski (Poland), Wojciech Kalocinski (Poland), Victoria Khasson (Estonia), Olesea Kovali (Moldova), Mateja Kovav (Slovenia), Viktoria Lovenberg (Hungary), Andreas Magnusson (Sweden), Corneliu Manole (Moldova), Lilet Nikoghosyan (Armenia), Anders Nordeng (Norway), Heidi Olli (Finland), Dragos Penca (Romania), Anna Platonova (Latvia), Ave Poom (Estonia), Marika Popp (Estonia), Audrius Poviliunas (Lithuania), Ilija Psaltirov (Macedonia), Dessislava Raykova (Bulgaria), Marcus Stober (Sweden), Rosalia Stoyanova (Bulgaria), Julia Tomova (Bulgaria), Svetla Tomova (Bulgaria), Vassil Touhtchiev (Bulgaria), Viera Uhlarova (Slovakia), and Catherine Hall Uttenthal (Denmark). My assistants at the American University in Bulgaria were very helpful in improving my chapters on the Balkans and Southeastern Europe. They are Gorica Atanosova (Macedonia), Sokol Lleshi (Albania), Milena Mihajlovic (Serbia), Andrei Rusanovschi (Moldova) and Christina Simona (Romania). My colleagues and friends, Professor Krzysztof Jasiewicz and Prof. Dieter Mahncke, offered advice for the Poland and Germany chapters. Alan Corwin carefully critiqued the chapter on Norway. I thank the Headquarters of U.S. European Command, especially my former student at the Air War College, Captain R. Scott Saunders (USN), for an invitation to visit U.S. peacekeeping installations in Bosnia in March 2002. I am grateful to the Kosovo School for European Integration, especially Sihana Xhaferi and Fatmir Curri, for inviting me to Kosovo numerous times to lecture. These visits have helped me write and illustrate the chapter on Kosovo in this book. My friend and former colleague, M. Wesley Shoemaker, wrote the earlier versions of the central and eastern European chapters in this book and continues to update the Russia and CIS book in this series. Michael Nix did a wonderful and meticulous job in 2007 of reading every word of this book and making copious editorial changes based on his decades of experience as a Canadian government editor. Finally I would like to thank my partner at Stryker-Post Publications, David T. Wilt, who supports my work in countless ways.

DEDICATION

To the memory of Philip F. Stryker, Dreamer, Founder, Friend

Philip F. Stryker with Ambassador Luba Acevska, Republic of Macedonia

Introduction: Nordic, Central, and Southeastern Europe

With the collapse of communism in Europe, the unification of Germany, and the dissolution of the Soviet Union, Europeans are faced with the most significant alteration of their continent's political map since World War II. Because two hostile Europe's—created at the Yalta Conference in February 1945 and subsequently hardened by the Cold War—no longer face each other, democratic Europe has doubled its size from 382 to 700 million people. From Moscow to Lisbon and Dublin to Skopje, democracies exist in which free elections provide the only legitimate claim to power and which are basically committed to freedom, individual rights, and some variant of capitalism. The result is a new Europe that is free and undivided.

Newly independent and sovereign nations have emerged, all in varying states of economic difficulty, some with borders in dispute, ethnic scores to settle, and millions of discontented and frightened citizens. The August 1991 putsch in the former Soviet Union destroyed central authority and dispersed power among its various republics. Western European countries led the way in recognizing the newly independent Baltic States of Estonia, Latvia, and Lithuania, which are reaching out to the West. Moldova, carved out of Romania at the beginning of World War II, may one day find its way back into union with that struggling state. In the Southeast, Yugoslavia came unglued and became the scene of the first full-scale warfare in Europe since 1945.

Political boundaries on the European continent, which extends from the Atlantic Ocean to the Ural Mountains in Russia, have become less sharp and more open. Our book on Western Europe includes countries with a total population of approximately 274 million. Russia and the Commonwealth of Independent States (CIS), former Soviet republics (minus the Baltic States) from Belarus, Ukraine and Moldova through the Caucasus to the Central Asian Republics, are presented in a separate volume.

In between is a 500- to 800-mile strip of countries with a total population of approximately 238 million and extending about 2,400 miles from the Nordic countries southward to the Greek border. The geographic center of Europe runs through Ukraine. Therefore, all the countries included in this volume are located in the western half of Europe. All look primarily westward for their trade, almost all feel Western in their political and cultural orientation, and most are clamoring for admission to the plentiful Western European table, to the European Union (EU) and to a place under the Atlantic Alliance's security umbrella.

Most European countries are too small to defend themselves alone. Therefore, the majority has joined or seeks to join the North Atlantic Treaty Organization (NATO), also known as the Atlantic Alliance. Created in 1949, NATO links the power of the United States and Canada, and the geographic position of Iceland (which has no army) with the military resources of Belgium-Netherlands-Luxembourg (BENELUX), Great Britain, Norway, Denmark, Germany, Italy, Portugal, Turkey, Greece, France and Spain. Since 1999 Poland, Hungary and the Czech Republic are members, joined in April 2004 by Estonia, Latvia, Lithuania, Slovakia, Slovenia, Romania and Bulgaria. In 2009 Croatia and Albania entered. A few major European countries prefer to remain non-aligned, including Ireland, Switzerland, Austria, Sweden, and Finland.

In 1991 NATO was transformed into a more political organization seeking to reach out to its former enemies. It created the Euro-Atlantic Partnership Council (EAPC, known until 1997 as the North Atlantic Cooperation Council—NACC) comprising 46 countries by the beginning of the century. The EAPC provides for regular consultations between NATO and the former Soviet republics and Central, Eastern and Southeastern European nations on subjects ranging from security issues, arms control, and the conversion of defense industries. In 1994 NATO initiated the Partnership for Peace (PfP), which links 20 countries, including Russia, in bilateral treaties with NATO. The purpose is to expand and intensify political and military cooperation and to strengthen stability and peace, primarily through training forces for peacekeeping operations. A special NATO-Ukraine Commission was established to deepen cooperation with that important country.

Many countries regard PfP as a crucial stepping-stone to full NATO membership. In principle, the alliance is prepared grad-

ually to accept new members, on the condition that they have solid democratic credentials, including a firm civilian grip on the armed forces, and can make a genuine military contribution to the common defense. The door remains open to a select group of European democracies who ask to join.

NATO planners fear the effects an increase in membership would have on already complicated decision-making mechanisms, which require unanimity and consensus. Also, Russia was uneasy about enlargement, especially insofar as former Soviet republics, such as the Baltic States, are concerned. To assuage Moscow's fears, the Atlantic allies signed with Moscow in 1997 a NATO-Russia Founding Act. This is not a legally binding treaty, but it states that NATO has no need, intentions, or plans to create additional capabilities or permanently to station troops or nuclear weapons in the new member states. NATO also created a Permanent Joint Committee, strengthened and renamed the NATO-Russia Council in May 2002, at its headquarters in which Russian officials can discuss, though not veto, NATO policies and decisions.

NATO's outdated doctrine of containing Soviet power through "forward defense" and "flexible response" was replaced by one that gives NATO a reason to exist in the changed European environment. Smaller, highly mobile, conventional, and multilateral forces are being created that can be deployed on short notice anywhere within NATO territory and that can help manage unpredictable crises and instability in Central and Eastern Europe, the Balkans, the Mediterranean area and beyond. NATO chose at its 2002 Prague summit to create a multinational rapid deployment force of 21,000 troops for use against enemies far outside of Europe.

The countries treated in this book are also linked in the 55-member Organization for Security and Cooperation in Eu-

Candidates become members, April 2004, joined in 2009 by Albania and Croatia

Source: *The Washington Post*

1

Introduction: Nordic, Central, and Southeastern Europe

... in 1921

rope (OSCE, known until 1994 as the Conference for Security and Cooperation in Europe—CSCE), to which all European states, former Soviet republics, and the United States and Canada belong. It meets irregularly to consider how to defuse threats to peace through mediation, crisis management, and the dispatch of observers, and it makes decisions by consensus. It has a Conflict Prevention Center in Vienna and an Office for Democratic Institutions and Human Rights (ODIHR) in Warsaw.

The Council of Europe was created in Strasbourg in 1949. Its 40 members include all Western European countries and most newly independent countries discussed in this book. Its assemblies of parliamentarians from the member states serve as a forum for discussing political, economic, social and cultural issues of interest to all European countries. Perhaps its main contribution has been its various conventions, especially its Convention for the Protection of Human Rights and Fundamental Freedoms (known as the European Convention on Human Rights—ECHR), adopted in 1950. All aspirants to EU membership must accept the Convention's principles. Since 1991 it has been particularly active in trying to strengthen democracy and human rights in Central and Eastern Europe. The United States requested and was granted observer status

in 1996 in order to be able to promote democracy more effectively in Central and Eastern Europe.

The 27 EU member states (with about 505 million citizens in 2010, two-thirds more than the U.S., with a little over 300 million) have agreed to pool a portion of their national sovereignty to the union. The irresistible logic of European unity has affected countries all over the continent. Most European countries formally applied for EU membership. Norway was offered membership in 1972 and 1994, but its voters rejected it both times. Switzerland could join at any time.

Longstanding members of the EU include the BENELUX countries, France, Germany, Italy, Great Britain, the Republic of Ireland, Denmark, Greece, Spain, Portugal, and since 1995 Austria, Finland, and Sweden. In May 2004 they were joined by Estonia, Latvia, Lithuania, Poland, the Czech Republic, Slovakia, Hungary, Slovenia, Malta and the Greek-speaking part of divided Cyprus. On December 21, 2007, all of these but Cyprus joined the EU's Schengen zone, which eliminates systematic border controls between member states. Romania and Bulgaria were admitted to the EU in 2007. Turkey was readmitted to candidate status, and Croatia is first in line to join, followed by Macedonia and Albania. Others joined in the lengthy process of accession, including Serbia in 2002 and again

in mid-2009. Entry into the EU is infinitely more complicated than joining NATO. New countries must accept 80,000 pages of EU regulations, half of them relating to agriculture. They must reach consensus with other states on complicated matters, such as banking laws, taxation, and a common currency.

The European countries treated in this book are also active in such international economic treaties or organizations as the General Agreement on Trade and Tariffs (GATT), the World Trade Organization (WTO), which since 1995 attempts to resolve disputes relating to the GATT Treaty, the International Monetary Fund (IMF), which provides funds for countries with balance-of-payments problems, the International Bank for Reconstruction and Development (World Bank), and the European Bank for Reconstruction and Development (EBRD). Headquartered in London, the EBRD was created after the collapse of communism to help Central and Eastern European countries make successful transitions to free-market economies.

The Nordic Countries

We begin our survey with the prosperous, peaceful, harmonious Nordic countries, which encompass Iceland, Norway, Denmark, Sweden and Finland. These lands are comfortably set apart from the rest of Europe, and for most of the postwar period they have enjoyed enviable prosperity and political stability. They are at the top of many international measurements: quality of life, women's opportunities, education, environmental protection, competitiveness, research and development, foreign aid and absence of corruption.

Most have been spared many of the continent's violent conflicts. They have had the wealth and the leisure to develop generous social welfare systems that are the model for many persons in the former communist countries who yearn for both the wealth of the Western world and the economic security offered at a minimal level by their ex-communist regimes. All are in the Nordic Council, which meets regularly to discuss nonmilitary problems they have in common. Two of them—Norway and Finland—border on Russia, and Finland has a half-century of valuable experience in close cooperation with Russians. Finland, Sweden and Denmark have been especially active and important in supporting the Baltic States, which were the first former Soviet republics to win their independence in 1991.

Transition from Communism

Most of the countries presented in this book had communist regimes until 1989–91 and are undergoing the difficult

Introduction: Nordic, Central, and Southeastern Europe

transition to democracy and free-market economies. Residents in all former communist countries had unrealistic expectations about the difficulties in converting planned economies to competitive free-market ones. The dramatic changes from 1989 to 1991 had created an exhilaration of victory and high expectations of quick improvements in people's lives through reforms. Dreams of instant prosperity quickly proved to be illusory. In the painful and protracted transition eastern Germans and other Central and Eastern Europeans find themselves in a similar situation.

All countries experienced economic decline at least until 1994. People began to sense that the results they had expected in the short term could be achieved only in the distant future, if at all. Struggling with a wide array of unexpected and unfamiliar problems, their political leaders came to realize that only part of the problems facing their countries had been caused by communism and would not disappear automatically once the old systems had been dismantled. They have to confront centuries of backwardness, which could take decades to overcome. In the meantime, social services are cut, economic inequality grows, and crime rises dramatically, especially organized crime. To some, it is the market economy, with its emphasis on free enterprise, which enables organized crime to flourish.

Many people who grew up under communism and were threatened by reform lost hope in the free market experiment. Since socialism remains an attractive idea in principle, they sometimes support socialist parties that would restore the social welfare system, which is still valued in their political culture. The anticommunist governments that first assumed power failed to achieve widespread prosperity. This changed the political environment and fostered the rebirth of discredited communist parties, whose demise almost everybody had predicted. They could succeed only by redefining socialism in more modern terms and by embracing pluralist democracy and, with reservations, a market economy. Their offer of more economic security in a time of painful transition is very appealing.

The Party of Democratic Socialism (PDS, changed in 2005 to the Leftists. PDS and in 2007 to the Left Party, which linked East and West) in Eastern Germany, the rechristened and reformed successor to the former ruling Socialist Unity Party of Germany (SED), skillfully benefited from the same disappointments and yearnings observable elsewhere in the former communist world. But there are some differences in the eastern German circumstances. Whereas reformed and renamed commu-

nist parties can rule in national governments elsewhere, although they seldom win majorities, the PDS remained a regional party until becoming the merged Left Party, able to thrive because of Germany's federal system.

The unlikelihood that it will ever be in a ruling national coalition enabled it to espouse populist views to attract voters. It has largely forfeited this advantage after participating in coalition governments at the land level. Most similar Eastern European parties have had to bear the burdens of ruling responsibility and risk the inevitable criticism and loss of support. The Left Party operates in an eastern area that was economically advanced before the communist era and benefits from the largess of one of the richest economic powers on earth, the FRG. Since the early 1990s eastern Germany received annual transfer payments of more than $100 billion.

Eastern Germans have one of the world's hardest currencies in their pockets and enjoy great buying power, even though the currency reform in 1990 eliminated many of their traditional export markets, most of which were in the East, especially Russia. Other Eastern Europeans can only envy them. Their incomes and living standards have grown noticeably, and they can count on steady cash infusions from the central government. Despite 18.5% unemployment in 2006

(and over a fifth if one considers make-work schemes and retraining programs) and productivity only 60% of that in western Germany, eastern Germans had by the end of the century tripled their household wealth in only seven years. As in the West, one out of two persons owns an automobile. The average eastern factory worker earns only 75% as much as his counterpart in the western part of Germany, but that is almost as much as an American factory worker earns.

Resentment of the West's role in the transformation process is strong all over the region. But Western tutelage is felt most immediately in eastern Germany, where the people face a swarm of western Germans who rule in the state governments, collect their taxes, control their banks, buy up their economic assets, manage their companies, and reorganize their universities and school systems. They dislike the visible external steering of their modernization process from western Germany. Eastern German woes are fundamentally subjective and psychological, not economic.

As in the rest of Central and Eastern Europe, citizens in eastern Germany are not willing to disregard their own lives during four decades of dictatorship, as many Westerners seem to want them to do. The German Democratic Republic (GDR) was the setting in which East Germans went

. . . and today

Introduction: Nordic, Central, and Southeastern Europe

Author and his wife in Old Town Tallinn, Estonia

to school, embarked upon careers, had their families, found their happiness in life. They cannot simply discard their own biographies and say that their earlier lives had been wasted during communist rule. This is also true of the three-quarters of eastern Germans who are not "losers" after unification.

The Baltic States and Kaliningrad

Estonia, Latvia and Lithuania can be counted among the winners of the Cold War although they continue to share a common fear and mistrust of Russia. Through the Baltics one can observe how the West will deal with an uncertain and diminished Russian colossus, which continues to instill fear and wariness in all other Baltic Sea states. This region is the gateway to Russia and contains one of Europe's most complicated geopolitical challenges: how to provide protection for Estonia, Latvia and Lithuania. Their security is a kind of political and moral litmus test for the extent to which Russia has genuinely changed and has shed its age-old imperial aspirations.

The Soviet Union dominated the Baltic States from 1940 to 1941 and again from 1944 to 1991. All three faced myriad challenges in 1991 and after: they were severed from their traditional markets and had to introduce new currencies, establish from scratch their own military forces, negotiate the departure of former Soviet troops, start cleaning up the environmental damage they had caused, adopt new constitutions and sets of laws, and organize their first democratic elections in a half-century.

This dramatic turn in history did not automatically eradicate the legacies of an overbearing Soviet empire. In order to maintain control over a sprawling multinational state and promote its own socialist industrialization, the Kremlin had intentionally mixed peoples and capriciously changed borders. When Soviet rule ended, sizable Russian minorities were left in both Estonia and Latvia. The Baltic States hold Russia responsible for their loss of independence in 1940, for the disappearance of about a fifth of their populations due to deportation, execution, or exile, for the reminders of Soviet rule in their countries, such as gray, unaesthetic buildings and environmental destruction, and for the fact that they fell far behind the other Nordic countries economically during a half-century of subjugation.

Although Balts strive to work constructively with Russia, they are not inclined to show the kind of fealty to which Russia is accustomed. Many Russians have difficulty adjusting to the new reality and claim the right to obedient ex-dependencies, who should adopt a deferential attitude. Some are not yet ready to tolerate the prospect that the Baltic States are free from Moscow's sphere of influence. Article 61 of the Russian Federation's constitution includes a right of intervention and

a role as protectress of 25 million Diaspora Russians, whom it officially calls "compatriots." The Baltic States are troubled by such claims of special privileges in Russia's "near abroad."

These three states have as many differences as similarities. They are all small in geography and population, have a history of repeated foreign domination and of only a few decades of independence in the 20th century, and have experienced humiliation and exploitation by the Soviet Union. Nevertheless, they are three very different nations with separate languages. Estonian is a Finno-Ugric language related to that of Finland, a country with which Estonia has very close relations. Latvian and Lithuanian are ancient Indo-European languages. The three are mutually incomprehensible. There are differing ethnic mixes, as well as cultural heritages. For example, the Catholic Church has played a special role in Lithuania, while religion is less important in Protestant Estonia. Finally, these three countries had little experience or inclination to cooperate closely with each other before the late 1980s. Even today their cooperation, although extensive, is pragmatic and has its limits.

All three newly independent states proceeded rapidly to hold free elections and to establish the kind of institutional and legal conditions that place them within the Western political model. They have all developed multiparty systems in which democratic procedures are respected. Despite frequent changes of coalitions and cabinets, they have maintained underlying political stability while demonstrating that power can be transferred peacefully from one coalition government to another. In Latvia and Lithuania, but not in Estonia, parties of former communists have been able to win power. However, they relinquished it when they no longer had the voters' support.

They have entered a network of international governmental organizations (IGOs) to internationalize their security concerns until they became NATO members in April 2004. They joined the UN and CSCE (now OSCE) in September 1991, and the Council of the Baltic Sea States (CBSS) in 1992. The 11-member CBSS, which has a rotating presidency, a secretariat, and working groups and committees, also embraces the Nordic states (including non-Baltic Norway and Iceland), Germany, Poland and Russia. It is a forum to discuss a variety of common issues ranging from the environment and trade to cross-border police cooperation. It is of declining importance, even as the Baltic region is watched keenly by the West because of resurgent Russia's energy clout and spending power. The Baltic States entered

Introduction: Nordic, Central, and Southeastern Europe

the NACC (now EAPC) in 1992 and the Council of Europe in 1993.

In 1994 Lithuania became the first to apply officially for NATO membership, followed shortly later by the other two. Lithuania also forged a "strategic partnership" with Poland in 1997 and created with it a joint battalion, LITPOLBAT, which is interoperable with NATO and prepared to contribute to its security interests. These are only a few of the increasingly tight relationships Poland and Lithuania are forging with each other. Because Lithuania provides the only logical "land bridge" between Russia and its enclave in Kaliningrad, Moscow viewed NATO application as a provocative act. But all three Baltic States noted the wording in the NATO summit declaration in 1994 that "we expect and would welcome NATO expansion." With quiet American encouragement, Denmark became the most visible champion of Baltic applications to NATO. The three quickly joined NATO's Partnership for Peace (PfP) as a concrete means for integrating Baltic defenses, achieving NATO standards and demonstrating the value of their contributions to Western security efforts.

Together they created the Baltic Airspace Surveillance Network (BALTNET), a radar monitoring system, steered by Norway. After the three were admitted to NATO, BALTNET was included in NATO's integrated air-defense system, NATINADS, and that of Finland, a country with whom Estonia operates a joint coastguard and marine-surveillance service. The Baltic Squadron (BALTRON), led by Germany and headquartered in Tallinn, Estonia, was interoperable with NATO and organized to clear mines and engage in such international naval exercises as "Open Spirit '98." It also became integrated into NATO's naval forces. The Baltic Battalion (BALTBAT), with support and guidance from Britain and the Nordic countries and with a rotating tri-national command structure, was trained to participate in UN peacekeeping operations, such as in Bosnia with Danish soldiers. Having fulfilled its mission, it was terminated in the fall of 2003.

A permanent Baltic Defence College (BALTDEFCOL), supported mainly by the Nordic countries to provide Baltic officers with interoperable training in English, is located in Tartu, Estonia. Upon acceptance into NATO, it became the main education institution to train Baltic soldiers in NATO standards. In 2002 Baltic liaison officers began serving at the headquarters of a multinational corps in Szczecin, Poland, commanded by Poland and including a German and a Danish division.

The military forces of all three countries participate in NATO maneuvers. In 1998 Lithuania hosted 5,000 soldiers, including

Americans, Danes, Norwegians, Germans and Balts, with Russians, Ukrainians and Belarusians present as observers. Lithuania's deputy defense minister, Povilas Malaksuskas, underscored the goal of all these cooperative efforts: "to make Baltic membership in NATO a logical inevitability."

The U.S. has communicated that it would like to see Russia and the Baltics develop good neighborly relations. This was made most explicit on January 16, 1998, when the American president endorsed in principle the desire to join the Atlantic Alliance by signing with the three Baltic presidents a "Charter of Partnership." It was not a guarantee of future NATO membership or American protection, and it set no timetable for such membership. But it put on record Washington's "real, profound and enduring interest" in Baltic security and the conviction that the three new democracies had as much right to join NATO as did the three ex-communist countries that joined in 1999: Poland, Hungary and the Czech Republic. In return, the Baltic nations committed themselves to work toward good relations with all neighbors, including Russia.

Russian leaders expressed no objection when in December 2002 all three Baltic States were offered EU membership for May 2004. However, NATO was another matter. For a long time they had rejected assurances from Baltic governments that NATO was not directed toward Russia. Russians are divided on how they should react to NATO enlargement. Nevertheless, many moderate and extremist political elements in Russia maintain that NATO presence so close to Russia is undesirable. They directed a stream of threats to the Baltics. But by the time of NATO's November 2002 meeting in Prague, when

NATO offered membership to all three, plus Slovakia, Slovenia, Romania and Bulgaria, the Russian government had accepted Baltic membership in the Atlantic Alliance as inevitable. However, in June 2003 Russia was still worried, insisting "on clear and unambiguous guarantees that arms and armed forces of other countries will not be deployed on the territory of the Baltic States." NATO issued no such assurances although it has no plans to deploy troops there.

A particularly delicate problem is posed by the Russian enclave of Kaliningrad, located on the southwest border of Lithuania. It is the northern third of the former East Prussia containing the earlier German city of Königsberg. After the war, all 1.2 million German citizens were expelled. The region has the potential for economic growth. It has a deep-water harbor that is Russia's only warm-water port in the North, over 90% of the world's amber, rich farmland, modest crude oil reserves, and a well-educated work force. However, foreign investors were scared away by endemic corruption, powerful organized crime, a drug epidemic, and Russia's highest HIV infection rate. Its future looks a bit brighter as Russia is taking a greater interest in its development. But its prospects remain uncertain and depend on general developments in Russia proper, located 300 miles away across Lithuania and Belarus.

The Baltic States do not face an immediate threat from Russia. Never before have they been as secure as in the present environment. Along with Russia, they desire outside help in many forms to solve economic, environmental, and security problems. Therefore, they cannot overlook the views of major foreign countries or international organizations, like NATO or

Baltic Defence College, Tartu, Estonia

5

Introduction: Nordic, Central, and Southeastern Europe

Slovak electoral poster favoring NATO and EU

had recovered from the economic devastation of the war, it rekindled its involvement in the East through trade (*Osthandel*) and its policy of political cooperation and tension reduction (*Ostpolitik*). Very quickly the FRG became the "East bloc's" most important trading partner. It is through its economic prowess, not the fact that it has Europe's largest military force outside of Russia, that Germany is so important in the area.

By 1989 Germany's "economic miracle" had become the model for eastern transformation. At the same time, eastern countries looked at Germany's Basic Law (constitution), political institutions, and central bank (*Bundesbank*) for examples. A host of semiprivate foundations, including those sponsored by Germany's political parties and subsidized by the state, fanned out to help teach Germany's political, economic, and social values and experiences. Alone among Western nations, Germany demonstrated a real commitment to strengthen political stability in the region through economic assistance. It provided far more aid than any other country, including the United States, mostly in the form of loans issued at favorable interest rates.

Germany's motives are a mixture of guilt over past mistreatment of some nations in the region, the desire to strengthen the foundations of peace, and economic and social self-interest. As a large, open, wealthy and tolerant magnet in the middle of Europe, Germany is one of the desired destinations for the "huddled masses" of the East. Germans fear that instability there could prompt a massive influx of immigrants and refugees. A former adviser to Helmut Kohl put it this way: "German foreign policy these days is driven by a simple priority: to prevent poor foreigners from swamping our prosperous country. Given the dangers of right-wing extremism, the idea is to do whatever is necessary to keep would-be immigrants from leaving their homes and heading for Germany."

The economic and political foothold that Germany gradually regained in the four decades after the war gave it a running start in the post-Cold War era. As the Central European countries' (and eastern Germany's) trade with the former Soviet Union collapsed, their trade relations were rapidly reoriented westward. Germany's trade with the region jumped by 30% between 1993 and 1995 and soon surpassed its trade volume with the United States. By the end of the century it exceeded its trade with France, Germany's single most important trading partner. Germany is the most significant trading partner for Poland, the Czech Republic and Hungary, conducting a tenth of its foreign commerce with them.

the EU, who counsel compromise in their own interest and for the purpose of peace and political stability in the region.

The Baltic Sea has become one of the most important and complicated areas in the new Europe. It links nine European countries, including the continent's largest (Russia and Germany) and some of its smallest. Democracy is practiced in each, but in some, particularly Russia, it is new and fragile and is accompanied by a weak rule of law and much corruption. Economic and informal ties are thriving all around. Along the western coast are some of the world's most prosperous nations; along the eastern is poverty, especially in Russia, but also in the Baltics and Poland. Eyes are on the Baltic States because the ways they grapple with fundamental problems of economic transformation and modernization provide insights and inspiration for other ex-communist countries.

Germany in Central Europe

No Western country has such long-standing historical, political and economic ties to Central and Eastern Europe as does Germany. For the first time since Germany's initial unification in 1871, this "land of the middle" is surrounded by nine friendly neighbors, more than most countries have. Before 1945 Germany's relationship in and with Central Europe (*Mitteleuropa*) was ambivalent. Germany's central position had always dominated discussions about it. Some Germans perceived *Mitteleuropa* as a cover for German cultural imperialism. Any notion of it as bringing Germany and the East together in some beneficial way perished in the Second World War. Everything changed after that, and many Germans have negative memories of the expulsions, the flight, the homelessness, the missing loved ones. Most Central Europeans also find the earlier notion of *Mitteleuropa* repugnant because it was identified with German hegemony and violence; therefore the term practically disappeared from usage.

Germany's defeat in the Second World War temporarily diminished its influence in the region. The Yalta agreement of February 1945 left the area within the Soviet Union's sphere of influence. Once the FRG

Introduction: Nordic, Central, and Southeastern Europe

Germany also became the region's main source of foreign investment, even though by 1998 only about six percent of Germany's total flowed into the area; 80% went to only three states: Poland, the Czech Republic and Hungary. In that year, a fifth of all foreign direct investments in the region were from Germany, as compared with 14.6% from the United States, 10.4% from the Netherlands, 7.7% from France and 7.5% from Austria. This focus on the four Visegrád states (Poland, Czech Republic, Slovakia and Hungary) reveals the important distinction Germany makes between these countries, which have successfully introduced economic reform and recovery and political stability, and the former Soviet republics (except the Baltics) and Balkan countries, which have not.

Germany has been one of the most energetic promoters of eastward enlargement of both NATO and the EU. Both of these organizations provide protection both for and from Germany. Because Germany enjoys close ties with the United States, Central and Eastern Europeans see it as an important bridge to the transatlantic alliance. NATO is widely regarded in the region as the only credible guarantor of the new democracies' independence from Russia. In 1993 Germany became the first NATO ally to advocate the alliance's eastward enlargement, even before the Clinton administration embraced it. America's leaders soon followed suit as a result not only of intense lobbying on the part of Presidents Lech Walesa of Poland and Vaclav Havel of the Czech Republic.

In 1993 an intoxicated Boris Yeltsin let slip during a visit to Warsaw that Russia would not object to Poland's joining NATO. Despite rapid corrections by the Russian president's advisers, doubt had been cast on the previous assumption that Russia would never accept NATO expansion into its former empire. Germany's motives are obvious. As countries to the east join NATO, the alliance's eastern front shifts eastward away from Germany. The result is that Germany is encompassed by friends, not foes, and its new capital becomes the geographic center of NATO.

No country influences the transformation of Central Europe more than does Germany. Yet its predominance does not extend to the cultural sphere even though its cultural presence is increasing. English has become the undisputedly dominant second language, except in the Czech Republic. There is an increasing demand for business German, and the Goethe Institute estimates that three-quarters of the 20 million foreigners learning German live in east-central Europe. A 2002 EU survey determined that in the eight new central European member states that joined in 2004, 17% claimed to be able to carry on a conversation in German. The Slovenians had the best command (36%), followed by the Czechs (27%) and the Slovaks (22%). One in five claimed to speak English. Nevertheless, it is American popular culture that reigns, both in the region and in Germany itself.

What are developing are not the old unequal, unstable, bilateral relationships with Germany, but rather multilateral relationships linking both the Central European countries and Germany to an increasingly integrated Europe and the Atlantic Alliance. German predominance is diminished by these supranational arrangements. Germany's special task is to be the bridge to these organizations, a role it consciously plays. Former Chancellor Gerhard Schröder noted in 1999, "Berlin has always served as the bridge to our Central and Eastern European partners. We are convinced that the European Union should not be limited only to the western part of the continent." For that reason Germany took the lead in sponsoring early EU membership for Poland, Hungary and the Czech Republic.

For the new democracies to the east, Germany is a source of both assistance and concern. Because of its trade and energy dependence on Russia (it gets 40% of its gas and 35% of its oil from Russia), Germany attempts a difficult balancing act to satisfy both its desire for good relations with Russia and its support for new allies in the Baltics and Central Europe who fear a resurgent Russia. There are fears that it tilts too much toward Moscow. Smaller allies are reminded of Bismarck's declaration in 1863: "A good treaty with Russia" is the secret to politics.

Although intended to apply only to Czech circumstances, the words of former President Vaclav Havel expressed in 1995 apply to all Central and Eastern European nations, who must deal with a new but always large, dynamic and economically powerful Germany. Referring to the complicated tangle of expectations and fears, combined with the differences in size and prosperity, he said: "Germany is both our inspiration and our pain; a source of understandable traumas and many prejudices and misconceptions, as well as the standards against which we measure ourselves; some see Germany as our greatest hope, others as our greatest danger."

Austria

Austria sees itself as especially qualified for the role of a "bridge-builder" between East and West. Until its collapse in 1918 the Austro-Hungarian empire encompassed most of Central Europe, much of the Balkans, northeastern Italy, and the western part of Ukraine. From 1945 to 1955 it was occupied by the four victorious allied powers, and it regained its full sovereignty after agreeing to remain a neutral country. It did not join the EU until 1995, and it still remains outside of NATO. At least since the Congress of Vienna in 1814–15, it has been the location for important international meetings. In 1990 NATO and the Warsaw Pact (the former military alliance binding the Soviet Union with its Eastern European satellites) signed the Conventional Forces in Europe (CFE) agreement, which reduced

Source: *The Economist*

7

Introduction: Nordic, Central, and Southeastern Europe

conventional weapons between the Atlantic and Urals and established confidence-building measures to give each side advanced notice of troop movements and missile launches. Russia refused to renew the treaty in December 2007.

Since the collapse of communism in Europe Austrians see themselves in a totally new situation. Before 1989 they were in a kind of *cul-de-sac*, surrounded on three sides by the communist bloc; now that dead end has been transformed into an intersection with a bustling thoroughfare opening into the East. One Austrian diplomat put it this way: "We used to be on the eastern fringe of western Europe; now we are in the center of Europe again." Leaving from Vienna, one travels *westward* to get to the Slovene capital of Ljubljana or the Czech capital of Prague. Austria and Hungary liberalized their border relations so much that in 1989 Hungary dismantled the electronically monitored fences and watchtowers along the Austro-Hungarian border. This opportunity to render a dramatic humanitarian gesture was a key link in the chain of events that led to the unification of Germany.

As communism was collapsing, Austria helped form the Pentagonale, joined by Italy, Hungary, Czechoslovakia, and Yugoslavia, to foster a project-centered approach to issues of international affairs, such as the environment, where more progress can be made through regional negotiations. The former Yugoslav Republic of Slovenia, which borders on Austria and formerly belonged to the Austro-Hungarian empire, has strengthened its economic and political ties with Austria. Because of the tension between the Czechs and Slovaks, the latter, whose capital Bratislava is close to Austria, is increasingly turning more to Vienna. Involved in more than 8,000 joint ventures with its eastern neighbors (4,000 in Hungary alone), Austria is becoming more deeply integrated with Eastern Europe.

Central Europe

Central Europe, whose history has been determined by the rivalries of great powers—Germany, Austria-Hungary and Russia—is more complicated than Western Europe. In the 20th century it was the source of conflict from which the Second World War and the Cold War emerged. Culturally it has always belonged to the West, but it was chained to the East after 1945. The U.S., Britain and Soviet Union agreed to this division at the Yalta Conference in February 1945, and thereafter the word "Yalta" became in the minds of Central Europeans shorthand for the artificial and unwanted division of Europe. The victorious powers imposed a heavily armed deterrence system on the region

that precluded any choice on the part of the countries themselves.

There is no universally accepted meaning of the term "Central Europe," which has been changing over time. In some ways, it is more a state of mind and expression of sentiment than a geographic reality. Its borders in all directions are open to dispute. The preference for the term "Central Europe" is a reflection of the sense of belonging to the West rather than to the East. In 1983 a well-known Czech writer, Milan Kundera, wrote a famous article entitled "The Tragedy of Central Europe." He argued that Central Europe had always belonged spiritually and culturally to the West, rather than to the East. It had participated completely in the major cultural movements of the West, including the Reformation, the Renaissance, and the Enlightenment. But the area had been "kidnapped, displaced and brainwashed" by the Soviet Union after 1945 and had been forced to become "Eastern Europe." Kundera's rejection of the loaded term, "Eastern Europe," was a direct challenge to the legitimacy of Moscow's control over the region, and he was joined by many dissidents, intellectuals, and Pope John Paul II from Poland.

In the midst and wake of the 1989 revolutions in the Soviet Union's European empire, the term, "Central Europe," was used by those who wanted an alternative to a Europe split into two blocs and who wished to see their small countries as subjects, not mere objects and captives, of European politics. Recognizing this sentiment, former U.S. Assistant Secretary of State, Richard Holbrooke, declared in 1994 that Poland, the Czech and Slovak Republics, Hungary, Slovenia and Croatia would henceforth be called by that designation. Over time, "Central and Eastern Europe" came into vogue among Western countries in order to make the countries of the former Soviet Union feel more wanted in the new Europe.

In this book, the term, "Central Europe," will refer to the Czech and Slovak Republics, Hungary and Poland. Slovenians prefer to be ranked in this category, but their relatively well-developed country will be treated with ex-Yugoslavia because of its pre-1991 history. The first three and the southern strip of Poland had been parts of the Austro-Hungarian empire and had enjoyed a limited amount of self-rule and greater tolerance than the subjects of the other empires that exercised control in the region, especially Russia and Ottoman Turkey. Always aware of being located between Germany and Russia, they have experienced repeated invasion and occupation throughout the centuries. This was facilitated by geographic factors. The area between the Baltic Sea and the northern

Carpathian Mountains (which generally extend in a west-east direction in southern Poland, western Ukraine, and northern Romania) and the Tatra Mountains in northern Slovakia is a plain that offers no natural barriers to invasions from the east and west. To this is added the absence of large rivers that could slow down invading armies.

Today all the Central European countries are on the fast track into the coveted Western European institutions. As a prelude, Poland, Hungary and Czechoslovakia (which in 1993 split into the Czech and Slovak Republics) signed a "Declaration of Cooperation on the Road to Europe Integration" with each other in the Hungarian city of Visegrád. This "Visegrád Group," joined by Slovenia in 1996, became the basis for the Central European Free Trade Association. This has no organizational structure but is a platform for ongoing consultation aimed at multilateral cooperation, harmonization of social and economic policies, and preparation for EU entry.

All were in the front of the line, along with the Baltic States, Malta and Cyprus, for admission to the EU, which happened in May 2004. The EU holds out the prospect not only of Western European prosperity, but it offers the small states in the region a kind of equality with larger states they never had experienced before. Poland, the Czech Republic and Hungary were admitted to NATO in 1999. Seven more followed in 2004 and two more in 2009. Membership in the Atlantic Alliance is prized because it offers security from a potentially resurgent Russia, which all of the countries in the region north of the Balkans continue to fear. The EU's and NATO's magnetic attraction on countries to the east makes the region's western frontier more fluid and blurred than ever before.

The region's new powerhouse is Poland, whose 39 million inhabitants constitute the largest population in the entire region outside of Germany. Before the collapse of the Soviet Union in December 1991, Poland had only three neighbors, none of which exists today: the Soviet Union, Czechoslovakia, and East Germany. Now it has seven. For the first time in a millennium Poland is at peace with all its neighbors, and for the first time in more than a century it feels safe on its eastern and western borders. It has developed particularly close relations with Germany, the Czech Republic and Slovakia. Its rapid political and economic transformation makes it an especially important model and trading partner for Lithuania and Ukraine. It is not afraid to threaten to use its veto in EU councils if it thinks its interests are being disregarded.

Introduction: Nordic, Central, and Southeastern Europe

Poland has established a link with both Germany and France called the Weimar Triangle, named after the venue of its first meeting in 1991. It wants to widen its Western contacts in order to reduce its possible dependence on Germany. The Weimar Triangle, which brings together the three countries' heads of state and government, ministers and parliamentary representatives for informal talks on fundamental matters of mutual interest, does just that.

Another innovative institution located on the Polish-German border, in Szczecin, is a Northeast Multinational Corps consisting of Polish, German and Danish troops, commanded by a Polish officer. This military cooperation, supplemented by a dramatic increase in German-Polish exercises and interaction (second only to that between the U.S. and Poland), is symptomatic of a new spirit in Polish-German relations. Together the two countries provide the bulk of NATO forces in the East, even though Poland insists that the U.S. is and will remain its key military partner. NATO membership gives Poland and other Central European countries the confidence to deal with their eastern neighbors, especially Russia. Nevertheless, they are mindful of a possible Russian resurgence. Therefore, Poland unequivocally supported the admission of the Baltic States into NATO.

Southeastern Europe

South of Central European is a cluster of countries that we call Southeastern Europe, despite the countless differences that exist among them. Most of them are relatively new states that have nevertheless been shaped by important historical factors as well as by geography. One of Europe's earliest divisions emerged a millennium ago between Roman Catholicism in the West and Eastern Orthodox Christianity in the East. The differences between these two religions' ideas led to a fundamental variance in political and social institutions. Most Southeastern European countries were Eastern Orthodox; only Slovenia and Croatia were Roman Catholic.

Beginning in the 14th century another defining influence came with the Ottoman Turkish conquest and occupation, which finally ended only in the early 20th century. The Turks imposed their own political and social institutions, which cut the area off from the political and economic developments occurring in the rest of Europe. Among the many cultural legacies such long Oriental rule left in the region was Islam, which is the prevailing religion in Albania and the Serb province of Kosovo and a significant minority religion in Bosnia-Herzegovina and Macedonia. All these cultural, political and religious features provided barriers from those parts of Europe to the west and north.

The same role was played by geography. The mountainous terrain of the Balkans (whose name is derived from the Turkish word for mountainous area) south of the broad Danube plain, combined with the enclosure formed by the Black, Aegean and Adriatic Seas, partially sealed the area off from the West. There are few navigable rivers that could serve as trade corridors as the Rhine River does in Western Europe by connecting five countries to the Atlantic Ocean. The Danube traverses the whole region, but its flow is not toward the west but southeasterly from Germany into the Black Sea. Until 1992 it was not navigable all the way and was iced over during the winter. Also the Turks always controlled its lower reaches. The Main-Danube Canal, completed in 1992, has connected the Danube to the Rhine River. But until 2003 manmade barriers prevented the uninterrupted traffic from western Europe to the Black Sea and back: in the 1999 Kosovo war, NATO planes destroyed some of the bridges in Serbia, and the ruins prevented ships from passing them. In mid-2003 the last debris was cleared from the Danube's navigation channels, and large ships can now pass. Other rivers in the region are navigable only for short distances.

Southeastern Europe also has fewer essential raw materials, such as fuel, coal, and iron ore, than does Central Europe. The facts that such resources were located in places like northern Bohemia (Czech Republic) and southern Poland and that good transport links connected Budapest with markets and materials helped those areas develop economically. Despite some oil fields in Romania and coalfields in Serbia, the absence of adequate quantities of raw materials hampered the industrialization of Southeastern Europe and helps explain the continued economic gap that exists between it and other parts of Europe.

Greece, Turkey, Romania, Bulgaria, Albania, Russia, Ukraine, Georgia, Moldova, Azerbaijan and Armenia founded the Black Sea Economic Cooperation group in 1992, with Poland and Slovakia having observer status. Deeply rooted historical animosities among some of its members, as well as a fragile economic and political environment in the region, have prevented the group from being as effective as its founders had hoped.

We shall first deal with the Balkans, where some countries are progressing well in their post-communist transformation, such as Slovenia and Croatia after the death of Franjo Tudjman, and most others are having severe difficulties. The 1999 war in Kosovo and the peacekeeping that followed it have brought the EU into the region in an unprecedented way. It has assumed important responsibility for the reconstruction of the Balkans. Kosovo, which declared its independence in February 2008, appears to have become a long-term protectorate of the EU and NATO. We will then turn to Romania and Bulgaria, which gained admittance to NATO in 2004 and joined the EU in 2007.

In order to present Mediterranean Europe together, we have moved Greece and Cyprus (which entered the EU in May 2004 despite its continued division into Greek- and Turkish-speaking sectors) to our Western Europe book. This is not to say that Greece plays no role in the Balkans despite the acute danger in 2010 that it would default on its debts. As the only country in the Balkans, except Slovenia, that belongs to both NATO and EU, it not only bears special responsibility in the area, but it was a model for the prosperity and stability that could come with European integration

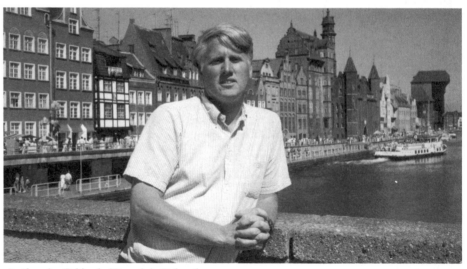

Author in Gdánsk (Danzig), Poland

The Nordic Countries

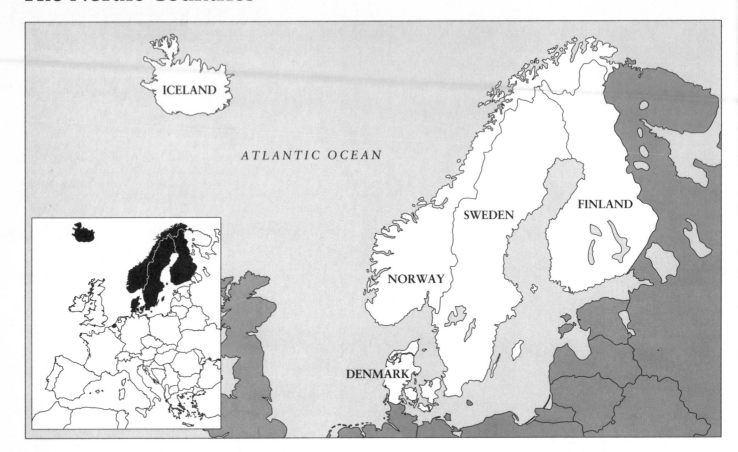

ICELAND

ATLANTIC OCEAN

SWEDEN

FINLAND

NORWAY

DENMARK

The People

Prosperous, peaceful, harmonious, with a stable, democratic political order and beautiful, unspoiled and sparsely populated territories on the outskirts of Europe are words that typify this area of the world. These are things that are often associated with the Nordic area, which encompasses Sweden, Norway, Denmark, Iceland and Finland, or, more narrowly, to Scandinavia, a term generally applied to the first three. Indeed, at first glance, these countries seem to have escaped many of the most severe problems that have afflicted postwar Europe. Yet, a closer look reveals that they share some important economic and social problems with the rest of Europe. Further, they are by no means so isolated from the world as many people often think.

Although the Nordic countries have chosen to take different paths on many matters, they have many things in common. Geographically, they are all located on the same latitude as Alaska and Siberia, but they are warmed by Atlantic currents, which make them more habitable. Also, they are comfortably set apart from Europe, and Iceland, Sweden, Norway (except for a short stretch at the northern tip) and parts of Denmark are separated from Europe by water. Thus, they have been spared many of Europe's violent conflicts. For at least two centuries

their populations have been too small to permit any grand-scale political activity outside their sphere. They have therefore had the luxury of being able to concentrate on their own affairs and to develop, to a great extent, at their own speed and in their own preferred way.

The 24.4 million citizens of the Nordic countries have minimal language problems among themselves. Except for Finnish, which is related to Estonian and distantly to Hungarian, all other Nordic languages are of northern Germanic origin. To help maintain a lingual tie to the other countries, Finland retains Swedish as an official language together with Finnish. Danes, Swedes, Norwegians and, to some extent, Icelanders can read each others' languages, and with patience and good will they can make themselves understood when speaking although Danish presents some difficulties to Swedes and Norwegians, and Icelandic presents greater problems to all three. These language ties and close proximity enable Nordic officials to pick up the phone and talk to each other in order to discuss everyday problems.

English is becoming the Nordic countries' *lingua franca*. At the University of Copenhagen 84% of the doctoral theses in the natural sciences are being published in English, and many universities throughout the region offer a multitude of courses and programs in English. Many large com-

panies, such as Finland's Nokia, use English as their official language. Nevertheless, laws in most Nordic nations promote the use of the local language in official publications and broadcasting.

The Nordic peoples also share many cultural values. One of the most important is Lutheran Christianity, to which most, at least nominally, belong. Lutheranism in Scandinavia is void of religious fanaticism. Although most citizens are baptized and married in the church and voluntarily pay their church taxes in some countries (no longer in Sweden since 2000), few attend church regularly. For instance, in Norway today only 3% above the age of 15 attend weekly. Another 6% go once every couple of months. All of the Nordic countries are highly secularized in that religious dogma or considerations play a very small role in the everyday lives and politics of the people. By the middle of the 19th century, religious freedom and tolerance were practiced in all Nordic countries and helped to bolster tolerance in the political and social spheres as well.

Most persons in these countries tend to take a practical, unemotional approach to politics that stresses compromise, stability and continuity. Compromise is necessary because all have proportional representation electoral systems, which always grant parliamentary seats to a large number of parties. Therefore, a single party almost never wins a majority of parliamentary seats, and the countries must be ruled by either minority or coalition governments. These lands do have fewer social tensions than some other European countries, and over the years, most of their citizens have developed a kind of immunity to totalitarian ideologies or unrealizable political demands.

All of the Nordic countries entered the second half of the 19th century as relatively poor agricultural societies and experienced the industrial revolution rather late. Industrialization brought greater wealth, but it also brought many problems. At the same time that they underwent fundamental social and economic changes, they adopted democratic political practices. As a result of many compromises between the traditional ruling elites and the newly developing or increasingly self-confident middle, working and farming classes, more people were allowed to vote, and the governments became answerable to popularly elected parliaments, rather than to the Swedish, Danish and (after 1905) Norwegian monarchs. In characteristic Nordic style, this process of democratization took place largely without violent revolutions or *coups d'état*. These peoples generally have had a good sense of timing in changing outdated practices or structures in order to be able to preserve that which is worth preserving. Also, they have had a genius for solving political, social and religious issues in such a way that the losers are never left permanently unreconciled to the system and with bitter determination to revive the dispute later.

The Earliest Period

The common ties among these countries did not emerge overnight, but in the course of centuries of mutual collaboration. In Denmark there is evidence of human settlements as early as 50,000 B.C., and by 10,000 B.C. communities began to be established all over Scandinavia. Although some trade gradually developed with the rest of the continent, Europe did not take much notice of the Nordic area. The Romans did not bother with this region at all, except for a small volume of trade in amber. Tacitus did refer to a tribe of people in Sweden known as the *Svear*, from whom the name *Sverige* (Sweden) was derived. The Romans also engaged in combat with Cimbri, Vandals and other Scandinavian groups.

The Vikings (Norsemen, Northmen, Normans)

This inconspicuous existence ended abruptly in the beginning of the 9th century, when the Vikings burst out of Scandinavia and began venturing in sturdy ships far from their own lands. They sometimes established colonies and traded peacefully, but they often pillaged and plundered, leaving wastelands in their wake. Most Europeans learned to pray for protection from the Viking's ravaging, and the institution of feudalism was, in part, a response to the widespread willingness of a common people to exchange their liberties for protection.

A notable twist probably occurred in Russia. In the 9th century, warlike Slav tribes were weary of rampant strife. The Vikings were using Russian rivers for trade. They, according to *The Primary Chronicle* of the 12th century, actually *invited* the Vikings to become their rulers. The "Varangian Russes," called Variagi in Russian, were Norman (Norsemen, Northmen, Vikings), who founded the first Russian dynasty. This part of the *Chronicle* is vigorously disputed in Russia today—the idea that *outsiders* had to be called in to bring order to the area is distasteful. It is indisputable, however, that the Vikings ventured all the way to the Black Sea, Constantinople and the Mediterranean Sea during this period.

The Vikings sailed to the British Isles, (establishing settlements in England, the Hebrides Islands, Shetlands and Isle of Man), Ireland (whose capital of Dublin was a Viking fortress), Normandy and Iceland. From the latter island, Eric the Red discovered and named Greenland in 981 or 982 A.D., where he established a settlement on the southwest tip. His son, Leif Eriksson, sailed from Greenland to the northeast coast of North America around the year 1000 A.D., beating Christopher Columbus to the New World by about five centuries. In the U.S., Leif Eriksson Day is celebrated on October 9th of each year. By the middle of the 11th century, the Vikings had reached their peak and dominated most of the sea shipping routes around Europe and Orkney. The boldness and restlessness of such modern Norwegian explorers as Roald Amundsen and Thor Heyerdahl show that some Scandinavians still have the adventuresome spirit of their forebears.

Christianity

Viking marauding had brought considerable wealth to the Nordic area. But it also caused a serious drain on the tribes' manpower and threatened to make the Nordic lands vulnerable to outside attacks. They began to settle down, and the regional tribal communities gradually gave way to larger kingdoms. Christianity, which had been introduced to Sweden as early as 830 A.D., along with other European influences, began to filter more and more into the Nordic area through the peninsula of Jutland. Norway's national hero and symbol of its nationality, St. Olaf, was a commander who brought Christianity to the land in the 11th century. By the 12th century, Christianity had spread to all corners of the area, and with the Pope's blessing, the Swedes conducted crusades in Finland, which became a part of the Swedish realm.

Medieval Norway

In the 13th century Norway, which had been united into one nation by the end of

The Nordic Countries

1397: Union of Kalmar (under Denmark)

1523: Swedish independence

the 9th century, reached the peak of its power. It took possession of Greenland and Iceland. Norwegian culture also reached its high point and was described vividly and imaginatively in the sagas of Snorre Snurrlasson. The terrible bubonic plague, known in Europe as the Black Death, from 1349–50 struck the region with full fury. One-half of Norway's population perished. This accelerated the economic and cultural decline of Norway, which became a predominantly peasant nation during the following centuries.

Contests for Supremacy

Throughout the ensuing centuries, Denmark and Sweden vied for domination over the Nordic region. Not until the 20th century were Norway, Finland and Iceland able to win full independence. Every Nordic nation was at one time ruled, at least in part, by another Nordic neighbor. The only exception was Denmark, which had experienced German rule. By the end of the 14th century it appeared that Denmark would control all of northern Europe. In the late 12th and early 13th centuries it had already begun to expand to other territories along the northern and southern Baltic coasts. In 1380 it acquired Iceland and the Faroe Islands and by 1387 its domination extended over Norway. Denmark's political domination over the region was formalized in the Union of Kalmar, which was established in 1397; it linked all five Nordic nations together in a single kingdom under Danish leadership. It also helped to curtail German commercial predominance in the region, which had threatened to lead to German political domination as well, especially in Sweden.

The Union of Kalmar began to break down after Queen Margrete died in 1412. Swedish nationalism had begun to grow, and by the middle of the 14th century, Swedes had developed a set of laws that applied to the whole nation. In the 15th century they increasingly resisted Danish domination and in 1434, a peasant uprising, supported by some noblemen, was directed against Danish rule. This event led to the convocation of the first *Riksdag* (Swedish Parliament) in 1435. King Christian II of Denmark sent an army against the Swedes and in 1520 had himself crowned in Stockholm as the hereditary monarch. There was a good chance that he could pacify the Swedes after he had promised a general amnesty for all rebels.

However, he broke his promise and ordered the decapitation of 80 leading Swedes. This disgusting and politically unwise bloodbath prompted the young Swedish nobleman and first genuine national hero, Gustav Eriksson Vasa, to lead a successful rebellion against the Danes. In 1523 Vasa was declared the first truly Swedish king, taking the name of Gustav I and exercising authority over all of Sweden except the southernmost provinces, which continued to belong to Denmark until 1658. The Union of Kalmar ceased to exist although the Swedes and Danes continued for another century and a half to struggle for supremacy in Scandinavia.

The Reign of Gustav I and the Emergence of Sweden

This is generally known as the Vasa period and was extremely important for Sweden's later development. Not only did

The house of King Gustav I in Delecarlia

he establish Swedish independence, but, like Henry VIII of England, he severed Sweden's ties with the Catholic Church in 1527, creating the Lutheran State Church and supported the Reformation. In fact, all over the Nordic area, the Reformation succeeded quickly and with little resistance. Therefore, these countries were left with only tiny religious minorities and were spared the kind of religious divisions and tensions that continued to plague many European countries for centuries. Gustav I also created a centralized national administration, which was an essential for Sweden's era as a great European power from 1611 to 1718, generally referred to as the Age of Greatness. During this period, Sweden flourished economically, culturally, politically and militarily.

Today, it is difficult to imagine that a nation of only a million inhabitants could conduct successful military campaigns against the then great powers of Denmark, Poland and Russia. When the Thirty Years' War began to rage in the heart of Europe in 1618, Sweden initially kept out of the struggle and instead continued to concentrate on broadening its foothold in the eastern Baltic. The result of this policy was that the Baltic became a Swedish lake that could be used only under Swedish terms.

By contrast, Denmark rushed headlong into the tragic, ostensibly religious, Thirty Years' War and sought to expand its influence southward. Its military adventures in northern Germany provoked the ravishing of Jutland by marauding Catholic troops. In 1630 a battered Denmark was

forced to sue for peace; in the same year Sweden decided to enter the bloody struggle because of the Catholic armies' advances toward the Baltic area and the serious reversals that the protestant princes had suffered in the first half of the war. King Gustavus II Adolphus, grandson of Gustav Vasa, led his Swedish troops brilliantly. He marched them all the way to Bavaria, and by the winter of 1631–2, he could hold court in Mainz and Frankfurt am Main. He was killed in 1632 while leading his troops to victory against Catholic forces at Lützen.

His death sapped the initiative and dynamism from Sweden's policy. Nevertheless, when Denmark attempted to take advantage of the new political void in Sweden by launching a renewed attack, the Swedes were able to respond quickly and successfully. The Danes were forced to accept a peace, at Brömsebro in 1645, which underscored and solidified Sweden's predominance in Scandinavia. Not only did Denmark lose much of its territory to Sweden, but it had to renounce its right to levy customs on Swedish goods in Øresund, the narrow strait between the two countries.

Sweden emerged as a great power from the Peace of Westphalia, which formalized the end of the terrible Thirty Years' War in 1648. It received German holdings in Pomerania, the bishoprics of Verden and Bremen and the island of Rügen. When Denmark sought revenge in the Danish-Swedish War from 1657 to 1660, during which Sweden occupied Jutland and other

Danish islands several times, it suffered even further losses. In the Peace of Copenhagen in 1660, Denmark lost all its Swedish provinces and thereby all control over the Øresund Strait. The borders between Sweden and Denmark, which were established in this settlement, remain essentially unchanged today.

This peace signified the end of Danish dreams of being a great power. It bankrupted the country and laid waste to much of its territory. The outcome of the conflict underscored Sweden's position as the leading power in Northern Europe although Denmark occasionally disputed this status in the following decades. Swedish authority extended over Finland, Estonia, Latvia, Ingermanland (in which Leningrad is now located) and several coastal towns, and its empire continued to grow in later years. Sweden fought many wars to expand its empire, but it was fortunate in being able to fight them mostly on foreign soil.

During the 17th century Sweden also was able to acquire a colony in America that it called *Nya Sverige* ("New Sweden"). In 1638 it purchased from Indians a large tract that encompassed southeastern Pennsylvania (including the present city of Philadelphia), a chunk of New Jersey and most of Delaware. The capital of this colony was Christina, which was later renamed Wilmington, in Delaware. Swedish and Finnish Lutheran priests, merchants, soldiers, settlers and convicts were sent to New Sweden. The residents had relatively good contacts with the local Indians and were possibly the first settlers to introduce a particular Swedish invention into the New World: the log house. In 1655 the Dutch seized the colony following an intense border dispute, but Swedish continued to be spoken in some communities there until the late 18th century, and the Swedish Lutheran Church established its foothold in America.

The Swedes acquired from France the Caribbean island of Saint Barthélemy in 1784. Very few people settled on this island, whose major population was Black slaves, but the capital was named Gustavia after the Swedish king. In 1878 the island was sold back to France. The Swedish also established temporarily a colony called Cabo Corso in what is now Ghana in Africa. The capital was called Carlsborg, and the present-day city of Accra was the site of a Swedish factory. There were very few Swedes in this colony, beyond a governor, soldiers and merchants.

By the beginning of the 18th century Sweden's empire had so aroused the resentment of Denmark, Russia, Poland and Saxony (in Germany) that the latter powers decided to help themselves to some of the Swedish holdings. Despite some ini-

1660: Swedish dominance

The Nordic Countries

tial successes by the young king, Karl XII, the Swedes revealed that they had neither the manpower nor the resources to resist for long. The country had become exhausted by constant war, and at least by 1718 Sweden's decline could no longer be denied. Its northern German territories were ceded to Prussia and Hanover by 1720, and during the Great Northern War (1709–21) the Swedish armies were defeated in Russia, which resulted in Russian occupation of the Baltic countries and of southeastern Finland.

The Napoleonic Wars

These battles from the end of the 18th and beginning of the 19th centuries brought significant territorial changes to the region, and the ideas of the French Revolution influenced political developments in certain Nordic countries, especially Denmark and Norway. In the struggle that gripped all of Europe, Denmark tried in vain to remain neutral. However the English feared that the country might eventually side with Napoleon, so they challenged the Danish fleet a short distance from Copenhagen in 1801 and forced Denmark to enter a formal non-aggression pact with Britain. Six years later the British again grew nervous. They demanded that Denmark hand over to them its high seas fleet and threatened to shell Copenhagen if this ultimatum was not accepted. The Danes understandably balked at this impudence, but after British ships had bombarded the capital city for four days, the disheartened Danes handed over their navy. Out of spite, they then cast their lot with Napoleon against the British, but Denmark ultimately had to pay a high price for this folly. By 1813 it was bankrupt, and in the Treaty of Kiel a year later, it was compelled to hand Norway over to Sweden, which had fought on the side of the victors.

But the Norwegians, who wanted full independence, went to war against Sweden in order to prevent one form of domination from being exchanged for another. A Norwegian national assembly had adopted one of the most liberal constitutions of its time and had selected a Danish prince as its new king. But a combination of Swedish leniency and military power during the armed confrontation of 1814 persuaded the Norwegians to accept a new arrangement. The newly selected Norwegian king abdicated, and the first Norwegian Parliament (*Storting*) accepted the Swedish monarch as the king of Norway. Sweden assumed overall predominance in foreign policy and the right to appoint a Norwegian viceroy, who performed the normal duties of a prime minister. All Norwegian titles of nobility were abolished.

Norwegians were left with wide powers over their own affairs and with their own constitution, navy, army, customs and legislature. In effect, Norway had complete liberty and independence within its own boundaries. In the course of the 19th century, Norwegians solidified their sense of national identity and resisted any closer relations with Sweden. Finally in 1905 they requested in the form of a plebiscite complete independence. In response, troops on both sides of the border mobilized. However, after some internal debate, Sweden backed off and granted Norway its independence. The outcome was peaceful largely because Norway's departure from the union did not deprive Sweden of vital resources and wealth, and there were no Swedish communities left on the Norwegian side of the border. At the end of that year, Prince Carl of Denmark was chosen king and took the name Haakon VII.

Sweden's acquisition of Norway in 1814 was mild consolation for its loss of Finland five years earlier. Because Sweden had sided with Britain against the French, Napoleon had granted Russia in the Peace of Tilsit a free hand against Sweden. Thus, in 1809 Russia took Finland, a land it had dominated for a century. This bitter loss of a province that had belonged to Sweden for many centuries cost the Swedish king, Gustav IV, his crown in a bloodless *coup*. In the same year, the Swedish elite adopted The Instrument of Government (*Regeringsformen*), which, after the U.S. Constitution, is the second oldest written document of government in the world and which is one of the four that makes up Sweden's present constitution.

In 1810 the Swedes chose one of Napoleon's field marshals, Jean-Baptiste Bernadotte, as regent. Turning on his former leader, Bernadotte led Sweden into the struggle against France, a decision that secured allied support for the Swedish acquisition of Norway. After the short campaign against that country in 1814, Sweden withdrew from European conflicts and has not been at war since. Bernadotte was crowned king in 1818 with the title of King Karl XIV Johan; he ruled until 1844 and his descendants still hold the throne. It is an irony of history that the king had once been an ardent opponent of the monarchy in France and had even reportedly had the words indelibly tattooed on his arm: "Death to Kings!" It can be assumed that he never wore short sleeves while he occupied the throne of Sweden.

The 19th Century

The 19th century was for the Nordic countries one of major political, economic and social changes. Except for the war of Prussia and Austria against Denmark, which resulted in Denmark's loss of Schleswig and Holstein, containing about one-third of Denmark's European holdings (see Germany), this was a century of peace for the Nordic area. The French Revolution had produced a spark of democracy all over Europe, and the Nordic countries, especially Norway and Denmark, were touched by that spark. However, unlike many European countries at that time, the northern peoples already had traditions in which some groups had political representation, parliaments had some powers and monarchical authority

1814: Sweden loses Finland to Russia, gains Norway from Denmark

14

was limited by constitutions and other barriers.

These foundations for modern democracy were strengthened in the course of the 1800s. Following a short outbreak of civil unrest in 1848, Denmark proclaimed a *Grundlov* (charter) that formally declared the country to be a constitutional monarchy, with guaranteed civil liberties and with a parliament that shared power with the crown. In Norway, municipal self-government was introduced in 1837, and in 1884 the Swedish king recognized the principle of parliamentary government in Norway by agreeing to appoint a prime minister who had the approval of a majority in the *Storting*. In Sweden, political power passed gradually from an aristocracy of birth to a prosperous elite of common birth, and ultimately to the middle and working classes. By the 1870s all Nordic countries had functioning representative assemblies although full parliamentary government was not introduced into Norway until 1884, in Denmark until 1901 and in Sweden and Finland until 1917.

Democracy and Industrialization

This progress toward political democracy took place at a time of extremely rapid industrialization. It had come late to the region and created wrenching social problems, such as the breakdown of many rural communities, too rapid urbanization, excessive population growth, the weakening of family ties and alcoholism. Nevertheless, the democratic transformation came about without any mass violence. This peaceful change was due in part to the existence in these countries of political institutions and attitudes that could more easily adapt to changing conditions and to increasing demands for greater democratic participation in politics.

More and more citizens were granted the right to vote. Finland achieved universal suffrage in 1906, followed by Norway in 1913, Denmark in 1915 and Sweden in 1921. The absence of mass violence also was due to the steady increase in literacy and to the success of mass movements, such as those for workers' rights or temperance, which could articulate and channel important demands on the political system.

Emigration to America

A further factor that alleviated social tensions in these countries was emigration, which reached massive proportions by the 1860s and which enabled the most desperate to begin new lives elsewhere, especially in the U.S. The possibility of leaving for the New World helped to diminish militant discontent, which could have been seriously disruptive at a crucial

time when these people were adjusting to the modern age. Sweden produced the greatest waves of emigration—in the 1880s at least 325,000 out of a total population of 4.5 million left for the U.S., and in the following two decades, from 10,000 to 20,000 Swedes left for America each year. By the year 1900 one-fifth to one-fourth of all native-born Swedes were already living abroad. Nordic immigrants decisively shaped parts of America, particularly the northern midwestern states around and west of the Great Lakes, where the climate and landscape were very similar to the home country. The lives, problems and successes of these people in America were movingly portrayed in the three volumes on this subject written by one of Sweden's outstanding novelists, Vilhelm Moberg. The Swedish director, Jan Troell, filmed his story. Edna Ferber's moving "So Big" attested to the hardiness and strength of character of these emigrés. This flood to America is also evoked in the Emigrants House museum at Växjö.

Finland experienced waves of emigration to the U.S. and, later, to Sweden. Many Norwegians also set their sights toward the New World. In fact, no country, except for Ireland, sent such a large percentage of its people as emigrants to the U.S. as did Norway. The first shipload landed in New York City in 1825, and in the years 1866 to 1873, over 100,000 left Norway. In the course of the 19th century almost a third of all Norwegians resettled in America. From 1900 to 1910 more than 200,000 departed. By 1910, roughly 880,000 Norwegians had left their country for greener pastures in America, especially in the northern Midwest. Today more than five million Americans claim to be of Norwegian descent, more than the total population of Norway.

World War I

All Scandinavian countries were able to remain neutral during World War I, but the 1917 revolution in Russia gave the Finns the chance for which many had waited for centuries: the opportunity to declare their country's complete independence. The Danes were able to observe that the wartime threat to shipping was so great that their hold on some faraway islands was simply too tenuous. Thus, Denmark sold its part of the Virgin Islands to the United States in 1917. Denmark also profited from Germany's defeat in the war by winning international approval for a plebiscite in 1920 to determine to which country the population of the province of Schleswig wished to belong. In the North, 75% of the people voted to return to Denmark, but in southern Schleswig, 80% voted to remain with Germany. This latter

Statue of Norway's King Haakon VII

vote left a small, Danish-speaking minority in Germany that still exists today. For decades afterwards, the Danish monarchs would not accept this final loss of southern Schleswig, and they showed their resentment by refusing to set foot in that part of Germany. However, the present Danish queen, Margrete II, discarded this antiquated prejudice of her predecessors and enters the province as a welcomed foreign guest.

Depression and World War II

The citizens of the Nordic countries were not so successful in isolating themselves from the economic shockwaves that were generated by the 1929 stock market crash on Wall Street. Everywhere in the region the 1930s were lean times, filled with bankruptcies, unemployment and anxiety. They were also politically and militarily frightening times, with democratic experiments failing in many European countries, and with the European giants, Germany and the Soviet Union, awakening from their own internal chaos and diplomatic and military paralysis.

During this period all four main Nordic countries, like Nazi Germany, introduced eugenics laws, some of which remained in the statutes until 1976. From 1934 to 1974, 62,000 Swedish women were sterilized, often against their will, because they were judged to be rebellious, promiscuous, of low intelligence, or even of mixed blood. The purposes were to prevent "degeneration of the race" and to save the state the heavy cost of welfare for inferior human

The Nordic Countries

beings. Officials who believed in the science of racial biology and thought they were helping to construct an enlightened, progressive welfare state openly carried out the policy. Norway and Finland confirmed that each did the same to about 1,000 women.

As the clouds of war gathered in the skies over Europe, the Nordic countries tried to maintain a policy of neutrality. All tried to avoid any steps which especially Hitler, the German dictator since 1933, could interpret as being the slightest provocation. They harbored the hope that the League of Nations, the impotence of which had already been demonstrated on repeated occasions, would somehow be able to maintain the peace. Even after the Soviets attacked Finland at the end of 1939, which temporarily drove the Finns into the arms of the Germans and ultimately created an extremely precarious situation from which the Finns have never been able entirely to extract themselves, the Scandinavian countries did not consider themselves to be mortally threatened. Denmark had entered a ten-year nonaggression pact with Germany in May 1939 and declined thereafter to make any military preparations. Norway ordered that military precautions be taken only in the northernmost part of the country, which touches Russia. Sweden peered nervously into the horizon.

The Danish during the War

Denmark's strategic location astride the exits from the Baltic Sea to the North Sea, as well as its proximity to Germany, made the small nation perched on top of the continent's most dynamic and aggressive power at the time an irresistible victim. Hitler sent his troops to occupy it in April 1940; with the ominous tones of German heavy bombers in their ears, the Danes offered no significant resistance to the forceful occupation of their country. In return the Germans promised to respect Denmark's independence, integrity and sovereignty and to allow the Danes to have their own government. It was the only occupied country placed under the authority of the German foreign ministry, and for a while it could hold the only elections in occupied Europe. The Danish government remained in the country, and King Christian X went horseback riding every day in Copenhagen in order to demonstrate that the leaders were still there.

Nevertheless, they had to bend to many unpleasant German demands, and the Germans selection of the Hotel D'Angleterre in the heart of Copenhagen as its military headquarters served as a constant reminder to the Danes of who exactly was in charge. They had to orient their economy exclusively toward German needs, to

Denmark is free! 1945

join the anti-Comintern Pact, to crack down on communist political activity within Denmark and ultimately to tolerate the official Nazi persecution of Jews. Hitler called it a "model protectorate."

After a wave of strikes and sabotage in August 1943, Germany ordered the deportation of Danish Jews, who were never required to wear a yellow Star of David. But historians believe that the German leader in Denmark, Werner Best, leaked the plans to Danish politicians, who could alert the country's 7,800 Jews to go into hiding. With a haven just a couple of miles across the sea, all but 500 were able to escape to Sweden. Unlike elsewhere in occupied Europe, Danes who helped Jews were not sentenced to death, and thousands hid and helped Jews to flee. The Danish government continued to feed and diplomatically protect several hundred Danish Jews in Theresianstadt concentration camp. In the end, only 116 Danish Jews, or 1.5% of the total, perished in the Holocaust.

The Danish population practiced a policy of giving the cold shoulder toward the occupation forces. Sometimes they chose not to hide their sentiments, such as in 1943 when it became fashionable to wear knitted caps with the colors of the British Royal Air Force. Quite early a Danish resistance movement sprang up, but for a while the Danish government opposed it out of fear that its policy of cooperation in order to save the country from destruction would be undermined. However, the government's position became increasingly untenable, and in August 1943 the Danish king and parliament stopped functioning. The center of resistance activity became the

"Freedom Council," whose membership included former politicians and officers.

The German occupation forces struck back by arresting resistance fighters, police and Jews, but they could never eradicate the Danish opposition, which enjoyed the sympathy and support of almost all Danes. For this resistance activity the alliance against Hitler recognized Denmark as a victorious power after the British had liberated the country on May 5, 1945. After the war Denmark punished those Danes who had collaborated too closely with the Germans. Sixty years later, in 2005, half (51%) of Danes admitted in a poll that their relationship with Germans is still influenced by the occupation.

At the same time, the 60th commemoration unleashed vigorous public criticism of all the political parties that had cooperated with the German occupation authorities. Some historians now argue that there was more collaboration than resistance during the war. This tension is also reflected in contemporary Danish literature. Some authors, such as Thorkild Hansen in his three-volume biography of Knut Hamsun, have dealt with Denmark's experiences under Nazi occupation as seen through the eyes of the resistance movement. By contrast, Ulrik Gräs published in 2000 the first Danish novel, *Berusede by* (*Dizzy City*), which approaches the occupation period from the point of view of a grandson of a provincial town mayor who, like many of the political establishment during the war, collaborated with the German authorities in order to minimize Danes' suffering.

Britain occupied Denmark's possession of Iceland and the Faroe Islands at the beginning of the war in order to prevent them from falling into enemy hands. In 1941 the U.S. relieved the British in Iceland and, with the approval of local authorities, has retained a military base on the island ever since. The long severance of Iceland from the mother country after the outbreak of the war enabled the Icelanders, who in 1918 had already been granted an autonomy statute for domestic affairs, to declare their complete independence from Denmark in 1944. Greenland was occupied by American troops and was made a temporary protectorate under U.S. authority. After the war it was returned to Danish jurisdiction although American troops continued to be stationed there by agreement with Denmark.

Norway and the War

Norway, with its long coast facing not only Britain, but also the North Sea and North Atlantic also presented an irresistibly tempting target for German expansion. Unfortunately, Norway had made military preparations only in the

North, and its troops were inexperienced and poorly equipped. Therefore, it was not well prepared when Hitler sent his forces against the country on April 9, 1940, the same day on which his troops occupied Denmark. To the Germans' surprise, the Norwegian government rejected the German ultimatum to surrender peacefully and to cooperate, as the Danes had chosen to do. The king, government and parliament withdrew from Oslo toward the North, from where they conducted war against German troops. Further, by sinking the German cruiser, Blücher, Norway was able to transport its entire gold reserves out of the country.

In the confusion of withdrawal to the north, the chief of the Norwegian National Socialist Party (*Nasjonal Samling*) and former defense minister, Vidkun Quisling, read a proclamation to the Norwegian people in the afternoon of April 9. Quisling criticized the government for turning down Germany's "peaceful" offer of cooperation, and he declared himself prime minister and foreign minister. His call to the Norwegian troops to lay down their arms merely stiffened the army's resolve to fight. The Norwegians so despised him that the Germans had to dismiss him as prime minister on April 15 although he was reappointed in 1942. The name *Quisling* is now inseparably associated with the very concept of treason against one's own country.

Not until May 5 was the southern part of the country conquered. With the help of Polish land forces and British naval forces, the Norwegians fought bitterly against German troops in the northern part of the country, and the Germans, unused to the bitter cold, suffered considerable losses in

Norway's Quisling returning the salute of a German officer

taking such strategically important objectives as the port of Narvik from which Swedish iron ore was shipped to Germany. By June 7, the Germans had conquered the northern part and had become the undisputed power in Scandinavia.

Once it was clear that the Germans would win, the Norwegian Parliament gave King Haakon VII full powers, and the latter, accompanied by the crown prince and the cabinet left the country for London, where he established a government in exile and directed lively resistance against the occupation forces throughout the war. His family found refuge in the U.S., and Crown Princess Märtha was a frequent guest in the White House. The current king, Harald V, spent the war years in Bethesda, Maryland. Norwegian ships protected allied convoys on their perilous Atlantic crossing, and Norway lost 200 ships and 1,300 seamen from 1940–2. Americans showed their gratitude in 1945: when Germans sank the SS Henry Bacon in the Arctic Sea, there was not enough space in the lifeboats. American crewmembers relinquished their seats so that the 19 Norwegian refugees aboard would survive.

Within Norway, the German commissioner, Josef Terboven, governed with the assistance of some cooperative Norwegian civil servants. Others were not cooperative, as so vividly depicted by John Steinbeck in his novel, "The Moon Is Down"; active and passive resistance was widespread. A few small units of the Norwegian Army were also evacuated to Britain, and they subsequently absorbed other Norwegians who fled by boat through icy seas or were already abroad. These highly motivated units, as well as local resistance movements, conducted sabotage and small attacks against the alien regime.

Their number grew in 1944 when they were permitted to equip Norwegian refugees in Sweden, who could then join in the attacks against the Germans and Norwegian collaborators. They received a steady stream of weapons, ammunition and materials from Britain. Unfortunately, these bold actions often provoked Nazi reprisals against civilians, and about 35,000 Norwegians were sent to prisons or concentration camps during the occupation. These included 1,000 teachers who, like most of their colleagues, refused to teach Nazi principles in the schools. Also, 95% of the pastors either were dismissed or they voluntarily gave up their positions because of their almost universal rejection of the "new order."

Not until May 7, 1945, did the unwanted foreign domination come to an end. On that day the joy and relief of the people, who had won their independence

only 40 years earlier, was almost boundless. Quisling was tried and quickly executed in September, and general elections were held in October. In 1946 Trygve Lie of Norway became the first Secretary-General of the United Nations; his successor was a Swede, Dag Hammarskjöld.

When Thorbjørn Jagland became prime minister in 1996 his first official act was to commit Norway to pay compensation for property stolen from Jews by the Quisling government during the war. Despite the difficulties of identifying, locating, and allocating the repayments, Norway became the first European country, except Germany, to make this commitment.

In 2002 parliament voted overwhelmingly to remove another black spot by offering compensation for the offspring of Norwegian mothers and German soldiers. These children suffered serious discrimination and scorn in school and at work. They were often forced to live under terrible circumstances after the war, and many of their mothers were deported or interned as collaborators. As an apology the government offered $3,276 to 12,000 of them in 2005, but 154 took their case for adequate compensation to Europe's human rights court two years later.

Sweden

Only Sweden escaped foreign occupation and active participation in the war. However, it was isolated from the outside world, and, because of its obvious military inferiority to Germany, it made concessions that created some animosity among Danes and Norwegians. Many Swedes themselves quietly resented these compromises, but most saw no reasonable alternative at the time.

Sweden conducted trade with Nazi Germany, which relied especially on Swedish iron, steel and ball bearings. In some cases, the Swedish police shared information with the *Gestapo* (German secret police), and in the early war years the government tried to muzzle the press to prevent stories unflattering to Nazi Germany. Swedes suppressed most communist activity in their own country in order to please Berlin's leaders. The Swedish government gave in to pressure to permit a German division to move across Swedish territory in order to reach the Russian front. It tolerated German violation of Swedish airspace for military purposes. Finally, the Swedish central bank and the wealthy Wallenberg financial empire bought looted gold from Germany, which provided Germany with additional funds to engage in profitable trade with Sweden and other neutral countries. The Swedish government agreed in 1996 to launch an investigation into allegations that looted Nazi gold had been deposited in Swedish banks, that

The Nordic Countries

Holocaust victims had deposited money in Sweden of which their heirs received only a part, and that Swedes had extended loans and other financial help to Nazi Germany. The Wallenberg family, which continues to dominate Sweden's business sector today, agreed to open its files to examiners.

After denying refuge to fleeing Jews in the early war years, Sweden dispatched the 31-year-old Raoul Wallenberg to Hungary in July 1944 under diplomatic cover on a mission funded by the United States to distribute Swedish safe-conduct passes to Jews. He courageously bribed, tricked and bullied Nazi officials in Budapest to spare the lives of 20,000 Hungarian Jews. In January 1945 invading Soviet forces wrongly arrested him on espionage charges while he was traveling to meet their commander. He died mysteriously in Soviet captivity. Not until 2000 did Russian authorities acknowledge publicly that he had been held in a Soviet prison two and a half years until his death, and a Russian investigative committee concluded that in 1947 he had been executed in the infamous Lubyanka prison in downtown Moscow.

Despite these unfortunate compromises, it should not be forgotten that Sweden granted refuge to thousands of Hitler's opponents, who would otherwise have ended in Nazi prisons or death camps. Such important postwar political leaders as Willy Brandt of Germany and Bruno Kreisky of Austria were able to live and work in Sweden during the war. As victorious powers, both Denmark and Norway took part in the occupation of Germany, and Brandt even returned to Germany as a Norwegian citizen and wearing a Norwegian officer's uniform. Undoubtedly they brought back to their own countries, which between the wars had been severely polarized politically, lasting impressions of Scandinavian moderation, tolerance and democratic spirit. These were qualities that were badly needed in the new beginning that Europe made after 1945.

Because neutrality had failed to protect all of the Scandinavian countries from armed aggression, Denmark, Norway and Sweden discussed the possibility of forming a Nordic Defense Community after the war. However, these talks collapsed over the question of whether this alliance should seek the backing of the Western powers, as Norway wished, or whether it should try to remain free of all Great Power conflicts, as Sweden wanted. Although there was and remains a strong emotional attachment of the Nordic region to neutrality, Norway, Denmark and Iceland decided to break with a long tradition and join NATO. Sweden and Finland chose to move away from their strict neutrality in 1994 and join NATO's "Partnership for Peace," a form of affiliation short of full membership.

Postwar Attitudes and Cold War

All Nordic countries espouse political values oriented toward the rest of Europe and North America. All had spoken or unspoken fears about Soviet military power and about a possible Soviet military threat to the Nordic area. All are aware that the region has considerable strategic importance. The exits from the Baltic Sea lead through narrow straits between Sweden and Denmark. Two of the countries—Finland and Norway—border on Russia, and Norway and Russia had different opinions as to exactly where the border between their territories in the North should be. Norway is the northern flank of NATO. It is astride the waters which separate the northwestern part of Russia from most other NATO countries and which lead to the Atlantic Ocean, where the NATO countries' most important shipping lanes are located. Finally, all are economically advanced countries with valuable industrial resources and high levels of technology.

Although the Nordic countries share common values and defense needs, they have chosen different roads to military security, while retaining a common objective of preserving stability in the region. There is no strategic bloc or single military alliance in the Nordic world. Iceland has no army at all, but relies on the American Icelandic Defense Force for its own protection. All four other countries have compulsory military service. Norway and Denmark are founding members of NATO, but neither permits the stationing of nuclear weapons or foreign troops on its soil during peacetime. The only exception is Greenland, where an agreement between the U.S. and Denmark enables the U.S. to station conventional (non-nuclear) forces.

Sweden pursues a policy of nonalignment in peacetime and armed neutrality in wartime. Finland is also nonaligned, but it entered a treaty of friendship and mutual assistance with the Soviet Union and agreed to limit the size and quality of its armed forces. That treaty is no longer valid. None permits the stationing of nuclear or chemical weapons on its territory. However, Norway and Denmark prefer not entirely to tie their hands on the question of deploying nuclear weapons on their soil in time of war, even though both plan to defend themselves by means of conventional weapons.

All Nordic nations had the goal of mutual restraint toward the Soviet Union, but not of total accommodation with that country, whose political values the Nordics abhorred. A central guideline in all Nordic foreign policies is to maintain the established equilibrium and low level of tension in the area. They would never be able to rely on their own strength for protection. This is a rather large area with an extremely small population. If one disregards Greenland, the world's largest island, the Nordic area is still larger than Great Britain, France, Germany, Portugal and the BENELUX countries combined. But its population, at 24.4 million, is only one-tenth that of those countries. Also, the Nordic countries would have to have enormous navies and mobile land and air forces in order to protect such far-flung possessions as the Faroes, Jan Mayen, Svalbard, Greenland, Bouvet and Peter I (tiny South Atlantic islands, not far from Norway's claim in Antarctica).

The Kola Peninsula

The collapse of the Soviet Union changed the threat to the Nordic Region, which was under the shadow of the Kola Peninsula, an area at the northwestern tip of Russia saturated with nuclear weapons. At Murmansk (60 miles east of the Norwegian border) and the small, ice-free coast next to the northern tip of Norway, Russia has its only naval and air bases with open access to the Atlantic. The late Sir Winston Churchill described Russia's problem of access to the open sea as "a giant with pinched nostrils." It contains early warning and air defense facilities, as well as major naval bases in every fjord between Pechenga on the Norwegian border and Murmansk. The peninsula is the home port of the Northern Fleet, one of four main Russian fleets and one with a Kiev-class aircraft carrier, about a dozen Kresta missile cruisers and 155 submarines, including more than 65% of the strategic missile bearing subs and 60% of its nuclear powered ones.

The nuclear threat to the Nordic region has shifted from one of weaponry to one of waste: 71 of the submarines were judged in 1995 to be derelict and still have their nuclear fuel on board because there is no place else to put it. Two-thirds of the nuclear waste ever dumped into the world's seas lies off Kola, and much more radioactive waste is stored in ships so rickety they cannot be moved from their moorings near downtown Murmansk. The Kola Nuclear Power Station, which provides 60% of the peninsula's power, is one of the world's least safe and suffered a near meltdown in 1993. Norway and the other Nordic nations show a great interest in clearing the area of nuclear waste. Norwegians sought in 1998–9 to confront another danger to stability in the North: desperation on the part of a million Russians in the impoverished Kola Peninsula, the only place other than Poland where Russia borders a NATO member. Norway provided tons of food, warm clothing and medicine.

In 1988 Sweden and Russia settled their long-standing dispute over their economic zones in the Baltic Sea, which separates their mainlands by 200 miles. The agreement, which deals with fishing and exploration rights, gives Sweden 75% of the disputed area and the Russians 25%. In 1993 Russia and the Nordic countries demonstrated their willingness to work together, particularly on environmental protection, by signing an agreement on cooperation in the Barents region.

All Nordic countries exercise restraint. Norway, not the U.S., or other NATO countries, patrols the Norwegian and Barents seas. No NATO maneuvers take place in the northernmost Norwegian county of Finnmark, thus always leaving a distance of at least 480 miles (800 km.) between any NATO maneuver and the Norwegian-Russian border. Both Norway and Denmark insist that attacks against their own territories can best be prevented if the aggressor can be persuaded in advance that both would call in foreign reinforcements very early in any conflict.

To underscore this, the Norwegians signed an agreement with the U.S. in 1981 providing for the advanced storage of heavy equipment and for Norwegian support of an American marine amphibious brigade, which could be rushed to Norway in an emergency. Reflecting the restraint Norway always exercises, its leaders decided at the same time that the depots would be located in central—not northern—Norway, where any military confrontation would, at least initially, take place. They did permit the construction in 1999 of a powerful American-made radar in Vardo, 40 miles from the Russian border. Its purpose is ostensibly to monitor space debris, but Russia complains that it could track its missile launchings and be linked to an American missile defense system. Russia is still a major worrying presence on the edge of the Nordic world. How it develops economically, politically and militarily greatly influences security in the North. No country there can ignore Russia.

Military Restraint and Preparedness

The fact that the Scandinavian states exercise military restraint does not mean that they are unprepared to contribute to their own defense. All except Iceland have compulsory active military service for males, lasting 9 months in Denmark, 12 months in Norway and 7–15 months in Sweden (depending on the branch), and followed in all three countries by reserve duty. In Sweden's case it ends at age 47. In 2003 Sweden's female defense minister, Leni Bjorklund, ordered the military to study the possibility of compulsory military service for women, something that only Israel has. "In an equal society, I see no obstacles to a sex-neutral military service. With modern technology, there are tasks for which women are well suited."

Norway's 24,000-soldier active peacetime force, supported by 45,250 home guard, could be increased rapidly to 219,000. Its armed forces are being streamlined and restructured to enable it to shift from its traditional focus on contributing UN peacekeeping forces to deploying combat units and special operations forces

for NATO and to protecting their vulnerable oil rigs and infrastructure from terrorist attacks. Its lack of rapid reaction capability was brought home in 1999 when the troops it sent to Kosovo arrived three months after the war was over. In 2003 NATO opened a Joint Warfare Center near the port of Stavanger to operate alliance training programs and to develop doctrine making NATO more agile and lethal. In 2009 it moved its operational command north of the Arctic Circle in order to boost its northern presence.

Sweden's 13,000 regular force could be increased over tenfold to 242,000 in wartime 14 days after mobilization. Since 1965 Denmark's armed forces have been roughly halved to 26,585 troops with 53,500 home guards, and Finland's comparable figures are 22,600 active duty and 435,000 (declining over time to 340,000) reserve soldiers. Denmark deployed 690 troops to Afghanistan, Norway 480, Sweden 430 and Finland 165.

The navies of Sweden, Norway and Denmark are equipped with submarines, frigates and torpedo and fast boats. These craft are designed for the defense of their very long and meandering coastlines, which offer so many hiding places for friendly and enemy ships alike. Since 1986 women are permitted to serve on Danish combat ships. A Danish general or admiral always heads a special Baltic Approaches Command, which must try to control the entrances to and exits from the Baltic Sea in wartime. Denmark has a limited number of troops stationed in northern Germany. It has troops in a Northeast Multinational Corps, composed also of Polish and German soldiers, located in Szczecin, on the Polish side of the German border. The air forces of both Denmark and Norway are equipped with American F-16 aircraft, parts of which are produced in Denmark and other NATO countries. In 2006 Norway deployed several of them in Afghanistan, joining 400 Norwegian soldiers already there.

Because it is in NATO, Denmark allowed itself the luxury of spending only about 2% of its GDP for defense, which prompted some critics to speak of "Denmarkization," a term which referred to the alleged inclination of a small country to assume that larger and more powerful countries will come to their rescue in time of emergency, regardless of what the smaller country spent on defense during peacetime. The Danes resented the charge of "Denmarkization" because they do not, in fact, neglect their country's defense. Both Denmark and Norway sent combat and mine-clearing troops to Afghanistan in 2001–2002, and their special forces joined in fierce battles to mop up powerful pockets of al Qaeda and Taliban fight-

The Nordic Countries

ers. To help stabilize and rebuild the war-torn country, Denmark sent 500 troops to Iraq, and 164 Norwegian soldiers were stationed in the British-controlled area around Basra, Iraq. In 2005, Norway announced the withdrawal of all of its military forces from Iraq, but it continued to train senior Iraqi security personnel at the NATO Joint Warfare Center outside Stavanger.

Nordic reactions to the Anglo-American war that unseated Iraq's dictator Saddam Hussein in March–May 2003 differed. Public opinion was solidly critical in all the countries. However, then Danish Prime Minister Fogh Rasmussen announced: "As a small European country we would rather rely on a superpower's security guarantees than on a European one based on a French, German and British security balance." Denmark sent a submarine and a ship to support its NATO allies. This was the first time since 1864 that Denmark was a belligerent. It deployed troops to Iraq after the war to supplement the policing efforts of the U.S., Britain and Poland. Iceland also approved of the military action, while the other three Nordic countries expressed regret that armed force had been used.

Although two-thirds of NATO member countries have women in their armed forces, and Belgium, the Netherlands and Norway theoretically allow women in all assignments, only Denmark has made real steps toward imposing full equality in all branches. This move was prompted by passage of a comprehensive equal rights law in 1978, and the military was compelled to comply with it. A four-year experiment with assigning females to naval combat duties indicated that male-female crews outperform single-sex units and that women recruits are more highly motivated than men. Therefore, Danish women are now assigned to all naval billets but submarines, and similar experiments are being made in the army and air force. Because of the country's declining birthrate, women may become a crucial factor in maintaining Danish force levels.

Within NATO in 2003 Norway was second only to the U.S. in per capita defense spending ($920). Sweden spends more on military security than Denmark; it expends over 2% of its GDP (down from 5% in the 1950s), or about 10% of the total state budget. Its policy of nonparticipation in alliances in peacetime and neutrality (which it retained upon entry into EU in 1995) during wartime is still supported by many Swedes. They are willing to underscore this policy by maintaining a strong total defense capacity, backed up by a well-organized civil defense. The aim of the Swedish defense is to raise the costs to an aggressor to such a level that an at-

tacker, though possibly defeating Sweden in the end, would ultimately lose more than it would gain from such an attack. Such preparedness would, the Swedes hope, dissuade any power from attacking the country in the first place.

There were some real problems with this strategy. If an unprincipled power with vastly superior armaments were to achieve overwhelming victory in Europe, it would be able to attack Sweden successfully after initially ignoring it. Swedish military strength has declined: its air force has lost half its military aircraft, and its navy has lost a third of its ships. In 2001 it scaled back its around-the-clock naval operations to a 9 a.m.-5 p.m. shift as a result of budget cuts. This partly explains why the Swedes cannot track submarines effectively and why their antisubmarine force can operate only in one area at a time. Of course, the Swedish military still packs quite a wallop. After the Soviet Union's demise, Sweden continued to modernize its military. However, in 1995 the defense budget was cut so severely that the country was by 2010 left with only 13,000 active-duty soldiers. Its top commanders fear that Sweden might have to abandon all pretence that it can repel an attacker without calling for outside help.

Both Sweden and Finland are reconsidering their policies of nonalignment. If Baltic entry had occurred without antagonizing Russia, then both states would have seen less danger in joining. Swedish forces already participate in NATO exercises and deploy forces to northern Afghanistan. Both countries send peacekeepers to the Balkans. The majority of citizens in these two Nordic neighbors still oppose NATO entry; a 2004 poll revealed that 44% of Swedes oppose membership, 22% favor it, and 34% were undecided. But that may change over time, especially if conflict were to break out close by.

In order not to be dependent upon other powers in wartime, Sweden produces about 80% of the weapons (and all the fighter aircraft) that its own armed forces need. In 1987 it unveiled a new Gripen supersonic fighter. Swedish manufacturers may no longer be able to produce the bulk of the country's weapons, and the government is faced with a situation where it is often cheaper to buy abroad than at home. To lower unit costs for its weapons and to earn foreign exchange, Swedish arms industries do sell abroad, despite widespread domestic opposition. Arms constitute 2% of its exports. SAAB exports aircraft, Hägglunds tanks and Kockums submarines. With Swedish defense spending inching downward, Bofors and other Swedish companies hoped to receive lucrative orders from other countries as well, especially from those in NATO.

Sweden creates difficulties for itself by pretending that it sells arms only to countries that would be unlikely to use them and which do not violate human rights. Sales to war zones are against the law. However, many of the 40 or so countries to which it sells arms do not meet those standards. By the turn of the century Nordic arms companies are cooperating with each other more and more, co-producing, for example, ammunition and gunpowder and procuring jointly such big-ticket items as helicopters and submarines. This would have been unthinkable for neutral Sweden and Finland during the Cold War.

Foreign Policies

Even if the five Nordic countries have different answers to questions related to defense, their foreign policies are similar in the sense that all are very active members in international organizations, especially the UN, and all but Iceland participate in UN peacekeeping operations. Norway provides more UN peacekeepers, in proportion to its population than any other country. Each of the countries maintains a permanent quick-response stand-by force that can be placed at the disposal of the UN for deployment to world trouble spots.

A joint Nordic battalion operated in the Balkans to prevent war in Macedonia. As did all Nordic peacekeepers in Bosnia and Kosovo, it served under NATO command even though Sweden and Finland do not belong to that alliance. Sweden maintains a permanent delegation accredited to NATO headquarters in Brussels. In 2003 NATO established a Joint Warfare Center in Jåttå in Stavanger, Norway, to help in the transformation of NATO's European forces.

All but Denmark participated in the EU-led peacekeeping force in Macedonia after the EU assumed command from NATO in 2003. Denmark sat it out because it had opted out of the EU's European Security and Defense Policy (ESDP), whose Headline Goal calls for a 60,000-troop rapid reaction force to be used when NATO and the U.S. choose not to be involved in a crisis. Both Sweden and Finland made troops available to this EU force; Sweden offered 2,000 soldiers including air and naval components. However, as neutrals, both resisted a mutual defense clause in a new EU constitution that would have forced them to come to the aid of a partner under military attack. Since 2004 all five help Balkan countries modernize their military training and tactics.

All were active proponents of East-West détente and vocal opponents of South Africa's *apartheid* policy. In 1988 Sweden, which has a tradition of mediating between Arabs and Jews, played a crucial role in establishing a dialogue between the U.S. and the Palestine Liberation Organization (PLO).

In 1993 Norway brokered a landmark agreement between Israel and the PLO that paved the way to the beginnings of Palestinian autonomy in 1994. In 1999 Oslo again became the venue for two days of meetings between Israeli Prime Minister Ehud Barak, Palestinian leader Yasir Arafat, and Bill Clinton, who became the first U.S. president to visit Norway. Norway had also hosted a historic cease-fire deal in 1996 between the Guatemalan government and rebel guerrillas. It subsequently played a mediator role in Myanmar. In 2000 its foreign minister was appointed to a fact-finding inquiry into the causes of the Palestinian-Israeli upheaval. In 2002 Norwegian government officials led the negotiations that resulted in a cease-fire and peace agreement in Sri Lanka. It also lent a hand in Sudan, and in Zimbabwe its monitors remained in place during the 2002 elections after the EU staff was thrown out. However, in 2002 it turned down a request by Chechen guerrillas to broker a peaceful end to a Moscow theater siege. In March 2008 the UN selected as its new envoy to Afghanistan a senior Norwegian diplomat, Kai Eide.

Following the devastating tsunami in Indonesia at Christmas time 2004, the Finnish government invited to Helsinki representatives of that country and of the rebellious Aceh province for peace talks, mediated by former President Martti Ahtisaari, to find a solution to that deadly insurrection. In July 2005 they agreed to end their three-decade conflict.

All strive to maintain especially close relations with developing countries and are among the world's most generous donors to development aid, as measured by percentage of GDP. In 2010 Norway and Sweden were the world's leaders at .96% and .93%, with Denmark in third at .82% and Finland in 10th place at .40%. The UN goal is .7% of GDP, and the U.S., while the world's largest donor in total funding, gave a paltry .16%. In 2007 the OECD placed the Nordics at the top in terms of the effectiveness and impartiality of their relief efforts to crisis-affected nations. The Swedish government shifted its priorities to newly independent democracies in the Baltics and Eastern Europe. It reduced aid to Vietnam and cut it to Cuba altogether.

Nordic Cooperation

A major emphasis of all their foreign policies is revealed by the fact that each has a minister for Nordic cooperation. The nerve center of this broad regional collab-

Scandinavian students at the College of Europe, Bruges

oration is the Nordic Council, which began its work in 1953. In all, it has 78 members elected by the national parliaments from among their own ranks, and it is broken down into several standing committees, which submit proposals to the plenary sessions. Members of the various governments also take part in the discussions, but they do not have the right to vote. The Nordic Council has no sovereign authority; its decisions, which must be unanimous, are merely unbinding recommendations to the five governments. Critics charge that member governments ignore the council's advice unless they planned to do it anyway. Also, with 23 committees, 74 Nordic institutions, 152 committees of inquiry and working groups, and 2,000 ongoing projects, the exasperated Danish minister for Nordic cooperation declared in 1988 that the system had gone mad.

Nevertheless, the Council does discuss many important pieces of legislation before they are passed by national parliaments. This has created a greater uniformity than is found in most other regions in a wide variety of laws dealing with such matters as marriage and child custody, contracts and commercial practices, copyright and patents, transportation and maritime law. The Council has a presidium with a standing secretariat in Stockholm, a secretariat for general affairs in Oslo and one for cultural affairs in Copenhagen.

The five countries decided in 1954 to form a single labor market, in which a citizen of one member country can work in any other country without a work or residence permit and can travel within the region without a passport. In 1955 all agreed that citizens from other Nordic countries should receive the same pension, unemployment and health and welfare benefits as each country's own citizens. The result is that almost a million persons have emigrated from one Nordic land to the other,

and in Sweden 60% of all immigrants are from other Nordic countries.

The move toward greater unity received a setback in the late 1950s when a Nordic Customs Union and a wider Nordic Economic Union failed to materialize. Nevertheless, these nations continued to tighten their links with each other. In 1971 a Nordic Ministerial Council was set up to provide a basis for closer practical collaboration among the five governments. In 1973 a treaty dealing with transport affairs went into effect, and for many years a single airline, SAS, has been operated by private and public funds from Sweden, Norway and Denmark. Finally, a Nordic Investment Bank, with its seat in Helsinki, was created in 1975 to finance investment and export projects of common Nordic interest.

The economic interests of the countries are by no means identical. As Iceland's former president, Vigdís Finnbogadóttir, commented, we "are a family, not quintuplets." By 1995 only Norway and Iceland remained in EFTA (European Free Trade Association), which had been founded in Stockholm. The five have different approaches to Europe and its integration although all abide by the EEA agreement with the EU, which involves free trade in everything but farm and fish products.

The transfer of sovereignty involved in EU membership challenges the strong national identity that each Nordic nation feels. Danish scholar Lykke Friis put it this way: "All Nordic countries are struggling to find a credible fit between their national identity and the EU. This fit is especially difficult because Nordic identity is about being better than Europe."

In a host of international comparisons, Nordic countries regularly come out on top: Finns are said to be the world's most competitive (followed by the U.S., Sweden and Denmark) and least corrupt. Norwegians have the highest quality of life; all are the most generous donors of development assistance. Women are treated equally more than anywhere else. For instance, a planned soccer game between Muslim imams and Swedish priests had to be cancelled in 2007 because the Swedes could not accept their opponents' demand that women priests be kept off the field. In a 2006 study of the success countries have had in closing the gender gap, the Nordic countries were on top, with the U.S. at 22d place. Sweden and Norway achieved the highest level of child welfare in a 2007 study. Transparency International's Corruption Perceptions index places the Nordic countries at the top for lack of corruption; the U.S. ranks 20th. Sweden was ranked in 2007 as the best EU country for innovation, followed by Finland, Germany and Denmark. In terms of global competitive-

The Nordic Countries

ness, Finland, Sweden and Denmark were ranked in 2006 at the top, right behind Switzerland, and Nordic productivity is 17% above the OECD average. Finally, in the Yale and Columbia universities' index of environmental performance, Sweden was first with the other four Nordics in the top 11; the U.S. was 66th.

Finns are the most enthusiastic about being in EU and are proud of being the only Nordic country to adopt the common currency, the euro. Denmark has the most nuanced attitude about the EU, to which it belongs. It has won a record four "opt-outs," including from the euro. In a 2000 referendum, Danes voted 53% to 47% to remain outside the euro zone. The Swedes joined the EU, but are divided over whether it was a good idea; they have rejected the euro for now. The Norwegians voted twice to stay out of the EU, and only a small minority in Iceland wants to join.

Sweden had second thoughts about going through with a plan it made with Denmark to build a 16-kilometer (10-mile) tunnel and road-and-rail bridge over the sound from Malmö to Copenhagen. This is the realization of a centuries-old dream to link the Scandinavian peninsula to mainland Europe. It enhances the growing sense among 700 million Europeans that they all belong on a single continent. The Oresund (UHR-ah-sohnd) double-decker bridge, completed in 2000, is a world-class technological achievement and an admirable aesthetic success. The upper deck is a four-lane highway, and the lower level is for rail traffic. From the Swedish coast it arches for five miles over windswept waves before descending to a 2.5-mile-long artificial island. Finally it drops beneath the sea into a 2.3-mile tunnel at the Danish end. Drivers and passengers must then cross two other bridges linking Denmark's main islands to arrive at the northern tip of the European mainland.

This $2 billion project created a city region of 3.5 million people, which is now one of the fastest growing regions in Europe. In the seven years after the bridge's completion, 20 billion euros of investment flowed in, especially in the biotech and pharmaceutical fields. Encompassing a 60-mile radius, it produces half of Denmark's and a tenth of Sweden's combined GDP. Within that region are a dozen Danish and Swedish universities with 10,000 researchers and 120,000 students. Long a depressed area, Malmö is now Sweden's fastest-growing city, in part because of the influx of foreigners. For years Denmark had stalled the plans until its own project to build a bridge linking the island of Zealand to the Jutland peninsula was underway. Although only a disappointing 9,000 cars carrying 14,000 commuters use the bridge each day, largely because of the

steep expense (62 euros round trip, half for commuters), it does provide the kind of easy access across the border to facilitate smuggling. An estimated one-third of beer consumed in Sweden has been brought in from outside, and smuggling and unregulated work account for an estimated 5%–10% of Sweden's economy.

Swedish opponents openly expressed another concern: that the moral environment of Malmö could be undermined by Copenhagen's laxer policies on drugs, alcohol and prostitution. A concrete focus of their fears is the "Free City of Christiania," founded by squatters in 1971 who took over a former army barracks near Copenhagen. Occupied by anarchists, hippies, drug pushers and "down-and-outs," this settlement became so dangerous that most Danes, the police and municipal buses usually avoided it. In 1993 the government failed to persuade the Danish parliament to evict Christiania's "citizens." In 1989 the leftist experiment established its own liaison office with the Danish Ministry of Defense, which owns the site, provides water, power and other services free of charge, and accepts Christiania as permanent. Two-thirds of the residents of this settlement live on public welfare.

Although still seedy by Danish standards, Christiania had become somewhat bourgeois and gentrified by the 21st century. Its aging hippies and counterculture residents are less dangerous now. By 2004 it had become Copenhagen's second-most popular tourist attraction, with an eccentric assortment of cafes, clubs, restaurants, weird architecture and open-air concerts. However, it remained Europe's largest and most visible cannabis market, with stalls along the streets. When Denmark's center-right government decided in 2004 to crack down on both the use and sale of illegal cannabis, police raided Christiania, seized assets and arrested dozens of people.

Some of the same concerns may weigh on Danish and German leaders, who decided in 2007 that a 20-kilometer bridge linking the two countries from Rødby to Puttgarden over the Baltic Sea should be constructed and completed by 2018. This is one of the largest infrastructure projects ever untaken in Europe.

A problem that plagued all Scandinavian countries is a long-lasting motorbike-gang war between the Hell's Angels and Bandidos. Violence involving machine guns, bombs and antitank missiles had by 1998 left 12 dead and more than 80 injured and had terrorized citizens everywhere. In an attempt to control such warfare, Denmark suspended the right of biker gangs to assemble and put accused offenders on trial. However, it erupted again in 2009 with Hells Angels and immigrant gangs in Copenhagen settling their turf griev-

ances with guns. The worst violence occurred in the Norrebro district, which is largely Turkish and Pakistani. Leaders in all the countries have met to discuss how this threat to the public can be eliminated.

Economics and Welfarism

All five Nordic countries have highly productive economies and have experienced rapid economic growth since 1945. In all the five lands economic prosperity depends greatly upon foreign trade in view of their small domestic markets. This means that all need the kind of industry and agriculture that are competitive. They are more vulnerable to changes in the world economic climate than are larger countries. Nevertheless, a 2008 BBC poll showed that the Nordics peoples had the most positive attitude toward globalization.

All have, in varying degrees, the general goal of economic egalitarianism (equality). All have developed elaborate social welfare systems, which many people outside the region greatly admire and which include largely free medical treatment, high unemployment benefits and generous child allowances. These many benefits are coupled with a widely spread high standard of living. There is perhaps less economic inequality and poverty in the Nordic states than anywhere else in the world. This was achieved by peaceful reform, not by violent revolution. The economic prosperity has helped create the high level of political harmony and consensus within the countries, and it is therefore an important ingredient in the overall political stability.

At the same time, these countries also presently face a common dilemma: taxes have been raised to stratospheric levels in order to pay for the welfare states. The average tax bite is around 50%. Nevertheless, despite the difficulties in paying for them (except in oil-rich Norway), no determined attack against the welfare state could succeed because most citizens are unwilling to sacrifice the social services and security that have been created. Nordic prosperity challenges the conventional wisdom that high taxes and large safety nets undermine competitiveness.

The "Nordic Model"—a large welfare state with coordinated wage negotiations, the world's most egalitarian wage distribution and maintenance of high productivity—is being powerfully challenged by external and internal forces. Swedish Foreign Minister Carl Bildt provides a tongue-in-cheek reminder that there is no single perfect "Nordic Model." It would have to be a composite: "Finland's education, Estonia's progressive tax policy, Denmark's labor market, Iceland's entrepreneurship, Sweden's management of big companies and Norway's oil."

The Kingdom of Sweden

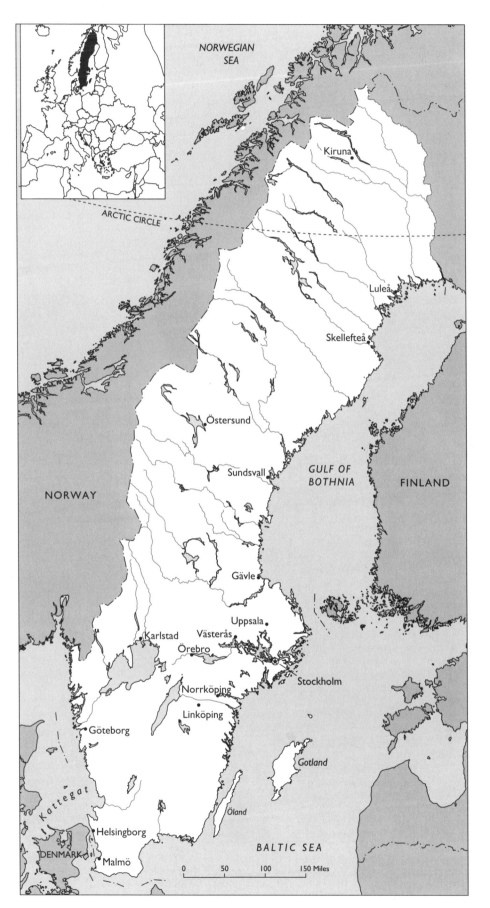

Area: 173,654 sq. mi. (449,793 sq. km.), approx. 1,000 miles from north to south and 300 miles at its widest point; somewhat larger than California.

Population: 9.1 million

Capital City: Stockholm (Pop. 1.56 million, estimated).

Climate: In the south and central portions the climate is rather like New England. The summers are warm and dry and long hours of daylight extend from late spring through early autumn; winters are cold, bitterly so in the northern regions.

Neighboring Countries: Finland (East); Norway (West); Denmark (Southwest); Germany, Poland (South across the Baltic Sea), Baltic states (Southeast across the Baltic Sea).

Official Language: Swedish.

Other Principal Tongues: Nordic tongues of the region.

Ethnic Background: Scandinavian. (North European).

Principal Religion: Lutheran (Swedish Church), 95%.

Main Exports: Machinery, motor vehicles, processed chemicals, wood pulp, paper products, finished iron and steel products, metal ores, telecommunications and biotechnology.

Main Imports: Machinery, motor vehicles, petroleum and petroleum products, chemicals, foodstuffs, textile raw materials and fabrics, iron and steel,.

Major Trading customers: EU (61.2% of exports and 70.9% of imports), Germany (10.4% of exports and 18.4% of imports), Norway (9.4% of exports and 8.3% of imports), United States (7.6% of exports), Denmark (7.5% of exports and 9.2% of imports), UK (7.1% of exports and 6.8% of imports), Finland (6.1% of imports).

Currency: Krona.

National Holiday: June 6. One of the many flag days celebrated is April 30 (1946), birthday of the king.

Chief of State: His Majesty King Carl XVI Gustaf, b. 1946. Ascended the throne September 19, 1973. Married Silvia Sommerlath (German) June 19, 1976.

Heiress Apparent: Her Royal Highness Princess Victoria, b. 1977.

Head of Government: Fredrik Reinfeldt, Prime Minister (since September 2006).

National Flag: A deep blue field crossed by a yellow stripe horizontally and another vertically, the latter being closer to the pole rather than dead center.

When one thinks of postwar Sweden, one tends to conjure thoughts of many things: enviable prosperity, dynamic industry producing well-designed products, assured future economic progress, an absence of strikes and debt, sky-high taxes,

Sweden

which the Swedes willingly pay in order to maintain one of the world's most advanced social welfare systems, permanent rule by a moderate, pragmatic parties, open arms to political refugees from all over the globe and, finally, leadership in the sexual revolution.

Some of these things have changed by now, and the last point was always grossly exaggerated anyway. Sweden is still a country where a majority of the people relish social experimentation whenever it promises a more just and egalitarian society. It has done away with grades and programs for the mentally gifted in the lower classes, outlawed spankings in every institution of the society, including the family, and introduced the use of first names between students and teachers (including most professors). It has done away with many titles, erased the distinction between the formal and informal words for "you" (a means for maintaining social distance, which virtually every other European language retains except English). It has also extended postnatal maternity benefits to 14 months—12 for one parent and two for the other. The state pays up to 80% of his or her salary.

It remains a healthy, democratic political system that is totally immune from any internal shift toward authoritarian rule. Nevertheless its political consensus is splitting a bit at a few seams. It is visibly prosperous, but it faces serious challenges to its economic health, as well as to its way of life and its way of perceiving itself. At a time when many citizens of former communist countries' regimes look to the "Swedish model" of the welfare state as the most humane alternative to their former stultifying centralized autocratic systems, that very model has changed on its home turf.

Sweden is still the heart of the Nordic region and the keystone for the Nordic balance. It is the largest and most populous nation in the area. It had also been the richest for a long time, and it is accustomed to being regarded with a blend of expectation and envy. But it is now oil-rich Norway that is reaping most of the envy, and for the first time ever, Sweden must approach its western neighbor as a needy suitor, not as a rich and slightly condescending patron. In terms of GDP per capita, the Norwegians and Danes have surpassed the Swedes in wealth. Sweden has no oil resources. The poorer neighbors to the east, the Finns, have made considerable economic progress, and many of those Finns who had moved to Sweden to find a better economic life returned home.

Sweden is the third largest country in the European Union and is roughly the size of France or slightly larger than California. It is very sparsely populated, with fewer than 20 inhabitants per square kilometer, which is somewhat lower than in the U.S. Such overall figures are misleading because the Swedish population is distributed very unevenly. More than 90% live in the southern half of the country and more than half live in the lower third. For many decades the northern people have migrated southward, and from the countryside into the cities, although there are recent signs that this latter process may be reversing itself slightly. In the year 1880 only 10% of the people lived in towns, and even 100 years ago Sweden was predominantly rural. During the second half of the 19th century the move into the cities accelerated. By now about 83% live in cities or towns. About a third of the people live in the large urban areas of Stockholm (1.56 million), Göteborg (761,000) and Malmö (498,000).

Sweden has been an independent kingdom since 1523, and its relative isolation from the political and military storms that have swept the rest of Europe have created a firm national identity and unity, symbolized by the king. For most of its existence Sweden had a homogeneous population, and this was a key factor in the Swedes' ability to create such a sturdy social and political consensus. But this homogeneity has begun to change. This former country of emigrants, which once poured a fourth of its population into the U.S., has itself become a country of immigration. Immigrants and their descendants make up 1.2 million out of a total population of 9 million. This means that more than 13% of the population is non-

Four generations in a 1946 photograph: King Gustaf V (d. 1950, age 92), his son, Crown Prince Gustaf Adolf (who succeeded his father in 1950 as King Gustaf VI Adolf, d. 1973), his grandson, Prince Gustaf Adolf (who died in an air accident in January 1947), and his great-grandson, Sweden's present monarch, King Carl XVI Gustaf.

Swedish in origin. If one adds those with at least one parent born abroad, then nearly a fourth of the population would be outsiders. Their percentage is steadily rising since immigrants' birth rates are higher than Swedes', who until 2005 were in a state of negative population growth when the birth rate again began increasing. Also by 2003 asylum-seekers were entering the country at the rate of 40,000 per year. The Iraq war prompted a couple of million Iraqis to leave the country, and 80,000 ended up in Sweden, where they constitute the second largest immigrant group, after Finns. In 2006 alone, more than 9,000 Iraqis applied for asylum, and 80% received refugee status.

Sweden always had a small Finnish-speaking minority in the north, numbering about 30,000. It also has had a *Same* (pronounced sa-may and sometimes incorrectly called "Lapp") minority, which now numbers about 17,000 and which has its own language and culture. The degree to which Same are integrated into Swedish society varies. The most traditional are the approximately 2,500 nomadic Same, whose livelihood is derived from raising reindeer. Sweden requires all Same children to attend the minimum nine years of school although it permits the Same language (a Finno-Ugric language) to be used and Same culture, which has only a limited written literature, to be preserved. It even provides eight nomadic schools for the children who are constantly on the move, and there is a folk school at Jokkmokk where Same of all ages can study their own culture. The state also broadcasts the news and special programs in the Same language.

Partly because of the rising concern in the world for the rights of minorities, a somewhat more aggressive consciousness has arisen among some Same, who maintain contact with Indian groups in North America. Some even raised a claim for possession of their people's native lands, but in 1981 the Swedish Supreme Court ruled that the Same can no longer claim possession of those lands although they still have preferential hunting and fishing rights. The Court also ruled that they could not interfere with energy projects or tourism in the mountainous Skattefjällen region of northern Sweden. In 2003 Sweden had still not signed the UN Declaration of Aboriginal Rights because of a domestic court decision.

Since the 1945 Nordic agreement to allow free emigration within the area, Finns poured into Sweden. Finns in Sweden are not visible to the outsider, and they do not have the kinds of adjustment problems many other immigrants do. In Finland, about 5.5% of the population speaks Swedish as the first language and has

Swedish language newspapers, schools and universities.

Stockholm, which was founded in the 13th century as a fortress to seal off the inland waterways from Baltic intruders, is the cultural, financial and government center of Sweden. Unlike Copenhagen, Paris or London, though, the Swedish capital does not overshadow the rest of Sweden, which is a decentralized country. Göteborg has Sweden's largest port and is in many ways as oriented toward such foreign cities as Oslo, Copenhagen and London as it is toward Stockholm. Malmö is situated on the Öresund sound directly across from Copenhagen and its residents often cross a bridge to the Danish capital to do some of their shopping.

Approximately 15,000 years ago Sweden was covered with ice, the movement of which cut deep scars into the land, leaving a long mountain chain along the Norwegian border. These mountains, which cover a fourth of the country, are the source of numerous rivers that flow eastward through the forests into the Gulf of Bothnia.

These rivers are sources of hydroelectric power, which provided the energy for Sweden's industrialization. They also offered rapid and inexpensive transportation for logs from the immense Swedish forests, which cover half the country's territory. Many of the indentations cut during the great ice age are now filled with almost 100,000 lakes, which occupy about 8% of the country's surface. Boats can travel all the way from Stockholm to Göteborg via lakes linked by rivers and the Göta Canal. Along the jagged coast of this country, which stretches 1,000 miles (1,600 km.), are thousands of islands. The average width of the country is 250 miles (400 km.).

As in Norway, all open land that is not cultivated or not part of a residence can be used by anyone for camping, hiking, skiing or other outdoor recreational activities, regardless of who owns the land. Swedes are very proud of this *allemansrätten* ("every man's rights"). The vast forests have long provided one of the three most valuable natural resources—wood. The other two are waterpower and mountains of Europe's highest grade of iron ore, found in the Bergslagen area in central Sweden and in the Kiruna and Skellefteå areas in the north. It also has sizable deposits of ferrous alloys, pyrites, fire clay, zinc, silver, lead, copper and shale uranium. Its greatest poverty is in oil and coal, but with its people's proven ingenuity, it has been able to achieve almost unparalleled prosperity, even without "black gold." A heavy dose of this ingenuity was necessary to make Sweden basically self-sufficient in food, even though its soil is

generally not good, its rainfall undependable and its growing season short. Less than 10% of its land area is suitable for agriculture, but Swedish farmers, who now make up only 3% of the active population, know how to apply a high level of mechanization and scientific farming techniques.

The climate is far milder than would be expected if one merely glanced at the globe. It is on the same latitude as Siberia and Alaska, and Stockholm is as far north as southern Greenland. Yet the Gulf Stream from the Caribbean is able to penetrate, bringing warm water that heats the air and produces a climate in the most populous half of Sweden that is similar to that of northern New England.

The country has a varied landscape. The south, or *Götaland*, which includes the islands of Öland and Gotland off the eastern coast, is a region of fertile plains and rolling, verdant hills, dotted with clean, red and yellow barns and farmhouses, freshly painted and surrounded in summer by fields of yellow flowers. Here is the heart of Sweden's industry and agriculture and the home of half the Swedes. Central Sweden is called *Svealand*, from which was derived the name of the entire country, *Sverige*, or *Svea-rike*, which means "Kingdom of the Svear." This region contains the capital city as well as the old university town of Uppsala. It also has many farming communities and countless lakes. The northern half of the country, or *Norrland*, is a rugged, mountainous frontier area of wilderness, timber and mining. In short, Sweden is a beautiful land of many scenic contrasts and of water everywhere.

RECENT POLITICAL HISTORY

For a half-century Sweden had been governed by the Social Democratic Workers' Party (SAP), which now calls itself the Social Democrats (S). The election in 1976 of the first non-SAP government since 1936 was a turning point. Swedes had decided that it was time to have a government that proposed a policy to stimulate the dynamism of the market place, increase productivity in the private sector by stimulating investment and slow the growth of government. It was never a question of dismantling the social welfare net. No Scandinavian government has a mandate from its people to do that. However, the conditions were not favorable for a shaky coalition government with a razor thin majority in parliament. It took over the helm after 44 years of SAP rule and at a time when the country was plunging into its worst economic crises in three decades. As the 1982 elections showed, it was a bad time to try to change the direction of economic policy.

Sweden

View of Stockholm, with the Royal Palace (center-top)

The non-SAP governments did accomplish a few things, but it failed to cope with runaway public spending and to stimulate investment in industry. The Center Party was far too obsessed with the nuclear power issue, and the Liberals were constantly worried about their decline in the public opinion polls to devote full attention to the pressing problems. The coalitions that ruled after 1976 simply shied away from truly decisive policies that would have been necessary to begin to solve the country's economic problems.

Olof Palme's SAP reaped the electoral rewards of this failure. Palme knew that in the minds of many Swedish voters his party was closely associated with the prosperity and full employment of the past. He also knew that his party's program was in harmony with the electorate's desire to maintain at all costs the social welfare system, which most Swedes have come to regard as permanent.

Palme stood at the zenith of his career when tragedy struck in 1986. Walking home unguarded with his wife late at night, he was killed by an unknown assassin's bullets. He was the first Swedish leader to be murdered since King Gustaf III, who was shot at a masked ball in 1792. Evidence emerged in 1996 that the assassin might have been dispatched by the *apartheid* regime of South Africa, which was known to be greatly angered by Palme's vociferous opposition to *apartheid*. Sweden also had a policy of funneling hundreds of millions of dollars into the

antiapartheid movement within South Africa. In 2001 a friend of Christer Pettersson claimed that the latter had privately confessed to the killing. Mrs. Lisbet Palme had identified Pettersson as her spouse's murderer, but his 1989 conviction was overturned on appeal because the police could not locate the murder weapon. Considered mentally deranged and an alcoholic, Pettersson's confession carried no legal weight, and the South African connection has been dismissed. There are even theories of CIA involvement, but nothing has been proved. The crime remains unsolved.

Swedes mourned not only the loss of this talented, controversial leader, but the loss of Sweden's totally open society. Scandinavia is one of the last regions in a violent world where close, informal contacts between political leaders and common people were possible. As Ulf Adelsohn, the conservative leader, lamented, "Sweden will never be the same after this."

This tragedy repeated itself 17 years later just a few blocks from where Palme had been murdered. In September 2003 Foreign Minister Anna Lindh, one of Sweden's most popular politicians and an oft-mentioned future prime minister, was shopping at a department store in downtown Stockholm when a 25-year-old Swedish citizen of Serbian descent, Mijailo Mijailovic, stabbed her ten times in the stomach and chest. He later confessed to the crime, claiming that when he saw

Lindh, voices in his parents' native Serbian, including that of Jesus, ordered him to kill her. He said it happened so fast that he had no memory of the act. He was given a life sentence, which in Sweden usually ends up being a total of 15 years. In June 2004 Mijailovic was found mentally ill and sent to a mental institution rather than prison.

This irrational act again challenged Swedes' sense of security and view of their country as exceptional, one that is tolerant and relatively free of crime. Only the king and prime minister have regular bodyguards. They were again reminded of their vulnerability in June 2004, when two teenagers in Malmö were discovered assembling an arsenal of guns and explosives they intended to use against their classmates on the anniversary of the 1999 shootings at Columbine High School in Colorado.

New Prime Ministers

Palme's personal deputy, Ingvar Carlsson replaced him as prime minister and leader of the SAP. His state visit to the U.S. in 1987, the first such trip in almost three decades, revealed how much the two countries' relations had improved since 1972, when Palme had compared U.S. bombing of Hanoi with Nazi Germany's extermination policy. That dubious statement prompted a mutual withdrawal of ambassadors for more than a year. Carlsson tried to be even-handed in his criticism of the U.S. and Soviet Union. His successor in 1991, Carl Bildt, had always opposed Sweden's foreign policy moralizing and its support for Vietnam during the war. After visiting U.S. military cemeteries in Belgium, he wrote: "Swedes ought to take the time to go and see the row after row of the hundreds of white crosses." In 1994 Carlsson replaced Bildt as prime minister. In March 1996 Göran Persson assumed the prime ministership and ruled for a decade before handing the reins to conservative Fredrik Reinfeldt in September 2006.

GOVERNMENT AND POLITICS

As in other Scandinavian states, politics in Sweden is characterized by great stability despite the existence of many political parties competing for power. It entered a democratic age without revolution, and violence is an element that has almost never raised its ugly head in Swedish politics until recently. This does not mean that there are no political conflicts or disagreements in the country's political life. It does mean that they are fought out verbally and in the democratic arena and with restraint, and that they are almost invariably resolved by the Swedish talent for cool-headed, pragmatic negotiations and compromise.

The Swedish constitution consists of four separate documents (Basic Laws), not just one as in the U.S. The first is the Act of Succession, which deals with the present royal family and which was amended, effective 1980, to permit the *oldest child* of the reigning monarch, not the oldest son, to succeed to the throne upon the death of the monarch. This meant that King Carl XVI Gustaf's son, who had been born crown prince, was moved behind his older sister, Victoria, in the order of succession. The second document is the Fundamental Law on Freedom of Expression. The third is the Freedom of the Press Act of 1949. The most important document is the Instrument of Government, which went into effect on January 1, 1975, replacing the 1809 Instrument of Government. This change brought no radical reform, but it formally incorporated into the constitution the current governmental practices that had evolved since 1809.

This last document explicitly sanctions popular sovereignty, representative democracy and parliamentary government. Thus, while most other constitutionally governed countries have gradually developed actual political practices that are not clearly spelled out in a constitution, Sweden has tried to bring its constitution and actual political practices into harmony. In 1976 and 1979 parliament again passed laws amending the document in a way that strengthened the protection of human rights and fundamental freedoms. Thus, its existing observance of these rights and freedoms now has documentation.

Constitutional Monarchy

Sweden is a constitutional monarchy with a parliamentary form of government. As a result of the recent constitutional changes, the monarch does not have sweeping political powers on paper, as do other European monarchs. He is in theory and fact a symbolic figurehead who exerts no influence on politics and takes no part in it. A Swedish monarch never actually wears a crown, and he performs only purely ceremonial functions, such as opening the annual session of parliament each October and conferring four of the five Nobel Prizes. (The Norwegian government confers the Peace Prize.) The Swedish chemist and inventor, Alfred Nobel, had donated the money for these prestigious prizes. He had made a fortune from his invention of dynamite, blasting gelatin and smokeless explosives, which made the development of firearms and artillery possible.

The monarch does not formally sign government documents, and his former fictitious power to select the prime minister has been taken over by the speaker of the parliament. Also, the formal power of government now rests with the cabinet, not with the monarch. The Swedes have stripped their monarch of all his duties and powers and collect taxes from him as they would any other citizen. Carl can certainly afford to pay his taxes without too much pain although, with an estimated net worth of about 38.5 million euros, he is by no means the wealthiest European monarch. The royal family receives approximately 9.7 million euros each year, around half of which is used to maintain castles and art treasures. All of his income is now subject to public scrutiny based on the country's transparency principle.

This stripping of the monarch's formal powers does not mean that the Swedes are indifferent to their royal family. Opinion polls reveal that the king and his German-born queen, Silvia, a commoner who was serving as a guide at the 1972 Munich Olympics when Carl met her, are by far the most popular public figures in Sweden. In fact, they are far more beloved and respected than are any of Sweden's present political leaders. Silvia, who still speaks with a noticeable German accent, is patron of over 60 charitable organizations.

Their popularity is not due exclusively to the fact that many have become cynical

(Right to left) King Carl XVI Gustaf, Queen Silvia, Crown Princess Victoria, Prince Carl Philip, Princess Madeleine, and the King's aunt, Princess Lilian

Sweden

Sweden's Royal Children—Madeleine, Crown Princess Victoria and Carl Philip

and disillusioned about their leadership, however. Having no political responsibilities, the king usually cannot be accused of doing anything wrong, since in this area he does nothing. That was not the case in February 2004, when Carl praised the Sultan of Brunei for his openness during a visit to that oil-rich country. Swedish diplomats had long called the sultan a dictator and criticized Brunei for human rights violations. To prevent such a gaffe, a cabinet minister now accompanies the king on all state visits, and only the government can decide which countries should be officially visited. The monarch can determine only his personal travel. The parliamentary foreign affairs committee demanded that the king concentrate only on his representative functions.

The royal family strives to be very near to the people, sending their children to normal public schools and taking a great interest in such charities as those seeking to improve the lot of handicapped children. Without a doubt, their popularity is the best protection against the voices that are sometimes heard on the political left to abolish the monarchy altogether. A change in the constitution permits the oldest child, regardless of sex, to ascend to the throne. At the turn of the century Crown Princess Victoria was preparing herself to be queen by studying history and political science at Yale University. In June 2010 she married a commoner who owns a gym. Her younger sister, Madeleine, is Stockholm's glamour girl even though she lives in New York. A 2004 poll revealed that 72% of Swedes favor the monarchy. Nevertheless, many

young Swedes, including the youth groups of all parties, oppose it.

Parliament

Since 1971 Sweden has had a unicameral parliament (*Riksdag*). At one time, almost 90% of Swedes 18 years of age or over went to the polls to elect 349 members by proportional representation; turnout had fallen to approximately 78% in the 2002 elections. For the election of 310 of the members, the country is divided into 28 constituencies, each of which chooses an average of 11 members. The remaining 39 are selected from national ballots in which all of the country constitutes a single constituency. A substitute deputy is selected simultaneously for each member so that there need not be a by-election if a deputy dies or resigns. In 2002 women captured 45% of the *Riksdag* seats and were awarded half of the cabinet posts.

Parliamentary elections are held at least every four years in September, although the prime minister can decide to call earlier ones. Such earlier balloting is very rare, and if it does take place, the newly chosen deputies merely serve out the remainder of the four-year parliamentary term. Many had found that three-year terms, in effect until 1994, were insufficient for a parliament; a government can act more decisively if it does not have to worry about elections so often. Therefore, parliamentary terms were lengthened to four years.

Sweden has a highly organized society. Each occupation group and such categories of citizens as consumers, members of co-

operatives, environmentalists, women, tenants and landlords have their own organizations, which deal directly with the government. Before an important piece of legislation is introduced into the *Riksdag*, the government calls together a royal commission composed of members of that body (except communist members), experts from the concerned interest groups and independent specialists to examine the proposals thoroughly and to develop, if possible, a consensus behind the new laws. Representatives of the groups also belong to many administrative agencies. The participating organizations, therefore, are a part of the democratic system itself, and not merely lobbyists.

Once the legislation is presented to the *Riksdag*, one of the 16 standing committees gives it another look, so that when a law is finally adopted, it usually enjoys a broad consensus. This process certainly helps to promote stability, but it has been severely criticized by some Swedes since the late 1960s. They charge that the process takes place behind closed doors and over the heads of most normal citizens and persons within the various occupations. This is mere "democracy at the top," they say. The parties have taken this criticism seriously and have developed some new proposals on the subjects of decentralization while continuing to practice the traditional method for achieving a consensus.

There is no institutional separation of power between the legislative and the executive branches in Sweden. Nevertheless, since the early part of the 19th century, Sweden has had a tradition controlling the governmental administration. The first form of guarantee against the abuse of power by judges, governmental officials and civil servants is the requirement that all documents be made public (a principle Swedes call *Offentlighetsprincipen*), except in rare instances where secrets vital to the nation's welfare are concerned.

The second guarantee is the election by the *Riksdag* of ombudsmen, a specifically Swedish invention, who have the independent authority to act on their own initiative or on the basis of written complaints from individual citizens, newspapers or other organizations. The Justice ombudsman sees whether any public official, except a government minister, has acted illegally or improperly. If he finds evidence of misconduct, he can admonish the erring official or initiate corrective steps, although prosecutions are infrequent. If he finds that the laws are vague or faulty, he can recommend to the parliament a change in the law.

There are also other, more specialized ombudsmen. The press ombudsman deals with complaints about journalistic ethics.

The antitrust ombudsman watches over the economy to see that competition is not stifled. The consumer ombudsman protects the consumer from unfair marketing methods and the equality ombudsman primarily is responsible for insuring that there is no discrimination against women on the job or in public life. It is scarcely surprising that a woman normally occupies the latter office. In 1999 an ombudsman for gays and lesbians was created. The ombudsmen can invoke a well-developed body of Swedish law, which is a synthesis of Roman and common law and which is interpreted by courts at three levels: Courts of the First Instance (*Tingsrätter*), Appellate Courts (*Hovrätter*) and a Supreme Court (*Högsta Domstolen*).

In practice, the *Riksdag* is subordinate to the cabinet (*Statsråd*), usually composed of 18 to 21 ministers and led by the prime minister. Together they are called "the government" and must be able to win a majority in the *Riksdag* for their important policies. The government is collectively responsible for policy, but parliament can force individual cabinet members to resign. Of course, the prime minister can dismiss them. Cabinet members are normally leading politicians in the governing parties and had won seats in parliament, although their substitutes occupy their seats while they serve as ministers. Occasionally, specialists who are not professional politicians and who were not elected to parliament are included in the cabinet.

The *Riksdag* majority has the last word on whether a matter becomes law or not. That majority may choose to allow the people to express, through a referendum, their opinion on a particularly important subject, but the results of such a nationwide vote, which occurs very seldom, are not binding on the government. In 1979 the constitution was amended to allow another kind of referendum. If a third of the *Riksdag* deputies desire it, a binding referendum on a proposed constitutional amendment can be held at the same time as a general election.

Provincial Government

Sweden is a unitary, not a federal state. But it does have provincial and local governments that have considerable responsibility. Each of the 24 provinces (*län*) is formally led by a governor (*landshövding*), who is appointed by the cabinet for a six-year term and who presides over a 14-member provincial administration (*länsstyrelse*), which is appointed by an elected provincial council (*landsting*). As in the municipalities, the provinces have plural rather than single person executives; such collective leadership encourages collaboration among all parties, and it

therefore fosters nonpartisan, compromising and practical leadership. The provinces lack the independence that the U.S. states have, and since 1971 there is no upper house in the national parliament that would be in a position to guard provincial interests.

Local Government

There are 284 municipalities (*kommun*), each with an elected assembly. The *kommun* does not have the same measure of autonomy as does an American city and is largely occupied with administration on a day-to-day basis of services that have been mandated by the national government. The *kommun's* responsibilities extend to housing subsidies, roads, sewerage and water supply, elementary education, public assistance, health care, child welfare and cultural, social and athletic activities. They have the right to levy income and property taxes. They not only charge fees for some of the services they render, but they receive subsidies from the national government for the services they are required to perform for it.

Absorption into the National Government

Provincial and local governments have been progressively transformed into administrative extensions of the central government. The provinces apply national policy and have primary responsibility for health care, hospital services, for certain types of education and vocational training. They have the right to impose an income tax to pay for their services. To make things even more complicated, there are also church councils at the local level, which are popularly elected and which look after church financial affairs.

Until the Church of Sweden was separated from the state in 2000, the church levied taxes, which about 90% of all Swedes chose to pay, rather than leaving the church and lowering their tax burden. The state still collects membership fees for all registered religious organizations. The average Swede pays income taxes to nation, provincial, and municipal authorities. Fortunately for him or her, however, only a single tax return that covers all three must be filed.

Political Parties

As in other democracies, political parties are very much a part of Swedish government. The proportional representation electoral system produces a multiparty landscape, which is kept within manageable bounds by the requirement that no party can win seats in the *Riksdag* which does not win at least 4% of the vote nationwide, or 12% of the vote in any one electoral district. Those parties who are able to win at least

one seat receive state subsidies to cover a portion of their expenses.

There are several different ways of approaching the party scene. One is to see it as a four- or five-party system, with generally coherent and stable groups that are closely linked to specific occupation groups in the well-organized Swedish society. In a land with no traditional language, ethnic or confessional differences, it is understandable that the parties would form along occupational or class lines. These close ties, which most parties have, make it more difficult for them to broaden their bases and become mass representation groups, which could single-handedly win a parliamentary majority. The one exception is the Social Democratic Party (S), which has dominated Swedish politics for a half a century.

Thus, Sweden has a stable, multiparty system that is divided into two roughly equal blocs: one contains a unified, dominant party; the other is fractured into three parties, which have difficulties ruling the country together. Since a hard-line, antisocialist front never developed, and since the major parties tend to be unideological and pragmatic, both blocs were always able to cooperate in the political middle. Most electoral shifts are among parties within each bloc, not between the two. Thus, electoral landslides are completely unknown.

The Social Democratic Party (S)

In 1989 S celebrated its one hundredth anniversary. Since the early 1930s, it ruled Sweden almost continually, with a three-month interruption in 1936. It won a majority five times. Sometimes it has coalitions with the Center Party (1936–39 and 1951–57), but it tends to dislike coalitions and is happier to rule as a minority government with the tolerance of another party, whenever it cannot win a majority. In 1976 it went into the opposition, returning to power after the 1982 elections. It reentered the opposition in 1991, but it came back to power in 1994. Ingvar Carlsson stepped down as prime minister in 1996 and was replaced by his finance minister, Göran Persson, who had won few friends by implementing painful budget cuts in order to reduce the gaping budget deficit. S's greatest strength is among the elderly, those living in small towns, and public sector workers.

September 2006 spelled the end of S's rule. The public increasingly perceived Persson as arrogant and bullying, whose aggressive manner contrasted with Fredrik Reinfeldt's affable, soft-spoken demeanor. Many Swedes had grown tired of the Social Democratic Party, which had ruled the country for 65 of the prior 74 years. Only 46.2% of the voters gave S the nod; that fig-

Sweden

ured out to 130 seats. Although S is still the largest party, it now occupies the opposition benches. Persson left no crown prince to succeed him as party leader. Instead, a crown princess, Mona Sahlin, emerged in 2007 to become the new Social Democratic leader. She shows greater voter appeal than Persson had, and she enters the September 2010 elections as the favorite.

The secret of the S's success was its close ties with the Trade Union Federation (*Landsorganisationen*—LO), which links 25 unions and organizes about 90% of all Swedish workers. Sweden is a highly unionized country, and since the founding of the LO, most of its members must also belong to S. This is not merely formal membership; most Swedish workers actually vote for the SAP in general elections. The LO supports S financially, organizationally and through the trade union press, such as the popular *Aftonbladet*, a tabloid newspaper whose circulation is by far the biggest. S revived its morning tabloid, *Stockholms-Tidningen*, which concentrates on local Stockholm news and on low-keyed presentations of the party's policies. The LO and S have a common committee during election years, and the LO chairman has a seat in the party presidium. S also has good relations with the Union of Employees (TCO), but its links with S are not nearly as close, and its influence not so important as is the case of the LO.

S's party programs since 1897 have always contained some radical elements such as presenting socialism as the long-range goal of the party, but these elements have been disregarded in practice. The party supported socialist economic reforms, but it always took a gradualist approach to change and was willing to cooperate with other parties and with private enterprise. It left private property untouched and allowed Swedish companies to make high profits, as a reward for financing full employment, a tight social welfare system and an ever-increasing living standard for all groups within the society. In 1959 it changed its party program so that it would be in harmony with its moderate, pragmatic politics.

The benefits for Sweden that flowed from this realistic approach were revealed in the country's undeniable prosperity. Some people began to talk of an "end to ideology," but in the late 1960s and early 1970s a "new left" emerged, composed mainly of young, middle class university students, which began directing its sharply pointed arrows at the Swedish political and economic system, admired by so many abroad. New left critics hammered at the inequalities that still existed and at the highly developed process of compromise at the top, which it claimed,

Göteborg, Sweden's second largest city and Scandinavia's largest port

took place over the heads of, and therefore beyond the control of the people. The critics also charged that Swedish society was becoming stultifyingly bureaucratized. They demanded more ideology in politics.

These more radical elements never made up a majority within S, to say nothing of the overall electorate, but their attacks jolted the party into taking a noticeable left turn. Olof Palme's outbursts against the U.S. were not enough to pacify these tenacious critics, and the party changed its program in 1975 in order to incorporate more ideological content. The program states that the "struggle for equality is directed against all kinds of class differences—economic, social and cultural." It declared that the existing freedoms and rights should be used to attain economic and social liberation and that economic democracy "should be an immediate goal."

Property Distribution

S's programs had contained such verbiage before, but this time the party was confronted with untiring critics on its left and a trade union partner, which was also thinking along lines of a more radical move to achieve a form of economic democracy. At the LO Congress of 1975 a trade union economist presented a bombshell report that called for a "distribution of the wealth," and the LO chairman even went a step further and spoke of a "special Swedish brand of socialism," which would have the goal of "abolishing capitalism and private property in industry." Indeed, while Sweden has gone a long way in redistributing income, it had done

little to redistribute wealth. Property ownership had changed very little from the 1930s to the end of the century. In a 1982 study, 89% of Swedish households owned no stock in corporations. But Sweden has now become one of the most progressive countries in Europe insofar as distributing stock and ownership is concerned. It reformed its pension system to include a stock portion.

LO proposed a concrete plan of "workers funds" which Swedish employers justifiably called a confiscation policy. A certain percentage of the firms' profits and payrolls would be turned over annually to five government-nominated boards, dominated by the trade unions. Each of these boards could purchase up to 80% of a company's stock. Individual wage-earners would neither own the shares nor draw dividends, but within a couple of decades the trade unions would gain control over every sizable company in Sweden.

In 1978 S also embraced the idea of the "funds," despite their unpopularity. In its campaign for the 1982 elections, it pledged to introduce these funds, to protect the large public sector, to restore full employment and to put an end to what it calls a dismantling of the social welfare state, which S was chiefly responsible for building. In 1983 Palme submitted the question of the "funds" to a vote in the *Riksdag*, a decision that had prompted 100,000 Swedes to march on parliament, the country's largest demonstration in recent history. The *Riksdag* approved the funds with a narrow majority. In 1991 the newly elected conservative government promptly abolished the funds altogether.

The Communists and Greens

One party that advocates a leftist ideological course is the Left Party (V), which split from the SAP in 1917. It transformed itself into a "Eurocommunist" party in the 1960s by scrapping its advocacy of a "dictatorship of the proletariat." It also changed its name in 1967 in order to make itself more appealing to left-wing socialists and the SAP (now S). It cut its ties with the Soviet Union, a move that led some elements in the party to split off and form other communist groupings. None has mustered more than the feeblest support at election time nor has ever won a single seat in the *Riksdag*. The V became a political home for a part of the "new left" in the 1970s, and it defines itself as "socialist-feminist" today. It now rejects any identification with communists.

The V finds its major strength is in the industrial centers. It actively opposes EU membership, as well as austerity and cuts in the welfare budget. It has never been included in a Swedish governing coalition although it is sometimes willing to support S's programs as the best alternative to "bourgeois" governments. Its leader in the 2002 elections, Gudrun Schyman, had helped make the party less communist although there are still communists in its ranks. She described the V as socialist-feminist, not communist. She demanded much more spending on welfare and jobs, a slowing down of national debt repayment, higher taxes on wealth, and an end to nuclear power and privatization.

Although the party won enough seats in 2002 to remain crucial for the S government, Schyman was forced to resign as V leader because of a bout with alcoholism and a clash with tax authorities, who said she had manipulated her expenses. In 2005 she emerged as leader of a new women's party composed largely of disgruntled Left Party feminists. She had once accused Swedish men of being no better than the Taliban even though 45% of members of parliament and half of government members are women. That party was irrelevant in the 2006 elections, but the Left Party managed to win 5.8% of the

votes and 22 seats. It sits on the opposition benches with no ability to help or harm the majority government.

The Greens had in 1988 become the first new party to win seats since Sweden introduced universal and equal suffrage in 1917. It maintained its position in 2006, winning 5.2% and 19 seats, but it is in the opposition. Greens advocate strict environmental controls, the extinguishing of nuclear power, the transfer of politics from professional politicians to amateurs and laymen, and a clear distancing from the EU. Both it and V oppose the euro.

The "Bourgeois" Parties

The second block of parties in Sweden is often called the "bourgeois" or "nonsocialist" bloc. In the 2006 elections, the four largest conservative parties named themselves the "Alliance for Sweden," based on a commonly agreed platform, and were able to form the first majority government since 1981. None of the parties in this group advocates a dismantling of the social welfare system, although all favor some correction of its excesses and abuses. They are not against collective action, which has deep roots in Sweden's heritage, but they do lay more emphasis on individualism and the rights of private property than does S.

This is why all advocate a greater degree of decentralization as a barrier against excessively centralized authority and bureaucracy. They also call for lower taxes in order to stimulate and liberate individual initiative again, but they disagree about the precise form of such reductions. In questions of foreign policy they have no fundamental disagreements either with each other or with S, especially insofar as Swedish neutrality is concerned. However, the leaders tend to favor more amicable relations with the NATO countries. The four-party "Bourgeois Alliance" created a shadow cabinet in parliament in anticipation of the September 2006 elections.

The bourgeois coalition ruled from 1976 to 1982, but it was stricken with disunity and problems from the very beginning. Its failure stemmed in large part from its response to the economic problems that had befallen the once fabled Swedish model of quiet compromise. In the 1988 elections it again lacked unity and suffered its worst defeat since the Second World War. It won the 1991 elections, finding its greatest strength among youth and middle-class voters in big cities. It formed a minority government, but it cracked apart on the delicate issue of nuclear power. In 1994 S replaced it. Voters disliked the bloc's budget cutting and attempts to reform the welfare state to make it solvent. This brought too much pain and too few im-

mediate benefits. Voters longed to return to the snug security they had enjoyed earlier.

The second largest party after S is the Moderate Unity Party (M). Taking a page from "New Labour's" game book in the UK, it renamed itself "New Moderates" for the 2006 elections. M had changed its program and name in 1969 in order to reverse a constant loss of voters, but most Swedes still refer to it as The Right Party (from its pre-1969 name *Högerpartiet*). It has always appealed more to the upper class, but it never was a reactionary party of the extreme right. Like other parties of the bloc, it had to adjust to Sweden's changing social structure and to extend its appeal into the urban areas, where it receives almost half of its votes. Its key supporters come from large and small businessmen, big farmers, the upper civil service, and in 1991 from young Swedes. It receives financial assistance from the Confederation of Employers (SAF) and from industry, as well as some sympathy from the union of academics and upper civil service (SACO/SR), but these forms of support are not nearly as significant for it as is LO support for S.

Many Swedish newspapers support the party, the most important being the respected Stockholm morning daily, *Svenska Dagbladet*, a well-informed, low-keyed paper whose circulation is declining. This newspaper does retain its independence and it does not hesitate to criticize M. The party has always had relatively strained relations with the other three parties in the "bourgeois" bloc. Its former leader, Ulf Adelsohn, summed up his party's position tartly by remarking that "things are pretty crazy if a man is taxed so much that he can't pay his rent, but the government is willing to pay him a rent subsidy to make up the difference." That kind of remark sounded like a serious threat to the welfare system and to the role of the state in the nation's economy. In a country in which the majority of voters derive their livelihood from public funds or employment, political assaults on the public sector and calls for a "change in the system," however logical they may be, are highly risky.

Its next leader was Carl Bildt. In his inaugural address to Parliament in 1991 he called the vote "a question of a revolution in freedom of choice," and declared, "the age of collectivism in Sweden is over." As the first Swedish prime minister in this century who is a passionate European, he pressed hard for his country's admission to the EU, which Sweden formally entered in 1995. His victory did not mean that he had a mandate completely to transform the welfare state. He aimed to stop its growth and trim it around the edges.

2006 Riksdag Elections

A new model for the Nordics?

Balance of power in the Riksdag

Centre party (7.9%) — Christian Democrats (6.6%)

Folk Liberal party (7.5%)

29 24

28

Social Democrats (35.2%)

130

Moderate party (26.1%)

Left party (5.8%)

97

22

Green party (5.2%)

19

Alliance for Sweden: 178 seats

Others: 171 seats

Source: *Financial Times*

Sweden

Hon. Carl Bildt, Foreign Minister

Swedes did not like this and voted his government out in 1994. Bildt returned to Sweden with the aura of an international leader and foreign policy heavy weight after serving two years as UN High Representative to Bosnia.

In 2006 he became foreign minister. He no longer uses the word "neutral" to describe his country's foreign policy, and the center-right government in which he serves is sympathetic to closer links with NATO. It cooperates closely on airspace surveillance and intelligence exchange with its NATO neighbor, Norway. It also provides training and equipment to the Baltic states, which are NATO members since 2004.

He stepped down as party leader in 1999 and was replaced first by Bo Lundgren and then in 2004 by Fredrik Reinfeldt, who made the New Moderates more inclusive, including to gays. In fact, as prime minister he appointed the first black—Burundi-born Nyamko Sabuni, a female model of integration, as minister for integration and equality—and the first openly gay ministers in the country's history. In preparation for the September 2006 elections, Reinfeldt edged the party toward the center without compromising its basic principles of individual freedom, free markets and rule of law. He revitalized the party by ousting a third of its staff and hiring a young team of economists to draw up gentler plans that do not scare voters.

These became his alliance's platform, and they include tax cuts that are half of what were demanded in 2002, a lowered tax burden for low- and medium-wage earners, reduced payroll taxes, and an end to the wealth tax. The latter accounts for only .3% of total revenues, but it drives rich Swedes like IKEA founder Ingvar Kamprad and Björn Borg out of the country. The government also seeks to strengthen incentives to work. Although

the official unemployment rate was low—5.7% at the time of the elections—Reinfeldt reminded Swedes that the more accurate figure is 15%–17% because of all the make-work and early retirement schemes. Youth unemployment is about 25%, and the growing number of immigrants have severe difficulties finding work. His government implemented policies to boost employment, wean citizens off welfare benefits, and help them reenter the workforce.

Reinfeldt promised to sell off some of the government's stakes in the 55 companies the state owns. It began in 2007 with six companies, including the Scandinavian airlines, SAS, the Nordea bank, Telia-Sonera communications company and the stock market operator, OMX. However, support for privatization dropped sharply, and the world financial market turmoil in 2008 prompted the government to delay the sell-offs.

Reinfeldt is seen as rather colorless, and even he admits that he is "not a media star." Within a year in office, his coalition had declined in popularity from 48% to 40%. M is more pro-EU than the Social Democratic opposition.

The 2006 elections gave the Alliance for Sweden the majority to launch these reforms. It won 48.1% of the votes, to the Social Democrats' 46.2%. The New Moderates won 26.1% and 97 seats, its best result since 1928. It is the second largest party.

The Center Party (C) also responded to the structural changes in Swedish society by changing its name in 1957 from the Farmer's Party. It now draws more votes from workers than from farmers, but its strength is still located largely outside the cities and mainly in southern Sweden. It receives about 70% of the farmers' votes, and farmers dominate its membership, leadership and parliamentary group. It

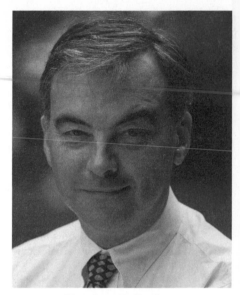

Hon. Lars Leijonborg
Leader, Liberal People's Party

also receives financial, organizational and political support from the Farmer's Organization (LRF), with which it has an overlapping leadership. The Center has ruled with S in the past, and its goal of a "guided market economy" is still very compatible with the traditional economic policy of the SAP. In fact, it was its cooperation with S over the tax cut scheme in 1981 that prompted M to leave the governing coalition.

There has always been tension between the Center and M, and this tension was made worse within the government by the Center's antinuclear energy policy and by its strong ecological appeals, which from 1976 on were able to attract many protest votes. It now has a fragile and mixed electorate that merely intensifies its traditional difficulty in deciding,

Prime Minister Fredrik Reinfeldt meets President George W. Bush

SVERIGES STÖRSTA MORGONTIDNING

I DAG MED
Bostad
Resor
Jobb

NUMMER 39
VECKA 6 · 4

DAGENS NYHETER.

SÖNDAG 10 FEBRUARI 2002

www.dn.se

VARDAGAR 10:- FREDAG/LÖRDAG/SÖNDAG 11:- TEL: 08-738 10 00

first, whether and with whom to form a coalition and, second, to what extent it should compete for votes at the expense of M or the Liberals. In 2006, it halted its downhill slide and won 7.9% of the votes and 29 seats. It is in the government.

The third party in the nonsocialist bloc is the Liberal People's Party (FP), which has its main strength in the larger cities, especially Stockholm and Göteborg. Its voters are a very heterogeneous group, and unlike all other major parties, it is not backed by any large economic organization, although it does receive some financial support from the employer's organization, SAF. Traditionally it also has been supported by the nonconformist religions and by the antialcohol organizations. It does have a strong foothold in the press, especially the largest national morning newspaper, *Dagens Nyheter* and the afternoon daily tabloid, *Expressen*, which had Scandinavia's largest circulation until it was overtaken by the Social Democratic *Aftonbladet*. The *Göteborgs'-Posten* is liberal. None of these papers is directly connected with the party, though, and all criticize it freely.

For a while the FP successfully attracted nonsocialist voters by stressing both the virtues of a market economy and of social responsibility through welfare policies. It had been losing ground in elections until 2002, when it tripled its vote to over 13%. Its leader, Lars Leijonborg, won votes by proposing that foreigners applying for citizenship be required to speak Swedish. The purpose, he explained, was not to discourage immigration, which Sweden needs, but to aid it by ending the marginalization of newcomers. It did well in 2006, winning 7.5% of the votes and 28 seats and entering the government. The only genuine anti-immigration party won a puny 2% of the votes and no seats at all.

The staid, God-fearing Christian Democrats, led by Alf Svensson, had soared to 11.8% of the votes and 42 seats in 1998, but they slipped back in 2002. In 2006 they garnered 6.6% of the votes and 24 seats to round off the seven-seat majority of the governing Alliance for Sweden.

ECONOMY

Like the U.S., Sweden had entered the postwar era with its factories, cities and economic structure intact. This was a great advantage, especially since it had an ample supply of raw materials and was located close to western Europe, which had been ravished and partly destroyed by the war. It made full use of its advantages and soon had a highly productive and growing economy that created unimagined wealth and generosity.

Sweden has a market economy. One-third of the labor force is employed by the state. It is also very dependent upon exports, which account for half the country's GDP; 80% of its exports consist of industrial products. It must also import heavily, especially oil. This reliance on foreign trade makes Sweden vulnerable to international economic conditions and prices.

The economy is not socialist, since most of the enterprises and means of production remain in private hands. This percentage had traditionally been about 95%, but it was lowered to 92% as a result of state takeovers under the non-S government between 1976 and 1982. In the 21st century, one family alone, the Wallenbergs, in their fifth generation as bankers and philanthropists, control about a third of the value of the companies listed on the Swedish stock exchange. Their holdings include such icons as Electrolux, Ericsson, Scania, ABB and AstraZeneca. With their vast and diversified holdings, little happens in business without their involvement. About 10% of the work-force is employed by state-owned enterprises, which include the railroads, iron ore mining in Lapland, post and telephone services, and a large part of the domestic energy production, primarily hydroelectric. All are in the process of privatization. Sweden has a modern economy, with 76% of its workforce in the services sector, producing 70.3% of GDP, and 22% in industry, creating 28.3% of GDP.

It may seem ironic that the non-S coalition nationalized more Swedish industry in four years after 1976 than S had done in the previous 40. In the worst postwar economic crisis (1975–77) the new government decided that some key ailing industries, especially steel production and shipbuilding sectors, could not be saved through increased state subsidies and mergers. Therefore, it boosted public spending and added more formerly private firms to the State Company (*Statsföretag*), which comprises the major part of the state-owned companies. The result

Volvo assembly plant, Göteborg

Sweden

was rapid wage inflation, a loss of international competitiveness and gaping current accounts deficits.

After 1982, S returned some state-owned firms to private hands. The Bildt government carried this on in 1992 by launching the privatization of 35 such companies. S had returned to the non-interventionist rules of the "Swedish model." Subsidies to lame-duck industries were abolished, and ailing firms are allowed to die. In 2006, Reinfeldt's conservative government turned its attention to the 55 state-owned companies, which employ 190,000 workers, and announced plans to begin with privatizing six of them. Market forces decide which Swedish firms thrive or fail, and many industries from telecommunications to airlines and banking have been deregulated. Whatever financial assistance it gives is concentrated on research and development and on incentives for high-tech investment. Its overall investment in R & D is 4.3% of GDP, the world's highest, followed by Finland (3.5%) and the U.S. (2.6%). Almost 60% of this is financed by private industry.

An impressive example of the growth of the knowledge sector and a new entrepreneurial culture is the expansion of Kista Science Park situated on a former waste site near Stockholm. Started by Ericsson and IBM in the early 1970s, it is now a sprawling complex with 600 technology companies and 27,000 workers. Even the Royal Institute of Technology and the Swedish Institute of Computer Science relocated there. Stockholm has become a breeding ground for Internet companies, and Sweden has more industrial robots per capita than any other country. Research and imagination help explain the country's continued development of modern products that sell well abroad.

S had always tended to leave the private character of the economy untouched, focusing instead on state influence over private industry and heavily taxing the profits. For S it was always more important for the state to be able to gather the eggs rather than to own the hen. What are some of the ways in which the state has influenced the economy and maintained the fabled "Swedish model"?

During its decades of rule, the priority of full employment was established so firmly that the other parties did not dare to challenge it. Unemployment had never risen above 3% since the 1930s, but it was officially 6% in 2008 before shooting up to 9.1% in 2010. It is somewhat higher among women and young people. The actual total figure would be 15%–17% if the state did not "hide" unemployment through temporary work programs, broad retraining possibilities, early-retirement schemes and students unable to find work. The *Financial Times* estimated in 2005 that as many as 1.6 million Swedes, or 30% of the potential workforce, are not working. The average Swede retires at age 63.7. However, it has a higher female workplace participation than most countries.

Among the reasons for low unemployment formerly was an active policy of tackling unemployment, involving imaginative job retraining and other measures to make Swedish workers more mobile. It offers inducements to firms to locate in the north where employment possibilities have always been limited. To add a stick to the carrot, generous unemployment benefits (about 80% of normal pay) are cut off if an unemployed worker refuses to accept either the training or the job he is offered. It was therefore better at reducing long-term unemployment. Even though employees are still protected from layoffs, the government now allows companies to hire temporary workers who can be released at the firm's will. The result is a dramatic expansion of temporary employment companies. Fighting inflation, which stood at 1% in 2010, usually had a low priority. Yet, the fairly tight fiscal and monetary policy that the government pursues helps keep inflation low.

Sweden has a large public sector, high taxes, a generous welfare state, low wage differentials and powerful labor unions. It has one of the world's highest living standards, and a 2007 UN report cited it as having the lowest incidence of poverty in the world. The 2004 UN human development index ranked Sweden second only to Norway as the most attractive place in the world to live. Its vigorous private companies, such as Ericsson (which alone accounted for 8% of GDP in 2002), Volvo and SAAB (except for their automobile divisions, which were put up for sale by Ford and GM respectively), Electrolux, ASEA, SKF and Alfa-Laval, are world leaders in their main products. SAAB's car division was bought in 2000 by GM, which produced its cars in Germany before being put on the auction block in 2009. The Swedish government refused to buy it. As enterprise minister, Maud

Timber cutting

Olofsson, put it, "The Swedish state is not prepared to own car factories." SAAB sells Gripen fighter aircraft not only to the Swedish forces, but also to the Czech Republic, Hungary and South Africa. Many of these large companies are cutting their manufacturing work-force to remain competitive.

With an annual growth rate of 3.2% from 1998 to 2002, but temporarily plunging to minus 6.5% in the midst of the 2009 global downturn and plus 1.5% in 2010, it cannot be called an economic sick man of Europe. It did suffer in 2009–10 as a result of the world recession. Its banks had lent the three Baltic states an equivalent of 18% of Sweden's GDP, so when those three economies contracted by over 10%, they dragged Swedish banks down with them. Fortunately Sweden had learned a lot about rescuing desperately troubled banks in 1992, when the government temporarily nationalized them, cleaned them up with a "bad bank," and then reprivatized them. Other countries, including the U.S., looked at this model in 2008–10 in their efforts to save their banks.

Sweden has a predominantly industrial and service economy, not an agricultural one. Its agricultural population has shrunk rapidly to 2% (producing 1.4% of GDP), but its modern farming methods have led to such increases in productivity that it can supply about 90% of the country's needs. EU entry has helped to keep food prices down.

Sweden is no longer the land of lumberjacks; the number making a living from forestry has dramatically decreased in the past half-century. This is one reason for the shortage of employment opportunities in the North. The immense forests still can supply the raw material for the wood processing industry, which is competitive on world markets despite the rather small size of the companies and the stiff competition from abroad, especially from North America. A fourth of all wood pulp and paper materials sold in the world is from Sweden. The export of other forms of raw materials has lost much of its former importance for the Swedish economy, although it still accounts for a seventh of total exports.

It is a country with many large and multinational firms. The top 20 accounted for half of the country's total sales. Many of these giants, such as Electrolux, Volvo and SAAB-Scania export far more than they sell in Sweden. The large companies have also invested heavily abroad, especially in the U.S., Britain, France and Germany, in order to get closer to their markets. In 1999 Volvo kept its profitable truck, construction equipment, and airplane and marine engine operations when Ford Motor Company acquired Volvo's

passenger vehicle operation. In 2010 Ford sold the car known for its safety to Geely of China, which pledged to keep Volvo's production sites in Sweden and Belgium. At the same time GM put lossmaking SAAB on the auction block again and threatened to shut it down if no buyer could be found. Sweden's foreign subsidiaries employ more workers than do the home companies in Sweden. In 1996 the 25 largest Swedish companies had 75% of their employment, production, and sales abroad.

The best-known industry has traditionally been iron and steel. Sweden's iron ore is of high grade and its steel production is also high. It has actually become a net importer of iron and steel products at present. Too much steel is produced in the world, and the steel industry everywhere is in dire need of restructuring.

Machinery, automobiles, ships, armaments, metal processing, electronics (the fastest growing Swedish industry) and other engineering products have a lion's share of Swedish production and exports. The weakest at the present time is shipbuilding, a traditional Scandinavian specialty. After the mid-1960s, Sweden had been building more ships than any country but Japan and was selling three-fourths of this production to foreigners. This reached a peak in 1976, but then it declined rapidly. There is no hope that the industry will ever fully recover from this crisis. Beginning in 1977 Svenska Varv (Swedish Wharf) absorbed all the big shipyards and began introducing a rigid program of automation. By 1985 these shipyards had a work-force about one-third of their size in 1976. They were also put on notice that they would have to get along without subsidies. Each shipyard specializes on a particular market, such as that for offshore rigs and platforms, tankers, cargo carriers or ferries.

About 80% of Sweden's exports goes to the industrialized world, with the Germany, Norway, the U.S., Denmark, Great Britain and Finland receiving almost half. Swedish companies want to be in the U.S. market because of its size and so that they can absorb new trends in research and marketing. It buys most of its imports from Germany, Denmark, Norway, Great Britain and the Netherlands. Taken together, the other Nordic countries account for roughly a fifth of its foreign trade. Because the workforce is geared to the world market, speaks English and is thoroughly computer literate (Sweden has one of the world's highest number per capita of computers), Sweden is one of the few rich European countries that sees globalization as an opportunity, not a threat.

Those who believe that Sweden has a charmed economic existence received evi-

dence of that in 2007. Two lady friends in the northern Swedish town of Overturingen were scouring the countryside in search of blueberries when they noticed something strange in the soil exposed by upended trees. They happened to have geologists' hammers and magnifying eyepieces with them. They dug for six hours and came upon what may be one of Europe's richest gold deposits. Sweden has some gold, but it has never been among the major gold mining countries.

European Union

The EU accounted for 61.2% of its exports and 70.9% of its imports in 2010. This offers the best explanation why Swedes voted 52.3% to 46.8% in 1994 to enter the EU in 1995. A united front of most of the country's business and political establishment supported entry. They argued that Sweden needed the EU to bolster its exports, keep companies from moving more jobs and investments abroad, improve its lagging international credit rating, and shore up its troubled economy. Farmers, environmentalists and leftists, especially in rural areas in northern and central Sweden, led the opposition, arguing that Sweden's voice would be drowned out in the European cacophony.

Even after entry, opposition remained strong, especially to monetary union. The government held a referendum on the question in September 2003. All major parties, the business elite and the media broadly favored the euro, with former communists, far right, environmentalist Greens and young Swedes against. Taking place only three days after the popular foreign minister and spokesperson for the "yes" campaign, Anna Lindh, had been stabbed to death in a Stockholm department store, proponents expected a heavy sympathy vote in favor.

The results were a landslide defeat. With over 80% voting, 56% said "no" and only 42% said "yes." Voters under age 30 voted more heavily against it than any other age group. Swedes were persuaded by economics, not sentimentality. Sweden was performing better than in the euro zone. Its budget was balanced, its growth rate twice as high, and its unemployment rate much lower. Its economy has also benefited in the past from competitive devaluations of the krona against the dollar. There was much resentment about France's and Germany's disregard for their obligation under the euro rules to limit their budget deficits to 3% of GDP. This seemed to enable large countries to bend the rules to suit themselves while holding small ones to their commitments. Finally, the vote expressed the worry of many Swedes that European integration was creating too much centralization in Brussels.

Sweden

Dissatisfaction over some other changes also played a role, such as the EU demand that Sweden liberalize its restriction on alcohol. This had been one of the cornerstones of Swedish social policy throughout the 20th century. It had to drop state monopolies on the import and wholesale distribution of spirits.

Energy Dependence

Energy is one of Sweden's economic Achilles' heels. Like the other Nordic countries, which are sparsely populated and situated in a cold climate, its energy consumption per capita is among the highest in the world (but behind that of Norway, Canada and the United States). It is very dependent upon OPEC countries, especially Saudi Arabia, for a particularly vital import: oil. Slightly over half of its energy needs must be covered by imports (down from 78% in 1973), especially by oil. Accounting for 15% of its overall needs, water power is its most important domestic source, providing half of its electricity generation; nuclear power produces the other half. Wood accounts for 2% of overall needs, nuclear power for about 15%, and coal, coke, wastes and other domestic sources for 12%.

Efforts are being made to reduce reliance on oil. Sweden is continuing its effective conservation measures. Between 1976 and 1986, it halved its oil consumption in response to the "oil shock," despite a growing number of automobiles. It has begun to serve clusters of homes with heat produced centrally in nearby heat plants and also is increasing its use of imported coal, peat, its own wood, water power and nuclear power. Sweden produces Europe's second highest percentage of renewable energy as a proportion of its total energy needs (29.6% in 2007, EU average is 6.5%) after Latvia.

Sweden dived deeply into nuclear energy. S had developed plans during its last years in power before the 1976 election to build a total of 24 nuclear plants that could provide over half of all the country's energy. The Center Party placed the issue squarely in the political limelight during the 1976 election, and in power it refused to permit the fueling and starting up of the seventh and eighth plants. After two years of wrangling within the center coalition and countless demonstrations by the powerful environmentalist groups, the government collapsed on the issue.

When the nuclear accident occurred at Three Mile Island near Harrisburg, Pennsylvania, the government decided to put the issue of nuclear power to a referendum in 1980. The results represented a kind of compromise: Sweden would complete the construction of 12 reactors, but it would shut down all nuclear plants by 2010. This defused the issue for a while. The Chernobyl accident in the Ukraine in 1986 caused limited but highly publicized radioactive contamination in northern Sweden. The heat of the public debate over nuclear power in Sweden again reached meltdown levels.

Sweden is on the horns of an energy dilemma. To buy more time, the government announced in 1991 that plans to abolish nuclear power would be postponed while energy-saving and pollution-free alternatives were sought. The Persson government closed down one plant in 1999 and another in 2005, leaving only 10 plants running in 2006, producing 52% of the country's electricity. In August 2006 one of them was temporarily shut down after its emergency systems were activated. The same thing happened again in October 2008 when cracks in some control rods were discovered in the Oskarshamm 3 plant.

Sweden's energy problems will increase in the future. The country's estimated uranium reserves of over 300,000 tons made it tempting to stick with this important source of domestic energy rather than to scramble to supply an even greater percentage of its total needs with expensive carbon imports. Already it generates slightly over half of its electricity from nuclear power, a percentage that is steadily rising—in 1986 it used twice as much nuclear energy as it did in 1980.

No adequate substitute sources have been found. This is why Prime Minister Reinfeldt announced in February 2009 a plan to reverse the 30-year ban on building new nuclear power plants. Legislation sponsored by his government calls for a renewal of building additional reactors beyond the current ten providing that permanent storage space for the radioactive waste be created beforehand. He moved slowly to give all parties the chance to develop a consensus. Polls in 2009 indicated that Swedes support the idea: 57% agreed that it should be possible to replace old nuclear plants with new ones, and 70% think the government's energy package is good.

The return to nuclear power facilitated the development of safer nuclear reactors. The Swedes, with their "Process Inherent Ultimately Safe Reactor" (PIUS), are pioneering in the newest nuclear technology and could turn a bitter necessity into a commercially profitable virtue. Sweden has an excellent record of nuclear safety. An unfortunate consequence of continued shutdowns could be that Sweden would have to increase its use of electricity generated by Russian and Baltic nuclear plants, none of which meet Swedish safety standards.

Labor Unions

Since 1938, when an agreement between the employer organizations and trade unions was reached at Saltsjöbaden, relations between management and labor have, on the whole, been characterized by cooperation rather than by confrontation. All Swedes benefited from this. Every year or two the highest representatives of the LO (*Landsorganisationen*), which represents 15 unions with 1.8 million members, and the SAF met to establish general wage guidelines which were then normally observed down the line. The LO was able to insist upon the principle of "solidarity wages," which means equal pay for the same kind of work regardless of the profitability of any specific firm. Thus, struggling firms could be strained even further by having to pay the same wages as the more successful companies.

The concept of "solidarity wages is under attack by skilled workers' unions and employers. Also, the unions, to which 90% of the labor force belongs, carefully guard the pay differentials between certain categories of jobs. When these pay differentials are not observed, rare but serious nationwide strikes can break out. Centralized wage negotiations, abandoned in 1984, often brought stability and labor peace. The nonsocialist government proposed in 1991 to dismantle centralized wage bargaining (which has all but disappeared), deregulating the labor market and lowering corporate wage bills. But Swedish unions resist the steep decline suffered by trade unions elsewhere by accepting necessary technological change. They traditionally are innovative, not reactive. They still run the country's unemployment benefits schemes. In 2006 the top LO boss was a woman, Wanja Lunby-Weden.

National Debt

To pay for its imports, its budgetary deficits and the foreign travel its prosperous citizens have come to love, Sweden went deeper and deeper into debt. High wage costs and tax rates deprive industries of investment funds they need to maintain their productivity. Any drop in productivity strikes at the very heart of Sweden's "middle way." That model, by which social welfare and income redistribution would be paid for by a robust private sector, now seems to work only in times of economic growth.

Sweden's high public consumption is vividly reflected in its comprehensive social welfare system, which some admirers contend make it the most just society in the world. Some observers have called it the perfect "postindustrial" society that has effectively solved its problems of production and can now concentrate on distributing economic and social benefits widely and justly. In other words, the consumption and distribution of wealth had allegedly replaced the *production of it* as the society's major problem. The resulting economic difficulties showed how the "postindustrial" situation is by no means static, if it ever existed at all, and that there are great dangers in focusing too much on consumption and losing sight of production. Welfare spending was significantly trimmed in the 1990s, bringing by 2005 the total national debt down to 49.9% of GDP and creating an annual budget surplus of an impressive 2.4% of GDP in 2008. That ballooned to a 4.7% deficit in 2009, as the government provided a hefty stimulus to revive an economy hurt by the global recession.

Welfarism and Taxation

Swedes understandably do not wish to give up a welfare system that pays almost all doctors' bills and at least half of dental bills, which provides invalids with about 90% of their normal pay until age 65 and which pays the unemployed 80% of their former income. It provides five weeks of paid vacation time and allows the employee to save up his vacation time and take it all in one extended period. By 1995 the average workweek for a full-time employee was 36 hours, one of the lowest in all Europe; the average time off work, for all reasons including vacation, is about 25%.

Sick pay of 80% of normal earnings after the first day of illness (for which one receives nothing) encourage the average Swede to be officially absent from work for reasons of illness 25 days (more than a working month) per year. In the sparsely populated North, this sickness absenteeism rises to 70 days per year. Even though the average Swede smokes less, drinks less, weighs less and lives longer than other Europeans, on any given workday, over 10% of the 4.5 million workforce (500,000) is absent due to illness. Such sickness costs Sweden roughly as much as it spends on defense, foreign aid, higher education and research put together. A 2002 poll revealed that two-thirds (62%) believe it is all right to be off sick even when one is feeling fine. Needless to say, this can play havoc with production schedules that depend upon the presence of key employees. Another 528,000 Swedes had by 2005 retired on sickness pensions.

One poor soul was diagnosed in 2007 as being "addicted" to heavy metal music and was therefore declared eligible to receive income support. The state pays 20% of his salary, and he is permitted both to listen to such music while he works and take time off at any time to attend concerts as long as he makes up the lost time. No wonder there is a perception of widespread fraud.

This welfare system is generous, but many Swedes agree that it is impossible to pay for. Costs of maintaining the system have expanded annually more rapidly than has economic growth. But as conservatives experienced in the 1994 elections, it was risky to reduce social programs that Swedes have grown to regard as their birthright. For more than 50 years they had been taught that state and society were the same things and that the function of government was to attempt to solve all problems. The Bildt government's message was that "the state ought not to strive after doing what a free society can manage better or as well." It no longer saw a need for welfare services to be entirely under public management and control; private initiative enjoyed more encouragement. Even S, which built the welfare state, supported crisis measures to save Sweden's economy and currency. These included reducing housing subsidies, sickness benefits, and foreign aid, making employers and employees share health benefits and sickness insurance with the state, raising gasoline and cigarette taxes.

Old age pensions were changed to begin at age 67. Considering that the average Swede retires at 63.7 years of age, this requires an adjustment. The population is rapidly ageing: in 2008, 17% were over 65, and that will rise to an estimated 24% by 2040. About 93% of elderly live at home. To secure the solvency of the system, Sweden radically restructured its basic taxpayer-funded retirement system and even permits a portion of the funds to be invested in the stock and bond market. It moved its pension system from defined benefits to defined contribution, meaning that what one receives in retirement varies according to how much one paid into the system. Thus Swedes lost their guaranteed generous state pensions. Not surprisingly, the private pension market is booming.

Unlike Norway, Sweden has no oil revenues that can pay the difference. The national, regional and local governments employ almost 40% of the Swedish workforce (compared to the OECD average of one-fifth). By 1995 public spending represented a whopping 70% of Sweden's GDP, compared with 45% in 1973. The bulk of government spending can only be paid for by direct and indirect taxes, which are over half (51.4% in 2005) of the average Swede's wages, the highest in the OECD.

Income taxes are steeply progressive. The top marginal rate in 1989 was 72%, which Swedes paid when their incomes reached about $50,000. The tax code appeared unjust because rich Swedes learned how to use the complex system of deductions to lighten their burden. In 1989 Finance Minister Kjell-Olof Feldt

called it "rotten." The major parties agreed to simplify the income tax structure by introducing a differing rate structure: 34% for the average payer who earns under $43,000 per year, and 56% for those earning more. Corporate tax was reduced from 50% to 30%. Many loop-holes were eliminated. Taxes on capital gains were made more equitable with other forms of income. Swedes still pay a VAT of 25%.

The extremely high tax level has had many negative consequences. It drove such wealthy Swedes as tennis star Björn Borg and skier Ingemar Stenmark into tax exile in Monaco. It drives some business out of the country. For example Ericsson, a telecoms supplier, moved key corporate and production functions abroad; in 1999 it opened a big headquarters in London in order to help it recruit foreign managers who would refuse to settle in high-tax Sweden. It has encouraged tax evasion and "barter work," one of the most primitive forms of work whereby Swedes swap services with each other behind the backs of the tax officials. For instance, a carpenter builds a cabinet for a mechanic who repairs his car in return. By 2003 it was estimated that such an "underground economy" combined with smuggling equals 5%–10% of GDP.

The tax system also discourages some Swedes from seeking promotions because most of the added pay would be collected by the state anyway. Working overtime is less attractive for the same reason. For example, in 1979 an employer offered his workers a bonus of $2,000 if they worked between Christmas and New Years, but it

One of Sweden's many rivers—every fifth family owns a boat

Sweden

was turned down because taxes would make the bonus negligible. Also, a fourth of the total labor force now finds it more attractive to work half-time than full-time because of the tax structure.

The welfare system would not have some of these negative effects if the former Lutheran work ethic had remained intact. As late as the early 1970s one's social status and self-esteem was still largely established by one's occupation and position. However, as in many other industrialized countries, many Swedes' drive to have individual success has weakened, and the importance attached to financial rewards and status has decreased. Fewer people obtain job satisfaction, partly because much work has become automated and routinized, and partly because prosperity created leisure-time activities that became increasingly attractive. In other words, Swedes have fewer qualms about being absent from work.

The Reinfeldt government sought to crack down on welfare cheating by creating a fraud squad to investigate criminal misuse and passing legislation making it easier to prosecute cheaters. It also ended the previous practice of simply trusting without checking claims that are filed. A government-appointed commission concluded in 2007 that up to 6% of total social welfare payments result from fraud or abuse. Considering that 12% of the population are foreigners, many of whom cannot find work, an increasing number of Swedes believe the traditional welfare system is unsustainable.

Finally, the social welfare system, which distributes 15% of GDP, has not evened out the differences in income, as many of its proponents had hoped, although these differences are certainly narrower than in most countries, including the U.S. Nor has the welfare system led to a diminution of crime, alcoholism, suicides, juvenile delinquency, vandalism or other antisocial activities, as many of its supporters had argued that it would. In fact, crime has risen so much, especially in the cities, that Sweden became one of the first countries in the world to provide financial compensation to victims of violent crimes.

CULTURE

The Equality Goal

Perhaps no nation in all of Europe has tried so hard to establish equality in so many segments of its society as have the Swedes. They have been willing to experiment, and their reforms are regarded with great interest from abroad. In many ways they have fallen short of this goal; there are still noticeable differences in wealth, income and social status, and not all Swedes agree that every single effort

and policy designed to achieve the goal of equality has been a good one. Many of the policies are being criticized on the grounds that they are unrealistic or that they place limits on the ability of an individual to use his talents to the fullest and to reap the benefits of his own capacity and effort. Critics contend that the result is often mediocrity, omnipresent and suffocating bureaucracy, or worse, a restriction of human freedom. But Swedes are a tolerant people with a strong pluralistic tradition. They debate these matters openly and do not try to hide the problems or the failures. Also, they have always had a pragmatic inclination and are able to undo those reforms, which most might agree have created more problems than they have solved.

One distinction among people that has almost entirely disappeared involves the word "you." The person who speaks English uses the same word for all individuals he addresses, remnants of this lingual distinction having disappeared from English in the last century (the formal usage was "thee," "thou" and "thine"). But all other European languages have preserved different words for "you"—a formal one (in Swedish, *ni*) for persons whom one does not know well, whom one wants to keep at arm's length or whom one wants to show particular respect, and an informal one (in Swedish, *du*) for friends, family or often those beneath one's own social station (such as a maid or gardener). More than in any other European country, the formal *ni* has fallen into disuse, and almost everyone is simply addressed as *du*. The only exceptions are elderly persons who cannot accept such a modern equalizing step in their last years and the king and queen, whom only journalists dare to address in public as *du*.

In addition to dropping the formal "you," they are also casting off many of the academic and occupational titles that used to adorn so many persons' names. Swedes were traditionally a very title-conscious people, with many persons attaching to their name a "Dr.," "Mr. Director," "Mr. Chief Postal Inspector," or, of course, a title of nobility in this monarchical country. One uses the titles less often now because they no longer fit easily into the egalitarian movement. Pupils do not call their teachers "Mr.," or "Mrs.," and students at the universities seldom address their professors or instructors as "Professor" or "Doctor." An American professor is surprised to hear his Swedish students calling him by his first name. In fact, the few persons who acquire Ph.D. degrees in Sweden today can look forward to a life in which only their families and employers will even know that they have achieved this academic distinction.

The Family

More equality has seeped into the Swedish family, where few fathers are stern disciplinarians who are treated with a combination of love, respect and fear by other members. With one of the world's highest female participation rates in the labor force, the patriarchal character of the Swedish family declined or disappeared and the position of both sexes was equalized. Family members have a more relaxed, comradely relationship with each other, especially in urban, middle class families.

As in most advanced industrialized societies, the extended family no longer lives under one roof. The elderly are financially independent since they receive at age 65 pensions that amount to two-thirds of their earlier working incomes and that are regularly adjusted for inflation. At present, 16% of Swedes receive old age pensions. The state provides them with an array of social services if they are needed. These services include the cleaning of their apartments or bodies in order to keep hygienic standards high, delivery of complete meals, chauffeuring and even special subsidies to enable them to remain in their own homes as long as possible. When they need full care, they can move into state-operated homes for the elderly. This usually occurs at about age 80. This involves many Swedes, since the life expectancy is 78.7 for men and 83 for women.

Fewer and fewer persons are in the work-force to support them because the nation's population is growing only because of immigration. By 2003 the total fertility rate of Swedish women had fallen to 1.29 per woman, whereas the rate needed to match the number of people dying is 2.1. One baby in four being born is from an immigrant family. The modest annual population increase is almost entirely due to immigrants' high birth rate, but by 2006 Swedes' birthrate was again rising. Sweden has the lowest infant mortality rate in the world. Contrary to a popular misconception, it does not have Europe's highest suicide rate; Finland, Denmark, Austria, Switzerland and Germany all have higher rates.

There are some persons who find drawbacks in the breakdown of the extended family under one roof, but the absence of the elderly from the homes of their children's families has undoubtedly brought greater freedom to most of those families and has eliminated an authority pattern which tended to bring more hierarchy and less equality into the family.

Not only the Swedish extended family has changed, but the very institution of the family is undergoing radical alteration. By the end of the 1980s the Swedish marriage rate had fallen to the lowest in the industrial world. Nonmarital cohabitation, which is now regarded legally and culturally as an accepted alternative rather than as a prelude to marriage, is the highest. Two-thirds of all couples have lived together before marriage; among the young, the rate is close to 90%. Half the babies are born out of wedlock. The average ages for first marriages are 30 for men and 27 for women (vs. 25.5 and 23.3 in the U.S.).

A growing number of Swedes are not marrying at all. In today's cohabitation environment, even the arrival of children is no longer a strong reason for marriage. Gone for the most part are engagement parties and elaborate weddings. Divorce is also reducing the number of families, although the Swedish rate is slightly lower than the American one and stopped rising by 1991. Thus, an ever-larger percentage of Swedish families have only one parent.

In 1994 homosexuals were granted the right to enter civil partnerships. Since 2004 they are allowed to adopt children or to have them by artificial insemination in Sweden. Most gay couples who opt for the latter go to Denmark for the procedure. In 2009 gays received the same right to marry as heterosexual couples. Individual churches retain the right to decide if they want to wed gay couples. There is an ombudsman for gays and lesbians to ensure that homosexual rights are respected.

In a country in which 70% of adult women have full- or part-time jobs (encouraged by the tax system, which taxes each partner separately), having children can cause certain strains. The state provides certain payments and allowances to families with children so that their living standards will not fall below those of families in which there are no children. These payments vary; the less the parents earn, the more such assistance they receive. When a child is born, both the mother and the father have the right to divide 14 months of almost fully paid vacation (80% of lost wages up to SKr24,562 or $3,425 per month) in order to care for the infant. An additional 90 days could be taken off for a token sum.

Even nonworking parents can receive a per diem allowance for 14 months to care for the child. Or, they can put aside six months of this childcare vacation and use them at any other time for any reason until the child is eight years old. Mothers take 85% of all parental leave. Both the father and the mother have the right to take up to 60 days paid sick leave per child not only if they are ill, but if their child is ill. Thus, while the law encourages both parents to work, (an undeniable factor in national and personal prosperity), it has to provide benefits to enable them to perform the mother's traditional chores.

The child enjoys a legal protection against being spanked or hit by his parents: "A child may not be subjected to physical punishment or other injurious or humiliating treatment." One Stockholm youth police officer explained, "if grownups don't hit each other, then they can't hit children either." The main argument in favor of the law is that it might limit child abuse; most child abusers were once abused themselves as children. Swedish children are very aware of the law, and there is considerable discussion among parents and children on how parents can discipline children without hitting them. In any event, the law reflects the extent to which the child's role in the modern Swedish family has changed. By 2000 only 6% of parents under age 35 supported the use of physical punishment. Seven European nations have followed the Swedish example, and more are considering doing so.

The woman's role in the family has also changed; 60% work outside the home. The law protects her equality at the work place. A special equality ombudsman, who is usually a woman, is empowered to investigate complaints of discrimination. There are numerous visible signs of women's changed role in society. They can now perform sentry duty at the Royal Palace in Stockholm, a place where the head resident can be a woman now that the law of succession was changed. Sweden's UN Peacekeeping Forces include women. In 1999 the government proposed that the equality of women be recognized by subjecting them to military conscription. This requires a change of the constitution, which forbids gender discrimination except in cases of military service or affirmative action. Since 1980 females are allowed to join the officer corps and constitute 2% of the total. They have entered the priesthood of the Swedish State Church. Women's wages still are less than men's, and in 2004 only two out of 282 chief executives in the top companies were female.

Although the women's role as equals in family decision making is rather secure, they must still do more of the housework than do men. The government-sponsored Equality Commission reported that in families where both partners had full-time jobs, 51% of the women worked 20 hours or more in the home and 10% did more than 40 hours of work, compared with only 18% of the men, who did 20 hours or more and 2% who did more than 40 hours. As one expert said, "we are still a long way from achieving real equality in Sweden. In the home there is not a lot else we can do, except by keeping the debate alive." For a while, at least, men will continue to be able to take it a little easier at home than will women. Nevertheless, in 2005 the World Economic Forum ranked Sweden first in the world in terms of women's position in society, followed by the four other Nordic countries.

Sexual Revolution

Sexual liberation was one form of emancipation that the Swedish woman was reputed to have since the 1950s, at least in the eyes of many foreigners. The outward evidence seemed to be clear. Films such as "She Danced Only One Summer," starring Ulla Jacobson, Ingmar Bergman's "Virgin Spring," or Vilgot Sjöman's two films, "I Am Curious–Yellow" and "I Am Curious–Blue" revealed nudity and sexual activity with a vividness that was shocking and sensational by the standards of the times. People did sometimes bathe publicly in the nude. Almost all limitations on pornography were dropped, and it could be displayed almost anywhere, including gasoline stations. In 1955, sex education was introduced as a required subject in the schools, teenage girls were able to get birth control pills,

Swedish student at College of Europe, Bruges

Sweden

and condom machines were put in many public places, including student union buildings.

Those who actually came to Sweden expecting to find a society where all sexual inhibitions had disappeared were badly disappointed, though. As in other European and North American countries, sexual attitudes had begun to change, but the changes in Swedish sexual mores never meant promiscuity, and the Swedes were not *avant-gardes* in the sexual revolution. In fact, observers who know Sweden well note that the Swedes are rather prudish compared to other northern Europeans. Nude bathing was mainly a family affair, and although it is practiced somewhat more widely in Sweden today, it is by no means more prevalent than in most other European lands, especially in Germany, where this is frequently seen in public parks.

The lead in the production and sale of pornography soon passed to such countries as Denmark and the Netherlands (which never acquired a reputation as sin centers), and pornography is openly available in most European countries. In short, the image of Sweden as the land of sexual license is one that the Swedes neither deserve, nor particularly desire to have. The constitution protects freedom of expression, including adult pornography. While the publication and distribution of child pornography is banned by law, the fact that Swedes are unique in Europe in being permitted to own and view it prompted Queen Silvia to break with tradition and attack it in an outspoken television interview in 1996. Although most Swedes agree with her opinion, the audacity of a monarch to intervene in political debate was surprising.

The public manifestations of changed attitudes toward sexual matters in Sweden were a reflection of the Swedes' fundamental tolerance. There are many Swedes today who think that tighter limits should be drawn. Many voices have been raised against the law that was liberalized in 1975 to permit abortions until the 12th week with no questions asked and until the 18th week under certain circumstances. For a couple of decades abortions have been legal under certain circumstances, but many people are distressed by the fact that one-third of all pregnancies are now terminated by abortion. There have also been calls to place limits on prostitution, although no government has attempted to outlaw this ancient profession.

Sweden has made the fight against the international trafficking in women a high-priority foreign policy issue. It is perhaps the only Western country to pass a pilot law making the purchase, not the sale, of sexual services illegal. In other words, the prostitute is regarded as the victim, and it is not the prostitute, but those who buy or organize the sexual services, who break the law.

Education

Since the 1960s increasing stress has been placed upon achieving social equality and less on competition. The general idea is that all persons are born with talent and capabilities, but an unequal social environment creates the differences among human beings. The schools are seen as an important socializing agent to counteract the unequal environment in other parts of the society. Put in an oversimplified way, the schools should focus more on social development than upon learning.

Most children attend the same basic school (*grundskolan*) for nine years. New teaching methods have been introduced, including group work, individualized curricula and special activities, such as learning chess in the fourth grade. The issuing of grades is strictly limited in the first six years, and there are no final examinations during the first nine years. After the nine compulsory years, about 80% continue for two or four years in an integrated high school called *gymnasieskolan*. This combines more than 20 different curricula under one roof. Some pupils take a more rigorous academic course, preparing one for university studies, while others take a more practical course preparing one for a trade or commercial career.

Over 10% of pupils go to the 600 independent schools that are funded by the state but are operated privately and permitted to select students according to their own criteria. Children attend them free, but the schools must meet national educational standards.

All pupils who finish a course of study at this integrated high school are eligible to apply for a place at one of the more than 30 state institutions of higher educa-tion, integrated in a single system of higher education (*högskola*). The major universities are in Uppsala, Lund, Stockholm, Göteborg, Örebro, Växjö and Umeå. There are only a limited number of places in each field. Rather than distributing these places strictly on the basis of previous academic performance, a fourth of them are reserved for people over age 25 with four years of work experience or two years at the high school and knowledge of Swedish and English. The rest of the openings are given to those applicants with the best academic records. Women dominate the lecture halls in some fields: 59% of the university graduates are women. Most law and theology students are female, as are four-fifths of students enrolled in medical and diagnostic treatment programs. Men still predominate in departments of engineering, national science and math, and business administration.

Many critics argue that the preferential treatment given to those who did not prepare for the university, but who entered later in life creates at best an equality of mediocrity. They say that the academic standards have gone down considerably, that the university has become easier and that the students cannot write well any more. There are almost no critics against the fact that there is no tuition at the universities and that most students receive loans to help finance their studies. The borrowers must pay back a sum to which intervening inflation has been added. Nor is there any criticism against the well-developed system of adult education, which was created in the 19th century. These kinds of equal opportunity are seen to be good. But the kind of equality which subordinates academic talent and performance to class or social considerations and which thereby lowers the quality of scholarship has not been accepted. In general, there is something of a backlash forming against what many Swedes see as

The changing faces of Sweden

a lowering of standards and discipline in schools at all levels. Societies have been formed to press for changes in what they see as a trend toward mediocrity. However, it is too early to say what long-term effect this undercurrent of protest and dissatisfaction will have.

Ethnic Diversity

Further compounding educational (and economic) problems is Sweden's growing ethnic diversity. Unlike some other European nations, Sweden had no colonial possessions in the past several centuries that exposed its society to foreign influences. In the 1960s, Sweden's booming industry was starved for labor, so immigrants were attracted to it from outside the Nordic area. But it never adopted a "guest worker" policy that foresaw immigrants returning to their countries once their jobs ended. The percentage of Nordics among the total foreign population in Sweden fell from about two-thirds in 1971 to less than half today.

The influx is greatly influenced by conflicts in the world. The crack-down and declaration of martial law in Poland at the end of 1981 brought many Poles to the country. A wave of "boat people" from Vietnam also drifted ashore. They were callously driven from their homeland by a regime the Swedish government and many Swedes had passionately supported during the Vietnam War in the 1960s.

After 2003 Iraqis became the second largest immigrant group after Finns. By 2008 Iraqis numbered 80,000, a third of whom were unemployed. The governments of the two countries reached an agreement in 2008 allowing some of them to be returned home forcibly. Swedish attitudes are changing, and the government is altering the asylum requirements. Seekers must now prove that they are being singled out for persecution, and only one in five can do that (down from 80% earlier). Those denied entry can either accept a little money and a free plane ticket home, or they can be ejected by the police.

Nordic immigrants can become citizens after only two years; for others the minimum is five, and there are inhibiting costs and complications. About 60% of the more than one million immigrants have acquired Swedish citizenship, but even non-Swedes with work and residence permits by law are treated on the basis of equality with native Swedes. This means that immigrants receive all welfare benefits for which they have contributed but little, that they are not forced to go home if they lose their jobs and that they can even vote and stand for election in local and regional elections, as long as they have been residents there for at least three years.

A night-time scene of *The Nutcracker* performed at the Stockholm Opera

Government offices distribute information materials in 14 languages explaining residents' rights and duties, taxes, insurance, employment and educational possibilities. The state also publishes an immigrant newspaper in six languages. Employers are required to provide foreigners with up to 240 hours of Swedish language instruction on company time. In 2010 a new immigration policy took effect paying immigrants to attend full-time language classes, civic orientation courses, or job training for two years after they obtain residence permits. The chief aim is to get women into the labor market.

Schools are required to give auxiliary Swedish lessons to immigrant children for as many years as are necessary to make the child completely competent in the language. They must offer special instruction to an immigrant child in his own mother tongue for as long as the parents desire such instruction. For adults who desire it, the schools also arrange for home study of the non-Swedish native language. The basic principle is that the state should be committed to helping any person residing in the country to maintain his own language.

The extent to which Swedish officialdom has gone to accommodate immigrants is perhaps unparalleled in the entire world. Public opinion surveys also underscore the fact that, while there is widespread opposition to further immigration, there is still considerable toleration toward those immigrants who already are in Sweden. There are no race riots as there have been in certain other countries, such as Britain and the U.S. There are also no strong vote-catching anti-immigration parties as in Norway and Denmark.

Many Swedes are having difficulties learning to live with the large number of foreigners within their midst, especially in the larger cities. By 2003, a tenth of the residents are non-Nordic. Assimilation of the one-fourth of the population that is either foreign-born or have a least one parent born abroad has not succeeded. Therefore, a new Integration Office reflects a changed government focus on insuring that individuals in diverse groups have equal rights and opportunities and are not subjected to racism and discrimination.

This difficulty is made worse by the fact that the visible increase in non-European and Southern European immigrants and asylum seekers has coincided with a frightening rise in unemployment and crime. Immigrants, who most often, but not always, work at the dirtiest, noisiest or most monotonous jobs, are increasingly confronting Swedish prejudice and anxiety about the changing ethnic composition of Swedish cities.

In some cities, such as Malmö, the immigrant population (either born abroad or having two foreign parents) had reached 37% by 2008 and will be a majority within a decade. In the suburb of Rosengard it exceeded 90%, compared with the national average of 15%. Half and rising of the children in Malmö schools have at least one foreign-born parent. Malmö, one-fourth of whose population is Muslim, has become one of Europe's most racially divided cities, and there is little interaction between the communities. This is made worse by a Danish marriage law that forbids a foreign spouse under 24 from living in the country; to get around this couples live in Malmö and commute to Copenhagen to work.

Sweden

In Europe today, any immigrant minority that approaches or exceeds 10% of the city's population usually spells trouble in one form or another. In 1989 a parliamentary commission of inquiry against racism and xenophobia judged the danger to have grown sufficiently that it recommended a law banning racist organizations. The extraordinary campaign to block the 2004 Olympic Games from coming to Stockholm demonstrated the problem. An extremist organization calling itself "We who build Sweden" asserted that it would "never allow a large number of niggers, Latinos and Eurotrash to come here, paid for by the Swedish taxpayer." Two bombs went off, and dozens of explosively racist threats were made. Partly because of this obnoxious campaign by a determined minority, Stockholm was not even among the top three contenders for the games.

Neo-Nazis were very active in 1999. They "executed" two policemen in southern Sweden, killed a trade-union official who had exposed a colleague as a neo-Nazi infiltrator, wounded an investigative journalist and his son in a car-bomb attack because of his reporting on far-right groups, issued death threats to scores of prominent people and their families who have supported immigrant-related causes, and threatened history teachers whose syllabi include the Holocaust. Research by Swedish newspapers revealed that nine of ten policemen and six of ten prosecuting attorneys and their families had received threats.

The problem of rights violations does not stem only from extremist locals. Swedes were stunned in 2002 when a Kurdish father in the university town of Uppsala fatally shot his daughter in the head in the presence of her mother and younger sister for refusing an arranged marriage with a stranger from Turkey. The victim had been an outspoken champion for second-generation immigrants seeking their own way of life.

The killing called into question Sweden's capacity to integrate its growing ethnic minorities, which in 2004 included 400,000 Muslims. Authorities moved to close a legal loophole that permitted foreign girls to marry at age 15, when others may wed only at 18. They also granted more money to crisis centers for young women trying to avoid arranged marriages or leave violent partners. Such incidents have lessened Swedes' readiness to allow foreigners to remain in the country: in the 1970s and 1980s about 80% of applicants were permitted to stay, but that percentage had fallen to 40% in the 1990s.

Concern is mounting that Sweden is accepting more than its fair share of immigrants. In this charged atmosphere a cartoonist, Lars Vilks, published in 2007 a crude sketch of a dog with the head of Muhammad in a provincial newspaper, *Nerikes Allehanda*, igniting protests in the Muslim world. Only a timely response from Prime Minister Reinfeldt, who expressed regret for the bad taste and met with a delegation of Muslim ambassadors, prevented the kind of violent outcry when Danish artists had produced similar drawings in 2005. But police had to hide Vilks after a radical Muslim group offered $150,000 if he were "slaughtered like a lamb." In 2010 seven persons, including two American women, were charged with plotting to murder him.

Swedes are very hospitable towards guests whom they invite in their homes, but as one observer, Richard F. Tomasson wrote, "There is general agreement on the Swedes as stolid and stiff, shy or reserved, formal and conventional, inhibited—even dull, nonexpressive, more interested in things than in people." Even Olof Palme stated in the precise English he learned as a student at Kenyon College in Ohio that "we're probably shy and reserved, . . . and the humor of hell would have the humor of Sweden. We are distant and perhaps rather dull." Thanks to the influence of immigrants and the fact that Sweden is more open to Europe, that "distance" and "dullness" is changing, especially among the well-traveled youth.

This is still a country with much public decorum, and many Swedes are inclined to withdraw into quiet anonymity. The content of much of Sweden's contemporary literature and of many of its films is the problem that individuals have in establishing meaningful contacts and relationships with others. It is therefore not surprising that many immigrants perceive their official treatment as fair and generous, but on the personal level such treatment is not always warm and friendly, and is sometimes even aloof and hostile.

A Stockholm University ethnographer, Åke Daun, confirmed these traits of coolness, shyness and introversion in a 1989 study. He reported that only 24% of adult Swedes admitted being moved to tears when hearing of Olof Palme's assassination, compared with 44% of first-generation immigrants to Sweden. Swedes see shyness as a positive trait and talkativeness as a negative one; they prefer being silent and alone. There is, of course, a positive side to all this: they shun conflict and do not like to say things for the sake of teasing others. Half as many Swedes as Italians and Finns admit to losing their temper easily if they cannot get their way.

The growing Swedish anxiety has been reflected in much tighter Swedish regulations for newcomers. Almost no one coming from outside the Nordic area can now receive a work permit, and, as a rule, only family members of immigrants already in Sweden are allowed to settle there. Further, Swedish authorities are making faster and stricter decisions on applications by political refugees and are immediately deporting those who are denied this status. Sweden, like most other wealthy European nations, has begun to close its open door.

It turns away people with unfounded claims to asylum. Nevertheless, 40,000 asylum seekers were arriving in Sweden each year by 2003, in part because other European countries had applied greater restrictions. It was estimated in 2005 that about 10,000 persons whose asylum had been rejected had simply gone underground in Sweden. In the face of furious demands from churches, parties and immigration organizations that they be legalized, the government allowed such illegal residents to reapply for asylum. With EU enlargement in 2004, Sweden at first announced temporary restrictions on the free movement of workers from the eight new members from Central Europe. But parliament decided that these measures were too restrictive, and Sweden became one of the few EU15 members to keep its doors open.

Sweden is a tolerant and generous country and wants to remain a refuge for the politically oppressed. But it is not willing to be a land of unlimited opportunities for outsiders. Swedish idealism has its limits, especially in time of economic distress.

State Goals in Culture

Sweden has an ambitious cultural policy and devotes more than 1% of state expenditures to it. One journalist, Anders Ehnmark, told why many Swedes think such an effort to support Swedish culture is necessary: "Sweden is a small country, with a low threshold of resistance to banality arriving from outside. For many years it has been a thoroughly Coca Colonialized country. American soap opera culture holds hegemony in the public mind." The Swedish parliament spelled out in 1974 the objectives in the state's cultural policy. In principle, cultural equality is considered to be just as important as economic and social equality. That means that any individual who so wishes should have the opportunity to develop whatever talents he possesses and to enjoy cultural experiences, regardless of geographic, educational or other hindrances. This policy is underscored in practice by plentiful subsidies for cultural activities at all levels of government.

In order to aid authors, book publication is subsidized. Because the Swedish language is spoken by only about 10 million persons, the market is simply too small to make most books commercially viable. Also, in order to provide authors with a greater measure of economic security, the libraries pay the Swedish Author's Fund a small fee for every book that is lent out. These funds are used to pay the authors a guaranteed basic income, pension or special scholarships. This is an effort to keep the Swedish literary tradition alive, which includes many fine writers.

In the second half of the 18th century, Carl Michael Bellman wrote poetry that could be sung. These songs describe the peculiarities and interests of the people of Stockholm in his day and give Swedes both entertainment and insight into their own past. He helped to establish a tradition of concentrating on the country's people and their folk culture, a characteristic of much Swedish literature before 1945.

The end of the 19th and the beginning of the 20th centuries were times of economic poverty and mass emigration, especially to the U.S. However, it was also a rich time for Swedish literature. Gustaf Fröding was a poet who wrote in the dialect of the common people and whose works were filled with folklore. Selma Lagerlöf was a romantic novelist who won a Nobel Prize. Perhaps the greatest literary figure in Swedish history, August Strindberg, produced dramatic works that were deadly serious, deeply psychological, invariably antifemale and often downright depressing. His plays are still presented on stages throughout the world.

The 1930s were also times of economic crisis, and Ivar Lo-Johannsson, one of Sweden's best-loved authors, wrote several books, including *Good Night Earth*, about the landless peasants during these discouraging years. The 1940s were years of disillusionment among many Swedish intellectuals and writers, caused, at least in part, by the destructiveness of World War II and by the feelings of guilt and shame on the part of some Swedes at having been spared from this horrible conflict while other Europeans had suffered so much. This malaise was reflected in the works of such writers as Stig Dagerman and Karl Vennberg.

After the war, many writers tried to come to grips with the effects of a materialistic society on the individual, who can easily become alienated in an environment of cement and individual affluence. Other writers looked back at the Swedish past. Vilhelm Moberg produced a monumental series of books on Swedish emigrants to the U.S. that included *Unto a Good Land*, *The Immigrants*, and *The Last Letter Home*, all of which have been translated into English. Moberg committed suicide in the late 1970s, but his literary description of Swedes in America was filmed by the Swedish director Jan Troell.

Author's daughter (l) with Swedish students in Stockholm

Another author, Astrid Lindgren, created unforgettable children's books with such figures as Pipi Longstocking. For decades they have helped children inside and outside Sweden to imagine the countryside, the people, the customs and the spirit of Sweden's past.

Vastly different but similarly lucrative books are being written by crime-writer superstars Henning Mankell and Stieg Larsson. Mankell's nine Inspector Kurt Wallander mysteries have been translated into 40 languages and have sold 30 million copies, in addition to having won many international prizes. Married to a daughter of the late Ingmar Bergman, he is a self-confessed workaholic: "Swedish people don't go to church anymore, but they're still Lutheran: work, work, work." Larsson was such a workaholic and tobacco addict (smoking 60 self-rolled cigarettes a day and writing through most of the night) that he died of a heart-attack in 2004 at age 50. His masterpiece Millennium trilogy, finishing with *The Girl with the Dragon Tattoo*, sold 27 million copies in over 40 countries and topped the bestseller lists in the U.S. Both probe the dark underside of Scandinavia's cradle-to-grave welfare societies.

In keeping with the country's objective to bring culture to as many people as possible, the state helps to finance theaters in many regions and has frequently subsidized independent theater troupes, which perform in the streets, in schools or in factories and which help to bring theater to many groups of people, including children.

When one thinks of Swedish film, such performers as Greta Garbo and directors as Bo Widerberg, whose films focused on the industrial worker in modern society,

come immediately to mind. The film giant, Ingmar Bergman, defined an entire genre of stark movies about the human condition. They included three titles that won Academy Awards as best foreign-language films: "The Virgin Spring" (1960), "Through a Glass Darkly" (1961) and his final film, "Fanny and Alexander" (1982). He also produced "The Seventh Seal," "Wild Strawberries," "The Silence" and "Personal." He helped to make the 1960s a golden decade for Swedish filmdom. He passed away in 2007 at age 89.

To shore up this art form in Sweden, the state assumed more of the costs of production and a 10% surcharge on all movie tickets flows to the Swedish Film Institute to help finance new films. Nevertheless, the industry remains in serious financial difficulties, and even the Swedes seem to show less and less interest in their own films. The average citizen goes to the movies only three times a year; 75% of all visits to the cinema are to see American films, whereas only 15% concern Swedish ones. The film, "Lilia-4-ever," directed by Lukas Moodyson, won an Oscar nomination in 2002 as Best Foreign Language Film. With groups like ABBA, Sweden is one of the world's top three exporters of pop music.

Performing Arts

Sweden's newest concert hall is named after Franz Berwald (1796–1868), Sweden's most famous composer of romantic music. The voice of another Swede, Jenny Lind, captured the ear of the musical world at the end of the 19th century, and in the 1980s a versatile pop group called Abba carried the Swedish banner throughout the world by entertaining millions of rock fans with their English-language songs.

Sweden

Since the late 1940s the choreographer and ensemble director, Birgit Cullberg, has been the towering figure in Swedish ballet. As in theater and dance, the symphony orchestras in Stockholm and in the various regions receive generous and essential state financial assistance.

Artists

Swedish art gained an international reputation, especially through the works of Carl Larsson, who died in 1919, and Anders Zorn, who died one year later. Larsson painted idealized and unproblematic scenes of middle-class daily life. Zorn was a pioneer in new art techniques and also painted many outstanding portraits, including ones of American President William Howard Taft and the steel magnate and philanthropist, Andrew Carnegie. As elsewhere in the Nordic countries, modern, abstract art has been popular in 20th-century painting.

One of the eight cultural guidelines established by the *Riksdag* in 1974 was that commercialism was to be resisted in the country's culture. Nevertheless, Swedish art is a realm in which commercial and artistic objectives have blended to create well-designed objects for use in the home. They include furniture, textiles, glass and porcelain, which are often in bright, fresh colors and are practical and beautiful. In Sweden, where skies are often gray and where the sun sometimes fails to shine for

weeks, such objects in the home can have a particularly refreshing and therapeutic effect on the individual.

Sweden's neutrality cannot protect it from difficulties caused by the intrusion of politics in the arts. When the Israeli ambassador visited Stockholm's Museum of National Antiquities in 2004 and saw a work by an Israeli-born artist, Dror Feiler, which depicted a Palestinian suicide bomber in a sailboat floating on a pool of blood-red water, he threw a spotlight into the pool causing the exhibit to short-circuit. He was ejected from the museum.

Religion

Most Swedes (85%) consider themselves members of the Swedish (Lutheran) Church. An overwhelming majority of Swedes paid the optional church taxes, (less than 1% of the average income) until they were abolished in 2000 with the separation of church and state. The state does collect membership fees for all faiths in addition to the Lutheran one. This makes sense in a country that has more than 200,000 Muslim residents, 160,000 Roman Catholics, 100,000 Orthodox Christians, and 16,000 Jews. Nevertheless, Sweden is a secular country, and only about 5% of Swedes attend church regularly. They generally attend only for special occasions, such as Advent, Christmas, Easter, baptisms, weddings and funerals. The church faces a shortage of priests and has

had difficulty organizing new parishes to keep up with the migration from rural to urban areas. In 1989 the church shed its legal obligation of recording all vital statistics, passing that function over to the Social Insurance Service. It retained its state financial support, though.

In 1995 the Lutheran Church agreed to a government-sponsored separation of church and state beginning in 2000; all political parties accepted this, and it went into effect as the new century was rung in. Before the change, the monarch had not been the head of the church, but he was required to belong to it; now he may be of any faith. The rights of the church are enshrined in the constitution under a law guaranteeing freedom of religious expression. Religion plays little role in politics, although the church does offer more than mere liturgy. Its preschools are crowded, and its youth movement is Sweden's largest youth organization. It has many summer camps and alternative programs, and it still attracts close to 70% of all teenagers for confirmation, providing it with a nine-month opportunity to influence a young person's thinking. Swedes in small towns tend to feel an attachment to the church building, which serves as a meeting hall, theater, nursery school and finish line for ski races.

Religious veins can be tapped to win support for such policies as development aid to the "Third World" or stricter controls on the use of alcohol. The latter movement gained momentum in the second half of the 19th century, when the Swedish nation seemed to be destroying itself through alcoholism and emigration. Legislation sought to control the use of spirits. Alcohol was rationed until 1955; the prices were kept very high in order to discourage its consumption. In 2005 it still had the EU's highest taxes on spirits. Official figures in 2002 suggest that this policy reduced intake. In the 19th century, the average adult Swede consumed 49 quarts of alcohol per year, compared with only 9.5 today.

Because these restrictions violate the EU's fair competition rules, they are being relaxed. Alcohol consumption has risen by 30% since EU entry in 1995 and reached by 2004 its highest level in a century. Despite widespread fears of the damaging effects on health and of alcohol-related crimes, some liquor stores of the state monopoly, *Systembolaget*, now stay open late and on Saturdays. Travelers are permitted to bring alcohol into the country. In 2007 the European Court of Justice ruled that Sweden had no right to bar its citizens from importing alcohol from other EU states. Taxes on alcohol are being reduced, so the price is falling. Experts say the previous strictures did little to change Sweden's real problem: the tradi-

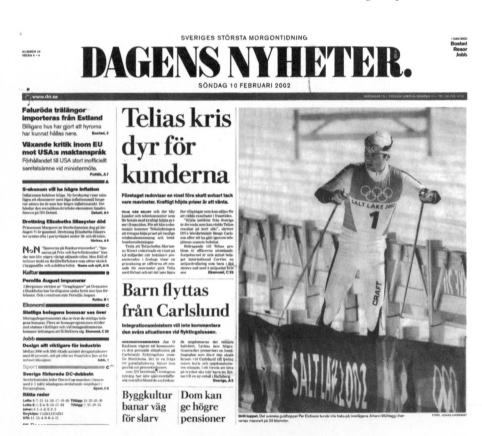

tion in Sweden and other Nordic countries to drink less often but to do so with the intention of getting drunk, rather than to combine moderate drinking with eating, as is the practice in Southern Europe.

Religious motives play almost no role in the popular campaign to stop smoking. The movement's slogan is "A Non-Smoking Generation"; English is used for the slogan because this language is quite fashionable today in Sweden where it is learned by all schoolchildren. As the American discovers to his pleasure, most Swedes under age 45 usually speak English well.

The Media

Swedes buy more newspapers per capita than any other nation except Japan and Iceland. It has about 100 dailies and 85 weekly newspapers, with a total circulation of 4.5 million. The number of newspapers has declined in recent years, and in most localities there is only one. Most have a definite political line; about three-fourths support the bourgeois parties, and only about a fifth back S. *Ny Dag* is the major communist paper and is published twice weekly. About a quarter of daily newspapers are distributed free. At the end of 2006 the world's oldest newspaper, *Post Och Inrikes Tidningar*, published since 1645, stopped printing and now publishes only on line. The print media's influence remains great. In 1997 a series in *Dagens Nyheter* broke the embarrassing story about Sweden's eugenics policy from 1934 to 1976.

In the 1970s the *Riksdag* passed a series of laws designed to strengthen the economic base of the press and to ensure that there is a diversity of views. Except for the market leaders, all newspapers receive direct and indirect (tax breaks) subsidies, with the money distributed roughly equally between the socialist and nonsocialist press. Such state assistance appears not to make the recipients more docile since subsidized papers are generally as outspoken about government policies as are those that are not. Those newspapers that appear in areas with few inhabitants receive especially significant financial support, and those newspapers that utilize the unified distribution system developed for magazine subscriptions also receive state assistance. There were 46 magazines in 1989, but there is no nationwide weekly news magazine such as *Time* or *Newsweek*.

Sveriges Radio AB is responsible for radio and television activities, which it coordinates through four independent subsidiaries: one for television, which operates two channels, one for national radio programs, which operates three stations, one for local radio and one for educational radio and television programs. The pan-European satellite channels ended the state monopoly over the broadcast media and have changed public attitudes about Sweden's role in Europe. They add an international perspective to debates and contribute to greater diversity of opinions. Private industry, the press and various popular movements own the stock in Sveriges Radio AB. In effect, though, it is state-controlled, since the government appoints the director and half of the board of overseers. Also, its budget must be approved by parliament, which grants some subsidies and which determines the amount of the user's fee, which all persons who own radios or television must pay.

One new pleasure for some Swedes will be professional boxing, which was reintroduced in 2007 after being banned for almost four decades. Only Norway and Iceland still prohibit it.

FUTURE

In 1994 Swedes decided to join both NATO's Partnership for Peace and the EU. Lotta Forsman of the Foreign Ministry explained that "the collapse of the communist dictatorships in Eastern Europe has changed the military map and consequently the basis for Sweden's neutrality." Defense Minister Sten Tolgfors and other politicians argue that NATO is a natural source of Swedish security: "The Nordic countries cannot by themselves generate sufficient political and military weight." Tolgfors suggested in 2008 that Sweden and Norway share airbases. The army

Sweden

chiefs of Sweden, Norway and Finland produced a report identifying 140 areas of possible military cooperation, which would save costs and help deal with the growing threat of Russia in the region.

Opposition to the European single currency has weakened, but it could take years before Sweden again seeks euro entry. However, the conservative government is more pro-EU than the Social Democratic one that preceded it. The end of 2009 Sweden completed the six-month rotating EU presidency with much to show for its efforts. It won plaudits for its levelheaded and professional presidency and its part in the approval of the EU's ground-breaking Lisbon Treaty. At the top of its priorities were fighting against the global recession, which hit Sweden harder than most European countries, and overseeing the writing of new EU rules on financial regulation. It designed a common EU position for the Copenhagen climatechange conference in December 2009. Sweden has a good record: it has cut carbon emissions by one-tenth since 1990, while its economy grew by 50%. It organized and supervised the election of the

first ever president and foreign minister of the European Council. Swedes are more favorable toward EU enlargement than almost any other people, and Foreign Minister Carl Bildt was a strong supporter of Turkish admission.

The Social Democrats, who had ruled for 65 of the past 74 years, lost the September 2006 elections. The New Moderates, led by Fredrik Reinfeldt, set the political agenda leading up to the election. His coalition, Alliance for Sweden, won a sevenseat majority and could proceed with its program of improving the economy and reforming, though not replacing, the welfare state. However, Sweden suffered one of Europe's worst economic downturns, and when economic times are bad, voters' center-left instincts get stronger. With 52% support going into the September 19, 2010, elections, 11 points ahead of the government, Mona Sahlin's Social Democrats are poisted to reclaim power.

Swedish troops remain in the northern part of Afghanistan. In November 2005, they suffered their first combat fatality when one of its peacekeepers was killed by a roadside bomb. The Reinfeldt govern-

ment's tenuous approval rating prevented the prime minister from making any bold foreign policy moves, such as joining the euro or NATO, which he favored.

As a major exporting country, Sweden was bound to be negatively affected by the global recession in 2008–10. Though technically still in recession in 2010, it worked its way out of the worst of it, keeping its budget carefully under control with a deficit of only 2.4% of GDP. It has an economy that is transforming itself to meet the challenges of the 21st century. It remains a remarkably comfortable, steady, decent, peaceful and egalitarian land.

In June 2010 Crown Princess Victoria married a commoner, Daniel Westling. He is the founding owner of a small chain of Stockholm fitness clubs, where they met. The pompous ceremony cost the taxpayers $2.6 million. This pricetag offended some Swedes at a time of economic recession. One Facebook group calling itself "Refuse to pay for Victoria's wedding" counted almost 60,000 members. A 2010 poll revealed that just over half of Swedes want to retain the monarchy. In 2003 that figure was more than two-thirds.

Swedish crime-writer superstar Henning Mankell.

Source: *Maclean's*

The Kingdom of Norway

Area: 125,182 sq. mi. (324,219 sq. km., not including Svalbard and Jan Mayen; slightly larger than New Mexico).
Population: 4.7 million (estimated).
Capital City: Oslo (Pop. 500,000, estimated).
Climate: From late spring to August the nights are very short, with hardly any night in June and July, and the sun shines constantly during the summer above the Arctic Circle. The flow of the Gulf Stream keeps the climate temperate along the coast. There are bitterly cold winters in the north and higher altitudes.
Neighboring Countries: Sweden (East); Finland and Russia (Northeast); Denmark (South, across the Skagerak), Scotland (Southeast, across the North Sea).
Official Language: Norwegian.
Other Principal Tongues: Sami (Lapp), other Nordic tongues, English.

Ethnic Background: Germanic, Scandinavian.
Principal Religion: Lutheran (80%).
Main Exports: Crude oil, natural gas, metals, machinery and transport, foodstuffs, fish and fish products, pulp and paper, ships, chemicals.
Main Imports: Machinery and transport equipment, metals including iron and steel, chemicals, processed petroleum

Norway

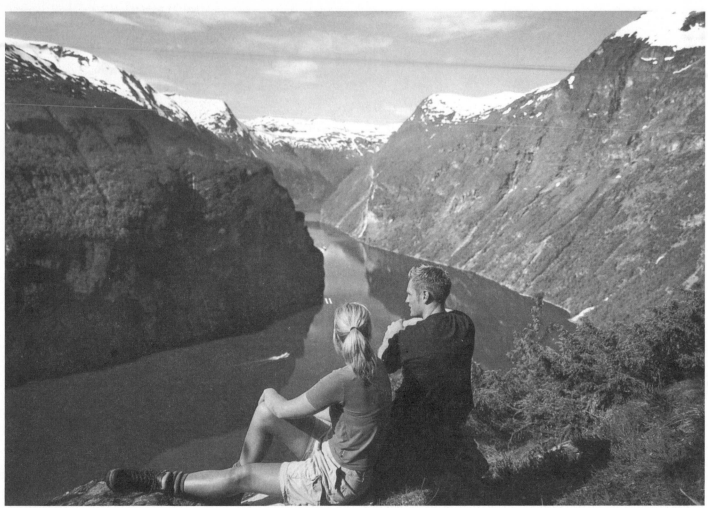

Source: *News of Norway*

products, motor vehicles, textiles, food-stuffs.

Chief customers: EU (80.8% of exports and 68.8% of imports), UK (25.3% of exports and 7% of imports), Germany (13.9% of exports and 13.6% of imports), Netherlands (9.8% of exports), France (7.9% of exports), Sweden (7% of exports and 15.9% of imports), United States (5.9% of exports and 4.6% of imports), Denmark (6.7% of imports), China (5.6% of imports).

Currency: Krone.

National Day: May 17, Constitution Day.

Chief of State: His Majesty King Harald V, b. 1937.

Heir Apparent: His Royal Highness Crown Prince Haakon Magnus (b. 1973).

Head of Government: Jens Stoltenberg, Prime Minister (since October 2005), leader of the Labor Party.

National Flag: A red field crossed horizontally and vertically by blue stripes (cross), bordered by thin white stripes.

In many people's minds, Norway is a sparsely populated nation somewhere in the frozen North, with a tortured land-scape filled with many majestic, snow-capped mountains, glaciers, isolated valleys, and a long coastline, which is dotted by small, quaint fishing villages and countless beautiful fjords. This image is certainly true, as far as it goes. This is a long, narrow country, with a 2,125-mile (3,200 km.) coastline washed by the Arctic and Atlantic oceans as well as the North Sea. It is the fifth largest country in Europe and occupies 40% of the Scandinavian Peninsula.

Half of Norway is located north of the Arctic Circle, and even the capital city of Oslo in the south is on the same latitude as southern Alaska. This means that many Norwegians are able to experience the midnight sun in the summer, but they must go without much daylight in the winter. In the extreme north, it shares a 118-mile (196 km.) border with Russia and a 430-mile (716 km.) border with Finland. Flanked most of the distance by the Kjølen mountain range is a long, 972-mile (1,619 km.) common border with Sweden, a now friendly country to which Norway belonged until 1905.

Almost two-thirds of Norway are covered by mountains although they do not give the country an Alpine character. Most of them are barren—without forests—in fact, only a fourth of the entire country lies *below* the timberline. One mountain range, the Dovre, divides the country into a northern and southern part, whereas the Langfjell chain separates the eastern from the western part of the country. The Kjølen chain marks the country's eastern border. In the highlands are countless cold, clear lakes and ponds, including the Hornindalsvatn, the deepest inland body of water in all of Europe. The rivers that originate in these mountains either flow gently in an easterly direction or precipitously into the sea. Its rivers provide Norway with a seemingly endless source of hydroelectric power, which was the basis for the country's industrialization.

Over a fifth of Norway is covered by forests, which supply wood, one of its most important raw materials, and 7% of its area is composed of 50,000 islands, only about 2,000 of which are inhabited. Lakes and rivers cover 5% of the territory and only about 3% of the land is arable farmland, the lowest percentage in all of Europe. Despite its extreme northern latitude and the fact that 1.4% of its surface is covered by 1,700 glaciers, Norway is not a gigantic deep freeze. This is due to the North Atlantic Current, which is warmed by the Gulf Stream from the Caribbean and which makes Norwegian winters mild, especially along the coast. Because of the effects of global warming, by 2005 its glaciers had shrunk four years in a row at the fastest rate since 1900.

Norway has the lowest population density in all of Europe (except Iceland). It has 13 inhabitants per square kilometer, compared with 372 in the Netherlands, 225 in Britain and 90 in France. Its population is also very unevenly divided, with about half concentrated in the southeastern corner around Oslo and its fjord, with very few inhabitants in the northern part of the country. Four out of five live within 10 miles of the sea. Almost three-fourths of the country is uninhabitable.

There are many small villages, and a third of the population lives on the land or in towns with fewer than 2,000 inhabitants. Norway has no large cities and only three have a population of over 100,000. Oslo, in which the government and much of the industry and cultural life are concentrated, has about a half-million residents; Bergen has about 215,000 and Trondheim about 135,000. A fourth city, Stavanger, with close to 90,000 people, has the headquarters for the state-owned oil company, StatoilHydro, and is the center

for the petroleum extraction activities in the Norwegian sector of the North Sea.

The country's leaders have long recognized the danger that many Norwegians living in the large tracts of sparsely inhabited areas might move into the larger cities. For this reason, an important element of the government's agricultural and industrial policy is to provide incentives for the people to remain in the less densely populated sections of the country. There is no possibility that Norwegians could settle these areas since the fertility rate declined to 1.8 in 2005; estimates are that there will be one million fewer Norwegians by the year 2050.

Norway was once an almost completely ethnically homogeneous country. There is an increasingly large number of foreign workers, some of whom came to Norway before the mid-1970s and who have either received Norwegian citizenship or are remaining with permanent residence permits. Except for those coming from other Nordic countries, no additional foreign workers are allowed to work in Norway. However, Norway has been an attractive goal for hundreds of thousands of immigrants and asylum-seekers although the country is no longer as hospitable toward newcomers as it once was. By 2003, the foreign-born made up approximately 7% of the total population.

In the northern part of the country are two ethnic minorities. The largest are the 45,000 Sami (formerly called Lapps) whose language and culture are completely different from those of the Norwe-

Crown prince Haakon

gians. About two-thirds of all Sami live in Norway and the remaining one-third live in northern Sweden and Finland. Only about 10% of the Norwegian Sami are now reindeer breeders, who lead a nomadic existence and who cling most tenaciously to the traditional Sami culture. The majority of Sami now lead a settled existence.

The second minority is composed of about 7,000 descendants of a Baltic people who also entered Norway earlier via Finland. They are called *kvener* and have retained many of their original physical and cultural characteristics.

Norwegians call their country *Norge*, a word derived from the earlier name *Nordvegr*, "the Northern Way." The country is indeed on the northern extremity of Europe and appears on the map to be geographically isolated. But since the 19th century it has been finely attuned to developments in the rest of Europe and the world. As a nation facing westward and southward across three seas, it has developed a merchant marine that not only helps it maintain its links with the rest of the world, but also helps other countries maintain links with each other. It does have weather-beaten fishermen, strapping lumber-jacks and ruddy-faced farmers, but these groups account for less than a tenth of the population.

POLITICAL SYSTEM

Norway is a country in which there is a deep consensus supporting the democratic process and institutions. The individual's personal and civil rights are widely respected, and Norwegians are ba-

Princess Märtha Louise weds Norwegian author Ari Behn

Norway

sically inclined to be very tolerant toward other viewpoints and manners of living. They enter into sharp debates with each other over political, economic and social questions, but these debates are always kept within a framework in which recognized rules of the game are respected and observed. The result is a high degree of political stability.

The Monarchy

This is a constitutional monarchy with a parliamentary form of government; there is no aristocracy. Harald V was sworn in as king in 1991, coronations having been abolished in 1908. He is only the country's third monarch since independence in 1905. In 1937 he was the first Norwegian monarch to be born on native soil in 566 years. After the royal family fled occupied Norway, Harald lived with his mother and sister in the U.S., where he attended two years of elementary school. After liberation in 1945 he continued his schooling in Norway, and he pursued a military career; in 1977 he was promoted to general of the army and air force and admiral of the navy. His wife, Sonja, was the daughter of a Norwegian textile merchant and is the country's first queen since 1938. Harald's older sister could not succeed to the throne because of a law, now repealed, which favored male succession.

Since the new law of succession applies only to those born after 1990 (the year of the act), the current crown prince, Prince Haakon (born before 1990) is the heir apparent, not his older sister, Princess Märtha Louise. Haakon graduated from

The proud parents of Princess Ingrid Alexandra

the Norwegian Naval Academy and completed a bachelor's degree in political science from the University of California at Berkley. He also studied law and political science at the University of Oslo. In 2000 he announced his entry into the training program for the foreign service.

His decision was reported to be satisfactory both to the royal palace and to Mette-Marit Tjessem Høiby. Both the press and the public had reacted positively to the crown prince's confirmation of his romantic relationship with Høiby, a commoner, single mother and former waitress. After her tearful public admission that she had been a "wild child" who had lived a "dissolute life," she and Haakon were married

August 25, 2001. Her four-year-old son served as a page. In a country where half of the children are born out of wedlock, Norwegians accepted her with as much grace as they accepted their finance minister, Per-Kristian Foss, who revealed in 2002 that he had formalized his long-standing gay partnership under Norwegian law.

In 2008 parliament granted gay and lesbian couples the same right to marry, to adopt children, and to receive artificial insemination as heterosexual couples. Oslo's chief commissioner, Erling Lae, announced that "no longer will there be different classes of love" before proceeding to marry his own male companion of 26 years.

Princess Märtha Louise married Norwegian writer Ari Behn. Cannons fired salutes and flags were hoisted in April 2003 when she gave birth to a girl, Maud Angelica Behn. She was the first Norwegian royal baby in three decades, and she soon moved with her parents to New York. Only a year later the crown prince and princess had a daughter, Ingrid Alexandra, who became third in line for the throne. She could become the first reigning queen in Norway since 1412. Märtha Louise created quite an international stir when she claimed in 2007 that she had been making "contact with angels." This provided an understandable boost for her just-published book, *Princess Märtha Louise's Wonderful World.*

The monarch performs mainly ceremonial functions, even though the constitution formally grants him considerable executive powers. Even decisions of the State Council (*Statsråd*), or cabinet are denominated decisions of the "King-in-Council," although the king is seldom involved in their deliberations. Thus, the government merely acts in his name.

The king can play a role in facilitating the formation of a government when no party or coalition of parties receives a clear mandate in parliamentary elections. In times of extreme crisis, as was the case during World War II, the parliament can allow the king temporarily to perform the governmental and military functions, which are formally granted to him in the constitution. But no Norwegian king would dare attempt to do so under normal circumstances. The crisis during World War II also demonstrated the major function the monarch can perform: he serves as an important symbol of the nation's unity and this can be extremely important, especially to a nation that did not become entirely independent until 1905. The king is the head of the state (Lutheran) church, and at least half of the cabinet members must also belong to that church. The royal castle in the middle of

The late King Olav V in his sailboat. He competed in the Olympics in 1964, 1968 and 1972

The late King Olav V opening the Norwegian Parliament

Oslo and the other properties used by the royals belong to the state, not to the royal family. They are lent to the monarch and are maintained by the taxpayers.

The king cannot be accused in a court of law for any misdeed. Since he is not permitted to make decisions in normal times, he is protected from making political mistakes. This protection, along with the personal qualities of those who have reigned since independence, made the monarchy a rather popular institution. Despite the glitter of royal matrimony, polls in 2001 indicated that support for the monarchy had declined sharply, from close to 90% a decade earlier to 62% on the eve of the royal wedding. But the king's bout with bladder cancer in 2003–4 dramatically restored his popularity. Kings are buried in the Trondheim cathedral, where the crown jewels are kept.

The Parliament

Real political power lies in the Norwegian people, represented by the 169 members of the parliament, called the *Storting*. Over a third of its members are women. Elections are held every four years, and all citizens 18 years of age or older are eligible to vote. The electoral system is a complicated form of proportional representation, which enables many political parties to function. This makes the creation of a workable coalition in the *Storting* difficult, despite a method of distributing seats that favors large and medium-sized parties. A party must win 4% of the votes nation-wide in order to receive any seats at all. A newly elected *Storting* is obligated to serve the full four years, since the constitution forbids early elections. Even by-elections are very rare, since vacated seats are filled by replacements who are elected at the same time as the deputies. Thus, substitutes are almost always available at all times.

The inability to call early elections forces the various party leaders to negotiate very seriously with each other in order to produce a government whose programs can win majorities in the *Storting*. No party has won an absolute majority since 1961, and from 1983 until 2005 there was not even a majority governing coalition. Therefore, the Norwegian talent for moderation and compromise, along with the basic political consensus in the country, has been essential for the maintenance of political stability. Most other countries would have failed the test and fallen into political chaos.

Deputies are elected from 19 counties (*Fylker*) in such a way that 38 representatives are elected from the northern counties, 49 from western and southern Norway and 68 from eastern Norway (of which 15 are from Oslo). In order to try to prevent any domination by the large cities, the rural areas are represented by a slightly greater proportion of deputies than the urban areas.

Voters elect only one parliament, the *Storting*, but after each election, it is divided into two parts. One fourth of the members are assigned to the *Lagting*, or second chamber, and the rest constitute the *Odelsting*, or lower house. These two houses deliberate separately only when the *Storting* must deal with questions touching on the constitution, such as the rights and duties of citizens. However, most matters, including constitutional amendments, are discussed in joint plenary sessions. Once a majority in the *Storting* approves a piece of legislation, it automatically becomes law.

The *Storting* also has standing committees that correspond to the various government ministries and which perform most of the detailed work of the parliament. Unlike in the U.S., seniority plays very little role in the assignment of seats and chairmanships in the committees; party membership and special skills are the decisive factors.

The *Storting* has the responsibility of electing a special five-person committee representing parties from across the political spectrum that selects and awards the prestigious Nobel Peace Prize. Its selection in 2009 of American President Barak Obama, who had been in office less than a year, elicited much criticism throughout the world, as well as disbelief on the part of Obama himself. But 43% of Norwegians thought that the young American leader deserved the award. He donated the $1.4 million prize money to charity.

When Norwegian economists Ragnar Frisch and Trygve Haavelmo were named in 1969 and 1989 laureates in economics,

Norway

they had to travel to Stockholm to receive the award and prize. In 2004 Finn E. Kydland shared the Nobel Prize in economics with an American for their work explaining business cycles. Six other Norwegians have received Nobels, including the Peace Prize won by Christian Lange in 1921 and Fritjof Nansen in 1922 and the chemistry prize by Odd Hassel in 1969.

Storting deputies can be elected only if they represent parties; no independents can be elected, although one may leave his party after the election and retain his seat until the next election. As a rule, deputies vote with their parties, but they do have the right to vote against their parties. On some moral issues, such as abortion, the parties announce that deputies will be permitted to vote according to their consciences, although the party's position on such an issue would be well-known. In order to encourage them to be conscious that they are supposed primarily to represent their constituents, not their parties, deputies are seated according to the alphabetical order of their counties, not according to their party affiliation, as is the custom in most European parliaments.

The Norwegian government is headed by a prime minister and a cabinet of at least seven ministers, the foreign minister being the highest in the hierarchy after the prime minister. The government meets in cabinet meetings at least once a week (usually on Fridays), although the various members meet informally several times during the week.

The Judiciary

Norway has an independent judiciary, with courts at four levels. From the lowest to the highest, they are the Conciliation Councils (*Forliksrådene*), the local courts (*Herredsrettene og byrettene*), the courts of civil and criminal appeals (*Lagmannsretten*), and the Supreme Court of Justice (*Høiesterett*), composed of a Chief Justice and 17 justices, of which only five sit for any one case. The framers of the 1814 constitution adopted the American innovation by granting the Supreme Court and the inferior courts the authority to declare as null and void any law they deem to be incompatible with the constitution. However, the Norwegian courts have exercised this right of judicial review very infrequently, preferring to leave it to the government and the *Storting* to make certain that the constitution is observed.

Constitutional Amendment and Referendums

The *Storting* also has the power to amend the 1814 constitution; all proposed amendments must be presented to the parliament, but in order to prevent the ba-

sic law from being changed too quickly or by a simple majority that might be available at any moment, any amendment must be approved by a two-thirds majority in a newly elected *Storting*.

There is no constitutional provision for a referendum. However, in a few instances, the *Storting* has declared that nonbinding referendums could be held in order to give the people the opportunity to express an opinion about an important issue.

For instance, in 1972 a national referendum was held on the question of whether Norway should enter the EU. In this vote, 53% said "no," and the government chose to honor this result and not to enter the EU. This rejection was due more than anything else to a general reaction by the periphery (rural) people against a move that, it was feared, could seriously affect the unique and traditional life and culture of the nation (see Culture). The EU was widely seen as a potential danger to Norwegian society. In 1992 the *Storting* voted both to accept EEA and, for the fourth time, to seek entry into the EU. But in a November 1994 referendum, 52% of the voters, citing many of the same arguments as in 1972, again voted EU membership down. This time prosperity and concerns for the structure of its economy tipped the balance.

In 2008 the governing and opposition parties agreed to amend the constitution in order to loosen the official ties between the government and the Lutheran Church,

to which more than 80% of Norwegians formally belong. Some links remain, but the Lutheran faith is no longer the official state religion, and the government relinquishes to the church the right to appoint bishops. The monarch is still obligated to be Lutheran, but Lutheran parents are no longer legally required to raise their children as Lutherans. The state continues to provide funding for the church, but it is now required to give financial support to other faiths, as well as to atheist and agnostic communities.

As in other Scandinavian countries, the institution of the ombudsman guards citizens' rights. There is an ombudsman for consumer affairs who ensures fair advertising and marketing practices, a civil ombudsman who sees to it that the administration does not treat any citizen unjustly, and an ombudsman for the armed services who deals with grievances of military personnel. All are appointed by the *Storting*.

Regional and Local Government

It is not surprising that a country so spread out and cut up by mountains, fjords, lakes, rivers and other natural barriers that make transportation within the country so difficult would have a lively tradition of local and regional government. There are about 50 municipalities (*bykommuner*) and about 400 rural communities (*landkommuner*), with their own councils elected every four years midway

Their Majesties King Harald V and Queen Sonja

between the national elections. Non-Norwegians who have resided in the country for at least three years can vote in these local elections. The councils appoint a local government and a mayor, their authority extending to schools, churches, health care, social welfare, zoning and local construction, fire fighting, traffic and a host of other matters.

Between the national and local governments are 19 counties (*fylker*), each of which is headed by a governor appointed by the central government. The counties deal with tasks for which the national and local governments share responsibilities, such as hospital construction, public instruction, health care and electricity supply. Each county has its own parliament, which is elected at the same time local elections are held. Although much political responsibility is assumed at the local and regional level, it should not be overlooked that the nation's major political priorities are established by the central government in Oslo.

Overseas Territories

The government in Oslo rules over far-flung territories around the world. It has a large tract of land called Queen Maud Land on the continent of Antarctica, which could one day have great economic significance. It also has two uninhabited islands near Antarctica: Peter I Island and Bouvet. Situated between Greenland and Iceland is Jan Mayen Island, which covers 380 square kilometers, on which the Beeren Mountain surges 7,400 feet (2,277 meters) into the air. First discovered by the Dutch, Jan Mayen became Norwegian in 1930 and now serves as a meteorological station and as a post in the NATO early-warning system.

Closer to home is the Svalbard archipelago, lying halfway between the North Pole and the tip of the Scandinavian peninsula. It is about 575 miles (959 km.) by air from the northern Norwegian city of Tromsø, from which regular civilian air service commenced in 1975. The largest and only inhabited island is Spitsbergen. This rugged area, with mountains rising to 5,585 feet (1,717 meters) and dangerous cliffs overlooking a landscape covered with ice and glaciers, exists in total darkness 112 days per year and in total daylight 127 days. Nearly two-thirds of Svalbard is covered by ice and provides an ideal habitat for polar bears, which outnumber humans two to one.

Spitsbergen's cold climate and remoteness make it an ideal place to store the seeds of almost three million different essential crops. Opened in February 2008, the intention is to protect mankind's future food supply in the event of a nuclear, asteroid or epidemic catastrophe. It would

NORTH POLE
SVALBARD

Source: *News of Norway*

contain the means to restock the Earth's agriculture. The "doomsday vault" is located 60 meters (almost 200 feet) below the permafrost and far away from potential intruders. The Norwegian government maintains them at its own expense, assisted by private donations, including $6.5 million from the U.S.

These islands were first mentioned in Icelandic journals in the year 1194, and for centuries they were a meeting point for whaling crews from all over the world. At the beginning of the 20th century they became economically significant because of their sizable coal deposits, which continue to be exploited today. Until 1920 the archipelago was a "no man's land" in international law, but in that year a complicated treaty was worked out. The other great powers in the Arctic liked the idea that a small seemingly harmless country like Norway would control the Spitzbergen Archipelago.

The treaty conferred on Norway sovereignty over the islands in 1925, while at the same time giving all nationals of the contracting parties the right to carry out maritime, industrial, mining and commercial operations on the basis of absolute equality. It also explicitly prohibited the establishment of naval bases or fortifications on the islands, which could never be used "for warlike purposes." Norway was granted responsibility of ensuring adherence to this treaty. The only other country that showed any appreciable interest in Svalbard is Russia, which did not sign the 1920 treaty. The instrument granted the Russians predominance over four of the 40 islands, covering about 6% of the total land area. Norway's expansion into the Arctic temporarily went to its head. It occupied Greenland in the early 1930s until the International Court of Justice ruled it illegal.

Only one Norwegian and one Russian company maintained permanent mining operations on the islands, even though both Norway and Russia lose money on them. In the mid-1990s Russia extracted about 500,000 tons of coal a year, while Norway gets about 400,000. Almost certainly, the real reason for both countries' presence there is strategic. Each is scared of allowing the other to gain exclusive use

Norway

of the harbors, which are so close to the sea lanes between Russia's northern ports and the Atlantic. No wonder that the British used to call Spitsbergen an "Arctic Gibraltar."

Russia's settlement at Berentsburg is larger than Norway's at Longyearbyen, located a short boat trip away. Out of a total population of around 4,000, about half are foreigners, mainly Russian. Contact between the two nationalities is frosty, and it is still the Norwegians who take the initiative. Spitsbergen remains the only place on earth where a person can walk into a Russian settlement unannounced and without a visa. But the difference in prosperity is striking. Longyearbyen (named for the American who founded it a century ago) is lively, and its 2,000 residents enjoy restaurants, night clubs and shops where almost everything can be bought. Total darkness prevails from mid-November through January, and summer temperatures average 43 degrees Fahrenheit. Well-heeled tourists are lured by polar-bear trips into the wild interior. Barentsburg's residents are largely poor miners who put plastic sheets over their windows to keep out the cold, have very little money, and eat food that caused an outbreak of food poisoning in 2004.

The Russians have always had difficulty accepting the idea of Norwegian sovereignty over the islands and have frequently challenged the scope of its authority. They have advanced the view that Norwegian regulations are subject to prior Russian agreement, a view that is wholly unacceptable to the Norwegians, who have established a hearing procedure for Russian citizens on Svalbard to air their grievances, and, on the whole, the two nationalities on the islands get along rather well. But Oslo retains the right to make final decisions.

Russia also takes exception to Norway's position that the 1920 treaty deals only with the islands themselves and not to the waters around them. Norway, for which fishing is its third largest export earner, has established a 200-mile fishing zone that gives it primary rights. It also has raised the claim that the Norwegian continental shelf includes Svalbard and that Norway therefore has the final authority over mining and drilling in those waters. In October 2005, two Norwegian coast guard officials who suspected illegal fishing boarded a Russian trawler on a routine inspection. However, instead of cooperating, the crew of the Russian ship changed course and sped toward Russian waters with the Norwegians onboard. It was chased across the Barents Sea by four Norwegian armed coast guard vessels. After a five-day "cops and robbers" chase, the two inspectors were freed.

Until 2005 Norway did not dare begin any drilling operations in these waters until some kind of mutually acceptable agreement could be reached with Russia, which refused to accept the Norwegian position on how the Barents Sea should be divided between the two countries. The maritime boundary disputes extended much farther than the relatively short 118-mile land border with its powerful eastern neighbor. Both countries filed their claims with the International Commission on the Limits of the Continental Shelf.

The fact that the geological indications for oil in the area are positive made the Russians impatient for a settlement. Norway's need for future oil and gas extraction prompted it in 2005 to begin boring test wells 230 kilometers north of Hammerfest after the government lifted the ban on drilling in the Barents Sea. Russia had already announced that it would begin prospecting in the Barents Sea, but drilling was to begin off the island of Novaya Zemlya, well outside the disputed area. Norway supplied some of the equipment for the Russian oil rigs and discussed with Russian officials the possibility of joint offshore projects in the Barents Sea outside the disputed waters.

Norway is intensely interested in the future development of the Arctic region. As the Arctic ice pack recedes, these waters become more open to increased shipping and the exploitation of offshore oil and gas reserves. Along with four other countries that border on the Arctic Ocean—Denmark, Canada, United States and Russia—it is determined to secure rights to the natural resources in the area. Competition is fierce, and the Russians raised the tension level in 2007 by sending two minisubmarines to place a titanium national flag 14,000 feet below the ice at the North Pole. However, in May 2008, after a frenetic year of Arctic activity, the five countries met in Ilulissat, Greenland, and agreed to observe existing international laws, such as the Law of the Sea Treaty, to resolving their disputes in the Arctic.

In April 2010 Norway and Russia resolved their four-decade dispute over how to divide the Barents Sea and a portion of the Arctic Ocean into clear economic zones extending to the edge of Europe's northern continental shelf. The line they drew splits the disputed area approximately in half. It extends their 122-mile land border northward beyond all the islands in the Barents Sea and into the Arctic Ocean up to the continental shelf just short of 85 degrees latitude. Because of its experience, Statoil, Norway's largest oil and gas company, agreed to help Russia's state gas company, Gazprom, to develop the huge offshore field called Shtokman.

POLITICS AND POLITICAL PARTIES

There are two ways of looking at Norway's party system. One is to see it as a multiparty system, perpetuated by an electoral system of proportional representation that always favors the proliferation of parties. Such division was further stimulated by the bitter debate over entry into the EU. This emotional conflict hammered Norway at many of its social fault lines. It cracked some of the country's traditional parties wide open and created the conditions for some entirely new ones to spring up. In the 2005 elections, 20 parties threw their hats into the electoral ring. They included the Beer Unity Party, which won the votes of 65 drinkers, and the Abortion Opponents' List, which captured a couple thousand votes.

Another way of looking at the country's party system is that it is made up of two clusters of parties, one socialist, or at least social democratic, and the other nonsocialist. The votes of each cluster remain more or less equal from one election to the next, although there are noticeable, often dramatic shifts among the various parties within each cluster. However, these shifts are not such that a two-party system would be likely to develop. This existence of two rather firm blocks lends stability to the political system. Nevertheless, competition for votes within each cluster sometimes makes parties less willing to cooperate with each other than one might expect. Each must always think about the next election.

Parties are undergoing changes. Their total membership has declined by half since the early 1990s, thereby depriving leaders of a large recruitment base. Turnout is falling, especially in local elections; in the 2005 national elections, 77% cast ballots. The link between parties and social class has been broken as the middle class dominates the various channels of political participation. Finally, the fact that most governments are minority ones tends to diminish the importance of elections and raise the importance of postelection negotiations. Therefore, parties' accountability to the voters is weakened.

The Nonsocialist Parties

The Conservative Party (Høyre or merely H) strongly supported Norway's entry into the EU and experienced dizzying growth during the 1970s, climbing to 50 seats in 1985. Since then it has steadily lost ground. Led by Erna Solberg in the September 2009 elections, it won 17.2 % (up from 14.1%) of the votes and 30 seats, up from 23. It tends to draw the votes of the better-educated and the better-paid, and since these groups grew in prosperous Norway, Høyre grew also.

Høyre does not encompass the entire conservative spectrum. Its voters tend to be concentrated in the industrial, urban centers of the southeast, and it does not appeal to the populist, pro-prohibition Nynorsk, or religious movements, which are so strong in the periphery (see Culture). It is a modern, urban movement, which defines itself as a "conservative party of progress." It demands protection of individual rights and of private property. It is strongly oriented toward NATO, the U.S, and Europe.

In contrast to the other Norwegian parties, *Høyre* is not ridden with internal divisions, and ideological debates within the party are almost unknown. Like the Labor Party, Høyre is secular, and supports economic growth and a high level of oil and gas extraction. It has basic differences with the other major conservative parties on a range of thorny subjects that include alcohol policy, abortion, environmental protection and oil policy. The pro-European Conservatives are wary of their former nonsocialist partners after a serious spat over European policy caused their coalition government to collapse in 1990. It is in the opposition.

Also in the opposition is the Christian People's Party (KrF), which in 2009 won 5.5% of the votes (down from 6.5%) and 10 seats (a loss of one). As its name indicates, it seeks to place Christian concerns in the political spotlight. It led a furious battle against the abortion law, which permits abortion on demand. It also appeals to many supporters of strong, antialcoholic legislation. Another policy it thinks is in harmony with the biblical spirit is a rise in Norway's development aid, which is already .96% of GDP. Even though Norwegians are overwhelmingly baptized Lutheran, the KrF's strong whiff of pietism and serious commitment to the values of the Bible has hampered it in attracting a considerably larger following in this largely secular country.

The hard core of KrF's votes mainly lives in the south and the west and is Zdistrustful of the secular, cosmopolitan Høyre. The KrF is strong in the periphery and attracts about two-thirds of those who support the movement to elevate the social status of *Nynorsk*. The party's leader is Dagfinn Høybråten, who replaced longtime chairman Kjell Magne Bondevik, a Lutheran pastor with much parliamentary and cabinet experience. He is popular and a skillful coalition builder. He first became prime minister after the 1997 elections, forging a ruling minority coalition with the Center and Liberal parties. The party is firmly opposed to EU entry. It stresses human rights, family values, higher welfare spending, and Norway's religious and cultural heritage.

Many politicians talk about values, but KrF puts its money where its mouth is. Noting that divorce ends half of marriages and is four times commoner than three decades ago, that a fourth of women aged 20 to 44 live with men to whom they are not married, and that 48% of children are born out of wedlock, the earlier KrF government instituted payments to a mother of 80% of her salary for 12 months or full pay for 10 months to stay home with her baby. Either parent can take the leave although it is almost always the woman. When the year is up, she or he may return to her job with at least the same pay as before.

Three-fourths of women work, the highest percentage in the developed world after Iceland. She also has the right to two hours of work each day to breastfeed her baby either at home or in the office; 80% of women continue to breastfeed after six months. Each parent can take ten days off work per year when their kids are ill. This approach appears to boost the birth rate, which at 1.8 children per woman is one of the highest in Europe. Men pitch in to do their share: they perform an estimated 40% of household tasks, one of the highest rates in the world.

The earlier KrF government also unveiled a male equal rights program that allows for preferential treatment to men in industries like childcare, preschool and primary school teaching, and child welfare in order to provide male role models. Citing the need to strengthen the family, the KrF pushed through a law stopping larger shops from opening on Sunday. It adopted in 1999 a $57.7 million package to compensate Jewish families for some of the property that was plundered by the Nazis and to finance projects for the Jewish community.

The only conservative party to join the government in 2005 and 2009 is the Center Party (Sp), led by Liv Signe Navarsete. It has fallen on bad times although it captured 6.2% of the votes (down from 6.5%) and retained its 10 seats. Earlier called the Farmers' Party, it did not change its name and move from an overtly anti-industrial position until 1959. Nevertheless, it is still wary of industrial growth, and, like the KrF, it is a party of the periphery.

Like some elements within the KrF, the Center adamantly opposed Norway's entry into the EU out of fear of the damage that membership might do to traditional Norwegian society. Also like the KrF, it calls for a reduction in oil production and it is hard-line in its support of environmental protection. This issue also creates a kind of wedge between the conservative heart of the party and the younger members. The young wing is even more radi-

Prime Minister Jens Stoltenberg with two cabinet members, Kristin Halvorsen and Aslaug Haga.

cal on environmental issues and is especially wary of any form of collaboration with the Conservative Party.

Seldom in contention as a member of the government is the Progress Party. In 2009 it had its best ever result, climbing to 41 seats (up from 38) and 22.9% of the votes, up from 22.1%. It is the last remaining protest party, which arose in the early 1970s, and it opposes the heavy tax burden and the growth of state control over the economy. Its early growth, especially in the Oslo area, reflected many Norwegians' opposition to the extremely high tax level in Norway, which siphons off close to half of the income that the average person earns. Its new leader since 2006 is Siv Jensen, a young firebrand lady, who insists that the government lower taxes but also spend more of the country's oil revenues to fix roads, shorten waiting lists for hospital treatment and take better care of the elderly. The party offers simple remedies for every problem. Progress appeals to anti-immigrant sentiments and portrays itself as the defender of the traditional welfare, health and educational systems and generally the Norwegian way of life. It is in the opposition.

The final nonsocialist party is the Liberal Venstre Party (V), often called "the Liberals." This is one of Norway's oldest parties, but it was never tightly organized, and split in 1973 over the EU issue. In fact, it was the chief victim of the EU battle, and it never recovered. Only that part of the party that opposed entry remained in parliament, and the entire debate drove the party to the left. It now defines itself as a "radical social-liberal party," and it presents itself as committed to environmental protection and more careful exploitation and utilization of Norway's natural resources. In the 2009 elections it failed to garner the minimum 4% of the

Norway

votes, so it lost all but two of its seats. It is in the opposition.

The Socialist Parties

The largest party in Norway and in the government is the Labor Party (A), which in 2009 captured 35.47% of the votes, up from 32.7%, and 64 seats, up from 61. From the 1930s it has dominated Norway and has been the only party since then ever to win a parliamentary majority. Beginning as a democratic reform party, it took a temporary radical turn in the 1920s, but then moderated its course again and now defines itself as a "socialist reform party." The pragmatic character of this group is such that one could hardly call it a true socialist party, even though its party program calls for the creation of a socialist society and the nationalization of large parts of the economy as long-range goals. In fact, its immediate goals are full employment and expansion of the social security net.

After World War II the party broadened its base to include employees, small farmers, fishermen and foresters, in addition to its traditional working class base, which remains the backbone of the party. Geographically, the party is strongest in the North and in the Oslo area. In contrast to most social democratic parties in Europe, the Labor Party has never been wholly dominated by academically trained persons.

As in Sweden and Denmark, Labor sees itself as the political arm of the trade union movement, and it is formally linked to the Trade Union Confederation (LO) through interlocking leadership, collective membership and organizational ties. The LO traditionally has two seats in the party's presidium, and two party representatives sit in the LO directorate. Also by tradition, the LO leader is given a Labor seat in the *Storting*, and the trade union apparatus is used at election time to support the party.

The Labor Party has been plagued by internal division. The youth wing of the party tends always to oppose the more pragmatic economic orientation of the middle-aged and older members. But the worst division arises from foreign policy disputes. There is an element in the party that never fully digested Norway's NATO role.

Polls indicate that support of NATO membership remains strong in Norway. During the 1991 Persian Gulf crisis it sent a coast guard vessel and a supply and support ship to the Gulf, and a minesweeper to the Mediterranean, as well as financial assistance to countries affected by the crisis. In 1993 it dispatched 220 peacekeeping troops to Macedonia as part of a UN tripwire to prevent the conflict in Bosnia from spreading. It also sent humanitarian aid to Bosnia. In 2001–2 it sent special operations forces to Afghanistan. Former Deputy Foreign Minister Jan Egeland noted: "Norway has two feet—one Atlantic foot and one European foot. This makes us feel very strongly that we need NATO for the Atlantic leg."

It was the firm tie with NATO that convinced many Norwegians in 1994 that they did not need the EU for security. Nevertheless, Norway promised to assign 3,500 troops to the planned EU rapid reaction force. It contributed forces to the EU's command of peacekeeping forces in Macedonia in 2003. In Afghanistan its 400 soldiers are engaged in the stabilizing of Kabul through ISAF, and its special forces are involved in the US-led Operation Enduring Freedom, which combats al-Qaeda terrorists. Its six F-16 fighter aircraft completed their mission in 2003 and returned home, but four more were sent in 2006. Because the UN had not sanctioned the war against Iraq in 2003, Norway could not lend its support to the actual fighting. But after hostilities ended, it sent humanitarian aid and 164 troops to assist in the reconstruction of the country; all troops were withdrawn after the 2005 elections.

In 2000 Jens Stoltenberg became Norway's youngest ever prime minister. An ex-finance minister and son of a former foreign minister, he is competent, good-looking, modern-minded, media-friendly, cosmopolitan and enthusiastic about taking Norway into the EU. He has an M.A. in economics from the University of Oslo. Once the head of a government-appointed commission on the male role in society, he set an example by taking a full paternal leave while he was state secretary at the Environment Ministry. He was voted out of the prime minister's office in 2001, but he again attained that post in October 2005. Although the left parties combined won only 47.9% of the votes to the opposition parties' 49.5%, Stoltenberg was able to create a comfortable majority of 86 seats in 2009 with the Center and the Socialist Left. In 2005 this had been the first majority government in two decades, and 2009 was the first time in 16 years that a Norwegian government won reelection. It is one of Europe's few center-left governments.

He won again in 2009 because of his stewardship of the economy; Norway managed the recession better than any country in Europe, holding unemployment to 3%. Many voters still did not understand why the welfare system, which for example provides full disability payments to alcoholics, seemed to have so many defects, kindergarten spaces so short, hospitals understaffed, taxes high, pensions barely adequate, and gasoline costs as high as elsewhere in Europe, despite the Government Pension Fund Global (formerly known as the Government Petroleum Fund) worth over $444 billion and rising with the price of oil and gas; it is worth about as much as the nation's entire economy and $85,000 per citizen. He promised lavish government

Bergen

spending, including for childcare, kindergarten spaces, free fruit for school pupils, and extended maternity and paternity leave. He pledged to stop tax cuts, and he used more of Norway's oil wealth to improve welfare programs. Even though it is a parliamentary rule that the government should not use more than 4% of the fund to cover a budget deficit in normal times, he used 7%. This insulated the economy from the global downturn. Stoltenberg's government heavily subsidized day care for any child and produced a law allowing same-sex marriages.

The Labor Party requires that 40% of its candidates for public office be women, and 40% of the *Storting's* members since 1993 are women, as are four out of five leaders of the parties that received the most votes in 2009. Thus, Norway has a higher percentage of women in top governing positions than any other nation in the world.

Until recently this did not carry over to the corporate world, though. In 2003 no women were at the head of any of the country's large companies, and only 8.4% of corporate board and executive positions (compared with 12.4% in the U.S.) were held by women. The former center-right government sponsored legislation in 2002 to change that by forcing private companies to allot at least 40% of their boardroom seats to women, as was already the case in state-owned companies. Penalties began to be applied in March 2008, but by that time the percentage of women on top boards had already jumped to 44%, far above the Nordic average of 29%, the Western European average of 9% and America's 15% for the Fortune 500. Over 80% of Norwegian companies had complied by the deadline. In unlisted companies not subject to the law, fewer than 20% of board members are female. Some of the most talented ladies, known as "golden skirts," accepted as many as 35 directorships each, and this helped enable so many companies to reach the 40% target.

A further step was taken by introducing gender-neutral crosswalk signs. Pedestrians now watch for stick figures rather than little men in hats crossing a road.

The Socialist Left Party (SV), led by Kristin Halvorsen, won 6.2% of the votes, down from 8.8% and declined from 15 seats to 11in 2009. This sufficed, however, to be invited to remain in the government with Labor despite differences of opinion on NATO, exploration in the Barents, and EU membership. This partnership is something that had been considered almost unthinkable a decade earlier although it had been willing to support Labor minority governments in the *Storting*.

SV had emerged from the political battle against EU entry and was at first an electoral alliance of several socialist groupings, including elements from the Labor Party. It preserves an old tradition within Labor, especially strong in the 1920s, of radical socialism (albeit within a democratic framework). Its program calls for a radical change of Norwegian society and places much emphasis on problems related to the environment, natural resources and the "Third World." Until 1992 it opposed Labor's backing of NATO. Unlike Labor, its leaders are almost all from the intelligentsia.

Communists receive very few votes and are politically insignificant. The Beijing-oriented Red Electoral Alliance and the Norwegian Communist Party remain unrepresented in parliament, having won only about a thousand votes in 2009.

ECONOMY

Norway's geography has always greatly influenced the economic activity of its people. Its long coastline has made the country reliant on fish and now, offshore oil. Facing westward, Norway has directed its trading activity toward other lands with access to the North Atlantic. Its mountains have enabled Norwegians to produce more hydroelectric power per capita than any other country and twice as much as the United States or Canada. Almost 99% of its electricity is hydro. This cheap, available electricity was the basis for Norway's industrialization, which gradually changed it from a country so poor at the end of the 19th century that 20,000 of its people chose to emigrate to the U.S. each year into a nation with one of the highest standards of living in the world. The economic growth has been especially dramatic since World War II, a conflict that destroyed 20% of the national wealth, half of its merchant tonnage, 40% of its fishing fleet and a third of its industry.

The small size of the Norwegian domestic market of 4.7 million inhabitants has forced Norway to export many goods and services abroad in order to maintain its high standard of living and social welfare system. It must also import many raw materials to keep its industries operating, as well as many consumer goods to satisfy the rising demands of its prosperous people. Over four-fifths (80.8%) of its exports now go to the EU countries, compared with less than half in 1974, while over two-thirds (68.8%) of its imports come from those nations. As a member of the European Economic Area (EEA), Norway enjoys all of the EU's free-trade privileges, but it does not have a voice in EU decision making.

Its exports and imports represent more than 40% of its GDP, a higher figure than in many industrialized countries. This heavy dependence upon trade makes Norway particularly vulnerable to international economic fluctuations, though. Presently, 20% of the labor force works in manufacturing and related activities, producing 41.3% of GDP. The service industry employs 77% and produces 56.4% of GDP. Only 3% earns a living in agriculture, and 2.4% of GDP is generated in this sector.

Hydroelectricity, Oil and Gas

No other industrialized country has such an abundant supply of domestic energy for its inhabitants as does Norway. Its waterpower is almost endlessly renewable, and it has developed only about half of its potential for hydroelectricity. Its energy abundance saves it from that painful decision facing most other European countries: nuclear power. It neither has nuclear power plants nor plans to construct any. With its long coastline, it will perhaps be possible for it someday to generate power from waves. It has other riches of enormous immediate value right now: in 2005 oil and gas accounted for 17% of Norway's GDP. Oil alone provided 76,000 jobs.

As a result of an international agreement reached at the 1958 UN Law of the Sea Conference in Geneva, Norway received possession of a sector in the North Sea three times the size of its mainland. The offshore oil and gas resources in the North Sea are expected to be commercial throughout the 21st century. Less than a third of its estimated petroleum resources

Towing a concrete oil structure out from Stavanger

Norway

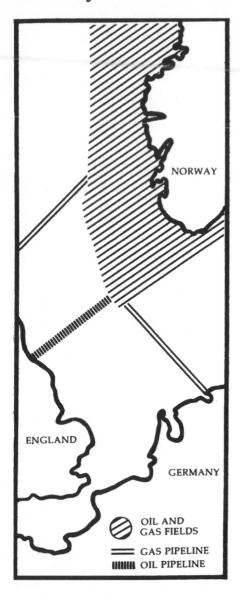

Legend:
- ⊘ OIL AND GAS FIELDS
- ═══ GAS PIPELINE
- ▭▭▭ OIL PIPELINE

have been depleted. It exports most of the 2.8 million barrels it produces per day. However, its oil production has peaked. It will increase until 2011 and then gradually decline, perhaps to around 1.5 million barrels a day by 2014. It is the world's fifth-largest petroleum producer and exporter of oil and the third-largest exporter of gas.

Drilling began in 1966, and in 1971 production started on the Ekofisk field in the southwest corner of the Norwegian sector. By the end of the decade, more fields had begun production, but in line with its policy of restraint, petroleum activities north of the 62nd parallel in the North Sea were delayed. One reason for this was the fact that two offshore disasters stung the nation. The first was in 1977 when a well in the Ekofisk field blew out of control, spilling thousands of tons of oil into the sea. The second occurred when a hotel platform capsized in 1980, killing 123.

This latter tragedy occurred on the first anniversary of the nuclear plant failure near Harrisburg, Pennsylvania, which had ignited a serious debate in all of Europe over nuclear power, even though the incident did not cause a single death.

In 1980 drilling started north of the line, and production continues there slowly, concentrating on the promising discoveries already made, not on prospecting for new fields. The government wants to make sure that oil keeps flowing when the old offshore fields of Ekofisk, Frigg and Statfjord become exhausted. It also wants the population north of the 62nd parallel to have the economic benefits of oil-related activities. Much of Norway's economic policy has always revolved around keeping citizens from leaving the sparsely populated parts of the country.

Norway's continental shelf contains around half of Europe's oil and gas resources. A gas platform named TROLL came on line in 1996, which doubled Norway's gas output and enabled it to provide 29% of European imports (half comes from Russia), including a third of Germany's and France's gas needs. By the turn of the century Norway's enormous offshore gas reserves accounted for 15% of combined oil-and-gas income. Norway exports all of its gas to the EU through underwater pipelines directly from the North Sea fields to a terminal at Emden, Germany. Its oil is delivered by underwater pipeline to Teeside, Scotland. Because of a deep underwater valley just off the Norwegian coast and the resulting precipitous rise of that coast, it is difficult to construct pipelines to the mainland. About 70% of its oil finds its way to Europe, and one-fourth goes to the U.S., which consumes 40% of the world's petroleum products. On the world stage, it is the third-largest exporter of gas and the fifth-biggest exporter of oil.

Norway must cover about 85% of its own oil requirements through imports, which is why prices at the pump are the same as in the rest of Europe. But its oil needs remain relatively small, comprising only about 41% of its total energy consumption. About 2% is provided by coal, some of it from Svalbard. A whopping 57% is provided by hydroelectricity, and Norway hopes by 2010 to produce 90% of its electricity from renewable sources. With its electricity prices half those of oil, it is no wonder that Norway can afford to consume more electricity per capita than any other country in the world. For example, the average Norwegian heats his home with it and uses twice as much electrical power as the average American. In 2002 the average Norwegian used 25,240 kilowatt hours, compared with 6,050 in Germany, 4,080 in Greece, and 2,770 in

Poland. It is also able to sell electricity to Sweden and Denmark.

Norway supplies over 10% of the EU-15's requirements of oil and about 29% of European gas requirements. At a time when Russia's energy shipments are becoming less certain, Norway is in a good position to fill European partners' need. In 2007 its two energy giants, Statoil and Norsk Hydro, merged to form StatoilHydro (62.9% state owned), the country's largest company and one of the world's biggest offshore productive capacities. Almost all of increased production will go to Europe. But the formation of such a large company and the northward movement of extraction into the Barents Sea, north of the Arctic Circle, make for tricky negotiations with Russia.

The Russian state-controlled Gazprom chose StatoilHydro as one of its foreign partners to help develop its massive Shtokman gas field off Russia's north coast; this may prove to be the world's largest offshore gas reserve. This is especially true since April 2010, when Russia and Norway settled their maritime border dispute in the Barents Sea. Norway is already the first company to commence deliveries of gas from an offshore field inside the Arctic Circle: its Snøhvit project.

Norwegians got a reminder in January 2008 of the kind of hard-ball politics the Russian government is willing to play in order to get competitors' attention. It sent the aircraft carrier Admiral Kuznetsov, escorted by other ships and submarines, including at least one nuclear attack submarine, into the center of Norway's vast Gullfaks oil field, crowded with over 40 big oil platforms. There it conducted provocative aggressive air operations that grounded all offshore helicopter flights. An accidental crash into an oil rig would be a catastrophe. Norway had already suffered its second-worst oil spill ever a month earlier in its Statfjord oil field and was very worried about a repeat. Equally worrisome was a mock Russian bombing run against Norway's northern command center at Bodo. Norway wants to cooperate with Russia, and it hopes to experience no further use of the Russian navy and air force to exert not-so-subtle pressure. This is a major reason why Norway is increasing its defense cooperation with Finland and Sweden.

Norwegian governments restricted maximum extraction to 90 million tons of oil and gas annually (extraction is far below that figure). Norway wants to preserve its reserves as long as possible and feared that too rapid exploitation could seriously disrupt Norwegian society and its economy. Because of the important interests it shares with oil-importing countries, Norway has not joined OPEC. Norwegians also debate whether their country should take advantage of global warming by drilling for more oil in "the High North" above the Arctic Circle while knowing that the consumption of that oil outside of Norway would accelerate climate change.

Official thinking in Norway is permeated by green considerations. Almost all of its electricity comes from hydro power, and it was the first country to capture carbon dioxide and store it underground. It was also one of the first lands to levy a carbon tax, and it has pledged to make the nation carbon neutral by 2030. However, it has a bad record of reducing greenhouse gas emissions: they have grown 15% since adoption of the carbon tax despite its ambitious target of being 30% below its 1990 emissions by 2020. Norway emits more than many other European countries.

Oil and gas are very important for the country's economy. Through taxes and royalties the state collects about 80% of the revenues from oil and gas production, and in 2006 it accounted for 36% of total central government revenue, compared with only 1% in 1975 and 5% in 1988. More than a third of overall investments is in the oil and gas sector. Improving technology steadily opens up previously inaccessible fields.

Since World War II, Norway, under the tutelage of Labor governments, always centrally planned and steered the country's economy more than did most other Western European countries. The goal always was to distribute income more evenly, and to maintain full employment and stable prices. The state holds about 40% by value of the Norwegian stock market. One in three workers is on the public payroll. It is no surprise that the Norwegian state took control of all phases of petroleum activity, and sought to maintain its control through Statoil.

Although foreign companies continue to be active in exploration and drilling, their services are used only as the Norwegians decide they are needed. Such discrimination ran afoul of the EU competition policy, and Norway had to restructure its entire natural-gas industry to satisfy EU authorities. Those foreign firms are preferred that invest money into mainland industries, including the ones that are related to petroleum activity, such as those involved in the production of petrochemicals or of platforms and other offshore equipment. This is particularly important because the weak link in the Norwegian economy is its mainland industry. Norway itself invests heavily abroad, and in 1996 this exceeded foreign investment in Norway for the first time. The bulk of its investments go to Sweden, France and Ireland.

StatoilHydro, which wants about a third of its output to come from international operations, is investing in operations in the Gulf of Mexico, where it is participating in many of the largest discoveries and projects. More than 100 Norwegian companies are located in Houston, Texas, employing around 6,000 Norwegians. This is the highest number of Norwegian expatriates outside of Scandinavia. Four out of five of these companies are in the energy sector. It is not surprising that the two countries' energy capitals—Stavanger and Houston—are sister cities that engage in many forms of cooperation.

Norway sets aside 80% of its oil earnings in the Government Pension Fund Global (formerly Petroleum Fund), a national nest egg that is invested in international equities in order to prevent inflation at home. It was valued at over $444 billion by 2010 (an average of $85,000 per Norwegian), making it the world's second-largest sovereign wealth fund after the United Arab Emirates. It owns 1% of all global stocks. But it lost 23% in the 2009 recession, or $100 billion, prompting the government to review the fund's operations. According to law, the government can in normal times spend up to 4% of it each year to plug a budget deficit. However, the Stoltenberg government stimulated the economy in 2009 by withdrawing 7%, and the fund bounced back.

The largest retirement savings plan in Europe, it is an investment fund the country can use to spread oil wealth between generations. It is also there for a rainy day in the future. By 2030 pensions will account for 15% of GDP, and the fund would be able to pay about half of that. As one expert put it, "we will continue to receive our free lunch for many years after the oil itself has gone." Many voters in 2005 and 2009 agreed that some of it ought to be spent now.

This "sovereign fund" sets the standard in the world for transparency and responsibility. It is invested only in 3,000 to 4,000 overseas enterprises in 40 countries. One-third of the funds are in the United States. It is overseen by the finance ministry and managed by an arm of the Central Bank of Norway. A philosopher advises the bank on how to steer clear of morally questionable investments. For example, it divested its stock in Lockheed Martin, because that firm produces cluster bombs and land mines, and in Wal-Mart because of its controversial labor practices. It increased its holdings in environmentally responsible companies in order to combat climate change.

Nonpetroleum Industries

Although Norway is a highly industrialized society, it remains within a nonin-

Fjord water   Source: *News of Norway*

dustrial landscape. This is because Norwegian industries tend to be rather small. Only a few hundred of the more than 14,000 companies have more than 200 employees, although those large companies employ about 40% of the work force in manufacturing. Industries are 91% privately and largely Norwegian owned. They are geographically spread out and are often located in beautiful fjord or coastal districts where they can be close to hydropower sources and ports. In 1997 Norway was ranked as the fifth country in the world in overall economic competitiveness.

Hydroelectric power is very important for industry in general, and especially for industries that produce chemicals, iron, steel and ferro-alloys, aluminum and other metals. The latter are very power-consuming and the approximately 30 companies in these sectors consume about a fourth of all electric power produced. Few other countries could supply such industries with cheap electricity to keep them alive. The largest of these electricity consumers by far is the primary production of aluminum for further processing into finished goods. In this sector Norway is the world's second largest exporter after Canada, although all of Norway's bauxite must be imported. It is the largest producer of aluminum in Europe. Much of the other metal industry can be supplied either by domestic ores, which are generally of poor quality and are mined predominantly in the northern half of the country, or by importing the needed ores

Norway

with money earned from exporting unneeded ores. In the northern mountains new deposits of gold have been discovered in such massive sizes that they could influence the world price of this precious metal.

Iron ore resources can be mined for at least another century, and Norway has considerable deposits of titanium (used in paints), sulphur, pyrite, copper, zinc, lead and nickel. The sad fact remains, however, that without state subsidies many of its metal producing industries would fail. In order to maintain high employment, aluminum production is maintained at 90% capacity although the industry loses money on every ton it produces. Other metal industries have been pared down to close to 50% capacity and are still losing money.

About the only industry that is not in trouble in Norway is the tourist business. Thanks to the beauty of its scenery and to the friendliness of its people, Norway normally attracts as many foreign tourists as its entire population. About 70% come from other Nordic countries. A major benefit of tourism is that it stimulates economic activity in the outlying regions, both in the mountains and along the coast. Tourism and the economy as a whole received a major boost in 1994, when the town of Lillehammer hosted the Winter Olympics.

Shipping

There are about 80 shipyards in Norway, most of them very small, although the industry is dominated by two large groups, Kvaerner and Aker. As orders for traditional ships declined, many companies converted to constructing offshore rigs and specialized ships. This adjustment has temporarily compensated for the loss of orders for regular ships, but many observers fear that even the market for specialized craft will soon be saturated. The state does subsidize this industry to keep it internationally competitive. But it stopped making new subsidy commitments to shipping companies in the 1980s, and it supported efforts to make the shipbuilding industry more efficient through rationalization.

Like Denmark, Norway has one of the world's largest merchant marine fleets. By 2007 it possessed 1,600 ocean-going merchant vessels, 5% of the world's fleet (down from 10% in 1967). About 60% fly the Norwegian national flag. Norwegians also own about a fifth of all ships used for offshore oil drilling. Well over 90% of these ships never dock at Norwegian ports, though. Oil tankers account for more than 60% of the total tonnage, and Norwegian shipping companies operate many oil drilling platforms.

The deep-sea expertise Norwegian divers have acquired made Norway the logical provider of the Regalia seagoing platform and trained personnel to help rescue and then recover the bodies of 12 out of 118 Russian sailors trapped in the submarine Kursk in August 2000. Norwegians operate many of the cruise ships that circle the Caribbean Sea. Further, the world's largest passenger ship, "France," was purchased by a Norwegian ship owner and rechristened "Norway." Its fleet is very modern and is entirely privately owned. There are very few large shipping companies and most are small or medium-sized. Maritime activities account for 11% of gross exports, making shipping the third largest export industry.

Forestry and Agriculture

Norway's forests in the central and southern part of the country provide a good part of the raw materials for a wood processing industry, although it does have to import some wood from Sweden. This industry traditionally exports 80% of its products, but heavy competition from its Nordic neighbors and Canada has also forced it to face fundamental reorganization. Much of the wooded area is owned by the farmers, many of whom derive supplemental income from forestry. Regardless of who owns the forests, they can, according to Norwegian law, be used by everybody for recreational purposes.

The country has not been self-sufficient in food for many decades, and Norway's agricultural production covers less than half of the people's food consumption. It is self-sufficient in dairy and meat products, but it must import 90% of its food grains. The problem, of course, is that only about 3% of the land can be used for farming, and the terrain is so rugged that the predominantly small farms make it difficult to combine them in a way which would permit large-scale and more efficient farming, although the state is making an effort to encourage this. Also, the northern climate means that the growing season is very short. The very best agricultural land is around the Oslo fjord, in the large valleys in the south-central region, and around Stavanger in the south and the Trøndelag area in central Norway.

The state's coffers have been open to Norwegian farmers for years, to the tune of $1.7 billion annually, in an effort to preserve the present pattern of settlement in the country. Every two years the government negotiates an "Agricultural Agreement" with both major farmers' organizations that fixes price levels, subsidies and marketing rules. Many farmers could never hope to survive without such assistance. The state also controls the quantity and price of imported foodstuffs, allowing in only what is in short supply in Norway. This is done to protect Norwegian agriculture, and it is certainly one reason why Norwegians were wary of joining the EU, which would prohibit such practices.

Fishing

Even Norway's most picturesque industry, fishing, could hardly survive with-

Fishing boats

out state help. The number of fishermen has declined from about 60,000 in 1960 to 26,700 by 1995, a figure that is less than 1% of the country's total workforce. However, during these two decades, their catch doubled, largely because of more efficient fishing and the declaration of a 200-mile economic zone along the Norwegian coast and around Jan Mayen and of a separate fishery zone around Svalbard. Measured by quantity of catch, Norway is the second-leading fishing nation in Europe, behind Russia. Its fish farms are highly efficient, and it has the world's largest farmed salmon industry. Fishing accounts for 14% of nonpetroleum exports and is still important because it supplies raw materials for the country's large fish processing industry.

Fishermen are strongly unionized and have well-developed cooperatives that buy the fish at fixed prices; they do not have to sell their catch by auction. Only 2% of the catches are sold fresh, and close to 80% is reduced to oil and meal, while about 10% is frozen and 8% is salted or dried. About 90% of the entire catch is ultimately exported. Norway suspended its commercial whaling after the 1987 season, but in 1993 it announced a resumption. Norway, Iceland and Japan are the last two countries in the world to hunt whales in violation of the 1993 ban by the International Whaling Commission. In 2006 Norway set its own catch quota for minke whales in the North Atlantic at 1,052, but it killed only 546 to November.

In many coastal communities, especially in the north, these mainly small or medium-sized companies represent the only possible industrial element. Therefore, the state has long given subsidies to them to keep them alive and to keep persons in those communities from migrating south into the larger cities. This form of subsidy may make little sense from a purely economic point of view, but as in so many other instances in Norway, political objectives outweigh economic ones. In the North, the once feared start-up of offshore oil operations north of the 62nd parallel is now eagerly awaited as the only means of averting the Arctic region's depopulation and subsequent decline.

Economic Problems and European Union

Oslo has become one of the world's most expensive cities in which to live. Its prices are, on average, 29% higher than the average within the EU. Only Switzerland and Iceland, both non-EU members, have higher prices. Food costs a third more in Norway than in Sweden, which explains the vibrant cross-border trade in Sweden. This is a strong argument for joining the EU. Inflation disturbed the tra-

ditional labor peace, and sparked strikes, which many are experiencing for the first time in their lives. It also drove up public spending. From where did the inflation come?

The extremely lucrative oil and gas activity brought lots of money into the country, which ended up more and more in the form of public spending rather than investment in private industry to raise productivity and to develop new technology. The oil operations also attracted much of the country's skilled labor and created a very tight supply in the rest of the country. Despite appeals by the government, employees in the petroleum sector successfully forced the oil companies to pay ever-increasing wages. To fill some of the labor shortages, 75,000 migrant laborers worked legally in Norway as of 2007, about 20,000 of whom from the Nordic world. They make up 3% of the labor force.

As in all Nordic countries, the guidelines for wage settlements covering the entire country are established in summit meetings between the LO and the employers associations every two years. Since these unified wage guidelines apply to all sectors of the economy, the unions (to which two-thirds of the labor force belongs) have succeeded in insisting that all wages rise with those in the petroleum industry, regardless of whether a company in the non-oil sector is profitable or not. That is where both government subsidies and inflation come into the picture. The government pays much of the costs of higher wages in the form of subsidies.

In the 1980s the government created two-thirds of the new jobs. By 1995 public sector employment had doubled since 1972, while industrial jobs had fallen by 100,000. Rising wage costs increase the price of products that Norwegian companies are trying to sell abroad. To make matters worse, Norway's sale of oil and gas greatly increased the strength of its currency, the krone (crown). Such a "hard" currency raises even more the actual prices of Norway's goods to foreign buyers. This caused Norway to lose some of its markets abroad.

No government could risk a dramatic rise in unemployment or a deep cut in the social welfare system. Any substantial dismantling of the social welfare system in a Scandinavian country could be fatal to any politician who would propose it, regardless of whether the system could be paid for or not. Unlike other Nordic countries, Norway can pay for its tightly-woven social security net. It introduced a National Insurance Scheme in 1967, which by 1971 had replaced all private pension or insurance programs. It protects all citizens against sickness, unemployment, in-

validism and many other unforeseen calamities. At age 67 a person receives a pension which for the average Norwegian amounts to about two-thirds of the income he earned during his working years. Employers' contributions pay 60% of the costs of the scheme, members' 20% and appropriations from the central and local governments the remaining 20%. As in other Scandinavian countries, welfare assistance is given as a right, not as an alm, and the objective is that neither personal calamity nor old age should endanger the living standard to which the citizen had become accustomed.

Things looked bright in the 21st century until the 2009 recession jolted the country. Real estate fell by 15% before beginning to rise again. There was no real estate crash since there were few mortgage lending excesses. Banks remained generally healthy and prudent in their lending. The government set up two stimulus funds (one for banks and the other for business and industry) to try to mitigate the effects of the global crisis. Norway's annual economic growth averaged almost 4% (falling to 1.5% in 2009 and minus .9% in 2010). Inflation in 2010 stood at 3.3%. Unemployment was 3.5% in 2010, one of the lowest in Europe. It would be slightly higher if persons in training and employment programs were included, but essentially all Norwegians who want to work are employed. Per capita GDP in 2008, at $79,200, was the second-highest in the world after Luxembourg, and it topped the Nordic nations. A study in 2009 found that Norwegians work the fewest hours of the citizens of any industrial democracy.

It is one of the few countries in Europe that is not reducing its welfare state. Its competitive position has improved because of productivity improvements following a shakedown of labor in manufacturing. It has made its tax system simpler to administer and understand. Although the real tax level stayed the same for the business sector, it reduced the highest marginal rate from 57.8% to 48.8%, and the middle class pays no more than 35.8%.

Its most important decision was whether to join the EU, to which it formally applied in 1992. In 1994 voters went to the polls, and 52.2% rejected EU membership. Its strong economy, low unemployment, and overall feeling of security allowed Norwegians an alternative to the EU. One explanation seemed to sum up the majority's attitude: "We know what we have, but we don't know what we'll get."

In many ways it enjoys most of the advantages of EU membership without most of the disadvantages. It is part of the internal market through the European Economic Area (EEA), which it joined in 1994 and which does not cover agriculture and

Norway

fish. It had to restructure its natural-gas industry, accepts all the EU environmental and social legislation, and even makes as large a financial contribution to EU coffers as a comparable-sized EU member, such as Denmark or Finland. However, it does not have to adopt the euro; is not bound by the Common Foreign and Defence Policy (CFSP); does not pay into the wasteful Common Agriculture Policy (CAP) while subsidizing its own farmers more than would be allowed in the EU; and finally does not have to abide by the EU's common fisheries policy, thereby maintaining its own 200-mile coastal exclusion zone, which remains well stocked with fish. Norway has agreed to pay 225 million euros to the EU over five years to help fund improvements in the 10 new countries that joined in 2004.

But it has no voice in EU decisions, being what former Trade Commissioner and now WTO President Pascal Lamy called "a fax democracy": it receives instructions and legislation from Brussels, but it has no input into the decisions. For example, in 2005 the EU slapped a 16% duty on Norwegian salmon, arguing that Norway "dumps" its salmon inside the EU at below the cost of production. Such rulings breed distrust toward Brussels, and the irritated minister of fisheries, Svein Ludvigsen, said: "If Norway was a member of the EU, this salmon issue would never be on the agenda." The matter was resolved by both sides accepting a minimum price for salmon sales.

In the 21st century, Norway's public is still divided on the EU. Aware that four-fifths of Norway's exports are sold in the EU, industry supports behind membership. Many realize that the EU is expanding eastward and will soon encompass most of Europe; this makes it harder to stand outside. There is the some desire to take part in the invigorated EU discussions concerning a European Security and Defence Policy (ESDP), for which Norway already provides troops. Belonging would help Norwegians shape the European decisions that ultimately affect them. Nevertheless, Prime Minister Jens Stoltenberg announced after the 2005 and 2009 elections that there would be no referendum on joining the EU during the lifetime of his government. Majority opinion in 2005 was against entry, but the government still favors membership.

Norway is moving steadily closer to Europe whether its people are fully aware of it or not. It is Europe's top oil producer, and a third of its export revenue is derived from North Sea energy sources. It maintains its economic performance and energy production in a way that does not unduly pollute the environment. In a 2008 study, experts at Yale and Columbia universities ranked Norway in third place after Sweden and Switzerland on its Environmental Sustainability Index, which takes into consideration 21 ecological factors. The U.S. was ranked 66th.

Norwegians are rich because of their oil, but they are confronted with the problem of how to use their wealth. All European countries have oil problems, but Norway has one of a different kind. The more they earn from oil, the more two different economies develop: one a flourishing energy production in the high seas, and the other a traditional mainland industry. They are still torn between wanting to keep their industry alive by avoiding a predominantly oil-based economy and wanting their standards of living to keep on rising as a result of oil wealth.

The major parties know that oil revenues can bankroll the expanding welfare state and bureaucracy. For example, in 2003 the government announced plans to dip into the huge Government Pension Fund Global to cover its budget deficit although a parliamentary rule allows no more than 4% of the fund to be used to cover a budget deficit. Prime Minister Stoltenberg tapped 7% of the fund's assets. However, the issue was not too contentious since there was a budget surplus of 17.5% in 2008, falling to 9.4% in 2010, and the state is free of debt.

Government subsidies can keep specific, weak industries alive and thereby fight unemployment. But such use of Norway's riches shelters its industry from change and real competition and robs it of the discipline that would be needed to make its mainland economy healthy again. The government subsidies that flow to industry are handouts to pay workers, not investments to improve production techniques. Thus oil and gas help to freeze the status quo, while Norway's competitors gear up for the future. What will happen, though, when the oil and gas run out, or if those two things would lose much of their value due to future technological developments in the energy field? The Midas touch obviously creates problems, as well as opportunities.

CULTURE

Rural-Urban Traditional Distinctions
A major characteristic of Norwegian politics and society remains the contrast and tension between the periphery and the center. The center encompasses the leaders of the country's civil service, military, Lutheran Church, industry and shipping in and around Oslo and the major cities. In this political and social center one speaks a Norwegian dialect now called *Bokmål* (earlier *Riksmål*), whereas in the periphery most persons speak another dialect now called *Nynorsk* (which means "New Norwegian" and which was earlier called *Landsmål*). Both dialects have equal status in the state administration and schools, but the use of one dialect or the other reveals important social distinctions. Until the end of the 19th century the only official dialect was *Riksmål*, which had been influenced by the Danish language during the long period of Danish domination over Norway. Thus, it was the language of the more cosmopolitan and middle-upper class city dwellers.

In the course of the 19th century the dialect of *Nynorsk* was developed by a nationalist, Ivar Asen, from many diverse rural dialects that Asen judged to be un-

Winners of the Award for Design and Excellence　　　Source: *News of Norway*

tainted by Danish. Now spoken by only 12% of the population, *Nynorsk* was much closer to the speech used by the common people, who at that time lived mainly in rural areas of the south and west. Among these people, class distinctions were minimal, since most were fishermen or small, independent farmers who owned their own land. They were much more religious than their compatriots in the cities, and their respect for state authority was much weaker. They also spoke a dialect that was looked down upon by the city folk. The people in the periphery were much more supportive of movements calling for popular religious revival, the widened use of *Nynorsk* and the prohibition of alcoholic beverages.

From 1917 until 1927 they were able to have all liquors and strong wines banned entirely, and they still are inclined to support politicians who call for tightened controls on alcoholic consumption. In the sparsely populated north the contrast with the center was less pronounced, since the society there was more fragmented, with more prosperous trade families having a greater economic influence or control over the small farmers and fishermen. The tensions between the center and the periphery still influence Norwegian politics and parties today and were crucially important in the debate over possible Norwegian entry into the EU in 1972 and in 1994. But the mobilization of the periphery against the center has been replaced by a noticeable rebellion of the center against the periphery on many issues.

Norway is experiencing another form of tension: toward darker-skinned refugees and immigrants. They now constitute about a quarter of Oslo's population. This traditionally white nation of 4.7 million had never regarded itself as a melting pot. The influx of as many as 16,000 such people every year has created a groundswell of unease. The Progress Party, whose support is important for the minority government elected in the 2001 parliamentary elections, easily exploits animosity against them. To gain favor from the growing Muslim population one Luther-an pastor proposed in 2004 that empty churches be converted into mosques. But this idea was rejected by ex-Prime Minister Bondevik, himself a church pastor.

Feelings ran especially high when two neo-Nazis stabbed a black teenager on a lighted Oslo street in 2001. This brutal and senseless act outraged thousands of Norwegians, who took to the streets to demonstrate against racism in their traditionally tolerant country. The two were convicted in 2002, and the government appointed a panel to recommend ways of strengthening anti-hate laws, including a ban on the public display of Nazi and racist symbols.

Beginning on the east side of Oslo, a dingy area with about 130,000 immigrants, and now all over the capital, many frightened parents are taking their children out of their neighborhood schools because immigrant children constitute an overall majority in them. Parents fear that the quality of education is dropping. With the blue-collar class shrinking, immigrants now comprise the new lower class, and their numbers are rising, thanks largely to family reunification. They are divided among themselves on ethnic lines and are in constant demographic flux. They have gone to the bottom of a sort of minority hierarchy, with the Sami at the top, favored because of their status in international law as an indigenous people and their own Sami parliament. Immigration and integration have become emotional and controversial issues among established parties and organizations. Only one candidate from an immigrant background, Labor's Saera Khan, won a parliamentary seat in 2005.

The Arts

The two principal dialects of Norwegian, *Bokmål* and *Nynorsk*, are spoken by only four and one-half million persons, and in contrast to the Swedes, who allow English words to seep freely into their language, the Norwegians try very hard to prevent their language from being anglicized in any way, even though most Norwegians learn English in school. Despite the fact that so few people in the world speak the Norwegian language, Norway is a very active literary nation. It has the world's highest book sales per person, and book publishing is supported by sizable state subsidies.

It has had three Nobel Prize winners in literature: Bjørnstjerne Bjørnson in 1903, Knut Hamsun in 1920, and Sigrid Undset in 1928. Hamsun is particularly perplex-

"The Scream" by Edvard Munch

Norway

Edvard Munch by himself

ing because he had welcomed the brutal Nazi occupation of his own country. He gave his Nobel Prize to propaganda minister, Josef Goebbels, and flew to the Eagle Nest retreat to meet Hitler. He wrote an article for a collaborationist newspaper on May 7, 1945, glorifying Hitler, who had just committed suicide a few days earlier. Until his death at 92 in 1952, Hamsun was shunned and punished by his countrymen for his shocking betrayal. But his revered novels, like *Hunger*, *Pan* and *Growth of the Soil*, are still on the nightstands and school reading lists of many Norwegians.

The earliest Norwegian literature is Eddic poetry from the 9th or 10th centuries, and many fairy tales and folk poems survive from subsequent centuries. After the country's links with Denmark were broken in 1814, Henrik Wergeland won the reputation as the most significant Norwegian lyricist with his visionary romantic poetry. He ignited a literary renaissance in the country. Bjørnson was the first writer whose works became widely known beyond the country's borders; his earlier plays and short stories are infused with nationalist ideas and enthusiasm, but his later works are more characterized by modern realism. Also well-received abroad were the plays of Henrik Ibsen, whose serious, penetrating works explore man's ethical and psychological dimensions. Ibsen, Bjørnson and two other writers in the realist school, Jonas Lie and Alexander Kielland, are generally considered to be the most significant Norwegian authors, although Arne Garborg, Undset and Hamsun should not be overlooked.

Just as the liberation from Denmark sparked a literary outburst, the emancipation from German occupation in 1945 had the same effect. For a while poetry and exciting narratives were produced, but Nor-

wegian literature quickly moved from the optimistic enthusiasm of national emancipation to pessimism, intellectual indecision, fear and powerlessness. Literature became more experimental. As Norway began its economic flowering and a wealthy consumer society developed, Norwegian literature turned to the alleged absurdity of society and the difficulties that individuals have in establishing their own identity and meaningful contacts with other persons in a cold, consumption-oriented society. Much Norwegian literature became thereby politicized, as authors pointed to a need for radical change.

A particular pride of contemporary Norwegian literature is Herbjørg Wassmo, who in 1987 won the Nordic Literature Prize for her 1986 novel *Hudløs Himmel* (Sensitive Sky). She is the first Norwegian woman to win it. Her writings depict women's psyche, chiseled in drastic realism. She commands a sensitive, poetic language.

The society those authors criticized so mercilessly was, however, a very tolerant one, which not only bore criticism well, but which even chose to pay for such literary attacks against itself. As few Norwegian books could be financial successes on the tiny Norwegian market, the state created a cultural fund that purchased 1,000 copies of each work of Norwegian literature so that every public library could have a copy to circulate. The state also grants three-year scholarships to young authors in order to provide them with the financial wherewithal to work undisturbed.

An author who does not need the state's hand is Jostein Gaader, a high school philosophy teacher. His novel, *Sophie's World*, is a highly readable history of Western thought told in a compelling mystery. After reaching the bestseller lists in Scandinavia and Germany, it was introduced to the American market in 1995. Also avidly read in the U.S. is crime novelist Jo Nesbø, whose *Nemesis* was nominated for an Edgars Award and whose novel, *The Devil's Star*, appeared in English in 2010. Also riding this wave are K.O. Dahl and Karin Fossum.

The state and the municipalities also subsidize all cultural activities with a view to making culture largely decentralized and thereby available to as many persons as possible. It maintains six regional theaters, in addition to the National Theater in Oslo, the country's main stage, and the National Stage in Bergen. Oslo also has the Norwegian Theater, which presents plays only in *Nynorsk*, and the Oslo New Theater. Plays are also televised once a week so that Norwegians can have the chance to experience theater performances in every corner of the country. In

Edvard Grieg

1988 the theaters found themselves in dire financial straits, due to a top-heavy organization, too many employees with too little work, and the fact that government subsidies, which amount to 85% of the total outlays, had not been adjusted in 15 years. Without such subsidies, a single ticket would cost $125, instead of only $15.

State subsidies also keep the Norwegian film industry alive, so that it can produce about 10 feature and 80 short films per year; most are aimed primarily at a Norwegian audience. These subsidies, amounting to $100 million in 2009, cover 45% of the production costs for black and white and 55% for color films. The state will also guarantee loans for up to 90% of the total production costs. All films shown in Norway must, however, be approved by a state film censor, a requirement that is highly controversial today.

Perhaps the internationally best known Norwegian film figure is the actress Liv Ullmann, who often appears on stage in the U.S. and in many films directed by the Swede, Ingmar Bergman, who died in 2007. Because of her fame and activism for the UN Children's Fund, she was named as the UN's first goodwill ambassador to various parts of the world, especially Africa. Bergman's and Ullmann's daughter, Linn Ullmann, who studied literature in the U.S. from age 16 to 22 before returning to Oslo as a literary critic for the daily newspaper, *Dagladet*, won rave reviews in both countries for her debut novel in 1998, *Before You Sleep*.

Recommended in 1997 for an Oscar for best foreign film was Norway's *The Other*

Side of Sunday, directed by Otto Nesheim. Set in 1959, it is a delightful portrayal of the maturing of a young girl who grows up in a pious family living in a rural part of Norway where almost everything was forbidden. Another Norwegian film won an Oscar nomination in 2002: *Elling*, based on Ingvar Ambjørnsen's novel, *Blood Brothers*. At the Seattle International Film Festival, it was voted as the audience's favorite film out of 230 movies.

And 2008 was a banner year: 23 Norwegian films were premiered, attracting 22.5% of movie goers. Topping the list was the World War II drama, *Max Manus*, based on a true story of the resistance hero. Close behind was *The Kautokeino Rebellion*, which chronicles a Sami uprising in northern Norway in 1852, directed by a descendant of the rebellion, Nils Gaup.

Norwegian art and music cross Norway's borders more easily since they appeal to human senses and intellect without the restriction of language. The best-known composer was Edvard Grieg, who composed intimate, soothing romantic pieces. Another widely acclaimed composer, Johann Svendsen, produced symphonic music, which, like that of Grieg, drew inspiration from Norwegian folk music. The country has many active composers today, and there are four symphony orchestras in the major cities. The Norwegian Opera was created under the directorship of the renowned singer Kirsten Flagstad in 1958 in order to provide a suitable setting for both opera and ballet. In 1994 the world heard one of Norway's most popular song artists, Sissel Kyrkjebø, open and close the Winter Olympics in Lillehammer. Many of her CDs and cassettes were released in the U.S. Also popular in America in the late 1990s were country music star Bjoro Haland and his band. A teen female duo, M2M (Marit Larsen and Marion Raven), won a large following not only at home, but in Europe and the U.S. Maria Mena, an 18-year-old singer-songwriter from Oslo with a New Yorker father, toured America and snagged a top 15 spot on the singles chart in 2004. Higher-brow stars are opera singers Kjell Mangus Sandev and his wife Kjersti Sandev.

The giant of Norwegian art is Edvard Munch, who is considered to be one of the fathers of expressionism around the turn of the century. The product of a family with a history of insanity, he created paintings that scream at the viewer and reveal how some human beings can be alienated, desperately anxious and torn inside. Unloved and misunderstood in the Norway of his time, he gained his fame in Germany. He moved back to his native country in 1909 and had an uneasy relationship with it until his death in 1944.

Most of his works are displayed in the Munch Museum in Oslo, and other works of his are scattered among the 320 art museums and art collections throughout the country.

On the day the world's attention was focused on the opening of the Lillehammer Winter Olympics, his (and Norway's) most famous painting, *The Scream*, painted in 1893 and worth at least $75 million and of which there are four versions, was stolen from the National Gallery in Oslo by thieves who brazenly left a postcard reading, "Thanks for the poor security." Norwegians heaved a sigh of relief in May 1994, three months later, when the police recovered it undamaged in a sting operation. In 1996 four Norwegian men were sentenced to six years in prison.

However, the luck was not to last. In 2004, another version of *The Scream*, along with an additional Munch masterpiece from 1893–4, *Madonna,* valued at $15 million and like *The Scream* uninsured, were violently ripped from the walls of Oslo's Munch Museum in a daytime raid while stunned visitors looked on. The paintings were whisked off in a waiting car. In February 2006 six suspects went to trial in Oslo for the theft. Three were convicted and given sentences from 4 to 8 years. The paintings were found in August only slightly damaged.

In March 2005 a watercolor called "Blue Dress" and two lithographs by Munch were pried with crowbars and stolen from the walls of an upscale restaurant of the Refnes Hotel at Moss, south of Oslo. Police recovered the three works less than 24 hours later. Only five months later two masked thieves stormed into Oslo's Hotel Continental and stole from the lounge wall three paintings they thought were by Munch. But the hotel had replaced its originals with worthless photocopies, so one can imagine the Munch-like screams out of the robbers' mouths when they got home and inspected their booty.

Norwegian Special Forces

Norwegian artists have been leaders in the production of "monumental art," and as in the other Scandinavian countries, abstract art has become a dominant form. It also has produced recognized sculptors, such as Carl Nesjar, Odd Tandberg, Arnold Haukeland and Nils Aas. The sculptor best known internationally, however, is Gustav Vigeland.

Education

At age seven, Norwegian children enter school, and for at least nine years they must attend an elementary school, which is financed and operated by the municipal governments. About 80% continue their education for an additional three years in schools that are operated and financed by the counties. A recent reform under an earlier Labor government combined in 1976 the separate tracks of secondary schools that had prepared young people for the university, for a trade or for some other job, which did not require a university education. The problem with such separate schools was that it was very difficult to change from one secondary school to another type; many critics also believed that such separate schools established and hardened class differences within Norwegian society.

Therefore, comprehensive schools, similar to the American high schools, were created, which combined various tracks under one roof and which eased the difficulty of switching from one track to the other. Those who follow the college preparatory course in the new comprehensive schools usually qualify for entrance into one of the four state-funded universities in Oslo, Bergen, Trondheim and Tromsø, into one of several specialized universities (which teach, for example, engineering, agriculture, architecture, business administration, physical education or music), or one of seven regional teachers' colleges. Education is free at all levels, and needy students in the secondary schools can receive extra scholarships. Students at the universities or colleges receive both scholarships and loans that must be repaid within ten to fifteen years. As elsewhere in Europe, the universities are experiencing severe overcrowding.

As in all Scandinavian countries, Norwegian schools have been laboratories for experimentation, especially the kind that seeks to eliminate social differences. Many of these changes have not been well received, and one of the first things the earlier Conservative government changed was reevaluation of grades in schools, which had been deemphasized or done away with on the grounds that they were discriminatory and were hindrances to learning. The new administration also enhanced the financial basis of private

Norway

schools and gave them more freedom to run themselves as they chose.

The Media

Considering its small population, the Norwegian press offers both variety and a considerable number of individual publications—in all there are 161 daily newspapers. All are in private hands, although all receive state subsidies in one form or the other. Most generally support the political line of one party or the other without having formal ties to it. It was estimated in 1989 that 40% of the newspapers support leftist parties, and a majority supports the center and right. The only exceptions are newspapers linked with the Labor and Communist parties. The largest newspapers are the independent to conservative Oslo dailies, *Aftenposten* and *Verdens Gang*, as well as the liberal dailies *Dagbladet* from Oslo and the *Bergens Tidende* from Bergen. Favorite weekly magazines are *Allers, Hjemmet* and *Norst Ukeblad*, which are all family publications. The favorite monthlies are *Reader's Digest,* entitled *Det Beste* in Norwegian, and *Donald Duck Co.*, whose hero is very familiar to American and European readers. In 2002 the international organization, Reporters Without Borders, rated the Norwegian press the world's fourth freest after those of Finland, Iceland, and the Netherlands.

Local radio and TV stations compete with the state-owned Norwegian Broadcasting Company. Its activities are free of direct government control, although it is run by a council composed of representatives of the *Storting*, the public service and certain public groups. The government also appoints the director. Financing comes from public funds since no advertising is permitted (except on some foreign stations); radio and television must

compete with one of the most beautiful natural settings for the people's attention. Norwegians are outdoors people, and they tend to spend their four weeks of paid vacation hiking, fishing, swimming, camping and boating in the summer and cross-country skiing or skating in the winter. Prosperity has also enabled one out of six families to buy its own seaside cottage or mountain chalet. This is a striking proportion when one considers that 53% of the families own the houses or apartments in which they live.

The Native Population

One group that lives especially close to nature is the 60,000 or so Sami, about two-thirds of whom live in Norway's far north, and about a third of whom live in the north of Finland and Sweden. It is believed that about 45,000 Samis live in Norway. Isolated for centuries in the northern periphery of Scandinavia, they preserved their unique Finno-Ugric language, broken down into three broad dialects by region. Until after the Second World War they were forbidden to use their language. Their exclusive identity with the Sami culture is breaking down as most Sami are being assimilated with the other Scandinavian cultures to one degree or another. They do not have facial features or skin color that distinguish them visually from other Norwegians. They can therefore blend into Norwegian society if they choose to do so, abandoning their language and changing their last names to disguise their origins.

The most tightly knit Sami are the reindeer-raising nomads, who now constitute only a tenth of the total Sami population. Each receives an annual subsidy of $14,400 from the central government. However, their grazing areas have been greatly reduced by fences erected along

the Norwegian-Swedish border and by the construction of hydroelectric plants at the waterfalls in the north. The tundra in the northernmost province of Finnmark, may cover huge mineral deposits, and the central government wants the profits from mining to go into its own treasury. The Sami, who are a minority in the North, are contesting this, as they are other irritating regulations from Oslo, such as a new rule that only a veterinarian can castrate reindeer.

The extension of the social welfare system to every corner of Norway has made practices of helping each other largely unnecessary, and therefore a part of the glue within the nomadic community has been destroyed. Of course, many Samis want to become partially or wholly assimilated into the Norwegian culture, but an emotional debate is still taking place in Norway concerning the future of this minority within the larger society. Expressed in a simplified way, some Norwegians argue that the Samis' standard of living should be elevated to the prevailing Norwegian level, while others argue that their cultural independence should be preserved at all costs, even though their culture scorns individual advancement and permits many social inequalities within its own society.

The Norwegian state does finance a Sami school at Karasjok for those children whose parents want them to learn in the Sami language. Other special schools and university courses are also provided. It is certain that the most effective means for the survival of this unique minority is to preserve its language, and subsidized radio and TV programs are aired. There are also Sami book publishers, newspapers (such as *Min Aigi*—Our Times—published twice weekly) and recordings of traditional Sami chants. Nevertheless, the Sami culture will continue to lose its grip on the lives of most of the group.

The lives of this faraway people was so vividly portrayed in the first Sami film ever made, *Pathfinder*, that it won an Oscar nomination in 1988 for best foreign film. This film was half financed by the Norwegian government and directed by a 32-year-old Sami, Nils Gaup, under appalling conditions. It was shot above the Arctic Circle in temperatures which reached 40 degrees below zero and when there were only two hours of daylight. Cameras had to be stored in a freezer to avoid condensation inside the mechanisms, and sound equipment had to be defrosted with electric hair dryers. The message was worth the extreme effort.

Through councils (called *Siida*), composed of representatives of the various families, the nomads regulate the use of grazing land. The council also tradition-

Sami with reindeer

ally had the function of guiding the community and of arranging for the provision of food and other necessities for the socially weak within the group. In 1989 Samis elected for the first time 39 representatives from 13 constituencies to their own Sami People's Congress. It is elected every four years on the same day as the national parliament in Oslo. It convenes in the Finnmark town of Karasjok, where a park (named Sameland, or Sápmi in Sami) offers visitors a poetic and magical trip through Sami culture. The congress has advisory as well as decision-making powers in matters related to the Samis.

At the third opening of this parliament in 1997, King Harald V publicly expressed regret to the Sami people for the repression inflicted on them and their culture: "Today we must apologize for the injustice the Norwegian state once imposed on the Sami people through policies of Norwegianization." In 2002 the Sami People's Congress demanded more self-government, although there is no consensus what that exactly means and for whom such a government would speak. Its electoral register contained only 10,000 names in 2002, and only two-thirds of them actually voted in the previous election. In Sweden a similarly elected *Someting* was created in 1993.

A major issue was how to gain control of the Sami region's natural resources. In 2003 the government in Oslo introduced the "Finnmark Bill," which grants the Sami no special rights in their homeland and gives the federal government control over the management of Finnmark's resources and lands.

FUTURE

The most difficult and most critical political question facing Norway today is how to find a healthy balance between the North Sea economy and that of the mainland, a balance that would protect traditional industry, environment and society, while providing a stable base for continued elevation in the standard of living and for maintenance of the social security net, which the country created for all citizens.

Norway's chief problems will continue to be economic ones. In the long run, though, the country's large oil and gas revenues will continue to help it economically and will enable it to maintain its comprehensive social welfare net through the rest of the century. The country is studying the lessons from the BP oil spill in the Gulf of Mexico before deciding whether to open Arctic waters to oil and gas drilling. Russia, which exports many of the same things as Norway—oil, gas, timber—will be an increasingly formidable competitor.

In general, Norway's problems will be the kind that most countries would be happy to have. Its democratic system functions well, its elites are accommodating and responsive, the citizens have a decent level of trust in government and enjoy channels for input in local government, organizations, schools and the workplace, there is very little corruption and crime, the population is well educated, and the prosperity is widespread and visible, with a $444 billion rainy day Government Pension Fund Global nest egg to fall back on. In the February 2010 Vancouver Winter Olympics it proved again that it is a winter games superpower, tying the U.S. for most gold medals at nine.

The public remains divided on the issue of joining the EU. One skeptic said, "it is no good telling people here that we should join the EU because other European countries want to do the same. We have to find strong Norwegian reasons why we should do so." Also, proponents could not argue that the country would be devastated economically if it stayed out; they made the same argument in 1972, but Norway prospered. Norway is still a young country, only one century old in 2005, whose independence and sovereignty is defended fiercely. Norwegians share a reluctance to reopen the acrimonious debate, which cannot be put off forever. Polls show a majority against EU entry. Although the government of Jens Stoltenberg, which narrowly won reelection in September 2009, remains in favor of membership, it is unlikely in the near future to make a major push to bring the question back on the political agenda.

Its support of the U.S. after September 11, 2001, was unconditional. Former Defense Minister Bjørn Tore Godal asserted, "the United States is Norway's most important ally." Norwegians all over the country observed a three-minute silence on September 14, and the government moved quickly to share intelligence with the U.S. When the war in Afghanistan began, Norway dispatched some of its best soldiers— Royal Marine Commandos and Army Special Operations Commandos—respected internationally for their expertise in winter warfare. These soldiers fought alongside American and other allied troops to flush out al-Qaeda and Taliban fighters from their caves. It also sent mine-clearing specialists and armored vehicles, and it dispatched F-16 fighter jets in 2006.

Perhaps most touching to Americans was the fact that 16 Norwegian officers formed part of the AWACS crews that monitored U.S. airspace during the 9-11 crisis. This was the first time since the American Revolutionary War that the U.S. needed the protection of foreign troops on its own soil.

In 2005 Norwegians celebrated their centennial of independence. The Norwegian-American community honored this occasion with a life-sized statue of the late Crown Princess Märtha, wife of the late King Olav V and mother of the reigning King Harald. She and her children had fled to the U.S. during the Second World War and had lived in the White House for part of the time. This statue was installed outside the Ambassador's residence in Oslo.

Lørdag
Aftenposten

Aftenposten - markedsplass for Vinter-Norge - hver lørdag

Morgenutgave. Lørdag 9. februar 2002. Uke 6. Nr. 67. 143 årg. Kr. 12,00. Flyekspr: Vest-/Midt-Norge kr. 13,00. Nord-Norge kr. 14,00.

Vi har idag
710 annonser i
Bolig SPESIAL

SALT LAKE 2002

MED GULL I BLIKKET

SALT LAKE 2002

1

Landets mektigste butikksjef:

Norske poteter uegnet til mat

Uspiselige. Norske poteter egner seg knapt som mat, tordner konsernsjef Sverre Leiro i Norges-Gruppen. Svarte, støtskadede eksemplarer skjemmer ut butikkene og skremmer vekk kundene – Blir ikke noe gjort, kommer norske potetbønder til å tape i konkurransen med utlandet, sier Leiro. Landbruksminister Lars Sponheim er enig. Nå vil han sørge for at dyktige potetbønder tjener bedre. Side 11

Vil språkteste 4 år gamle barn

Alle innvandrerbarn skal språktestes før de fyller fem. Snakker de for dårlig norsk, må de på språkkurs. Lars som kombinerer læring og lek, ser en kommunikasjonsekspert. Erna Solberg tvilende. Samtidig

The Kingdom of Denmark

Area: 16,629 sq. mi. (43,069 sq. km., slightly more than twice the size of New Jersey, excluding Greenland and the Faroe Islands).

Population: 5.5 million (estimated).

Capital City: Copenhagen (Pop. 1.4 million, including the commune of Frederiksberg. Now called "Greater Copenhagen.")

Climate: Due to the flow of the Gulf Stream, the temperatures dip to below freezing for about 100 or so days during the winter, and summer days are sunny and bright, with cool nights.

Neighboring Countries: Germany (South); Norway (North); Sweden (East and Southeast).

Official Language: Danish.

Other Principal Tongues: There is a small German-speaking minority in the south (approximately 30,000); English.

Ethnic Background: Germanic, North European.

Principal Religion: Lutheran protestant.

Main Exports: Machinery and transportation equipment, meat and dairy products, chemicals, energy, minerals, fuels, ships, pharmaceuticals, electronics, textiles, furniture.

Main Imports: Industrial machinery, automobiles, grain and foodstuffs, chemicals, minerals, petroleum, textile raw fibers, yarns, metals, wood.

Major Trading Customers: EU (70.3% of exports and 73% of imports), Germany (17.7% of exports and 22.2% of imports), Sweden (14.8% of exports and 14.7% of imports), UK (8.1% of exports and 5.8% of imports), U.S. (6.2% of exports), Norway (5.8% of exports and 6.1% of imports), Netherlands (6.8% of imports), China (5.4% of imports).

Currency: Krone.

National Holiday: April 16, birthday of the queen.

Chief of State: Her Majesty Queen Margrethe II (pronounced Mar-*great*-a), b. 1940. Ascended the throne January 15, 1972. Married (1967) Count Henri de Laborde de Monpezat (France), named Prince Henrik of Denmark from that date.

Heir Apparent: His Royal Highness Crown Prince Frederik (b. 1968).

Head of Government: Lars Løkke Rasmussen, Prime Minister (since April 2009).

National Flag: A red field, crossed in the center by a white stripe, and from top to bottom, by another, the latter being off-center, closer to the pole.

A thousand years ago the Danes were among the roving Vikings who terrorized most of Europe. Even after these marauders settled down, Denmark was a powerful country ready and willing to assert its domination over much of the Nordic area. Today the Danes are a peaceful and inventive people, who spend less than 7% of their budget on defense. Characteristically, it was a Dane (Piet Hein) who thought of a way of constructing a super elliptical peace-negotiating table which can seat participants in such a way that all have a sense of prestige.

This does not mean that they are not patriotic. As in the other Nordic countries, one sees more national flags displayed than in any other Western European country, with perhaps the exception of Switzerland. Also, foreign flags can be displayed in Denmark only with special police permission and only as long as the Danish flag is displayed also. It is true that the Danes feel free to criticize their own state and society. But when any such discussion is over, most still remain firmly convinced that Denmark is by far the best place in the world to live.

Because the country is very poorly endowed with natural resources, Danes for centuries had to make a living primarily

Denmark

from agriculture and fishing, when they were not raiding various other lands during their medieval history. In this peninsula with its islands, scarcely larger than Vermont and New Hampshire combined, there are still almost five pigs for every human, and Denmark remains the world's largest exporter of pork. It is also the second largest exporter of butter and the third largest of cheese. Since 1945, though, Denmark has become an increasingly dynamic and innovative industrialized country, and its agricultural population has fallen from almost a fourth in 1945 to about 6% today. Danes have learned to make up for their lack of raw materials by know-how and ingenuity, and by the 1970s no more than a third of their exports were derived from agriculture.

Denmark is made up of the Jutland Peninsula that shares a 41-mile-long (68 km.) border with Germany, which always exercised much cultural, economic, political and military influence on Denmark. Since 1815 the only military actions directed against Denmark have originated from Germany, and Denmark's economy has always been considerably oriented toward its neighbor. In spite of World War II, Danes bear little hostility toward Germans although a 2005 poll revealed that half (51%) of Danes said their relationship with Germans is influenced by the wartime occupation. But they do tend to view their southern neighbors as Canadians view the Americans: near, numerous, not intentionally threatening, but a bit too powerful economically and culturally.

Germany is Denmark's major creditor and customer today, and for Jutlanders, Hamburg is almost as important economically as is Copenhagen. The 30,000 Danes who live south of the border in Schleswig-Holstein have guaranteed representation in the state parliament there without having to win 5% of the votes. In 2005 their votes enabled the Danish minority's party (SSW) to play a crucial role in determining the victors of the provincial elections.

The rest of Denmark is composed of 406 islands, and no Dane lives further than 31 miles (52 km.) from the sea. The numerous islands (not including Greenland) give the country a total coastline of 4,380 miles (7,300 km.). This is equivalent to about one-sixth the way around the world at the equator, or the distance from Copenhagen to Mumbai, India. In fact, Denmark has more total coastline than India. Danes keep that coastline in their own hands. They won from the EU a permanent ban (derogation) on other EU citizens buying up coastal holiday homes; none of the new member states was granted this concession. With such a long coast, it is not a surprise that Denmark has always been a leading fishing and maritime shipping nation.

Close to a fourth of all Danes live in the capital city. In fact, few countries are so dominated by their capitals as is Denmark. Copenhagen is the governmental, administrative, economic and cultural heart of the country. To the delight of almost all who see it, it has old streets and elegant buildings, a stately royal residence with colorfully dressed guards, and charming canals crisscrossing the city. It is also a vibrant, growing city that almost appears to be bursting at the seams. Copenhagen has a very active free port and a busy airport, which makes it one of the world's major transportations hubs. By opening in 1990 the first international air-link and ferry services to Latvia's capital city of Riga, it is reviving historical ties with other Baltic neighbors. It is hoped that this will stimulate economic growth to help counterbalance the powerful Ruhr-Paris-Milan triangle. As a small and highly prosperous nation with a very open society, this country is inescapably tied in with a heavily interdependent world, and is vulnerable to all major political, military and economic developments in Europe. Its people, therefore, know well that they could never hope to imitate the prince in Hans Christian Andersen's fairy tale, The Swineherd, who "went back into his own country and locked the door behind him."

GOVERNMENT

Following the collapse of Nazi Germany, Denmark quickly reverted to its old pattern of leftist-socialist parliamentary government under its constitutional monarchy. Communists were never a major element and all but disappeared. The welfare state was gradually enlarged, as in other Nordic countries. A new constitution abolished the upper house of parliament in 1953, leaving a unicameral legislature. Government was predominantly by minority coalitions of the left.

Danish politics is characterized by a great measure of underlying stability despite a multiparty system, which makes it both impossible for a single party to win a parliamentary majority and difficult for a combination of parties to form a majority coalition. Such stability is due in large part to the Danes' tradition of tolerance and compromise and to the overall consensus about political aims and democratic means.

The Monarchy

Denmark has Europe's longest-standing monarchy, established in 985. In 1848 a peaceful revolution put an end to the absolute monarchy, and the constitution that was adopted the following year and

The Danish Royal Family: (left to right) Prince Joachim, Her Majesty Queen Margrethe II, Prince Henrik, Crown Prince Frederik.
Photo by Klaus Møller

69

Denmark

Princess Mary with son Christian. His sister, Isabella, followed on April 21, 2007, and is the first girl to be born into the Danish royal family since 1946

which has been revised several times since, is still valid. Today, the monarch continues to symbolize the unity of the nation. The last major revision of the constitution in 1953 permitted females to succeed to the throne if there is no male; this was supposed to be changed by the time Crown Prince Frederik and Princess Mary had children. This was rendered temporarily moot on October 15, 2005, when Mary gave birth to her first child, a son named Christian.

When King Frederick IX died in 1972 his daughter, Margrethe II, became queen. She is a hardworking and intelligent woman, who is the first Danish monarch to give press conferences. She is the most educated monarch in Europe, having studied law, social sciences and archeology in Copenhagen, Århus, Cambridge, the London School of Economics and Sorbonne in Paris. Using a pseudonym, she has translated French works, including Simone de Beauvoir, into Danish and has illustrated books, including those by Tolkien and Hans-Christian Anderson. Despite an annual budget of about $3 million, the queen lives relatively modestly and is far less wealthy than the queens of Britain and Holland.

She did away with much of the court etiquette at Amalienborg Castle in the center of Copenhagen, as well as the clumsy addition to her royal title, Queen of the Vends and Goths, Duchess of Slesvig-Holsten, Stormarn, Ditmarsken, Lauenburg and Oldenburg. Like the Danish government, which in 1946 wisely accepted the permanency of the 1920 border between Denmark and Germany even though the British gave it the chance to reopen the question, Margrethe fully accepts the loss

of part of Schleswig to Germany. Unlike her father, she does not hesitate to travel to the lost province, where Danes vote in Schleswig-Holstein state and local elections and can determine which party would rule, as they did in 2005.

Her function is chiefly ceremonial. She does not attend cabinet meetings and none of her acts is official without being countersigned by the responsible minister. She is so concerned to be perceived as being politically neutral that she does not even vote in Danish elections. Her only political function is to oversee the formation of a government that can have its program accepted by a majority in parliament. This is, of course, a frequent and important task in a country in which new elections now normally have to be held every other year. But she always must accept the advice of the nation's parliamentary leaders. Since no Danish monarch is permitted to make an important political decision, the crown is kept safely out of the political fray; this insulation from political criticism helps to maintain the popularity of the royal family.

After having driven a dog sled across Greenland for three months, the athletic Crown Prince Frederik had a strip of land on that huge island named after him. On May 14, 2004, he married an Australian from the island of Tasmania, Mary Donaldson, a commoner whom he had met in a Sydney bar during the 2000 Olympic Games. He reportedly introduced himself to her as "Fred from Denmark." A professor's daughter, she has learned Danish well and is widely popular. She is in line to become the first Australian to be a queen in Europe. Within months of the wedding, Frederik's brother, Prince Joachim and his

wife Alexandra separated. Public opinion polls at the time of Frederik's marriage revealed that 82% of all Danes favor the monarchy. There is no republican movement.

The Parliament

Real political authority originates from the popularly elected parliament, called the *Folketing*, which since 1953 has been unicameral. The *Folketing*, which meets in Christiansborg Castle, is composed of not more than 179 members, of which two each must come from Greenland and the Faroe Islands. For electoral purposes, Denmark is divided into three zones—Greater Copenhagen, Jutland and the islands—which are subdivided into 17 districts with a total of 103 constituencies. Four seats are reserved for Greenland and the Faroe Islands. All Danes are eligible to vote if they are 18 years of age or older. The electoral system is complicated, with proportional representation enabling many parties to win seats in the *Folketing*, despite a requirement that a party must capture at least 2% of the total vote in order to gain any seats.

The fact that so many parties are represented in the parliament prevented any party from gaining a majority of seats during the entire 20th century and into the 21st. A majority coalition is a rarity. Most governments are now minority coalitions protected by a special provision that permits a new government to begin to rule without a parliamentary vote of confidence and to continue to rule until a majority can be mustered against it. Since the late 20th century, Danish parliaments nor-

Mary and Frederik on their wedding day

mally survive the full four years for which they are elected.

Parliamentary sessions are quiet and most civilized. Applause and any form of interruption to show disapproval are strictly forbidden. At one time, members honored extraordinary oratory by quietly handing the person a ten øre coin (a little more than one cent, but now out of circulation). Members often meet together in coffee clubs to make many preliminary decisions and usually address each other by using the familiar form of the word "you." The formal word for "you" is now reserved for the queen and very old people, or when writing an application letter.

The growth of government, especially of the welfare portion, has led to the strengthening of the prime minister and his cabinet, whose members are usually, but need not be, members of parliament. The cabinet introduces most bills. It would be a mistake, however, to underestimate the power of the ordinary membership. Because of the absence of steady and reliable majorities, governments must constantly count possible votes in the *Folketing* before making any decision. Further, one-third of the members can demand a referendum on any piece of legislation. This potent weapon is very seldom used, but it is a safeguard against possible disregard by the majority for the concerns of the minority. The constitution also requires a referendum in any case were Denmark agrees to transfer a portion of its sovereignty to an international body. Thus, in 1972, Danes were asked to approve their country's entry into the EC (now EU), and about two-thirds of them did so.

Since 1955 the *Folketing* has also had the power to appoint an ombudsman, who, with a staff of 12 full-time lawyers and eight clerks, can process the claim of any citizen who thinks he has been treated unjustly by any government official or institution, except the legal courts. The ombudsman may also investigate a matter on his own initiative. He seldom uses his power to initiate legal action, but he frequently makes recommendations to ministries, and they are always acted upon. He can also recommend free legal aid to persons who wish to bring a case against an official, as long as the ombudsman believes that there are good grounds for such proceedings.

A second ombudsman, for consumer affairs, was created in 1975 with a staff of 22 to process complaints that goods or services were sold through false advertising or unfair marketing methods. In most cases, solutions to these problems have been found through negotiation, rather than through litigation. Whenever businesses are in doubt about the propriety of

an advertising or marketing technique, they can request the advice of the ombudsman for consumer affairs in order to find out in advance what might be considered impermissible. Thus, in Denmark public and business officials alike must be aware that their practices could be investigated by one or the other ombudsman, elected by the *Folketing*.

POLITICAL PARTIES AND GROUPS

Until well into the 1960s parliamentary seats were distributed basically among four parties: the Social Democratic, the Radical-Liberal, the Liberal and the Conservative. But the 1960s were in Denmark, as elsewhere in Western Europe and North America, years of ferment. Taxes rose to pay for rapidly expanding social welfare programs. The number of employees in the changing Danish economy threatened the livelihood of some farmers and small merchants. Added to this was a youth revolt that led many persons to ask fundamental questions about the increasingly comfortable technical and materialist society.

In March 2007 Danes had a reminder of their tradition of nonconformism and tolerance for rebellion against the authorities when some of the worst riots in their history, lasting three nights, raged in Copenhagen. At issue was the clearing out, sale and ultimate demolition of a building, dubbed "Youth House," which had been occupied by squatters since the 1980s. The young rioters engaged in running battles with the police, tore up cobblestones to throw at the authorities, and set dozens of cars and a school on fire. Even the famous but much-abused Little Mermaid was painted pink. The unrest re-erupted in October 2007, leaving many Copenhagen

**NATO Secretary General
Anders Fogh Rasmussen**

residents weary of seeing their cars burned and their property defiled or smashed.

These developments gave rise to new parties on the left, while the uneasiness toward rising taxes and budgetary and balance of payments deficits led many Danes to support other unconventional parties. The explosion came in the 1973 elections when five previously unrepresented parties got 36% of the vote, and their percentage has not sunk significantly since. The result is difficulty in producing a stable government.

Danish voters are divided roughly evenly between left and right, but the sheer number of parties that win seats in the *Folketing* makes it difficult to maintain a governing coalition with a stable majority. Ex-Prime Minister Poul Schlüter, the first Conservative prime minister since 1894, conceded on New Year's Day 1991: "One certainly can say we don't have Europe's strongest government!" Nevertheless, there is an underlying stability.

The Parties of the Left

From 1924 to 2001 the Social Democratic Party (S) was Denmark's most important party. It has always been a relatively unideological reform party with a working class character and close ties to the labor union. In 1961 it eliminated all references to Marx in its party program, and began attracting more and more votes from public servants and employees. One result is that the party became quite heterogeneous, and the intra-party splits between its left and right wings inclined the major trade union federation (LO) to become slightly cooler in its support of the party.

It faces difficulties as a working-class party in a country in which fewer and fewer people have blue-collar jobs. Also, it is split between leftists who want to move leftward to compete with the Socialist People's Party, and those on the right, who wish to move back toward the center. Its leader tried to capitalize on his government's popularity after the September 11 terrorist attacks by calling early elections in 2001, but the results were a disaster. For the first time since 1924 it failed to emerge as the largest party. It became the major opposition party. In 2005 it suffered its worst electoral defeat in 32 years, winning only 25.9% of the votes and 47 seats. In an attempt to resolve the internal split between left and right, the party held Denmark's first internal primary leadership election. Helle Thorning-Schmidt, an attractive newly elected MP, emerged as the winner, becoming the first woman to head the Social Democrats. In the snap election in November 2007, with a turnout of 86.6%, she ran a good campaign, but her party slid even further, capturing only

Denmark

25.5% of the votes and 45 seats. This was its worst result in 100 years.

The Socialist People's Party (SF) was founded in 1959 by a former head of the Danish Communist Party (DKP) and originally was joined mostly by disaffected communists, who nevertheless advocated a more radical program than that of the Social Democrats. (The DKP has meanwhile practically disappeared, with only about .1% of the votes.) The SF is composed mainly of academics and pacifists, and about 60% of its members are employees and civil servants. Its major policies include unilateral disarmament, withdrawal from NATO, an atomic-free zone in Scandinavia and increasingly close Nordic economic cooperation rather than Danish orientation toward the allegedly more capitalist EU. It climbed steadily in the 1980s, and in 2007 it doubled its votes and seats to 13% and 23 respectively.

Social Democrats have tried to shun this party, but they do depend on its votes on some important issues. By the same token, even limited cooperation with the Social Democrats in the past was too much for the SF's left wing, which broke away from it in 1967 and formed the Left Socialist Party. The latter reemerged under the banner Unity List Red-Green (EL), which won 2.2% of the votes (down from 3.4%) and four seats (down from six) in 2007.

One of the four traditional parties and one that is a regular coalition partner of the Social Democrats is the Radical Venstre Party (RV). The RV was founded in 1905 and is composed of liberals who see themselves as being a little closer to the left than the other nonsocialist parties. They advocate the maintenance of an efficient private economy, as well as social reform without socialism. They vote with the conservatives on economic issues, but with the left on foreign and defense policies. Although small, RV wielded power beyond its size since it often had the role of "kingmaker," determining which coalition will rule. In 2007 it slipped badly, from 9.2% and 17 seats to only 5.1% and nine.

The Parties of the Center-Right

In recent years the parties of the center and the right have gained ground by promising to reduce taxes and to curb welfare spending. The Conservative People's Party (KF), founded in 1916, is a pragmatic party that defines itself as a party of the political center. It is a staunch advocate of private property and free enterprise, a strong defense and, since the onset of the energy crisis of 1973, of nuclear power. It draws its votes mainly from the middle class and self-employed. Following the 2001 elections it joined the center-right government. Its leader is

Prime Minister Lars Lokke Rasmussen

Bendt Bendsen. In 2007 it held steady, winning 10.4% of the votes and 18 seats. It remains the junior member of the governing coalition.

The Liberal Venstre Party (V) was founded in 1870 and was traditionally a farmer's party; now it draws half its votes from cities and towns. It advocates a restriction of the government's activity in the economy, and since the 1970s it has pressed for a reduction of public spending and private consumption in order to cope with the economic crises that have beset Denmark.

Its leader until April 2009 was Anders Fogh Rasmussen. At age 25 he had been Denmark's youngest member of parliament. For more than two decades he had been a right-wing ideologue and had written a book, *From Social State to Minimal State*, describing the welfare state as "developing a slave mentality in the people." But when he took over the party's leadership in 1998 he was aware that power is won through the political center, and he developed appealing positions on social affairs and the environment. He posed as a guardian of the welfare state and favored the euro and EU enlargement although he wanted to get rid of the EU's wasteful Common Agricultural Policy and reduce Brussels' handouts to poorer regions. He is charismatic but was never known as a "man of the people." He has a serious air and is known for his sharp mind rather than great oratory.

Following the landslide victory in 2001, he formed a center-right minority government. In 2005 the Liberals lost four seats to a total of 52, and it slipped further in 2007, garnering 46 seats based on 26.3% of the votes. The governing minority coalition of Liberals and Conservatives, supported by the Danish People's Party and the New Alliance, has 94 of the 179 seats in parliament while the leftist opposition

has 81. Rasmussen became the first Liberal leader ever to win a second and third consecutive term.

After only one year in office, Rasmussen's approval rating had soared to two-thirds. He had avoided scandal. He kept his campaign promises to freeze taxes, cut foreign aid (down from .96% of GDP in 2005 to .82% in 2010, the third-highest in the world), curb immigration and pare down the civil service. Despite the global recession that struck Denmark in 2009, the economy is one of Europe's strongest, and its budget surplus had grown to 3.6% in 2008 before falling to a 5.8% deficit in 2010. Voters viewed him as the best guarantor of their social system. They still regard free education, free health care, inexpensive childcare and high-quality services for pensioners as their birthrights. But they are reluctant to pay for them with high taxes, currently the EU's second highest after Sweden. They liked the tax cap, tax cuts, and reduction of duties on alcohol and cigarettes, as well as longer maternity leave and shorter hospital waiting lists. Although two-thirds of Danes had come to oppose the Iraq war by election day, the issue of Denmark's 501 troops there was largely absent during the campaign. Voters also seemed unconcerned about the international black eye the country has gotten because of its restrictions on immigration; most of them favor fewer foreigners.

During its EU presidency in 2002, the prime minister was an impressive European leader. Its Copenhagen summit in December approved the greatest enlargement in EU history—ten countries. In a departure from tradition, then Prime Minister Fogh Rasmussen allowed a cameraman to record his country's presidency. When Danish TV showed largely undoctored riveting documentary on Rasmussen's EU activities, complete with a host of embarrassing off-the-cuff remarks by various leaders, there was an outcry in several capitals. Nordic transparency has its costs, but the prime minister was unrepentant: "We must become accustomed to greater openness about what goes on in politics."

His name was frequently mentioned as the possible first Danish secretary general of NATO. Although he coyly denied that he desired such a high international position, that is exactly what he became in April 2009. He was replaced as prime minister by the third Rasmussen in a row, all unrelated: Lars Løkke Rasmussen, the earlier health and finance minister. Affable and approachable, he had had much domestic political experience but little international exposure, and his approval rating was a miserable 16%. The vice-prime minister, Lene Espersen is more popular with voters. The Liberal-Conservative coalition remains the government, and in 2010 the prime minister shuffled his cabinet, changing more than a dozen cabinet posts and appointing Denmark's first female defense minister, Gitte Lillelund Bech. Denmark did a credible job of hosting the largely unsuccessful climate-change summit in Copenhagen in December 2009, which attracted 100 heads of government and 15,000 delegates.

In 1995 the Danish People's Party (DF), led by Pia Kjaersgaard (pronounced "caresgore"), was formed. With slogans like "Denmark is for the Danes," it did very well in 1998. Three years later it doubled its seats, and it won two more in 2005. It kept on climbing in 2007, capturing 13.8% of the votes and 25 seats. Its campaign posters in 2001 portrayed a photo of a young blond girl and the slogan: "When she retires, Denmark will have a Muslim majority." The DF also wins support because of its anti-European views. Because of its extremist views on immigration, ex-Prime Minister Fogh Rasmussen kept the DF out of his center-right minority coalitions, well aware that a growing number of Danes, including in business circles, are embarrassed by Kjaesgaard's uncompromising hostility to immigrants. But he needs its votes sometimes in parliament. For instance, DF support was required in 2002 for legislation to tighten immigration rules making it more difficult to seek asylum and receive welfare benefits and residence permits. By 2005, asylum applications had plunged by 75% in only three years' time, and the proportion of applicants granted asylum plummeted from 53% to only 10%. By election time in 2007, the number of immigrants granted asylum had been slashed by 80%.

In 2008 the DF advocated that Islamic headscarves be banned for public employees. The government decided it had to support this, but it broadened the law to prohibit the wearing of all religious symbols by judges, be they Islamic, Christian, Jewish or Sikh. Public opinion supported this, with 48% in favor and only 39% against it.

The 2007 election did not focus on the economy, but instead on the ideas of a new party on the center-right, formed only six months before the voting and calling itself the New Alliance. It is led by Naser Khader, a Palestinian immigrant and non-practicing Muslim from Syria, who rose to prominence during the furious controversy about anti-Muslim cartoons in 2005. His was a voice of moderation, urging his fellow immigrants to put the values of their adopted country, such as freedom of speech, first. He is charismatic, likeable and clever. He advocates an end to so-called *blok politik*, which sees

Syrian-born Naser Khader enters parliament

the party landscape sharply divided between right and left, instead of the traditional governments clutching the center ground. With a dead heat predicted in the 2007 election, he had hoped to be the king maker, but that did not happen. His party won only 2.8% of the votes and 5 seats. As a center-right party, it supports the government from the outside on most important issues. It is fiercely opposed to the appeals of Pia Kjaersgaard's DF. Khader asserts that "the veto power must be taken away from the People's Party."

Immigration Problems

Kjaersgaard and her party successfully exploit and fuel an explosive issue: growing discontent over a flood of refugees, particularly Somalis and other Muslims (Turks, Kurds, Pakistanis, Iranians and Iraqis), into Denmark. By 2008 foreigners and their descendants made up 6.5% of the population. They are blamed for exploiting the welfare system, crime, and harboring terrorists. By 2002 half were on welfare, a figure that rises to 90% among such ethnic minorities as Somalis.

In 1984 parliament introduced a law preventing border police from turning back people who claim political exile. As a result, the flood of refugees soared from several hundred in 1984 to 9,000 in 1985. By 1986 they were pouring in at a rate of 1,000 per week. This resulted in insulting

graffiti on Danish walls and unpleasant racial incidents. One early sign of discontent was that during the first nine months of 1986, some 15,000 Danes resigned from the Red Cross, the organization responsible for taking care of new arrivals. This dissatisfaction prompted parliament to amend the liberal asylum law.

By the year 2000 Denmark had approximately 260,000 immigrants and refugees from outside the EU and Nordic region. In 2010 roughly 200,000 (3.5% of the population) were Muslim. They come chiefly from Turkey, Pakistan, Morocco and Bosnia-Herzegovina. The government tried to spread them out in the kingdom, but that failed. They remain concentrated, and 60% of them are unemployed. Denmark's inability to integrate them has exposed the ambiguity of Danish attitudes toward cultural diversity and the fragility of its famed social tolerance. A 1998 poll revealed that almost half of all Danes admitted to being "racist" or "fairly racist," the second-highest ratio in Europe (after Belgium) and the largest in the Nordic world. Polls a decade later confirmed that Danes remain solidly in favor of tight immigration controls.

The DF's party program states that Denmark "is not and never was a land of immigration," and it rejects any form of open borders. In 2000 it placed a controversial advertisement in a national newspaper showing a white homeless man,

Denmark

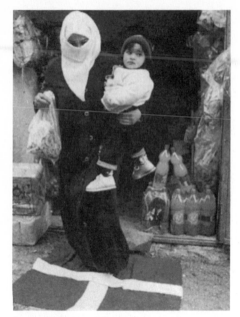

Protesting Danish cartoons

with the caption: "When I become a Muslim, I'll have a home." This refers to the widespread opinion that immigrants jump to the front of the line for state housing and live off the country's generous welfare system.

The government has responded by introducing the strictest immigration laws in the EU. Family unification has been made more difficult. When a Danish court ruled in 1999 that a man of Turkish origin be expelled from Denmark, a gang of young immigrants and anarchists went on a rampage on Nørrebrogade, a major shopping thoroughfare in a district popularly know as "Mini-Mogadishu" because of the concentration of immigrants who live there. There was also a row over a decision by shop owners to prevent female employees from wearing the Muslim headscarf while on duty. These controversies blow wind into the DF's sails.

Ex-Prime Minister Fogh Rasmussen found it politically expedient in his 2001 campaign to recognize the xenophobia that is in the air in Denmark by declaring, "we have to make stricter laws so that fewer foreigners come to Denmark." This policy helped him secure unprecedented electoral victories in 2001, 2005 and 2007. His government tightened legislation restricting family reunification, reduced welfare benefits for foreigners, and extended the waiting period for permanent residency from three to seven years. It reduced the country's acceptance rate of asylum-seekers to 10%, the lowest in the Nordic region. Their numbers have diminished dramatically.

If a Dane and a non-Danish spouse want a residence permit, both partners must be 24 years or over, have a minimum annual income of $50,000, put up a deposit of 53,000 crowns (approximately $8,700) until the foreign spouse is able to get citizenship, not have drawn on welfare benefits for the past 12 months, have their own apartment, meaning that they cannot sublet or live with parents, and be judged to have stronger ties to Denmark than to any other country. As of 2005, immigrants who seek a residence permit must first take a loyalty oath promising to fight terrorism. These requirements led about 1,000 couples to live on the Swedish side of the strait and ferry or commute across the bridge to work in Copenhagen. A May 2008 poll showed how unwelcome many young Muslim students in Denmark feel: two-thirds of the respondents were considering emigrating after graduation, mostly because of "the tone of the Danish debate about Muslims."

In 2005 the government announced plans to boost its antiterrorism security police by about 40%. A 2002 law forbids instigation of terrorism or offering advice to terrorists. Newer laws ban the financing of radical groups and give police the powers to eavesdrop on suspected radicals electronically. Suspected radicals are subject to close surveillance, and intelligence officers work closely with Danish universities to look out for suspicious activity and to monitor students from abroad. In September 2006 police conducted a sting operation in Odense, the birthplace of Hans Christian Andersen.

They found chemicals used to make bombs in several homes and arrested nine men, all Danish citizens and (except one) of immigrant origin. This created jitters in the entire country. Eight more Islamic militants, suspected of planning a bomb attack, were arrested a year later. In 2008, two men secretly filmed mixing explosives were convicted of preparing a terrorist attack.

A 2005 poll found that 80% of Danes support new laws to battle terrorism and control immigration. That these laws contain restrictions on free speech is perhaps surprising for a nation famous for its toleration. But it is typical of Denmark that the public debate about how to balance individual freedoms with society's protections against terrorism is at the top of the political agenda.

In 2005 Denmark faced its worst international crisis since the Second World War. For some time a polemical war had been raging between anti-immigrant nationalists and fundamentalist Muslims among Denmark's 200,000 Muslim immigrants. Many Danes have come to view Islam as a threat to the survival of Danish culture. For two decades, Muslims had been forbidden to build mosques in Copenhagen, and there are no Muslim cemeteries.

In September 2005, a Danish newspaper, *Jyllands-Posten*, commissioned and printed a dozen cartoons portraying the Prophet Mohammad in an unflattering way. One of them showed bombs tangled

"The Situation is out of control"—Muslim fury over Danish cartoons (from Austria)

in the prophet's headgear. In October Rasmussen declined to meet with 11 ambassadors from Muslim countries, who wanted to discuss the offensive drawings, and some subsequently withdrew their ambassadors. A February 2006 poll revealed that 58% of Danes believed that the problem was not the newspaper's action, but that imams living in Denmark had exploited the situation for their own purposes.

By February 2006 the situation snowballed out of control. Danish products were (and to some extent still are) boycotted across the Muslim world and even in some European stores that were afraid of losing their Muslim customers. Denmark's embassies in Damascus and Lebanon were attacked and burned by angry mobs, and police in Afghanistan fired into a crowd trying to storm a Norwegian base. The Danish consulate general in Dubai described what was happening as a "nightmare scenario." "I don't think anyone in their wildest imagination would have expected an escalation like what we have seen." More than 50 persons died in the demonstrations.

Some European newspapers fueled the flames by defiantly publishing the cartoons in solidarity with *Jyllands-Posten*, and the EU and U.S. President George W. Bush publicly defended their ally's right of free speech. More disappointing were its Nordic partners, especially Sweden and Norway (whose embassy in Syria was also burned). They sought to distance themselves from the Danes, who were reeling from global protests and boycotts. In Denmark itself the government, which refused to offer any apology for the publication, was riding high in the polls, and the popularity of Pia Kjaersgaard's Danish People's Party shot up from 13% to almost 18%. But the country had much work to do to win back its reputation and markets in the Islamic world. In 2009 the Copenhagen municipal council granted permission for the first mosque to be built. It was constructed with private funds on a site purchased by the embassy of Iran.

A sensational best-selling book in Denmark entitled *Islamists and Naivists* equates Islamic fundamentalists with Nazis and Communists. The authors, Karen Jespersen and Ralf Pittelkow, wrote: "The reality is that nobody in Denmark bats an eye anymore when people talk about the threat that Islam poses to Danish values because this is viewed, however wrongly, as a fact of life." The work reflects the extent to which skepticism about Islam has become a part of the European political mainstream.

In February 2008, when it was reported that the police had arrested three men suspected of plotting to murder one of the artists, 17 Danish newspapers decided to republish one of the offending cartoons to reiterate the principle of free speech. This sparked riots in the streets of Copenhagen, mainly in immigrant neighborhoods, where schools and cars were torched. Osama bin Laden denounced the publication and warned all Europeans of a strong reaction to come. The cartoon might have prompted a suicide bombing four months later outside the Danish embassy in Islamabad, Pakistan, which killed eight people and wounded 20.

The artist who drew the most offensive of the dozen drawings, Kurt Westergaard, was forced to move nine times to escape assassins. In January 2010 a Somali fanatic broke into his home outside of Aarhus with an ax. He was prevented from completing his bloody mission only when Westergaard took refuge in a specially reinforced bathroom. He could communicate with the police, who arrived quickly and shot and wounded the assailant.

Prime Minister Rasmussen called this outrage "an attack on our open society." Even American citizens have been implicated in death threats against cartoonists and newspaper editors.

In April 2009 this entire lamentable cartoon affair came back to haunt Fogh Rasmussen, whose last hurdle to becoming NATO secretary general was the threatened veto of Turkey, a Muslim country. Rasmussen and Denmark are perceived by many Muslims as insensitive to Islam, an important issue considering that NATO's biggest challenges at the time were Afghanistan and Pakistan. He had reformulated his earlier statement about free speech, saying that it had to be balanced with a deep respect for personal religious convictions. After the Turkish government again objected to his nomination at the NATO summit in Strasbourg, President Barack Obama took Turkish President Abdullah Gül aside for a half-hour chat. He then called Rasmussen into the

Denmark

back room, and the three leaders discussed privately. A phone call to Turkish Prime Minister Recep Erdogan was needed to break the deadlock, and Rasmussen was approved. This was a masterful diplomatic success for the new American president. After racing home to resign as prime minister and then off to Turkey for a NATO meeting, Rasmussen fell down the stairs in Istanbul and dislocated his shoulder.

Provincial and Local Government

There are several other levels of government in Denmark. Since the 2005 reform, it is divided into five provinces, each led by elected provincial councils headed by a mayor (*Amtsborgmester*) elected by the council from among it own members. There are also about 150 primary municipalities led by elected municipal councils. Two other major areas under Danish jurisdiction have complete authority in domestic affairs, with only foreign and defense policy emanating from Copenhagen: Greenland and the Faroe Islands. Each is allowed to send two MPs to the *Folketing*.

Outlying Lands: Greenland

Greenland is at one point only 14.5 miles from Canada. In 2005 Denmark became embroiled with Canada over ownership of Hans Island, a patch of Arctic rock each country claims. The Danes even sent a warship to back up their sovereignty over the island. The two countries soon called a truce and agreed to disagree over its possession.

Greenland is the world's largest island and is 50 times the size of Denmark, three times larger than France and about one-third the size of the U.S. Over 80% of its majestic but dangerous area lies under permanent ice and snow that continually breaks off into the ocean forming many of the world's icebergs. This is the earth's second-largest ice sheet after Antarctica and contains nearly 10% of the planet's frozen water. By 2000 it was melting on the margins at a rate of about 12 cubic miles per year. This shrinkage accounts for 7% of the world's sea-level rise. By one estimate, if all of Greenland's ice were to melt, the seas around the world would rise by 23 feet. While the ice in the higher elevation appears to be stable, the thinning of the ice is occurring around the coast. The dilution of the surrounding ocean with fresh water threatens to disrupt currents that keep Europe warm.

The narrow coastal strip around much of the island (a strip that itself is eight times the size of Denmark) is tundra, on which trees cannot grow higher than knee level. Only about a fifth of Greenland's population of 56,500 is Danish. The rest are natives of Inuit (Eskimo) or mixed back-

grounds, who speak an Inuit dialect although they learn Danish in schools. Since 2009 Inuit (also called Greenlandic) is the official language. Most live in the 120 or so towns or settlements located chiefly along the southwestern coast, the largest being the capital, Nuuk (formerly Godthaab). Nuuk is a modern city of 15,000 inhabitants with first-class Danish hotels and five-story apartment houses, which differ little from European dwellings, except that cod and seal skins often hang on lines from balconies along with jeans and fashionable Danish clothes.

Greenland (which the natives call Kalaallit Nunaat or "Land of People") became a Danish colony in 1775 was made an integral part of Denmark in 1953, but a new generation of Greenlanders wanted more direct control over their island's destiny. Denmark made it known that it would respect the people's wishes. In 1979, following a referendum in Greenland, the island was granted self-government as a "distinct community within the Kingdom of Denmark." The native population determines its own domestic affairs through a 21-member locally elected assembly called the *Landsting* and an executive called the *Landsstyre*. Denmark continues to determine foreign and defense matters and is represented in Greenland by the queen's high commissioner.

The autonomy status does not affect the island's inclusion in NATO or the status of the Danish-American air bases at Soendre, Stroemfjord and Narssarssuaq, nor of the installation in Thule. A giant radar installation is located there roughly halfway along the shortest route between the U.S. and Russia. Thule therefore plays a crucial role in the American early warning

A fish vendor in the olden days

system and in its missile defense system. In 2003 both Denmark and Greenland agreed in principle to permit the upgrade of the radar, essential for tracking missiles. Greenlanders were reportedly delighted when the newly inaugurated President George W. Bush responded quickly to Premier Jonathan Motzfeldt's congratulatory message. Bush expressed his country's eagerness to work with Greenland's government on matters of common concern, such as the Thule base.

In 1999 the Danish prime minister apologized to the native Inuit people for forcing them out of their homes in 1953 so that an American airbase could be expanded. For years they had demanded such an apology. But in 2003 the Danish Supreme Court rejected demands by Inuit hunters in Greenland for increased compensation for having been forced off their land in 1953. It also rejected the right of resettled people to return to the area around the airbase and to displace the Americans there. Danish and American officials were embarrassed in 2000 by new evidence that an unarmed hydrogen bomb on board a crashing B-52 bomber in 1968 might still lie on the seabed in the frozen Baffin Bay off the Thule air base.

Three years after receiving limited self-rule, Greenlanders voted against remaining in the EU. It thereby became the first element to ever leave the EU. In the first referendum over the membership in 1972, over 70% of the Greenlanders had voted against entry, but they were swamped by the Danish majority. Ten years later, after haggling with Brussels over fishing rights and with Danes over mining rights on the island, and after having achieved political autonomy and more self-confidence, the islanders decided to leave the EU, which had poured from $10 million to $20 million worth of investments into Greenland every year.

The 1983 electoral victory of the two parties that were committed to withdrawal from the EU—the socialist Forward Party and the leftist Inuit Movement—was the prelude for Greenland's final decision in 1985 to leave the EU. It entered partnership negotiations with the EU in 2005 centering on fishing rights. Denmark continues to send it costly subsidies, amounting to about $700 million per year ($11,300 per person or 60% of government revenues). It also sends thousands of technicians and advisers, without whom the island could not hope to survive in its present form. With economic and social modernization having only begun in the 1950s, Greenland is very dependent upon Danish expertise to build and operate housing units, hospitals (which have helped double average life expectancy since the 1950s), schools, power plants and communication and transportation facilities. The last is particularly difficult because there are no trains or roads between towns and settlements.

The essential services that Danes perform should not, in the opinion of some islanders, give the Danes control over the island's economy and resources. The people live primarily from fishing and sealing, as well as from jobs in the public sector, and they raise sheep, lambs and reindeer. Under the ice there are also such minerals as zinc, lead and cryolite, which are already mined, as well as gold, rubies, diamonds, iron ore, uranium, nickel, molybdenum and perhaps oil, which may be extracted one day, mainly offshore. Melting ice provides rich potential for hydropower, which the native government hopes will one day supply 80% of electricity. With the Northwest Passage through Canada's North opening up, Greenland is well positioned to be a major shipping center. It is already enjoying booming tourism.

The compromise to which the Danes and Greenlanders agreed during the negotiations over autonomy was that each side would have a veto right over the exploitation and sale of Greenland's natural resources. Also Greenland is granted half of any future proceeds from oil and minerals. This compromise was necessary, but it brought many disagreements.

In November 2008, over three-fourths of Greenlanders, with a strong sense of righting historical wrongs, voted in a referendum to loosen their ties with Denmark, and the home country accepted this. This went into effect on the national holiday, June 21, 2009. They took control of security, police, education and justice affairs, made Inuit the official language, and took a larger percentage of future profits from minerals, including gold, diamonds, rubies and oil although much of this wealth is still inaccessible under ice. Denmark retained the last word on foreign and security matters.

The people went to the polls on June 21. The left-leaning Inuit Ataqatigiit (IA), led by Kuupik Kleist, won 44% of the votes and 14 of 31 parliamentary seats. It unseated the ex-governing Siumut (Social Democratic) party, vowing to lead the government to complete independence. He promised that his country would act as an "equal partner" with Denmark, and the Danish prime minister responded with a pledge that Greenland can choose full independence whenever it wants it. Never has there been a more amicable separation.

Full independence will not come quickly. Dominated by fishing, the economy cannot stand alone. Greenlanders and their Danish helpers must cope with

The Little Mermaid

many social problems that have emerged as a result of the extremely rapid movement of most natives from an isolated existence at the edge of civilization into modern life. This sudden change risks the collapse of the old way of life before a new one emerges. The results are heavy unemployment among the young, venereal diseases, child abuse and the familiar scourge of alcoholism. Today, nine out of ten crimes on the island stem from the latter, and any visitor sees its presence in Greenland almost everywhere he looks. The suicide rate is nearly 17 times as great as in 1960 and four times that of Denmark, which itself has one of the world's highest levels of suicide. Education and nutrition are bad. Social challenges to Danes and native islanders are very great and will require more than Danish subsidies to solve.

The Faroe Islands

The Faroes, an archipelago of 18 islands in the North Atlantic between Norway, Scotland and Iceland, have a rough and beautiful landscape of mountain peaks, high plateaus, valleys and fjords. The 43,000 Faroese are descendants of the Norse settlers who came during the Viking era, and they still speak their own language, which is related to Icelandic and certain western Norwegian dialects. Of course, all Faroese also speak Danish.

These islands are not well suited to farming, but they are ideal for sheep and cattle grazing. Their waters were also full of fish, which provided work for a fourth of the labor force and comprised over 90% of the islanders' exports. Fish were the foundation for the islanders' economy until the industry collapsed due to over fishing. This dragged the rest of the islands' economy down with it. By 1994 unemployment had reached 20%, and about 9%

of the population had been forced to emigrate. Only a series of emergency aid packages from Copenhagen have staved off bankruptcy.

The islands have been self-governing within the Kingdom of Denmark since 1948. The ancient, locally elected parliament, the *Lögting*, and the executive, the *Landsst´yri*, are responsible for all matters except those involving foreign policy, defense, the police, the courts and, until 2004, church policy and the "People's Church." The Faroese have their own flag, postage stamps and paper money. They do use Danish coins. Denmark pays for about a third of all public spending. Such support enabled the islanders to have a higher average income than the Danes themselves until the islands' economy turned sour in the 1990s.

The local inhabitants do not allow the Danes to make the most important economic decisions for them. They decided in 1974 not to be a part of the EU, fearing that the EU's fish policy might threaten that industry. They have also resisted all temptations either to permit the search for oil within their 200-mile economic zone or the establishment of what could be a lucrative tourist industry in the islands. They are in NATO, though, and have a small radar station. While the Faroese do not want to seal themselves off from the outside world, they do wish to avoid anything that could disturb their quiet island life, their cultural independence or their native language. In a May 2001 referendum they rejected independence from Denmark.

ECONOMY

Denmark has long ceased being a primarily agricultural country, although its production in that sector is generally effi-

Denmark

cient and is an important component of its foreign trade. Denmark is now highly industrialized, even though it almost totally lacks raw materials, except salt and newly discovered North Sea oil and gas, which may eventually be capable of supplying up to a third of the country's energy needs. What the Danes lack in raw materials they must make up for in highly skilled labor and high quality production. They must work with their brains and they must have a sharp eye for niches in the world market that they could fill quickly and with a minimum of materials. This requires imagination and adaptability to customers' tastes, and these requirements are well suited to Danish ingenuity and the small size of Danish firms. In Denmark's modern economy, 73% of the work force is employed in services (producing 72.4% of GDP) and 24% in industry (creating 26.5% of GDP).

Danes specialize in finished goods and have moved in on highly specialized markets. For example, Denmark is the world's largest supplier of insulin for diabetics and of industrial enzymes. It also has a large share of the world market in marine diesel engines, hearing aids (especially those attached to eye glasses), and radio telephones. Danish furniture is known for quality, design and flair. It produces Lego toys, which can be found in children's playrooms all over Europe and North America; 98% of its sales are abroad. By 2005 Lego was suffering losses due to the falling dollar, inexpensive Chinese toys, and modern kids' preferences for mobile phones and computers. Legoland Park outside Copenhagen continues to attract more than a million visitors a year and is Denmark's biggest tourist attraction. There are similar Legoland Parks in the UK, Germany and the U.S.

Denmark also has become the world's largest exporter of a particularly familiar product throughout the world: beer. This is primarily because of the Carlsberg-Tuborg brewery group, which also has sizable operations in the U.S. Carlsberg patronizes the arts, grants scholarships, and owns famous Danish brands such as Georg Jensen silver and Royal Copenhagen porcelain. In 2000 it sold one of the national jewels, Tivoli Gardens, to a consortium led by the Scandinavian Tobacco Corporation, which promised to improve the beloved park without disturbing its tranquil character. In 2005 an economic icon for Danes was sold to Nordic Telephone: TDC telecommunications, a former state-owned monopoly that dominated the home market.

As a highly prosperous nation with a small domestic market, Denmark is extremely dependent upon foreign trade. Indeed, it has one of the highest levels of foreign trade per inhabitant in the world. Industrial exports constitute from 35% to 40% of its total production, and few Danish farmers could hope to survive if the country's foreign agriculture markets were lost. Over two-thirds of its industrial exports go to other EU countries (mainly to Germany and Sweden). With such dependency upon exporting, it is no surprise that Denmark pursues a liberal (free) trade policy and chooses to remain in the EU, despite lingering opposition to membership. After Sweden and Finland joined in 1995, and with enlargement deep into Eastern Europe in 2004, a Danish exit from the EU would seem no longer to be a feasible option.

In a September 2000 referendum, voters by 53% to 47% rejected the common currency, the euro. A disappointed Foreign Minister Mogens Lykketoft noted ruefully, "there is a general animosity in Europe toward the EU bureaucrats issuing all these regulations, and that is particularly strong in Denmark. What we saw today was a political vote here, not an economic one." Danes feared that greater EU harmonization might have threatened their welfare state and maybe even their sense of national identity. The krone nevertheless remains tied to the euro (as it was linked to the German mark after 1982). Danes denied themselves the possibility of influencing EU policies regarding the new currency.

A May 2008 poll revealed that 55% of voters favored adopting the euro, while only 38% opposed it. Danes have already gotten used to euros because they flow over the border from Germany and are widely accepted in restaurants and shops. After his third electoral victory in November 2007, Ex-Prime Minister Rasmussen promised a referendum to give Danes a chance to express their opinions about the euro and the four opt-outs Denmark had won from EU dealing with defense, citizenship and justice and home affairs. Polls in 2008 suggested that Danes are ready to adopt the euro, join European defense efforts, and scrap the opt-outs, which are fundamental powers for a sovereign state. It seems unnecessary, for example, for them to have to pull their soldiers out of a NATO operation when it becomes an EU one, as was the case in Bosnia. Danes, who are notoriously independent-minded on EU matters, are now among the most pro-European in the union; 66% agreed in 2007 that membership in the EU was a good thing.

Industry is overwhelmingly privately owned. The central or local government authorities operate only the postal service, gas works, electricity generation, ports, certain transportation companies and some other services belonging to the coun-

Daily changing of the Royal Life Guard in Copenhagen

try's economic infrastructure. The state does not engage in industrial production and it is seldom willing to subsidize lame-duck industries. Also, only about one-twelfth of its industry is foreign-owned. Firms are of small or medium size, with an average of 60 employees. Almost half employ less than 20. It is nevertheless true that most industrial exports stem from medium or large-sized firms, but Danes have never tried to build up gigantic industries, such as steel, automobile or aircraft production. Anticipating the single EU market in 1992, mergers took place in basic Danish industries like foodstuffs, sugar and alcohol that amounted to be the most far-reaching restructuring of Danish industry in a century. Finally, industry is geographically dispersed—there is no one concentrated industrial region.

Labor and Employers

Labor and employers are highly organized. The Confederation of Danish Employers (DA) represents 159 employer and manufacturer organizations. The National Organization of Trade Unions (LO) links

1,699 unions, which organize about 85% of all wage earners, one of the highest percentages in the free world. DA and LO collectively negotiate wages and working hours every two years, and the government intervenes only if the two sides cannot agree. In that case, the *Folketing* legislates the final proposals presented by an impartial mediator. Strikes are forbidden while a valid agreement is still in force, and there are relatively few strikes.

One difference of opinion that exists between employers and the trade unions is the latter's wish to introduce what they call "economic democracy." There are already forms of employee participation in the firms' decision-making, but this does not extend to sharing profits. Supported by the Social Democratic and other leftist parties, the LO maintains that the unions should be given a portion of the businesses' value, which the employees helped to create. There are many different proposals, but all call, in general, for 5% of all wages to be put into special funds under the control of the unions. These funds, provided by the employers, would be used to buy shares in industries, which would then be owned by the unions, not individuals, who would nevertheless derive some kind of financial benefit from this upon retirement.

Employers quickly noted that such a practice would enable the unions to gain quickly a controlling share in most industries, despite the fact that the Danish constitution would forbid this share to exceed 49%. The specter of the trade unions controlling the economy horrifies businessmen and others, but it delights some persons who think that such a measure would make Denmark a more just society. By the end of the 1980s, these funds were already cash-rich and were even being invested in a variety of ways, including agriculture. In 1990 the Conservative government initiated moves to restrict the unions' power to maintain closed shops and to pass on union dues to political parties, in effect to the Social Democrats.

Every year a fifth of workers lose their jobs. But most find a new job quickly, and the unemployment rate in 2008 was the lowest in three decades (1.8%), rising to 3.5% in the following recessionary year. The secret is called "flexicurity," a Danish model that protects the worker, not the job. It is a blend of a flexible labor market, generous social security, and training and high benefits during bouts of unemployment. Since they can fire unneeded workers, Danish firms have a competitive advantage over their rivals. However, this model is expensive and requires the world's highest tax level: the average tax rate is 53%. Not all countries would choose to imitate it.

Agriculture

The percentage of Danes engaged in agriculture and fisheries has fallen to only 3%. They produce a total of 1.2% of GDP although the food industry provides between 12% and 18% of domestic employment. Two-thirds of farms have been merged or converted to other use since the Second World War. About two-thirds of the land is still used for farming, almost entirely by single families, and non-farmers are not allowed to own farmland. However, there are fears similar to those in the U.S. that many family farms may fail. Favorable climate, good soil, and careful, but intensive land use, result in the country's having two to three times as much farmland per inhabitant as do its more densely populated, but less efficient, EU partners—it maintains the highest productivity and export of farm produce per capita in all Europe.

Agriculture accounts for 25% of its merchandise exports. This has helped Denmark produce three times as much food as its own citizens need and it sells about 70% of its produce abroad; these sales account for about a third of its foreign currency earnings, making Denmark the world's fifth-largest exporter of food products. EU countries purchase about two-thirds of its farm exports, which is an important reason why Danes chose to join the EU in 1972. Americans, who have developed a taste for Danish cheese and canned hams, are the second largest purchasers. In 2002 Danes were incensed by the EU decision that only Greek cheese can be labeled "feta" when three-quarters of the world's feta is produced outside of Greece, 25,000 tons of it in Denmark. Denmark set an EU precedent in 2004 by publishing the names and amounts of EU cash received by its farmers. Embarrassingly, it turned out that Mariann Fischer Boel, the EU's agriculture commissioner from Denmark, and her husband had received an annual EU farm subsidy of $100,000.

About 90% of the farmers' total income is derived from animal products, and only 10% from grain. Denmark's major livestock is the pig, 24 million per year, making it the world's largest exporter of pork. Almost 80% of it is exported, primarily to Germany. Because of the growing size of pig farms, which cause strong unpleasant odors over large distances, pork farmers are under attack from the tourism industry, environmentalists and animal-welfare activists. A few farmers have discovered that mink-raising can be quite profitable, and Denmark is now one of the world's main suppliers of these skins. Farmers have retained powerful clout through the Agricultural Council. The farmers themselves came under severe attack by ecolo-gists, who claim agricultural methods and materials pollute the earth.

Shipping and Fishing

All Danes are surrounded by the sea and understandably have always been a seafaring people. Except for such "flag of convenience" states as Liberia, only Norway and Greece have more shipping tonnage per capita than does Denmark. Most of the fleet never docks in Danish ports, but 85% of all ships sailing Baltic waters have Copenhagen as their homeport. Shipping provides close to a tenth of the country's total foreign currency earnings, ranking behind industry and agriculture, but ahead of tourism and fishing.

Two of the world's largest shipping companies, A.P. Møller and the East Asiatic Company, are Danish. The crisis in world shipping has undeniably been felt in Denmark. Since 1973 its fleet has declined in numbers, and its share of the world's merchant shipping dropped from 1.76% in the early 1960s to 1.36% at the beginning of the 1980s. Fewer new vessels are on order in Danish shipyards than at any time since 1950, but in the 1990s it remains the world's largest shipbuilder after Japan and Korea. A major reason for the decline in the competitiveness of Danish shipping is, without question, the wage levels, which doubled from 1972 to 1978.

Denmark is among the top ten fishing nations in the world. An unusual feature among fishing nations is that company activity is almost unknown in Denmark. The captains own almost all fishing vessels; each ship's earnings entirely depend upon the catch, and the crews share in the distribution of profits. It is not surprising that there are no strikes in this sector. Vessels fish mainly in the North and Baltic seas, but there is an important problem: access to Norwegian, Swedish, or EU countries' waters has been restricted or eliminated. Danes face a general problem in these waters—there are too many fishermen chasing too few fish. The Danes' most important fish for use as food is cod. For industrial use, it is the sand eel. Their major buyers are the EU (especially Sweden), Switzerland and the U.S. About six hundred inland trout farms have sprung up, made possible sometimes by spring water and a cool climate.

Energy

Like most industrialized countries, Denmark underwent a major conversion in the 1950s and 1960s from coal to oil, and by 1972 its dependence on imported oil had swelled to 93% of its energy consumption. Thus, when the first oil crisis shook the world in 1973, Denmark was unprepared. This was especially so since it had seemed

Denmark

to have obtained very little from the portion of the North Sea that had been carved out for it. Danes have so far resisted nuclear energy, but they have switched many power plants from oil to coal, with the goal of fueling at least 80% of them with coal. Power plants are also being geared to provide district heating (whereby heat is pumped into individual dwellings from a central plant) for about 40% of households. About 30% are heated by gas, either in individual furnaces, or from district heating systems. The country is self-sufficient in gas, but it has very little hydropower.

Despite its heavy use of hydrocarbons and abstention from atomic power, Denmark has been admirably successful in reducing its carbon dioxide emissions by almost 15% below its 1990 level. It has an effective carbon tax that requires polluters to pay for their environmental damage and then recycles the proceeds back to industry to subsidize research and environmental innovation.

It is fitting that Copenhagen was chosen as the host for the UN's summit on global warming in December 2009, which failed to achieve a global agreement. The country has a vital stake in slowing global warming. Its average elevation is only 31 meters (105 feet) above sea level. Nowhere in Denmark is more than 32 miles from the ocean. Red flashing lights on walls around Copenhagen remind residents where the water would reach if sea levels raised by seven meters (23.6 feet).

Finally, energy conservation measures help Danes continue to reduce their oil consumption. Wind energy supplies a fifth of Denmark's total power, the highest proportion in the world. The 80 offshore windmills near Esbjerg and Copenhagen harbor make up the world's largest wind farm. The country is an international powerhouse in this field. Its companies, of which Vestas is the biggest, control about half the industry worldwide and supply windmills, for example, to the New England coast. Further building of windmills practically stopped in 2007 when subsidies were reduced. Nevertheless, Danes hope to expand their use of renewable energy sources from 17% in 2005 to 30% by 2020. Of their waste, 42% is recycled, 54% is incinerated to generate heat and electricity (vs. 13% in the U.S.), and only 4% (compared with 54% in the U.S.) is buried in landfills.

Prosperity, Welfare Benefits, Taxation

Any visitor to the country can see that the average Dane lives a very prosperous life and that there is very little visible poverty in the country. Average per capita income is among the highest in the world. Almost 60% of households own the houses and apartments in which they live. The average Dane spends only a sixth of his income on housing and a fourth on food, drink and tobacco. In 1992 the Washington-based Population Crisis Committee concluded that of 140 countries it studied Denmark has the highest quality of life; Sweden and Finland were not in the top ten.

Most Danes have supported the development of a comprehensive social welfare system, whose underlying philosophy is that a society should be judged by the way it treats its weakest members and that individuals are very seldom personally responsible for the social problems from which they might suffer. Therefore, the public should support any person unable to support himself. As a rule, these assistance funds come directly from tax revenues, not from insurance schemes to which the beneficiaries must contribute. Also, one qualifies for benefits merely by being a resident of Denmark, which means that foreigners can receive roughly the same benefits as can citizens. The fact that the state pays the cost of childbearing, funerals and burials indicates that the country literally has a cradle-to-the-grave welfare system.

Danes work an average of 37.5 hours a week, have four weeks of paid vacation, receive 90% of their previous income for up to three and a half years as well as retraining and relocation expenses in case of unemployment, and can claim a state prepension at age 60 (55 for widows), which pays 60% of the normal pension, and one is limited to only 200 hours of work per year. In 2005, half of all workers were taking advantage of this by retiring early at age 60. The government's decision to raise the retirement age from 60 to 65 (60 for military) was understandably unpopular, as is a 2005 proposal to up it to 67.

Medical care is free (paid through taxes), and the patient can choose his own doctor in his own town or area. If he goes outside his town of residence, he cannot choose his doctor. Maternity benefits were raised beyond the earlier 14 weeks. Parents who have children under age nine can get sabbaticals of up to 52 weeks per child and receive a weekly allowance worth $315. Over four decades of welfare legislation culminated in a comprehensive assistance act of 1976, which guarantees every resident in need economic aid not merely to survive, but also to maintain the standard of living to which the person had become accustomed.

Many foreigners greatly admire such a complete welfare system, but the reverse side of the coin is one of the world's highest tax levels and the highest of any EU country. The income tax, which constitutes about two-thirds of all taxes, is heavily pro-gressive, and even those with middle incomes feel the bite. The marginal personal income tax rate is 63% (lowered by 8% in 2009), and the minimum marginal rate is 43%. Corporate rates are 28%. Denmark also has the EU's highest taxes on many consumer goods; for instance, the VAT stands at 25%, the highest in the EU. Tax revenues in 2004 came to 49.6% of GDP, second in the world only to Sweden's 50.7%.

Many Danes have begun to wonder whether welfare assistance and other forms of government spending have gone too far. Unemployment pay is higher than the minimum wage, so many Danes prefer to collect the unemployment benefits than to go back to work by taking a low-paying job. To stem this trend, parliament passed a reform package in 1996 that declares that persons below the age of 25 are no longer permitted to collect full unemployment benefits. Demonstrating how far some people want to extend the welfare state, one prominent Social Democrat proposed in 1989 that the six-week maternity leave should be supplemented by a special leave to *propagate* (albeit only for those in jobs with a high risk of low fertility). These kinds of questions and abuses have fueled both tax evasion and tax revolts. High taxes on electronics, alcohol and tobacco sent Danes (whose alcohol consumption is the highest in the Nordic world) over the German border in droves to shop for these items. To prevent this and to lower the prices, the government significantly lowered taxes on alcohol and cigarettes in 2003.

In 2005 one-third of working-age Danes were drawing state transfer payments, such as student grants, sick or unemployment pay, or early retirement entitlements. The costly welfare system has not rid Denmark of some seemingly intractable problems, including homeless who were usually alcoholics or drug addicts and who were entirely dependent on welfare payments for survival. Also, the suicide rate is one of the highest in the world. Nevertheless, a 2005 poll revealed that two-thirds of Danes agreed that their welfare model needed only minor adjustments in the coming years.

The desire for a high standard of living despite high tax levels has also contributed to the inclination of more and more women to work; 71% of Danish women between the ages of 16 and 66 have jobs, compared with 37% in 1950; this is the highest percentage of any nation after Sweden. Of members of parliament, 37% are female. In 2005 the World Economic Forum ranked Denmark number four in the world (the top five were all Nordic countries) for gender opportunity. Only one in five children is cared for by a full-time parent. One social by-product of the enormous increase in working wives is that the fertility rate has declined to 1.8. Denmark will increasingly be facing the demographic problem caused by growing numbers of older citizens being supported by a shrinking working population.

Economic Reform

Like many other people, Danes lived beyond their means. Only a partial sacrifice of the high standard of living could put the country's financial books back in order, and that is exactly what the government did from the early 1990s on. It made sweeping cuts throughout the economy, including the social welfare programs. It abolished the automatic indexing for wages and welfare benefits that tied them to inflation, and imposed severe statutory limits on wage rises in both the public and private sectors. It also cut public borrowing and vowed to maintain the value of the currency. It consciously slowed down economic growth and placed a higher priority on combating inflation than on reducing unemployment.

The medicine worked and saved Denmark from the financial abyss. By 2010 it had inflation of 2.4%, reduced the national debt to 66% of GDP, limited its annual budget deficit to 5.8% of GDP, improved exports and maintained a current accounts surplus of 2.6% of GDP, one of the largest in the OECD in relation to size of economy. Denmark's financial institutions were also strengthened through mergers, and it escaped the serious problems facing banking in the other Nordic countries. Its economy was growing in 2010 at a rate of .9%. Also, unemployment, which had surged to 12.5% in 1994, had declined to 4.2% by 2010. In 2005 the World Economic Forum ranked Denmark fourth in the world in terms of growth competitiveness, behind Finland, the U.S. and Sweden. In 2007 the same organization put Denmark in first place in terms of exploiting information technology; the U.S. dropped to seventh. In September 2007 *The Economist* magazine ranked Denmark as the world's best place to do business.

The 2009 global economic downturn did not spare Denmark. Economic growth contracted by 4.1%, unemployment rose slightly, property prices declined sharply, the budget balance went into a 2.5% deficit, and the government had to produce two rescue packages for the banks. Prices remained stable.

An ambitious austerity program is not easy for governing coalitions that had no majority in parliament and ruled a nation long-accustomed to annual increases in real wages and welfare spending. But many Danes are encouraged that their country has begun to overcome the addiction to borrowing.

CULTURE

Literature

It is difficult for a small country with its own language to gain the world's attention to certain aspects of its culture. Although the Danish language is understood, albeit with some difficulty, by other Scandinavians, it cannot be understood at all by German and Dutch speakers, although all three languages are of Germanic origin. The geographically restricted reach of Danish has meant that most Danish literature remains unknown in the rest of the world even though Denmark publishes more books per capita than any other nation in the world except Iceland.

The major exception is the literary giant, Hans Christian Andersen (1805–1875), whose folk tales filled with fantasies and down-to-earth moral insights have delighted children (and adults) for generations. The 200th anniversary of his birth was celebrated throughout the world in 2005 by appointing Hans Christian Andersen ambassadors. His mind has become a part of many persons' childhood: "The Princess and the Pea," "The Emperor's New Clothes," "The Steadfast Tin Soldier" and "The Little Mermaid" (memorialized by a four-foot-tall 385-pound statue created by Edvard Eriksen in 1913 in Copenhagen harbor, which is one of the city's most beloved landmarks) and many other delightful tales.

In 1998 the maiden's statue was beheaded for the second time in 33 years. After three days a hooded figure dropped the head off at a television station, and police suspected that the culprits were to be found in the feminist protest milieu. In 2003 vandals blew her up, but officials repaired and returned her. She also lost an arm, which was later recovered and reattached.

In 2010 she was sent abroad to the Shanghai World Expo in China. This was the first time she had traveled, and she was sent by a secret route to foil any plots to "Shanghai" her. As the centerpiece of the Danish pavilion, her assignment was to help boost Danish trade and tourism. However, her voyage created an uproar: six out of ten Danes thought she should stay home. The future of "mermaid diplomacy" is uncertain.

Andersen has by far the greatest international reputation of any Danish author, but Denmark has many other writers of which it can be proud. In the 18th century Ludvig Holberg wrote many comedies and a novel of fantasy, *Niels Klim's Journey to the World Underground*, which is a delightful plea for religious tolerance. A more intensive Christianity was presented in the lyrics of Johannes Ewald (1743–1781), especially *Ode to the Soul*.

In the 19th century other Danish authors dealt with spiritual matters. Perhaps the most profound and the one with the greatest impact upon philosophical and theological thinking in the Western world was Søren Kierkegaard (1813–1855), the father of existentialism. He attempted to get people to reflect on their own existence and to realize that human life is a problem and demands choices and self-creation.

N.F.S. Grundtvig pointed to the spoken, live word as the key to a human and Christian community. He founded the current national state and Volk high schools. Frederik Palundan-Müller's novel *Adam Homo* is now translated and accessible to the English-reading audience. Another important Danish work, *Seven Gothic Tales*, appeared first in English in 1934 under the pen name of Isak Dinesen, a year before it was rewritten in Danish by its author, Karen Blixen. Her work dealt with man's religious life, and she argues that man is a mere marionette of God and that he should simply live out the destiny to which God assigns him. Blixen is best known throughout the world for her book, *Out of Africa*, later made into a hit film, an engaging portrayal of her two decades living and farming in Kenya. Peter Høeg more recently gave Danish literature a worldwide audience with his best-selling novel, *Miss Smilla's Feeling for Snow*.

Several Danish writers won Nobel Prizes in Literature in the 20th century. They include Karl Gjellerup and Henrik Pontopiddan (1917), as well as Johannes V. Jensen (1944). Many Danes call Jensen's novel, *Kangens Fald* (*The Fall of the King*) the Danish "book of the century."

Religion has played very little part in post-World War II Danish literature, with the notable exception of Martin A. Hansen's *The Liar*. Some authors, such as Thorkild Hansen, in his three-volume biography of Knut Hamsun, have dealt with Denmark's experiences under Nazi domination. Others, such as Villy Sørensen, Niels I. Meyer and K. Helveg Petersen, focus on the problems arising from the individual's life in a prosperous, materialistic society and offer moderate left solutions to contemporary problems. Dea Trier Mørch, Elsa Gress and Suzanne Brøgger have produced sensitive literature focusing on women's roles in society. They also produced a satirical response by one of Denmark's most popular contemporary authors, Klaus Rifberg, in his 1978 novel *Dobbeltgænger* ("The Double"). Others, such as Peter Seeberg and Ole Sarvig, have written modern experimental novels and Thorkild Bjørnvig, Marianne Larsen and Henrik Nordbrandt, have written lyrical poetry that commands an attentive audience in Denmark today.

Denmark

The 1930s brought three outstanding Danish playwrights to public acclaim. Kaj Munk was a clergyman deeply influenced by Kierkegaard. He wrote about strong men who tried to accomplish great things, but who were doomed to failure by man's inherent sinfulness. The German occupation force executed Munk for resistance activities. Soya produced realistic drama, and Kjeld Abell in his plays rebelled against the boredom and mediocrity of bourgeois society.

The Arts

It cannot be said that the Danes are passionate theater fans. A 1975 survey revealed that only 16% of the population ever attends a performance. Also, theater in Denmark is not commercially viable. The state provides a variety of subsidies to keep the 15 theaters in Copenhagen and ten in the provinces alive. In general, the state gives financial support to most of the arts, on the principle that it has a duty to provide an economic foundation for Danish culture without interfering with it. Artistic freedom is always to be respected. The Ministry of Cultural Affairs also supports efforts to bring traditional culture to Danes who have little education in order to try to close what some Danes see as a "cultural gap." It finances activity centers and events in working class areas, but the efforts to expand cultural opportunities have not yet proven to be very successful. Such costly programs, as well as financial support for art and artists, are increasingly criticized by many Danes, who feel that tax money could be better spent for other more immediate economic needs.

The only theaters open during the summer months and comprehensible to non-Danish speaking persons is the Pantomime Theater, which has a long tradition of artistic excellence. The Tivoli Gardens, in which this theater is located, is filled with amusements and cafés and is certainly one of the world's most famous and delightful parks.

A Dane, Carl T. H. Dreyer, was an early film pioneer, with such films as "Jeanne d'Arc." No Danish filmmaker today would dare try to produce a film without state aid. Because of such aid, about 20 films a year are made, most of them focusing on everyday life in a very realistic way. Film directors Henning Carlsen and Lars von Trier have international reputations, and such directors as Henning Kristiansen, Morten Arnfred, Astrid Henning-Jensen, Anders Refn, Edward Fleming, Bille August, Hans Kristensen and Jørgen Leth, create films for an avid Danish audience.

The towering figure in Danish music was Carl Nielsen (1865–1931), who gained a wide international public. Other composers, such as Per Nørgård, Ib Nørholm, Hans Abrahamsen, Erik Norby, Bo Holten and Poul Ruders have also been creative and successful. Thanks to such American artists as Thad Jones, Copenhagen has become one of Europe's major jazz centers. Denmark is also a European ballet center. The Royal Danish Ballet's international fame was established in the 19th century by August Bournonville. It is housed in the Royal Theater in Copenhagen and has its own school, where talented youngsters from age seven to sixteen are trained. It has been particularly successful in producing great male dancers, such as Erik Bruhn, Peter Martins and Peter Schaufuss.

At the forefront of Danish artistic achievement are the sculptor, Bertel Thorvaldsen (1770–1844) and the painter C.W. Eckersberg (1783–1853). Thorvaldsen achieved an international breakthrough in Rome and came to be the most renowned sculptor of his day. Eckersberg also made his breakthrough abroad as a pupil of Jacques Louis David in Paris. From David he learned to observe nature very closely and to reproduce it honestly. His numerous paintings of the Danish coasts, countryside and prominent citizens of Copenhagen provide the modern viewer with a valuable look at 19th century Denmark. He also taught at the Academy of Art, which had been founded in Copenhagen in 1754. There he was able to launch an entire school of Danish painters.

This included Christen Købke, often regarded as the country's greatest painter. Born in 1810 the son of a master baker, he was a contemporary of Hans Christian Andersen. He preferred to paint Danish churches and the outskirts of Copenhagen, where town and country met. He died early in 1848, only 37 years of age.

In the 1940s, daring Danish painters and sculptors, such as Richard Mortensen, Mogens Andersen and Robert Jacobsen, experimented in modern styles in non-figurative art. Contemporary Danish artists, such as Jørgen Haugen Sørensen, Egon Fischer, Willy Ørskov, Niels Strøbek, Per Kirkeby, Stig Brøgger, Paul Gernes and Tonning Rasmussen, have continued the experimentalist tradition. This has had an important impact on industrial products and furniture, in which Danish design has been very innovative, as well as commercially successful. Scientist Niels Bohr won the Nobel Prize in 1922. World-class architects include Jørn Utzon (the Sydney Opera House) and Johan Otto von Spreckelsen (the Grand Arch at La Défense in Paris).

Religion

The focus of some of Denmark's greatest literature on religious subjects should not leave one with the impression that Danes are a deeply religious people today. They are not. A poll indicated that only 45% of the adults believe that there is a God. Even a Lutheran pastor declared in 2003: "There's no heavenly God, there's no eternal life, and there's no resurrection." In 2003 the government announced that it would begin allowing a group that worships Norse gods to conduct legally recognized marriages. Regular church attendance on Sundays had by 2003 fallen to 1%–3% of the population.

Danes are obviously not a people greatly concerned with religious questions and matters. A 1987 survey revealed that more Danes believe in reincarnation than in the Christian doctrine of the resurrection of the body and that there are more full-time teachers of new, non-Christian religions in Denmark than there are priests in the Evangelical Lutheran Established Church, which receives financial support from the government and which is called the People's Church, not the State Church. Anybody can opt out of paying the church tax, but around 12% of the church's income still comes from a direct state subsidy.

Nevertheless, the official church is so enmeshed in Danish society that 84% of all Danes belong to the church, although they are free to leave it. In fact, only one person in Denmark is required to belong: the reigning monarch, who is the head of the church. Working with the government's church minister, it is she, not the bishops or a synod, who decides about liturgy, ritual, Bible translations, and the outer appearance of the psalm book. More than half of the marriages take place in a church, and over 80% of Danish children are baptized; over 95% of Danes are buried at local churches. Danes admit that theirs is now a "four-wheeler religion": they come in a baby carriage to be baptized, are driven to the church in a fancy car to be married, and are transported in a hearse to their own funeral. The church is there when desired—sometimes Christmas, Easter, and for family needs.

A 1988 law granted homosexuals the legal status of married couples, including inheritance, tax deductions and alimony, but excluding the right to adopt children. This was the first such law in the world. The social event of 1989 was a group marriage of ten gay couples in Copenhagen's city hall.

Education

All children are required to attend at least nine years of school, from ages seven to sixteen. All public education, which is administered and largely financed by local governments, is free from elementary school through the university. About 5% of the Danish children at the primary or lower secondary level attend private schools. It is very easy to found a private school in Denmark, and the local government authorities ask very few questions about the proposed schools' educational philosophies before granting them the usual 70% state subsidy for nonpublic schools.

The egalitarian goal of many Danes is revealed by the facts that during the first seven years of schooling, numerical grades and required tests cannot be given. Many Danes fear that lasting social distinctions among citizens could be created if younger children received such grades and tests. However, from the eighth grade on, voluntary examinations can be given to those pupils who want to enter institutions of higher education, and pupils also can be issued grades if the parents desire this to be done. Attempts by some left-wing politicians and educators to abolish all grades and examinations have not yet found a political majority.

After the 7th grade, about 30% of the pupils choose to pursue vocational studies, while the rest follow courses that lead to the grammar school (gymnasium or "high school") and, after a three-year course, to university or higher technical studies. A grammar school diploma automatically entitles a student to entry into a university without an entrance examination although one's grades do help determine what one may study.

The oldest is Copenhagen University, established in 1479 and others are in Århus, Odense, Roskilde and Alborg. Separate colleges, such as the dental colleges of Copenhagen and Århus, the Royal Danish Conservatory of Music, the Royal Danish College of Pharmacy and the Royal Academy of Fine Arts, teach specialized subjects that are not normally taught at the Danish universities. As a sign of the times, there has been a shift in the subjects that students choose to study. In 1976 half of them chose liberal arts majors leading to teaching or civil service, while only a fifth of them selected majors targeting the private sector. By 1991 less than a fifth opt for majors relevant to the public sector, while more than 40% prepare for employment in business, computers, and engineering. Men are predominant in these fields, while most of the law and theology students and 80% of the medical students are women. Among the only professions in which women match or exceed their share of the general population are medicine and diplomacy; the foreign service makes sure that half of its new recruits are women.

The Media

Radio and television programming is the responsibility of Radio Denmark, a publicly-owned corporation managed in-

dependently by 27 persons chosen by the *Folketing*. License fees finance all broadcasting, and in 1988 a new second television channel became operational on which commercial advertising is permitted for the first time. This broke the state-run TV monopoly, and almost all observers agree that the presence of a second channel has improved the quality of the government-run station. In 1996 Danes were glued to their televisions watching their Olympic team win more gold medals than anyone expected and the first Dane ever to win the Tour de France bike race, Bjarne Riis.

Many Danes still rely on the 55 daily newspapers, almost a dozen of which are published in Copenhagen, for much of their news. The most respected of the larger newspapers are *Politiken* and *Berlingske Tidende*. The latter is one of Europe's oldest newspapers. It was the first European newspaper to publish the text of the American Declaration of Independence. It is a conservative and middle-class newspa-

per, which has come very close to bankruptcy in the past, due in part to its employees' resistance to any measures of economic restraint. Many Danes wanted the latter to survive because it is the major nonsocialist voice in a predominantly left-oriented mass media landscape. It is now profitable. Both decided in 1986 to launch Sunday editions.

Most Danish newspapers have severed their ties with political parties. The Social Democratic Party's *Aktuelt* and *Det Fri Aktuelt* folded. There are specialized newspapers, such as *Børsen* for businessmen, and the fast-growing *Information*, for the intellectual left. One non-Copenhagen newspaper has a national outlook and circulation: the slightly conservative *Jullands-Posten*, published in Århus.

FUTURE

Denmark is much surer of itself now that its economy has become one of Europe's strongest despite the 2009 global re-

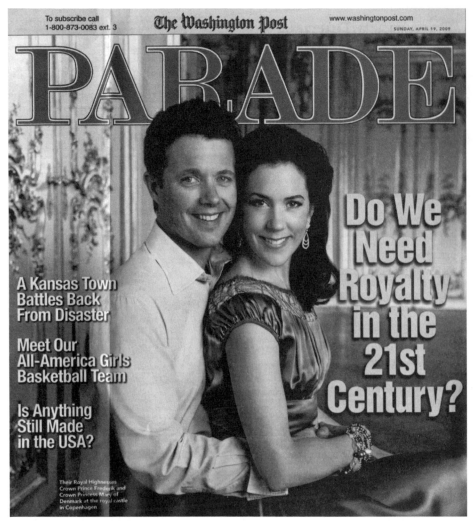

Crown Prince Frederik and Crown Princess Mary of Denmark

Denmark

cession. It enthusiastically endeavors to establish and tighten links with the Baltic states, especially Lithuania. It helped create a Danish-German-Polish corps that has its headquarters in the Polish city of Szczecin (Stettin) along Germany's border.

Denmark supported the war against al-Qaeda terrorists and the Taliban in Afghanistan; in 2010 it still had 690 troops there. It diplomatically supported the U.S.-UK war in Iraq in 2003 although two-thirds of Danes opposed it. It deployed a submarine and naval destroyer to support the allies. After the war Denmark provided 501 troops under British command to help the allies police postwar Iraq. They included a light reconnaissance squadron, mine-clearing experts, special operations forces and a civil affairs unit. The prime minister resisted demands for the premature withdrawal of Danish troops. "That would be a victory for the terrorists and be a fatal signal that terrorism pays." All but 27 of its troops were withdrawn from Iraq in mid-2007. In 2009 it sent a naval vessel to the Indian Ocean to join allied efforts to prevent pirate attacks from Somalia.

Denmark had been openly uneasy about the Maastricht Treaty. Referring to the EU, Foreign Minister Niels Helveg Pe-tersen said: "We are not ardent integrationists." In 1993 Danes nevertheless decided that their future belongs in the EU. In the previous year, a very narrow majority had rejected the Maastricht Agreement in a referendum, expressing concerns heard in other EU countries: unelected bureaucrats in Brussels were concentrating too much power and acting with a heavy hand. Worse, they operated outside of democratic control and were rushing Europeans into greater unity by fiat.

After having negotiated four "opt-outs" from the EU, meaning that Denmark would not take part in the monetary union, common citizenship, cooperation in domestic and justice affairs, or defense, the government again took the question to the people, this time actively campaigning for a yes vote. Also in the yes camp were virtually all of Denmark's political, economic and media establishment. Although 57% of voters said yes, Denmark was left deeply divided.

On May 28, 1998, voters decided not to adopt the euro in the first round. But Denmark agreed to keep the krone in a band within 2.25% of the euro and follow the European Central Bank's interest rate moves. Thus it is ready to join whenever its people choose to do so. The government held a referendum on the issue on September 28, 2000. It failed to pass by 53% to 47%. However, by 2008 a majority of Danes favored both the adoption of the euro and the scrapping of the four opt-outs. Danes have become much more pro-EU.

The center-right minority government, now under new Liberal Prime Minister Lars Løkke Rasmussen since April 2009, gets much credit for cutting taxes, curbing immigration, improving pensioners' welfare, and cracking down on violent crime. He promises to stick with his predecessor's broad policy agenda while Fogh Rasmussen gives the small country much international visibility as NATO secretary general. Denmark is scheduled to assume the EU presidency the first half of 2011.

With elections due in 2011, the prime minister has many challenges, not the least of which is a rock-bottom 16% approval rating in the face of rising popularity of the opposition Social Democratic leader, Helle Thorning-Schmidt, with 37% popular backing. It helps that the Danes are the happiest people in the world, according to a 2008 World Values Survey conducted by the University of Michigan.

Tivoli Gardens

NORWEGIAN SEA

LANGJÖKULL
HOFSJÖKULL
Akureyri

REYKJAVÍK
Keflavík
Hafnarfjördur
Kopavogur
Thingvellir

VATNAJÖKULL

MT. HEKLA

Vestmannaeyjar
MYRDALSJÖKULL

ATLANTIC OCEAN

Note: jökull means "glacier"

Area: 39,768 sq. mi. (102,952 sq. km., slightly smaller than Ohio and half the size of Great Britain.)

Population: 320,000 (estimated).

Capital City: Reykjavik (pronounced RAKE-ya-vic; pop. 161,300, estimated). Over half of the country's population lives in Greater Reykjavik.

Climate: Considering its northern position, the climate is cool, yet moderated by the Gulf Stream, with the summers in the mid-50°s (13°C) and the winter about freezing.

Neighboring Countries: Iceland lies alone in the North Atlantic, just touching the Arctic Circle, and is about 335 miles northwest of Scotland and approximately 425 miles from the coast of Norway. Greenland lies about 100 miles to the west.

Official Language: Icelandic (based on Old Norse).

Ethnic Background: Nordic, Celtic

Principal Religion: Lutheran (95%); other Protestant and Roman Catholic (3%); no affiliation (2%).

Main Exports: Fish and fish products, animal products, aluminum.

Main Imports: Machinery, transport equipment, petroleum, food, textiles.

Major Trading Partners: EU (70%), UK, Germany, U.S., Japan, Denmark, France.

Currency: Krona.

National Day: June 17, anniversary of the establishment of the Republic.

Chief of State: Olafur Ragnar Grímsson, President (since July 1996).

Head of Government: Johanna Sigurdardottir, Prime Minister (since February 2009).

National Flag: Red Cross, lined in white, upon a blue field.

Hidden beneath the Myrdal Glacier is a treacherous volcanic fissure. When it erupts, the glacier melts instantly, changing from a benign sea of ice to a roaring wall of water racing across the flatland below it. In 1963 an underwater eruption off the southern coast resulted in the birth of a new island (named Surtsey) accompanied by exploding showers of hot lava, clouds of steam and black smoke. These instances only help explain why Iceland is known as the battlefield of fire, ice and steam.

Glaciers cover 12% of the country and its major icecap is the world's third largest. They provide an almost endless water supply for hydroelectricity. There are uncounted geysers and hot springs. The colors in Iceland's flag reflect these elements: red for fire, white for ice and dark blue for the sea. Some 30 of its 100-odd volcanoes

have erupted since the island's settlement in the late 9th century, and one-third of the world's lava production over the past half-millennium has flowed in Iceland.

Icelanders were dramatically reminded of this in 1996 when a new volcano (subsequently named Loki after the Nordic god of fire) erupted under the Vatnajokull glacier; the ice pack is the largest in Europe, measuring 1,800 feet in some places and covering 10% of the island's surface. It melted vast volumes of ice and formed a huge lake under the ice. Smashing through the ice, the volcano spewed black clouds five miles in the air and sent bursts of red lightning over the six-mile-long fissure. Then came a torrent of black sulphurous water, ice and mud at times five meters high onto the deserted coastal plain 120 miles east of Reykjavik. Along its 20-kilometer-wide path to the sea, it destroyed roads, bridges, tunnels and power and telephone lines. Ex-Prime Minister David Oddsson said: "In the space of three or four hours our transport system has been put back 30 years."

In March and April 2010 the Atlantic world was once again reminded what an oversized influence tiny Iceland has on our lives. One of its least powerful volcanoes, Eyjafjallajökull (pronounceable only by Icelanders and mercifully shortened in

Iceland

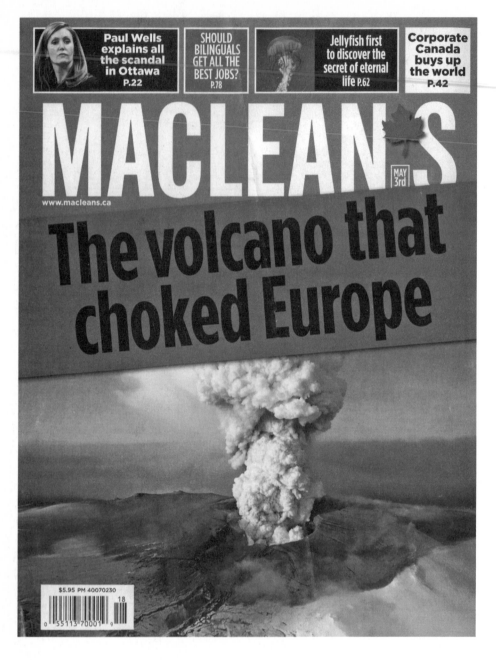

be expected to increase in the coming decades. One volcanologist put it this way: "You can't really predict what Icelandic volcanoes will do. . . . It could go on for years."

Iceland stands at the northern end of the Atlantic, guarding the boundary between that ocean and the Arctic. The Denmark Strait is to the west, the Greenland Sea to the north and the Norwegian Sea to the east. The island is squarely on the "great circle" air routes between American, Scandinavian and East European cities. The northernmost tip of Iceland touches the Arctic Circle.

It is half the size of Britain and somewhat larger than Ireland. Ohio and Iceland are about equivalent in size. The island is oval-shaped, with many peninsulas extending from the western and northern coasts. The maximum east to west distance is about 300 miles (480 km.), and from north to south it extends about 200 miles (320 km.).

Iceland is the result of thousands of lava flows and volcanic eruptions. Most of the island is plateau, typically 1,500 to 2,000 feet (457 to 610 meters) in altitude, with volcanic peaks and high tablelands rising above it. Along the north and west coasts, steep cliffs border deep fjords, most of which have good natural harbors and from which broad valleys reach far inland. The largest plain is in the southwest and is Iceland's most fertile grassland.

Although the Polar Current chills the north coast, the Gulf Stream warms the south, bringing a surprisingly mild climate to a land on the doorstep of the Arctic. The average winter temperature is higher than that of New York City, although the almost constant winds greatly intensify the chill factor.

When the first settlers arrived, the lower elevations were covered with forests, but they were cut for firewood and prevented from regrowing by sheep grazing and the cooler climate. Moss and grass cover many of these same areas today. Seals, walrus, and arctic foxes were the only native wild mammals, but humans introduced rats, mice, mink and reindeer, deliberately or otherwise. Iceland's coastal waters were teeming with fish.

HISTORY

Some explorers, especially Irish monks, had previously visited Iceland. Norsemen and some Celts settled the island between 870 and 930 A.D. The ninth-century settlers noticed steam rising from the ground on a spot they called "Smokey Bay" or "Reykjavik." They came mostly from the coastal areas extending from Trondelag to Agder in western Norway, especially the part known as Gulathing, today's Sognog

the press to "E-15" for the eye-crossing number of letters), which had been quiet since 1821–23, when it blew off and on for two years, erupted. It spit a plume of steam and ash about four miles into the air. The cloud quickly covered most of Europe and North Africa. Since airplanes cannot fly through a volcano cloud without damaging their engines, air traffic largely stopped for five days. This cost the airlines over three billion dollars at a time they could least afford it. The resulting chaos was a reminder of how interconnected we have become through the crisscrossing of airline routes and how central Iceland's location is in the Atlantic world. Since the volcano was located 75 miles southeast of Reykjavik and the winds

were blowing southeast toward Europe, few Icelanders were affected by it, and their planes continued to fly.

The frightening thing is that other volcanoes, especially Katla, located only 16 miles away from E-15, pack a wallop a hundred times more powerful. Katla is decades overdue to erupt. Even more intimidating are Oraefajokull, whose 1362 eruption was worse than Mount Vesuvius in 79 AD, and Laki, which covered Europe with poisonous gases in 1783. Iceland is a geological infant that is still in the state of formation. It was hard to laugh at the jokes going around the financially battered island that "it was the last wish of the Icelandic economy that its ashes be spread over Europe." Volcanic activity can

Iceland

Thingvellir—solemn and windswept, ancient site of democratic ideals

Fjordana, Hordaland and Rogaland, as well as from the ethnically mixed Viking colonies in Scotland and Ireland. Only the interior, which has always been largely uninhabitable, remained unsettled. The presence of the Celts probably explains the higher percentage of dark-haired people than in other Nordic countries.

Regardless of the original ethnic mix, the population soon became homogeneous. There was little additional immigration. In modern times there has been a steady increase in population because of the low death and high birth rates.

Icelanders continued their explorations beyond their home island in the 10th and 11th centuries. Eric the Red settled Greenland in 986. About 1000 his son, Leif, who was born in Iceland, led the first proven expedition to the American continent, but attempts to settle "Vinland" failed.

At the foot of a great cliff and overlooking a broad lava plain, the *Althingi*, the oldest parliament in the world, began its annual sessions in the year 930, 60 years after the arrival of the first settlers. Recently, a member of parliament suggested that if the British insist on calling their country the "Mother of Parliaments," then Iceland should proclaim itself the "Grandmother of Parliaments." In 1000 that body decided that Icelanders would thereafter be Christians. Although the *Althingi* now meets in Reykjavik, the original location at Thingvellir is the most celebrated historical site in Iceland. Contacts with Norway remained strong through the first four centuries of Icelandic history. Around

1020 Iceland entered its first agreement with a foreign country: the *Althingi* and King Olav Haraldsson (St. Olav) reached an accord on reciprocal rights. The Icelanders' memory of their earlier independence outlasted centuries of foreign domination, famines, plagues and natural catastrophes. Many of their legends and sagas hark back to the times when they were masters of their own fate.

Iceland was independent until it came under the control of Norway in 1262, then Denmark in 1380. When the Icelandic chieftains (the Godar) accepted the king of Norway as their sovereign under the "Old Covenant" in the years 1262–1264, Iceland became a part of the Norwegian realm. However, it retained its own parliament (*Althingi*), laws, and self-government in most internal matters. The kingdoms of Denmark and Norway (including Iceland) were united in 1380. But Iceland continued to enjoy considerable self-government throughout the Middle Ages. The 15th century has been referred to as the "English Century" in Icelandic history due to the many contacts between the countries, including much trading and some skirmishing.

With the Reformation, enforced by the Danish Crown in the 16th century, Danish royal power took firm hold, and the introduction of the trade monopoly in 1602 and absolutism in 1662 reduced Iceland, in effect, to the status of a Danish colony. The *Althingi* itself became increasingly powerless and was finally abolished in 1800. The trade monopoly, which meant

that Icelanders received low prices for their products and paid high prices for the goods that they had to import on Danish ships, merely stimulated Icelandic resentment toward Copenhagen.

From 1835–1847 Jónas Hallgrímsson and other patriots edited the periodical *Fjölnir*. They advocated a return to the virtues of a golden past, the commonwealth of 930–1262, and the reestablishment of the *Althingi*, which occurred in 1843. In the middle of the 19th century, the Icelanders, led by longstanding *Althingi* president Jon Sigurdsson, continued this campaign finally to sever their ties with Denmark. The Danes were receptive to the idea of loosening their hold on Iceland, but their concessions seldom went far enough for the Icelanders.

Home rule was granted finally in 1904. During the First World War Icelanders bolstered their self-confidence by being able to solve their own problems at home without Danish help. In December 1918 an agreement called the "Act of Union" between Iceland and Denmark granted the island full independence. It agreed to continue recognizing Denmark's king as the king of Iceland on the condition that this arrangement be reexamined after 25 years. Until 1944 the state was called "The Kingdom of Iceland."

When the 25 years had elapsed, Denmark was in no position to influence the Icelanders' decision to sever all royal ties between the two countries—it had been overrun by German troops in 1940. The British occupied Iceland that same year.

Iceland

In July 1941 the United States and Iceland concluded an agreement that provided for the stationing of American troops to protect the island. On June 17, 1944, following a referendum, the Republic of Iceland was proclaimed at Thingvellir, the venerated spot where the *Althingi* had been first assembled more than a thousand years earlier. The U.S. was the first country to recognize Icelandic independence.

GOVERNMENT

Iceland is a parliamentary democracy in which the most powerful political figure, the prime minister, must have a majority in the parliament, the *Althingi*. At least every four years, citizens at least 18 years of age elect 63 members of parliament by a system of proportional representation. In 1991 the upper house (*Efri deild*) was abolished, leaving only a unicameral lower house (*Nedri deild*). The prime minister is the head of government.

Political Parties

There is no majority party, and since the 1930s successful government has depended on the formation of a coalition. There are five main political parties now represented in the *Althingi*. All of them have "open primaries" in which even nonmembers can have an influence on their leadership.

The Social Democratic Party (SDP) is major ruling party. It was the earliest party to call for Iceland to commence negotiations on entering the EU, but no other party supported this until now. It was damaged by a split and formation in 1995 of a breakaway leftist Awakening of the Nation (also called the People's Movement). The SDP has its own newspaper, *Althydubladid*.

In 2003 the SDP formed an electoral partnership called the Social-Democratic Alliance with the most vociferous party of the political left, the United Left. Some opponents claimed that communists dominated it. Indeed, it must contend with severe internal conflicts between hard-line socialists and more moderate members. It opposed NATO and the stationing of American troops on Icelandic soil. Since 1978 it has not made the realization of these objectives a condition for its entry into a coalition government.

The earlier conservative government of Geir Haarde collapsed in January 2009 in the midst of Iceland's worst economic disaster in history. The caretaker government until elections could be held later in April was led by Johanna Sigurdardottir of the Social-Democratic Alliance. The daughter of a prominent labor leader, she had been

Prime Minister Johanna Sigurdardottir

an Icelandair flight attendant for 30 years and union organizer for its employees. She served as social affairs minister in several governments since 1987, strengthening the social welfare system and widening housing opportunities for the poor. She has two sons with her former husband, but she later formed a civil partnership with another woman in 2002. She is Iceland's first female prime minister and the world's first openly gay head of government. That appears to be fine with her

View of Reykjavik

President Olafur Ragnar Grímsson

fellow citizens. Gay sex was decriminalized already in 1940, and civil partnerships were made legal in 1996.

The April 2009 parliamentary elections were an opportunity for voters to take revenge on all politicians who had been tainted by the economic meltdown that laid Iceland low beginning in the fall of 2008. Electoral turnout is always high in Iceland, and this time it was 85.1%. It brought a sharp swing to the left. Sigurdardottir's Social-Democratic Alliance was the big winner, capturing 29.8% of the votes (up from 26.8% in 2007) and 20 seats (up from 18). In the campaign she had presented the European Union (EU) and the euro as Iceland's panacea and pledged to apply for EU membership within 18 months and to adopt the euro within four years.

The partner in the narrow governing coalition is the Left-Green Movement. Led by former truck driver and geologist Steingrimur J. Sigfusson, it garnered 21.7% of the votes (up from 14.3%) and 14 seats (up from 9). Prime Minister Sigurdardottir must deal gingerly with this partner since it is skeptical about entry into the EU for reasons widely shared in the country: that it would lose control of its exclusive fishing waters and of its other natural resources. Nevertheless, in July 2009 parliament voted narrowly (33 to 28) in favor of seeking EU membership.

Two other parties also made gains: a new Citizens' Movement, born out of the sometimes violent protest demonstrations in the streets of Reykjavik in January 2009, captured 7.2% of the votes and 4 seats.

The Progressive Party (PP) won 14.8% of the votes (up from 11.7%) and 9 seats (up from 7). It is a slightly left-of-center party, which has traditionally represented agrarian interests. It supports NATO although it sought the removal of American troops from Iceland as soon as "conditions" permitted; they left in 2006. It opposed entry into the EU but may reconsider in light of the economic catastrophe. It maintains a daily newspaper, *Timinn*. It was the first Icelandic party to use TV advertising. Both parties are in the opposition.

The undisputed loser in April 2009 was the Independence Party (IP-Conservatives), which was in power as the economy disintegrated. It lost a third of its voters and 9 seats, capturing only 23.7% of the votes (12.9% fewer than in 2007) and 16 seats (down from 25). This was its worst result since the party's founding 80 years earlier and the first time in 18 years it was not in the government. Its leader, Geir Haarde, was diagnosed with esophagus cancer and passed the baton on to Bjarni Benediktsson, who put on a brave face: "We lost this time, but we will win again later." IP's program is based on the market economy and on membership in NATO, but it staunchly opposed joining the EU. It is supported by Iceland's major newspaper, *Morgunbladid*.

Another victim of IP's wipeout was the colorful former mayor of Reykjavik, David Oddsson, a comic playwright, who had been Europe's longest-serving prime minister (13 years) and then foreign minister. Oddsson ultimately became Central Bank Governor. But he had the bad luck to be in that post when the hinges holding the economy together broke, sending it into freefall. The government cannot dismiss the holder of this position. But the Sigurdardottir coalition was so determined to get rid of him that it legislatively redefined the qualifications for the post: the holder must now have a master's degree in economics. Since Oddsson had studied law, he had to go. Along with another former prime minister, Geir Haarde, he faces charges of "extreme negligence" in Iceland's 2008 banking crisis. He was nevertheless hired as editor of the influential daily, *Morgunbladid*.

Gone is the Women's Alliance formerly called the Feminists. Their general message was that because of women's experience in child-bearing, they have different values than do men. But despite their crucial contribution to society, they have little influence in a male-dominated country. Although 80% of all women work, their pay is 40% lower than that of the average man. Nevertheless, in 2005 the Swiss-based think tank, World Economic Forum, ranked Iceland third in the world (behind Sweden and Norway and ahead of 17th-place U.S.) in terms of gender opportunity.

The President

The president of the republic is the head of state and performs primarily ceremonial functions. However, he or she can play an important role in coordinating coalition talks after a parliamentary election.

A swimming pool in Reykjavik with thermal baths

Iceland

Presidents are elected directly for a four-year term, and there have been only five presidents since the establishment of the republic in 1944.

Ragnar Grímsson won his third term in June 2004 with almost 86% of the votes. Nevertheless, turnout was only 64%. This was 20% below that of the previous election, and more than a fifth of the ballots were cast blank. In January 2010 he revealed the reserve power a president has when he vetoed a law adopted by parliamentary vote the last day of 2009 requiring a $4 billion reimbursement to Britain and the Netherlands. This was only the second time in history an Icelandic president has withheld his signature from a law. This opened the way to the country's first referendum in March 2010.

Local Government and the Judiciary

Iceland is a unitary state. For administrative purposes, it is divided into 23 rural districts. There are also 215 parishes and 14 incorporated towns. A subject of hot debate is the unceasing influx of rural Icelanders, especially the young, into the capital city of Reykjavik. About 70% of the total population lives in or around the capital.

The judiciary consists of district and lower magistrates appointed by the minister of justice. The Supreme Court, with eight permanent members, is the highest court in the land.

NATO AND DEFENSE

Although in 1918 the newly independent Iceland intended to follow a policy of "eternal neutrality," the tense world political situation in the late 1940s prompted it to join NATO. Polls indicate that about 80% of Icelanders are in favor of NATO membership; it has no army, navy or air force of its own, but it is an important member. It occupies a strategic position on the maritime and air routes between the northern seas and the North Atlantic sealanes so critical to NATO.

Its geo-economic significance is enhanced by the reality of global warming, which will open up the North to increased shipping as ice melts. It sits at the mouth of the Arctic Ocean and is ideally located for the transhipment of cargoes to the Barents Sea or through the Northwest Passage in northern Canada to the Bering Sea. It has at least three potential deep fjord sites. Perhaps it is no accident that China maintains the largest embassy in Reykjavik.

As its contribution to the common defense, Iceland permitted the stationing of U.S. forces on its territory at the NATO air base of Keflavík, located 30 miles (48 km.) from the capital city. The size of that force

General Secretary Gorbachev and President Reagan in Reykjavik White House photo by Terry Arthur

continuously dwindled after the end of the Cold War. In 1993 the Americans announced the withdrawal of their F-15 interceptors and Orion P3Cs, and a year later eight more F-15 fighters were brought home. When the Pentagon, citing Iceland's reduced importance as a strategic outpost, announced in 2003 a decision to withdraw its four remaining F-15s, along with five rescue helicopters and two refueling planes, the Icelandic government strongly objected. Iceland saw them as essential to its air defense and, more important, a symbol of America's commitment to defend the nation. Feelings were also bruised because Iceland's leaders were informed of the decision but not consulted about it.

In 2004 this Iceland Defense Force (IDF) numbered 1,658 U.S. troops (of whom 960 were Navy, 650 Air Force and 48 Marines). There were also 16 Dutch naval troops to man one P-3C surveillance airplane. In 2006 the Pentagon announced as a part of its worldwide base reductions and troop redeployment the final withdrawal of four Air Force fighter jets and a rescue helicopter squadron. More than 1,200 military personnel and 100 Defense Department civilian employees were brought home. This move put over 600 Icelandic employees' jobs in danger.

Such equipment and troop reductions hurt the Icelandic economy since the U.S. paid about $260 million in annual rent, which amounted to 8% of Iceland's total foreign earnings, and employed many local people. The Icelandic government was considering picking up the tab for the costs if the Americans remained. The redeployments leave the country with no military defenses, and this created understandable tension between the two allies.

While the IDF had the responsibility of defending Iceland from foreign attack, Ice-

landers are responsible for maintaining order at home. There are two groups of personnel who protect the cities. They do it well because there is less crime within the country than in the U.S. These forces are the unarmed 300-member police force and the 12-member "Viking Squad." This squad is the Icelandic equivalent to the American Delta Force. Its troops are heavily armed and well-trained as antiterrorist commandos. Iceland also has a coast guard of 130 sailors operating three patrol craft.

The IDF had the mission to patrol the strategically important waters 140 nautical miles from its coasts. The American aircraft there included AWACS. Submarine detection devices (SOSUS) under the water were maintained from the base. American forces have two radar stations in southern Iceland, and Icelandic civilians man two new radar stations in the north.

The Icelandic government long ago established several important limitations on the U.S. base: there could be no nuclear weapons, even on U.S. ships that enter Icelandic waters. In 1985 the Icelandic parliament declared the coast to be a "nuclear free zone." Reports in 1985 that there may have been American contingency plans to deploy such weapons in time of crisis and that Marines who guard the base have manuals dealing with the handling of atomic weapons created some concern. Then Secretary of State George Shultz went to Iceland to assure the government that no measure of any kind would ever be taken without its permission. A second limitation was vague: the weaponry at the base had to be defensive, not offensive. When the two modern AWACS radar planes were introduced to the base, some critics feared that they could be used as command posts of an offensive war.

Until the late 1990s the stationing of American soldiers in Iceland was a continuous bone of contention among the Icelanders. A vocal minority regarded their presence as a limitation of Icelandic sovereignty and openly advocated a termination of the bilateral agreement of 1951 providing for the American defense of Iceland. In 1973 the government of Olafur Jóhannesson even considered closing the American-manned NATO base, but nothing came of the matter. Some Icelanders feared the *cultural* influence of American soldiers and dependents on Icelandic life although this fear diminished as American force levels were scaled down.

In order not to irritate the sensitive and nationalistic Icelanders, the U.S. maintained a low profile, although Americans were given considerable freedom of the country. American TV at the base was once available to Icelanders, but the opposition to it was such that cable TV was installed on the base. American radio could still be heard in Reykjavik, though. U.S. forces and their families had to live within the military compound. Unless one of the spouses was an Icelander, soldiers could not leave the base in uniform or remain outside after midnight without special permission. All jobs that were not strictly military had to be given to Icelanders. Also, Iceland was perhaps the only country in the world in which the only banned alcoholic beverage was beer. Until this ban was finally lifted in 1989, American GIs had to be careful not to violate that unusual prohibition off base.

Instead of the usual military guards at base gates, there were Icelandic customs officials charged with protecting the country's stringent import restrictions. Americans could leave the base with no more than two packs of cigarettes, and one had to be open. Picnickers were not allowed to bring raw meat off base for barbecues and had to file a list of edible goods they took out of the installation. Said one Icelander: "We don't want Reykjavik to be a Norfolk or a San Diego."

Some Americans showed little understanding for the particular sensitivity of Icelanders. A land with only 300,000 inhabitants, with just over a half century of independence, but with a long tradition of relative isolation, is perhaps more inclined to overreact to outside influences that are not entirely wanted. Yet most Icelanders see no alternative to NATO membership and protection by allied forces. They would never dream of creating the kind of well-armed military units that would make foreign help unnecessary.

By the end of the century almost everybody favored the bilateral relationship. But the American flag was lowered for the last time at the U.S. base on September 30, 2006, and the last U.S. forces were with-

A fishing catch

drawn after 65 years of military presence on the island. This leaves Iceland with no military defenses and a coast guard of only 130 persons. The Americans promised to defend it as a NATO ally. One unpleasant legacy was left behind: cockroaches. They existed only in the U.S. base, and now there is fear that they will escape and migrate throughout the island.

The Icelandic government has decided, however, to change its traditionally passive role within NATO. It has had very little military expertise and has therefore been unable to make competent assessments of the strategic situation as it affects Iceland. It has not sent representatives to the NATO Military Committee or Nuclear Planning Group, and the U.S. has always paid its required contributions to the NATO Infrastructure Fund. On April 1, 1985, it reorganized and upgraded its Defense Department of the Ministry of Foreign Affairs, which not only handles relations with the IDF, but also with NATO

headquarters and defense ministers. This reorganization, which is the greatest change in Iceland's military affairs since 1944, met with no public controversy.

Foreign Relations

Since World War II Iceland has established diplomatic relations with more than 76 countries. It was the first country in 1991 officially to recognize the independence of the Baltic States and was among the first to recognize the Yugoslav breakaway republics of Slovenia and Croatia. It sent a medical team to Bosnia, development aid to Africa, and food via the Red Cross to Russians around Murmansk. It has joined a number of international organizations. In 1946 it became a member of the UN. It is also a charter member of the Council of Europe, the OECD and many of the institutions associated with the UN, such as the IMF. It joined EFTA in 1970, and has had a free trade agreement with the EU since 1972.

Iceland

Iceland's geographic position has, for the most part, placed it out of the normal travel routes. This may change as the Northwest Passage through international waters in northern Canada opens up to shipping. In the recent past, there have been a few occasions when the world turned its eyes toward the island country. In 1973 then presidents Nixon of the U.S. and Pompidou of France met with Soviet leader Brezhnev to discuss world issues. Once again, in 1986, the leaders of the world's two most powerful countries came together in the Reykjavik summit. Ronald Reagan and Mikhail Gorbachev pushed diplomats aside and met face-to-face to discuss breathtaking visions of nuclear disarmament. In 1991 Iceland exercised some moral authority by supporting independence moves in the Baltic States within the USSR. It has contributed to peacekeeping operations in Afghanistan, where it took responsibility for air traffic control, and in 2003 it quietly approved of the U.S.-UK war effort in Iraq and subsequently pledged nearly $4 million in humanitarian and reconstruction assistance to Iraq.

In 1972 Bobby Fischer defeated Boris Spassky in Reykjavik in the most celebrated chess match in history. While Spassky was advised between games by 35 Russian grand masters, Fischer had only his notebook. It was the first time since 1945 that a world champion was not from the Soviet Union. He gained such hero status in Iceland that parliament granted him citizenship and a passport in 2005 to protect him from deportation to the U.S. This allowed the eccentric chess genius to immigrate to Iceland, whose government refused to notify the U.S. when he traveled abroad. Washington had issued a deportation order because Fischer had disobeyed international sanctions in 1992 by playing an exhibition rematch with Spassky in Yugoslavia earning $3 million while Serbia was engaged in a bloody war in Bosnia. This was his last public match. He had become increasingly unbalanced, spewing anti-Semitic rhetoric (although he himself was Jewish) and praising the September 11 attacks in 2001 as "wonderful news." He passed away in Iceland in January 2008.

ECONOMY

Fishing and Agriculture

The most prominent characteristic of the Icelandic economy has always been its lop-sided dependence upon the fishing industry, itself heavily dependent upon cod. Exports accounted for over half of its GDP, and since 1945 almost half of its export earnings were from fish and fish processing, which provided 10% of employ-ment. Cod accounted for 40% of fish exports. Its major fish markets are the EU, which takes about 60% of its fish and fish products, and the United States, which imposes almost no tariff duties on the fish. Fish now account for less than 10% of GDP. The importance of this single product has been so great that Iceland has a separate Ministry of Fisheries. A decline in fish prices and the government's slashing of fishermen's quota for cod by half in 1994 in order to protect stocks and allow the fish population to recover inevitably hurt the economy in the short term. Iceland has handled its marine resources adeptly and has prevented excessive overfishing.

In 1986 another segment of Iceland's fish industry was highlighted: saboteurs from an environmentalist group called "Sea Shepherds," operating primarily out of the U.S. and Canada, wrecked Iceland's only plant for processing whale oil and byproducts and sank two of Iceland's four whaling ships. They charged that the country conducts illegal commercial whaling under the guise of scientific research. In 1992 Iceland left the International Whaling Commission and announced plans to resume commercial whaling. It rejoined in 2001 after concluding that it could best influence the whaling debate from within the organization. It resumed whale hunting, arguing that stocks of minke and fin whales in its coastal waters are robust enough to support it.

Whaling is economically unimportant for Iceland, but it remains a controversial issue. Icelandic fishermen contend that the protected whales compete with them for the decreasing fish stocks in their wa-ters. Marine scientists analyze the stomach contents of the whales scheduled for killing to determine how much fish minke whales eat. They estimate that the 43,000 whales living close to the island eat a total of one to two million tons of fish each year. A more precise figure would help Iceland manage its fish stocks better. In 2006 Iceland's authorities issued permits to catch 30 minke whales and nine rarer fin whales on top of the 40 minkes already killed annually for "scientific purposes."

The giant mammals have spawned a lucrative new industry in Iceland: whale watching. In 1949 only a hundred tourists came to observe them, but in 2004 that figure had soared to 62,000. Some estimate that this specialized tourism produces more income than whaling and that killing whales could discourage them from coming. However, tourism continues to grow.

The country so depends upon fishing that it was understandable for it to want to extend its fishing limit around its own coasts in order to reduce the fishing activities of other countries in these waters. It did so, first to four nautical miles in 1952, then to 12, 50 and finally 200 miles (350 km.) in 1975. Each extension resulted in conflicts called "cod wars" with Britain, whose fishing fleets also worked in Icelandic waters.

In 1976 the third "cod war" flared up with particular intensity; Iceland sent coast guard gun boats against British trawlers, and warning shots were fired, boats were rammed and trawler wires were cut. Britain responded by sending two naval frigates and surveillance flights in and over Iceland's self-declared waters. Iceland even temporarily broke diplo-

80 SÍÐUR B/C/D

Morgunbladid

STOFNAÐ 1913

276. TBL. 85. ÁRG.   MIÐVIKUDAGUR 3. DESEMBER 1997   PRENTSMIÐJA MORGUNBLAÐSINS

Jeltsín boðar mikla fækkun kjarnaodda

BORÍS Jeltsín, forseti Rússlands, og Karl Gústaf Svíakonungur í botvagni konungs á leið til hallar hans í Stokkhólmi.

matic relations with London. Finally an agreement was reached in the summer of 1976 when Britain accepted Iceland's conditions on cod fishing. Bilateral tensions remained, and not until 2006 did an Icelandic prime minister visit the UK. Although the economy has become more diverse and less vulnerable, branching into tourism, manufacturing and financial services, the fishing industry is still important. The size of the catch varies, and foreign demand and currency values are in constant flux.

Agriculture is still important although it provides employment for only 4% of the workforce. Sheep raising was formerly the nation's most important economic activity, and there are still some 800,000 sheep. In addition, there are over 50,000 cattle. Few grains are grown, although some can thrive in the climate. Geothermally heated greenhouses are a growing business, producing especially tomatoes, cucumbers and flowers. Although the climate is too harsh for grapes, an increasingly popular (though expensive at $20 a bottle) wine, Kvöldsól (Midnight Sun), made of wild bilberries and crowberries picked in the summer, is made.

Energy and Living Standards

Much of the rest of Iceland's energy needs are derived from two renewable sources: hydroelectric and thermal. Indeed, about 80% of its total energy and all of its electricity comes from such sources. That enables Icelanders to use twice as much electricity per capita as Americans and still not harm the economy or environment. As an island, its electrical power cannot be exported easily. Icelanders have learned to tap the hot lava and waters under their soil. Today, 99% of the home and hot water heating in Greater Reykjavik,

where over half the country's population lives, comes from these sources. Four-fifths of all Icelandic homes are heated geothermally with hot water being piped around towns and villages from nearby bore-holes.

A pleasant byproduct of hydro and geothermal energy is that these are "clean" and "green" sources. Therefore, Iceland is free of the air pollution and urban grime that are produced by fossil fuels. The country has established the goal of eliminating the use of fossil fuels entirely by perfecting hydrogen fuel cells, which produce energy by combining hydrogen with oxygen from the air. This would make Iceland the first nation in the world to derive all of its energy from clean, renewable sources. One pilot program involves three buses powered by such cells into the Reykjavik city transport system.

Industry now employs more people than agriculture and fishing combined. Some of it still processes fish or agricultural products. Machine and building industries are increasing in importance, but the country's almost total lack of wood and metals hampers the operations of such industries.

With about 90% of its energy potential unused, Iceland is well equipped to house energy intensive industries such as aluminum production. The Icelandic Aluminum Company, a wholly owned subsidiary of the Swiss firm Alusuisse, imports ore from abroad and processes it into finished metal. By 1991, aluminum exports constituted about 15% of Iceland's merchandise exports. International competition has not dampened hopes of expanding this industry.

Icelanders are divided. Environmentalists oppose the construction of hydropower to fuel the aluminum smelters,

which require enormous amounts of electricity to operate. For example, to build the Kárahnjúr Dam to block the Jökulsá á Dal River in 2006, 22 square miles of wilderness had to be flooded so that electricity for a new Alcoa Fjardaal smelter could be produced. The emotional issue of how to balance nature and development dominated the 2007 elections. Proponents argue that such economic activity is revitalizing the underpopulated East and providing jobs for 15% of the region's workforce. Polls indicate that a majority of Icelanders support it for that reason. Proponents also point out that Iceland has lots of clean energy and is therefore uniquely able to produce aluminum. To sweeten the pill, the government created the huge Vatnajökull National Park in 2007 to offset the wilderness lost to Kárahnjúr.

An Italian company helped build a $2 billion hydroelectric system and aluminum smelter, completed by 2008. The world's largest aluminum company, Alcoa (American), also built a smelter. This was the largest single private-sector investment in Iceland's history.

Traditionally when fish catches and markets were good, the country experienced booms that encouraged the strong trade unions to demand higher wages. Indeed, Iceland loses far more working days to strikes per 1,000 employees than any other industrialized country in the world. When the economy turns sour, then Icelanders tend to continue living beyond their means. They did not want to give up their relatively high standard of living, which was generally on a par with other Nordic countries. Before financial disaster struck, it had the world's fourth highest per capita GDP ($63,000 in 2007, ahead of the U.S. with $45,600). But since GDP in 2009 declined by almost 10% and the public debt ballooned to about 120% of GDP, Icelanders find themselves considerably poorer. Almost 90% of all homes are owned by those who occupy them. This is perhaps the world's highest percentage of owner-occupied buildings, despite skyrocketing real estate prices, which doubled between 2004 and 2006. However, the economic crisis left many homeowners struggling to hang on to their dwellings. Real estate values plummeted, and many have mortgages denominated in foreign currencies. An estimated fourth of households are said to be on the brink of bankruptcy. Even in the best of times, the maintenance of prosperity is a challenge for a largely barren country of active volcanoes, lava fields and glaciers, which must import almost everything it consumes.

After having experienced the highest inflation rate in Europe (12% in 2009), it abolished the indexing of wages (which tied them to the inflation rate) to help

Author and daughters sitting on the spot in Thingvellir where first Althingi was located.

Iceland

BAILING OUT ICELAND WOULD APPEASE THE WRATH OF THE VOLCANO

NZZ am Sonntag CHAPPATTE

Source: *NZZ am Sonntag*

bring it under control. The continuing volatility of the krona was a major reason why 59% of Icelanders said in a 2003 poll that they favored the adoption of the euro. Tourism grew fast and more than doubled since 1990 to about 350,000 visitors a year by 2005, more than its own population. The collapse of the krona in 2008 stimulated foreign tourism even more. The boom in this sector helps provide some Icelanders with work, while unemployment reached 10% in 2009.

EU Membership and the Euro

In the 1990s interest in full EU membership came alive in all Nordic countries, which heavily depend on trade with Europe. Iceland was always the most wary of the EU, fearing that the sole prop for its economy—fishing—could be endangered. It has a 200-mile marine boundary and manages its fish stocks well. Through EEA Iceland is not isolated from the EU because it enjoys free trade in all things but fish and agriculture. There was growing interest in full EU membership, especially in the business community.

Iceland made a move in the direction of harmony with the EU by deregulating its banking industry to permit more competition; in 1990 its first privately owned bank, Islandbanki, came into existence. Shares in state banks and telecoms have been sold to the private sector. The last two state banks and Iceland Telecom were put up for sale in 2001. The result for a while was that the economy steadily grew. Icelandic

banks, led by the three largest (Glitnir, Kaupthing and Landsbanki), aggressively supported a wave of Icelandic takeovers all over Europe, acquiring companies at an astonishing rate. They overexpanded into Scandinavia and the UK and opened branches in China. Iceland became a friendly place for financiers and was not subject to EU tax-scrutiny. Corporate profits are taxed at only 18% (personal income at 36%), the third lowest in the OECD behind Ireland and Hungary. Some Icelanders were uneasy about the impact such huge economic changes had on the country. One observer argued: "The law of the jungle has been dominating our business life." This fear was justified.

Membership in the EEA provided an important impetus to liberalize the economy and temporarily blunted the debate on actually entering the EU. EEA membership enables Icelanders to live and work across the EU. Support for EU membership grew. Critics point out that Iceland must abide by many EU laws and regulations without having any input into them.

Polls in 2008 showed that 70% favored joining. One of the most convincing arguments in favor was currency stability. This was especially true in 2009, when the kronur was worth about 40% less than in the previous year. No wonder the parliament voted 33 to 28 in July 2009 to begin accession negotiations immediately. One year later after prolonged financial turmoil and banking crisis, 60% opposed EU membership, and only a third favored it. Even 60%

of the business community was against it. Hostility toward what was perceived as an uncaring Europe was focused on the EU. The European Commission's recommendation on February 24, 2010, to begin accession talks failed to change the majority opinion. Opposition parties exploited disputes with EU countries, especially Britain and the Netherlands, to stoke anti-EU sentiment. Icelanders' famous spirit of independence reasserted itself.

Kreppa: the Bottom Falls Out

The economy was ripe for a correction. But the credit crunch stemming from the U.S. and infecting Europe in 2008 triggered a crisis in Iceland even though Icelandic banks had not acquired the kind of mortgage-backed investments that shook up the American and European banking system. The banks did build up an excessive level of foreign debt equivalent to 10 times the tiny country's GDP. This overextension went far beyond the small depositor base at home and was a catastrophe waiting to happen. Standard and Poor reduced its credit rating to junk status, and investor confidence in the country fell sharply.

Since it must import almost everything, it has always had a huge current account deficit (the difference between the import and export of goods and services), that in 2008 amounted to 16% of GDP (down from 26% in 2006). In the spring of 2008 the krona lost almost 30% of its value compared with the euro, and the slide continued in the next year to 40%. Inflation ballooned to 12% in 2009, and the central bank had to raise interest rates to an astonishing 15.5% in order to curb such inflation and shore up the currency. Unemployment stood at 1.5% in 2006, but in 2009 it reached a shocking 9%.

Dangerous recession was in the air. Although Iceland has never defaulted on its debts, the Nordic central banks took the unprecedented step of setting up a 1.5-billion-euro emergency fund for Iceland's central bank to use to save its banks. The government appealed to the banks to rein in their expansion plans, cut back acquisitions and build a stronger deposit base.

In October 2008, the country's wealth engines, the banks, collapsed, and they took the currency down with them. According to the International Monetary Fund (IMF), this was the largest banking failure in history relative to the economy's size. Panic spread. To avoid national bankruptcy, the government groveled abroad and borrowed about $11 billion: $2.1 billion from the IMF and $8 billion more from the Nordic and other countries. This amounts to about $33,000 for each of the island's residents. The government even considered borrowing $4 billion from the Russians, the first nation to offer Iceland help. Said the former prime minister: "When our old friends didn't help us, we had to find new friends."

Icelanders will be increasingly wary of the success of high-flying businessmen and bankers who seem to build up financial empires overnight and then leave the island in financial turmoil. The three main commercial banks—Kaupthing, Glitnir and Landsbanki—had been aggressively buying Scandinavian and British companies, and by 2006 Icelandic businesses employed more than 100,000 people abroad, 70% of them in Britain. They have had to learn to restrain their expansionist impulses to conform more closely with the small domestic economy. The government seized them in October 2008, when they had accumulated more than $60 billion in overseas debt. It negotiated a deal to recapitalize them in July 2009 with an injection of $2.1 billion. They are new banks now. Control of two of them (Islandsbanki and New Kaupthing) was given to creditors while the third, New Landsbanki, was more complicated.

Few Icelanders could believe how far and how fast their country had fallen. Their self-confidence was shattered, and thousands of them went into streets to join the only mass demonstrations to shake the country since the debate about NATO membership in 1949. These brought down Geir Haarde's conservative Independence government, which was blamed for the mess. They became the first leader and

government to lose power as a direct result of the global economic crisis. Haarde and former prime minister and central bank governor, David Oddsson, along with other officials and regulators, were charged in an official April 2010 report with "extreme negligence" in the run-up to the crisis. A summary of the 2,000-page report was handed to the special prosecutor for use in a criminal investigation. A group of actors publicly read every word of the report aloud and around the clock from the stage of the Reykjavik City Theater; it took five days to finish. The chief executive of Kaupthing Bank was arrested in May 2010.

In the fall of 2009 the Sigurardottir government agreed to restructure or write off the $70 billion debt. On December 30 a bare majority (33 to 30) in parliament agreed to pay Britain and the Netherlands about $5.4 billion for the money their governments had reimbursed to their own 400,000 depositors when Kaupthing's online bank, Icesave, went under. This amounted to half the country's annual GDP.

That was the last straw. In January 2010 President Grimsson cast only the second legislative veto in Iceland's history and ordered that the question be submitted to the country's first ever referendum. Critics claimed this huge payment would penalize taxpayers for the recklessness of a private bank and that Icelanders would be saddled with higher taxes and budget cuts for decades in order to pay off the debt. It

is not surprising that in the March 2010 referendum turnout was 63%, and more than 93% of voters rejected the plan. Only 1.6% approved.

This vote was non-binding. But the fact that the prime minister and government had appealed to their countrymen not to vote in the referendum helped sap their authority even further. This was just at a time when Iceland needs strong leadership to push through painful budget cuts. In the meantime, a fourth of households are on the brink of bankruptcy, unemployment is 9%, burglaries have doubled, hospitals and police are downsizing, and almost a third of all adults and half the 18-to-24-year-olds are considering emigrating, according to polls.

Investments and Transport

Foreign investors are still attracted by its huge untapped reserves of hydroelectric and geothermal power. The welfare system remains generous though more modest than elsewhere in the Nordic world. Some reforms are bound to be unpopular, such as requiring contributions to pensions and the prospect of raising the official retirement age from 67 to 70. Bright spots in the economy are immense renewable energy resources, a well-educated skilled work force, a work ethic that makes the 40-hour week almost unheard of, an open and transparent democracy, a predictable legal system, and a convenient mid-Atlantic location.

Iceland has a rather good transportation system for a country of its size compared to population. It has over 7,500 miles (12,343 km.) of roads. Although efforts are being made to pave more roads, about 6,750 miles (10,893 km.) are still dirt. The country has four major and about 50 minor ports and over a hundred usable airfields. Iceland's best-known transportation is a fleet of airplanes that transport passengers over the North Atlantic between Europe and North America. Operating outside of IATA regulations, Icelandair (called Icelandic Airlines until its merger in 1973 with the country's other airline, Loftleidir) flies passengers for bargain prices. Skyrocketing fuel prices and fierce competition from the major commercial airlines and other cut-rate companies temporarily threw Icelandair's financial balance into the red. But it survives. A smaller airline, Eagle, also has some international routes.

CULTURE

Icelanders are proud of their Nordic heritage and in many respects are closer to their Viking forebears than any of the other Nordic countries. Their language (which has given the world such words as

The spectacular waterfall Godafoss in northern Iceland

Iceland

Kristján Jóhannsson

"saga" and "geyser") is so close to Old Norse that Icelanders can read the 13th- and 14th-century sagas in their original form. It was Icelanders who carried out the most dangerous Viking sea voyages of all, those through Greenland and beyond to Newfoundland and Labrador. That heritage, combined with 680 years of rule by distant kings and their own isolation and hardships, has made Icelanders fiercely protective of their independence and their cultural purity. An American ambassador to the country, Marshall Brement, who translated and published Icelandic poetry, characterized Icelanders as "inward-looking, perhaps introverted. But above all, they are fiercely devoted to the preservation of their language and culture."

They create their own words for modern things: *simi* (telephone); *ratsjá* (radar); *rafmagn* (electricity); *tolva* (computer). The latter is taken from two words meaning number (*tol*) and female soothsayer (*volva*). There are no dialects in Icelandic. Most of the Nordic literature of the Middle Ages, and all of it, which is truly world class, came from Iceland. Much of our information about the Viking Age and later centuries in Scandinavia itself comes from those Icelandic writings. The people are fascinated with their own past, and there is scarcely a social conversation that does not touch on their history or genealogy. In fact, many families can trace their family tree back almost 30 generations; few peoples in the world are able to give such a complete picture of their heritage. The fact that two-thirds of all births in Iceland are now out of wedlock may make this more difficult in the future.

The vehicle for preserving their national identity and past is their literature, especially their sagas, which tell stories of their gods, heroes and ancestors. The 40-odd Icelandic sagas are a towering mixture of history, fiction, genealogy and encyclopedia that are shrouded in mystery. While it is known that they were produced in 13th- and 14th-century Iceland, it is not known who wrote them. Ex-President Vigdís, a former language teacher, asserted, "if we lose this identity, which is the language, a great treasure will be lost. We don't have anything from the past except the word." This is why there was such an outpouring of joy in 1966 when the Danish decided to return the body of ancient writings collected by the Icelandic professor, Arni Magnusson (1663–1730). The Danish decision prompted hundreds of Icelanders to assemble before the Danish Embassy in order to praise Denmark and at the same time to sing patriotic songs. When the writings arrived, the inhabitants streamed into the streets to celebrate.

After the sagas, Icelandic literature declined, not to revive until the 19th century. In the 19th and 20th centuries there appeared a long line of fine poets and novelists. In 1955 an Icelander, Halldór Laxness, won the Nobel Prize for chronicling the life of modern Iceland. Among his most important works is *Independent People*, written in 1946. In 2005 Arnaldur Indridason's *Silence of the Grave* won the British Crime Writers' Association Gold Dagger award.

Iceland is the home of world-renowned tenor Kristján Jóhannsson, who has performed in every major opera house including Italy's La Scala, New York's Metropolitan Opera, the Vienna State Opera, the Royal Opera House, and Covent Garden. Icelanders are avid readers. They publish more books per capita than any other country, and three daily newspapers serve only 244,000 people. The largest, a morning edition called *Morgunbladid*, has a circulation of more than 40,000. The other two are *Frettabladid* and *DV*. Three-fourths of the newspapers distributed daily are now free.

Iceland occasionally produces internationally acclaimed films such as "When the Raven Flies" by the Icelandic director Hrafn Gunnlaugsson. This brutally authentic Viking film about violence and revenge captures both the mood of the Norsemen and bleak beauty of the Icelandic landscape. An international celebrity, whom some tourist guidebooks call the most famous Icelander since Leif Ericson, is the pop star Bjork Gudmundsdottir. She won the best actress award at the Cannes film festival in 2000 for her role as a near-blind factory worker in the film "Dancer in the Dark."

The country has no daytime TV. It has a state-run radio station. It also has a national television network (RUV), which aims to protect the national culture through higher Icelandic content. It charges a monthly fee that includes radio. It does not broadcast on Thursdays. The reason given is that this weekly blackout encourages more reading, chess-playing and spending time with the family. Network employees admit that the tradition also is designed to give them a day off each week. A live broadcast of President Reagan's arrival in October 1986 was the first time in two decades that Icelanders could watch TV on a Thursday evening.

Private radio and television stations are now permitted. A private TV network, the Icelandic Broadcasting Corporation (IBC), maintains two commercial channels that, for a monthly fee of 3,000 krona (about $30), compete with the state-backed Channel 1, which some critics call dull. They have at least one advantage: they broadcast on Thursdays. So does BSkyB, a satellite TV service beamed from London. It has no license to broadcast to Iceland, use of its output is therefore piracy. But by installing a satellite dish, Icelanders can receive its multi-channel offering of entertainment, news, films and sports. With hefty monthly fees of $75 to receive RUV and IBC, it is hardly surprising that many Icelanders choose to tune into Sky for free.

The Danes brought Lutheranism to the island, and the church is the official one. Ninety-five percent of the people profess to be Lutherans, although few attend church regularly. The state supports it, and the *Althing* must approve any change in its organization. There is religious freedom, and other churches are active in the major towns.

Education is compulsory between the ages of seven to sixteen and most pupils continue on. All students learn English and Danish. The University of Iceland, with 4,000 students, provides all of the higher education on the island, and includes departments or schools of law, medicine, engineering, science, theology, philosophy and economics; 8,000 study abroad each year, with America the most popular destination. Given the bitter winters, it is remarkable that 90% return, keeping Iceland dynamic, modern and open to new ideas. The country's literacy rate is 99%.

Special insurance is mandatory and covers old age, disability, maternity, sickness and unemployment benefits. Some health costs are, however, paid by the individual. There is one physician for every 750 inhabitants. In 1996 Dutch sociologists at Erasmus University conducted a study to determine which European people live the longest and happiest lives. They concluded that Icelanders top the list.

Iceland has Europe's highest birth rate after Albania (2.0 children per woman) despite the fact that it also has the developed world's highest rate of female employment. The nation is experiencing a baby boom since the onset of the financial crisis of 2009. One theory is that with unemployment at 9%, couples have more time to produce "Kreppa babies." However, marriages are down by about 50%, as hard-pressed couples lack the funds to get married. Nevertheless, the record-setting bearing of children is praised as a sign of this hardy nation's optimism for the future.

Its population is so small and homogeneous, and such complete medical and family records have been maintained since the First World War, that it decided in 1999 to become the first country in the world to permit this information to be combined into a single linked computerized database. The aim was to create a genetic inventory that traces the likely chromosomal sites of the genes for a number of inherited diseases. A biotechnology company, deCode Genetics, was set up to search these linked databases for clues into the nature of diseases. Considerable controversy preceded the decision, but 58% of Icelanders were in favor of the database in 1998.

By 2004 the project was in trouble because of concerns that it infringed on the privacy rights of Icelanders even though 20,000 people chose to opt out. But 140,000 had already offered family records and blood samples, enough to keep the project going. Another problem was that the company never turned a profit. When the devastating financial crisis hit the country in 2008-9, the company went quickly through $676 million and was bankrupt by 2010 even though its database made it one of the world's leading players in biotechnology. It is emerging from bankruptcy, but it remains to be seen if it will develop a feasible business model.

FUTURE

Iceland celebrated its 60th year of independence from Denmark on June 17, 2004. Its wariness toward EU membership has reappeared because of the crushing debt obligations to European countries. Icelanders' famous spirit of independence has reasserted itself, and a solid majority now opposes membership.

The nation still has much going for it. In 2006 the UN ranked it first in the world (tied with Norway) for quality of life. In 2005 the World Economic Forum placed it seventh in the world for economic competitiveness. A new Global Peace Index was introduced in 2008 to test countries against 24 "peacefulness" criteria, including the crime rate and potential for terrorism within its borders; Iceland was ranked first in the world. Also in 2010 researchers at Yale and Columbia Universities ranked it first in the world in terms of environmental performance, with the U.S. number 61. It was praised for its renewable energy sources and its green efforts. But the glory days are at an end for the time being. Of concern to citizens in Atlantic countries, volcano activity in this young geological island can be expected to continue for at least four decades.

The EU alone would not have saved it from the collapse it experienced. But it might have helped to have had the euro and to have been able to call on Brussels for aid rather than crawling to the IMF. Its currency lost 85% of its value against the euro. It did not default on its debt and is living with inflation and interest rates over 12%; its taxes are ready to soar.

Social Democratic Prime Minister Sigurdardottir has an uphill struggle to convince many parliamentarians and the general populace that EU membership will not destroy their way of life and the foundation of their economy. One Icelandic sociologist put it this way: "Many people would not be able to tolerate a minister in Brussels deciding how many pounds of cod a fisherman was allowed to catch each year." Many EU laws already apply to Iceland, but it is things like fishing and how to deal with crushing debt that will be the challenge.

Sigurdardottir got high marks after her first half year in office: she steadied the country's wavering self-confidence and gently put an end to the first street demonstrations in six decades. However, the passionate debate on reimbursing Britain and the Netherlands $5.4 billion met with overwhelming public opposition. This was expressed in the March 2010 referendum, in which 93% of voters ignored the government's appeals. This has sapped the authority of the prime minister, just at a time that Iceland desperately needs strong leadership.

The hardy optimist can always find some good news among the bad. The average age in Iceland is only 37, the birth rate is among the highest in the developed world and rising, the workforce is highly educated and trained, and the pension funds, though battered, are probably safe in the long run. Finally there are abundant natural resources. But one Icelandic ambassador had to admit: "Young families are threatened with losing their houses, and elderly people their pensions. This is catastrophic."

Demonstrators protesting Iceland's financial collapse, 2009.

The Republic of Finland

Area: 130,119 sq. mi. (338,144 sq. km., about the size of Washington state).

Population: 5.3 million (2009).

Capital City: Helsinki (Pop. 500,000, estimated).

Climate: Temperate in the south, but rapidly ascending into Arctic temperatures in the northern areas.

Neighboring Countries: Russia (east); Norway (north); Sweden (west).

Official Languages: Finnish (92%), Swedish (5.5%).

Ethnic Background: Finn 92%, Swede 5.5%, Gypsy .12%, Sami .11%

Principal Religion: Evangelical Church of Finland (Lutheran, the official religion, 84%); Orthodox Church of Finland (1%), other and nonreligious 15%

Main Exports: High technology (especially electronics) 26%, paper and pulp products 19%, machinery and metal products 19%, iron and steel, timber, ships, clothing and footwear.

Main Imports: Foodstuffs, petroleum, chemicals, autos, textile yarns, fabrics.

Major Trading Customers: EU (56.8% of exports and 64.1% of imports), Germany (10.9% of exports and 16% of imports), Sweden (10.7% of exports and 13.8% of imports), Russia (10.2% of exports and 13.7% of imports), UK (5.8% of exports and 5% of imports), U.S. (6.4% of exports and 4.2% of imports), Netherlands (5.6% of exports and 6.8% of imports), China (5.3% of imports).

Currency: euro

National Day: December 6 (1917), Independence Day.

Chief of State: Tarja Halonen, President (since March 2000).

Head of Government: Mari Kiviniemi, Prime Minister (since June 2010).

National Flag: White field crossed horizontally, and then vertically by bright blue stripes, the latter being off center, closer to the pole.

In the ancient past, Finland was regarded as a cold land of legendary witchcraft, far off Europe's beaten path. It was very thinly populated by a silent and complicated people, who spoke an extremely baffling language when they chose to speak at all. Now the country is dynamic and forward-looking and is very much in the mainstream of both Western and Eastern Europe.

With a land area about the size of Italy, but with less than one-tenth of the population, the Finns call their rugged and strikingly beautiful country the "land of lakes and marshes." Indeed, with 60,000 lakes, one-tenth of the country is under water. But outsiders would probably say "the land of forests, lakes and marshes." The ever-present forests provide the country with its most valuable natural re-

Finland

source. They cover 70% of the surface area and are actually growing, not shrinking. Only Russia and Sweden have larger forested areas in Europe. An additional 22% is unforested peat land or marsh. Only 12% of the land area is used for cultivation, pasture and urban settlement. Finland has few mountains.

This country is at the head of the Baltic Sea in the northeastern corner of Western Europe and is the northernmost of the world's industrialized countries. Except for Norway's North Cape, which touches Finland, the country extends farther north than any other mainland area of Europe. In fact, one-third is north of the Arctic Circle. It also extends farther east than any other Western European country and shares an 800-mile (1,280 km.) border with Russia. On the south it faces the Gulf of Finland with Estonia beyond, and on the west are the Gulf of Bothnia and Sweden. With 130,000 square miles, Finland is the seventh largest country in Europe, with only Russia, Ukraine, France, Spain, Sweden, and Germany being larger. There are some 20,000 coastal islands, most of which are in the southwestern archipelago, merging into the Åland Islands in the west. Finland extends about 700 miles (1,120 km.) from north to south and 400 miles (640 km. east to west).

Glaciers miles thick completely covered Finland during the great ice ages. That is one explanation why the country is relatively flat with thousands of lakes filling the low spots. It also partly explains why much of the land, still recovering after the release 10,000 years ago from the unimaginable weight of the ice, is rising about one foot every 50 years. Where the Baltic is shallow, that uplift movement is giving Finland more land at the expense of the sea. The glaciers are the reason that the most common land type is moraine, a mixture of rocks and soil transported from other locations by the ice.

Finland has three major topographic regions, based on altitude. The uplands north of the Arctic Circle average 600 feet to 1,000 feet (183–305 meters) above sea level and include all the high points in Finland, the highest being 4,357 feet (1,328 meters). The coastal plain is less than 300 feet (91 meters) above sea level and extends inland from the Baltic 20 to 60 miles (32 to 96 km.) The lake district fills the remainder of the country south of the Arctic Circle and is intermediate in altitude. The entire country averages about 500 feet (152 meters) in altitude, only half of the average for Europe as a whole.

Although Finland lies between 60° and 70° north latitude, it has a much milder climate than most countries so far north. The Gulf Stream and the prevailing winds are welcome benefactors for the Finns,

giving them a climatic advantage over southern Greenland, Canada's Northwest Territories and most of Siberia, which lie in the same latitudes, but which have much more severe weather. A better comparison is Alaska, also between 60° and 70° North, and partly favored by warming ocean currents. The length of the day varies greatly, even in the south, which has six hours of sunlight daily in December and 19 hours in June. In northern Lapland, however, the sun never sets for 73 days in summer and never rises for 51 days in winter.

HISTORY

The Early Periods

When the Indo-European tribes pushed into the Baltic area about 4000 B.C. they found people already there who are believed to be related to the present-day Finns. These early inhabitants probably had moved into the area soon after the continental ice sheet began to melt about 12,000 years ago. As the Indo-Europeans moved up the shores of the Baltic Sea, they pushed some Finns ahead of them. About 2000 B.C. and again at the beginning of the Christian era, waves of immigrants came to Finland from across the water to the south and land to the southeast and gradually pushed the Lapps, who had arrived earlier, into the northern portions of the country. All of these early Finnish tribes moved west from north and central Russia. Finnish is related to Estonian and to the languages of isolated parts of northern Russia. It is also distantly related to modern Hungarian.

Scandinavian influence in Finland began during the era of great migrations,

about 400 A.D., and continues to the present. Christian missionaries first entered southwest Finland in the 10th century, and the Catholicized Finnish aristocracy developed close links with Poland. The king of Sweden and the bishop of Uppsala made a crusade into Finland 200 years later, establishing a foothold in the southwest, which was expanded in the following centuries to include all the northern shore of the Gulf of Finland. Swedes colonized the southwestern and southern coastal areas and the Åland islands, areas where Swedish language and culture is still very strong. The Swedes slowly annexed the remainder of Finland and ruled it as a Swedish province, though not as a colony, until 1808.

Following a successful Russian invasion, Finland was declared an autonomous Grand Duchy of Imperial Russia, a status that continued until 1917. During the 19th century Finns were permitted to continue to practice the rudimentary representative government the Swedes had created. This early period of Russian rule saw very little effort at Russification. It actually gave the Finns a chance to overcome the heavy Swedish cultural and lingual influence and to assert their Finnishness, while retaining those elements of Scandinavian traditions and values, such as the structure of society and the judicial system, which Finns found valuable. Not until the mid-19th century did the educated classes and the country's major newspapers begin to use the Finnish language. But in 1899 a Russification campaign began. The Finns were no longer permitted to practice the Swedish form of government, and Finland was required to provide troops for the Russian army. This

A typical countryside panorama

99

Finland

provoked Finnish resistance to Russian rule, and in 1905 a general strike paralyzed the country.

In 1906 the Russian government, badly shaken by an unsuccessful revolution, agreed to a Parliament Act for Finland, providing for Finland's system of proportional representation voting and a single-chamber assembly. At the same time, Finnish women became the first in Europe to be permitted to vote. When the tsar renounced these concessions in 1910, Finns again mounted determined resistance. Such opposition to Russian domination made it logical after the outbreak of World War I in 1914 for Finnish nationalists to cooperate with the most powerful country opposed to Russia, namely Germany.

A Nation is Born

The Russian Revolution occurred in early 1917. When Lenin's Bolsheviks overthrew the Kerensky government in November 1917, the majority of Finns demanded full independence, and the Finnish parliament declared it on December 6, 1917. But the radical left was determined to unleash a revolution in order to establish a socialist state. Known at the time as "Reds," they seized Helsinki and southern Finland in early 1918, causing the parliament to move north to Vaasa.

Thus, Finland's independence was followed almost immediately by a civil war. Led by the former Finnish general in the tsarist army, Gustav Mannerheim, Finnish government forces, known as "Whites," won a decisive victory over the Reds at Tampere early in April. Mannerheim's forces were later supported by a German division that landed on the southern coast and recaptured Helsinki early in the month. The rebellion was thus put to an end; Finnish society was able to remain western, not Soviet, but the costs of Finland's struggle for independence were enormous. Not only were 20,000 Finns killed, but the nation was split into two hostile halves. Not until the Russians invaded the country two decades later was this wound healed.

In the struggle between monarchists and republicans, the former won a temporary victory. Two weeks before the end of World War I the Finns chose a German to be their king, but the defeat of Germany made such a monarchy utterly unrealistic. Therefore, Finland adopted a democratic and republican constitution in 1919 that is still in effect.

Finland joined the League of Nations in December 1920. As the power of the League began to deteriorate in the 1930s, Finland unsuccessfully attempted to ally itself with Sweden and other Scandinavian countries. Therefore, when the Soviet Union attacked Finland in November

General Mannerheim

1939, the Finns had no friends who would or could help.

The Red Army attacked on the ground in the east and southeast and by amphibious assaults across the Gulf of Finland. It threw almost one million men into the attack, who were opposed by about 300,000 white-clad Finns, 80% of whom were reservists. The Finns, regardless of their numerical inferiority, put up a fierce and effective defense, often fighting on skis. All the amphibious assaults were repulsed as was the main Russian attack against the Finnish fortifications on the Karelian Isthmus.

Russian drives into Finland from the east proved to be disastrous. They came expecting an easy victory and were pitifully ill-prepared. They were equipped neither with field tents nor with portable woodstoves. Finnish troops, attired in warm white winter clothing, often on skis and familiar with the terrain and cold, cut the Russian columns into small pieces and destroyed them. The Russians were scarcely able to cope with the Finnish "invisible wall"—white-clad soldiers who appeared suddenly, fought fiercely and then disappeared in the landscape of drifting snow. The Battle of Suomussalmi was the most dramatic example, with two Finnish divisions completely destroying two enemy ones, resulting in 27,500 Russians killed or frozen to death and 1,300 captured. The Finns lost only 900 men.

The British government sent two air squadrons and allowed its soldiers to leave its army to fight for Finland. As described in a well-known book in Finland, *The Help That Never Arrived*, Britain and France were planning a large-scale mili-

tary intervention when a Soviet breakthrough induced the Finns to make peace. The Soviet Union's overwhelming manpower eventually proved too much for the brave but outnumbered Finns. After three months they accepted the peace terms offered by the Soviets, which at the time were cooperating with Germany and which were reportedly nervous that the British might come to the aid of Finland via Norway and Sweden. In the end, Finland had sustained 25,000 killed and 43,000 wounded, while Soviet casualties were eight to ten times as high.

One of the principal costs of the Winter War was the loss of most of the Karelia. The entire southeastern corner of Finland, containing 10% of the country's territory and people, went to the Russians in the peace settlement. Much of the Karelian population had to be resettled in the West. A further consequence of the war was that the Germans and many others concluded that the Red Army would be a pushover in any future conflict. This fatal misperception enticed the greedy Hitler to attack the Soviet Union only two years later.

When they did attack in mid-1941, Finland, desiring to regain the territory it had so recently lost, went to war on Germany's side. The Finns tried to keep relatively independent of Germany, however, and did maintain peaceful relations with the U.S. throughout the war. They also refused to participate in the siege of Leningrad and to cut the rail lines linking the vital north Russian port of Murmansk and Moscow. It did take the opportunity to reconquer its lost territories and to seize Eastern Karelia, which had always belonged to Russia, although it was populated by Finns. Sensing the way the wind was blowing after the crushing German defeat at Stalingrad, the Finns began to explore ways to a separate peace in 1943, but they were not permitted to extricate themselves from the war so easily.

Things were, on the whole, very quiet on the Finnish front from late 1941 until the allied landings along the coast of France in June 1944. At that time, the Soviet Union decided to launch another attack on Finland through the Karelian Isthmus. It directed some of the most concentrated artillery fire in history toward the Finnish positions, and the Finnish front cracked very quickly. It rapidly became clear that Finland could not withstand this furious Soviet onslaught, so it again sought material German help. Together, the two nations' forces brought the Soviet attack to a standstill.

However, General Mannerheim, who became president in the late summer of 1944, sued for peace with the Soviet Union. The latter placed very hard conditions on Finland. The most immediate demand was for Finns to expel the 220,000 German soldiers who had been stationed in northern Finland. The Germans nevertheless put up very stiff-necked resistance—during their retreat, the Germans destroyed everything in their path, leaving Finns the postwar task of reconstructing the northern part of their country.

The September 1944 treaty with the Soviets forced it to accept the loss of the same areas as in 1940, and almost 400,000 Finnish refugees were set in motion once again. Further, Finland had to relinquish Petsamo and to allow the Soviet Union to establish a naval base for 50 years on the Porkkala Peninsula, immediately southwest of Helsinki. It had to pay the Soviets heavy reparations (ultimately almost $445 million), which by 1952 it had paid in full. Finally, the Finns were required to reduce their army to its peacetime level within two and one-half months.

The strains of war had helped the Finnish people to draw together and to set aside some of the social and lingual differences that had continued to divide them since independence. Finland was fortunate in that it had been the only belligerent country in continental Europe that was not occupied during the war. But the Finns paid a very high price: about 2.2% of their population had been killed in action, and an equal number had been permanently maimed. They lost 12.5% of their territory and were forced to resettle more than 400,000 refugees, 14% of their population.

Finally, they found themselves in a radically changed strategic situation. Germany had been totally defeated. The Soviet Union, with an 800-mile Finnish border, had emerged as the most powerful country in Europe and virtually the only great power in the Baltic area. Soviet troops had important base rights on Finnish territory within a few miles of Helsinki. Looking south, the Finns saw how the Soviet Union had simply annexed the Baltic states of Estonia, Latvia and Lithuania in the course of the war. They were very aware that Finland was the only lost part of the pre-1914 Russian Empire that had not been reabsorbed by a revived Soviet Russia. There was worse: Finland realized that there was not a single country in the world that would risk a war with the Soviets to keep Finland independent. What should a small, western-oriented country do in such a situation in order to maintain its national independence and its right to determine it own domestic political and economic order?

A Balancing Act

The Finns have always been noted for a quality known in Finnish as "*sisu*," variously translated as perseverance, tenacity, steadfastness, diligence, courage, or simply "guts." This was a quality necessary for a people that always had to struggle to survive in a harsh natural environment. At the same time, they are a very realistic people whose main political problem since World War II has been one of foreign policy. Like other small countries that share borders with big powers, Finland did and now does have various options. It could disregard the security interests of its powerful neighbor and pay the price for that. Or it could recognize those security interests and see how it could adjust its policies to them without sacrificing its own national sovereignty. More and more Finns realized that the latter option was the only realistic one, and their leaders have long established the country's foreign policy on that foundation.

In order not to irritate the Soviet Union after World War II, Finland was forced to turn down all offers of Marshall Plan assistance from the United States. Moscow had suspiciously viewed such aid as a trick designed to undercut its influence and to establish an American predominance over Europe. Therefore, it forbade all of its newly developed client states in Eastern Europe from accepting this aid. Finland's subsequent economic recovery and prosperity and the fact that it was the only European country fully to repay its war debts from both world wars are all the more astonishing when one remembers that it received no economic aid from the U.S.

A Finnish peace treaty with the Soviet Union came into force in 1947 that placed maximum limits on Finland's armed forces. This was followed in 1948 by a more important step, the signing of a Treaty of Friendship, Cooperation and Mutual Assistance with its powerful neighbor. The Soviets had already entered into such treaties with the satellite states of Eastern Europe, and so when it was announced in February 1948 that the Soviet Union had also invited Finland to work out a mutual assistance pact, many Finns thought that the end of their independence was near.

Yet Finnish leaders acted quickly and skillfully. They politely rejected Stalin's offer to sign a treaty identical to the ones signed with Hungary and Romania, countries that had fought against the Soviets during the war. Instead, Finnish leaders drafted their own treaty, tailored to their own particular needs and circumstances. They drew on earlier proposals that the Russians had made to Finland in 1938 and 1939. Perhaps justifiably suspecting foul play in 1939, the Finns had rejected the Soviet proposals, and the Winter War had resulted.

The Soviet-Finnish Treaty

The Treaty of 1948 obligated Finland to defend itself in the case of an attack "with the help, if necessary, of the Soviet Union or together with the Soviet Union." Such "assistance" would "be supplied as mutually agreed between the Parties." Article 2 adds that both countries "will consult together in case there is found to be a threat of the military aggression referred to in Article 1."

The decisive part of the treaty, as far as the Finns are concerned, is the preamble in which "Finland's desire to remain outside the conflicting interests of the Great Powers" is recognized. This granted Finland a privilege not extended to the Soviet Union's Eastern European satellites: the right to be neutral. It is certainly true that the Russians only chose to use this word in reference to Finland in 1970 and, indeed, until the Soviet Union had withdrawn its troops from the Porkkala Peninsula in 1956, one could hardly speak of genuine neutrality. In large part, this Soviet decision stemmed from its buildup of adequate naval facilities on its own soil. It stemmed also from the changed strategic situation, which moved critical points from the waters south of Finland toward the Baltic area closer to Denmark and the straits leading to the North Sea, as well as toward the northern Norwegian and Bering Seas.

The Finns' basic assumption was that the Soviet Union did not want to conquer the entire world, but that its policy was basically defensive and essentially oriented toward stability along its borders. Without question, the Soviets had in Finland a more stable and less threatening

Finland

Finnish soldiers—the "invisible wall"

neighbor than anywhere along the entire huge Soviet border in Europe or Asia. From the standpoint of the Russians' self-interest, the treaty was also advantageous in that direct Soviet control of Finland, which no country in the world could prevent, would undoubtedly cause the neutral but extremely well-armed Sweden to join NATO and would eliminate Norway's policy of restricting NATO activity on its soil. Such an unpleasant event would immensely strengthen an enemy alliance by moving NATO several hundred miles closer to the Soviet Union and by strengthening the NATO presence in the Baltic Sea. Thus, like all good and lasting treaties, the 1948 one rested on a firm foundation of mutual interest.

For this reason, President Koivisto traveled to Moscow in 1983 to renew the treaty for another 20 years. It was not scheduled to expire until 1990, but the early renewal was an expression of the desire for continuity despite leadership changes in both countries. Immediately following the failure of the Soviet coup in August 1991, the Finns decided to renegotiate the treaty. Esko Aho was the first Finnish leader to question it. His government did not want it and the neutrality it imposes to be obstacles to entry into the EU, which occurred in 1995.

In 1990 Finland unilaterally abandoned clauses of the treaty that limited the size of its military forces and relations with Germany. In 1992 Finland and Russia replaced the 1948 treaty altogether and forged independent Russia's first political treaty with a Western country. Both nations committed themselves to respect the other's borders, to protect the other's citizens on their territories, and to renounce the use of force against each other. The treaty is valid for 10 years and renewable for five-year periods unless annulled by either country.

Neutrality and Foreign Policy

Finland's foreign policy, which did not enjoy a widespread consensus even within the country until a generation had passed after World War II, depended upon almost constant Finnish reassurances to the Russians that it would never again present a threat to their security. J.K. Paasikivi, Finland's president from 1946 to 1956, devoted almost his entire effort to eradicating traditional anti-Russian views within Finland, lest they place Finland's security in danger. This policy, known as the "Paasikivi line" was reinforced and expanded by his successor, Urho Kekkonen. The "Kekkonen line" was based upon the realization that the worse East-West tensions are, the greater the ominous prospect that Finland would be obligated to support the Soviet Union. Therefore, Finland took a very active role in reducing such tensions.

For instance, it hosted the initial Strategic Arms Limitation Talks (SALT) between the U.S. and the Soviet Union that resulted in a milestone agreement in 1972. Further, it actively organized, promoted and hosted the Helsinki Conference on Security and Cooperation in Europe in 1975, which was attended by virtually all the highest political leaders in Europe. The "Helsinki Agreements" were a central element in all superpower and European dialogues.

Some observers in the West distrusted Finland's policy of bending over backward not to irritate the Soviet Union. In the late 1960s, the term "Finlandization" entered the international political vocabulary to refer to a condition in which a country is so frightened by Soviet power that it is no longer able to control its own foreign policy. It implied a loss of sovereignty and a kind of remote control of a country from Moscow. Finland's example was often presented as a warning to other Western European nations, although the Finns never pretended that the relationship they maintained with the Soviet Union should be adopted by other nations. "Finlandization" was viewed as an ideal solution for Eastern European countries, since the Soviet Union decided in 1989 to permit democratic revolutions there. During a highly symbolic visit to Helsinki in 1989, Gorbachev praised Finnish neutrality, stating that "for me, Soviet-Finnish relations are a model for relations between a big country and a little one." The word "Finlandization" now sounds better.

Neutrality was a way of saying no to military cooperation with the Soviet Union. The rationale for this disappeared with the Soviet collapse. Finland's foreign policy is undergoing significant change, and it now has options. It no longer defines its approach in terms of neutrality, but of nonalignment, since it is firmly anchored in the Western family of nations. It declines to enter NATO, a position supported by half of Finns, even though in 1994 it joined the Partnership for Peace. It believes that the kind of nonalignment is best for Nordic regional security that is backed up by growing cooperation with NATO, by a credible national defense, and by implicit collective security provided by the EU. Unlike Denmark it is willing to participate in a common EU defense arrangement, and a blueprint for this was adopted at the EU summit meeting in Helsinki in December 1999.

Earlier Relations with the USSR

Finns bristled with anger when they heard the expression "Finlandization." The term implies indirect criticism of their earlier foreign policy. It was normally used by people who lacked deep knowledge of Finland and its history, and who were referring to political situations that had nothing to do with Finland itself.

The Finns practiced careful self-censorship toward unpleasant actions of the Soviet Union. Finnish newspapers were expected to be discreet and wholly accurate when criticizing the Soviet Union and such criticism could never be sensationalized. As one Finnish historian wrote, "The Finns deny themselves the luxury of making emotionally satisfying gestures." Another noted, "If we bow West, we present our bad sides to the East. We just can't afford to do that." Where self-censorship was practiced, former President Kekkonen openly appealed to the press to show "responsibility."

In 1986 a case of censorship involved a Finnish film entitled *Born American*, which depicts the imprisonment and harsh treatment of three Americans who cross the Soviet border. The Finnish government's response was to ban it because of its hostile portrayal of the Soviet Union. Such censorship did not determine Finns' personal attitudes toward their powerful neighbor. Opinion surveys in 1987 among high school pupils indicated that the USSR was viewed as an Orwellian society with no freedom and miserable living standards. However, two-thirds believed that the Soviet Union was not a threat to peace.

Finland's response to the Soviet Union's invasion of Afghanistan in 1979 was an example of restraint. This brutal venture was a severe shock to the Finns, especially since Moscow had often referred in official declarations to Finland and Afghanistan as "neighboring, non-aligned" countries with which it could entertain good relations. Although Finnish leaders publicly called on the Soviet Union kindly to withdraw its forces from Afghanistan, Finland, unlike most other nations of the world, abstained from condemning the invasion by vote in the United Nations. Further, in the aftermath of the Soviet Union's shooting down of a South Korean passenger jet with hundreds of persons aboard in mid-1983, the Koivisto government appealed to Finnish ground crews not to join an international boycott of flights in and out of the USSR. Finland avoided taking a stand whenever the interests of the great powers, including the United States, were in conflict. Thus, unlike some of the U.S. allies, Finland almost never criticized American foreign policy in public.

Finland is always extremely sensitive to any development in Northern Europe that might provoke a Russian reaction toward it. Finnish tempers flared in the spring of 1986 when the Soviet Union waited three days to inform the Finns officially about the Chernobyl nuclear disaster. Soviet leaders subsequently reached an agreement that such information would be exchanged immediately.

While Western leaders could understand Finnish concerns in these matters, they had greater difficulty understanding Kekkonen's respectful allusions to Lenin, who had lived in Finland, had expressed sympathy and friendship toward the country and had been the first leader to recognize Finland's independence. His visit to Lenin's birthplace and his willingness to stand with communist dignitaries on top of the Lenin Mausoleum in Moscow on the occasion of the 50th and 60th anniversaries of the Bolshevik Revolution were puzzling. After the failed August 1991 coup in the USSR, Tampere's Lenin Museum, which is independent of the Finnish government, offered to take Lenin's embalmed body if it were forced out of its Red Square Mausoleum. The museum's director said: "We always gave Lenin a hiding place when times were difficult in Russia."

Western observers asked why the Finns had constantly to repeat their loyalty to their treaty with the Soviet Union. A former Finnish foreign minister explained that such monotonous repetitions are like declarations of love in marriage: "the latter have no news value either, but their omission can give the partner cause for unwarranted suspicion." In the Koivisto era this tedious liturgy of assurances to the Soviet Union was heard less often, but Finns still genuinely accepted the "Kekkonen line." True consensus had replaced repetition. The benefit of Finland's good relations with both superpowers was shown in 1990, when Mikhail Gorbachev, worried about the Baltic states' drive for independence, asked Koivisto to help. Koivisto informed President George Bush of the former Soviet leader's concerns.

The turbulent events in the former Soviet Union in the 1990s created heightened anxiety in Finland, whose leaders feared that the gigantic multi-national neighbor might head inexorably toward dissolution and catastrophe. Such a prospect fills most Finns with horror. It could drive hundreds of thousands of desperate and starved Russians across the 1,200-kilometer border with Finland.

Finnish uneasiness was heightened by the 1993 Russian parliamentary election campaign, in which ultranationalist candidate Vladimir Zhirinovsky spoke of reincorporating Finland into a new Russian empire and banishing Helsinki's Finnish residents to Lapland so that Russians could move into their apartments. In January 1994, the Russian ambassador in Helsinki sent a note to the Finnish Foreign Ministry complaining that the existence of two right-wing groups violated the 1947 Treaty of Paris, which bans fascist activity in Finland. Finns regard this treaty as obsolete and were incensed that Russian leaders would try to influence Finland's presidential election in this crude way.

Nevertheless, with Russian nationalism on the rise and with thousands of Russian troops deployed in the region of St. Petersburg, Finns want to avoid upsetting their giant neighbor. This is why President Martti Ahtisaari warned in 1995 against an eastward expansion of NATO, instead recommending opening the EU to Central and Eastern European membership. As the only EU state sharing a land border with Russia, Finland has a special interest in promoting what it calls a "northern dimension" of deeper cooperation with Russia. The idea is to assist Russia to settle down and prosper in the region with sympathetic and helpful Nordic states. When Finland assumed the rotating EU presidency in July 1999 it made improvement of relations with Russia one of its main themes. But in 1999 Finland's foreign minister, Tarja Halonen (who became president in 2000), openly criticized Russia's brutal military policies in the Caucuses, particularly in Chechnya and Ingushetia.

Worries about Russia increasingly directed Finns' attention toward Western Europe, especially the EU. Many fear being isolated in a rapidly changing world. As former Conservative Party leader, Ilkka Suominen, asked, "If the world changes from confrontation to more cooperation, then where does neutrality lie?" The government applied in 1992 for entry into the EU. In October 1994, 57% of the voters accepted their country's entry into the EU. This historic event took what had been a Western European bloc right up to the gates of Russia. Finland's Swedish-speaking Åland Islanders, who enjoy a self-governing status, initially voted not to follow Finland into the EU, but they changed their minds in 1994 and voted to go along with the rest of the Finns. Finland is the Nordic area's biggest enthusiast for the EU and is proud to be the first to adopt the euro.

Defense

Remembering that the Western democracies had left it to fight alone against the Soviet Union, the Finns try to maintain sufficient military preparedness in order to be able to cope with any potential aggressors. Its military doctrine is based on self-reliance and territorial defense. It aims to mobilize at short notice a well-equipped force of a half million soldiers who can retain control of strategically important areas, delay and wear down an attacker until it can concentrate the necessary force to defeat him in areas of Finland's own choosing.

Finland has compulsory military service for all males over 18 years; about 90% of all men serve. If males prefer to perform civilian service, they may do so but remain a few months longer. Since 1995

Finland

women may also volunteer, and 500 are in the active forces. They are trained for the same duties as men and have the same opportunities and responsibilities. There are 22,600 active duty troops, of which the majority are conscripts. Finnish men must serve on active duty for 6 to 12 months. Most serve six months, but officers, non-commissioned officers, and certain technical specialists must remain a year. A Finn is in the reserves until age 60. There are 16,000 soldiers in the army, 3,800 in the navy, 2,750 in the air force, and 2,750 para-militaries; all have conscripts.

In wartime, it could mobilize 435,000 trained and equipped soldiers: 347,000 in the army; 35,000 in the air force; and 12,000 in the navy. This total is being reduced gradually to 340,000. Most serve in the southern part of the country, but efforts are now being made to shift more of the country's military capability northward into Lapland, where an eventual violation of Finnish territory would most likely occur. Finland's defense spending is 1.6% of GDP. Spending on 3,100 active and 22,000 reserve border troops and civil defense is included in other ministries' budgets. Finns show a strong affection for their military. Former Prime Minister Paavo Lipponen stated, "the army is the most popular institution in Finland."

Because of the country's policy of non-alignment, Finnish troops are also welcome participants in UN peacekeeping missions, particularly in the Middle East. That this form of duty is not without risk was demonstrated in 1985 when 21 Finnish soldiers were captured in southern Lebanon and held for eight days before being released by their Christian militia captors. The commander of the UN troops in southern Lebanon was a Finnish major-general. In 1995–7 Finland dispatched a 450-man peacekeeping force to Bosnia to help enforce the Dayton Accords. In 1999 Finland provided forensic scientists to investigate massacres in Kosovo. In 2010 it had 407 troops in Kosovo and 165 in Afghanistan.

Former President Martti Ahtisaari was a key mediator with Russia and NATO in the search for a peaceful settlement of the Kosovo conflict. In 2006–7, he again took the lead in guiding negotiations to find a formula for Kosovo's independence that would be acceptable to Serbia. Former Prime Minister Harri Holkeri, who was once president of the UN General Assembly, served 10 months as the UN administrator for Kosovo from July 2003. In 2000 Ahtisaari had helped secure Namibia's independence from South Africa. In 2005 Ahtisaari had brokered a truce between the Indonesian government and the tsunami-devastated Aceh province. He directs the Crisis Management Initiative in

Helsinki. For his brilliance as a negotiator and mediator, he was awarded the Nobel Peace Prize in October 2008.

Most Finns and all political parties still favor conscription. Polls in 2002 indicated that 80% were willing to defend their country "even if the prospects of survival are dim." But in a 2007 poll half were opposed to joining NATO, and only a fourth favored it. Even a majority of military officers were against membership. An ex-foreign minister noted: "In order to join NATO, we have to change the people first."

Nevertheless, Finland's ties with NATO are warming as the EU is divided on Russia. Finland is worried about a resurgent and assertive Russia, and it has committed itself to removing the landmines along its long common border by 2016. The very fact that there is talk about NATO membership is a radical departure. President Tarja Halonen, who supported unilateral disarmament in her youth, opposes joining, but the newly revised constitution requires that she cooperate with the government in foreign affairs. Many Finns were furious when in 2007 she described Estonia and Russia as friends of equal importance. This was at a time when Russia was putting frightful pressure on Estonia and was besieging its embassy in Moscow. In reality the prime minister holds the keys. If he and a majority of the cabinet change their minds, Finns are likely to follow their lead.

About a third of its military equipment is produced in Finland. It purchased arms from the Soviet Union (MIG jet fighters), Sweden (Draken interceptor aircraft), Britain (Hawker Siddeley jets), America (64 Hornet F-18C interceptors produced in Finland) and France. In 1992 it bought Russian tanks, artillery, and ammunition from the stockpiles of former East Germany. It sends its officers to the U.S., France, Britain (and earlier, to the Soviet Union) for specialized training. Finland has assumed a special role in assisting the Estonian military. It sends advisers to Estonia, including instructors to the National Defense and Public Service Academy in Tallinn and Baltic Defense College in Tartu. It provides specialized training to some Estonian troops on its own soil. Backed by a well-deserved reputation for fierce and imaginative defense on their own territory, the Finns are able convincingly to show their teeth to any potential attacker.

GOVERNMENT

What the Finns gained from their particular brand of foreign policy was the privilege to have a domestic political and economic order far different from that which the Soviet Union required of its

Dr. Urho Kekkonen

Eastern European neighbors. Until March 1, 2000, Finland had the same constitution it had adopted in 1919. Unlike three of its Scandinavian neighbors—Norway, Sweden and Denmark—Finland is a republic and the only country in Europe that never had a king or a home-grown aristocracy.

The President

At the time the 1919 constitution was written, supporters of a monarchy reached a compromise with advocates of a republic: the president would not be a mere figurehead who cuts ribbons and gives parties for foreign dignitaries. Instead, he or she would be the leading figure in the political system and would be required to sever all ties with a particular political party. Finns elect their president directly by universal suffrage for a six-year term. When no candidate receives 50% of the votes on the first round, a runoff election between the top two candidates takes place three weeks

President Tarja Halonen

104

later. Presidents must give up party affiliations when taking office.

In March 2000 the constitution was amended to reduce the president's powers. Finland essentially moved to parliamentarianism after strong presidential power. The prime minister is now clearly the most important political figure. Added authority was shifted to parliament, which decides who should represent Finland at international gatherings. Both the president and prime minister represent Finland in the EU's European Council, but that could change. The president continues to play a part in foreign affairs "in cooperation with" the government. She commands the armed forces although declarations of war and important treaties require parliamentary approval. The government negotiates treaties.

She no longer has the right to dissolve parliament, to call new elections, to initiate and delay legislation, or to appoint the cabinet. She is obligated to work with the prime minister to achieve the government's goals. She still has the power of pardon and signs all laws approved by parliament. She formally appoints all bishops for the state-supported Lutheran and Orthodox churches, all university professors and the governors for Finland's five regions. The only exception is the predominantly Swedish-speaking island of Åland, which has been self-governing since 1921. Finland's 448 municipalities are administered by their own popularly elected municipal councils, which exercise the municipalities' power to collect taxes, maintain public order and attend to education, culture, health and social welfare.

The office of the presidency was once so powerful that some observers jokingly referred to Finland as the only real monarchy in Scandinavia. This seemed particularly appropriate because of the man who occupied the office from 1956 until 1981, Dr. Urho Kekkonen. Thanks to his own efforts, most Finns accepted his foreign policy views until the Cold War ended in the early 1990s. Because of Kekkonen's strong personality, the presidency grew even more powerful. This high office is rewarded by a special right to be exempted from taxes. The president's 262,000-euro annual salary is both gross and net income. Members of parliament earn 5,340 euros per month.

In the 1982 presidential elections a record 86% of Finns chose the highly popular Mauno Koivisto. His modesty and unpretentiousness contrasted strongly with Kekkonen's sometimes brash and almost authoritarian style. Further, he was a man who was far less inclined to intervene excessively in domestic politics. His presidency brought a gradual transfer of more responsibilities to the prime minister, the cabinet and parliament. Under his leadership, the Finnish political system began to resemble more closely that of the other Scandinavian countries where the chief focus is on parliament, not on the head of state.

In 1994 Finns elected a new president, Martti Ahtisaari, a Social Democrat. A career diplomat and former U.N. undersecretary general, Ahtisaari had never before run for public office. That fact proved to be his strength because he had not been associated with the economic disasters that had overtaken Finland. Actually, the president has very little constitutional power in the economic sphere; his or her power once lay in foreign policy, which was Ahtisaari's area of expertise.

His successor in March 2000 is Tarja Halonen, who brought much political experience into the presidential palace. A former labor lawyer, she had been minister of foreign affairs, justice, social welfare and health. As was every president since 1982, she is a Social Democrat, but her politics are farther to the left than any of her predecessors. She has a reputation as an antichurch, pro-gay feminist who has always struggled for the rights of minorities and the expansion of the welfare state. Because of her down-to-earth manner and consistent defense of women's rights, she is exceptionally popular and won the votes of many conservative women, especially in her hometown of Helsinki.

In January 2006 she was reelected in the second round by a close vote of 51.8% to 48.2% for her Conservative rival Sauli Niinistö. Turnout was 77.1%, down from 80.2% in 2000. The key issue was Finland's defense policy. After the Baltic states entered NATO in 2004, Finland and Sweden are the only remaining nonaligned countries left in Russia's northwestern border area. But only Finland has a long common border with Russia. With a sense that Moscow has become more aggressive in its foreign and economic policies, some Finns' wariness toward the eastern neighbor has grown.

President Halonen argued that the EU offers Finland sufficient security against an external threat, whereas Niinistö spoke of a need to prepare for new challenges by embedding Finland more securely in the West, meaning NATO. Although polls show that only about a third supports NATO membership, Niinistö's strong electoral performance indicates that opposition may be weakening. In her swearing-in ceremony, Halonen emphasized foreign policy continuity and stronger EU ties with Russia.

Parliament

There are various reasons for the frequent parliamentary deadlocks. The 200-seat unicameral chamber, the *Eduskunta* (42% members are women, only exceeded in Sweden with 46%) has many powers. They include the power to amend the constitution, to force cabinets to resign and to approve legislation, which is not subject to judicial review. Its members are elected by a system of proportional representation. This kind of electoral system always permits a large number of parties to win seats in parliament. The greater the number of parties, the greater the difficulty of forming a stable governing coalition that can count on a parliamentary majority. Winning a vote on certain kinds of legislation, such as important or urgent economic measures, is particularly difficult. Such measures require majorities of two-thirds or even five-sixths of the members. This is a requirement that is unique to Finland and one that some leading political figures are determined to change.

At the present time, three big parties occupy most of the seats in the *Eduskunta*. None is a mass, "catch-all" party that attracts voters from all social and occupational groups. Therefore, there is no prospect of a parliamentary majority being won by any one party, or even by the two left-wing or the two nonsocialist parties. This is especially true since the voting strength for all major parties has, on the whole, remained remarkably stable for the past 60 years. In practice, coalitions can be held together only if a minimum of three of the four largest parties participate in them.

Parties of the Left

In the March 2007 elections the Social Democratic Party of Finland (SDP) won 21.4% of the votes and 45 of the 200 seats, down from 53. This was the first time since 1962 that it was reduced to third place. The SDP is the chief spokesman for organized labor and for lower-level employees. Although not a heavily ideological party, it is one of the most leftist members in the Socialist International. The party officially favors an expansion of the social welfare system. The latter objective is particularly difficult, however, because of the requirement for especially large parliamentary majorities to enact economic measures. Social Democratic prime ministers, who must always lead coalitions that include nonsocialist parties, have shown themselves to be pragmatists who are very willing to pursue a conservative economic policy if Finland's well-being seems to require it.

In 2003 it entered a three-party government with Center and the Swedish People's Party, but Paavo Lipponen had to relinquish the prime minister's chair. For the first time in 1995, a woman (Tarja Halonen) was foreign minister, and she

Finland

became Finland's first female president in 2000. For the second time Finland had a female defense minister, Anneli Taina. It is now in opposition.

The other traditional leftist party was the Communist Party of Finland (SKP), a workers' party. In order to attract a larger following among intellectuals, youth and others who favored a radical change of society, but who did not wish to belong to a rigidly structured communist party, the SKP operated within a broader united group called the People's Democratic League (SKDL). The SKP broke away from the SDP and declared itself a separate party in Moscow in 1918. It was banned from politics in the 1930s, and though legalized in 1944 the party spent the years from 1948, when it was widely suspected of having planned a *coup d'état*, until 1966 in opposition. It remained organized along the Leninist lines of democratic centralism, requiring absolute obedience to the party line once the party had made a decision. The program dropped the Leninist concept of dictatorship of the proletariat, which granted a communist party, as the allegedly true representative of the people, the right to rule a country without free elections.

In the second half of the 1960s, an intra-party quarrel between an orthodox and a revisionist wing of the party erupted, and the chasm between them was opened wider when the Soviet Union invaded Czechoslovakia in August 1968. The more moderate, majority wing of the party embraces the idea of "Eurocommunism," or that branch of communism in democratic countries that is tailored not to the needs of the Soviet Union, but to the needs of the home countries. Under chairman Arvo Aalto, the leadership launched a new slogan: "Socialism with a Finnish face." This wording is strikingly reminiscent of the former Czech communist leader's call for "socialism with a human face," a call that provoked the Soviet invasion.

Backed by the Soviet Union, the orthodox wing, headed by Taisto Sinisalo, opposed this direction taken by the majority within the party. Therefore, Aalto's revisionist majority expelled the hard-line faction of the party in 1985, leaving Finland with two communist parties, including the break-away hard-line faction called Democratic Alternative.

They joined forces under the banner, Left Alliance (VAS), which won 8.8% of the votes and 17 seats in 2007. Although the Communists are often exasperatingly shifty partners, who maneuver to avoid responsibility for unpopular programs, observers generally agree that their sharing of government responsibility has been good both for them and for Finland. They are now in the opposition.

Downtown Helsinki

The Green League (VIHR) captured 8.5% of the votes and 15 seats in 2007. They entered the governing coalition. Environmental issues, particularly global warming, played a leading role in the electoral campaign.

Parties of the Center and Right

The National Coalition Party (KOK, also called "the Conservatives") is a conservative party that stresses the values of nation, private property and enterprise, religious principles and restraint in expanding the social welfare system. It comes the closest of all Finnish parties to being a mass party, and it draws over 60% of its votes from skilled workers and employees. Led by 35-year-old Jyrki Katainen, it did well in the 2007 elections, climbing to 22.3% of the votes and 50 seats. It entered the government, with Katainen as finance minister.

Although it supported the "Kekkonen line" in foreign policy, it was distrusted by the Soviet Union as being too nationalist, although it must be remembered that all Finnish parties are nationalist in the sense that their policies are oriented toward Finnish interests. It is open to NATO membership, but it does not push the issue due to popular opposition. The KOK's support for some of the government's legislation has been crucial in the past when the governing parties were unable to agree. Thus, the KOK has long been an essential feature of Finnish politics. Little separates the major rightist parties doctrinally.

The fourth and largest major party is the Center Party (KESK). It changed its name in 1965 from the Agrarian Union and attempted to expand its base to include more than the farmers. This effort was only partially successful, and although one-fourth of its voters are workers, about a third are farmers. The party advocates protection of Finnish agricultural interests, private property, individual rights and economic and governmental decentralization. It seeks to balance out the political left and right in Finland.

In 2003 and again in 2007 the Center Party narrowly emerged as the largest party. In 2007 it won 23% of the votes and 51 seats to remain the senior member of the four-party governing coalition. It was led in 2003 by a tough, no-nonsense farmer's daughter and lawyer from rural western Finland, Anneli Jaatteenmäki. Her party constructed a three-party governing coalition with the SDP and SFP with 117 of 200 parliamentary seats. Center was victorious because of its strength in rural areas, winning only two seats in Helsinki.

For two months, Jaatteenmäki became the country's first female prime minister, and Finland became the first European democracy to have both a female president and woman prime minister. She had criticized the 10% unemployment rate, the third-highest in the EU, and accused Lipponen of having been too cozy with the Americans and having failed to take a firm enough stand against U.S.-British

Prime Minister Mari Kiviniemi

policy on Iraq. However, the information she used to pursue the latter line of criticism caused her resignation as prime minister in June 2003. She was accused of lying about the leak of Foreign Ministry documents used to blame Lipponen of compromising the country's neutrality by supporting the war against Saddam Hussein. Lipponen, who became parliamentary speaker, was furious.

Since most Finns opposed the war, this played well to voters. However, Finns are even more insistent that their politicians tell the truth, and they were shocked. Transparency International cites Finland as the world's least corrupt country. After denying that she had the documents, extracts from them showed up on her website, and a leak from inside her party revealed that she had the papers in her possession. The police interviewed Jaatteenmäki, and her government was paralyzed by a media frenzy. Although she admitted to no wrongdoing, she concluded that the scandal made it impossible for her to remain as prime minister. After 63 days in office, she resigned. In May 2004 she was tried on charges of illegally obtaining and leaking secret documents and was acquitted. The trial was broadcast on national TV and attracted record attention.

She was replaced as prime minister in June 2003 by ex-Defense Minister Matti Vanhanen of the Center Party. A teetotaling former journalist, he is a specialist on the EU. He was the country's most popular politician. With his unassuming manner and clean-cut good looks, he harvested the female vote handsomely, and a women's magazine named him the sexiest man in Finland. A divorcé, his popularity was only burnished by a book, *The Prime Minister's Bride*, written by a former girlfriend, Susan Kuronen (who changed her last name to Ruusunen, Finnish for "Sleeping Beauty"),

and published just before the March 2007 elections, exposing lurid details of their nine-month love life. Like a stoic Finn, he ignored it until after the election when he sued her and the publisher for invading his privacy. Both Sleeping Beauty and her publisher were acquitted after the court ruled that different standards of privacy exist for public figures like politicians.

Plenty of women remained in the government, including a former Miss Finland, Tanja Karpela, as culture minister, and the youngest minister (of foreign trade and development aid), Paula Lehtomälo, a 30-year-old linguist from the North. They must remain on guard while working in parliament. An internal report on sexual harassment, published in 2008, revealed that a third of female employees had received inappropriate comments from men, 15% had been subjected to improper advances, and 7% had received propositions for sex. In 40% of the cases, the advances or comments had been made by a member of parliament. In April 2008, Foreign Minister Ilkka Kanerva was dismissed after a magazine published some of the 200 text messages he had sent to an erotic dancer.

The Swedish People's Party (SFP) is the third party in the government. Over the years it has declined steadily due to the decreasing percentage of Swedish-speaking voters to the present 5.5%. To counter this decline, the SFP disassociated itself in 1964 from its purely Swedish language base and proclaimed a socially progressive national policy. Still, the great majority of its voters are found in the Swedish-speaking minority. It won 4.5% of the votes and 10 seats in 2007, and it entered the government.

Among the eight parties that won seats in 2007 is the Christian League (SLK), which won 4.9% of the votes and 7 seats. The True Finns captured 4.1% of the votes and 5 seats. Both are in the opposition.

From among the many parties, the parliament must put together a cabinet, called the Council of State (*Valtioneuvosto*), and appoint and dismiss the prime minister and up to 17 cabinet ministers. The latter need not be members of the parliament, but, as a group, must enjoy a majority in the legislature. Cabinets tend to be very short-lived, and the country had 60 governments before it had celebrated the sixtieth anniversary of its independence. There were 12 governments in the 1970s alone, and Finland now has almost a dozen living ex-prime ministers. Yet, new governments are usually created by merely shuffling around a few cabinet seats. Vanhanen resigned in 2010.

Thus, there is somewhat more cabinet stability than meets the eye. The Center Party and the Social Democratic Party are crucial participants in almost every government. Until 1995 the National Coalition was consistently excluded, and the major nonsocialist parties cannot assemble a majority in parliament. Of course, neither can the two leftist parties, so there is no alternative to the delicate broad coalitions that have become the rule.

ECONOMY

After World War II had ended, the Soviet Union handed the exhausted and defeated Finland a reparations bill that could only make the Finns shudder. They had to give the Russians a large part of their merchant marine and to deliver heavy indus-

Finnish-designed products are known worldwide

Finland

trial products—ships, metal and engineering equipment—at prices that the Russians had established arbitrarily. This seemed like a terrible demand to make on a country that had always been primarily agricultural and whose industry was limited almost exclusively to wood products.

In the end, the Soviet demands proved to be a great blessing in disguise for the Finns. The sums to be paid were not impossible, and they were paid by 1952. But by having been forced to create a heavy industrial base and thereby to diversify its industry in order to pay the reparations, Finland established the very foundation for its present economic prosperity. The Finns have a habit of paying what they owe. They were the only Europeans to pay off all of their debts from both world wars. Finland experienced an extraordinary economic transformation in the second half of the 20th century. Shortly after the war its GDP per capita was a third below that of Sweden, but today it is roughly equal; 70% of its people worked the land, but now that latter figure is only 5%. Its modern economy employs 70% of the work force in services, producing 64.3% of GDP, and 25% in industry, creating 32.6% of GDP.

Economic Links with Russia

It established significant trade patterns with the Soviet Union, which was until 1991 Finland's most important single trading partner. Not only did the Soviet Union provide 90% of Finland's oil, half of its electricity, and all of its natural gas, but it was a guaranteed market for Finnish exports, even though this two-way trade declined somewhat in the 1980s, and both Finns and Soviets increased their trade with the West. As the USSR diversified its trade with the West under Mikhail Gorbachev after 1985, Finns began to worry about losing business and about their ability to compete. Nevertheless, when the average Finn thought of the Soviet Union, he thought perhaps as much of economic opportunity as of political danger.

The Finnish shipbuilding industry was one of the greatest beneficiaries of the Soviet reparation demands. Finland had to replace its own fleet and it then turned to production of ships for export. Until the 1990s sales to the Soviet Union accounted for more than 8% of Finland's total exports. The Soviet Union was particularly interested in Finnish-made ships suited for Arctic conditions, and more than 80% of the shipyards' orders came from that country. Russia was also an especially good customer in that it pays for these ships as soon as they leave the slipway. Further specialties include high-technology shipping, such as liquid gas carriers, cable layers and Arctic oilfield vessels. Most of the "love boats" cruising in the Caribbean, half of the world's icebreakers and the drilling rigs used to bore a fourth of the offshore wells in the North Sea, were constructed in Finland.

The Soviet Union was an avid buyer of products from its only immediate neighbor that has an advanced Western economy and technology. It bought ships, machinery, paper, chemicals and large quantities of food and drink, tobacco products, clothing and footwear. It also welcomed the large-scale production projects that Finland conducts just over the Soviet border. These include the construction of a wood processing complex at Pääjärvi, the enlargement of a paper and pulp complex at Svetogorsk and the largest of all—the Kostamus project involving construction of an open-cast iron ore mining complex 30 miles (48 km.) inside the Soviet Union. Such projects are far more attractive than similar Finnish projects in the Middle East because Finnish workers can return home on weekends, and the projects stimulate economic activity in the nearby northern and eastern parts of Finland, which badly need economic stimulation.

The USSR gave Finnish firms contracts to build 50 villages deeper in the Soviet Union along the gas pipeline being constructed to transport natural gas from Siberia to Western Europe. By 1991 Finnish companies had signed about 260 joint-venture agreements with the USSR, but only a handful went into operation.

Finland is one of the highest per capita energy users of the world and has to worry particularly about its supplies. Its electrical consumption is third in Europe behind Norway and Sweden. It is one of the richest countries in peat resources, and it does fire some power plants with this material. With no oil, gas or coal of its own, and with hydroelectric resources that do not come close to those of Sweden or Norway, it must import about two-thirds of its energy. Over a fourth (29%) of its energy is renewable, compared with the EU average of 6.4%. About half comes from Russia, including not only oil, gas and electricity, but also nuclear fuel services.

In contrast to the Swedes, the Finns have not been paralyzed over the question of nuclear power. There is a powerful Green movement that has to be persuaded. Two of Finland's four reactors are from the former USSR, and the fuel for its two Swedish-built ones is enriched in Russia. The Russians also promised not only to provide nuclear fuel, but also to dispose of much of the nuclear wastes, thereby largely freeing the Finns from that frightening problem. Nuclear power plants produce a third of Finland's electricity and a seventh of all its energy. Again, Finns saw that the Soviet Union not only gave them headaches, but aspirin as well.

Finland is one of the few EU countries to expand its nuclear power after the Chernobyl accident in 1986. It is constructing its fifth power plant, Olkiluoto 3, on the site of two existing safe and well-run reactors at Eurajoki on the western Bothnian coast. Financed privately and using cutting edge technology, it is Finland's largest investment project to date and is expected to be completed in 2010.

Finnish paper-making machines sold throughout the world

The Finnish energy company, Fortum, has submitted an application for a sixth reactor. Finland is at the forefront of nuclear waste disposal; an underground repository bunker for its highly radioactive waste is being built on the site. Its expansion of nuclear power is desirable since it limits excessive energy reliance on Russia. Plans to build a cable between Finland and Sweden will make it easier for the latter to import electricity from Finnish nuclear plants.

After the arrival of *perestroika* in the USSR the former certainties of trade with a reliable Soviet Union vanished. Finns no longer could be sure who on the Soviet side was making key business decisions, and they complained that they were no longer being paid on time. Because of violence and economic shortages in the USSR, Finnish workers were no longer eager to go there to work, even for short periods of time. The Soviets curbed oil and gas deliveries to Finland. Finns received a particularly rude shock in 1991 when the Soviet government ended the bilateral clearinghouse system based on semibarter trade and replaced it with a normal trade arrangement financed through convertible currencies. This had a temporarily devastating effect on trade with the Soviet Union. Finnish exports to its neighbor dropped 34% in the first month alone to a level of 8% of Finland's total exports, a far cry from the 25% only two decades earlier. Overnight Finland was running a balance of payments deficit with the Soviet Union and was becoming far more dependent upon its markets in Western Europe.

This turn of events plunged Finland into its deepest recession since 1945 and

Building ships

revealed a prominent Achilles heel in the Finnish economy. In 1991 its GDP declined by 5% and its industrial production by 15%, and it faced record unemployment and bankruptcies. However, Finnish efforts to boost trade with Russia succeeded, rising by a third in 1994. By 2008 Russia accounted for only 11% of Finland's exports and 13.9% of its imports. Nevertheless, Finnish exports to Russia have grown by 25% per year in the 21st century. Half of its imports were oil and gas, and a growing percentage of its exports were luxury goods for newly rich Russians. Countries use Finland as a conduit to Russia for goods because the two countries' common border functions well.

Profiting from this burgeoning trade are the ports of *Hamina and Kotka*, located 36 and 66 kilometers respectively from the Russian border. These are the EU's most

easterly ports and are becoming increasingly important hubs for lucrative Russian traffic. St. Petersburg's affluent bourgeoisie are welcome guests, and Russian is replacing English as the first foreign language taught in local schools in those communities.

Other Sectors of Economy

Although only about 7% of its land can be used for agriculture, Finland was traditionally a farming country. But the percentage of Finns who earn a living from the land or from forestry has decreased steadily from almost 70% in 1880 to almost 50% on the eve of World War II, to 36% in 1960 and to 14% by 1978. In 2009 farming employed only 5% of the population and contributed 3.1% of GDP.

Almost 90% of farms are still operated by families. They have grown in size by 44% since joining the EU in 1995 as farmers seek economy of scale. Because of the small size of most farms, the short growing season and the bitter weather conditions in winter, productivity in agriculture is relatively low. Farm income has declined by 35% since accession because the country's high food prices fail to keep pace with rising production costs. Many farmers can survive only by engaging also in forestry, often in the wooded areas that they themselves own. Yet, Finland remains self-sufficient in all foodstuffs except fruits and vegetables, and, if the harvest is bad, in grain. Dairy and meat products are in surplus and are therefore exported.

The rapid flight from the farms created serious economic and social problems for Finland. From the 1950s to the 1970s many Finns either emigrated to other countries, especially to Sweden, or poured into the urban centers in the southern part of Finland. In the *Economist* of London, one observer described the development this way: "Finland is roughly a jug-shaped

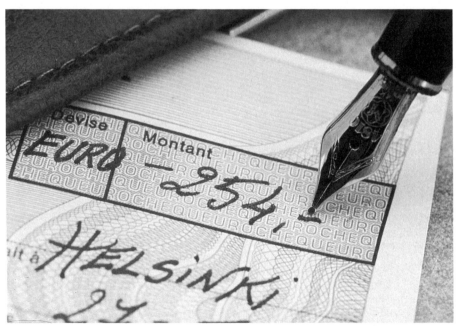

The Euro comes to Finland   Courtesy: Central Audiovisual Library, European Commission

Finland

TORSTAINA 31. TAMMIKUUTA 2002

HELSINGIN SANOMAT

country. Imagine the jug filled with the kind of liqueur that has tiny golden specks floating in it. Left alone, nearly all the Finns would, like those specks, drift slowly down to the bottom. Three out of five of them already live in the southernmost fifth of the country." The results of this southward drift were urban problems of tight and expensive housing, a proliferation of concrete suburbs, and above all, unemployment.

Finland used to be called a country short on investment capital and long on labor, but many of its citizens who left to find work abroad, especially in Sweden, are returning home. Further, Finland has larger direct investments in other countries than foreign firms have in Finland. It has poured large sums of money into developing and diversifying the economic base in the northern four-fifths of the country. This is especially difficult given the transportation impediments caused by the great distances, sparse population and cold climate. The only favorable transportation factor is the long water routes branching in many directions.

The main objective is not to make farming more attractive, but to offer tax relief and other subsidies to businesses that locate there and train or retrain rural inhabitants. It does this primarily through the Regional Development Fund, shortened in Finnish to Finvera. Though state-owned, it refuses to rescue lame duck industries. It encourages risk-taking, but it also demands profitability. The Finnish government promotes social, health, cultural and educational services in the North and attempts to shift a portion of administration and decision-making away from the Helsinki area.

It looked to its neighbors, especially Sweden for help; Sweden provided half the foreign capital invested in Finland. However, by the mid-1990s Finland had become more of an equal economic part-

ner with Sweden. Many foreign investments in Sweden are now of Finnish origin. The Nordic Investment Bank has helped to finance joint Finnish-Norwegian and Finnish-Swedish projects in the north of Finland.

Nokia (named after a town and river of that name in southwest Finland) is Finland's biggest high-tech company and the world's biggest producer of mobile phones, once accounting for 40% of the global market for mobile telephones. It is still the world's leading handset maker, but it is losing ground due to stiff competition and the global economic downturn. Although less than 1.5% of its global sales are in Finland, it finds an enthusiastic market in its very own neighborhood. Finland now has more mobile phones than fixed-line telephones: 92% of households have one or more cell phones, the highest percentage in the world. It is normal for seven-year-olds to begin using them. A 2001 UN report placed Finland on the top of 18 world technology leaders, ahead of second place U.S., in terms of number of patents granted, receipts from royalties and license fees, internet hosts per capita, and education and training in science, mathematics and engineering.

Although foreigners, primarily Americans, own about 90% of its shares, Nokia's economic predominance in Finland is almost unique in the world. With $35 billion in annual sales make it the engine of the economy, accounting for two-thirds of the value of the Finnish stock market, a fifth of Finland's total exports, and 5% of GDP. Its earnings roughly equal the total Finnish government budget. Only one of its nine plants worldwide is in Finland. About 22,000 of its 54,000 employees work in Finland, and another 20,000 Finns work for companies that depend on Nokia for contracts. A company located in the U.S. comparable in size in proportion to the overall population would employ about

one million persons. Some Finns worry that their economy might be too dependent upon this one giant company. No wonder one Helsinki hotelier noted, "We pay more attention to the chief executive of Nokia than to the prime minister." The firm uses English as its official language.

This country is fortunate to have many valuable raw materials. The most plentiful, and luckily renewable, resource is wood—lots of it. Two-thirds of its forests are privately owned. This, together with its paper products, accounts for 23% of its exports and almost a fifth of its gross production. The wood and paper industry also provides employment for 19% of the work force. Although the financially strong U.S. and Canadian paper mills now meet half of Western Europe's wood pulp needs, Finland's new highly efficient paper plants still find their major market in Western Europe. In general, Finland's wood and paper industry is thriving, but Finns must watch very carefully the less desirable by-product of paper mills: pollution.

Finland is not overly dependent upon its wood industry. About half of the iron ore needed for its domestic market is produced locally, and it has rich deposits of nonferrous metal as well. It is one of Europe's leading producers of nickel and copper and also mines zinc, chromium and cobalt and produces 10% of the world's vanadium. These generous mineral deposits, along with its forced diversification after 1945, have enabled Finland to build an efficient metal and engineering industry. This sector now produces 19% of exports and a fifth of the gross production. It also employs 34% of the labor force. Diversification has further spread to the chemical and textile sectors, which now produce 9% of exports and provide work for 19% of the labor force.

As might be expected, the economy is very export-oriented. More than a third of total production must be exported, and a quarter of total consumption must be met by imports. Of course, some industrial branches are even more dependent upon exportation than others. For instance, the forest industry exports 80%–90% of its production, the textile and clothing factories about 45%, and the metal and engineering industries about 40%. This is one important reason why Finland is very sensitive to any changes in the international trade or political climate, and why it has a special minister for foreign trade. Its major market is Western Europe; about two-thirds of its trade turnover is with EU and EFTA countries. Germany, Sweden and Great Britain are its major Western European trading partners.

Great Britain's and Denmark's entry into the EU made it advantageous for Finland to sign in 1973 an industrial free trade agreement with the EU effective in 1977. Although it did not become a member of the EU's Common Agricultural Program, it enjoyed complete duty-free trade with the EU countries since 1984. Its economic ties with the West were also facilitated by its associate membership in EFTA and its full membership in the WTO, the OECD and the Nordic Council.

The sensitivity on the part of the Soviet Union had earlier dissuaded Finland from seeking EU membership. That changed in the 1990s. In 1992 the Finns formally applied, and in 1995 it joined. A Finn, Jacob Söderman, became the EU's first ombudsman in 1995. The Finnish government regards full membership as an essential economic and political anchor for the country in the post-Cold War era, especially given the economic problems at home and the instability in neighboring Russia. In 1999 it became the first Nordic country to adopt the euro.

Unlike in most other European countries, labor unions are gaining members and now represent 80% of the labor force. They are politicized and strongly support the SDP. Nevertheless, they usually have been willing to enter general income agreements with all governments and industries that are designed to keep the economy efficient and competitive. Finns' success also stems partly from a high degree of economic pragmatism. They used to view Sweden as their model, but much of their recent economic success was due to their willingness to deviate from that model.

Finns were concerned about unemployment, but it had declined to 7% by 2008; however, the real figure would be as high as 15% if early retirement, training programs and subsidized work were included. The problem remains, though, that job losses from low-tech plant closures almost match the number of new jobs created by high-tech successes. Finland has been hesitant to use public funds to shore up inefficient and unprofitable industries. Further, they have not shirked cutting public spending or taxes and introducing stringent monetary control and financial restraint to protect their overall economic health.

The May 2004 entry into the EU of Estonia, whose wages and corporate tax rates are far lower, caused unease. But Finland responded by cutting corporate taxes from 29% to 26% and by gradually lowering income taxes though the top end is still close to 50%. The wealth tax was abandoned in 2006. The fact that a fifth of all alcohol consumed in Finland comes from Estonia compelled the Finns to reduce the price of alcohol by a third in order to compete. For two years it also required Estonians and other east Euro-

peans to have work permits in order to stem the flow of cheap labor. The Finns maintain a visa office in Tallinn. In 2007 it lifted the restrictions on migrant workers from the new EU member states.

Finland in the early 21st century has one of Europe's steadiest economies, increasing an average of 3.4% per year from 1994 to 2005, a blazing 6% in 2006 and 2.7% in 2008. According to the Global Competitiveness Report 2003, Finland has the greatest business efficiency and prospects for economic growth in the following few years among the 75 economies studied. It scored high in every category, including macroeconomic policies, public institutions and technology usage. A year later the World Economic Forum's (WEF) annual review of 101 countries put Finland on top in terms of growth potential. In 2005 the WEF ranked it number one in competitiveness, right ahead of the U.S., Sweden and Denmark. *The Economist* in 2007 ranked its business environment second in the world after Denmark. It does this while protecting its environment. A major 2008 study by Yale and Columbia universities placed it sixth on an Environmental Performance Index along with the other Nordic and Baltic countries; the U.S. was in 66th place.

High technology and a research and development commitment of 3.5% of GDP (70% from the private sector) per year (compared with 4.3% for Sweden and 2.6% for the U.S.) are among its secrets of success. Among the promoters of technology research in Finland are a national technology agency, called Tekes, which supports basic and applied research at universities and other research institutes (40%) and to businesses (60%); the Finn-

ish National Fund for Research and Development; and the Finnish Academy of Science and Letters.

Technology is so prevalent that students at the Helsinki University of Technology devised a computer program in 2005, called the Virtual Air Guitar Project. It enables literally anybody to create rock solos by simply wearing a pair of wired gloves and strumming an imaginary guitar, while a computer registers the hand movements and adds musical accompaniment to match the player's finger work precisely. Other Finnish computer geeks made their own full-length galactic animation film that millions of viewers around the world downloaded free.

Finland maintains one of the highest levels of prosperity in the industrialized world. It is also one of the most inclusive societies, with economic inequality and a poverty rate among the world's lowest. It recovered well in 1991–3 from its deepest recession since 1945, during which it suffered the worst decline of any Western European country in recent times. Foreign trade by 2005 had doubled to 40% of GDP in only a decade and a half. Exports were booming, investment was high, growth was positive, and inflation was 1.3% in 2008. Total public debt was down to 58% of GDP, and the government maintained a budget surplus of 3.5% of GDP in 2008. Its earlier attempts to meet the convergence criteria for the EU common currency succeeded.

Finland did not escape the global recession that has shaken countries in 2009. In the first quarter of 2009 its economy contracted by 7.6%. This is the first time since 1993 that this has happened. But recovery was well underway by 2010.

Finnish student (m) with Norwegian (l) and Polish classmates at College of Europe, Warsaw

Finland

CULTURE

For centuries Finnish culture was heavily dependent upon influences from abroad. Eastern Finland was always exposed to cultural trends from Russia, and Sweden was a conduit for such trends from the rest of Europe. Not until the 19th century did a specifically Finnish identity really awaken, and this was led by the elite's increased use of the Finnish language in literature, journalism, education and politics.

Literature and Arts

A central figure in the break from the tradition of using Swedish was J.V. Snellman, a prominent university professor and statesman. Although of Swedish background himself, he was the first great author to write in Finnish. In 1835 the first part of Finland's greatest literary work, the *Kalevala*, was published. This monumental national epic by Elias Lönnrot presents traditional Finnish folk poems that tell of myths and legends. It gave a powerful boost to Finnish nationalism and to a yearning for independence. In 1870 another epic, *Seven Brothers*, was published by Aleksis Kivi, who portrayed the Finns of his time with great humor and realism, but with very little romanticism. He established the standard for Finnish prose and drama and soon became universally recognized as Finland's national author.

Both of these epic works, the *Kalevala* and *Seven Brothers*, capture the importance that Finns attribute to common people and their identification of man's fate with mysterious, impersonal forces, often associated with forests and nature. This identification gives Finnish literature a sober, almost tragic and often heroic tone. In most Finnish works, though, the reader senses an unmistakable national enthusiasm.

Since 1945 Finnish literature, as well as film, has reflected an intense national self-examination, with much social consciousness and criticism. It has been experimental and "modernist," with much use of loose imagery and collage. Finns have developed a particular passion for the spoken theater; it has more than 40 professional theaters and countless amateur ones as well.

Domestic film products make up a quarter of all distributed films, up from 4% at the end of the 20th century. A few directors have an international reputation, such as Aki Kaurismäki and Aku Louhimies. The latter's film, *Frozen Land*, hardly puts his country's best foot forward; it is intended to remind the viewer of what a cold, dark, hopeless and depressing country Finland is. Louhimies would probably have understood the motivation of the teenage gunman who in November 2007 posted a video on YouTube predicting a massacre several hours before opening fire at a Finnish school, killing eight persons including the principal.

In 2007, at age 50, Kaurismäki announced his retirement with 22 other Finnish film producers when the government reneged on a promise to raise film subsidies by $1.6 million. They need the money. His 2006 film, *Light in the Dusk*, sold only 38,000 tickets at home, compared with 460,000 tickets sold for *Pirates of the Caribbean: At World's End*. Finns still prefer Hollywood fare.

Finland publishes more books per capita than any other nation in the world except Iceland. Because of the complexity of the Finnish language, much of its literature and drama remains untranslated and unknown outside of Finland. Other forms of cultural expression lend themselves better to international audiences. The music of Jean Sibelius (1865–1957), who drew much inspiration from the *Kalevala*, opened the way for a national romantic style and introduced Finnish music to a world audience. Finland trains more musicians per capita than any other country, and the Sibelius Academy in Helsinki is the country's highest institution for musical studies.

The Finnish opera receives particular support through the annual Savonlinna Festival, which draws large numbers of visitors from outside Finland and which presents important national works with high standards of international artistry. The Metropolitan Opera of New York was so impressed with the quality of the Finnish National Opera that it invited the latter to perform in New York during the 1983 season. This was the first time the "Met" ever invited another opera company to perform in its own home. The Finns also have established a worldwide reputation for imaginative modern design in architecture, industrial arts and city planning.

Ninety percent of Finns belong to one of the two official Finnish churches, the main one being the Evangelic Lutheran Church. However, fewer than 5% attend church services outside the Christmas and Easter holidays. The two churches receive subsidies from taxes paid by registered members, but that income has dwindled so much that the Evangelic Lutheran Church had to dismiss a fourth of the people on its payroll.

Languages and Minorities

Finnish is a Finno-Ugric language related linguistically only to Estonian, Hungarian, and a couple of dozen dialects spoken in isolated communities in Russia and the far North. Finnish and Estonian are very close, but the linguistic roots with Hungarian are meager. Philologists have identified only about 200 words that Finnish and Estonian, on the one hand, and Hungarian, on the other hand, have in common: 55 of them concern fishing, 15 deal with reindeer, and only three with commerce. One noted philologist came up with only one mutually comprehensible sentence: "The living fish swims in water." Finnish remains mysterious to the outsider. Finns keep it largely free of foreign words; they prefer inventing words, such as *puhelin* (telephone) or *norsu* (elephant), to borrowing them. They can make up words to be more precise. Finnish has no masculine or feminine, so they do not say "he" or "she." They have no articles ("a" or "the"). Unlike the Estonians, they have resisted modernizing their spelling, so their words seem bafflingly long.

The percentage of citizens whose primary language is Swedish has declined in the last century from 15% to about 5.5% although both remain official languages. There are no longer serious social differences or tensions between the two language groups. In fact, aside from language, very little distinguishes the two groups from each other. Swedish-speaking Finns are still granted a great measure of cultural autonomy. There are 41 Swedish high schools in 31 cities and a Swedish university in Turku. Most Swedish speakers now also speak Finnish, but not vice versa, despite the fact that all Finnish children learn some Swedish in school, but few are able to speak it well. Most Finnish school children (91.7%) choose to learn English as their first foreign language, whereas 7.7% choose to learn Swedish as their first foreign language. Only a tiny percentage of pupils ever enroll in Russian language courses.

There is a third population group in Finland, which has a culture and Finno-Ugric language of its own: Sami (pronounced Sah-meh) a short but strong people toughened by a hard life. They should not be confused with "Laplanders," anyone who lives in the North (Lapland), the majority of whom are not Sami. Their origins remain obscure, but scholars believe they were Finland's first inhabitants. Finland has only about 3,800 Sami; there are far more in Norway (40,000) and Sweden (17,000). To the disappointment of tourists, they no longer wear their colorful blue, red, yellow and white costumes except on festive occasions; they are mostly settled and make their living chiefly from timbering, farming and tourism. One enterprising tour company tried to create a bonanza by sponsoring honeymoon stays in Lapland during the winter months. The attraction: 24-hour night-time! Surprisingly, the venture failed.

A fourth category of residents is immigrants and refugees. Finland still maintains a tightly restrictive refugee policy, insisting on evidence of political, religious or racial persecution. Amnesty International had criticized Finland for returning Soviet seekers of asylum. Laws and regulations also discourage immigrants, who comprised 2.3% of the total population in 2008. Of its 108,346 foreign-born residents in 2005, Russians, Estonians and Swedes represented 43%, and fewer than 25,000 (23%) came from nonwhite countries and were visible minorities. Its net immigration is only about 10,000 per year. It has the EU's lowest percentage of immigrants. This explains why it is the only major European country that has not generated a far-right, anti-immigrant party.

Because of its low birthrate, Finland wants to attract more immigrants, and it is seeking ways to find the right kind and to make them welcome. The country's image as being cold (both in its people and climate), its remote location, its difficult language, its lack of established foreign communities, and its sky-high costs and taxes are not luring. For centuries Finnish identity has been based on ethnic homogeneity, so the natives are not overtly welcoming. The government provides free Finnish lessons and help with job retraining. Nevertheless, an estimated quarter of foreigners are unemployed.

Among the 15 former Soviet republics, Finns are culturally closest to their kin 50 miles across the Gulf of Finland in Estonia. They are from the same ethnic stock and can understand each other's language, with a bit of effort. The Estonians have much more practice since they have watched Finnish television for years, thereby making them the former Soviet citizens best informed about the outside world and most familiar with Western problems, pornography and advertising. In fact, their favorite Finn was a jovial TV character who did commercials for sausages and meat, reminding them of how prosperous life could be with a capitalist economic system.

In the Gorbachev era, Finns' interest in Estonia increased. Finnish farmers sent shiploads of used farming equipment to Estonia to help in the agricultural reform, and Finnish paper was donated for use in greater book publication. Finnish and Estonian firms have established numerous joint ventures. By 1994 half of the foreign-owned businesses had Finnish partners, and 13 of 22 commitments made by the government financing corporation, Finnfund, were to Estonia. In characteristic fashion, the Finnish government had kept its distance from the enthusiasm toward Estonia, not wishing to appear to be undermining Soviet rule there. Finland had recognized *de facto* Soviet annexation of the Baltics in 1940. But in 1991 it joined other nations in recognizing the newly independent Baltic states.

Finns arrive in Tallinn by the ferry load to cash in on low prices in Estonian stores and bars. Some Finnish tourists' free-spending and heavy-drinking behavior has given Finns a bad reputation in Estonian eyes. Very few Finns behave that way at home. They are ingrained with modesty and find it difficult to self-promote in this consensus-driven society. It is sometimes said only half-jokingly that "anger in Finland is a bigger taboo than sex." It is normal to see people in restaurants eating in silence. Many consider silence to be a sign of wisdom and good manners, not boredom.

There is a Finnish-speaking minority in Estonia and in the St. Petersburg (Russia) area called Ingrians. About 30,000 of them have emigrated to Finland. They are among the most popular immigrants in Finland, but their integration is not easy. Those from Russia often no longer speak Finnish and are indistinguishable from Russians, who are much less liked. Russian immigrants complain that they are discriminated against on the job market and that the media view them all as gangsters, spies or prostitutes.

Looking east, Finns also see Slavicized brethren in Karelia, who after the collapse of the USSR are pressing for greater independence from Moscow or, in some cases, outright annexation by Finland; 8,000 Finns from there have already moved to Finland. But not wanting to assume a huge economic burden, Finland wants neither a further influx nor any talk of annexation. Of the 716,000 people who live in Karelia, only about 80,000 are Finno-Ugric-speaking Karelians, of which only 18,000 (2.3%) are Finns and 6,000 (.8%) Veps, another nationality related to Finns. Thus, Finns and their relatives represent less than 15% of the population; most of the rest (73.6%) is Russian.

To discourage more emigration to Finland, whose wage level was 100 times as high as that in Russia in 1993, Finnish organizations are founding schools in Karelia and supplying books in Finno-Ugric languages. Also, Finnish companies have two-thirds of the 120 joint ventures there. In general, unlike in the rest of Scandinavia, immigration to Finland is almost unknown, and there are few resident aliens. Finns fear an influx of drugs, organized crime and prostitution through the Baltic states, but that anxiety is directed toward Russians rather than Balts.

The Media

Finnish-Swedish bilingualism is practiced in the mass media. The Finnish Broadcasting Company (YLE), a state-owned organization, operates or supervises all radio and television broadcasting. It has no radio advertising and two of its television channels have none. It broadcasts Swedish TV programs in western and southern Finland, and there are Swedish-language radio stations. A Sami radio station broadcasts in Lapland, and Radio Finland transmits in various European languages. Domestic production accounts for 57% of all programs, and 54% of foreign programs are from Europe and 29% from the U.S. Foreign programs are transmitted in the original language with subtitles. The Finnish Broadcasting Company gets the large part of its revenues from license fees. There is a privately owned MTV Ltd (having nothing to do with American MTV), which finances its operations through advertising. There are also private local radio stations (most owned by newspapers and publishers),

The Estonians are coming!

Finland

cable TV companies, and a few local TV stations.

More than 200 Finnish-language and more than 20 Swedish-language newspapers are privately owned. In the decade following independence, Finnish newspapers were mainly tied to political parties, but now more and more are independent of parties. The *Helsingin Sanomat* has become by far the largest in circulation, followed by *Ilta-Sanomat*, *Aamulehti*, *Turun Sanomat*, and *Maaseudun Tulevaisuus*. In 2002 an international professional organization, Reporters Without Borders, placed Finland first in the world in terms of press freedom; the U.S. was 17th.

Education

All Finnish children must attend nine years of school. They have completed the transition to non-tracked comprehensive schools at the secondary level. The goal in establishing such unified schools, similar in some ways to American schools, was to equalize educational opportunities. After completing the comprehensive school, about half of the pupils enter a three-year senior secondary school that prepares them for a matriculation examination and access to the universities. There are no private schools or universities.

The country's largest university is the University of Helsinki with approximately 20,000 students. To create a new innovative world-class university, three universities in the metropolitan area were merged: the Helsinki University of Technology, the Helsinki School of Economics, and the University of Art and Design. It is following the example of Oulu University, which was the country's first integrated multidisciplinary university, combining a traditional university, a technical university and a business school. Similar plans are being made for Tartu. There are further universities at Jyväskylä, Tampere, as well as Swedish-language universities in Turku and Vaasa. Lapland University in Kovaniemi on the Arctic Circle teaches in Finnish.

Because of the flood of students to the universities and polytechnic schools today, many applicants used to be turned away, but they are now able to accommodate 70% of high school graduates. Those who are admitted receive free (tax-paid) tuition and a monthly stipend for the full 55 months (six years) of study. To attract more foreign students, several universities offer degree programs in English. Many students who finish their studies are unable to find employment in jobs for which their studies prepared them.

Finland adopted an Arena 2000 project that hooked up all Helsinki schools to the Internet. In a cold country like Finland, people will be able to meet by Internet when they cannot go physically from one place to the other. By 1997 Helsinki already had twice the number of Internet subscribers per 1,000 inhabitants as the U.S.

International comparisons of 31 countries, sponsored by the OECD in 2004 and 2007, ranked Finnish schools the world's best: first in science and second in literacy and math. One OECD education expert estimated that Finnish pupils, on average, were more than one school year ahead of American 15-year-olds thanks in part to the "highly effective way of recruiting, training and supporting teachers." The quality and social standing of teachers are key to this success, despite the facts that they are not better paid than their counterparts elsewhere and that class sizes approach 30. Teachers' pay in 2005 varied from $28,344 to $45,216, compared with $32,364 for a nurse and $82,032 for a physician. That they are respected helps persuade some of the best university students to go into teaching; there are ten applicants for every place at the university that trains teachers. Pupils do not enter school until age seven, with preschool available through age six. All must learn at least two foreign languages: Swedish by law and usually English by choice. The successes tend to cover up the problems: there is a high drop-out rate, and youth unemployment is high.

A sign that all is not well in this country with the world's best schools were two tragic events. In November 2007, a pupil murdered eight at Jokela high school in Tuusula. Another deranged student did the same in September 2008 at a trade college in Kauhajoki, western Finland, killing 10 and then himself with a semi-automatic pistol. Finland ranks fifth in the world in per capita gun ownership behind the U.S., Yemen, Switzerland and Serbia. Prime Minister Vanhanen called for stricter gun controls, and the nation is debating this.

Social Welfare

There is an extensive social welfare system as sweeping as that in neighboring Sweden. Finland's social welfare is certainly expensive: one fifth of the national budget is devoted to it, and it is one reason why the average Finn spends over a third of his income in taxes. The people receive generous unemployment benefits and pensions. Medical care is not totally free. Finns must pay for the first visit to a doctor, but they are free thereafter for the rest of the year. They do not pay for many medicines, and hospital care is usually not more than $10 per day in public institutions. The economic crisis in the 1990s adversely affected the welfare system. There have been cuts in social benefits and public health care.

Its universal and generally good health care system costs the country 7% of its GDP, compared with 15% in the U.S., which cannot finance universal care. The ban on smoking in bars and restaurants in June 2007 will make some Finns even healthier.

Finns have average life expectancies in Western Europe (76.2 years for men, 83 for women). Some observers attribute this to a predominantly meat and dairy diet that lacks sufficient vegetables. It confronts—as do many nations—a continuing problem of excessive alcohol consumption. One of the first things independent Finland did was to attempt to prohibit the drinking of alcohol. Prohibition was in effect from 1919 until 1932, but, as in the U.S., its only effect was that of creating a

President Halonen celebrates her reelection

new and prosperous occupation: bootlegging. Alcohol consumption, including binge drinking, doubled in the first decade of the 21st century. This has made the substance the number-one killer in Finland.

It has one of the lowest birth rates (1.7 replacement rate) in Western Europe and will be the first to experience a demographic shock. One group of parliamentarians found the situation so desperate in 2008 that they proposed a law to give Finns an additional week off work in order to go on a "love vacation." The sponsors explained that this would help stressed-out Finns revive passion and reduce their high divorce rate.

The percentage of the population over age 64 will jump from 17% in 2010 to 27% in 2035. By 2030 there will be one employed worker for each welfare or pension benefit recipient. This is due only partly to a very liberal abortion law. But it puts a squeeze on the economy and pension system as fewer workers will support an aging population. Finland expects to have the EU's oldest population by 2017. The average Finn retires at age 61.7, but a 2005 reform phased out early retirement, raised the pension age to 63, and created incentives to keep working.

Sports and Relaxation

One will hardly find a Finn who does not engage in the favorite national sport: cross-country skiing. The loggers' paths through the pine forests are ideal for skiers, When the snow melts, then Finland's long-distance runners attract the world's attention and have done so since the legendary Paavo Nurmi. "The Flying Finn" had built up such a lead in the 1,500-meter run in the 1924 Paris Olympics that he could walk the last 50 meters and still take one of his six Olympic gold medals. In the 1970s Lasse Viren carried the banner by becoming the first person ever to win gold medals in the five- and ten-thousand-meter runs in two successive Olympics.

Americans blink their eyes in disbelief to see Finns playing Pesäpallo, a very popular modified form of American baseball although the players dress like race drivers. Golf is increasingly popular. Most Finns dream of spending part of their year at a country cottage, preferably on one of the many lakes. A fourth of the population owns one and uses it in both summer and winter. There in solitude they enjoy spiritual renewal and such pleasures as sauna bathing.

One pleasure that bears an expensive price tag in Finland is speeding on public roads. Traffic fines are based partly on an offender's income. When in 2004 a wealthy heir to a local sausage factory was clocked at 50 miles per hour in a 25 mile per hour zone in downtown Helsinki, he was given a 170,000 euro ($221,000) fine. Even Nokia's president had to shell out 35,000 euros for running a red light. It should not be surprising that two of the country's candidates for the European Parliament in 2004 were race car drivers.

Perhaps the most widely known Finnish tradition is the sauna, one of the only Finnish words that have become part of the international vocabulary. Of the 5.26 million Finns, 1.5 million own saunas. Many Finns build them in their basements or in little wooden sheds outside their houses, and there is now one sauna for every five Finns. After sitting in temperatures from 180°F to 210°F (80°C to 100°C), they jump into ice-cold water or take a roll in the snow. They claim that there is nothing better for a person's health or frame of mind.

A sauna bath is also a meeting point for friends or business associates. In fact, the cabinet even conducted a working session once a week in the sauna. If former President Kekkonen had particular difficulty getting the various political leaders to agree on a policy, he merely took them into the sauna, where problems could be ironed out in a more relaxed style. This is no longer possible since the late 1980s because women are now in the cabinet. In Finland, men and women who are not in the same family or are not close friends traditionally do not steam together. In 1992 former Defense Minister Elizabeth Rehn ended the practice of conducting national security debates in the sauna once and for all by declaring: "I believe in making decisions when I am fully clothed, and not when I'm naked. That way I have my notebooks in my hand, and everybody knows what has been decided!" Helsinki's first female mayor, Eeva-Riïta Siitonen, a modern former TV announcer, President Tarja Halonen, and ex-Prime Minister Anneli Jaatteenmäki, no doubt agree.

FUTURE

Finland is the most prosperous country in the world, according to an index introduced in 2009 by Legatum, a London-based think tank. Close behind were the other Scandinavian countries, with the U.S. in ninth place. Because of earlier skill shortages in some sectors of the economy, Finland opened its door to immigrants from new EU partners in Eastern Europe in 2006. This especially benefited Estonians, who can speak the language and had already enjoyed visa-free travel. More and more Estonians and others worked in Finland. Unlike many Europeans, Finns are not obsessed with the uncertainties of globalization since they seem to benefit greatly from it. But they have not escaped the ravages of the world economic downturn in 2009, which has shaved 7.6% off its GDP. This temporarily limited Estonians' and other foreigners' work possibilities in Finland.

Finns are proud of being the only Nordic country to adopt the EU's single currency, the euro. There is some uneasiness. Many Finns think that too much power has been transferred to Brussels. An example is a regulation from the far-away European capital ordering member states to protect wolves and other endangered predators. The 7,000 reindeer herders in northern Finland protest against having to watch the growing wolf population decimate their herds relentlessly while having to get a permit to kill the well-fed predators. Even President Halonen asked an interviewer from the *Financial Times*: "Do you really think that in Brussels they know how many wolves we should have?"

Former Prime Minister Matti Vanhanen celebrates his reelection in 2007.

The Baltic Republics

Due to their shared histories as well as frequent geographical and cultural similarities, there is necessarily some repetition from one entry to the other.

changed borders. All three Baltic states were left to deal with the residual problems.

The three republics of Estonia, Latvia, and Lithuania are located along the eastern shores of the Baltic Sea. Finland lies to the north, separated from Estonia by the Gulf of Finland, while Sweden lies to the west, across the Baltic Sea. Estonia, the most northern of the three republics, borders on Russia to the east, though the two countries are physically separated along most of the border by a series of lakes that stretch from just north of Pskov to the Baltic Sea. Tallinn, the capital, major port and largest city, lies on the Gulf of Finland, 50 miles across from Helsinki, the capital of Finland. Estonia has 1,000 islands off of its coast, while Latvia and Lithuania have none. Latvia, to the south of Estonia, shares borders with Belarus and Russia on the east. Its capital, Riga—located on the Gulf of Riga at the mouth of the Daugava [Western Dvina] River—is its largest city and best port.

Lithuania, the most southern of the three republics, borders on the Kaliningrad enclave of the Russian Republic to the south and the Republic of Belarus on the east. Its shoreline, only 99 kilometers long, is relatively narrow and it has only one good port, the city of Klaipeda. Vilnius and Kaunas, its two major cities, lie considerably inland, Kaunas along the upper reaches of the Nemunas [Niemen] River and Vilnius on the Neris River, a tributary of the Nemunas. Vilnius, the current capital and the ancient capital of the Grand Principality of Lithuania, lies quite close to the current border of Belarus and was actually part of Poland between the first and second world wars.

The entire Baltic coastal area is a plain with occasional higher elevations, particularly as one moves away from the sea, but the highest of these elevations are never more than about 900 feet in height. Nevertheless, they are the reason why a number of small rivers flow through the Baltic Republics and into the Baltic Sea. The shoreline itself consists mostly of low dunes running along the beaches. There are plenty of sandy beaches, but the water is extremely shallow for a good distance into the sea, making swimming difficult. Pine forests, which predominate throughout the Baltic coastal area, often come down almost to the shore.

It is these pines that help to explain amber, the symbol of the Baltic. Fifty million years ago, the Baltic Sea was a vast marshland covered by pine trees. The resin oozed out of the pine trunks and dripped into the silt of the marsh where it eventu-

Imagine pushing against a locked door for 50 years—and suddenly it opens! The disintegration of the Soviet Union in 1991 enabled the Baltic States to be the first Soviet republics to regain independence. All three faced myriad challenges: they were severed from their traditional markets, introduced new currencies, established from scratch their own military forces, negotiated the departure of former Soviet troops and started cleaning up the environmen-

tal damage they had caused, adopted new constitutions and sets of laws, and organized their first democratic elections in a half century.

This dramatic turn in history did not automatically eradicate the legacies of an overbearing Soviet empire. In order to maintain control over a sprawling multinational state and promote its own socialist industrialization, the Kremlin had intentionally mixed peoples and capriciously

116

ally hardened, and then petrified over succeeding millennia. Today, amber is often found along the shore, washed up by the sea.

Most of the area was originally a combination of marsh and forest and even today farms give the appearance of having been cut out of the forest. Small lakes are very common, with an estimated 3,000 in Lithuania alone. Soils, which are usually gray, are relatively poor, and most farming is dairy farming. One arm of the Gulf Stream reaches into the Baltic, making the climate milder than it would otherwise be. Summers tend to be cool with frequent light rains. Winters are cold and damp.

Languages

The Estonian language belongs to the Finno-Ugric branch of the Ural-Altaic family, though it contains words taken from Swedish, German and Russian. It is closely related to Finnish. Because most Estonians watched Finnish television during Soviet time, they understand Finnish much more easily than Finns understand Estonian. The Estonians, along with the Finns, are the remnants of tribes that once lightly peopled much of the northern two-thirds of what is today European Russia. Although still existing in a couple dozen small pockets in Russia, particularly in the Karelian Peninsula, most were absorbed into the larger Slavic population over the centuries.

The Lithuanian and Latvian languages belong to the Letto-Lithuanian family of Indo-European languages. Lithuanian was heavily influenced by Polish, however, while Latvian shows influences from Swedish, German and Russian, the tongues of peoples who once controlled the country. Although Latvian and Lithuanian are related to each other, the three Baltic languages are mutually incomprehensible.

HISTORY

Balts have occupied this same area for over 2,000 years. The first historical reference is in Tacitus's *Germania*, where he praises the Lithuanians for their talents in farming. The Baltic area had some contact with the civilizations to the south because of amber, which is found along the Baltic coast and became the basis for a trade route that came into existence as early as the second millennium B.C. The decline of the Roman Empire turned this area once more into a back-water, however, and nothing more was heard for several centuries.

The next historical reference dates from the 7th century, when Viking raiders swept down out of Scandinavia and launched a series of raids along the coast and up the rivers. These invasions, continuing for the next 200 years, eventually resulted in some Viking settlements along the rivers. Most of the Baltic Sea area was under the control of the Vikings at this time, but their main interest was on expansion of the trade route across Russia down to Constantinople. Accordingly, they only levied an annual tribute on the Baltic peoples and otherwise left them alone.

On the periphery, the Baltic peoples all remained pagan even as their neighbors to the west and the south embraced Christianity. That led, at the beginning of the 13th century, to a Christianizing effort by German missionaries. These first were peaceful, and a bishopric was actually established at Riga in 1201. This peaceful penetration was soon followed by an invasion of crusading knights, the most significant being the Knights of the Sword and the Order of Teutonic Knights. The Teutonic Knights conquered present-day Latvia in 1225. Gradually, the area of Estonia was also brought under the control of the Knights of the Sword, who subsequently turned it over to the Order of Teutonic Knights. The Latvians and Estonians were made serfs and converted to Christianity, but they managed to retain many of their customs and their own languages.

Meanwhile the Lithuanians, who up to this time had been organized into separate tribes, formed a federation. Gediminas [1316–1341] founded the Jogaila [Jagellon] dynasty and laid the basis of the Grand Duchy of Lithuania. During his lifetime, Gediminas extended his conquests southward, fighting both Russians and Tatars until his kingdom extended from the Baltic to the Black Sea. He thus freed the western part of Kievan Rus from the control of the Tatars, including the city of Kiev itself.

Gediminas was slain in 1341 while once again attempting to drive back the Teutonic Knights. He was succeeded by his son, Jagellon [Jogaila], who married Hedwige, queen of Poland. Jagellon, having converted to Roman Catholicism, took over as ruler of Poland and turned over the Grand Duchy of Lithuania to his cousin, Vytautas. Christianity was adopted in 1387. Vytautas died without an heir in 1430, however, so the crown reverted back to the Jogaila line. From that time, the Grand Duchy of Lithuania was increasingly tied to Poland until, in 1569, the two kingdoms were merged in the Union of Lublin. In its heyday in the 16th century, the Grand Duchy of Lithuania was a huge multiconfessional empire, extending all the way to the Black Sea, with six legal languages, including Hebrew and Armenian.

Lithuania continued to have its own laws and army. But the upper classes became increasingly Polanized, and most of them became Roman Catholic. Polish replaced Russian as the language of administration in the 16th century.

In 1772, 1793 and 1795, Poland-Lithuania was partitioned among its neighbors. As a result, Russia obtained the Ukrainian and White Russian territories plus all of Lithuania proper up to the Nemunas River. Russia obtained the remaining Lithuanian territories in 1815.

The spread of the Protestant Reformation in the 16th century led to the creation of the two secular states of Courland and Livonia and the dissolution of the Teutonic Knights in 1560. The former knights converted to Lutheranism and became a secular nobility. Their Estonian and Latvian serfs were also converted at this same time.

Courland and Livonia became takeover targets of their neighbors. The Russian tsar, Ivan the Terrible, wanted to gain control of ports along the Baltic and launched his Livonian War in 1558. He was successful in the beginning, but when the Teutonic Knights collapsed in 1560, Poland stepped in and stole his conquests, annexing Livonia and Courland to Poland-Lithuania. At the beginning of the 17th century, the Swedish King, Gustavus Adolphus, intervened and seized most of Livonia in 1626. The Swedish territory, which included most of modern day Estonia, was given a relatively liberal regime. The privileges of the German nobility—the so-called Baltic Barons—were curtailed somewhat and a university was established at Dorpat (now Tartu). It was also as a result of Swedish rule that the Lutheran Church continued as the established church in Estonia.

Modern Nordic solidarity. Estonian (l) and Swedish students at the College of Europe.

Baltic Republics

At the end of the 17th century, Peter the Great came to the throne in Russia and launched his Great Northern War against Sweden in 1700. The war lasted until 1721, but Riga fell to Russia in 1710 and Tallinn [Revel] soon afterwards. Russia obtained Livonia and Estonia by the Peace of Nystadt. Courland gradually became a Russian protectorate during the 18th century and was formally annexed in 1795.

The Baltics under Russian Rule

Peter the Great allowed his new Baltic subjects to retain their own laws and the autonomous status they had enjoyed under the Swedes. There was no attempt to introduce Russian institutions or to encourage the spread of the Orthodox religion. Peter's second wife, Catherine, was actually a Baltic peasant girl whom he took as a mistress during the Baltic campaign and later married. It was the German-speaking nobility that benefited most from this autonomy; the Letts and Estonians were still mainly serfs. There were some economic benefits to the area, however; in the 18th century, Riga became Russia's second major port after St. Petersburg, a position it would continue to hold in the 19th century.

A major change occurred at the beginning of the 19th century when Alexander I became tsar. He detested serfdom and as early as 1803 issued a decree permitting the voluntary emancipation of the serfs. Later in his reign, Alexander abolished serfdom in the Baltic provinces, in Estonia in 1816, Courland in 1817, and Livonia in 1819. In Lithuania, which was under a separate administration, serfdom continued. It was abolished there in 1861, as part of the general serf emancipation throughout the Russian Empire.

In the Baltic Provinces, the short-term consequences of emancipation were mainly negative. The Baltic serfs were freed without land. Having no alternate means of employment, they found themselves working as day laborers for the same large landowners who had been their masters before emancipation. But the long-term consequences were both positive and far-reaching. The presence of free labor made Estonia and Latvia logical places to locate manufacturing plants when foreign capital began pouring into Russia after Alexander II launched his great reforms in the 1850s.

Russian rule also had its negative aspects in the 19th century. In Lithuania, in particular, the Russian government resented the role of the Roman Catholic Church and actively fostered the spread of the Orthodox Church in this area. It did not help that Lithuania participated, along with Poland, in the uprisings of 1830 and 1863. The University of Vilnius was closed down after the 1830 uprising, and the Russian lan-

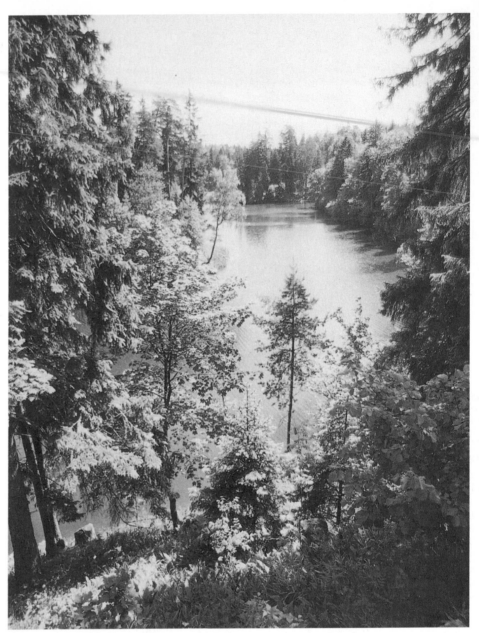

Lachemaa National Park, Estonia

Courtesy: NOVOSTI

guage was introduced in all schools. After the 1863 uprising, land ownership was limited to adherents of the Orthodox faith.

Perhaps the greatest sustained effort at Russification came during the reign of Alexander III [1881–1894]. Alexander, a Slavophil and strong adherent of Russian Orthodoxy, extended previous Russification efforts to the areas of Estonia and Latvia and even applied them to the previously exempt German-speaking upper classes.

The industrialization process, begun by Alexander II, was continued by his son, Alexander III. One result was the creation of both an urban working class and a middle class, including professionals and intellectuals, in the Baltic provinces. All this

provided the basis for the beginning of Estonian and Latvian national movements.

In Lithuania, a similar development occurred, though on the basis of a different class, the peasant landholders who emerged as a result of serf emancipation in 1861. Many of these peasant proprietors sent their sons off to be educated in Russian universities, and they came back as doctors, lawyers, teachers and engineers. This led to the creation of the first specifically Lithuanian nationalist movement in the 1890s.

By 1905, illegal nationalist political parties existed in Estonia, Latvia and Lithuania and took an active part in the Revolution of 1905. The Lithuanians were perhaps the best organized, having suffered longer from repression, but similar activities were carried in all three areas. A provisional revolutionary government was established in Riga and two separate congresses met in Vilnius in December 1905. With the collapse of the revolution, widespread arrests were carried out, but government repression only succeeded in forcing the more prominent nationalist leaders to emigrate while the nationalist movements themselves went underground.

The beginning of World War I provided a new opportunity for the nationalists. Although the majority of the Baltic peoples loyally supported the war effort in the beginning, the subsequent course of the war brought disaffection here as it did in other parts of the Russian Empire. After March 1917, the Baltic nationalists backed the democratic aspirations of the first Russian Revolution of 1917, but began pressing for their own governments. The Bolshevik Revolution of November 1917 further alienated the Baltic peoples because the vast majority favored the creation of democratic states.

Creation of the New Baltic Governments

Developments in the Baltic provinces followed a fairly similar pattern after March 1917 although the fact that almost all of Lithuania and the southern half of Latvia were occupied by German troops obviously made for differences. The most important factor between March and November 1917 was the attitude of the Russian Provisional Government. Although not sympathetic to independence movements, it authorized establishment of an autonomous Estonian government in April 1917, which led to elections for an Estonian National Council in July. Konstantin Päts, leader of the Farmers' Union, was installed as president of the National Council on July 14.

Lettish delegates to the Russian Duma had organized a Latvian Refugees' Committee even before the March Revolution. After March 1917, they began urging the Provisional Government to establish an autonomous administrative district for the part of Latvia still under Russian control. Local elections were held in the north, but the fact of German occupation in the south militated against any further developments at this time.

The situation in Lithuania was even worse because almost the entire country was under occupation. Nevertheless, Lithuanian deputies to the Duma organized a Lithuanian National Council in Petrograd and began to demand political autonomy from the Provisional Government.

The Bolshevik seizure of power in November 1917 proved to be a turning point. The national movements rejected Bolshevism and tried to break away from the new Communist government. The Bolsheviks, in turn, rejected the national movements and tried to suppress them.

A Latvian National Council, established after the November Revolution, declared Latvian autonomy on November 16 and called for election of a constituent assembly to form a Latvian government. The Estonian government proclaimed its independence on November 28 and also called for elections to a constituent assembly.

The Bolsheviks not only refused to recognize the Latvian National Council; they also abolished the local government bodies set up by the Provisional Government. In Estonia, they arrested President Päts and dispersed the National Council. The Bolsheviks did permit elections to a new constituent assembly, but when the parties of the old government won a majority of the seats in January 1918, the Bolsheviks moved to suppress the winners. A civil war broke out and lasted about a month before German troops moved into Estonia, and the Bolsheviks were forced to flee. The Lithuanian National Council, split between radicals and moderates, did not take a specific stand against the Bolsheviks, but they moved to suppress the Lithuanian National Council anyway.

The Bolsheviks soon lost control of the Baltic provinces, first, because of advances of the German army, and then through agreement to the Treaty of Brest-Litovsk. The Bolsheviks had wanted to retain the Baltic provinces, but one of the results of the Bolshevik seizure of power in 1917 was disintegration of the Russian army. Unable to stop the German advance, the new Communist government signed the Treaty of Brest-Litovsk with Imperial Germany in March 1918, thereby giving up all claims to the Baltic provinces. The entire Baltic coastal area was at this time occupied by the German army. Baltic nationalists now faced the threat of annexation by Germany and again found themselves suppressed and their leaders imprisoned. The collapse of the German Empire in November 1918 put an end to that. But as the German armies began to pull out, the Bolsheviks poured back in, and the Baltic peoples had to fight another round with the Bolsheviks in order to establish their independence.

The armistice called for the German army to begin evacuating the Baltic provinces, a process that eventually stretched over several months. In the meantime, the nationalist leaders began organizing independent governments. Estonia, which had had an operating government once before, began reconstituting itself immediately after the armistice. The Estonian National Council met on November 20, President Päts was released from prison soon afterwards. The new government

began operating on February 24, 1919. Two months later, Päts was replaced by Otto Strandman, a member of the leftist Workers' Party. A few months later, Strandman gave way to Jaan Tonisson, the leader of the *People's Party*, who served until 1920.

Governments had to be created in Latvia and Lithuania, but the nationalist leaders had been active for some time and so were well known. An All-Latvian Council of State met at Riga on November 18, 1918, formed a Provisional Government and appointed a president and prime minister. Karlis Ulmanis, leader of the Peasants' League, became the first president. He held this office until 1920.

In Lithuania, a Provisional Government was also set up in November. A National Assembly met in Kaunas in January 1919, and the first Lithuanian president was elected on April 4. Even as they were organizing their governments, the nationalists found themselves again under attack as Bolshevik armies reopened the war following the German surrender. By February 1919, Latvia had been completely overrun and most of Lithuania was under occupation by Bolshevik forces. Estonia, which had begun to form its own army, was a little luckier. It managed to drive the Bolsheviks back to the border.

The situation in Latvia was more complicated. A Latvian army was created and began driving back the Bolsheviks, with some assistance from German army units still in the country. Once they had regained control of most of the country, however, the German army supported a *coup d'état* against the Latvian government, installing a new one controlled by Baltic Germans. The Estonian and Latvian armies first joined to drive out the Bolsheviks, then turned on the puppet Baltic German government and overthrew it. The Latvian government was reinstated on July 7, 1919. Riga, the Latvian capital, came under attack again by German forces in October, but managed to hold out. Meanwhile, part of Latvia was still held by Bolshevik forces until they were driven out in January 1920.

The Bolsheviks had invaded the new Estonian state in March 1919 to take power in Northeast Estonia. However, the Estonians defeated them in January 1920 and signed with Soviet Russia the Treaty of Tartu on February 2, 1920, which drew the border along the military frontlines and recognized Estonia's independence, sovereignty, and neutrality "forever." It represented a major victory over Bolshevik Russia and was one of the few military victories in Estonian history. Similar treaties recognizing Baltic independence were signed with Lithuania on July 12, and with Latvia on August 11, 1920,

Baltic Republics

Baltic Area – 15th to Early 18th Centuries

Swedish Possessions	
Teutonic Order (about 1400) / Prussia (1561, 1660 and 1721)	
Republic of Novgorod (about 1400) / Muscovy (1561) / Russia (1660 and 1721)	
Lithuania (about 1400) / Poland-Lithuania (1561, 1660 and 1721)	
Duchy of Courland: Dependency of Poland-Lithuania (1660 and 1721)	

Mindaugas

several months after the last Bolshevik forces had finally been withdrawn from the Baltic area. International recognition soon followed, and all three states were admitted to the League of Nations in 1922.

Reoccupation and Sovietization

Like other European countries, the Soviet Union peered anxiously at a restless and expansive Germany, and it sought to protect itself. On August 23, 1939, the USSR and Germany signed a nonaggression pact that contained a secret protocol dividing Europe into spheres of influence; Finland, Estonia, Latvia and (one month later) Lithuania were assigned to the Soviet Union. This freed Moscow's hand to attack Finland in November 1939 and ultimately force it to make territorial concessions, while remaining independent. It also enabled Stalin to issue an ultimatum to the Baltic states in 1939 and again in 1940 to accept Soviet troops on their soil. It then demanded governments loyal to the Soviet Union. With a small number of their own troops surrounded on their own territory by superior numbers of Soviet Army troops, and noting that 25,000 Finns had died in the unsuccessful effort to thwart a Soviet invasion, they did not dare resist.

Believing he could temporarily stave off disaster for the Estonian nation until the frightening political situation improved, President Päts signed a document accepting Stalin's demands. He and most other Estonian leaders were then deported to the Soviet Union. The new Moscow-controlled government, aided by local Estonian Communists (numbering only 133 in the entire country) staged elections to parliament, during which no mention of any impending annexation by the Soviet Union was made. Only Communist-dominated organizations were allowed to

nominate candidates. Deputies obedient to the Communists won 92.8% of the votes. The new parliament formally asked to join the Soviet Union on July 22, 1940, and was accepted on August 6, 1940. The other Baltic states were led through the same procedure and met the same fate in August 1940.

Russia today adamantly denies that the Soviet Union had ever "occupied" the Baltic states and that their joining was involuntary, despite some admitted pressure at the time. In May 2005 the Russian ambassador to the European Union asserted: "One cannot use the term 'occupation' to describe those historical events. At that time the troop deployment took place on an agreed basis and with the clearly expressed agreement of the existing authorities in the Baltic republics." Asked if the Russians were lying about this part of Baltic history, Latvian President Vaira Vike-Freiberga answered, "Through their teeth."

Although a very different regime rules in Russia since the collapse of the Soviet Union, the United Nations acknowledged the Russian Federation as the successor to the USSR. Therefore Russia is cautious about renouncing what was done under Communist rule. It fears that concessions could open Pandora's box of claims against it and provide a precedent for other newly independent republics and even nations

within the present borders of Russia, such as Chechnya. It has never apologized for the Soviet Union's actions in 1940 or subsequent crimes, even though the Baltic states demand such an apology. Nor has it ever hinted that the occupation might have been illegal. The fact that the Balts accepted their fate without armed resistance in 1940 lends some credibility to the Russians' interpretation. Interrupted only by German occupation from 1941 to 1944, the Baltic states spent the next half-century as disgruntled but relatively prosperous republics of the Soviet Union.

Independence

Encouraged by Mikhail Gorbachev's reform proposals, which permitted more free discussion and toleration than ever in Soviet history, the Baltic states seized the opportunity first to enlarge their self-determination within the Soviet Union and then to gain complete independence. In 1988 "popular fronts," composed of both Gorbachev Communists and non-Communist democrats and nationalists were formed, first in Estonia and then in Latvia and Lithuania. On August 23, 1989, the 50th anniversary of the German-Soviet nonaggression pact, two million Estonians, Latvians and Lithuanians formed a human chain from Tallinn to Vilnius to dramatize their demand for freedom.

On the way to church, Estonia (19th century)

Baltic Republics

Courtesy: George Skudos

With large and articulate exile groups, especially in the U.S., the three peoples were able to mobilize considerable international sympathy and diplomatic support for their aspirations. This was especially facilitated by the fact that all Western democracies, except Sweden and briefly Australia, had refused to recognize the Soviet Union's annexation of the Baltics in 1940.

Lithuania became the first Soviet republic to declare its independence on March 11, 1990, followed by Estonia on March 30 and Latvia on May 5, 1990. On May 12 the heads of all three countries signed the Declaration of Concord and Cooperation reestablishing the 1934 Council of the Baltic States.

Gorbachev indignantly rejected these demands for independence and even ordered that Interior Ministry troops use force against dissidents in the streets of Vilnius on January 13, 1991, killing 15. A week later six persons were killed in Riga, and the threat of violence also hung over Estonia. Russian President Boris Yeltsin supported the Balts' calls for freedom, and Gorbachev ultimately joined him in agreeing to sign a new union treaty on August 19, 1991. This treaty, along with the prospects of Baltic independence, precipitated the Moscow coup attempt against Gorbachev on that day. The

insurrection's failure after only three days prompted most countries in the world to recognize the Baltic states' independence.

The Nordic countries and the European Community (EC, after 1994 called the European Union—EU) were first, followed by the United States on September 2 and the post-coup Soviet government on September 6, 1991. On September 17, 1991, the Baltic Republics, which had belonged to the League of Nations, were admitted to the United Nations. With strong Western support, all three Baltic states negotiated the withdrawal of Russian troops from their territories—by August 1993 for Lithuania, and by August 1994 for Estonia and Latvia.

All three states entered NATO in April 2004 although they have no significant armed forces. Their three top commanders form the Baltic Military Committee, which meets twice a year to review their NATO requirements and joint defense projects. In an important speech in Warsaw in June 2001, President George W. Bush had given the signal by saying, "all of Europe's new democracies, from the Baltic to the Black Sea and all that lie between, should have the same chance for security and freedom."

Before then it had been assumed that Russia would never have permitted Baltic participation in NATO, but much had

changed under the leadership of former President (now Prime Minister) Vladimir Putin. Russia's past threats and bluster had been counter-productive by merely underscoring the Baltic states' need for protection from an overbearing neighbor. It had also become clear to the Russian government after the September 11 terrorist attacks against the U.S. that its real security threats come from the south and east, not the west. It needed Western, especially American, help in defending itself from those threats and in shoring up its battered economy. Finally, Putin realized that there was little he could do to stop NATO enlargement into the Baltics. Lithuania's President Valdas Adamkus made it unmistakably clear why the Balts wanted to join: "Accepting Lithuania into NATO is a signal to Russia that never will Lithuania be taken over by Russia again. This is a formal declaration to Russia politically that we are free, and declaring ourselves free forever."

At NATO's Prague summit in November 2002 that signal was given, and all three Baltic states were formally invited to join, which they did in April 2004. Nevertheless, the warnings did not go away. A senior Russian general warned NATO in March 2004 against deploying weapons and aircraft close to the Russian border. The NATO Secretary-General responded by assuring the Balts, who possess no fighter jets, that "it will be NATO airspace, and NATO airspace will be policed." Some NATO nations rotate in providing air cover for the Baltics.

Even before joining NATO, the three states had acquired an advanced radar system, called Baltnet, which looks deep into Russia. The Russians try continually to test it, as one unfortunate pilot did in September 2005 by penetrating Lithuanian airspace. When his Su-27 fighter bomber's electronics failed, he had to bail out 120 miles northwest of Vilnius. The Lithuanians held him and his wrecked plane in custody until they had fully investigated the incident.

The three states responded differently in 2005 to Russia's invitation to attend the 60th anniversary of the victory over Nazi Germany on May 9, 1945. The entire affair reopened old wounds. The presidents of Estonia and Lithuania boycotted the ceremony, refusing to celebrate their countries' own occupation. The Latvian president agreed to go, but she stated that while victory over Hitler meant freedom for many, "for others it meant slavery, it meant occupation, it meant subjugation and it meant Stalinist terror." All three were appalled by Russian President Vladimir Putin's statements that the collapse of the Soviet Union was "the greatest geopolitical catastrophe of the 20th century" and that the 1939 Molotov-Ribbentrop pact had been a measure to enhance Russia's security. In light of Moscow's policy of intimidation toward the Baltics, it is little wonder that in 2008 all three avidly supported Ukraine's and Georgia's bid to join NATO.

Putin was irritated by ex-President George W. Bush's decision to "bookend" his own trip to Moscow by visiting Riga beforehand and Georgia afterwards. In Latvia on May 7, 2005, Bush, whom many Balts saw as the world's most potent symbol of freedom, met all three Baltic presidents and received Latvia's highest medal, the Three-Star Order. He granted all three visa-free travel to the U.S. He repeatedly spoke of the earlier "occupation," while acknowledging that the U.S. and Britain shared some blame for the division of Europe and the annexation because they had caved in to Stalin at the February 1945 Yalta conference. Recognizing Russian sensitivities, he gently urged all three countries to respect the rights of their Russian minorities. In 2008 the U.S. reached bilateral agreements with Estonia and Latvia to open the way to visa-free travel, with Lithuania only a step behind. It is galling to Russians that they need visas to enter the three Baltic states.

The fact that the three Baltic states did not act like a unified bloc was a reminder of how different they are. Ex-President Vike-Freiberga of Latvia put it like this: "Don't expect us to dance out onstage in a line like the little swans in Swan Lake." The specific reference to a Russian ballet was intentional. She noted that their accession to NATO and the EU has diminished their need for cooperation. EU membership means that they have to compete over benefits from Brussels. It is significant that former Lithuanian President Valdas Adamkus's active role in helping to defuse the election crisis in Ukraine in 2004–5 was not a Baltic initiative. In turn, the three states, together with Poland, urge their EU partners to be cautious about an intrusive Russia. The three countries' parliaments agreed in 2005 to pass on many functions of their own Baltic Assembly to a Pan-Scandinavian Nordic Council. Their economies are the fastest-growing in the EU, but their different economies are producing increasingly different societies.

Russia always looms menacingly next door. Like most countries in central Europe, all three Baltic states are nervous about President Barack Obama's talk of pushing the "restart" button with Russia. President Medvedev's references to a "sphere of privileged interests" in former Soviet states do not sound good in their ears even though President Obama rejected such a notion. A open letter in July 2009

signed by former Baltic presidents and ministers, among other central European leaders, warned that "all is not well either in our region or in the transatlantic relationship.?. . . NATO today seems weaker than when we joined," and "Russia is back as a revisionist power pursuing a nineteenth-century agenda with twenty-first-century tactics and methods." The Russian attack on Georgia in August 2008 reverberates, especially since it prompted no clear and determined western response from the NATO allies. In 2009 Russia conducted its largest military maneuvers for years along the Baltic border. Estonia's president Toomas Hendrik Ilves noted: "What we have seen is a complete paradigm shift in the security architecture of Europe. Everything we have done has been based on the assumption that Russia won't engage in aggression. . . . That premise is no longer operable."

A new Russian law outlawing any identification of Nazism with Soviet Communism criminalizes the way the Baltic states view their post-WWII experience. Perhaps worst, opinion polls in many European NATO countries reveal that a majority of citizens strongly oppose the use of their national armies to defend east European and Baltic nations from a Russian attack. Only in Britain and France do more people support defending the Baltic states than oppose it. NATO foreign ministers met in Tallinn in April 2010. Secretary of State Hillary Clinton assured the leaders of all three Baltic states of America's commitment to defend them and that "we believe there is no sphere of influence, no veto power that Russia or any country has over any country in Europe concerning membership in NATO." The U.S. pushed its NATO partners to agreeing to develop military contingency plans to defend the Baltic allies.

Economies

The Baltic states have been the most successful former Soviet republics in transforming their economies from socialism to market economies. They had always been the most prosperous republics within the Soviet Union and the most enthusiastic practitioners of Gorbachev's *perestroika*, so they were well poised to reform their economies when the opportunity came in 1991. They were the first to

introduce their own currencies, to free prices, wages and trade, to reduce government subsidies and inflation, and to sell off state enterprises. The visitor now finds increasing signs of prosperity everywhere.

This change has not been experienced at equal rates, and the diminution of many citizens' living standards, especially of those on fixed incomes, cannot be ignored. High inflation in the early postcommunist years, affecting such essentials as rent, heat, food, day care, and such free-time activities as cultural entertainment, caused many persons grudgingly to change their lives and, at times, reflect on the ways things were materially better in the old regime. In Latvia and Lithuania, resentments caused by shock therapy have helped former Communists occasionally win elections.

Young and well-educated persons, along with some well-placed former Communist elites who could benefit from privatization, are doing well. Elderly persons, large families, and single women are struggling. The social welfare net that most Western European democracies have built up over the past few decades does not yet exist, mainly because their states cannot afford it and, in the case of Estonia and Latvia, because their constitutions mandate balanced budgets.

The global recession hit the Baltic states very hard, shaving 17% off Estonia's GDP in 2009, a stunning 24% off Latvia's and 15% off Lithuania's. This downturn began two years earlier when reckless credit and real estate bubbles began popping. It will take several years to return to the stability and growth they had experienced.

At the beginning of the 21st century, the Baltic states enjoyed the fastest economic growth rates in Europe. Estonia's grew by 11.4% in 2006 alone. No wonder they were called the "Baltic tigers." By 2008 that growth was slowing down. If their 8%–12% growth rates would have continued, they would have doubled their standard of living in a decade. This was the result of good luck and good policies. They are stable, business-friendly, inexpensive and close to rich markets. They have free trade agreements with each other. Unemployment was low in all three although it has climbed with the recession. A thriving shadow economy and the fact that by 2007

Baltic Republics

several hundred thousands of young Balts had found work in the UK and Ireland and later in Sweden and Finland meant that real unemployment was even lower. But this migration created serious labor shortages.

Such rapid growth and westward migration have created problems. Every country worries about a brain drain of its educated youth. Remittances drive up inflation, including for housing, whose prices rose in Estonia by 28% in 2005 alone and at a rate of 10% to 15% annually from 1999 to 2007. Tallinn especially became a magnet for foreigners eager to speculate on property, particularly in the medieval old town. Soaring lending fueled this rise in property prices until they fell sharply in 2008. Annual wage growth of 20% (30% in Latvia) was good news for the employed, but it exceeded productivity increases and added to inflation. All three countries have a long way to go to catch up with Western Europe. The richest, Estonia, is only two-thirds of the EU average GDP per capita. The overheated economies are cooling sharply. With high inflation and sky-high current account deficits (23% of GDP in Latvia, 16% in Estonia and 13% in Lithuania in 2008) hopes of qualifying for the euro before 2012 were

dashed for all but Estonia, which is determined to enter January 1, 2011.

Unlike Russia, they produce a variety of goods that Western consumers want to buy, from cars, ships and clothing to medicines and beer. They have dramatically shifted their trade from the ex-Soviet Union toward the prosperous West, especially the Baltic Sea area, with some 70 million consumers. For example, between 1991 and 2007 Estonia's foreign trade with Russia had declined from 95% of total trade to well below 10%. About two-thirds of its trade is now with the EU, a figure that grew after 10 new countries, including the Baltic states, entered the EU May 2004.

Few Balts fear an imminent Russian military invasion, but many are anxious about Russian political and economic interference. Baltic trade with Russia remains important even as all three struggle to minimize their energy dependence on Russia. They are scrambling to prevent their major power industries from being gobbled up by much larger Russian energy companies, which seek to increase their control over pipelines and the supply and distribution of natural gas and electricity. For example, Gazprom owns 37% of Estonia's Eesti Gaas, 34% of Lat-

via's Latvijas Gaze and 34% of Lithuania's Lietuvos Dujos. Lukoil gasoline stations are all over the Baltics.

The Baltics face such common problems as trying to minimize pollution in the Baltic Sea, a particularly sensitive body of water because of its shallowness, its semi-enclosure, and its brackish waters that are renewed only every 30 years. The Baltic Sea had been used as a weapons dump for the Soviet, American and British militaries after the Second World War; entire German ships full of captured weapons, including bombs, blistering agents and nerve gas, and 14 chemical agents, were scuttled. These toxic substances are returning from the depths to haunt fishermen and the littoral states. Pointing to this danger, Estonia became the first Baltic Sea country to reject a request by the Russo-German company, Nord Stream, to make preparations in its waters for a gas pipeline on the sea floor between Russia and Germany.

The Baltics are making relatively good progress toward establishing rule of law, including established and impartial commercial law. Among 155 countries ranked in a 2004 Economic Freedom Index, Estonia was sixth, Lithuania 22nd and Latvia 29th. A whiff of corruption hangs over the privatization program, which is largely finished. Such corruption exists in the political and economy sectors in all three, and all are experiencing organized crime and high crime rates in general. Latvia, Lithuania, Estonia and Russia in that order have the world's highest suicide rates. But these problems are far below the level found in CIS countries. In 2009 Transparency International ranked Estonia 27th among 133 countries in terms of corruption, Lithuania 41st and Latvia 59th. Indeed, one reason why Estonia, Latvia and Lithuania were invited to join the EU was that they were judged to have the cleanest public administrations in the former communist world.

EU membership brings challenges. Per capita GDP in the Baltics is far below the EU average, and Latvia and Lithuania have three times the proportion of farmers and one-third of the EU's average agricultural productivity. They are creeping up in the UN human-development ranking: Estonia 41st, Lithuania 45th and Latvia 50th. EU membership does not in itself bring wealth. *The Economist* estimated that it could take more than a half-century for them to draw level with the earlier EU members. But it will certainly bring all three more stability and security, trade and investment, freedom of movement for their citizens, and the opportunity to act as bridges between East and West.

Newspapers from Estonia, Latvia, and Lithuania. *Diena* folded in 2009.

Republic of Estonia

The 15th century City Hall, Tallinn

Courtesy: NOVOSTI

Area: 18,370 sq. mi. (45,227 sq. km. Larger than either the Netherlands or Switzerland, and bigger than New Hampshire and Massachusetts combined).

Population: 1.3 million (UN, 2007).

Capital City: Tallinn (430,900).

Climate: Temperate with cool summers and cold winters, somewhat tempered by an arm of the gulf stream that reaches into the Baltic.

Neighboring Countries: Russia (east); Latvia (south).

Official Language: Estonian.

Other Principal Tongue: Russian.

Ethnic Background: Estonian is linguistically close to Finnish. There is some German influence as a result of being ruled by German Knights from the 13th to 17th centuries, and extensive Russian influence as a result of being part of the Russian Empire 1709–1918. Estonians currently make up about 67.9% of the population.

Other Ethnic Groups: Russians (25.6%); Ukrainians (2.1%); Belarusians (1.3%); Finns (.9%).

Principal Religions: Lutheranism, Russian Orthodox Christianity.

Chief Commercial Products: Machinery and equipment, wood and paper, food

products, furniture, clothing and footwear, chemicals, transport equipment.

Main Trading Partners: EU (70.2% of exports and 78.6% of imports), Finland (17.9% of exports and 15.8% of imports), Sweden (13.2% of exports and 10% of imports), Latvia (11.4% of exports and 7.5% of imports), Russia (8.8% of exports and 10.1% of imports), Germany (12.7% of imports), Lithuania (5.8% of exports).

Currency: kroon (The euro is used as of January 1, 2010).

Former Political Status: Conquered by German and Danish Knights in the 13th century, it came under Swedish control

Toomas Hendrik Ilves
The President of Estonia

125

Estonia

in the 17th century. Peter the Great annexed it in 1710 and it remained part of the Russian Empire until 1918. Independent state, 1918–1940. Annexed to the Soviet Union by Stalin in 1940; declared its independence in August 1991.

Independence Day: February 24.
Chief of State: Toomas Hendrik Ilves, President (since October 2006)
Head of Government: Andrus Ansip, Prime Minister (since April 2005)

ESTONIA SINCE WORLD WAR I

Independent Estonia, 1918–1940

Estonia had elected a constituent assembly charged with drawing up a constitution for the country in April 1919. The left dominated the assembly, so that the constitution that was eventually produced was what might be called "radical liberal" in orientation. Approved by the assembly in June 1920, it went into effect on December 21, 1920. All power was vested in a single-body legislature of 100 members called the *Riigikogu*. This was a modified parliamentary system. The "commission of the legislature" was essentially a cabinet, while the presiding officer, called the *Riigivanem* ["Senior Statesman"], performed the functions of a premier. There was no separate head of state, however, so the "Senior Statesman" performed all ceremonial functions as well. Another unusual feature of the constitution is that it provided for popular participation in decision-making by means of the referendum and the initiative.

A survey taken in 1922 gives us a good picture of the country. The total population was 1,107,300 with Estonians making up 87.6% of the total. Another 8.2% of the population spoke Russian, while 1.7% spoke German. Estonia was thus the most homogeneous of the Baltic states at this time, and its minorities enjoyed full citizenship rights. It was also religiously homogeneous, with 78.3% of the population declaring themselves to be Protestant, with another 19% professing Russian Orthodoxy. And it was rural, with 58.5% of the population earning their living from agriculture.

In 1918, two-thirds of the rural population had owned no land whatsoever but, instead, supported themselves by working as day laborers for the large estates that made up 58% of the land. Land reform legislation, passed in October 1919, expropriated nearly all the estates and distributed the land to the landless rural laborers. An additional 56,000 small holdings were created. This undoubtedly made political sense, since Baltic Germans owned a majority of the estates. But the plots turned out to be too little, so that a majority of the new owners were unable

to survive without extensive governmental assistance. The eventual solution was to organize the small holders into cooperative societies, which were able to buy modern machinery that could be used on several farms.

An economic crisis began in 1929 and then turned into what the Americans called the "Great Depression." Estonia was heavily dependent on agricultural exports, and the sharp drop in the international price of these products led to great distress in Estonia, particularly in the countryside. As in many other European countries, the depression placed unbearable burdens on democracy.

It was at this time that a new political grouping, the Association of Estonian Freedom Fighters, began to grow in significance and power. It had been organized in 1929 as a veterans' organization espousing patriotism, nationalism and anti-communism. By 1932 it was beginning to show increasing tendencies toward anti-parliamentarianism and anti-liberalism. The Freedom Fighters, organized into paramilitary organizations, wore gray-green shirts, with black and white armbands bearing a hand grasping a sword and the dates 1918–1920.

Their most important demand was for the creation of a separate executive power that would be independent of the legislature. The Freedom Fighters' proposal for constitutional reform was submitted to referendum in October 1933 and passed. This constitutional change created the office of president of the republic, to be popularly elected for a term of five years. It also vested executive power in the president rather than the legislature. The president could appoint and dismiss governments, declare states of emergency and dissolve the legislature. The revised constitution went into effect on January 24, 1934, and elections were set to fill the new presidency. Among the candidates was General Andreas Larka, president of the Freedom Fighters. Another candidate was Konstantin Päts, then serving as premier. The Freedom Fighters swept urban local elections at the beginning of 1934, and it appeared that their man would win the presidency as well.

Päts decided to take preemptive action by pulling off his own coup before elections could occur. He therefore gave the commander-in-chief of the army special powers to maintain law and order and then banned the Freedom Fighters as a "threat to the security of the state." He also banned all political assemblies. The Estonian legislature met, approved Päts's emergency legislation, then was dismissed. Päts issued a decree postponing presidential elections indefinitely. The legislature met for a short time in September 1934, but it

**Early Estonia:
outdoor museum in Tallinn**

was dissolved when it did not prove to be completely pliant. Päts continued to rule by decree. In February 1935, another decree dissolved the political parties. In their stead, a number of "corporations" representing various interest groups were formed to represent the interests of the people.

In February 1936, Päts began moving to "legitimatize" his authoritarian regime by submitting a referendum to the people asking them to approve calling a constituent assembly. This passed and the assembly met in February 1937 to ratify a new constitution drafted by the Päts government. This constitution, which went into effect on January 1, 1938, provided for a strong presidency to be elected by a special electoral chamber, not by popular vote. The new parliament also consisted now of two chambers, with the upper chamber partially appointed by the president. The electoral chamber met in April 1938 and confirmed Päts in office.

A small oppositional group was permitted to exist in the lower body of the legislature, but it held only seven out of 80 seats. This was the structure that was still in operation in 1939 when Stalin entered a pact with Hitler putting the Baltic states in the Soviet sphere of influence.

Second World War

Hitler launched his invasion of Poland on September 1, 1939, and Soviet troops entered to occupy the eastern third of Poland on September 17. On September 19, the Estonian government was informed that the Soviet fleet had extended its defense perimeter to include the Estonian coastline. Six days later, the Soviet Foreign Ministry presented the Estonian government with a treaty for a military alliance between the two countries, which included the establishment of Soviet bases in Estonia. Left with no alternative, the Estonian government signed the agreement. On September 28, the first Soviet troops entered Estonia.

Nothing happened for several months, probably because the Soviet Union was tied down in its "winter war" with Finland. The 25,000 Finnish deaths in that war convinced Estonia's leaders that resistance to the Soviet Union was futile. Once that was resolved, the Soviet Union turned its attention back to the Baltic States. Toward the end of May 1940, the Soviet Foreign Ministry accused all three states of violating the 1939 mutual assistance pacts with the Soviet Union. Then all three were pressured into installing popular front governments. These did not last long, however. In July all political parties other than the Communist Party were banned, and most noncommunists were dismissed from office.

This was followed by waves of arrests in all three countries, and Päts was deported to the Soviet Union. In one night alone, on June 14, 1941, 10,000 Estonians were deported to Siberia. With only communists, organized as the Working People's League, permitted to stand for office,

new elections were held on July 14. The newly elected legislatures met on July 21. Their only piece of business was to vote to join the Soviet Union, which they did by acclamation. The following month, the USSR Supreme Soviet acceded to their request. They thus became Soviet Socialist Republics. This created the myth that the Baltic states had voluntarily joined the Soviet Union, a position the Russian government continues to maintain.

Germany's invasion of the Soviet Union beginning on June 22, 1941, temporarily reversed this situation. German troops overran and occupied the three Baltic Republics later in 1941. Such occupation lasted until 1944. Because of the mass arrests, the deportations to the Soviet Union, the drafting of 33,000 conscripts into the Red Army, the collectivization of farmland, and the scorched-earth withdrawal policy ordered by the Soviets, many people initially welcomed the German soldiers as liberators.

Many remember having more to eat and less fear of arrest under German rule, despite the activities of the German secret police. Whereas the Soviet occupiers immediately destroyed Estonian national symbols, the Germans did not forbid them. The Estonian flag could be flown, subject to some controls, and Estonian soldiers could wear it on their uniforms. In general, the Germans left the impression that Estonians could have some self-government after the war whereas the Soviets left no doubt who would remain in complete charge. Many Estonians were drafted into the German army and fought against the Red Army. For that reason many Russians referred to Estonians for decades as "fascists."

With the German retreat, the Baltic Republics once again fell under Soviet control. A fifth of the Estonian population either fled to the West or was deported to Siberia. After the end of the war in 1945, guerrilla fighters, known as "Forest Brothers" because they fled to the woods from where they conducted their "war of the woods," continued to oppose Soviet control in the three republics for a decade. They hoped in vain to receive help from the West. The movements got no outside assistance, and they were eventually suppressed.

The Soviet Era

Many changes occurred in the three republics over the next 45 years. Soviet policy was to integrate the republics so thoroughly that there would be no question of their ever leaving the union. To that end, the Soviet government first carried out policies of nationalization and collectivization. Next it sought to bind the Baltic Republics to the rest of the Soviet Union economically by locating branch factories of Soviet industry in the three republics. Such factories received most or all of their raw materials from other parts of the Soviet Union and delivered most of their finished products to customers in the other republics.

After becoming part of the Soviet Union, Estonia's demography began to change dramatically. By the time Soviet rule ended in 1991, 2.3 million Russians were left behind in the Baltics, over a half million in Estonia alone. Estonians had constituted 97% of the country's population in 1945 (after Russia had incorporated predominantly Russian-speaking areas in eastern Estonia totaling 5% of its territory). As a result of Moscow's policy of moving and mixing nationalities, Estonians constituted only 72% in 1953, 64.7% in 1979, and 61.5% in 1989. By 1996 this had risen to 64.2% due to Russian outmigration after independence, leaving an ethnic mix of 28.7% Russians, 2.7% Ukrainians, 1.5% Belarussians, 1% Finns, and 1.9% other nationalities. In 2001, 46% of Tallinn's population was Russian-speaking. Massive inward migration of Russians seeking employment in industry, mining, and the civil service, and preferences in housing, combined with outward deportation of native Estonians in 1941 and again from 1944 to 1949 (totaling at least a fifth of the native population) had dramatically changed the demographic mix. In the opinion of many Estonians, this threatened their national survival.

Among non-Estonians resettled in the republic were employees of the Soviet government, particularly its security agencies and military. Many were part of projects to develop Estonia's lignite and brown coalfields and branches of the

Tallinn's harbor in Soviet times

Courtesy: NOVOSTI

Estonia

Celebrating Independence Day beside the Parliament in Tallinn   Courtesy: NOVOSTI

Soviet military-industrial complex in the Narva area. As a result, the population in northeastern areas such as Narva was eventually more than 95% non-Estonian.

This program of economic integration was accompanied by a program of "Soviet Russification," aimed at transforming the cultures of the three republics. All students received Russian language training in the schools, plus general indoctrination lectures on the nature of Soviet culture. In addition, there was a systematic effort made to settle non-Baltic nationals in the republics. When a new factory was built, most of the workers would be transferred there from elsewhere in the Soviet Union. They were given priority in the assignment of scarce housing, a practice that greatly irritated native Estonians. The heavy industrialization carried out after 1945 meant that the standard of living in Estonia was above that of any part of the Soviet Union. However, the polluting effects of Soviet industries cast an unhealthy gray and dull shadow over Estonia. Combined with the unaesthetic Soviet-style buildings that were thrown up and the general dilapidation that accompanies all communist life, Estonians and the other Balts remain surrounded by reminders of the unfortunate Soviet legacy.

Estonia Regains its Independence

The Estonian people accommodated themselves to Soviet rule, but they were never happy with it. When, therefore, Gorbachev launched his programs of *glas-*

nost (openness) and *perestroika* (restructuring) after coming to power in 1985, Estonians were the first to take advantage of them.

In enunciating his policy of glasnost, Gorbachev called on the Soviet peoples to speak out against negative tendencies in the society and to support his reforms. This became a manifesto that led to the creation of thousands of "unofficial" organizations all over the Soviet Union. Formed originally in support of Gorbachev's policy of reform, many of them soon began to push their own agendas. For Estonians, his policies were a welcome breath of fresh air, and they were among the first to throw their enthusiastic support to him. At the same time, and almost from the beginning, the Estonian people used *glasnost* for their own purposes.

The first unofficial Baltic organization was the Estonian Heritage Society (EHS), founded in December 1987. Ostensibly aimed at preserving the national heritage and environment, the EHS very quickly became a vehicle for Estonian nationalism. It stressed Estonian history; it honored Estonian heroes killed while fighting for Estonian independence; and it resurrected the old Estonian blue-black-white flag. Opposed by the government at first, its programs proved to be so popular that the Estonian Communist leaders eventually endorsed some of its positions. For example, the Presidium of the Estonian Supreme Soviet legalized the pre-revolutionary flag in June 1988.

An organization destined to play a much larger role than the EHS was the Popular Front of Estonia (PFE), first suggested in April 1988 by Edgar Savisaar, a sociologist and planning official. Many reform communists threw their support to the idea so that the PFE quickly won preliminary approval both from the Estonian Communist Party Central Committee and the Estonian Soviet government. This gave the PFE access to the public media, and it rapidly began to build up public support.

This led to a split in the Estonian Communist Party. Karl Vaino, party secretary since 1978, began to fear the challenge presented by the PFE and sought to limit its influence. Reformers within the party challenged him, however. Moscow sided with the reformers, and Vaino Valjas replaced Vaino.

Valjas officially addressed the first congress of the PFE, held in October 1988, and expressed his support for the goals of the PFE. With 22% of the delegates also belonging to the Estonian Communist Party, it appeared that the PFE was merely a popular arm of the party. That was misleading, however. Although communists made up a significant percentage of the membership, it was overwhelmingly reform communists who joined the PFE. Increasingly, the PFE was used to allow reform communists to take control of the Estonian Communist Party and the Estonian government. For example, Savisaar, head of the PFE, was appointed deputy chairman of the Estonian Council of Ministers and head of the State Planning Committee.

Another Estonian unofficial organization was the Estonian National Independence Party (ENIP), established in August 1988. Political parties other than the Communist Party were illegal at this time, so in the beginning the government gave the ENIP a hard time. It was undoubtedly the existence of the ENIP that helps explain the significant communist support for the PFE. Other unofficial organizations that were formed in 1988–89 were the Estonian Green Movement, the Estonian Council of Churches, and a Rural Movement. In addition, the Social Democratic Party was revived in 1989, and a Christian Democrat movement came into being.

Meanwhile, there was a further split in the Estonian Communist Party. Faced with a choice between nationalism and communism, more and more Estonian communists opted for nationalism. Valjas tried to control this tendency by specifically catering to it. He reduced the size of the Central Committee, purging mainly non-Estonians, and he carried out a similar purge of the Estonian Supreme Soviet, increasing the number of Estonians to two-thirds of the membership. In January 1989 the government declared Estonian to be the state language and required knowledge of it for recruitment to certain government and professional posts.

The goals of the Popular Front of Estonia were also shifting during this period. The original emphasis had been on breaking the control of the "centralized administrative-bureaucratic system" and establishing the right of Estonians to decide their own affairs without outside interference. This had been symbolized by the call for sovereignty. Increasingly, however, the argument was made that these goals could not be achieved without political pluralism and that this was not possible without a break from the communist system. For people who accepted this argument, independence became the necessary goal.

The elections to the USSR Congress of People's Deputies in March 1989 gave the PFE the chance to test its strength although the results were somewhat obscured by the fact that many PFE-endorsed candidates were also members of the Communist Party. Nevertheless, PFE candidates basically swept the slate, winning 18 out of 21 seats they contested.

A new test came in February 1990, when republic elections were scheduled. The Popular Front of Estonia adopted a platform in October 1989 calling for sovereignty and independence. Thus the PFE went on record for the first time as publicly favoring independence.

Responding to these developments, the Communist Party of Estonia began moving in the same direction. In February 1990, Prime Minister Indrek Toome, a former head of ideology for the CPE, founded the Free Estonia Group as his vehicle for reelection. He ran on a platform of experience and competence. Arnold Rüütel, president of the Supreme Soviet, also maneuvered to assure his reelection. As presiding officer for the Full Assembly of People's Deputies—a meeting of deputies at the local, republic and union levels of government—he steered through a resolution declaring that Estonia's independence should be restored on the basis of the 1920 Tartu Treaty with Soviet Russia. Thus Rüütel was also on record as supporting Estonian independence.

Reform communists who had endorsed Estonian independence did well in the February 1990 elections. But it was the candidates endorsed by the Popular Front of Estonia who made the best showing, winning a clear majority of the seats. When the new Supreme Soviet met at the end of March, it first passed a resolution declaring that it did "not recognize the legality of state authority of the USSR on the territory of Estonia." The next day, it

Estonian Cadets

elected Edgar Savisaar, head of the Popular Front of Estonia, as the new prime minister. Since he had resigned his membership in the Communist Party some months earlier, he became the first noncommunist to be elected head of Estonia's government since 1940.

Savisaar's government now began taking on many of the trappings of independence. Postage stamps were issued and plans were announced to issue an Estonian currency, the kroon. The government also launched a campaign aimed at privatizing service industries and state distribution networks. In addition, the Estonian Supreme Soviet passed a law prohibiting the drafting of Estonian youths into the Soviet military.

On May 8, 1990, Estonia became the third Baltic republic to declare its independence. Six days later, Gorbachev issued a decree invalidating the declaration. Vadim Bakatin, Soviet minister of the interior, ordered troops into Estonia to enforce the decree. However, Prime Minister Savisaar telephoned Bakatin and got the order reversed. Bakatin later signed an order guaranteeing the Estonian government control over law enforcement in Estonia. His leniency was probably an important reason why he was later dismissed as interior minister and replaced by a hardliner, Boris K. Pugo, one of the plotters of the August 1991 coup. Estonia was to remain in a state of suspended animation for another year before its independence would be recognized.

Periodically, Gorbachev condemned Baltic demands for independence and continued to insist that the Baltic States could only obtain their independence by complying with legislation passed by the Supreme Soviet on the issue. This was out of the question for the Baltic states since their legal position was that they were re-

asserting an independence that, under international law, had never been lost. Meanwhile, the Communist Party of Estonia, which had voted the previous March to separate from the Communist Party of the Soviet Union, carried through its break in September 1990. One more connection was thus severed.

During the fall of 1990, Gorbachev sought to enforce a more hard-line position. This lasted until May 1991, when it finally became clear to him that his policy had alienated reform-minded individuals without producing anything positive. Moreover, he now began to realize that he could not achieve a new union treaty without reaching an accommodation with reformers. This included accepting a major transfer of power and authority to the individual republics. Negotiations for a new union treaty went on during the summer and it was due to be signed on August 17, 1991.

Hardliners opposed to the new union treaty launched their *coup d'état* against Gorbachev on August 16. The failure of that coup finally broke the logjam on recognition. Estonia and Latvia declared their independence while the coup was still in progress. After it had failed, most of the world rushed to extend recognition to all three Baltic republics. The post-coup Soviet government granted its own recognition in September.

Estonia as a Sovereign State

Edgar Savisaar remained as prime minister of an independent Estonia for approximately five months. In January 1992, he came increasingly under attack for the state of the economy. The parliament approved his request to impose a state of emergency to deal with the economic situation. However, criticism of him continued, and he resigned.

Estonia

Tiit Vähi was selected as the new prime minister of a government of experts. Individuals entering the cabinet dropped their party membership while in the cabinet. One of his first acts was to repeal the state of emergency and to promise to work closely with parliament. He said that he expected to remain in office only about six months. His political agenda included a new constitution and a new law on Estonian citizenship, to be followed by new elections to the parliament. The Supreme Council approved the new citizenship law on February 26, 1992.

In April 1992, another law restructured the government by replacing the Supreme Council by the *Riigikogu*, a single-chamber assembly consisting of 101 members. The same law created a president of the republic to replace the chairman of the Supreme Council. The new constitution was submitted to a referendum in June 1992. The question of denying citizenship to individuals who had moved to Estonia after 1940 was also included on the ballot. Both measures were approved overwhelmingly. The new legislative elections that took place in September were therefore limited almost exclusively to ethnic Estonians.

That helps explain why the right-wing Pro Patria "Isamaa"/ERSP Bloc became the dominant group in the new legislature. The new prime minister, Mart Laar, headed a coalition government made up of the Pro Patria electoral alliance, which controlled 51 out of the 101 seats in the *Riigikogu*. The elections also included a popular vote to fill the office of president of the republic. Arnold Rüütel, who had steered Estonia to independence as head

Ex-Prime Minister Mart Laar

Hon. Lennart Meri
The Former President of Estonia

of the Estonian Communist Party, actually came in first with 43% of the vote. Because he failed to win an absolute majority, however, the *Riigikogu* elected the new president. Their choice was Lennart Meri, candidate of the Pro Patria "Isamaa" Bloc, even though he had came in a poor second in September with only 29% of the vote.

Meri was a former foreign minister and ambassador to Finland. The son of a diplomat, he was educated in Berlin and Paris and speaks a half-dozen languages fluently. His family was among those deported to Siberia in 1941. They were permitted to return to Estonia in 1946. An ironic reminder of that dark past was given in 2007 when President Meri's 88-year-old cousin, Arnold Meri, a highly decorated Soviet soldier, was charged with genocide for assisting in the deportation of hundreds of Estonians to Soviet camps in 1949.

During the Soviet time, Meri had a varied and distinguished career as a translator, writer, and filmmaker. He was best known for his histories of Estonians and other Finno-Ugric peoples. He had a reputation for his bluntness. Once when he was in the White House with other Baltic presidents, President George H.W. Bush asked him if he liked to fish. Meri answered by reaching for an indelible pen, circling Estonia on an expensive electronic map, and saying that the biggest fish can be caught there. At another occasion he was asked to speak to a group of Russian leaders. Speaking in perfect Russian, he began his remarks by saying, "I hate Russia!" There was a hush in the startled audience. Then

he continued: "The Russia of Lenin. But I love the Russia of Pushkin [Russia's beloved 19th century poet]." In 2001 he was replaced as president by Arnold Rüütel. Meri passed away in March 2006 and will be remembered as a uniquely erudite and amiable but blunt statesman who firmly stood against Russia at a critical time and ably steered his country toward partnership with the West.

Even though the government of Mart Laar had a right-wing orientation, it was outflanked on the right by the Eesti Kodanik (Estonian Citizens). This was a rightist-nationalist movement headed by Jüri Toomepuu, a U.S. citizen and retired U.S. Army colonel, who repeatedly attacked the government for being too lenient toward residents who are not ethnic Estonians.

Citizenship Laws

No irritant is as persistently troublesome as the citizenship issue. Estonian independence in August 1991 did not automatically eradicate the legacies of the Soviet empire. All three Baltic states were left to deal with important residual problems: who belongs to the restored sovereign states and who does not? Concretely, who should be granted citizenship? Can a democracy deny full rights to a sizable minority who were living and working in the country at the time of independence?

For Estonia the question of citizenship became vital. It faced the prospect of continued heavy Russian influence on most aspects of policy if all residents were granted automatic citizenship (called the "zero option") or dual citizenship, as Russian-speakers and Russia demanded. Thus it refused to grant either.

Estonians see this not only as a question of control over their nation's affairs, but also as a matter of principle: In the Estonian view, the majority of Russians had been permitted to settle in Estonia in order to implement a Soviet policy of occupation after it had forcibly annexed Estonia in 1940. On what basis could occupiers and their descendants expect to be recognized as citizens? For example, Germans who had been part of the occupation forces in various European countries during the Second World War would not have been permitted to claim citizenship rights there merely because they were residing in the country at the time when Hitler's Reich collapsed. Why should Russians be permitted to claim that right today? A 1949 Geneva convention declared that the settlement of occupied territory under the aegis of a military occupation regime is impermissible.

Russia adamantly denies that the Soviet Union had ever "occupied" the Baltic states and that their joining the USSR was involuntary, despite some admitted pressure at the time. It regards the Estonians' acceptance of their situation without armed resistance and the signing by a democratically-elected president of the agreement ratifying the changes as justifying the Russian interpretation. Therefore, Moscow's political leaders have never apologized for the Soviet Union's actions in or after 1940. Nor have they ever hinted that the occupation might have been illegal. They remember the effect their admission had in 1989 that there had been secret protocols to the Molotov-Ribbentrop Treaty consigning the Baltic states to Soviet rule. This public confession galvanized the Baltic independence movements and accelerated their achievement of freedom.

A majority of Russians in Estonia agree with the position that the country had voluntarily joined the Soviet Union and had never been annexed. They do not regard themselves as "occupiers" or "colonialists," even though they did enjoy certain advantages during Soviet rule in terms of housing, employment and education. Most had moved within their own country, the Soviet Union, in order to seek a better economic standard of living, and many of their children were born in Estonia. They do not consider it fair to blame them for any injustices that were committed by the discredited and now-abolished Soviet Union.

Many Russian-speakers find themselves in a dilemma. For them, return to Russia or any other former Soviet republic, where there is considerable economic and political turmoil, is unthinkable because their jobs, residences, friends and relatives are in Estonia. Their roots in the rest of the former USSR have been broken after decades of residency in the Baltics. Most want to stay: a 1995 poll revealed that only 1% was willing to leave Estonia although a third is keeping open the option of repatriating.

Estonians based their citizenship laws on the notion of legal continuity of their prewar republic. They insisted that severe restrictions be introduced. They granted citizenship automatically to pre-1940 residents and their descendants. In Estonia a sixth of the Russians qualified on this basis; subsequent naturalization raised this to over a third by 1998.

Confronting criticism that Russian-speakers were being made permanent noncitizens, Estonia opened citizenship to all persons who met certain criteria, including residency in Estonia for two years and the willingness to take a loyalty oath to the Estonian Republic. Applicants must demonstrate competence (though not fluency) in Estonian, a difficult language unrelated to Russian. Applicants for Eston-

ian citizenship must answer questions in Estonian about the constitution and political system, and they are permitted to look up the answers in the text of the constitution (which is written in Estonian). In 2003 the Supreme Court ruled that the 7,000 Soviet veterans and their dependents living in Estonia may receive permanent residency permits, but the parliament's Constitutional Committee vowed to ignore this ruling.

All peoples show a special interest in how their countrymen are treated abroad. Russia is no different, and its leaders were incensed by Estonia's citizenship laws. They pointed to the Agreement on the Bases of Interstate Relations of January 12, 1991, signed by Boris Yeltsin and Estonian leaders. Article 3 obligated Estonia to offer citizenship to any Russians wanting to be Estonian citizens and living in Estonia on that date. Since this was signed eight months before Estonia became independent, at a time when it was not yet clear that Estonia could become a separate state and when the citizenship issue was still largely irrelevant, the new leaders of a free Estonia decided not to implement it. Russia believes that Estonia's reneging on a formal signed agreement created the conditions for subsequent bad relations between the two countries.

Estonians claim that their citizenship law does not discriminate on formal ethnic grounds. However, since the immediate effect was the disenfranchisement of most ethnic Russian residents, many Russians, as well as some persons in the international community, see it that way.

Few Russians can meet the language requirement without major effort. In 1989, when Estonian was declared to be the only official language of Estonia, only 13% of Russians in Estonia had a good command of the local language. The others had seen no need to learn Estonian because Balts were expected to speak Russian well if they wanted to work or study, and most did so. There was an outcry after independence in 1991 that the new language restrictions were "unfair" and "human rights violations."

Estonians reply that the rights of those who do not speak Estonian are greater than in some other small nations, such as Quebec province in Canada, which fear absorption and destruction of their cultures. Parents are free to send their children to Russian-language schools. Parliament rejected a law in 2003 that would have required Russian-language secondary schools to switch to Estonian in 2007. They face no restrictions on using their language at the work place although it is an advantage to speak Estonian and although the defense forces and many categories in the civil service are blocked to noncitizens.

Estonian authorities point out that the success rate of those who take the Estonian exam is high. After the test's standards were raised in 1995, over 80% still passed it, and 92%–93% succeeded in the constitution and citizenship exam. To raise these figures even further, a new category of teacher was introduced. The "Teacher of the State Language" received special training in Estonian-language teaching and

Estonian and Russian students mingling at their professor's home in Tallinn

Estonia

twice the pay of other teachers. This is open to any nationality, including Russians. Finally, when certain aspects of the Estonian citizenship create special difficulties and tension, authorities have demonstrated a willingness to be flexible and to make the requirements more feasible. Deadlines are routinely extended. But success over time is undeniable. By 2007 the percentage of Russians speaking Estonian had climbed from 15% in 1991 to 40%; among 18- to 24-year-olds, it is nearly 60%.

Critics counter that such success statistics are deceiving since only persons confident of passing are willing to pay the $25–$40 fee and take the all-day exam. Also, in areas where the population is overwhelmingly Russian, such as Narva, the success rate is only 60%. Many Russian-speakers complain of a lack of state funds for language classes, poor instructional materials, absence of clear guidelines for what needs to be learned for the language test, mystifying application procedures, needless delays, unfriendly and unhelpful Estonian officials, and generally an unspoken conspiracy to make it as difficult as possible to acquire Estonian citizenship.

Article 50 of the Estonian constitution states that where more than half of the permanent residents in a locality are members of an ethnic minority, such as in the overwhelmingly Russian-speaking Northeast of Estonia, they have a right to deal with the state and local authorities in their own language. Legal resident aliens in Estonia are permitted to vote in local elections. Although all candidates must be citizens, they are not required to speak Estonian. State radio and television are broadcast in Russian, as well as Estonian. There are Russian-language theaters and a wide variety of Russian newspapers and magazines available. Many university courses are taught in Russian, and almost all examinations at Estonian universities may be written in Russian if the student prefers.

Russian nationals residing in Estonia resent several aspects of the citizenship policy as demeaning and unfair: being ascribed the status of "aliens," with the implicit risk of deportation even though they do not feel like aliens, having lived much or all of their lives in Estonia; the necessity to choose between two nationalities (either Estonian or Russian) or accept an "alien's passport"; the need to take formal steps to secure residency permits even though they may have lived all their lives in Estonia; and, of course, the need to learn the Estonian language, spoken by only a little over a million people in the entire world.

The Estonian government argues that its citizenship laws, adopted by elected

Marja Bussov   Photo by Hermine Dreyfuss

parliaments, are reasonable by Western standards. While a fifth of the adult population in Estonia is disenfranchised in national elections, other democratic countries, such as Luxembourg and Switzerland, have similar percentages of resident aliens. It claims that its policies toward minorities have been more successful in easing ethnic tensions than in most former communist states. Unlike such ex-Soviet republics as Moldova and Georgia, Estonia (and Latvia and Lithuania) has experienced no ethnic violence. Like the other Baltic states, it has maintained a democratic regime in an ethnically diverse society by applying a rule of law. This has helped it gain international support.

International organizations have issued mixed reviews of Estonia's citizenship law, in part in response to Russia's energetic efforts to have Estonia condemned for human rights violations. In April 1992 the Human Rights Watch Helsinki published a policy guideline for all former Soviet republics supporting the granting of citizenship to all legal residents at the time of independence. It recognized that international law gives great freedom to sovereign states in setting citizenship requirements. Nevertheless it found that Estonia's citizenship law, based on the principle (called *jus sanguinis*, "blood law") that one is considered a citizen of a country if his forefathers were also citizens of that country, seemed to violate several international conventions.

Both Russia and Estonia have used international organizations to international-

ize their bilateral problems, rather than to cooperate in finding solutions. They first aired their differences at the Conference (later "Organization") for Security and Cooperation in Europe (CSCE, now OSCE). At Russia's initiative, the CSCE appointed a high commissioner to monitor human rights developments in the Baltics; in December 1992 the Estonian government invited a CSCE mission to come to Tallinn to evaluate its citizenship laws.

That mission became permanent in February 1993. It proposed the formation of a presidential roundtable, an advisory body composed of five members of parliament, five persons from the Russian Representative Assembly, and five representatives from the Estonian Union of Peoples, an umbrella group for diverse minorities. This roundtable has functioned effectively. In December 1995 it recommended a relaxation of the language and citizenship laws to help the non-Estonian population integrate. The OSCE published a report in late 1995 concluding, "one could not speak of a consistent pattern of human rights violations in Estonia."

Undeterred, Russia took its grievance to the United Nations (UN), distributing a memorandum on human rights violations in the Baltics. President Yeltsin personally called on the Secretary-General to look into the matter. In 1995 the UN Committee on Human Rights issued a report criticizing Estonia's citizenship and naturalization policies. Russia also raised the issue in the Council of the Baltic Sea States (CBSS); in May 1995 the CBSS authorized a commissioner to monitor Russian-speakers' civil rights in the Baltic states.

Russian President Boris Yeltsin charged in 1993 that Estonia's citizenship law was an act of "ethnic cleansing and the imposition of an Estonian version of apartheid" (terms first used by one of the leaders of Estonia's independence movement, Edgar Savisaar, who opposed the strict citizenship law). Estonian officials counter that every person is free to choose his own citizenship. Article 49 of the Estonian constitution declares, "every person shall have the right to preserve his or her ethnic identity"; no one is forced to integrate or to learn Estonian. At the same time citizenship is open to every person, regardless of nationality, who is not an active duty member of foreign armed forces, who had not worked in such Soviet intelligence and security organizations as the KGB, and who goes through the proper procedures and learns a modicum of Estonian; there is no ethnic requirement for citizenship.

Whatever one's citizenship, residents of Estonia are permitted to criticize the government and its policies openly, organize rallies or form organizations. Since 1995 deputies of the Russian coalition of three political parties, "Our Home is Estonia," voted into parliament by the one-third of Russian-speakers who are citizens, represents Russian-language citizens of Estonia in parliament and serves as a voice for Russian residents' concerns. In close parliamentary votes, such as the election of the Estonian president in August 1996, the votes of six Russian deputies can be decisive. These heterogeneous Russian parties usually support the ruling coalitions.

The absence of political prisoners and martyrs gives a hollow ring to charges from Russia of "human rights violations," "genocide," and "fascism" (a particularly favorite tag for Estonians, stemming from the German occupation from 1941–44 and the fact that many Estonians had served in the German army). The result is that Russians with diverse and moderate views have come to the forefront as spokespersons for the immigrant community. Talk of rebellion and "fifth columns" has subsided. Although Russian-speakers and Estonians lead largely separate lives in Estonia, they bear little hatred or deep aversion toward each other.

Resentments both in Russia and in the Baltics stemming from citizenship laws adversely affect bilateral relations. Former Russian President Boris Yeltsin warned: "If the Russian-speaking population expresses the natural desire to protect itself from crude discrimination, Russia will not be able to remain in the position of an indifferent onlooker." They burden sensitive negotiations. Russia denies it normal trade status, temporarily cut off all gas shipments to Estonia, and doubles its customs charges on imports from Estonia. Russian propaganda attempted to portray Estonia to the international community as a rogue state. Most important, in order to protest Estonia's citizenship laws, Russia protracts the signing of a border treaty satisfactory to Estonia. It thereby burdened Estonia's efforts to join the EU and NATO.

In 1995 the government speeded up the process of issuing residence permits and gray noncitizen passports (citizens carry blue ones) to replace old Soviet passports that many ethnic Russians carried. These new passports guarantee that noncitizens, whose numbers are down to about 100,000, may return to Estonia after visiting their relatives in Russia. Former Russian President (now Prime Minister) Vladimir Putin's call to Russians residing in Estonia to return to Russia permanently fell on deaf ears.

In response to EU concerns about Estonia's treatment of non-Estonian nationals expressed when it issued its 1997 invitation for Estonia to join fast-track negotiations for membership, the government announced an amendment to the citizenship law. It grants citizenship to all children born in Estonia of noncitizens if the parents had been residents for at least five years. Finally passed in December 1998, the amendment also stipulated that the children's parents must apply on their behalf and be themselves stateless. This does not apply to those who have already chosen to accept Russian citizenship. Estimates vary on how many of them are in Estonia: the Estonian government says about 120,000, but its Russian counterpart puts the number at about 147,000.

The amended law went into effect in July 1999 and opened Estonian citizenship to approximately 3,500 children. In spite of the small numbers involved, the EU hailed the action as "a forward-looking approach which promotes the stability of Estonian society and is consistent with the principles and aims of the European Union." The Estonian government actively encourages noncitizens to make the effort to acquire citizenship. In order to present role models and to show that the effort can pay off, it sponsored a television series involving interviews with Russian-speakers who became citizens. In 2010 there were still approximately 100,000 stateless persons in Estonia, about 8% of the total population.

POLITICAL SYSTEM

Estonia is a multiparty, parliamentary democracy that has enjoyed political stability since 1991. It established the kind of institutional and legal conditions that place it within the Western political model. It developed a multiparty system in which democratic procedures are respected. Despite frequent changes of coalitions and cabinets, it has maintained underlying political stability while demonstrating that power can be transferred peacefully from one coalition government to another. In contrast to Latvia and Lithuania, parties of former communists have been unable to win power in Estonia.

It proceeded rapidly to establish a democratic regime and to hold its first free elections since the 1930s. An Estonian constitutional assembly with a wide popular and political base and led by the democratic nationalist segment of the independence movement prepared a new constitution. Remembering the autocratic government that emerged in the tumultuous 1930s, the majority rejected the former 1938 constitution, with its strong executive, and adopted instead a parliamentary, rather than a presidential system. The new constitution and a law denying automatic citizenship to non-Estonians who had moved to the country after 1940 were submitted to a referendum on June 28, 1992, three months before the first parliamentary elections. They were accepted overwhelmingly.

The President

The president is elected for a four-year term indirectly by parliament. An exception was made for the first post-Soviet presidential election, when citizens cast the first round of votes. An amendment to have the president elected by the *Riigikogu* stipulated that a candidate needed a two-thirds majority to win. It also created an electoral college to take over, should no candidate be able to obtain the required 68 votes. Following this procedure in 1996, the *Riigikogu* deadlocked between Meri and Rüütel. President Meri stood for reelection and was opposed by Rüütel. Neither was able to command the necessary 68 parliamentary votes to become elected. The matter was then referred to the electoral college, which reelected Meri by a vote of 196 to 126.

The prestige of the only president in the 1990s, Lennart Meri, was so great that the presidency gained a level of importance and authority that the drafters had not intended. A multilingual philologist and specialist in Finno-Ugric languages, he was the son of a prewar diplomat. He and his family had been deported to Siberia from 1941–46, an experience that helped him decide never to join the Soviet Communist party. He was foreign minister and ambassador to Finland before winning the presidency.

The constitution barred Meri from seeking a third term in 2001. Arnold Rüütel, an earlier leader in Estonia's drive for independence, edged out Toomas Savi, to become president. As in 1996, the parliament was unable to decide on a candidate, so an assembly of 101 members of parliament and 266 local government delegates met to vote in the new president. In 2003 the government endorsed a constitutional reform for the president to be elected directly by the people, but it had not been enacted in time for the September 2006 presidential election.

Toomas Hendrich Ilves narrowly beat out Rüütel. Born in Sweden in 1953, his family moved to Leonia, New Jersey, when he was three. He lived in the United States for 23 years and got a degree in psychology and literature at Columbia University. He became a commentator for the Estonian service of Radio Free Europe in Munich until 1993. When Estonia won its independence, he renounced his American citizenship and returned to Estonia. He was its first ambassador in Washington and served as foreign minister from 1996 to 1998 and again from 1999 to 2000. During this time, he led the negotiations for entry into the EU and NATO. He later became deputy chair of the European Par-

Estonia

liament's foreign affairs committee. He left government service in order to engage in electoral politics.

He is one of his country's only senior politicians with first-hand experience in Brussels and the U.S. He is cultured and invariably elegantly dressed, wearing a bow tie. He is cosmopolitan, Western oriented and relaxed in an Anglo-Saxon manner. He is also not afraid of hardship, which he demonstrated in April 2010 when the Icelandic volcanic ash in the air prevented him and his 14-member delegation from flying home from Turkey. They simply rented a bus and made their way for four days through central Europe, stopping at convenience stores for food. He arrived in Tallinn just in time to host a dinner for visiting dignitaries.

The Parliament and Government

The political heart is a unicameral 101-seat *Riigikogu*, elected by proportional representation every four years. In order to limit the number of parties in parliament and thereby increase the chances that stable governments can be formed, a party must win at least 5% of the total votes cast to be represented in the *Riigikogu*. The politician who can assemble a majority coalition in this parliament becomes prime minister, the most important political figure. The prime minister presides over the cabinet and oversees day-to-day operations as head of government. Although formally appointed by the president, he must be approved by, and maintain the support of, a majority in the *Riigikogu* in order to remain in office. The prime minister's cabinet must also be approved by the legislature made up of numerous political parties. Since no one party ever controls a majority of the seats, governments are always coalitions.

Prime Minister Andrus Ansip   Source: BBC

Only Estonian citizens can vote in national elections, but noncitizens who are legal residents are permitted to vote in local elections. Although only citizens can stand as candidates, noncitizens can have an input into that level of government closest to them. This is important especially in areas with large Russian-speaking populations, such as the Northeast around Narva, and in the capital city of Tallinn, where 46% of the residents are not native Estonians. It led to a change in the leadership of the Tallinn City Council after a Russian-oriented party, the People's Trust, won four seats on the Council in 1999. The nationalist-oriented parties of the Estonian ruling coalition had wished to oust the Center Party-dominated city government, but it lacked a majority. It got its majority by negotiating a coalition agreement with the People's Trust.

Perhaps no country in the world has gone as far into "e-government" as Estonia. The buzz words are "faster, more effective, more transparent, and more favorable." Every Tuesday the prime minister meets with his 13-member cabinet. Each follows the agenda on a flat-screen monitor. No papers and pens are used (at a savings of 200,000 euros each year). All items for discussion and necessary documents are on computer for study in advance. Votes are done by mouse click. Ministers who are abroad can vote through their laptop computers. Like all public documents, all cabinet decisions are put on the Internet. All draft legislation is publicized online so that citizens can read them, express their opinions and offer suggestions. An estimated 5% of all ideas citizens express through this channel find their way into legislation.

Government services are offered to citizens 24 hours a day via computer so that they can avoid bureaucratic hassles. Since government offices are linked by Internet to each other, quicker action is possible. Parliament approved Internet voting for the October 2005 Tallinn local elections and the 2007 parliamentary elections. Voters only need an official electronic ID card, which a million residents already had by 2005. No wonder every Estonian citizen has a legal right to computer access.

Parliamentary Elections

Estonian prime ministers always face the difficulty of holding shifting party coalitions together. Mart Laar, chairman of the Pro Patria Bloc and prime minister in 1992–95, assumed power in 1999. He abolished the corporate tax and introduced an across-the-board 26% flat tax for companies and individuals. The constitution requires a balanced budget.

Laar's government, the longest-serving in Estonia's post-Soviet history, collapsed

in 2002. He was replaced by Reform's leader, Siim Kallas, who became prime minister in a minority government with the Center Party. He pursued the major objectives of the previous government, namely to steer Estonia into NATO (successful in April 2004) and the EU (entry in May 2004). In August 2004 he became Estonia's first EU commissioner (for administrative reform) and one of the five vice presidents of the European Commission.

After the elections of March 2003, the Center Party got the most votes, but it could not form a government. That was done by a newcomer, Res Publica, a conservative, business-oriented party that campaigned on an anticorruption and anticrime platform. It was led by 36-year-old Juhan Parts, former chief state auditor, who became prime minister in a three-party coalition with the Estonian Reform Party and the People's Union. In the opposition were the Center Party, the Pro Patria Union and the Moderates. No other parties cleared the 5% hurdle.

In April 2005 Parts stepped down after parliament had expressed no confidence in his justice minister over proposed anticorruption measures. He was replaced as prime minister by Reform Party leader Andrus Ansip, former manager, banker, mayor of Tartu and economics minister in Parts' government. He had once joined the Communist party. His governing coalition, the eighth since 1990, included the center-left Center Party and the centrist People's Union. He promised to continue guiding Estonia toward euro membership, to lower taxes, and to increase social welfare spending.

In the March 2007 elections, Ansip's Reform Party emerged as the largest party, winning 27.8% of the votes and 31 seats. This was a rare case of a government being reelected in Central Europe; in fact, he is the first Estonian prime minister to be returned to office since independence in 1991. The Union of Pro Patria and Res Publica (which merged in 2006) captured 17.9% of the votes and 19 seats. The People's Union garnered 7.1% of the votes and 7 seats. On the left, the Center Party won 26.1% of the votes and 29 seats. The Social Democratic Party (formerly the Moderates) got 10.6% of the votes and 10 seats, and the Greens captured 7.1% of six seats. No other parties cleared the 5% hurdle.

The governing coalition is composed of the Reform Party, Union of Pro Patria and Res Publica, and Social Democratic Party. Prime Minister Ansip promised that Estonia would become one of the EU's five wealthiest countries in 15 years.

Of importance is the number of exiles who returned to play important political, military and economic roles. However,

Balts who lived in comfortable Western exile during the Soviet times sometimes experience resentment among certain segments of the population. They must learn to be tactful in offering more efficient foreign ways of doing things. In Estonia the top vote getter in early parliamentary elections was an American, Jüri Toomepuu. A loser in the first presidential election was an American political scientist, Rein Taagepera, who was founding dean of Tartu University's School of Social Sciences. Estonia's first defense minister was Hein Rebas, a Swedish reserve officer, and a retired American colonel, Alexander Einseln, commanded Estonia's defense forces.

Foreign and Defense Policy

The U.S. government, having always refused to recognize the 1940 incorporation of the Baltic governments into the USSR, was an early and enthusiastic supporter of their efforts to regain their independence. One example of just how far the U.S. government was willing to go in that regard relates to Aleksander Einseln, recruited by the Estonian government to head the newly created Estonian Defense Forces. An Estonian native who had fled with his family to America in 1944, Einseln was a former tank commander and Vietnam veteran who retired from the U.S. Army as a colonel. Not wanting to jeopardize either his U.S. citizenship or his army pension, he requested permission from the U.S. Army to accept the assignment. When permission was denied, he accepted the assignment anyway, and his pension was suspended.

It soon became clear that the American action was being interpreted as being anti-Estonian. To deal with an embarrassing issue, Washington reversed itself, granting Einseln's request and reinstating his pension. To legalize the situation, Senator John McCain introduced a bill allowing retired officers, with the permission of the Secretary of State and the relevant service secretary, to serve in the armed forces of newly democratic countries. Einseln became involved in domestic Estonian politics in 1995 when he criticized Defense Minister Andrus Oovel in public. As a result, President Meri grudgingly demanded his resignation as chief of Estonia's army.

Estonia became a member of the World Trade Organization in November 1999 after the parliament had ratified the accession protocol by a vote of 48 to seven. A number of opposition political parties abstained during the vote on the grounds that the terms of admission were against Estonia's national interests. In 2004 Estonia's foreign minister, Kristiina Ojuland, was the most interesting of the three candidates to become Secretary-General of the Council of Europe.

Estonia has worked to establish close and friendly relations with Scandinavia, and it was involved in intensive negotiations to become a member of the European Union, which occurred for all three Baltic states in May 2004. Estonia's early invitation was well merited. It has been consistently in the vanguard in reforming its economy since 1991. It has also been the recipient of the largest amount of foreign investment of any of the Baltic states. In fact, Estonia is Europe's largest recipient per capita of foreign investment. With a turnout of 63.4% in September 2003, 66.9% voted yes and only 33.1% no in the referendum approving membership. No political party opposed it, and a common refrain to the one-third that opposed it was: "A no to the EU is a yes to Russia." Then Prime Minister Juhan Parts exclaimed: "Spring has arrived in Estonia; we're back in Europe!" Foreign Minister Ojuland asserted: "This decision will guarantee the future of Estonia."

Estonia joined NATO in April 2004, along with the other two Baltic nations. Estonians do not discuss NATO with Russia on the grounds that every state has the right to choose its own security arrangements. As a NATO member, Estonia needs a very different kind of military than it now has. Its troops would have to be mobile and useful for peacekeeping missions, rather than being a citizen's army with secret arms dumps in forests waiting to fight a territorial war on its own soil.

It has 4,750 active forces, including 1,310 conscripts, who serve terms of eight months (11 for officers, NCOs, some specialists, navy and border guards). There are about 25,000 reservists, 10,766 of whom are in 15 Defense League (*Kaitseliit*) units. Of the active forces, approximately 4,200 (including 2,000 conscripts) are in the army, 300 in the navy (with 5 ships) and 250 in the air force (with 7 aircraft). It has 2,600 border guards, including 170 conscripts. As in all Baltic states, women are permitted to serve in the armed forces.

NATO is advising all new members to shift their forces from territorial defense based on conscripts to a professional army with mobile units trained for NATO operations. The government expressed support in 2003 for the Defense Ministry's plan to reduce the number of conscripts by 50% and to raise the number of professional troops. It also committed the country to preparing troops for NATO's rapid response force by 2006. However, there is resistance among parties and the military to eliminating conscription altogether.

In 2002 it had 46 peacekeepers in Bosnia, and in March 2003 it deployed 120 peacekeepers to Kosovo for six months,

Major General Aleksander Einseln, Former Commander, Estonian Defense Forces

replacing a Latvian unit that had served there since September 2002. In August 2004 it sent 95 peacekeepers back to Kosovo, again replacing a Latvian unit. It also dispatched a mine-clearance team and a canine unit to Afghanistan in August 2002 to enhance security around airfields used by American forces. They stayed one year, but its 12-member mission was extended to March 2005. In 2010 it had 150 soldiers in Afghanistan.

Estonia supported the U.S.-British war effort in Iraq in March 2003. Then Prime Minister Siim Kallas emphasized the importance of the U.S. for Baltic security by stating: "I do not want war. But I believe we must pick a side. And I believe it is the side where the United States is." Aware that many Estonians did not agree with his policy, he continued, with a potentially threatening Russia in mind: "Isn't it absurd to imagine that hiding behind the wardrobe and wagging a reproaching finger at America would better ensure our defense from Stalin Jr. than being an outright and public friend and ally of the United States?" After hostilities ended, Estonia dispatched 55 soldiers for peacekeeping duties in Iraq, and in 2004 it sent a 32-member Estpla-8 infantry platoon and a 13-member CT-2 cargo team. By 2010 it had no soldiers deployed in Iraq.

It was on America's side at the 2008 NATO summit in Bucharest when it supported membership for Ukraine and Georgia against Russia's vehement objections. President Toomas Ilves argued: "The main reason for saying no is a Russian veto, and that's the most dangerous thing about all of this." The U.S. compensates Estonia for some of the expenses and upon entry into NATO unblocked its military aid to all three Baltic states. It had been frozen because they had not signed

Estonia

Christmas with the Angelstok family in Tallinn

bilateral agreements with the U.S. to exempt each other's citizens from prosecution by the International Criminal Court.

Estonia's allies rate its British-trained intelligence service as one of Eastern Europe's best; it has an iron-clad rule not to spy on politicians. It was good intelligence work that led to the arrest in November 2008 of Herman Simm, a former security chief in the Estonia defense ministry who sold 3,000 top secret NATO and EU documents to Russia's SVR Foreign Intelligence Service for about $131,000. This made him one of the top spies in NATO history. The Kremlin denied any involvement in the case.

Border and other Disputes with Russia

Border disputes belong to the most complicated and serious international conflicts in which any country can be involved. Agreements concerning them are especially important because they are of such long duration. Two friendly countries, such as Estonia and Latvia, who do not threaten each other and who genuinely want good neighborly relations, can solve their border disputes relatively easily, after dealing with technical issues and sorting out conflicting economic interests. It is very different with negotiations between a small, proud country that possesses few power resources and a long memory of domination by the negotiating partner and a large power that has controlled or strongly influenced the small country for two and a half centuries. Such negotiations are highly political and emotional. They go to the core of each country's definition of themselves and of their security needs. They are affected by each nation's attempts to come to grips with the past and to adjust to the present.

A small country like Estonia has few borders to fix. Russia has them all around it. The rapid unraveling of the USSR, which enabled Estonia and the other Baltic states to become independent in August 1991, left numerous border uncertainties throughout the former empire. They extend from the most contentious (the Kurile Islands claimed by Japan) and run along the long-disputed Chinese frontier, past the new Central Asian and Caucasian republics, the Ukraine, and even inside the Russian Federation itself, where a few ethnic minorities, such as the Chechens, are determined to carve out their own sovereign states. Thus, compromises in any one set of border negotiations could be invoked as precedents in countless other talks.

It made no sense to discuss borders while all were ruled from Moscow. Internal borders within the highly centralized Soviet Union were largely irrelevant. But frontier disputes now affect the neighbors' foreign relations and are charged with symbolism and emotions, especially in Estonia. Few issues are more important for sovereign states than their borders. Most consider their inviolability to be vital interests, for which they would be willing to go to war. A small state like Estonia yearns for secure, internationally recognized borders. It is nervous about the fact that it could hardly defend them by military force against a large nation like Russia. Not being a member of a powerful alliance, like NATO, it has no allies who would come to its rescue if its borders were violated, as it learned in 1939 and 1940.

In 1945 Estonia lost territory to Russia, but it could do nothing to prevent it. Estonia's losses east of the Narva River and

in the southeast Petseri district amounted to 5% of its total land area. Independence in 1991 raised the question of where the permanent border should be drawn. On September 12, 1991, Estonia declared the border changes forced on it in 1945 to be invalid. Specifically, it argued that its border along the Narva River in the northeast corner of the country and in the southeast corner of Estonia, south of Lake Peipus, be moved eastward to where it was before 1945. Also, the frontier running through Lake Peipus before 1945 should be recognized.

Estonia realizes that it does not have the power to restore the old border. It is also nervous about accepting back more than 2,000 square kilometers of territory now inhabited almost entirely by Russians. The Estonians repeatedly suggested that it was prepared to renounce this territory if Russia recognized the Tartu Peace Treaty, an important 1920 agreement with Russia. That is, it would accept Moscow's redrawing of the border in 1945 in exchange for an important Russian political concession that would legitimize Estonia's restrictive citizenship law. In November 1995 the Estonian government announced that it would treat the current demarcation line as the *de facto* state border. This ignited a storm of criticism from Estonian nationalists.

Negotiating Estonia's maritime borders was easier than dealing with land borders because negotiators are drawing new lines, and there exists much international law that can be applied. By October 1996, the major differences over Estonia's maritime border with Russia had been resolved. An agreement between the two countries was reached, and Finland, which had to agree to any lines drawn in the Gulf of Finland, approved. But Russian negotiators announced that no sea agreement would be signed until the thornier land negotiations are completed. It is on the land border between the two countries that a settlement is especially urgent for Estonia. But despite the fact that only a few minor issues remained unresolved, the talks are at an impasse.

Estonia knew that the EU and NATO were hesitant to accept it as a member as long as it had an outstanding border dispute with a powerful country like Russia. Neither of these international organizations ever officially stated this, but representatives offered unmistakable hints. NATO Deputy Secretary for Political Issues, Gebhardt von Moltke, said in Tallinn that "Estonia's outstanding border issue with Russia would have to be solved peacefully . . . before membership would be possible." The EU communicated the same message in May 1996.

The U.S. had communicated that it would like to see the two countries de-

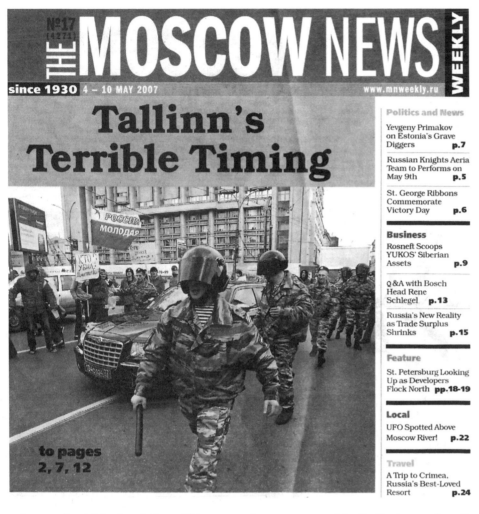

№17 (4271) THE MOSCOW NEWS WEEKLY

since 1930 4 – 10 MAY 2007   www.mnweekly.ru

Tallinn's Terrible Timing

to pages
2, 7, 12

velop good neighborly relations. This was made most explicit on January 16, 1998, when the American president endorsed in principle the Baltic states' desire to join the Atlantic Alliance by signing with the three Baltic presidents a "Charter of Partnership." Though not a guarantee of future NATO membership or of American protection, it put on record Washington's "real, profound and enduring interest" in Baltic security and the conviction that the three new democracies have as much right to join NATO as do the three ex-communist countries that were invited in 1997 to enter: Poland, Hungary and the Czech Republic.

The overriding desire to join first the EU and then NATO made it clear to the Estonian government that a change in its negotiating strategy toward Russia was essential. Estonia was ready not only to concede territory lost to Russia after minor border adjustments were made, but also to back away from its insistence that Russia accept the validity of the Tartu Treaty "for even a half an hour."

A reexamination of the international legal aspects of the border treaty led Estonian officials to conclude that there was no

longer any need to tie the issue of continuity assured by the Tartu Treaty to the signing of a border agreement. An announcement from the EU in 1997 that Estonia is a front-rank contender for admission, successful negotiations to establish visa-free travel with the Nordic countries, and the absence of any serious international objections to Estonia's citizenship laws outside of Russia indicated that almost no countries questioned the continuity of Estonia's statehood or its sovereignty. Thus there was no need to underscore this fact by insisting that Russia recognize this in the context of the border treaty. In effect, it would have meant that it was Russia's right to decide whether Estonia was a sovereign state that could make its own laws, including those regarding citizenship.

Therefore, with most of the technical border questions and all the general questions already solved, Estonia accepted an agreement with Russia on November 7, 1996. The text made no mention of the Tartu Treaty, and it placed the border where Moscow had fixed it by unilateral decree in 1945. However, in January 1997 then Russian Foreign Minister (later Prime

Minister) Yevgeny Primakov announced that Russia would not sign the agreement until the two countries could hold bilateral talks aimed at changing certain pieces of Estonia's domestic legislation. This no doubt included the citizenship law, which the OSCE, the UN and the Council of Europe had basically approved.

Estonia and Russian negotiators met three times during 1997 to finalize the border maps to accompany the border treaty. But Russia insisted that the November 1996 agreement be reopened, adding, for example, a clause concerning the point where Estonia, Latvia, and Russia touch each other. It haggled for an hour and a half over the color of the folder for a treaty. It contested the names of places on the maps, insisting for example that Pskov not appear in its Estonian spelling, Pihkva. Tallinn concluded that these stalling tactics revealed that Russia lacks the political will to implement the treaty. There are also political dangers for Russia's leaders. A treaty with Lithuania in November 1997 ignited controversy in the Duma, and they do not want to risk that again.

By 1998 bilateral relations with Russia had improved. The two governments reached a gentlemen's agreement that the OSCE must be the channel for all citizenship questions; Estonia no longer accepts advice on these matters directly from Russia. Having gone through the door to Western integration, Estonians themselves are not in as much of a hurry to sign a border treaty with Russia. Current President Toomas Hendrik Ilves said to the Estonian parliament on February 12, 1998: "The government is awaiting the settling of this issue calmly since 1997 proved that Estonia can achieve its foreign policy goals, regardless of whether it has or does not have a border agreement with the Russian Federation."

The EU, which Estonia entered in May 2004, provided $77 million to help it secure its border with Russia, as required by the EU's Schengen Agreement, which all three Baltic states entered in December 2007. The EU has always regarded Estonia's and Latvia's border treaties with Russia as purely bilateral matters and has given little diplomatic assistance despite the fact that those borders are its only non-demarcated external borders. On May 18, 2005, the foreign ministers of both Russia and Estonia signed a treaty governing their sea and land borders. All parties in the Estonian parliament ratified the treaty after adding a preamble referring to the founding of the Estonian Republic in 1918 and to the Treaty of Tartu. Russia refused to ratify the treaty and withdrew its signature.

In April and May 2007 relations between the two countries reached their lowest point since independence. The newly elected government decided to move a Soviet war monument, known as the "Bronze Soldier, along with about a dozen nearby graves of unknown soldiers, from the center of Tallinn to a military cemetery outside of town. Designed six decades earlier by an Estonian sculptor, using an Estonian model, the statue meant totally different things to resident Russians and Estonians. The former saw it a memorial to the wartime sacrifice to defeat Nazi Germany. The latter saw it as a symbol of the hated occupation after 1944; some Estonians even dubbed it the "tomb of the unknown rapist." However, fearing violence and perceiving political motivation only two weeks before parliamentary elections, 49% of Estonian respondents said in an *Eesti Päevaleht* poll at the time that they opposed the movement of the "bronze soldier," while only 37% favored it.

The relocation, which the Russian government called a "sacrilege" and "blasphemy," sparked the worst riots Estonia had seen since becoming free. Ethnic Russians attacked the Academy of Arts and the main theater, and they looted businesses. One man was stabbed to death, and a dozen police officers and 44 protesters were injured. A youth group close to then President Vladimir Putin, *Nashi*, attacked and besieged the Estonian embassy in Moscow. This was an action that, along with Russia's generally aggressive behavior, prompted U.S., NATO and EU protests and unified Estonia's allies in support of it. Estonia later retaliated against *Nashi* by barring its young members from entering Estonia. By putting them on an immigration blacklist, Tallinn prevented them from traveling elsewhere

in Europe because of Schengen restrictions. Russia discontinued passenger train service between St. Petersburg and Tallinn, banned heavy trucks from using the main bridge across the border at Ivangorod, and terminated gas and oil shipments to Estonia. Estonia is not dependent upon energy from Russia, and only about 8% of its foreign trade is with Russia. Moscow lifted all these measures after the crisis dissipated.

Ex-President Bush invited President Ilves to the White House in a show of support. Suspecting political motives on the part of the prime minister, who was facing a close reelection at the time, Ilves, like Tallinn's mayor, Edgar Savisaar, had opposed the moving of the memorial. In November 2006, Bush had been the first sitting American president to visit Estonia. He visited all three Baltic states, where he found congenial audiences for his message of promoting democracy.

ECONOMY

Estonia has been hit very hard by the global recession that began in the fall of 2008. It will take several years to work its way out of the hole it is in and become again the acknowledged tiger among the Baltic states, and indeed among all 23 countries emerging from communism. Its GDP declined a depressing 14.1% in 2009 before bouncing back in 2010. At 15% in 2010, unemployment is the next target. But Prime Minister Ansip is the only Baltic head of government to have remained in power as the boom turn to bust. Estonia's politics are more solid than its fellow Baltic countries, and this helps it through the hard times.

Estonian bank lures customers

It resumed positive growth in its GDP in 1995. It was the first former Soviet republic to introduce its own currency, the kroon, which it tied to the German mark until the euro came into being in 2002. To keep its money stable, it created a currency board, which takes monetary policy largely out of the state's hands. Upon entry into the EU in May 2004, it pledged to adopt the common currency as soon as possible. It already permits the use of euros within Estonia if both parties agree to the transaction. It joined the EU's exchange-rate mechanism (ERM2) in 2004, and it has the privilege of designing its future euro coins. It is one of the few EU countries that meets the common currency rules. It is the model of financial virtue. In 2010 its public debt was only 7.2% of GDP, and its budget deficit a mere 1.7% of GDP. Its currency was stable throughout the recession, and its wages and prices remained flexible. With the support of the European Commission and

IMF, it qualified to adopt the euro on January 1, 2011.

The structure of its economy reveals how modern it is. Sixty-three percent of the workforce is employed in the services industry, producing 66.8% of GDP. Industry employs 32% and produces 30.4% of GDP. Estonia reduced its inflation rate from a dizzying 1,000% in 1992 to 5% in 2007 and 10% in 2008 due to fast economic growth and a fixed exchange rate. It declined dramatically in 2009. As in the other ex-Soviet-bloc countries, the rising price for Russian energy drives up inflation since they use power less efficiently than in western Europe. Wages grew faster than productivity. Although the gap between rich and poor has increased, it is obvious especially in the cities that prosperity has reached a large part of the population.

Its economy grew by 7% every year throughout the 1990s and by about 6% annually after a slump in 2003; in 2007 it shot up 11.5%, which some analysts saw as a sign of dangerous overheating. By 2008 economic growth and property prices had declined sharply. Tallinn had become a magnet throughout Europe for property speculators, driving values up by 10% to 15% annually for eight years in a row. Property values doubled between 2004 and 2007. Apartments in the city's medieval old town had shot up to 5,000 euros ($7,500) per square meter. Real estate prices plummeted in the subsequent recession and are only slowly recovering.

Estonian law requires governments to maintain a balanced budget and to deposit the surplus into a currency-stabilization reserve fund. In 2005 it had an astounding state net asset of 6% of GDP, rather than a national debt. This nest-egg enabled it to weather the recession better and hold its debt to 7.2% of GDP in 2010.

It quickly privatized the bulk of its economy. It began immediately to dismantle the command economy inherited from the Soviet Union, setting up a privatization agency modeled on Germany's trust agency (*Treuhand*) in 1992. By the end of 1994 privatization was 90% complete. Rejecting tariffs and bail-outs, cutting off subsidies to industry and allowing wages to rise freely stabilized the value of the Estonian kroon and gave a great spurt to both foreign investment and exports.

As a result, new stores, restaurants and other service enterprises sprouted while foreign investment, particularly from Scandinavia, led to additional jobs in private industry, replacing the ones lost in the crumbling state enterprises. Retail shops have all been privatized. The number of foreign companies opening headquarters has ballooned. By 2006 a third of

Estonia's total economy was wholly or partly owned by foreigners, who produce half its exports. Three-fourths of those investment funds come from Finland and Sweden. By the end of the 20th century, three-fourths of its GDP was generated by the private sector, including privatized businesses and startups, so its privatizing agency could be closed at the end of 2000. Railways, ports, and energy utilities were placed on the auction block and sold.

New factories had been built during the Soviet era. Constructed on the Soviet model, many have had to sharply cut their labor forces in order to become even marginally competitive. Therefore the Estonian government's policy of privatization affected these factories the most. This is particularly true with regard to the area of Narva, located in the northeastern part of Estonia. Narva is inhabited almost entirely by Russians, the result of the fact that the Soviet government decided in the 1960s to build a branch of its industrial-military complex there.

In spite of the numerous factories built in the 1960s and 1970s to serve as suppliers of the Soviet arms industry, Estonia's largest industry is still that of primary extraction, the production of oil from oil shale. Two other major industries are the manufacturing of mineral fertilizers and shipbuilding. It also has consumer industries such as textiles and medium industry such as electrical and mechanical equipment. Most of the rest of its industry is concerned with the processing of forest products (timber, wood pulp for paper manufacturing, peat) or food processing. Fishing is another major industry.

Among the former communist countries, Estonia enjoys the highest foreign direct investment (FDI) per head and the highest credit rating. Its per capita FDI in 2004 was 115.7 euros, compared with 47.8 in Latvia and 54.7 in Lithuania. It is appealing to investors, among other reasons, because of its flat tax rate of 23% for both personal and corporate income, its lack of tariffs and general openness, and habit of treating foreigners and Estonians alike in business. Eight other Eastern European countries, including Latvia, Lithuania and Russia, followed the Estonian lead on the flat tax. Only 3.6% of total tax revenues fall directly on corporations. A country that is three-fourths urban, it is on its way to becoming a predominantly information-based service economy, with native Estonians constituting the minority of the work force in industry. Despite severe financial limitations, its university system produces a high-tech work force. But Estonia spends less than 1% of its GDP on research and development.

Estonians use the Internet more than any other post-Soviet country and twice as

"Grease" opens in Tallinn

much as do French and Italians. Some speak of "e-stonia." This is an addiction it has in common with its most important trading partner and source of investment, Finland, a country with which it shares close and unique linguistic and cultural ties. Half of all Estonian bank customers manage their money online. In a new parking system, 25,000 use their mobile phones (of which there are 89 per 100 people) to pay for parking. Four out of five taxpayers file their annual returns online, and it takes the authorities only five days to process them. Estonia is the European programming base for Skype, owned by eBay.

This growing use of the Internet also exposes a worrisome vulnerability. This was seen in April and May 2007 in the aftermath of an emotional dispute with Russia over moving a Soviet war monument out of the center of Tallinn. For three weeks a flood of unwanted data and hits on its computer systems came pouring in mainly from Russia. It quickly clogged the Web sites of the government, businesses and newspapers. NATO, the EU and the U.S. sent experts to try to help deal with this near Internet shutdown and electronic blockade. Some saw this as the first real war in cyberspace, and it raised questions about whether NATO's collective defense commitment applies to such cyber harassment. In 2008 the U.S. announced that it would sponsor an Estonian institute to work on computer defenses and international security.

Giant Finnish firms, such as the state oil company Neste, department store chains, such as Stockmans, and hundreds of medium- and small-size businesses find

Estonia

Estonia a congenial place to do business. About 500 Finnish companies, including Nokia, operate in Estonia, employing 22,000 Estonians. Sweden is also an important nearby partner. Swedish banks control most of Estonia's banking system.

Despite a host of political problems between them, Russia still plays a significant role, though much reduced from 1991, when 90% of Estonia's exports went into the Soviet economy; by 2010 that figure was 8.8% to Russia. However, Russia's 10.1% share of Estonia's imports includes some of the energy Estonia needs. This directly affects inflation. Its trade patterns look westward. About 80% of tiny Estonia's GDP is generated by foreign trade, and it was rising by 25% per year. The bulk of its trade (70.2% of exports and 78.6% of imports) is with EU countries.

Determined to minimize its economic dependence on Russia, Estonia relies far less on its eastern neighbor for energy than do Latvia and Lithuania. It buys more from the West and continues to extract oil from shale, which is an infamous polluter, but which still is its largest industry, ahead of mineral fertilizers, shipbuilding, and the processing of forest products. It is the only country in the world to exploit oil shale deposits. Its desire to protect its oil shale industry, which supplies 90% of its energy needs, delayed its closing of the energy chapter with the EU. However, it is Estonia's major resource. It is also a main employment source for Russian-speakers concentrated in the northeast, which already has the country's highest rate of unemployment.

It has no nuclear power plants. To give both Germany and Russia a stake in its prosperity and stability, it granted Russia's Gazprom and Germany's giant Ruhrgas partial ownership in its gas industry, a move that slightly warmed Estonia's chilly relations with Russia. Estonia

is struggling to keep its state-owned electricity company, Eesti Energia, alive and out of Russian hands. Since 40% of its sales go to 500 industrial clients, it is vulnerable to losing those clients through price wars. To reduce its energy dependence, it derives 18% of its energy from renewable sources, hoping to raise that to 25% by 2020.

Agricultural land occupies 37.4% of Estonia's surface, forests 48.7%, swamp and wetlands 7.4%, water 4.6%, and artificial surfaces 1.9%. Five percent of the work force is engaged directly in farming, and they produce 2.8% of the country's GDP. This is one sector in which privatization has been slow. Nationalist pressure postponed the free sale of land. Only persons who can trace their Estonian citizenship to before 1940 can buy land although there is a legislative effort to change this. By 2000 most agricultural land was individually owned. Most of it is still organized into collective and state farms, but all supervision by the state has been removed. Farmers have been the hardest hit by Estonia' almost totally open economy. Consumers must look hard in grocery stores to find Estonian-grown products. Much of its agricultural sector is still organized into cooperative units.

Estonia wins rave reviews from private business and bank people, as well as from such international governmental organizations (IGOs) as the London-based European Bank for Reconstruction and Development (EBRD) and the EU. Because of its economic progress and democratic political stability, it entered the EU in May 2004. Foreign businesses consider Estonia the least corrupt of all former communist countries, and investment is pouring in, especially into Tallinn. Estonia benefits from membership in the EU, the target of over 70% of the country's foreign trade. But ironically because it has virtually no

trade barriers, its belonging to the EU actually raised them.

CULTURE

Estonia's culture is very much associated with its historic cities, the most important of which are Tallinn (the capital), Tartu and Narva. Tallinn, historically known as Reval or Revel, was first mentioned in written sources in 1154 and has played an important role in Estonian history ever since. The town's fortress was built by King Waldemar II of Denmark beginning in 1219 on the site of an earlier fortress. The city became a member of the Hanseatic League in 1284 and a major trading center. Over the centuries, it belonged to the Danes, the Teutonic Knights, the Swedes and, from 1710 onward, Russia.

The old city was surrounded by a wall, about two-thirds of which still stands. Half of the guard towers and some of the gates also remain. Medieval buildings include the Dom Castle and the Long Hermann Watchtower. The oldest of the churches is the Domkirk [cathedral, originally called *Toomkirik* in Estonian], which dates from 1232. Other churches of interest are St. Nicholas, built in the 14th century, St. Olaf's, built in the 15th century with a Late Gothic spire from the 16th century, and the Bremer Chapel of St. Mary, built in the 16th century. Most Estonians are nominally Lutherans, but there are also many Russian and Estonian Orthodox churches, including a Russian Orthodox Cathedral, St. Alexander Nevsky's in Tallinn, built in 1902–4. In 2003 President Rüütel gave the visiting Patriarch of Moscow and All Russia Aleksii II, who had been born in Estonia, the highest state award, the Terra Mariana Cross, 1st Class. Aleksii passed away in 2008.

Other cultural treasures include the Town Hall, built in 1402–4 on the site of an earlier one-floor building dating back to the beginning of the 14th century, and the Blackheads' Club, which dates from the 14th century. The Academy of Sciences, established in 1946, Estonian State Opera House, numerous Estonian-language theaters, and the Russian-language Russian Drama Theater are located in Tallinn. The capital city also has an art institute and conservatoire, founded in 1919, the Tallinn Pedagogical University, and the Tallinn Technical University. In 2005 a new Tallinn University united these existing institutions of higher learning, after years of discussion. The aim is to unite resources and faculty, as well as to create synergy and efficiency. The country boasts dozens of institutions of varying quality that offer competitively priced, multilingual courses.

Tartu, known historically as Dorpat, was founded in 1030 by Grand Prince

Estonians at "Old Town Days Festival," Tallinn

Yaroslav of Kievan Rus. Then called Yuriev, it was built at the site of an earlier Estonian settlement, Tarpatu. Yuriev was conquered by the Teutonic Knights in 1212, and it later became the seat of the Livonian bishops. The Germans gave it the name of Dorpat. Fought over numerous times throughout the centuries, it passed back under Russian control in 1710 when Peter the Great took it from Sweden. The modern name dates from the first period of Estonian independence following World War I.

Tartu, also a member of the Hanseatic League, was a major trading center; its chief claim to fame is its university, founded in 1632 by King Gustav II of Sweden. Transferred for a time to the city of Parnu during the 18th century, it was returned to Tartu in 1802. Today Tartu University, Estonia's most prestigious, has seven faculties and 4,000 students. The university library, once housed in the Cathedral of Peter and Paul, contains over two million volumes. The cathedral, in ruins in 1802 when it was reconstructed as a library, is probably the oldest building in Tartu. Most of the other university buildings date from the 19th century.

Although the ancient Estonians had an oral literature, very little of that survived the centuries of domination by other cultures. The roots of modern Estonian culture can be traced to the formation of the University of Tartu in 1632 because that marked the beginning of a small educated Estonian elite. The first book of Estonian grammar appeared in 1637, followed by an Estonian translation of the Bible in 1739.

Little more happened until the 19th century when an attempt was made to revive a folklorist tradition. Many songs, sayings and fairy tales were eventually collected, most strongly reminiscent of Finnish folklorist survivals. Somewhat later, Friedrich Reinhold Kreutzwald used many of these oral works to create an epic he called *Kalevipoeg* [The Son of Kalev]. It was published by the Estonian Learned Society in 1857–1861. This nascent Estonian literature slowly replaced German culture, which was preeminent in Estonia for centuries. Many Estonians today have German names, a reminder of earlier times when a people that traditionally had no last names was given them by a Germanic upper class.

Kreutzwald's epic marked the beginning of an Estonian national literature, exemplified by the appearance of poets such as Lydia Koidula, Friedrich Kuhlbars and Jacob Tamm, novelists such as Eduard Vilde and Juhan Liiv and Ernst Scrgava, and the playwright August Kitzberg. Estonian writers worked under a great handicap, however, for the Russian government enforced a censorship down to 1905 that attempted to suppress themes that might encourage Estonian nationalism.

The Revolution of 1905 forced a number of writers to flee abroad. But the constitutional regime established in 1906 led to the abolition of most censorship and the appearance of a vigorous Estonian press. It also marked the birth of a new literary movement called Young Estonia, whose chief representative was the poet Gustav Suits. Suits, who had fled to Finland in 1905, continued to live abroad until after the Russian Revolution of 1917. He eventually became a professor of Estonian Literature at Tartu University.

The greatest novelist of the first Republic (1920–1940) was Anton Hansen Tammsaare, whose most important work, *Truth and Justice*, is about rural life. Another figure from this period was Friebert Tuglas, a writer of short stories and novels. Suits and Tuglas, along with Ernst Enno and the poet Marie Under, became the dominant figures in Estonian literature during the period of independence down to 1940. Tuglas, a member of the Social Democratic Party prior to 1917, succeeded Suits as professor of Estonian literature at Tartu in 1944, after Estonia had come under Soviet domination. However, Tuglas made no literary contribution after that time except for a travelogue, *The First Trip Abroad*, which appeared in 1945, and a volume of musings called *Thoughts and Moods*, published in 1960.

A number of Estonian writers made their way abroad during World War II. These included Marie Under, Karl Rumor,

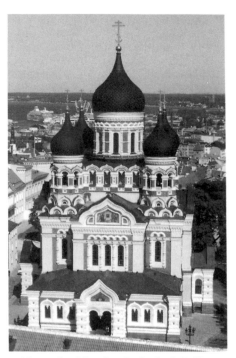

Alexander Nevsky Cathedral, Tallinn

Artur Adson, and August Gailit. These and other writers kept Estonian literature alive as emigre literature even as the Soviet occupation regime was imprisoning figures such as Hugo Raudsepp, Estonia's greatest playwright, and exiling others, such as the poet Heiti Talvik and former President Lennart Meri, to Siberia. Most of these figures are too well integrated into their new environments to resettle in Estonia, but their influence on the new generation of emerging Estonian writers is likely to be great.

During the communist era, Jaan Kross, who has been a frequent nominee for the Nobel Prize in Literature, wrote allegorical short stories (e.g. *Conspiracy and Other Stories*) and historical novels, such as *Between the Three Plagues* and *The Czar's Madman*. Alexander Solzhenitsyn wrote large parts of his epic on Stalinist crimes, *The Gulag Archipelago*, in the Estonian winter resort, Otepää. Tõnu Õnnepalu became famous after independence in 1991 through such novels as *Border State*, which deal with non-national subjects and always with homosexuality.

The nation has produced well known artists, such as the late Medieval painter Michel Sittow, the 19th-century exponent of the Estonian national awakening Johann Köler, and the 20th-century bohemian artist Eduard Wiiralt, who spent most of his life abroad. Johannes Pääsuke is regarded as the father of Estonian cinema and produced the country's first full-length film in 1924. Probably the best-known Estonian work is the cloak-and-dagger film set in the 16th century, *Viimne Reliikvia* (*The Last Relic*). Priit Pärn initiated a school of animated film producers.

The collapse of communism and the Soviet Union enable Estonian culture and language to thrive and develop again. Polite formulations and expressions reentered their vocabulary after having fallen into disuse during foreign rule. Even treasured traditions, such as celebrating Christmas publicly, are again possible. During the Soviet era, December 25 and the Orthodox Christmas Day were normal workdays, and Estonians had to pull their window shades and celebrate in the privacy of their immediate families.

Estonia has again become itself. The Museum of Occupations and the Fight for Freedom opened in 2003. It chronicles the trauma the nation endured during the war and the half-century of Soviet rule that followed. A long line of old suitcases honors the thousands who had disappeared into Soviet gulags. In 2007, Estonia's Jewish community of 3,000 opened its first synagogue, located in Tallinn, since the Holocaust.

There is probably no other country in the world in which music and politics are

Estonia

more closely linked. As is true of all of the Baltic states, folk songs had for centuries been a means for the people to express their national culture and identity. During Soviet rule huge song festivals were the only legal way for large numbers of Estonians to gather and to express their national feeling. Indeed Estonia's movement to become independent is often referred to as the "singing revolution." Its choral music remains excellent. Other forms of music are also popular. Arvo Pärt, who was born in 1935 and spent many years in Berlin, is one of the most frequently performed composers in the world. In the 1970s he was a symbol of musical dissent in Estonia. He achieved world fame with large-scale religious works. This is especially remarkable given the fact that Estonia is a very secular nation; only 29% indicated in the 2000 census that they are followers of a particular faith.

Conductor Neeme Järvi has lived in the United States since the 1980s. Nevertheless, he tirelessly promotes Estonian classical and contemporary music, and his repertoire always includes Estonian pieces. Tanel Padar and Dave Benton (a native of Aruba living in Estonia) won the 2001 Eurovision song contest with their soul song spiced with a touch of hip-hop, "Everybody." In 2004 the country put its best face forward when supermodel, Carmen Kass, ran unsuccessfully for a seat in the European Parliament.

The sport in which Estonia is a true superpower is "wife-carrying," invented in Finland. A man has to carry his wife or partner over a rough 253-meter obstacle course that includes two timber hurdles and a chest-high water pool. The Estonians devised the winning "Estonian carry" upside-down position, which permits the man to run and use his arms freely during the race. In 2007 Estonians ran off with the title for the tenth year in a row. One of the contestants revealed their secret: "Estonians win because they have thin and beautiful women."

FUTURE

Estonians are optimistic about their future. While 43% of non-Estonians in the country said in 2004 that they were pessimistic about their personal welfare in the future, only half that many Estonians expressed this view. This optimism is reflected in the dramatic rise in the Estonian birth rate. This is crucial for a nation whose birth rate had fallen to only 1.2 children per woman and whose divorce rate is one of the world's highest, with two-thirds of marriages breaking up.

The Parts government, which was replaced in April 2005 by Estonia's eighth government since 1990, now led by Prime Minister Andrus Ansip, made population increase a priority. It introduced one of the world's most generous state-funded maternity leaves: mothers (or fathers) receive as much as 15 months leave at full pay. Non-working mothers get $200 per month, known as the "mother's salary." But greater economic stability and membership in the EU have also strengthened parents' willingness to bring children into the world. One Tallinn gynecologist said: "These are EU babies." It is a sign of the times that one sees more baby carriages on the sidewalks. Ansip's Reform Party was reelected in March 2007 and continues this successful maternity policy despite a 12% cut in public finances.

A less encouraging development is the shockingly high HIV epidemic. Estonia now has the highest infection rate in Europe—15,000 or over 1% of the overall population; this is more than three times the EU average. Fewer than half are intravenous drug users, and officials fear it could get worse through unprotected sex. Due to excessive drinking, other unhealthy habits, and a run-down health care system, the life expectancy of Estonian men has fallen to 67.6 years, the shortest within the EU. The average woman can expect to live to age 78.5. Estonia has the world's third-worst record for suicide after Latvia and Lithuania, with Russia trailing close behind.

All three Baltic states entered the 21st century with some major challenges left to be faced. For the sake of their prosperity and security, all three successfully sought economic and military integration with the West. Estonians voted two-to-one in favor of EU entry, and in 2004 Estonia joined both NATO and the EU. Their need for the security that western integration provides stems from the long-standing Russian claim to predominance over the nations on its periphery. None faces an imminent threat to its newly regained independence, but all must remain on guard, to ensure that they do not lose a part of their sovereignty. That would be the case if Russia were able to restrict their ability to make their own decisions, such as on joining a military alliance. All three Baltic states constantly remind their EU and NATO partners to be wary of a resurgent Russia. This appeared justified after Russia attacked Georgia in August 2008.

Estonia is a small state with a well-educated population. It quickened its steps to join the eurozone to avoid currency problems. The ongoing world recession is a short-term headache. Its long-term prospects are bright. With its economy developing briskly, its greatest remaining problem is how to deal with the large Slavic minorities that make up almost a third of its population and much of the industrial work force. Like Latvia, Estonia faces both foreign and domestic political problems that are sometimes in conflict with each other. To preserve its language and culture and to survive as a nation, it has chosen to restrict its citizenship and create strong motivation for members of ethnic minorities to recognize the Estonian character of the restored republic.

While pursuing this policy, it must always calculate Russia's response and adjust it to what Moscow would be willing to tolerate. How Estonia resolves this problem will strongly influence not only its own domestic tranquility, but also its relations with its eastern neighbor. Tension is always present. In March 2004 a Russian fighter jet ventured into Estonian airspace. Three years later the two countries clashed over the relocation of a Soviet war monument from Tallinn's city center to a military cemetery outside of town. Estonia finalized a border agreement with Russia in order to live at peace with it and to deepen Estonian integration into the Western world. Russia withdrew its signature and refused to ratify the treaty when the Estonian parliament added language critical of the 1940 occupation by the Soviet army. Russia retains powerful leverage over the Baltic States.

Estonians and Russian speakers honor victims of 2004 Beslan school tragedy at doorstep of Russian embassy in Tallinn

Republic of Latvia

Dressed for a festival on a street in Riga

Courtesy: NOVOSTI

Area: 25,400 sq. mi. (65,786 sq. km.).

Population: 2.3 million.

Capital City: Riga (800,000).

Climate: Temperate with cool summers and cold winters, somewhat tempered by an arm of the gulf stream that reaches into the Baltic.

Neighboring Countries: Estonia (north); Russia (east); Belarus (southeast); Lithuania (south).

Official Language: Latvian

Other Principal Tongues: Russian.

Ethnic Background: Latvian belongs to the Baltic family of Indo-European languages. It is closely related to Lithuanian, but contains words taken over from Swedish, German and Russian, the languages of peoples that controlled the country at various times in the past. Latvians currently make up 57.7% of the population.

Other Ethnic Groups: Russians (29.6%), Belarusians (4.1%), Ukrainians (2.7%), Polish (2.5%), Lithuanian (1.4%), Others (1.9%).

Principal Religions: Lutheran, Russian Orthodox Christianity, Roman Catholicism.

Chief Commercial Products: Wood and wood products, machinery and equipment, metals and mineral products, chemicals, transport equipment.

Main Trading Partners: EU (72.5% of exports and 77.4% of imports), Lithuania (15.8% of exports and 13.9% of imports), Estonia (14.4% of exports and 8.1% of imports), Germany (8.7% of exports and

15.2% of imports), Russia (9.6% of and 8.4% of imports), Sweden (7.7% of exports), Finland (5.1% of imports).

Currency: lat.

Former Political Status: The Latvian lands were part of the territory governed by the Teutonic Knights from the 13th to the 16th century. They were subsequently ruled by Poland, then Sweden. Peter the Great annexed Riga in 1710; the remainder of the country fell to Russian rule in the 18th century. With the collapse of the Russian Empire, Latvia declared its independence in

Hon. Valdis Zatlers
President of Latvia

1918. Occupied by Soviet forces in June 1940, it was annexed by Stalin in August 1940; declared its independence May 4, 1990.

Independence Day: November 18.

Chief of State: Valdis Zatlers, President (since July 2007).

Head of Government: Valdis Dombrovskis, Prime Minister (since March 2009).

Latvian national identity has been shaped by the desire to be liberated from foreign domination and to protect the small nation's language and culture from

143

Latvia

absorption. Like the other Baltic states, it experienced a succession of foreign masters—Danes, Germans, Swedes, Poles and Russians. During the Great Northern War, which began in 1700, Russian Tsar Peter the Great conquered Riga and what is now Estonia in 1710. Estonia and Livonia (a state consisting of what is now southern Estonia and northern Latvia) officially became a part of the Russian empire in the 1721 Treaty of Nystad and remained so for more than two centuries.

Latvians had passed down innumerable folksongs, legends and fairytales. Many were recorded in written form in the 19th century, when the consciousness of Latvian nationhood solidified. The concept of the Latvian nation sprang not from the reality of an independent political state, but from its national culture. There were Latvian fraternities and student organizations at the universities of Tartu (in Estonia) and St. Petersburg (in Russia). Toward the end of the century a national organization, Jauna strava, thrived; one of its later members was Janis Rainis, Latvia's most famous poet.

For most of this time, the tsars supported those reforms that enabled Latvians and other Balts to develop their national cultures. This ended in 1881, when Alexander III came to power. Sensing a danger from their national revival, he tried to stop it. He ordered a policy of Russification. Russian was declared the official language and the medium of instruction, and the Russian Orthodox religion was imposed. This strict Russification program was terminated after the 1905 Russian Revolution. This was a great emotional event for Latvians, who began struggling against German landlords and the Russian police. Their nationalism grew progressively stronger in the 20th century.

The First World War created the conditions for Latvian independence; it was the first time the Latvian national flag was raised. Latvian rifle regiments were formed to fight against the Germans, and many were killed in 1915 when the front line ran right through Latvia. When the Bolshevik revolution occurred in 1917, many Latvians supported the new Soviet government, hoping thereby to win their freedom. On November 18, 1918, Latvia declared its independence, but it had to continue to fight against German troops and the Red Army in order to secure it. Russia signed a treaty recognizing it on August 11, 1920. However, this lasted only two decades.

Latvia after World War I

Latvia's history as an independent state after World War I bears many similarities to that of Estonia. That is not surprising, since the two countries were alike in many respects. The next decade and a half witnessed political instability, as many different political parties and such extreme nationalist organizations as Perkonkrusts (outlawed by the government) struggled for control.

Like Estonia, Latvia created a 100-member single-chamber parliament (called the *Saeima*) based on proportional representation. Latvia's use of this electoral system made it more difficult to form stable governments, since it increased the number of political groups vying for seats. In the 1931 elections, for example, 27 different political groupings won representation in the legislature. Twelve of the groups managed to elect only a single member. At the other end, only two groups had more than 10 members.

The Latvian constitution, approved in February 1922, provided for the election of a president of the republic to a fixed five-year term. The president, who was made commander-in-chief of the military, was also authorized to issue decrees when parliament was not in session, subject to parliamentary confirmation when it reconvened. The first president of the republic elected under terms of the new constitution was Janis Cakste. A lawyer and early nationalist leader, he had headed the Latvian delegation to the Paris Peace Talks.

Latvia's population at this time was approximately 1.9 million, with Latvians making up about 75% of the population. The largest single minority was Russian, which comprised about 7.8%. Another 8.1% were other Slavs, mainly White Russians and Poles. Other minorities included Jews (5.2%), Baltic Germans and Lithuanians.

Like Estonia, Latvia had an agrarian-based economy, with two-thirds of the population supporting themselves through agriculture. One difference is that Latvia had significantly more industry, particularly in and around the city of Riga. The majority of the population was Protestant (57.2%), but there were significant Russian Orthodox (13%) and Roman Catholic (22.6%) populations.

Latvia also began its independent existence with a land reform that expropriated the old landed estates and provided for their distribution to landless peasants. As a result of the reform, small holders who had obtained their land at this time held 22.2% of the total. In general, Latvia had better luck with its land reform than Estonia, and food production, particularly of beef and dairy cattle, continued to grow through the 1920s and 1930s.

Latvia's Move toward Authoritarianism

The inability to reach consensus was made worse by the world economic depression that began in 1929. It led to a growth of anti-parliamentarianism in Latvia, mainly led by right-wing, nationalist forces. The Nationalist Association, then a small and relatively insignificant right-wing party, proposed giving additional political powers to the president of the republic. A number of fascist or semifascist groupings also emerged at this time advocating anticommunist, antisocialist, anti-Jewish and antiforeign policies. The Latvian government outlawed most of these, but the mainline political parties began to take a more nationalist and antiforeign stance as well.

Karlis Ulmanis, leader of the Peasants' League and one of the founders of modern Latvia, having served as first provisional president from 1918 to 1920, could not get sufficient support from among the other members of the legislature, however, so his constitutional proposals were tabled at this time. On March 16, 1934, he was made premier. Claiming that he had discovered a communist plot to overthrow the government, Ulmanis declared a state of emergency, suspended the parliament, banned party political activities, and outlawed the Thunder Cross Association, a fascist organization. Two months later, Ulmanis organized a separate government committee to take on certain of the functions of the parliament, that is, to handle matters that would normally require legislation. President Kviesis gave his approval to this new arrangement in June.

Most Latvians quietly accepted this new authoritarian regime, apparently convinced by Ulmanis's argument that he needed the additional powers to defend Latvian democracy. Two years later, Kviesis' term came to an end. When he stepped down, Ulmanis took his place. Since Ulmanis continued to hold the office of premier, the effect was to merge the two offices from this point onward. In 1934 Prime Minister Karlis Ulmanis, supported by the army and the paramilitary organization, Aizsargi, dissolved parliament and ruled without it.

The Soviet Union Annexes Latvia, 1940

The authoritarian direction of the Latvian government after 1934 weakened it internationally, especially insofar as the Western democracies were concerned. When the leaders of Nazi Germany and the Soviet Union negotiated a "nonaggression" pact in August 1939, their stipulation that Latvia fell within the Soviet sphere of influence caused less of a reaction than it might otherwise have done. Following this pact, the Soviet Union tightened the noose around the Baltic states' necks.

Hitler launched his invasion of Poland on September 1, and Soviet troops entered to occupy the eastern third of Poland on September 17. With Poland settled, Stalin moved to bring the remaining areas of the Soviet "sphere of influence" under his control. In September 1939 Latvia was forced to accept Soviet troops in Liepaja and Ventspils numbering more than Latvia's own army. Latvia was compelled to sign a mutual assistance pact with the Soviet Union on October 5, 1939.

Nothing happened for several months, probably because the Soviet Union was tied down in its "Winter War" with Finland. Once that was resolved, the Soviet Union turned its attention back to the Baltic states. In May 1940, the Soviet Foreign Ministry accused the Latvian government of violating the 1939 mutual assistance pact signed with the Soviet Union. Almost immediately thereafter, the Latvian government was forced to resign and a popular front government was installed in its place.

This government remained in power for just a little over a month. It came to an end in July, when the Communist Party was made the sole legal party. Most noncommunists were dismissed from office, and a considerable number of them were arrested. New elections were then held on July 14, with only communists permitted to stand for office. The freshly rigged legislature met on July 21. Its only piece of business was to vote on a resolution asking to join the Soviet Union. With all noncommunist voices having been suppressed, it was passed by acclamation. The following month, the USSR Supreme Soviet acceded to the communist request made by their Latvian stooges. Latvia thus became a Soviet Socialist Republic. Russia continues to insist that all three had voluntarily joined the USSR. From August 1940 to June 1941, the communist government nationalized the land, then launched a program of "land reform" whereby larger estates were turned into state farms while smaller parcels were distributed to landless laborers.

Germany's invasion of the Soviet Union beginning on June 22, 1941 temporarily reversed this situation because German troops overran and occupied Latvia later in 1941. Latvia remained under German occupation until 1944. During the German occupation from 1941 to 1944, Latvians fought on both sides. Although most Latvians who wore German *Wehrmacht* uniforms were conscripts who served in normal military units, some became members of the SS. During the 1990s a few hundred of them marched through Riga every year on March 16 to commemorate their fallen comrades. Such displays were forbidden in 2000, and a few Latvians face trial in Latvian courts for alleged war crimes. At the same time, Latvia began at the turn of the century to bring to trial a handful of Soviet military veterans accused of wartime atrocities against Latvians.

Soviet Rule

With the German retreat in 1944, Latvia once again fell under Soviet occupation. A guerrilla movement known as the "Forest Brothers" arose to oppose Soviet control after the end of the war in 1945, but such efforts were ineffectual. Latvia got no outside assistance, and the opposition was eventually suppressed. The Baltic states spent the next half-century as disgruntled but relatively prosperous republics of the Soviet Union.

Many changes occurred in Latvia over the next 45 years. Soviet policy was to integrate the Baltic republics so thoroughly that there would be no question of their ever leaving the union. To that end, the reestablished Latvian communist government reinstated its 1941 nationalization decree, then carried through a general collectivization of agriculture. Meanwhile, the Soviet government sought to bind Latvia and the other two Baltic Republics to the rest of the Soviet Union economically by locating branch factories of Soviet industry in the three republics. The first factories in the 1950s emphasized primary extraction, but a much larger range of factories was built there in the 1960s and 1970s. Such factories received most or all of their raw materials from other parts of the Soviet Union and delivered most of their finished products to customers in the other republics. This economic integration was so successful that Latvia and the other two Baltic republics became more integrated into the Soviet economy than any other area of the Soviet Union.

Economic integration was accompanied by a program of "Soviet Russification," aimed at transforming the cultures of the Baltic republics. All students received Russian language training in the schools, plus general indoctrination lectures on the

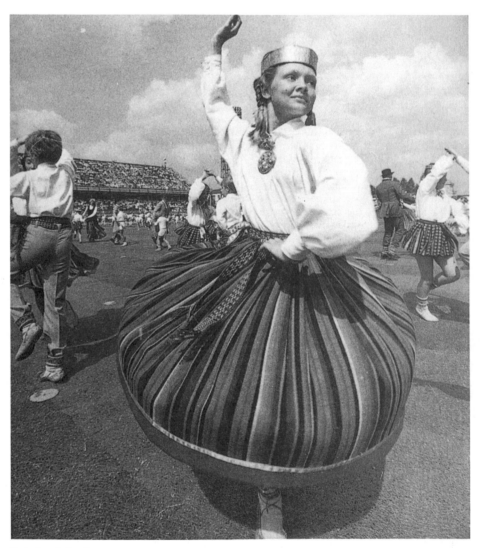

Latvian folk dancer

Courtesy: NOVOSTI

Latvia

Latvian student reading this book

nature of Soviet culture. In addition, a systematic effort was made to settle non-Baltic nationals in the republics. When a new factory was built, most of the workers would be transferred there from elsewhere in the Soviet Union, and scarce housing was allotted to them.

The effects of this policy can be seen by examining the figures of the 1989 Soviet census. Ethnic Latvians made up only 52% of the population of the republic. They had become a minority in the country's seven largest cities. Latvians had nearly become a minority in their own country. These overall figures also masked the fact that, in certain industrial regions near the border, Latvians had become a tiny minority. In many urban areas, including the capital city Riga, it was more common to hear Russian spoken than Latvian. Russians also tended to monopolize many types of jobs, particularly in management and in parts of government. Everywhere, the Russian way of doing things became dominant. On the positive side, the heavy industrialization carried out after 1945 meant that the standard of living in Latvia and Estonia was above that of any other part of the Soviet Union.

Latvia Regains Its Independence

The Latvian people accommodated themselves to Soviet rule, but they could not forget their brief period of independence between the wars. When Gorbachev launched his programs of *glasnost* (openness) and *perestroika* (restructuring) after coming to power in 1985, Latvians were therefore among the first to take advantage of them. Latvians seized the opportunity first to enlarge their self-determination within the Soviet Union and then to gain complete independence. In 1988 a "people's front," composed of both Gorbachev communists and non-

communist democrats and nationalists was formed. In the late 1980s nationalist fervor was fanned by the conference of Latvian writers. On August 23, 1989, two million Estonians, Latvians and Lithuanians formed a human chain from Tallinn to Vilnius to dramatize their demand for freedom.

With large and articulate exile groups, especially in the U.S., Latvia and the other two Baltic nations were able to mobilize considerable international sympathy and diplomatic support for their aspirations. This was especially facilitated by the fact that all Western democracies, except Sweden and briefly Australia, had refused to recognize the Soviet Union's annexation of the Baltics in 1940.

In enunciating his policy of *glasnost*, Gorbachev called on the Soviet peoples to speak out against negative tendencies in the society and to support his reforms. This became a manifesto that led to the creation of thousands of "unofficial" organizations all over the Soviet Union. Formed originally in support of his policy of reform, many of them soon began to push their own agendas.

Latvians were among the early supporters of Gorbachev's policy of *glasnost* and *perestroika* restructuring, and Latvian unofficial organizations also sprang up, taking advantage of the new atmosphere. One of the first such organizations was Renaissance and Renewal, a religious rights organization. The Popular Front of Latvia (PFL), organized in October 1988, incorporated many of these earlier unofficial organizations into its overall structure. The leader of the PFL was Dainis Ivans, a journalist. Within a year its membership had grown to 250,000, about 85% of whom were Latvians. This provided an important contrast with the Latvian Communist Party, which had a membership of 184,000, only 39.7% of whom were Latvians.

The ethnic issue was a greater one in Latvia than in either of the other two Baltic republics because of the larger percentage of non-Latvians in the republic. Conservatives were particularly disturbed by what the front represented and managed to get the PFL decertified in January 1989. This did not stop the front from continuing to operate, however. In the March 1989 elections to the USSR Congress of People's Deputies, front-supported candidates won three-fourths of the seats.

Like Estonia, Latvia had a political party specifically committed to independence, the Latvian National Independence Movement (LNIM). Labeled an extremist organization, it nevertheless exercised influence on the PFL. Under the prodding of the LNIM, the Popular Front of Latvia went on record in June 1989 as favoring "Latvia's independent statehood."

Russians and other non-Latvians had become very concerned about Latvian nationalism, and there were rising fears of ethnic strife. The Popular Front of Latvia sought to alleviate these anxieties by advocating equal rights for all persons living in Latvia, regardless of nationality or other affiliation. The front specifically supported the right of other nationalities either to receive instruction in their own language in the public schools or to set up their own schools. It also advocated political pluralism. This defused a lot of the opposition and helped to win additional support for independence from among the non-Latvian sections of the population.

The Latvian Communist Party, which had more Russians than Latvians among its membership, proved to be the most conservative of the Baltic communist parties. However, even it came under pressure from its Latvian members to take a more nationalistic stance. In September 1989, Janis Vagris, the First Secretary, endorsed the concept of a sovereign Latvia, including republican economic autonomy.

The overlap between the Latvian Communist Party and the Popular Front of Latvia can be seen in the list of delegates to the second congress of the PFL, held in October 1989—24% of the delegates were members of the Latvian Communist Party, while 45 out of 100 of the members of the steering committee were LCP members. They obviously represented members of the reform wing of the party, however, for the congress not only endorsed Latvian independence and creation of a multi-party political system, but called upon the Latvian Supreme Soviet to declare illegal Latvia's 1940 incorporation into the Soviet Union.

New elections to the Latvian Supreme Soviet were scheduled to take place in March 1990. Hoping to co-opt the nationalism issue, the communist members of the old Supreme Soviet adopted a declaration on February 15 endorsing an independent Latvia. That statement proved to be too weak for the new delegates elected in March. On May 4, the new Supreme Soviet proclaimed Latvian independence with a transition period before implementation. Although the declaration got 138 positive votes, 57 deputies refused to participate in the vote, claiming that the declaration was unconstitutional. Most of the delegates abstaining had been elected by the large non-Latvian element within the population. On May 12 the heads of all three Baltic countries signed the Declaration of Concord and Cooperation reestablishing the 1934 Council of the Baltic States.

On May 14 Gorbachev issued a decree invalidating Latvia's declaration of independence. The Soviet military also became involved in the issue when it began dropping leaflets on Riga, accusing the Latvian government of counterrevolution. The next day, several hundred Soviet army troops, accompanied by cadets from an officers' training school in Riga, joined a protest march against Latvian independence. By June 1990, however, the Soviet government had begun ignoring the situation in Latvia, even as it began easing off on its pressure on Lithuania and Estonia. The negative international reaction to the Soviet moves in the Baltic was clearly a factor in this change of policy.

Gorbachev indignantly rejected continuing demands for independence and even ordered that Special Force Units of the USSR Ministry of Interior (OMON) use force against dissidents in the streets of Vilnius, Lithuania, on January 13, 1991, killing 15. Latvians from all over the country came to the capital to defend their democratically elected parliament. Nevertheless, on January 21, 1991, OMON troops killed six persons in Riga.

Coup in Moscow and Latvian Freedom

In May 1991, Gorbachev threatened the new union treaty for the USSR, which he wanted to get negotiated and signed over the summer. He began a rapprochement with Boris Yeltsin, which led to nine of the republics agreeing to sign a new union treaty on August 17. This became the signal for conservative hardliners to organize a coup with the aim of overthrowing Gorbachev and reasserting centralized control.

The August 1991 coup failed, but even as it was going on, the Latvian government again declared its independence. The postcoup Soviet government temporized for two weeks, but it soon found the number of states granting recognition to Latvia and the other Baltic republics to be irresistible. In early September, it, too, recognized the independence of the Baltic Republics. On September 17, 1991, the Baltic states, which had belonged to the League of Nations, were admitted to the United Nations.

Ugolnikov family in Riga

Numerous exiles returned to play important political, military, and economic roles although Latvians who had lived in comfortable Western exile during the Soviet times sometimes experience resentment among certain segments of the population. They must learn to be tactful in offering more efficient foreign ways of doing things. The United States' first ambassador to Latvia was of Latvian heritage. Gunars Meierovics was a leader in what was then one of the country's most successful parties, "Latvia's Way." It was wiped out in the 2002 elections.

A major preoccupation of the Latvian government for several years after that time was the continuing presence of ex-Soviet troops in the republic, plus the problem of an extremely large non-Latvian population. These troops were originally under the jurisdiction of the Commonwealth of Independent States (CIS), but the Russian government assumed responsibility for Russian troops stationed in the ex-Soviet republics in the summer of 1992 after establishing its own Ministry of Defense. Subsequent negotiations between the Latvian and Russian governments elicited a Russian promise to have all troops out of Latvia by the summer of 1993; however, President Yeltsin rescinded this agreement in September 1992 after the Latvian government stripped non-Latvians of citizenship.

Demography and Citizenship

The Latvian government had taken this action because it was under pressure from nationalists within its ranks concerned with the extremely large non-Latvian element in the population. Latvia has a small population: 2.3 million, 800,000 of whom live in Riga. In 1934, ethnic Latvians had constituted 75.5% of the country's population. Russians were the largest minority in Latvia (12%), and they enjoyed citizenship, language guarantees, their own schools, and cultural autonomy. After being bullied into the Soviet Union in 1940, Latvia's demography changed. Indeed, when Soviet rule ended in 1991, 2.3 million Russians were left behind in all the Baltic states, with the lion's share in Latvia.

Russia and Russians living in Latvia demanded automatic citizenship ("zero option," adopted by most former Soviet republics). In Latvia the non-Latvian population had reached almost half by 1991 and an astonishing 63% in the capital city of Riga (and a majority in the six next largest cities). By 2005, 57.7% of the country's residents were Latvian, 29.6% Russian, 4.1% Belarussian, 2.7% Ukrainian, 2.5% Polish and 1.4% Lithuanian. Massive inward migration of Russians and outward deportation of native Latvians had dramat-

Enjoying their work: Chimney-sweeps, Riga   Courtesy: NOVOSTI

ically changed the demographic mix and threatened its national survival.

According to Latvia's postindependence citizenship law, automatic citizenship could be claimed only by persons who were Latvian citizens—or their direct descendants—prior to Latvia's incorporation into the Soviet Union in 1940. This rendered about 48% of the population of the republic "stateless." These regulations were subsequently incorporated into a new electoral law passed in October 1992. Under the terms of this new law, non-Latvians needed to establish competency, though not fluency, in the Latvian language and permanent residence in the republic for at least 16 years extending back into the Soviet era in order to qualify for naturalization. An important exception was ex-Soviet military and security personnel and their families stationed in the country. Their 16 years of residency requirement did not begin until after independence.

In December 1992, the government announced the first partial results of a citizen registration that it had begun carrying out. About 67% of the inhabitants of the republic had been registered by that time. Of those registered, 1,339,530 were classified as Latvian citizens, while an additional 452,378 persons were classified as noncitizens. However, the government also announced that 405,124 of these noncitizens—or 89.5%—had expressed a desire to become citizens.

Latvia subsequently reduced the minimum permanent residence requirement to five years. According to figures published in 1995, 40% of nonethnic Latvian population had passed Latvian-language and history tests and qualified as citizens. Nevertheless, more than one-quarter of Latvia's adult population remains without the franchise. In 1998, 53% of Latvians voting in a referendum approved of giving automatic citizenship to all children born in Latvia since 1991. Adopted by

Latvia

elected parliaments, the citizenship laws appear reasonable by Western standards. Latvia's policies toward minorities have been more successful in easing ethnic tensions than in most post-communist states. International organizations, such as the UN and Council of Europe, have also generally accepted the laws despite Russia's energetic efforts to have Latvia condemned for human rights violations. In 2001 the OSCE declared that its language and citizenship rules meet European standards, but that the government could do more to ease the naturalization process, such as lowering the $50 fee and offering Latvian language classes.

Devising citizenship policies that are both acceptable to Latvians and tolerable for Russians is the most persistent political problem in relations with Russia and the one that elicits the most visceral resistance from Moscow. For Latvia the question of citizenship is of vital importance. With a large Russian-speaking minority, it faced the prospect of continued heavy Russian influence on most aspects of policy if all residents were granted either automatic or dual citizenship. Thus it rejected these options.

This was not only a question of control over Latvia's affairs. It was a matter of principle: in the Latvian view, the majority of Russians had been permitted to settle in Latvia in order to implement Moscow's policy of occupation after it had forcibly annexed the two lands in 1940. On what basis could occupiers and their descendants expect to be recognized as citizens? Russia adamantly denies that the Soviet Union had ever "occupied" Latvia and that its joining was involuntary, despite some admitted pressure at the time. It has never apologized for the Soviet Union's actions in 1940 or subsequent crimes. Nor has it ever hinted that the occupation might have been illegal. The fact that Latvians accepted their fate without armed resistance in 1940 lends some credibility to the Russians' interpretation.

Determined to remain masters in their own house, Latvians based their citizenship laws on the notion of legal continuity of their prewar republics. They imposed severe restrictions, granting citizenship automatically to pre-1940 residents and their descendants. Subsequent naturalization raised this by 1998 to about 40% in Latvia. Confronting criticism that Russian-speakers were being made permanent noncitizens, Latvia opened citizenship to all persons who met certain criteria. They include the willingness to take a loyalty oath and a language test. Few Russians can meet the language requirements without major effort. In 1989, only 22% had a good command of the local language. The others had seen no need to learn them because Balts were expected

Latvia's parliament

to speak Russian well, and most did so. There was an outcry after independence in 1991 that the new language restrictions were "unfair" and "human rights violations." Latvia's citizenship laws do not discriminate on formal ethnic grounds, but since the immediate effect was the disenfranchisement of most ethnic Russian residents, many saw it that way.

A 1998 law in Latvia calls for the phasing in over a decade of Latvian as the sole language of instruction in public schools. The *Saeima* (parliament) passed a new language law in 1999 that mandated the use of Latvian in most aspects of public life and in areas of the private sector such as first aid and public safety. Ex-President Vike-Freiberga vetoed an earlier version of the law after the U.S. government and the EU criticized it. However, she signed a watered-down version after it had received the approval of the OSCE and the Council of Europe.

The Russian government remained critical of the new legislation, which went into effect on September 1, 2000. Its anger was again provoked in 2004 by a law that reduces the use of the Russian language in secondary schools. It requires that at

least 60% of teaching at minority schools be in Latvian beginning in 2004 with the tenth grade. Latvian education experts traveled to Moscow to explain the new law and provide assurances that Russian is not being banished from the schools. Thousands of ethnic Russians rallied in the streets of Riga to protest against it, shouting "Hands off our schools!" The most radical antireform organization (Shtab) called on students to boycott classes until the law is abolished. Some Shtab organizers even went on a hunger strike. The government organized a concert with the popular Russian rock band Mummy Troll in Riga's old town to siphon off support for the protests. The OSCE High Commissioner on National Minorities judged the law reforming minority education to be "necessary."

Nevertheless, the rights of those who do not speak the local language are greater than in some other small nations, like Quebec province in Canada, that fear absorption and destruction of their cultures. Parents are free to send their children to Russian-language schools. Russians face no restrictions on using their language at the workplace. It is an advantage to speak

Latvia

Latvian, and the defense forces and many categories in the civil service are blocked to non-citizens. State radio and television are broadcast in Russian. There are Russian-language theaters and a wide variety of Russian newspapers and magazines available. Many university courses are taught in Russian, and most examinations at Latvian universities may be written in Russian if the student prefers.

The Latvian position on citizenship is grounded in notions of citizenship widely held in the rest of the world. Like most countries, they chose *jus sanguinis* as the principle for conferring citizenship: descent from an individual of a particular nationality. Every child with at least one parent who is a Latvian citizen has the right, by birth, to citizenship. Thus, Latvia offers citizenship to anybody who follows certain procedures and learns the local language and demonstrates a basic knowledge of its political system. This latter requirement points to a deeper aspect of genuine citizenship: it should involve more than merely endowing an individual by law with certain rights and the expectation that he or she will perform certain duties. In the fuller sense, a citizen is a person who feels a moral commitment and loyalty to the state and who is willing to put aside some aspects of self-interest in favor of the interests of the community at large. In ancient Greece and Rome this was called "civic virtue." Alexis de Tocqueville wrote that good citizenship needs to be underpinned by "habits of the heart." Latvia wants citizens whose primary loyalty is to Latvia (where 71% were Latvian citizens in 1996), not to any other state. By 2009 there were about 370,000 non-citizens or nearly 20% of the population.

Russian leaders are incensed by these laws. Complaints from some of the 25 million Russians living in the newly independent former Soviet republics do not fall on deaf ears in Moscow, where a wide assortment of political leaders and groups are ready to exploit them for their own purposes. Although Russian-speakers lead largely separate lives in Latvia, they bear little hatred or deep aversion toward Baltic nationals. According to a 1995 poll, two-thirds (63%) of Russians living in Latvia found relations with the majority nationality to be good; only 43% found that minorities were being "badly treated." Clearly ethnic tensions are not only far below the threshold of violence, but they are diminishing as non-Latvians are adjusting to the eased requirements established in the citizenship laws.

POLITICAL SYSTEM

Like the other Baltic republics, Latvia has established the kind of institutional

Hon. Vaira Vike-Freiberga
Former President of Latvia

and legal conditions that place it within the Western political model. It has a multiparty system in which democratic procedures are respected. Despite frequent changes of coalitions and cabinets and a series of embarrassing political scandals, Latvia has maintained underlying political stability while demonstrating that power can be transferred peacefully from one coalition government to another. Former communists have been able to win power since Latvian independence, but they relinquished it when they no longer had the voters' support.

With some alterations, Latvia readopted on July 6, 1993, its 1922 constitution, which calls for a stronger president than in Estonia. He or she is elected to a three-year term by the unicameral legislature, the *Saeima*. Its 100 members serve three years and are elected by proportional representation in five constituencies. Parties must win at least 5% of the votes to obtain seats. Unlike in Estonia, non-citizens are not permitted to vote in national or local elections.

President
Perhaps the most famous returned exile is Vaira Vike-Freiberga, whom parliament elected as president of the republic after President Guntis Ulmanis's second term had ended a month earlier. She was sworn in on July 8, 1999. At age seven she had fled Latvia before the advancing Red Army. A linguist and psychologist by training, she became a psychology professor at Montreal University. While in exile she had lobbied the Canadian government never to recognize the Soviet annexation of the Baltic states and had organized the émigré effort to scan thousands of Latvian folksongs into a computer database. One of the reasons she is so admired is that she is steeped in Latvian folklore.

Prime Minister Valdis Dombrovskis

After retiring from teaching, she returned to Latvia in 1998, became the head of the Latvian Institute, relinquished her Canadian citizenship, and became one of eastern Europe's first female heads of state. One of her first acts as president was to send back to parliament a new language law she deemed too harsh because it would have required that private commercial transactions be in Latvian. A tenacious and energetic political leader, her overwhelming reelection in June 2003 underscored the fact that she was Latvia's most popular politician ever.

Because of the two-term limit, she had to step down in July 2007. She was succeeded by Valdis Zatlers, an orthopedic surgeon with little political experience. He ran against Aivars Endzins, who was more popular with the public. But after a secret backroom deal in parliament, Zatlers came out on top 58 to 39.

Prime Minister and Parliament
Executive power is exercised by the prime minister and his cabinet, who govern on the basis of majority support in the legislature. Because of the extremely fragmented nature of the *Saeima*—100 members divided among more than a half a dozen political parties or blocs plus a dozen or more independents—it has often been impossible to form a majority-backed coalition government.

In October 2002, an entirely new party emerged as the winner, Einars Repse's New Era. He formed a center-right coalition that endorsed a generous maternity leave law that grants mothers (or fathers) monthly subsidies up to her (or his) salary to care for a child. With 33,000 annual deaths and only 20,000 births, Latvia faces a severely low birth rate. Repse lamented,

Latvia

"The Latvian nation is dying out, there will be no one to work soon."

Although he was awarded the Quadriga-Prize as "European of the Year" in Berlin, Repse ran into troubles almost immediately. He was accused of violating government ethics standards and of conflict of interest for accepting preferential loans from banks that had benefited from his earlier policies as central bank director. He resigned in February 2004 and was replaced by the amiable Indulis Emsis of the Greens, which in Latvia are conservatively oriented. He became Europe's first Green prime minister. But he resigned after only eight months when parliament rejected his draft 2005 budget.

Emsis was replaced as prime minister by Aigars Kalvitis of the center-right People's Party. His four-party coalition was the country's 13th government in 14 years. In October 2006 it became the first Latvian governing coalition to be reelected since Independence. Kalvitis's People's Party captured 23 seats while his coalition partners, the Union of Greens and Farmers and the First Party won 18 and 10 seats respectively. To enlarge their majority of one, they invited the conservative Fatherland and Freedom Party, which won 8 seats, to rejoin the government.

However, after three years in office, the longest-surviving government since independence, he ran into trouble when he clumsily tried to fire the chief of the anticorruption bureau, Aleksejs Loskutovs, for what were widely perceived as political reasons. In what was dubbed the "umbrella revolution" in October-November 2007, the largest protest rally in free Latvia took place in the rain outside of parliament to demand Kalvitis's resignation. In December his successor, Ivars Godmanis, interior minister and earlier prime minister at the time of independence, was sworn in as prime minister with the charge to steer the country through its economic turmoil. He too was brought down by the plummeting economy that in mid-January 2009 had provoked the worst rioting in Riga's Dome Square since independence. President Valdis Zatlers remarked that "trust in the government and officials has collapsed."

In March 37-year-old Valdis Dombrovskis was sworn in as prime minister. He is a physicist by training and former finance minister and Member of the European Parliament for the ERA party. He showed great courage in introducing the kind of painful austerity measures needed to secure EU and IMF help in overcoming Latvia's worst economic crisis since independence. The medicine proved to be too strong for the People's Party, which left the governing coalition in March 2010. The remaining shaky four-party coalition is a minority government.

This underscores the difficulty any democratic government has in trying to win support for brutal spending and wage cuts and tax increases. Diplomatic observers argue that Latvia is not as politically mature as the other two Baltic states because of the strength of business oligarchs, deep Russian economic interests, growing Russian political influence, and the tense social divisions between ethnic Latvians and the 30% of the population with Russian roots.

Foreign and Defense Policy

Since 1991, three ideas have guided Latvia's foreign policy—building Baltic solidarity, reorienting the economy toward the West, and protecting Latvian sovereignty from Russia. The Latvian government has had to spend a great deal of its time on its relations with Russia. In theory, Latvia would like to have good relations with Russia, and it sees the necessity of a continuing, if diminished, economic relationship as well. The large number of ethnic Russians in the country is a major concern, and the Latvian government's decision rendering them "stateless" had an extremely negative effect on its relations with Russia. In 2007 there were 400,000 such noncitizens, 17.5% of the total population. Latvia's language law mandating the use of the Latvian language in most facets of public life, passed in December 1999, was also denounced in Russia, so the problem continues.

Perhaps nothing is more divisive than trials of former Soviet secret police, almost all of whom are Russian. In 2002 an 81-year-old retired former agent was accused of helping organize deportations of Latvians to Siberia and put on trial for genocide. In 2004 the law lapsed that had banned former collaborators from public office and sensitive jobs, such as in the judicial system. In 2006 parliament passed a bill to publish the names of almost 4,500 persons suspected of having been Soviet secret police informants.

One way of punishing Latvia for both the language laws and trials was not to sign a border agreement. Russia had planned to sign such a treaty with Latvia on May 10, 2005. However, it postponed this indefinitely when the Latvian government issued a declaration saying that such a border treaty did not mean that it had given up other issues, such as compensation for former Gulag inmates, or holding Stalin and Hitler equally responsible for causing the Second World War. Vike-Freiberga demanded that Russia "express its regret" for its "subjugation" of Eastern and Central Europe. In March 2007 the two countries finally signed a treaty demarcating their border, but the Russian Duma (parliament) delayed ratification.

When the European Union decided in 2000 to open membership negotiations with Latvia and Lithuania, Vike-Freiberga commented that "Latvia has left behind for good the post-Soviet period and has become a democratic and open European state." She proclaimed that "justice has been done" when Latvia was invited in December 2002 to join. It entered in May 2004 after 72% of voters turned out for a referendum in September 2003 and voted 67% to 32% in favor of entry. The country's government and business community strongly supported entry. Latvia's constitution requires such a double majority (of turnout and of approval) for a measure to pass in a referendum. The largest daily newspaper, *Diena* (which collapsed in 2009), ran a banner headline: "Latvia returns to Europe!" Parliamentary Speaker Ingrida Udre became Latvia's first EU commissioner. In May 2008, polls showed 72% popular approval of the EU, and parliament approved the quasi-constitutional Lisbon Treaty.

Latvian school chorus breaks out in song in Siena, Italy

With strong Western support, all three Baltic states negotiated the withdrawal of Soviet troops from their territories. Since August 1994 Latvians are undisputed guardians of their own nation. Feeling insecure and knowing that no Western power would defend them militarily without a formal guarantee, Latvia and the other Baltic states made it known that they wish to enter NATO. Latvia's trade has already shifted from about 80% to the other Soviet republics to 90% toward the West. Latvians regard NATO as the only alliance capable of thwarting any future Russian expansionist temptations or attempts to restore "spheres of influence." It joined in April 2004. The importance of the NATO decision at its Prague Summit in November 2002 was underscored by Vike-Freiberga: "Latvia lost its independence for a very long time and knows the meaning of independence and the loss of it, knows the meaning of security, and the loss of it."

Riga again hosted a NATO summit meeting in November 2006. Then French President Jacques Chirac decided to use the occasion to humiliate Latvia and irritate the U.S. by invited Russian President Vladimir Putin to join him for dinner the last day of the conference to help him celebrate his 74th birthday. He did not bother to inform or consult the Latvian government. No Russian president has ever visited the Baltic states since the collapse of the Soviet Union, and a visit while ignoring the Latvian government would have meant that Russia did not regard Latvia as sovereign. Then President Vike-Freiberga informed Putin that he could come only if he made an official visit to the presidential office first, thereby recognizing Latvia's sovereignty and equality. Putin decided not to come.

Membership requires changes in Latvia's armed forces. It currently has 5,745 active forces. Women may serve. There are 11,034 paramilitary forces that include 551 full-time National Guard and 10,483 part-time. Its army numbers 1,058, its navy 587 (and 12 ships including coastal patrol craft), and its air force 319 (with 24 aircraft). A Joint Staff has 3,202 soldiers. Most of its forces are geared for territorial defense, but the government decided in 2003 to shift to a volunteer army and to end conscription. The resulting military is better trained and more able to carry out NATO missions outside of Latvia. It once sent 97 peacekeepers to Bosnia, and it had 11 soldiers in Kosovo. The Latvian government supported the 2003 American-British war in Iraq although the majority of Latvians opposed it. After the end of initial hostilities, the government authorized the deployment of 125 soldiers to help stabilize Iraq. It dispatched a 36-troop unit to Kirkuk in northern Iraq to serve under Polish command. The U.S. provided assistance to these forces before they were withdrawn. But 175 Latvians are still deployed in Afghanistan. In 2008 Latvia entered a bilateral agreement with the U.S. that led to mutual visa-free travel.

ECONOMY

Latvia, the most industrialized of the Baltic states, lags behind Estonia in terms of overall economic success and foreign investment, and its privatization program had greater problems. On the positive side are the Baltic States' best port (Riga, which increased its tonnage by 20% in 2003) and a corporate income tax rate of only 15. On the negative side is a catastrophic downturn of the economy in 2008 and 2009 caused by the global credit squeeze and recession. It had seen a 30% annual increase in wages (bad for businesses but good for the people), and a current accounts deficit of almost 23% of GDP.

The economic statistics in the midst of its worst recession since independence are depressing: The budget deficit has soared to 9.2%. This is a disaster for a country that aspires to adopt the euro. It adamantly refused to devalue its currency, choosing instead the stronger medicine of deep cuts in public spending and wages. Salaries of public sector employees were cut up to 50%, pensions were reduced by 10%, and hospital budgets were lowered by 40%. GDP fell by 18% in 2009 (24% since the recession began), the worst performance in the EU. Imports and exports fell by more than 40%, a magnitude rarely seen in peacetime. Its credit rating was downgraded to junk before being raised again in 2010 in recognition of the country's bold efforts. The government's painful austerity program, introduced as a condition to gain IMF and EU support, sparked the worst riots since independence in the streets of Riga in January 2009. Its government became the second in Europe (after Iceland) to fall because of the global recession.

Its official unemployment rate was 19.7% in 2010, double the EU average. But because of the underground economy and the fact that many young Latvians found work in the UK, Ireland and other Nordic countries, the real rate is perhaps somewhat lower. Real estate values have drastically declined with the rest of the economy. Housing prices are down two-thirds from their peak, and the banks are hesitant to lend. Latvia experienced a soaring 49% growth in tourism and business travel to and from it since 2004, triggered by EU membership.

As a step toward adopting the euro, it was admitted to the EU's exchange-rate mechanism (ERM2) in 2005. In the midst of the crisis, the government fought fiercely to prevent a devaluation of the lat, which is pegged to the euro. It did so through drastic public and private-sector salary cuts and a reduction of public spending. Since almost 90% of Latvians' borrowings are in euros, such devaluation would be a disaster. The European Commission agreed to provide Latvia with $10.5 billion (7.5 billion euros) to help it through the crisis. It has already decided that its future euro coins will include the freedom monument, the national coat of arms, and the same picture of a Latvian girl that had been on the interwar 5 lat coin. The former target date of 2012 for

Latvia

adopting the euro will be postponed until mid-decade. All of this has taken a toll on residents' confidence in institutions. Support for the EU is lower than in any other member state.

Latvia has a modern economic structure: 63% of the workforce is employed in the services sector and produces 73.2% of GDP. Industry employs 26% of the workforce and produces 23.3% of GDP. Its major industries include machinery, metalworking, electrical equipment, light industry, agricultural equipment, chemicals, and pharmaceuticals. Forestry products and extractive industry are also important, including timber, paper, peat, limestone, dolomite and clay. Riga, a major center for industry, manufactures consumer goods like radios and other electrical appliances, cars and trucks, and agricultural equipment. Light industry, including food processing and woodworking, is also important.

Only 11% of the workforce remains in agriculture, producing 3.6% of GDP. Most of the old collective and state farms have been turned into cooperatives, but there are still very few private farms. This has, in part, been because relatively few peasants favor a return to private agriculture. Another factor has been the lack of any political will to pass the necessary legislation. Agriculture no longer has the significance in the economy that it formerly had, but Latvia still has an important dairy industry. Dairy products, one of Latvia's important exports, have been redirected to the West since 1991 although this has been somewhat hindered by a worldwide surplus.

The government used its decree-issuing authority to carry through a general denationalization of domestic retail trade in 1992. However, the privatization process slowed after the government announced in 1992 that it would not sell any more state-owned facilities for Latvian rubles. Latvia has yet to privatize many large enterprises, and it has carried out much less restructuring than neighboring Estonia. As a result of this slowness to privatize, relatively little foreign private investment flowed into Latvia. In 2004 foreign direct investment per capita was 47.8 euros, the lowest in the Baltics. It did not help that by 2005 Latvia had 13 different prime ministers in 14 years. The top investors are Sweden and Germany tied for first, followed by Denmark and the United States.

The government has worked at establishing ties with the Scandinavian countries. After implementing a comprehensive policy of privatization, foreign private investment has begun to grow, much of it coming from its Nordic neighbors.

In 1995, the economy suffered a setback when about one-third of the country's 67 commercial banks collapsed. Although Latvia has a well-run central bank, Riga

Downtown Riga at end of Soviet era. Building on the right is now the stock exchange

has become a significant offshore financial center for Russians seeking a safe home for their money. One Latvian bank (Parex, which was rescued through nationalization in November 2008 to prevent a bank crisis) even ran an advertisement on Russian TV showing a dollar bill and the words, "We are closer than America." Many influential banks have uncomfortably close links with Russia. Parex's two Russian founders were able to acquire Latvian citizenship without having to pass the normal Latvian language exam. In general, about three-fourths of Latvia's banking assets are owned by foreign banks, especially ones from Scandinavia. Swedish banks were hurt by the recession in Latvia. But Latvia accounts for less than 5% of Sweden's largest lender in the region, Swedbank. Despite losses, no foreign bank pulled out.

Latvia's trade has shifted from about 80% to the other Soviet republics to 90% toward the West, particularly the EU (72.5% of exports and 77.4% of imports). It moved more slowly than Estonia to redirect its trade from Russia, which provides 8.1% of Latvia's imports, largely energy. One reason is that the majority of the population in the major cities plus most workers in industry are non-Latvian, usually Russian.

The main northern route for Russia's oil exports ran through Latvia to the main oil port of Ventspils. This has supported a powerful commercial group in Latvia that favors close ties with Russia rather than with the EU. Russia's leverage was demonstrated in 2003 when it stopped pumping oil to Ventspils. Some Latvians saw this as a move to gain complete control over the port. The Latvian government hopes to sell its stake in Ventspils and to privatize the oil terminal there so that it

would be co-owned by European and Russian investors.

It wants the port to serve as a key connection between Russia and an enlarged EU. However, the lack of oil supply led Latvia to postpone such privatization. Like other new EU members, Latvia fears Russian domination of its energy supplies. Russian energy groups supply more than three-fourths of Eastern Europeans' oil and gas, compared with only one-fourth of that needed by Western Europeans. They prefer buyers in the West if possible. Latvia is second in Europe behind Sweden in the production of renewable energy: 33% of its needs are covered by this, compared with an EU average of 9%. Latvia hopes to raise this to 40% by 2020. It is highly committed to green politics. In a 2008 index of environmental performance compiled by Yale and Columbia universities, Latvia placed fifth in the world, one notch below Lithuania and far above the United States, which was ranked 66th. Nevertheless, Latvia must still import more than 40% of its energy.

Latvia has other problems it must tackle. Its dismal Soviet-era hospitals must be modernized. Its poor rural areas must be developed. Corruption is so rampant that the respected Berlin-based organization, Transparency International, ranked Latvia as the second-most corrupt country among the 10 that joined the EU in 2004. The U.S. ambassador, Catherine Todd Baily, warned that Latvia was in danger of becoming "a playground of a few individuals where they go to line their own pockets and those of their friends."

CULTURE

Latvian culture was historically the culture of the peasantry, the upper classes being mainly German. The same was also true of the cities, for that was where the German and Jewish merchants and tradesmen lived. Thus a great deal of Latvia's historical culture is not Latvian at all, though as Latvians became educated and entered the middle class in the 19th century, they tended to adopt elements of that earlier culture. Modern Latvian culture is no longer a peasant culture and it is, in fact, mainly an urban culture.

Approximately a third of the population lives in the city of Riga, Latvia's capital, its chief port, and its largest industrial center. In the 12th century, German merchants of the Hanseatic League began trading with Latvian tribes living along the Daugava [Western Dvina] River. In 1201, Bishop Albert of Bremen, who had been given the title of Bishop of Livonia by the pope and dispatched to the area accompanied by the Teutonic Knights, built a fortress along the right bank of the river. Bishop Albert also founded his own militant Order of the Brethren of the Sword, and he used it to spread Christianity among the Latvians.

A town grew up around the fortress, and Riga quickly became a major center for trade. It joined the Hanseatic League in 1282. But Bishop Albert's religious order controlled the city until the Reformation. Riga became an independent merchant city-state in 1561, but it was soon taken over by the Polish king. It passed back and forth between Poland and Sweden until 1710, when Peter the Great captured it, and it became part of the Russian Empire.

Riga remained mainly a city of foreigners until the late 19th century. Today it is not only the political and cultural center of the republic, but the industrial center as well. Riga University, founded in 1861, is now called Riga Technical University. The country's main university is the University of Latvia in Riga, with a large student body. There are numerous colleges and technical schools as well. The Latvian Academy of Sciences and its 14 affiliated research institutes are also located here. The city has an opera and ballet theater, numerous other theaters for plays, and four concert halls. It is therefore the center for higher Latvian culture.

The city itself is full of historic buildings, including guildhalls, medieval warehouses and private residences, dating back as far as the 14th century. One of the oldest buildings is the Riga Castle itself, headquarters of the Livonian Order in Riga, which dates from 1330. There are also many churches, a few of which are from this same period, though most of them were at least partially rebuilt in subsequent centuries. The oldest of these is the Dome Cathedral, a brick church con-

Riga University Student

secrated in 1211. For centuries the seat of the archbishop of Livonia and Prussia, it has been rebuilt or remodeled many times and shows evidence of many architectural styles, stretching from the Romanesque to the Baroque. The Reformation reached Riga in the middle of the 16th century and the Domkirk became a Lutheran Church at that time. Today it is a museum. The city also has many operating churches representing various denominations: Ro-

man Catholic, Russian Orthodox, Baptist, and, of course, Lutheran. There is also one remaining synagogue.

Latvia has a strong folklorist tradition, but because most Latvians lived in the countryside, the bulk of the early collections of Latvian folk tales was made by Germans resident in the cities. Most were translated into German before being published. A written literature by Latvian writers first appeared in the 19th century as the number of educated Latvians began to grow. The man usually given credit for laying the foundation stones for a Latvian literature was Juris Neikens, a 19th century author of numerous short stories. A contemporary, Juris Alumans, was the first Latvian poet, but he helped to start a school of poetry, represented by Krisjanis Barons, Fricis Brivzemnieks, and Atis Kronvalds. Another 19th century figure, Adolfs Alunans, is considered to be the father of Latvian drama. The novel was given Latvian form by two brothers, Reinis and Matiss Kaudzites, who jointly wrote *The Times of Land-Surveyors,* published in 1879.

Two novelists of the early 20th century were Augusts Deglavs, author of *Riga,* a three-volume work published between 1912 and 1921, and Jekabs Jansevskis, author of *The Native Land,* a six volume work published in 1924–25. Realism is represented by the dramas and short stories of Rudolfs Blaumanis and the poems of Vilis Pludonis. Romanticism is represented by the dramas of Janis Rainis, whose greatest work, written in 1905, is an epic tragedy dealing with early Latvian history entitled *Fire and Night.* Rainis was also a social reformer who spent several years in tsarist prisons before 1905. He participated in the

Old Town Riga

Latvia

1905 revolution and subsequently had to escape to Switzerland, where he lived until 1920. *Fire and Night* became the basis for an opera written in 1921 by the composer Janis Medins.

Literary figures of the period of Latvian independence include the novelist Janis Akuraters, the poets Karlis Skalbe and Edvards Virza, the short story writer Janis Ezerins, and the novelist Janis Jaunsudrabins. Jaunsudrabins is unusual in that he also made a reputation for himself as a painter.

Some good writers of the Soviet period managed to make their way abroad. They include the playwright Martins Ziverts, the essayist and novelist Zenta Maurina, and the novelists Anslavs Eglitis, Girts Salnais, and Antons Rupainis.

FUTURE

Latvia is a small state about the size of Ireland with a well-educated and disciplined population. This has helped make the transition to a market economy more successful than in any of the other ex-Soviet republics except Estonia. However, it has two problems for which it has found no solution: a fragmented electorate that has often meant that there was no majority for any specific action, and a large non-Latvian population that threatens the political stability. The two problems are interrelated because part of the political fragmentation results from disagreements over how to treat the non-Latvian population. Both problems will diminish as more and more non-Latvians acquire citizenship.

Its long-term prospects are bright although the boom times are temporarily over, including in the real estate sector. The slowdown triggered a frightful recession and property crash. It did not bring a devaluation of the lat although it postponed entry into the eurozone until mid-decade. Latvia's government was the second in Europe (after Iceland) to fall due to the effects of the global recession. Former finance minister and now prime minister, Valdis Dombrovskis, who took office in March 2009, has shown courage and skill in managing the economic crisis. But his medicine drove the People's Party out of his coalition, and now he must rule with a four-party minority government. The worst is over. However, there will be an uphill struggle to regain anything resembling normalcy in terms of real wages and living standards.

Latvia's greatest remaining problem is how to deal with the large Slavic minorities that make up a third of its population and much of the industrial work force. Like Estonia, Latvia faces both foreign and domestic political problems that are sometimes in conflict with each other. To preserve its language and culture and to survive as a nation, it has chosen to restrict its citizenship and create strong motivation for members of ethnic minorities to recognize the Latvian character of the restored republic. While pursuing this policy, it must always calculate Russia's response and adjust it to what Moscow would be willing to tolerate.

Some major challenges must be faced. For the sake of their prosperity and security, Latvians sought economic and military integration with the West. Their need for the security that such integration provides stems from the long-standing Russian claim to predominance over the nations on its periphery. They face no imminent threat to their newly regained independence. But they must remain on guard to ensure that they do not lose a part of their sovereignty. That would be the case if Russia were able to restrict their ability to make their own decisions. NATO entry occurred in April 2004. EU membership followed a month later. Both offer Latvia reassurance for the future.

Republic of Lithuania

Wedding Day at Trakai Castle

Area: 25,174 sq. mi. (64,445 sq. km., twice the size of Belgium).

Population: 3.4 million

Capital City: Vilnius (580,000)

Climate: Temperate with cool summers and cold winters, somewhat tempered by an arm of the gulf stream that reaches into the Baltic.

Neighboring Countries: Latvia (north); Belarus (southeast); Poland (southwest); Russia (Kaliningrad Enclave) (west).

Official Language: Lithuanian.

Other Principal Tongues: Polish, Russian.

Ethnic Background: Lithuanian belongs to the Letto-Lithuanian family of Indo-European languages. It is the oldest Indo-European language still spoken and maintains many of its ancient characteristics. It is closely related to Latvian and contains some influences from the Polish language. Lithuanians, mentioned in Tacitus's *Germania* as excellent farmers, have occupied the southern shores of the Baltic for over 2,000 years. A dynastic union with Poland in the 14th century brought a Polanization of the Lithuanian upper classes. Russian influence began in the 18th century when Lithuania became part of the Russian Empire. Lithuanians currently make up 80% of the population.

Other Ethnic Groups: Poles (7.1%), Russians (7%); Other (4.3%).

Principal Religion: Roman Catholic Christianity.

Chief Commercial Products: Mineral products, transport equipment, machinery and equipment, textiles, chemicals.

Main Trading Partners: EU (64.8% of exports and 68.3% of imports), Russia (15% of exports and 18% of imports), Latvia (12.9% of exports and 5.4% of imports), Germany (10.5% of exports and 14.8% of imports), Estonia (6.5% of exports), Poland (6.3% of imports and 10.5% of imports), United Kingdom (4.6% of exports), Netherlands (4.2% of imports).

Currency: litas

Former Political Status: An independent Principality in the 13th century. A dynastic union with Poland in 1385 led to an increasing closeness between the two countries until they were merged in 1569. Lithuania became part of the Russian Empire in the 18th century and remained so until 1918. Independent state 1918–1940; annexed to the Soviet Union

Lithuania

President Dalia Grybauskaite

in 1940; declared its independence again in March 1990; took control of its borders on August 26, 1991.

National Day: February 16 (Independence Day).

Chief of State: Dalia Grybauskaite, President of the Republic (July 2009).

Head of Government: Andrius Kubilius, Prime Minister (December 2008).

National Flag: Three horizontal stripes—yellow, green, red.

LITHUANIA SINCE WORLD WAR I

Independent Lithuania, 1919–1939

For centuries Lithuanians dreamed of again being masters in their own house. The cataclysm that shook and reordered Europe from 1914–18 provided that long-awaited opportunity. Elections to the Lithuanian Constituent Assembly took place in April 1920. A new constitution went into effect August 1, 1922, which created a parliamentary system with a single-body legislature, called the *Seimas*. It also created a ceremonial president of the republic, elected for a five-year term. Aleksandras Stulginskis became the first president under the new constitution.

Lithuania was overwhelmingly rural at this time with 79% of the population earning their living from agriculture. It was also relatively backward; according to the 1923 census, approximately a third of the population was illiterate. There was no individual agriculture among the peasants since their holdings were organized into communes similar to the *mirs* of Russia and farmed in common. The large estates were mainly in the hands of either Poles or Russians, though the Poles were mainly descendants of individuals of Lithuanian extraction who had been Polanized in the 16th to 18th centuries, when the Polish monarchy and Polish culture dominated the united Poland-Lithuania.

A 1922 land reform program expropriated the land of Russian estate owners and limited the size of other estates to 375 acres. These lands were subsequently redistributed to peasant small holders. The land reform also provided for the break up of the peasant communes and the distribution of the land to the peasants to create private farms. Turning the peasants into individual farmers brought increased prosperity to the countryside. But the plots of land carved out from the large estates were so small that these peasant small holders had great difficulty making a go of it. In the 1930s, many either sold or abandoned their land and then sought employment in the cities or emigrated.

Lithuania was the most densely populated of the three Baltic States. With 2,035,121 in 1923, it also had the largest population of the three. Its people were mixed ethnically, with approximately 80% speaking Lithuanian. Jews were the single largest minority (7.6%), followed by Poles (3.2%), Russians (2.5%) and Germans (1.4%). There were also a few White Russians and Latvians. Religiously, Lithuania was rather homogeneous, with 85.7% professing Roman Catholicism. The remainder was either Jewish or Protestant.

Source: *The Economist*

Lithuania's Border Disputes

Lithuania's chief problem in the period of the 1920s was in securing acceptable international borders. Although there were a number of border disputes, its most significant problem by far was the city of Vilnius, the historic capital of Lithuania. Some of the leaders associated with the new Polish state, including Joseph Pilsudski—sometimes called the father of modern Poland—had strong ties to the Vilnius area. Pilsudski was a descendant of a Polonized Lithuanian noble family and had been born in Vilnius. When the Lithuanian leadership opted for a separate, independent Lithuania, Pilsudski decided that the Vilnius area ought to be part of Poland. His real aim was to recreate the old Polish-Lithuanian Empire.

The background of the dispute is extremely complicated. The original Lithuanian proclamation of independence had been made in the city of Vilnius, but the newly proclaimed Lithuanian government was forced to abandon that city in January 1919 as Bolshevik forces approached. They fled to Kaunas, which became the provisional capital. The Bolsheviks were forced out in April 1919 by Polish forces, who then occupied the city. In the summer of 1920, the Bolsheviks launched a counteroffensive, driving the Poles back.

Soviet Russia and Lithuania signed a peace treaty on July 12, under which the Bolsheviks recognized Lithuanian independence. Three days later, they offered to restore Vilnius to Lithuania if it would ally itself with Soviet Russia against Poland. This required Lithuania to grant Soviet troops transit rights during their invasion of Poland. In the process, they occupied Vilnius. The Soviet invasion force continued westward toward Warsaw and was only stopped by a major battle at the Vistula River in August. As the Soviet forces retreated, they turned Vilnius over to the Lithuanian government, which took possession of the city on August 26, proclaiming it once again the national capital.

Meanwhile the Polish forces pressed farther and farther eastward. They hoped to fulfill Pilsudski's dream of restoring the ancient borders of Poland-Lithuania. Since the Polish government was desirous of Allied support against Soviet Russia, it gave in to Allied pressure to end its border dispute with Lithuania. On October 7 Poland signed the treaty of Suwalki granting Lithuania the city of Vilnius and the surrounding district.

By this time, however, the Polish invasion force, defeated by the Soviets, was beginning its retreat westward. Two days later, a Polish unit under General Lucjan

Zeligowski broke away from the main Polish force and advanced into Lithuania, apparently acting under secret instructions from Pilsudski. Vilnius was quickly occupied. General Zeligowski then moved farther into Lithuania, apparently intending to conquer the entire country. Lithuanian troops counter-attacked, however, and General Zeligowski was forced to withdraw to Vilnius.

The Polish government disavowed Zeligowski, but that was only for international consumption. Zeligowski, acting on orders from Pilsudski, proceeded to create a Central Lithuanian Republic, supposedly independent of both Poland and Lithuania. All attempts to solve the matter diplomatically failed. Then General Zeligowski arranged for rigged "elections" to take place in January 1922, which were won by pro-Polish candidates. The puppet legislature voted for union with Poland.

The Polish Sejm proceeded to annex the Vilnius area. The Allied ambassadors, tired of the whole thing, accepted the annexation, thereby recognizing the existing line as the final frontier. Refusing to accept the annexation, Lithuania broke diplomatic relations with Poland. These were not resumed until 1938. In the case of Vilnius, Lithuania waited a long time to achieve an acceptable international frontier. Lithuania got Vilnius back in 1940, but Poland did not officially relinquish it until 1994, and even then without apology.

The second boundary question was with regard to Memel, located on the Lithuanian coast a short distance from the mouth of the Nemunas, Lithuania's largest river. Memel had been part of Prussia since the 18th century, but it was taken from Germany at the Treaty of Versailles. The Allies had intended that Memel go to a reconstituted Poland-Lithuania. Although Lithuania's decision to seek its own independence ended that possibility, the Allies, refusing to recognize Lithuanian independence because of its border dispute with Poland over Vilnius, could not bring themselves to turn Memel over to Lithuania. Instead, Memel was placed under French military administration, and the matter was put on hold.

Memel itself (now Klaipeda) was a town of only about 20,000, most of whose citizens were German nationals. Lithuania's interest in the city was that it needed a seaport, and Memel was the only good one along the entire Lithuanian coast. Its interest in Vilnius was much greater, however, so it did nothing until it had become clear that the international community had recognized Poland's annexation of Vilnius.

With nothing further to lose, the Lithuanian government decided to seize Memel by force. On January 7, 1923, days after the French had begun their own occupation of the German Ruhr area, Lithuania sent troops accompanied by a large number of "volunteers" to invade and occupy Memel. The Lithuanians lost 20 men, while two Frenchmen and a German policeman were killed. With the French tied down in Germany and the German and Soviet governments supporting Lithuania, the Allies decided that nothing could be done and agreed, in February 1923, to transfer Memel to Lithuanian sovereignty.

Thus, in this dispute, Lithuania got both the desired seaport and international recognition of its acquisition. The government immediately gave the Lithuanian name of Klaipeda to the city and the region and established it as an autonomous province with its own government. With all of Lithuania as its hinterland, it flourished in subsequent years although it continued to have a significant German population. That would become a diplomatic issue between Germany and Lithuania after Hitler came to power in 1933.

Lithuania's Move Away From Democracy

The May 1926 elections resulted in a political transformation when the Christian Democrats, who had dominated every government up to this time, were defeated. A new coalition government under the premiership of Mykolas Slezevicius now took power, composed of the Social Democrats and the Peasant Populists. One month later, in June 1926, the coalition's candidate, Dr. Kazys Grinius, a prominent leader of the Peasant Populists, was installed as president.

Among the changes introduced by the new government was a different attitude toward the Soviet Union. This was symbolized by a nonaggression pact, which the two countries signed in September 1926. The Christian Democrats and the Nationalists had opposed an agreement with the Soviet Union from the beginning, and they began planning a counterstroke. On the night of December 16, with the support of the army, they carried out their *coup d'état* against the government. Entering the parliament building accompanied by a group of officers, they seized control. Then they dismissed the cabinet, adjourned the session of parliament, and deposed the president. Antanas Smetona, leader of the Nationalists and first president in 1919–20, was reappointed.

The coup having succeeded, the left decided to cooperate to save what they could of Lithuanian democracy. Grinius submitted his resignation as president, and Slezevicius resigned as premier. The parliament met and elected Antanas Smetona as president. The coup had thereby been legalized. One of Smetona's first acts was to name Augustinas Voldemaras, a prominent Nationalist, as the new premier. Voldemaras formed a cabinet com-

Ornamental cats

Courtesy: NOVOSTI

Lithuania

posed of Christian Democrats, Nationalists and members of parties of the center.

The Social Democrats and Peasant Populists continued to control a majority in the legislature, however. When, after a period of cooperation, they challenged the government in April 1927, the latter dissolved the legislature. Smetona ruled for approximately a year by decree, then proclaimed a new constitution in May 1928, which formalized the new structure. From that time onward, Smetona and his Premier, Augustinas Voldemaras, ruled the country by decree. Lithuania was thus the first of the Baltic countries to abandon democracy and replace it with a form of authoritarianism.

The Lithuanian Authoritarian Regime

Lithuania differed from its two Baltic neighbors in that its authoritarian regime involved two figures, Smetona and Voldemaras, and because some political organizations continued to operate. The Nationalist Party was the most significant of the political groups at this time although Voldemaras created a semi-fascist group, Iron Wolf. It was forced out in September 1929 after he came under clerical criticism and became the target of a failed assassination attempt by three Lithuanian students. J. Tubelis, President Smetona's brother-in-law, succeeded him as premier. Tubelis remained premier until 1939.

In 1934, spurred on by worsening economic conditions, a number of military officers attempted a coup to restore Voldemaras to power. When it failed, he was arrested and sentenced to several years in prison. Released in 1938, he left the country and settled in southern France.

There were also numerous peasant revolts in 1934 that were put down by force. Believing that the revolts were the result of political agitation, Smetona banned all political parties other than the Nationalists. The government permitted the election of a new legislature in 1935, but this was largely meaningless since the government nominated all electoral candidates. A new constitution was also approved in 1936. In essence, it legalized the authoritarian presidency that had existed since 1926. In one innovation, Smetona was henceforth to be addressed as Tautos Vados, or "Leader of the People."

Lithuania under Soviet Rule, 1939–1991

Although the Lithuanian people had failed in some respects with regard to domestic policies, their greatest mistake was in foreign policy. Perhaps nothing they could have done would have made any difference, but they were at odds with almost all of their neighbors and had no friends. Thus when Nazi Germany and the Soviet Union got together to negoti-

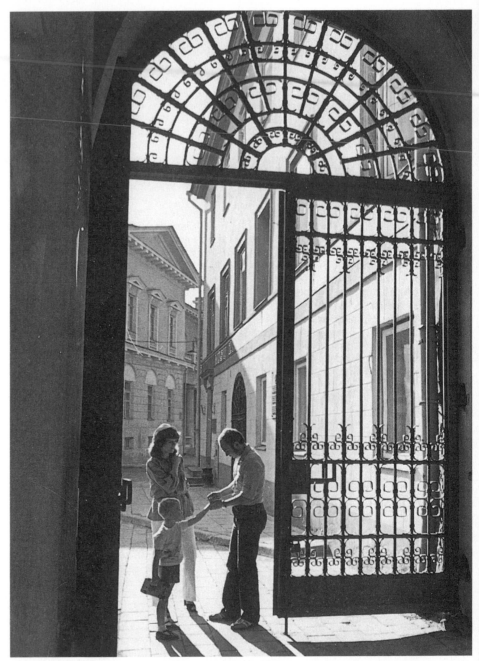

The old part of Vilnius, the Lithuanian capital whose "sister" city is Madison, Wisconsin
Courtesy: NOVOSTI

ate their "nonaggression" pact in August 1939, Lithuania was among their victims. Dividing Eastern Europe into spheres of influence, the original agreement assigned Estonia and Latvia to the Soviet Union, while Lithuania fell within the German sphere of influence. However, a protocol signed on September 23, 1939, reversed this. Lithuania was placed within the Soviet sphere of influence, while Nazi Germany got an extra piece of Poland.

Hitler launched his invasion of Poland on September 1, and Soviet troops entered to occupy the eastern third of Poland on

September 17. With Poland under control, Stalin moved to cash in his other chips. In October all three Baltic States were forced to sign mutual assistance pacts with the Soviet Union. As an aside, Lithuania was the only one to get anything out of the agreements. The Soviet Union transferred the city of Vilnius and surrounding area, which it had just taken from Poland, to Lithuania.

Nothing happened for several months, probably because the Soviet Union was tied down in its "Winter War" with Finland. Once that was resolved, the Soviet

Union turned its attention back to the Baltic States. Toward the end of May 1940, the Soviet Foreign Ministry accused Lithuania of violating the 1939 mutual assistance pact. Then, on June 14, Soviet Foreign Minister Molotov demanded the arrest of the Lithuanian interior and security ministers and the creation of a new Lithuanian government capable of supporting the 1939 treaty. In addition, Molotov demanded that Soviet troops be authorized to enter the country and to occupy "the most important centers."

Lithuania had no choice but to give in to the Soviet request. After the Red Army had entered the country, Molotov demanded the right to name a new premier. A government front government was now established. The Social Democrats and Peasant Populists were given ministerial seats, but the Communists controlled all the important ministries.

The popular front government had a remarkably short life. In July, all political parties other than the Communist Party were banned, and most non-Communists were dismissed from office. This was followed by a wave of arrests. With only Communists, organized as the Working People's League, standing for office, new elections were held on July 14, 1940. The newly "elected" legislature met on July 21. Its only piece of business was to vote on whether to join the Soviet Union, which it did by acclamation. The following month, the USSR Supreme Soviet completed the charade by "acceding" to this request. Lithuania thus became a Soviet Socialist Republic.

The new Communist government immediately began to implement general Soviet policies. A government decree nationalized all of the land. Larger estates were taken over directly and turned into state farms, but there was also a promise of land to landless laborers. Smaller farmers were permitted to retain up to 75 acres, though technically they did not own it any longer. Nationalist elements now began to organize opposition to the new policies. In retaliation, the Communists began rounding up oppositional elements and deporting them to Siberia.

Germany's invasion of the Soviet Union beginning on June 22, 1941, reversed this situation after German troops overran and occupied Lithuania later in 1941. It remained under German occupation until 1944. With the German retreat, however, Lithuania once again fell under Soviet control. The murder of the city's Jewish population by the Nazis and Stalin's deportation of most Poles meant that Vilnius lost 90% of its population during the Second World War. An anticommunist resistance movement arose, often consisting of individuals who had been active in guerrilla actions against the Germans.

By the summer of 1945, this movement had approximately 50,000 members and was operating throughout Lithuania. Units functioned mainly in rural parts of the country, with their encampments in the middle of a forest. Guerrilla units would move out to attack centers of communist control while, back at the encampment, others worked to organize popular resistance. The reconstituted Lithuanian Communist government countered the resistance movement by creating its own "People's Defenders" although the main struggle against the guerrillas was carried out by the NKVD (secret police). This war between the Lithuanian resistance and the NKVD went on until 1947. Such efforts were ineffectual. Lithuania got no outside assistance, and the resistance movement was eventually suppressed.

Many changes occurred in Lithuania over the next 35 years. Soviet policy was to integrate the Baltic republics so thoroughly into the Soviet system that there would be no question of their ever leaving the union. To that end, the Soviet government first carried out policies of nationalization and collectivization. Next it sought to bind the republics to the rest of the Soviet Union economically by locating branch factories of Soviet industry there. Such factories received most or all of their raw materials from other parts of the Soviet Union and delivered most of their finished products to customers in the other republics.

Economic integration was accompanied by a program of "Soviet Russification," aimed at transforming the cultures of the three republics. All students received Russian language training in the schools, plus general indoctrination lectures on the nature of Soviet culture.

It was Estonia and Latvia that became the chief victims of this policy, however. According to the figures of the 1989 Soviet census, Lithuania was still 80% ethnic Lithuanian. By comparison, ethnic Estonians by this time made up only 61.5% of the population of the republic, while in Latvia the figure was only 52%. On the positive side, the heavy industrialization carried out after 1945 meant that the standard of living in the three Baltic republics was above that of any part of the Soviet Union.

Lithuania Moves toward Independence

The Lithuanian people were a little slower to get organized than the Estonians and Latvians, but once organized they proved to be even more determined to split with Moscow than either Estonia or Latvia. Sajudis, the Lithuanian Popular Front, traces its origins to a commission established by the Lithuanian Academy of Sciences on May 23, 1988, to propose

Vytautas Landsbergis

changes to the Lithuanian constitution to accommodate Gorbachev's policies of *glasnost*, *perestroika*, and democratization. The commission brought together party and nonparty intellectuals and professionals who, in turn, decided that the times demanded something more. On June 3, they created an "initiative group," which subsequently took the name of Sajudis.

Over the summer of 1988, Sajudis organized mass meetings and demonstrations on issues such as the 1939 Molotov-Ribbentrop Pact, the status of the Lithuanian language and the possibility of some form of economic autonomy. From the beginning, the animating spirit behind Sajudis was a nonparty intellectual, the musicologist Vytautas Landsbergis. Sajudis held its founding congress in October 1988. A resolution was passed calling on the republic's government to issue an assertion of Lithuanian sovereignty.

Algirdas Brazauskas, who had just been appointed First Secretary of the Lithuanian Communist Party, was one of the invited speakers at the congress. He supported the measure initially, but was then forced to reverse himself on orders from Moscow. The Lithuanian Communist Party lost much of its credibility as a result, as can be seen by looking at the results of the March 1989 elections to the USSR Congress of People's Deputies.

Sajudis candidates won 36 out of 42 seats to the Congress and might have won even more had they not deliberately refrained from challenging certain top communists, including First Secretary Brazauskas, who was liked personally, in spite of his having toed Moscow's line on the sovereignty issue. In fact, there was an overlap in the electoral positions of Sajudis and the Lithuanian Communist Party, for the latter

Lithuania

advocated economic autonomy, pluralism of opinions, democracy and *glasnost*.

The Lithuanian Communist Party came under tremendous pressure after it had lost to Sajudis in the spring elections. In an attempt to create nationalist credentials, the party began in mid-1989 discussing a split with the Communist Party of the Soviet Union. Another indication of the way opinion within the party was evolving came on August 22, 1989, when a commission of the Lithuanian Supreme Soviet, at that time still controlled by communists, voted to condemn the 1940 Soviet annexation of Lithuania and to declare it invalid. The party's formal split with Moscow came in December, at the Lithuanian Communist Party Congress. It became the first republic party to split with the CPSU.

Even so, the Lithuanian Communist Party still found itself following along in Sajudis's wake. On August 23, 1989, the governing council of Sajudis voted unanimously that Lithuania should "take the peaceful course to becoming an independent democratic republic once again." In December 1989, Brazauskas, going further than he had ever gone before, could only bring himself to advocate a "sovereign Lithuanian state in a new union of free republics." Even that position caused a split in the Lithuanian Communist Party, when a faction claiming to represent one-fourth of the membership broke away and reaffirmed its ties with Moscow.

It was against this background that elections were held to elect a new Lithuanian Supreme Soviet. The elections took place on February 24, 1990, with runoff elections on March 10. The Sajudis slate, which included reform communists as well as representatives of the newly legalized Christian Democrat, Social Democrat and Green parties, won an overwhelming majority.

The newly installed parliament elected its chairman of the presidium, it chose Vytautas Landsbergis, head of Sajudis and a noncommunist. Lithuania had its first noncommunist government since 1940. On March 11, 1990, the Lithuanian Supreme Soviet adopted a declaration of Lithuanian independence.

The Soviet Union not only did not recognize Lithuanian independence; it also organized a partial economic boycott against the republic. Orders went out to all state enterprises in the republic to obey only orders from Moscow. There was public discussion about presenting Lithuania with a bill for Soviet capital investments over the years—estimated at 21 billion rubles—payable in hard currency. There were also Soviet military maneuvers held in March 1990 in and around the city of Vilnius, though Gorbachev claimed at the

If you don't help Lithuania, who will? Be socially active!

same time that force would not be used except to prevent bloodshed.

The Lithuanian response to the Soviet demand for indemnities was to raise counterclaims for goods and services extracted from the republic, environmental damage and for the tens of thousands of Lithuanians killed by Soviet officials over the years. The rhetoric escalated still further in April when Gorbachev threatened to reduce sharply the flow of gas and oil to Lithuania if it did not immediately retract its declaration of independence. The Lithuanian government offered to discuss the question of the effective date of independence, but not the question of independence itself. Oil shipments to Lithuania's sole refinery were then cut off, and reductions were made in the delivery of other raw materials.

Meanwhile, Lithuania got some support of sorts when the Estonian and Latvian governments joined Lithuania in issuing their own declarations of independence, though the declarations were not to take force immediately. In addition, the United States threatened to withhold most-favored-nation trading status from

the Soviet Union if it blockaded Lithuania. As a result, after some further threats, the Soviet Union lifted its partial embargo on Lithuania.

Things remained quiet for several months, but Moscow hardliners made a new move against Lithuania in January 1991. Gorbachev claimed no advance knowledge when USSR Ministry of Interior troops seized a television tower in Vilnius, but he did not repudiate the action.

The issue of Baltic independence was one of the issues that precipitated the coup against Gorbachev in August 1991. Its failure led most of the world to extend recognition to the Baltic States and led the postcoup Soviet government to extend its own recognition in September 1991. Lithuania was admitted to the United Nations in October 1991.

Sovereign Lithuania

In a surprise, the electorate gave Sajudis, the party of Landsbergis, only about 22% of the vote in the first parliamentary elections in 1992. The winner was the Democratic Labor Party, the successor party to the Lithuanian Communist Party, led by Algirdas Brazauskas. It got over 40% of the vote and a majority of the seats in the Seimas. This result was reaffirmed in the subsequent presidential elections that were won by Brazauskas, who then took office in February 1993. He succeeded the first post-Soviet prime minister, Kazimira Prunskiene.

It would be misleading simply to say that the communists returned to power in Lithuania in 1992. In fact, Brazauskas is a nationalist, first and foremost. It was he who was responsible for the Lithuanian Communist Party's split with Moscow in 1990 and its subsequent support for Lithuanian independence. Moreover, when Brazauskas founded the Democratic Labor Party after independence, many communists became politically inactive, with the result that only about 5%–10% of its membership in 1992 were formerly members of the Lithuanian Communist Party.

It was not politics but economics that was responsible for Brazauskas' victory. By 1992, the economy was in relatively poor shape, with salaries frozen and many people being paid up to three months late. Moreover, Lithuania had been forced to cut its imports of oil and gas beginning in July 1992, after Russia began charging world prices payable in hard currency for exports to areas outside the ruble zone. By October Lithuania did not have sufficient fuel to heat most buildings. As one commentator explained the vote, "the simple people know only that before it was warm, and now it is cold."

After his victory, Brazauskas asked: "Can you imagine how a person receiving

Lithuania

Presidential Palace, Vilnius

a small salary can survive, with world prices coming down upon their heads? A government has to reply to the people's cries." His win did not bring about a change in direction although it did involve a change in style. In an attempt to cushion the transition to private enterprise, for example, the government made a point of working out its policies in close consultation with factory managers. This slowed the process somewhat, but it did not reverse it.

The newly independent Lithuanian government initially concentrated mainly on domestic problems although it also pressed for the removal of Soviet troops from Lithuania as soon as possible. That presented a particular problem as long as the troops remained under the aegis of the Commonwealth of Independent States (CIS). The Russian government set up its own Ministry of Defense in the summer of 1992 and subsequently negotiated an agreement with Lithuania for the removal of the troops as soon as possible.

There were approximately 20,500 troops in Lithuania at this time. Some small token force withdrawals began in September 1992, and Russia promised that all would be out by sometime in 1993. President Boris Yeltsin suspended the troop withdrawals in October, asserting a "profound concern" over the treatment of ethnic Russians in the Baltic Republics. Since Lithuania, unlike the Estonians and Latvians, had extended citizenship to all persons who were resident prior to mid-1990, it is not immediately clear why Lithuania was included in the decree. Moscow wanted guarantees concerning the pensions and status of retired Russian military personnel living in Lithuania. In any case, new negotiations with Russia led to

the evacuation of the last Russian troops from Lithuania in the summer of 1993.

National Minorities

Lithuania has also had some problems with minorities within the country, mainly Poles and Russians. District governments in and around Vilnius where Poles were in a majority were suspended, apparently because the Poles elected communists to office. In spite of nationalist demands to the contrary, the government eventually ended up extending citizenship rights to its minorities. Around 80% of the population is ethnic Lithuanian. Only about 7% of the residents are Russian, living mainly in cities. Through its acquisition of Vilnius and the surrounding area in 1940, Lithuania acquired a sizable minority of Poles. They are the largest minority, numbering about 260,000, or a little over 7% of the total, and they reside principally in Vilnius and in the rural Southeast. The republic's Soviet leaders had skillfully prevented a large influx of Russian-speakers. This had been made easier by the fact that Lithuania was not as industrially developed as Estonia and Latvia. This condition enabled independent Lithuania to grant almost universal citizenship to all residents in 1991 without risking a loss of control over the nation's destiny. This was the kind of automatic citizenship ("zero option") adopted by most former Soviet republics and demanded by Russia in Estonia and Latvia, where the demographic situation is dramatically different.

POLITICAL SYSTEM

Lithuania completed its transition from the earlier communistic system in October 1992 when the Lithuanian people approved a new constitution in a national referendum. It is now a multiparty, parliamentary democracy. The constitution calls for a semi-presidential system. Although the president formally oversees both foreign and domestic policy, in fact the president takes the lead in foreign policy, and the prime minister conducts domestic policy. He or she may issue decrees, declare a state of emergency, and return laws passed by the single-chamber legislature, the *Seimas*, for reconsideration. Next in order of importance is the Chairman of the 141-member *Seimas*. Its deputies are elected for terms of four years; 71 are elected by direct vote and 70 by proportional representation. Second-round run-offs take place in constituencies where no candidate wins a majority the first round. The president appoints the prime minister, who must retain the support of a majority in parliament and who is responsible for day-to-day operations, as well as maintaining diplomatic relations with foreign countries and international organizations.

The President

The president of the republic is the highest official of the state. Popularly elected for a term of five years, he represents the country internationally and provides general political leadership domestically. He appoints and dismisses state officials. He may issue decrees under certain circumstances, and only he may declare a state of national emergency. Laws passed by the *Seimas* may either be approved and published or returned with remarks for reconsideration.

In 1998 a former senior official of the US Environmental Protection Agency, Valdas Adamkus, was elected president. In the runoff election he narrowly defeated the

Lithuania

son of a KGB colonel, Arturas Paulauskas, who had the endorsement of the sitting president, Algirdas Brazauskas. Adamkus, who was 71 when first elected, had spent most of his life in the United States as an émigré. Because of that background, he had to fight a lawsuit to get on the ballot. His émigré past was an important issue in the election. In the end, the Lithuanian people, forced to choose between an outsider and Paulauskas, opted for the outsider. They hoped that Adamkus would be able to lead Lithuania westward and that his know-how and international connections would firmly root their future in the West. In his words: "I want to see Lithuania as a democratic country so that the younger generation will grow up under western cultural influence." The primary function of a Lithuanian president is to represent the country abroad, and he speaks excellent English and German and knows American ways.

The Lithuanian constitution gives the president only a limited domestic role, but Adamkus got around this limitation after his election by building a working relationship with the parties of the government coalition. By 2003 he seemed tired and was often ill. Ineffective at home and surrounded by a weak team, he appeared to be increasingly out of touch. Nevertheless, he sought reelection as the favorite. But twice former prime minister and Vilnius mayor, Rolandas Paksas, conducted a well-organized and well-financed campaign hammering at the country's corruption, poverty, and bad government. Paksas did well in rural areas, which have not shared equally in Lithuania's increasing prosperity. Fascinating voters by such stunts as flying his own plane under a Kaunas bridge, he scored an upset victory, winning 54.9% of the votes to 45.1% for Adamkus. Turnout was 52%.

Paksas's presidency was engulfed by scandals and lasted only 15 months. In April 2004 he became the first European leader to be impeached and removed from office. He was accused of improperly restoring Lithuanian citizenship to a Russian businessman and crony with connections to organized crime, Yuri Borisov, who had financed his campaign with a $400,000 contribution. The State Security Department reported that Paksas had leaked classified information by tipping Borisov off that Lithuanian authorities were investigating him and tapping his phone. In a brazen move, Paksas even hired Borisov as a presidential adviser while the impeachment proceedings were going on. Quickly realizing the stupidity of that act, he reversed his decision within hours.

The Constitutional Court ruled that he had "grossly violated" the law. By the required three-fifths majority, parliament

Andrius Kubilius
Prime Minister of Lithuania

voted narrowly to convict him of improperly granting citizenship and influencing a privatization deal. Prime Minister Brazauskas, most politicians, the Roman Catholic Church and 60% of the people favored his removal. To the end Paksas denied the charges, portraying himself as the victim of a corrupt system and accusing his opponents of exacting political revenge for his unexpected victory a year earlier.

Although embarrassed, many Lithuanians viewed the way with which the scandal was dealt to be evidence of how strong the country's democracy has become. The turmoil it caused at the very time that the country was entering NATO and the EU also revealed the undercurrent of fear about Russia's meddling in Lithuanian affairs and the determination to finalize its break with Moscow. Given the country's past, this is a very sensitive issue.

Since Lithuania has no vice president, Parliamentary Speaker Arturas Paulauskas became interim president until elections could be held in June 2004. In the two electoral rounds, five candidates vied for the presidency. The chief election commission refused to register Paksas as a candidate. The election was marred a few days before the voting by police raids on the offices of four parties supporting Adamkus. They were undertaken by the Special Investigation Service, headed by Paksas sympathizers. The action was so frightening that the mayor of Vilnius, who backed Adamkus in the election, took temporary refuge in Poland for fear of arrest.

The frontrunner emerged from the second round as the victor—former President Valdas Adamkus, who in 2003 had been appointed as a goodwill ambassador for UNESCO. With 52.5%, he defeated Kazimira Prunskiene, the leader of the pop-

ulist Peasants' Party and first post-Soviet prime minister, who had the backing of the still-popular Paksas.

In May 2009 Dalia Grybauskaite was elected president by a landslide with 68% of the votes. Born in Vilnius in 1956, she studied political economy in Leningrad, working at a fur factory to pay her way. A tough politician with a black belt in karate earned while she was a diplomat in Washington, she is a former finance minister who speaks four languages. The five preceding years she had served as the EU's budget commissioner, where she acquired a reputation as hardworking, incisive, and successful. Her nickname is "Iron Lady." Perhaps because of her EU experience, she does not share the fervent Atlanticism one finds among most Lithuanian politicians. She ran as an independent candidate. Although her powers on paper are relatively limited, she has a powerful personal mandate and dares to use it. There are limits, though. A controversial law she inherited bans the "promotion" of homosexuality through education to the young. Her predecessor had vetoed it, but parliament overrode that action. Although she opposes the ban, she is unable to overturn it.

Parliament and Prime Minister

The *Seimas* is a single-body legislature with a total of 141 members elected for a period of four years. Under Lithuania's voting system, 71 of the seats are filled by direct vote; the remaining 70 seats are awarded on a proportional basis, each political party being assigned seats on the basis of its share of the popular vote. A party must receive at least 5% of the votes to gain parliamentary seats. The *Seimas* has the power to amend the constitution, enact laws, control the activities of the government, approve the budget, appoint and dismiss chairs of the state institutions, and settle other issues pertaining to state power. Its chairman is one of the republic's top three political figures.

As the constitutionally designated head of government, the prime minister and his cabinet are responsible for the day-to-day operations of government. He is also charged with implementing of laws and resolutions of the *Seimas* and decrees issued by the president of the republic. He maintains diplomatic relations with foreign countries and international organizations.

Formally appointed by the president, the prime minister must be confirmed by the *Seimas* and must retain the support of a majority of that body to remain in office. Thus, among his other functions, the prime minister must maintain a close working relationship with the *Seimas*. Ministers are appointed and dismissed by the president of the republic upon the recommendation of the prime minister.

The 2004 parliamentary elections pitted Algirdas Brazauskas's Social Democrats against an entirely new party with a radically different leader, Viktor Uspaskich. A Russian entrepreneur who had lived two decades in Lithuania, he made a fortune importing gas from Russia in the 1990s. Because he owns a pickling factory, he acquired the nickname of "Mr. Gerkin." A populist with considerable charisma, he and his Labor Party attracted votes from disgruntled Lithuanians who were not among the winners of the transition from communism: pensioners, farmers, unemployed and others with gripes against the government and the free-market economy. He campaigned against corruption (a third of Lithuanians admitted in a 2004 poll to having paid a bribe within the past year) and for sharply increased pensions and living standards for poorer people. Ironically his party was supported by more multimillionaires than any other party or bloc. One editorial summed up his campaign: "promise, promise, promise." Labor emerged from the election as the largest party. But no party or bloc won a majority. After exploring all alternatives Brazauskas agreed to remain as prime minister.

Next came Gediminas Kirkilas, who led a four-party minority government. His was the 14th government in the preceding 15 years. He had the misfortune of being in power when the global recession hit Lithuania with a vengeance. New elections were held in October 2008, and with a meager turnout of 48.5%, the winning party was the conservative Homeland Union, led by Andrius Kubilius, which captured 19.7% of the votes and 45 seats. He formed a government with the National Resurrection Party, which won 15% of the votes and 16 seats, and the Liberals' Movement of the Republic of Lithuania, which garnered 5.7% of the votes and 11 seats. Thanks to the double-digit inflation rate, the fear of an end to economic growth, and anxiety over increasing Russian aggressiveness, Kirkilas' Social Democratic Party, which had ruled since 2001, had to settle for 11.7% of the votes and only 25 seats. It moved into the opposition, along with Roland Paksas' Order and Justice Party (12.7% and 15 seats), Viktor Uspaskich's Coalition Labor Party and Youth (9% and 10 seats), and the Liberal and Center Union (5.34% and 8 seats).

Kubilius' austerity program, which called for 10% to 20% pay cuts for all state employees, 30% reduction in public spending, and up to 11% lessening of pensions, was no more popular than that of his predecessor. Even Prime Minister Kubilius took a 45% pay reduction. Fortunately the opposition parties and the trade unions (which are extremely weak) grudgingly supported the government's emergency measures.

Foreign and Defense Policy

Former President Brazauskas managed to annoy Russia when he announced in January 1994, in a television address, that the Lithuanian government had submitted a formal request for membership in NATO. Lithuania was the first Baltic republic to do so. Moscow was especially sensitive to Lithuania's entry into NATO because its only land bridge linking Russia proper and its troops in Kaliningrad runs through Lithuania. Therefore, its reaction was swift and negative, with a spokesman for President Yeltsin warning that any moves to expand NATO could "trigger military-political destabilization in the region."

Foreign policy did not change significantly under President Adamkus, who took office in 1998. He favored better relations with Russia and all of Lithuania's neighbors. Lithuania is warming up especially to one of its oldest rivals, Poland. In June 1997 it forged a "strategic partnership" with Warsaw. It also created with Poland a joint battalion called LITPOLBAT that is interoperable with NATO. In July 1998 Lithuania hosted 5,000 soldiers at a maneuver on its territory. The participants included units from the United States, Denmark, Norway, Germany and all other Baltic states, with Russians, Ukrainians and Belarusians present as observers. Its Deputy Defense Minister Povilas Malakasuskas underscored the goal of all these cooperative efforts: "to make Baltic membership in NATO a logical inevitability."

Backed by the lobbying activities of more than 700,000 Lithuanians living in the U.S., these diplomatic and military efforts succeeded. Lithuania joined the Alliance in April 2004. All parties supported membership, and some leaders rejoiced that NATO membership will enable the country to deal with Russia from a position of strength. A NATO meeting in Vilnius in April 2005 to coordinate policy toward Lithuania's volatile neighbor, Belarus, demonstrated how dramatically Europe had changed since the end of the Cold War. Russian naval forces pay friendly calls to the main port of Kleipeda.

In preparation for NATO membership Lithuania began raising its defense budget, to reach 2% of GDP at the end of 2004. Its military forces are small, numbering only 8,850 active forces, including conscripts who serve 12 months. Women are permitted to serve in uniform. It has a total of 6,700 reservists plus 14,600 paramilitary that include coast and border guards. Its army has 7,190 troops, including 3,027 conscripts. Its special forces have reaped particular praise from NATO. The navy has 470 sailors (including 120 conscripts) and 14 ships. The air force numbers 950 troops and 16 aircraft. It has 5,000 border guards and 540 coast guard. To adapt to NATO requirements the structure of the armed forces is being reformed.

In 2008 the number of senior officers increased, with generals and admirals climbing from four to seven, colonels and naval captains from 30 to 40, and lieutenant-colonels and majors from 105 to 120. In 2004 Armed Forces Commander Major General Jonas Kronkaitis, who had served in Vietnam as a young American officer, was replaced by Brigadier General Valdas Tutkus, who along with 5,000 other Lithuanian soldiers had fought in Afghanistan as a Soviet officer.

Lithuania deployed 37 peacekeepers in Kosovo and 250 in Afghanistan. It had 53 infantrymen in southern Iraq in a Danish battalion and 45 in the international division in Iraq commanded by Poland. It still maintains a provincial reconstruction team in central Afghanistan and 14 soldiers in Iraq. It purchased 60 shoulder-launched Stinger missiles from the U.S. to defend major installations like nuclear power plants from terrorist attacks. ABC News reported that Lithuania, along with Poland and Romania, hosted a secret CIA prison. The government spokesman denied any knowledge of the jails or having approved of them.

As Lithuania entered NATO in 2004, tensions with Russia heated up. All three Baltic states had just expelled Russian diplomats accused of spying on NATO activities. Within days of its enlargement, NATO dispatched four Belgian F-16 jets, supported by 100 Belgian, Danish and Norwegian troops, to Siauliai Air Force Base outside of Vilnius. It had also sent an AWACS electronics plane in February on a demonstration flight to Rumbula Airfield in Latvia and then to Siauliai. The F-16s' assignment was to police the skies over the Baltic states and to underscore the new border being drawn between Russia and Europe. A hundred Germans in the NATO Baltic Air Policing unit operate six F-4F Phantom II jets out of Lithuania.

Although Russia had grudgingly accepted NATO's eastward enlargement, its leaders were furious about the deployments and denounced them. Nationalist firebrand, Vladimir Zhirinovsky, even warned that the Baltic capitals would be the first bombing targets on Russia's list if there were ever a confrontation with the U.S. The largest Russian TV channel in Lithuania, ORT, which is known to be under direct Kremlin control, aired a show on August 31, 2004, questioning the historical grounds of Lithuania's independence. It specifically accused Lithuanians

Lithuania

Mass is celebrated in Kaunas

Courtesy: NOVOSTI

of collaborating with the Nazi regime. In 2005 the Russian ambassador in Vilnius called Lithuania a "nation of scandalmongers" where "everyone is dirty."

Two weeks after the Lithuanian government outlawed the display of Soviet symbols, Russian hackers attacked about 300 Lithuanian websites, including those of government agencies, political parties and businesses. They littered them with Soviet symbols like hammers-and-sickles and five-pointed stars, as well as anti-Lithuanian slogans and profanities. It is this kind of rough behavior that prompts Lithuania to take a tough line when the EU talks about improving ties with Russia.

Such bellicose and insulting talk merely enhances the Balts' comfort and pride in joining the Atlantic Alliance. Some even compared the welcomed roar of the F-16s' engines to the rumble of Soviet tanks that rolled into Vilnius in January 1990. Colonel Edvardas Mazeikas, Siauliai base commander, said it this way: "For us, history is close. We are in a very dangerous place. All through our history, war has passed through here, from Napoleon to the Nazis to the Soviets. Lithuania is a very good place for tanks. That's why collective security is so important to us."

Adamkus placed a greater emphasis on Lithuania's joining the EU, a position also endorsed by his predecessors and successor in the presidency. Formal entry occurred in May 2004, following a successful referendum in May 2003 when Lithuania became the first former Soviet republic to vote itself into the EU. Virtually every party supported EU entry.

The country's leaders and clergymen pulled out all the stops to get voters to the polls since the constitution requires at least a 50% turnout for a referendum result to be valid; 63% voted. Mayors organized buses and offered gifts to voters; priests in this largely Catholic country urged people to examine their consciences and vote; the largest supermarket chain, VP Market, even offered a bottle of beer, a soft drink, chocolate or washing powder to persons who could prove they had voted. When it was announced in parliament that 91% of Lithuanians had voted "yes," lawmakers sang the national anthem, some with tears in their eyes. Former President Paksas announced, "Lithuania now starts a new stage of its history in a European family. Hello Europeans!" Celebrations lasted into the morning.

In order to polish the country's international image as a prelude to admission to the EU, the Lithuanian parliament passed a law in 2000 enabling trials of former Nazi collaborators to take place even if the individual is too old and weak to attend the proceedings, as long as the charges are for genocide and war crimes. During the German occupation of the Baltic states from 1941 to 1944, some Balts had participated in the eradication of 99% of the 300,000 Jews who lived in the three republics; of Lithuania's prewar Jewish population of 235,000, only 9,000 remain.

The law allowed proceedings to continue against Aleksandras Lileikis, a 92-year-old man who had lived a half-century in the United States before his U.S. citizenship was revoked in 1996. As chief of the Lithuanian security police, *Saugumas*, during the German occupation, he approved of "death cards" for up to 70,000 Jews. After his forced return to Lithuania in 1996, he had enjoyed widespread sympathy in the population as a hero in the struggle against the Soviets. Others sympathized with him because he was an old and broken man. But the winds changed as Lithuania became more desirous of EU entry. In 1999 Algirdas Brazauskas addressed the rethinking of public opinion in this way: "I am not in favor of Lileikis going to jail. But there must be some kind of judgment pronounced against him." Lileikis died soon thereafter. Brazauskas passed in 2010.

Kaliningrad

Lithuania has no land disputes with its neighbors (Belarus, Poland, and the Russian enclave of Kaliningrad). Its major dispute with Russia was Russian transit rights for its military forces in Kaliningrad. Earlier post-Soviet Lithuanian foreign policy had tended to be confrontational toward Russia. This was partly because of the continuing presence of Russian troops after Lithuania reestablished its independence in 1991. With the election of President Brazauskas in 1993, there was a significant change in foreign policy. During the campaign, he had pledged himself to work for a closer working relationship with Russia, particularly in the economic area, and in general he succeeded. He also managed to negotiate an agreement with Russia whereby it agreed to remove the last of its troops by September 1993. Lithuania was thus the first of the Baltic republics to be totally free of Russian troops.

It refused to grant Russia a corridor for transporting Russian troops to and from the Russian enclave of Kaliningrad. However, it accepted an informal agreement in 1991 to allow Russian troops to cross Lithuania by rail only, with a maximum of 180 soldiers on any one train and their weapons in a separate car. Lithuanian soldiers could inspect these rail transports to ensure that these stipulations are being followed. This agreement was renewed on a year-by-year basis until eminent EU entry required new transit regulations in 2003.

Lithuania's invitation in 2002 to join the EU necessitated a new transit agreement for the 950,000 Russians living in the Kaliningrad enclave who want to travel to Russia through Lithuania. Russian President Vladimir Putin had warned of a new "Berlin Wall" around Russian citizens. Since July 2003 they can receive a "facilitated-transit document" (STD), which is basically a simplified multiple-entry visa valid for three years. It costs only five euros. Visa holders can travel through Lithuania either by train or by automobile, and they have 24 hours to complete their transit. The Lithuanian government opened a second consulate within the Kaliningrad Oblast in the city of Sovetsk to deal primarily with Russians living in the eastern part of the enclave. To circumvent the visa requirement, many more Russians fly to and from Kaliningrad.

Both countries are studying the possibility of a high-speed, nonstop train link connecting Kaliningrad and the Russian mainland. The travel compromise was linked to the Russian Duma's ratification in May 2003 of the Lithuania-Russia border treaty that had been signed in October 1997. This included the land border, the exclusive economic zone and the continental shelf in the Baltic Sea.

Kaliningrad depends upon Lithuania and Poland to provide for many of the daily needs of its residents. They are the chief foreign investors, and foodstuffs, clothing, furniture and other consumer goods from these two countries are prominent in stores; 80% of its electricity comes from Lithuania.

Lithuania's Communist leader, Antanas Snieckus, had wisely refused an offer made in the 1950s by Soviet party chief Nikita Khrushchev that Lithuania take control of the Kaliningrad region. Snieckus feared that his republic would invite the same problems with a large Russian minority that were mounting in Latvia and Estonia. Nevertheless, having lived within the USSR for a half-century, Lithuanians are particularly familiar with Soviet behavior and mentality and can collaborate with Kaliningraders even more effectively than can Poles. Nevertheless, Lithuanian public opinion was incensed in November 2008 when Moscow threatened to deploy missiles in Kaliningrad; it later withdrew that threat.

ECONOMY

Lithuania has felt the full force of the global economic downturn. It was particularly hard hit because sales to its largest export partner, Russia, were reduced by

Founded in 1570—Vilnius University Library with over 4 million volumes

Courtesy: NOVOSTI

half in 2009. The economy contracted by 22% in 2009. Its currency, the litas, was also under severe attack. However, the government was determined to keep it pegged to the euro and to continue its bid to adopt the European currency by middecade. Unemployment leapt to 14%, while corporate taxes were raised from 15% to 20% and the VAT from 18% to 21%. The budget deficit ballooned to 9.5% in 2010. The real estate bubble burst, leaving many Lithuanians holding mortgages denominated in foreign currencies for property worth far less than earlier. At best, the country faces several painful years as it tries to regain competitiveness.

Lithuania is the least industrialized of the Baltic republics. However, the fact that 59% of its workforce is in the services sector, which produces 62.7% of the GDP, indicates that it has an increasingly modern economy. Industry, including mining, employs 29% of the people and produces 32.8% of GDP. It is clearly no longer a predominantly agricultural country: agricultural employment has fallen to 12% of the workforce creating 4.5% of the GDP.

Most of Lithuania's industry is located in or near its major cities. Kaunas, Lithuania's second largest city, has metal and woodworking industries as well as light and food industries. Kleipeda, Lithuania's third largest city and its major seaport, is the largest ice-free port in the Baltic area and a major hub for trade between Scandinavia, Western and Eastern Europe. It is home to a large deep-sea fishing fleet, and it has one of the largest shipyards in the Baltic. The main local industry is fish pro-

cessing. The town also has a pulp and paper mill, a woodworking factory, textile mills, plus a large plant that manufactures radios and telephones. In addition, it is a traditional center for the working of amber. Vilnius, Lithuania's largest city and its capital, is a center for computer manufacturing, machine tools, electric meters, drills, farm machinery, building materials and food processing. There is also a small amount of industry located in smaller towns.

There has been little privatization of agriculture. Collective farms still are the rule although the state's role in them has dwindled and the old collective and state farm structure has largely been dismantled. Nevertheless, there are still very few private farms. The government of Vytautas Landsbergis had favored the privatization of agriculture, but most individual peasants were unwilling to accept the responsibility of private farming.

Brazauskas, who was installed as Landbergis's successor in 1993, had actually been elected president on the promise that he would slow down the process of reform. He argued that it was "a mistake to get rid of the remaining collective farms . . . by giving their property to individuals." He then added that farmers who "wished and were able to keep their private farms should be provided with all the necessary facilities for it" but that those still on collective farms should be allowed to choose their own form of privatization. Valdas Adamkus, who succeeded Brazauskas as president in 1998, favored private farming, but he did not make it a high priority. There appears

Lithuania

to be no momentum for any significant changes in the countryside. Many farmers do receive agricultural subsidies from the EU.

Forestry products are another source of income for persons residing in the countryside. With approximately 25% of the land covered by trees, Lithuania produces both timber and pulpwood, and wood is its main export. There are also considerable deposits of peat plus materials used in construction such as limestone, chalk, dolomite, clays and gravel, whose exploitation provides additional jobs in the countryside.

Before 1991, about 55% of Lithuania's exports went to other parts of the Soviet Union. Negotiations with Russia and some of the other republics extended those arrangements. But postindependence Lithuanian governments have been committed to reorienting Lithuania's trade more toward the West. Currently 64.8% of its exports and 68.3% of its imports go to and come from the EU. Russia now accounts for 15% of its exports and 18% of its imports. Lithuania joined the World Trade Organization (WTO) in 2001, with the U.S. leading the WTO accession negotiations.

Approximately one-third of the republic's industrial workers work in engineering or metal-working factories created during the Soviet period. Built to serve customers located mainly in the other republics, they were particularly hard pressed in the first three or so years of independence, but they are doing much better today. Until it cooled down in 2008, the Lithuanian economy had been growing at a blistering pace: by 9.7% in 2003, 7% in 2004–5, and 8% in 2006–7.

In June 1993, Lithuania began issuing its own permanent currency, the litas, to replace the talon, an interim coupon issued after independence. When this did not bring inflation under control, it introduced legislation in 1994 to establish a currency board system, modeled after the one successfully tried in Estonia. The essence of the system is that the currency board issues only as much currency as is backed by the country's reserves of gold and foreign exchange. What that meant in practice is that the Lithuanian central bank had to curtail credits to state-owned industries and failing enterprises and stop issuing paper money to cover government budget deficits. As the system began working, inflation dropped drastically and prices, wages, and pensions stabilized. Immediately upon entering the EU in May 2004 its government announced that it would move quickly to join the eurozone. It joined the Exchange Rate Mechanism (ERM-2) and is working toward qualifying for the euro to which the litas is pegged. Due to the terrible global recession, it will not meet its original target date of 2012 for adopting the euro.

The government began on a program of general privatization, which was largely implemented by the end of 1996. In 1998 it completed one of the biggest privatizations in Eastern Europe, selling off 60% of Telekomas, the country's fixed line telecoms monopoly. At the end of the century it confidently turned its privatization efforts to shipping and ship repair, oil refining, gasoline station networks, and television and radio.

Investment is pouring into the port of Klaipeda, a free economic zone catering to much of the former Soviet Union. From 1995 to 1999 its cumulative foreign direct investment doubled every year, with the U.S. as the leading source. In 2004 it attracted 55 euros of foreign direct investment (FDI) per capita, less than half what Estonia received but slightly more than Latvia. The litas has become steadily more solid. Unemployment was declining due to the approximately 450,000 Lithuanians (a tenth of the population) who had left to work abroad. This is a worrisome brain drain that has caused labor shortages in certain sectors of the economy. Average monthly wages climbed by 2005 to 354 euros, less than Estonia's 474 but more than Latvia's 316.

A major impediment to entry had been the Soviet-era Ignalina nuclear power plant, which once supplied 80% of the country's electricity. With promises of EU financial support, Lithuania shut down the first plant in 2004. It pledged to decommission by the end of 2009 the safer and more modern second reactor, which produced three-fourths of the country's electricity and provided enough to export to neighboring countries. Polls indicated that 70% of the population would have liked to postpone the shutdown. In a 2009 referendum 90% voted for such delay, but the low turnout invalidated the result. Therefore a few hours before midnight on New Year's Eve, 2009, the reactor was shut down. This loss of its main electricity source came at a bad time. It drives electricity prices up by 30%. It also means that Lithuania is now a net importer rather than exporter of energy. It thereby has become more dependent upon Russian gas and oil. Prime Minister Kubilius warned that this makes Lithuania "very sensitive to anything that happens on Russia's borders."

To minimize that risk, Lithuania is negotiating with the other two Baltic states and Poland to construct a modern 3,200-megawatt nuclear power station at the Ignalina site. Difficult technical and ownership issues must be worked out. Vilnius complicated the talks by passing a law in 2006 calling for Lithuania to have a 34% share in the plant and each of the other three only 22% apiece. The new plant would start producing electricity in 2018 at the earliest. It also began in 2010 to construct a new undersea cable between Sweden and the Baltic states to draw energy from the Swedish grid by 2016. A similar cable is planned with Poland. Lithuania also hopes to raise its use of renewable energy sources from the present 15% to 23% by 2020.

Lithuania's largest oil refinery, Mazeikiu, dominates the country's gasoline supply and contributes a tenth of its GDP. The 2006 sale of control of it to a Polish company, PKN Orlen, was an effort to protect its largest industrial enterprise from the Russians. Russia promptly closed the sole pipeline that supplies the refinery in order to force the Lithuanians to reconsider the sale. It was never reopened. The only thing the country could do in retaliation was to veto EU negotiations with Moscow in 2007.

Ex-President Adamkus suggested only half seriously that the only Russian railroad supplying Kaliningrad runs through Lithuania and could perhaps be shut for what the Lithuanian media termed "political repairs." That did not happen. But it became necessary for Mazeikiu to bring in more expensive crude oil by ship. In order to try to reduce its dependency on Russia, Lithuania agreed to form a consortium with Ukraine, Poland, Georgia and Azerbaijan to extend the Odessa-Brody pipeline through Ukraine as far as Gdansk in Poland. It is uncertain whether the extension will ever be built.

Oil had become a key symbol of the country's independence since the Soviets had shut off its pipeline to Mazeikiu in 1990 after Lithuania became free. With this memory in mind, the Lithuanian state invested $300 million to construct a Baltic Sea tanker terminal in order to have an alternative to Russian crude oil. Lithuania showed in 2004 that it feared dependency even on smaller Estonia by resisting efforts of Eesti Energia, the state-owned electricity company, to buy all or part of Lithuania's electricity-distribution industry.

CULTURE

Lithuanian culture was essentially a rural, peasant one until the end of the 19th century. After that, it developed an urban culture, based on the rising professional and middle classes, though the population of most Lithuanian cities remained largely non-Lithuanian until the latter part of the 20th century. Vilnius, the capital and largest city, continues to have a large Polish population. It was, in fact, part of Poland until 1939, and only became Lithuanian shortly before Lithuania itself was incorporated into the Soviet

Union. In one sense, then, Kaunas, the second city and the capital of Lithuania during the interwar period, is more Lithuanian than Vilnius.

Vilnius has Gediminas Castle, the fortress-residence of the Grand Dukes of Lithuania, the Gothic Church of St. Anne that dates from the 14th century, the university building in the oldest part of the city, and the "Medininku vartai" ("The Gates of the Dawn"), all that is left of the nine gates in the former wall that surrounded the city when it was the capital of the Grand Duchy. There are also some houses that date from the 15th to the 17th centuries. But the city became Polanized after the Union with Poland in 1569. Vilnius University, the republic's greatest center of learning, was originally founded in 1579, but the Russian government closed it in 1832. When it reopened in 1919, Vilnius was part of Poland, so the university was located in Kaunas until after World War II. Vilnius is home to the Lithuanian State Opera and Ballet Company and to numerous drama theaters, as well as the republic's main philharmonic orchestra.

Kaunas also has its own philharmonic orchestra and numerous theaters, though it lacks an opera and ballet company. It has numerous churches and museums. There are five institutes of higher education in the city, including a medical college. Another is Kaunas' Technological University, founded in 1951 after the university was shifted to Vilnius. A number of scientific research institutes are situated in Kaunas.

The foundation of Hungarian-born American billionaire George Soros has expended $65 million in Lithuania to support research, scholarships, book transla-

Lithuanian student reading this book

tions, school texts and such social actions as fighting AIDS and drug addiction. Nevertheless, in 2005 the maverick Labor Party, which is in the governing coalition, began to attack him through the leading tabloid, *Respublika*, as an evil foreign meddler involved in "financial schemes and networks." Many of the best-known intellectuals published an open letter demanding that the tabloid cease its "destructive attacks."

Literature

Although the Lithuanian people had a strong oral folklorist tradition, a written literature was rather late in developing. In fact, the first book published in the Lithuanian language was a religious text, *Simple Words of the Catechism*, which appeared in 1547. The religious controversy associated with the reformation led to the translation of the *Bible* into Lithuanian in 1590. As a result of the triumph of Catholicism in Poland–Lithuania, it was never published, but remained in manuscript form in the library of Königsberg University (now in Kaliningrad in Russia). The Jesuits, who were primarily responsible for the triumph of Catholicism, did produce several things in Lithuanian, including a catechism, a collection of sermons, and a dictionary, the latter published in 1629.

The first example of secular literature in the Lithuanian language, a translation of 10 of Aesop's fables, appeared in 1706. The first Lithuanian author, the poet Kristijonas Donelaitis, lived in the 18th century, though his epic poem, *The Seasons*, circulated only in manuscript form during his lifetime and was not published until 1818. Donelaitis was a Protestant pastor in the town of Tolminkiemis, and parts of his poem appear to be paraphrases of his sermons. Yet the poem also presents a realistic portrayal of the life of the peasants, at that time still struggling serfs. The German poet Goethe, who was familiar with the poem, compared Donelaitis to Homer.

A second poet, Antanas Baranauskas, who lived and wrote in the 19th century, had a background similar to that of Donelaitis in that he also followed a religious avocation, and in later life became the Catholic bishop in Seinai. Baranauskas wrote his poems during his youth before being ordained as a priest. His most important poem, written during summer vacations at home in 1858–59, was *The Forest of Anyksciai*. Baranauskas projects a mystic oneness with nature that is almost pagan in its orientation:

Forest and peasant knew no discord,
Grew up together, aged in accord.
To the Lithuanian, caveman of yore,

The forest gave a strong wooden door;
And since he never would hew the wood,
Till aged it fell, the dry trees still stood.

Lithuania became a part of the Russian Empire at the end of the 18th century, along with parts of eastern Poland. At that time, there was no separate Lithuanian nationalism, but Lithuanians supported Polish attempts—in 1831 and again in 1863—to throw off the Russian yoke. As a result, the Russian government attempted to stamp out Polish-Lithuanian nationalism by Russifying the people and the culture. The University of Vilnius was closed after the 1831 uprising; then the Latin alphabet was replaced by the Cyrillic alphabet following the 1863 upheaval. These efforts to stamp out the local culture were unsuccessful.

Lithuanian political and cultural leaders arranged to have Lithuanian-language books and newspapers published in East Prussia, then smuggled them across the border. The first Lithuanian-language newspaper, *The Dawn*, began publishing in Tilset in 1883. In addition, increasing numbers of Lithuanians entered universities either in Russia or abroad and subsequently added their literary output to the stream. Jonas Maciulis Maironis studied at Kiev and St. Petersburg and later became a professor and a priest. His collection, *The Voices of Spring*, published in 1895, glorified the Lithuanian countryside. He also wrote ballads and satires and even a drama in verse, *The Death of Kestutis*, which was not published until 1921. Another dramatist, Vilius Storasta, who wrote under the name of Vydunas, produced *The Shadow of Ancestors* in 1908, *The Eternal Flame* in 1912, and *Bells of the Sea* in 1914. A fourth play, *The World on Fire*, appeared in 1928.

Vincas Kreve, another playwright, produced his first dramas before World War I, but his most important plays appeared in independent Lithuania. They include *Skirgaila* (1922), *On the Roads of Destiny* (1926), *The Death of Mindaugas* (1930), and *The Son-in-Law* (1939). Kreve served for a short time as minister of foreign affairs in the Soviet-dominated government in 1940, then went into hiding before fleeing abroad. In 1947, he became a member of the faculty of the University of Pennsylvania and remained there until his death in 1954.

The second major figure of the period of Lithuanian independence was Vincas Mykolaitis, who wrote under the *nom de plume* of Putinas. Extremely versatile, Putinas, who was also an ordained priest, produced poetry, novels, and plays. His two best novels are probably the autobiographical trilogy, *In the Shadow of Altars* and *The Crisis*, both written in the 1930s.

Lithuania

Putinas, who died in 1967, continued to write after the Soviet occupation of the country in 1940, but these works, favorable to the new regime, are lesser works.

There is also a body of writings done by Lithuanians in emigration. Antanas Vaiciulaitis taught at several American universities after World War II, then joined the Voice of America. His books include three volumes of short stories, legends and myths. Jurgis Gliauda, who also made his way to America after World War II, is the author of *House Upon the Sand* (1951), *Ora pro nobis* (1952), and *The Sonata of Icarus*. Other writers in emigration include Nele

Mazalaite, Alfonsas Sesplaukis, Henrikas Radauskas, and Stepas Zobarskas.

FUTURE

Lithuania's greater ethnic unity and the strong unifying role of the Roman Catholic Church help stabilize the country. It has shown that it can have many peaceful changes of government. It even became the first European country to impeach its head of state. In May 2009 the country's got its first female president, Dalia Grybauskaite. The parliamentary elections in October 2008 produced a center-right government led by Prime Minister Andrius Kubilius. Both president and prime minister are supporting austerity policies to bring the country out of the recession. Their measures will work after several painful years.

Lithuania had farther to go to qualify for membership in the EU than the other two Baltic states, but all three entered in May 2004. It moved quickly to adopt the European currency. However, the EU ruled in May 2006 that its inflation was slightly above the limit. Then came the global economic meltdown, which battered the litas. Its entry into the eurozone will be delayed beyond the original target date of 2012.

Until the slowdown in 2008 and 2009, Lithuania had one of Europe's highest economic growth rates, booming exports, a budget surplus and shrinking unemployment. It worried that too many of its best workers were leaving the country. Officials estimate that as many as 450,000 Lithuanians, or a tenth of the population, left to work abroad, especially in Britain, but also in Ireland and Scandinavia. Privatization proceeded briskly, tax collection has been improved, and governmental spending had fallen to 32% of GDP. The country is highly committed to green politics. In a 2008 index of environmental performance compiled by Yale and Columbia universities, Lithuania placed fourth in the world, one notch above Latvia and far above the United States, which was ranked 66th.

Like the other two Baltic states, Lithuania entered the 21st century with some major challenges. For the sake of its prosperity and security, it sought economic and military integration with the West. It joined NATO in April 2004. Its need for the security that such integration might provide stems from the long-standing Russian claim to predominance over the nations on its periphery. Lithuania faces no imminent threat to its newly regained independence, but like the other two Baltic states, it must remain on guard. If Russia were able to restrict their ability to make their own decisions, such as on joining a military alliance or hosting allied fighter jets on their territory, Lithuania, Latvia and Estonia would no longer be fully sovereign states. Former President Adamkus warned in 2008 that a resurgent Russia may spark a new cold war. He said he understood Moscow's desire for a big voice in world politics, but it creates "unnecessary tensions" and "wants to dominate and dictate."

The country has been in the international spotlight. Lithuanian film fans mourned the death of Hollywood star Charles Bronson, who had been born in Pennsylvania of Lithuanian immigrants.

Kaliningrad (Russia)

University where philosopher Immanuel Kant taught

Kaliningrad (Russia)

The Kaliningrad Oblast (Russian region) is the northern third of the former East Prussia; the southern two-thirds went to Poland after the Second World War. Renamed in 1946 after a former president of the USSR, Mikhail Kalinin, who never set foot in the area, it contains the earlier German city of Königsberg, founded in 1255 as a fortress of the Teutonic Knights. It joined the Hanseatic League in 1340, and in 1457 it became the seat of the Teutonic Order's grand master after the knights had lost Marienburg to Poland. From 1525 until the union of Brandenburg and Prussia in 1618, it was the residence of the dukes of Prussia, and in 1701 it became the coronation city of the Prussian kings. It was there that the philosophical giant, Immanuel Kant, had lived and worked from 1724 to 1804.

In the Second World War it was the scene of determined German defense against the Red Army that was driving westward to conquer Germany. The furious warfare left the city devastated, and the Soviet Union made no effort to rebuild Königsberg in its former style. It demolished the ruins of the old castle. On its site Soviet officials began to construct a municipal city and Communist Party administration building, the "House of Soviets," that was never completed. Its towering empty shell stands as a symbol of this re-gion's uncertain future. The city and surrounding countryside are sad testimony to the aesthetic and environmental degradation that Soviet communism brought to the lands it conquered.

Before the war the city was admired for its architecture, wealth and culture. East Prussia was a breadbasket for all of Germany. After the war, all 1.2 million German citizens were expelled, and the region became a Soviet garrison and deployment area for the Soviet naval, land and missile forces. It was closed to outsiders from 1948 to 1992. Some of its skilled labor force produced or serviced advanced weapons systems during the communist era. A fifth of its workforce is still paid by the military. The number of soldiers has dramatically diminished to 24,000 (U.S. estimate) or 40,000 (Polish estimate), roughly a tenth of the 1991 strength. A Soviet space mission control center was located there. While Moscow still has 66 Lenin statues standing, only one remains in Kaliningrad—on Victory Square, earlier Hansa Square, renamed Hitler Square in 1933. Its agriculture declined so far that the oblast must import food to support its residents.

The Post-Soviet Era

After the Baltic States gained their independence in 1991 and the Soviet Union collapsed a year later, Kaliningrad became a Russian enclave that continues to belong to the Russian Federation. But it is separated from the rest of Russia by independent Lithuania and Belarus. Its nearly one million people increasingly call themselves "Euro-Russians" and travel to nearby Warsaw (280 kilometers away in Poland) and Vilnius (195 kilometers away in Lithuania) much more often than to St. Petersburg or Moscow. One survey in 2002 found that 80% of its youth under age 25 had traveled in Western Europe (including Poland), while only 15% had been in other parts of Russia.

Source: *The Economist*

Although Lithuania has no land dispute with Russia over Kaliningrad, a sensitive issue existed concerning Russian transit rights for its military forces in Kaliningrad. An informal agreement was reached in 1991 to allow Russian troops to cross Lithuania by rail only, with a maximum of 180 soldiers on any one train and their weapons in a separate car. Lithuanian soldiers can inspect these rail transports to ensure that these stipulations are being followed. This agreement is renewed on a year-by-year basis.

When Lithuania's joined the EU in May 2004, a new transit agreement was needed for the 950,000 Russians living in the Kaliningrad enclave who want to travel to Russia through Lithuania. Russian President Vladimir Putin (whose wife hails from Kaliningrad) had warned of a new "Berlin Wall" around Russian citizens. He called the issue a "litmus test" for Russia-EU relations and warned of a "blue curtain," referring to the color of the EU flag.

Neither Poland nor Lithuania would hear of "corridors" across their territory. In the words of former Polish President Aleksander Kwasniewski, "talk about corridors takes us back in history to the start of the Second World War, which began with demands from Hitler's Germany to enjoy free access to Danzig across Poland." The EU had never made any exceptions to its requirement for a strict visa regime toward nonmembers, and it clearly did not relish the idea of having a criminal haven located inside the EU, with no control over its borders.

An agreement was reached. Since July 2003 Kaliningrad residents can receive a "facilitated-transit document" at the cost of five euros, which is basically a simplified multiple-entry visa valid for three years. Visa holders can travel through Lithuania either by train or by automobile, and they have 24 hours to complete their transit. Those residents wanting to travel elsewhere, including to Lithuania

Abandoned and unfinished House of Soviets, Communist Party building.

169

Kaliningrad (Russia)

or Poland, must pay 35 euros, present a work ID or invitation, and wait 10 days to receive their visa. The Lithuanian government opened a second consulate within the Kaliningrad Oblast in the city of Sovetsk to deal primarily with Russians living in the eastern part of the enclave.

To circumvent the visa requirement, many more Russians fly to and from Kaliningrad; nine daily flights connect it with Moscow. The government has modernized Khrabrovo airport and constructed one of the most modern air traffic control systems in the hope of making the airport a hub for air travel between Europe and Russia. Both countries are studying the possibility of a high-speed, nonstop train link connecting Kaliningrad and the Russian mainland. The travel compromise was linked to the Russian Duma's ratification in May 2003 of the Lithuania-Russia border treaty that had been signed in October 1997. This included the land border, the exclusive economic zone and the continental shelf in the Baltic Sea.

Kaliningrad's strategic importance for Moscow was enhanced by Russia's weakened position in the Baltic area and by the fact that Kaliningrad is Russia's only warm-water port in the Baltic Sea. It remains home to the Russian Baltic fleet, a motley collection of 112 rusting vessels, including submarines and warships, rotting in the dirty water of Baltisk (formerly Pillau). Russia hopes to find a way someday of transforming the region into a trade window open both to the West and the East. Russia has already begun building a terminal at Baltisk for large cruise boats traveling to St. Petersburg, Scandinavia and Germany. It also hopes someday to improve the old "Reich Road One," called "Berlinka," into a major interstate highway connection to the future Via Baltica. The road that leads to Poland is being improved. Moscow worries about the fact that the enclave is located about 250 miles from the rest of Russia and borders on Poland, which was admitted to NATO in 1999, and Lithuania, which entered in 2004. Many in Russia, especially in the military and security agencies, regard Kaliningrad as a precious war trophy and military bastion that must be protected from outside interference.

Relations with Germany

From 5,000 to 15,000 of the approximately two million Russians of German heritage (*Volksdeutsche*) remaining in Russia were permitted to resettle after 1990 in Kaliningrad. From 60% to 70% of these Germans later emigrated to Germany. The enclave is the size of Connecticut and has 950,000 residents, 435,000 of whom live in the city of Kaliningrad. The overwhelm-ing majority (80%) is Russian; the rest come from various parts of the former Soviet Union. By 1994 there were also as many as 100,000 military forces, many left there after the Soviet Army withdrew from Poland, the Baltic states and eastern Germany. At the time of the Two-Plus-Four Agreement, which unified Germany in 1990, Germany unmistakably emphasized that it makes no territorial claims to Kaliningrad.

In fact, about the only German involvement today is the brisk trade of German tourists, who visit their former neighborhoods and farms and usually return to Germany saddened by the dilapidation and catastrophic environmental pollution they witnessed. Approximately 40% of the 100,000 tourists who visit annually are German. In 2004 the direct rail connection with Berlin, the "Königsberg Express," was restored after three years inactivity. The 650-kilometer trip takes 16 hours. This makes Kaliningrad the only Russian city with direct access to the western rail net. Since 2007 the rail ferry "Vilnius" provides the first non-stop ship connection from Sassnitz-Mukran in Germany to Kaliningrad's Baltijsk port.

It is a reassuring signal to Russia that Germany shows little political interest in and makes no claims to Kaliningrad. Former Russian President Boris Yeltsin had felt it necessary to declare during an election visit to the enclave in 1996 that the "Kaliningrad Oblast is Russian soil. Nobody should have any doubts about that." Germany has supported multilateral European efforts to stimulate economic development and the creation of a special economic zone. It created a "German-Russian House" in 1997 to help coordinate cultural and economic exchanges. In 2001 a thousand Russians were learning German there, and 600 were getting training in manual trades.

Germany's request to establish a German consulate was refused until 2004. In 2002 Russia permitted the first Western country to open a consulate: Sweden. This was followed by two Lithuanian consulates in Kaliningrad and Sovetsk. By 2005 Denmark and Poland had opened consulates, with more to follow. Moscow jealously guards its own authority to establish taxes and approve joint ventures. It even requires all outgoing mail to be processed first in Moscow.

Political Situation

No foreign government makes any claim to the territory, and there is no internal support for separation from Russia. Germany renounced any demands in the 1990 treaty of German reunification, and Poland has also signed treaties with both Russia and Germany abjuring any territo-rial claims against either country. A few right-wing Lithuanian politicians still contend that parts of Kaliningrad, roughly those parts between the Pregel and Nemunas Rivers, should belong to Lithuania, but their views carry little weight. This was obvious when the country signed border treaties with Russia in 1991 and 1997 and an agreement of cooperation in 1999. The Lithuanian government is aware that its country received a significant portion of East Prussia after the Second World War, namely the former Memel and (with the port city of Klaipeda). Any suggestion that Lithuania should have part of Kaliningrad would be answered by Russian claims against present Lithuanian territory.

Washington's position since the 1945 Potsdam Conference is that the Soviet Union earlier and Russia today possess only administrative, not *de jure*, control of the region and that the question of its status remains to be decided. However, wishing to integrate Russia into the Euro-Atlantic community, the U.S. government has shown no inclination to press this interpretation. It adopts a low-profile approach as an unassertive supporter, not leader, of Western efforts to help the exclave.

Vladimir Putin asserted: "Kaliningrad will always remain Russian. This soil has become particularly near and dear to Russia." In 2005 he appointed a former tax minister and entrepreneur, Georgi Boos, as governor with orders to "organize the area like a German enterprise: everything must be effective." With Putin's backing, the energetic Boos made the enclave one of the most dynamic regions in Russia. The cathedral was restored, a Russian-Orthodox church was constructed, and a commitment was made to rebuild the royal castle, dynamited in 1969, at a cost of 100 million euros.

However, the falling standard of living, economic crisis, cut in subsidies, excessive bureaucracy, higher taxes, and autocratic rule by appointed governors and officials raised tensions to a breaking point in December 2009 and January 2010. An estimated 10,000 citizens, bearing buttons and signs reading "Putin resign" and "No Boos" poured twice into a central square to demand Boos's resignation. This forced the disliked governor to hold serious talks with opposition leaders for the first time. An opposition editor noted with regret: "There is the will to change something, but not the means to change anything. That is the problem." "We have no say in anything."

Economy

The region has the potential for economic growth. It people have the highest standard of living in Russia. It has a well-educated work force, a deep-water harbor that is Russia's only warm-water port (although its deepest part remains off limits for commercial trade), over 90% of the world's amber, rich farmland, modest crude oil reserves, and an industrial infrastructure that produces ships, machinery, food products, processed fish and wood. However, despite the highest per capital level of foreign direct investment in Russia, many investors are scared away by endemic corruption, powerful organized crime, a drug epidemic out of control, and Russia's highest HIV/AIDS infection rate.

Up to 70% of its GDP is generated by medium- and small-sized enterprises. There are over 2,000 joint ventures in Kaliningrad—400 Lithuanian, 360 German, and also American. Gas-guzzling Hummers are assembled in the enclave, as are KIA, BMW and General Motors vehicles for the Russian market. The Chinese state company, Chery, which acquired Volvo from Ford in 2010, has plans for an auto plant.

Unemployment averages 10%–15% but is over 50% in some areas. Because of the boom, however, these percentages are falling. Per capita GDP is more than one-third below the Russian average and even much farther below that of its neighbors. The average monthly pay is less than 250 euros ($310), but four in ten live below the poverty line of $100 per month. Surprisingly, one in three residents owns a car, compared with one in ten in the rest of Russia. Kaliningrad has Russia's highest crime rate; 2,000 homeless children survive from petty crime. The disastrously low level of health is shown by the fact that life expectancy for men is only 59, one of the lowest in the world; for women it is 71 years.

Until Poland and Lithuania joined the EU, citizens of Kaliningrad enjoyed visa-free travel there and were permitted to import goods duty-free that they could then resell in Russia. Thousands eked out a living by crossing the border with sacks full of cut-rate cigarettes, black-market CDs and other wares to sell to their relatively prosperous neighbors. That had to stop once Poland and Lithuania were EU states. At least half of its commerce is transit trade to and from the Russian mainland, and its travel agreement with Lithuania in 2003 will not hinder that. This mixture of legal trade and smuggling has been a crucial benefit for the local economy. It is estimated that the underground economy accounts for 40%–60% of Kaliningrad's total trade. However, with Poland (its leading trading partner) and Lithuania in the European Union, the open borders slammed shut, and the enclave could become even poorer and more isolated than it is now.

Located so far away from the rest of the Russian Federation, it must depend on its immediate neighbors, Lithuania and Poland, to provide for many of the daily needs of its 950,000 residents. They are the chief foreign investors, and foodstuffs, clothing, furniture and other consumer goods from these two countries are prominent in stores; 80% of its electricity came from Lithuania until the Ignalina nuclear power plant was shut down the end of 2009.

Lithuania's Communist leader, Antanas Snieckus, had wisely refused an offer made in the 1950s by Soviet party chief Nikita Khrushchev that Lithuania take control of the Kaliningrad region. Snieckus feared that his republic would invite the same problems with a large Russian minority that were mounting in Latvia and Estonia. Nevertheless, having lived within the USSR for a half-century, Lithuanians are particularly familiar with Soviet behavior and mentality and can collaborate with Kaliningraders even more effectively than can Poles.

Kaliningrad's government and the provincial legislature (*Duma*) look to Brussels for help. Ex-Governor Vladimir Yegorov said in 2001: "Our unique geographical position is a reason for the leaders of Russia and the EU to create a special agreement on the Kaliningrad region." According to a 2001 poll, 80% of the enclave's citizens trust the EU, but not the mother country. In the six years from 2001 the EU provided more than 100 million euros to projects in Kaliningrad.

This troublesome exclave needs outside help to prevent it from exporting its many problems to its neighbors and to deal with economic decline worse than in the rest of Russia. However, the worst economic problems are home grown: the persistence of Soviet-era practices, corruption, and the Russian Duma's failure to pass laws to meet the concerns of foreign investors about the security of their ventures. All of these helped foil attempts to create a free economic zone (FEZ) in the oblast and put an end to any talk of its becoming a "gateway." But a "Special Economic Zone" involving a preferential customs and tax regime was put in place and has boosted the local economy. Both the EU and the surrounding states feared that it could become the "black hole" of the Baltic Sea region, but that may not happen.

FUTURE

In July 2005 the city celebrated its 750th anniversary, and this seems to have prodded Moscow to take a greater interest in it. Past attempts to polish up the city were only partially successful although some streets were repaved, sidewalks improved, and concrete facades covered or painted. The German weekly news magazine, *Der Spiegel*, financed the digging out of the remaining walls of the razed castle, which became a sort of outdoor museum. There are now plans to rebuild it. Kaliningrad University was renovated and renamed Immanuel-Kant University.

Given the continued influence of nationalist voices in Russian domestic politics and Russia's concerns about NATO enlargement, it is unlikely that Kaliningrad's military status will change. Indeed, this very fact added urgency to the Polish and Baltic desire to join the Atlantic Alliance. These concerns were enhanced in 2007 and 2008 when the Russian government warned that it could deploy Iskander cruise missiles in Kaliningrad if the U.S. were to build a missile shield in Central Europe. It already has shorter-range Tochka missiles in Kaliningrad. In January 2009 the Russian threat was dropped.

The enclave's future remains uncertain. It depends on general developments in Russia proper. Kaliningrad's citizens are disillusioned. Public protests in 2009 and 2010 against autocratic and insensitive rule underscore the tensions that exist between Moscow and its westernmost outpost. Also, 60% favored changing the name back to Königsberg, according to a 2001 poll. One naval captain expressed the sentiment this way: "Kalinin was nothing more than a tool of the devil, Stalin. Why should we be reminded of that daily?"

Statue of Immanuel Kant at Kaliningrad University

The Federal Republic of Germany

Midnight, October 2–3, 1990: UNIFICATION as throngs converge on Berlin's Brandenburg Gate which for over 40 years symbolically divided East from West of the restored capital city of Germany.

Area: 137,691 sq. mi. (357,050 sq. km., slightly larger than the combined size of Ohio, Pennsylvania and New York).

Population: 80.9 million (2008)

Capital City: Berlin (became official capital by parliamentary vote in June 1991, following German unification on October 3, 1990), Pop. 3.39 million.

Climate: Northern temperate.

Neighboring Countries: France, Luxembourg, Belgium, the Netherlands (West); Denmark (North); Poland, the Czech Republic (East); Austria, Switzerland (South).

Official Language: German. The German language, structure and pronunciation vary widely according to region.

Ethnic Background: Indo-Germanic: Saxon and Teuton, plus an admixture of Slav and other tribes such as Goths.

Principal Religions: Protestant (Evangelical Lutheran), and Roman Catholicism, Islam.

Chief Commercial Exports: Road vehicles, chemicals, machinery, telecoms technology, electrical devices, fuels.

Major Customers: EU (64.79% of exports and 64.6% of imports), France (9.7% of exports and 8.6% of imports), U.S. (7.5% of exports and 4.5% of imports), UK (7.3% of exports and 5.6% of imports), Italy (6.7% of exports and 5.8% of imports), Netherlands (6.4% of exports and 12% of imports), Belgium (5.3% of exports and 7.8% of imports), Austria (5.4% of exports and China (6.2% of imports).

Currency: euro.

National Day: October 3 (Day of German Unity).

Chief of State: Christian Wulff, President (June 30, 2010).

Head of Government: Angela Merkel, Chancellor (since November 22, 2005).

National Flag: Three horizontal stripes of black, red and gold.

Few people of the world have such a rich and varied past as do the Germans. Yet theirs is a history full of mountains and valleys. Without German science, theology, philosophy, music, literature and the other arts, Western civilization would have been left with gaping holes. But Germans have known times of shame and destitution so deep and dark that many could not be sure that the sun would ever shine again.

German history is one of religious, class and territorial division. Austria's foreign

173

Germany

minister, Prince Klemens von Metternich, said in the early 1800s that Italy was merely a *geographical conception*, but he could have said exactly the same about Germany. For many centuries there existed the fiction of a unified, almost universal German empire stretching from the North Sea to Sicily. Yet, until 1871 Germany was, in fact, a highly fractured scene of independent and rival kingdoms, principalities, ecclesiastical states and independent cities. Even though most of their subjects spoke one of hundreds of German dialects, few considered themselves Germans; rather they felt themselves to be Saxons, Bavarians, Prussians, Rhinelanders, or Frankfurters.

When political unity finally came in 1871, many Germans were left outside the new German Empire, such as the German-speaking Swiss and Austrians. This unity lasted only three-quarters of a century and ended in disgrace and destruction. Not until the Berlin Wall came tumbling down on November 9, 1989, did reunification become possible; on October 3, 1990, Germany became one country again, and that date is now celebrated as the national holiday.

Germany is populated by a dynamic, talented and imaginative people who for centuries have defied definition. Two thousand years ago, the Roman historian Tacitus called the Germanic tribes (which later migrated to most other parts of Western and Eastern Europe) warlike, but until the 20th century the Germans brought war to other nations far less frequently than did others. Germans were deeply involved in tragic wars in the 20th century, and even in 1950, the U.S. High Commissioner for Germany, John J. McCloy, joked: "Just give me a brass band and a loudspeaker truck. Then let me march from Lake Constance in the South to Kiel up North, and I will have an army of a million men behind me—all eager-eyed."

He was badly mistaken. Germany is, in fact, now a country in which pacifist sentiment is perhaps stronger than in any other European or North American country. Surveys in 2000 also showed that Germans have the lowest level of national pride of any European nation except the Slovaks. They rarely sing the national anthem, probably because only half of all Western Germans and less than a quarter of those in Eastern Germany can recite even its first line. One young German noted with pleasure and with some exaggeration that "Europeans have always wanted a pacifist Germany; well, now they have one!" Indeed, a major source of American irritation toward Germany after the Second World War was the unwillingness of many Germans to defend themselves.

The French-Swiss writer, Madame de Staël, described the Germans almost 200 years ago as a pacific, poetic and romantic people, but Germans also acquired a reputation for diligence and order. German politics has often been described as romantic and irrational. But it was a German statesman (Bismarck) with whom one most directly associates the term *Realpolitik*, which describes a carefully measured, rational policy based on a realistic assessment of a nation's interests and means. The Germans' road to democracy was very bumpy and they have made several wrong turns. But today Germany is one of the world's most stable and tolerant democracies, about which former Chancellor Willy Brandt could say in the early 1970s: "Germans can again be proud of their country."

Germans are still, to a degree, haunted by their history. No people today tries so hard to come to grips with its own past, and almost no one is more critical of Germany and its past than is the German himself. But the Germans' critical eye to their own past has brought some undeniable benefits to the present. It has helped to harden both the democratic consensus in Germany and the determination to bend over backwards to respect and protect human rights and dignity.

Clichés are never more than half-truths, but those relating to Germans are much more in need of revision than those about most other peoples. Germany is a country in the process of rapid change, in part because of industrialization familiar to Americans and other Western Europeans, and in part because of a lingering reaction to their own experience under Hitler, a dictator almost universally regarded outside and inside Germany as the most evil and brutal individual in recorded history. One can witness change in Germans' attitudes on politics, social problems, religion and work and in almost all German societal institutions, including the family and the schools. The process of integrating the former German Democratic Republic (GDR), which had been ruled by a Communist dictatorship for 40 years, is altering Germany even further. In short, Germany is a country that one must approach with a fresh and open mind.

The People and Place

Germans are the largest nationality in Europe west of Russia, where more than 1.5 million ethnic Germans still live. The FRG has almost 81 million inhabitants after absorbing 17 million East Germans. Germany is a very densely populated country, with 250 inhabitants per square mile. The only European countries where the people live more closely together are the Netherlands and Belgium. The FRG's population is unevenly dispersed, though. The most thickly settled part is the Ruhr-Rhine area around Düsseldorf, Cologne (Köln), Dortmund and Essen (a conglomeration of cities and heavy industry often called "Ruhr City").

Other large urban concentrations are the Rhine-Main area around Frankfurt, the Rhine-Neckar area around Mannheim and Ludwigshafen, the Swabian industrial concentration around Stuttgart, as well as the cities of Berlin, Leipzig, Dresden, Bremen, Hamburg, Hanover, Nurem-

Germany's highways

174

Crop fields in a medieval pattern radiate from a Bavarian village

Jon Markham Morrow

berg and Munich. There are, however, very thinly settled areas in the Northern German Plain, the Eifel Mountain region, the Upper Palatinate, the Bavarian Forest and the peripheral areas adjacent to the earlier border with the GDR. Those latter areas on both sides of the former dividing line are experiencing rapid growth in unified Germany as they become the new heartland.

The FRG, like other countries, has experienced a rapid flight from farms into cities and towns; the rural population dropped from 23% in 1950 to less than 5% today. But about half of all Germans live in towns or villages of less than 20,000 inhabitants. Unlike countries such as France, Britain, Italy or Denmark, no single German city dominates the political, cultural and economic life of the entire country, although Berlin may gradually assume this position in the 21st century.

For centuries Germany has been called the "land of the middle" because it occupies the heart of Europe. This is a major reason why other European powers have often sought to keep Germany divided and weak. It has no natural frontiers, and the North German Plain, which is interspersed with hills, has always been and remains an ideal invasion route. Only the Alpine foothills in the Southeast offer uninviting terrain for invading commanders. Because the altitude rises from the North Sea to the Alps, most of Germany's rivers, which provide the country with an excellent inland waterway system, flow north

and empty into the North Sea via the Rhine, Ems, Weser and Elbe rivers. The only exception is the Danube, which flows southeast toward the Black Sea.

The visitor to Germany now looks in vain for physical traces of the pauperized and demolished land that in 1945 began to dig itself out from under a pile of rubble. In the Western part one sees a highly prosperous country with a well-fed, well-clothed, well-cared-for and predominantly middle-class people. Germans in the Eastern part enjoy roughly the same prosperity. The FRG is ribboned by highly modern superhighways traveled by millions of private automobiles with no speed limit on most. Its modern cities in the West show few signs of urban blight, but cities in the East show their four decades of mindless and tasteless urban renewal or neglect. It is an economic giant in the world and now operates in European politics with far more confidence, effectiveness and respect than almost any other nation dreamed would be possible after Germany's total collapse in 1945.

The FRG has even become a less tense and far more pleasant place to live. With high incomes in the West, a short workweek, lots of vacation and a commitment to "quality of life," Germans have become world champion travelers abroad. When they stay home, they enjoy "free-time centers," which have proliferated everywhere. Their cities contain museums, concert halls and pedestrian zones filled with

sidewalk cafes, street-shows and pleasant street life. They enjoy their comfortable lives with a spontaneity that invites a much closer look at this modern country.

HISTORY

Roman Penetration

Around four centuries before Christ, Germanic tribes, which were of Indo-European extraction, began entering from the North and East of what is now Germany and displacing or mingling with the Celtic peoples whom they found there. These tribes were, however, not the only people to be attracted by the soil, rivers and strategic importance of this area in the heart of Europe. In 58 B.C. Julius Caesar led a Roman army that defeated the Germanic tribes in Alsace and in other Germanic areas west of the Rhine River. A good cultural observer as well as a good commander, Caesar wrote the earliest description of the tribes that he had just defeated and thereby sparked the interest and imagination of other Romans who later came to colonize or develop the area.

The Romans extended their frontier eastward toward the Elbe River in 9 B.C., but this expansion survived only two decades. A German chieftain, Arminius, (later known to Germans as Hermann) in 9 A.D. led an army that practically decimated the Roman occupation forces during a furious battle in storm and rain in the Teutoburg Forest, which is said to be located southeast of the present-day city

Germany

of Bielefeld. The remnants of the Roman forces withdrew westward and southward again beyond the Danube and Rhine rivers. Thenceforth, the Romans remained behind their heavily garrisoned frontier stretching from Cologne (Colonia) to Bonn (Bonna) to Augsburg (Augusta Vindelicorum) and all the way to Vienna (Vindobona). Here the Romans built beautiful cities such as Regensburg (Castra Regina) and Trier (Augusta Treverum) with their stone structures, warm air heating underneath their floors, aqueducts, baths, coliseums and even running water in some villas and public buildings.

They introduced advanced Roman agricultural methods, a money economy and Roman law, administration and culture. Trier even served temporarily as a seat of the Roman emperor, especially for Constantine the Great from 306–312 A.D. What we now know about the Germanic tribes at that time came to us from Romans such as Tacitus, who in his book *Germania* described the tribes' legends, customs, appearance, morals and political and economic systems. His characterization of these tribesmen as particularly warlike helped launch a cliché about Germans that is by no means an inherent trait nor is valid today.

In the latter half of the 2nd century A.D., Germanic tribes began hammering away at the Roman front and, attracted by stories of great wealth in the Italian peninsula itself, actually invaded the heartland of what had become a decadent Roman Empire in the 5th century, causing it to collapse in the West. For centuries the Roman cities were left largely to decay, and much of the legal, administrative and cultural advancements of the past were forgotten. Yet the Romans left their traces in the grammatical structure and some words of the German language, in the German concept of law and the cities that after the first Crusade in 1095 began to gain significance in Germany again.

Some historians have dated the beginning of German history at 9 A.D. when Arminius defeated the Romans at Teutoburg, but the various German tribes he led against the Romans certainly felt no common identity among themselves as *Germans*. There can hardly be a *German* history without a *German* people and some kind of German state. It is a mistake to identify Germany with the various tribes that began to enter what is presently Germany before the arrival of the Romans and with those such as the East and West Goths, Vandals, Burgundians and Langobards which swept into the area during the great migrations before and after Roman supremacy. Those migrations almost completely changed the racial makeup of Europe from the 2nd through the 5th

Roman-built *Porta Nigra* in Trier

centuries A.D. The German nation was formed only very gradually over many centuries through the conquest and integration of a great number of Germanic tribes. Of course, some such as the Angles, some Saxons, the Danes, Swedes and Norwegians never became a part of the German nation. Others were initially conquered, particularly by the larger tribes—the Friesians, Franks and Swabians, Bavarians, Saxons and Thuringers—and ultimately grew into a community larger than any single tribe.

It is highly doubtful that a German nation would ever have emerged if a Carolinian empire had not taken shape after the Roman rule had effectively ended. This far-flung empire, composed 80% of Germanic peoples and encompassing those speaking Latin-based languages in the West, reached its peak under Charlemagne ("Charles the Great"), who ascended the throne in 768 A.D.

During his rule the empire extended from Northwestern Europe south to Rome and from Hungary to northern Spain. Charlemagne was a leader of extraordinary personal qualities who spent half of his time in the saddle holding his vast territory together. His empire survived only a few years after his death in 814. It was divided in 817 into Kingdoms of East and West Franconia and Lorraine. After bitter and complicated inheritance quarrels, two realms faced each other along roughly the same line as the present border between Germany and France. By 843 this border had become more or less fixed, and in the year 925 it became firmly established. Only in the East could subsequent German expansion take place.

Although Charlemagne's huge empire had been considerably reduced after his death, he had created the indispensable

foundation for the formation of a German nation and a German consciousness. There were no other geographic, racial, cultural or strictly linguistic factors that could have pulled Germany together without Charlemagne's political and military acumen. During his reign some persons began to refer to the tongues spoken in the Eastern part of the empire as "Deutsch" (*Doich*)—German, a word derived from "Diutisk," meaning "common" or "popular." In the following three centuries more and more inhabitants of what is now Germany developed a consciousness of being German.

The Eastern Franconian realm in 919 became the German Empire. "Empire," however, is a somewhat misleading word, since it connotes a centralized, unified power. In Germany there was a strong degree of unity, but until almost the end of the 19th century, rule was by a multitude of heads of local states and independent cities. However, by the 11th century these states and cities had become the most powerful in Europe and were able to claim the title "Roman Empire." In the 13th century this was dignified to the title "Holy Roman Empire," and in the 15th century "Holy Roman Empire of the German Nation." The reach and power of this empire expanded and contracted, but it always retained certain organizational features: the highest nobility (usually called "electors") actually *elected* an emperor.

Although this position was not hereditary as was the case with other European monarchies, there was a dynastic element in that, with very few exceptions, the new emperor had to be a blood relative of his predecessor. There was no capital city; he moved around continually, ruling from wherever he happened to be. He usually resided in various bishoprics or in a col-

Germany

Charlemagne's Empire in 814

lection of buildings known as a *Pfalz*. As one can now see in the charming medieval city of Goslar in the Harz Mountains, the *Pfalz* contained a royal residence, buildings and stables for the emperor's retinue, at least one church or chapel and surrounding farms, mines and businesses from which the emperor could derive his income.

Since no taxes were levied, he was compelled to finance his activities from the various imperial estates throughout the empire. Finally, the major and minor nobility met infrequently in an imperial diet called the *Reichstag*, a body whose work cannot be compared to a modern democratic parliament, but one that displayed how much the emperor depended upon the lesser noblemen if he wanted to conduct a war, increase his revenues or the like.

Germany always has been a mixture of central and regional power, of unity and disunity. There were endless struggles over who should lead in the empire, and the emperor's actual power was never assured, even after he had been elected. He had to maintain a powerful army and forge delicate alliances among the rival dukes in the realm and powerful archbishops who ruled such important cities as Mainz, Cologne and Trier. This is why German provinces and cities became much more important in Germany than in other countries.

During the 8th and 9th centuries the Hungarians posed a constant threat to the German Empire. The fortresses Romans built had long since fallen into ruin. To cope with this threat, the German kings and emperors erected fortresses around the imperial estates, royal and ducal palaces, abbeys and cities with the treasured right to maintain a market place. Erfurt, Meis-

sen, Merseburg, Frankfurt, Ulm, Gosler and Aachen originated from fortified royal estates and palaces, and Augsburg, Passau, Strasbourg, Trier, Worms, Cologne, Mainz and Speyer, originated from fortified abbeys and monasteries. Martin Luther's characterization of God as "a mighty fortress" specifically refers to the safety found in these walled cities. The Hungarians were decisively defeated in 955 and were rooted out of what is now Austria, thereby permitting Bavarian settlers to pour into this "East March" (whence the German name for Austria: *Österreich*).

The Zenith of the Empire

The German emperors focused their attention far beyond what is now the German-speaking world, particularly on Italy. In 962 the Saxon King Otto I was crowned emperor by the Pope in St. Peter's Cathedral in Rome, a tradition which was to last over 500 years. This unique privilege, which was bestowed on no other ruler, entitled the German monarch to be called "emperor." It also gave the German Empire a universalistic claim to rule over the entire Western world as the protector of Christianity. This claim never became reality.

The special relationship established between the emperors and popes proved to be of questionable value for both. German emperors became embroiled in Italian and papal affairs for more than three centuries, a costly diversion from the more important task of creating a unified Germany. Emperors became active in papal selections and on occasion succeeded in driving popes right out of Rome. At the same time, popes often connived with Germany's enemies and bitterly fought again emperors' attempts to gain control of the Catholic Church within Germany.

A showdown between the two occurred in 1077 when Emperor Heinrich IV replaced Pope Gregor VII when the latter refused to permit Heinrich to appoint bishops and other high Church officials in Germany. Gregor struck back by taking away Heinrich's imperial crown, releasing all of Heinrich's subjects from their loyalty to the emperor and excommunicating Heinrich. The latter soon realized how much he had overreached his power and authority and felt compelled to go to the fortress of Canossa, where the Pope had sought protection. Dressed in the simple garb of a penitent, Heinrich pleaded three days for forgiveness. Then with outstretched arms, he threw himself at the Pope's feet, who had no alternative but to forgive him. Heinrich's act of prostration at the feet of the Pope was a turning point in German history. Soon thereafter, a revengeful Heinrich drove Pope Gregor into exile and lonely death in southern Italy. For centuries the German emperors could always count the popes among their enemies, even though they continued to influence their election until about 1250.

The perennial activity of the emperors in Italy tended seriously to weaken their ability to contend with the domestic challenges to their authority. One of the few exceptions to this was Emperor Friedrich I of the Swabian dynasty of Staufen, which from 1138 ruled Germany for about a century. Known as Barbarossa because of his red beard, Friedrich was a strong monarch from the moment he ascended the throne in 1152 at the age of 30. He was a handsome and imposing man, intelligent and well-educated. A highly charismatic figure who attracted loyalty and devotion like a magnet, he was a model knight whose martial skills he continued to display by participating in tournaments until age 60. Despite a determined challenge within Germany by the Saxon duke, his aims were clear: supremacy in Northern and Central Italy without suppressing the Italian cities' freedoms, and continued influence over the papacy without directly controlling Rome. He wanted to crown his reign with a triumphant crusade, but after forging a mighty army and guiding it toward the Holy Land, he drowned in a river in Saleph in Asia Minor.

After his death bards circulated a legend throughout Germany that the red-bearded emperor was not really dead, but instead had sunk into a magic slumber within the mountain of Kyffhäuser, sitting on an ivory throne, his head resting on a marble table. He would leave Kyffhäuser only when his land signaled that it needed his help; if, however, all was in order, ravens would fly around the mountain, and Barbarossa would return to his sleep

Germany

for another 100 years. Those ravens are still circling the mountain.

The Decline of "The Empire"

The German emperors' attention had become so fixed on Italy that the last Staufen emperor, Friedrich II, an erudite and farsighted ruler, tried to rule the enormous empire from Sicily. Yet, by the time he died in 1250 and his successor, Conradino, had been executed in 1268, the German emperors could hardly pretend anymore to control large areas outside Germany. They had lost much of their power and influence within Germany as well. Due largely to the emperors' obsession with crusades and Italian campaigns, rather than for consolidating and increasing their power within Germany itself, a process of erosion of their power set in which left some free cities, several hundred German noblemen and the Church largely free of imperial control.

By 1268 no one could speak any longer of a powerful and supreme emperor over all of Germany. He could not call on the princes to support him in wartime without their approval; there was no common foreign policy, nor was there an imperial army. The only imperial laws that had any chance of being obeyed were those that had been approved by all three segments of the *Reichstag*—the "electors," the other princes and the cities—which the emperor convened infrequently in Worms, Frankfurt, Regensburg, Augsburg or some other important city in southern Germany.

From the 13th century on, the parts of the empire predominated over the whole,

The *Bamberg Knight*, one of the 13th century's finest examples of statuary

Romanesque Friedrich I

the regions over the empire, the princes, kings and high clergy over the emperor. The absence of any strong, centralizing power in Germany prevented for six centuries the development of a unified German nation, as the French and English had been able to do. For six centuries, German politics was largely characterized by conflict between ruling houses. After 1438 the imperial crown practically became the sole possession of the House of Hapsburg, and Austria gradually became the predominant German-speaking territory and one of the most powerful countries in Europe.

The Rise and Fall of "City Power"

By the end of the 14th century the population of Germany had risen from less than a million in the year 500 A.D. to 13–15 million, despite the great plague, which had reduced the European population by about a third. Most Germans lived on the land or in villages, and many were tied to the ground they worked and were compelled to deliver a considerable part of their produce to large landowners. Cities had begun to sprout up everywhere by the 10th century, primarily to provide protection. They also provided peasants with a place of refuge from the bondage that was widespread in the countryside.

The Crusades also had provided a mighty stimulation for cities, whose prosperity was often reflected in the mighty cathedrals that were built. Ulm built one, for instance, which could hold two and a half times as many people as lived in the city. Tradesmen and craftsmen in the cities began to develop guilds to protect their economic existence and to maintain a good reputation by assuring that quality work was done. These guilds also sometimes forcefully challenged the elite, patrician rule of the cities.

The power and influence of German cities was greatest when they joined together in leagues. The most important league was that of the Hansa cities. In 1241 Lübeck and Hamburg forged an alliance in order to protect the land and sea lanes between them from robbers, and gradually more and more cities along the North and Baltic Sea coasts, and even deep within the interior of Germany, Poland, the Baltic area and Scandinavia, joined. By the time the Hansa League had reached its height in the first half of the 15th century, it embraced such cities as Cologne, Brunswick, Bremen, Wismar, Rostock, Danzig, Königsberg, Breslau and Cracow, and the League had large trading colonies in London, Bruges, Gotland and Novgorod. Seldom did the Hansa cities conduct traditional military warfare; they preferred the far more effective trade war. Not until the end of the 15th century was the Hansa League's dominance over the North and Baltic Sea area broken.

By the 15th century, Germany had become a comparatively rich part of Europe, but, like today, its economic strength far outstripped its political influence. Although they remained far smaller than the leading cities in Southern and Western Europe, German cities had very much to do with such prosperity. The wars that were to ravage Germany in the 17th century, and especially the shift of the trade routes westward following the discovery of America, brought about the decay of the great German cities. This stagnation tended to clip the wings of the middle classes, which cities produce and strengthen, and therefore tended to stifle the development of democracy in Germany. It also left Germany primarily an agricultural country until the middle of the 19th century.

Intellectual Awakening

The 15th and the early 16th centuries were ones of intellectual awakening. This discovery of man and the world was the focus of humanism, which has remained controversial to this day and age, and the *Renaissance*. The latter was an Italian creation of the 14th and 15th century and for Europe signaled an important turning point. It meant an inclination on the part of a few to question all previous religious, scholarly, scientific and political authority that had placed limitations on man. It was a time when Leonardo da Vinci showed that natural science must be based on exact observation and experimentation, when Christopher Columbus dared to cross the ocean to disprove previous theories about the shape of the earth, when a Florentine political figure named Niccolò Machiavelli ripped the idealized cloth from politics to show it in its raw, non-ethical reality.

Germans were very much a part of this burst of discovery. Nikolaus Kopernicus, a clergyman from Frauenburg in Prussia, showed that the Earth was not the center of the universe and was merely one of the many bodies in a much larger planetary system. Martin Behaim constructed the first globe of the earth. Peter Henlein produced the first pocket watch. Berthold Schwarz discovered shooting powder quite by accident and thereby revolutionized warfare. An ingenious goldsmith from Mainz, Johannes Gutenberg, developed the first printing press using movable type, which was a prerequisite for taking the written word out of the libraries of the rich, the noble and the clergy and into the reach of the masses. In art, Albrecht Dürer, Hans Holbein and Mathias Grünewald achieved deserved recognition throughout the civilized world. Universities sprouted up all over Germany in this time of inquiry and became important centers of research and learning to the present day.

In this time of serious questioning it is not surprising that the practices and teachings of the Roman Catholic Church were also examined by critical minds. The master of all humanists was Erasmus of Rotterdam (1465–1536), who lived a part of his life in Germany and has amused the educated world with his *Praise of Folly*, in which he pointed to the grotesque difference between what men profess in this world and what they actually do. He also challenged the theologians to reexamine the New Testament in light of "the original sources." He criticized the abuses, pomp and ceremony of the Church and demanded a rational basis for the Catholic faith and a return to the "simple, pure Christ." He never broke with the Catholic Church, nor joined forces with those who later did, but he helped establish the theological foundation from which a Catholic monk in the provincial town of Wittenberg launched a powerful attack that shook the Church to its very roots.

Martin Luther

Martin Luther was the son of a minister from Thuringia who was able to save enough money to send his gifted but brooding son to the University of Erfurt to study law. Luther was reportedly shocked by a sudden flash of light and decided instead to become a monk, pastor and professor in Wittenberg. In 1511 he left for a long-awaited voyage to Rome as a firm believer, but he returned to Germany with his faith in the Church badly shaken. His

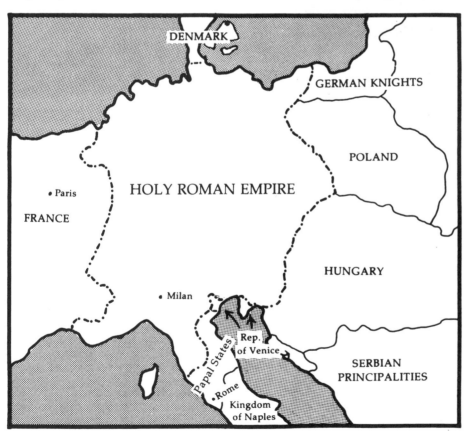

The Holy Roman Empire, mid-14th century

Germany

ET SPE ERIT VESTRA.

Martin Luther

anger and frustration built up as the Roman pontificate devised a method for raising its own revenues by selling to Catholics forgiveness for their sins.

In countries with strong central rulers, such papal financial maneuvers could be resisted, but until 1517 the Church's agents needed not fear resistance in the weak and fragmented Germany. When a papal representative knocked on Martin Luther's door to present the scheme one day, the glowing kettle boiled over. On October 31, 1517, he published his "95 Theses" branding the Catholic Church as an insult to God and challenging it to an open debate over fundamental theological issues. It is not certain that he tacked this highly explosive writing on the cathedral door at Wittenberg. What is certain, however, is that the Vatican was never the same after this angry monk rolled his weighty stone in its direction.

The Church decided to enter into a three-year debate with Luther, but this merely stimulated the interest that curious and critical Europeans paid to the stream of speeches and writings that poured from Luther's mouth and hand. When the Pope finally decided to silence this troublesome monk, it was too late. Martin Luther merely burned the papal bull (writing) in public and defiantly proceeded to the Reichstag in Worms. There he presented his views on April 18, 1521 to Emperor Charles V and to the leading German nobles, clergy and bourgeois in Germany. Luther held firmly to his views and asserted, "as long as I am not contradicted by the Holy Scripture or by clear reasoning, I will recant nothing since it is difficult and dangerous to act against one's conscience."

In order to protect this renegade with an enormous following in Germany, sympathizers captured him during his journey back to Wittenberg and took him to the Wartburg fortress outside of Eisenach. There he lived for a year under the as-

sumed name of "Junker Jörg" far away from the furious controversies of the day. In 1522 he completed a German translation of the New Testament. This was not the first translation of the Bible into German; over 170 handwritten ones in the same language had appeared in the Middle Ages, and since the invention of the movable type printing press there had been 14 previous High German (northern Germany) translations. But Luther, the scholar, was able to penetrate deeply into the Greek and "Vulgata" texts and produce a translation, which, as he himself said, forced the prophets and apostles to speak a comprehensible German. Only such a text could enable the Christian to read and understand the Bible on his own, without the guidance or interpretation of the Church. In 1534 he published his final translation of both the New and Old Testaments, which found its way into enthusiastic hands all over Germany. In this way, Luther's German became the standardized *High German* spoken by the educated in every corner of Germany. Although a multitude of dialects continue to be spoken in Germany, Luther gave a land that was fractured into many tiny splinters a common language, which is essential for any collection of people hoping to be called a nation.

His call for a liberation from the theological confines of Rome unleashed demands for change and other forms of liberation that seriously shook the social structure of Germany. In all of these conflicts, the ultimate victors were the German princes.

There was a rebellion of knights in 1522 led by Franz von Sickingen, about whose origins we shall read later. Compared with the growing bourgeoisie (middle-upper class), which was becoming more and more prosperous in the cities, the economic importance of that portion of the lower nobility that had also been knighted (barons, etc.) was steadily declining. Also, armored knights on horseback had become militarily obsolete since Swiss infantry armed with halberds (a wide-shaped axe on a long pole) had learned to decimate their opponents with relative ease. Because of this, Swiss foot soldiers, not knights, became the treasured military mercenaries in half of Europe. The knights had lost most of their income and all justification for existing. Their rebellion was a desperate attempt to turn the clock back in Germany, but the princes crushed it. The status of knighthood was thereby eliminated once and for all as a power factor in Europe.

Although the princes became powerful, the people also became more assertive. In 1524–5 an idealistic priest, Thomas Müntzer, led a futile revolt of poor artisans and day workers against the princes in order to establish a "Christendom of the poor." A far more serious convulsion occurred when thousands of German peasants, primarily in the southern part of Germany, revolted. This was the largest and most forceful revolution in the history of a people who have manifested very little attraction to revolutionary causes. Almost four centuries later, the professional Russian revolutionary, Vladimir Ilyich Lenin, remarked scornfully that if would-be German revolutionaries wished to storm a train station, they would first buy a ticket before setting foot on the platform.

Revolt

The peasants revolted against the remnants of serfdom that still bound many of them to the higher nobility. The nobles tended to despise all simple people who worked the land as persons without rights. The peasants resented the steady increase in payments and workdays owed to the lords, and they demanded protection for fishing and hunting rights, as well as a return to community use of much of the grazing and watering facilities the lords had simply appropriated for themselves. They demanded a reestablishment of earlier institutions, which had granted them some self-rule, and they insisted on a return to "the earlier justice," to German law, rather than Roman law. The lords preferred the latter because it denied peasants any freedom whatsoever.

Those who joined this revolt found in Luther's words about the "freedom of a Christian man" a divine justification for their goals and actions. Initially, Luther sympathized with the peasants' demands and encouraged the lords to take their pleas seriously. But when the bands of rebels began to attack fortresses and churches and to dispatch with bloody swiftness those who wielded earthly authority, Luther became furious and lashed out against those whom he accused of turning Germany into a battlefield.

When it came to "things belonging to Caesar," Luther did not hesitate to decide in favor of order and princely authority. His reaction to this social revolution and its ultimate cruel suppression had serious consequences for Germany. Peasants remained poor, despised, unfree and without political influence for almost 300 years, until reforms in the wake of the French Revolution finally eliminated the formal chains that had been placed on them. Perhaps more important, Luther's stand left a legacy of freedom in Germany, which was interpreted only as inner, purely mental freedom, but not political freedom. Thus, this man who had led the charge against the limits placed on man through Catholic theology actually justified external obedience to the princes and thereby strengthened the hierarchical political order within Germany. This helped to retard the victory of democracy within Germany until the middle of the 20th century. It even allowed some Germans who strongly disapproved of National Socialism (Nazism) after 1933 to remain within a brutal dictatorship, but nevertheless to persuade themselves that they could embark upon an "internal emigration."

The new Protestant faith spread quickly throughout northern Germany and Scandinavia. By 1555, about four-fifths of all Germans had embraced the new belief. In that year the Peace of Augsburg was reached, which recognized that the Protestant faith had an equal status with the Catholic and that each territorial prince and free city would decide which faith all residents under their control should practice. *Cuius regio, eius religio* ("whoever rules chooses the religion") was the formula for a kind of religious freedom that was restricted to the rulers. Those subjects who could not accept their rulers' preference had to move to another territory or city, and thousands of Germans did just that. Thus, the religious division of Germany was sealed for centuries.

The Time of Troubles

The Peace of Augsburg did not permanently settle the religious question in Germany. A Catholic counterreformation, set in motion in Rome and supported by the Hapsburg emperors, heated tensions between German Protestants and Catholics, who formed a Protestant Union and Catholic League in 1608 and 1609 respectively. All that was needed was a spark in Bohemia to ignite an almost indescribably destructive "Thirty Years War" on German soil that ravaged this weak and divided land from 1618 until 1648.

In the early years of the war the Catholic states, particularly Austria and Bavaria, won brilliant victories, penetrating northern Germany to the Baltic Sea and reconverting by the edge of the sword many Germans to Catholicism. Catholic successes stemmed largely from strong internal friction within the Protestant camp between Lutherans and Calvinists and from extraordinarily capable generals, Tilly and the dashing and overly ambitious Wallenstein.

These initial successes under Hapsburg leadership prompted other European powers to enter the war. It was soon obvious that this war was not even primarily a religious struggle for the souls of Germans. Fearing Hapsburg control over a strategically important part of the Baltic Sea, and noting suspiciously a Hapsburg alliance with Catholic Poland, the Danish king, Christian IV, and then the Swedish king, Gustavus Adolphus, took over leadership of the Protestant cause. They received financial support from England and Holland. More importantly, the Swedish king was able to receive aid from Catholic France, which was always determined to prevent the Hapsburgs from growing too strong, especially when in control of Spain as well as Austria.

Document signed in 1529 by Charles ("Carolus") V, the Holy Roman Emperor

Germany

Thus, Germany was crisscrossed by marauding foreign armies that lived off the land in a manner summarized by Wallenstein: "The war must feed the war." No door, wall or fortress could protect the civilian population from the armies that cut wide swaths through the countryside and cities, followed by hordes of often disease-ridden camp followers, and leaving a trail of wreckage, ashes and corpses behind them. Ironically, some of the powerful, comforting and assertive Lutheran hymns were written during this devastation. An example of how arbitrary such destruction could be was Rothenburg ob der Tauber, today one of Germany's most beautifully intact medieval cities. Field Marshal Tilly offered in 1631 to spare the town and its leaders only if one of the city councilmen could drink about a gallon of wine *in one draw*. The elderly mayor stepped forward and accomplished this incredible feat, thereby saving his city and colleagues.

The Treaty of Westphalia

Who won this 30-year nightmare? A quick glance at the Treaty of Westphalia in 1648 gives the answer. Sweden took control of the city of Wismar, the Dukedom of Bremen-Verden (except the city of Bremen), the islands of Rügen, Usedom and Wollin, and part of Pomerania, thereby depriving Germany of the outlets to the sea via the Elbe, Weser and Oder rivers. France got most of Alsace, the cities of Metz, Toul, Verdun, Breisach and the Rhine, and achieved protector status over ten German imperial cities. Germany's western border, which had existed since the 9th century, was thus fundamentally altered. Switzerland and the Netherlands were granted full independence from Germany.

The German princes' official right to determine the religious beliefs of all of their subjects was withdrawn, at least in theory. But the German princes were granted full sovereignty within their own territories, including the right to make treaties with foreign powers. The proviso that these treaties could not be directed against the emperor or the empire remained valid only on paper. Germany was left with almost 2,000 sovereign states ranging from the large territories of Brandenburg, Austria, Saxony and Bavaria, 83 free and imperial cities (including Hamburg and Frankfurt am Main), countless ecclesiastical and other small units, some of which included as few as about 2,000 inhabitants. The map of Germany now looked more than ever before like the face of a child with measles. At a time when centralizing, centripetal forces were at work in England and France, centrifugal forces were prevailing in Germany, throwing it farther and farther away from national

Contemporary drawings of the Thirty Years War

unity. There could no longer be any serious talk of "imperial politics."

Germany was left breathless, devastated and demoralized from the plunder and destruction. In some areas such as Württemberg, the Palatinate, Thuringia and Mecklenburg, two-thirds of the inhabitants had been eradicated, and overall losses in Germany ranged from a third to a half of the total population. The total population dropped from about 20 million to 10–14 million. Thus, Germany, which at the beginning of the 17th century had the largest number of inhabitants in all of Europe, fell behind that of France for the next century and a half and behind

that of Russia to the present day. It was more than a century before it reached its pre-1618 level. In addition to human deaths, 1,600 cities and 18,000 villages had been totally demolished, and livestock, farmland and the rest of the economic infrastructure had been left in shambles. In comparative terms, the destruction to Germany was far greater in 1648 than in 1945. One could say that only an atomic war could produce comparable damage today.

Alien Forces Move In; Germans Leave for America

It is not surprising that the Turkish Ottomans and the French took advantage of

Germany's plight to try to enrich themselves further. While Prince Eugene of Savoy was able to stop the Turkish invasion at the gates of Vienna in 1683, the French were far more successful under King Louis XIV to acquire what Cardinal Richelieu called *une entrée en Allemagne* ("a gateway into Germany"). In several campaigns France snatched about 600 cities, villages and fortresses in Alsace. It took Strasbourg and a large tract of territory between Alsace and Lake Geneva, and its decision to "burn the Palatinate" left such lasting traces as the ruins of Heidelberg Castle.

One of the many consequences of the seemingly perpetual war and religious strife in this era was that many beleaguered sects, such as the Mennonites, Quakers and Dunkers, decided to seek their peace and happiness in the New World. There they could escape the political and religious hierarchy, as well as the earthly corruption into which the European nobility had apparently fallen. The first German immigrants to America tended to settle in New York, Maryland and Virginia, but in 1681 William Penn established the first religiously free state in Pennsylvania. The German exodus to

Pennsylvania began with 13 Mennonite families from Krefeld in Westphalia, who landed in Philadelphia on October 6, 1683, a day still celebrated in some parts of the United States as "German Day." They created Germantown on the outskirts of Philadelphia. They were followed by the Moravians, so-called because they came from the Hapsburg province of Moravia, and the Amish (erroneously called Pennsylvania "Dutch") from the area of Bern, Switzerland, who have retained to this day, in large part, most aspects of a life style characteristic of pious Germans in the 17th century, including the Bern dialect of German.

Not all Germans found in America the "quiet, honest and God-fearing life" of which they had dreamed, but their reports back to Germany helped open the flood gates for further waves of refugees from religious persecution in the 18th century. One Protestant group from the area of Brunswick set sail in 1707 for New York, but unfavorable winds forced them to land in Philadelphia. They decided to settle in New Jersey, which in 1733 became the home of an immigrant named Johann Peter Rockefeller, who founded what later became one of the richest families in the

world. By 1776 there were more than 250,000 Germans living in the thirteen colonies. Germany's religious quarrels were America's gain.

It was at this time that one of the most durable legends in Germany was born. To this day many German pupils learn in school that in the early years of the American republic a vote was taken in Congress to determine which language the nation should officially adopt, and German lost by only one vote. That deciding vote was supposedly cast by the Speaker of the House of Representatives, Frederick Augustus Conrad Muehlenberg, himself a German immigrant.

The fact is that no such vote was ever taken, either in Congress or in the Pennsylvania legislature (1828 according to another myth) or any other state legislature. The misunderstanding stemmed from a petition presented to Congress in January 1794 by a group of Germans from Virginia demanding that laws be translated into German for the benefit of the large German population. The appropriate committee rejected the proposal by a vote of 42 to 41. As Speaker, Muehlenberg abstained, but he proclaimed afterwards: "The sooner Germans become Americans, the better."

Even though German was never to be the leading language in America, the Germans introduced many words into the American vocabulary: angst, blitz, dachshund, delicatessen, flak, frankfurter, glitz, hamburger, hinterland, kaput, kindergarten, kitsch, leitmotiv, pretzel, realpolitik, rucksack, sauerkraut, schadenfreude, wunderkind, zeitgeist and zigzag among hundreds of others.

Movement to the Northeast

By the middle of the 17th century, the Germans had been reduced largely to mere spectators and objects of European politics. However, the next 50 years saw this situation change; a highly dynamic state arose on the sandy soil in the Eastern part of the empire, which forced its way into the ranks of world powers by sheer force of will, hard work and discipline: Prussia.

Before the 12th century Germany had consisted of two basic parts: a Romanized Germany west of the Rhine and south of the Danube and a Germanic territory east and north. After the 12th century a third part began to take shape: in the Slavic and Baltic East which came to include Mecklenburg, Brandenburg, Pomerania, Upper Silesia and East Prussia. This development involved the often-violent conquest of Slavs and Balts and the partial absorption of these peoples. With the conquest and colonization of the East, the Empire's center of gravity slowly began to move eastward.

The extremely fragmented Holy Roman Empire after the Treaty of Westphalia: 1648

Germany

The motives of those Germans moving east were by no means nationalistic, but rather materialistic and idealistic. German farmers sought land and more independence from their earlier masters; noblemen wanted to open new ground and to gain income from it; skilled craftsmen and businessmen sought new opportunities and markets. However, none of these desires could have been fulfilled if another powerful motive had not been at work as well: the Christianizing of "heathen" peoples.

Medieval Knights

The Crusades that began at the end of the 11th century sparked the imagination of a class of persons that had begun to emerge before the 10th century: the knights. Warfare had been revolutionized in such a way that foot soldiers were replaced by well-armed knights who often fought on horseback. Therefore, the high nobility required knights to live in their vicinity or in fortresses or estates that the lords placed at their disposal. Most of the knights in the earlier days were not of noble birth, so they attempted to make up for their humble status by developing certain virtues such as bravery, courage, loyalty and consistency. The highest virtue was moderation in every situation but battle.

One of Friedrich Barbarossa's sons founded a "German Order of Knights" in 1198, whose mission at first was to care for pilgrims and crusaders in the Holy Lands. It soon joined the active military struggles against the Islamic disbelievers who had laid an allegedly unjust claim to the Holy City of Jerusalem. The Order took in both knights, priests and other brothers who could perform useful services, and its uniform was a white cloak with a black cross on it. Their rules were as strict as those in a monastic order. Since they saw themselves as fully dedicated to the service of Christ, they did not marry. They were also forbidden to own property and swore to maintain absolute loyalty and personal poverty.

The Rise of Prussia

Less than a quarter of a century after the Order was founded, its sights were cast in an entirely different geographic direction. A Polish duke, Conrad of Masovia, asked for the Order's help in 1226 to assist in crushing a hardy tribe of "heathens" called "Prussians." This was a Baltic people related to the Lithuanians and Latvians and regarded by Germans and Poles alike as barbarians. They had no written language, but they had strange customs such as polygamy and placing unwanted babies out to die. The conquest and Christianizing of such a tribe received the bless-

The German Order of Knights at its pinnacle

ing of the Pope and the approval of the Holy Roman Emperor. With such encouragement and advancement under the call of "Death to Disbelievers," this conquest was bound to be a cruel one.

The German Order crossed the Vistula River in 1231 in order to engage the Prussians. Not until 1283 was the bloody job completed and the entire territory from the Vistula to the farthest border of East Prussia (that portion of Prussia east of the Vistula estuary) brought under the Order's control. The struggle had devastated much of the land and almost completely eradicated the Prussian tribe. The remnants were converted to Christianity upon the threat of death and were ultimately absorbed by the German conquerors. Their language disappeared completely, and all that remained of them was the name "Prussia," by which the territory came to be known and which became the official name of the state in 1701.

It created a holy republic over the land, and in 1309 the Order's Supreme Master, who was elected by the other knights, moved his seat from Venice to the fortress of Marienburg in Prussia (now in Poland). From there commands were issued to fortresses and cities throughout the entire area. It became a German-led, rigidly organized land administered by the knights,

who since they were forbidden to own property, possess wealth or marry, were more like ascetic civil servants than feudal lords. They directed the systematic colonization of the land and were responsible for the establishment of more than 1,000 villages and 100 cities, including the major ones, Danzig (now Gdansk in Poland), Elbing and Königsberg (now Kaliningrad in Russia). Until well into the 15th century, the history of Prussia is the history of colonization, and in some areas this was more violent than in others.

Nowhere were the Slavic or Baltic populations forced to move, and Germans, Slavs and Balts lived side by side, although in most places Germans occupied the key political and economic positions. The nobility and bourgeoisie were predominantly German, but the agricultural population was mixed. This condition continued more or less to exist until Hitler and Stalin launched massive exterminations and expulsions in the 20th century to homogenize the ethnic composition in these areas.

The German Order of Knights reached its pinnacle in the 14th century, but its hold over the area was broken in the 15th century. Poles and Lithuanians attacked Prussia in 1410 and delivered the knights a crushing defeat on a wet and stormy day in the woods of Tannenberg. This was the first major military defeat the Order had ever suffered, and sensing the way the wind was blowing, many German noblemen sided with the Poles. Only Marienburg remained unconquered, but new battles eventually drove the Order out of all the area except East Prussia, which in 1466 became a tributary of Poland. The Order was compelled to swear loyalty to Poland.

One area in the German East that had resisted domination by the Poles was the Elector Principality of Brandenburg, a relatively insignificant, poor and backward territory on the periphery of the German Empire, and ruled by a dynasty from southern Germany, the Hohenzollerns. Brandenburg and East Prussia had become linked in 1525. Taking advantage of the severe turmoil caused by the Reformation, the last Supreme Master of the German Order, Albrecht von Brandenburg-Ansbach from the family of Hohenzollern, simply assumed in 1525 the earthly title of "Duke of Prussia," and in 1660 the last ties that bound East Prussia to Poland were severed.

The Hohenzollern dynasty, which had made its residence in Berlin and whose heartland remained Brandenburg, was able to gain control of West Prussia, Pomerania and Silesia, and ultimately it acquired huge chunks of territory in the Rhineland and Westphalia as well. From a poor land known derisively as "the sandbox of the Empire" with no raw materials and a population of little over a million persons grew a huge and powerful kingdom ultimately embracing about two-thirds of all Germans and serving as the foundation for the first truly unified German Empire in 1871.

Perhaps more than any other European state, Prussia did not evolve, but was made by the human hand. A series of extraordinarily able rulers in the 17th and 18th centuries enabled Prussia to rise like a meteor to the ranks of the major European powers. From 1640 to 1688, Friedrich Wilhelm, "the Great Elector," laid the cornerstone for a powerful Prussia. He had spent three years in the Netherlands during his youth, and there he had been deeply influenced by the Calvinist dynamism and sense of obligation. He married a woman from the ruling House of Orange. From the Thirty Years War he had drawn the lesson that his state needed to enhance its military prowess. He said "Alliances are good, but one's own power is even better; one can more safely depend on that." He therefore enlarged the Prussian army from 3,000 to 30,000 soldiers.

He also established an oft-forgotten Prussian tradition which lasted for a century and a half and which was both humanitarian and strengthened Prussia.

When the French king invalidated the Edict of Nantes in 1685, which had granted considerable religious and civil liberty to the Huguenots (French Protestants), Friedrich Wilhelm responded with the Edict of Potsdam opening the Prussian gates to the religiously persecuted. More than 20,000 French Huguenots, most of them skilled craftsmen and businessmen, poured into Prussia, and by the year 1700 one out of three residents of Berlin was French. Far from attempting to Germanize these newcomers, foreigners were permitted to retain their own language and customs.

The Huguenots built their own schools and churches and powerfully contributed to the arts and to the vibrant economic life of Prussia. Many of the area's greatest names until the present day are of French origin. More than 20,000 Protestants from Salzburg fled the Counter-Reformation and in the course of the 18th century there was a steady stream of emigrants and religious refugees to Prussia: Mennonites, Scottish Presbyterians, Jews and sometimes Catholics. In some ways, Prussia in the 18th century was to the persecuted of Europe what America was in the 19th century: a religiously tolerant land that offered enormous opportunities to the talented and hardworking.

Prussia Becomes a Center of Culture

Friedrich I ascended to the throne in 1688. He was a well-educated and cultured man who maintained a glittering, but excessively extravagant court. He established another Prussian tradition that is also frequently overlooked today: he established Prussia, especially Berlin, as a leading home for science and the arts. He founded the Academies of Art and Science, and he ordered the building of many edifices, such as the Charlotte burg Palace, which changed the face of Berlin from that of a peripheral and provincial town to that of one of the most dignified cities in Europe. He also achieved through patient and skillful diplomacy an important political goal: in 1701 he won the emperor's approval for the Prussian Elector to bear the title of "king." This was a considerable boost for the prestige of a still poor country on the outskirts of the German Empire.

The Soldier King

When Friedrich Wilhelm I (so numbered because the earlier Friedrich Wilhelm had not been a king), was crowned in 1713, Prussia gained a ruler who was capable, but greatly different from his predecessor. What one now most often associates with Prussia was largely due to the new king's influence: the spirit of Spartan simplicity and the conscientious fulfillment of one's obligations to the state,

which was to be ruled by the king alone, but for the good of the subjects. As he told his son, "The dear Lord placed you on the throne, not in order to be lazy, but in order to work and to rule his lands well." He discarded the luxurious court life his father had conducted to compete with the glittering courts of France and Austria, and introduced an austere court. He also created a first-rate civil service staffed by duty-conscious, highly respected, but poorly paid officials.

His popular name, "the Soldier King," indicates where his primary attention was paid. Although during his entire reign he led his country into only one short war, he poured four-fifths of all state income into the army, whose size he doubled to 70,000 men. The stunningly rapid growth of the Prussian army in size and importance prompted the Frenchman Mirabeau to remark shortly after the death of Friedrich Wilhelm I: "Other states possess an army; Prussia is an army that possesses a state!"

Located in the middle of Europe with a conglomeration of often-unconnected territories and no natural frontiers and a relatively small population, Prussia had to have a strong army to maintain itself in the kind of international setting that prevailed at that time. One could argue the Prussian army was disproportionately large in relation to the country's population and financial strength. But it must be remembered that the new army was still considerably smaller than those of Austria, France and Russia and that "militarism" was by no means restricted to Prussia during this "Age of Absolutism." Further, the Prussian army never "possessed" the state, as Mirabeau charged. It was the most disciplined army in the world and never made the slightest attempt to rule the state.

The army was, without a doubt, first rate. Carlyle once wrote that Prussia had a shorter sword than Austria, France and Russia, but that it could draw it out of the sheath much more quickly. It was open to the newest military technology. Also, the Prussian army became more and more a national army and less and less a mercenary army. Prussia was one of the first countries in the world to learn that its own citizens serve better than the troops of a foreign country. Its discipline and well-planned supply system was also a blessing for the civilian population in those areas where the army operated. In an age of undisciplined armies that "lived off the land," the civilian population was constantly subjected to plunder, murder and rape. Civilians seldom needed to fear such horrors from the new Prussian army.

Friedrich Wilhelm I was interested solely in establishing the best-organized, most modern and efficient state and mili-

Germany

tary in the world. Unlike his father and his son, he was utterly disinterested in art and education. This brought him into violent conflict with his son. The father was a stern ruler who was wholly absorbed in enhancing his state's power. In 1758 his son, who in 1740 had become King Friedrich II, wrote this about his father: "Books, flutes, writings—if he could ever get his hands on them, they were thrown into the fireplace, and the burning of my books was always accompanied by several blows or by very emphatic rebukes."

Friedrich "The Great"

The son was a sensitive, highly intelligent humanist, who composed flute concertos, which are still played in concerts, and who preferred all his life to use the French language. He even wrote thoroughly respectable poetry and essays in French. Most of his writings, which now fill 25 volumes, are in French rather than German, which he never learned to write without numerous mistakes. He was a close friend of the French philosopher and satirist Voltaire, whom he invited for prolonged visits to Berlin and Potsdam. In general, the young Friedrich was open to all the cultural, philosophical and liberal political ideas of his day. He was an enlightened man with a strong sense of taste, as his favorite residence in Potsdam, Sans Souci (French for "carefree") manifested his nature. He despised the absolutist government of his father, even if it was aimed for the good of the people. Once, at age 18, he even tried to flee his father's kingdom with a close friend, but they were caught and delivered back to an irate parent and placed in prison.

What should his father have done? Have the heir to the throne and his friend both hanged for treason? Disregard the law of the land and forgive both for a treasonous act? The father's solution: he had the friend executed for treason right in front of Friedrich's eyes. This paradoxical mixture of strict justice, mercy and reason of state has troubled many people ever since.

Finally, at the age of 28, Friedrich II ascended to the throne in 1740. The young king's reaction to this event was characteristic: "How I abhor this job to which the blind coincidence of birth has condemned me!" Many persons saw in the new king the first philosopher to ascend a throne since the Roman Emperor Marcus Aurelius. Friedrich announced, "any man who seeks the truth and loves it, must be treasured in any human society." Within the first week of his rule, he abolished torture in all cases but high treason. Throughout his 48-year reign, he demanded of every subject a strict performance of his duty. But he was always inclined to permit any-

Voltaire's room at Sans Souci

thing else that did not directly hurt the interests of the state. This tolerance was applied not only to religious practices and intellectual and artistic pursuits, but to personal behavior as well. For instance, when a case was reported to him of a cavalry officer who was caught committing a heinous act of sodomy upon his horse, Friedrich merely ordered that the poor man be transferred to the infantry.

After Friedrich became king, he for all practical purposes put his flute away forever. Before he had been crowned, he had referred to a military uniform as "a gown of death," but afterwards he was scarcely ever seen wearing anything else. His transformation from a sensitive humanist

to "the first servant of the state," as he later called himself, is one of the intriguing mysteries of history. Few would have ever guessed in 1740 that he would become known as "Friedrich the Great" as a result of his leadership.

As king, he had become a lonesome figure with a tortured soul, inwardly unhappy, but restlessly active, working 18 hours per day. He was always unkempt and ungrounded, and he loved nobody and was loved by nobody. He had especially troubled relations with women and preferred the company of men in his beloved Sans Souci palace in Potsdam. Against his will, he was pressured by his family to marry Elisabeth Christine von

186

Braunschweig. He relented, but no sooner was the ceremony over than he packed her off to a separate palace and saw her only a few times the rest of his life. It need not be said that their marriage was childless.

The first half of his reign was a time of almost constant war, which at times seemed to threaten his country's very existence, but which in the end elevated Prussia to the rank of a great European power. The newly crowned king had just published an elegant attack on Machiavelli's immorality and duplicity in politics; within weeks Friedrich unleashed an unprovoked and unjustified attack on Austrian-owned Silesia. Certainly he was no more unscrupulous than most other rulers of the time, but in this and in almost all other wars during his reign, justice happened to be on the side of his enemies.

Friedrich later said that he had started what was known as "The War of the Austrian Succession" because "the satisfaction of seeing my name in the newspapers and later in history had seduced me." However, one should not take very seriously such remarks made by a cynic such as Friedrich. What really motivated him was a unique opportunity: in the same year he had become king (1740), a young and politically inexperienced woman, Maria-Theresia, had ascended the Austrian throne. He calculated that she would not have known how to respond to such a brazen act on Prussia's part. There were few Austrian troops in Silesia, so the venture promised to be a military cakewalk.

Perhaps surprisingly, the young Austrian empress rejected Friedrich's ultimatum to withdraw from the province, so the latter unleashed his troops in late 1740. The two armies clashed in furious battle at Mollwitz, and things looked so hopeless for the Prussians that the young ruler actually fled from the battlefield, an offense normally punishable by death. But he was saved by a Prussian victory later that day. Ultimately, two campaigns were necessary to secure Prussian domination of Silesia, and by also taking a substantial portion of land from the Poles, Friedrich was able to unite East and West Prussia into a single territory.

Friedrich tried to justify his action in 1743: "I hope those who will later judge me . . . will be able to differentiate in me the philosopher from the prince, the honorable man from the politician. I must confess that whoever is dragged into the mess (*Getriebe*) of high-level European politics finds it very difficult to preserve his own character frankly and honestly." He wrote that the art of politics appears in many ways "as the opposite of private morality. However, it is the morality of the princes, who . . . do only that which promises to be to their advantage." The Prince had no alternative to "following the practice which authorizes deceit and the abuse of power."

His qualms were not such that he could resist the temptation in 1756 to swoop into Saxony and thereby to become embroiled in the "Seven-Years War" with Austria, which lasted until 1763. Friedrich's troops met with initial success. He published Maria-Theresia's secret plans that were found in the Saxon state archives, which the Prussian troops had captured. These plans showed that the Austrian empress was by no means above duplicity when her state's interests were at stake.

This war provided clear examples of the extent to which the fate of whole nations depended at that time upon the personal preferences and whims of their absolutist rulers. When the Russian Tsarina Elizabeth, the daughter of Tsar Peter the Great, was informed that Friedrich had cracked a joke about her at the dinner table in Sans Souci, she exploded with rage, and joined Austria, France, Bavaria and Saxony in a war against Prussia. Her decision almost dashed Friedrich's kingdom to its destruction. Soon the Russians were at the gates of Königsberg, the French were approaching the Elbe, and the Austrians reentered Silesia. Friedrich tirelessly led his almost hopelessly outnumbered troops from one edge of his kingdom to the other, meeting first one enemy and then another. He was imaginative and bold, and his administration in Potsdam, which his predecessors had built up, worked like a perfectly constructed and oiled machine.

Though he received money from England, which as usual was very interested in weakening France, the Prussians stood alone against all the great European continental powers. Friedrich's army had lost almost all of its artillery by late 1760. Berlin had fallen to the enemy and En-

Friedrich the Great

Germany

gland had stopped sending money to a ruler so near to defeat. But in early 1762 a wonder occurred when Tsarina Elizabeth died. Her successor was Peter III, a glowing admirer of Friedrich the Great. He not only left the enemy coalition, but he entered into an alliance with Prussia, thereby saving that country from certain defeat. Peter III was assassinated a year later, and his wife, who was later called Catherine the Great, quickly withdrew Russia from the war entirely. But by that time Austria was physically and financially exhausted and had to sue for peace in 1763.

Peace for 23 Years

In the Peace of Hubertusburg, the situation seemed to revert to that which it had been prior to the start of the conflict, with Prussia retaining Silesia and East Prussia, and with Saxon independence being reestablished. But in reality this was a great triumph for Prussia. By maintaining itself successfully against three great powers in Europe, it won recognition as a great power in its own right. Prussia also learned that good relations with Russia were absolutely essential, and until 1890 such relations remained a primary goal of every Prussian leader.

After the war's end, Prussia under Friedrich the Great enjoyed 23 years of peace. Prussia was able, however, to continue to enlarge itself by participating in the partition of Poland with Russia and

Austria. Seeing that Russia was perfectly willing to intervene militarily in Poland in order to prevent any strengthening of the Polish state, Friedrich suggested the first partition in 1772. Maria-Theresia had serious qualms about such a dastardly act of political immorality, and Friedrich gleefully reported later, "she wept, but she took." In 1793 and 1795 these three powers partitioned Poland again, creating a potentially dangerous domestic political situation within Prussia by rendering the Poles a majority of all inhabitants within the borders of Prussia.

Friedrich II was one of the most brilliant military leaders of all time. It has been said that one of Adolf Hitler's favorite films was one about Friedrich the Great. It can only be considered unfortunate that one obvious lesson Hitler learned from the Hohenzollern ruler's almost miraculous victory in 1763, despite overwhelming material and manpower superiority of the enemy coalition and crushing military defeats, was that an iron will and bitter determination not to surrender can ultimately carry the day. His tragic attempt to repeat Friedrich's feat almost two centuries later brought scarcely describable death and misery to Germany, its people and its neighbors.

Friedrich II was called "the Great" during his own lifetime. This was not only because of his wars and his successful, if sometimes morally questionable, foreign policy, but also because of his reforms, his

intellectual and cultural achievements as a young man, and the kind of state he helped to create. The Prussian state was feared by its neighbors because it was militarily strong and prepared and because of its qualities as a state. It had an uncorrupted administration, an independent judiciary, and a state of law (*Rechtsstaat*) in which there was more legal equality for all citizens than could be found in most other European states at the time. Journalists could write relatively freely, although Friedrich did have a newspaperman beaten who once wrote uncomplimentary things about the king.

Prussia's tolerance toward all religions was considered in Europe to be a very bad example during most of the 17th and 18th centuries. It was also very tolerant toward the different nationalities within its own borders and toward enlightened learning of all kinds. By the standards of the 18th century, which are those that should be used to judge the state ruled by Friedrich the Great, Prussia was a modern and enlightened state. It was certainly no democracy, but enlightenment in politics at first meant basing the affairs of state on reason. Such manifested itself in Europe initially in the form of absolutism, and France under Cardinal Richelieu was an early model. Not until the French Revolution, when a brand of enlightenment which stresses human rights and popular sovereignty and when the call of "liberty, equality and fraternity" caught fire in Europe

Middle Europe in 1740 when Maria Theresia (22) became Empress of Austria and Friedrich the Great (28), King of Prussia

Legend:
- First partition (1772)
- Second partition (1793)
- Third partition (1795)

BALTIC SEA

RUSSIA

PRUSSIA

EAST PRUSSIA

Warsaw

AUSTRIA

Poland: A Land Devoured

(outside Holland and England), was Prussia challenged by a state and by ideas that were clearly more modern than its own. Indeed, after Friedrich's death in 1786, the newly risen Prussia had only two more decades before it crumbled in the face of Napoleon's France.

The years 1789 to 1815 were for the German states years of unrest, of war, but also of almost unparalleled genius, talent and productivity in literature and philosophy. It was a time of openness to new ideas, including political ones.

Admiration of America

The American Revolution had sparked the imagination of many literate Germans. The Americans were celebrated as the "Hellenes of our time," who, by challenging the exclusive rule of the "breed of the nobility," had shown feudal Europe the way to "sweet equality." The greatest German poet of all time was Johann Wolfgang von Goethe, who along with Friedrich Schiller was the greatest exponent of both the impetuous Storm and Stress (a literary age when writers rebelled against the restraints of classicism and the enlighten-

ment) and of the restrained Classical period in German literature during the second half of the 18th and early part of the 19th centuries. Goethe wrote in *Poetry and Truth* that the youthful United States was "a magnificent country," "a magnet for the eyes of the whole world." He wrote: "America, your lot is fairer than ours."

In 1781 Friedrich Klopstock wrote a hymn to the new nation entitled "The Present War." It said, *inter alia*, "You are the rose dawn of a great new day . . . that will last for centuries." Two years later an anonymous poet gave expression to the popular feeling: "The nations of all Europe will respond with echoes of this holy victory."

While many Germans were inspired by the American ideas and events, it was the French Revolution in 1789 that brought the spark of democratic revolution to Europe. Prussia had been a state well-ordered from above; France was now a nation whose most powerful inspiration came from below—from the people. Revolutionary France was able to fuse ideals, whose force had already been put into practice in America, with national power

to an extent that no country on the continent of Europe could resist. The French Revolution was a declaration of war against the old Europe. To underscore this, French revolutionary leaders promised in the early years of the revolution to help any people that rose up against despotic rulers, and Napoleon's Grand Army later carried the message through the heart of Europe and all the way to Moscow.

Napoleon—Admired and Despised

Some leading Germans greeted Napoleon and the French Revolution. The philosopher Friedrich Hegel called this mighty convulsion "the end of history," while his compatriot Immanuel Kant admired the idealism of the French masses as did Friedrich Schiller, whose admiration, like that of many others, diminished when the guillotine began doing its grisly work. Goethe went to meet Napoleon in Erfurt, where the masses and princes greeted the Frenchman with such flattery and servility that Talleyrand wrote disgustedly: "They kiss the hand which could destroy them today or tomorrow." In Germany, Napoleonic power was recognized and, for one reason or another, respected. Wherever it was not, Napoleon sent his armies, and by 1807 all German states had been compelled one by one to make peace with France.

French domination over most of Germany brought an enormous territorial reshuffling at the expense of the smaller territories, which he eliminated. He abolished all religious rule over sovereign territories, gave the medium-sized states more territory and elevated Bavaria and Wurttemberg to kingdoms. In 1806 he grouped 16 medium-sized states, including Bavaria, Wurttemberg and Baden into a Rhenish League with one of Napoleon's brothers as the monarch, all under French protection. They were obligated to supply 64,000 troops to Napoleon, who assumed control over their armies. All were compelled to declare their exit from the German Empire, which thereby lost a third of its territory. This, combined with Napoleon's defeat of the Austrians and Russians at the battle of Austerlitz, 60 miles (100 kilometers) north of Vienna in 1806, spelled the end of the German Empire, which had existed for almost 1,000 years, although it had been weak and very divided. Shortly thereafter, Emperor Franz II cast off the German imperial crown, and the Holy Roman Empire of the Germans came to an end.

Napoleon's objective was clear: he wished to create states in Germany that were strong enough to support France but too weak to constitute a threat to it. The French occupiers were loved no-

Germany

Napoleon on campaign

where in Germany, and French rule was absolute, in the sense that all orders came from above. Yet it was in some respects very progressive and liberal. Everyone was equal before the law, class privileges were reduced or abolished, schools were taken over by the state, the legal systems were simplified and the churches' active hand in politics was reduced or eliminated. This liberal influence was most lasting in the Rhineland, where it henceforth always outweighed the absolutist tradition.

Prussia had made peace with Napoleon in 1795. This gave it a decade without war, but also permitted Napoleon a free hand in Germany. When Prussia finally had to act against France, it stood alone. At first Napoleon had been friendly toward Prussia in order to keep it out of any coalition directed against France. There was no need for such friendliness once Austria had been defeated, so Napoleon simply marched his troops through Prussia. When the Prussian king, Friedrich Wilhelm III, protested this, Napoleon unleashed his armies against Prussia, delivering humiliating defeats in the battles of Saalfeld, Jena, Auerstädt and Friedland.

At the end of October 1806 Napoleon led his troops into Berlin, where he declared his continental blockade against England. He also helped himself, as he did in every land he dominated, to art treasures, including the four horses on top of the Brandenburg Gate, and shipped them off to Paris. In the summer of 1807 Prussia was compelled to join France and Russia in the Peace of Tilset. This peace treaty permitted Prussia to continue existing as a state, but it lost half its territory, including all Prussian lands west of the Elbe, and was compelled to provide France with money and troops. In short order, Prussia had been reduced to an insignificant country completely in the hands of Napoleon.

Partial Reform

After this devastating defeat, the Prussian king declared that the Prussian state must replace through intellectual and cultural strength what it had lost in material strength. He knew that Prussia had to reform and modernize itself, so he appointed such men as Karl vom und zu Stein, Karl August von Hardenberg, Neidhart von Gneisenau, Gerhard von Scharnhorst and Wilhelm von Humboldt to make all Prussian citizens, in von Gneisenau's words, "free, noble and independent so that they believe that they are part of the whole."

Prussia now experienced a burst of reform activity, brought to a head by the misery of defeat. The overall strength of that country seemed to indicate the strength of the new ideas coming out of France. The social, political, military and educational reforms were not sufficiently democratic in the modern sense, and some of them were undone after 1815. But they were without a doubt steps in the right direction, and they aroused much enthusiasm throughout Germany at the time.

Serfdom was abolished, although the serfs were obliged to pay for their emancipation by incurring debts or by ceding much of land they had tilled to the former landowners. Thus, many Junker (aristocratic landholder) estates actually grew larger, and many former serfs became landless agricultural workers whose lot in life had improved very little, especially since the landowners still maintained control over police and the lower-level judiciary within their districts. Still, it was an important turning point which allowed peasants to win back much of what they had lost in 1525. Noblemen were allowed to practice bourgeois professions, such as law and commerce, and the bourgeoisie was permitted to acquire former knightly estates. Also, Jews were granted social and economic equality, though they still did not gain equal political rights.

The cities were given a greater measure of self-rule in that public officials were to be elected by all property owners. Right into the 20th century, local government in Prussia was admired throughout Europe, even though it stood in sharp contrast to the semi-absolutism in the countryside.

General von Scharnhorst wrote in 1798, "we will not be able to win battles until we learn like the Jacobins to awaken the community spirit." The model was the new French army, and the goal was to create an army motivated by patriotic spirit. All degrading punishments were abolished. Universal military service was introduced "to unify the army and the nation," and foreigners were no longer permitted to serve. Ability was to become the sole criterion for advancement, so the officer ranks were opened up more to non-noblemen. The change was slow, but the percentage of commoners in the officer corps rose from 7% in 1806 to 21% by 1848.

The farsighted minister of culture, Wilhelm von Humboldt, introduced educational reforms aimed at opening up the system to the talented from all classes. Elementary schools were created for all, and humanistic high schools (each called a *Gymnasium*) were created for those destined to rise to higher positions. In 1810 the University of Berlin was created. This was the first university in Germany to combine free research and teaching, and it was permitted to administer itself in order to guarantee it continuing freedom.

From 1807 until 1812, the Germans experienced a peace that was really more like a slow preparation for war. In 1812 the great part of Napoleon's Grand Army, which at the time included some 30,000 Bavarians, 30,000 Austrians and 20,000 Prussians, froze in the snows of Russia. German statesmen stuck their wet political fingers in the air and began to make secret preparations for a change of alliances. Napoleon feared that the worst was ahead of him. In mid-1813 he called the Austrian Chancellor Metternich to his headquarters in Dresden and announced that he "would not withdraw from a single inch of territory. . . . I was brought up on the battlefield, and a man like me worries little about the lives of a million persons." Metternich asked icily why he said such a thing behind closed doors instead of announcing it from one end of France to the other. Napoleon replied: "It may cost me my throne, but I will bury the world underneath its rubble." Just 132 years later another defeated dictator who had brought war and destruction to all of Europe would say the very same thing from an underground bunker in Berlin.

Within four months after his meeting with Metternich, Napoleon's hold on Germany, Italy and Spain had been broken. Napoleon suffered a crushing defeat in late 1813 at the "Battle of the Nations" near Leipzig, a battle that brought a scarcely believable carnage: 70,000 Frenchmen and 52,000 allies lost their lives. On March 31, 1814, the Russian tsar and the Prussian king marched into Paris at the head of their troops. The following year an English army under Wellington and a Prussian army under Generals Blücher and Gneisenau played the key roles in defeating Napoleon once and for all at Waterloo.

Napoleon's occupation of Germany was not a total disaster—he left the German nation far less fragmented than it had been before—about 300 German states, cities and territories had been joined into 50, and the Vienna Congress would reduce that number even further. This paved the way for a united and aggressive Germany in the future. The French also brought a valuable reform impulse.

As in 1918 and 1919, it was most unfortunate that democratic ideas had been brought into Germany by the troops of an alien occupation power. The French Revolution therefore ultimately created in the minds of many influential Germans considerable enmity toward France and toward democratic ideas. Initially, some leading Germans greeted this momentous event, and in Mainz a revolutionary republic inspired by France was established briefly. However, the excesses of the Revolution became increasingly visible and it progressed from civil war within France to an international struggle for power, largely on German soil. These excesses led some important Germans, such as Goethe and Schiller, to reject revolution as a valid means of change, and it therefore strengthened the traditional German allergy toward revolution. The bloody excesses in France also led many to doubt that the French Revolution was in fact a step in the direction of eliminating political tyranny and social injustice.

The French occupation of Germany also spawned German nationalism by enabling persons in all parts of Germany to put aside some of their local patriotism and to struggle side by side to rid Germany of a foreign power. From then on, German nationalism became an increasingly important factor. Since no unified German state yet existed, German nationalism took on an idealistic and romantic character. Also, since it was born in reaction to a conqueror who seemed to understand how to achieve French national interests under the cover of high-sounding calls for "liberty, equality and fraternity," German nationalism and the struggle against alien rule became linked in the minds of far too many Germans with resistance against the ideals of the French

The Rhenish League, or *Confederation of the Rhine*

Germany

Revolution, known in Germany as the "ideas of 1789."

This unfortunate link helped conservative rulers throughout Germany to water down or undo reforms Napoleon had introduced or promised before 1815. It also established in many German minds a strong resistance, which lasted until at least 1945, to the ideas of democracy, equality, civil rights, popular sovereignty, mass participation in politics and representative government legitimized by the consent of the governed.

The Congress of Vienna

The statesmen at the Congress of Vienna were tired of revolution and were interested in restoring much of which had existed a quarter of a century earlier. None wanted a unified Germany and none wanted the dissolution of his own state. Their chief objective was to protect Europe from a renewal of the kinds of shocks and challenges that had come out of France. None talked of popular sovereignty, but all spoke of legitimate monarchy. In the end, Prussia gave up some land to a newly created Kingdom of Poland, but received the northern part of Saxony, Swedish Pomerania and the island of Rügen, as well as territory in the Rhineland and Westphalia. These new territories were separated from the rest of Prussia by Hanover, Brunswick and Hesse-Cassel, but they placed it along a common border with France. Its job was one that was earlier performed by Austria—to prevent France, whose 1789 borders remained practically unchanged, from threatening Central Europe. As a result of the settlement, Prussia grew into Germany, while Austria grew out of Germany toward Northern Italy and the Balkans. The mineral resources in Upper Silesia and the Rhineland provided Prussia with the potential to become the greatest industrial power in Germany and ultimately in Europe.

The Congress of Vienna had, as we saw, no interest in a unified Germany, but it did create a German Confederation to replace the old empire that had died a quiet death almost a decade earlier. The Confederation was a loose association of 35 sovereign German principalities (including the five kingdoms of Prussia, Hanover, Bavaria, Wurttemberg and Saxony) and four free cities. Its sole institution was a Federal Parliament (*Bundestag*) in Frankfurt, whose chairman was always an Austrian and whose delegates were not elected, but were appointed by the member states. In other words, it was a diplomatic organization, not a real parliament. It was dominated by Austria and Prussia, whose main goal by now was to prevent all change. They were not alone.

The violent events that had shaken Europe in the past quarter-century had left many Germans and non-Germans alike longing for peace, order and authority. All members of the Confederation pledged, however, to introduce constitutions, which, if they were observed, would always place limits on rulers. Such constitutions never saw the light of day in most German states until more than three decades later. This included Prussia and Austria, where absolutism was quickly restored and which joined with Russia in a "Holy Alliance" in 1815 to suppress signs of revolution anywhere in Europe. Only in southern Germany were constitutions introduced that established monarchies and brought more citizens into political life. The most shining example was Baden where the first signs of parliamentary democracy in Germany became visible.

Conservatism and Obedience

After 1815 there was an ultraconservative reaction led by the governments of Prussia and Austria, a development that sorely disappointed many Germans, especially the youth. Many had hoped during the wars of liberation from French domination that Germany would become democratic and united. Indeed, they believed that the despotic power of the individual German sovereigns could be broken by creating a unified Germany. Until the 1860s the aims of unity and freedom went hand in hand. Nowhere were these hopes stronger than at the universities, where idealistic students formed highly politicized fraternities under the banner of "honor, freedom, fatherland." The frater-

nity members dressed in clothing fashionable in Germany in much earlier days, and their colors were black, red and gold, which had been the colors of volunteers during the wars of liberation, and which thereafter became the symbolic colors of republicanism in Germany. They are Germany's colors today.

The fraternity at the University of Jena sponsored in 1817 a mass assembly at Wartburg Castle for persons from all over Germany on the fourth anniversary of the Battle of Leipzig and the 300th anniversary of Luther's Reformation. Thousands came, and passionate speeches were given calling for individual liberty, constitutional government and German unity. Reactionary policies of the leading German states were criticized. At the end of this nationalistic rally, the father of the popular gymnastic associations, Friedrich Ludwig Jahn, organized a particularly unfortunate ceremony which was repeated 116 years later in Berlin: not only the symbols of authority, such as a pigtail and a Prussian corporal's cane, but "un-German" books were thrown into a huge bonfire.

Among the books thrown to the flames were those of a playwright, August von Kotzebue. Two years later a deranged and fanatical theology student assassinated him, calling him a "traitor of youth." This senseless act was just what the leaders of most German states needed to declare the "Carlsbad Acts" in 1819. They called for rigid censorship, prohibition of any political activity directed against the authoritarian order in most states, the outlawing

Prussia and Austria after the Congress of Vienna: 1815

Caspar David Friedrich's *Two men gazing at the moon* (1819)

of fraternities (which continued to operate underground), and close scrutiny and supervision of the universities. The Prussian king dismissed all his reformist ministers, and Prussia and Austria remained the centers of conservative reaction.

Romanticism

For the next three decades, Germans were intellectually as divided as ever. This era has been called the "Biedermeier" period: a time of relative peace and security in which the bulk of Germans passively did not look very far beyond their family and village lives. This view of life is well-portrayed by the paintings of Carl Spitzweg and the operas of Albert Lortzing. Another artistic and philosophical movement, romanticism, emerged at roughly the same time. Romanticism stressed feelings and was a reaction against the rationality of the enlightenment. The romantic sought to break all barriers, including those of reason and sought refuge in the past, in nature, in art or in fantasy. He was drawn to legends and fairy tales, especially following publication by Jacob and Wilhelm Grimm of German fairy tales in the years 1812–1814 and of legends a few years later.

Romanticism in art was best portrayed by the painter Caspar David Friedrich, whose superb landscape paintings showed the links between man and nature; in literature the Schlegel brothers, E.T.A. Hoffmann, Clemens Brentano, Ludwig Tieck, Joseph von Eichendorff and Eduard Mörike; in music by Franz Schubert and

Carl Maria von Weber. At first romanticism was not political. But by the end of the 19th century it had seeped into the political thinking of many Germans and lent their views an often unrealistic and immoderate air.

A third and expressly political trend was liberalism, that longing for the previously promised, but largely undelivered, constitutional government and individual freedom. The uprising in Paris in 1830 spread to cities all over Germany and forced the introduction of constitutions in Brunswick, Hanover, Hesse-Cassel and Saxony. There were further uprisings in 1832.

Queen Victoria ascended the British throne in 1837, which nominally included the Hanover crown. The linkage had been established in 1713 when the Hanover monarch George became king of England. Tradition, however, forbade women from ruling Hanover. The new Hanoverian king abolished the constitution, an act publicly opposed by seven prominent professors at the University of Göttingen, including the Grimm brothers. When the seven were promptly dismissed and given three days to leave the kingdom, loud voices of protest were heard throughout Germany.

It was in reaction to the reestablishment of authoritarian rule in a politically fragmented Germany that gave rise in the early 1830s to the "Young Germany" movement, to which a number of German writers belonged, most notably Heinrich

Heine and Ludwig Börne. These young writers were convinced that literary figures should become politically active and socially critical. Their influence was so feared by the authorities that the German Confederation forbade their writings in 1835 and their leading exponents were driven into exile, particularly to Paris.

Like most German intellectuals of their time, these writers saw German nationalism and liberalism as goals that went hand in hand. It was in this spirit that Hoffman von Fallersleben wrote a song, "Deutschland, Deutschland über alles," ("Germany, Germany above all others") in the 1840s. The melody had earlier been written by Austrian Joseph Haydn and was a well-known hymn in Protestant churches. This song, which became the national anthem for a united Germany in 1871 and whose third verse is Germany's anthem today, is often misunderstood as having been a call for German domination over the whole world. In fact it was directed against the disunity of Germany. It was a call for placing the goal of a united and democratic Germany above all provincial loyalties and above all inclinations to find happiness in one's own private corner. The final verse sums up the song's message: "Unity and Law and Freedom for the German Fatherland." It was assumed that all these goals were inseparably linked.

A final powerful intellectual force at the time was the Berlin philosopher, Friedrich Hegel, whose almost encyclopedic work gave rise to at least two contradictory traditions: one supporting authoritarian rule and one supporting revolution. In some of his writings Hegel described the state as an organism that is not a mere instrument in the hands of the citizens, but which grows and has needs of its own. Such growth, he argued, was completely rational; in fact, he maintained that reason reaches its highest perfection in the state. Which state had reached the highest existing perfection? The Prussian state, he answered. A state's power reflects the rationality of the state. "What is rational is actual and what is actual is rational," he wrote. The life of the individual human being has meaning only within the state, he argued. Authoritarian rulers could not have been more pleased with a philosophical doctrine than with this one.

However, Hegel also developed a doctrine called the dialectic, which involved the clash of opposites and the development of something entirely new. Hegel meant the clash of ideas, but one of his bright German Ph.D. students, Karl Marx, converted this concept of clashing ideas to one of clashing economic forces. The explosive implications of this theory became clear very soon. Marx, who was born in

Germany

Trier, the son of a Prussian customs official, and who married a woman of minor nobility, was forced to flee Germany in 1843 because of the biting social and political criticism that he wrote in his Cologne newspaper, *Rheinische Zeitung*. In his London exile he wrote in 1848 the *Communist Manifesto*, which predicted a violent revolution as a result of which the working (proletarian) class would replace the capitalist overlords who owned the land and factories. This powerful tract ended with the words: "Proletarians of the world, rise up; you have nothing to lose but your chains!" Such a rising never came in England or in Germany, but Marxism became a far more significant intellectual and political doctrine in Germany than in the United States.

Closer to Unity

The German Customs Union was established in 1834 by all German states except Austria, Hanover, Mecklenburg, Oldenburg, Holstein and the Hansa cities. This farsighted move, which created a unified inland market, not only became the cornerstone for a united Germany 37 years later, but it became an important model years later for the EC. The German Customs Union greatly stimulated the industrialization of Germany, whose population at the time was three-fourths agricultural. At the same time it diminished the position within Germany of Austria and enhanced the economic predominance of Prussia.

The authoritarian German princes seemed to be firmly in their saddles when they were severely shaken in 1848 by a spark of revolution, which had started in Sicily and southern Italy and which, as usual, arrived in Germany via France. But the rebels' objectives in Germany and France were different. What many Germans wanted was unity and freedom, things that had already been realized in whole or in part in France a half-century earlier. As a student in Bonn, Carl Schurz, wrote in his memoirs, "The word democracy was on all tongues and many thought it a matter of course that, if the princes should try to withhold from the people the rights and liberties demanded, force would take the place of mere petition."

Few Germans wanted a revolution as in France in 1789, but many wanted the traditional authorities to approve of more freedom for the people and of a constitutional monarchy that would include the principle of popular sovereignty. What specific demands were made became clear very quickly. In frightened response to the spontaneous demonstrations and assemblies in the first week of March 1848, many princes granted freedom of press and assembly, the creation of citizen's

Courtesy: Irmgard M. Baylor

militias, jury trials, reform of the electoral system and collaboration in constructing a federal German state.

In Prussia, King Friedrich Wilhelm IV waited a little too long to make concessions. Not until he had been informed that Metternich had been driven out of Austria did he decide to grant Prussia a constitution and to support the move toward a united Germany. An unfortunate incident in the square before the royal palace, where nervous troops fired a volley of shots into a crowd that had presumably assembled to applaud the king's concessions, touched off a rampage of violence in Berlin that was not to be duplicated until the end of World War I. The Prussian troops, which had not engaged in combat since the Battle of Waterloo, were baffled and quickly demoralized by fighting street battles against snipers, who fought from rooftops and from behind barricades and who disappeared into side streets and alleys when regular troops closed in on them.

After one day of such fighting, the army was compelled to withdraw from the city, but the king valiantly chose to stay with his "dear Berliners." He was thus a sort of captive of the revolutionaries and was forced to call together bourgeois and intellectual groups to discuss reforms. He later looked back with regret on that humiliating time: "We were on our bellies then." It seemed that the death knell for the loosely organized group of mainly authoritarian states called Germany had

been rung, but time would reveal that the princes had just temporarily lost their nerve. By the end of March 1848 all German states, including Austria and Prussia, had concluded that there was no alternative to allowing representatives to be elected by universal manhood suffrage to a national parliament to draft a liberal constitution for a German federation. This first German national parliament convened on May 18 in the Paul's Church in Frankfurt on the Main.

The Parliament of the Professors

This has often been called the "parliament of the professors" because of the fact that an overwhelming number of delegates were professors, lawyers or university-educated civil servants who had little practical experience in politics, and in typical German scholarly fashion spent weeks on end discussing abstract notions of law, freedom and the state. The delegates had good intentions and produced an admirable document called the Fundamental Rights of the German People. However, they were unable to unite on the question of parliamentary control of royal power. Gradually, their slow, deliberate and discursive work was overtaken by events outside the Paul's Church. The demands for reform were not quite strong enough to realize themselves. The resulting frustration led to outbursts of violence in Vienna, Frankfurt, Berlin and elsewhere that discredited the entire reformist movement in more and more Germans' eyes.

The reestablishment of firm monarchical control in Vienna stimulated a longing for order. Suspicions among the states and the classes began to reassert themselves. Nowhere was this more evident than in Prussia, where the king soon began resisting any diminution of his power. The king's disposition was strengthened by a renewal of mob violence in Berlin in June 1848, in which weapons in the state armory were seized and distributed among the rebels. This violence frightened the middle class citizens and played into the hands of the king.

He ordered the troops back into their Berlin barracks in November, an order that ignited more resistance and that could be carried out only by force. But this order ended the revolutionary activity in Prussia. Friedrich Wilhelm caught many of his critics off guard by decreeing a constitution. Revised in 1850, this document provided formal safeguards for Prussian subjects' liberties and established a bicameral legislature that was clearly designed to prevent truly innovative action by more radical elements. The upper house was composed mainly of the nobility and the lower house was elected in a complicated way based on the amount of taxes the citizens paid; two-thirds of the seats were thereby elected by 15% of the population, which paid two-thirds of the total taxes.

This strange electoral system remained a thorn in the side of the Prussian working class and liberal reformers until it was finally abolished in 1918. Despite its many shortcomings, though, this constitution was a step away from absolute government and toward constitutional, parliamentary government in Prussia.

After entirely too much debate, the Frankfurt Parliament made two fundamental decisions: first, the majority recommended a "small German" solution to German unity, with close links to Austria, rather than a "large German" solution under the Hapsburgs of Austria. It was decided that it would be nonsense to establish a German nation-state that would include Milan, Venice, Budapest, Prague and Krakow. Second, it offered the German imperial crown to the Prussian king in 1849.

Friedrich Wilhelm IV brusquely rejected this gift with the words "If the thousand-year-old crown of the German nation, unused now for 42 years, is again to be given away, it is I and my likes who will give it!" No doubt, it was not his idea of monarchy to see it based on the sovereignty of the people and offered by lawyers and professors who had been elected by the people. It is possible that he would have accepted it from other princes. But the king was aware that accepting such a crown might

very well have meant war with Austria, which, as later events showed, was not prepared to accept German unity under Prussian domination without a fight. He could also not forget his heritage nor muster enthusiasm for a new state in which the Prussian identity might ultimately disappear.

His rejection of the crown sealed the fate of the revolution. Nevertheless, for the rest of the year he continued to send diplomatic feelers to some other German princes to explore the chances of establishing a form of German unity more to his liking, but these came to nothing. More successful was his troops' suppression of the last acts of rebellion in Saxony in 1849, where they restored the Saxon king to the throne, and during the summer in Baden and the Rhineland-Palatinate, where they crushed a ragtag "people's army" of intellectuals, poets and professional and amateur revolutionaries. That last victory enabled the king of Wurttemberg to disband the Frankfurt Parliament, which had dwindled to about a hundred die-hards, who had fled to Stuttgart. His comment: "Against democrats only soldiers will do. Adieu!"

Migration to America

As was the case after Hitler jolted Germany with his brutal intolerance after

19th Century Hamburg

Germany

1933, America greatly profited from the events that had shaken Germany in 1848–9. Revolutionaries and sympathizers fled by the thousands to the United States, which had been one of the few countries in the world to send a message of encouragement to the Frankfurt Parliament. These German exiles brought their ideals and their zeal with them, and many of them spoke out elegantly against slavery, streamed into the new Republican Party and fought mainly on the side of the North during the Civil War. Frederick Hecker organized an all-German regiment for Lincoln; the young Graf (Count) Ferdinand von Zeppelin made his first ascent in a balloon in America and acted as an aerial observer for the North in the Civil War.

The former leaders of the Baden Revolutionary Army, Franz Siegel and Carl Schurz, fought for the North. Siegel led an army in the Battle of New Market on May 15, 1864, against Confederate units that included the Virginia Military Institute corps of cadets. Partly because of the young cadets' legendary bravery, Siegel's forces were badly beaten. Schurz was a particularly towering figure among the "1848ers." He campaigned for Lincoln in the 1860 election, was named by the winner as ambassador to Madrid, but he resigned this post later in order to return to America to command a division in the Union Army.

Under President Rutherford B. Hayes he was Secretary of the Interior and introduced civil service reform and advocated the integration of the Indians into American society. New Yorkers today can stroll in the Carl Schurz Park on East End Ave and 86th Street. In the 19th and early 20th centuries, 86th Street from Lexington to Second Avenue was popularly known as "Sauerkraut Boulevard" and the "German Broadway." It was during the Civil War that the cartoonist Thomas Nast, who had emigrated from Landau to New York in 1846 and later to Morristown, NJ, drew the rotund, red-nosed Santa Claus who became firmly anchored in the American imagination. He was also responsible for many other American caricatures: the Democratic Party's donkey, the GOP's elephant and Uncle Sam.

The end of the American Civil War stimulated even greater numbers of Germans to seek a better life in America. In the years between 1866 and 1896 Germans were the largest immigrant group to go to America, reaching a peak of a half million in 1882, or more than two-thirds of all immigrants in that year. In fact, Germans led in overall immigration between 1820 and 1920, and in 1907 alone 1.3 million Germans arrived in the United States. Most settled in the quadrangle of New York-Minneapolis-St. Louis-Baltimore, where they established German communities with their own schools, newspapers, churches, hospitals and clubs. They also opened breweries and beer gardens.

Their habit of engaging in more pleasant Sunday activities, such as sponsoring band contests, festivals, or simply walking with the family or chatting in a beer garden, contributed to lightening the Sunday severity found all too often in 19th century America. In the 21st century some 49 million Americans (17% of the total population) consider themselves to be of German descent. There are actually more since many Americans identified themselves as "Western European" and "Northern European" in the 2000 census, rather than specifying countries. Americans of German descent are the largest ethnic group in 23 U.S. states ranging from Alaska to Florida. In Wisconsin and the Dakotas, they constitute more than 40% of the populations. Unlike Poles, Italians or Irish, they are not a cohesive group influencing political life.

Carl Schurz

The history of these German-Americans is traced by the German-American Heritage Museum, which opened its doors in Washington D.C. in March 2010. One learns, for example, that the forebears of Elvis Presley immigrated to America in 1710 under the name Pressler. Also the inventor of blue jeans, Levi Strauss, hailed from Germany. The museum was funded mainly by an umbrella group of many contemporary German-American fraternal and social clubs.

Prussian Power Emerges

The 1848 revolution was over. It has often been said that the Germans' main problem was that they had never had a successful revolution. Of course, as the case of England demonstrates, revolutions are not absolutely essential in the establishment of democratic government, as long as reform is possible. However, Germany was to experience too little reform in years to come. Many liberals who had participated in the "March Revolution" became very self-critical after its failure and became convinced that they had to adjust their political objectives much more to the prevailing political conditions. They thus became more open to ideas associated with Otto von Bismarck, who was to become the Prussian minister-president a few years later: *Realpolitik* (politics that recognize the hard facts of the world) and the inclination to tone down the demand for freedom if the possibility of national unity is at stake.

During the two decades following the events of 1848–9, Prussia not only steadily increased its industrial base and power, but it moved aggressively to establish the preconditions for German unity under Prussian domination. One step was the submission by the new king, Wilhelm I, of a bill to reorganize and double the size of the army, a measure hotly opposed by a majority in Prussia's lower house. The majority did grant a large sum to strengthen the existing army units, but when Wilhelm simply used this money to finance his desired reorganization, the Parliament refused to grant any more funds until the king canceled his unauthorized army reform. The result was such a serious deadlock and tension that the king reportedly considered resigning. Only a person of extraordinary skill could lead Prussia out of this crisis. That man was soon found: Bismarck.

Bismarck's background and reputation seemed to be just what a conservative king like Wilhelm I would have wanted. An East Elbian aristocrat, his disdain for scholarly things and his youthful love for beer-swilling and disorderly conduct had caused him to be banished from the city limits of Göttingen where he had been sent for an unsuccessful year of university study. Yet, since 1850 he had gained much diplomatic experience, first as the Prussian representative to the Parliament of the German Confederation in Frankfurt, then as an envoy in St. Petersburg and Paris. These assignments helped him to broaden his scope beyond Prussia and to conclude that Prussia should become the heart of a unified Germany without Austria. Already in 1856 he had written: "Germany is clearly too small for us both. . . . In the not too distant future we shall have to fight for our existence against Austria . . . since the course of events in Germany has no other solution."

Appointed Prussian minister-president in 1862, Bismarck was unsuccessful in persuading parliament to accept the king's plans for reforming the army. For a while

Kaiser Wilhelm I

he simply ignored parliament, but he knew that he could not continue to do so forever. Thus, he decided to initiate a bold foreign policy, which would capture the imagination of nationalists and liberals alike and which would ultimately achieve German unity. The success of this policy won the admiration of many of his countrymen for generations to come.

Bismarck's first years as Chancellor of Prussia were ones of armament and war. In 1864, 1866 and 1870, he conducted short but significant wars against Denmark, Austria and France. The war conducted by both Prussia and Austria against Denmark in 1864 over Danish control of the predominantly German-populated territories of Schleswig and Holstein gave Prussian commanders useful battlefield experience. The Prussian victory at Düppel in Jutland also stimulated patriotic feeling in Prussia and in other German states. It weakened liberal opposition to

Otto von Bismarck

the army reform bill, and inclined more and more Germans to look to Prussia for leadership.

It is hardly surprising that the joint administration of Schleswig-Holstein agreed upon by the Prussian and Austrian victors did not go well. Friction was inevitable, and Bismarck was very astute in exploiting it to force a show-down with Austria, which would never have peacefully acquiesced to his designs for German unity. In mid-1866 Bismarck ordered Prussian troops to occupy Holstein, and after declaring the German Confederation dissolved, he declared war on Austria. It lasted only seven weeks. With new breech-loading rifles, which had just been used so successfully in the American Civil War, and with the capacity to move their troops to the battlefield on new railroads, the far better prepared Prussians were able to deliver a stinging defeat to the Austrian and Saxon armies at the Battle of Königgrätz. This victory eliminated Austria from the soon-to-be unified Germany.

North German Confederation

In mid-1867 a North German Confederation composed of 22 German states north of the Main River came into existence, with the king of Prussia as its president. Bismarck's very moderate treatment of the defeated Austrian Empire enabled Prussia to gain in Austria a trustworthy ally for a half-century. When in 1870 Prussia launched its final war to establish German unity, Austria did not support that last active opponent to a united Germany: France.

With increasing nervousness the French looked east across the Rhine where Bismarck had created momentum toward German unity. Feverish French diplomatic activity in the south German states and Austria failed to create determined opposition to Prussia. The crisis erupted in midyear when the Prussian government announced that Prince Leopold of the House of Hohenzollern had accepted the Spanish throne, which had been vacant since 1868. As Bismarck well knew, the French would never tolerate a Hohenzollern on the Spanish throne, since they would then face a hostile dynasty on their eastern and southwestern borders. The French ambassador to Prussia, Benedetti, persuaded Wilhelm I at the spa Bad Ems that it would be a good idea to withdraw Leopold's candidacy.

Wilhelm politely refused to assure the French diplomat that the Hohenzollern candidacy would not be renewed in the future. The king wired his description of the talks to Bismarck, who then published the telegram after intentionally shortening it in such a way that Wilhelm's reply to Benedetti seemed far more abrupt and

impolite than it actually had been. The French were infuriated by this "Ems Telegram," and in an atmosphere of inflamed emotion, the French government declared war on Prussia on July 19th.

The Birth of the German Empire

To French surprise, the south German states immediately joined the Prussians in the war. Never known for indecision, the Prussians struck quickly and fatally. Smashing through Lorraine, the Prussian Army cut Paris off from the two main French armies and delivered a devastating blow to the French at Sedan on the Belgian border. By January 1871, all resistance ended. A humiliated France looked on as the German Empire was proclaimed in the Hall of Mirrors in the Palace of Versailles on January 18, 1871. For the first time in history, there was a united Germany. The Prussian king became Kaiser Wilhelm I.

Bismarck was probably mistaken in acquiescing to pressures from the kaiser (Caesar—i.e. "emperor"), Prussian military leaders and others by imposing a harsh peace on a prostrate France. Germany annexed Alsace and most of Lorraine, with their advanced industry and rich iron deposits. Also, France was required to pay a very large indemnity and to allow German occupation troops to remain in France until the sum was paid. For the next half-century, French policy would revolve around undoing these terrible losses, and the pigeons that German leaders had turned loose in 1871 would in 1919 come back to roost with a vengeance.

These limited wars were models of the primacy of political over military objectives. Military actions ceased the moment Bismarck's political objectives were achieved. Faced with demands to crush entire armies or to humiliate defeated enemies by way of triumphant marches through their capitals, Bismarck always insisted that the business at hand was the conduct of Prussian or German politics, not an attempt to administer "justice" or to humiliate or destroy great powers. Bismarck strove after 1871 to protect what Germany had gained. Above all, he guarded Germany's most vital interest, the European center. He did not allow Germany's attention to be dangerously diverted by numerous colonial adventures. He once said, pointing to a map of Europe: "Here is Russia and here is France, and here we are in the middle. That is my map of Africa."

To insure Germany's protection, Bismarck built up one of the most complicated and delicate alliance systems ever known in peacetime. He saw Germany threatened from two sides and sought to eliminate this threat by preventing the French and Russians from forming a co-

Germany

alition against Germany. He accomplished this by maintaining friendly relations with Britain, by isolating France diplomatically, by establishing a "Dual Alliance" with Austria in 1879 and the "Reinsurance Treaty" among Austria, Russia and Germany in 1887. The latter obligated Germany to stand by whichever partner was attacked by the other, thereby discouraging potential aggression from either Austria or Russia. Bismarck did not regard this treaty as incompatible with the Dual Alliance with Austria because in neither agreement was Germany obligated to aid any aggressor. Of course, one factor gave Bismarck great flexibility: he alone could determine guilt for any outbreak of hostilities, and this decision would always have been in accordance with German national interests.

Of course, the legacy Bismarck left Germany was not all positive. His alliance system was exceedingly complicated, and he failed to train successors to continue the policy. His followers, who wished to simplify the alliance system, did not renew the Reinsurance Treaty in 1894. Also, his style of *Realpolitik* demanded great skill, the sober and unimpassioned recognition of the limits of power, the exercise of moderation and the respect of other nations' vital interests. His successors often imperfectly understood his policies, and they tended to remember the gestures of his statecraft and not its substance. Bismarckian *Realpolitik*, if understood only in fragments, could be a dangerous inheritance for any nation.

The legacy that Bismarck left German domestic politics was also by no means entirely positive. The German Empire had the outward appearance of being democratic. However, while some other European countries, such as England and France, were in the process of becoming more democratic in practice, Germany was not. It remained a country in which the most important decisions were made by people who were not elected and not directly subject to popular or parliamentary control. Bismarck's skill as a politician prevented a process of democratic reform from gaining any momentum.

The chancellor, like many of his countrymen, felt uncomfortable about political and cultural pluralism in Germany. This was especially revealed in laws Bismarck introduced to limit the influence of the Catholic Church and the Social Democratic Party of Germany (SPD). His campaign against the Catholic Church, called the "Cultural Struggle," was similar to campaigns conducted in many European countries in the 19th century to limit the church's influence over education and other social affairs. Bismarck also resented the growth of the Catholic Center Party

Germania, **overlooking the Rhine Valley, commemorates the unification of 1871.**

Courtesy: Jon Markham Morrow

and suspected that the Vatican was trying to stir up opposition to the Imperial government among the Polish minority within Germany and among the other Catholic countries in Europe. A series of laws whittling away at the church's privileges was passed starting in 1873, but these laws unleashed such an outcry among Catholics and Protestants alike that Bismarck was forced to repeal most of them by 1881.

The leader was also unable to view German socialists as loyal citizens because of their Marxist revolutionary program and their talk of internationalism. He blamed the socialists for two unsuccessful assassination attempts against the Kaiser in 1877, and in October of the following year he succeeded in persuading Parliament to pass an Anti-Socialist Law forbidding all associations that aimed to subvert the ex-

isting order or that showed "socialist tendencies." This law forced the SPD to operate underground, crippled the growing labor unions, deprived socialists of the customary protection of the law and drove many of them into exile abroad. Like the laws against the Catholic Church, these antisocialist laws also backfired and actually stimulated an increase in the membership and overall strength of the SPD.

At the same time, Bismarck linked these repressive measures with progressive social welfare laws to help the needy and working classes. The first social insurance laws were introduced in 1881, and in 1883 there came a Sickness Insurance Law, one-third of the premiums for which were to be paid by the employers, and an accident insurance financed entirely by the employer; finally in 1889 old-age disability insurance financed by employees, employers and the government was introduced. These laws were far in advance of those of any other nation and were the model for the National Insurance Act of 1911 in Britain; not until the 1930s were such programs introduced in the United States by the federal government. Even today, Germans are proud of their social welfare legislation.

Industrialization and Urbanization

Some Germans hoped for an era of liberal reform when Wilhelm I died in 1888. But his son, Friedrich III, who was known to favor such reforms, died of throat cancer only 99 days after his coronation, and a young, inexperienced and impetuous Wilhelm II became kaiser. The new ruler hoped to become popular by canceling the Anti-Socialist Law, introducing some domestic reforms and conducting an energetic German foreign and colonial policy. Noting that Bismarck had wholly differ-

ent ideas, he fired the "Iron Chancellor" in 1890. He was then free to take the lead over a people who were enthusiastic about the prospects for Germany's future. The kaiser, who was rather intelligent and superficially interested in many different things, but who was unable to focus his attention on anything very long, was boastful about Germany's power. He also had a way, as one of his biographers noted, of approaching every matter with an open mouth. Although in actual crises, the young kaiser tended to be cautious, he seemed to many non-Germans to represent a restless country with more power than it could use well.

German unification and rapid economic and population growth had given Germany a strong hand to assert its claims in the world. By the end of the 19th century the extremely rapid industrialization and urbanization had transformed Germany into one of the world's foremost industrial, trading, banking and urbanized

countries. All Western countries experienced difficulties in adjusting to the social consequences of industrialization. However, the suddenness of German economic and population growth had no equal in Europe.

Between 1816 and 1913 Germany's population almost tripled from 25 to 67 million, and more and more Germans moved into the cities. In 1830, four-fifths of the population lived outside of towns and engaged in agriculture, but in 1895 barely one-fifth did so. Berlin's population alone grew from three-quarters of a million in 1870 to over two million in 1910. The increasingly urbanized people were hard at work making Germany the most economically powerful country in Europe. With Alsace-Lorraine, Germany became the leading producer of iron and steel. It almost quadrupled its domestic rail net between 1871 and 1914, and it built one of the world's largest merchant marine fleets. Its industries were very diversified,

The unification of Germany, 1871, showing only the major states and areas

199

Germany

Capt. Alfred Thayer Mahan

ranging from armaments producers such as Krupp and electrical plants such as those of Siemens, Halske and the General Electric Company (AEG), to chemical industries such as Bayer, Agfa and I.G. Farben. Overall German industrial production had already surpassed that of the French in the 1870s, caught up with that of Britain in 1900 and had overtaken it by 1910, when only the United States outproduced Germany.

Imperial Germany also exploded with artistic and scholarly creativity. Its universities and research laboratories became places where the most imaginative thinking in the world was being done. For instance, Wilhelm Konrad Roentgen discovered X-rays, Max Planck the quantum theory and Albert Einstein the theory of relativity. Robert Koch did groundbreaking research on tuberculosis, cholera and sleeping sickness, Paul Ehrlich on syphilis and Rudolph Virchow on pathology. The work of such great professors as Theodor Mommsen and Heinrich von Treitschke in history, Wilhelm Dilthey in philosophy, Ferdinand Tönnies, Georg Simmel and Max Weber in sociology, and Adolf Wagner, Lujo Brentano and Werner Sombart in economics, is still admired today.

Berlin also gained a reputation as an exciting cultural center. Johannes Brahms and Richard Strauss composed their music there. The sympathetic Prussian social critic, Theodor Fontane, wrote his novels, focusing on the Prussia that he loved, but that he saw in decline. Also, after the opening of *Die Freie Bühne* (The Free Stage), such talented playwrights as Gerhard Hauptmann and Frank Wedekind were able to introduce a new element of criticism and expressionism into the German theater. Unlike France then and to-

day, Germany's culture and scholarship was not concentrated in the nation's capital, but was also distributed among such cities as Hamburg, Cologne, Leipzig, Munich and Frankfurt on the Main. Despite the cultural creativity of the time, many educated Germans were gripped with a kind of cultural pessimism. They looked around themselves and saw what they considered to be excessive materialism and consumerism, values they viewed as British and American. German spirit was in decline, they lamented, and many agreed with the philosopher Friedrich Nietzsche, who in 1888 claimed "German spirit: for the past 18 years a contradiction in terms."

Social Division, Foreign Adventurism and Nationalism

Industrial and population growth changed the face and character of German society. The German Empire, which had become united territorially in 1871, became increasingly divided socially. Expressed in an oversimplified way, German society became more and more polarized. A class conscious, somewhat doctrinaire and fairly well-organized proletariat confronted a ruling class that was, in the main, stubbornly conservative. Nationalism grew to be very strong in Germany, but it could never overcome the extreme antagonisms that arose out of this split in German society.

The robust and assertive foreign policy on which Wilhelm II embarked in the 1890s, when Germany enjoyed relatively good relations with the other major countries in the world, led Germany by 1914 into a diplomatic situation in which it felt encircled and distrusted. By building a powerful navy, pursuing colonial ambitions in Africa, and frequently brandishing the sword, Germany's rulers created more problems than they were able to solve.

Bismarck had kept the German Empire within the limits its geographic position in the middle of Europe imposed upon it. He had avoided colonial adventures, which would only have antagonized the other European powers, especially Britain. However, supported by German public opinion, his successors changed this, and by the turn of the century the German flag flew in Africa (Cameroons, South-West Africa and Tanganyika), there was a tiny foothold in China and a smattering of Pacific islands (named, ironically, the Bismarck Archipelago).

In order to try to protect this usually unprofitable empire, Germany decided to build a battle fleet that would enable it to conduct a major naval war against the great powers. Kaiser Wilhelm II announced in 1898: "Our future lies on the

water." This decision was a major factor in the deterioration of good relations between Britain and Germany. A German navy that challenged Britain, which, as an island, was completely dependent upon open sea-lanes, was bound to be destabilizing and to drive the English into the arms of Germany's potential enemies.

Undoubtedly the chief influence on German naval thinking was Captain A.T. Mahan of the United States Navy. In *The Influence of Sea Power on History* he argued that mastery of the oceans is identical with world domination and that any strong land power fighting against an amphibious master that also has land forces is destined to lose. Mahan visited Germany in 1893 and was received like a hero. He was invited to dine aboard the Kaiser's yacht. The ruler wrote in 1894 to a friend "I am just now not reading but devouring Captain Mahan's book and am trying to learn it by heart . . . It is on board all my ships and constantly quoted by my captains and officers."

What worried the British and the French was that Germany was willing to use its new navy. In mid-1911, Wilhelm sent a gunboat to Morocco's Atlantic port of Agadir in response to France's dispatch-

Mata Hari, executed German spy, 1917

ing a military mission to Fez. France's action was a clear violation of the 1906 agreements of Algeciras, but the German overreaction to this move caused other Europeans to overlook this point. German bellicosity concerned Europe more than a questionable French interpretation of a treaty. Thereafter, German political calculation had always to include the possibility of a war with Britain, which was now firmly on the side of the Entente (France and Russia).

The German chancellor's chief foreign policy advisor, Kurt Riezler, who later emigrated to the U.S., viewed with concern the kind of nationalism that was gripping his countrymen. He wrote in 1913 that too many Germans exaggerated the "power of force." Due to their craving for international recognition, they lacked political sense, judgment and goal orientation. Their nationalism showed "the manners of a young dog" and was laden with "envy and resentments," both of which were poor advisors for an "upstart" who did not know how to "let things ripen." The most vocal spokesman for this kind of impatient nationalism was the Pan-German Union, about which Chancellor Bethmann-Hollweg declared in 1912 almost in despair: "Politics cannot be made with these idiots!"

World War I

Long before June 28, 1914, the day on which the Austrian archduke Franz Ferdinand was assassinated in Bosnia, there had been much dissatisfaction in the capitals of Europe. The preceding decade had produced numerous crises that could have served to ignite a war. However, in order for a crisis actually to lead to war, several powers must conclude that they are in a favorable position to gain from such a conflict. That feeling of confidence prevailed in many European capitals in July and August 1914.

Within six weeks after the assassination of the archduke, all of Europe's major nations were locked into a war that was to last four years and that far exceeded all previous wars in terms of casualties and destruction. Of course, no European leaders had contemplated, let alone wanted, the kind of war that actually came in August 1914. In the minds of most statesmen at the time, war was a relatively violent action lasting a month or six weeks and conducted as a part of intricate diplomatic games. The memory of the Napoleonic wars having faded, they had not yet had the opportunity to observe the consequences of wars that unlocked powerful emotions stemming from nationalism and democracy. They also vastly underestimated the capacity of countries in possession of modern industry and technology

The combatants in World War I, 1915–18

to conduct theretofore inconceivably destructive wars for long periods against one another.

There was general shock and indignation in all of Europe when Archduke Franz Ferdinand's assassination was announced. On July 5 and 6 Germany granted its ally, Austria-Hungary, a free hand to deal with the matter, and Russia (and indirectly France) gave the Serbians a similarly free hand. Only in the final days of the crisis did the German Chancellor desperately try to regain control of the situation. Subsequent events revealed that a tighter German rein on Austrian policy would have served German interests better. However, in the eyes of German leaders, there appeared to be no alternative to their policy of allowing Austria to deal harshly with Serbia at this time.

On July 28 Austria-Hungary declared war on Serbia, and two days later Russia made the critical decision to order general mobilization, thus indicating its unwillingness to allow the Austrian-Serbian war

to remain localized. German leaders had for a long time made it clear that they perceived a Russian general mobilization to be a direct potential threat to Germany itself. When Russia refused to withdraw its call to arms, Germany sent a last warning to both Russia and France, but when the German note remained unanswered by August 1st, Germany declared war on Russia. It did not immediately declare war on France, but France mobilized its army anyway on August 1st. With Russia, Germany and France carrying out general military buildups, a European war had become unavoidable. When Germany violated Belgian territory in order to gain easier access to France, Britain also entered the war, thereby transforming the European war, which Germany probably would have won, into a world war.

All of the European powers shared the responsibility for the outbreak of World War I. Some, such as Austria-Hungary and Serbia, bore the greatest responsibility. Germany, Russia and France must be blamed for not having sufficiently re-

Germany

General von Hindenburg, Kaiser Wilhelm II, General Ludendorff

strained their respective allies and thereby having allowed a local Balkan squabble (where there had already been two wars in 1912 and 1913) to ignite a world war. Without doubt, Britain bears the least responsibility for the war that came. Nevertheless, crowds of people in all belligerent countries greeted the outbreak of war with a gaiety that is usually reserved for carnival time. Two million German, more than a million French, a million British, a million Austrian, a half-million Italian and countless Russian soldiers were to perish in the four-year bloodletting that followed. The war also destroyed the old Europe, and what could be pieced back together collapsed a mere two decades later.

Almost immediately after the start of hostilities, German troops knifed through Belgium and into France according to a carefully laid "Schlieffen Plan," but by mid-September at the Battle of the Marne, they had been stopped in their tracks before reaching Paris. For four years two opposing armies faced each other in trenches stretching from the English Channel to the Swiss border and protected by mazes of barbed wire, machine-gun nests, mortar and heavy artillery batteries. Chemical warfare (gas) was also introduced during the grisly conflict. Occasionally massive attacks were launched against the opposing trenches that sometimes brought infinitesimal gains and always huge human losses. For instance, in the inconclusive Battle of the Somme in 1916, the Germans lost 650,000 men and the Allies 614,000.

It was a different story in the East, where warfare was highly mobile and brought huge gains and losses of territory. After an initial Russian advance into East Prussia, German forces scored stunning victories against the Russians at Tannenberg and the Masurian Lakes. Out of these victories was born the legend of military genius and invincibility that surrounded the victorious Generals Paul von Hindenburg and Erich Ludendorff for the remainder of the war. By 1916 their authority over military and political questions alike exceeded even that of the kaiser and the chancellor.

The German successes in the East enabled their armies to march right into the heart of Russia. Still, the badly shaken tsarist empire managed to put up stiff resistance. It became clear to the Germans that the two-front war was a vice that could eventually crush Germany. This became especially apparent when the United States entered the war on the Allied side in the spring of 1917. President Woodrow Wilson had been determined to keep the Americans out of the war, but the Germans made several blunders that drew the United States into the conflict. A high official in the Foreign Office, Arthur Zimmermann, sent a telegram to the Mexican government promising territorial rewards north of the Mexican border if it would support Germany in the war. This telegram was intercepted by the Americans and understandably antagonized American leaders and public opinion.

The most serious German mistakes involved its naval warfare against neutral shipping. By the spring of 1915 German surface ships had been swept from all of the major seas except the North and Baltic Seas. It had been built up with so much fanfare and political sacrifice. But because of the ever-tightening British blockade of the North Sea and English Channel outlets, the bulk of the German Navy remained bottled up in Germany's northern ports. This blockade also brought increasing hunger and deprivation to the German population and gradually led German leaders to use submarines to strike at Allied shipping. Submarines were regarded as a particularly hideous weapon at the time since they torpedoed ships without warning and without any capacity to help survivors. A particular outcry had gone up in the United States when a large passenger liner, the Lusitania, was torpedoed off the coast of Ireland in mid-1915, with a loss of 1,198 lives, including 139 Americans. The indignation in America was such that the Germans promised not to repeat such attacks.

For a while German submarine activity died down, but by early 1917 generals Hindenburg and Ludendorff, backed by their immense popularity, forced the adoption of unrestricted submarine warfare on the unwilling chancellor. The head of the German Admiralty misjudged the ultimate effect of America's entry into the war to be "exactly zero"; in any case, it was widely believed that Britain would be forced to its knees before Americans would arrive. Although the first American divisions did not arrive in France until almost a year later, the immediate boost to Allied morale and the military contribution American soldiers made in the final months of the war were decisive in the defeat of Germany.

Ending the War on the Eastern Front

American entry into the war made it essential that the Germans eliminate the Eastern front. Because the weapon of war had not worked entirely, they selected another weapon: that of revolution. On March 15, 1917, the Russian tsar abdicated, but to the Germans' surprise, the new government decided to continue the war. Therefore, German leaders decided to transport a group of Russian revolutionaries from their exile in Switzerland through Germany to Scandinavia from where they could return to Russia. This group was composed of Marxists who were known to favor Russian withdrawal from the war and included most predominantly Vladimir Ilyich Lenin. The Germans incorrectly figured that Lenin would be an ideal marionette for Germany, since

he and his faction-ridden Bolshevik party would presumably be unable to hold power more than a few weeks without German support.

Neither the Germans nor Lenin had any concern for each others' interests. As Leon Trotsky wrote in his memoirs: "In the case of Lenin's trip two opposite plans crossed at a definite point, and this point was a sealed [rail] car." The train, which departed from Zurich with 32 Russian revolutionaries, had such high traffic priority that the German crown prince's own train was kept on a side track in Halle for two hours until Lenin's train had passed. The group arrived at Petrograd's (now St. Petersburg) Finland Train Station on April 16 and was greeted by thousands of supporters. It cannot be doubted that the transport and subsequent German financial assistance was vital to the Bolsheviks before their seizure of power in Petrograd on November 7, 1917.

Lenin did indeed announce Russia's withdrawal from the war, but the Germans imposed an extremely harsh peace treaty upon the new Bolshevik leadership at the Russian border town of Brest-Litovsk in early 1918. The Soviets, as the Bolsheviks had come to be called, were forced to relinquish huge chunks of territory from the Russian Empire. This treaty, along with the reparations demanded of Russia in August, set a most unfortunate precedent. It merely stimulated the Entente's will to resist and reinforced the enemy's moral self-confidence to impose on the Germans nine months later a peace no less dreadful than this one. That moral self-confidence was also strengthened by a weakness Germany demonstrated during both world wars: its lack of moderation. Without such moderation, no negotiated settlement was possible, only a dictated one. German occupation authorities after 1871 tended to mistreat or try to "Germanize" conquered nations, which could have been potential allies. The highest German diplomat in Russia in the summer of 1918 made a bitter comment about his own people: "Never was a *Volk* more capable of conquering the world and more incapable of ruling it!"

Collapse of the War Effort

Early in 1918 Hamburg, Leipzig, Cologne, Munich and the heavily industrialized Ruhr area had experienced serious strikes, and in Berlin 200,000 munitions workers struck. Hunger was causing the "home front" to collapse—the average rations for German civilians had been cut to only 1,000 calories per day. The tensions were greatly increased by a worsening of the military situation. Large numbers of fresh American troops began arriving in France in the spring of 1918. Germany's last great offensive was launched on March 21, 1918, but the exhausted German troops were unable to cope with the Allied counteroffensive, which began on July 10. On August 8, known to Germans then as "Black Friday," British infantry broke through the German lines at Amiens and threw the German troops in France into a mass retreat. On August 14 Ludendorff was forced to admit that the war could not be won militarily, and on September 29 he communicated to Supreme Headquarters that "the present condition of our army demands an immediate cease-fire in order to avoid catastrophe." On October 3, von Hindenburg told the chancellor that "under these circumstances it is necessary to break off the fight in order to spare the German people and its allies needless victims."

Despite such calls of desperation at the time, these men and many others had the audacity to claim later that it had been

Labor unrest in Germany's Ruhr area

Germany

the civilian leadership, especially those who had founded the new republic, who had "stabbed Germany in the back" by losing nerve and suing for peace at a time when Germany's armies had allegedly not been defeated in the field. This legend placed an unbearably heavy burden on Germany's postwar democratic leadership.

Its armies retreating, its allies crumbling, its people starving, Germany sent a delegation to seek peace with the Entente. It met French Marshal Foch at Compiègne in a rail car Hitler used to conduct the French surrender ceremonies almost 22 years later. There the French Marshal delivered nonnegotiable conditions which Germany could take or leave: the 34 articles included the withdrawal of the German Army from France, Alsace-Lorraine and Belgium to the Rhine, Entente occupation of the left bank of the Rhine and delivery to the Entente of all German submarines and heavy military and transport materials. The disheartened Germans had no alternative but to accept. The war officially ended on November 11, 1918.

Collapse of the Empire and Birth of the Republic

Even before the cease-fire could be signed, the German Empire ceased to exist. Kaiser Wilhelm simply could not bring himself to abdicate, as the victors had demanded, so Chancellor Max von Baden simply announced the kaiser's abdication on November 9. A short time later, the Social Democrat Philip Scheidemann, was informed that German communists were about to declare a republic, so he rushed to the window of the Reichstag building and announced "The emperor has abdicated. . . . Long live the German Republic!"

The new Social Democratic Chancellor, Friedrich Ebert, made no secret of the fact that his emphasis would be on creating order and a parliamentary-democratic political structure in the badly shaken country. But no sooner had the republic been declared than demands began to be made for a second, more radical revolution. The Polish revolutionary theorist and activist Rosa Luxemburg remarked sarcastically: "Oh how German this German Revolution is! How proper, how pedantic, how lacking in verve and in grandeur."

It was not long before some groups chose to use force against Ebert's government, and Germans witnessed significant events that threatened the Republic in its infancy. In late 1918 the Communist Party of Germany (KPD) was formed, and on the same day the Steel Helmet League, a right-wing paramilitary organization of disenchanted war veterans, was created. The fatal split in German society, which would paralyze and ultimately destroy the republic, continued to widen. The re-

gime clearly found itself in a crisis from which it would never be able to extricate itself.

The communists made two unsuccessful violent attempts to seize power in Berlin. More than 1,000 lives were lost in defeating the first attempt from January 6–12, 1919. The second erupted during the first two weeks of March 1919 and caused 2,000 deaths and considerable destruction to the city of Berlin. The government crushed a leftist uprising in Munich in May 1919 with such brutality that many observers accused the new republican government of being "blind in the right eye." That later right-wing strikes against the republic were not suppressed with equal brutality stemmed from the fact that the postwar German Army of only 100,000 soldiers (*Reichswehr*) and the Free Corps troops, which were hastily assembled to cope with the crises were, on the whole, anti-republican and far more sympathetic to the right; they were never successfully transformed into reliable instruments of the Weimar Republic.

The government found itself in the predicament of having no alternative to the use of troops to restore and maintain order who were, in the main, unruly, disillusioned freebooters who had become far too accustomed to violence during a war that had severely shaken their sense of values and proportion. Such troops were extremely difficult to control, and the blemish of partiality toward the right was placed on the new republic itself.

The Weimar Republic and a Disastrous "Peace" Treaty

In the spring of 1919 delegates to a National Assembly met in Weimar, a city chosen because it lay outside the storm of

revolution that raged in Berlin and because of its association with the humanists Goethe and Schiller, who had lived and worked there. This assembly, whose venue gave the new republic its name, had three tasks: to form a government of Germany, to sign a peace treaty and to draft a new constitution. It legitimized the "Weimar Coalition," composed of the SPD, Center and German Democratic parties, which had ruled Germany since the November Revolution of 1918. However, the necessity of fulfilling the second, highly unpopular task of signing a peace treaty caused this coalition of the republic's supporters to lose its parliamentary majority in 1920, which it never regained.

The first major problem with the Versailles Treaty was the manner in which it was written. In contrast to all previous peace settlements in Europe, the vanquished (in this case, the Germans) were not included in the negotiations. If the Germans had been included, perhaps they would have felt some responsibility for the treaty, but as it was, it represented a dictated peace towards which the Germans never felt any moral obligation to subscribe to its terms. The settlement had a strong whiff of "victor's justice."

Prior to American entry into the conflict, President Woodrow Wilson had proposed a "peace without victory" and later issued a written document containing "Fourteen Points" as a basis for European peace that contained very lofty language. The Germans later accepted the text, but it faded into the background at Versailles as French Prime Minister Georges Clemenceau ("the old tiger") virtually dictated the terms of what turned out to be an attempt at revenge. Little did he know that he was helping to sow the seeds of

The colossal *Reichstag*, Berlin

204

German territorial losses to the Allies following World War I

disaster, particularly in the mind of a wounded Austrian corporal, Adolf Hitler.

The Germans could hardly believe their eyes when the terms were forwarded to Berlin in mid-May 1919, with the warning that nonacceptance would result in an immediate resumption of hostilities. They had expected to lose all territory conquered during the war, as well as Alsace-Lorraine, but they also lost a tenth of their prewar population and an eighth of their territory. The city of Danzig and the province of Posen were ceded to Poland, and a narrow corridor was cut right through West Prussia to connect these areas with Poland. Worse, the coal-rich Saar region was placed under League of Nations and French control for 15 years.

This, combined with the loss of practically all its merchant marine fleet, made it far more difficult for Germany to pay the shockingly high reparations demanded of it. The Rhineland was occupied by Allied soldiers and was to be demilitarized permanently. Germany's high seas fleet was to be turned over to the Allies, a requirement that prompted the Germans to scuttle all their naval ships, which had been interned at Scapa Flow in the Orkney Islands north of Scotland in mid-1919. The future German Army was to be restricted to 100,000 career officers and men with no military aircraft, tanks or other offensive weapons.

Perhaps worst of all, Article 231 of the "Treaty" placed sole responsibility for the outbreak and therefore for all destruction of the war on the shoulders of Germany and its allies. This article had been written by a young American diplomat, John Foster Dulles, as a compromise to the French, who had wanted to annex the Rhineland and to have even higher reparation payments from Germany. But Dulles had to admit later, "it was the re-

Goethe and Schiller Monument in Weimar

vulsion of the German people from this article of the Treaty which, above all else, laid the foundation for the Germany of Hitler."

At the time of the treaty, Adolf Hitler was only beginning to emerge from the political shadows. Born in Austria, he drew around himself a growing circle of enthusiastic admirers. Soon he helped found an energetic and anti-democratic party, the National Socialist Workers' Party of Germany (NSDAP), abbreviated "Nazi." Although he had little formal education, Hitler was a fiery speaker, capable of stirring his listeners with haranguing, emotional tirades. For the next quarter of a century he never ceased to rail against the weak Weimar government and the wickedness of the Versailles Treaty.

The document actually made a mockery of many of Woodrow Wilson's Fourteen Points, such as "open covenants openly arrived at," freedom of the seas, the "impartial adjustment of all colonial claims," and of course the self-determination of nations. The victors permitted this latter right only where people wanted to detach themselves from Germany, such as in northern Schleswig and part of Upper Silesia. Wherever an area's population clearly wanted to join Germany, such as Austria or northern Bohemia, no referendum was permitted. Such hypocrisy stimulated within Germany cynicism toward both the treaty and toward any German government that would sign it. Of course, Germany's harsh policy toward a collapsing Russia at Brest-Litovsk had provided a disastrous precedent. Nevertheless, Germany's short-sightedness in 1918 could not reasonably be invoked to justify an equally short-sighted Allied policy a year later.

As Chancellor Scheidemann said to the National Assembly in 1919, "Which hand would not wither up which put itself and us into these bonds?" The treaty was a millstone around the neck of the new republic. It not only helped create a deep division in German society, but it seriously hampered the normalization of Germany's relations with the outside world. It could only be maintained by force, but the United States quickly withdrew from Europe's military affairs, and Britain and France gradually lost the will to enforce it energetically. One day a spellbinding demagogue would be able to untie the "fetters of Versailles" right before the eyes of a weary and lethargic Europe and reap much applause within Germany for this.

An Attempt at Democracy, Runaway Inflation and Anarchy

It was unfortunate that national humiliation coincided with the birth of the first democracy in Germany. When at last it

Germany

had adopted the political organization extolled by the victorious allies, it had become an international outcast. The new German constitution reflected the democratic spirit of the "Weimar Constitution." The delegates sought to accomplish what the delegates of the Frankfurt Assembly had tried to do in 1848: to combine liberty with national unity and strength. It guaranteed basic individual rights and created a strong lower house of Parliament (*Reichstag*) that had the right to initiate legislation. It also maintained certain traditional German political institutions, such as a federal form and a strong presidency elected every seven years (as a republican substitute for a strong kaiser).

The Weimar Constitution did include several weaknesses. In order to give parliamentary representation to as many different groups as possible, it established the proportional representation electoral system. The unfortunate result was that not only anti-republican splinter groups, such as the Nazi Party, could publicize their causes in parliament, but the large number of parties that could win parliamentary seats made the formation of a majority almost impossible. The result was predictable: parliamentary instability and ultimately paralysis.

A second weakness was the provision for initiatives and referendums. While such instruments of direct democracy often appear progressive, they can frequently be manipulated by enemies of the democratic order as Hitler did after 1933. The third mistake was the inclusion of emergency powers in Article 48, which could be invoked in the event that "pub-lic order and safety be seriously disturbed or threatened." As we shall see, this article was later used to circumvent parliament and thereby to undermine the democratic intentions of the framers. This constitution on the whole was an admirable document, but the German nation was too divided on fundamental political values to be able to live by it. To be respected and observed, a constitution must fit a nation and a society well. If it does not, then it will ultimately be cast off like an ill-fitting garment.

The Weimar Republic experienced continuous crisis. The population had been impoverished by the long war and postwar chaos. The republic saw no other way of keeping up its reparations payments than to borrow money abroad and to produce new money as fast as it could be turned out by the printing presses. The devastating result was inflation. At the beginning of 1922 the German mark was worth only one-fiftieth of its prewar value; one year later it was worth one ten-thousandth. In 1914 the U.S. dollar had been worth 4.2 marks; in 1923 it was worth 25 billion marks.

The hero in Erich Remarque's novel, *Three Comrades*, gave an idea of what this meant in personal terms: "In 1923 I was advertising chief of a rubber factory.... I had a monthly salary of 200 billion marks. We were paid twice a day, and then everybody had half an hour's leave so that he could rush to the stores and buy something before the next quotation of the dollar came out, at which time the money would lose half its value." There finally was a currency reform in 1923 in which one new mark (*Rentenmark*) was equal to a trillion old marks. But this dizzying inflation had already had the effect of a second revolution in Germany. It had financially wiped out millions of Germans and had spread fear and cynicism throughout the land, which merely weakened the republic further.

The republic was continuously battered from the left and the right. During the night of March 12–13, 1920, Free Corps troops marched on Berlin, singing military songs and flying the black-red-white flag of Imperial Germany. On their helmets was a popular Free Corps symbol: the swastika, the distorted cross that was also the Nazis' chief symbol. The troops faced no armed resistance since the majority of generals in Berlin refused to allow their soldiers to fire on former comrades from the front. The leader of the *coup d'état* was Wolfgang Kapp, who had been brought up in the United States. He installed himself as chancellor and forced the government to flee the city. Virtually all groups in Berlin observed a general strike called by the government before departing was observed by: socialist labor unions, radical leftist militants, shopkeepers and the government ministries. Factories, schools, banks and stores were closed, streetcars and buses ceased running and water, electricity and gas were shut off. This resistance finally forced Kapp and his supporters to flee Berlin only five days later. Almost immediately after the Kapp effort, the communists staged disorders in Berlin, Münster and the Ruhr area, especially Düsseldorf.

Former Finance Minister Matthias Erzberger, who had signed the Versailles

Rampant inflation in the Weimar Republic's darkest days: a thousand marks is hastily overprinted to make it worth a million... then a billion mark note!

Caricaturist George Grosz catches the cynical attitude of the times as he satirizes the wealthy in the badly divided, economically hard-pressed Weimar Republic: (left) "The Landlord" and (right) "View of Tauentzienstrasse," which depicts a blindman, prostitute, and a corrupt capitalist.

Treaty, was gunned down in the Black Forest in 1921 by a right-wing squad, and the following year Foreign Minister Walter Rathenau was felled by assassins' bullets. The next day, Chancellor Joseph Wirth declared in the *Reichstag*, where Rathenau's body lay in state: "The enemy is on the right!" He was correct. Although the radical left tried to destroy the republic, the right did present a greater danger, primarily because it was so well-placed in the civil service, the judicial system and the army.

Stagnation and Loss of the Ruhr

The year 1923 saw the suppression of a Nazi attempted coup in Munich and of communist disorders in Hamburg, Saxony and Thuringia. It also saw the French military occupation of the Ruhr area, Germany's industrial heartland. The German government temporarily suspended all reparations payments and called upon Rhinelanders to practice passive resistance by refusing all cooperation with the French, but this form of retaliation merely meant more hunger and inflation for Germans. The French action was partially a reaction to Germany's signing the Rapallo Pact with the Soviet Union in 1922, call-

ing for a normalization of political and trade relations between the two countries. The two armies began to maintain secret contacts with each other, and German officers began training in Russia with weapons that the Versailles Treaty forbade: tanks, airplanes and submarines. The Soviet Union was also an international outcast at the time and was seeking some support against the Western Allies.

That the storm over the Ruhr finally blew over was the work of the man who became chancellor for a few months in August 1923 and who served as foreign minister until his untimely death in October 1929: Gustav Stresemann. Before and during World War I, he had been a fervent nationalist who had strongly advocated German expansion. But he was one of those persons who had learned from Germany's past and who had concluded that its future was best served by cooperating with the West, not by fighting it. Like Konrad Adenauer after World War II, he helped to restore Germany's position in the world without having much military power at his disposal. However, unlike Adenauer's policy, Stresemann's foreign policy failed to win much domestic support and legitimacy for the Weimar Republic.

The Golden Twenties: Satisfaction and Dissatisfaction

Stresemann ended passive resistance in the Ruhr, and he set out to reach an international agreement that would enable Germany to pay its reparations. In 1924 the American banker Charles Dawes led a committee of experts that drew up a plan to regulate German reparations payments and to channel foreign credit into Germany to stimulate its recovery. This plan set the stage for a remarkable increase in German living standards and wages in the second half of the 1920s. The results were so promising that five years later the Young Plan, also of American origin, sought even further economic stimulation by scaling down the payments scheduled in the Dawes Plan.

The overall result was that more than 25 billion marks worth of foreign capital was poured into Germany, mainly from the United States. This inflow of capital actually exceeded the outflow of reparations payments from Germany. Thus, in the long run, the payments did not have as adverse an economic effect on Germany as agitators constantly charged.

Stresemann also reached out to France. In the Locarno Treaty of 1925 Germany

Germany

agreed to recognize the permanence of its borders with France and Belgium, to foreswear (with France and Belgium) the use of force against each other except in self-defense, to submit any disputes to arbitration or conciliation, and finally to enter the League of Nations, which Germany did in 1926. Although Germany did not recognize the permanency of its eastern borders, it agreed to seek their modification only by peaceful means. It underscored this commitment by signing in 1926 a pact of friendship, the Berlin Treaty, with the Soviet Union. The foreign minister's main focus remained on the West, though. His cooperation with the British and French leaders created considerable enthusiasm in Europe and greatly cooled tensions for the rest of the decade, which because of its increasing prosperity, optimism and cooperation was known as "the golden twenties."

The second half of the 1920s was also a time of relative political stability, thanks not only to Stresemann's influence, but also to another event: the election in April 1925 of Field Marshal von Hindenburg, the "Wooden Titan" and "Hero of Tannenberg," as president of the republic. At the time, many democrats threw up their hands in despair that such a man, who was mentally embedded in the imperial past, could become the highest political leader in Germany. But he actually took seriously his pledge to defend the Weimar constitution, and with this war hero in the presidential palace as a kind of substitute monarch, many German conservatives began for the first time to accept the legitimacy of the republic and to tone down their attacks against it.

This was also a period of extraordinary cultural achievement, although the roots of "Weimar culture" no doubt were planted during Imperial Germany. It was a time in which the Mann brothers, Thomas and Heinrich, Gerhard Hauptmann, Bertold Brecht, Kurt Tucholsky, Erich Kästner, Oskar Kokoschka and Gottfried Benn were reaching huge audiences and were producing works that in some ways supported the new political order.

Still, many writers continued to capture the attention of those whose ideals had been crushed by the fall of the empire and the loss of the war and who could not view civilian life in the new democratic republic as a satisfactory replacement. Erich Remarque's novel *The Road Back* portrayed a disillusioned returning soldier, who asked: "what are we doing here? Look about you: look how flat and comfortless it all is. We are a burden to ourselves and others. Our ideals are bankrupt, our dreams are *kaputt*, and we wander around in this world of rotten opportunists and speculators like Don Quixotes in a foreign land." Such feelings were intensified by the immensely popular battle-front novels by authors such as Ernst Jünger, Werner Beumelburg and Edwin Erich Dwinger, which called for a return to heroic virtues.

Some of Germany's most respected academic minds, such as Martin Heidegger and Carl Schmitt, focused on the shortcomings of liberalism and democracy. Also, many antiliberals were able to sooth their consciences by reading such best sellers as Oswald Spengler's *The Decline of the West*, which decried the republic and the alleged death of culture in the materialist West, and Arthur Moeller van der Bruck's *The Third Reich*, which called for a new and better political and social order.

For the first time in its history, Germany had a city that was not only the political, but also the cultural and intellectual center of the country. In fact, Berlin in the 1920s equaled or even surpassed Paris as the cultural center of Europe. Painters, writers, dramatists and film makers from all over Europe found Berlin to be the most stimulating place to work and live, and entertainers like Marlene Dietrich and American-born Josephine Baker found wildly enthusiastic audiences there. However, some Germans were repelled by the experimentalism in art, sexuality and living styles that were taking place in Berlin and rejected the city as a center of decadence. In fact, one of the first things to be swept out of Germany when the Nazis came to power was the Weimar culture.

Two things brought the "golden years of the twenties" to an end. First, Stresemann died of a stroke in late 1929. He had been the only leader who had made parliamentary government work acceptably well, had brought about compromise between labor and capital, and had enabled Germany to take an equal place among the nations of the world. His death was an untimely tragedy for a nation entering a grave crisis, for he was perhaps the only leader who could have successfully competed with Hitler for control of Germany's destiny. Only ten days after his death came the second blow to the republic: the American stock market collapsed and overnight the chief source of credit for Germany dried up. Germany was thrown into a fatal economic crisis.

By 1930 the Weimar republic was practically dead, although it limped on for another three years. Dr. Heinrich Brüning became chancellor and attempted to master the economic crisis by reducing government spending, rather than by trying to stimulate the economy through decisive government economic programs. This policy earned him the name "hunger chancellor." He had no parliamentary majority. The SPD sometimes supported him begrudgingly in the absence of any acceptable alternative, but Brüning was compelled to resort to the emergency powers granted in Article 48 of the Weimar Constitution, which had been designed originally to enable the president to "restore public safety and order" in times of crisis.

Article 48 was never intended to enable a president or chancellor to rule for long periods of time semi-independently of the Parliament, as all chancellors did during the imperial time and which all did again after March 1930. When the *Reichstag* voted its no confidence for the government for this violation of the constitution, Brüning dissolved Parliament and called for new elections for September 1930. He disregarded all warnings that elections in the middle of such an economic depression and widespread unemployment could only benefit the extremist parties of the left and right. After all, unemployment had risen from 1.37 million in 1929 to 3.15 million in 1930. Such warnings were absolutely correct.

The Communist Party increased its number of seats in Parliament from 54 to 77, and the Nazi Party grew from 12 members to 107, thereby becoming the second largest party after the SPD. The Nazis were thereafter in a position to hammer

President von Hindenburg's signature (actual size)

208

away at the Republic through parliamentary obstruction. Unemployment continued to rise to over 6 million in 1932, while production by 1932 had fallen to barely half the 1929 level. Such economic desperation and governmental paralysis gave a man with a small, socially unpolished minority of followers, but with great demagogical skill, the power to sway the frightened masses—the chance he had awaited for a decade.

Throughout the 1920s the Nazi Party had great difficulty gaining political momentum and a significant following. It had first taken shape in the confusion and frustration following the end of World War I and had aimed its appeal toward the disillusioned and impoverished, first in Austria and shortly afterwards in Germany. Its official name indicated the wide spectrum of groups it tried to encompass: National Socialist German Workers' Party. Throughout its entire existence, it was not a party that aimed to serve one particular class, as the Communist, Social Democratic or Conservative parties tried to do. Instead, the Nazi party was one that attracted the social scrap of all classes. This is why it was and is difficult to put a political label on the party or movement. It was not exactly conservative because it attacked the capitalist economic system and the *status quo*, and, as a rule, German business leaders did not support the party financially or otherwise until after it had actually come into power in 1933.

In a famous speech before the Industrial Club in Düsseldorf in 1932, Adolf Hitler made it unmistakably clear that he considered German business leaders to bear a heavy share of the blame for the 1918 disaster and that business interests would never achieve primacy over political interests in the soon-to-be Third Reich. He always kept this promise. Hitler sought many social changes. In many ways he advocated and introduced a revolution (called by many a "conservative revolution") against bourgeois and industrialized society. National Socialist policy and aims were not leftist either. They were blatantly nationalist, a fact that attracted many conservative supporters who abhorred his means of gaining power. Also, he openly attacked the Communist Party and Social Democrats as un-national and, in the case of the communists, as handmaidens of the Soviet Union. He detested liberalism, democracy and the Weimar Republic, aversions he of course shared with the communists.

An Early Attempt in Bavaria

Hitler made an almost comical attempt to seize power in Bavaria in 1923 by having his followers "arrest" government leaders in the Munich Bürgerbräu beer

Adolf Hitler leaves a Nazi party meeting

hall (now razed). He had hoped this brazen act would set in motion events that would result in the crash of the Weimar Republic. Instead, he was arrested and there was a highly publicized trial that gave this well-practiced demagogue the opportunity to capture the attention of all of Germany and to articulate his attack against the Weimar Republic. He was sent to Landsberg prison for a five-year sentence, although in the end he served less than one year. While in prison he produced his rambling, often raving, book *Mein Kampf* ("My Struggle"), put into writing by his loyal follower, Rudolf Hess.

Hitler's unsuccessful "beer hall putsch" and his imprisonment convinced him that he must try to gain power by means of the ballot box. While in prison, he told a friend: "It will be necessary to pursue a new policy. Instead of working to achieve power by an armed coup, we shall have to hold our noses and enter the Reichstag against the Catholic and Marxist deputies. If outvoting them takes longer than outshooting them, at least the result will be guaranteed by their own constitution. Any lawful process is slow. . . . Sooner or later we shall have a majority—and after that, Germany."

Ten years later he accomplished his goal, but it is mistaken to argue that Hitler came to power entirely legally. When the critical elections came in the years 1930–1933, he unleashed his two private armies, the *Sturmabteilung* (Storm Division—SA) and *Schutzstaffel* (Protective Troop—SS), to break up other parties' rallies and meetings, to beat up opponents in the streets, to terrorize those who manifested an inclination to vote for another party, and to make other kinds of unnerving demonstrations, such as throwing up blockades around Berlin at election time. No person with democratic convictions and a rudimentary knowledge of the Weimar Constitution could call such tactics "legal."

Party Organization

In the 1920s Hitler set about the reorganization of his party from top to bottom. He divided all of Germany into districts, each called a *Gau* and led by a hard-core Nazi called a *Gauleiter*. These districts were subdivided into circles (each called a *Kreis*) and groups. Such units were also created for Austria, Danzig, the Saarland and the Sudetenland, which at the time were not even a part of Germany, but which gave a clue as to what Hitler had in mind for the future. At the top of this party organization was the leader (*Führer*), Hitler himself. Such rule from the top was called the "leadership principle."

Germany

Until he committed suicide in 1945, Hitler's leadership within the party was only once seriously challenged by a group of military officers who sensed that Germany was committing suicide under the *Führer* during the waning days of World War II. Indeed, it is inconceivable that the party would have been so successful without Hitler's powerful will and his ability to coordinate a diverse collection of ambitious Nazis.

Throughout most of the 1920s the Nazi Party found members and votes primarily among fanatical, nationalistic patriots, anti-Semites and social misfits fascinated by militarism. They had a psychological need for rabble-rousing rhetoric that was well supplied by party rallies and a daily reading of the party's newspaper, the *Völkischer Beobachter* ("People's Observer"). But the party was getting nowhere fast, with 32 parliamentary seats in 1924 and only 12 in 1928. However, after the economic disasters of 1929 and 1930, more and more Germans began to look to the former corporal from Austria, who had gained German citizenship through the back door of Bavarian citizenship only shortly before becoming chancellor of all Germany in 1933. As the novelist Erich Kästner wrote: "people ran after the pied pipers down into the abyss."

When Brüning was dismissed as chancellor in May 1932 because of his inability to muster a parliamentary majority, the senile octogenarian von Hindenburg and three intriguers—Hitler, General Kurt von Schleicher and Baron Franz von Papen—dominated German politics. The latter had been the German military attaché in Washington during the first part of World War I who later was expelled from the U.S. for spying. In the twilight of the Weimar Republic, many Germans had the impression that there were only two alternatives: the conservatives, with their established position in the army, coupled with the civil and diplomatic service on the one hand, and Hitler, who stood at the head of a dynamic mass movement on the other. It turned out that Hitler, who had a much clearer idea of what he wanted than did his political opponents, had the clear advantage.

He was no democrat, but he was a populist, whose power was based on the masses, not upon the country's elites. It is true that Hitler was in some political trouble: in the parliamentary elections of November 1932 his party had lost two million votes. In this last free election in prewar Germany, two out of three Germans voted *against* Hitler, and most of those who voted for him in that election had not voted for all that he was to do in the following 13 years. Hitler refused to participate in any coalition in which he

was not chancellor, and von Hindenburg wearily tried every conceivable conservative combination to prevent the chancellorship from going to Hitler, whom he personally despised. But all efforts were to no avail. Von Papen finally persuaded the aged president that he, von Papen, could control the upstart Hitler. So on January 30, 1933, von Hindenburg, backed to the wall, appointed Hitler chancellor in a cabinet containing only three Nazis.

Political responsibility usually moves radicals and ideologues to more practical viewpoints, a historical fact that must have quieted von Hindenburg's worries at the time. In any case, Hitler came to power by miscalculation, rather than by overwhelming popular demand. His ascension to power in Germany was neither inevitable nor a culmination of a thousand years of German history as he asserted; such an evaluation honored Hitler far too greatly. In some unsteady situations such as in 1933, power is like a ripe piece of fruit waiting to be picked by that person who is most ready to act decisively. On January 30, 1933, in Germany that person was Adolf Hitler.

Hitler Seizes Total Power

For a few weeks, Hitler had to be cautious because he had no parliamentary majority, by coalition or otherwise, and because von Hindenburg, who was still very cool toward him, had not given him permission to exercise emergency powers. But an incident during the night of February 27, 1933, gave Hitler the chance to throw off most of the restraints on his power and to fire the *coup de grace* into the drooping head of the Weimar Republic. In that night the *Reichstag* was gutted by fire. Controversy still surrounds this incident, but it is probable that the Nazis themselves set the fire. Hitler acted "quickly as lightning" (which along with "ice cold" was one of his favorite expressions). He declared that this had been an act of communist violence and won von Hindenburg's formal approval the next day to suspend constitutional guarantees for individual and civil liberties.

During the first four weeks of Hitler's chancellorship the courts had dared to reject many of the high-handed methods employed by Hermann Göring's Prussian police force to victimize the Nazis' political opponents. That was no longer possible because Hitler now wielded emergency powers and thereby had the ability to terrorize Germans through instruments of the state. His storm troopers were able to race through the streets arresting socialists, communists and liberal party leaders, taking sledge hammers to newspaper presses, breaking up all opposition political meetings and terrorizing the entire na-

tion. Neither von Hindenburg nor the German army resisted these moves.

In this atmosphere of violence and intimidation, the last election of the Weimar Republic was held on March 5, 1933, in which the Nazis were still unable to receive more than 44% of the popular vote. Yet, by scaring and arresting enough members of Parliament, Hitler was able to manipulate a majority in the Reichstag in favor of the so-called "Enabling Act," which in effect suspended Parliament's power and made Hitler the sole leader of Germany. Only the SPD dared to vote against this. Only a few more steps were necessary to give him full dictatorial power.

Anti-Semitism and Repression

Hitler and his party proceeded to enforce a so-called *Gleichschaltung*, an untranslatable German word meaning the destruction or restructuring of all independent groups or institutions so that none could exist without supporting Nazi rule. In March and April 1933 he abolished the federal organization of Germany, and for the first time in its history, Germany became entirely centralized, with governors (*Reichsstatthalter*) carrying out Hitler's policy in the various regions. By June all independent labor unions had been outlawed and a Labor Front was created under the leadership of the invariably intoxicated Robert Ley, with the task of keeping labor under firm control. By July all political parties except the Nazi Party had been abolished and concentration camps were established, where alleged enemies of the state could be "concentrated" and controlled.

By October, all communications media, including film, were brought under Nazi control and all newspaper editors were required to be Aryans (non-Jewish members of an ancient race to which, according to Nazi doctrine, Germans belonged). They could not even be married to Jews. This was only one of the first of a steadily growing number of measures directed against Jews within Germany, who, according to Nazi ideology, were social parasites who weakened the German nation. Many Jews, including brilliant intellectuals and scientists, began to flee Germany during the ensuing years. One of them was Albert Einstein, who came to the United States. These anti-Jewish measures reached a prewar crescendo in the night of November 9–10, 1938, when hundreds of Jewish homes, stores and synagogues were systematically damaged and plundered. The amount of broken glass this senseless and criminal rampage left gave the event the name of *Kristallnacht* ("Crystal Night"). Although many Germans were sickened by this incident, none dared to resist.

Germany

This event increased the tempo of the stampede of Jews from Germany, which started in 1933 when all non-Aryans and people who were "no longer prepared to intercede at all times for the National Socialist state" were excluded from civil service and ultimately from posts in the universities. Many young Germans had streamed into the Nazi student organization and assumed the right to control the lectures and writings of their professors for "un-German" or other politically revealing utterances. Youthful idealism can sometimes have a beneficial effect in politics, but it can also be disastrous. In 1933–1934 an estimated 1,684 scholars, including 1,145 professors, were dismissed from the universities. At the universities of Berlin and Frankfurt am Main, about a third of the faculty was fired, and in all of Germany the size of the student body fell by about one-third, due largely to the inclusion of Nazi Party membership in the admission procedure.

This policy of *Gleichschaltung* issued an almost fatal blow to the cultural and intellectual preeminence of Germany. But there was one country that benefited enormously from this self-defeating and shortsighted policy: the United States. Before the outbreak of war, approximately 200,000 Germans, half of whom were Jewish, had fled to the U.S. American immigration quota restrictions, which had been tightened during the economic depression of the 1930s, were such that a large portion of the German refugees to the United States were intellectual or cultural leaders who could find sponsors more easily. They were attracted by such universities as the New School for Social Research in New York, Princeton University, the University of Chicago or to such magnetic cultural centers as Hollywood or New York City.

Even an abbreviated list of these refugees gives an idea of the enormous loss to Germany: in addition to scientists Albert Einstein and Edward Teller, in literature practically the entire Mann family (Thomas, Heinrich, Klaus, Erika and Golo), Bertold Brecht, Stefan Zweig, Carl Zuckmayer, Alfred Döblin, Leon Feuchtwanger and Erich Maria Remarque. In film there were Fritz Lang, Marlene Dietrich and Otto Preminger, in theater Max Reinhardt, in music Arnold Schönberg and Kurt Weil, in art, Georg Grosz and Max Ernst, in architecture, Walter Gropius and Ludwig Mies van der Rohe; in publishing, Frederick Praeger and Kurt Wolff, and in scholarship, Paul Tillich, Erich Fromm, Hans Morgenthau, Theodor Adorno, Ernst Bloch, Leo Strauss, Erich Vögelin, Hannah Arendt, Ernst Cassirer and Kurt Riezler. By 1938 the New York columnist Dorothy Thompson could claim with justification that "practically everyone whom the

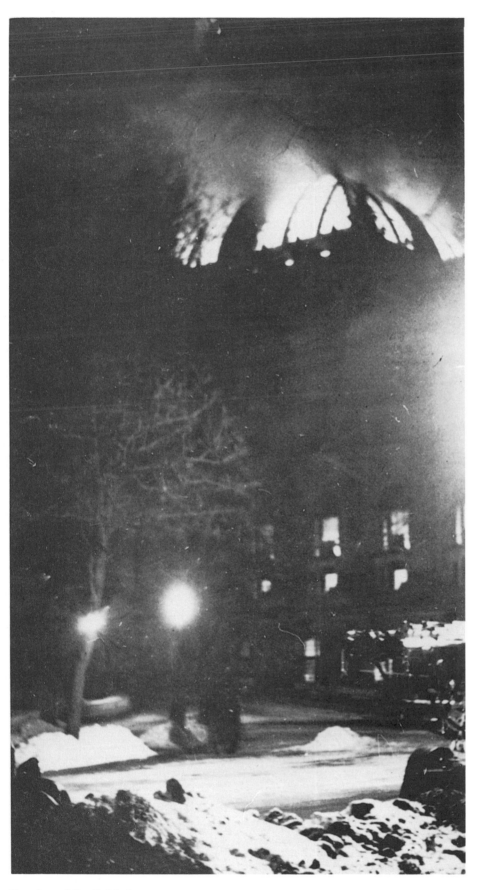

Burning of the *Reichstag*

Germany

world considers to be representative of German culture before 1933 is now a refugee." Of course, some stayed in the United States only until Hitler was defeated, but most stayed for good.

"Night of the Long Knives"

In the dark hours of June 30, 1934, known as the "night of the long knives," Hitler had hundreds of potential challengers to his authority within his own party murdered, especially the SA leadership, including Ernst Röhm. While his assassination squads were at work, he also eliminated many prominent non-Nazis, such as von Schleicher and some of von Papen's closest aides, as well as leading authors, lawyers, civil servants, Catholic politicians, and harmless citizens who at some time had caused irritation to one or the other Nazi bosses. Von Papen and Brüning escaped by the skin of their teeth, the latter eventually landing in a professorial chair at Harvard. These cold-blooded acts were enough to intimidate most resistance to Hitler within or without the Nazi party until his death in 1945.

The senile von Hindenburg died August 2, 1934, and Hitler simply combined the offices of president and chancellor and declared himself the absolute *Führer* of party and state. He then required that the nation give retroactive approval of this unconstitutional act in a plebiscite, a favorite maneuver of dictators whereby one may vote "yes" or "no" under the watchful eyes of party henchmen. Despite intimidation measures, five million Germans voted "no" to this act. Hitler then proceeded to require all officers and soldiers to take an oath of allegiance not to Germany, but to him alone. Many German officers had grave misgivings about taking such an oath. But Hitler's shrewd treatment of the army gradually eliminated it as an immediate threat to his power, although high-ranking officers would later prove to be his most daring, though ill-fated, foes.

The Third Reich

By fall 1934, Hitler stood as the undisputed leader of a dictatorial state he called the "Third Reich." This name was used to remind Germans that he had created anew a Germany worthy of the two earlier German empires: the one created by Heinrich I in 919 and the one formed by Bismarck in 1871. His path to power had been washed by blood and strewn with corpses. Many of his subjects had been driven through fear to passivity. Yet in 1939 he could claim with justification that he ruled a people that generally supported him. How was this possible? In the first half of his 12-year rule he was able to achieve certain things that many Germans

and non-Germans alike regarded as little less than miraculous. His accomplishments confused and disarmed his opponents, who in 1933 were still the majority within Germany. But their numbers had dwindled considerably by 1938, even if most of them did not actually become Nazis.

Before 1933 Hitler had shown himself to be an unparalleled organizer and hypnotic speaker, but few Germans expected him actually to succeed in conducting the complex affairs of state. Before he came to power, he remained largely in the realm of fuzzy generalities. For example, he made no concrete suggestions on how to combat the problem of unemployment. He also seemed to reveal his cards very quickly after coming to power, inflicting a heavy dose of terror on the German people. Indeed, that his rule always rested in part on terror indicated that the whole German people never entirely embraced National Socialism. But terror gradually declined and remained at a level just sufficient to keep the population in a state of fear without driving them into desperate resistance. His orchestration of terror within Germany and his skillful use of his own undeniable charisma were psychological masterpieces from which all would-be dictators could learn.

In retrospect, some professionals have diagnosed Hitler as clinically paranoid. Continuously tense and expectant, he was sensitive and suspicious. He had no close relationship with anyone, not even with his mistress, Eva Braun, whom he finally married moments before committing suicide. Untrusting, he always felt that his failures resulted from the enmity or failure of others, even those close to him. He was able, however, to maintain his conduct within nominally acceptable bounds, and some persons considered him to be no more than a "crank."

Initial Successes

What were his specific accomplishments? By far his most important and popular was his dealing with the economic crisis. In early 1933 there were more than six million Germans out of work; by 1936 Germany achieved full employment without creating inflation. Germans had been put to work building an admirable network of superhighways known as *Autobahnen*, as well as other public works. Industries were given tax relief, and the government's financial leaders, especially Dr. Schacht, channeled investments to desperately needy economic sectors and successfully manipulated government funds and the money supply so that the economy would not be choked for lack of money. Hitler also revitalized the arms industry in Germany.

This provided an important stimulus for the economy, but it should be noted that most of Germany's unemployed found jobs in civilian industries, not in arms industries. In the three years after Hitler had assumed power in Germany, the country's GNP and national income had doubled, and Germans had begun to enjoy a modest prosperity.

Within Germany the mood had changed from one of hopelessness to one of confidence in the future. Of course, the facts should not be overlooked that by 1939 many Germans had become soldiers and approximately 300,000 were in concentration camps. Hitler's economic performance was so successful that many persons in and out of Germany gained the impression that this man could indeed perform wonders. Others in countries all over Europe began to see totalitarianism, cooperation with and imitation of Germany as attractive.

A second accomplishment was that he accelerated a process begun several decades earlier in Germany, namely the breaking down of class differences. The Nazis were officially in favor of this *Volksgemeinschaft*. They did not speak of a "classless society," as do communists, but of "community." This latter term had become very attractive to many Germans who were sick and tired of conflict and who wanted to see central authority established in Germany. "Community" as interpreted by the Nazis required a high degree of social mobilization of youths, women, farmers and other groups. In fact, Germans were expected to become so active in politically dominated groups that they could not possibly go their own way and be individually free. Still, in the Third Reich there was much upward and downward mobility, mixing of classes and open opportunity for the talented (so long as they were not Jewish or openly critical of the new political order).

It is certainly incorrect to say that Hitler's rule was "class rule," because no one social group dominated the party and state. For that reason, it is technically incorrect to call National Socialism fascism, which in Southern Europe meant upper class domination over the other social classes and groups, all bundled together and cemented by artificially produced mass enthusiasm. No social groups fared badly in Hitler's Reich. Yet it would be indeed wrong to argue that Hitler eliminated class conflict entirely. Despite the rapid economic recovery, the problems between capital and labor, big and small business, or industry and agriculture were not solved. But the important fact is that there was less social inequality in Germany during the Third Reich than there had been before, and both East and West

Autographed portrait of the *Führer*

Courtesy: David W. Staton

pre-1914 great European powers, Austria-Hungary, had been destroyed, and another, Russia, had been excluded from the victorious coalition. The United States refused to help enforce the treaty, so only Britain and France remained to hold the dictated settlement together. In the course of the 1920s Britain grew tired of its role and began to seek a policy of moderation and accommodation toward Germany. French leaders did not favor such a policy of appeasement, but France had become so weakened by pacifism and political division from within that it could no longer oppose Germany energetically.

Hitler violated the Locarno Treaty in 1936 and remilitarized the Rhineland. In March 1938 Germany swallowed up Austria in the face of virtually no opposition from it or any other country. Six months later, Germany obtained French and British approval at a conference in Munich for Germany's absorption of the Sudetenland, the predominantly German-speaking western part of Czechoslovakia. Hitler's appetite was whetted, so in 1939 he declared Bohemia (capital: Prague) and Moravia to be German protectorates and occupied the Memel area. He had marched his troops a long way while the rest of Europe slept, but when his troops entered Prague, Britain woke up and resigned itself to the bitter fact that it would have to prepare for war against Germany. France reluctantly agreed.

The Start of World War II

By the spring of 1939, Britain and France had already allowed Germany to become the dominant power in Europe. Hitler's greatest mistake was that he cast this enormous accomplishment away by leading Germany into war. After 1938 he had no further diplomatic victories. From 1939 to 1941 he led Germany to dazzling successes, but all were of a military nature. With relative ease his newly created army (*Wehrmacht*) rolled over part of Poland, Denmark, Norway, Holland, Belgium, Luxembourg, Yugoslavia and Greece.

The most miraculous victory, in the eyes of the world, was the victory over France. Most German generals shuddered at the thought of attacking France, remembering the failure of the 1914 advance and the four-year war of attrition, which had sapped Germany's strength and will. But Hitler had great faith in the tank warfare tactics developed by General Heinz Guderian and in the brilliant strategic plan devised by General Friedrich Erich von Manstein. He also recognized the most important factor: France was simply unwilling to fight a war even before German tanks crossed its border.

In six weeks, Germany had rolled into France via a flank attack around its famed

Germany greatly profited from and continued this process after 1945.

A third accomplishment that won the admiration of many of his countrymen was Hitler's rapid rearmament of Germany. In January 1933, Germany had a 100,000-man army without an air force and modern weapons. By 1938 it had a conscript army and was the strongest military power in Europe. Hitler also made the significant decision, against the advice of many military experts, to integrate armored units with other combat forces. This later proved quite successful in overrunning most of Western Europe. The military buildup may have been a curse for the rest of Europe, but many Germans approved it. They saw it as a means for revising the despised Versailles Treaty.

A fourth accomplishment was a string of almost stunning diplomatic and military victories. Until 1942 Hitler had always been a master of recognizing when houses of cards were about ready to collapse and then of acting decisively while others wavered. He had the instinct of a buzzard that told him when to swoop in on that which had been already dying. He had seen when the Weimar Republic had reached the end of its road, and Hitler merely gave it the *coup de grace*. He also could see that the international system that had emerged from Versailles was collapsing. At that conference, one of the four

Germany

Maginot line of supposedly impregnable fortresses. The amount of French military activity is vividly evident even to this day. If one inspects the war memorials in the towns and cities of France, the names of those who perished in World War I outnumbers by ten-, twenty- and even thirty-to-one the names of those victims of World War II.

By the summer of 1940 Germany controlled Europe from the Arctic Circle to the Pyrenees and from the Atlantic Ocean to the Soviet Union. If Hitler had made a generous peace offer to France, he might have destroyed Britain's and other countries' will to resist, but Hitler never thought of such a possibility. He could not grant a magnanimous peace because, as he himself later wrote, the victory of the stronger always involved "the destruction of the weaker or his unconditional subservience." He had a knack for seeing the weakness in his enemies, but he was unable to build anything lasting. Also, because he considered himself to be infallible and irreplaceable, he insisted on doing everything quickly; he could not plant anything that required time to grow.

Based upon his writings and actions, one can say with reasonable certainty that Hitler sought to establish German hegemony in Europe and direct domination over the Soviet Union, which along with the older European powers' overseas colonies, would occupy the bottom of Hitler's power pyramid. Above them would be the rest of the European countries, divided into Germanic lands bordering on Germany, servant peoples, such as the Poles, and satellites and quasi-independent states. On top would be an all-powerful Germany. This German-dominated order would place Hitler in a good position later to struggle against America and Japan for world domination. That he did not accomplish this stunning goal was due in large measure to serious mistakes he himself made after such stunning successes.

The Beginning of the End

In 1940 he launched an aerial attack against Britain, which left rubble piles throughout the kingdom, but which also inspired heroic British action in what Prime Minister Winston Churchill called Britain's "finest hour." While still involved in this furious struggle, violating the treaty whereby Germany and Russia had split up Poland between them, Hitler unleashed his armies against the Soviet Union in mid-1941, against the advice of his generals, thereby creating a two-front war that had been such a nightmare for Germany during World War I. The attack was launched too late, so in a repeat of Napoleon's humiliation, "Mother Winter"

saved the weaker Russians. Cold weather and snow closed in on the German troops, many of whom had not been issued proper winter equipment. After initial victories against an enemy Hitler had grossly underestimated, the German advance slowed to a freeze. Hitler saw his dreams of grandeur buried under Russian snow and ice.

In the midst of this truly desperate situation, Hitler compounded his difficulties even further. On December 7, 1941, Japan attacked the U.S. fleet at Pearl Harbor in Hawaii, and the U.S. responded by declaring war on Japan, but not on Germany. Germany had no treaty obligation with Japan, but inexplicably and without conferring with anyone, Hitler declared war against the U.S. Germany had no military means for conducting military operations against the Americans, but this step decisively tipped the scales in favor of his opponents and ultimately sealed Germany's defeat. Thereafter, he had no idea how to extricate Germany from ruin. For example, he could not follow up on General Erwin Rommel's victories in North Africa in

the summer of 1942, and, of course, he excluded the very idea of a political settlement. His only order was "Hold at all costs!" In 1942 Germany began losing territory in the East, especially after a disastrous defeat at Stalingrad in early 1943.

After 1941 Hitler withdrew more and more from public view and spent most of his time in military headquarters. Since his first goal—to dominate Europe—was slipping out of reach, he turned toward a second goal—the eradication of the Jews. He began astonishing the world not with diplomatic and military victories, but with crimes the extent of which the world had hitherto not known and the extent of which would only be discovered at the end of the war. Earlier and contemporary dictators or would-be world conquerors such as Alexander the Great, Napoleon and Stalin, had caused thousands or millions of deaths. But whether one agreed with them or not, they usually had political or military motives for their brutality. Hitler had none. Strictly speaking, his crimes were not war crimes, because his murder campaign of the Jews worked

German Expansion, 1935–39.

German officers examine a captured Polish banner

against his political and military objectives. This campaign was not only morally repugnant, but it sapped further the strength of a weakening Germany.

The "Final Solution"

From the time he first began making public speeches, Hitler left no doubt that he was intensely anti-Semitic. He put this in writing in *Mein Kampf* and underscored it with anti-Jewish legislation after coming to power in 1933. On January 30, 1939, the sixth anniversary of his acquisition of power, he spoke publicly of "eradicating the Jewish race in Europe." This actually was another manifestation of his paranoia. His delusion was that the Jews were responsible for Germany's failure in World War I and were a threat to his current ambitions for Germany. Sometimes, a paranoid's delusions are directed against one person, but Hitler's were directed toward millions.

In mid-1941 Hitler began having Polish and Russian Jews rounded up and shot beside mass graves. At the Wannsee Conference at the outskirts of Berlin on January 20, 1942, the decision was made to extend this policy to Jews in Germany and other occupied countries as well. Special extermination camps were constructed in Treblinka, Sobibor, Maidanek (Lublin), Belzec, Chelmno (Kulmhof) and Auschwitz for this grisly purpose.

By the spring of 1942 the "final solution," which of course "solved" nothing but caused the needless death of about six million innocent people by 1945, was in full swing. This policy was pursued with such single-minded determination that the German war effort itself was greatly hampered. Manpower badly needed at the front or in domestic industries was either sent to extermination camps as victims of this policy or to SS units or other special military units (called *Einsatzgruppen*) as executors of this policy. Railroad rolling stock was diverted and rail lines were clogged. Also, this policy of murder prompted the Western Allies to declare as a major war aim the "punishment of those persons responsible for these crimes"; the Soviet Union proclaimed the same in November 1943. This new war aim made any kind of compromise peace with Germany unthinkable and prompted Hitler's enemies to demand Germany's "unconditional surrender."

The Jewish Museum in Berlin documents this lamentable tale: of 560,000 German Jews before the war, 276,000 emigrated to safety; 25,000 in mixed marriages with non-Jews survived; 8,500 escaped over the German border; 10,000 went into hiding, of which only 1,500 survived; 200,000 were deported from Germany and occupied countries and perished. After the war, 50,000 German Jews were homeless. They were joined by 150,000 Jews from Eastern Europe, who poured into the American occupation zone. Most ultimately emigrated.

How much did the German people know about this ghastly policy at the time? Certainly all Germans of a sound mind knew that their country had adopted an official policy of discrimination against Jews, and all had been informed that their government was "resettling" Jews in the East. However, for a variety of reasons, the regime did not reveal to the German population details about the policy. The most important reason, no doubt, was that Hitler did not trust his own people and suspected that they would not approve. He had noted that most Germans had supported neither the nationwide boycott of Jewish businesses in 1933 nor the "Crystal Night" of 1938, which actually produced more pity for Jews, shame and irritation (but no more than that) among non-Nazis than anything else.

Further, in mid-1941 Hitler had to suspend a policy he had introduced publicly in 1939 to eliminate 70,000 to 80,000 patients in convalescent and nursing homes, 10,000 to 20,000 sick and invalids in concentration camps within Germany, all Jewish patients in mental hospitals and about 3,000 children between the ages of three and 13 in orphanages and special schools for the handicapped. One of the major reasons for the suspension was the increasing unrest within the German population and the active opposition of the churches.

Hitler spared the Jews no misery, but he was careful not to allow most Germans to know for sure what was happening to the Jews. The exterminations were conducted in Eastern Europe, outside Germany, and careful precautions were taken not to enable unauthorized persons to witness what was happening within the camps.

Germany

He even took the special measure, whenever possible, of sending German Jews first to large ghettos such as Theresienstadt in Bohemia, where they were able to write postcards back to Germany for awhile before being transported to death camps. Of course, rumors about what was really happening filtered into Germany, but the absence of confirmation enabled anyone to reject the rumors or to remain in doubt if he chose to do so. Most Germans did just that, as did most non-Germans in the other occupied areas, for that matter. In Germany and in other occupied areas there were persons who took risks by hiding or helping Jews. But nowhere was there the kind of mass uprising that would have been necessary to put an end to that shameful policy. In fact, only the military power of Hitler's enemies brought the Third Reich to its knees.

Other Genocide

Hitler's policy of liquidating people whom he considered to be racially inferior was, of course, not restricted to the Jews. The Jews were not the only group that fell within his definition of *Untermensch* ("subhuman"). Only about a fifth of the 25,000 Gypsies living in Germany in 1939 survived by 1945, and estimates of the total number of European Gypsies murdered at Hitler's order range up to a half-million. In October 1939 German leaders began a five-year campaign to destroy the entire Polish elite and culture. Polish priests, professors, journalists, businessmen and earlier political leaders were systematically liquidated. When one considers that the Soviet Union conducted a similar policy against the Poles in those areas under its domination, most dramatically in the Katyn Forest in 1939, when Soviet forces murdered 10,000 Polish officers and elites and dumped them into mass graves, it is almost miraculous that Poland was able to survive the war as a nation. In the end, Poland had lost about six million countrymen, about half of whom were Jews and not more than 300,000 of whom had fallen in battle.

The German treatment of the Russians and of subject peoples under Russian control was even worse than that of the Poles. German policy in the Soviet Union revealed the extent to which Hitler's racial theories thwarted Germany's national interests. Many peripheral peoples in the Soviet Union who had never joined with it voluntarily greeted invading German soldiers more like liberators than conquerors. A farsighted German policy to transform these people into allies might have been successful and extremely beneficial to Germany.

Instead, Russians and non-Russians alike were treated with the same brutality.

Hitler addresses a Nazi rally

Unlike in Poland, the German Army was involved in the actions directed against the civilian population in the Soviet Union. The Germans especially mistreated Soviet prisoners of war. According to German military records, by May 1, 1944, the Germans had captured more than five million Russian soldiers, mostly in 1941. However, at that time, fewer than two million remained alive. Almost a half million had been executed, 67,000 had fled and almost three million had died in the camps, mostly of hunger. German mistreatment of the Soviet population helped Stalin to unify the population in the war effort against the Germans. The many acts of brutality committed later by Soviet soldiers in occupied Germany, as well as the strong distrust that the Soviet Union showed toward Germany after 1945, must be seen against this background, although nothing can excuse the bestial acts committed by these two peoples against each other.

Minimal Internal Resistance

There were, of course, some symbolic acts of resistance to Nazi rule within Germany. In early 1943 two young Christians in the Catholic youth organization, Hans and Sophie Scholl, brother and sister, passed out flyers on the streets of Munich for a few minutes calling Hitler a tyrant and demanding acts of sabotage in the arms factories before they were whisked away and promptly executed.

The most serious opposition to Hitler came from within the German Army, supported by a unique coalition of aristocrats, civil servants, trade unionists and clergy-

men from both churches. The German military traditionally had considered itself superior to Nazis, whom it tended to regard as uneducated, rowdy troublemakers. On July 20, 1944, this coalition made a bold attempt to assassinate Hitler, but the bomb placed under the table during a meeting in Hitler's eastern headquarters miraculously failed to harm the *Führer* seriously when it exploded; it had been placed there by Colonel Claus Schenk von Stauffenberg, a decorated war hero who had lost an arm and an eye in battle. Assuming that the Nazi leader was dead, the plotters moved to take control of the major governmental and military command centers in Berlin. However, Hitler quickly went on the air to announce that he was alive, and he ordered that the plotters be arrested. Within hours the leaders were executed. Hitler suffered nerve damage to an arm and appeared shaken by the incident.

The assassins were without question prompted to act by information they had of Hitler's grisly extermination policies. When asked about his motive before the "People's Court" following the attempt, Count Yorck von Wartenburg said, "I thought about the many crimes," before he was shouted down by the hated Chief Justice Roland Freisler. But there were other motives as well. Germany was entangled in a war it could not win, and there was no attempt on the part of Germany's leaders to reach a political settlement. It was characteristic that after the July 20 plot Hitler ordered mass arrests of more than 5,000 former cabinet ministers, mayors, parliamentarians and civil ser-

Germany

vants (including such important postwar figures as Konrad Adenauer and Kurt Schumacher), whom the enemy coalition could have viewed as a possible alternative to the Third Reich. For Hitler, the only conceivable alternatives were Germany's holding on under his own leadership or facing total destruction.

The Allies Close In

By the fall of 1944 enemy armies were advancing on Germany from the East and West, and more and more Germans saw the hopelessness of the situation and began to regard conquest by the Western Allies as liberation. But Hitler did not share this secret war aim of many Germans. He had personally assumed command of the German forces. He had unleashed a torrent of powerful rockets on London and its suburbs using technology only recently developed. These attacks by what he called his "wonder weapons" merely served to harden even more the determination of the British and their American ally.

Disregarding warnings from military advisers that the Red Army was poised for a massive strike from the East, Hitler ordered his last military offensive against the Western Allies in the Belgian Ardennes Forest in late 1944. The element of surprise and extremely bad weather that kept Allied aircraft grounded for a few days helped the Germans to gain initial success and to stop the Western powers' advance on Germany in its tracks. However, once American and British air power could be brought into the action, the German offensive was stopped, and by the first week of January the German forces were being decimated or rolled back.

As some of Hitler's generals had warned, the Red Army crashed through the German line in the East and in one violent movement pushed from the Vistula to the Oder rivers. Because Hitler had squandered his last reserves in the Ardennes offensive, he had nothing left to stop the Russian advance.

Hitler's decisions that had slowed down the Western Allied advance and favored a rapid Russian advance into the heart of Germany had unfortunate consequences for postwar Germany. In the first half of February 1945, President Roosevelt, Prime Minister Churchill and General Secretary Stalin met in Yalta in the Crimea area to discuss the postwar control of Germany and to divide Germany into zones of occupation. The lines they drew were heavily influenced by the calculations of where exactly the Allied armies would be in Germany at the end of the war. At the time, it appeared that Russian troops would be somewhat farther within Germany than was actually the case when hostilities ceased. However,

based on the decisions made at Yalta, U.S. troops had later to be pulled back from Saxony and Thuringia, which were within the designated Soviet zone. Also, the collapse of cooperation among the four Allies after the war left the temporary line drawn between the Soviet zone of occupation and the zones of the Western Allies as the dividing line between East and West Germany until 1990.

Seeing enemy armies advancing within his own country's territory and with no hope for stopping them, any rational and responsible leader with a concern for his own people would have done anything to salvage whatever would be necessary for his people's survival. Hitler was not such a leader. In late 1941 he had made a chilling statement to the Danish and Croatian foreign ministers: "If ever the German *Volk* is no longer sufficiently strong and willing to sacrifice its own blood for its existence, then it should fade away and be destroyed by another, stronger power.... In that situation, I will lose no tears for the German people."

The Collapse

On March 18 and 19, 1945, he gave two orders that demonstrated he had not changed his mind and he now thought it was time to carry through with the end of Germany. He ordered all Germans in areas threatened by the invasion forces in the West to leave their homes and set out on what could only have been a death march eastward. The following day he gave the so-called "Nero order": "to destroy all military, transport, communications, industrial and supply facilities as well as anything of value within the Reich

that could be used by the enemy for continuing its struggle either immediately or in the foreseeable time." When Albert Speer, his trusted confidant and munitions minister, objected to this policy, which would have completely eliminated the Germans' ability to survive after defeat, Hitler answered "ice-coldly": "If the war is lost, then the people will be lost also.... In that case the people will have shown itself as the weaker, and the future would belong solely to the strengthened Eastern people. Whoever survives this struggle would be the inferior ones anyway since the superior ones have already fallen."

Hitler himself chose not to be among the survivors. On April 30, 1945, a few hours before his underground bunker in Berlin was captured by Soviet troops, he stuck a pistol in his mouth and pulled the trigger. Speer and others did their best to prevent these orders from being carried out. But the important effect of these orders was that most Germans, at least in the Western part of Germany, viewed the enemy occupation of Germany as liberation. While the occupation forces expected to find a nation of fanatic Nazis, they found instead a shell-shocked, seriously disillusioned people. They had been more thoroughly "denazified" by Hitler's treatment of Germany in the closing months of the war than the carefully planned denazification and reeducation program would ever have been able to accomplish. The occupation powers interpreted Germans' passivity and willingness to cooperate as typical German servility. Instead it was a reflection of the extent to which Germans felt themselves to have been deceived and betrayed by Hitler.

Divided Berlin

217

Germany

The Early Postwar Period

Hitler had unwittingly strengthened the chances for democracy to succeed after he had left the stage. Thirty-three years after Napoleon had been defeated in 1815, a new Napoleon was elected president of France. By contrast, in post-1945 Germany, no one who invokes the name and legacy of Adolf Hitler would have the slightest chance of gaining power. Thus, one can be thankful that Hitler and his party had so thoroughly discredited themselves in German eyes. But what kind of Germany did Hitler leave behind? Seven million Germans had perished; only the Russians suffered greater human casualties as a result of the war. Germany lost a fourth of its territory, and what remained was divided into two German states.

Not since the Thirty Years War from 1618 to 1648 had the Germans suffered so much destruction or loss of life. Not a single great German city survived the war undamaged by saturation bombing by the Western Allies and, later, artillery shells. One-fifth of the nation's housing was destroyed, and in the larger cities the situation was genuinely desperate. Only 47% of the buildings in Hamburg were left standing and most others were severely damaged. In the commercial city of Frankfurt, only about a fourth of the houses survived, and in Nürnberg, where Hitler had held some of his most impressive party congresses and rallies, only about one-tenth of the dwellings remained unscathed. Shocked and hungry Germans without shelter were cramped in houses and apartments belonging to others, in hotels, in makeshift structures, or even in former bomb shelters. Everywhere were mountains of rubble with narrow paths cut through them to enable pedestrians, carts and vehicles to pass. Bridges, viaducts, water mains and power lines were cut. All bridges over the Rhine, Weser and Main rivers had been destroyed, and these three key waterways were closed to shipping. Power facilities, even if left intact or repaired, were often unable to function for lack of coal. Home heating was almost nonexistent for all but the occupation forces, and often the only warmth the Germans could get was at warming stations in certain places in the city, where they could go for a few minutes a day.

The German population had suffered frightful losses in the war, which for the first time since 1814 had been fought in the heart of Germany. Over two million German soldiers had been killed in action, two and a half million had been taken prisoner, over a million and a half were missing and at least an equal number had been crippled by the war. Civilian deaths and injury were in the hundreds of thou-

In Germany . . . desolation

sands, and far more than a million German children had been orphaned.

There was very little food, especially in the Soviet and French sectors, where occupation troops and authorities were compelled to "live off the land." Prewar Germany had never been self-sufficient in food, and during the Weimar Republic it had to import about 20% of its needs. Because of the economic disruption and the loss of extensive agricultural areas in the East, this figure rose to 50% in the three Western zones after the war. In those zones, the official target in the immediate post-war years was a mere 1,550 calories per day, but in the heavily populated British zone in 1946 the actual rations sank to 600 to 1,000 calories per day. Malnutrition was especially harmful to the young. Hamburg reported 10,000 cases of hunger edema (abdominal swelling), and in towns and cities in Hesse 90% of the children developed rickets. The mortality rate for infants and young children rose to 154 per thousand in the Ruhr area and 160 in Berlin.

For most Germans, finding the next meal was immensely more important than the political future of their country. The defeated country had suffered economic collapse. For a couple of years the Allied occupation powers restricted production, delayed recovery and decentralized or dismantled industrial plants in order to reduce the power of industrial leaders or to provide reparations to some of the victorious Allies, particularly the Soviet Union, which transported whole factories to mother Russia. As a result of this economic turmoil, the great majority of the population had become pauperized. Many were

reduced to selling or swapping their most treasured heirlooms for a pittance in order to obtain food or other necessities, often on the thriving black market and at exorbitant prices. In some cases, honorable women actually had to resort to prostitution among the occupying forces in order to provide food for their families and relatives. Former President Herbert Hoover reported in February 1947 that the situation in Western Germany was worse than in any other part of Europe. He told President Truman bluntly: "You can have vengeance, or peace, but you can't have both."

Migration from the East

The available food, housing and jobs had to serve not only the prewar residents of the three Western zones, but also the flood of refugees who poured in from the East. Million of Germans were expelled from Southern European countries or from former German lands east of the Oder and Neisse rivers, which now form the border between Germany and Poland. These lands in 1938 had amounted to about 44,000 square miles (70,400 sq. km., or 24% of Germany's entire land area), and they had supplied a large part of Germany's food and coal. Most of these areas became a part of Poland to compensate Poles for their lands the Soviet Union had seized. Germany officially relinquished these lands to Poland within weeks after it regained its unity and full sovereignty in 1990. The rest (a part of East Prussia, including the city of Königsberg, now Kaliningrad) was absorbed by the Soviet Union.

These expulsions of ethnic Germans from Eastern Europe reached a height in

Germany

A demoralized population

the winter of 1945–46. Those affected were often given 24 hours notice and were able to take with them only 50 to 60 pounds of baggage apiece. Other Germans fled the Soviet occupation zone in order to escape the kind of authoritarian political order that was being established there. These refugees placed severe strains on the Western occupation authorities and on the previous residents, who were required to share their meager incomes with the often highly unwelcome newcomers in order to distribute the nation's material burdens more fairly. By the time the Berlin Wall was erected beginning August 13, 1961, approximately 12 million refugees had poured into West Germany.

Adding to the refugee problem was that of the displaced persons (DP's), whom the Nazis had brought to Germany to perform forced labor. They numbered about six and a half million persons by the end of the war, and about two million of them refused to return to their homelands in the Soviet Union or in the Baltic states, which had been annexed by the USSR. They were fed and clothed largely by the U.S. through the UN Relief and Rehabilitation Administration, but they often occupied jobs and housing that were denied to Germans.

The German people were largely disgraced and demoralized. Hitler had greatly changed German society, having reduced or eliminated permanently the power and influence that, for example, noblemen, military officers or large Prussian landowners had wielded earlier. Unlike 1918, the collapse of the Third Reich eliminated the nation's entire political

elite. Germany's highest surviving Nazi leaders were placed on trial in Nuremberg from November 1945 until October 1946, and most were given either death sentences or long prison terms in Spandau Prison in West Berlin. Only one prisoner, Rudolf Hess, remained there. Blind and crippled, he died in August 1987 at age 93, and the prison was razed.

The controversial denazification programs of the occupation powers required that those Germans who had held positions of obvious authority or influence under the Nazis be jailed, fined or demoted. Others, such as civil servants, teachers, journalists or industrial leaders, most of whom had no choice about joining the Nazi Party, were temporarily removed from their jobs. In the end, all of the elites under the previous regime had been deprived of their status, except church leaders. *Mein Kampf* was outlawed although unofficial copies can be obtained on the Internet, and its copyright date ends in 2015. It is questionable that most of the denazification measures were necessary at all. Defeat and utter destruction under the leadership of Hitler had been the best antidote to Nazism. Although it took several more years to convince many Germans that even the general idea of National Socialism had been wrong, their approval of the concrete form Nazism had taken had disappeared almost completely by the end of the war.

The German army was completely disbanded, and when the Federal Armed Forces were created in 1956, the military's influence and prestige in political and social life had been almost entirely eliminated. The various classes had not been eradicated, but they had been brought more closely together during the Third Reich and the aftermath of the war. Germans now mingled more easily with one another. Although an end to hostilities brought no political revolution or social upheaval, as had been the case in 1918, the quiet social and political revolution that culminated in 1945 was much more far-reaching than that of 1918.

Germans were now divided territorially, but they were no longer so divided domestically. The old conservatives had been discredited and the romanticism of war, assertiveness in the world and ideas about German national unique superiority had been extinguished. Ideologies had little appeal anymore, and most Germans had become convinced that a flight from the much debunked "bourgeois values," including especially parliamentary democracy within a rule of law, solves no problems, and can bring immense suffering to human beings. Many Germans emerged from the war politically apathetic, but important changes in their political attitudes had occurred which would augur well for a new German democracy.

Collapse of Allied Cooperation

The Soviet Union and Poland annexed large chunks of German territory in the East, and Germany was reduced to about three-fourths its prewar size. What remained of Germany was divided into four occupation zones: the Soviet zone was former East Germany; the British zone was in the North; the French zone was in the Southwest and the American zone was in Bavaria, Hesse and the port of Bremerhaven in the North. Berlin was also divided into four sectors. Full power was in the hands of the four Allied commanders, who bore enormous burdens in bringing order to the chaos, feeding the population, reestablishing a tolerable economic situation and creating political conditions that would make the return of National Socialism impossible.

The Allies tried to work together, and the United States even pulled its troops out of Saxony and Thuringia in July 1945 in order to honor its agreement on occupation zones established at Yalta in February 1945. Also in July, the leaders of the three major Allies—the Soviet Union, the United States and Great Britain—met at Potsdam, outside of Berlin, to discuss Germany's future. France had not taken part in the Yalta Conference and, to the ire of General de Gaulle, was not invited to the Potsdam meeting.

There were many disagreements on details, but the three basically agreed that Germany should be denazified, that the Oder-Neisse frontier would temporarily be

Germany

the border between Germany and Poland, that Germans in Hungary, Czechoslovakia and Poland would be transferred to Germany, that Germany would be required to pay reparations as long as these payments would "leave enough resources to enable the German people to subsist without external assistance," that "during the period of occupation Germany shall be treated as a single economic unit," that the German political structure would be decentralized and, finally, that German political life should be reconstructed on a democratic basis.

It soon became obvious that Allied cooperation was impossible, given the differing definitions of such terms as "democratic" and the four victors' greatly different security and political objectives in Europe. The Allies' disharmony was West Germany's opportunity that permitted it to rise so quickly from the ashes of defeat. Talks involving the political and economic future of Germany stalled, and American soldiers became impatient to go home. At the end of 1945 there were spontaneous GI demonstrations in Paris and Frankfurt which left no doubt in the minds of American leaders that the large part of the three million U.S. soldiers in Europe had to be demobilized very quickly. GI's were sent back to the U.S. at a stunningly fast rate; clearly a long occupation of Germany was not in American plans. Nor was a permanent feeding and economic subsidy of a part of the German people among those aims. Despite the agreements at Potsdam, Germany was not operating as an economic unit. It had become increasingly clear to U.S. leaders that the resulting prolongation of German poverty and economic stagnation would not only greatly harm Germany's neighbors, who were traditionally dependent upon trade with Germany, but would perhaps make it vulnerable to communist appeals.

The Beginning of Political Activity

The excessive political indoctrination and activity during Hitler's rule had extinguished political interest in the minds of most Germans by the spring of 1945. Most Germans' thoughts were directed toward food, warmth and privacy, and this fact helped divert their attention both from a horrible past and the very uncertain politics of the present. Still, political activity began to bubble from below, on the municipal and land (state) level and always under the surveillance and supervision of the occupation authorities. The future direction of German politics was far from clear. German communists had high hopes, and a number of right-wing parties began to take shape. Anti-democratic attitudes among some Germans also persisted for a while. But there was also a

democratic movement, which gathered steam and which was especially encouraged by the three Western occupation powers. The memories of National Socialist crimes prompted many thoughtful Germans to reintroduce morality and religious principles into politics and to construct a new political order around basic human rights and democracy.

American leaders soon became convinced that U.S. policy should shed all its punitive aspects and shift toward wholehearted support of the democratic potential in Germany. President Roosevelt's treasury secretary, Henry Morgenthau, had advocated the former aspects. He had wished to change Germany forcefully from an industrialized nation back to an agrarian society. His proposals had never become official U.S. policy, but elements of it had been incorporated in the official American occupation guideline, JCS 1067. However, U.S. Secretary of State James Byrnes announced in Stuttgart on September 6, 1946, a significant change in U.S. policy. In the opera house of that bombed-out city, he aimed to quiet German fears by assuring them that "as long as an occupation force is required in Germany the army of the United States will be part of that occupation force." He went on to propose a greater measure of German self-government and, as a first step, the merging of the American and British zones. A British observer commented on the dramatic effect of this speech: "At the time

they were spoken these were bold words and they came to the millions of Germans who had heard or read them as the first glimmer of dawn after a long, dark night. Their moral impact was incalculable."

One month later the Berliners revealed in their first municipal elections how receptive they were to a democratic direction. Despite the Soviet presence in East Berlin and the Soviets' open support of their German communist creation, the Socialist Unity Party of Germany (SED), which ruled the GDR, communists received less than one-fifth of the votes. The Soviets and East German communists quickly saw that they dared not agree to any settlement of the German question that involved free elections.

Secretary of State and ex-armed forces Chief of Staff George C. Marshall foresaw that Europe would economically stagnate for an unnecessarily long period of time unless massive American aid were poured into the war-ravaged countries. The generous American offer, known as the "Marshall Plan," even included the Soviet Union and what were slowly developing into its satellite states it had occupied militarily.

The year 1947 saw the end of any possibility that the four victorious Allies could work together in harmony and good faith. The failure of the Foreign Ministers Conference in Moscow in April, the refusal of the Soviet Union to allow itself or those countries under its domination to accept

Germany after World War II

220

The Berlin Airlift   A/P Wide World Photo

mans had a de facto "cigarette economy," in which American cigarettes, not old German Reichsmarks, were the country's actual currency. After several years, many Germans could actually begin smoking cigarettes again rather than hoarding them as a money substitute. The economic improvement was so dramatic that in 1949 Erhard's party could enter the first West German elections with the convincing slogan *Es geht wieder*! ("It's working again!")

The Cold War Begins—The Berlin Blockade

The "Cold War," which resulted from the severe differences between the Soviet Union and the Western Allies, ultimately helped to seal Germany's division, but it also offered the three Western zones the chance to regain a large part of German

The Air Bridge Monument in Berlin which commemorates the land blockade of the city in 1948/49

Marshall Plan assistance, the break-down in June of a meeting of all German land government chiefs in Munich, and the founding in October of the *Cominform* in Moscow, calculated to coordinate a communist propaganda offensive against the "imperialism of the United States and its Western Allies," all reflected a degeneration of East-West relations.

The year 1948 brought no improvement. In February the British and Americans created a sort of economic government, which was joined in the summer by the French zone (except the Saar, which was not reunited with Germany until 1957 following a plebiscite). This union, at first called "Bizonia," tightened the links that had already emerged between the two zones. This new body brought together leading German political figures who began discussing future German government and thereby established an early foundation for the FRG.

Leaders of Bizonia elaborated the future guiding West German economic principle of the "social market economy." This combined a free market approach (which helped West Germany rapidly to become prosperous in contrast to its counterpart in East Germany) with a commitment to the social welfare of its citizens, which was crucially important for social peace within Germany and, more important, for democracy. Bizonia also used the Marshall Plan assistance to improve its citizens' well-being. In July 1947 representatives of 16 European countries receiving Marshall Plan aid had declared in Paris, "the German economy should be integrated into the economy of Europe in such a way as to contribute to a raising of the general

standard of life." It is, of course, possible that with this measure the other nations sought through economic means to insure that Germany could not again become an aggressive political enemy.

In the next few years West Germans received almost $4 billion in money and supplies from the Marshall Plan. This not only enabled West Germans to rebuild their industrial plants with the most modern tooling, but it established the foundation for West European cooperation, which the Plan required and which culminated in the European Community (EC), now called EU. It also introduced a long-range liberalization of European trade and payments, which has been a key to the economic prosperity of many European nations.

Further Economic Progress

West German economic recovery also got an important shot in the arm from a bracing currency reform in mid-1948 through which the increasingly worthless Reichsmark was replaced by a new *Deutschmark*. Every German started at the same point, with only 40 marks in his pocket. This reform was followed by a scrapping of all rationing and price controls—a bold move widely criticized at the time, but one that the chairman of the Bizonal Economic Council, Professor Ludwig Erhard, and the U.S. occupation governor, General Lucius Clay, considered essential.

They proved to be right. Suddenly goods reappeared in the stores and markets. One witnessed a disappearance of the black market, whose more treasured items had come from the U.S. military post exchanges (PXs). For a while Ger-

Germany

sovereignty. The sense that the Western Allies and the West Germans had important common objectives was stimulated by the communist seizure of power in February 1948 in Czechoslovakia, although the country had functioned since 1945 as a parliamentary democracy.

Especially revealing was the blockade of all road and rail routes to West Berlin from June 1948 until May 1949. This was in response to increasing political and economic unity among the three Western zones, most visible in the currency reform. No doubt the Soviets expected that the Western Allies could be forced to relinquish their rights in Berlin and to abandon the city.

The American reaction was to organize an aerial supply line between the Western zones and the besieged city. This seemingly impossible task (which even included transporting coal) sparked American, British and West German imagination and admiration. Several hundred American and British aircraft carried up to 12,000 tons of supplies to Berlin each day. The success of this heroic operation, combined with the effect of adverse world opinion, forced the Soviets to lift the blockade. Although more than three-quarters of the freight was carried on American planes, the action claimed more British lives (39) than American (32). The operation was the first time the Western allies signaled in no uncertain terms that they would resist the creeping Soviet

takeover of the eastern part of Europe. For Germany it signaled a shift from being a defeated and distrusted enemy to being an inseparable friend and ally of the Western partners. It further cemented West German-American solidarity. A Berlin city referendum in May 2008 failed to save Tempelhof airport, where most of the flights landed. This monument was closed the end of that year, and Berlin shifted its air operations in 2011 to a refurbished Berlin-Brandenburg International Airport at Schönefeld, southeast of Berlin.

The Federal Republic of Germany— Konrad Adenauer

From the winter of 1948–49 on, the great majority of West Germans would accept no foreign policy that did not merit the confidence of the U.S., whose protection over Berlin and West Germany were considered indispensable.

The disagreements among the four occupation powers reached such a low state that the three Western Allies decided in the summer of 1948 to permit German leaders in their three zones to write a constitution and to found a West German state. The Constituent Assembly met in Bonn under the chairmanship of the elderly former mayor of Cologne, Konrad Adenauer, and under the watchful eyes of the three occupational authorities. Things were finally settled in May 1949, almost four years to the day since the capitulation of the Third Reich.

What was created was seen to be strictly "for a transitional period." The document was called a Basic Law, not a constitution, a word that might connote something more permanent. The founders wrote into the preamble that they had acted also on behalf of those Germans living under Soviet occupation and that "the entire German people is called upon to accomplish, by free self-determination, the unity and freedom of Germany." Thus, West German leaders imposed upon themselves the obligation to bring the two parts of Germany back together, even though that goal seemed to be slipping farther and farther into the distant future.

On August 14, 1949, most of the eligible voters in West Germany went to the polls to elect their first parliamentary representatives. Adenauer's Christian Democratic Union (CDU), along with the Bavarian Christian Social Union (CSU), captured 31% of the votes, and the SPD 29.2%. Several other parties also won seats, and Adenauer was able to patch together a coalition government with only a one-vote majority, his own vote. Adenauer was to serve as West German chancellor until 1963, longer than the entire Weimar Republic had existed. The voters saw this shrewd politician as a comforting father-figure (*Der Alte*—"The Old One"), who took a firmer control of West German politics than any other chancellor since. As a confident (some say authoritarian) ruler, he was able to place his imprint on the young democracy. The Soviet Union responded to the creation of the Federal Republic of Germany by converting its occupation zone into the German Democratic Republic (GDR), ruled by the communist-led SED.

The FRG's new capital was not established in a major West German city such as Frankfurt on the Main. That might have appeared as a permanent capital city for a state that was expressly intended to be provisional. Instead, the sleepy Rhenish university town of Bonn was selected as the "temporary" seat of government, and an architecturally unattractive former teacher's college became the new Parliament and governmental center. Until late 1987, West Germany's capital remained the least impressive governmental seat in all of Europe. Some liked to call it "the federal village." The new government ordered that the gutted *Reichstag* building, located a few meters within the Western sector of Berlin, be reconstructed so that it could again serve as the capitol of a "soon to be" reunified Germany. Work on the renovation was finally completed in the 1970s.

NATO is Created

The Cold War froze the division of Germany, but it also provided West Germany

Konrad Adenauer (r) with SPD leader Kurt Schumacher (l) and Carlo Schmid (m)

the opportunities its crafty first chancellor knew how to exploit for the benefit of his country and his party. There were intense fears in Western Europe and North America that the Soviet Union sought direct or indirect domination over all of Europe. This fear led to the establishment of the North Atlantic Treaty Organization (NATO) on April 4, 1949, several months before the creation of the FRG. When NATO planners began working on plans for defending Western Europe, it was quickly apparent that the Western Allies and smaller West Europe countries alone could not provide the necessary forces. This was especially true since the United States had no intention at that time of permanently maintaining large numbers of American troops in Europe. Western European defense was conceivable only with the help of Germany. In the fall of 1949 the U.S. General Staff drafted a plan for the inclusion of German troops in NATO.

Adenauer listened very carefully to the message coming from Western capitals: "No NATO without Germany; no Germany without NATO." He reflected on his country's three principal goals and the best way it could achieve them: 1) West Germans, painfully viewing the plight of their countrymen in East Germany, wanted protection from Soviet domination; 2) they wanted political and economic recovery from the ashes of disgrace, to regain much of their national sovereignty, to create jobs, to rebuild their cities, to share in international trade and thereby to acquire material prosperity and to be respected as equals in the Western world, whose values they shared; 3) finally, they wanted their country to be reunified within the German borders of 1937.

The chancellor decided to strike a bargain with the NATO countries. On November 11, 1949, the 31st anniversary of the cease-fire ending World War I, Adenauer announced in an interview with the French newspaper, *L'Est Republicain*, that "if a common Supreme Command could be created, the Federal Republic would be willing at an appropriate time to integrate itself into a European defense system." He presented this decision to his own people as the "politics of necessity," and he stated the issue very simply: "We are faced with a choice between slavery and freedom. We choose freedom." In the years to come, Adenauer was successful in getting an important political advantage for each increase in German activity or responsibility in NATO. He helped to establish the United States as the permanent guarantor of West German security and to counteract the goal that many American leaders had well into the 1950s of withdrawing U.S. troops from Western Europe. He set

a course that was never fundamentally changed by his successors in the chancellor's office until the end of the Cold War.

There was, however, a problem with Adenauer's bargain with the West, which the opposition Social Democrats simply could not get out of their minds: how would this integration with the West, especially the military part of it, affect the goal of German reunification, a goal that most Germans at that time wanted very much and that was an obligation placed on all West German governments by the framers of the Basic Law? Social Democrats strongly sensed at the time that by seeking to achieve the goals of security and recovery through political, economic and military integration with the West, the FRG was greatly reducing the chances that the Soviet Union would permit the reunification of Germany.

Social Democratic Opposition to NATO

The SPD's order of priorities was almost the complete reverse of Adenauer's. Throughout the 1950s, reunification was its top priority. The party was not in principle opposed to reconciliation and integration with the West, nor was it ever opposed to a military defense for Germany. It believed that the military and economic commitments the FRG had assumed in or-

der to achieve Adenauer's goals would reduce or eliminate the chances that the pieces of Germany would find their way back together again. With the FRG integrated economically in Western Europe, with NATO and Soviet troops facing each other along the Elbe River, and with each part of a divided Germany serving as an essential element in the European balance of power, the Soviet Union would be far less inclined to withdraw its troops from East Germany. This would especially be the case if a reunified Germany were free to join NATO, as Adenauer always insisted it should be. The SPD feared that the military balance in Europe would require a perpetually divided Germany and therefore showed much greater willingness than the Adenauer government to examine closely Soviet proposals for reunification and to assume that the Soviets were acting at least partly in good faith.

Adenauer continued to argue that his policy was not hostile to the aim of German reunification. He, like the Social Democrats, aimed toward German reunification "in peace and freedom." He argued that in return for the FRG's entering the Western Alliance, the three Western powers had formally committed themselves to seek German reunification. He also cast an eye on the West's greater in-

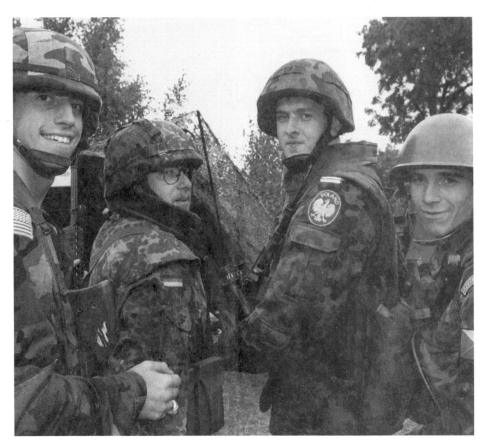

American, German, Polish and Czech soldiers in NATO maneuver in Poland

Germany

dustrial capability to arm itself quickly, on the high degree of Western political and economic integration in the future, and on the prospects of unrest in Eastern Europe, which would be directed against the Soviet Union's tight and self-serving grip on its satellites.

He therefore predicted that in time the balance of power would shift in favor of the West, and this shift would make possible negotiations "on the basis of strength" with the Soviet Union. He argued that the Soviets held the key to reunification and would ultimately be compelled to settle the German question on Western terms. This latter element of Adenauer's reunification policy was, as the SPD correctly foresaw, an illusion. With the Soviet Union's acquisition of nuclear weapons, there could be no serious talk of rolling back what Churchill had so aptly named "The Iron Curtain" through demonstrations of military strength.

Adenauer was right in his assessment of what West Germans wanted most and of the enormous advantages for his disgraced and impoverished country, which Western European unity, crowned by the creation of the Common Market (EC) in 1957, offered: the FRG would be an equal member of such a community. It would derive all of the economic benefits the trade and pooling of raw materials would bring. Although it appeared to be grounded on the desire of many Germans for reunification, the position of the SPD actually caused an erosion of the SPD's domestic political position within the FRG. Social Democrats had to watch with dismay and bitterness how Adenauer's party grew progressively stronger while the SPD stagnated.

Political Tensions of the 1950s

The domestic battle over the crucial foreign and security policy decisions made in the 1950s was so intense and emotional that it is almost a wonder that the young democracy survived them. The issues were serious ones related to the future of Germany and the German nation. These bitter controversies of the 1950s never completely disappeared.

German rearmament was a truly explosive issue that dominated West German politics until the FRG's formal entry into NATO in 1955. From the point of view of the Western Allies and the Adenauer government, the major problem was how to place international controls on West German troops. The FRG's future allies, who had fought against Germany only five years earlier, wanted security *from* West Germany, as well as security *for it*. Well aware of these fears, which he found entirely justified, and desiring German integration and equal status with the West, Adenauer also stubbornly refused to consider establishing an independent German national army. In an effort to solve this problem, the French had presented the "Pleven Plan" in 1950, calling for the establishment of a European Defense Community (EDC). West German military units would be completely fused with a larger European army, and no German generals would command German corps. The FRG would technically not have NATO status, but it would be included de facto since the EDC itself would belong to NATO.

The link between the FRG's entry into the EDC and the regaining of West German sovereignty was clear from the very beginning. In 1951 the FRG was permitted to establish a Ministry for Foreign Affairs and to establish diplomatic relations with other states. Also, the *Deutschland Vertrag* (Germany Treaty, also known as the Bonn Conventions) was drafted and was to be signed together with the EDC Treaty. The Bonn Conventions provided for the abolition of the Occupation Statute and of the Allied High Commission, which formally ruled Germany, and prepared the way for West German sovereignty, with certain restrictions.

The issue of a German military role became acute again when in 1954 the French National Assembly rejected the EDC, which an earlier French Foreign Minister had proposed. Surprisingly quickly, however, the foreign ministers of Great Britain, Canada and the U.S. met with the prospective members of the EDC to discuss alternatives. In October these powers signed the Paris Treaties calling for the direct entry of the FRG into NATO, an end to Germany's occupation status and the restoration of full German sovereignty. The three Western powers retained their authority on matters relating to German reunification, Berlin and a final German peace treaty. In late 1955 Adenauer traveled to the Soviet Union to establish full diplomatic relations with that victor and to negotiate a trade treaty and the release of the last German prisoners of war remaining in Soviet hands.

The West German debate over foreign policy remained very polarized. In January 1956, less than a year after the FRG had become a full member of NATO, the first thousand volunteer soldiers entered the Federal Army (*Bundeswehr*), whose creation the SPD had opposed. There was a powerful pacifist strain within the SPD that opposed all forms of German rearmament. This element was a part of an emotional mass movement known by the slo-

Willy Brandt as Mayor of West Berlin hosting President John F. Kennedy

gan (*ohne mich*—without me). Because of the recent memories and the direct experience that Germans had with the war, the *ohne mich* movement enjoyed widespread support among the general population. For instance, one opinion survey in 1955 revealed that while 40% of the respondents were in favor of a West German army, 45% were opposed. Among those respondents identifying with the SPD, only 21% were in favor of the Federal Army and 71% were opposed. Opinion polls also indicated that West Germans were not happy about the stationing of American nuclear weapons on German soil or about the Federal Army's acquisition of dual capacity weapons that could fire or deliver nuclear warheads.

Minimal SPD Gains at the Polls; Continued German Division

The SPD went into the federal parliamentary elections of September 15, 1957 confident that it could make significant gains, but the results stunned the Social Democrats and probably Adenauer as well. The SPD vote did rise from 29% to 32%, but this rise was partially due to the fact that the Communist Party of Germany (KPD) had been ruled unconstitutional a year earlier and was therefore not permitted to participate in the election. However, the CDU/CSU vote rose from 44% to over 50%, and it gained an absolute majority in the *Bundestag*, the only time this has ever happened since the founding of the FRG. The election was widely interpreted as approval of Adenauer's foreign and economic policies.

This election disaster, plus another Berlin crisis in 1958, convinced the SPD to change its foreign policy tack and to support Adenauer's policy of rearmament and integration with the West. Although there were quarrels between the parties occasionally, by the time of Adenauer's retirement in 1963, a foreign policy consensus had taken shape in the FRG that continued to exist throughout the 1960s.

With the FRG firmly planted in the Western alliance, West German leaders began to look eastward to see how they could improve West Germany's relations with the Soviet Union and its satellites. The construction of the Berlin Wall in August 1961 had made it clear that the two Germanys would not be reunified for a long time. Before August 1961 East and West Berliners could pass freely from one part of the city to the other. But the ugly wall, which cut right through Germany's largest city, destroyed the last hope of national unity.

From the very beginning West Germany's foreign policy was heavily influenced by the fact that Germany was a divided nation in the middle of Europe.

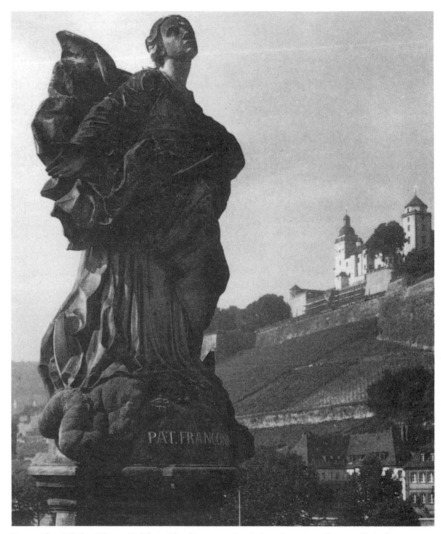

From the Main River Bridge, the Franconia statue ignores the castle of Würzburg
Photo by Jon Markham Morrow

After 1955 the FRG did not pursue a determined policy of German reunification, preferring instead to focus on Western economic and military integration, while preventing the legitimization of the *status quo* in Central Europe.

Once the signals for a relaxation of tensions between East and West began to be given by France and the U.S., culminating in such agreements with the Soviet Union as the nuclear test ban treaty in 1963, German Foreign Minister Gerhard Schröder began in the early 1960s a "policy of movement." This involved a loosening of the "Hallstein Doctrine," which had forbidden West German diplomatic contact with any country except the Soviet Union that officially recognized East Germany. The FRG established trade missions in Warsaw, Budapest, Sofia and Bucharest. This policy was an important beginning, but it did not go far enough. The FRG neither discarded the Hallstein Doctrine altogether, nor recognized the Oder-Neisse

border between the GDR and Poland. Worst of all, it still aimed to isolate the GDR diplomatically.

The FRG had always worked closely with East German officials on practical, day-to-day questions, especially involving economic matters. For instance, the FRG insisted as a condition for its entry into the EU that trade between the two Germanys be conducted as if there were only one Germany. Such free trade was enormously beneficial for the GDR, providing it with an open entry to the EU and serving as a basis for the relatively high economic prosperity in the GDR as compared with other Eastern European countries. Yet, top-level political contacts were studiously avoided.

In 1966 the FRG's two largest parties formed a "Grand Coalition," with Kurt Georg Kiesinger of the CDU as chancellor. Although the parliamentary system was operating very smoothly and although the war damage and mass poverty had given

Germany

way to visible prosperity, the major parties' leaders saw economic troubles ahead. The SPD also wanted to participate in such a coalition government in order to demonstrate that it also was capable of ruling the FRG.

The Grand Coalition stimulated considerable domestic opposition, especially in 1968 when its majority in the *Bundestag* passed a series of constitutional amendments and laws granting the government certain emergency powers in times of crisis. Although it argued that any truly sovereign state had to be able to take special measures in times of emergency to defend the democratic order, many West Germans pointed out that similar emergency laws had been misused during the Weimar Republic to undermine democracy. This controversial issue, combined with doubts about American policy in Vietnam, sent thousands of mainly young Germans into the streets. They employed confrontation tactics, which they had learned from the civil rights and antiwar movements in the U.S., even using the American terms for these tactics, such as "sit-in" and "go-in." They called themselves the "extra-parliamentary opposition" (APO), which they claimed was necessary since the opposition within Parliament had sunk to a negligible 5%.

Far less controversial in the eyes of young Germans was the Grand Coalition's policy of seeking improved relations with the East. This received a particular push from Foreign Minister Willy Brandt and the crafty Minister for All-German Affairs, Herbert Wehner, both of the SPD. The Kiesinger government took steps toward overcoming the impasse in German reunification. It announced that it was prepared to accept the East German regime as a *de facto* government, and it even exchanged letters for the first time with East German leaders on a semiofficial basis. It established a trade mission in Prague in 1967, and its diplomatic recognition of Romania in 1967 and Yugoslavia in 1968 indicated that the Hallstein Doctrine was in fact dead, even if not wiped off the books.

The Brandt Government

In 1969 the SPD and Free Democratic Party (FDP) won a razor-thin victory in parliamentary elections, and Willy Brandt became chancellor. The new government had no intention to change the FRG's policy toward the West, but it was determined to conduct a dynamic and innovative policy toward the East. Fundamentally, the Brandt government decided to overturn two decades of West German foreign policy and to recognize the territorial *status quo* in Europe, including the division of Germany. The word "reunifi-cation" was dropped from the government's terminology.

The first dramatic step in August 1970 was a German-Soviet treaty in which both states renounced the use of force in Europe. West Germany also declared that it had no territorial claims against any country and that the borders of all European states are inviolable, including the Oder-Neisse line and the border between East and West Germany. This treaty was the first West German recognition of East Germany's international legitimacy. Brandt was no doubt correct in commenting that in actual fact, "nothing is lost with this treaty that was not gambled away long ago."

The GDR before German reunification

The second step was a German-Polish treaty in late 1970, containing basically the same points as in the German-Soviet treaty, but underscoring the acceptance of the Oder-Neisse frontier. The treaty also provided for normal diplomatic relations and, in a separate accord, Poland agreed to exit permits for some ethnic Germans living in Poland. To demonstrate his sincerity in introducing a new era of Polish-German relations, Brandt dropped to his knees in reverence before a monument in Warsaw honoring the Polish Jewish victims who were killed or mistreated by Germany during World War II. The Poles have never forgotten this electrifying gesture.

A third step, not involving the FRG directly, but strongly encouraged by it, was the Four-Power Agreement on Berlin in 1971. The FRG had linked its ratification of the German-Soviet Treaty with a successful resolution of the Berlin problem. Brandt reasoned that if the FRG was willing to recognize the status quo in Europe, the Soviet Union should be willing to recognize the *status quo* in Berlin. The Four-Power Agreement contained a Western Powers' acknowledgment that West Berlin was not a constituent part of the FRG and the Soviet Union's recognition that there were ties between the FRG and West Berlin. Further, the FRG would perform consular services for West Berliners and represent them in international organizations and conferences. The Soviet Union also promised that transit traffic to and from West Berlin from the FRG would proceed unimpeded. That was deemed necessary since the East German government had frequently hampered access to the city it surrounded in order to place pressure on the Bonn government. The Soviet Union admitted that West Berlin was neither located on the territory of the GDR nor was it an entity entirely separate from the FRG.

The last significant step was the Basic Treaty between the two Germanys themselves. Bonn knew that it could not bypass East Berlin despite the fact that the East German regime was defensive, rigid and determined to exact a very high price for any concession. After many months of frustrating negotiations an agreement was signed in late 1972 and ratified in mid-1973. It normalized the access between the FRG and West Berliners and made it possible for West Berliners to visit both East Berlin and the GDR. By signing the Basic Treaty the FRG publicly accepted the GDR as a legitimate state and agreed to deal with it as an equal. Yet, Bonn continued to insist that there was only one German nation (even if there were two German states) and that the GDR would not be treated like any other foreign country. To

underscore this, the FRG maintained a permanent liaison mission in East Berlin, not an embassy, and Bonn's dealings with the GDR were conducted by the Chancellor's Office, the Ministry of All-German Affairs or a special office in the Interior Ministry, but *not* by the Foreign Office. The official relations between the two Germanys improved as a result of the Basic Treaty. But the two countries' relationships remained ambiguous and tense, charged with conflict and suspicion.

A major scandal occurred in 1974 when it was revealed that one of Brandt's chief aides, Günter Guillaume, was an East German spy who had access not only to top secret information, but also was privy to knowledge of Brandt's intimate private life, which was reported to be spicy. This embarrassing revelation and intraparty criticism against Brandt's leadership led to his resignation from the office of chancellor in May. Helmut Schmidt took his place. This was during a time of global economic difficulties associated with tremendously increased oil prices. The energy crisis and the resultant economic problems began increasingly to replace the Eastern policy focus of the government. Although Schmidt signed the Helsinki Accords at the Conference on Security and Cooperation in Europe (CSCE) in 1975, his attention became more directed toward the West and away from the East. His goal was to maintain what had already been achieved, and to preserve or reestablish the economic health and military security of Western Europe.

Plagued by continual dissension within the SPD and recurrent coalition crises with the FDP, the Schmidt government collapsed in 1982, when the Free Democrats switched partners and enabled the CDU, led by Helmut Kohl, to take power.

The following year, voters confirmed this *Wende* (change) by giving the new CDU/CSU-FDP coalition government a solid endorsement in the *Bundestag* elections. The Kohl government set about tackling the problems of unemployment and the emotionally charged deployment of American Pershing and cruise missiles on German soil.

The Schmidt government had agreed to do the latter in the 1979 NATO "Twin-track" decision, which was designed to counter a renewed Soviet nuclear missile threat. At the same time, the Kohl government pursued the policy of detente with the GDR and the USSR with as much vigor as had the SPD while in power. Like most West German leaders, Kohl no longer believed that German reunification could be achieved in the present era. In 1987 he stated in Moscow that he personally would never live to see the day when the two Germanys would become one country. Like virtually everybody else, he was caught completely by surprise as the GDR collapsed before his unbelieving eyes, and the elusive German unity fell into his lap.

HISTORY OF THE GERMAN DEMOCRATIC REPUBLIC (GDR)— EAST GERMANY

At first the Soviet Military Administration governed the Soviet Zone of Germany. But the Soviet authorities had long-range plans for Germany that involved reeducating the people and eventually winning them over to communism. German communists who had spent the Nazi years in the Soviet Union were brought back, put in charge of local governments, and given control over the press, radio, and book publishing. Their instructions

A "freedom train" to the West: October 5, 1989

Germany

were to educate the people in antifascism and to gain their cooperation for Soviet occupiers. On April 30, 1945, Walter Ulbricht returned from the USSR in a Soviet aircraft and in June announced the reestablishment of the Communist Party of Germany (KPD). It combined with the CDU, SPD, and Liberal Democrats to form an "Antifascist Democratic Bloc," which was soon dominated by the KPD. The Soviets had expected that the communists' long record of antifascism would make the KPD popular among workers, but the latter clearly preferred the SPD. In April 1946 this prompted the forcible uniting of the two parties into a Socialist Unity Party (SED), with Ulbricht as general secretary. The other parties declined in significance until they were little more than a facade.

In 1948 work on a new constitution began, and on October 7, 1949, the GDR came into being. Industry was nationalized and agriculture was collectivized, creating a state-controlled economy. SED domination was tightened through a pervasive state police (*Stasi*) that spied on the citizenry and stifled dissent in every form. On May 26, 1952, the border between the two Germanys was sealed by barbed wire, minefields, watchtowers, and free-fire zones.

Revolt and Suppression

Stalin's death in March 1953 and the gradual rise of a new Soviet leadership undermined the positions of all orthodox leaders in Eastern Europe. Although he was Stalinist from the beginning, Ulbricht managed to hold on to power until 1971. He faced occasional challenges to his leadership. Almost immediately after Stalin's death, the Politburo disregarded Ulbricht's will and adopted a "New Course," which moved toward greater political and economic pluralism. Enraged by onerous reparations to the USSR, higher production quotas, and the lack of personal freedom, workers revolted on June 17, 1953. But Soviet forces brutally put down the insurrection. Until German unification in 1990, this date was commemorated in the FRG as the "Day of German Unity." The revolt may have saved Ulbricht's career; the Soviets now backed him against the moderates, who found themselves removed from their positions of authority.

On January 29, 1956, the GDR joined hands militarily with the Soviet Union by creating a National People's Army (NVA) and joining the Warsaw Pact. In 1956 Soviet leader Nikita Khrushchev delivered a dramatic speech attacking the Stalinist heritage. This message emboldened communist intellectuals in the GDR who wanted to make the SED more responsive to the people and to create a more popular, humane form of socialism. Their chief spokesman, Wolfgang Harich, was

Young Germans on the Wall: November 9, 1989. Sign attached to the wall: "Cement Demolition Technique"

arrested and sentenced to ten years. Other reformers were branded as "revisionists" and forced to retreat.

Ulbricht met his most serious political challenge on August 13, 1961, when, backed by the Soviets, he authorized the sudden construction of a wall between West and East Berlin, where hundreds of thousands of East Germans had continued to flee. This sealed the last escape route and forced East Germans to come to terms with their plight and their government; there was no longer any alternative. This was the only historical instance in the world that a wall was erected to keep an entire people confined, rather than to keep enemies out. The constant drain on manpower, particularly skilled persons, had been an important economic reason for the wall. Despite the devastating blow it delivered to the international prestige of this socialist state, which presented itself as the model for Germany's future, it led to greater prosperity in the GDR after 1961 and helped provide East Germans with the highest standard of living within the Soviet empire.

Ten years later the Soviet Union concluded that its interests required closer relations between the two Germanys. When Ulbricht opposed this, he was replaced in 1971 by Erich Honecker, a roofer who had grown up in the Saarland. In 1935 he was jailed by the Nazis and spent ten years in a Berlin prison. After the war he became chairman of the communist Free German Youth. Following political training in Moscow, he oversaw the military and security services. He had opposed any form of "revisionism" and was totally loyal to

the Soviet Union. He strongly supported the erection of the Berlin Wall and was deemed responsible in 1990 with the orders to shoot to kill along the dividing line between East and West Germany.

About 350 persons were killed trying to cross the border. For this he was charged with manslaughter in the newly united Germany. To rescue him from German justice and the embarrassment he might cause the USSR by his testimony, Soviet leaders first protected him in a military hospital outside of Berlin and then whisked him off to the USSR in March 1991, violating German sovereignty in the process. When the Soviet Union itself ceased to exist at the end of 1991, he was told he would have to leave. He took refuge in the Chilean Embassy. On July 29, 1992, he was forced to return to Germany to face charges of manslaughter, corruption, and breach of trust. East German bosses are the only leaders in the ex-Soviet empire to face justice in Western courts. His trial began in November, but in January 1993 he was proclaimed terminally ill and was released. He immediately joined his family in Chile, where he died a year later.

When Mikhail Gorbachev launched his reformist policy of *perestroika* in 1985, Honecker and other members of the SED leadership resisted introducing it in the GDR on the grounds that the East German economy had already been reformed in the 1970s and was allegedly working well. Their rejection of a market economy was ideologically motivated. They argued that if the GDR adopted a market economy, then little or nothing would distinguish it

228

from the FRG; consequently there would be no further justification for the GDR to exist as a separate state. They also resisted introducing more freedom in the political realm and even prevented the distribution of some free-thinking Soviet newspapers, such as the *Moscow News*. It was extremely embarrassing for a party that had been so servile to the Soviet Union to be in a position of having to resist its leadership. The SED found itself in a fatal dilemma from which it could never extricate itself.

Collapse of GDR

In 1989 one of the most dramatic postwar developments began taking place before the very eyes of a stunned world public: German reunification. In early summer a human hemorrhaging westward commenced, as East German vacationers began crossing the newly opened border between Hungary and Austria. Budapest informed the irate East German leaders that the human rights agreements accepted at the Helsinki Conference in 1975 superseded earlier bilateral treaties preventing the free movement of peoples. The next avenue of escape was through Czechoslovakia. After thousands had taken refuge at the West German embassy in Prague, "freedom trains" took East Germans through the GDR into the West. The stampede grew when Czechoslovakia opened its western borders.

Under enormous stress, the GDR celebrated its 40th and final anniversary on October 7, 1989. The SED's slogan for the event was "Ever Forward—Never Backward!" The prediction was accurate, but the communist chiefs were badly mistaken about which direction was forward. The honored guest was Gorbachev himself,

who at that time was the most popular political figure in Germany. However, rather than lend his prestige to the struggling East German leaders, he made it known that they would have to pay a high price if they did not learn the lessons of history and adopt timely reforms. He informed them that they could not expect the support of Soviet troops in the GDR to prop up their rule against the people. Without Soviet military backing communist rule could survive nowhere in Germany.

This was a very important message in a country in which public demonstrations had been going on for some time. An umbrella opposition group, New Forum, had come into existence a few weeks earlier, and huge demonstrations had spread to all major East German cities. Things came to a head on October 9 in Leipzig. Honecker reportedly issued an order to security forces to put down the demonstration by any means. Communist leaders in Leipzig, fearing a massacre such as had occurred in China the previous June, decided to prevent such a bloodbath in their city. With Kurt Masur, director of Leipzig's Gewandhaus Orchestra, as spokesman, and joined by Protestant Church leaders, they issued an appeal for calm. They coupled this with a call for non-violence and "a free exchange of opinions about the continuation of socialism in our country." Such a dialogue would occur "not only in the Leipzig area, but with our national government." On October 18 Honecker was ousted from power and replaced by Egon Krenz.

The End

The Berlin Wall came tumbling down on November 9. It is ironic that a wall

constructed in 1961 to keep East Germans in was opened in 1989 for the same reason. Within minutes millions of East Germans began pouring over the border. Germans, who for decades had suppressed displays of national feeling, experienced a deeply emotional outpouring. While millions sat in front of their televisions and wept, Berliners danced together on top of the Wall, embraced each other on the streets, and chiseled away at the ugly barrier. When word arrived at the *Bundestag*, many members, including some Greens, stood up and spontaneously sang the third verse of the national anthem, which stresses "unity and justice and freedom." The rest of Europe looked on with mixed feelings, uneasily remembering a frightening German past, but stirred by the sight of people casting off their shackles and demanding freedom and self-determination.

Krenz proved to be only an interim figure. Unable to put an end to either the demonstrations or the continued emigration to the West, he promised "free, democratic and secret elections," a move toward a market economy, separation of party and state, freedom of assembly, and a new law on broadcasting and press freedom. He also appointed as prime minister Hans Modrow from Dresden, one of the very few East German communists who was personally popular. Honecker was arrested, but he was released for health reasons and was soon taken under the wing of the Soviet Army in the GDR.

Krenz could not save his party or himself. He and the other members of the East German Politburo resigned on December 3. Five days later, a special SED party congress met and installed Gregor Gysi, a lawyer who had made a name for himself by defending dissidents and the opposition New Forum. Upon accepting the leadership, Gysi admitted that a complete break with Stalinism and a new form of socialism was needed and that the SED was responsible for plunging the GDR into crisis. Feeling betrayed, 700,000 of the 2.3 million party members quit within two months the party, which renamed itself the Party of Democratic Socialism (PDS) in an attempt to escape the impending doom.

There was an outpouring of disgust and rage among East Germans as massive corruption on the part of their former leaders was revealed. They had enriched themselves while in office. Television broadcast images of the "proletarian" leaders' luxury compound in Wandlitz, estates with as many as 22 staff members, hunting lodges, deer parks, well-stocked wine cellars, and satellite dishes for better reception of Western broadcasts. Their living standards had been totally removed from

Discussions on German reunification, Bonn, May 5, 1990

Germany

the meager everyday existence of normal GDR citizens long fed on exhortations for austerity. Even worse were revelations of shady financial dealings totaling millions of marks, involving illegal arms sales to Third World countries and foreign currency maneuvers, the profits of which ended up in personal Swiss bank accounts. One rank-and-file SED member said: "We did not expect this of communists and their creed of equality."

At the last moment, Honecker was whisked out of Germany on a Soviet military plane, an act that the Kremlin admitted was a "technical violation of German sovereignty." The FRG tolerated the incident with little more than bland diplomatic protests because it did not want to antagonize the declining superpower. An American diplomat put it this way: "The Soviets have done things that are not nice, but the Germans have their eye on the ball, and the ball is a timely troop withdrawal. The German interest is to smooth over any bumps." The arrest of the GDR's former premier, Willi Stoph, Defense Minister Heinz Kessler (who was planning to flee to the USSR) and two other SED leaders was ordered.

Reunification

Suddenly German reunification was back on Europe's and the superpowers' agenda, and developments toward it raced faster than any government's ability to react. The rapid collapse of communist rule left a political vacuum in the GDR. Demonstrators in East German streets unfurled banners pronouncing "Germany—One Fatherland!" Aware of his constitutional mandate to seek German unity, and wishing to calm the waters and head off right-and left-wing extremists, Kohl announced on November 28 a 10-step plan for reunification, which included humanitarian assistance to refugees, freer travel between the two Germanys, massive economic aid contingent on free elections in the GDR, and ultimately reunification if that was the will of

the German people, especially of East Germans. He applied no timetable. To reassure his NATO and EU allies, he stressed that any reunified Germany would be embedded in the Western community of nations and NATO. To those who fear for stability in Europe, which until now has been guaranteed by a divided Germany, he asserted, "freedom does not cause instability." West Germans no longer needed to sacrifice unity for freedom, as they had done since 1949.

In March 1990 the last communist government, led by Modrow, collapsed. East Germans had conducted the only successful revolution in German history, and it was a bloodless one. The pace of the reunification movement quickened with the first free elections in East German history on March 18, 1990. The surprise victor was the conservative coalition, "Alliance for Germany," led by the CDU-East, which won 48% of the vote by promising prosperity and union with the FRG. The SPD-East was a distant second. The communists, running under a new name—PDS—won only 16% and sank temporarily into irrelevance. As in 1949, Germans turned to the CDU as the party of prosperity and assured democracy. A "grand coalition" of conservatives and SPD formed a government and entered negotiations with the Kohl government to overcome the political, economic, and military obstacles to "One United Germany."

The train was speeding toward unity, and the best the Bonn government could do was to make it an orderly, legal process. There was no time for a transition, no pause to "study the problems." A breathless Kohl saw a unique opportunity and had announced in February: "We are jumping with a single leap!" He waved aside Social Democrats' call for a more deliberate process and the demand of many intellectuals for a "better" East Germany treading a "third path" between capitalism and socialism.

The next steps toward unity on October 3, 1990, were taken with dizzying rapid-

ity. On July 1 the West German mark was introduced in the GDR in a currency reform without precedence on such a large scale. In a stunning diplomatic breakthrough, Kohl went to the Soviet Union July 14–16 to get Gorbachev's assurances that he would not stand in the way of German unity and that a united Germany could decide "freely and by itself if, and in which alliance, it desires membership"; in other words, Germany would not have to leave NATO in order to be united. Returning to Moscow on September 12, Bonn's leaders joined GDR Minister President Lothar de Maizière and the foreign ministers of the four Allied Powers to sign the "two plus four" treaty granting full sovereignty to Germany and suspending the four powers' rights. The Conference on Security and Cooperation in Europe (CSCE) endorsed the agreement in New York on October 1. It went into effect at midnight on October 2, when a "Liberty Bell" the U.S. had given Berlin four decades earlier rang in unity.

Unity left much unsettled business for a part of Germany in which the economy had to be privatized and in which the secret police, *Stasi*, supported by 85,000 officers and over a half million informants, had penetrated every niche of GDR society and maintained files on six million persons. This frightening phenomenon was portrayed in film director Florian Henckel von Donnersmarck's international hit, *The Lives of Others*, which won an Oscar in 2007 as Best Foreign-Language Film. It is a gripping tale of a *Stasi* officer who begins to doubt his work as a spy and ends up protecting his victims.

Germans were left to wrestle with the problem of what to do with such files, which had been assembled with complete disregard for the individual's privacy. They hold many of the keys to rooting out and punishing those persons who suppressed citizens' freedom, but their misuse could again endanger that freedom. They shed light on the GDR's extensive contacts with and training of terrorist or-

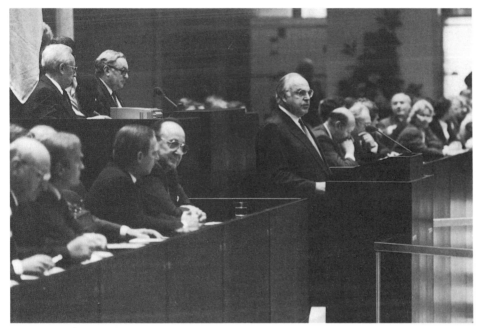

Former Chancellor Kohl addresses the opening session of the *Bundestag* of a united Germany: December 22, 1990

ganizations, the sheltering of fugitive West German Red Army Faction killers, and the staging of anti-Semitic attacks in the FRG to discredit Bonn. They also help Bonn uncover spies who had infiltrated the FRG more thoroughly than had ever been imagined. Still, after the 2009 federal elections the *Bundestag* had as members more former *Stasi* agents than human rights activists. Roughly 17,000 former *Stasi* informants work openly in the nation's bureaucracy. Considering that *Stasi* employed more than 90,000 agents and 200,000 "unofficial collaborators" constituting one out of 50 GDR citizens, this is not surprising.

One set of files the German government did not receive is that containing identities, code names and other vital data of thousands of *Stasi* foreign agents, most of whom worked in Western Germany. The CIA spirited them away after the fall of the Berlin Wall. Until 1999 it refused to turn them over to the Germans, saying that the archives would expose many friendly agents still operating in the West to retaliation by their victims. This became an emotional test case for the German government, which considers the files to be its property, as it seeks to reassert the full sovereignty of a reunited Germany and establish a more equitable partnership with Washington. Most of the files were returned; only those relating to foreigners who worked for the *Stasi* in the U.S., Europe, the Middle East, Africa and elsewhere were not given back.

Not wishing to announce open season for witch hunts, but wanting to protect the

rights of citizens, the government decided in 1991 to allow individuals access to their own files, while threatening journalists with three-year jail terms if they published information from them without permission. Joachim Gauck, former director of the agency that investigated the *Stasi* files, admitted: "Charges, accusations. The memories, the pain and sadness, the failures—that will last very long. We must face it. We must show ourselves that injustice, and especially injustice in high places, does not pay."

This prompted charges of press muzzling by civil liberty advocates, who called the decision the most serious effort at limiting freedom of the press since the Hitler era and a repetition of earlier times

The 16 states (Länder) of the FRG

in the FRG, when many prominent Nazis were permitted to resume their careers after 1945 without a review of their histories in well-kept Nazi records. Other former GDR citizens must confront their own troubled past. The legendary former head of East Germany's foreign intelligence service, Markus Wolf, returned to Germany from exile in the Soviet Union and was released on $30,000 bail, a paltry sum for a man who is paid at least that much for interviews with the sensation-hungry Western press. When his treason trial began in 1993, he asked: "What country am I supposed to have betrayed?"

Because such cases had the hint of retroactive justice since the defendants were fairly operating under the laws of their country at the time, the Constitutional Court ruled in 1995 that former East German spy masters like Wolf cannot be prosecuted for conducting Cold War espionage against the West. His conviction was overturned, but he was tried and convicted again in 1997 on charges of kidnapping three Germans on both sides of the Berlin Wall 30 years earlier. His sentence was suspended. In 1998 he was jailed once more for refusing to identify a Western informer during a spy trial. Again he was freed quickly. In 2006 he died in Berlin, age 83.

Amnesty applies neither to East German agents caught in the West (although the court urged mercy in such cases), to West Germans who committed treason by spying for the GDR, nor to former East German spies accused of such offenses as kidnapping or bribery, crimes condemned by the GDR's own laws. Thus, prosecution continues.

In 1996 appeals by the GDR's former defense minister, Heinz Kessler, his aide, and top party boss Hans Albrecht, convicted for killing people attempting to escape across the Wall, were denied. By 1997, more than 30 former GDR officials and border guards had been convicted of shootings. In August 1997, for the first time, former members of the GDR political elite were held accountable for deaths along the border. Its last leader, Egon Krenz, and his co-defendants, Guenter Schabowski and Guenter Kleiber, were convicted of manslaughter. Krenz was sentenced to six and one-half years in prison and was released in 2003 after only four years. The other two received three-year jail terms. Krenz defiantly shouted: "The political persecution is revenge for the fact that East Germany existed!"

The prelude for the first free all-German elections in almost six decades, scheduled December 2, 1990, were state elections in the five newly recreated lands in the East; on October 14 the CDU won in four of them. Therefore, few observers were sur-

Germany

prised to see the CDU/FDP coalition win a resounding victory in December and Kohl reap the electoral reward for presiding over the mending of Germany's division.

Columbia University historian Fritz Stern noted that "Germany had been given something uncommon: another chance. The century ended as it began, with a major German lead in Europe based on economic clout, technological advance, and human efficiency and performance . . . [but] under much more favorable circumstances than in the pre-1914 age of rough-hewn nationalism." Prussia has not been recreated, despite the reburial of Frederick the Great at his beloved Sans Souci Palace in Potsdam outside Berlin and the return of the Prussian eagle and iron cross to the newly restored statue of the victory goddess atop the Brandenburg Gate in 1991.

Kohl and Foreign Minister Hans-Dietrich Genscher knew that while no European country wanted to thwart German unity, there was uneasiness about the possibility that an economically powerful Germany, 43% larger than before and more populous than any country west of Russia, would dominate Europe. Most European leaders were too polite to express these fears publicly—not British Prime Minister Margaret Thatcher and French President François Mitterrand. Thatcher bluntly told Soviet leader Gorbachev two months before the wall fell that "we do not want a united Germany." Her own foreign office disagreed with her. In January 1990 Mitterrand expressed his fear that reunification would turn Germans into the "bad" people who once dominated Europe. He thought this would require a Russian-British-French alliance to counter it. It was astonishing after a half century of partnership how quickly both leaders fell back into antiquated 19th century thinking. Both were dramatically wrong in their judgment. Mitterrand settled his nerves by persuading Chancellor Kohl to trade the German mark for the euro, thereby binding Germany more tightly to its European allies.

To minimize these fears, Germany signed landmark treaties with the USSR and Poland. On November 9 it signed a friendship treaty with the Soviet Union that amounted to the closest links the Soviets had with any major Western nation. It contains a section affirming that both nations "will refrain from any threat or use of force which is directed against the territorial integrity or political independence of the other side." Neither country would aid an aggressor against the other. Bonn insists that this agreement, ratified in the USSR in March 1991, was aimed at forging a new relationship with the USSR

in a way consistent with Germany's obligation to NATO, which is a defensive alliance.

The ink was hardly dry when Germany signed a treaty with Poland on November 14, 1990, fixing their mutual border along the Oder-Neisse Line. The former German land to the east of this demarcation constituted a third of Poland's territory. Genscher stated bluntly, "we Germans are aware that the treaty does not surrender anything that was not lost long ago as the result of a criminal war and a criminal system." But he also admitted that settling this last major dispute of the war hurt: "For those who have lost their homelands, who suffered expulsion [after 1945], it is an especially painful one."

POLITICAL SYSTEM

In 1949 West Germany's founders called their new constitution a Basic Law in order to emphasize that it would apply only temporarily until reunification. But in 1990 the newly formed Eastern German states chose to be absorbed by the FRG through Article 23, which was then scrapped to assure neighboring countries that no other former German territories could enter the FRG that way. Thus, the Basic Law became, in effect, a permanent constitution. It reflects several objectives that the founders hoped to achieve: individual freedom, political democracy, stability (to prevent a repetition of the Weimar experience), built-in safeguards against the emergence of another dictatorship and links with some aspects of the German political tradition.

In contrast to the U.S. Constitution, which has a Bill of Rights attached at the end, the Germans placed in the first 20 articles of the Basic Law guarantees for unalienable rights and liberties and the protection of life. Also in contrast with the

U.S. document, the Basic Law explicitly grants Germans, who had never experienced a successful democratic revolution, the right of revolution. Article 20 reads in part: "all Germans shall have the right to resist any person or persons seeking to abolish the constitutional order, should no other remedy be possible."

A Powerful Court

To underscore its commitment to the principles in this document, the founders, with the full support of the American occupation authorities, created the Constitutional Court, which would have the power of judicial review and therefore would be the final arbiter in constitutional questions. With two chambers located in Karlsruhe, where founders thought it could remain freer from political influences, the court reviews legislation, adjudicates disputes between the national and *Land* (state) political institutions, rules on questions concerning individual rights, and can even ban groups or parties if it believes that their activities are not in harmony with the principles of the Basic Law. For instance, in the mid-1950s it banned the neo-Nazi Socialist Reich Party and the Communist Party for this reason.

The court has a clearly political character, as the selection of the justices reveals: half of the 16 justices are chosen by the lower house of parliament, and half are selected by the upper house (in order that state interests are not overlooked). Each serves one 12-year terms. The parties nominate candidates. For example, on March 5, 2010, the SPD nominee, Andreas Vosskuhle, a 46-year old law professor, was elected President of the Federal Constitutional Court. The FDP's nominee, Andreas Paulus, was elected on the same day as a justice on the court.

Because of its powerful affect on the law, it is often called the third chamber of

Sie haben 2 Stimmen

hier 1 Stimme
für die Wahl
**eines/einer Wahlkreis-
abgeordneten**

Erststimme

1	**Reinhardt, Erika** Hausfrau S-Wangen Ludwig-Blum-Straße 5	**CDU** · Christlich Demokratische Union Deutschlands
2	**Conradi, Peter** Bundestagsabgeordneter, Architekt Ostfildern 4 Im Haurer 1	**SPD** · Sozial-demokratische Partei Deutschlands
3	**Kiesswetter, Ekkehard** Rechtsanwalt S-Ost Plettenbergstraße 14	**FDP/DVP** · Freie Demo-kratische Partei/ Demokratische Volkspartei
4	**Rühle, Heidemarie-Rose** Hausfrau S-Süd Römerstraße 13	**GRÜNE** · DIE GRÜNEN

hier 1 Stimme
für die Wahl
einer Landesliste (Partei)
– maßgebende Stimme für die Verteilung der
Sitze insgesamt auf die einzelnen Parteien –

Zweitstimme

CDU	Christlich Demokratische Union Deutschlands Dr. Wolfgang Schäuble, Matthias Wissmann, Dr. Lutz Stavenhagen, Anton Pfeifer, Udo Ehrbar	1
SPD	Sozialdemokratische Partei Deutschlands Dr. Herta Däubler-Gmelin, Harald Schäfer, Hans-Martin Bury, Wolfgang Roth, Dr. Liesel Hartenstein	2
FDP/DVP	Freie Demokratische Partei/ Demokratische Volkspartei Dr. Helmut Haussmann, Georg Gallus, Martin Gruner, Dr. Wolfgang Weng, Dr. Olaf Feldmann	3
GRÜNE	DIE GRÜNEN Christa Vennegerts, Oswald Metzger, Ursula Eid-Simon, Dr. Thilo Weichert, Monika Knoche	4
LIGA	CHRISTLICHE LIGA Die Partei für das Leben Karl Simpfendörfer, Bettina Schega, Ewald Jaksch, Wilhelma Schmidts, Marion Gotthardt	5
CM	CHRISTLICHE MITTE Anny Stark, Peter Bella, Michael Platt, Erna Schonstein, Werner Keller	6
	DIE GRAUEN Initiiert vom Senioren-Schutz-Bund „Graue Panther" e.V.	7

"YOU HAVE 2 VOTES"

the legislature." Like the U.S. Supreme Court, it can judge laws or parts of laws to be unconstitutional, but it had done so only in 611 cases in 60 years. Unlike the U.S. court, it seeks consensus and seldom writes dissenting opinions. Any citizen may bring a constitutional case, and about 6,000 do that each year. The court is administratively independent and cannot be impeached by the parliament.

It has not been afraid to lock horns with the government. For example, it struck down Chancellor Adenauer's attempt in the mid-1950s to create a second television channel under national control because this would have clearly violated the states' constitutional jurisdiction over mass communications media. In 1983 it decided to postpone the national census on the grounds that the questions the state intended to ask would have violated the citizens' right of privacy. The next census was not scheduled until 2011 when the EU requires all member states to collect data that includes profession, household size, family status and housing. In 1995 it struck down Bavaria's requirements for schools to hang crucifixes in every classroom, and it prevented the punishment of pacifists caught shouting the slogan, "soldiers are murderers." The first female chief justice, Jutta Limbach, faced further parliamentary criticism for agreeing to rule on parliament's power to restrict political asylum, as it did in 1993.

The court sometimes upholds the government's policies, as it did in 1993 when it ruled that the Maastricht treaty for European unity and the FRG's participation in UN-sponsored peacekeeping operations outside of Europe are not unconstitutional. In July 2009 it gave the green light for the EU Lisbon Treaty (constitution), but it concluded that Germany's sovereignty could be endangered by some parts of the treaty. However, it ruled in only one month earlier that the parliament should pass a new law giving itself more authority over EU decisions. It made clear that there are limits to the powers the German parliament can turn over to the EU. The European Parliament is not a proper legislature, and the EU is not a democratic state. It ruled out some forms of participation, such as the establishment of a single EU military command. The new limitations have not been fully tested, and they were known to have made Chancellor Merkel more careful about contributing money to a eurozone loan package for financially distressed Greece in 2010.

All parties in disputes before this powerful court, including the national government, have always complied with its decisions. Almost 80% of citizens trust the court, while less than half have faith in the federal government and parliament.

State Government

More than any other state in Europe with the exception of Switzerland and Belgium, Germany has decentralized and fragmented political power. Such decentralization is traditional in Germany, which consists of what had been a myriad of states and free cities. The only experience with highly centralized government—the Third Reich and the GDR—left a bad taste in Germans' mouths. The FRG is now broken down into 16 states (each called a *Land*). Most of these states were newly created after 1945 and the five in the former GDR, plus a unified city of Berlin, were recreated in 1990. In May 1996 Eastern German voters rejected unequivocally an effort by all major parties, except the PDS, and the governments of Brandenburg and Berlin to merge these two states.

Reichstag seen from Brandenburg Gate

Germany

The massive influx of refugees into the Western occupation zones did much to break down the formerly strong regionalism of the various areas of Germany. But Bavaria has retained its own unique character, visually, culturally and politically, more than any other state. It proudly calls itself the "Free State of Bavaria" and, curiously, has never formally ratified the Basic Law although it has abided by it since 1949. The Eastern German states also have different political cultures.

Each state has its own government, and it is free to choose the form it prefers. The state constitutions differ considerably in some respects, but they all call for forms of parliamentary government. A government, led by a minister president, is chosen by a unicameral parliament, called a *Landtag*, elected by proportional representation. State issues play the dominant role in such state elections, but since the early 1960s these elections, which are seldom held at the same time as national elections, have increasingly become indicators or bellwethers for citizens' approval of national policies or leaders. Therefore, national leaders lend their active support in local campaigns, an important reason why the voter turnout is very high by American standards, averaging about 70% since the early 1950s.

In accord with German tradition and to prevent a single leader or group of leaders in the central government from gathering all strings of power, the founders granted specific exclusive power to the states: education at all levels (although the national government does contribute to the financing of universities, and it is responsible for constructing all school buildings), law enforcement and internal security (although the central government does maintain an Office for the Protection of the Constitution, roughly equivalent to the FBI in the U.S., and a Federal Criminal Office, which maintains data that is useful to the state police authorities), the administration of justice and mass communications and media. Only in the areas of defense and foreign policy is the national government largely free of the state governments. As in the U.S., all powers not expressly granted to the national government belong to the states. In 2004–5 all 16 ministers president accepted the need to reform the federal structure, but they failed to agree on the powers they should cede to the central government, especially regarding education.

States used their powers over regional broadcasting to resist a unified national satellite television policy. State leaders travel around the globe and conduct their own foreign policy to a degree. Some have even opened offices in Brussels to influence EU policy and seek financial favors.

The new Chancellor's Office in Berlin, dubbed the "washing machine"

The upper house (*Bundesrat*), which the states control, has been used to force the federal government to consult with them on any foreign policy deals that affect them. The states wield great powers in Brussels, particularly over budget contributions and the ability to block the European Commission from imposing anti-trust (competition) and industrial policy on the states. All these trends underscore the fact that regional politics is more significant in the FRG than in any other European country. Almost all important political figures in federal politics rose from a strong base in the states.

Two factors prevent the states from being as individualistic as American ones: legal uniformity and shared taxation. German law, which was decisively influenced by Roman law and by the Napoleonic Code, was codified in the last three decades of the 19th century. Since the 1950s the criminal code has been in the process of revision. The point is that German law is the same in every state. In general, the national government wields the most legislative power while the state governments have most of the administrative power. The staffs of most federal ministries are relatively small. Indeed, if one excludes the employees of the Federal Railways and the Federal Postal Service (both of which are being privatized), only about 10% of public employees work for the national government, whereas roughly a third work for local governments and over half work for the states.

The states finance and set operating rules for local governments in the communities (*Gemeinden*). Local government differs from state to state, but all communities have an elected council (*Stadtrat* or *Gemeinderat*). Also, each county (*Kreis*) has an elected council (*Kreistag*) led by an executive officer (*Landrat*).

Germany's decentralization has its positive and negative consequences. The great number of decision makers and the necessity for consensus are mighty barriers to tyrannical government. On the other hand, it makes reform exceedingly difficult. The levels of government are so intertwined that they often block each other. The 16 *Länder* have as many elections, and on average there is a *Land* election every three months. This fact enables the opposition in Berlin to gain control of the upper house of parliament, the *Bundesrat*, and thereby to block reform. Anticipating approaching *Land* elections, a federal government is inhibited in introducing radical reform. Finally the largest political parties themselves are organized federally with powerful regional leaders. This makes it hard for central leaders to impose changes.

Parliament—the Second House

The states' interests are also guaranteed by their legislative role at the federal level. The second house of parliament, the *Bundesrat*, is composed of delegates from the state governments and, like all upper houses in federal states, exists primarily to protect states' rights. Seats in the *Bundesrat* are apportioned on the basis of each land's population; each of the most populous states (including North Rhine-Westphalia, Bavaria, Baden-Wurttemberg and Lower Saxony receives five seats; each of

234

Former Chancellor Dr. Helmut Kohl

the medium-sized states (such as Hesse, the Rhineland-Palatinate, Schleswig-Holstein, and the five new lands in the East) receive four, and each of the three smaller states (Hamburg, Bremen and the Saar) receive three. The lands send specific delegates depending upon the subjects being discussed; sometimes they are administrators and other times they are leading politicians, including the minister presidents. Delegates are always bound by instructions from the state governments, and each delegation must cast all of its votes for or against a matter.

The *Bundesrat* can initiate legislation, and it must approve all legislation relating to the states' constitutional or administrative responsibilities. Also it must approve any legislation affecting state boundaries, national emergencies and constitutional amendments. Presently, about 60% of all legislation falls within the *Bundesrat's* veto power. In many cases, party lines do not decisively affect votes in this body. For instance, smaller or poorer states often have more in common than do larger or wealthier ones, regardless of which parties rule in the state capitals.

Parliament—the Lower House

The lower house of Parliament (*Bundestag*) is the most important chamber. It is normally composed of 598 members elected at least every four years by Germans 18 years of age or older. The electoral system is a complicated mixture of proportional representation and single-member districts. Half of the members are elected by plurality vote (more votes than any other single candidate) in 299 constituencies with an average size of approximately 250,000 residents.

The other half is elected by proportional representation from land party lists. Each voter casts two ballots, one for the constituency candidate and one for his preferred party. The party vote is the more important because it determines the percentage of total seats in the *Bundestag* each party will receive.

A further complication is the concept of "overhang votes." If a party wins more seats in the "first vote" than it would be entitled to under strict proportional representation, it keeps the extra seats, and the size of the *Bundestag* expands accordingly. Thus, after the 2009 elections the *Bundestag* was enlarged to 622 seats. However, in 2008 the Constitutional Court ruled that these extra seats were unconstitutional and that the *Bundestag* would have to change the law after the 2009 federal elections. The rule had never decisively influenced an election outcome. But with five parties now winning parliamentary seats, they would have enhanced significance if they were allowed to continue.

With German unity, Berlin became the official capital, but that did not automatically mean that the seat of government would be transferred to Berlin. Faced with the daunting costs of integrating and modernizing the bankrupt economy of the GDR, many shirked from the price tag of moving all their operations to Berlin. A massive move severely affected the economic livelihood of Bonn and its suburbs. There were also political considerations. Some Western German politicians did not want to transfer the capital from Bonn, which is located close to Brussels and other EU centers, to a faraway city with a reputation for past militarism and present rebelliousness and a thriving counterculture. Also, until 1994 Berlin was surrounded by a large number of Soviet troops, who could possibly have intimidated the German government if relations between the two countries were to become strained.

On June 20, 1991, in one of the longest (12 hours) and most emotional debates ever held in the *Bundestag*, a narrow majority (338–320) voted to make Berlin the seat of government. Younger legislators tended to favor Bonn, whereas those old enough to remember the earlier Berlin and its grandeur, such as Kohl and Brandt, favored Berlin. The outcome was a powerful message of reconciliation to Eastern Germans. But the latter played a decisive role in the vote: whereas narrow majorities in both the two largest parties, the CDU/CSU and SPD, voted for Bonn, it was the 25 members from the small Eastern German parties, the PDS and Alliance 90, who tipped the scales for Berlin.

Seven ministries, including defense and agriculture, remain in Bonn and maintain offices in Berlin. But the rest, along with at least 20,000 government workers, were transferred to Berlin in 1999. Some 140 embassies had to move, along with countless organizations, such as lobby groups and industry representatives, who must be close to the center of power. By 2009 one found 8,732 officials working in Bonn, while 8,931 were based in Berlin. The additional cost for maintaining two capitals is about 8.8 million euros per year: 751 tons of official mail is shipped back and forth annually, and 132,000 plane tickets are booked for shuttles.

Confounding expectations, Bonn not only survived the change, but it is thriving after remaking itself into an international R&D campus and convention center for everything from research into

Chancellor Angela Merkel: a new beginning

Germany

alternative energy and medical science to a locale for UN offices. It has created 12,000 jobs since the move, and one in 10 jobs in its environs is now in health care. It used to be called a sleepy bureaucrats' town, but now it is a living growing city.

On April 19, 1999, former Chancellor Gerhard Schröder spoke at the inaugural session of the newly renovated Reichstag building, with its massive glass dome that symbolizes, in his words, "the openness and the transparency of our democratic politics." He emphasized that "equating *Reichstag* with *Reich* makes no sense," given the strong and stable democracy in today's FRG. But exactly what to call the new capitol, if not *Reichstag*, consumed months of debate. Finally the all-party Council of Elders declared a solution that satisfied no one: *Deutscher Bundestag—Plenarbereich Reichstagsgebäude* (German Federal Assembly—Plenary Area, Imperial Assembly Building). Modern glass structures to accommodate the members of parliament and their staffs were constructed adjacent to the *Reichstag*.

For the first time in German history, the parliament in 1949 was granted exclusive control over the country's government and bureaucracy, and it has supervisory power over the military. It elects a military ombudsman, who is unique in the world. He or she has access to all military facilities at all times and can speak with any armed forces member. Even the highest-ranking officers cannot block access. Although most legislation originates with the government, the *Bundestag* must debate and approve all. Debates in the *Bundestag* plenum are conducted in a very free and relaxed atmosphere. They are punctuated with humorous or pointed quips, boisterous interruptions, laughter, applause and desk pounding.

Major debates are televised in order to bring the activity of the parliament closer to the attention of the citizens. The *Bundestag* combines the role of a debating parliament, such as the British House of Commons, with that of a working parliament, such as the U.S. Congress. Most of the work is actually done in the 19 standing committees, which though not as powerful as U.S. congressional and senatorial committees, thoroughly examine and amend legislation.

They also increasingly use their investigatory and information-gathering powers quite effectively to perform their function of being a responsible critic of the government. An interesting feature is that seats and chairmanships in the committees are distributed according to party strength in the *Bundestag* itself. Thus, the opposition party will occupy many committee chairmanships, and by tradition will always occupy that of the finance committee.

President Christian Wulff

The *Bundestag's* function as a "working parliament" is enhanced by the fact that almost half of its members are civil servants, who, in contrast with U.S. civil servants, are freed from their normal jobs while serving in political positions and can return to the civil service at any time. Even their promotions and pay raises are continued while they are in political office. Civil servants are represented in the *Bundestag* at a rate ten times higher than their proportion in the larger population, and workers, farmers, housewives and those in business and professional occupations are greatly underrepresented. A third of *Bundestag* members are women.

The FRG is a parliamentary system and the most important of the functions of the *Bundestag* is to choose a government. A majority chooses the chancellor, the most powerful political figure in the FRG, from among its own members, and she then chooses her cabinet, most of whom have seats in the *Bundestag* and who are then directly responsible to the chancellor, not to the *Bundestag*. The chancellor is always responsible to the lower house. However, in order to prevent the continuous cabinet instability that plagued the Weimar Republic, she can be voted out of office only if a majority is immediately able to choose a replacement. This requirement for a "constructive vote of no-confidence," which has been attempted very infrequently, insures that Germany will always have a government.

Ex-Chancellor Schröder's decision in May 2005 to call federal elections a year early was constitutionally questionable. To prevent the instability that had plagued the Weimar Republic, Germany's founding fathers made it hard to dissolve parliament and call early elections. Only if there is no majority in the *Bundestag* behind the chancellor can it be done. Since Schröder had a majority, albeit a narrow one, he had to engineer his own defeat in a no-confi-

dence vote on July 1, 2005, by persuading some of his supporters to defect to the opposition.

The federal president has the power to refuse early elections if he thinks there is no need for them. Ex-President Horst Köhler decided to permit them, but parties or MPs can challenge his decision in the Constitutional Court. This was done, but in an August 2005 ruling, the court gave chancellors broad latitude in deciding when to cut parliamentary mandates short. It argued that the erosion of the *Bundestag's* confidence in the chancellor "cannot be established in a court of law." The judges thereby opened the path for more frequent votes of confidence to bring about early elections. If after an election no chancellor candidate wins the majority of votes in the *Bundestag* after three rounds of voting, as seemed possible in November 2005, the president can decide whether to allow a minority government or to call new *Bundestag* elections. The 2005 elections reminded Germans that the presidency is a more powerful office than they had realized.

The chancellor's office (*Bundeskanzleramt*)—the equivalent of the U.S. Executive Office of the President, has a staff of about 500 in six departments. It is located in a new and modern structure with much glass (dubbed by Berliners as the "washing machine") opposite the *Reichstag* building in Berlin. The chancellor directs the work of all governmental ministries, which answer to him. Since Konrad Adenauer, chancellors have been very powerful figures, whose popularity almost always runs ahead of that of their own party or challengers. Some observers have even called the FRG a "chancellor's democracy."

The President

The federal chief of state is the president. Remembering how the powerful Weimar presidency had overshadowed and, to a certain extent, undermined parliament, the founders decided to grant the president largely ceremonial powers, such as formally naming the chancellor and his cabinet, signing all laws and appointing and dismissing national civil servants and federal judges. In each case, however, he merely carries out the will of the government or parliament. He could possibly be an important mediator and conciliator in the event of a parliamentary crisis, but that has not yet occurred in the FRG. The president has a villa in Bonn, but he resides in Dahlem (Western Berlin) and works in Bellevue palace in central Berlin.

Former President Richard von Weizsäcker was a patriarchal Christian Democrat whose style and substance have earned him almost universal respect by transform-

Germany

Last GDR Minister President Lothar de Maizière with author

Photo by Heinrich Bortfeldt

ing the presidency into a post of real authority. He used the office to describe broadly the direction in which he believed the FRG should go. He spoke out at carefully chosen moments on the meaning of Germany's past, the potential dangers of nuclear power, the importance of trade unions in the society, the significance of German unity, and the need to move the seat of government to Berlin. Weizsäcker strengthened the nature of the presidency as a kind of conscience of the nation. He showed that the president's power lies in his use of the "bully pulpit." A president's success is thereby measured by the quality of his speeches.

His successor in May 1994 was also a Christian Democrat, Roman Herzog, former president of the Constitutional Court. Herzog was followed in May 1999 by Social Democrat Johannes Rau, popular ex-minister president of the FRG's largest *Land*, North Rhine-Westphalia.

In May 2004 Horst Köhler, former head of the International Monetary Fund (IMF) and Christian Democrat, was elected as the ninth federal president. Virtually unknown in Germany at the time of his nomination, he was the first economist and only the second opposition political figure to be elected. In May 2009 he won re-elected. He provided a respected economic voice at a time of national economic uncertainty.

However, it was his economic focus that caused him to resign in May 2010. Köhler unleashed a barrage of criticism when he said in a radio interview in Afghanistan that Germany, as "an export-oriented nation," might sometimes need to "defend

our interests, for example open trade routes." Critics interpreted his message to be that German soldiers are sent abroad to secure German economic interests. That was not what he meant. He had made repeated efforts to encourage Germany to conduct a debate about its global role. This was the first time a president quit his post.

The regional chiefs of the ruling CDU and FDP replaced him with an active and experienced politician, someone with a thicker skin than Köhler to survive the savage German political environment. They selected the Minister President of Lower Saxony, Christian Wulff, who was narrowly elected on June 30, 2010. Since Chancellor Merkel had wanted Labor Minister Ursula von der Leyen, Wulff's selection damaged Merkel and her position within the party and coalition government. The opposition Social Democrats and Greens nominated the former head of the *Stasi* files, Joachim Gauck, to run against Wulff.

In order to prevent the president from claiming a superior role based upon a popular mandate upon direct election by all the people, the founders decided to have the president selected every five years by a Federal Assembly (*Bundesversammlung*) composed of all members of the *Bundestag* and an equal number of delegates from the various land parliaments. In fact, no national political figure is elected directly by all voters.

The founders also distrusted elements of direct democracy (such as initiatives, referendums or plebiscites) at the national level. They did not wish to create a useful tool for a popular demagogue like Hitler

who could undermine the authority and responsibility of parliament, the very heart of democracy. Although the Basic Law does not explicitly forbid them at the national level, the *Bundestag* never enacted laws to permit them to take place. However, since reunification in 1990 they are possible in all states and municipalities and are conducted with increasing frequency; almost 300 are held at the local level each year. For example, almost every power project must suffer a referendum, as do some private-sector investments. Schleswig-Holstein sponsored a referendum that rejected the German spelling reform although the state legislature overturned the result. Bavarian voters abolished their state senate in 1998. Advocates of direct democracy argue that this mechanism has become necessary since membership in parties and trust in politicians are falling. A 2008 poll indicated that 80% of respondents want referenda at the national level.

Political Parties

A crucially important point is that a person can be elected to the *Bundestag* only as a member of a political party. In the past, Germans had regarded parties with distrust. They allegedly divided the body politic, and their log-rolling and pursuit of particularistic interests had an undignified and illicit air in the eyes of the average German. This condescension before 1945 had greatly weakened the prestige of parliament and therefore of democracy. Also, so many parties had seats in the Weimar parliament that it was almost impossible to construct a stable and lasting majority.

Therefore, the Basic Law (in contrast to the U.S. Constitution) granted political parties official recognition and status, as well as the responsibility to organize the country's political life. Also, the Basic Law requires any party to receive a minimum of 5% of the votes cast nationwide (unless it can win three seats directly) in order to receive any seats in the *Bundestag*. In the first election in 1949 many parties cleared this hurdle, but since 1953 only five parties have been able to accomplish this. But five is a crowd when it comes to forming stable coalition governments. Electoral arithmetic makes the classic governments of center-left or center-right almost impossible. The only alternative to a grand coalition of the two largest parties is an agreement among three parties to rule together. Given the differences among the parties, this is very difficult. The parties are increasingly incapable of delivering working coalitions. It is a recipe for policy paralysis.

The *Bundestag* is made up of parliamentary parties (each called a *Fraktion*) that

Germany

practice a high degree of party discipline; almost nine out of ten votes are straight party votes. Many observers have called the FRG a "party state" and they are largely correct.

Since 1959 the major political parties have received increasing amounts of financial subsidies from the national treasury. Direct corporate donations account for only 5% of party revenues, donations by individuals for 15%, and state financing and membership fees for the bulk.

The Christian Democrats and Christian Socials

The largest party in the grand coalition following the 2005 elections is the CDU, which is linked in parliament and in federal elections with its Bavarian sister party, the CSU. The CDU/CSU is the first successful political party in German history that did not rest on a single confessional or class base. It is a union of diverse groups who after the Nazi catastrophe wanted to put Christian principles back into political life and to take ideological rigidity out of it. They wished to give Germany a new moral, democratic and socially just beginning. Adenauer's economics minister, Ludwig Erhard, introduced a brand of capitalism with a social conscience (called the "social market economy") that brought not only prosperity, but a broad net of social assistance for the uprooted, the hungry, the unemployed, the old and the sick.

Germans are very proud and protective of their generous social legislation, and the creation of the FRG's modern social net is primarily the work of the CDU/CSU; the SPD-FDP coalition only tightened this net in a few places during the 1970s. It is thus a democratic, reform-oriented party, which attracts votes primarily from Catholics, independent business people, white-collar employees and civil servants. It would not be considered a conservative party in the U.S. political sense, even though it does win the votes of most conservatives in Germany. However, this does not weaken or embarrass the CDU/CSU since almost all conservatives in the FRG, in contrast to the Weimar Republic, support the democratic system. For years the party grappled with the problem of how to put aside the internal struggles within its talented and experienced leadership in order to present a picture of unity.

Catholic Bavaria is the FRG's most conservative state and the CSU is therefore also conservative. The CSU, which especially appeals to Catholics, rural and small city dwellers, craftsmen, small business groups and, increasingly, those in the service industries, easily wins land elections in Bavaria (though not in Munich, the state capital). Its leader was Edmund Stoiber, who was chosen as the combined CDU/CSU chancellor candidate in the 2002 *Bundestag* elections. He lost, thereby continuing the tradition that no Bavarian can become federal chancellor. In 2007 he stepped down. When in the 2008 state election the CSU lost its absolute majority in Bavaria for the first time in 46 years, he was replaced by Horst Seehofer. Many of their supporters were lost to a new party of CSU rebels that focused on local issues, the *Freie Wähler* (Free Voters), who took a tenth of the vote. The CSU had lost its aura of invincibility. One of Chancellor Merkel's most popular ministers stems from this regional party: handsome 37-year-old Baron Karl-Theodor zu Guttenberg, the party's foreign policy expert and defense minister in the cabinet. His illustrious family joined the resistance against Hitler, and one member was executed for involvement in the 1944 plot to assassinate the Führer. His independence streak appeals to voters, and at times his popularity have exceeded Merkel's.

The political and economic success of Kohl, the first German chancellor to have been too young to have played any role in Nazi Germany, helped restore in many citizens an interest and pride in being German. Kohl and his party believed that Germans have atoned enough for the nation's past sins. Former President Weizsäcker occasionally deflated such self-satisfaction by reminding Germans of the seamier side of their past, while encouraging them to be proud of what they have accomplished since 1945. Kohl frequently spoke of the "Fatherland" and the *Heimat* ("Homeland"). He also encouraged displays of patriotism and the frequent playing of the national anthem, the third verse of the *Deutschlandlied* (Germany Song, often mistakenly called *Deutschland, Deutschland über Alles*).

Before Germany's dramatic move toward unity, it appeared that Kohl's party, which was ridden with dissatisfaction about what appeared to be a bumbling chancellor, was heading for defeat in the December 2, 1990, federal elections. However, Kohl instinctively knew that, faced with the challenges of melding two Germanys into one, German voters would choose that leader who was decisive and exuded confidence that future problems could be solved. Therefore, the Union parties adopted the slogans, "Yes to Germany, yes to the Future!" At each of its election rallies, a campaign song was sung in English: "Feel the power, touch the future, reach the heart!"

The first all-German election in 58 years was a plebiscite on unity, after the fact. Those parties that had seized the opportunity to bring it about were handsomely rewarded, and those that seemed petty and afraid and who cast doubt on unity were punished. With voter participation falling to a new low of 77.8% (74% in the East), the governing CDU-CSU-FDP coalition won 55% of the votes. It actually performed better in the East than in the West. The CDU-CSU captured 44% of the votes and 319 seats. It won big in the former GDR, where few Catholics live. Half of East German workers voted CDU, and it was the preferred party for young voters in both parts of Germany.

The CDU's standing in the East was troubled after the election by the cabinet resignation of the GDR's last minister president, Lothar de Maizière. As a lawyer and high lay official in the East German Protestant Church, he was shown to have maintained contacts with *Stasi* from 1981 to 1988. He maintained credibly that these were necessary for his efforts to defend his clients and church. He was cleared of allegations that he had actually spied for *Stasi*, but he was forced to relinquish his party vice-chairmanship to another Eastern German, Angela Merkel, who became the party's general secretary in 1998. Other leaders of the old Eastern CDU, one of the bloc parties that had co-operated with the Communists, were gradually forced out of their posts.

The CDU/CSU won a narrow victory in October 1994. In 1996 he surpassed his political hero, Konrad Adenauer, as the longest-serving chancellor in the 20th century: 14 years. Both had sought to bring Germany greatness, not through military strength and *Realpolitik*, but by making it liberal, democratic, trusted and prosperous. In some ways Adenauer's job was more difficult. He had led a defeated, despised, divided, and impoverished country that was occupied and partly ruled by foreign troops. His compromises prompted critics to call him "chancellor of the allies." By contrast, Kohl led a Germany that was unified, rich, and powerful, with a mature democracy and the third-largest economy in the world. He almost completed Adenauer's dream of "a free and united Germany in a free and united Europe."

No one could deny Germany's strength under Kohl. But by working closely with Germany's European allies, especially France, as well as with the U.S. and by pressing for a unified Europe more vigorously than anybody else, he helped solve the perennial problem that had vexed European statesmen for years: how to make Germany strong without terrifying the rest of Europe.

By September 1998, voters had grown tired of Kohl, who had not been able to solve Germany's main problem: unemployment. For the first time in the FRG's history, they voted to throw out an incumbent chancellor and to remove from power all the parties in the ruling coalition. Kohl was gracious in defeat, took full responsibility for the fiasco, and announced that he was stepping down.

He was replaced as party leader by Wolfgang Schäuble (later finance minister), who was almost killed by an assassin's bullets in 1990 and who is confined to a wheelchair. His tenure was cut short by a scandal that came crashing down on the CDU. Kohl confessed to accepting $1 million in illegal campaign funds. The press was filled with lurid reports of corruption, party slush funds, secret bank accounts, and bribes by shady international arms dealers. Kohl made matters worse by refusing to reveal the names of donors, claiming that he had given his "word of honor" to keep them confidential. He also ordered the destruction of a huge number of key documents and two-thirds of his government's chancellery computer files. Not only public opinion and voters, but the party itself turned on the formerly unassailable leader. Schäuble admitted that the CDU was in "the worst crisis of its history."

The first party notable to dare call for an end of the Kohl era was Angela Merkel. He never forgave her for this, and she prevented his being named subsequently as the honorary party chairman because of his historic achievements. However, on his 80th birthday in 2010, she said: "You will go into the 20th-century history books as a great statesman." The public is more forgiving. A 2010 TV poll showed that 59% now rate him as a good chancellor, ahead of his successor, Gerhard Schröder, at 47%.

Merkel is a pastor's daughter and Eastern German doctor of physics who had entered politics in 1990 in order to fight for democracy in the former GDR. A quick learner and a good administrator who is unpretentious and shows courage, integrity and coolness under fire, she is the only Easterner to survive an entire decade near the top of the CDU. Her asset is that she is a female Ossi who is free of the unsavory cronyism and backroom dealing that had tarnished the party elite. At the 2000 party congress she was endorsed as leader by a resounding 90% of delegates. However, in 2002 her party decided that CSU leader Stoiber had the better chance of leading the CDU/CSU to victory in the September 22 elections, so it chose to back him as chancellor candidate instead of Merkel. She became the party's parliamentary leader.

Merkel reestablished her grip on the party and began to recast herself as a radical reformer. Because of her courage to advocate fundamental change, willingness to take risks, and ability to become leader against the will of the party establishment, she was often compared with Margaret Thatcher. She finds this comparison tiresome because she is not a radical reformer. The CDU/CSU won only four more seats than the SPD in the federal elections on September 18, 2005, but they were enough to make her chancellor, the Federal Republic's eighth, over a grand coalition with the SPD. She is many firsts: the first female, East German and Russian-speaking chancellor; the youngest German chancellor ever (age 51 in 2005); a Protestant leader of a predominantly Catholic party. She is a childless remarried divorcee, a fact that cost her among traditional Catholic CDU and CSU voters. She had made the decision to conduct a "gender-neutral" campaign and was rewarded by only 35% of women votes nationwide. Most Germans voted for change, but not the root-and-branch kind.

Her first four years in office were a foreign and domestic policy success. In late 2009 *Forbes* magazine called her the "most powerful woman in the world." She was seen as having steered Germany relatively safely through the greatest global economic storm in seven decades. She persuaded voters that the superiority of Germany's post-war model of consensus, wealth, wage discipline and a social market had been demonstrated. She blamed America's subprime mortgage crisis and freewheeling capitalism for the catastrophe. Her grand coalition government had saved 1.4 million jobs through short-time work schemes and a "cash for clunkers" boost for the auto industry.

Entering the September 27, 2009, federal elections, the CDU/CSU was certain to win more seats than any other party. The big question was whether its favorite coalition party, the FDP, would do well enough that they could together form a majority government. With a turnout of 70.8%, the CDU/CSU captured 33.8% of the votes, a loss of 1.4% since 2005 and its lowest share since the FRG's first federal election in 1949. It did capture 239 seats, a gain of 17 and enough to form a majority "black-yellow" coalition with the FDP, which had its best ever result.

Nevertheless, in the new five-party political constellation, the large parties (CDU/CSU and SPD) are steadily getting smaller. Their combined vote was only 56.8%, a far cry from 91.2% in 1976 and around 80% thereafter. It is the small parties that are getting bigger. Even a whacky "Pirate Party," which favored free access to everything on the Internet, captured 2% of the votes, almost exclusively from

For Peace, Against Blind Obedience

Right turn

Seats in the Bundestag, 2009* (2005)

SPD 146 (222) — CDU 194 (180)

Greens 68 (51) — CSU 45 (46)

Left Party† 76 (54) — FDP 93 (61)

2009
2005
COALITION

Source: Federal returning officer

German federal elections
Party share of total votes, %

CDU/CSU
SPD
FDP
Greens
Left Party†

1980 85 90 95 2000 05 09

*Provisional result †PDS before 2009

Source: *The Economist*

Germany

Guido Westerwelle, Foreign Minister and Leader of FDP

young voters. The 2009 elections were the first with the participation of a generation that knew of the fall of the Berlin wall only from hearsay.

The FDP—"Liberals"

For a long time, the FDP (called the "Liberals" or "Free Democrats") was the only small party to survive in the Bundestag. It had never received more than 13% of the vote, and at times it danced dangerously close to the 5% line. Yet the FDP played a role in German politics far out of proportion to its size or voter strength. Only once (in 1957) has a single party ever won an absolute majority of seats in the Bundestag. Thus, German governments must almost always be coalitions of at least two parties, and for a long time the FDP was the linchpin for almost every governmental coalition. This changed after the *Bundestag* had to accommodate five parties; ruling coalitions must sometimes have three.

The FDP sees itself as the heir to the traditional German liberal movement, which was always composed of two strains: a strong nationalist commitment and the protection of individual rights through minimizing state intervention in the economy and society. In the early 1970s the nationalist strain largely left the party, so throughout the 1970s the FDP could be more comfortable in the center-moderate left coalition with the SPD. From 1969 to 1982, the FDP was in the governing coalition with the SPD. However, it is economically more conservative than the SPD. The FDP attracts most of its votes from the middle class mainly in urban areas. It always wins many strategic second votes from Christian Democrats or Christian Socials who want to boost it over the 5% hurdle in order to be a coalition partner in the government.

When it sensed a conservative wind blowing, it decided in 1982 to change partners, thereby enabling the Christian Democrats to rule. The FDP was widely criticized for the way in which it brought the Schmidt government tumbling down. Thousands of its members and some of its parliamentarians left the party in protest.

The buzzards seemed to be circling in the lead-up to the 1998 elections, but its dynamic party secretary general, Guido Westerwelle, succeeded in scaring some of them away. This experienced survival party arose from the dead. But for the first time in almost three decades the FDP found itself neither in the government nor in possession of the foreign minister's post. That did not change in 2002.

In September 2005 federal elections, it climbed to a new high of 9.8% of the votes and 61 seats. It had committed itself to a governing coalition with the CDU/CSU, but together they had not won a majority of seats. It declined to join a "red-red-yellow" coalition with the SPD and Leftists.PDS or a "Jamaica coalition" (a term coined for a country whose flag is black-yellow-green) with the CDU/CSU and Greens. Therefore it became the largest party in the opposition. It had its best result ever in the 2009 federal elections, and it emerged as the junior partner of Chancellor Merkel's CDU/CSU. It captured 14.6% of the votes, an increase of 4.8%, and 93 seats, an increase of 32. The party was ecstatic.

A trained lawyer 47 years of age in 2009, Westerwelle dominates his party as few other leaders. He also has the personal self-confidence to be openly gay. He became foreign minister, the usual top job for the junior coalition member even though foreign policy is not his strong suit. He calls himself a "committed Euro-

pean," but he admits he "can't shed my Atlanticist skin," meaning his strong support for the U.S.-German relationship. He does advocate the removal of all American tactical nuclear weapons from German soil. Also entering the cabinet for the FDP was Health Minister Philipp Rösler, a 36-year-old physician born in Vietnam; he is the first Asian to occupy such a high office in Germany.

Westerwelle gets along well with Chancellor Merkel, who call each other "Du." But the party returned to power determined to put its stamp on government. His strong advocacy of tax cuts, health care reform, and the delayed closing of nuclear power plants have clashed with Merkel's more cautious ideas about coping with the economic downturn. His lashing out at "welfare scroungers" diminishes respect toward him. Their coalition government got off to a bad start with lots of public bickering, and it is not a model of harmony. That has cost the FDP and Westerwelle popularity.

The Social Democrats

The SPD is a traditional working-class party that is the only one in the FRG having had a continuous existence since before the German Empire. In the Weimar Republic it was one of the regime's staunchest supporters, and during the Third Reich its leaders either found themselves in concentration camps or went into exile. After the war it fully expected to become Germany's governing party because of its former opposition to the Nazis, but its leaders badly misread the voters' minds. West Germans, gripped by poverty, were less interested in the SPD's socialist solutions than they were in the prosperity its opponents promised and actually produced. Also, Social Democrats' focus on strong national policy directed against all four occupation powers and especially aimed toward German reunification proved to be far less appealing than Adenauer's policy of winning West German sovereignty, international respect and military security through military and economic integration with the West.

In order to break out of the "one-third ghetto" (winning only a third of the votes) within the electorate and in order to attract more Catholic and middle-class voters, the SPD changed its program at the party congress in Bad Godesberg in 1959. It cast off the Marxist ballast in its party program and made the basic decision not fundamentally to challenge the capitalist order, but instead to seek to correct its flaws through social reform. The following year the party's chief strategist, Herbert Wehner, announced in the Bundestag that the SPD would accept Adenauer's foreign policy of integration with the West.

Having become in theory as well as in fact a mass social reform party anchored in the democratic West, and with a new young chancellor candidate, Willy Brandt, who remained the party's chairman until 1987, the party began attracting increasing numbers of middle class voters. These included gains among civil servants, white-collar employees in industry and the service sector, and especially youth; these groups soon gained a far greater share of the party's leadership positions than workers. This opening of the party to the middle class was crucial to the SPD's gaining power in 1969, but it also converted the SPD into a broad-spectrum party whose main problem became that of unifying such diverse groups behind a common leadership.

In 1990 the SPD picked as its chancellor candidate its biggest vote-getting provincial politician, Oskar Lafontaine, ex-minister president of the Saarland and one of the party's most outspoken leftists. He belonged to a new generation of politicians who did not directly experience Nazism or the onset of the Cold War. His political outlook was significantly shaped by the student rebellion of the 1960s, and his politics are postindustrial, postmaterialist "new politics" emphasizing environmental issues. He was brought up in a divided Germany and showed no emotions toward the idea of a united country, to which he derisively referred as a "provisional entity" until the nation-state became superfluous. He hated words like "fatherland," and on the occasion of Germany's unity at midnight October 2 to 3, 1990, he alone among political leaders refused to sing the national anthem. He was unable to notice, let alone tap, the emotions released by the opening of the Berlin Wall. This antagonized many of his party comrades, including former chancellors Brandt and Schmidt.

In his campaign, during which he was almost killed when a deranged woman slit his throat with a butcher knife hidden in a bouquet, he harped on the problems and costs associated with unification and was perceived as a prophet of doom. His message was depressing, and his leftist themes did not interest German voters in 1990, especially those in Eastern Germany, who wanted prosperity within the FRG. *Die Zeit* called him "the wrong man at the wrong time," and the electoral disaster proved this. The SPD dropped to 33.5% of the vote and 239 seats. Its 24.3% in the East, which had been the party's electoral fortress before Hitler's take-over, was shocking. It got the votes of only a fourth of East German workers.

Having led the SPD back into the "one-third ghetto" from which it had worked so long to escape, Lafontaine left his party to rebuild itself. Rhineland-Palatinate Minister President Rudolf Scharping assumed leadership. He was the first national party leader in Germany to be selected by means of a poll of 870,000 party members throughout the country. He was a moderate, hard-working, but uncharismatic leader. Voters ignored his calls for change in the 1994 federal elections although the SPD was able to increase its votes to 36.4% (37.6% in the West and 31.9% in the East) and seats to 252. In the aftermath Social Democrats began bickering among themselves, and many blamed the party's deep malaise and plunging popularity on Scharping's vacillating policies and weak leadership. In 1995 Oskar Lafontaine replaced him as party leader.

Lafontaine was a traditional left-wing politician who enjoyed enthusiastic support by many of the party's rank-and-file.

Former Chancellor Gerhard Schröder

But another Social Democrat was showing himself to be a more promising vote-getter in general elections, and this became very important for a party that had lost four straight Bundestag elections in 16 years. When Lower Saxony's minister-president, Gerhard Schröder, won an impressive re-election victory in March 1998, the SPD turned to him as chancellor candidate, while Lafontaine continued as chairman of a party that had historically been prone to self-destructive divisiveness.

Schröder came from humble origins, the son of a widowed cleaning lady. Born in 1944, he is the first chancellor with no memory of the war. As a student he was a Marxist who took part in the student rebellion and became chairman of the Young Socialists, the SPD's youth organization. However, being ambitious and a skilled political tactician, he saw that his dreams could be fulfilled only in a "new center." Despite an insecure private life (four wives) and criticism that he lacked deeply rooted convictions and vision, he made full use of his extraordinary speaking abilities, his telegenic good looks, and his pragmatic bent. He had forged close ties with Germany's business community. In the 1998 *Bundestag* elections, Schröder led the SPD to a decisive victory, capturing 40.9% of the votes and 298 seats. For the first time in FRG history, the combined parties of the left won both a majority of votes and of seats in the lower house.

Many observers, including Schröder himself, had expected a grand coalition of SPD and CDU/CSU to rule Germany after the elections. But the SPD's dramatic

Author (l) with Deputy Speaker of the Bundestag Wolfgang Thierse (m)

Germany

gains and the conservatives' shocking loss of 8% of its votes enabled the Social Democrats to form a coalition with the Greens that enjoyed a 21-seat majority. That coalition turned out to be divided during its first one-half year. Traditionalists (led by Lafontaine, who took the post as finance minister), advocated anti-business neo-Keynsian policies. They clashed with modernists (led by Schröder) who wanted to work with business to overcome unemployment. Schröder seemed not to be in full control.

This perception was strengthened by serious conflicts with his Green partners, who pushed hard for a quick timetable for phasing out Germany's nuclear power. In March 1999 the boil was lanced. Lafontaine resigned all of his political posts and seat in the *Bundestag* and re-emerged six years later as an effective populist co-leader of the ex-communist Left party. Schröder assumed the chairmanship of the SPD and set about to establish order.

In the September 2002 elections, it seemed almost certain that he and his party would be soundly defeated because he had failed to lower unemployment. But he pulled out a card never before played in elections in the Federal Republic since the war: he openly criticized U.S. policy, declaring that Germany would not support Washington's "adventures" in Iraq and that "the German way" leads in a different direction. He apparently believed that the transatlantic relationship was sufficiently strong to survive a few weeks of campaign effrontery against the U.S. Worse was an alleged statement by his justice minister comparing President Bush's approach to Iraq with Hitler's tactics. Schröder called Bush to apologize for this outrage, but the furious American president refused to take the call. A diplomatic ice age followed. Given the fact that 80% of Germans, including three-fourths of conservative voters, opposed warfare against Iraq, these opportunistic declarations, along with an unexpectedly strong performance by his Green partners, provided Schröder and his party with just enough votes to win.

One thing about the 2002 election was very American: for the first time, the chief rivals squared off in nationally televised debates. It was a setting that well suited the silver-tongued, telegenic Schröder. This practice has been followed in subsequent elections.

Halfway into his second term, Schröder had become one of the most unloved chancellors in FRG history. The grassroots discontent stemmed from his Agenda 2010 reform program, approved in 2004, which called for adjustments in the social welfare system by reducing pensions, weakening job protection laws and introducing co-payments for state health care. It did not challenge the basic need for generous social protection. Nevertheless, leftist and trade union critics saw it as betrayal of social democratic principles. Voters welcome the abstract notion of reforms, but they tend to oppose any specific measures. A frightening exodus of members from the party (180,000) prompted Schröder to recognize his failure as party chief.

When the SPD was trounced in a May 2005 election in Germany's largest *Land*, North Rhine-Westphalia, Schröder had had enough. Without consulting with his party or his Green coalition allies, he called for *Bundestag* elections a year early. His party was furious, and a widening rift opened up between Schröder and his SPD.

All signs pointed to a crushing SPD defeat in September, 2005, but Schröder again proved to be a tireless and resourceful campaigner. *Der Spiegel* called him a "testosterone bomb." In a way, he campaigned as an old-style leftist against his own reforms and railed against "Anglo-Saxon liberalism" (the free market). He succeeded in making his party seem like the protector of Germany's social achievements. He emerged from the TV debate with Angela Merkel as the clear favorite in the polls to be chancellor.

Given pre-election predictions that the party might get little more than a quarter of the votes, the SPD's final result was almost sensational: 34.2% of the votes and 222 seats, only four fewer than the CDU/CSU. This was the first time in FRG history that a government had been voted out of power, but no alternative government was elected to take its place. Nevertheless, in his euphoria on election night, Schröder went over the top. In the so-called "Elephant Round" of the top party leaders on TV, he condescendingly told Merkel not to be provincial and that she could not expect him to recommend that his party enter a coalition with her as chancellor. He claimed that the voters' message was that he should remain chancellor. This insensitive behavior was widely criticized and helped undermine his leadership. He underestimated Merkel's ability to maintain her party's backing and to prevent him or anybody else from taking her place in the top job, despite her poor electoral performance.

After a few weeks he realized that he had to go. He decided to earn big money on companies' boards of directors, including the Russian-German pipeline consortium led by Gazprom. Only 10 days before the elections, he had signed a controversial deal with President Vladimir Putin to ship gas to Germany via an undersea Baltic pipeline that bypassed and therefore infuriated Poland. His one-million-euro annual salary with Gazprom so soon after leaving office stirred up a firestorm of criticism. He left the SPD in turmoil. A new generation of leaders moved into the leadership positions of both large parties. Those who had come of age during the social tumult of the 1960s, like Schröder, were giving way to younger, potentially more pragmatic and less ideological leaders, who entered politics after the collapse of the Berlin Wall in 1989.

His chief of staff, Frank-Walter Steinmeier, became foreign minister. He was the first vice-chancellor not to have a parliamentary seat. He is the second-most popular politician after Merkel and increasingly disagreed in public with her foreign policy directions. He was positioning himself as the party's chancellor candidate for the 2009 federal elections.

Witnessing the creation of a strengthened unified Left opposition party, SPD leaders were unsure whether they should shun the new party, ally with it, or shift leftwards to undercut it. One wing in the party, led by chancellor candidate Steinmeier and Finance Minister Peer Steinbrück, wanted to depart from the proletarian party image and adjust to a "new center." Temporary party leader Kurt Beck and left-wing leader Andrea Nahles wanted to win back lost voters on the left. Others including Beck abandoned the party's categorical ban on alliances between the SPD and the neo-communist Left party. The furor over this U-turn

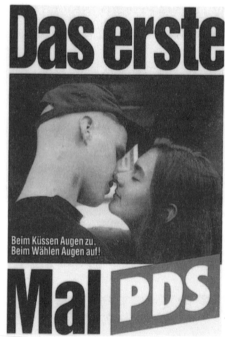

"The first time—Close your eyes when kissing. Open them when voting," Left.

threatened to tear the party apart. No one could keep the peace between the feuding wings.

The polls were not kind to the party as it entered the September 2009 federal elections. Once Europe's most successful and influential center-left party, the SPD struggles to find a new path between Markel's pragmatic center and the Left Party's hard-left course. With Steinmeier as chancellor candidate, the party suffered its worst defeat in almost 80 years, plummeting to 23% of the votes (a loss of a breathtaking 11.2%) and only 146 seats, down 75. The party was in disarray, and there was nowhere for it to go except into opposition, with Steinmeier as its head in parliament. But his star has clearly fallen.

A party gathering was convened in Dresden a couple of months after the election under a cloud of humiliation, depression and aggression. The question in the air was not when the party would get back on its feet, but whether it would survive as the main leftist political force. It was time for a new generation of leaders. Sigmar Gabriel, a 50-year-old former minister president of Lower Saxony and federal environment minister, was elected chairman. He belongs to the reformist "Seeheimer Circle" and is a good speaker. He vowed to create a new "left-wing center." Andrea Nahles, a leader of the party's left wing, became general secretary.

The SPD will spend the next few years discussing whether to cooperate with the ex-communist Left Party. For that reason, Berlin Mayor Klaus Wowereit is a rising star in the party. He already rules the capital city as head of a successful SPD-Left (red-red) land government.

The Left Party

The Party of Democratic Socialism (PDS), renamed Left Party.PDS for the 2005 federal elections and then simply The Left (*Die Linke*) in 2007, is a credible electoral and parliamentary political force, especially in the former Eastern Germany, but now also in the West. It is burdened by its own history, being the heir to the SED, which misruled the GDR for 40 years. Antipathy against the party was kept alive by continuing revelations about financial scandals and outrageous *Stasi* activities, such as its harboring and training former West German terrorists in the GDR. Prosecutors issued arrest warrants for former top East German leaders for ordering that persons attempting to escape from the GDR be killed. From 1961 to 1989, about 350 lost their lives.

Some view it as the heir to the discredited SED and as representative of the interests of former SED members, who make up a majority of its membership. Of its 72,000 members, about half are Eastern

Gregor Gysi, "Left Party"

Germans over age 65. It capitalizes on the problems felt in the East: disappointment, insecurity, unemployment, comparatively lower wages, and the view that Eastern Germany has been taken over by arrogant West Germans and their uncaring capitalist economic system. It receives many protest votes against the established national parties, which seem to focus their attention mainly on the West. At the same time it has successfully broadened its demagogic appeal in Western Germany by playing on anxieties about globalization, wealth distribution, welfare cuts and fear of losing a job. It calls for a shorter workweek, restoration of full welfare benefits, a minimum wage, a "wealth tax" and "wealth for all." It opposes Germany's deployment in Afghanistan and elsewhere, favors closer ties with Cuba and Venezuela, and takes a critical stance toward the United States, whose former President George W. Bush Lafontaine called a "terrorist."

The Left's appeal is no longer restricted to the Eastern parts of reunified Germany and Berlin. It casts itself as a party that has purged itself of Stalinism, but not of socialism. In most of its federal electoral campaigns, its leader was the only media star in a very mixed bag of socialists. Gregor Gysi is a witty, brilliant East Berlin lawyer who, being Jewish, is a rarity in modern German politics. He had made a name for himself by defending dissidents in the GDR. He tried to give the party a modern, fresh image, and his followers wore buttons in 1990 reading in English: "Take it easy Gysi!" He filled halls whenever he appeared in the West, and the visitors were predominantly young people who liked his unconventional and open style and refusal to speak in communist "functionary's Chinese."

For the 1990 federal elections it formed a "Left List/PDS," of which it was the senior partner. This alliance garnered only .3% of the votes in the West and 11.1% in the East, for a total of 2.4% nation-wide. For this election only, the 5% hurdle was waived for new parties, so the PDS was given 17 seats in the Bundestag. Gysi won a directly elected seat in East Berlin's Hellersdorf-Marzahn, a very unusual feat for a candidate from a small party.

The party's momentum continued in 1994. It captured 19.8% of Easterners' votes (but only .9% among Westerners). More important, by capturing four of the five directly elected seats in its stronghold of Eastern Berlin, it benefited from an almost forgotten route around the 5% clause into the Bundestag: to give regional parties the possibility of gaining a significant parliamentary presence, the founders decided that any party that can win at least three direct mandates should receive a number of seats proportional to its overall percentage of votes. Thus, the PDS, which won 4.4% nationwide, was awarded 30 Bundestag seats in 1994.

This was a very colorful mixture of representatives, which included nine Westerners, about half women, a lesbian activist, the great grandson of Otto von Bismarck, an author of steamy short stories, and several nonparty members. One

Former Leader of the Greens Joschka Fischer

Germany

was Stefan Heym, a former Jewish émigré to the U.S. He fought as an American soldier against Germany and then settled in the GDR in 1952 to become one of its most acclaimed novelists. He died in 2002.

In 1998 it continued its climb by winning 5.1% of the votes, almost all in the East. Although it again won four direct seats in Eastern Berlin, this is the first time that it cleared the 5% hurdle and would have entered the *Bundestag* anyway. It gained five seats for a total of 35.

In January 2002 the PDS entered the mainstream of reunified German politics by joining the Berlin city government headed by Social Democrat Mayor Klaus Wowereit. In the 2002 federal elections, it lost its star vote-getting leader, Gregor Gysi, who resigned over a trivial air-miles scandal. It saw its share of votes in Eastern Germany fall from 22% to only 16.9%. In the West it got a paltry 1%, adding up to only 4% nationwide, well below the 5% threshold. What was especially devastating was that it won only two direct seats. Thus it had only two seats in the *Bundestag*. The PDS's political influence seemed to be on a downward slide.

The party is determined not to be branded as a social democratic party, but rather as Germany's only true socialist party. In a report on threats to the constitution, the federal security service categorized it in 2009 as having "extremist aspirations." It keeps its eye on parts of it, such as "Communist Platform."

The PDS entered the 2005 elections as the part of a left-wing ticket with the Western-based Electoral Alternative Labor and Social Justice party (WASG). The team called itself Leftists in the West and Leftists-PDS in the East, and it was co-led by populists Gysi and Oscar Lafontaine. The latter was the populist unifier, who tied together very different followers in East and West. The strongholds are in the East, where a core of the people remains uncomfortable with the free market. Its followers there are more pragmatic and are interested in sharing in rule. Western followers tend to like more radical Marxist models and prefer protest to responsibility. What brought them together was dislike of Schröder and "neo-liberal" (free-market) thinking. With a base in both Eastern and Western Germany (something the PDS lacked) and with star power at the top, it was able to attract disgruntled leftists in East and West and to clear the 5% hurdle needed to win parliamentary seats.

The alliance's hatred of the former SPD-Green government's reforms and its message of preventing any diminution of the welfare state resonated with voters. It captured 8.7% of the votes and 54 seats. In the East, it got 25.4%, an increase of 8.5%, and

German soldier in Kabul, Afghanistan

in the West it shot up to 4.9% of the votes, an impressive 3.8% more than in 2002. A fourth of Germany's unemployed voted for it. It was clearly a successful electoral alliance.

The two parts formally merged to form The Left in 2007. Whether this combination of power-conscious ex-communists, who have an effective grassroots organization in the East, and idealistic Western trade unionists and disappointed Social Democrats, who formed an ad hoc milieu party (WASG) in the West, can ever become a permanent fixture in German politics is uncertain. However, their prospects look much brighter after winning legislative seats in West German states: Hesse (with 5.1% of the votes), Lower Saxony (7.1%), Hamburg, North Rhine Westphalia and Bremen. These results stunned the mainstream parties and shook the entire political system. The Left became the largest opposition party on the federal level winning the support of one out of seven Germans. Its gains were mainly at the expense of the SPD.

Since no other party will form a coalition with it at the federal level, it practices total opposition to the grand coalition's policies. Such parties thrive in opposition. The newly created Left strengthens a trend within the *Bundestag* that power is now divided among five national parties, making coalition-building trickier.

In the September 2009 federal election it won a stunning 11.9% of the votes, a gain of 3.2%. Most of its votes came from the East. It also added 23 seats for a total of 76.

It constitutes a serious opposition force in parliament. It is divided over what its relations with the SPD should be. A major barrier was Lafontaine himself, who was regarded by many Social Democrats as a harmful renegade. Battling prostate cancer, he retired from federal politics in January 2010 and opened the way to new party leadership. Gysi remained as head of the parliamentary party. But the party elected two new largely unknown co-chairpersons. Gesine Lötsch, who is on the academic staff of Humboldt University, won the most votes: 92.8%. Bavarian union functionary, Klaus Ernst, received a more modest 74.9%.

Greens

The Greens were the first new party in over 25 years to find its way into the federal parliament. Their presence affected not only the ability to form stable governments, but also the tone and style of parliamentary government. The key to their earlier success was their focus on environmental problems, which most Germans view as very important. This is why all parties turned their attention to this issue and robbed the Greens of their monopoly on it. Ecological problems are particularly acute in Eastern Germany, where the former Communist rulers showed appalling disregard for the environment.

In their early days the Greens showed their ability to mobilize hundreds of thousands of persons for mass demonstrations against the federal government's defense policy, or against a state government's

Germany's Foreign Office in Berlin

plans to build a nuclear power, or reprocessing plant or to expand the Frankfurt airport. Some feared that it could threaten the democratic regime. In the past, mass movements had weakened and ultimately destroyed the Weimar Republic. For this reason, the founders of the FRG created a purely parliamentary democracy, rather than one in which a plebiscite is possible.

In 1990 their eternal in-fighting, rejection of German unity, absence of a positive program, and ambivalence toward taking responsibility in government caught up with them. Grossly misreading the popular mood supporting unity, Western Greens adopted the slogan, "Everybody talks about Germany; we talk about the weather!" Failing to unite their parties for the *Bundestag* elections, Western German Greens received only 4.8% of the votes in the West and were therefore ejected from parliament, to their shock and dismay. An election coalition of Eastern German Greens and Alliance 90, a collection of Eastern German grassroots groups that organized the 1989 revolution, won 6% of the votes in the East (1.2% nationwide) and eight seats under the special election law that applied only to the 1990 elections.

The party was split between realists (*Realos*), who favored accepting government posts to achieve the party's goals, and the fundamentalists (*Fundis*), who argued that the party had tarnished its image by ceasing to be an exclusively opposition force and by entering an "arrangement with capitalism." In 1991 the inevitable occurred: The *Fundis* broke away from the Greens and formed their own Ecological Left/Alternative List, which vowed to concentrate on strengthening non-parliamentary opposition, but it became politically irrelevant. This split made the *Realos* more respectable in the eyes of some voters. In 1993 the Eastern and Western parties merged, calling themselves Alliance '90/Greens, or Greens for short. They staged a political comeback in 1994, winning 7.3% of the votes and 49 seats. In 1998 the party dipped slightly to 6.7% of the votes and 47 seats. But this was sufficient to enable the Greens to enter the federal government for the first time.

Its leader at the time, Joschka Fischer, a school dropout and activist, who once gave his profession as "street-revolutionary," became foreign minister. He is a brilliant and humorous speaker with great political skill in forging unity in a party that was created to oppose party discipline and establishment politics. He proved himself to be a reliable partner to Gerhard Schröder, even though his party was forceful in pressing on the SPD its ideas concerning ecological taxes and a rapid shut-down of Germany's 19 nuclear power plants.

Fischer's greatest challenge was to reconcile the Greens' antiestablishment roots with a yearning to prove that they are capable of serving as responsible ruling partners. He labored to keep his party unified behind the NATO bombing of Yugoslavia to stop ethnic cleansing in Kosovo. He argued that Germany had emerged from the Second World War with two firm convictions: "never again war" and "never again Auschwitz." Recognizing the contradiction, he reasoned that in order to prevent crimes against humanity, Germany must sometimes be prepared to put aside its pacifism, which runs deep in German society and especially in the Green party.

Not all of his party comrades agreed. In a raucous special party conference called in May 1999 to discuss a bombing halt in Kosovo, Fischer was pelted so hard by red paint that he suffered a perforated eardrum. A human chain tried to block delegates' entry into the hall, and posters depicted Fischer and Schröder with Hitler-style mustaches. Stink bombs were set off in the arena, fights for control of the microphone broke out, and one man strolled naked in front of the dais to mock the leaders' efforts to maintain some decorum. Fischer was decried as a "warmonger."

In the 2002 elections the Greens ran on little else than Fischer's popularity. He

Germany

was an effective foreign minister, and he tried hard to maintain good ties with the United States when it was not popular in Germany to do so. Although he and Schröder actually campaigned together, a first in German elections and a practice that was not repeated in 2005, he was more careful in his language about Iraq and the partnership with the United States. The Greens' votes in 2002 leaped by 30% to 8.6% and 55 seats. As usual, the Greens performed better in the West.

The Greens entered the September 2005 elections uncertain of its future role in federal politics. The party did well, winning 8.1% of the votes overall and 51 seats. It is no longer an overwhelmingly Western party, winning 5.1% of the votes in the East (up .4%) compared with 8.8% in the West (down .6%). Unable to coax the FDP into joining a "traffic-light coalition" (red, yellow and green) and unwilling to join the CDU/CSU and FDP in a "Jamaica coalition" (black, yellow and green), it entered the opposition. This is particularly satisfying to the *Fundis* in the party. In May 2008 in Hamburg it entered its first-ever state-level coalition with the CDU. Fischer initially retired to the back benches. But he soon vacated his *Bundestag* seat and accepted a visiting professorship at Princeton University.

Leading the party into the September 2009 federal elections were Claudia Roth and the first German party chairman with an immigrant background: Cem Özdemir (a *Realo*). His Turkish parents had come as guest workers. Because of his youth (early 40s) and good looks, some party members call him the "Green Obama." The party captured 10.7% of the votes, up by 2.6%, and 68 seats, a gain of 17. They are in the opposition. In the past, the Greens were almost always on the political left. However, many of its voters have become well-to-do city dwellers with lots of education. For them, coalitions with the CDU/CSU or FDP are no longer unthinkable. This new flexibility bodes ill for the SPD, which used to be the only acceptable partner for the Greens.

Right-Wing Parties

The past two decades witnessed a strengthening of parties on the far right, a development that causes anxiety in both the FRG and abroad. They range from illegal neo-Nazi groups to legal parties that feed on myriad dissatisfactions, including hostility toward immigrants, tight housing, high unemployment, globalization and rising crime. Some Germans bemoan what they see as a breakdown in law and order caused by the leftist alternative subculture. The domestic intelligence service estimated in 2008 that there are 4,400 neo-Nazis in Germany.

The Republicans claim to be a nationalist, not a neo-Nazi party. But in 1992 the government ordered intelligence surveillance of it to determine if it is antidemocratic. It found a warm reception in Western Berlin, where more than 10% of the population is foreign. The Turks living there constitute the largest Turkish community outside of Turkey and the third largest in the world. The Republicans call for repatriation of foreign workers in stages and for tough measures to stem the flow of asylum seekers into the FRG, noting, "a multiracial society is a red flag to our party." Its image has been tarnished by unpopular skinhead violence against foreigners, including the American national sledding team in the Eastern German city of Oberhof. The Republican's .4% showing in the 2009 Bundestag demonstrated its electoral irrelevance.

The same cannot always be said of the National Democratic Party of Germany (NPD), Germany's oldest neo-Nazi party and a refuge for unreconstructed Nazis. It is more conservative than the Republicans and won 1.5% of the votes in the 2009 federal elections and no *Bundestag* seats. Its headquarters are in East Berlin, and the party has 6,000 members. In 2004 it stunned Germany by capturing 9.2% of the votes and 10 seats for the state parliament in its electoral fortress of Saxony. In the 2009 state elections it retained 8 seats.

Every February thirteenth it mobilizes 6,000 demonstrators in Dresden to protest the terrible bombing of that city in 1945, which it describes as a "bombing Holocaust." Its deputies in the Saxon parliament walked out of the chamber during a ceremony to honor the victims of Auschwitz, saying they would only honor German war victims. The intelligence service considers the party to be "racist, anti-Semitic and revisionist," aiming to destroy democracy in order to create a Fourth Reich. Nevertheless, one voter in four in Saxony considers it to be a "normal" party.

It has found a fertile new recruiting ground: the unorganized young skinheads and neo-Nazis linked to a wave of far-right violence. About half of those violent crimes occur in the East, the only part of Germany where the NDP thrives. It has modernized its strategy by no longer seeking merely to defend the Third Reich. It has broadened its appeal to resist global capitalism and to oppose Turkey's entry into the EU, the Iraq war and labor-market reforms. It has also sprung beyond the skinhead scene to find a place in the world of youth music. In 2005 it handed out 200,000 copies of a CD called "School Yard," which contained nationalist ballads and rock songs.

Also fishing for votes on the rightist fringe is the German People's Union

(DVU), which in 2009 captured only .1% of the votes in the federal election. The three parties' puny total of less than 2% in 2009 was a relief to the FRG. However, their ability to score as high as 12.9% in certain Land elections, as they did in Saxony-Anhalt in 1998, where they won many young persons' votes, shows that they can be useful collectors of protest votes.

In 1992 the government outlawed six neo-Nazi groups, including German Alternative, which was involved in anti-foreigner violence. In 1995 it banned the small, militant Free German Workers' Party. The German cabinet asked the Constitutional Court in 2000 to ban the NPD. However, that effort failed in 2003 when the Constitutional Court refused to hear the case because the government had cited as evidence inflammatory statements and writings by party members who turned out to be paid informants of state security services. A 2005 poll revealed that 73% of Germans support a ban on the NPD. In 2009 the German Youth Faithful to the Homeland was banned for spreading Nazi propaganda to young people after two other far-right organizations had been banned the year before.

The scores of right-wing nationalist and neo-Nazi groups do not follow one leader. But they are better organized, more dangerous, and in closer contact with each other than most Germans had thought they were. Their effect on Germany's international image can be devastating despite their electoral impotence. That is a major reason why the federal government introduced legislation in 2005 banning far-right demonstrations at Holocaust memorial sites and at the commemorations of the end of the Second World War. The Constitutional Court determined that the right to assembly does not apply to groups glorifying Hitler's regime.

A Past that is not Past

The American novelist William Faulkner once wrote, "the past is never dead. It is not even past." This is certainly true for Germany today. More than a half-century after the Second World War ended, the government had to decide on a Holocaust memorial in the heart of Berlin close to the Brandenburg Gate. After much emotional debate, it was agreed that there would be a toned-down memorial with a wall-shaped library containing a million books, and a research center for scholars. Designed by New York-based architect, Peter Eisenman, the memorial is an undulating field of 2,711 concrete slabs the size of two football fields.

The memorial is right behind the American embassy, which was renovated and reopened on July 4, 2008. Many critics found the building, which had been redesigned after the deadly 1998 terrorist attacks on the U.S. embassies in Kenya and Tanzania, too fortress-like, unimaginative and "coldly dismissive." "Too much like Alcatraz," "overbearing mediocrity," and "insultingly cheap and feeble," moaned the critics. The reactions varied from mockery to outright rejection. Nevertheless, 350,000 Berlins showed up at a street festival to welcome the new embassy the day after it was officially opened.

Before the memorial could be completed, controversy erupted again. It was learned that the material to be used as an anti-graffiti coating on the 2,751 concrete slabs to prevent swastikas or other neo-Nazi slogans from being spray-painted on them was produced by a German chemical company, Degussa, which had once owned the firm (Degasch) that had produced the Zyklon B gas used to murder Jews in the concentration camps. After much soul-searching discussion, the product was approved. The memorial opened to the public on May 10, 2005. It is a red flag to neo-Nazis, and only federal law prohibiting right-wing demonstrations near Holocaust memorials keeps them away.

The Schröder government had to confront the multibillion dollar demands to compensate foreign laborers who had been forced to work for German companies during the war. A settlement was finally reached in 2000 whereby Germany would create a special foundation that will pay up to $5 billion to nearly a million forced laborers. Each receives payments of between $2,500 and $7,500.

In April 1999, a chastened Chancellor Schröder reflected on whether his generation has a different attitude about the Holocaust: "No. This event will always influence the way German politicians think and act. Even if one says there is no such thing as collective guilt, it is still our task to see to it that people remember what happened because by remembering we can assure it will not happen again." Such remembering remains part of Germany's future. In a mutual act of reconciliation, Schröder joined other leaders in Normandy in June 2004 to commemorate the 60th anniversary of the D-Day invasion. A 2005 poll revealed that 80% of Germans now see May 8, 1945, as a day of liberation, not of surrender.

In 2008 additional memorials were dedicated in Berlin that honor others in the broad spectrum of victims. In January ground was broken on the long-delayed Topography of Terror center at the site of the former Gestapo and SS headquarters; it is now completed. April 2008 saw the unveiling of a memorial and documentation center concerning Germans forcibly expelled from Central and Eastern Europe after the Second World War. This had antagonized numerous countries, especially Poland, which argued that this was an attempt to rewrite history and mitigate German war crimes.

However, Germany was still prosecuting perpetrators of war crimes in 2010. In March a former SS soldier, Heinrich Boere, was convicted of killing three Dutch resistance fighters. Court proceedings also began in November 2009 against 89-year-old John Demjanjuk, charged with aiding in the murder of 27,900 Jews. He was a former Red Army soldier captured by the Germans and recruited for concentration camp duty. After the war, he fled to America and worked as an auto worker before being extradited to Germany in May 2009. Because of the age of the defendants, these may be the last such trials. One German newspaper called the men "fragile, doddering and deaf."

In May a memorial dedicated to gay men and lesbians persecuted and killed during Nazi rule and located on the edge of the Tiergarten near the Jewish memorial was inaugurated. It features a concrete slab with a window that shows clips of men kissing and women kissing alternating every two years. Berlin Mayor Klaus Wowereit, who is gay, attended the ceremony. Only one month earlier, the former Kochstrasse was renamed Rudi-Dutschke-Strasse (street) after the leftist student leader in the 1968 student rebellion, who was assassinated.

The FRG: A Stable Democracy

The significance of the current problems facing the established political parties in the wake of unification should not be exaggerated. The FRG has weathered many serious problems in the past: moral, political and economic regeneration after 1945, a student rebellion in the late 1960s, urban terrorism, fundamental political changes such as the Eastern Treaties and the economic shocks of the 1970s.

The democratic order of the FRG has over the years earned and received a reservoir of good will from its citizens to help it survive serious crises. This springs not from the actual constitutional structure, but from Germans' political attitudes. That is, it depends on the political culture—those political ways of thinking that provide the basis for a workable political system. The FRG has become more than a fair-weather democracy that would collapse quickly if confronted with a crisis.

One sometimes heard of radical criticism of "bourgeois society" and of the allegedly "pseudo-democratic" and "illegitimate" political order. Such criticism was very audible and was also scribbled on the walls. Yet, there was and is no "legitimacy crisis" in Germany. During its entire existence as a state, it has not faced a single truly serious challenge to its legitimacy; this stands in stark contrast to the Weimar Republic, which was born into such a crisis and never extricated itself from it. It made remarkable strides to win the approval and support of its citizens.

Sensible observation of Germany, combined with an examination of relevant public opinion surveys, indicates that the German political culture had changed considerably since 1945 and that it is a stable and democratic country with a politically interested, informed, involved and tolerant citizenry. Immediately after the war, after excessive political mobilization and propaganda under Hitler, Germans tended to withdraw from public affairs and to seek refuge in private and family circles. Now Germans in both parts are no less active in public or political affairs than their counterparts in older democracies such as the U.S. and the Netherlands. In terms of voting, they are even more ac-

Holocaust Memorial in Berlin

Germany

tive than those counterparts. Germany has been accurately described as a country that has a strong and activist civil society and a relatively weak state. More and more direct democracy, involving referenda and initiatives, is practiced on the state and local level.

A few facts help demonstrate Germans' overall satisfaction with their regime, at least in the Western part. In 1951, 90% of all adult West Germans believed that Germany had been better off during an earlier German regime, and a third even favored restoration of the Hohenzollern monarchy. By 1976, however, 90% thought they were better off under the present scheme, and almost no one wanted the restoration of the monarchy. This was due to many Western citizens' positive experience under democracy. Their country has had a high level of accomplishment. Prosperity and the expanded social welfare system smoothed class conflicts and allowed all groups in the society more benefits from the system and a greater opportunity to advance.

Germany is a functioning democracy in which only a small percentage of Germans are asking whether it should remain a democracy. In a 2007 *Spiegel* poll, only among East Germans over the age of 35 was there a majority that admitted to being "little" or "not at all" satisfied with the way democracy is practiced in Germany today. The criticism that Germans have become very materialistic is certainly valid. But while materialism might be rejected in principle (but seldom in practice) by some leftists and intellectuals, it has no doubt made Germany far more governable and respected as a political democracy.

FOREIGN AND DEFENSE POLICY

The FRG became more independent and critical of the U.S., and it is more willing to side with its European allies on some issues. It is less restrained by the embarrassing German past and has been confronted with a diminution of Russian, French, and British power in Europe. Also, Washington was absorbed during the 1960s and early 1970s with Vietnam and a new relationship with the Soviet Union and the People's Republic of China. The FRG increasingly shouldered political responsibilities and exercised diplomatic flexibility throughout the world. Because of its past, the FRG prefers a low-key, quieter diplomacy, which would be least likely to arouse fear or envy in other countries. For the first time in its history, Germany has clearly defined borders not disputed by any nation. It has neither destabilizing minorities abroad nor any claims to former German territories. The cliché that the FRG was an

German soldiers arriving in Mogadishu, 1993   Courtesy: German Information Center, New York

"economic giant and a political dwarf" is outdated.

In his first policy statement in the all-German *Bundestag*, ex-Chancellor Kohl pledged that "there is no comfortable niche in international politics for us Germans, and we must not shirk our responsibility." The united nation would, he promised, not be a "restless Reich." A new Germany in a new kind of Europe has emerged, and it is realistic that the continent's largest and richest democracy bears more responsibility in a world with a considerably weaker Russia. This is not a role Germany seeks, but one that is thrust upon it.

The new Germany displayed its willingness to use its new political clout in 1991 when it muscled its EU partners to recognize the independence of the Yugoslav republics of Slovenia and Croatia, despite serious misgivings in London, Paris, Washington, and the UN. It was especially noteworthy that Bonn did not even reply to a formal U.S. request to withhold such recognition. Uncomfortable with bad feelings that unilateral action caused, Germany was careful to get allied backing before recognizing Macedonia in 1993, a move Greece bitterly opposed.

Germany and the First Gulf War, 1991

Germany dealt clumsily with its first test as a strengthened power. When fighting broke out in the Gulf on January 17, 1991, it took a week for the government to

show solidarity with its allies. The fear that Germany would be dragged into the war by joining a defense of Turkey, one of Germany's NATO allies, prompted the government to insist that it would not become involved. No other ally had disputed Turkey's right to be defended by the full force of NATO.

While it was paralyzed, opponents of the war efforts took over in the streets and denounced the U.S. and Iraq both as aggressors. "Say no!" and "No blood for oil," read the posters. The mayor of tiny Pfedelbach in the Black Forest was forced to withdraw his invitation to General Norman Schwarzkopf to visit the town from where his ancestors came when angry antiwar residents branded the war hero as a "mass murderer." An exasperated finance minister, Theo Waigel, exclaimed: "Again and again we see a misconceived pacifism which does not restore peace but puts up with the aggressor!" The *Frankfurter Allgemeine Zeitung* agreed: "What distinguishes the Germans from other peoples is not that they fear war, but that they fear war more than they love freedom." Polls a few days after hostilities commenced revealed that four out of five Germans indeed agreed with the allies' war effort and were critical of the anti-American rallies, but three out of four opposed German participation in the war.

After regaining its composure, the Kohl government acted decisively by criticizing the "one-eyed" protestors, cracking down on firms breaking its arms export laws, and sending emissaries to Israel. It agreed to deliver weapons, including Patriot missiles, to the Jewish state, violating Germany's long-standing policy of not sending weapons into "areas of tension."

The German government went even farther, crossing some important thresholds: It dispatched 1,000 soldiers to Turkey equipped with 18 fighter aircraft and Roland and Hawk missiles to protect NATO airbases. This was the first time since the Second World War that German military forces had been sent abroad in response to a threat of war. It also sent 2,200 naval forces with minesweepers and frigates to the Eastern Mediterranean and offered more than $11 billion to aid the allies. It served as the hub of the resupply effort, provided doctors for allied military hospitals in Germany freeing allied doctors to serve in the Gulf, gave precision-guided weapons and vehicles to its allies for use there. It gave the U.S. Army alone 1,000 vehicles, including Czech-made tank transporters, which former East German soldiers had to instruct the Americans how to use.

Arguing after the conclusion of hostilities for the need to render humanitarian aid to the war's victims and to open up the Persian Gulf to free trade, Germany sent 2,000 troops and airlifted assets to Iran to help Kurdish refugees, as well as minesweepers to the Gulf to help clear out Iraqi mines. Although these measures met with almost no protest in the FRG, it emerged from the crisis damaged by the charges that it had shown ingratitude for the diplomatic help it had received to achieve unification and had let its allies down in time of emergency.

The Right to Deploy Abroad

Kohl's intention to amend the constitution to allow Germany to join in international coalitions was successfully blocked by the SPD; it refused to allow *Bundeswehr* troops to participate in anything more than UN peacekeeping forces. Germany seeks a permanent seat on the UN Security Council, not for itself but for the EU. In 1992 it sent three spotter aircraft and a naval destroyer to help enforce the UN sanctions against Serbia and Montenegro, and it sent a *Bundeswehr* unit with a UN mission to Cambodia, where Germans suffered their first fatality since joining peacekeeping operations. In 1993 it assisted in the American airlift of humanitarian aid to Bosnia. That same year the Constitutional Court ruled in a landmark decision that it was not unconstitutional for German airmen to serve in AWACS reconnaissance planes supporting NATO enforcement of a no-fly zone over Bosnia.

They became the first *Bundeswehr* soldiers to take part in a potential combat mission since 1945.

In 1993 the FRG dispatched 1,700 troops to join the UN effort in Somalia; these were the first German soldiers to serve in Africa since General Rommel's *Afrikakorps* in the Second World War. In 1994 the Constitutional Court ruled that German troops may join military ventures abroad as long as they are acting under the aegis of the United Nations or another international group (such as NATO) to which Germany belongs and provided that a majority in the lower house of parliament approves. In 1995 the FRG dispatched 14 Tornado fighter jets for duty over Bosnia. This was the first German combat unit deployed since 1945. It also sent peacekeeping forces to help implement the Bosnian peace agreement later in the year. Each of these "out-of-area" operations was subjected to intense and emotional debate within Germany. But when the government agreed to commit 3,000 troops, including armored infantry, to the 30,000-soldier "Stabilization Force" in Bosnia in 1997, almost no one in Germany raised any objection. The Social Democrats and Greens, then in the opposition, backed the plan.

Germany is cautiously but steadily overcoming its postwar aversion to the use of military force. With the Balkans as a testing ground, the *Bundeswehr's* emergence as an international intervention force helped to diminish Germany's subordinate role within NATO. When the alliance launched an air war against Yugoslavia in the spring of 1999 to stop brutal ethnic cleansing in Kosovo, Germany was a full participant. It sent eight combat aircraft and a warship, and it dispatched several thousand troops to neighboring Macedonia, where in 2002 it had 586 peacekeepers deployed. This was the first time since World War II that Germany engaged in warfare against a sovereign state.

In former Chancellor Schröder's words, "we are trying to contain the ongoing human catastrophe—to stop the killings and deportations. . . . NATO has to win this military conflict." It assigned 6,000 troops to KFOR (down to 2,486 by 2007, along with up to 900 in Bosnia-Herzegovina), which maintains the peace in Kosovo. The total of 44,000 soldiers from 35 different nations were commanded in 1999–2000 by German General Klaus Reinhardt, a scholarly man with a doctorate in history, who completed some of his military education in the United States.

According to opinion polls, most Germans agreed with the military action in Kosovo. One survey even suggested that a stunning 90% of young Germans aged 18 to 24 supported NATO. But there was a clear split between Western Germans

and those in the East: 64% in the West back the bombing, compared with only 40% in the East. The PDS was the only major political party that opposed the war. The war over Kosovo helped Germans, who emerged from the Third Reich with a powerful aversion to any use of force, to cross a large and significant psychological boundary.

Germany's willingness to support a military effort on the other side of the globe in Afghanistan in 2001–2 was a sensation, but it followed a steady development since 1994 to shed the country's postwar psychological and constitutional inhibitions about using military force for anything but territorial defense. Only a decade earlier, former SPD leader Oskar Lafontaine had said in reference to the Persian Gulf War that requesting Germans to take part in any military action was "like offering brandy chocolates to a reformed alcoholic." But Volkmar Schultz, a member of the Bundestag's foreign relations committee, said that that was over: "We have reached the end of the postwar period in German history. We cannot automatically run away from military action. Since 11 September most of the political class in Germany accepts this as an unavoidable fact."

There are limits. Any hint that Germany's troops are fighting to support the country's economic interests is unacceptable to a population so ambivalent about war. This imprecision prompted the resignation in May 2010 of President Horst Köhler.

At one of the many public demonstrations in Germany supporting the United States in its hour of crisis, President Johannes Rau said: "No one knows better than the people here in Berlin what America has done for freedom and democracy in Germany. Therefore, we say to all Americans from Berlin: America does not stand alone." The first person ever convicted of aiding the September 11 hijackers was convicted in a German court. However, in 2004 he was freed upon appeal because the American government refused to provide evidence gained from an al Qaeda operative in U.S. custody.

In the aftermath of hurricane Katrina, which devastated and flooded New Orleans in August and September 2005, the Germans immediately sent three airplanes carrying food, 90 specialists from their Federal Agency for Technical Relief, who took 15 high-power pumps to help empty the floodwaters, 20 criminal investigation experts to identify victims, and a team of doctors. Even the Jazz Institute in Darmstadt collected donations for New Orleans musicians.

After cliff-hanging negotiations and threats within his governing SPD-Green

Germany

German protest against war in Afghanistan

coalition and supported by 59% of the German population, Schröder committed 3,900 troops to the war effort. It sent three transport planes to Incerlik Air Force Base in Turkey to support operations in Afghanistan, as well as two frigates and escort vessels with up to 1,800 sailors to patrol the waters off the east coast of Africa. Berlin offered up to 800 soldiers to operate Fuchs armored vehicles equipped to check soil for nuclear, chemical and biological contamination, 250 troops for evacuating wounded, 500 troops for air and ground transport, and 92 of its total of 1,000 special forces (KSK).

German soldiers are fighting and dying in Afghanistan even though they are not deployed in the more dangerous southern part. It has removed some of the troops' limitations. As of April 2010, 43 soldiers had been killed. In 2003 Germany doubled its contingent to 2,500 and, along with the Dutch, took over command of all peacekeepers in Kabul until August. In 2007 the German government dispatched six Tornado reconnaissance jets to Afghanistan to provide support for NATO and for its own troops there (raised in 2010 to up to 5,350). It also extended its commitment by another year even though

about two-thirds of public opinion had swung against the mission. However, the war never became a major issue in the 2009 parliamentary elections, in large part because the commitment had been initiated under the earlier SPD-led government. Only the Left Party demands an immediate withdrawal.

Germany also deployed 126 soldiers in Termes, Uzbekistan, from which it supplies its men and women in Afghanistan. After the U.S. was expelled from Uzbekistan in 2005, the future of that base is uncertain. Berlin ordered about 1,500 naval forces to the Horn of Africa and the coast off Kenya. It also deployed 880, many of them naval forces, to Lebanon to try to stable that country after a brief war in the summer of 2006. By mid-2008 it had approximately 8,000 soldiers deployed on foreign peace-keeping and anti-terror missions.

In addition to these military assets, Germany granted generous humanitarian aid, including $28 million for the American victims of the terrorist attacks donated by individuals and corporations in Germany. Finally, Germany hosted a UN-sponsored political summit during November-December 2001 in the famous Petersberg Hotel overlooking Bonn, which brought together representatives of the many Afghan factions to discuss the formation of a post-Taliban regime and government. The German government played an active and supportive role in helping achieve an agreement. For instance, then Foreign Minister Joschka Fischer phoned the leader in Kabul temporarily recognized by the UN, Burhanuddin Rabbani, who was

Stoppt den Krieg!

Demo für den Frieden

Sa., 03. 11. 01, 11.00 Uhr
Start Rathausplatz

Krieg verstärkt den Terror
und schafft neue Märtyrer.
Lassen wir uns nicht
in eine unkontrollierbare
Gewaltspirale hineinziehen!

Eine Veranstaltung des
Freiburger Friedensforums
Info-Telefon: 0761/ 56 125
www.friedensforumfr.de

"No blood for Hussein and Bush"—2003

dragging his heals, to remind him that the billions of dollars in promised international aid to Afghanistan would not be released until a broad-based government were in place.

The years 2009–10 brought rude reminders that German soldiers were engaging in warfare, not merely serving as peacekeepers and development personnel in Afghanistan. Just days before the 2009 federal elections, a German commander called in airstrikes against Taliban forces, only to learn later that scores of civilians had also perished. The bombing was especially delicate since it was the deadliest action by German troops since the Second World War. Because of the way he handled the incident, Defense Minister Franz Josef Jung was forced to resign. His replacement, Karl-Theodor zu Guttenberg, then fired the most senior general, Wolfgang Schneiderhan. Chancellor Merkel called this regrettable occurrence "a combat mission," and the government properly calls its activity in Afghanistan "war."

The War in Iraq

The 2003 Anglo-American war in Iraq showed to what extent Germany, under

Chancellor Schröder, had begun to assert itself more in foreign affairs. Some German politicians and diplomats were appalled by the strident tone and style of his diplomacy over Iraq although many were convinced that he had been right to stand up to the U.S. on this matter. In 2010 official documents revealed that on a visit to Washington on January 31, 2002, over a year before the outbreak of war, President Bush had told Schröder of his intention to topple Saddam Hussein. The chancellor's reply was that if he intended to do that, he should carry it out as quickly and decisively as possible. Never did the U.S. ask that German troops be sent to Iraq.

His later refusal to participate in any war and to sign up to any UN resolution that permitted military action was also supported by an overwhelming percentage of his countrymen. Polls at the time revealed that while 90% of German respondents thought the United States would continue to be an important partner, three-fourths believed that the U.S. has "too much power," and over half went so far as to consider it a greater threat to world peace than even Saddam Hussein's Iraq or North Korea. Schröder himself said his firm policy was part of his country's "coming of age," its "emancipation." For the first time it dared oppose the U.S. on a really important issue.

Germany, which began a two-year stint on the UN Security Council in January 2003, teamed with France, which saw an opportunity to limit U.S. power and influence in Europe, to lead the resistance to the war. They both quickly discovered that although most Europeans on the street agreed with their opposition to war in Iraq, their attempt to unify European governments behind their lead backfired and actually divided Europe. Official support of the transatlantic link remained very strong, especially in the new democracies in Eastern and Central Europe. A majority of European governments did not appreciate what they saw as a Franco-German attempt to isolate the U.S. in the name of Europe.

Germany nevertheless provided the United States with more indirect support than most other allies. It assigned 2,500 of its soldiers to special security duties guarding U.S. bases in Germany, thereby freeing about 5,000 American soldiers. German armed forces helped the U.S. ready and move its armored units out to Emden and Bremerhaven for shipment to Iraq. The U.S. military was granted unlimited use of installations and of Germany's airspace in order to support allied forces in Iraq and the Persian Gulf area. Germany dispatched a chemical and biological detection unit to Kuwait, sent troops to operate Patriot mis-

sile batteries in Turkey, and permitted its soldiers to serve in AWACS aircraft missions north of the war zone to protect Turkey. In 2004 it offered a hand to the struggling Iraq by writing off about 80% of that country's debt to Germany; this amounted to $5 billion. In 2005 it also expanded to about 250 the number of Iraqi security forces it trains in the United Arab Emirates (UAE). It also agreed to send 70 million euros in assistance.

In the aftermath of the 2003 Iraq war, Germany and France joined with Belgium and Luxembourg to create a joint rapid reaction unit built on the existing French-German brigade. The four said they would set up a multinational headquarters and a separate military center in Belgium to command and plan EU military operations when NATO is not involved. They invited other European nations to join their effort, but sensing that its real purpose was indeed to weaken the transatlantic alliance, none did. The four found themselves isolated in Europe, and they abandoned the plan. However, in June 2004 Britain joined with France and Germany to create the EU's first planning cell and to speed up the creation of effective rapid reaction units. Based in Brussels, the planning cell was used by the EU to back up its takeover from NATO of the 12,000-strong mission in Bosnia in late 2004.

Germany

Poesie des Augenblicks

Meisterwerke der französischen Genremalerei im Zeitalter von Watteau Chardin Fragonard

French Painting Visits Germany

Franco-German Collaboration

In January 2013 the two neighbors, Germany and France, who are each other's most important trading partners, will celebrated the 50th anniversary of the Treaty on German-French Cooperation. The 40th was remembered in grand style. President Jacques Chirac and Schröder met at the Elysée Palace, and 603 German parliamentarians joined 577 counterparts in the palace of Versailles. The next day, the two leaders met in Berlin. In their "Elysée Declaration," the two leaders agreed to increase the frequency of their special meetings to every six weeks, to appoint in each other's capital a "secretary-general for Franco-German cooperation" who would coordinate, prepare and follow up their common European policies, to dispatch the relevant minister to the other country's cabinet meetings when discussing a subject of interest to the other, and to propose common Franco-German legislation to each other's parliaments. They hope that such integration at the top, along with partner relationships between cities and combined military units, will help warm their citizens' hearts toward the other.

France made an important gesture to Germany by inviting Schröder to the 60th anniversary of the D-Day invasion in June 2004. He was the first German leader to attend the celebration, and he interpreted the invitation as a sign that "the postwar period is finally over" and that as a "tested democracy, we can now be accepted by the former Allies as a full-fledged partner whose foundations lie in the same fundamental values." At the same time he felt obligated to say: "We Germans know that we unleashed this heinous war. We recognize the responsibility our history has laid upon us, and we take it seriously." Remembering that his own father was killed four months after D-Day, he noted that the German people also suffered in the war.

On November 11, 2009, Merkel became the first German leader to commemorate on French soil Armistice Day ending World War One. She was invited to the Arc de Triomphe in Paris for a full military ceremony, where she publicly held hands with French President Nicholas Sarkozy. She said in her speech: "When there is antagonism between us, everybody loses. When we are united, everybody wins." Sarkozy called for "an ever closer association of French and German policies." He well understands that the special relationship between the two countries has traditionally multiplied French influence in Europe and the world. A deepening of their relationship could make Europe "one of the principal players of the 21st century," as he told his ambassadors. Merkel is more cautious of such grandiose statements.

The reality is that French and Germans are not particularly attracted toward each other. One can see that in the choice of languages schoolchildren take. Fewer than a million French secondary pupils learn German; 9% learn German as a first foreign language and 14% as a second. Only 5% of German children are still learning French in their final year.

Nevertheless, polls in both countries indicate that the strengthened Franco-German relationship rests on popular approval. A 2004 poll published by *Le Figaro* showed that 82% of French respondents believed Germans had become their best allies, with the UK and U.S. second and third. A 2004 Ipsos poll in Germany revealed that 56% of Germans regarded France as Germany's most reliable ally, compared with 28% who said it was the U.S.

However, as transatlantic tensions cooled down in 2004, more and more German foreign policy specialists had second thoughts about the notion that France and Germany should be a "counterweight" to the U.S. Germany had always sought to prevent France from transforming the EU into an instrument of French policy against the U.S. German foreign policy swung back to its traditional position of equidistance between France and America, of being a "counterweight" to the French dream of being a "counterweight" to the United States. Many German analysts began again to regard close Franco-German relations as necessary, but not sufficient, for an effective foreign policy.

French President Sarkozy seemed to agree, writing in his autobiography: "If the Franco-German understanding is still necessary, it is not a strong enough motor for Europe today." For the partnership to work well, there have to be good personal and working relationships at the top, and that is lacking. Sarkozy and Merkel are known to get on each other's nerves. They have different temperaments and leadership styles. Sarkozy is impulsive and wants the credit for actions that he often takes unilaterally and without consultation. The physicist Merkel weighs arguments and assembles allies before deciding. The Germans' main rules are "no surprises" and "nobody wins" in the Franco-German relationship. Sarkozy plays by different rules. As a French diplomat put it: "Franco-German co-operation is hard work. We are very different. There is nothing natural to it and yet it works."

The continent-wide debate on a new EU constitutional treaty in 2005 revealed that the two partners were going in different directions. While the Bundestag ratified the constitution on May 28, French voters turned it down a day later. Thoughtful Germans realize that in the enlarged EU of 27 states, Franco-German agreement is no longer sufficient to determine EU policy and move the Union ahead. France is not in a position to lead, and because of its history, Germany must be careful about stepping forward as Europe's leader. But there can be little doubt that on economic issues, Germany now dominates.

The 2010 euro crisis over Greek debts exposed a wide rift in the two countries' economic philosophies. Germany wants strict rules on budget deficits with tough penalties, whereas France stresses more government involvement in other member states' policies. The crisis, one of the most serious in EU history, highlighted Germany's growing isolation within the EU. It no longer things automatically that what is good for the EU is good for Germany. Its government asserts its national interests more forcefully, as France and Britain have always done.

Without changing its position toward the Iraq war, Germany restored normal relations with the U.S. It also renewed its call for its own permanent seat on the UN Security Council. The U.S. does not support this bid, focusing instead on more major reform of the UN and its Security Council. Most Germans want the UN to play a role as sole provider of legitimacy for the use of force. But that requires, in their opinion, that the Security Council be reformed to reflect the momentous global transformations after the end of the Cold War, including the weight of a unified Germany.

By supporting French policy over Iraq so strongly in 2003, Germany also sharply diminished its influence in Eastern Europe. Like most new members of NATO from the East, Poland tends to look to the

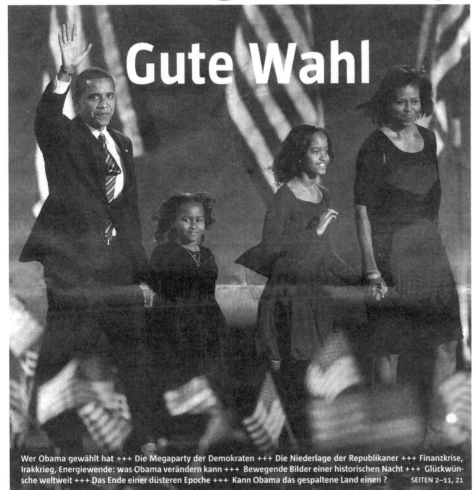

IR. B728
5. WOCHE
0. JAHRGANG
ISGABE BERLIN
1,70 AUSLAND
1,00 DEUTSCHLAND
ONNERSTAG, 6. NOVEMBER 2008

ZWÖLF SONDERSEITEN ZUM SIEG VON BARACK OBAMA

die tageszeitung

Gute Wahl

Wer Obama gewählt hat +++ Die Megaparty der Demokraten +++ Die Niederlage der Republikaner +++ Finanzkrise, Irakkrieg, Energiewende: was Obama verändern kann +++ Bewegende Bilder einer historischen Nacht +++ Glückwünsche weltweit +++ Das Ende einer düsteren Epoche +++ Kann Obama das gespaltene Land einen ? SEITEN 2–11, 21

Dienstagabend in Chicago: Familie Obama, die neuen Bewohner des Weißen Hauses, bedankt sich bei ihren Anhängern für die Unterstützung FOTO: TIMOTHY A. CLARY/AFP

| taz muss sein | Wir sind Obama | KOMMENTAR VON BERND PICKERT ◼ verboten |

Good choice

U.S. as the key guarantor of its security. Berlin turned down Poland's invitation in 2003 to contribute troops to serve under its command in postwar Iraq. Polish-German reconciliation has been very important for post-Cold War Europe. Four hundred city partnerships have been established, twice as many as between Germany and the U.S. Germany was the most important sponsor for Poland's entry into the EU in 2004 although half of the Germans opposed Polish membership. They fear the competition from Polish workers, who were forbidden free entry into the German labor market for seven years until 2011.

The German government resented strong and critical Polish positions within the EU on such matters as the EU constitu-

tion. At the same time, Poles no longer universally regard Germany as a model. A climate of mistrust reentered Polish-German relations for a few years. It was fueled by differences over the Iraq war and former Chancellor Schröder's special relationship with Russia. A Polish scholar noted: "Always at the moment when Berlin and Moscow get too close, we have been threatened." Donald Tusk was elected Polish prime minister in October 2007 on a promise to mend ties with Poland's neighbors, especially Germany, and he largely succeeded.

U.S. as Ally

The U.S. relationship has always been and remains very important for the FRG;

indeed, no ally supported German unification more resolutely than did the U.S. Like most Europeans, Germans are generally mystified by the American political system. The U.S. is a large, highly decentralized country whose national powers are separated and distributed to competing and sometimes almost hostile institutions in the nation's capital. Such separation of powers is particularly significant in foreign policy because it often makes it impossible for a president to produce that which he had promised foreign leaders. The American political system enables unknown persons of various professional backgrounds to rise to the highest national political offices through a painfully long and complicated electoral system largely unfathomable in Europe. Because of the parliamentary system in the FRG, aspirants for the highest offices must enter politics at an early age and deal with a wide variety of political problems while they slowly work their way to the top.

In stark contrast, the unique American selection system permits a person to arrive in the White House who had pursued a nonpolitical career and who might have little political experience. This is why many Germans are so shocked to see that a former peanut farmer or actor could almost suddenly appear in the White House. Since Europeans focus almost exclusively on American national politics, they are often unaware of presidents' prior political activity at the state or local level.

Germans are particularly troubled by the fact that a newly elected president may have notably little experience in foreign affairs and that it is he who has the power to select a maze of foreign policy advisers, secretaries and under-secretaries and agency chiefs, many of whom might also have had little or no foreign policy experience. Such a presidential "team" is often permitted to operate in what seems like an uncoordinated way and frequently sends off widely differing signals, something that inevitably creates doubts about American leadership capabilities and about the continuity of American foreign policy. Americans must remember that the image of the U.S. and its leaders is in itself an important factor in European politics.

After the 2003 Iraq war, Germany moved to salvage what Schröder called the "vital friendship" between Germany and the U.S. The chancellor said he regretted his "exaggerated remarks" during the 2002 election campaign. He rejected being forced into a "senseless choice" between its two key allies, the U.S. and France, and argued that the debate over creating a "multipolar world" (France's term for a checked America) is counterproductive. Ex-Foreign Minister Fischer called the

Germany

transatlantic relationship "indispensable." Germany and France both supported U.S.-British resolutions in the UN for the reconstruction of Iraq. Fischer argues that the debate over Iraq was always a matter of tactics, not goals, and that it is in Germany's interest for the U.S. to succeed there.

Europe and the world have changed, and the U.S.-German relationship will never be as close as it once was. Germany will be more independent and less compliant even after reconciliation. Most of the Social Democratic and Green leaders of Germany are not anti-American. But since they grew up after the war and did not experience the immediate postwar years, they are not as passionate Atlanticists as the generation of Helmut Kohl and Helmut Schmidt. They are at least as interested in European integration and the EU as they are in the transatlantic alliance. The percentage of Germans who want the EU to become a superpower rose in 2003 from 48% to 70%.

Public opinion is changeable and is strongly influenced by the popularity or unpopularity of incumbent American presidents. In a 2004 poll, 90.4% of Germans thought good transatlantic relations were important although 71% considered that the U.S. selfishly and inconsiderately defends its own interests. In the tense aftermath of the Iraq war in 2003 only 45% considered strong American leadership in world affairs to be desirable, vs. 68% a year earlier. Nevertheless, a large majority still believed that Europe and America should cooperate not compete with each other.

The extent to which public opinion is influenced by who sits in the White House was demonstrated by the election of Barack Obama in November 2008. During his campaign he had traveled to Berlin in July and attracted a crowd of 200,000 wildly enthusiastic admirers. German newspapers greeted the electoral result with headlines like: "The world celebrates Obama," "Good Choice!" and "Germany congratulates the new U.S. president. Yes, we can be friends!" In his April 2009 Germany trip to attend the NATO summit in Baden Baden and Strasbourg, he had an electrifying effect on crowds in the streets and in a town meeting. He was obviously far more popular than any of the European leaders, including Merkel. In polls at the time, 89% of German respondents said that with him the U.S. was again on the right path, and 76% wished Germany had politicians like him. France remained the Germans' most trusted friend, in the view of 87%, but the U.S. had risen dramatically to second place with 78%, followed by Britain with 71%. In 2009, 56% of western Europeans believed U.S. leadership was desir-

able (44% in central and eastern Europe); 63% of western Europeans saw America in a positive light (53% in the East).

Perhaps because Chancellor Merkel has such a different personality from the charismatic president and because so many Germans ask, "Why don't we have a German Obama?", she has a strained and stiff relationship with him. Many Germans sense that he has a closer affinity to French President Nicolas Sarkozy than with their own leader. It is the opposition Social Democrats who see him as a natural ally.

A broad consensus on foreign policy remains under Chancellor Angela Merkel's grand coalition of CDU/CSU-SPD, despite differences on Turkish membership in the EU. Germans are still committed multilateralists, and they cherish the thought of being a "civilian power," believing most conflicts can be settled by diplomacy. But it has become easier for them to press for their national interests. In a 2005 poll, 83% of German respondents found it desirable for Germany to exercise strong leadership in world affairs. They are not totally averse to power politics when it seems unavoidable and when its allies are involved.

As in previous governments, the main lines of foreign policy are made in the

chancellor's office, not the Foreign Ministry, led by Foreign Minister Guido Westerwelle. Merkel practices a different style in foreign affairs, seeking to pursue German interests without alienating allies, including the U.S. She is more Atlanticist and pro-British than Schröder, and she wants to be both Atlanticist and European. Nevertheless, if forced to choose, Europe would probably be for her the higher priority. Within days after assuming power on November 22, 2005, her aim for a swift transatlantic rapprochement was set back by embarrassing revelations that the U.S. had mistakenly detained a Lebanese-born German citizen and held him in Afghanistan for five months and that the CIA might have used air bases on German soil to transport detained terror suspects to countries that might torture them.

On November 3, 2009, a reelected Merkel gave one of the best speeches of her life before a joint session of the U.S. Congress. Not since Konrad Adenauer a half century earlier had a German chancellor been granted this high honor, and he spoke only before the House of Representatives. In an emotional speech, she thanked U.S. presidents from Kennedy to George H.W. Bush for standing by the FRG during the Cold War. "We know how much we owe you and we will—I will— never forget this."

Armed Forces

In 2005 the Federal Armed Forces (*Bundeswehr*) celebrated its 50th anniversary with the motto, "50 years resolutely for peace." Unification and the collapse of the Soviet empire in Central Europe profoundly affected the size and the mission of the *Bundeswehr*. Since 1991 the military's budget has been cut by 15%; by 2008 the FRG was spending only 1.5% of its GDP (compared with 4.1% in the U.S.) on defense. Half the expenditures are for personnel costs. More than half of its defense budget goes to salaries and benefits for personnel, a third of whom are civilians. Only 13% is spent on new equipment. However, it remains the largest NATO land army in Europe and also contains a formidable air force and a small navy that operates in the North and Baltic seas. Almost all German soldiers are assigned to NATO, the supreme commander of which is always an American general.

Soon after unification the *Bundeswehr* began a unique effort of merging two formerly hostile armies into one. About 25,000 professional East German soldiers who were judged to be reliable defenders of Germany's democratic order became a part of a combined force that, in compliance with an agreement made with the Soviet Union in July 1990, numbered 332,800 troops, 73,450 of whom were draftees. The agreement specified that no Western German units were to be deployed on former GDR territory until Russia had withdrawn its 375,000 troops by August 31, 1994, and that no foreign troops and nuclear weapons would ever be stationed there. On September 8, 1994, the last Allied soldiers departed from Berlin, leaving the city free of foreign troops for the first time since 1945.

In 2010, the *Bundeswehr* had a total of 250,613 active forces. The army had a strength of 163,962, including 112,000 conscripts. The navy had 24,407, including 3,720 naval aviation, 4,950 draftees and 490 women. The air force numbered 62,244, with almost 12,000 conscripts and 950 women. Germany has a reserve force of 161,812. Officer and NCO reservists must serve until age 60; other males until age 45. All these numbers continue to come down as Germany reshapes its military for new kinds of threats.

In 2004 ex-Defense Minister Peter Struck, supported by all major groups across the political spectrum, announced a change in strategy from a focus on territorial defense to overseas interventions and peacekeeping with lighter, more mobile forces. This change is in line with shifts occurring in U.S., NATO and EU security doctrines. The country remains committed to only multinational operations with a clear international mandate. Since the defense budget is being cut, with few prospects for increases in the near future, Struck emphasized the need for collaboration, role specialization and pooling resources with the European partners.

The *Bundeswehr* will be allowed to remain at 250,000 soldiers (and only 50,000 conscripts) in the hope of boosting spending for new weapons. This includes joint forces information systems, reconnaissance equipment and armored transport vehicles. It is divided into three groups: an "intervention" force of 35,000 troops, a "stabilization" force of 70,000 for peacekeeping, and a "support" force of 137,500. The army, air force and navy will be linked into a single force geared to rapid, long-range deployment. By 2010 the number of *Bundeswehr* installations had fallen by 105 installations to a total of about 400.

Germany has retained its conscript army on the principle that it is a vital link between the military and society. The founders of the *Bundeswehr* feared the creation of a "state within a state," as was the case during the Weimar Republic. This rationale is less compelling after 60 years of stable democracy. The reasons for retaining the draft now have more to do with the costs and the health-care system. Males in both parts of Germany are required to per-

Newspaper headline: How great is the danger for our soldiers?

form six months of military service. In 2010 this was lowered from nine months in order to maximize the number of young men who can be drafted.

If a man is judged to be conscientious objectors, he must perform 13 months of alternative civilian duty. In 2004, about 91,000 reported for civilian duty, while 82,000 were drafted for military service. This combined number was less than half of the young men of draft age. Many work in the health and elderly-care sectors of the economy, which would suffer greatly without them.

As more and more of its NATO allies abolish conscription and create professional armies, and as the shrinking *Bundeswehr* inducted progressively fewer young males making the system more and more unfair, more voices are being raised to advocate a professional army, such as those the U.S., UK, and France have. Although the Merkel government declared in 2005 that conscription remains an indispensable requirement, the issue is now under serious discussion. The Greens have taken the stand that there is no reason to continue it. In a 2007 opinion poll, two-thirds of Greens and Left supporters favored its abolition, an opinion shared by only 37% of the CDU, 49% of SPD and 45% of FDP. Taken as a whole, 48% of respondents favored scrapping against 48% who did not. In 2009 the CDU/CSU rejected an attempt by their FDP governing partners to abolish conscription altogether.

The armed forces are no longer among the least respected German institutions. A 2008 survey revealed that 89% of the population supports the German army although some would describe Germans' relationship with their armed force as one of "friendly indifference." It is important that the armed forces are always presented to the public as lightly-armed providers of humanitarian assistance. In April 2009, a surprising 84% have a positive view of NATO. Asked what institutions they most trusted, respondents listed the military third (after police, and the Constitutional Court), ahead of churches, parliament, government and far in front of political parties. Nevertheless, a 2007 poll found that only 42% of Germans were proud of the *Bundeswehr's* achievements, compared with 87% of Americans.

Thanks to this renewal of trust in the nation's soldiers, the country was able to award in July 2009 the first medals for bravery since WWII. They were received by four veterans of the Afghanistan war, who saved civilians and wounded comrades after an attack. The new Bundeswehr Cross has the shape of the original Iron Cross, but it is gold rather than black.

Nevertheless, no other NATO country has such a large percentage of its population that seeks to avoid compulsory 9-month military service by claiming status as conscientious objectors. This right is anchored in the Basic Law, but it was originally intended for a small group of truly conscientious objectors. There are scores

Germany

of C.O. organizations, and many churches and other groups are active in giving advice about how to apply and successfully to argue for such exemption.

After intense domestic debates, Germans, by and large, have come to accept military deterrence as a means to maintain peace. But until the war over Kosovo in 1999 few could accept the notion that the actual use of force is ever justified. There was little room in their minds for a concept of the "just war."

Many Germans had persuaded themselves that nobody knows the horrors of war better than they do and that they are therefore particularly sensitive to the victims. This is partly a result of Western Germany's efforts for decades to drive home the lessons of two world wars that militarism is wrong and war never pays. This black-and-white message is taught in the schools, propagated in the public media, and expressed on public monuments. Everywhere are "peace museums."

The idea that war is always wrong had become a kind of ideology in Germany and prevented many Germans from seeing parallels between Hitler's aggression and that of modern dictators. Such perceptions had changed considerably by the end of the century. Because of his persuasive justification for military intervention in Bosnia and Kosovo, ex-Foreign Minister Fischer played an important role in weakening Germany's traditional postwar pacifism. But Germany's NATO allies should never assume that Germans' caution and hesitancy toward using military force have disappeared.

Another aspect of military service is also being rethought and debated: the role of females. Among the NATO countries, only Germany and Italy had not permitted women to bear arms. They were traditionally permitted only to serve in the *Bundeswehr's* medical and musical corps. But in 2000 the European Court of Justice in Luxembourg ruled in favor of a German woman who claimed that Germany's constitutional ban against women in the military amounted to unlawful sexual discrimination. It upheld a complaint by Tanja Kreil, an electrical engineer, whom the Defense Ministry rejected as a weapons technician. The court left open the question of "where sex constitutes a determining factor for access to certain special combat units." This refers to the appropriateness of women serving in elite commando regiments specializing in hand-to-hand combat or on one of Germany's 14 submarines. The armed forces now include 11,380 women, 6% of the total.

Germany's Strategic Situation

NATO strategy has been reexamined in a fundamental way to adapt to the post-Cold War era in which the Warsaw Pact has ceased to exist. It was discovered in 1993 just how threatening and prepared that pact had been. Documents found in the former GDR revealed that East German and Soviet planners had drawn up detailed and regularly updated plans for a military invasion of West Germany. They had already made street signs for Western cities (renaming such streets as Düsseldorf's Königsallee "Karl Marx Allee"), printed money for their occupation government, built equipment to run broad-gauged Russian trains on Western tracks, stocked more ammunition for the 160,000-man National People's Army than was possessed by the half-million man *Bundeswehr*, and made up medals for officers who performed well in the conquest.

Germany's strategic situation dramatically changed in the 1990s. Its Eastern flank used to confront directly the Warsaw Pact countries with no buffer against a heavily-armed, suspicious and unpredictable Soviet Union. Now a larger Germany faces an unthreatening group of Eastern European democracies that desperately wanted to become NATO and EU partners; in 2004 seven of them joined NATO and eight the EU.

Beyond them is an unstable Russia with an elected government that is trying to restore the country's great-power status. The threat is chiefly an economic one. German must pay close attention since it imports 45% of its gas and 34% of its oil from Russia. No longer is the focus on blunting an all-out Russian attack on NATO forces concentrated in Germany, necessitating a "forward defense" by "layer-caked" NATO forces along an inter-German border. The future danger might come from a disruption of resource supplies or undetermined threats to any NATO member state, from Norway to Turkey. Threats might emanate from non-European countries or from unknown dangers springing from violent national unrest in Central Europe or the former Soviet Union.

The 2003–4 Defense Policy Guidelines declaring that crisis prevention and management have replaced territorial defense as the German armed forces' mission: "there is no conventional threat to German territory." The kinds of threats the country faces are the proliferation of weapons of mass destruction, international terrorism, ethnic conflict, genocide, massive human rights violations, and international criminal activity. Thus Germany needs to modernize its forces by making them more mobile and technologically adept. Since there is little prospect of greater defense spending, pooling of resources with other European and NATO partners is necessary, as is an international mandate (from the UN if possible) for any commitment of troops.

In 2010 Germany had about 8,000 soldiers deployed in a half-dozen places around the world, including 209 Eurocorps in France, about 5,000 in Afghanistan, 104 in Uzbekistan and others in Balkans (2,486 in Kosovo including 110 women and 560 in Bosnia including 47 women), the Horn of Africa, and the Congo as part of an EU peacekeeping force. A German admiral had overall command of the EU's first peacekeeping command in Macedonia. It is developing within its armed forces the capacity to deploy up to 35,000 troops outside its border at any time, and it is contributing forces to both the EU's and NATO's rapid reaction forces. To provide its military forces with the necessary lift and modern firepower, it is purchasing 60 Airbus A400M transport aircraft, to be ready in 2009 at the earliest, and is acquiring laser-guided bombs and air-launched cruise missiles. The admirable thing about all this is that the German military presence abroad neither frightens the Germans nor scares the rest of the world.

To respond to a wide range of threats in the 21st century, Germany has integrated some of its units into multinational divisions and corps within NATO: a Dutch-German corps under alternate command has been formed. British, German and Belgian troops constitute a lightly-equipped multinational rapid-reaction force with an airmobile brigade. A corps has been created with headquarters along Germany's Eastern border in Szczecin, Poland, that comprises Polish, German and Danish troops. This unit was modeled on the French-German "Eurocorps" in Strasbourg, France, created in 1992. A U.S. combat division serves in a German-led corps, while a German division is part of a U.S.-led corps. Like all these joint units, it can be used to defend member states, serve in peacekeeping missions, or operate under EU aegis.

For a long time the "German problem" had both an interior and exterior dimension. The inner problem, the failure of democracy, was solved long ago. However, the exterior one still existed: what role should Germany play in the European system of states, given the inability of other European powers to form a counterweight to the power of a reunified Germany in the heart of Europe? Many doubt that France could play that role. Since 1945 it was the United States that provided that counterweight. Any weakening of Germany's Atlantic ties could have stirred renewed fears of a Germany unbound in Europe.

American forces permanently stationed in Europe had shrunk by 2010 to about

Germany

100,000, with about 48,000 in Germany (still the largest U.S. military overseas presence outside of Afghanistan). This is a 75% reduction in Germany since the Berlin Wall fell in 1989. No European country, including Germany, wants the total withdrawal of American troops. No major German political party, except the Left Party, has campaigned for the withdrawal of U.S. soldiers. Berlin still contributes $1 billion per year to support U.S. bases. In addition to the U.S. soldiers, Germany also hosts 22,400 British troops (to be lowered to 17,400 by 2019, including the closing of three bases), 2,800 French, 300 Dutch and 287 Canadian.

The U.S. is conducting a complex worldwide shift in its overseas bases in order to be closer to potential crisis areas; to "deter forward" is the motto. This change, when it happens, would affect American troop levels in Germany. They would be reduced by 50% by 2015. Two heavy divisions (the 1st Infantry and the 1st Armored), as well as selected V Corps and U.S. Army Europe units, will be moved back to the U.S. Half of the installations in the country would be closed, including such important training grounds as Baumholder, which hosts 12,000 U.S. soldiers. In 2005, it shut down Rhein-Main Air Base, adjacent to Frankfurt Airport. It also announced the reversion in 2007 of 11 bases in southern Germany, especially in and around Würzburg. That would leave 62 American bases in Germany, over half of the total U.S. military installations in Europe. Some of its F-16 fighter jets would be reassigned from Spangdahlem Air Base to Turkey.

The divisions would be replaced by a much smaller light combat brigade, and other units would be rotated in and out for exercises and deployments. It would retain a few key facilities, such as Ramstein Airbase and its nearby military hospital in Landstuhl. Many of its units would be rotated on six-month unaccompanied assignments to countries such as Poland, Bulgaria and Romania, which are closer to the Balkans, the Middle East and Central Asia and where military stocks could be pre-positioned. The Pentagon insists that this future redeployment has nothing to do with tensions with Germany or its antiwar stance toward Iraq.

While insisting that "the Alliance and the presence of U.S. troops in Europe remains indispensable for our security," the German government believes that a common European foreign policy must, in the long run, include a common security and defense policy in some form. Europeans are discussing a distinct European Security and Defence Policy (ESDP). Karsten Voigt, in charge of U.S. policy in the Foreign Ministry, stated, "you cannot ask

European ambivalence toward U.S.
Copyright 1987 by Herblock in
The Washington Post

about a European identity if Germans don't take part." A consensus exists in the EU that such an identity is necessary, while preserving NATO in one form or the other. Americans have often called on Europeans to bear a greater responsibility for their own defense, but not in competition with NATO. Nevertheless, the U.S. government came to accept ESDP as a necessary European contribution to the common defense.

NATO still retains a diminished role for nuclear weapons. Traditionally, FRG governments have always supported a NATO defense strategy that calls for the use of nuclear weapons in the event that an enemy attack cannot be stopped by means of conventional arms. Since the FRG refuses to possess nuclear, chemical or biological weapons (although it does possess multipurpose weapons capable of delivering nuclear warheads), it must rely on its allies, particularly the U.S., to provide the kind of nuclear deterrence that might be necessary to dissuade a potential aggressor from either attacking the FRG in the first place, or from continuing such an attack.

To underscore its determination to defend the FRG, the U.S. maintains a drastically reduced number of nuclear weapons (about 20 free-fall bombs in Büchel) in the Western part of the FRG. They would be delivered by German fighter-bombers and

German pilots. Another 200 or so are stored in the BENELUX countries, Italy, Norway and Turkey. Even the presence of such a small number of bombs is a matter of controversy in German public debate. When a Pentagon report published in June 2008 found that security standards at most nuclear weapons sites in Europe fell short of requirements, critics called on the U.S. to remove all its nuclear weapons stored in Germany.

That call was renewed in 2009 by Foreign Minister Westerwelle of the co-ruling FDP although he opposes acting unilaterally to remove them. Polls consistently show that a clear majority of Germans opposes the nuclear presence. The CDU/CSU is the only party that wants to keep the bombs, but Turkey and the central European NATO partners want them as a deterrent to Russia, which has about ten times as many as NATO. Despite President Obama's rhetoric about nuclear nonproliferation, the U.S. government rules out removing the weapons unless Russia agrees to reductions in its own arsenal. Secretary of State Hillary Clinton made that clear in 2010: "As a nuclear alliance, sharing nuclear risks and responsibilities widely is fundamental."

ECONOMY

The FRG deserves its reputation as an economic giant. It is the world's second-largest exporter of goods after China, and 40% of its GDP is generated by exports. It has the largest economy in Europe, 30% of eurozone's GDP, and is economically the most important member of the EU, one-fifth of whose budget is paid by Germany. Its economic activity is guided by the principle of the social market economy. This means that while it does not permit unrestrained economic competition whatever the social costs, it does openly advocate and support a liberal (free) world trade.

It is the world's fourth-largest economy, having in 2009 been overtaken for third by China. Because of its dependence upon global export markets, it was inescapable that it would be severely shaken by the world economic downturn that began in the fall of 2008. At first its government was in denial, arguing that it was an American problem since the subprime mortgage crisis began there. In 2009, however, there was no more denying that Germany was in the midst of its worst economic recession since WWII. By the middle of the year, GDP had contracted by 6.9%, compared with 4.8% in the eurozone as a whole and 2.5% in the U.S. Unemployment had risen to 8.3% (13.3% in the East), and the OECD predicted it would rise to 5.1 million (from 3.3 million in 2008) by 2010. Its budget def-

Germany

"We calculate fairly" opposing euro price rises

icit ballooned to 4.6%, a record for a country that is deeply wary of debt. Borrowing is at a postwar high.

The government devised a couple of stimulus packages worth 64 billion euros ($90 billion), a 500-billion-euro ($700-billion) bank rescue, and a wildly popular "cash for clunker" bonus to drivers who scrapped old cars and buy new ones. Germany slowly worked its way out of its lamentable situation, which it shared with all its allies and trading partners.

Integrating Eastern Germany's Economy

Germany's unification in 1990 presented the FRG with difficulties and challenges. In a way, the problems were even greater than when the FRG had to rebuild a devastated land after 1945. During the 12-year Nazi regime, Germany had maintained the institutional infrastructure of a market economy, private property, a private sector legal code, and an administrative sector that understood the market system. Eastern Germans could not fall back on such continuity in 1990.

During 40 years of communist rule, the economy was continuously plundered, first by the Soviet occupiers in the form of war reparations, and then by the SED, who let the country's capital stock, housing, transportation network, communications systems, and environment degenerate. Enterprises had no resources of their own for investment; profits were sent to the central government, which was stingy in returning money for modernization. The economy was planned from the top, and the country was isolated economically from the capitalist world. Trade of generally shoddy goods was on a state-to-state basis and directed primarily toward the GDR's communist partners in Eastern Europe and the Soviet Union. This "command economy" created hopeless bottle-

The euro arrives

necks and shortfalls and robbed individuals and firms of the opportunity to apply their own initiative and creativity to improve their economic situation. Only 5% of the workforce worked independently in repair shops, small stores, and restaurants. Citizens were nurtured to be passive, obeying the leaders at the top in return for a guaranteed job and income, which was the highest in the communist world.

Thus, when Western Germans woke up from the initial euphoria of unification, they found an economy in the East in which roughly half of the workforce in the average company was unproductive, a majority of the companies were uncompetitive in the world market, a third of the

country's production had traditionally been exported to countries in the East which could no longer pay for poorly made and overpriced Eastern German goods, most of the property used for industry and farming had been taken out of private hands, environmental neglect had reached crisis proportions and citizens had huge pent-up consumer expectations they hoped would be gratified immediately. Perhaps worst of all, citizens had forgotten over the past four decades how a market system, a private company, and a Western legal system operate.

It was in this setting that ex-Chancellor Kohl, who like most German politicians genuinely underestimated the economic difficulties involved with the unparalleled merger of two so different economic systems and who wanted to win the first all-German federal elections, announced that "no one will be worse off" after unity. Such unjustified optimism rapidly instilled disappointment, pessimism, cynicism, fear, deep unrest and rage among Eastern Germans when they soon experienced the worst economic collapse in Germany since the Great Depression from 1929–33. Within a month after unification, Eastern German industrial output and employment (including short-time work) had fallen by more than a third and was getting steadily worse.

Why did this collapse occur? On July 1, 1990, the Western *Deutschmark*, one of the world's hardest currencies, was introduced in the GDR at an exchange rate of one-to-one, even though experts estimated the East mark to have only a quarter of a West mark's value. The Kohl government regarded this as a political necessity to keep the momentum of unity going, but it made no economic sense. Eastern Germany's former communist

Germany's largest banking center: Frankfurt/Main

trading partners could no longer buy its goods, so a third of its customers disappeared. These markets could not be replaced in the West because of the low quality of Eastern products. The problem was further aggravated by the fact that East Germans themselves wanted to buy higher quality Western goods, rather than goods produced in their own part of Germany. Thus, demand for their products declined even further, while Western Germany's economy boomed because of the huge demand in the East.

Production costs rose because pay was in a more valuable currency while output was going down. At the same time, wages also rose as East Germans desired to have the same pay level as their countrymen in the West. Within a year of monetary union wages had risen 50% to 80% in many Eastern firms, and East Germans' pay had risen to about half of that in the West and was steadily going up. These rises occurred despite drastic cuts in productivity; therefore, Eastern companies' competitive advantage from cheap labor was destroyed. Run-down East German companies that had to pay employees at Western German wage levels could not produce goods at prices that people are willing to pay. By mid-1991 fewer than one in ten companies in the East was economically viable. Unless productivity increases, the higher wages climb and more employees have to be laid off to meet the payroll. But to increase productivity enough to pay high wages, companies need to be dramatically modernized. That is, they desperately need investment, but this was perhaps the greatest disappointment.

It was expected that Western companies would invest heavily in the East and thereby cushion the shock of transition to a capitalist economy, but several factors held them back: first is precisely the fact that most Eastern enterprises were not economically viable. Investors do not want to buy companies that lose money, have antiquated equipment, bloated workforces, unrealistically high wage levels compared with productivity, and environmental liabilities that could bankrupt an investor. East German firms were so careless in polluting the air, soil and water that the clean-up costs could be prohibitive. Legal changes were necessary to relieve new owners of the responsibility for a firm's past pollution. East German factories used high-polluting energy sources, such as brown coal, with a high sulfur content, which will have to be replaced with cleaner fuels at high costs. In many cases it would be cheaper to create new companies rather than to take over problem-ridden old ones.

A second problem was a complicated jumble of property claims resulting from earlier expropriations by the Nazis, the Soviets, and the SED. Property taken and redistributed by the Soviets between 1945 and 1949 (called at the time "Junker Land") is not to be returned to former owners, in contrast to that confiscated before and after, with some qualifications. In 2005 the European Court of Human Rights in Strasbourg confirmed that families of expropriated landowners between 1945 and 1949 have no right to compensation beyond the financial indemnity offered by the Kohl government at the time of reunification. More than a million claims to such property were filed, but the litigation is complicated and time-consuming. This is especially true since local and land government administrations are understaffed and practically bankrupt, and since many East German judges were removed because of their earlier collaboration with the communist state.

Investors are fearful of time- and cost-consuming litigation involving property claims, and they are therefore inclined to wait until such problems are sorted out before sending in their money. Realizing the difficulty, the federal government, working together with the Eastern Land governments, finally agreed that property could be sold to investors rather than returned to prior owners (who would be compensated) if this were necessary to create jobs. Not only does the government want to protect jobs in order to quiet fears and unrest in the East, but in order to prevent a massive migration of East Germans into the West. Most want to remain in Eastern Germany, but in 1991 an estimated 10,000 persons a month, often those with dynamism and badly-needed skills, were moving westward; several hundred thousand more commute up to eight hours per day to work in the West. By 2000 most property claims had been settled.

A further problem in stimulating economic activity is that Eastern Germans are understandably mystified by the intricate complexity of Western German laws and regulations that have been introduced into the East. Anxious East Germans who suddenly had to live under totally different and unfamiliar rules are buying hastily published paperbacks with titles like *Your Rights as a Tenant*, *Your Rights as an Employee*, and *How to Deal with the Tax System*. Few know how a capitalist business works and how to start one up; they lack management and financial know-how and are unprepared to dive into a free-market system. Leipzig's mayor spoke of "a whole society far more complicated than any of us realized—everything here is new." Investors, as well as ordinary East Germans, are dismayed to see that management in struggling East German firms, at least below the top level, is still largely

Worker in the electrical industry: Siemens in Berlin

the same as during the communist era. Not only are there doubts about how much such managers know about a capitalist system, but also how much they believe in it. Although they may be well educated and experienced, their presence is a psychological blow to those East Germans who had dreamed of starting anew.

Finally, the infrastructure needed for modern business was antiquated: a 1920s vintage telephone and communications system, an absence of modern and pleasant office space, a road network that has barely been maintained since Hitler's time, and a largely non-computer-literate workforce.

To help guide the transition from an unproductive socialist economy to a modern capitalist one, a Trust Agency (*Treuhand*) holding company was established. With a staff of 3,000 by mid-1991, its job after unity was to try to privatize at reasonable prices and as quickly as possible the huge empire of former East German state assets, consisting of more than 8,000 companies, 60% of the forests, and 35% of the farmland. It also had to divide up state assets among the various levels of government, distribute liquidity cash, supervise the restructuring of companies not yet fit for sale, and prevent the creation of monopolies.

No agency could accomplish such a massive task easily. It assumed from the start that a third of the companies could

Germany

be privatized quickly, another third only after considerable restructuring, and a final third would have to go under. Some flagship East German companies were allowed to fail when the right kind of buyers could not be found, such as the Interflug airline and the Wartburg automobile manufacturer.

The Trust Agency's work went painfully slowly. By 1993 nearly 9,500 companies had been sold (95% to West German companies), and 435 had been closed. When large street demonstrations took place in the spring of 1991, the Trust Agency was instructed to shift its emphasis to making companies viable that were not ready for sale, while still officially aiming to transfer ownership of the Eastern German economy to private hands. This amounted to massive infusions from the federal treasury, including from a German Unity Fund, to keep the companies afloat and to save jobs.

This assistance could not prevent the Trust Agency, which in 1995 was broken down into smaller agencies, from becoming a scapegoat for the downturn in the Eastern economy and for capitalism's slow start. Amid mounting protests against unemployment and soaring costs for rent, energy, and transportation, its chairman, Detlev Rohwedder, was assassinated in his Düsseldorf home. His violent death eliminated the last hopes that the merger of two unequal parts into one harmonious whole could be done without upheaval.

In the meantime, the federal government sought ways to speed up the recovery. This was an unaccustomed challenge because West Germany had created its economic prosperity and strength by slow, steady, balanced growth, not by quick action, as is being demanded for the East, which produces only 10% of the FRG's GDP. From 1991 to 2009 the West transferred 1.6 trillion euros ($2.1 trillion) to the East, a sum equivalent to 4% of GDP annually. Those cash transfers continue in the 21st century in the amount of 80 billion euros ($104 billion) per year. This cash infusion provides buying power to Eastern Germans and replaces the decrepit communist infrastructure. Almost half of East Germans lives on state benefits. Although the jobs of about 850,000 Eastern workers depend on the transfers, they have failed to generate more work in the East and have left the Eastern German economy unable to function without subsidies. In some ways it merely papers over the cracks of unification.

Germany's commitments caused the federal government deficit temporarily to balloon to 7% of GDP (a flagrant violation of the EU's stability pact). This prompted embarrassing EU warnings that Germany was over the 3% limit, which could have

triggered stiff fines of billions of euros for having violated the euro's guidelines if the law had been strictly applied. It was not, mainly because several other key EU countries, including France, ignored their obligations. Many Germans had forgotten this by 2010 when they criticized Greece for running up a high budget deficit.

Because the German savings ratio is high, the federal government can draw on those large domestic savings to help finance the budget if necessary without borrowing abroad. By 2007 the German national debt had risen to 65% of GDP, up from 47.3% a decade earlier and higher than that of many European countries.

Healthy economic growth enabled Germany to lower its unemployment to 3.1 million, the lowest in a long time. The rate had declined by 2010 to an overall average of 7.8%. It remains twice as high in the east, and it is even worse in the northern part of the East. A tight money policy by the European Central Bank in Frankfurt held Germany's inflation to 1% in 2010.

In the city of Berlin, the overall unemployment rate was just under 16%, rising higher during the recession. Its economy is lifeless, and it staggers under a debt of $64 billion. It has Germany's highest rate of residents on welfare: 18.6%, and it receives $4 billion in subsidies annually. The capital city's boom is in tourism. During 2008 it lured 7.9 million tourists, breaking its own record for the fifth consecutive year. Low prices are a major reason, with hotels less than half the price compared with London or Paris.

There are encouraging signs: 300,000 new (mainly small) businesses created since 1990 survived. The fact that five-sixths of Eastern industrial firms, which cover a third of all industrial workers in the East, opted out of the practice of nationwide wage accords has meant that the work force there can protect some jobs by adjusting wages and working hours to what their companies can pay. By 2010 only half of west German workers were covered by nation-wide contracts, down from two-thirds a decade earlier. Much red tape has been slashed. Thus, Easterners are showing the kind of adaptability that all nations must have in order to thrive in the globalized economy. This and subsidies helped induce 1,700 foreign firms to invest in the East during the 1990s.

Few large companies have moved their head offices to Berlin; Sony and Coca Cola are exceptions, but the German Railway announced in 2005 that it was transferring from Berlin to Hamburg. In the East as a whole, there are hardly any major company headquarters, and successful Eastern firms have tended to move their head offices west. Noteworthy exceptions are

Jenoptik in Jena and DHL, a subsidiary of Deutsche Post, in Leipzig. The consequence is that Eastern cities lack a business elite, which means less spending and philanthropy. Nevertheless, the East's infrastructure has improved immeasurably.

The telecommunications network is better than that in the West. The East now has the world's most modern, efficient and clean brown-coal-fueled power stations. The government subsidizes new coal plants even though few of them have the capability of capturing carbon emissions. Much of the former pollution has disappeared. Roads are much improved, universities are being modernized, and crumbling city centers are being restored. On their outskirts are new factories, exhibition complexes and high-tech research centers. More than 750,000 new homes were built in the last seven years of the 1990s, and over 40% of Easterners own their own homes, compared with a national average of 58%. Car ownership has trebled since 1989. Per capita GDP remains at 70% of western Germany's. Any increase in the East is only because 4.3 million easterners had left and were only partially replaced by 2.7 million westerners moving in. Thus it has lost a tenth of its population since unification, disproportionally women.

Although average gross wages are 23% lower than in the West (10% lower for public-sector workers, who have to work 90 minutes longer per week than their Western counterparts), enormous progress has been made since unification. Real wages and pensions have almost doubled. Net household income has grown to 90% of that in the West, and productivity has jumped from 41% to 78% of Western levels. Labor costs are 62% of the Western German level, but they are still four times higher than in the neighboring countries to the East. More than three-quarters of all industrial plants have been replaced since 1990.

In general, economic prospects in the East are best in the southern part of the region encompassing the federal states of Thuringia and Saxony and located below the so-called "White Wurst Line" (named for the southern part of Germany where white sausage is eaten) extending 220 kilometers from Erfurt to Leipzig, Zwickau, Chemnitz and Dresden. A similar North-South divide exists in the West: greater prosperity is found south of the line extending from Cottbus, on the Polish border, to Aachen in the west. Of 31 self-sustaining industrial clusters in the East, 23 are in Saxony and Thuringia. They have more manufacturing jobs than many states in the West. East Germany is peppered with areas of growth, with Dresden having reached Western level.

The vast majority of Easterners are far better off materially that they were in the GDR. In a 2000 poll 60% admitted that their lives had improved over the preceding decade, but two-thirds complained that they still did not feel "totally at home" in unified Germany.

The rate of relative poverty, at 11.1%, is on the rise, especially among children. At least 300,000 Germans were without health insurance in 2004, a worrying development in a country that prided itself on universal coverage. One can expect some improvement since smoking was banned on public transportation, restaurants and bars in 2007. Germans question the old assumption that the East would simply meld into the West. Instead the economic, political and cultural divergence is becoming increasingly apparent.

Perhaps most distressing is Easterners' attitude toward democracy. Asked in a 2003 Eurobarometer survey whether they were "satisfied with the functioning democracy in Germany," 66% of Westerners answered yes, but the percentage of Easterners answering in the affirmative fell from 38% in 2000 to 32% three years later. (In 2007, 56% of East Germans over age 35 and 46% of those aged 14 to 24 were dissatisfied with democracy, as it is now practiced.) Fewer than half of Eastern Germans (49%) thought democracy was the "best form of government for Germany" (compared with 80% in the West). An astounding 76% (compared with 52% in the West) agreed that "socialism is a good idea that was poorly implemented." In 2007, 57% of Easterners and 45% of Westerners agreed with that statement. Westerns' reaction to these views is growing animosity.

A 2004 Forsa Institute poll showed 24% of West Germans wanting the Berlin Wall back. Three years later two-thirds of East German respondents said they remembered the GDR positively. Angela Merkel spoke of the tendency by westerners to reduce the old GDR to the dictatorship and secret police. "No one's life, even in a dictatorship, is completely formed by that dictatorship." Everybody still had some good experiences and fond memories, and no one wants to abandon all those aspects of their lives all at once. However only 18% still dreamed of its return; 71% did not want the Communist regime back. More encouragingly, 2009 polls showed that 91% of easterners and 85% of westerners support reunification. Four out of five East German 14–19 year-olds no longer see themselves as "Ossi" or "Wessi." Nevertheless, only one out of four (27%) easterners believe that all Germans have become "one nation." The gulf is revealed most visibly in the way they vote.

Taxation and Federalism

The federal government and the lands try to coordinate their policies through such advisory bodies as the *Konjunkturrat* (economic council) and *Finanzplanungsrat* (finance planning council). But the central government cannot order the lands to follow its policy, largely because it has no monopoly on taxing power. According to the Basic Law the living standards in all states must be uniform; this became a very problematic requirement after unification in 1990, which linked a prosperous West with a pauperized East. Thus, the complicated taxing system in the U.S., which permits the per capita tax receipts in some states to be three or four times as high as in other states, is not found in the FRG, at least not before unification in 1990.

In 2000 and 2003 the government won parliamentary approval for the most dramatic tax reform in a half-century. The top rate of corporate tax was cut from 52% to 38.7% to 25%. The top income tax rate was reduced from 51% to 42% by 2005. The bottom rate was lowered from 23% to 15%. The capital gains tax on the sale of company cross-holdings, theretofore 50%, was abolished. Since German banks and insurance companies held some of the largest shares of industrial companies, the latter measure provided a strong incentive for long-overdue corporate restructuring.

Banks got their costs under control by selling off much of their real-estate portfolios and nonperforming loans. The business and trade union communities greeted this historic reform.

Whereas in the U.S. prior to World War II the states were virtually financially independent, in the FRG the question has revolved around how to divide common tax revenues. The financial relations between the national government and the states is extremely complicated, but it involves roughly the following: federal payments to poorer states, the sharing of common tax revenues, payments by richer states (such as Hesse and Baden-Wurttemberg) to poorer ones (such as Schleswig-Holstein and the new lands in the East), intergovernmental grants and subsidies, and federal payments to states for administrative services rendered.

Individual and corporate income taxes, the biggest source of revenue, is divided in a way that the national government gets 40%, the states get 40% and the cities 20%. Thus, there is no need for a German citizen to file two different income tax returns. The states receive 44% of the second biggest source, the Value Added Tax, which rises from 16% to 19% in 2007. This tax means what its title literally says; thus, if, for example, parts from several companies are used to make an automobile, a tax

Käte Kollwitz with young Germans in Prinzlauer Berg, Berlin

Germany

is imposed on the value added to the parts after they have been assembled to manufacture the car. The federal government gets all taxes on gasoline and alcohol, the lands all on car taxes, and the cities all property taxes.

In all, the central government receives about 55% of all taxes, but makes less than 45% of all expenditures, including national defense. The states, on the other hand, spend more than they receive, and the federal government must make up the difference. No one is entirely satisfied with the present tax system, but as yet no one has found an acceptable alternative to the continuous haggling over the distribution of revenues. In 1986 the Constitutional Court demanded a fairer equalization of payments between richer and poorer states. In 1990 the controversy flared again, as cash-strapped new Lands in the East clamored for a full share of the pie. Some politicians in both parts advocated tax breaks for Eastern Germans during the difficult transition. In any case, the system of redistributing tax resources has not succeeded in evening out the economic gaps between rich and poor lands.

In the federal government a "dynamic tension" often exists between the separate ministries of Economics and of Finance. They receive expert advice from the FRG's five leading economic research institutes and from the government's own council of economic advisers, known as the "five wise men." To help maintain stability are two government banks. The *Kreditanstalt für Wiederaufbau* (Loan Corporation for Reconstruction) was founded in 1948 to channel Marshall Plan funds and now helps finance German trade, foreign aid and domestic investment. Owned 80% by the central government and 20% by the Lands, it receives funds from both the budget and the capital market to help provide long-term investment capital on favorable terms for small and medium-size companies, environmental protection, hard-hit sectors such as shipbuilding, and regional development.

The powerful and prestigious *Bundesbank* (Federal Bank), located in Frankfurt as are most German banks, was one of the world's most independent central banks. Since the introduction of the euro on January 1, 2002, it has lost much of its power to the European Central Bank, located across town and operating with a much smaller staff (600 vs. 2,600). The *Bundesbank* is no more influential now than the other 11 central banks in the eurozone.

The *Bundesbank* was charged with issuing bank notes and defending the currency's value against inflation. Remembering how political manipulation helped cause the hyperinflation in the 1920s, the FRG's founders ensured that the new cen-

tral bank would be impervious to government pressure. All presidents of the Land central banks are on its council, as well as up to 10 directors appointed for eight-year terms upon recommendation by the federal government. Also located in Frankfurt is the *Deutsche Börse*, which runs Germany's stock markets.

The Government's Role in the Economy

Before unification in 1990 FRG governments were more hesitant than many other Western European governments to intervene directly in the economy and to protect or prop up lame-duck industries. The state participated in the ownership and management of some public services such as the telephone, rail and airline systems. Federal and state governments have given financial assistance to service, aerospace, computer, automotive and energy related industries. The bulk of subsidies was paid to service industries, especially transport. The average farmer also receives handsome subsidies.

The central government moved not only to dismantle many of the controls and regulations that were characteristic of the traditional postwar German economy. It also fulfilled its promise to sell off a large part of its shares in private industry. The FRG had sold its stakes in such groups as Veba (energy), Volkswagen (although a fifth is still owned by the *Land* of Lower Saxony, from which it receives subsidies), Viag (metals and chemicals), and Salzgitter (steel and engineering).

In 1996 it privatized a part of Telekom, the post office's telecommunications corporation, which had been split from the postal service in 1989. This was Europe's largest public offering to date, and more than two million retail investors participated. By 1999 more than 1,500 companies were offering telephone-related services in Germany. Such competition has reduced phone charges and forced Telekom to improve its service. In 2000 the government sold off more shares of Telekom, Europe's largest wireless company, which was busy purchasing foreign firms, such as Voice-Stream in the U.S. It also privatized the government printing offices in 2000, to be followed by the state-owned postal services.

The state sold its 53% stake in Lufthansa and its 66% stake in the Rhine-Main-Danube waterway authority, which in 1992 completed the last canal, opening a maritime link between the Atlantic Ocean and the Black Sea. The Federal Railway (*Bundesbahn*), minus the rail network, was sold into private hands. Even the interstate highways (*Autobahnen*) are heading for the auction block; since 2004 tolls have been levied on truck traffic. Direct state aid to failing sectors in the West was

significant in the coal, shipbuilding and electrical industries. Polls in 2008 revealed that Germans are skeptical of privatization: 77% thought the states should take large equity stakes in energy companies; almost two-thirds thought financial institutions should be partly nationalized, and another 60% thought that Lufthansa, the postal service and the railways should be state-owned.

The states are also involved in such pragmatic (not ideologically inspired) intervention. For example, Bavaria offered BMW money not to create a new plant in Austria. Baden-Wurttemberg also offered Daimler-Benz, the country's biggest company, funds to keep a new plant within the state. In fact, Baden-Wurttemberg devotes one-tenth of its budget to science and research facilities to enable its companies to stay ahead in technology. These subsidies can create conflict with EU authorities, as was seen in 1996 when the government of Saxony insisted on providing assistance to Volkswagen plants despite objections that they violated EU guidelines. But without subsidies Eastern states are unable to attract large investments.

Natural Resources and Energy

The economy suffers from several important handicaps. Except for modest deposits of iron ore, of natural gas and especially of hard coal in the Ruhr and Saar regions, and of brown coal in the foothills of the Harz mountains, near Cologne, and in the East, the FRG is poor in natural resources. In general, it must import raw materials and export finished goods. Since raw materials are usually priced on the international market in U.S. dollars, the FRG's strong currency, the euro, lowers its bill for imported materials.

In no sector is the FRG's dependence upon imports as critical as in energy, especially oil, which accounts for 35.6% of Germany's needs. It has succeeded in reducing its dependence on oil imported from the Persian Gulf; its main supplier now is Russia, from which it gets 34% of its oil and 45% of its gas. Most of its natural gas, which provides 8.5% of its electricity, must be imported.

The only significant domestic energy source is coal, from which 37% of its total energy and half of its electricity is derived. It accounts for about 28% of the West's energy needs and a far higher percentage of the East's. However, German coal must be subsidized since its extraction costs are higher than the costs of importing foreign coal. By 1999 it cost about $60,000 in yearly subsidies to protect each of 85,000 jobs in the coal mining industry. In 2007 the government decided gradually to eliminate all subsidies by 2018 for the hard-coal mines in the West. The eight mines (seven of them in the Ruhr) will be shut down, and the 32,000 remaining miners will be retired early or given other jobs. Brown-coal production will continue in the East.

Alternative (renewable) forms of energy, including hydroelectric power, account for 2% of total energy consumption and an impressive 15% of electricity. Germany is the world's biggest producer of solar power, which provides 2% of its electricity, and it is a world leader in wind power.

Although conservation measures have had some success, total energy consumption continues to rise. The government had once planned to cope with this through nuclear power, which in the 21st century accounts for about a quarter of the country's electricity. Germany had 17 nuclear power plants by 2010. Earlier plans to increase them were stopped in their tracks by the intense domestic protest against the construction of nuclear power plants and of facilities for the reprocessing and storage of nuclear wastes. By 1991 the FRG government had shut down all Soviet-designed reactors in the East because they failed to meet safety standards. At Greifswald a meltdown almost occurred in the mid-1970s.

Germany's large and powerful antinuclear lobby regularly targets shipments of nuclear fuel or waste with massive, sometimes violent protests. The former SPD-Green government pledged to shut down Germany's remaining plants, but the two parties differed on timing and tactics, with the SPD wanting a longer phase-out period done with the collaboration of industry. Germany has contracts to use French reprocessing facilities and temporarily store wastes at the power stations. It also has nuclear commitments with Britain. Thus a quick shut-down of nuclear generation would create difficulties not only with allies, but with the industry within German itself. Also it is not clear how the one-fourth of electricity produced by atomic plants would be recouped by other means. Nevertheless, the earlier government agreed in 2000 that the last nuclear plant would go offline by around 2020. In 2003 it switched off its first nuclear plant in Stade.

Chancellor Merkel's CDU favored allowing some nuclear plants to remain in use for their full operating times, up to 15 years, closing down early only those that are prone to breakdowns. Its FDP coalition partners favored building new reactors. Facing a global energy shortage, more and more Germans were willing to consider the nuclear option. But two minor accidents at nuclear power plants in Schleswig-Holstein in June 2007 and a further one in Vattenfall in July 2009 shifted public opinion once again in support of the phase-out. In 2009 only 17% favored continued use of nuclear power. In February 2010 the CDU environment minister declared that the age of nuclear energy is essentially over. That is music to Greens' ears.

The inability to expand nuclear power generation at a more rapid rate and to develop alternative sources, despite the fact that many government research subsidies are devoted to energy-related projects, prevents the FRG from improving the structural weaknesses of its energy position. It remains the highest per capita importer of energy and food of any major industrialized country.

Foreign Trade and Investments

Foreign trade remains the essential pillar of Germany's prosperity. It is the world's second-leading exporter after China, with 10.4% of the world market share. Its exports account for over half of its manufacturing jobs; 40% of its GDP is derived from exports, a fact that makes the FRG very sensitive to world economic climates. It has the advantage of not being overly reliant on the U.S. market, to which 7.5% of its exports flow, versus 40% of Japan's and 80% of Canada's. In fact, its trade with Central Europe doubled in value in the decade following the end of communism and now far outstrips that with the United States. More than 2,000 American firms have invested in Germany.

Export success has provided the FRG with enormous amounts of investment capital, much of which is invested in the U.S. Of the $300 billion German foreign investments in 1999, nearly 60% was in the U.S., compared with 19% in Great Britain, 9% in Italy, 5% in France. In the 1990s there was a surge of foreign investment by German companies. By 1999 Germany had twice as much capital invested abroad as foreign companies had invested in Germany.

Auto manufacturers employ one in seven of all German workers. To avoid high production costs, German auto makers, which make a third of the EU-15's cars, are cutting jobs and shifting production abroad. BMW built a factory in South Carolina. Daimler-Benz, which laid off thousands of workers, had a training program in "southern American English" before opening its plant in Alabama. In 1998 it entered a super-merger with Chrysler to create the world's third biggest automaker after General Motors and Ford (both of which have major operations in Germany). Within two years it was clear that this was not really a merger, but rather a takeover. Germans replaced Chrysler's top American managers. Volkswagen, which purchased the Rolls Royce factory

Atomic power? No thanks!
The Greens

(while BMW acquired the famous RR brand name), is producing in the Czech Republic and Mexico.

An estimated one million Americans work for more than 3,000 German-owned subsidiaries. Many may not even know it: A & P is owned by Tengelmann; Budd Car Co. by Thyssen (now merged with Krupp); Scientific American, Henry Holt, St. Martin's Press, and Farrar, Strauss & Giroux by Holtzbrinck publishing company in Stuttgart; Chicago's Spiegel mail-order house by Otto Versand of Hamburg; Clorox and Loctite by Düsseldorf's Henkel; Allis-Chalmers' agricultural equipment division by Klöckner of Duisburg; Celanese by Hoechst in Frankfurt (which also acquired Marion Merell Dow, Cargill Hybrid Seeds of Minneapolis, and French Rousel-Uclaf pharmaceutical). Bertelsmann, which already owned Bantam, Doubleday, Dell, RCA and Arista records, seven American magazines (including *McCalls*, *Family Circle*, *Parents*, and *Fitness*), and half of Barnes & Noble Internet bookselling service, bought Random House in 1998 to become the world's largest publisher of English-language books. Siemens, the Munich-based electronics conglomerate, the majority of whose employees work abroad, owns Westinghouse's nonnuclear power plant operations.

Global integration has brought an unexpected negative by-product to German companies. As Swiss banks discovered, expansion into the U.S. market makes foreign companies vulnerable to suits filed in American courts. In 1999 more than two dozen class-action lawsuits were filed against German companies that had used

Germany

slave labor (90% of whom were not Jewish) and had reaped profits from the Holocaust during the Second World War. Deutsche Bank admitted that it had financed the building of Auschwitz, and marquee names like Daimler-Benz, Volkswagen and Siemens were called to the dock.

A year later the Schröder government reached a settlement that created a special foundation that will pay up to $5 billion to the million survivors. Each will receive from $2,500 to $7,500. The deal fell short of full corporate immunity, but it called for the American government to urge courts to dismiss all class action cases and to advise plaintiffs to seek financial redress through the foundation. A cap on attorney payments was set at $50 million. Not only German, but also American, British and other European companies are being pursued. Their subsidiaries in Germany also allegedly used slave labor. They include GM, Ford, Chase Manhattan Bank, and J.P. Morgan.

The FRG has undeniable economic assets. It is located in the middle of Europe and has an excellent net of road, rail, water and air connections that tie it to all the world's major markets. It continues to enjoy a tradition of efficiency and quality production and service. When after World War I the victors wanted to place the loser's goods at a disadvantage, they required the words "Made in Germany" to be stamped in English on all German products. However, this measure boomeranged: German goods and services were of such high quality that purchasers did not avoid, but instead sought goods with those words stamped on them. To such quality must be added a well educated and well trained workforce and excellent English-language skills.

Labor, Unions, Employers' Organizations

The supply and cost of labor is a problem for Germany. For years, the FRG had a shortage of labor and even brought in "guest workers" from southern Europe and Turkey, now numbering about four and a half million. While a majority of these guest workers remain indispensable for many sectors of the economy in which few Germans care to work, they do present the FRG with immense and potentially explosive problems of social integration that will tax German ingenuity and tolerance for years to come.

Also, labor costs exceed those in the U.S. and are among the highest in Europe. Employees receive a 13th months' pay at Christmas time. At 35 hours (42 in the East), Germany had one of the world's shortest workweeks, but it is easing upward again as workers sacrifice to save

their jobs. The actual work week in 2009 was 41.2 hours (EU average: 38.6%). The average American worker works longer hours (1,900 versus 1,557 in Western Germany each year), 25% more hours in a year's time, and he receives twelve days of paid vacation versus six weeks and 13 to 16 holidays for the German. Social benefits applied to each American job are half as high as in the FRG, where they add 80% to basic wage costs.

In the past, productivity was raised to match rising labor costs, but the country's ability to do this in the future is clouded. It has a higher percentage of its work force in industrial production (28%, producing 30.4% of GDP) than in most EU countries, but its products are mainly the high-end and high quality kind that do not face much competition from low-wage economies. Its service sector has grown to 70% of the workforce, who produce 68.7% of GDP.

The FRG has a highly skilled labor force, and equally important, a high degree of labor peace, despite restlessness among frightened Eastern German workers faced with unemployment and retraining, and despite periodic tensions between employers' and employees' groups, which are called "social partners." Both vigorously represent their members' interests, but since the early postwar period when these groups cooperated closely to help the FRG recover from the war, they have both assumed that they share responsibility for the economy as a whole. The success of this partnership is seen in the facts that strikes are relatively few: from 1992 to 2001 Germany lost only nine working days a year per 1,000 workers to strikes, versus 22 in Britain and 48 in the U.S. Also wage contracts increased wages above the inflation rate, but not so high that inflation would be seriously stimulated. The latter fact has helped produce and protect Germans' prosperity.

After unification, East German unions merged with those in the West. The structure of labor unions (to which about a third of all workers and employees belong) helps to assure a great measure of labor peace. The 17 major individual trade unions each follow the principle of "one union, one industry." For example, instead of metal workers in the entire country being organized by many different and competing unions, any one of which can paralyze an industry through a strike, all metal workers who wish to join a union, join only one labor negotiating partner, not with many. All 17 unions then belong to the German Trade Union Federation (DGB) that, like all individual trade unions, is independent of political parties and religious denominations. The DGB

helps to coordinate trade union goals and activities, and is listened to very carefully by all German governments on labor matters. In addition to the DGB there are a few other trade union organizations, such as the Union of Salaried Employees (DAG) and the German Civil Servants' Federation (DBB). By law the latter is forbidden to enter collective bargaining and to call strikes.

Unions are on the defensive. To save jobs from being shipped abroad, they have become more pragmatic and flexible. They are composed largely of blue-collar workers in a white-collar world and are harder to organize. They are not attracting enough young Germans, and they were weakened by the recession and downsizing of companies' workforces. Union membership has fallen from about 30% of the labor force in 1991 to 20% in 2004; by 2008 it had lost 44% of its members since 1991. In the East, it has halved since 1990. Although their power is eroding, unions retain some influence, especially when the Social Democrats rule. After the 2002 federal elections, three-quarters of their deputies in parliament were themselves unionists. The unions could not prevent the earlier Schröder government from introducing its Agenda 2010 reforms, but they supported its being watered down a few years later by raising unemployment benefits for older workers.

Firms may choose to opt out of collective bargaining if their works councils agree, and 56% of Eastern workers and are outside of it compared with 35% in the West. On the other side of the fence are several hundred employer organizations, many of which are part of a larger umbrella organization called the Confederation of German Employers' Associations (BDA), which coordinates fundamental employer interests.

Another institution that helps to insure labor peace is codetermination (Mitbestimmung). In all but the smallest firms (those with fewer than five employees), all workers, including foreigners, 18 years or older can elect representatives to a works council, which has many rights, especially in social welfare and personnel matters. Workers in large companies also send representatives to the supervisory councils that are the control organs for the companies' management.

The exact composition of these supervisory councils has been and remains a hotly debated issue since the 1950s because of its implications for policy-making within the various industrial units. Workers elect half of the members in the large mining and steel companies and slightly less than half in other large companies. Despite the many disagreements, codetermination did provide a far larger scope for worker participation in decisions made in German firms than in most other countries, including the U.S. It gave labor more responsibility in the firms' policies and served as an important stabilizing element in the economy and society.

They are beginning to be seen as a relic and an impediment in a global economy. Critics say they have too much power and block firms from making the kinds of decisions necessary to maintain competitiveness. Worker participation has turned into self-serving union bureaucracy. In 2005 Volkswagen found itself entangled in a scandal amidst charges that managers had bought union leaders' support by paying for their foreign holidays and even prostitutes.

Agriculture

A final economic advantage is a fairly efficient agriculture in the West, which was able to produce about three-fourths of Western Germany's food needs. This is remarkable when one considers that before the war the Western part of Germany was predominantly industrial, whereas the Eastern part was the country's agricultural breadbasket. The main crops are flour and feed grains, potatoes, sugar beets, vegetables, fruits and wine, and most farmers also raise livestock, mostly cattle. Government-sponsored land consolidation schemes have raised the number of large and medium-sized farms considerably, although small farms still predominate in the West. Cooperatives, which link together about three-fourths of the Western farms, strengthen small farmers' competitiveness. Western German farmers exercise impressive political clout; they have been able to prevent the government from accepting in GATT negotiations freer trade in agriculture, which the Americans especially demand.

Agriculture was collectivized in East Germany in 1958, creating large collective farms and fields. Many former owners retained title to their land, but it was non-negotiable and therefore worthless to them. In the GDR, 12% of the workforce was engaged in agriculture, compared with only 5% in Western Germany. In 2010 only 2% of the nation's workforce was employed in agriculture, and they produced a minuscule .9% of GDP. Farmers in the East enjoyed certain privileges, compared with their countrymen in industry: they escaped the worst pollution, many had their own homes and private plots, they were heavily subsidized, and they enjoyed the time off and sick leave that private farmers in the West do not have. De-

spite the large scale of their farms, East German farmers produced only 40% as much per capita as their Western German counterparts, although they had made the GDR self-sufficient in food. Like everybody else in the East, farmers are undergoing a tortured transition to other jobs or to a forgotten form of private agriculture.

Present Economic Challenges

The greatest challenge the country faces is the worst economic downturn since the war. The danger that a disappearance of economic success could threaten democratic values applies more or less to all countries. But in the case of Germany it applies to a greater extent. Germany's first real experiment with democracy during the interwar years was rocked from the beginning by staggering economic problems, and the Weimar Republic finally fell in January 1933 in part because an economic depression had left more than six million Germans out of work. The FRG was able to win and maintain legitimacy in the eyes of its own citizens largely through its almost stunning economic accomplishments.

It wrestles the daunting challenge of absorbing a once bankrupt, unproductive socialist economy in its Eastern lands, whose people had been deprived of prosperity for four decades. It has proven to be more difficult than expected to stimulate Western investment in the East in order to create jobs and raise the standard of living.

Some question whether Germany can remain a competitive producer in the world economy. Its labor costs are among the world's highest (though they began to come down in 2005), its working year one of the shortest, its productivity below its peers in America and Japan, its social spending enormous. Among Germans 55 to 64 years of age, only 38% were still employed in 2005. The Merkel government realizes that this cannot be sustained. It is estimated that if nothing changes, the government would need 80% of the state budget in 2050 just to support the state pension system. Therefore the retirement age was raised to 67 for Germans born after 1970. The call for some economic "rethinking" is being echoed by some and vehemently rejected by others, who regard the status quo as a birthright, regardless of global economic realities.

Despite the problems, Germans are unlikely to alter their economic system in a fundamental way. Asked what the fundamental purpose of an economy is, most would answer "for social stability," while most Americans believe it exists to raise the living standards of persons willing to work hard and imaginatively. Few Ger-

mans want the social consequences of America's emphasis on efficiency and individual economic freedom, especially after the debilitating 2009 recession. They are willing to pay the necessary taxes to enable the government to alleviate the pain that capitalism can create.

Under Merkel's leadership, Germany is not the sick man of Europe. There is some positive news. It is still the world's fourth-largest economy and the biggest in the eurozone, with almost a third of its GDP. It was also the world's leading exporter until China overtook it in 2009. The economy is changing more quickly than at any time since the "economic miracle" of the 1950s. Its corporations have taken the lead in restructuring, trimming down their workforces and cutting unit costs in order to remain competitive and profitable. More than 30% of the nation's workforce now has temporary or part-time jobs, and this gives firms more flexibility.

A euro crisis that began in Greece in early 2010 ultimately forced Germany to be the largest contributor to a $110 billion eurozone and IMF bailout package to prevent Greece's debt problems from infected the rest of Europe. Two thirds of German public opinion was against this bailout, with *Bild* proclaiming in its headline: "Once again we are the idiots of Europe." Another headline read: "Greeks want our money." The left-leaning prestigious *Spiegel* even called for an abolition of the euro.

The prevailing view was that Germans had saved and sacrificed while the Greeks had lived beyond their means. Why should Germans, in effect, extend their welfare state to the Mediterranean? Further, post-war German democracy had won the citizens' consent by offering thrift and monetary stability within a context of consensual capitalism. This was based up the folk memory of hyperinflation wiping out life savings after each world war.

This time, there was little sense of solidarity with Europe. It seemed like Germans were being forced to choose between economic stability and European integration. Critics in Brussels talked of German selfishness and nationalism. But after much hesitation the Merkel government saw no alternative to joining the effort. After all, Germany benefits greatly from the euro. Almost half its exports are to other euro countries, and they produce 15% of Germany's GDP.

By 2010 its economy was stronger than it had been a decade ago. It was growing by 1.7% in 2010, with only 7.8% unemployment (higher in the East) and 1% inflation. Its budget deficit was an oversized 5.6% of GDP. But a Constitutional Court ruling requires that the structural deficit be cut to .35% of GDP by 2016. Job losses

Germany

The relaxed atmosphere ...

to offshoring slowed, and one German company was returning to Germany in 2010 for every three going abroad. Many companies are abandoning China.

CULTURE

One German Culture?

Germany is politically and legally unified, but the two sides have not yet formed a harmonious blend, and the resentments that separate West from East are deep. For decades Germans on each side of the Wall had assumed that they were basically the same, speaking the same language, reading the same literature, sharing the same historical and cultural traditions. They thought they knew and understood each other, but they were wrong. Germans are not psychologically unified, and so far a sense of national solidarity is lacking to complete the unification process. *Ostpolitik* expert Egon Bahr remarked at the time of unity: "we Germans got married in a hurry and enjoyed it. Now we must get to know each other. Normally it is the other way around, but, then, what is normal in Germany?" Foreign Minister Genscher liked to tell the joke about the Ossi (Eastern German) saying that "We are one people!", to which the Wessi (Western German) replies: "So are we!"

Many Western Germans believe they have inherited an unknown, problem-ridden country populated by German-speaking strangers. Eastern Germans, in turn, are baffled by the new Germany of which they are now a part and had expected more sympathy from Westerners than they have gotten. They are stunned to see how little remains of the society in which they grew up; Western German laws and traditions are so much the norm that many Easterners agree with psychologist Margit Venner: "This is not unification, it's an annexation!" President von Weizsäcker always says it best: "We cannot deny how

much still divides us. . . . The form of unity has been determined: now we must give it substance."

Visually the two parts are beginning to look more like each other. Although the East is still drab and polluted by comparison, it has undergone a face-lift. Facades of shops are being freshly painted and city streets refurbished. Stores are bountifully stocked with consumer goods, and Western firms, banks, and gasoline stations are opening branches everywhere. But anyone visiting both parts of Germany hears an earful about the other and quickly realizes that misunderstandings abound: Ossis are allegedly petty bourgeois, narrow-minded, provincial, ungrateful despite their outstretched palms, and want all the benefits of capitalism now despite the fact that they are lazy (a questionable impression given the fact that Eastern Germans created 300,000 new businesses in the first seven months of unity). By contrast, Wessis are seen to be rich snobs, arrogant, inconsiderate, insensitive, egotistical, distrustful, and less kind toward children. Many Eastern Germans suffer

from an inferiority complex in comparison to Western Germans, whom they find to be more decisive, independent, more open to the world, more confident, and more able to achieve and to master problems.

The economic disparity is enormous, although it is narrowing gradually. In 1992 East Germans earned half as much as West Germans in an economy with about 40% of the real output per worker. Per household the Easterners had half as many cars (to say nothing about the low quality of East German automobiles), deep freezers, and color televisions, 7% as many telephones, and a seventh as many automatic washing machines. In 1991 the average East German household had financial assets valued at DM20,000 vs. DM100,000 in the West. The *Bundesbank* noted, "the financial situation of the population in the new federal states is similar to the situation in Western Germany in the early 1970s."

They had only 27 square meters of living space per inhabitant (compared with 35.5 in the cramped West) in decrepit housing, 40% of which was built before the First World War. Although about 42% of East German housing was privately owned before 1989, the bad effects of rent control and centralized allocation were visible. The poor condition of housing was the price East Germans had to pay for having to spend only 3% of their disposable income on it. Toxic pollution and poor medical delivery kept East Germans' life expectancy lower than in the West: 69 years for men and 75 years for women, compared with 70 and 77 years in the West respectively. In a 2004 study of the German cities with the highest quality of life (based on prosperity, employment, communal finances, etc.), Munich came out on top. Not a single Eastern city, not even Berlin, placed in the top ten. How-

... in German schools

Baby Party of Germany

ever, there are clear indications that easterners' quality of life has been enhanced: they live on average six years longer than before 1989.

A 2007 *Spiegel* poll revealed that Eastern Germans are generally satisfied with their new Germany. Asked if they considered themselves "losers" after unification, only 20% aged 35 to 50 and 15% of those between 14 and 24 answered "yes." Asked if they would rather live in the East if the Wall were put back up, 37% of the older group and 35% of the younger group answered in the affirmative. However, these figures reflect the fact that a minority would prefer to live at home regardless of the regime under which they would have to live. What they miss most from the GDR is social security, the school system and protection from criminality.

However, one should not dwell exclusively on the differences. East and West Germans voted in much the same way in 1990, and many polls revealed similar opinions after unification: Both prize the same thing: high income. A total of 71% of Germans see the environment as the top priority, with 82% of Eastern Germans and 87% of Westerners favoring increased spending in that area. Both sides reject any suggestion of increased spending on the military, although rising crime, drug use, violence against foreigners, and soccer hooliganism prompt 40% of Eastern Germans, but only 22% of Westerners, to desire more respect for state authority, and 65% and 25% respectively to want greater police presence.

Two-thirds of Germans in both parts were "proud to be German," although Western Germans had a greater sense of being European than did their Eastern countrymen, who had been kept largely isolated. They generally agree who their favorite nationalities are: French, American, and Austrian, although the Easterners put the Austrians ahead of the Americans. They also dislike the same peoples—Poles, Turks, and Gypsies—although Eastern Germans' antipathy is somewhat stronger. Asked what country should be the new Germany's model, 40% said Switzerland, because of its "wealth and independence," and 29% said Sweden; only 6%, 8%, and 2% respectively cited the U.S., France, and Britain as their models.

Family Structure and Life

German society was already in a process of change when two different German societies were grafted together in 1990. For the third time since 1933, Germans in the East must adjust to a very different kind of society. From an earlier German society characterized by authoritarian behavior and institutions and by great social and economic differences among citizens has emerged in the West a predominantly middle-class society with widespread prosperity and with more opportunities and education and upward social mobility. Some of these changes are clearly reflected in important social institutions.

Particularly since World War II, the authoritarian family structure has given way to a more relaxed family organization.

This breakdown actually started during the Third Reich, when children were mobilized in activities outside the family and were even encouraged to report on their parents' opinions and behavior, if they veered from Nazi ideology. One now sees more and more permissiveness in the contemporary German family, and it is also fashionable in some middle- and upper-middle-class families for children to call their parents by their first names.

That this trend toward a less rigid family structure will probably continue is indicated by comparative polls. In 1953 a third of all young respondents between the ages of 13 and 24 indicated they would like to raise their children "exactly the same as I was raised." In 1975 the figure was only 14%. Also, 28% of young respondents indicated in 1951 that independence and free will were the values that should be stressed in the family, whereas 25% believed that obedience and deference were the most important values; in 1976 the corresponding percentages were 51% and 10%.

The combined effects of weaker religious beliefs, Marx's attacks on the family as "legalized prostitution," the former practice of favoring single mothers in the distribution of apartments, and the fact that 91% of women in the East worked, compared with only 51% in the West, contributed in Eastern Germany to considerable family differences compared with the West. In the preunification GDR, 32% of children were born out of wedlock, compared with 9% in the West. The divorce rate was a third higher in the East. Among the thousands of legal and social issues that had to be resolved before unification, very few were so controversial that no agreement was possible.

The most celebrated example was abortion, and the GDR's law permitting legal abortion on demand within three months was left in place there, while the West's more restricted Paragraph 218 applied in the old FRG. Polls after unification revealed that 57% of East Germans favored legal abortion on demand, compared with only 28% in the West. In 1995 a single law came into effect: abortions are illegal, but a woman who has one anyway will not be prosecuted provided that the abortion takes place during the first 12 weeks of pregnancy and she attends compulsory counseling geared to "the protection of unborn life." Abortions on medical grounds and in the event of rape are legal and are paid by the national health system.

A decade and a half after unification there still are two societies. Easterners have lower incomes and higher unemployment. Westerners still dominate business and government. Immigration into Western Germany, especially by the well

Germany

educated and creatively talented, continues unabated. Combined with a drastically low birth rate, the Eastern population is becoming dramatically elderly. At the current rate, there will only be 12 million people left in the East by 2020, down from 17 million in 2005. Even East-West personal unions are rare. In Berlin only slightly more than 2% of marriages are between partners from different parts of the city. It is believed that there are more mixed romantic relationships than friendships because friendships are based on similarities and love on opposites.

The Education System

A similar breakdown of authoritarianism is taking place in the schools. One sees very few traces of the former stern discipline. The school environment is relaxed, and pupils' relations with their teachers are often close and warm. Discussion and the free expression of opinion are generally encouraged, and discipline and orderliness are far less evident than in most American schools. Americans' most probable reaction when visiting a German school is that it is considerably more permissive than the schools to which they are accustomed.

Reforms since the late 1960s have attempted to open up the school system in the West to permit more working and lower class children better educational opportunities, as had already been done in the East. The unspoken model for some of these reforms has been the American school system, which has always been more oriented upon providing equal education opportunity for all rather than producing an academic elite. Since education is a state responsibility, there is considerable diversity in the school systems within the FRG. Roughly half of the children between the ages of three and six attend kindergartens, which are not a part of the state school system and for which fees are normally charged.

All children at age seven enter unified primary schools (*Grundschule*), which they attend for four years (six in Hamburg, Bremen and Berlin). After this, children enter one of three different kinds of higher schools. About 30% (compared with two-thirds in 1969) complete a five-year short-course secondary school (*Hauptschule*) until age 15. This used to be followed by three years of part-time vocational school combined with on-the-job training. But fewer and fewer *Hauptschule* pupils can become such apprentices (called *Azubis*—trainees) that lead to a marketable skill. In an intermediate school (*Realschule*), Another 30% (compared with about 22% in 1969) complete a course lasting six years leading to a graduation certificate (*mittlere Reife*), which permits persons to enter cer-

tain advanced technical schools and the medium levels of business and administration. Some continue on for a "limited" *Abitur* (called a *Fachabitur*), which then allows university-level study in a limited number of subjects.

The third kind of school, the *Gymnasium*, offers a more academically demanding nine-year course (although an increasing number of states are eliminating grade 13), aiming toward a diploma acquired by 45% of pupils by 2009. It is called the *Abitur*, which entitles one to enter the universities; 42.3% of all girls and 36.4% of boys between the ages of 18 and 21 attend (compared with 10% and 15% in 1969).

Critics argue that such a tracked system merely hardens class distinctions within the society by favoring the children of civil servants, salaried employees and the independently employed. In contrast to workers, these groups traditionally encourage their children to enter the more academically demanding schools, and to make financial sacrifices by entering their future jobs much later in life. There is no doubt that class background does heavily influence educational results. A child whose parents went to the university is four times as likely to attend a *Gymnasium*. In credential-conscious Germany, the secondary school a child attends, the exams he passes, and the degree he obtains classify him for life. On the other hand, one can argue that because German secondary schools have only a 7% dropout rate (one-third for Turkish immigrants), compared with about 25% in the U.S. and 45% in the U.K., and therefore prepares young Germans better for the workforce, the school system actually narrows social and economic differences more effectively than do the U.S. and U.K. Nev-

ertheless, certain reforms have been introduced that are praised by some and severely criticized by others.

First, some pupils in advanced classes are given state financial support in order to reduce the monetary burdens for poorer families, which longer schooling entails. Second, a "second educational path" was introduced for those pupils who later conclude that they made the wrong decision at age 11 concerning what higher school they should attend. This path involves demanding evening courses for three to six years, but these pupils with determination can receive *Realschule* or *Gymnasium* certificates and gain access to higher educational institutions.

A third reform was the creation in some cities of "comprehensive schools" (*Gesamtschulen*). Like the American high school, the comprehensive school combines all pupils under one roof, but nevertheless permits certain interior tracking for pupils with different interests and objectives. These schools were never widely accepted and are attended by only 5% of all pupils. Fourth, a far greater percentage of students has been allowed to attend the formerly elite *Gymnasium*, which is the essential way station towards the universities and well-paid, prestigious professions. A third of student-age Germans now study at the universities, compared with only 6% in 1950.

Elementary schools teach the new simplified spelling and grammar rules finally agreed upon in 1996, after 15 years of discussion, by the culture and education chiefs from all German-speaking countries. The 212 spelling and punctuation rules were dropped, and the peculiar "s-z" character was replaced by a double "s." The official dictionary of the German language, the *Duden*, has been revised accordingly. Confusion has reigned ever since.

Not surprisingly, this reform unleashed furious criticism in the land of Goethe and Schiller. Hundreds of writers, journalists and publishers signed petitions against it, and the German Academy for Language and Poetry called on teachers, editors, publishers and writers to ignore the new rules altogether. That fury simply will not die. In 2000 one of Germany's most prestigious newspapers, the *Frankfurter Allgemeine Zeitung (FAZ)*, decided to ignore the reforms officially introduced in 1999. Scholars and writers, such as Günter Grass, praised the paper, and some polls indicated that most Germans reject the changes. In 2004, *Der Spiegel*, the *Süddeutsche Zeitung* and *Bild* joined the bandwagon by returning to the old way of spelling.

While the education system has been considerably opened up, criticism against it still abounds. Some argue that the reforms have left too many traditional elements in place. Others counter that the reforms have greatly lowered education standards. With Western Germany's earlier economic success in mind, some foreign observers focus on four strengths of the German school system. First, secondary school pupils are educated according to their aptitudes. Second, they avoid overspecialization. They must show competence in at least 10 subjects before graduation and must achieve a minimum standard, judged by authorities from outside each school, in the core subjects of mathematics, science, German, and for all but the least able, a foreign language. Third, teachers are treated as members of the professional middle class, with high social status, the best pay in the world, tenure as civil servants, and a short school day from 8 AM to 1 PM.

Fourth, future workers are given career training. Three-fourths of all graduates (most who are not going to the university) spend at least three years in a rigorous apprenticeship working for a fourth of the normal pay under the guidance of a qualified "master." At the same time, they go a day or two a week to vocational schools learning the theory of their chosen trade. They cannot get a good job until they have served their time as apprentices and have passed a difficult practical and theoretical examination. Unfortunately in the 21st century there are too few apprenticeships to meet the demand, especially in the East.

Germans' pride in their educational system was hurt by a 2002 international comparison (PISA) showing that the quality of German education had slipped alarmingly relative to many other nations. In the three subjects studied—reading literacy, mathematics and science—German 15-year-olds placed 21st among the 32 leading industrial nations, behind both the OECD average and the U.S. A follow-up poll in 2003 revealed that 60% of Germans were "alarmed" at the findings, and 25% refused to accept them. The 2007 test results showed some improvement in international comparisons.

East German schools always tried to narrow social differences by merging tracks within the old German educational system and giving pupils a "polytechnic" education: one that brings all pupils into the working world for practical experience. Unfortunately, those schools also included heavy doses of propaganda in their curricula. Therefore, after unification in 1990 a shakedown began. Many schools were renamed so that their original names replaced their communist-inspired ones. Former textbooks were discarded and replaced by ones from the West. Courses on communist ideology were dropped, and

German students at the College of Europe, Bruges

the approach in civics and history courses was altered. Former teachers who belonged to the SED had to fill out questionnaires and survive a screening process to continue teaching.

When Russian was made an elective, rather than a required course, 90% of the pupils dropped it and picked up English instead. East Germans had never liked Russian, and very few ever mastered it despite the years they were compelled to study it. Studies in 1990 showed that their competence in English equaled that of Russian, even though their exposure to English in school had been scant. Of course, thousands of teachers of Russian had to be hurriedly retrained to teach English. A study of schools in both parts of Germany a few weeks after unification revealed astonishing similarities in kids' attitudes and cast doubt on the effect of intense communist propaganda over 40 years. In both parts of Germany, children wanted an "interesting job," safe from economic ups and downs, and with maximum free time; both preferred free enterprise and believed that pay should be linked to performance; they were not interested in political activism; and English was their foreign language of choice.

A third of young Germans (36% in 2009, compared with 41% in the U.S.) attempt university studies, a fourth of them to universities of applied science (*Fachhochschulen*). The extremely rapid increase in pupils who finish the *Gymnasium* has led to serious overcrowding at the universities. For instance, the University of Mu-

nich has an official capacity of 25,000, but 63,000 are enrolled. At the Free University of Berlin 60,000 students occupy 29,000 places. No wonder 27% of all students (half in the social sciences) give up before graduation. Only 23% of an age group finish the university, compared with the OECD average of 36%. Those who finish at the M.A. level have an average age of 28.

Although more than 20 new universities have been built in the West since the mid-1960s, students have great problems receiving admission to the programs and universities of their choice. Budget cuts prevented the universities from expanding their staffs to cope with the high numbers of students. Many students are highly dissatisfied with the lack of sufficient facilities and staff. This problem is exacerbated by the fact that the average student now spends 13 semesters at the university before taking final examinations, thereby strengthening the *ewiger Student* (eternal student) image.

The university system, designed by Wilhelm von Humboldt in the early 19th century is not suited to an era of mass education. There is much justification for the students' complaints of declining higher education due to sharp spending cuts (from 1.32% of GDP in 1977 to only .92% in 1997), a doubling of university enrollment (to more than 1.8 million in 1998) in the same period, overcrowded classes in poorly maintained university buildings, understocked libraries and computer centers, and unconcerned professors, who in some institutions are outnumbered by as many as 600 students to one. The ratio of faculty to students is almost four times better in the U.S. and Britain than in Germany.

In an attempt to deal with some of these problems, a four-year degree similar to the American bachelor's was introduced as an alternative to the generally six-year *Diplom* (Diploma), which Germans claim is higher than the American or British equivalent. This was part of a Europe-wide decision, called the Bologna process, by 29 science ministers in 1999 to introduce the Anglo-American system of separating bachelor's from master's degrees. By 2009 most of the old diploma curricula had been changed.

Professors hired since January 2002 receive less pay than their older colleagues, but they are entitled to performance-linked bonuses to encourage them to do better. In 2004 the Schröder government launched an "innovation offensive" to try to improve the quality of research and learning. Discussion focused on how to develop the kind of "elite universities" one finds in the U.S. This is difficult to do in a country like Germany with a tradition

Germany

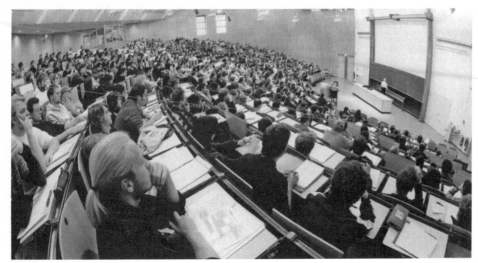

Overcrowded German Universities, Munich Technical University

of state funding and control. Fund raising and high tuition are anathema, as is the notion that all universities would not be equal in prestige and support. The government decided in 2004 to provide added funding for the country's 10 leading universities and research centers.

With the looming prospect of unemployment even if they complete their studies, students reject talk of paying tuition or shortening their study time. The states, which are responsible for education, complain that they lack the money to solve the problems. They call on the federal government to help, but it claims to have empty pockets because of the weak economy and the costs of unification. To spur students to finish on time, Baden-Wurttemberg introduced fees in 1999 of 500 euros (approximately $700) for every half-year of study after six-and-a-half years. This cut the number of long-term students in half. In 2005 the Constitutional Court ruled that universities are allowed to charge tuition. Most western German states have levied 500-euro annual tuition fees, but they remain controversial, and the universities never know if they will be dropped by nervous state governments. East German universities have no fees, but still only 4% of western students chose to move east to study. In part because of all these problems, only six German universities are among the top 100 in the Shanghai rankings; Munich is the highest in 55th place.

In order to offer an alternative to the crowded universities, the first private German universities were founded in Witten-Herdecke, Koblenz and Ingolstadt. Modeled largely after American private colleges, the future of these private universities remains uncertain, but 44 of them had been founded by 2004. An extension

of Touro College from New York opened its doors in Western Berlin. It is the first Jewish-affiliated college in Germany, and about half of its students are Jewish.

The increasingly restricted job market that awaits students after they finish their studies exacerbates their uneasiness. Until well into the 1970s, an economically booming FRG, with expanding industries and financially strong and generous state treasuries, could absorb almost all university graduates. In 1974–75, for example, 85% of university graduates were given public service jobs. Those prosperous years are gone, and the paucity of jobs in the East darkens employment prospects even further.

Religion

About 90% of Western Germans belong to Lutheran Protestant or Catholic churches. Protestants and Catholics are divided roughly equally in the Western part of the FRG although they are not evenly dispersed throughout the country. In general, the North is predominantly Protestant, whereas the South and the Rhineland are predominantly Catholic. The East was traditionally solidly Protestant; only 6% of East Germans are Catholic, compared with 43% in the West. Thus, a united Germany became more Protestant. The churches' hold over the school system has long since been severed, and there are few denominational schools left. Religious instruction is, however, offered in the schools on a voluntary basis and in separate classes for Protestants and Catholics. Beginning in 2010 Muslim pupils are required to attend Islamic religious education as a regular subject, taught in German by teachers educated at German universities.

There is no clean separation of church and state in the FRG as in the U.S. The

opening words of the Basic Law remind Germans of their "responsibility before God and mankind," and two-thirds of respondents in a 2000 poll favored keeping God in their constitution. Politicians take oaths invoking God although they are free to delete such references, as did Gerhard Schröder and half of his cabinet in 1998. Crosses are hung in all but 12 of Bavaria's 40,000 classrooms. Both major churches, and since 2002, the Central Council of German Jews receive funding from a church tax (a tax surcharge of 8%–9%) that the state collects with the income tax. This amounted to $7.8 billion in 2000. The state also pays the salaries of all bishops and archbishops, though not of priests, and about three-fourths of the teaching costs in church schools. Since German Jews were granted equal standing with Protestants and Roman Catholics, there is increased state financing for Jewish schools and other institutions.

A person may be excused from paying the tax if he officially leaves the church of which he is a member. Such a step used to bring a person social or professional handicaps. A doctor or a kindergarten teacher could be denied employment at a church-related hospital or kindergarten because he had formally left his church. But this is the exception today, and more people are formally leaving the churches. Nevertheless, about two-thirds pay the tax, which provides the Churches with two-thirds of their income.

By the 21st century the proportion of Catholics who attend church regularly had fallen to 14%, less than half as many as 25 years ago. Among Protestants, it had shrunk to only 4%. Attitudes sometimes change when it is time for a baptism, wedding, or funeral, or when children are being raised. However, the number of church weddings and baptisms had also declined by a third in both faiths over the last three decades of the 20th century. From 2008, couples who have a church wedding no longer have to undergo a second civil ceremony afterward.

The churches were the only institutions to survive the Third Reich practically unscathed although the Lutheran church admitted in 2000 that it had used forced laborers during the Nazi era. It agreed to pay $5 million to a compensation fund. The Catholic Church said that only two of its communities had used such labor in cemeteries and that it had no plans to pay into the fund. The churches have contributed significantly to establishing a moderate and compromising political culture. Mindful of the horrors of Hitler's rule, Germans still retain the Christian foundations of their society.

However, questions remain concerning the extent to which they should actively

Germany

enter the political arena. The Protestant Church was very visible in the "peace movement" in both parts of Germany. It was particularly important in the East, where the communists had officially encouraged atheism, but where churches were tolerated if they did not meddle in politics. Protestants could not agree with the latter stipulation, and their church became a sanctuary for growing oppositional groups in the 1980s; because of this, young people took a new interest in it. In the GDR it opposed the militarization of society through military education in the schools. It advocated a right of conscientious objection that did not exist in the GDR. Under the banner of "Swords to Plowshares" it opposed all countries' arms buildups.

It brought into the limelight the GDR's first massive, organized opposition to the regime by protecting it and providing it with meeting rooms and a podium for all persons interested in a critical dialogue. It supported civil courage to question the regime and urged dissidents to remain in the GDR to build a better country. It made bold and articulate demands for freedom. Perhaps most important, it succeeded in keeping the revolution against the SED regime nonviolent. The Leipzig demonstrations every Monday, which broke the back of the regime in the fall of 1989, always began in the Nikolai Church with a "peaceful God's service." It was there on the critical date, October 9, that the call for nonviolence, penned by symphony conductor Kurt Masur and five others including clergymen, was proclaimed. In the noncommunist government that ruled the last half-year of the GDR's existence, Protestant clergymen were the largest single professional group in it.

Catholic bishops and priests, especially in Bavaria, have not been above trying occasionally to influence the voting of their parishioners through messages from the pulpit. Yet the strength of religion as an influencing factor in politics and society has declined greatly. It has little bearing on voting. Only about a third of the Catholics and a tenth of the Protestants in the West attend church regularly, and most of those who do have become largely secularized. In April 2005 Cardinal Joseph Ratzinger from Bavaria was selected to be the new Pope, Benedict XVI. Many German Catholics rejoiced even though his doctrinal views are far more conservative than mainstream Catholic opinion in Germany.

That rejoicing has become much more muted as scores of cases of sexual and physical abuse are coming to light in Catholic institutions all over Germany. One of the most conservative Catholic leaders, Bishop Walter Mixa, resigned amid allegations he routinely flogged kids decades ago. Corporal punishment in Germany was banned in the 1970s. Over 200 former pupils of a prestigious Jesuit secondary school in Berlin, the Canisius-Kolleg, phoned a hotline to report prior abuse. The statue of limitations bars prosecution for abuse that occurred decades ago. But this has embroiled the pope since he had been an Archbishop in Germany while some of these offenses took place. Thousands of Catholics are leaving the Church. The diocese in Freiburg lost more than 5,300 parishioners in March 2010 alone, and 56% of German Catholics say they have lost all confidence in the Church.

There are differences in religious beliefs between Germans in the two halves of the country: Only 7% of Eastern Germans say they believe in life after death, compared with half of Western Germans. Two-thirds of Eastern Germans were either never baptized or left the church, compared with only 7% in the West. While most Western German children go through religious confirmation ceremonies, Eastern Germans had a secular "youth dedication" (*Jugendweihe*) ceremony. As a part of the Eastern nostalgia wave in the 21st century, the "youth dedication" has returned for about half of the young people (80% in some areas), albeit in de-ideologized form.

Before the Third Reich there were about 600,000 Jews living in Germany. At the war's end, there were 1,500 who survived in hiding, 9,000 were alive in concentration camps, and 15,000 survived by marrying non-Jews. There are now more than 200,000 Jews, 20,000 of them in Berlin. This constitutes Europe's third-largest Jewish population after France and Britain and the fast-growing. In Berlin there are seven synagogues, Jewish preschools and a high school, cemeteries, social service agencies and retirement homes. There are 89 synagogues in the entire country. As a further sign of the renaissance of Germany's Jewish community, its largest synagogue, with space for 1,200 persons, reopened in Berlin in 2007. It had not been fully destroyed in the November 9, 1938, Crystal Night anti-Jewish rampage because it was located in a courtyard surrounded by the houses inhabited by non-Jewish Berliners. The Nazi arsonists were afraid to completely torch the synagogue for fear of burning the houses too.

In 2002 Germany passed Israel as the leading destination for Jewish immigrants from the former Soviet Union, over 19,000 in a single year. Over time twice as many Jews from the former Soviet Union settled in Germany than in Israel. This prompted the government to limit the entry of such Jews from 2006 on. About half have joined an established Jewish community, and three-fourths depended upon welfare assistance.

They come because Germany offers them citizenship and automatic government benefits. They face challenges in integrating. Many do not speak German; many are near or past retirement age; and most of their academic degrees are not recognized. Some top physicians from Russia are not allowed near a patient. There are other complications because rabbis do not recognize as many as 30% of them as Jews because their mothers were not Jewish. When the head of the Central Council of Jews requested the government to remove "improper Jews" from the applicants, the Foreign Ministry refused,

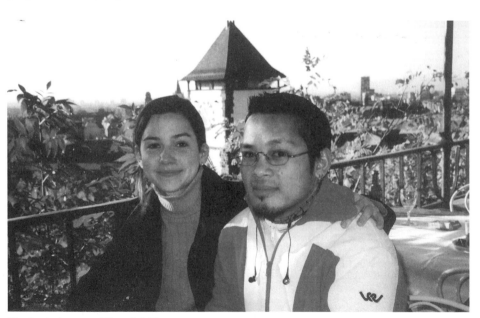
Students in a multi-racial Germany

271

Germany

THE NEW YORK TIMES, SUNDAY, SEPTEMBER 23, 2001

The people of Berlin stand by you.

In memory of September 11, 2001

Our hearts are with the victims and their families.

We feel solidary with all Americans in this dark hour.

We in Berlin will never forget what you have done for us.

You were there when we needed you.

And now we will be there for you when you need us.

Detlef W. Prinz, PrinzMedien Berlin
Klaus Groth, President and CEO of the Groth Group
Peter Dussmann, Chairman of the Board of Dussmann AG
Dr. Eric Schweitzer, Member of the Board of ALBA AG
Theodor Baltz, President and CEO of MedienKontor Berlin
Rafael Roth, President and CEO of Kurf rstendamm Karr e
Dr. Volker Hassemer and Dr. Wolfram von Fritsch, Partners for Berlin
Dr. Thomas Guth, Chairman of the Board of Dr. Joachim Schmidt AG & Co.
Dr. J rg Franke and Holger Timm, Chairmen of the Board of Berliner Effektengesellschaft AG

vowing that never again would Germans determine who is a Jew.

There are anti-Semitic graffiti and street attacks. Most appear to be committed by Muslim youths. However, the commander of the elite special-forces army unit was dismissed in 2003 for publicly agreeing with remarks made by CDU member of the *Bundestag*, Martin Hohmann, who argued that if Germans were a "race of perpetrators" because of the Holocaust, so too were the Jews because of their role in terror associated with the Russian revolution. Polls in 2005 revealed that 80% of German respondents are "angry" about how Israel treats Palestinians. An astonishing 50% even share the view that what Israel is doing to Palestinians today is "in principle" nothing else than what the Nazis did to the Jews during the Third Reich.

In an effort to prevent the two countries from drifting apart, Chancellor Merkel took eight members of her cabinet to Israel for a joint session with the Israeli cabinet in March 2008. In a highly symbolic gesture, she became the first postwar German leader ever to be invited to speak before the Israeli parliament. She said that "for me, Israel's security will never be open to negotiation. . . . Whoever threatens Israel also threatens us."

There are 3.2 million Muslims (about 4% of the total population). The 2.5 million of Turkish origin (120,000 in Berlin) are the largest. There are sizable communities from former Yugoslavia, Iran and Iraq. They worship in mosques all over the country although virtually all imams (religious leaders) active in Germany are foreigners, some holding short-term visas. In an attempt to defuse tensions, the German government supported the creation of a Central Council of Muslims to represent the interests of Muslims in the country. The Constitutional Court ruled twice in 2003 that a Muslim teacher in Stuttgart and shop assistants could not be fired for wearing headscarves to work. Nevertheless, three *Länder*, including Baden-Württemberg, passed laws in 2004 banning teachers from wearing Muslim headscarves in state schools.

Attitudes toward America

Perhaps nothing is more noticeable for visitors to the FRG than the attachment of Germans, especially youth, to anything that is American (except in politics). On the radio, one hears far less German music than American and British. For young singers, sales outside of Germany were more important than nationalist urges. Even the CDU's 1990 electoral campaign was sung in English: "Feel the power, touch the future, reach the heart!" However, by 2005, German-language groups had made a comeback, capturing 49% of music sales. When in February 2008 Germany's hottest young group, Tokyo Hotel, performed in New York, they were mobbed by frenzied female fans.

There is seldom an evening in which an American television show cannot be seen. Jeans, T-shirts and jogging shoes are worn by young Germans, who crowd into fast-food chains such as McDonald's and Burger King, which one finds in every city of any size. Their parents often shop in large supermarkets or shopping centers or fill their cars' tanks at gasoline stations that seem to offer everything from groceries and magazines to car washes. An estimated 85,000 Germans, inspired by Karl May's novels, belong to American Indian clubs. A "pow-wow" in Essen attracted 6,000 Germans in 1994. They came with native garb and paint on their faces, calling themselves names like "Old Powderface."

German is the most widely spoken native language in the EU and is the language of almost a fifth of all books worldwide. However, by the 21st century, only 1% of the world's published scientific

A Turkish grocer in Hamburg   Courtesy: German Information Center

VW ad about its cars' *"Fahrvergnügen"* (pleasure to drive) was riding high until a wise-guy added a "t" in the middle.

Many German protest movements, such as those against war, for women's and minorities' rights and in favor of environmental protection, are largely based on American examples. Yet, despite the undeniable and seemingly irresistible attraction which many Germans have toward aspects of American culture, there is anti-Americanism in the FRG. Traditionally it was only among the militant leftist circles that it would come blatantly to the surface. Anti-American sentiments were largely silent among a part of the politicized youth and left-leaning intellectuals. That has changed. Anti-Americanism is associated with criticism against certain American policies, such as high military budgets, seeming disregard for international institutions and law, the death penalty, the availability of handguns, apparent indifference to global warming, or the Iraq war, policies that are also criticized in the U.S. Anti-Americanism should not be seen in terms of a general aversion against the U.S. or its people.

Criticism of America is sometimes a general way of expressing anticapitalist, antigrowth attitudes. It can involve cultural rejection of globalization, "Anglo-Saxon liberalism" (free-market economics), and a scientific and technical civilization the U.S. seems to represent. It is also an outgrowth of a conflict between generations. On the one hand is an older generation in the West which admired American democracy and prosperity and which has never forgotten the Marshall Plan and the U.S. defense of

works are written in German. Thus German scholars publish their work in English if they wish to be read outside of Germany. More and more university classes are taught in English, theses and dissertations are being written in English, and colleagues at German-based research centers increasingly communicate with each other in English.

American slang has mightily invaded the German language, and young people, businessmen and scholars seldom express themselves for long without using some English words. But, unlike many French, most Germans do not seem to be distressed by this lingual invasion.

The Financial Times quoted the deputy editor of the daily *Die Welt*, who discovered that one could write German articles while using hardly any German words: "Unser Way of Life im Media Business ist hart, da muss man ein tougher Kerl sein. Morgens Warm-up und Stretching, dann ein Teller Corn Flakes und ein Soft Drink oder Darjeeling Tea, dann in das Office— und schon Brunch mit den Top-Leuten, meeting zum Thema: Sollen wir die Zeitung pushen mit Snob Appeal oder auf Low Profile achten? Ich habe den Managern ganz cool und businesslike mein Papier presentiert: Wir müssen News powern und erst dann den Akzent auf Layout und Design legen, auf der Front Page die Headline mehr aufjazzen und die Deadline beachten. Für jede Story brauchen wir ein starkes Lead. Der Cartoon muss gut plaziert sein. Das Editorial muss Glamour und Style haben, unsere Top Priority bleibt: Action und Service!"

The business community has accepted terms like "service center," "flat rate" and "fax" with no problem although a survey

revealed that 85% of Germans did not understand one company's slogan, "be inspired." Sometimes companies go too far in adopting English. For example, a cell phone is called a "handy." The first time they hear it, Anglo-Saxons invariably have to ask what that is. The Internet has brought many terms that have stuck, such as "log in" and "scan." But even Americans have adopted some German words that they mix with English, such as "love fests," "music fests" and "spin meister." "Ersatz" is used to describe a negative substitute. Some German words fail when introduced into English. For instance, the

273

Germany

Cem Özdemir, Green co-chair

West Berlin in the late 1940s and 1950s. One TV journalist said at the time of unification: "We had help from the Americans, who had thought carefully about what should become of Germany, and this enabled us to make something of ourselves." Helmut Kohl frequently told campaign audiences in the East that if the Americans had occupied them, their lives would have been as democratic and prosperous as in the West.

On the other hand, a younger generation grew up amidst material prosperity and talk of détente. Their political consciousness was shaped at a time when the shock waves of severe racial tension in American cities, the Vietnam War and Watergate were being felt outside the U.S. In Eastern Germany much propaganda had been directed against America, but polls reveal little anti-Americanism there.

Much of the anti-Americanism is rooted in protest against the prevailing culture of the westernized Germany. It has been linked with longings, observable in other Western European countries and the U.S. as well, to drop out of a highly competitive, urbanized society oriented toward comfort, economic prosperity and individual success, and to adopt alternative forms of living, which are poorly defined. More recently it has involved escaping the fierce economic competition globalization has created. Thus, anti-Americanism is less a political call to arms against the U.S. than it is a code word for a change of values among a part of contemporary German younger people that embodies a conflict among several cultures within the FRG itself.

Of course, emotional disagreements on international events and the unpopularity of an American president can color attitudes, at least temporarily. That was the case in the aftermath of the U.S.-British war against Iraq in March–April 2003, which was extremely unpopular in Germany and elsewhere in Europe. In a Pew Global Attitudes poll in May, only 45% of Germans expressed a favorable view of America, and 75% of those who disapproved cited as the reason personal animosity toward former American President George W. Bush, who was unusually unpopular in Europe. In 2007 only 19% said they had confidence in him. Almost 60% of respondents said they wanted looser ties with the United States. In 2005, only a third expressed gratitude for the help the U.S. had given Germany after the Second World War. The outrageously nonobjective films and books of U.S. filmmaker Michael Moore sold well in mainstream German society, and conspiracy theories flourished. A national poll in 2005 revealed that one of five Germans (one-fourth of the young) believed that the CIA was behind the September 11, 2001, attacks.

How rapidly such negative attitudes can change was shown after Barack Obama became president in January 2009. By April, 89% of Germans believed that with Obama the U.S. was "again on the right path," three-fourths "wished they had politicians like him in Germany," and 63% saw America in a positive light again.

One frequently hears clichés in Germany about Americans: that they always chew gum, are fat, loud, generally dress tastelessly (in loud colors), are fanatic joggers and sports addicts. Some Germans find that many Americans are shallow, unilingual, uncultured, slightly naive and politically uninformed about the rest of the world, even though Americans seem to have an almost missionary desire to spread the American way of life. Yet, opinion polls reveal different, more positive descriptions of Americans: that they have a good business sense, are individualistic, energetic, patriotic, progressive and technically talented. Less than a fifth of all Germans consider Americans to be ill-mannered or ruthless, and only 4% consider them to be insecure.

Americans and Germans mingle rather well with each other although there are differences between them. Like some other European nationalities, Germans tend to be more private than Americans. They often do not know their neighbors and are more apt to put fences around their houses to insure their privacy. They also observe certain social conventions that somewhat slow down the development of intimate social contact.

For instance, the German language has two different words for "you." The German says *Sie* if he wants to keep formal and at a distance and *Du* if he wants to be more familiar. The English equivalent of a formal "you," Thee, fell into disuse years ago, even among small religious sects that had retained it. In Germany, colleagues who have worked with each other for years might still address each other as *Herr* (Mr.) or *Frau* (Mrs.). *Fräulein* (Miss) has fallen into disuse because there is no male counterpart, and there is no German equivalent to Ms.

However, the usage of *Du* and *Sie* has changed over time. For example, everybody of student age says *Du* to each other. Employees at some relatively egalitarian companies, such as Ikea, or in left-wing parties use *Du*, whereas law firms, banks and the government bureaucracy prefer *Sie*. It was big news when the two top politicians in the governing center-right coalition, Angela Merkel and Guido Westerwelle, agreed to say *Du* to each other.

Europeans, including Germans, are uncomfortable about answering such personal questions when one first meets as where one works, for whom one voted or how one acquired a certain painting or piece of furniture in his abode, questions the American generally feels free to ask in order to open a conversation. This is not to say that Germans do not form firm friendships. They certainly do, even if it takes longer to do so. But while Germans seem to like the more relaxed American manner, they do generally recognize and mildly criticize the superficial aspect of Americans' personal interaction. Unlike most Americans, Germans tend not to call other people by their first names and to use casual expressions like "drop by sometime," unless they really mean it and wish to give an unmistakable signal of friendliness to a person.

Foreigners

The FRG was highly successful after 1945 in absorbing and integrating more than 14 million German refugees and expellees from East Germany and the former Eastern territories. Now Germany is faced with the very difficult problem of integrating racially and culturally diverse groups of non-Germans.

Because of Germany's economic prosperity, political tolerance, liberal asylum laws, and constitutional guarantee of asylum "for persons persecuted on political grounds," it has become a magnet for refugees, although it does not accept as high a percentage of immigrants per capita as does the U.S. Also, in the 1950s and 1960s, West Germany recruited southern Europeans, particularly Turks, in order to overcome severe labor shortages in low-paying jobs. Together with about 120,000 foreigners in Eastern Germany, foreigners now number about 6.7 million, or approximately 8% of the population (12.7% of the working age population); these figures are down because over a million took German citizenship from 2000–5 and are no longer considered foreigners. All but 3% live in the West. In 2005 the largest group was Turks (2.5 million), followed by a million from the former Yugoslavia, Italians (558,000), Greeks (346,000), and Poles (286,000). Their numbers are rising because of their far higher birth rate and because members of their families are arriving from their countries of origin to join them. One fourth of all newborns have a foreign parent. By mid-century half the population will have non-German origins.

Most foreigners intend to stay in the FRG forever. Relatively few of them accepted governmental bonuses to return to their countries. Of the children born in Germany in 2008, 38% have an immigrant background. In cities with more than 200,000 inhabitants, 45% of children under age 15 have such a background. Although an estimated 20% of foreigners were born in Germany, few were granted citizenship. For example, of the 2.5 million Turks in Germany in 2008, about a fourth (700,000) are German citizens; among the total immigrant population, 950,000 have acquired citizenship. Turks are especially hesitant to give up their Turkish citizenship because they would become ineligible for inheritances in Turkey.

The federal government vowed to change Germany's citizenship law. After a furious debate that focused especially on initial plans to permit dual citizenship, parliament accepted an amended law in 1999 that nevertheless represents a landmark overhaul of the 1913 citizenship law. It cuts the link between German blood ties and nationality. Beginning in 2000, children born in Germany to foreign parents were granted German citizenship if at least one parent has lived legally in Germany for eight years or longer. These chil-

dren can hold dual citizenship until age 23, when they must renounce their foreign citizenship if they choose to retain their German one. No naturalized citizens may hold dual citizenship. In gratitude for this law, about 95% of Turkish-German citizens vote SPD.

Foreigners are especially concentrated in certain large industrial cities, where they sometimes constitute a majority in poorer sections of the cities and serve as convenient scapegoats for certain alarming urban ills, most notably, rising crime. For example, foreigners constitute a quarter of Frankfurt's residents. Unemployment rates for them are double the national average and rise to 43% in Berlin; 40% of their youth have acquired no vocational qualifications; among Turkish men, that figure is almost three-fourths. A third of young children come from immigrant families. Although most Germans are disgusted by antiforeigner violence, most seem to believe that the number of foreign residents has become too high.

Glasnost in the Soviet Union seriously affected emigration. In 1989 alone, 377,000 ethnic Germans from Eastern Europe (especially Poland) and the USSR joined 344,000 Germans from the GDR and the steady stream of non-German refugees into the FRG. This was the largest wave of ethnic Germans entering the FRG since 1949, and the influx continued in 1995, when 218,000 entered. The sudden outpouring temporarily swamped the procedures in funds. All compete for limited accommodation and employment and, as polls and city elections show, are testing Germans' patience. About two million Germans remain in the former Soviet

Union. Many of these also wish to emigrate, even though it is not easy for them to adjust to working and living in a less protective state like the FRG.

Ethnic Germans from Eastern European countries, enjoy an open-door immigration policy, and 700,000 ethnic Germans from outside of Germany poured into the country in the year following the collapse of the Berlin Wall; many could speak no German. By 1997 the numbers of both asylum seekers and German resettlers had declined dramatically. In 2002 Germany received 91,416; this was about 7,000 fewer than the year before.

There is one group, numbering 60,000 (40,000 in Saxony and 20,000 in Brandenburg), that speaks a Slavic language but is not foreign: the Sorbs. They have lived in Eastern Germany since the 6th century. Their unique language and customs are legally protected. The extent of their successful integration was demonstrated in May 2008 when Stanislaw Tillich, a Sorb, was sworn in as Saxony's minister-president. He finished his oath of office by repeating the words "So help me God" in both German and Sorb.

Turks display a greater resistance to social integration than do other nationalities. This was not helped by Turkish Prime Minister Recep Erdogan's visit to Germany in February 2008. He urged them to remain aloof from German society, arguing that assimilation is a "crime against humanity." Turkish children should be able to learn in Turkish-language schools and at a Turkish-language university on German soil. Many Turks responded positively to this message, but he quickly wore out his welcome in other quarters.

View of Berlin's Unter den Linden boulevard with the Brandenburg Gate at upper left.
Courtesy: German Information Center

Germany

turn to their homelands when the GDR collapsed. It is noteworthy that xenophobia in the East is stronger among young people than among older, whereas the opposite is true in the West.

The former general secretary of the CDU, Laurenz Meyer, also made an unfortunate remark in 2000 that enflamed passions: "France has a predominantly French culture, Italy the Italian. Why shouldn't we have the German defining culture [*Leitkultur*] in our homeland?" German feelings on the subject of foreigners are ambiguous. A 2006 poll revealed that a third of respondents believed that "too many foreigners" are living in Germany. Another 27% "rather agreed." Asked if they were "very" or "somewhat" concerned by the rise of Islamic extremism, 82% answered "yes," compared with 77% in Britain and 76% in France. However, only 7% of Muslims agreed that suicide bombings were "often" or "sometimes" justified. In Germany 51% of Muslims thought "many" or "most" Europeans were hostile to them, compared with 42% in Britain and 39% in France.

Many Germans blamed the untenable situation partly on Article 16 of the Basic Law, which granted political asylum to all who claim it. It had been inspired by the fact that many German anti-Nazis had been saved during the Hitler era because they found asylum in democratic countries and by the fact that thousands of Jews perished because other countries had turned them away. In 1993 the government and opposition SPD agreed to revoke Germany's liberal asylum law. Asylum seekers arriving from countries Germany has declared to be free of political repression are automatically denied refuge. Border patrols have been tightened. Economic migrants are no longer treated as refugees, and illegal migrants are immediately expelled.

Germany no longer receives half of all asylum seekers in Europe. In 2003 for the first time in two decades, more foreigners asked for asylum in Britain than in Germany, whose number was about 50,000. By 2007 that number had fallen to 19,000, the lowest in 30 years. However, the numbers were up by 15% the next year, due mostly to an increase in Iraqi applicants. Only about 1% of the Iraqis are granted asylum, but about a third are given refugee status, meaning that they can remain temporarily. In general, only a small minority of applicants is granted permanent sanctuary. One political result is that the right-wing parties continue to be demolished at the polls. Like many other EU countries, Germany had, in effect, adopted a zero-immigration policy. The year 2008 saw the lowest number of immigrants obtaining German citizenship since unification in 1990.

The hesitancy to become an integrated part of German society creates particular problems in the schools, where the percentage of foreigners in classes sometimes rises to over 50%. Thus, Germans must tackle the problem of bilingualism in the schools, of resultant lowered standards in the classrooms, and of an increasing inclination on the part of German parents to avoid sending their children to schools in which there is a high percentage of foreign children enrolled. This is an extremely delicate problem for a country that tries very hard to be tolerant, compassionate and just. By the mid-1990s many Turks had ascended to the middle class, and 37,000 run their own businesses. 15,000 study at universities, and Turks have become lawyers, software experts, and a member of the *Bundestag* and now co-chairman of the federal Green party, Cem Ozdemir. He is the first person from an immigrant background to became a party chairman.

Fears that the FRG might become swamped by foreigners persist, and the federal and land governments have found it necessary to warn against xenophobia, which is strongest in the East, although only about 2% of the population there is foreign. The GDR was a far more isolated society, so its people had far less contact with outsiders. Also, the Communist regime in the GDR had never accepted responsibility for the crimes of the Second World War, so its citizens had not grown up with the same feeling of guilt toward wrongs done to other peoples, such as the Jews, as people in Western Germany had been. About 100,000 guest workers had been sent there from communist countries like Angola, Cuba, Vietnam, and Mozambique, and many refused to re-

This created serious long-term problems for Germany, which needs new immigrants each year to fill out its shrinking labor ranks. About half of university-educated females have no children, and 51.1% of university graduates are female. Nevertheless, in 2010, only 69.7% of women worked (more in the East), up 6% since 1990. However, of women aged 25–49, more work part time (39%) than full time (34%). Few make it to the top: only 10% of the board seats and 5% of senior management positions in the biggest companies are occupied by women. The wage gap is 23%, among the widest in the EU. They are hampered by the facts that only one in five children under three can get a place in a day-care facility (only 9% in the West) and that school ends at 1 PM.

Mothers may return to their jobs after three years, but they often find that they have lost ground to men, who earn one quarter more in full-time employment than women. Few top jobs in business are held by women. Every third woman with a job works part time, which is a serious career killer. The *Financial Times* of London estimated in 2005 that in terms of promotion equality in the workplace and work-life-balance, German women are a decade behind the rest of Europe and at least 15 years behind the U.S.

The worst thing is that the birth rate had fallen by 2008 to only 1.37 children per woman. In 1960 German women bore 1.3 million children, but only 680,000 in 2005.

"Cats" playing in Stuttgart

The average first-time mother is almost 30. By 2050, half of the population is expected to be of retirement age, and Germany's population could fall from the present 80.9 million to only 65 million. To help working mothers manage work and newborns and to encourage middle-class and well educated women to bear more children without abandoning their careers, "parents' pay" linked to their salaries is granted for 14 months; either parent can take up to 12 months off. Means of assisting unmarried couples and single mothers have also been devised. They still face problems with the schools, which are oriented around the stay-at-home mom: school is usually out at 1 PM, and provisions have to be made to care for the kids the rest of the day.

Two-thirds of Germans, according to a 2005 poll, favored tougher limits on immigration. This negative feeling is an important reason why two-thirds also opposed the eastward expansion of the EU. Their fears that they would lose their jobs to a flood of immigrants from the East prompted the government to negotiate a seven-year transition period before the labor market would be open to citizens of the new member states. The sentiment was so strong that politicians, most of whom supported EU enlargement, feared tackling it head on. Former Chancellor Kohl had spoken for many when he declared: "Germany is not a country of immigration." Chancellor Merkel did admit that Germany had become such a land. But to enable potential immigrants to integrate better, a new law in 2007 requires spouses from non-EU countries to acquire a basic knowledge of the German language before they are permitted to join their partners in Germany. Turks especially felt offended by this requirement.

In May 2004 Germany adopted its first-ever immigration law. Proponents argued that the country needed to attract educated specialists to keep the economy competitive and stimulate excellence in research. Former Chancellor Helmut Schmidt said in a 2004 interview: "There is almost no area where Germany stands out with its achievements." The law is a compromise that reflects the view that immigrants are risks and recognizes the widespread fear of opening the borders to political and religious militants. Although it makes it easier for skilled workers to come, it rejected a point system that would have permitted highly qualified foreigners to enter without an employment contract. Only those with a contract in hand may come. Employers must also continue to demonstrate that no German citizen can do the job that is being filled. It contains a long list of anti-terrorist and anti-extremist measures and gives the government greater leeway in ar-

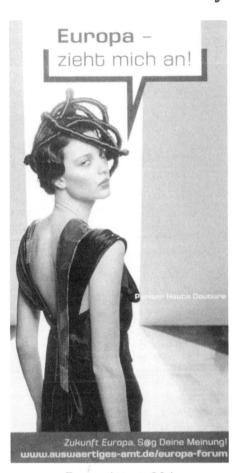

Europe Attracts Me!

resting and deporting undesirable foreigners. Thus although for the first time Germany has defined itself as an immigrant society, it remains difficult for foreigners to work or settle in Germany.

The Media

Germans are relatively well-informed. Roughly three-fourths of all adults read at least one of the wide range of daily newspapers although Germans under age 30 are less likely to read a daily than those over 40. The total number of independent dailies has declined. Most are regional papers; 76% of German readers by a local paper rather than a national one. More and more newspapers and magazines have become concentrated in publication groups, and the majority of dailies are no longer editorially independent.

The largest such group is that controlled by Axel Springer, who produces about 25% of the total national output of daily newspapers. This includes the most widely read daily, the *Bild-Zeitung* (literally "Picture Newspaper"), a sensationalist mixture of conservative politics, crime, sex and gossip, and read by more than a fourth of all adults. With a circulation of almost five million, it is the world's larg-

Germany

est-selling newspaper outside of Japan. Even this boulevard newspaper shares Germans' postwar restraint. When the German and English soccer teams faced each other in the semifinals of the European championships in 1996, British tabloids displayed headlines like "Watch Out Krauts!," "Achtung! Surrender," and "Filthy Hun!" German papers refused to respond in kind, and the Germans went on to win the cup.

The Springer enterprise also publishes one of the four informed, serious, nationally distributed elite newspapers, *Die Welt*. In a trial run it introduced a smaller tabloid format called *Welt-Kompakt*. The others are the best-selling among quality newspapers (with a circulation of 431,000 in 2008) slightly left of center *Süddeutsche Zeitung* (published in Munich) the next-best selling moderately conservative *Frankfurter Allgemeine Zeitung* (circulation 361,000 daily copies), and the outspoken left-liberal *Frankfurter Rundschau*, which has lost money for years and may not last long. The authoritative *Handelsblatt* is the German counterpart to the *Wall Street Journal*, and Britain's *Financial Times* has a German-language edition. The lively *taz* aims at an alternative audience. Most are having to shed staff, reduce pages, switch to tabloid formats (such as the *Berliner*), or be sold to other owners (*eg.* the *Süddeutsche Zeitung*) in order to survive.

The political party press no longer plays a significant role as it did in the Empire and Weimar Republic days. The CSU puts out its weekly *Bayernkurier*. Also, the PDS continues to publish the daily *Neues Deutschland*, which has changed greatly from its dogmatic SED days; it reports news more objectively and is free to criticize some PDS policies. All other newspapers in the GDR had been censored and controlled at least indirectly by the Communists. In 1991 they were put on the auction block, and all but two of the 15 Eastern German dailies were sold; the Trust Agency intervened to ensure that they did not all fall into the hands of the four major media magnates.

West German publishers bought the East German regional papers and gave them a new look. But none of Western Germany's newspapers caught on in the East; only one-eighth of the total circulation is Western. *Berliner Zeitung, Freie Presse* (Chemnitz), *Sächsische Zeitung* (Dresden), *Mitteldeutsche Zeitung* (Halle), and *Volksstimme* (Magdeburg) are widely read.

There are widely read weeklies. The highly influential *Der Spiegel*, with 5.9 million readers and one million copies sold weekly in 2008, originally modeled itself after America's *Time*. Now it is far more opinionated, investigative, critical and crusading in its reporting. In the words of

Child star in *Good bye, Lenin!*, Nico Ledermüller

The Economist, it "has probably done more to raise German blood pressure over the years than any other single publication." Its website has overwhelmed all rivals. Its staff controls the magazine and in 2008 dismissed its long-serving editor, Stefan Aust. *Stern*, with seven million readers and declining, is also investigative (some would say "muckraking"); since 1983 it has sported a black eye for publishing faked Hitler diaries, for which it had paid a fortune. *Die Zeit* is intelligent and politically moderate.

In 1993 three new weeklies entered the market to challenge the supremacy of the established news magazines. *Focus* has an American-style format and includes short news items and heavy use of graphics and glossy color photos; it has six million readers, but is slipping. *Die Wochenpost*, a serious journal founded in the GDR in 1953 and bought by *Stern* after unification, has been revamped. It emphasizes on-the-spot reporting and includes long articles. It is a favorite among intellectuals in Eastern Germany, where 80% of its copies are sold.

Public radio and television are administered by nonprofit public corporations that are financed chiefly by monthly fees paid by those who own televisions or radios and by limited advertising. There are nine regional radio-TV corporations, which combine to form the "Association of Public Broadcasting Corporations" (ARD) in the Federal Republic. The ARD sponsors the first TV channel, televised nationally, and the third channel, televised regionally. It also encompasses the two radio corporations, the *Deutschlandfunk*

(Germany Radio), which broadcasts within all of Europe in German and 14 other languages, and the *Deutsche Welle* (German Wave), which transmits on short and medium wave all over the world in more than 30 languages. *Deutsche Welle* also has a televised version in German, English and other languages.

A second German television channel, based in Mainz, transmits nationwide on the second TV channel. In order to insure that the radio and TV corporations remain politically independent, their legal basis is in state laws, and they are overseen by broadcasting councils composed of representatives of all important political, ideological, social and religious groups. Although they are duty-bound not to favor any particular political party, their programming and the appointments to their councils and management do sometimes become subject to controversies among the parties.

Since the 1980s ARD's and ZDF's ratings have dropped significantly as private TV channels capture a larger and larger share of the audience. For example, 56% of young people age 14 to 29 watched private channels in 1995. A growing number of adults watch a private all-news channel (N-TV) similar to CNN, and Phoenix, which is equivalent to C-Span. Private TV provides a lucrative market for U.S. companies; of the foreign programs purchased by German networks in 1997, almost 90% were American.

Artistic Traditions and Theatre

Germany has a glittering cultural tradition, but Nazi rule drove its cultural elite abroad, especially to the U.S. Germany has never regained its earlier preeminence. It can still claim a reputation for music, however. It has 72 orchestras and music theaters in the West, generously subsidized by the states or cities. Some are highly regarded internationally, such as the Berliner Philharmonik, the Sinfonieorchester of Munich, the Stuttgarter Kammerorchester, the Bach-Orchester of Munich and the Berlin Amati-Ensemble.

An American, John Cranko, who died in 1973, helped Stuttgart to develop into a ballet center equal or superior to Munich. In 2005, American John Neumeier became the managing director of the Hamburg Ballet, where he produced over 130 ballets and put Hamburg on the world ballet map. Carl St. Clair from a small Texas town became music director of the Komische Oper in Berlin in 2008. He had been music director of the Pacific Symphony in Orange County, California.

Many foreign musicians such as Ingrid Bjoner, Evelyn Lear, Jess Thomas, Tomas Stewart and, it should not be forgotten, the Beatles, received their first significant stage experience in the FRG. Since the 1980s Anglo-Saxon musicals, especially those composed by Sir Andrew Lloyd Weber, have become popular. For example, by 1995 three of his shows had run for eight years in specially rebuilt theaters: *Starlight Express* in Bochum and *Cats* and *Phantom of the Opera* in Hamburg. *Cats* and *Dance of the Vampires* played to full audiences in Stuttgart in 2002. Major cities in the GDR also enjoy an excellent quality of performing arts.

In painting and sculpture no postwar German artists have been able to establish a distinguishing German style that is internationally recognized as such. The FRG does have many artists who produce recognized works in styles coming from abroad. This is particularly visible in pop-art and hyperrealism, movements that emanated from the U.S.

In literature, German writers after 1945 strove to make a clean break from the past. In their writings they tried to come to grips with their nation's experiences under dictatorship, in war and in postwar misery. In the 1950s and 1960s, though, new themes emerged, which focused on the materialism and egotism of a prosperous society. Many German writers became unmistakably political in their writings and, in a few cases, in their public involvement. The best known of such writers in the West are Heinrich Böll and Günter Grass, a Nobel prize winner in 1999. Böll, who in 1972 became the sixth German to win the Nobel Prize in Literature and who died in 1985, wrote with grace and simplicity. He was an avowed moralist, who was in the forefront of the "peace movement."

Grass' German is full, rich and imaginative, and through his fantasy characters he bitterly criticizes the shortcomings of his society. He is a staunch if critical supporter of the SPD. He campaigned actively for the party and even wrote about his electoral activities in a book, *From the Diary of a Snail*. He was a man who relentlessly impressed upon his countrymen the moral necessity of not evading the memory of the Third Reich. It therefore came as a shock when he admitted in *Peeling the Onion* late in life that, as a 17-year-old boy, he himself had been a passionate Nazi and had even served in the Waffen-SS. His unit had the unusual assignment of trying to rescue Hitler from his Berlin bunker. He ended up in an American POW camp disliking his victorious and well-fed captors.

In 2009 Herta Müller won the Nobel Prize in Literature. She was largely unknown both abroad and outside of literary circles in Germany itself. Born in 1953, she grew up in a German-speaking city in the Banat region of Romania, where her thoughts and ideals collided with the rigid communist regime. She emigrated to Berlin in 1987. Her novels deal with the challenges of living in a dictatorship. Among her four novels translated into English are *The Land of Green Plums* and *The Appointment*. Her last book in 2009 published just before she received the prize is a masterpiece about life in Soviet labor camps: *Everything I Own I Carry With Me*.

Much of contemporary Western German literature is characterized by anxiety, malaise, self-doubt and social criticism. The German public had also been receptive to another kind of critical literature, namely that coming from Eastern Germany, where some of Germany's best postwar writing originated. GDR authors like Stefan Heym (who had been an American Army major during the war), Christa Wolf, Ulrich Plenzdorf, and Jurek Becker, were widely published in the West. They were popular enough to disregard the simplicity of "socialist realism," and to criticize certain characteristics of the SED state. Wolf was criticized for withholding some of her criticism of the regime until after the GDR's fall, when she published *Was Bleibt* (What Remains), written ten years earlier, describing how she was watched by the secret police.

German theatre survives because of massive state subsidies. They totaled 8.2 billion euros in 2003: 45% from the localities, 43% from the states, and 12% from the federal government. That comes to 99 euros per capita. Ticket sales yield only about 15% of theatres' income. Only about a fifth of Western Germany's 300 theaters are privately owned. While many persons argue that state support enables more artistic guidance, rather than commercial ambitions, government cuts are hitting the arts hard. In 1993 two of Berlin's most famous theaters, the Schiller and the Schlosspark, were closed. Several dramatists have won international recognition, such as Heinar Kipphardt, Franz Xaver Kroetz, Martin Walser and Peter Weiss.

Germany

NR. 41 1.10.2009 Deutschland € 3,20
Österreich € 3,50 / Schweiz CHF 6,–

Mit TV-Pro

Arme Sieger
Kein Geld für Wohltaten:
Wie Merkel und Westerwelle
das Land regieren werden

Paare erzählen: Wenn die Liebe im Schweigen untergeht

Merkel and Westerwelle, poor victors, no money for good deeds

Rolf Hochhuth's play, 'The Representative,' dealing with Pope Pius XII's attitude toward Hitler's extermination of the Jews stirred up much impassioned discussion after the war; this gives an idea of how Germans searched their souls to understand their recent past.

The works of several East German authors, such as Peter Hacks and Ulrich Plenzdorf, were played with much success on Western stages. East Germany had succeeded in maintaining a high standard of theater. Bertolt Brecht had returned there after wartime exile in the U.S. and provided an important impetus to it. Af-

ter 1989 Eastern German theater has been able to become more experimental.

Until the mid-1960s it appeared that the German reputation in film, established before the war by such directors as Fritz Lang, Ernst Lubitsch, F.W. Murnau, G.W. Pabst and Leni Riefenstahl (who died in 2003 at age 101) would be lost forever. The first two decades of postwar productions were mainly provincial, unproblematic entertainment films, which could be summed up in one German word: *Schmalz* (corniness). The need to compete with television for viewers helped keep the level of films low. Between 1956 and 1976,

the annual production of German films and the number of cinemas dropped by 50%. Even today, about a fourth of all films shown in the FRG comes from the U.S. and a fifth from Italy and France.

Partly because of the 1968 Film Promotion Measures Act and a Film Promotion Agency (FFA), which channels state subsidies to producers of feature, documentary, short and youth films, a wave of creative filmmaking, known as "the young German film," emerged in the 1960s. Federal funds, including its start-up loans, combine with a host of regional funds, to dispense more than 200 million euros ($260 million) each year. A federal fund created in 2007 provides about 60 million euros ($78 million) more.

German directors in this wave have succeeded in winning international recognition. They include Alexander Kluge, Volker Schlöndorf, Johannes Schaaf, the late Rainer Werner Fassbinder, Hans Jürgen Syberburg, Bernhard Sinkel, Margarethe von Trotte and two directors who particularly like to place their films in American settings, Werner Herzog and Wim Winders. However, since they often fail to attract sufficiently large audiences, the federal government decided to curtail funding for heavily experimental and purely artistic films after 1983.

A refreshing exception to social criticism in film is Doris Dörrie, a self-assured young director. She went to the U.S. to become an actress, but instead she studied film and theater in California and New York. In her box office success, *Männer* (Men), the characters laugh about themselves and each other, and their laughter is contagious for the audience. She reflects the waning ideological inclinations of contemporary Germans: "I grew up with pop concerts, not with political discussions. The fact that I do not deal with big political themes is directly linked to that."

Some German producers learned to thrive on the American market, such as Wolfgang Peterson, who did *The Perfect Storm*, and Roland Emmerich, who produced the ultimate American flag-waving film, *The Patriot*. In 2003 a film directed by Caroline Links, *Nowhere in Africa*, won an Oscar for best foreign-language film. This came 24 years after Volker Schlöndorff's film, *Tin Drum*, won the same award.

A banner year for German film was 2003 when two blockbusters hit German theaters. *Good bye, Lenin!* is a bittersweet comedy of a young man who recreates the former GDR in the bedroom of his sick mother. She had gone into a coma just before the Berlin Wall fell and would die of shock to know that her socialist paradise no longer existed. The fond memories of the GDR delight audiences, especially in the East. Directed by Wolfgang Becker, it grossed $40 million in one year and dominated the European Film Awards.

Germans had a different emotional experience in 2003 when they saw "The Miracle of Bern," directed by Sönke Wortmann. It retells the story of Germany's come-from-behind victory in the soccer World Cup in 1954. The victory had unleashed a tremendous wave of emotion in a Germany still recovering from defeat and devastation. It was the first time in decades that Germans were recognized in the world for nonaggressive achievement. It was a "feel-good" film with the message that one can feel proud of Germany and also sympathize with the millions of Germans who suffered during and after the war.

The same cannot be said about the 2004–5 international hit, *Downfall*, a troubling film by Oliver Hirschbiegel portraying a humanized Hitler in his Berlin bunker during the last five days of his life. Some Germans and Americans argued that it was inappropriate to show Hitler as a human being, who was polite and considerate toward his female staff and willing to kiss his mistress Eva Braun on the lips.

Another good year for cinema was 2007, when Florian Henckel von Donnersmarck's film, *The Lives of Others*, won the Oscar for Best Foreign-Language Film. It is about a Stasi officer who oversteps his orders and covers up for his victims. Von Donnersmarck lived six years as a child in New York and two later years in St. Petersburg learning Russian. In 2010 Michael Haneke's *The White Ribbon* won the Palme d'Or at Cannes and an Oscar nomination for Best Foreign-Language Film. This stark black-and-white film explores the culture and society out of which National Socialism grew.

Eastern Germany's film industry was centered in the DEFA film production studies in Potsdam-Babelsberg. Founded in 1946, it was the site of the entire GDR film industry and included a college for film and TV and an agency for film exports and imports. Before 1989 it had annually produced about 20 feature films, 25 TV films, 170 documentaries, and many animated films. In 1992 Volker Schlöndorf stepped in to rescue the Babelsberg studio, acting as its business manager and attracting investors. By 1996 it had again become one of the world's most advanced film facilities, producing more than one feature film a month, as well as soap operas and TV dramas. Its fortunes soared when the studio complex was sold in 2004 to Filmbetriebe Berlin Brandenburg. Two experienced media and real estate managers, Carl Woebcken and Christoph Fisser, took over the management.

In 2007 it had a record year, producing a dozen major feature films and lots of profit. Some movies with international stars were made there. They included Matt Damon in *The Bourne Supremacy*, Tom Cruise, who played Hitler's hapless assassin Claus Schenk von Stauffenberg in *Valkyrie*, and Clive Owen and Naomi Watts in *The International*.

FUTURE

Some of the myths that surrounded postwar Germany have been broken, such as an economic miracle and a prized education system. Social and economic conditions in the new Germany are more polarized than in the old West Germany, and the political environment is less settled and predictable. Some postwar certainties are disappearing: the U.S. is weaker, NATO and the EU are more unwieldy, and Russia is less predictable. Some are worried about unemployment and the prospect that their living standards will not be sustainable. Easterners are especially unsettled by economic uncertainty. Although most have a higher standard of living than before 1990, others are waiting for the upturn they were promised. Some Westerners have long since lost patience at having to shoulder the expense of unification, with no end in sight. The worst economic recession since the war exacerbates these fears, as does the government's unpopular decision to join in an expensive eurozone bailout of Greece.

Seen in perspective, Germany's problems are relatively minor compared with those it faced in the 1940s and 1950s. By world standards, it has an efficient economy, especially in the West, a good track record for achievement, and a well-trained work force in the East to fall back on. None of its current difficulties threaten to derail democracy. In an April 2009 poll, 68% judged the political system favorably.

As a fully sovereign, unified nation, it shows more independence in its foreign policy, as its refusal to support the U.S.-British war in Iraq demonstrated. Berlin's partners welcome the shift from restrained passivity to restrained activity. Germany is more active on the global stage than it has ever been since 1945. That will continue.

Germany's allies, including the U.S., will not always be happy with its stronger sense of independence and willingness to talk openly of the national interest now that the Cold War is over. But it will remain a conscientious partner in NATO at the same time that it promotes a unified Europe and some form of European defense identity.

Although "continuity" was the Merkel government's foreign policy promise, she focuses on Germany's international policy. She played a central role in breaking an acrimonious stalemate over the EU budget, thereby enhancing her prestige both abroad and at home. She repaired relations with the U.S., Germany's Eastern neighbors and Russia. Her foreign policy was more Atlanticist that it had been under her predecessor. It does not put the highly institutionalized Franco-German relationship so far above other bilateral links, especially with the UK and U.S.

In May 2008 Merkel was awarded the prestigious Charlemagne Prize of Aachen. She is a realist who cultivates a refreshingly unpretentious style both at home and abroad. As a negotiator, she has a very sharp eye for the common ground, the ability to break complex problems into manageable pieces, a command of obscure technical details, and the instinct to go for a deal rather than to risk failure by not budging from her own demands. She has shown the ability to put herself in the shoes of every player and to create the right atmosphere for cooperation. She listens to everybody, not just the leaders of the big states.

Her victories are impressive: she engineered an agreement on an amended "Lisbon Treaty" to replace the failed EU constitutional treaty. She got her EU partners to agree on goals for reducing greenhouse gas emissions, and she was able to narrow the gap between Europe and the U.S. on global warming. It is almost entirely because of her leadership that a poll by Britain's GlobeScan in April 2008 recorded a dramatic improvement in Germany's image in the world. An average of 56% in the 23 countries surveyed thought it was "mostly positive." This was the highest in the EU and higher than the United States. This was repeated in 2009, when a BBC survey found Germany to be the most popular country in the world: 61% of respondents found its global influence to be positive, and only 15% negative.

Merkel deals with the U.S. in a way that she can say no without alienating it. For example, she publicly criticized American detention policy at Guantanamo Bay while on an official visit to Washington. She would also never use opposition to the U.S. as an election ploy. In her first government declaration, she appealed: "Let the battles of the past lie. Those battles have been fought." She maintains a rather stiff but constructive relationship with the popular American president, Barack Obama.

Her government works with all its strength for a close, honest, open and trusting relationship in the transatlantic partnership. She is less forgiving of Russian leader Vladimir Putin than was her predecessor. But Germany's dependence on Russia for 34% of its oil and 45% of its gas limits her flexibility. She is the first

Germany

chancellor to speak Russian. She opposes Turkish entry into the EU as a full member, preferring instead a "privileged partnership."

Her greatest challenges are in economic and domestic policy. The Greek debt crisis that emerged in the spring of 2010 threatens both the euro and European banks, including Germany's. Her participation in the massive bailout of Greece is not appreciated by most Germans. Her Christian Democrat-Free Democrat coalition government suffered a stinging defeat in the country's largest state, North Rhine Westphalia in May 2010. The CDU there dropped 10 percentage points, and the FDP won less than half of its record 14.6% in the September federal elections. This ended her electoral winning streak and cost her government its majority in the upper house, the *Bundesrat*. Her party's minister president of Hesse also stepped down, while another minister president, Christian Wulff of Lower Saxony, vacated his position to become president after the sudden resignation of Horst Köhler. Since Merkel had supported another contender, Labor Minister Ursula von der Leyen, Wulff's narrow election after three rounds of voting could be interpreted as a sign of her growing weakness in the party apparatus.

In her first term, she was by far the most popular German leader in the history of the Federal Republic. By election time in September 2009, that popularity had declined somewhat. But she had been more consistently popular than any other chancellor since Konrad Adenauer. This is particularly remarkable considering that she was in power during the worst economic crisis in the Federal Republic's history. Polls in June 2009 showed that 78% thought she had done well as chancellor, and 58% wanted her to remain in her job. One year later, she was still Germany's most popular politician, with 48% satisfied with her. However, her party had fallen to 30% in the polls. The FDP was under 5%, thanks its tax-reduction proposals that few Germans think the country can afford. This compares badly with the 48% they received together in the 2009 federal elections.

The 1998 elections had brought an entirely new generation of leaders to power, one that has no memory of the Nazi era. The young rulers in their 50s governed from Germany's former imperial capital, a dynamic city that is steeped in history. All were graduates of the 1968 protest movement. A similar generational change occurred in 2005, when those same 1968 protestors, led by Schröder and Joschka

Fischer, were ushered out of the front ranks. They were replaced by younger, more pragmatic and less ideological leaders, who entered politics after the collapse of the Berlin Wall in 1989. This includes especially Angela Merkel. The 2009 elections were the first that saw an even younger generation of voters, one that had no personal memory of the fall of the Berlin Wall in November 1989.

Despite a popular Chancellor Merkel, many Germans still find themselves in the grips of a malaise. They realize that the formulas that worked so well for their country in the decades after the Second World War are no longer working as well. They cannot accept bold reform, and too many reject even timid change.

However, the year 2009 was one of glorious anniversaries. On May 23d, the Basic Law and the Federal Republic itself turned 60. Never in their history have Germans been so free, so peaceful, so prosperous and so admired in the world as during these six decades. And they can enjoy this success together: November 9th was the 20th anniversary of the fall of the Berlin Wall. Twenty-nine heads of state and governments from Europe and Russia gathered in Berlin to remember that world-changing event.

Cooperation at the top: Barack Obama and Angela Merkel

282

Republic of Austria

Area: 32,369 sq. mi. (83,835 sq. km.).
Population: 8.28 million (2006).
Capital City: Vienna (Pop. 1.55 million).
Climate: Alpine. Temperate, with rainy days from late October to mid-December. Snowfall begins in the mountains in mid-November, with the air clear and the days cold but sunny.
Neighboring Countries: Czech Republic and Germany (North); Switzerland and Liechtenstein (West); Italy and Slovenia (South); Hungary and Slovak Republic (East).
Official Language: German.
Ethnic Division: German (98.1%); Croatian (.7%); Slovene (.3%) other (.9%).
Principal Religions: Roman Catholic (85%); Protestant (7%); other or none (8%).
Main Exports: Machinery and transport equipment, consumer goods, chemicals, food, drink and tobacco, paper products.
Main Imports: Machinery and transport equipment, consumer goods, chemicals, raw materials, food, drink and tobacco.
Principal Trading Customers: EU (72.6% of exports and 79.3% of imports), Germany (31% of exports and 41.5% of imports), Italy (8.9% of exports and 8.2% of imports), U.S. (5.1% of exports), Switzerland (4% of exports and 4.4% of imports), France (3.2% of imports).
Currency: euro.
National Day: October 26 (1955), when U.S., Allied and Soviet occupation was ended.

Chief of State: Heinz Fischer, President (since July 2004).
Head of Government: Werner Faymann, Chancellor (since June 2008).
National Flag: Three horizontal bands—red, white and red. Flags may also have the national emblem, a double-headed, black eagle, centered in the white band.

Austria is a landlocked Alpine country. Three-fourths of its territory, particularly in the West and South, is covered by some of the most majestic mountains in the world. About the size of Maine and twice the size of neighboring Switzerland, it is but a small piece of the huge, multinational Austro-Hungarian Empire that collapsed in 1918. It was always a hub for North-South European traffic, and the Danube River, which flows from southern Germany through northern Austria and Vienna, through Eastern Europe and empties into the Black Sea, has always been an important transportation link between Eastern and Western Europe.

This nation borders more countries than does any other Western European land. About three-fourths of Austria is embedded geographically within what has been known since World War II as Eastern Europe; this fact made the former Soviet Union particularly interested in Austrian neutrality. It also has made Austria a natural meeting place for leaders of Eastern and Western Europe, as well as a land of refuge for several hundred thousand Eastern Europeans since 1945.

Austria is a country of truly extraordinary natural beauty. Its snow-capped peaks overlook lush green valleys, countless streams and lakes and picturesque mountain villages. Austria is filled with architectural reminders of its imperial past. Everywhere one sees elaborately decorated baroque churches, imposing castles and palaces, and large, serene monasteries and cloisters. Every major city, especially Vienna, has rich museums and elegant theaters that keep alive the artistic tradition of the country. Also, more than a dozen musical festivals take place in Austria every year, the most famous being in Salzburg. These testify to a creative musical past almost unparalleled in the entire world.

The visitor is greeted by a people who are relaxed, friendly, hospitable and strongly traditional, especially outside the capital city of Vienna, where about one-sixth of the country's population lives. Almost nine out of ten of its people are Roman Catholic, and 99% speak dialects of German that have a distinctive and pleasant musical ring to them. There are three small language minorities in Carinthia, where 20,000 Slovenes live along the border of Slovenia, and in the Burgenland along the southeastern border, where 25,000 Croatians and some Hungarians live. Small Czech and Slovak minorities have also survived in Vienna. There are about 750,000

Austria

foreigners in the country, 9% of the total population. Many are from former Yugoslavia and Turkey.

In some ways Austria is strikingly similar to neighboring Switzerland. Both are naturally beautiful and economically prosperous countries. Despite a high degree of cultural diversity, both are politically stable democracies. Both are federal states, although Austrian politics are more centralized than is the case in Switzerland. Both pursued neutralist foreign policies. Yet there are also undeniable differences. Whereas centuries ago the Swiss established a secure national identity, Austrians until recently lacked a clear consensus on what it actually meant to be an Austrian. Also, in Switzerland a stable democracy was able to evolve slowly and was therefore able gradually to gain the backing of the overwhelming majority of its citizens. By contrast, Austria remained a highly stratified and traditional country until well into the 20th century and has confronted an almost traumatic change of its political, social and economic practices and values.

HISTORY

The Early Period

Historical evidence indicates that what is now Austria has been settled since the late Ice Age almost 1,000 years before Christ. Indications of earlier human presence are uncertain. Between 35 and 15 B.C. the Romans conquered the Celtic inhabitants and divided the area among three Roman provinces. The new masters gave the region many of the same benefits they bestowed on other lands: Roman law and administration, a well-developed network of good roads, aqueducts and new forms of agriculture, including wine-making. They founded most of Austria's cities, such as Vienna, Salzburg and Linz, and between 150 and 350 A.D. they introduced Christianity.

When the Roman Empire began to crumble, the area that is now Austria became vulnerable to invasions by Germanic, Hun and other tribes, which brought much destruction to the area from the 5th through the 8th centuries. Not until Charlemagne established a bulwark in the extreme eastern part of his huge empire in 799 did the area become relatively stable and secure. He called this area his East March (frontier), whose present name in German, Österreich, reflects the area's earlier role. From 799 on, Austria's destiny was very closely tied to that of the rest of the Germanic world.

Part of the Holy Roman Empire and Hapsburg Rule

Austria became a part of the Holy Roman Empire in 962 and a few years later the House of Babenberg began its 270-year reign over the country. The Babenbergs gradually moved their capital eastward, and in the 12th century finally established it in the Hofburg (literally the court fortress) in Vienna. The last Babenberg ruler fell in 1246 in one of the countless struggles against the Hungarians.

Count Rudolf of a family from the "Habichtsburg" in the Aargau area of Switzerland was selected Holy Roman Emperor in 1273. This Hapsburg family ruled Austria for the next 600 years, and under its leadership Austria rose to be one of the grandest powers of all of Europe. This extremely rapid growth inevitably changed European politics drastically. The Hapsburg genius was to be able to expand its empire more by wise marriages than by war. By the 16th century they had acquired an empire over which the sun never set. Flanders and Burgundy had been gained through a marriage with Mary of Burgundy. In 1516 Spain came under Hapsburg rule, and in 1521 two Hapsburg brothers saw a need to divide administratively the last empire between themselves. This was not the end of growth; in 1526 Bohemia and Hungary were unified with Austria. Most of Latin America except Brazil came under Hapsburg rule, as did the Netherlands, the rest of Belgium, Naples, Sardinia, Sicily and a few provinces in eastern France. This huge empire was geographically divided with major centers as diverse as Vienna, Brussels, Zaragoza and Naples; it had no unifying elements except the ruling House of Hapsburg.

Defense against the Turks

Austria was often forced to perform its duty of defending Europe from the East. In 1529 and 1683 the Turks actually reached the gates of Vienna and besieged the city. Both times the Austrians pushed them back. But Turkish forces remained close by and occupied Budapest for a century and a half. The second time the Austrians were led by a foreign prince, Eugene of Savoy, a grand nephew of the French Cardinal Mazarin. Eugene drove the Turks out of Hungary, thereby stemming once and for all the Turkish tide westward. An influential national hero, Eugene ordered the construction of one of Vienna's most beautiful palaces, Belvedere, which served as his summer residence. His winter palace is now the office of the Austrian minister of finance. His time was an era of the Baroque, a style which reached its zenith in Vienna and Salzburg, and which can still be admired everywhere in Austria.

Maria Theresia

The Austrian Empire had become the envy of other rising European states, which looked for a chance to snatch attractive chunks of its holdings. When the Austrian Emperor Karl VI died in 1740, one rising power moved particularly swiftly: Prussia. In both Prussia and Austria, two young monarchs ascended to the

Young Maria Theresia

Mature Maria Theresia

thrones in 1740. They dominated much of the European scene for the next four decades and converted Germany into a loose bundle of many states with two dominant powers. In Prussia, a philosophically inclined 28-year-old Friedrich II was crowned king. Later known as Friedrich the Great, he had composed chamber music and written books condemning war and immorality in politics. In Austria a 22-year-old woman who had shown great interest in the arts, but virtually none in politics, became Empress—Maria Theresia. Preferring to reside in the more gracious Schönbrunn Palace rather than the Hofburg, she became a devoted wife and the mother of 16 children to whom she gave as much love and concern as any mother could.

She presented herself to her people as a happy, sincere, pious, philanthropic and folksy ruler, and she was loved and respected by almost all of her subjects. Yet she was a courageous and hard-working ruler who had a knack for choosing able advisers and was stubbornly determined to defend her empire and the Catholic faith. Calling herself the "first and supreme mother of her lands," the Austrians under her leadership tenaciously fought Friedrich in three wars and were forced in the Treaty of Hubertusburg in 1763 to concede only the province of Silesia to Prussia, which had risen to the status of a major European power as a result of the wars. She had moral qualms about taking advantage of some of the diplomatic opportunities that offered themselves, such as participating in the partition of Poland, but for reasons of state she did it anyway. It is no wonder that Friedrich the Great referred to her as "the only man among my opponents."

During her reign Vienna bloomed. Today both the works of Haydn and Mozart as well as the streets in the city that boasts palaces, fountains and statues, attest to the greatness of her era. Vienna became the cultural center of the German-speaking world. It also became the sole center for administering the far-flung Austrian Empire, and Austrian politics still reflects the high degree of centralization that Maria Theresia intensified. She was absolutely opposed to religious toleration and attempts to reform her Empire "from below." She herself introduced lasting reforms, though. She separated the judiciary from the administration, abolished torture, established elementary schools, and removed the universities from Church control.

Her son, Josef II, a liberal ruler, accelerated the reform process after her death in 1780 by eliminating all traces of serfdom and by granting his subjects the right to choose their preferred religion. Haps-

A salon in the Schönbrunn Palace

burg rule at this time was conscientious and in some respects farsighted, but it nevertheless was "enlightened absolutism." The principles of democracy and equality were greatly distrusted and persistently opposed, which is one reason why Austria was unable to resist the tide set in motion by the French Revolution in 1789.

Napoleon

When Napoleon created in 1806 a "Confederation of the Rhine," dependent upon France, Kaiser Franz (the title derived from "Caesar" meaning "Emperor") renounced the crown of the "Holy Roman Empire of the German Nation," and that long moribund entity ceased to exist entirely. Napoleon's Grand Army crushed the Austrian forces in 1809 at Wagram, and the French Emperor was able to dictate a humiliating "Peace of Schönbrunn" from the once beloved residence of Maria Theresia. Austria had its revenge after the bulk of Napoleon's experienced troops had frozen to death in the bitterly cold snows of Russia. An Austrian general, Prince Karl Schwarzenberg, commanded the victorious Allied forces at the "Battle of the Nations" against Napoleon near Leipzig in 1813.

The Congress of Vienna and the "Holy Alliance"

An Austrian Foreign Minister, Prince Klemens von Metternich, was a Rhinelander who led Austria from collaboration with Napoleon to an alliance with his enemies and therefore insured victory. He was able in 1814 to assemble six emperors and kings, 11 princes and 90 accredited envoys at the Congress of Vienna for eight months in order to reconstruct Europe after the fall of Napoleon. The flood of political figures

and their entourages provided many Viennese the splendid opportunity to rent out their houses at exorbitant prices and to escape to the countryside to count their windfall profits.

Those foreign notables who could not afford the high prices either slept in the city's beautiful parks or in or under their carriages. Most envoys spent their time in cafes, at balls, at receptions or at tournaments trying to amuse themselves while the major powers, Britain, Austria, Prussia, Russia and, surprisingly, the loser—France—were deciding Europe's fate behind closed doors. In the final settlement, Austria's hold over peoples in Eastern and Southern Europe was recognized. The Austrian monarch thus continued to rule over a multinational empire led by Germans and composed of Czechs, Slovaks, Poles, Hungarians, Italians, Croatians, Slovenes, Serbs and others.

Austria's attention now more than ever had to be directed away from the German world. Still, it was determined to compete with Prussia for dominance within Germany. Prussia had been granted German lands in the Rhine and Palatinate areas in order to help keep a potentially revengeful France from springing beyond its borders. This arrangement, which led Prussia into the heart of Germany and Austria out of it, ultimately helped Prussia to defeat Austria in the struggle for control of Germany.

Emerging from the Vienna Congress was a "Holy Alliance," which was dedicated to preventing further reform within Europe. Britain left this pact almost as soon as it had been created, but Russia, Austria and Prussia remained. All three ultimately paid very dearly for their determination to dig in their heels and to ignore the signs of the times.

Austria

The spirit of the "Holy Alliance" matched Austria's mood very well. It had a conservative elite, who ruled over a very hierarchically organized society. The nobility owned most of the land and provided the bulk of the army officers, diplomats and upper civil servants. Most of the peasants were poor and powerless while the bourgeois scrambled for whatever authority or titles they could obtain. To this day, Austrians probably remain the most title-conscious people in Europe. Fortunate is he who can attach a "Herr Doktor" or a "Herr Professor Doktor" to his name—and female spouses are permitted to borrow their partner's titles. Others use such titles as "Herr Engineer (or Businessman) with Diploma," "Herr Government Counselor," or "Herr Chief Postal Official."

Prince Metternich took the task of opposing change as seriously as did Kaiser Franz, who proclaimed in 1831, "I won't have any innovations!" The press was heavily censored, and mail was opened and read by government agents. Spies were sent into university lectures, and school authorities were obligated to report any sentiments that might be considered subversive. Students were forbidden from studying in foreign universities, and until 1848 all reading materials used in schools or universities required government approval.

Revolutionary Stirrings

Given the repression of individual freedoms and of the right of national minorities to manage a part of their own affairs, it is not surprising that the wave of revolution in 1848 also shook the Austrian state. A Hungarian nationalist, Louis Kossuth and others, demanded constitutional government for Hungary, but Kossuth admitted that this would be impossible as long as "a corrupting puff of wind that be-

Maximilian I of Mexico
Source: *Austrian Information*

numbs our senses and paralyzes the flight of our spirit comes to us from the charnel house of the cabinet of Vienna." Fighting soon broke out in Vienna, where a flabbergasted kaiser asked, when told that rebels were taking to the streets: "But are they allowed to do that?" The rebels had momentary success until the revolutionaries themselves became hopelessly disunited over the objectives that should be sought.

The Hapsburgs were forced to dismiss Metternich, and the incompetent kaiser abdicated in favor of his 18-year-old nephew, Franz Josef, a serious and hard-working monarch who ascended the throne with the words "farewell youth!" and who ruled for the next 68 years. His younger brother, Ferdinand Maximilian, ruled as Emperor Maximilian I of Mexico from 1864 until 1867, when he was executed by firing squad. A constitution, albeit authoritarian in character, was accepted, and Austria sent representatives to the Frank-

furt Assembly, which sought unsuccessfully to draft a liberal constitution for all German-speaking people. Ultimately the revolution failed in Austria, as it did almost everywhere else in Europe. Nevertheless, it had badly shaken the empire and revealed deep dissatisfaction with a form of government that was not democratic and did not recognize the rights of subject nationalities. Yet, once the revolutionary storm had blown over, the new ruler showed how little he had learned by enforcing a policy characterized by absolutism and tight centralization.

Competition and Partnership with Prussia

In 1866 Austria suffered a crushing defeat at the hands of the Prussian army at the battle of Königgrätz. With new breechloading rifles, which had been used so successfully in the American Civil War, and the capacity to move their troops to the battlefield on new railroads, the Prussians were far better prepared than the Austrians, whose wealth had been spent to construct the stately Ringstrasse in the center of Vienna rather than to modernize their army. This defeat finally wiped away any Austrian dreams of dominating or sharing power over all of Germany and cleared the way for a "small German" unification clustered around Prussia and excluding Austria.

For more than a century the dualism within Germany pitting Austria and Prussia against one another had powerfully influenced the European constellation of nations. That dualism was destroyed, and the relationship between the two states became one of partnership. The Prussian chancellor, Otto von Bismarck, refused his generals' request for permission to make a victory march straight through the heart

The Young Franz Josef

Seat of the Congress of Vienna (Foreign Ministry until 2005)

Archduke Franz Ferdinand and Emperor Franz Joseph

Crown Prince Rudolf

Empire, it stimulated yearnings for independence or autonomy on the part of the empire's other nationalities, especially the Czechs. From time to time there was talk in the empire of federal reforms that might extend the same privileges to all subject peoples, but these always foundered on the rocks of Hungarian and Austrian intransigence.

Despite a short-lived liberal era in the late 1860s and 1870s, the last decades before World War I displayed growing tension within and along the borders of the Austro-Hungarian Empire. As elsewhere, these were decades of rapid industrialization that not only increased the country's wealth, but also gave birth to a powerful working class movement and to a Socialist Party that demanded better pay and working conditions. Although the socialists were moderate in their aims and methods, they were bitterly opposed by conservatives who saw in them a mortal threat to the state.

The steady collapse of the Turkish Empire and growing Russian interest in Balkan affairs (clothed in idealistic terms of Pan-Slavism) seriously threatened the very existence of Austria-Hungary, which sought to preserve the status quo at all costs. In 1912 the Balkan states had fought against Turkey in order to enlarge themselves at Turkey's expense, and in 1913 the same Balkan states fought each other over the booty. To Austria's chagrin, the chief winner in both was the rising and highly ambitious Serbia, which began to serve as an attractive model for the Southern Slavs within the Austro-Hungarian Empire. Also, in 1913 a high military official, Col. Alfred Redl, was revealed to have been a

spy for the Russians for over ten years. This shocking revelation shook Austrians' confidence in their own governmental structure and weakened its international reputation.

World War I

Thus, the Austrians tended to overreact when one of the most important events in world history occurred on June 28, 1914, a Serbian holiday commemorating the assassination of the Turkish sultan in 1389 by a Serbian patriot. A Bosnian Serb student, Gabriel Princip, murdered Austrian Archduke Franz Ferdinand and his wife

of Vienna in order to humiliate Prussia's longtime rival. Bismarck remarked that it was not his aim to humiliate or judge, but rather to serve Prussia's interests. Prussia needed a trustworthy ally, and for the next half-century Austria played that role. For instance, in 1870 Austria did not try to prevent Prussia's unification of Germany by supporting the French in the Franco-Prussian War of 1870.

Continuing Nationalities Problems

The new German Empire, which was proclaimed in the Hall of Mirrors at the Palace of Versailles in January 1871, had acquired an ally that would become increasingly weakened by its nationalities problem. The 19th century saw the birth of nationalist movements all over Europe. A multinational state like Austria had to swim against the current of the age and could survive only by introducing timely reforms to satisfy the aspirations of national minorities. Austria was never able to do this.

The German-speaking minority of the Austro-Hungarian Empire was able to reach a compromise with the Hungarians in 1867 as a direct consequence of the defeat at Königgrätz. The Hapsburg Empire was converted into a dual monarchy, composed of two independent and equal states, with the Austrian emperor serving also as the Hungarian king. Military, diplomatic and imperial financial affairs were handled in Vienna, but Hungary had its own parliament, cabinet, civil service and administrative system. While this settlement did increase the efficiency of governmental operations within the

Balkan students visit Archduke's assassination site, Sarajevo, 2004

Austria

in Sarajevo, now Bosnia's capital. The archduke had become successor to the throne after the kaiser's only son, Rudolf, had become entangled in an extramarital love affair and killed himself and his mistress in 1889.

The shots of Sarajevo sounded the end of an almost 50-year absence of major wars among European great powers. Austria held Serbia responsible for this act and, ultimately, backed by Germany, made unacceptable demands upon Serbia. All over Europe, alliances were invoked, threats were made, "blank checks" and ultimatums were issued. In the end, all major powers had painted themselves into a corner with their many commitments, and could not get out. By the first week of August Europe was locked into a war that lasted four long years and far exceeded all previous wars in terms of casualties and destruction. Shortly before his death in 1897, Bismarck had correctly predicted, "one day the great European War will come out of some damned foolish thing in the Balkans."

During World War I Austria-Hungary primarily sought to retain some control over the Balkans. As Germany's military power ebbed, Austria became increasingly bewildered and confused. Proportionately, Austria-Hungary's losses of men were greater than those of Germany: 1.2 million killed and 3.6 million wounded.

By the fall of 1918 the various non-German nationalities within this empire had begun to mount opposition move-

Austrian Chancellor Dollfuss ("Mini-Metternich")

ments. An exhausted Austria simply ceased to fight in the face of such resistance and the quite imminent and predictable collapse of Germany in the fall of 1918. Another casualty of the war was the mind of wounded Austrian Corporal Adolf

Schickelgruber, a reject of the prestigious Austrian Academy of Art in Vienna. This mind was further inflamed by the Germanic defeat as he fumed in prison. It would come into full bloom in just 15 years when he would become master of Germany, using the name Adolf Hitler.

On November 11, 1918, Kaiser Karl abdicated. He had ascended to the throne upon the death of Franz Josef in 1916. The next day the Austrian republic was proclaimed. Karl's son, Otto von Habsburg (age 97 in 2010), was only six at the time and lived and worked most of his life on the German side of the border. Not until later in life was he allowed to enter Austria freely. He did not regret the demise of the Austrian monarchy. He passed on his passion for pan-Europe to his seven children: one (Gabriela, princess Imperial and Archduchess of Austria) became Georgia's ambassador to Germany in 2010. Her younger sister (Walpurga) was a leading conservative Swedish politician, while their brother Georg was ambassador-at-large for Hungary. Another brother had a seat in the European Parliament.

Soon a democratic constitution was put into effect. The new republic, at one-eighth the size of the former empire, was only the small German part. The Treaties of Trianon (with Hungary) and St. Germain distributed the rest of the territory to Romania, Poland and Italy, or were used to construct the new states of Hungary, Czechoslovakia and Yugoslavia. In the process, Austria

Austria-Hungary until 1918, showing the nations carved from its borders

Germany's Hitler enters Vienna, 1938

lost 4 million of its German-speaking population to Hungary, Poland, Czechoslovakia, Yugoslavia and Italy. It also lost access to the sea. Proportionately, it lost much more territory than Germany. Such fragmentation destroyed the Austrian economy. This was the worst possible atmosphere for an untried democracy, and for the next two decades Austria was unable to regain its balance. In desperation, many Austrians demanded in 1920 a referendum to join the newly formed German republic to the north, but the victorious powers vetoed such a combination, fearing that it would strengthen Germany.

Hopeless Internal Division

From the start, Austria was hopelessly divided into two hostile camps, represented politically by socialists, whose strength was in Vienna, and the Christian Social Party, which was strongest in rural areas. These camps not only created social institutions such as sports clubs, reading circles and youth groups, which isolated their members from those in the other camp, but they also created large and well-armed paramilitary units. The socialists had their *Schutzbund* ("Protective League"), and the opposing *Heimwehr* ("Home Guard") had become so heavily armed by 1933 that it reportedly had tanks and howitzers and enough material to equip 500,000 men for a military campaign of moderate length.

Inflation, unemployment and working class and rural poverty eroded the sympathy and patience for a formally democratic state, which could be kept alive during the 1920s only by loans from the League of Nations. The worldwide economic depression that shook Europe so violently in the early 1930s eliminated whatever shreds of stability were left in Austria and opened the door widely to political extremism.

Through that door stepped an authoritarian Chancellor Engelbert Dollfuss, a diminutive man of four feet eleven inches, who reportedly liked his nickname of "Mini-Metternich." A shrewd and competent politician who had been a lawyer and university lecturer in economics, he strongly opposed socialism and any talk of Austrian union with Germany. He sought to convert Austria into a corporatist state (one in which all citizens belong to highly organized groups bound together by the political leaders in order to achieve the state's goals) on the model of by then fascist Italy.

In 1933 he dissolved parliament, and in early 1934 he ordered the arrest of political opponents, especially socialists, liberals and trade union leaders. He even commanded that artillery fire be directed against workers' tenements in Vienna and that ruthless methods be used to suppress any resistance within the working class districts. The socialists were crushed in street fighting. He promulgated a constitution that allowed him to rule Austria as a dictator, but his time was very short. In July the Austrian Nazis attempted an unsuccessful *coup d'état* in Vienna. They were able to seize the chancellery for only a few hours, during which time they murdered Dollfuss.

"Union" with Germany

His replacement, Kurt von Schuschnigg, tried to retain Austrian independence, but he soon discovered that he had very little support. The socialists and trade unions had been crushed, and the middle classes liked more and more the idea of a union with the increasingly dynamic Germany. When Adolf Hitler, Nazi leader of Germany, decided that the time had come for Austria to become a part of Germany, there was little which Schusch-

nigg could do. Under orders from Berlin, the pro-Nazi Austrian interior minister, Arthur von Seyss-Inquart, assumed Schuschnigg's functions and called upon the German Reich to save Austria from alleged communist chaos. On the night of March 11, 1938, two days before a scheduled national referendum to determine whether Austria should become an integral part of Germany (which the unifiers were expected to lose), German troops entered Austria. The referendum was immediately called off. Two days later it became a province of the German Third Reich.

By the time that Hitler greeted the cheering crowds at the Heldenplatz in Vienna, 70,000 Austrians had already been put into jails or concentration camps. Schuschnigg was interned in various concentration camps until American troops liberated him in 1945. He emigrated to the United States and was a professor of law and politics at Saint Louis University from 1948 to 1967. He called these the best years of his life.

This *Anschluss* ("joining") of the two countries lasted seven years, a time of almost continuous war, destruction and suffering for the Austrian people. Loss of Austrian lives during the war, although not as severe as in World War I, nevertheless was substantial. Altogether 6% of the population, almost 400,000 Austrians, including 65,000 Jews, perished during the Nazi period. Of course, Austrians were both victims of and participants in the Nazi terror. In 1945 more than a half million Austrians were members of the Nazi party, a higher proportion of the population than in Germany. Also, about a fourth of the convicted Nazi war criminals were Austrian. On the other hand, Austria had, in fact, been occupied against its peoples' will in 1938 and had been forced to fight alongside the Germans. Beginning in 1944 the victorious allies emphasized that Austria would be treated as a victim of Nazism; they did this to encourage Austrians to surrender. After the war, many Austrians gladly accepted this interpreta-

Kurt von Schuschnigg

Austria

tion of occupation along with the collective absolution it offered.

Memories of this war experience helped to convince almost all Austrians that they had a destiny that could not be linked directly to Germany. In prisons, concentration camps and resistance groups, many Austrians who had earlier professed widely different political views learned to know and admire each other. This helped create a sense of tolerance and determination to work out political differences peacefully. Also, the need to rebuild the country after the war helped Austrians to put aside their ideological differences and to work together for the good of all Austria.

Thus, out of the ashes of destruction, a strong commitment to democracy was born. Also, the looting and raping for which some Soviet soldiers were responsible in the post-World War II period horrified and alienated most Austrians. This antipathy helped prevent the communists from winning the active support of the Austrian people and thereby from accomplishing the Soviet goal of quickly consolidating power in Austria and then of legitimizing this power through controlled national elections.

The Postwar Occupation Years

The four principal victors divided Austria into four occupation zones: the Russians occupied the eastern part of the country surrounding Vienna; the Americans occupied the north-central part, which included Salzburg; the British occupied the southern and the French the western portions of the country. In mid-1946 restrictions on interzonal traffic and trade were lifted. The inner city of Vienna itself was declared an international zone and placed under four-power occupation, a fortuitous factor that made it more difficult for any one power to coerce the Austrian government.

The Allies declared that Austria had been illegally occupied by Germany in 1938 and had been "liberated" in 1945. Therefore, on May 1, 1945, Austria's constitution of 1920 as amended in 1929 and all laws passed prior to March 5, 1933 (the date Dolfuss took power) went into effect. Unlike Germany, Austria was permitted to have its own civilian government from the very beginning, so allied control was always indirect, rather than direct, as was the case in Germany. In 1948 Nazis who had been purged or sentenced to death after the war were granted an amnesty.

At first, political conditions in Austria seemed to be just to the Soviets' liking: there was no strong and popular noncommunist partisan group to liquidate (as was the case in Poland) nor (or so it seemed at the time) was there a strong noncommunist political party that had to be intimi-

dated into submission. Despite the fact that the communist cadres, who had spent the war years in Moscow, were generally unknown and distrusted by most Austrians, they were aggressive and confident that they could control the political future of Austria. They thought their opposition to Hitler had increased their popularity and that the presence of Soviet troops could enhance their political status and influence.

The Soviet occupiers looked for a leader of a multiparty Austrian government that, they hoped, would be dominated by their compliant Austrian comrades. They thought that they had found just the right man—Karl Renner, a popular and highly respected socialist who had been the first chancellor of the earlier Austrian Republic. Because he had hesitatingly supported the *Anschluss* in 1938, the Soviets assumed that he could be blackmailed, if necessary. Best of all, they falsely assumed his old age would rob him of the stamina to deal with detailed problems of governing, and this would make him more amenable to compromise with the communists.

Renner skillfully and tactfully proceeded to dash the Soviet hopes. He formed a three-party government composed of the Communist Party, the Socialist Party of Austria (SPÖ), and the old Christian Socialist Party, now purified of its former authoritarian ideas and renamed the Austrian People's Party (ÖVP), which shared executive and administrative positions. The ministries of Interior, which controlled all police and security forces, and of Education, Public Information and Worship were given to communists, but Renner devised an ingenious way of minimizing the potential dangers of having such important ministries guided by communists.

He proposed that two undersecretaries be appointed to each ministry so that all three governing parties would be represented at the top of each ministry. The communists were delighted because they thought that this arrangement would enable them to exercise influence in every ministry. The real result, though, was general inefficiency and deadlock in most departments. If any undersecretary vetoed a matter, it was sent to the cabinet for consideration. To get the cumbersome 35-member body to act quickly on matters of importance, he established the policy of serving wine and food to the cabinet members after each session. Because normal rations in Vienna in 1945 were a near-starvation 400 to 800 calories, the meals that followed the meetings were often of greater importance to the participants than the business at hand.

Renner held the most controversial matters until the end, so that the cabinet could

reach an agreement very quickly and with a minimum of controversy. Further, after June 28, 1946, the Soviet authorities could no longer unilaterally reverse the decisions of the Austrian government. Austrian legislation was submitted to the Allied Control Council (ACC) for approval, but if a majority of the Allied commanders did not disapprove it within 31 days, the legislation automatically became law. The significance of this was that the Austrian government could continue to function even when the Allied powers were in disagreement. As was clear by 1947, an unfortunate single vote arrangement doomed the ACC in Germany to impotence.

In the fall of 1945 the Allied powers agreed to permit elections for the newly established Austrian Parliament to be held in November. Austrian communists confidently assured the Soviets that they could gain 25 to 30% of the votes, but Russian and Austrian communists were stunned by the results: the ÖVP received 49.8% of the votes, the SPÖ 44.6% and the communists a mere 5.42%, which gave them only four seats in Parliament. The Soviets had clearly misread the political temper in Austria, and the election was one of the most important events in postwar Austrian history. It brought to a halt the communist hopes to gain control of the country.

Until 1966 the ÖVP and the SPÖ ruled Austria together in a *Proporzsystem* (proportional system) whereby cabinet and administrative posts, and many other jobs down to janitorial positions, were distributed to leaders and members of the two parties according to their electoral strength. This system allowed the two largest to work together as a team rather than have to join with extremist parties. It also enabled the government to defend the

Dr. Karl Renner

country's interests against the Allied occupation forces and to combat attempts to destroy or pervert democracy in Austria.

After the election disaster, the Soviet Union had no consistent and clearly defined aims for Austria except economic exploitation. The Soviet Union originally had demanded that Austria pay it reparations because Austrian soldiers had served in the German army and had participated in the destruction of the Soviet Union. The other three Allies refused this, pointing out that this would be inconsistent with their agreement that Austria was to be treated as a liberated country. Therefore, the Soviets demanded and were granted the right to administer the many economic assets the German government had acquired in the Soviet zone in Austria.

In 1946 it assumed ownership of the Danube Steamship Company, which had come into German ownership after *Anschluss*. Through the Soviet Petroleum Administration (SMV), the Russians controlled most of Austria's petroleum reserves. The Administration of Soviet Property in Austria (USIA) operated 420 confiscated industries and agricultural holding by 1955 and employed about 10% of industrially employed Austrians.

Fearing further Soviet expropriations, which in the end would leave very few industries and resources in eastern Austria for the Austrians themselves, the Renner government dropped all ideological reservations and began in 1946 to nationalize the nation's three largest banks and all heavy industry, including all principal mines, the largest steel, iron and aluminum plants, most petroleum facilities, the main electrical plants, the automotive, locomotive and shipbuilding industries and the Danube Steamship Company. In 1947 they nationalized the power industries. The Russians, who controlled about 60% of these nationalized industries, were greatly angered and simply refused to recognize the Austrian legislation. In return, the Austrians refused to recognize most of the Soviet holdings. In the years that followed, the Austrian government nationalized the railroads, civil aviation, public utilities, radio and television, and the salt, tobacco, liquor and match monopolies.

By the early 1950s Austria had established a stable domestic political order, and Marshall Plan aid from the U.S. helped to create the conditions for the rapid reconstruction of the country and for the gradual return of prosperity. From 1945 to 1947, the U.S. financed 88% of Austrian imports and 57% in 1948. In the time period from July 1948 to June 1949 Marshall Plan aid alone accounted for 14% of the Austrian national income, a far higher percentage than in any other European country. In the early days, the Marshall Plan provided 88% of the foodstuffs and 73% of the coal. In 1961 the United States transferred to the Austrian government all the loans (counterpart funds) that had accumulated through Marshall Plan assistance ($11.2 billion by then).

However, the country was still occupied and divided, and it was therefore not yet sovereign. Austria was caught in the great power tensions that had replaced the unified Allied effort to crush Hitler. Leopold Figl said before Parliament in 1952: "The Austrian people know that it is not because of technical or objective matters that the treaty is being held up: it is purely power political considerations to which justice must give way."

Within the first decade after occupation of Austria, more than 300 meetings of the Allied deputy foreign ministers had been held to discuss a settlement in Austria, but the results were always the same. Suddenly in February 1955 an important break in the stalemate came when Soviet Foreign Minister Molotov announced that the Soviet Union would consider signing a state treaty with Austria. The following month it called on Austria to send representatives to Moscow to discuss the matter. When a rather skeptical Austrian delegation, which included the state secretary for foreign affairs and Bruno Kreisky (who later served as Chancellor of Austria), got off the plane in Moscow and was greeted by all the major Soviet leaders, it was clear that something good was about to happen. Kreisky whispered into Vice-Chancellor Schärf's ear, "If they receive us with such pomp and circumstance, they cannot send us home without pomp and circumstance."

The talks went extremely well, and the concluding "Moscow Memorandum" outlined the major provisions for the subsequent treaty. First, Austria was to adhere to a policy of neutrality on the Swiss model. Second, occupation forces would be withdrawn from Austria by the end of 1955. Third, all Soviet economic holdings in the country would be returned, for which Austria would pay over $152 million and ship a million tons of oil to the Soviet Union each year for ten years. The Western Allies accepted this settlement very quickly, since its terms were far more favorable than they had ever sought. On May 15, 1955, the Allied Foreign Ministers Molotov, McMillan, Dulles and Pinay, and Austrian Foreign Minister Figl signed the Austrian State Treaty in the Belvedere Palace.

Full Sovereignty Again

Austrian surprise and joy at this formal ending of Austria's occupation status was indescribable. In the West, reactions were a mixture of perplexity, pleasure and uneasiness. Why, after ten years of delay, did the Soviets leave Austria? There are many reasons, but the main one is probably that the Soviet Union wanted to make a final attempt to prevent West Germany from entering NATO, whose founding in 1949 Soviet leaders had been unable to prevent. Many Germans desperately wanted to see their country reunified, and by dangling before their eyes an attractive example of what a low price must be paid for national unity and a withdrawal of foreign troops, the Soviet Union hoped to persuade them to remain neutral and to work out a form of German national unity acceptable to the Soviet Union.

The *New York Times* noted: "The Kremlin is producing a little miracle play for the benefit of the Germans, not the Austrians." However, neither the Western Allies nor a majority in the West German Parliament could overlook the fact that the stakes in

The Austrian Parliament

Austria

Austria were not nearly as high as in Germany. Austria is a small country with little influence on that balance of power that had prevented the Soviet Union from seriously considering attacking Western Europe. By contrast, Germany is a key to maintaining that balance of power. This fact made many West Germans highly skeptical that the Soviet Union would be as willing to tolerate for long an independent and neutral Germany as it would an independent and neutral Austria.

POLITICAL SYSTEM

Military Limitations

As a fully sovereign state, Austria spelled out the precise status of its neutrality in a constitutional amendment enacted on October 26, 1955, now the country's national holiday. The amendment explicitly forbade Austria from entering any military alliances or permitting any foreign troops to be stationed on Austrian soil. It also pledged to use all the means at its disposal to maintain and defend its neutrality.

Austria formed no military links with the Soviet Union, but it has its own armed forces, which the treaty severely limited in size. All services are combined in the Army of 27,200 active duty soldiers, of which 13,600 (including 6,900 conscripts) are ground troops. There are 2,300 in the air force, of which 900 are conscripts. Conscripts must serve eight months after turning 17. They must participate in 30 days of refresher training (60–90 days for officers and NCOs) within eight years after discharge. There is a 72-hour reserve force numbering 195,000, backed up in an emergency by 990,000 reservists with training but no commitment. Officers, NCOs and specialists remain in the reserves until age 65; others until age 50.

In 2005 the Defense Ministry announced sweeping changes: 37% of its bases, barracks and other property would be closed and sold, numbering 51 out of 140 properties. In addition to cutting costs, the army would be streamlined and gradually converted into a reduced all-volunteer force. Conscription has been reduced to six months as a step toward a professional army. The idea is to build an international brigade that can take part in European operations engaged in conflict prevention.

The Austrian military is forbidden by the treaty to possess guns that fire farther than 30 kilometers or to possess nuclear or special weapons, including missiles. Although it is not forbidden to have an air force capable of protecting its own airspace, NATO and Warsaw Pact air-craft violated that airspace for more than three decades. As its army commander noted, the country's defense "stops ten meters

Austrian troops marching past the Hofburg imperial palace

above the ground." In 2000, for the first time in Austrian history, it decided to purchase American aviation equipment: nine Sikorsky S70 Black Hawk helicopters.

To improve its air defense, Austria ordered 18 Eurofighter Typhoons to replace its antiquated Draken planes starting in 2007. This was an extremely controversial decision that the new Social Democratic chancellor, Alfred Gusenbauer, supported by the Green and Freedom parties, vowed to cancel on the grounds that they are too expensive and are unnecessary for a neutral country. Even military persons in other branches argued that the money was needed for other defense purposes. Austria allots only .8% of its GDP to defense; in fact, it spends more of its national budget on opera than on its military. But cancellation of the contract would be too costly, and the People's Party made the acquisition a condition for entering the Grand Coalition.

Even with an improved air defense capability, it is still doubtful that Austrian troops could defend their country against a well-equipped and determined attacker, in contrast to the Swiss military, which would probably be able to do that. Probably it would never need to: except for Liechtenstein and Switzerland to the west, Austria is surrounded by NATO countries.

Foreign Policy

Austria's chief foreign policy goals are to preserve its independence and to promote peace and stability in the community of states. This called for a form of neutrality that Austria terms *active*. Austrians interpreted theirs as military, *not* political neutrality. From the beginning Austria rejected Swiss practices by seeking to join certain international political organizations. In December 1955 it

joined the United Nations, and the following year it entered the European Council (which does not deal with military questions).

Over the years, about 60,000 Austrians have participated in more than 50 UN peacekeeping missions in the Congo, Cyprus and the Middle East, especially on the Golan Heights between Israel and Syria. Since joining the EU in 1995, Austria has participated in practically all international missions in the Balkans. In 1997 it sent soldiers to Albania to help stabilize that country, which had temporarily fallen into chaos. In 2010 alone there were 462 Austrian soldiers serving in Kosovo, 99 in Bosnia and 378 in Syria, including the Golan Heights. Austria's commitment to the UN was particularly conspicuous while Kurt Waldheim served as UN Secretary General from 1972 to 1982. It was elected three times to serve two-year non-permanent appointments on the UN Security Council: 1973–4, 1991–2 and most recently 2008–10.

The policy of neutrality placed no muzzle on either politicians or private citizens. As Foreign Minister Leopold Gratz stated in 1984, "Our neutrality binds the State, but not the individual and not the press, and not our thinking. So we never left any doubt as to which political system we adhere to." Also, that neutrality did not necessarily prevent Austria from considering sanctions against other countries.

Austria also had no problems entering purely economic organizations. In 1960 it entered EFTA, a free trade organization whose economic importance is steadily declining. Its association with the EU, with whose members three-fourths of its trade is conducted, was much more problematic because of the EU's stated goal of political unity. The Soviet Union objected to the possibility of Austria's full member-

The Vienna Opera House

ship, but it was prepared to accept Austrian associate membership with no political role. After five years of difficult negotiations, Austria reached an agreement in 1972 that provided for the almost complete dismantling of customs and trade restrictions on industrial and agricultural goods between it and the other EU countries by 1977.

In the early 1990s Austria formally applied for full EU membership, and in June 1994 two-thirds of Austrians voted for it in a referendum. The EU required Austria to give assurances that its neutrality would not stand in the way of a common foreign and security policy. The entry of Poland, the Czech Republic and Hungary into NATO in 1999, followed in 2004 by seven other central European countries, affects Austria's security deliberations.

Although public opinion remains opposed, the People's Party supports NATO entry although that is unlikely to occur soon. Along with many Austrians, it argues that neutrality no longer makes sense after joining the EU, which has developed a security and defense policy with which Austria cooperates. Austria contributes to the EU's small ad hoc battle groups, and in the Balkans Austrian soldiers even serve under NATO command. However, more than 70% of the public still support neutrality, which in the country's security doctrine is defined as "nonaligned."

Austrians remember the humiliating EU sanctions against it in 2000. This is one

reason why it is the most Eurosceptic in the club. In the July 2007 Eurobarometer poll, only 36% of Austrians agreed that their country's membership was a good thing, and just 44% said it had benefited from joining, against 43% who maintained it had not. Only the UK registers lower approval. Support for the EU is strongly supported in the business community, and it is extremely unlikely that the people would ever vote to leave the club despite their disenchantment. Opposition to Turkish entry is intense.

Former Chancellor Wolfgang Schüssel strongly urged his countrymen to rejoin Western institutions: "European enlargement provides us with a huge opportunity. It marks the return of *Mitteleuropa* and puts Austria back at the heart of Europe. Hungary, Slovenia, Croatia, the Czech Republic, bits of Poland, have long been part of our economic and cultural area. We want to build on that to coordinate ideas and interests in a region of more than 40 million people." Austria has clearly benefited more from this opening to the East than any other country among the older EU members. Its trade and investment have boomed, and its stake is less in manufacturing than it was earlier and more in financial services and property.

Ex-Foreign Minister Benita Ferrero-Waldner of the Freedom Party, later the EU's commissioner for external affairs, agreed, stating in 2000: "It has become obvious that since Austria joined the Euro-

pean Union in 1995, the participation in European security structures has become more important to Austria than the preservation of its traditional policy of neutrality. The reasons for Austria's declaration of neutrality in 1955 have always been that by doing so, Austria's independence and security would be best served. Today these goals are best served by a full integration of Austria into a European and Euro-Atlantic security structure."

Austria joined the Partnership for Peace (PfP) in order to strengthen its ties with NATO. In 1998 it also hosted the Alliance's ex-supreme commander, General Wesley Clark, who stressed that its proximity to the Balkans and other flash points makes membership an attractive proposition to Austrians and to NATO. The country would provide a convenient land bridge to NATO peacekeeping forces in the Balkans. During the U.S.-British war in Iraq in March-April 2003 Austria did not allow American troops or airplanes to cross its territory because the action had not been authorized by a UN mandate.

Austria stands outside all military alliances and provides for its own security by making a contribution to peace in the world. At least since the Congress of Vienna in 1814–15, Austria has been the location for important international meetings. It sees itself as especially qualified for the role of a "bridge-builder" between East and West. President Kennedy and Soviet party chief Nikita Khrushchev met in Vienna in the early 1960s. From 1970–72 most of the meetings between American and Soviet negotiators to work out the SALT I Treaty were held in Vienna, and President Carter and Soviet President Leonid Brezhnev signed the Salt II Treaty there in 1979. After 1989 NATO and Warsaw Pact nations conducted Conventional Forces in Europe (CFE) negotiations in Vienna, aimed at achieving reductions of conventional weapons in Europe. The CSCE decided in 1990 to create a conflict prevention center in Vienna.

Austrians see themselves in a totally new situation. Before 1989 they were in a kind of *cul-de-sac*, surrounded on three sides by the communist bloc; now that dead-end has been transformed into an intersection with a bustling thoroughfare opening into the East. One Austrian diplomat put it this way: "We used to be on the eastern fringe of Western Europe; now we are in the center of Europe again."

Austria and Hungary liberalized their border relations so much that in 1989 Hungary dismantled the electronically monitored fences and watchtowers along the Austro-Hungarian border. Austrian officials fear a flood of refugees from other Eastern European countries and therefore deployed troops along the border to pre-

Austria

vent illegal crossings and speeded up the procedure for asylum applications.

Austria played a central role in the westward exodus of East Germans in 1989. This opportunity to render a dramatic humanitarian gesture strengthened its application to the EU by demonstrating that it is a useful and trusted Western country with excellent connections in Eastern Europe. Concerned that too many Bosnian refugees had arrived, it began in 1997 offering them monetary incentives to return home.

It helped form the *Pentagonale*, joined by Italy, Hungary, Czechoslovakia, and Yugoslavia, to foster a project-centered approach to issues of international affairs, such as the environment, where more progress can be made through regional negotiations. Austria looked nervously at the former Yugoslavia. Slovenia pressed for new economic and political ties with Austria. Because of the tension between the Czechs and Slovaks, the latter, whose capital Bratislava is close to Austria, is increasingly turning more to Vienna. Harking back to the earlier Austro-Hungarian empire, Austria shares an embassy in Montenegro with Hungary.

Involved in more than 8,000 joint ventures with its eastern neighbors (4,000 in Hungary alone), Austria is becoming more deeply integrated with Eastern Europe. For example, three of its major banks—Raiffeisen, Bank Austria Creditanstalt and Erste Bank—possess more than a fourth of the 62% of Eastern European banking assets owned by foreign banks. In 2008, 19.1% of its exports were heading east, and 14.8% of its imports were coming from there. The volume is growing. But it finds itself besieged by cheap imports and immigrants from the East. Therefore, it introduced protective measures against sensitive imports and, for the first time in decades, halted the flow of immigrants.

Vienna is the location for many permanent international organizations. For instance, the headquarters for OPEC is located there. The city is rapidly becoming one of the three major centers for activities of the UN. Austria built, at its own expense, a huge and ultramodern Vienna International Center, which it rents to the UN for a symbolic one Schilling per year. This "UN on the Danube" houses the International Atomic Energy Agency, the UN Industrial Development Organization (UNIDO), the UN Relief and Works Agency for Palestine Refugees, most UN offices dealing with drug traffic and abuse, the UN Commission on International Trade Law, and many others. Austria also sets aside public funds amounting to about .52% of its GDP for aid to developing countries; this is the world's eighth-largest percentage.

In 2005 the Foreign Ministry moved from its cramped quarters across from the Hofburg and five other locations into splendid new offices under one roof in the heart of the government district on Minoritenplatz. In 2007, upon the recommendation of ex-Foreign Minister Ursula Plassnik, the name was changed to Federal Ministry of European and International Affairs.

In sharp contrast to Switzerland, Austria never believed that its neutrality should prevent its political leaders from speaking out publicly on important international questions. For instance, Austria always sharply condemned the Soviet Union's disrespect for human rights and its use of military force in Eastern Europe and in Afghanistan. In 1983 it issued a blistering condemnation of the Soviet's shooting down of a South Korean civilian airliner.

Territorial Losses and Claims

In addition, Austria's neutral stance did not prevent it from defending its own territorial claims, which that it found entirely legitimate. After the end of hostilities in 1945, Yugoslavia again raised its claim to part of the Austrian province of Carinthia and underscored this by occupying the province. However, the British, in whose zone the province was located, ordered the Yugoslav forces out of the area. After the split between Yugoslavia and the Soviet Union in 1948, there was no major power that continued to support the Yugoslav claim. Therefore, in 1955 it recognized Austria's possession of the region in exchange for some promises to make cultural concessions to the Croatian minority located there.

Austria was less successful in gaining control of the largely German-speaking and traditional Austrian area of South Tirol, which the Treaty of Saint Germain had awarded to Italy in 1919. For more than two decades, Austria unsuccessfully demanded that the South Tirolians be permitted to determine in a referendum whether they wished to belong to Austria or Italy. After World War II none of the victorious allies supported Austria's claims. Therefore, it was forced to enter long negotiations with the Italian government to achieve the highest possible cultural autonomy for German-speaking residents of the area of Bozen, which the Italians combined with the overwhelmingly Italian-speaking region of Trentino.

These talks were periodically marred by bombings in South Tirol by German-speaking Tirolians who favored annexation by Austria. Finally, in 1969 an agreement was reached whereby the language rights of the South Tirolians would be respected, and certain governmental responsibilities would be transferred to

Bozen, which would become autonomous. Also, low-income housing, public service jobs, funds for kindergartens and schools and many other subsidies are distributed on a proportional basis depending on the size of the respective population groups. The formula has been German: 60%, Italian: 30% and Ladiner (a small minority isolated in two valleys, speaking a Latin-based language and related to the Romansch minority in southeast Switzerland): 10%. Though falling short of their original demands, South Tirolians approved this solution in a referendum, and Austria pledged to relinquish all of its claims over the area as soon as the language rights were fully realized. Although some South Tirolians assert that Italy has not yet fulfilled its promises, the problem is resolved.

The Emergence of Stable Democracy

Also like Switzerland, Austria is an economically prosperous and stable democracy with a federal form to help accommodate diversity and a consensus approach to political and economic problems, which helps guarantee political and labor peace. This contrasts almost completely with Austria before 1918; with numerous ethnic minorities demanding independence, a militant working class demanding a world socialist revolution, rampant anti-Semitism (which helped produce both Hitler's anti-Jewish ravings and Theodor Herzl's Zionist dream of a Jewish homeland), anticapitalism, anticommunism and anticlericalism, all dangerously blended to generate constant tension, hatred and violence.

In contrast to Switzerland, whose democratic system has evolved slowly over centuries, Austria has undergone radical changes in political and social values and practices. German-speaking Austrians often had no clear national identity. Did they belong to the German nation or to a separate Austrian nationality? In a poll taken in 1956, 46% indicated that they belonged to the German nation, but in 1991, three-fourths said that an Austrian nationality already exists, with only 5% rejecting Austrian nationhood. This explains why there was unease in Vienna in 1990, when the German government adopted plans to include Austria in the new German History Museum in Berlin. The polls reflect an important change, but one former U.S. ambassador still asserted that "there is no Austrian . . . The Austrians are the creoles of Europe. Look at the Vienna telephone book. It's like a final exam in Germanic and Slavic pronunciations."

During the first republic after 1918, far too few Austrians held firm democratic values. Most had formed their political views under the authoritarian empire, and many were outright antagonistic and scornful toward democracy. In addition, there was a weak liberal tradition. The chief enemy of the socialist and Catholic subcultures (called *Lager*) was liberalism, which stressed individual rights and free economic activity largely uncontrolled by the state. Finally, common experiences during and immediately after World War II had a great effect on the minds of many Austrians, in that extremist politics of the left and right were discredited. Of course, the basic subcultures did not immediately disappear after 1945, but most Austrians strongly supported their government, which sought to rid the country of foreign occupation and to establish a democratic Austria. They shared a widespread determination not to allow the country to devour itself as it once had.

Overcoming the National Socialist Past

A shadow hung over the 1986 presidential election. Kurt Waldheim was haunted by revelations that he had served on the staff of a German general who had been executed in 1947 for war crimes in the Balkans area. His election was not a vote for Nazism or anti-Semitism. Austrians had grown tired of 16 years of Socialist rule, which had been marked by political scandals, wasteful bureaucracy, money-losing nationalized industries and ineffective economic policies. Therefore, voters elected the first conservative president since 1945.

Indeed, Waldheim's past increasingly made him unable to perform his largely ceremonial duties. In his first year in office, he became known to some as the "prisoner of the Vienna Hofburg." He could not receive foreign heads of state. The most stinging rebuke came from the United States.

In 1987 Waldheim was put on the "watch list" after the Justice Department concluded that there was evidence that he had "assisted or otherwise participated in the persecution of persons because of race, religion, national origin or political opinion." This was the first time the U.S. had declared a friendly country's head of state an undesirable alien barred from entry. Not a single other Western government invited Waldheim. In spite of reassurances, many Austrians viewed the action as an insult to their nation; popular reaction within Austria was intense and negative at the time. The exact nature of the charges was made public in early 1994, and Waldheim was found to have aided and participated in the Nazi efforts directed against Jews and foreign nationals. Other inquiries produced no conclusive evidence that he had actually had a hand in war crimes, but they cast doubt on his claim not to have known what was happening. He died in 2007 at the age of 88.

Presidential palace flying EU and Austrian flags

More and more Austrians agree that their country must "come to grips" with its past. An ominous reminder was given in 1991 when a Gallop poll conducted for the American Jewish Committee revealed that 39% of Austrian respondents held the view that "Jews have caused much harm in the course of history"; 31% preferred not to have Jews for neighbors, but even higher percentages were averse to living near Poles, Slovenes, Croats, Serbs and Turks. Of the approximately 200,000 Jews who had lived in Austria in the 1930s, more than half emigrated before the 1938 annexation by Germany, and 65,000 perished. The total now is only about 10,000, many of whom are recent arrivals from the former Soviet Union.

Unlike the Germans, the Austrians have never engaged in a cathartic debate about their Nazi past, hiding behind the comfortable official interpretation that they had been Hitler's first victims. For the first time in 1991, Chancellor Franz Vranitzky acknowledged that many Austrians had supported Hitler and had taken a hand in his crimes; he apologized for the atrocities Austrians had committed. In 1993 he be-

President Heinz Fischer

came the first chancellor to visit Israel, where he acknowledged that Austrians had been not only victims but also "willing servants of Nazism."

Textbooks were subsequently changed to emphasize the complicity of many Austrians in Nazi crimes and the fact that Austria was not merely a victim of Hitler. Vienna's mayor decreed that the film, *Schindler's List*, be required viewing for all schoolchildren. In November 2005, British revisionist historian David Irving found out the hard way that it is against the law to deny the Holocaust. Austria had issued an arrest warrant against him in 1989 for denying the existence of gas chambers. While on his way to Vienna to give a lecture, Irving was arrested. In February 2006 he was sentenced to three years in prison even though he had pleaded guilty and said that he now accepted that the mass murder of Jews had taken place. In December 2006, he was released to serve the remainder of his term on probation, and he was deported to Britain.

In 1995 parliament voted for the first time to pay compensation to 30,000 victims of Nazi persecution. In 1996 the government finally agreed to abide by the terms of the 1955 Austrian State Treaty, which obligated it to return to the Jewish owners or heirs those art pieces that had been confiscated by the Nazis. In a gesture of atonement, it handed over 8,000 items to the Federation of Jewish Communities in Austria, which auctioned them for more than $14.5 million, donating the proceeds to Holocaust victims. After two paintings by Egon Schiele, which Austria had lent for a show in New York, were seized because of suspicions that they had

Austria

The Spanish Riding Academy with its world-famous Lipizzaner stallions being put through their paces

belonged to Holocaust victims, Culture Minister Elisabeth Gehrer ordered that once prior ownership is certified, all art confiscated by the Nazis would be returned to their rightful owners. In 1998 parliament unanimously approved this decision, which may ultimately strip more than 100 masterpieces from Vienna's leading museums.

The issue became more complicated in 2004 when the U.S. Supreme Court ruled that an 88-year-old Jewish refugee in California, Maria Altmann, could seek to recover $150–$250 million worth of art, especially five paintings by Gustav Klimt, which the Nazis had looted from her family in the 1930s. Altmann's aunt, Adele Bloch-Bauer, wife of a wealthy industrialist, had died in 1925 and had willed the five paintings, including two portraits of her, to her native Austria. But her husband Ferdinand, who fled to Switzerland during the war, revoked all their previous wills before his death in 1945 and willed

the paintings to his brother's three children; Altmann was the only surviving niece.

An earlier settlement negotiated with the Clinton administration had made payoffs contingent on the dismissal of all World War II-era lawsuits in American courts. Thus Altmann's case postponed until the following year the paying of $210 million in compensation to more than 2,000 claimants.

Finally in January 2006 an Austrian arbitration court ruled that the paintings, including the much reproduced gold leafclad portrait of Altman's aunt, Adele Bloch-Bauer, should be returned to her. Austrian art lovers waited in line for hours at the Austrian Gallery to get one last look at the paintings before they were shipped to their rightful owner in America. Benefactor Ronald S. Lauder promptly bought it for the Neue Galerie in New York for $135 million, the highest-known price ever paid for a painting. All five

paintings fetched a stunning $327 million. Crowds to see the paintings in New York have exceeded all expectations.

Ex-Chancellor Viktor Klima, the first Austrian chancellor born after the Second World War, emphasized in 1997 that his government is committed to confronting and studying the Nazi past; "it must teach us." He reiterated this in 1998 on the sixtieth anniversary of the *Anschluss*. Also in 1998 the government gave the go-ahead to construct a holocaust memorial in Vienna. Critics had decried the structure, which they likened to a "concrete bunker" located close to the spot where hundreds of Jews had committed suicide in the midst of an anti-Semitic pogrom in 1421. In 2003 the Wiesenthal Center in Vienna cited Austria as doing the least to pursue war criminals, relative to the number probably inside its territory.

Government Structure—The President

Austria has a parliamentary form of government. The head of state is a president, who is elected directly for a six-year term, with one reelection possible and with all citizens of voting age required to vote. The presidency is largely a ceremonial post. Austrians want in a president a moral authority who represents the country well internationally and who acts as a moderating influence at home. However, the office would potentially have significant power in times of political instability.

In the 1992 and 1998 presidential elections Thomas Klestil of the conservative Austrian People's Party won. A former ambassador to Washington and number two in the Foreign Ministry, he quickly succeeded in reestablishing ties with countries that had boycotted Austria and in enabling his country to assume a higher profile in international affairs.

He died the day before he was succeeded in July 2004 by Heinz Fischer, who had served as speaker or deputy speaker of parliament since 1990. A seasoned moderate politician known for his adeptness in mediating partisan bickering, Fischer is the first Social Democrat to be president in two decades. Winning 52.3% of the vote, he defeated Benita Ferrero-Waldner of the People's Party, who became the EU commissioner for external affairs. She was replaced as foreign minister by Ursula Plassnik, a lawyer and professional diplomat who had spent a high school year in Foxcroft, Virginia, and later studied at the College of Europe in Bruges.

In April 2010 Fischer was reelected by a landslide, winning 80% of the votes. His opponent was a right-wing firebrand, Barbara Rosenkranz, of the Freedom Party. Mother of 10 children and wife of a fundraiser for imprisoned neo-Nazis, she is nicknamed the "Reich Mother" because of her presumed Nazi sympathies. She suggested that all anti-Nazi laws be scrapped and that denial of the Holocaust be made legal. She captured only 15% of the votes.

In 1992 the Hofburg Palace, where the president has his office, was partly destroyed by fire. The 18th-century Redoutensaal ballroom and conference hall was gutted. The priceless National Library and Spanish Riding School were spared, and passers-by escorted 69 Lippizaner horses to safety in the middle of the night.

Parliament and Parties

In normal times, the most powerful political figure is the federal chancellor, who must control a majority in the National Council, by far the most powerful chamber in the bicameral legislature. By means of a complicated proportional representation electoral system in 25 districts, 183 members are elected. In 2007 the voting age was lowered to 16 and the term extended to five years. Despite this proportional representation system, which in other countries usually enables a large number of parties to win seats in the parliament, only five Austrian parties have been able to win any seats at all.

The SPÖ, which renamed itself in 1991 the Social Democratic Party of Austria, is the country's largest party, and it ruled alone from 1970 until 1983. Its socialist appeals have been increasingly moderated, and it has become a pragmatic, reform-oriented party. Some of its members are still attracted to "Marxist" doctrine, but its program stresses that it welcomes all supporters who embrace the party's ideals as a result of religious, philosophic, humanistic or "Marxist" analysis. The party is openly anticommunist and was often critical of the former Soviet Union. It refuses any form of political cooperation with the Communist Party of Austria (KPÖ), which has sunk to political insignificance. The SPÖ's strength is found mainly in urban and industrial areas, especially in Vienna. The SPÖ dominates the trade union movement and attracts the votes of most workers.

In the September 2008 federal elections, held at the onset of the country's worst economic downturn since the war and after a two-year grand coalition collapsed that was seen to have done nothing but bicker, the two main parties reached their lowest points in history. At the same time, two far-right parties enjoyed their greatest success ever. The SPÖ fell from 35% of the votes to 29% and 58 seats, but it emerged as the largest party. New party leader and chancellor, Werner Faymann, reaped the credit for this. A former Vienna city councilman in charge of housing, he

Chancellor Werner Faymann

rose rapidly to become chancellor at age 48. He assumed the powerful ministry of transportation and infrastructure in the last federal government. When a party rebellion broke out in the SPÖ in June 2008, Alfred Gusenbauer passed the party's reins and the chancellorship to his far more popular friend Faymann.

The latter has a down-to-earth eloquence and pragmatic and populist streaks. He never finished a university degree nor ever had a job outside of politics. But he is a clever tactician and an excellent campaigner, and that paid off. In December 2008 he retained the chancellorship in a renewed grand coalition with the People's Party. His 16-headed cabinet contains five women. As a symbol of the SPÖ's rejuvenation, the powerful post of party business manager was given to 28-year-old Laura Rudas, who has had a seat in parliament since she was 26.

The politically adroit Greens fell from 10.5% to 9.8% of the votes, losing a seat to end with 19 in 2008. Their green message is better suited to prosperous times. Their voters are predominantly prosperous, middle-class and younger than supporters of other parties. In their egalitarian manner, they distribute their seats equally among men and women. Their third-ranking candidate, Alev Korun, became the first member of parliament of Turkish origin. The Greens are the only party that favor's Turkey's entry into the EU. They are in opposition. Economics professor, Alexander Van der Bellen, passed the party leadership to Eva Glawischnig.

The Austrian People's Party (ÖVP) was founded in 1945 by the antifascist ele-

ments of the former Christian Social Party. The Catholic Church now abstains from direct political activity, but the ÖVP, which does not view itself as a specifically Catholic party, can usually count on the support of most practicing Catholic lay organizations. The party is also successful in gaining the votes of farmers, independent merchants and industrialists, lawyers and doctors, and generally the middle class. The ÖVP's program favors a social market economy and private property, but it also supports social welfare and workers' participation in the management of companies.

In the 2008 elections, it tumbled to its worst performance ever, capturing only 26% of the votes, down from 34%, and 50 seats, down from 66. The day after the election, party leader Wilhelm Molterer passed the leadership to the eloquent and affable Josef Pröll, who had been agriculture minister in the last government. He had just turned 40 at the time of the elections, indicating that the country's leadership is as young as it had ever been. He has proven himself to be an effective political operator. He occupies the dual positions as vice-chancellor and finance minister in the grand coalition. The latter post ensures him power but not popularity in a time of such economic distress. His party comrade, Michael Spindelegger, is foreign minister. It bodes well that Faymann and Pröll worked quite well together in the last grand coalition. The tone of this government is more amicable than in the previous one, but it has accomplished little.

The ÖVP and the SPÖ had ruled together until 1966. During this time, they devised a "proportional system," which called for the fair distribution of governmental and administrative posts to members of the two major parties. For instance, state secretaries who belonged to the opposite party often aided cabinet members. The Transport Ministry, with its patronage in the railways and highways, was a fiefdom of the SPÖ, while the Ministries of Agriculture and Defense were in the ÖVP's domain. Even jobs with the EU in Brussels were allocated according to this outdated practice. This system rested on a fundamental consensus about the nature of the democratic regime. It also encouraged Austrians to join parties so that they can be considered for these jobs. At 15% of the adult population, such membership is among the highest in the West.

Nevertheless, there is a widespread feeling that the "proportional system" has outgrown its usefulness and that it has encouraged corruption and inefficiency since jobs are distributed on the basis of political affiliation, rather than competence. Among its absurdities is the fact

Austria

that the Austrian Airlines (sold in 2009 to Lufthansa) and the Vienna Airport each had two presidents. It is already being phased out in the many state industries that have been privatized, and overall fewer jobs are handed out. But it has not disappeared and remains strong in banking. A growing number of voters think it should be abolished in the civil service. Jörg Haider hammered relentlessly and successfully against this outdated system of patronage. After his Freedom Party's stunning success in the 1994 elections, he boasted that "we have finally succeeded in putting postwar Austria behind us."

The Freedom Party of Austria (FPÖ) rose dramatically, winning an astonishing 26.9% and 52 seats in 1999, mainly at the expense of the ÖVP. This was one of the greatest electoral successes in recent years by a far-right party in Western Europe. Particularly potent were Haider's fulminations against EU eastward enlargement and the massive influx of Central Europeans that could unleash. All Austrian politicians concede more politely and privately that fears of being swamped make enlargement a hard sell domestically. The three neighbors, the Czech Republic, Hungary and Slovenia, have a combined population nearly three times larger than Austria's. The government estimates that five million foreign workers live within commuting distance of the main Austrian cities.

The FPÖ's main objective was to prevent the formation of a dominant, completely two-party system. Haider, who assumed leadership of the party in 1986, had branded the earlier grand coalitions as a "marriage of elephants." He was a fiery orator and a charismatic crowd-pleaser, who called for a more nationalistic policy and denounced corruption, privilege, and the influx of immigrants.

Haider also appealed to young Austrians who were fed up with politics being dominated by the two big parties and who wanted change.

In 1989 he was chosen as minister-president of Carinthia, a post he held until 1991, when provincial legislators voted him out for daring to compliment the Nazis by saying that "they had a sound employment policy in the Third Reich." In 1995 he again harmed his party by making sympathetic remarks to Waffen SS veterans. No wonder it was said that many ex-Nazis were attracted to the FPÖ. Right-wing politicians must walk a fine line when speaking about the Nazis since the law prohibits the Nazi Party, praise of its ideology, and attacks on Jews.

The government felt obliged to respond to Haider's calls for stricter controls on immigration by doing just that in 1993. It introduced some of Europe's toughest immigration laws. In 2003 plans were announced for even tougher asylum rules that would make it easier for the government to deport rejected seekers and restrict even further who could be entitled to claim refugee status. One of the FPÖ's election posters read: "Don't let Vienna Turn into Chicago!"

The influx of immigrants, including 60,000 from Bosnia alone in 1992, brought the number of foreigners living in Austria to over 750,000 or 10% of the total population by 2008. They experienced none of the violence that afflicted Germany, but the issue was propelled to the top of Austria's political agenda.

If immigrants are from a non-EU country and cannot speak German, they should take compulsory German-language lessons, paying half the costs. If they cannot pass a language examination after four years, their residency permits are supposed to be withdrawn. But that

happens only in about one-tenth of the cases. Welfare assistance for asylum seekers from places no longer deemed as a zone of conflict, such as Kosovo, was reduced. It was made easier for family members to join immigrants already settled in Austria, but in 2005 the waiting period to get citizenship was raised to at least six years.

Like all but three of its EU partners (UK, Ireland and Sweden), when enlargement took place in May 2004, Austria declared a transition of up to seven years before workers from the new central European member states could gain access to Austria's labor market. The country's labor shortage soon forced it to drop many of those restrictions. However, Central Europeans could come as students, tourists, or retirees, and they had the right to establish a business or be self-employed. Many Austrians regard East-to-West migration as a problem, and public hostility to immigration is strong. But given the country's low birthrate, it will accept such migrants in the medium- and long-term to fill gaps in the labor force. Also many of the immigrants from neighboring countries are well educated, speak fair German, and are willing to adapt to Austrian society.

Austrian politics had received a powerful jolt when the Freedom Party was invited to enter the ÖPV governing coalition in 2000. Before it was sworn in, the new government issued the fullest acknowledgment of Austria's complicity in Nazi crimes ever made by a post-war Austrian government. In power it did nothing to suggest that either democracy or minority rights were at risk in Austria.

Although Haider did not join the cabinet, there was an international uproar among all 14 EU partners, supported by the U.S. and Israel. All other EU members and the Czech Republic individually decided to ostracize Austria in their bilateral relations, even though Vienna had broken no EU rules. In an attempt to soften international hostility to Austria, Haider formally stepped down as party leader in March 2000, and Susanne Riess-Passer took his place. This did not defuse the crisis. But EU countries became increasingly embarrassed about the precedent they had set and the effect their sanctions had on Austrians. Polls in 2000 showed that nine out of ten Austrians of all political stripes opposed the EU's measures.

To get out of the corner into which it had painted itself, the EU asked the European Court of Human Rights to appoint a panel of "three wise men," led by former Finnish President Martti Ahtisaari to investigate. In September 2000 they completed their enquiry and called the sanctions "counterproductive." They con-

Poster in Vienna of the FPÖ's Susanne Piess-Passer; we have done it!

Feeding on the massive discontent due to the global recession, both the Freedom Party and the newer Alliance for Austria's Future achieved spectacular results in the 2008 elections, coming to within a whisker of the SPÖ if their votes are combined. Under its new chairman, Heinz-Christian Strache, the FPÖ won 17.5% of the votes, up from 11%, and 35 seats, up from 21. Strache is a dental technician by training and a sports fanatic by nature. His direct and approachable populism struck a chord with much of the electorate. At 39, he is the youngest of the country's young political leaders. He styles himself as a man of the people. He rails against Brussels, immigration and foreign competition, which he blames for the ongoing economic crisis. He advocates creating a ministry for the deportation of immigrants. He won votes from both large parties. But his most spectacular feat was to win the votes of over 44% of voters age 16 to 19 and more than a third among those under 30. This was especially important since the voting age dropped to 16 for the first time. It was "cool" to vote for him. He also attracted many blue-collar voters.

Haider and his BZÖ experienced a spectacular comeback in the 2008 elections. It captured 11% of the votes, up from 4.2%, and 21 seats, up from 7. Hardly had the celebration died down when three weeks later Haider was fatally injured in an automobile crash at age 58. He was racing back into Carinthia's capital of Klagenfurth along a road where he had almost died before. He was intoxicated and driving more than twice the speed limit (142 kilometers or 88 miles per hour in a 70-kilometer or 42-mile zone) when he struck a concrete divider and rolled several times. His death unleashed an outpouring of shock, emotion and grief seldom witnessed in Austria. Some observers compared the effect to Princess Diana's death in 1997. Even most of those who opposed him mourned the passing of one of Austria's most talented and colorful post-war political leaders.

One of his legacies will be his part in putting an end to the proportional system and the resulting dominance of the two largest parties. But more important is the way that he articulated Austrians' confusion about their past. They will remember in him their own mixture of defiance and repentance, victimhood and guilt, and the struggle to expel old ghosts.

The BZÖ moved quickly to fill the gap left by Haider's death. His 27-year-old press spokesman and reportedly homosexual partner, Stefan Patzner, was appointed party chairman. But no one can match Haider's popularity and charisma. It is possible that with him gone, the two far-right parties will merge.

cluded that the Austrian government's respect for the rights of minorities, refugees and immigrants is not inferior to that of other EU states and that its standards are often higher. They did find that the Freedom Party is a "right-wing populist party with radical elements" that exploited racist sentiments during election campaigns. An incensed Haider retorted: "Unlike in Germany and other European countries, asylum seekers' homes are not burned in Austria, and there are no neo-Nazi marches."

The People's Party-Freedom Party coalition chalked up some accomplishments. It pushed through laws to do away with the *Proporz* system, which had given the two largest parties an equal share of the patronage spoils. It introduced constitutional changes to give minorities more strongly guaranteed rights. It negotiated compensation for victims of the Nazi period in Austria. Tuition was introduced for students in its underfunded and overcrowded universities, something the SPÖ has vowed to rescind. Perhaps its greatest accomplishment was that it was able to force a reform of the pensions system through parliament in 2003.

The new system raises the retirement age, reduces the current pay-as-you-go pensions for future retirees by 10% for those now over age 35, and eventually abolishes the separate and more generous pensions for public employers. The issue had threatened to blow the federal budget apart in a few years. With a declining working-age population, the country faces a future pension crisis as Austrians tend to retire before the official age of 65 for men and 60 for women. Nevertheless, in 2009 *Forbes* magazine ranked Austria as the best place in the world for retirement because of its standard of living, good medical care, and beautiful cities and landscape. Vienna was ranked first in offering the best quality of life.

Unable to negotiate a coalition with the Social Democrats after three months, Schüssel turned again to the Freedom Party, which entered the new government in 2003 to secure a nine-seat majority. This time it was very much under the thumb of the victorious People's Party rather than being the more or less equal member earlier.

Haider decided to purge some of the party's most hardcore right-wingers, drop his nationalism and create in April 2005 a new party devoid of ideology—the Alliance for Austria's Future (BZÖ). He sought to moderate his anti-immigration rhetoric, but his message was still aimed against excessive foreign presence, immigration, "loss of identity," bureaucrats in Brussels, globalization and Turkey's EU entry, which only 10% of Austrians support. Most grass-roots activists remained with the old party.

The late Jörg Haider

Austria

Viennese housing designed by artist Hundertwasser

A Federal State

Austria is a federal state composed of nine provinces: Vienna, Salzburg, Vorarlberg, Carinthia, Upper Austria, Lower Austria, Burgenland, Styria and Tirol. Each province (called a *Land*) has a popularly elected legislature, which elects a governor and members who serve four to six-year terms in the 58-member Federal Council, the upper house of the Austrian Parliament. The number of seats allotted to each province depends upon its population. The smallest receives at least three seats, whereas the largest may receive no more than 12. Unlike the U.S. Senate, the Federal Council has far fewer powers than the lower house. It may only review and delay legislation, and it has the right to veto only the annual budget.

The provinces are not as powerful as states in the U.S., since most government authority, including police power, rests with the central government. The provincial governments do have certain authority over welfare matters and local government, and strong provincial loyalties persist. However, in general, Austria, despite its federal structure, is highly centralized politically. This condition prompted citizens in one province, Vorarlberg (which after World War I attempted to join the Swiss Confederation), to vote in a provincial referendum in 1980 for negotiation with the federal government to achieve more say over political decisions affecting its citizens, such as taxes and the allocation of funds.

Other Government Elements

The Austrian constitution provides for a Constitutional Court whose members are appointed by a number of federal institutions and leaders. This court has the task to review all cases involving constitutional questions and to decide on jurisdictional conflicts between the various levels of governments.

The constitution also calls for the election of chambers financed by taxes and representing various segments of the economy, especially the Chambers of Agriculture, of Labor and of Commerce. These have the right to present advisory opinions on government bills and actions affecting their particular interests. Such chambers are no doubt holdovers from the former corporate state. However, they do play an important role in bringing diverse interest groups into the governing process and they contribute to establishing a political consensus that helps to maintain stability. Thus, they reflect the nature of democracy in Austria today, which aims to reduce conflict and to promote compromise in a land that historically was tragically torn. The process of compromise places much responsibility on the shoulders of political and economic elites, who must tie together various groups in the Austrian society.

This is one rationale for the rule of proportionality, by which offices are distributed among members of both major parties. The Austrian system would be fundamentally changed if one party or group would take all of the spoils on the grounds that it won more votes in the last election. Of course, electoral campaigns are hotly fought and are filled with exaggerated rhetoric about how disastrous it would be if the other party won.

However, between elections the parties and economic groups cooperate with each other. To make this cooperation work effectively, political leaders must enjoy much freedom from their constituents or supporting subcultures. Some critics argue that this fact somewhat weakens popular control over the elites and weakens political participation of lower levels. Also, young protesters in the 1980s maintain that their actions are in part directed against a political system that leaves far too little room for young people to determine their own future. But the democratic experiment in Austria has been so successful since 1945 that very few voices demand a fundamental change of the political system.

ECONOMY

Austria is the fourth-richest country in the EU. It has basically a free enterprise economy in which the market determines what is produced and at what price. Economic competition exists and is encouraged, although it was traditionally not as highly valued as in the U.S. After 1945, it had a higher percentage of the economy under government ownership than in any other country in Western Europe. Almost two-thirds of all corporate capital belonged to the public sector, and a quarter of the entire labor force worked in nationalized industries or in industries controlled by nationalized banks. These were permitted to operate largely independently of government control and accounted for about one-fifth of the country's GDP and one-third of its total exports. However, large-scale privatization has changed all this.

The largest trade union, the centralized Austrian Trade Union Federation (ÖGB) represents about one-third (36% in 2006) of all wage and salary earners, somewhat above the European average. It has been steadily losing members, but almost the entire workforce is covered by collective bargaining agreements. The idea of "social partnership," whereby government, employers and employees cooperate over pay and economic policy, remains strong. The former Schüssel government from 2000–2007 weakened it by legislating reforms on matters the ÖGB thought were its prerogative, such as pensions and healthcare. The ÖGB is a nonpartisan, moderate labor organization that aims not toward revolution, but toward securing good pay and working conditions for its members. No doubt, memories of bitter social tensions in the past and the small size of the country help enable such cooperation to work.

There are other important results of close cooperation among labor, management and government. Strikes are almost unknown in Austria. Statistically, the average Austrian worker strikes a few seconds per year, compared with 192 minutes in the U.S., 215 in Britain and 553.5 in Italy. Second, Austria had relatively low unemployment (4.3% in 2009 rising to 4.9% in 2010) and inflation (1.9% in 2010). Employers are traditionally hesitant to lay off workers, a fact that helps maintain labor peace, but which sometimes hurts the financial situation of particular firms. However, the labor market is less rigid than in Germany.

Some restructuring in traditional branches is necessary. The national debt stood at 62% of GDP in 2007, and the budget deficit, at 5% in 2010, had shot up above the EU maximum of 3% because of the global recession. Before this the government had worked it down through pay freezes to the public sector, pension and welfare cuts, and reductions in subsidies to state-owned firms, railways and farmers. Overall, a third of the work-force in state-run industries was cut.

Ex-Chancellor Vranitzky announced plans to privatize many state companies: "In Austria, the shelter that the state has given to almost everyone—employee as well as entrepreneur—has led to a situation in which a lot of people think not what they can do to solve a problem but what the state can do. This needs to change. Once people have sniffed the fresh air of self-initiative, it will change." Shares were sold from the country's largest oil and gas company, the largest utility, and Austrian Airlines (sold to Lufthansa in 2009). The principle is to reduce the state's shareholdings and to remove day-to-day political interference in management.

But there are limits. When the government proposed in 2003 the sale of one-third of the Voestalpine steel group, there was an outcry. It had been founded by the Nazis in 1938 under the name of Hermann-Göring-Werke in Linz. After the war it was the flagship of state-owned industry and a fief of the Socialist party and trade unions. The government had to promise that the firm would not be split up or sold to foreigners. Because the Schüssel government decided there was not enough domestic capital to buy such companies as Telekom Austria or the state-owned postal service, privatization was put on ice. To make small savings, 300 of the 1,640 post office branches were closed in July 2005, and up to half the postal service was for sale in 2006.

A third reason for labor peace is that the real earnings of workers and employees have steadily increased. High labor costs affected Austria's trading position. Although wages are roughly on a par with those in Germany, the cost of fringe benefits, including payments for the very generous social security system, add about 80% to wage costs, as opposed to about 60% in Germany. Since 2000 unit labor costs have been reduced. The states' claim on the national tax income, in the form of taxes and other payments, now exceeds 40%.

Austria lowered its corporate tax to 25% (22% including allowances) in 2005. Since this is well below the EU average of 40% and is at Central European levels, it attracts investment and helps keep businesses from moving to low-tax neighbors. This hurts nearby Bavaria most, which is losing investment to Austria. The over-all tax burden, at 43% of GDP, is 3% higher than the EU-15 average. Austria is most immediately concerned by Slovakia, which has become a foreign investment hotspot. Industrial and prime office rents in the capital city of Bratislava are already higher than Vienna. Many Slovaks are buying up housing on the Austrian side of the border because it is much cheaper than in or around the Slovak capital.

Bratislava Airport could help service Vienna, with high-speed rail connections.

Austria is fortunate to have some important natural resources: gas, brown coal (peat), iron ore, zinc, aluminum, magnetite, lignite, copper, timber and others. These can be traded or used in their own diversified industries, which produce iron and steel, chemicals, capital equipment and consumer goods.

Exports account for 53% of Austria's GDP, up from 38% in 1990. About three-fourths of its trade is with the EU, which it formally joined on January 1, 1995. Germany is by far Austria's most important trading partner, with 31% of exports and 41.5% of imports. Unification greatly stimulated its sales to the FRG.

Austria likes to see itself as a bridge between East and West, and its trade with Russia and Central Europe grew rapidly. By 1998 its trade with Eastern Europe had more than doubled since 1989, and by 2009 its exports there amounted to 19.6% of Austria's total, and its imports 14.4%. Trade with the East was helping keep Austria's economy a step ahead of its neighbors even though it remains far less than with the EU-15. But such large economic exposure to the eastern countries can be a real risk in times of economic distress, such as 2009–10. Proportionally Austria is the most vulnerable country dealing with the East: its loans to Eastern Europe total three-fourths of its GDP, followed by Sweden (30%) and Greece (19%).

The U.S. accounts for only about 5% of the nation's foreign trade. One Austrian product that has become visible in American convenience stores is the high-energy drink, Red Bull, whose sales in dollar terms have overtaken Diet Coke and Diet Pepsi. General Motors is the single largest investor of any foreign company in Austria.

As in most other European countries, maintaining sufficient energy supplies is a major problem. Because of its mountain water, it is able to supply about two-thirds of its electrical power through hydroelectricity. Over the entire year, Austria is actually a net exporter of this kind of power, but in the winter when there is little water, it must import electricity. Its oil reserves are becoming rapidly depleted, so Austria must now import almost 90% of its petroleum, thus sometimes throwing its balance of payments into deficit. Its natural gas reserves are also declining, thus requiring Austria to import about 60% of its needs, largely from Russia and Eastern Europe.

In 2009 it signed a transit agreement joining the EU-endorsed Nabucco pipeline project that will bring gas from the Caspian Sea via Turkey, circumventing Russia. A year later it signed a pipeline

deal with Russia allowing the latter's South Stream project to penetrate farther into the EU. Both efforts remain years away from realization. It must import about 80% of the coal it needs. Overall net imports account for about two-thirds of its energy, up from 63% in 1974. About a fourth is supplied by Russia. Thanks in part to his plentiful hydropower, Austria gains 23% of its energy from renewable sources and hopes to raise that to 34% by 2020.

It was intended that nuclear energy would be able to supplant the country's needs, and a nuclear power station was built at Zwentendorf near Vienna, which could have supplied 11%–15% of the country's electrical needs. However, in a

Announcement of special exhibition in Kunsthaus Vienna

Newsstand in downtown Vienna

Austria

1978 referendum, a narrow majority voted against putting the power station into actual operation. Leaders of both industry and labor want to activate the plant, but the nation's political leaders and public opinion remain divided on the question. The nuclear disaster and subsequent discharge of radiation at Chernobyl in the former Soviet Union has increased the antinuclear power sentiment within the country. Austria intensely opposes Czech nuclear power stations, especially the one in Temelin, 40 miles (60 km) from the border, as well as Czech plans to expand its atomic generation and sell electricity to Germany. The Austrian government entered a treaty with the Czechs guaranteeing better safety measures at the plant.

The pictures of scenic mountain landscapes, Alpine villages or stately baroque cities, and of singing, yodeling and waltzing Austrians, dressed either in ballroom finery or in leather pants and Alpine hats, thoroughly enjoying life, have always attracted virtually millions of tourists each year. Austrians have the highest per capita income from tourism, which produces 9% of its GDP, in all of Europe, and without this source the Austrian economy would collapse almost immediately. Tourist receipts can no longer balance the trade deficit, however, as they once could, but it keeps such a deficit within bearable limits. As in Switzerland, it also helps retard the flight from rural to urban areas and stimulates businesses outside the major industrial areas that support the tourist industry. The economic drawbacks of tourism are that it is seasonal and very heavily dependent upon German, Dutch and British economic prosperity. Germans account for about three-fourths of the overnight stays and the Dutch for about 10%.

Austria's roads and ecology are also sensitive to the increasing number of trucks and cars that traverse the country and leave their exhaust fumes behind. As East-West traffic grows, the problem becomes doubly serious. The government failed to renegotiate an agreement with EU partners to limit heavy trucks. Limits and high fees on truck traffic in Switzerland redirects much of it onto Austrian roads.

Only 6% of Austria's work force is engaged in farming and forestry, and they produce 1.9% of GDP. By contrast, 28% of employment and 30.5% of GDP are derived from industry and mining, and 66% work in the services sector and produce 67.5% of GDP. Farms are predominantly small or medium-sized, family-owned, often fragmented and located in the northern and eastern part of the country. Mountains cover three-fourths of the country, and half of its farms are located in mountain regions. Generous subsidies from Vienna and the EU help make them viable. Austrian farmers can still supply about 90% of the country's food needs. Some items, such as cheese and beef can be exported. About 46% of Austria is covered by forests, which provide the country with a valuable natural resource: timber.

CULTURE

Austria is traditionally an overwhelmingly Catholic country, but the faith is rapidly losing its grip on the people. In 1900, 91.6% claimed to belong to the Roman Catholic Church; by 2007 that had fallen to barely 70% overall and less than 50% in Vienna. Only 13% attend weekly mass (17% among those claiming to be Catholic). The number paying the state-administered "church tax" of about $400 per year is also declining. Pedophilia and pornography scandals among priests have taken their toll. For example, Cardinal Hans Hermann Groër of Vienna was removed from office in the 1990s for molesting boys, but until his death in 2003 he never confessed or faced trial. Thousands

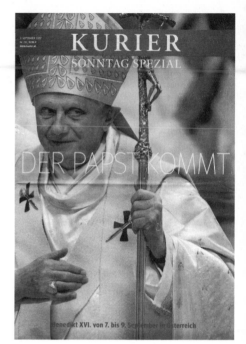

The Pope is Coming [to Austria]

of shocked Austrian Catholics left the Church because of this scandal.

A majority of the population favors abolishing the celibacy of priests, and 49% say they do not take to heart what the pope says about marriage, sex and birth control. A fifth of the churches no longer have a priest of their own, and the number of priests since 1990 has fallen from 5,100 to 4,262 in 2007; only 31 new priests were inducted in 2006.

To try to turn this decline around, Pope Benedict XVI traveled to Austria in September 2007. However, he was met by widespread indifference. In a poll at the time, 82% said the visit meant nothing or very little to them; among those under age 30, this figure was 96%.

Since 1912 Islam is considered an official religion, thanks to the minority policy of the Austro-Hungarian empire. However, fear of fundamentalist Islam today has created tense populist opposition to the construction of mosques and minarets within the country.

Despite its small size, Austria is a land with an enormously rich scholarly and cultural heritage. Europe's oldest remaining German-speaking university was founded in Vienna in 1365. During the empire it became famous the world over for learning and research, especially in medicine as exemplified by pioneering work in antiseptic and brain surgery of Theodor Billroth and Theodor Meynert.

Now there are 12 universities and six art academies in Austria, which charge low tuition for citizens of Austria or of countries in the "Third World." As in most

Horst Hiemer · Jörg Gudzuhn · Johanna Schall · Gudrun Ritter
DIE DREIGROSCHENOPER
Bertold Brech's "Three Penny Opera" announced in Vienna

European countries, the school system is tracked horizontally into general education, trade or commercial and basic education courses. The first two can provide access to the universities. In 2005 the European Court of Justice ruled that German applicants who wish to get around admissions quotas at home cannot be excluded from the overcrowded Austrian universities. Traditionally Austrian students can study whatever they want without restrictions as to major.

As elsewhere in the EU, the universities have undergone reforms. Shorter BA curricula have been set up, and modest fees have been introduced in an attempt to reduce the 40% dropout rate. Only 18% of the working population has higher education qualifications, substantially below the 25% OECD average. In order to promote high-level scientific study, the government is creating an "Institute of Science and Technology Austria" modeled on elite American universities and offering only PhD programs.

One can scarcely think about classical music without thinking of Austria. The first opera performance north of the Alps took place in Salzburg, and in Vienna opera and orchestra music thrived. Joseph Haydn, Wolfgang Amadeus Mozart, a child prodigy from Salzburg, and Ludwig van Beethoven, who chose Vienna as his second home, helped give Vienna the reputation as the music capital of the world, especially toward the end of the 18th century. Some critics argue that the American movie *Amadeus* completely distorted musical history. They maintain that Antonio Salieri was a good friend of both Haydn and Beethoven and was regarded as a top-flight conductor during his lifetime, although his compositions are seldom heard today. Although he disliked him, Salieri allegedly had nothing to do with the imagined poisoning of Mozart, who died of typhoid fever. His student and good friend, Franz Süssmayer, not Salieri, completed Mozart's *Requiem* after his death.

In the 19th century, Viennese-born Franz Schubert became one of the forerunners of the musical romantic movement. Twice a year in early and late summer, the "Schubertiade" festival is held in the tiny village of Schwarzenberg in western Vorarlberg. Anton Bruckner, Johannes Brahms and Hugo Wolf produced their musical treasures. Richard Strauss's opera, *Der Rosenkavalier*, whose words were written by Hugo von Hofmannsthal, premiered in Vienna in 1911. Light comedy became a particular Austrian specialty, with such masters as Johann Strauss, Karl Millocker ("The Beggar Student") and Franz Lehar ("The Merry Widow").

One has many reminders of Austria's musical past. There are many traditional musical festivals in the nine provinces and Vienna. Especially well-known is the festival in Salzburg, where many of the best conductors and musicians in the world assemble. One musical show that is not a part of the country's past is "The Sound of Music." It had never been produced at an Austrian theater until March 2005, when it began playing in German to sell-out and enthusiastic audiences at the venerable Volksoper. For decades it was believed that Austrians would resent a light American-style comedy set in the period when Hitler took over their country. Even the 1965 block-buster film version starring Julie Andrews and Christopher Plummer never got a theatrical release in Austria. There are, expectedly, some dour music critics who are not amused. One critic for the newspaper, *Kurier*, complained that the song "Edelweiss" is "an insult to Austrian musical creation."

Kaiser Maximilian I founded the Vienna Boys' Choir in 1498 to sing in daily masses and occasionally at the royal table. Some of its notable members were Haydn and Schubert. Since 1950 the boys, organized in four choirs of 24, have made many foreign tours and have become musical ambassadors for Austria. But in the midst of the choir's 500th anniversary, its artistic director, Agnes Grossmann, the first woman to hold that distinguished post, resigned in protest against the punishing concert and academic schedule. She argues that up to 100 annual concerts on top of demanding musical and academic studies overburdens the boys physically and emotionally. "When I arrived two years ago, the boys were emotionally dead. They wore masks and showed no sense of childhood joy." More bad news emerged in 2010 when eight former choir boys called a hot line set up by the choir to report sexual abuse.

Austria also has a rich literary heritage. In the 12th and 13th centuries the chivalrous and court poetry of Walther von der Vogelweide was admired throughout the

Austrians were gripped by eight-year captivity of this young girl in 2006

Austria

German-speaking world, and he remains one of the greatest writers of middle (high medieval) German. The greatest German medieval epic poem, the *Niebelungenlied* (about 1200 A.D.) was partly set in the Danube area. In the 18th and early 19th centuries, Franz Grillparzer was an especially important Austrian literary figure, and Adalbert Stifter's novel, "Indian Summer," written in the 19th century, is one of the greatest novels in German literature.

Around the close of the 19th century Vienna experienced a burst of artistic creativity. This time, known as the *fin de siècle*, was one in which Austria was experiencing social and political disintegration, a condition that created a fertile breeding ground for all that was new and for artists who wished to break with their past. So new and different were the young artistic products that one spoke of "Young Vienna."

"Viennese schools" developed in psychology, art and music and reached their full maturity by the outbreak of World War I. One poet described the city at that time as "the little world in which the big one holds its tryouts." Salons and cafes became lively places where intellectuals, professionals and businessmen met and discussed the issues of the day.

Sigmund Freud (whose 150th birth anniversary was celebrated in 2006) gave psychology a new direction he elaborated in his monumental work "The Interpretation of Dreams." Having moved man's sexual urges to the center of man's subconsciousness and behavior, he influenced

Christoph Waltz in Quentin Tarantino's "Inglorious Basterds" won the Oscar for Best Supporting Actor for portraying SS Colonel Hans Landa

the way humans view themselves and their motives as did few thinkers in history. Sigmund Freud Private University (SFU) opened its doors in 2005 in Vienna to train students in psychotherapy and psychology.

A contemporary of Freud, Konrad Lorenz, analyzed animal behavior to look for important clues to that of human beings. In art, the work of Gustav Klimt, Franz von Stuck and Kolo Moser was so unique that it was referred to as the "Vienna Secession." In music, Vienna became a rich terrain for the experiments of Gustav Mahler (who was allowed only one première in Vienna), Franz Schmidt, Alban Berg and Arnold

Schönberg. The last dispensed with traditional tonality and was perhaps the greatest musical revolutionary of the 20th century. His concerts often unleashed cries of "garbage!" and conspicuous rushes to the exits! The work of these experimentalists no doubt was partly a protest against the values of their society and was not very well received in their time.

In literature, Hugo von Hofmannsthal and Arthur Schnitzler appear as the very mirror of Vienna in their day. The first wrote mystical novels and a comedy in 1921, "The Difficult One," which vividly portrays the Austria that collapsed in 1918. Schnitzler's works, with their mixture of irony and sentimentality, were entertaining, but they also reflected the influence of Freud and contained effective attacks on the social ills of the day. Psychological insights into the human soul were also particularly revealing in the fascinating biographies of Stefan Zweig.

At the same time, Prague became an important German literary center within the Austrian Empire. Franz Kafka was a lonely figure who described man entrapped in a bureaucratic world. Rainer Maria Rilke, a master of German lyrical poetry, and Franz Werfel were also products of that intellectual crossroads between the Germanic and Slavic worlds.

World War I represented a true collapse with which the writers Joseph Roth and especially Robert Musil, in his fascinating portrait of Austria in "The Man without Qualities," tried to come to grips. In art, Austria showed its independence. It remained practically untouched by impressionism, but was deeply touched by expressionism and surrealism, as was shown by the works of Oskar Kokoschka and Alfred Kubin. The interwar years also produced one of the world's greatest movie directors: Billy Wilder.

The end of World War II signaled a new beginning for Austrian artists and writers. Many young and highly experimental authors, such as Gernot Wolfgruber, Franz Innerhofer, Peter Henisch and especially Peter Handke, have attracted serious attention. Handke's works are within the spirit of the anti-theater, which aims to break from the restraints of the traditional stage and to shock and teach the viewer. Some of Austria's talented authors and novelists chose to live and work in Germany. The 2004 Nobel Prize in Literature was awarded to Austrian novelist and playwright Elfriede Jelinek, who is especially known for her autobiographical novel, *The Piano Teacher*. Now as earlier, Austria provides a fertile home for traditional as well as *avant-garde* artistic movements.

Austrian film directors like Billy Wilder, Fred Zinnemann and Otto Preminger were Hollywood greats. The country still produces some internationally acclaimed films. An example, *38*, directed by Wolfgang Glueck, depicts a Jewish writer who searches desperately for a hiding place in Austria after the German invasion in 1938. *38* was nominated for Best Foreign-Language Film at the 1987 Academy Awards.

The 2008 Best Foreign-Language Film was won by an Austrian film, *The Counterfeiters*, directed by Stefan Ruzowitzky. Based on a true story described in a 2007 book by Adolf Burger, *The Devil's Workshop*, the film focuses on 140 Jewish prisoners in Sachsenhausen concentration camp who were forced by the Nazis to forge foreign currencies, stamps and documents. Burger was one of those prisoners who survived. In 2010 Viennese stage star Christoph Waltz won an Oscar for Best Supporting Actor for his role portraying the cultured multilingual "Jew Hunter," SS Colonel Hans Landa, in the *Inglorious Bastards*. The film is based on a true story.

With EU membership, Austria is unable to maintain the state broadcasting monopoly through the Austrian Broadcasting Corporation (ÖRF). Besides ÖRF's two television programs, about half of Austrian households can watch German channels through cable television. Private radio stations were permitted in 1994.

German newspaper concerns have purchased large stakes in some of Austria's largest publishing groups, and many newspapers depend on German money. Its quality newspaper market is led by the lively *Der Standard*, which was launched by the Axel Springer group in 1988. The second-largest daily is *Kurier*, which owns several important magazines and is itself partly owned by the German *Westdeutsche Allgemeine Zeitung*. They are followed by the stodgier *Die Presse* and the *Salzburger Nachrichten*. The powerful *Neue Kronen-Zeitung* dominates the tabloid market.

Most papers backed by political parties have folded.

The media had a field day reporting cases of cruel imprisonment to a stunned public in 2006 and 2008. First came the story of Natascha Kampusch, who was kidnapped as a 10-year-old girl and held in a miniscule dark underground cell for eight years until she managed to escape. Her captor killed himself within hours of her flight by throwing himself in front of a train. She gave TV interviews to an enthralled public on the riveting story of her abduction and captivity.

Natascha's case was widely considered to be the epitome of depravity in Austria's postwar history until the nation learned two years later about 73-year-old Josef Fritzl, who kept one of his daughters imprisoned for 24 years in a basement dungeon, where he subjected her continually to sexual abuse and incest. She bore him seven children, three of whom never saw daylight until they were liberated.

Fritzl admitted that "my drive to have sex with Elisabeth grew stronger and stronger." He was charged with rape and also murder for not providing medical care to the seventh child, who died. He pleaded guilty in 2009 and began his life sentence at a psychiatric hospital. He described himself as a product of Nazi-era Austria, with its obsession for discipline and order. Such statements sparked endless public psychoanalysis, as well as nervous assurances by the country's leaders that "it's not Austria that is the perpetrator" (ex-Chancellor Gusenbauer) and "there is definitely nothing fundamentally Austrian in this case" (President Fischer).

FUTURE

Since 1945 Austria has developed a stable and harmonious political and social order, which can be expected to survive all but the most devastating economic and political crises. This will enable it to survive the current economic crisis, its worst since the war although less serious than for many other European countries. Its 4.9% unemployment is among the lowest in the continent. Housing prices have fallen only slightly. Its banks have weathered the storm rather well. Economic prosperity, which has resulted from social peace, active cooperation of all economic groups, low defense budgets (.8% of GDP) and relatively productive industries, will be maintained. The policy of neutrality is being changed to become compatible with its membership in the EU, but NATO membership is unlikely anytime soon.

Public opinion is more skeptical toward the EU than in any other member state, and hostility toward Turkish entry is strong. But there is no likelihood that voters would choose to leave the EU. It and the euro are important supports in dealing with the global economic crisis that caused its GDP growth to plummet to minus 3.5% in 2009 and minus 1.9% in 2010. Its budget deficit ballooned to 5% in 2010. Overcoming the current deep economic recession will continue to be a challenge in the immediate future.

During the seven-year rule by the People's and Freedom parties, Austria underwent painful but necessary economic and political adjustments that made the country one of the EU's best economic performers. It rejected the traditional consensus politics and passed far-reaching reforms, including privatization and the pension system. The fact that the labor unions opposed them all, but could not prevent them, was a measure of their loss of influence.

The grand coalition partners had consistently strained relations and bickered constantly. A leadership crisis in the SPÖ in July 2008 prompted the People's Party to terminate the 18-month grand coalition. The fall was largely due to the poor leadership and lack of charisma on the part of Alfred Gusenbauer. He was replaced as chancellor by the more charismatic and popular Werner Faymann. New elections held on September 28, 2008, brought a dramatic surge of the two far-right Freedom and BZO parties and a decline in the two main ones, the Social Democratic and the People's parties. A renewed grand coalition of the two latter parties under the leadership of Chancellor Faymann went into effect in December 2008. It is operating smoothly even though the People's Party is running ahead of the Social Democrats in most polls. The next election will be in 2012.

The election in 2003 of native son Arnold Schwarzenegger as governor of California received top billing in Austria. It honored his 57th birthday with a one-euro stamp. No less than former President Thomas Klestil asserted that "we are proud of you. . . . Your repeated references to your youth in Austria have considerably raised the profile of our country in the United States . . . and demonstrates to America and the world how good Austrians are." Even the French intellectual newspaper, *Le Monde*, chimed in that Mozart is no longer the most famous Austrian in the world. Schwarzenegger is. He did get a black eye in his country of origin in December 2005 when he refused to save a convicted murderer, Tookie Williams, from execution. Like all EU countries, Austria has no death penalty. The Green Party even demanded that Schwarzenegger be stripped of his Austrian citizenship, something former Chancellor Wolfgang Schüssel called "absurd."

The Republic of Poland

A glimpse of the interior of the Royal Castle, Warsaw

Courtesy: Embassy of Poland

Area: 120,727 sq. mi. (312,683 sq. km.).
Population: 38.5 million.
Capital City: Warsaw (Pop. 1,688,000).
Climate: Temperate in the West; continental with colder winters in the East.
Neighboring Countries: Ukraine, Belarus (East); Lithuania (Northeast); Russia—Kaliningrad Enclave (North); Czech Republic, Slovakia (South); Germany (West).
Official Language: Polish.
Other Principal Tongues: Belarusian, Ukrainian, German.
Ethnic Background: Polish (98%) other (2%).
Principal Religions: Roman Catholic (ca. 90%; ca. 50% practicing), Uniate, Greek Orthodox, Protestant and other (5%).
Chief Commercial Products: Machinery and transport equipment, semi-manufactured goods, chemicals, agricultural and food products, mineral fuels.
Main Trading Partners: EU (78.9% of exports and 73.3% of imports), Germany (26.7% of exports and 29.8% of imports), Italy (7.1% of exports and 6.7% of imports), France (6.2% of exports), UK (6.1% of exports), Russia (9.1% of imports), China (5.4% of imports).

Currency: zloty
Former Political Status: Independent kingdom from the 10th century; joined with Lithuania in the 14th century, decline in power in the 17th century leading to partitions of Poland by Russia, Prussia and Austria at the end of the 18th century; independent from 1918 until German conquest in 1939; "People's Republic" within the Soviet sphere 1944–1989.
National Day: May 3 (marking the day in 1791 when Poland adopted the first democratic constitution in Europe) and November 11 (marking Polish independence after the First World War).
Chief of State: Bronislaw Komorowski, President (since July 2010).
Head of Government: Donald Tusk, Prime Minister (since November 2007).
National Flag: White and red horizontal bars.

An exasperated Stalin once remarked, "communism fits Poland like a saddle fits a cow." A Roman Catholic people whose hearts and minds have always pointed westward, Poles paid a heavy historical price for living between Europe's two largest nations, Russia and Germany, with

an expansive Austro-Hungarian Empire to the south until 1918. Unlike countries such as the United States or Britain, they seldom had the tranquility and luxury to determine their own place in the world and to manage their own affairs. That changed dramatically in 1989 with the end of communism in Poland and again in 1991 with the collapse of their Eastern nemesis, the Soviet Union. Poles have not only regained their sovereignty, but they find that the world around them has totally changed. Whereas they had three unfriendly neighbors until 1989, *none of which exists today*, they now are surrounded by seven peaceful (though not all stable) nations.

Poland is shaped in an uneven circle as a result of the boundary changes that occurred after World War II. The land is mostly a flat plain that rises to mountainous heights only along the southern border, where the Sudeten and Carpathian ranges are found. These mountains seldom exceed 2,000 feet in elevation within Poland. The soil is not very rich, and for this reason, agricultural yields are rather modest except in relatively small areas of black soil and wind-driven topsoil found in the center and south of the country. Eu-

Poland

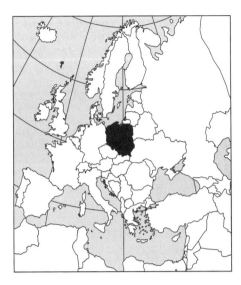

rope's fifth largest country, Poland is located at the crossroads of the continent, halfway between Brussels and Moscow or Stockholm and Athens.

The climate reflects the middle position of Poland between Western Europe, with its moist oceanic climate, and Eastern Europe with a dry, continental climate. The summers are warm and permit the cultivation of fairly good crops except during the years when there is not enough rain. The winters, on the other hand, can be bitterly cold.

Poland had significant Ukrainian, Belarussian, Jewish and German minorities prior to World War II. Today, as a result of events associated with that war, Poland is ethnically and religiously homogeneous. Almost every citizen is both an ethnic Pole and a Roman Catholic.

HISTORY

The Early Polish Kingdoms

Poland officially celebrated its millennium—a thousand years of existence as a state—in 1966. This date, observed with much pomp by the communist govern-

ment, is actually the thousandth anniversary of the introduction of Christianity into the area. Roman Catholicism was established in Poland in the year 966.

The Piast ruling dynasty was named after its semi-legendary founder, Piast, who brought together under his leadership a number of Slavic tribes living in the area between the Vistula and Oder rivers. The most important of these were the *Polanie*, which means "inhabitants of the plains" in Polish. It is from the name of this tribe that the name *Polska* (Poland in English) is derived. Prince Mieszko I (Mee-*ehs*-ko) adopted Roman Catholicism in 966, and it thereafter became the religion of the country as well.

Mieszko I's adoption of Christianity may have been genuine, but it was also a wise political move. A thousand years ago, it was an insurance policy against the continued pressure of German rulers who justified their incursions into Polish lands as a movement to convert the pagans.

The fact that Poland adopted Christianity in its Western form has been of great and lasting influence in Polish history. With Roman Catholicism came the Roman alphabet, to which were added letters designed to render some specific Slavic sounds. In contrast, the Russians and other

eastern and southern subbranches of the Slav family adopted the Cyrillic script, which is based on the Greek alphabet.

Because of the split between the Roman Catholic and the Eastern Orthodox churches, Poles later came to think of themselves as an outpost and frontier of Catholicism and Western culture. The Russians, being orthodox ("correct") Christians, viewed the Poles as "intruding Roman heretics." A

Shifting borders: c. 1150 . . .

and c. 1350

307

Poland

mixture of political rivalries and conflicting spiritual values resulted in a lasting hostility between the two leading Slav nations.

The consequences of this split did not fully appear for several centuries. Prior to that, the Polish state, linked in a dynastic union with the much larger Grand Duchy of Lithuania from the 15th century onward, was one of the most important European realms. The land that would later become known as Russia did not free itself from the long period of Tatar rule until toward the end of the 15th century. It did not emerge as a regional power until the 16th century.

The early history of Poland was marked by the struggle to create a stable national state while fending off incursions by German princes from the west and contesting with "Russian" princes for territory and power in the East. In addition, Polish kings sometimes had to block early Bohemian (Czech) rulers who claimed some of the areas held by the Polish crown.

One of the early Piast rulers occupied Kiev (now the Ukrainian capital) briefly, while another ruler, Boleslaw the Brave, extended his control toward the Black Sea. Important trade routes were brought under Polish control during this period. However, these successes were undermined by a method of inheritance called the *appanage* system, whereby the territory of a ruling prince was divided among all his sons. While destroying the unity of the kingdom, this led to endless clashes among brothers and cousins for the position of leadership. The same kind of inheritance system prevailed after 1054 in the early "Russian" state of Kiev, with similar results. The contenders were forced to rely on combinations of fighting men and on alliances with the higher clergy for support. This was paid for by land grants or by delegations of political power to the landed gentry (*szlachta*). The political power of the gentry thus grew, and this hampered the growth of a strong, centralized monarchy. It also led later to a concept of liberty almost bordering on anarchy, thus making orderly government practically impossible.

The most famous—or infamous—example of this development in later centuries was the concept of the *liberum veto*, which was never used from 1505 to 1648. By 1795, however, it brought the state down. By speaking the words *veto nie pozwalam*— "I do not allow," a *single* member of the national assembly could block legislation and force the assembly to be dissolved. In practice, these obstructive votes of minor gentry could be controlled or purchased by powerful magnates, or even by agents of foreign powers meddling in Poland's affairs. Although praised as a "democratic system," the constitutional freedoms and privileges were actually extended almost exclusively to the gentry, which was about 10% of the population. The city dwellers enjoyed some rights, but the peasants were reduced to serfdom. This oppressive system continued with little change during the existence of the Polish-Lithuanian "commonwealth."

The unity of the state was restored in the 14th century under Wladyslaw Lokietek, father of Casimir (Kazimierz) the Great, who strengthened the state. The cities now expanded as German artisans and Jewish traders moved eastward under official encouragement. Culture advanced. Jagiellonian University in Krakow was established in 1364. It later became a distinguished seat of learning and the alma mater of the astronomer Copernicus.

In spite of Casimir's wisdom and great contributions to government, law and culture, his rule was characterized by a loss of Polish territories in the west and southwest. The province of Silesia was ceded to semi-Germanized Czech rulers, while the Teutonic Knights, a militarized German religious order, was allowed to extend its control over areas adjacent to the Baltic Sea. Poland expanded eastward, setting the stage for future clashes with the Russian state once it had freed itself from Tatar domination. For a while, however, it seemed that the Polish state was safely launched on a course of greatness with its power embracing territory from the Baltic to the Black Sea.

The Jagiellonians

Casimir the Great was the last of the Piast dynasty because he had no male heir. The throne passed to his nephew, Louis of Anjou, who was also the king of Hungary, and then to the latter's daughter, Jadwiga.

A new era in the history of Poland opened when she married the grand duke of Lithuania, Jagiello, who converted to Roman Catholicism upon his marriage. He turned the grand duchy over to his cousin, Vytautas, and became king of Poland in 1386, founding a dynasty that lasted until 1572.

However, Vytautas also died without an heir in 1430, so the Grand Duchy of Lithuania reverted back to the line of Jagiello. It became increasingly tied to Poland until, in 1569, the two kingdoms were merged in the Union of Lublin.

One of the reasons for the union of Poland and Lithuania was joint defense against the Teutonic Knights along the Baltic Sea. Although Polish forces soundly defeated the Knights at Tannenberg (Grunwald) in 1410 and forced them to acknowledge the authority of the Polish king, they were never fully brought under Polish control. Thus when, with the advent of the Reformation in the 16th century, the Knights dissolved their religious order—becoming eventually the nucleus of the kingdom of Prussia—they became a standing menace to Poland's access to the sea. The Reformation also resulted in a widespread adoption of Protestantism in Poland. But this was reversed by the new order of Jesuits, which essentially won Poland back for Roman Catholicism during the counter-reformation.

Decline and Fall

The previously loose organization of Poland-Lithuania was transformed in 1569 into a more centralized state. However, soon thereafter, with the end of the Jagiellonians, the process of decline began. Until a final collapse at the end of the 18th century, there was a succession of elected kings, most of whom were foreign.

Shrine to the Virgin Mary, Czestochowa

One of these monarchs, Sigismund III of the Swedish royal house of Vasa, involved Poland in the "Time of Troubles" that raged in Russia following the death of Ivan Grozny ("the Terrible"). Polish troops occupied Moscow in 1610 and used false pretenders to the Russian throne to advance Polish policy. These attempts to profit from Russia's weakness were unsuccessful, but they created lasting resentment and distrust.

The rest of the 17th century was one of much misery for Poland. It was during this period, for example, that Poland lost most of Ukraine. Part of the territories of the Grand Duchy of Lithuania, which had been united under the Polish crown in 1569, this area was occupied mostly by Cossacks, nearly all of whom were Russian Orthodox. Intent on separating them from Russia in the 17th century, Poland alienated them by trying to force them all into a new "Uniate" church that recognized the authority of Rome. An economic factor was also present: in addition to encouraging Polish noblemen to settle in the area and to polanize the Ukrainian nobles there, the Polish crown had issued decrees that would have turned the mass of Ukrainian peasants into serfs.

Bogdan Khmelnitsky, whose own lands had been taken over by another Polish nobleman, now became a leader for Ukrain-

⫿⫿⫿	First partition (1772)
▨	Second partition (1793)
▧	Third partition (1795)

BALTIC SEA
PRUSSIA
EAST PRUSSIA
RUSSIA
Warsaw
AUSTRIA

POLAND: A land devoured

ian autonomy. Elected *Hetman* (chief) of the Zaporozhian Cossacks, Khmelnitsky launched an uprising in 1648 that cleared much of the Ukraine of Polish forces. However, a defeat by Poland convinced him that the Cossacks were not strong enough to achieve victory on their own. Believing that a Polish victory would mean the end of the Orthodox Church in Ukraine, Khmelnitsky sought Russian help to win independence for Ukraine. After helping the Ukrainians, however, Russia later controlled them.

Russia accepted the Cossack offer in 1653. War broke out the following year between Poland and Russia. A year later, Sweden took advantage of the situation to invade Poland. But it was too large for Sweden to control. It had almost destroyed Poland before the Swedish forces were stopped near a shrine to the Virgin Mary at Czestochowa. Tradition credits the rescue of the country to the miraculous intervention of the Virgin Mary.

The war between Russia and Poland had been "put on hold" during the Swedish invasion, but when the Swedes had

been driven out, that war started again. It ended in the Truce of Androsovo, signed in 1667. Under its terms Russia obtained all of Ukraine east of the Dnieper River and was permitted to occupy the city of Kiev for two years. Russia never gave back Kiev, however, and the terms of the truce were made permanent by a treaty of peace signed in 1686.

Poland's decline was briefly interrupted during the reign of Jan Sobieski, a native Polish ruler who led a Polish army to Vienna in 1683 to help lift the siege of that city by the Ottoman Turks. Although this victory bolstered the self-image of the Poles as a strong Christian power, the image was misleading.

After Sobieski's death, the Poles turned to a foreign ruler, Augustus, king of Saxony, and offered him the Polish crown. King Augustus II (his Polish title) offered the young Peter the Great an alliance against Sweden, suggesting that Charles XII, the new young Swedish king, would be unable to defend the extensive territories along the Baltic Sea that his grandfather had seized in the 17th century. The re-

Poland

sult was the Great Northern War that began in 1700.

Augustus was wrong about Charles XII although that young ruler made a mistake in concluding, after the battle of Narva, that Poland, not Russia, was the real enemy. Charles XII spent the next seven years waging a war against Poland, eventually defeating Augustus II and forcing him to abdicate as king of Poland. He then placed his own candidate on the throne. Augustus II was reinstated as king of Poland after Peter the Great's defeat of Charles XII at Poltava in 1709.

This marked the real end of Polish independent action, if not formal independence. From this time onward, foreign powers would dictate who sat on the Polish throne. The last king of Poland was Stanislaw August Poniatowski, a former favorite of Catherine the Great, empress of Russia. He was a man of great culture and charm, but he possessed only limited talents for governing a country in a state of disintegration.

Partitions of Poland were carried out in 1772, 1793 and 1795 by neighboring Russia, Prussia and Austria. They first diminished, then finally ended, the independent existence of the once glorious commonwealth. Before the final partition, there were still occasional expressions of Polish patriotism. Casimir Pulaski, the youthful leader of one such movement, eventually left Poland for the United States and died while fighting the English in America's War of Independence. Another Pole, Tadeusz Kosciuszko (Kos-*chewsh*-ko), led an unsuccessful uprising in Poland after fighting in the American Revolutionary War. There was also a final effort to reform the political structure that resulted in a proposed constitution, regarded with reverence even today as the May 3 Constitution (1791) although it was never actually put into effect.

"Not Yet Lost"

After the collapse of the old commonwealth, the struggle for the revival of Poland was continued mainly by trying to interest foreign powers in sponsoring restoration of an independent Poland. Poles also flocked to various armies fighting or preparing to fight one or the other partitioner. Many were attracted by the high-sounding slogans of the French Revolution. This led many to enlist in a Polish legion created by Napoleon in the Italian province of Lombardy. Their official song began with the words "Poland is not yet lost as long as we live." It became the national anthem in later years and still is today. Napoleon actually had little concern for the cause of Polish independence although he was glad to see Poles join his armies. He did create a symbolic "Polish"

state in 1807—the Duchy of Warsaw— which collapsed with the defeat of his forces in the historic battles of 1812.

At the Congress of Vienna, Alexander I of Russia demanded that the historic Polish lands be brought together to form a new Kingdom of Poland with himself as head of state. Adam Czartoryski, a Pole who was one of Alexander's advisers, had actually suggested the idea. Neither Austria nor Prussia was eager to give up Polish territories obtained as a result of the partitions, but they eventually agreed to Alexander's demands. The Kingdom of Poland thus came into existence in 1815 as a separate possession of the Russian emperor. Alexander took the title of king of Poland and not only granted the Poles a constitution, but also set up a separate Polish government and army. He then named his brother, the Russian Grand Duke Constantine, as regent and actual ruler of Poland.

Although Constantine's wife was Polish, and he ruled by all accounts both competently and fairly, many Poles were dissatisfied with this arrangement which, after all, implied Russian domination, even if indirect. They therefore rebelled in 1830 and attempted to expel the Russians. The attempt failed, and Nicholas I, who had in the meantime become tsar, punished the Poles by abolishing the constitution and making Poland an administrative unit within the Russian Empire. In spite of another unsuccessful Polish uprising in 1863, it remained part of Russia until World War I.

Throughout the 19th century, there were many expressions of sympathy for the cause of an independent Poland, especially whenever spectacular, but unsuccessful, uprisings occurred, such as in 1830 and 1863. But there was no occasion for outside intervention in "The Polish Problem" until the First World War. That war, which ended with the defeat of Germany, the collapse of the Austro-Hungarian Empire and the weakening of Russia through revolution and civil war, finally led to the rebirth of Poland as an independent state. Among those who advocated it even prior to the end of the war was President Woodrow Wilson, who made the argument that "statesmen everywhere are agreed" that an independent Poland was necessary as part of a reconstituted Europe.

Poland after World War I

Poland was officially reborn on November 11, 1918, but it enjoyed an independent existence for a little more than 20 years. The Treaty of Versailles, signed in June 1919, granted Poland access to the Baltic Sea through a narrow corridor that separated East Prussia from the main body of Germany. In addition, the city of Danzig (Gdansk), which had been designated as Poland's port, was organized as a free city with a League of Nations high commissioner. Although permitted internal self-government, its foreign relations

Signing the German-Soviet Pact (August 23, 1939) which divided Poland between them. L. to r.: Germany's Ribbentrop with Stalin, Molotov

were placed under Polish control. This clumsy arrangement was necessitated by the fact that the League of Nations did not want to put this largely German-speaking city under Polish rule, but believed that it had to provide Poland with a port. Hitler's demand for Danzig's return to Germany was later used to "justify" the Nazi invasion of Poland.

The reborn Polish state consisted of provinces that had been under the foreign rule of three different countries for over a century. There was much wartime destruction. Immediately following the end of the war, Poles experienced widespread hunger, alleviated to some extent by an American relief program. Politically, the nation was badly divided, with a number of groups and parties competing for power. In addition, the country was still largely agricultural, and its rapidly growing population made the economic situation even more difficult.

From 1918 to 1920 Poland fought six border wars—against Germany, Czechoslovakia, Lithuania, western Ukraine and Bolshevik Russia. The latter war was significant for all of Europe in that it prevented the Bolsheviks from linking up with communists in Germany. It thereby helped foil the communist revolution there and kept the Bolsheviks out of the heart of Europe. The Bolsheviks viewed Poland as the "red bridge" to Europe. Poles saw the struggle as a crucial test of whether the Bolsheviks could rebuild the Tsarist empire and whether the bordering countries could resist Russian imperialism disguised as socialism. The fighting lasted two years. Led by Marshal Jozef Pilsudski, a former socialist who had fought on the side of Germany and Austria in World War I, the Poles struck in the East and took most of Lithuania and Belarusia and entered Ukraine. The Bolsheviks drove them out of Ukraine in June 1920 and within six weeks were at the gates of Warsaw. But in August the Polish army delivered a devastating blow to the invaders, decimating three Soviet armies. Admitting his mistake in believing the Poles would welcome the Red Army, Lenin sued for peace. Before the fighting ended, Pilsudski took Vilnius from Lithuania in October 1920. In March 1921 the Treaty of Riga drew the line between Poland and the Soviet republics, established diplomatic relations between Poland and the USSR, and completed Poland's struggle for acceptable borders.

One of the first prime ministers, the world-famous pianist Ignacy Paderewski (Pad-er-*ev*-ski), left the country after a few months, disgusted with the constant political squabbles. Pilsudski, the provisional chief of state, temporarily retired from politics during this period as well.

Warsaw; 1945 and today

He was persuaded to return to power in May 1926, however, to rescue the country from disaster due to the political bickering. From that time until the end in 1939, the country was governed, first, by Pilsudski, who died in 1935, and then by his associates, especially a group known as "the colonels."

Parliamentary government was never fully abolished, but the system was "streamlined." Political parties were permitted to continue in existence, but only the candidates who had the approval of the administration could be elected to the parliament (*Sejm*, pronounced "same").

During this period, domestic affairs were dominated by continuing problems concerning the economy and ethnic mi-

norities with doubtful loyalties to Poland. The Nazis later recruited many Germans, while the Ukrainians had their own strong revolutionary movement, with a terrorist wing.

In addition, some young alienated Poles joined the illegal Communist Party, then an elite party. But filling the prisons with these disaffected youngsters only turned the jails into "prison universities" where the inmates received thorough indoctrination from fellow prisoners sometimes deliberately planted there by the party.

The fear of communism and the bitter relations with Soviet Russia, against which Poland had waged a war in 1919–20, forced Poland to maintain a large army. Aware of their dangerous location

Poland

Map legend:
- BALTIC SEA
- Kaliningrad
- Danzig
- U.S.S.R.
- Vilnius
- Bialystok
- U.S.S.R.
- Brest
- Minsk
- Warsaw
- East Germany
- Wrocław
- Jelenia Gora
- Kraków
- L'vov
- U.S.S.R.
- CZECHOSLOVAKIA
- U.S.S.R.
- N

Annexed to Russia, 1939   - - - - - - 1939 Boundary
Annexed from Germany, 1945   ——— 1945 to present
                                        ■ ■ ■ ■ Curson line

0   50   100 Mi.
0 50 100 150 Km.

between Germany and the Soviet Union, the Poles tried to maneuver between the two powerful neighbors. Although they signed a nonaggression agreement with Hitler in January 1934, they refused to enter into a closer, anti-Soviet association with the Nazis. In the end, neither the Germans nor the Soviets had any reason to side with the Poles against the other. Poland also alienated Western public opinion by participating in the division of Czechoslovakia, which occurred following the Munich Conference in 1938.

Poland during World War II

Undeterred by a guarantee of territorial integrity the government of Great Britain gave to Poland, Hitler made a series of brash demands on Poland during the summer of 1939 that were rejected by the Polish foreign minister. Then, on August 23, 1939, Hitler signed a Nonaggression Pact with the Soviet Union. The secret portions of the pact provided for a new partition of Poland. The Soviet Union received the eastern part of the country with its heavily non-Polish population. Poland's poorly equipped force proved un-

able to resist the massive attack launched by Hitler in September 1939.

The heroic, but futile Polish resistance to the German armies ended in mid-September 1939. Soviet troops marched into Eastern Poland on September 17 and stopped along an agreed-upon boundary, called the Ribbentrop-Molotov Line named after the German and Soviet foreign ministers. The Polish government had, by this time, already fled the country, making its way, first to Romania, then to France, where it set up a Polish government-in-exile. It finally moved to London in May 1940 after Hitler's invasion of France. The partitioning powers energetically tried to wipe out all traces of an independent Poland between September 1939 and June 22, 1941, when the short-lived cooperation between Hitler and Stalin came to an end with Hitler's invasion of the Soviet Union. A large part of Poland was directly incorporated into the Greater German Reich. The remainder was formed into a "General Government" under a Nazi governor, Hans Frank.

A systematic policy of exterminating Poland's political and intellectual leaders

reflected a Nazi plan to make the Poles a source of manual labor, working for the benefit of the "master race." Separately, Jews were herded into ghettos, then later shipped off to death camps and gas chambers. When only 60,000 were left in the ghetto, Jewish fighters rose up in April 1943 and valiantly battled against German soldiers for almost a month. There was no chance of military success, and it was crushed, as was the second Polish insurrection that broke out in Warsaw on August 1, 1944. The last survivor of the 1943 Ghetto Uprising, then 23-year-old Marek Edelman, said: "Humanity has decided that it is more beautiful to die with a gun in your hand than without." He passed away in 2009 aged 87.

One brave woman, Irena Sendler, was awarded Poland's highest honor, the White Eagle, in 2003 for having organized an elaborate and dangerous scheme that rescued more Jewish children from the ghetto than the Jewish workers Oscar Schindler had been able to save. She died in 2008 at age 98.

Many Polish families protected Jews. But in at least one case it was Poles themselves who perpetrated the crime. In a shocking book, *Neighbors*, published in 2000, New York University historian, Jan T. Gross, detailed how in July 1941 Polish townsmen beat, clubbed and drowned a hundred Jews in the small town of Jedwabne; then they forced 1,500 more into a barn, doused it with gasoline and set it ablaze. To postwar Poles, who for 60 years had been taught that their people had been heroic victims, never collaborators, in Nazi atrocities, this was a shattering revelation for which ex-President Aleksander Kwasniewski publicly apologized in 2001. In 2008 Gross published a second book, *Fear: Anti-Semitism in Poland after Auschwitz*, which recounts how some returning Jewish concentration camp survivors were killed by Poles who had occupied their property. An opinion poll taken in 2008 concluded that 36% of Poles still had a negative view of Jews and 46% had negative views of Muslims.

Meanwhile, an independent Poland continued to exist in the form of its government-in-exile in England. Many thousands of Poland's fighting men managed to make their way west in 1939 and formed military detachments pledged to fight side by side with the Western allies. Polish airmen, in particular, distinguished themselves during the Battle of Britain, the massive German air assault on England in August–September 1940. They fought anywhere the British fought, including in Narvik, Tobruk and elsewhere in North Africa.

The position of the Poles was complicated by the fact that, while the West was allied with the USSR in their joint strug-

Poland

Warsaw Uprising: Listening for Instructions

gle against Nazi Germany, the Poles saw the Soviet Union as an enemy as well, since it had obtained extensive Polish territories as a result of the Nazi-Soviet Nonaggression Pact of 1939. After Hitler launched his invasion of the Soviet Union in June 1941, the British attempted to mediate the breech. They managed to persuade the Polish government-in-exile to sign an agreement restoring relations between the USSR and Poland.

As a result, the Soviet Union permitted the formation of a number of Polish fighting units from among prisoners taken by the Soviet Union in 1939 and from among the many Polish citizens who had sought refuge in the Soviet Union. Because of the serious rifts between the Polish forces and the Soviet leadership, the troops, commanded by General Wladyslaw Anders, were placed under British command and trained in Palestine. Later, they served gallantly in Italy, especially at Monte Cassino, where they were the first allied soldiers to enter the ruins of the famed monastery.

The Soviet Union had always insisted that it intended to retain the territories obtained as a result of the Nazi-Soviet Nonaggression Pact. As Soviet war fortunes began to improve, it showed increasing dissatisfaction with the insistence of the Polish government-in-exile on regaining the prewar frontiers of Poland in the East.

The break between the USSR and the Polish government-in-exile occurred in 1943 when the Germans announced the discovery of a mass grave of 21,768 Polish officers in the Katyn Forest. Each had been murdered by a bullet to the back of the

head. Since many were only reservists serving in wartime, the victims included the military, political, intellectual, medical, scientific, legal and business crème of Polish society. The Soviets had slaughtered them and blamed the crime on the Germans. General Wladyslaw Sikorski, the Polish prime minister-in-exile, asked for an impartial inquiry by the International Red Cross. Claiming its total innocence, the Soviet Union accused Sikorski of helping Nazi propaganda and severed all ties to the Polish government-in-exile. Sikorski died in a 1943 air accident, and one theory holds that Stalin ordered his killing. His body was exhumed in 2008 to try to determine the cause of his death.

In the Soviet Union, a Union of Polish Patriots now emerged as spokesman for the Poles. A Polish "army" was formed as an auxiliary of the Soviet troops. These communist-led organizations became the nucleus of the Lublin Committee, which was installed July 22, 1944, as the new government of Poland after the Red Army had reached what the Soviet Union was willing to recognize as Polish territory.

On August 1, 1944, when the Soviet Army had moved to the eastern bank of the Vistula River, and it looked like the Germans were withdrawing from Warsaw, the underground loyal to the London leadership staged an uprising, assuming that the Allies would help them. It hoped to obtain control of the city before the Red Army captured it.

At the last moment, Hitler issued orders for his troops to make a stand, and the up-

rising was brutally crushed after 63 days, leaving 200,000 persons dead (including many of the country's intellectuals and leaders) and 80% of the city destroyed. The Red Army made no attempt to cross the Vistula and come to the aid of the Poles. Stalin called the fighters a "band of criminals" and made airlifts impossible by refusing to allow British and American planes to refuel in the Soviet Union. The Soviets later arrested some of those who had escaped through the sewer system.

The official Soviet explanation was that the Red Army had run out of steam after a successful push over the summer, and it needed time to pause and regroup before pushing on westward. The failed uprising added another lasting element of bitterness and resentment to the relations between the two countries. Stalin was, in fact, extremely suspicious of any Poles not under his control. Such individuals should never again be permitted to play a political role in Poland. At one point, sixteen leaders of the pro-London underground were lured into the open, supposedly for the purpose of negotiation with the Soviets. Instead, they were unceremoniously arrested and imprisoned. The psychological and physical magnitude of the catastrophe is almost unimaginable. In August 2004, on the 60th anniversary of the uprising, a museum commemorating it was opened in Warsaw.

Following the Yalta Agreement of February 1945, the U.S. and Great Britain "derecognized" the government-in-exile. This was after the Soviet Union had agreed to

First Secretary Wladyslaw Gomulka (left) chats with Chairman of the Council of State Aleksander Zawadzki AP/Wide World Photo

313

Poland

add a few noncommunist leaders to the communist government in Warsaw and to create a government of "national unity." The most prominent noncommunist addition was Stanislaw Mikolajczyk (Mee-koh-*wie*-chik), leader of the peasant party.

Stalin's vague promises of "free and unfettered elections," made at Yalta, offered little protection to noncommunist groups that tried to resume their political activities after the war. The fiction of "national unity" died as soon as the onset of the Cold War ended the illusion of postwar accord between East and West. Mikolajczyk had to flee the country in 1947.

From "People's Democracy" to "People's Republic"

Postwar Poland is, in many respects, an almost entirely new country. It is located about 185 miles farther to the west than it had been in 1939. At the expense of Germany, it gained a 325-mile-long coast on the Baltic Sea. This is a large coastline when compared to the narrow corridor of the interwar period. What had been East Prussia prior to the war was divided between Poland and the Soviet Union. It eliminated what many Poles viewed as a "dagger pointed at the heart of Poland." The former German city of Königsberg became the heart of the present Russian enclave of Kaliningrad [see separate entry]. The frontier with Germany was substantially shortened. The "recovered" lands taken from Germany are economically more valuable than those surrendered to the USSR.

Another basic change was in the demographic composition. Instead of having a population more than 30% ethnically non-Polish, the country today is inhabited by almost 39 million people, only about 2.3% of whom are ethnic minorities. Most of the Ukrainians and Belarusians who had lived in Poland were annexed into the Soviet Union. From 200,000–300,000 Ukrainians are left in the western part of Poland, where they had been forcibly resettled in 1945. In northern Poland about 200,000–300,000 Belarusian still live. Around 20,000 Lithuanians, 20,000 Slovaks, 3,000 Czechs, and 13,000–15,000 Russians live within Poland's borders. All the above minorities are well integrated into Polish society.

That does not apply to the heterogeneous collection of 23,000–25,000 Gypsies (Roma) who live in Poland. One also sees increasing numbers of Vietnamese and Armenians, who have crossed the border and settled. The Germans had exterminated the bulk of the more than three million Jews. This meant that half of the victims of the holocaust were Poles. The majority of Jews who managed to survive chose to leave the country, but between 6,000 and 15,000 remain. Only in the 21st century are Jews beginning to return to

Poland. Most Germans were expelled, and only an estimated 300,000–500,000 presently well-integrated Germans remain, mainly in Opole. Thus, Poland is more Polish and more Roman Catholic than it had been for many centuries.

Until mid-1947, during the period of "national unity," the official claim was that the system established in Poland was to be different from both the capitalist model of the West and the communist one of the Soviet Union. This claim could not survive the beginning of the Cold War, however. While the United States proclaimed a policy of "containment" of communism, the USSR sponsored creation of the Communist Information Bureau (*Cominform*) at a conference held in western Poland in 1947. Under the circumstances, Moscow compelled Poland to reject an offer of Marshall Plan aid extended by the U.S.A. Soon thereafter, the rift between Stalin and Marshal Tito of Yugoslavia led the Soviet Union to exert even more pressure to hold the line elsewhere in Central and Eastern Europe. In one country after another, communist leaders identified with the "national" road to socialism were removed from office, jailed, and sometimes executed.

For a variety of reasons, events in Poland did not lead to such extreme measures against leaders accused of "nationalist deviationism," but there were drastic changes. Wladyslaw Gomulka, who had been active in the pro-Soviet underground during the years of German occupation and who presided over the absorption of the territories "recovered" from Germany, was removed from office at this time and eventually imprisoned. Never tried, he was able to reemerge as a leader in 1956.

Communist domination over all aspects of social life and Soviet direction of Polish internal affairs were substantially strengthened in the late 1940s. Political parties that had kept their prewar names were brought under communist control. Some of the pre-1945 non-communist leaders were induced to merge either with the communists or with the communist-front groups. Thus, the Polish Socialist Party (PPS) was merged with the communists, who had been using the name Polish Workers Party, to form the Polish United Workers Party. It is important to note that the word "communist" had such a negative ring in the ears of most Poles that the ruling party never dared call itself by that name.

In spite of all of the changes in the wartime and early postwar period, the communists could not compete for the support of the workers against the traditional Polish Socialist Party. It was merged out of existence, largely with the help of one of its younger leaders, Jozef Cyrankiewicz (Tsee-*ran*-kay-vich). He was rewarded with the

Edward Gierek

job of premier from 1947–53 and 1955–70; he was later appointed chairman of the Council of State (1970–1972). The Peasant Faction, which had retained a large following under its prewar leadership, was forced to combine with a communist-front group to form the United Peasant Party. Independent social organizations were also herded together into "united" groups controlled by the communists.

The high point of Soviet meddling in Polish affairs was reached when Konstantin Rokossowski, a Soviet army marshal, was made commander-in-chief of Poland's armed forces, minister of defense and a deputy premier in the government. Important positions in the army were given to Russian officers, not all of whom could claim, as he did, to be of Polish descent. Economic transformation was reflected in stepped-up industrialization plans and an almost complete elimination of private enterprise in industry and commerce. There was also an attempt to shift land ownership from individual peasant holdings to a form of collectivized farms. However, in comparison with other countries of the area, the results of collectivization remained limited. Throughout the entire period of communism, agriculture in Poland remained the least collectivized of the communist-governed states, with the exception of Yugoslavia. Only about 15% of the land was removed from private ownership.

After 1947, increasing pressure was brought to bear on the Catholic Church, directed principally against its educational efforts. Church schools were secularized, Church lands were confiscated, and restrictions were placed on religious activities. This pressure reached its peak in 1953 when Cardinal Wyszynski (Vee-*shin*-skee) was placed under house arrest in a monastery and forbidden to carry out his functions as primate of Poland. How-

Author (m) with daughter (r) and Polish professor (l) in Warsaw at Christmas time

ever, the confiscation of Church lands and the general persecution probably had an effect opposite to that intended. The fact that the Church was no longer a landowner probably increased its prestige among the rural population. The general persecution mainly served to increase its hold over the masses, which always remained remarkably strong.

The Catholic University of Lublin and the Theological Academy in Warsaw topped the Catholic educational system. The communists looked upon the Church as a rival organization that competed for the allegiance of the people. No efforts were spared to make the position of the Church difficult. At the same time, the regime had great respect for the traditional power of the Church in Poland. This protected the Church from an all-out frontal assault. This also produced some anomalies as when, for example, the communist leadership publicized its endorsement of Cardinal Wyszynski in the 1956 elections, even though it had kept him under house arrest since 1953.

The Polish Struggle of October 1956

Following the death of Josef Stalin in 1953, the Polish government launched a "new course," which involved some relaxation of the old Stalinist norms. Workers were little affected, but there was a reduction in taxes for the peasantry and a slowdown in the process of collectivization. Intellectuals found they could be a little more critical in their comments about Polish life. Then an event occurred that had widespread repercussions.

Jozef Swiatlo, a high-ranking official in the Polish secret police, fled westward soon after Stalin's death. In 1954, Radio

Free Europe in Munich began a series of broadcasts of Swiatlo's memoirs. His well-documented disclosures of the terrorist activities of the UB, the political police organization, became widely known in Poland and led to the abolition of the Ministry of Public Security. This was followed later by the arrest of some leading secret police officials.

Several economic reforms were also introduced, especially with regard to labor discipline. Critical voices began to be heard, first among writers and students and then among the rank-and-file membership of the party. In the realm of communist political theory, "revisionist" views came to the fore, accompanied by a tendency to question some of the most basic tenets of Marxism-Leninism. Students and recent graduates began to organize discussion clubs in which pointed questions embarrassing to the government were raised in lengthy debates.

Poland was thus in a state of political turmoil when Soviet party chief, Nikita Khrushchev, made his famous "secret" speech at the 20th party congress in 1956 denouncing the evil deeds of Stalin. As luck would have it, Boleslaw Bierut, First Secretary of the communist Polish United Workers Party, died in Moscow two weeks after Khrushchev's speech. He was succeeded by Edward Ochab, a shrewd politician who recognized the need for reform. Gomulka was placed under house arrest in a villa on the outskirts of Warsaw that served as a secret police prison. It was mild incarceration in the sense that he was not tortured. He was freed in 1955.

A wave of strikes by industrial workers broke out in June 1956, accompanied by clashes between workers and troops in

Poznan. The regime tried at first to blame the outbreaks on "capitalist provocation." But it soon came to the conclusion that the entire structure of communist rule might crumble unless there was a dramatic change of direction in government.

The logical choice to accomplish this was Gomulka who, because of his insistence on a "Polish road to socialism," had become a symbol of independence from the Soviet Union. He was thought likely to satisfy the "revisionist" elements within the party, as well as the masses of workers and ordinary citizens.

However, his reputation as a revisionist worried parts of the Soviet hierarchy. As preparations were going on to elect Gomulka to the position of first secretary of the party in October 1956, a delegation of top Soviet leaders suddenly appeared in Warsaw. Rumors began to fly that Soviet troops were on the march toward the Polish capital.

In the end, Khrushchev and his comrades were reassured about continued Polish-Soviet ties and possibly impressed by the resolute stand of factory workers who had obtained arms and were converging on the airport. They agreed to Gomulka's election as party secretary and departed. The Soviet delegation also grudgingly accepted other changes in the Polish communist leadership, including the removal of Marshal Rokossowsky, a visible symbol of Soviet interference in Polish internal affairs.

The Aftermath of Turmoil

A tragic clash such as occurred about the same time in Hungary was avoided. As for Gomulka, many considered him to be a "liberal" who favored popular control of government because of the role he played during the "spring in October." Actually, he was a rather austere, conservative communist with a political sense for what could be done in Poland and with the Polish people. This kept him in power in Poland until 1970. However, as the "thaw" of 1956 passed into history, many of the more visionary hopes of the intellectuals were disappointed.

Nevertheless, the Polish regime continued to differ from those in neighboring communist-ruled countries. There was a reversal of the trend toward collectivization of agriculture. For example, there was a massive abandonment of even the token collectivization that had occurred after Gomulka returned to power.

Agricultural circles were about the only form of cooperative organization in the farmlands. Their main function was the joint purchase and use of farm machinery. This was a far cry from the practice of totally controlling agricultural production through a system of collective farms. Go-

Poland

mulka decided that the Polish peasant had to be left to discover for himself the blessings of socialism rather than be forced into it.

In other branches of the national economy, especially in industry, Gomulka saw less room for noncommunist management. Workers Councils, organized during the 1956 upheaval, were later discouraged, and industry was once again managed in a centralized manner. There were, however, some attempts to make central planning of the economy less rigid. For a number of reasons, industry continued to suffer from serious shortcomings. Various emergency measures occasionally resulted in unemployment and a halt in the movement of people from the overcrowded countryside to the cities. In commerce, a degree of private enterprise was permitted although it was overburdened by state controls and taxation. Individual craftsmen were also permitted to work alone or in small groups.

In the cultural sphere, there was a tremendous outburst of creative activity after 1956. The rigid rules of "socialist realism" were relaxed, and it became possible to experiment with new and nonconformist forms of artistic expression. Access to the Western press and literature was relatively free, and travel permits to areas outside the communist bloc were issued more generously than elsewhere in Central Europe.

In political life, an effort was also made to create a real function for the *Sejm* (parliament). The habit of debating proposed legislation in committee and attempts critically to evaluate the efficiency of government changed the legislature from a rubber stamp completely controlled by communist leaders to a reasonably authentic voice of some parts of public opinion. Polls and other studies of public attitudes also came into use. Polish sociologists point with pride to the fact that, under their influence, a revised interest in the social sciences spread to other nations of Central Europe and to the Soviet Union.

In 1964, the relatively tolerant Khrushchev was dismissed from office, and his successors began to retighten control. These Soviet events were mirrored in Poland, where the "spring" of 1956 was followed by a new freeze. Although the people continued in various ways to have "little freedoms," a sense of disappointment and distrust characterized the attitude of intellectuals, who had high hopes of basic changes under Gomulka.

The Events of 1968–1970

Dissatisfaction with the regime came into the open in early 1968 when students and intellectuals clashed with the police. The reason for the conflict was the sup-

December 1980: Lech Walesa with supporters

pression of a theatrical performance of a work by Poland's greatest poet, Adam Mickiewicz (*Mits*-kay-vitch). His 19th-century work, *Dziady* (Forefathers), contained anti-Russian themes that audiences lustily applauded. There also was dissatisfaction with the official attitude of the government. Following the lead of the Soviet Union, it came out in support of the Arabs in their conflict with Israel. This policy enabled one of the groups within the leadership, the so-called Partisans led by the ambitious General Mieczyslaw Moczar (*Mo*-char), to open an attack on "Zionist" elements supposed to be in the government and the party.

These charges appealed to a deeply rooted anti-Semitism in Poland. Although married to a Jewish woman, Gomulka decided to go along with what turned out to be a massive purge of Jews within the government, universities and cultural organizations. Many had to leave the country, renouncing their Polish citizenship and leaving most of their belongings, because they could not make a living in Poland. Thus, the once flourishing Jewish community, reduced by Hitler's destruction and postwar emigration from over three million to less than 30,000, almost ceased to exist.

Gomulka's political maneuvering and his obedience to the Soviet Union, demonstrated by his support for the invasion of Czechoslovakia in 1968, saved him temporarily from political defeat. In spite of pressure from Moczar and his Partisans, Gomulka was reelected party leader in 1968. He was supported by Edward

Gierek, boss since 1957 of the party organization in the important mining and industrial province of Upper Silesia. But Gomulka (aptly described as a "spent force" by one observer) could no longer control the conflicting trends within the party leadership. Moreover, the differences that arose reflected not only the direction of leadership, but, also, the generation gap between old-timers such as Gomulka and younger, better educated, technically minded elements demanding a share of power.

Gomulka's final downfall came after an apparently spontaneous outbreak of protests by workers expressing dissatisfaction over increased food prices on the eve of the Christmas holidays in 1970. In the party, a coalition of competing factions agreed to dismiss Gomulka and replace him as first secretary with Edward Gierek.

The Gierek Era, 1970–1980

Under the leadership of the initially popular Edward Gierek, an ex-miner, Poland embarked on an ambitious plan of rapid industrialization and economic growth. It was financed by heavy borrowing of capital from the Soviet Union as well as from a number of Western governments, international financial institutions and private banks.

The results seemed impressive until about the mid-1970s. The gross national product increased substantially during these years, and there was a striking improvement in the standard of living. Several factors brought this economic "miracle" to an end. The immediate cause was a dramatic change for the worse in the international economy. A second factor was the widespread graft and mismanagement within the government. But the most important, long-range reason was that Poland was borrowing money from abroad to finance domestic consumption. None of the new plants financed by the loans produced any significant amount of goods for export. Thus Poland lacked the necessary hard currency reserves to pay back the loans when they became due.

To service its foreign debt, therefore, Poland had to resort to increased exports of food products, thereby cutting into the supply of food for domestic consumption. While workers' wages had increased, less and less was available to buy. In 1976, an attempt to raise prices on basic food articles led to the outbreak of strikes as well as looting and attacks on communist party headquarters in many localities. The decision to cancel price increases barely 24 hours after they had been announced undermined the prestige of the government and the ruling party.

In addition, governmental attempts to prosecute workers who had incited strikes led to the creation of KOR, an organization for the defense of arrested and dismissed workers. In 1977, another organization called Movement of Defense of Human and Civil Rights (ROPCIO) came into being.

Gierek expressed a desire to "improve communication with the working masses" and sought a further normalization of relations with the Roman Catholic Church. Several antichurch measures were dropped,

permission was given to construct churches in the new industrial towns, and the church's debts to the state were cancelled.

The election of a Polish pope in 1978 added another destabilizing factor to this development. The election of Karol Wojtyla (*Voi*-tuwa), Archbishop of Krakow—who took the name of John Paul II—brought an outburst of national pride that extended even to many members of the Communist Party. Gierek himself sent a message of congratulations to Rome, and negotiations began immediately for a papal visit to Poland. This occurred in June 1979 and included a nationally televised meeting between the Pope, Gierek and other party and state leaders.

Gierek was more successful in his relations with the Catholic Church than he was in his second goal of improving communication with the masses. When he took over as party leader, he promised that workers would be consulted, that intellectuals would be heard, and that the party could not possibly regulate everything. The political thaw did not last long, however. By 1973, censorship had been fully restored, and it was soon clear that the party was instituting through a further centralization in the name of reform instead of reducing its intervention in national life.

Moreover, the party was granting its own members special pay and privileges that set them off from, and aroused the hatred of, the masses while claiming to be the "leading political force in society in constructing socialism." Isolated and filled with bureaucrats, the party became more and more a hollow shell, determined to "stonewall" just about anything.

Strikers and Dissidents

Dissatisfaction with the communist system had been simmering in Poland for a number of years. It resulted in the emergence of various political and intellectual dissident groups, ranging from barely legal to illegal organizations. While claiming a belief in the basic tenets of communism, some advocated reform of the system and removal of those who mismanaged it. Others, on the extreme right, advocated abandonment or overthrow of the system.

Illegal publications, study circles and "flying universities," often holding classes in church buildings, proliferated. The decisive change came when the small intellectual groups identified themselves with the plight of the workers, who had resorted to strikes to protest oppressive conditions in the factories and the undercutting of their living standards by hikes in the price of food.

Opposition in Poland derived substantial support from the outspoken position of the Catholic Church under the leader-

ship of Cardinal Wyszynski, who died in 1981. The election of a Pole as Pope was also a source of moral support. Nevertheless, it was the spectacular collapse of the economy after a decade of what looked like successful development that set off Poland's crisis in 1980–81.

Facing a rapidly deteriorating economic situation and a foreign debt that had grown to $28 billion, the government tried to appease both workers and political dissidents by promises of improvements that could not be kept. Matters came to a head when thousands of workers in the Gdansk shipyard went on strike and occupied the premises of the enterprise.

Confrontation, Confusion and Clumsiness

Under the leadership of Lech Walesa (Vah-*wen*-sa), an unemployed electrician who emerged from nowhere to a position of prominence, workers insisted that the government send a negotiator to deal with the *Twenty-one Demands* posted by the workers' strike committee. The main point of the demands was permission to establish independent trade unions in competition with the party-controlled official trade union organization. When the government accepted this demand, a new institution, Solidarity, was born. It claimed a membership of 10 million workers. Soon, an extension of the protest movement to the countryside resulted in the creation of a rural branch of Solidarity as well. Whether intended or not, this ultimately set into motion a confrontation of Polish workers, supported by the Roman Catholic Church, intellectuals and stu-

General Wojciech Jaruzelski

Poland

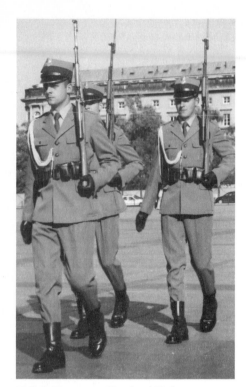

Polish Troops at Tomb of Unknown Soldiers, Warsaw

Father Popieluszko

dents, with the communist leadership and the Soviet Union.

What followed in Poland was a drastic shake-up of the party-state leadership. Gierek and his close associates were ousted, and the relatively unknown Stanislaw Kania was named party leader. The post of chairman of the council of ministers (prime minister) was assumed by General Wojciech Jaruzelski (*Voy*-check Ya-roo-*zel*-skee), a career military officer who was already defense minister and therefore head of the Polish armed forces.

For a while, negotiations involving the communist government, the independent Solidarity movement and the Catholic Church raised the hope that Poland might enter a new phase of its history. This would have involved a rather unusual triangular arrangement between the discredited communist authorities (with the Soviets in the background), the independent trade union movement, and the church (led until 2004 by Cardinal Wyszynski's successor, Cardinal Glemp). However, a worker movement independent of the Polish United Workers Party was, by its very existence, a challenge to the communist claim to be the party of the workers. It soon became clear that an independent Solidarity was unacceptable both to significant elements in the PUWP and to the Soviet leadership. The true picture was visible in October 1981 when Kania resigned as party secretary and was replaced by Jaruzelski, who added this party post to his other jobs.

During previous periods of unrest, the armed forces had not been used to restore order. On December 13, 1981, however, General Jaruzelski declared martial law throughout the country and ordered the military to begin a roundup of trade union activists and dissident intellectuals. Thousands were detained, including Lech Walesa and most of the other Solidarity leaders. A curfew was enforced throughout the country, and telephone communications between cities were restricted.

The government also sought to discredit Solidarity by attempting to show that the trade union was not merely seeking an improvement in the economic situation, as it claimed, but that it was interested in either sharing political power with the communists, or taking it away from them. Secret tapes made by the security police at a national conference of Solidarity in the city of Radom had Walesa and others stating that the time had come for "confrontation" with the government rather than "compromise." The tapes were probably altered.

In late 1982 Solidarity and the discredited old official labor unions were banned, and new official trade unions replaced them. According to the government, the new official unions had a membership of about seven million, of which 60% were former members of Solidarity. Since that figure represented slightly less than half of the total labor force, it was obvious that although Solidarity had been banned, it was by no means dead.

After being held in custody for several months, Walesa was eventually released without any charges being filed against him. His receipt of the Nobel Prize for Peace also strengthened his hand. As a result, he was permitted to continue to speak out publicly. However, the government closely monitored his actions, and he was continuously under the threat of harassment or worse. A 1984 amnesty resulted in the release of 652 Solidarity detainees, though a few were rearrested after meeting with Walesa. They, too, were subsequently released, but remained subject to government harassment when they attempted to speak out publicly. The final amnesty that freed all detainees was declared in September 1986. During this time, American labor unions were giving Solidarity important assistance, such as providing outlawed printing equipment.

There were those within the leadership of the PUWP who opposed the independent Solidarity movement. However, the decisive factor that led the Polish government to declare martial law and ban the movement was the strong pressure the Soviets were exerting at this time. Jaruzelski later maintained publicly that he had imposed martial law to prevent an invasion by the Soviet Union, and he defended this decision the rest of his life. Subsequently published documentation revealed that Moscow's leaders had, in fact, agonized over whether to crush Solidarity, but they had been dissuaded by their own military, who argued: "The Polish armed forces are battle-ready and patriotic. They will not fire on their own people." One Kremlin leader, Mikhail Suslov, warned that military intervention "will mean a catastrophe."

Notes of conversations between Jaruzelski and the commander of the Warsaw Pact, Marshal Viktor Kulikov, published in late 2009, revealed that the Polish commander had asked the Soviets for help in gaining control over Solidarity. He reportedly said that if demonstrations "sweep through the whole country, then you [the Soviet Union] will have to help us. We won't be able to deal with a crowd in the millions." This would seem to undermine his later assurances that he was acting only in Polish national interest to stop a Soviet invasion. By the time martial law ended in 1989, nearly 100 people had died, tens of thousands were arrested without charge, and about 10,000 were confined in internment camps.

The Roman Catholic Church

A major concern of the Soviet leadership under Leonid Brezhnev was the still important position of the Roman Catholic Church in Polish life. That concern appears to have increased after Karol Wojtyla, Archbishop of Krakow, was elected Pope in October 1978. It is for this reason that many scholars accepted the argument that there had been a connection between the Soviet KGB (secret police) and a subsequent attempt on John Paul II's life

A church courtyard's fence displays a banned *Solidarity* sign

while he was officiating at a ceremony in St. Peter's Square in Rome. The evidence is indirect because the man who actually fired the shot was a Turkish national who, the Italian government charged, was an agent of the Bulgarian secret police. Soviet involvement derives from the fact that the Bulgarian secret police would almost certainly not have been operating in such an important matter without the knowledge of the Soviet KGB. There is no evidence that the Polish government knew anything about the plan to kill the pontiff. At least up to 1985, it was under pressure from the Soviets to reduce the influence of the Church. The government was divided on the issue, with moderates arguing the value of cooperation with the Church and "hard-liners" arguing the danger of such an accommodation.

While the internal struggle was still going on, three members of the Polish security police, acting under orders of their superior officer, a colonel, brutally murdered Father Jerzy Popieluszko, a priest. He had become a target because he was an ardent and public supporter of Solidarity. Eleven days after he had been reported missing, his body was found, weighted, at the bottom of a reservoir. An autopsy showed that he could have been beaten to death

before being thrown into the water although that was never proved. The cause of death was not established in the trial, and he could have still been alive when he was thrown into the river.

This grisly act forced General Jaruzelski's hand. Disassociating himself and his regime completely from the killing, he ordered that the four implicated individuals be put on public trial, and extensive but selective television and radio coverage was permitted nationwide. All four were convicted and received long prison sentences. In addition, their superior in the Ministry of the Interior was fired. Jaruzelski himself took the further step of assuming direct responsibility for the police and the internal security forces, replacing two members of the party secretariat who had formerly been in charge of those activities.

In spite of Jaruzelski's actions, church and state relations reached a new low. They were charged with emotion arising out of the revelations during the trial of the dirty war the security police waged against the Church. Responding to these emotions, Cardinal Glemp began to take a more militant line, and Jaruzelski answered in kind. Speaking in a 1985 press interview about differences with the Church, the general was quoted as saying somewhat defen-

sively: "In Poland the Church has a vast, favorable opportunity to carry out its priestly mission. Regrettably, certain priests abuse this freedom to stage unlawful acts. We talk about it openly."

Church-state relations began to improve again in 1986. They climaxed in January 1987 when General Jaruzelski paid a state visit to Italy and was received by Pope John Paul II. A Vatican spokesman described the 70-minute private talk as "earnest, clear and profound." Symbolically, Jaruzelski's daughter, Monika, who accompanied him, was given a rosary and took another home to her mother. Equally symbolically, he invited the Pope to visit Poland. The most important visit took place in 1979, followed by return trips in 1983 and June 1987. According to press reports at the time, Jaruzelski also promised to grant the Church full legal status, a move that would allow the Church's youth organization and its various professional bodies to operate publicly. However, nothing was done to put this into effect before the papal visit in June.

Whenever the pontiff arrived, the fireworks began. Solidarity banners appeared everywhere he went. Crowds ultimately numbering into the millions attended the many masses he said, cheering him with wild enthusiasm. At each mass or appearance, he praised Solidarity with warm enthusiasm in order to show his disapproval of the government. Jaruzelski was unable to silence him. In 1987 the Pope kissed the tomb of Father Popieluszko, reviving all of the old emotions surrounding his death. Upon his departure, the general appeared at the airport to say relatively harsh words to the highly respected Pope. Usually "unflappable," Jaruzelski had been visibly disturbed and was shaking with undisguised anger. The damage had been done.

Although Jaruzelski had not gotten what he wanted from the Pope's 1987 visit, he was evidently impressed by the response of the Polish people to the Pope. From this, he concluded that some accommodation with the Church was necessary if he wanted to reconcile the Polish people to continued communist rule. As a result, the government began permitting the Church to enlarge its area of activities and to become, in the words of one Pole associated with the movement, "the most interesting independent intellectual and social center in Poland."

As in East Germany, the Church became a refuge for dissident artists. In September 1987, Wroclaw's large Gothic "Church of the Holy Cross" arranged an exhibit of the works of 151 artists from all over Poland under the title "National Biennial of Young Artists." The government permitted the exhibit, even though many of the 423 works of art on display had secular themes

Poland

Wilanow Palace in Warsaw, the summer residence of Polish kings

and, according to Polish law, could not legally be exhibited inside a church.

The Church was also permitted to expand its educational role. Church schools teaching secular subjects were established throughout the country, and the Catholic University in Lublin added faculties in law, economics, psychology and sociology. In addition, the Church established publishing facilities where it began printing its own textbooks. Many of the activities originally sponsored by Solidarity were thus given new life under the patronage of the Church.

In January 2007 the widely held view that the Church had acted as a courageous opponent of communism was badly shaken. Warsaw's new archbishop, Stanislaw Wielgus, announced just minutes before he was to be formally installed that he was resigning over disclosures that he had cooperated with the secret police during the communist era. Dozens of priests were then revealed as collaborators.

The Regime Loosens Up

Jaruzelski did not want the Church to be the sole intellectual alternative, and he accordingly moved to grant more freedom generally. This led the government to give approval to *Res Publica*, a privately owned magazine, to begin publishing in July 1987. Although allowed only 25,000 copies, it was important as the first of Poland's many underground magazines to achieve legal status.

An even more important move came in January 1988 when the government stopped jamming the broadcasts of Voice of America, Radio Free Europe, and the Polish language broadcasts of the BBC. Although Jaruzelski made the final decision himself, it was reportedly on the advice of Mieczyslaw Rakowski (Myekcis-lav Ra-*Kov*-skee). The latter was then deputy chairman of the council of ministers. Before joining the government he had for 24 years been the editor of *Poli-*

tyka. That was the most readable official publication in the Soviet block and is still today the best and most important political weekly newsmagazine in Poland.

All of this provided background for Jaruzelski's greatest gamble: his attempt to implement an economic reform that had much in common with what Gorbachev was trying to do in the Soviet Union. To obtain public backing, Jaruzelski submitted the plan to a referendum in November 1987. The three-year program contained elements such as increased private enterprise and a decentralization that was supposed to cut the number of government jobs by a quarter. It also included a cut in subsidies that would have brought an immediate, significant increase in prices. Whether for that reason or because they simply did not trust the communists, voters rejected the reform.

Stung by its defeat, the government decided to begin implementing the reform anyway, although more slowly than originally planned. The first price rises went into effect at the beginning of 1988 with food, rent, and fuel increasing by an average of 45%. It was the official party unions that first protested, and this led to a strike among transport workers in the city of Bydgoszcz. The government granted a 60% pay increase to the transport worker. In the meantime, the strike began spreading to other parts of Poland. Among those joining the strike were the workers at the Lenin Shipyard in Gdansk.

The August 1988 strike now became explicitly political. This was the birthplace of Solidarity, and Lech Walesa once again emerged as a local leader. Occupying the Lenin Shipyard and refusing to leave, the Gdansk workers demanded that, in addition to a pay increase, Solidarity activists dismissed in 1981 should be reinstated in their jobs. The government agreed to a wage increase, but it refused to bargain over the political issue. It soon became clear that this was not to be a replay of

1980–81. There was no national groundswell of support for the Gdansk workers. After eight days they ended their strike in return for a government promise to open a political dialogue with Solidarity.

The government had won a victory of sorts, but not one of much value. For its economic reform to have any chance of success, it had to have the active support of the workers, and this it did not have. A public opinion poll taken in early 1988 indicated that only 7% of those polled believed that the economic reform had any chance of success.

That is not surprising. After all, the political leadership had been pursuing a program of economic reform since 1980, all without tangible results. This bred a sense of pessimism exemplified by the comment of one Polish journalist in July 1988 that Poland had already been through reform, "and it did not work."

Inflation, already high, grew worse as the summer progressed and there were increasing shortages of all kinds of consumer goods. Later a new and different wave of strikes swept across Poland, spreading for the first time to the Silesian coalfields. Because coal exports were one of Poland's major sources of hard currency earnings, the government had always gone out of its way to keep the miners happy. But even they had seen their standard of living drop in the preceding months, and they were now demanding action.

In a final irony, it was the official trade unions, not the outlawed Solidarity, that declared a lack of confidence in the government and demanded that it resign. The government stepped down in September 1988, and Jaruzelski appointed Mieczyslaw Rakowski as the new chairman of the council of ministers (prime minister).

Determined to break the political-economic deadlock, Rakowski introduced a new phrase into the communist lexicon—the "constructive opposition"—and offered four cabinet seats to Solidarity supporters. He also called for roundtable negotiations with the opposition. But what he offered was the chance to participate in the economic reform; there were to be no political reforms. Solidarity was not to be legalized. In fact, Solidarity supporters were urged to repudiate their leadership, since "it is impossible to compromise with Walesa." Under the circumstances, no one in the opposition was willing to join the government, and the proposed roundtable negotiations never got started.

Rakowski was left with the alternative of either dealing with Walesa or of somehow discrediting him. The party decided to assign that task to Alfred Miodowicz (Meeo-doe-vitz), leader of the official trade unions and a member of the party Politburo. Miodowicz challenged Walesa to a television debate, which took place in November. With 70% of the nation watching, it was Walesa who came across as the statesmanlike leader. This point was conceded even in the USSR.

Reporting on the debate, *Komsomolskaya Pravda* wrote that some of Walesa's "recent speeches have been distinguished by a certain political balance and reasonableness. It would also be possible to agree with a number of his assertions made directly during the debate." The party next tried to co-opt Walesa personally by offering to make him a deputy prime minister. But he held out for formal negotiations and "laws, rights, positions offered by law, not by privilege."

By December 1988, it had become clear that all of Rakowski's efforts to push through economic reform while ignoring Solidarity had been a failure, as were the party's efforts to discredit Walesa. Yet conservatives in the top leadership of the party continued to oppose any compromise with the opposition.

To clear the way, General Jaruzelski called a Central Committee meeting just before Christmas. Six hard-liners were removed from the Politburo, and eight persons were added. This was followed by a second two-day meeting of the Central Committee in January 1989, which ended with a communiqué supporting the legalization of Solidarity. Even at this meeting, conservatives attacked the leadership decision to deal with Walesa. But Jaruzelski pushed through the decision against their opposition. Among those who opposed the decision was Alfred Miodowicz.

Roundtable Discussions with Solidarity

Roundtable negotiations between the government and Solidarity opened on February 6, 1989. Once the two sides began talking, they quickly carried their discussions beyond the question of the legalization of Solidarity and began to put together a historic compromise. As Tadeusz Mazowiecki, a leading Solidarity negotiator, commented, "both the communists and we crossed the Rubicon. It's really surprising how far things went."

In addition to legalizing Solidarity, an agreement in April called for creation of a Senate as a second legislative body, all of whose members were chosen by popular election in June. New elections to the *Sejm*, the old legislative body, also took place at the same time. In the latter case, however, the communists and their allies were guaranteed 65% of the seats, with the remaining 35% to be freely contested. To provide executive authority and to act as a counterweight to a more powerful legislature, the post of president was also created, to be chosen by the newly elected legislature.

Most of those in leading positions in the Solidarity movement decided to stand for either the *Sejm* or the Senate. Walesa declined, saying that he did not want to compromise his credentials as a trade unionist. He did, however, create a Citizens' Committee of approximately 100 opposition figures that took over management of the campaign for the opposition. He actively campaigned for Solidarity candidates.

In the June elections, the Polish United Workers' Party suffered a crushing defeat. Solidarity took 99 out of 100 seats in the Senate, plus all of the open seats in the Sejm. In addition, most of the top communist leadership, running unopposed for Sejm seats, was rejected because they failed to get 50% of the valid votes.

The newly elected legislature agreed to install Jaruzelski as president. But the failure of the communists at the polls meant that they were unable to form a government. Their allies, the United Peasants' Party and the Democratic Party, refused to support the PUWP candidate for chairman of the council of ministers and opened discussions with Solidarity. This led Lech Walesa to propose a Solidarity-led coalition government that would include representatives of the PUWP. Then a second decisive Soviet intervention occurred. After Mieczyslaw Rakowski, the new head of the Polish United Workers Party, announced his opposition to such a coalition, he got a 40-minute telephone call from Gorbachev. Tadeusz Mazowiecki, Lech Walesa's hand-picked candidate, was installed as chairman of the council of ministers at the end of August.

Smart young Poles in Brussels

Poland's First Postwar Non-Communist Government

In December 1989, the legislature made several changes in the constitution. The adjective "People's" was dropped from the official name of the country, making it is once again the Republic of Poland. All references to socialism and the leading role of the People's United Workers' Party were also deleted.

On January 1, 1990, the government instituted its plan to bring about Poland's transition to a free-market economy. Prices were freed, subsidies to industry were canceled, the currency was set free to float, and the draft budget showed a surplus. The plan, named after Leszek Balcerowicz (later president of the Polish National Bank), produced hardships throughout the society, but it also began the process of transforming the economy. Unemployment rose as inefficient state industries lost their subsidies and had to begin laying off employees in order to cut their costs. However, individual Poles began establishing thousands of small businesses, and small amounts of foreign investment began to pour into the country. For the year, foreign investment was estimated at $100 million.

As the year progressed, however, a split became evident in the Solidarity ranks. In particular, Walesa began publicly attacking specific policies of the Mazowiecki government. His first target was the program of economic reform, which, he argued, was being implemented in a way that made it harder on the Polish people than it needed to be. His main objection was that the government was not moving fast enough in clearing communists out of key positions. Poland was, by this time, the only country in Central or Eastern Europe other than Albania that still had a communist as head of state. Communists also held 45% of the seats in the *Sejm*, though the results of the June 1990 local elections suggested they would not be able to retain most of those seats in a genuinely free election.

When Walesa first raised the issue of his becoming president, many of his supporters in Solidarity tried to dissuade him from running. He backed down at first, then changed his mind and declared his candidacy on September 17. Two days later, General Jaruzelski, sensing the direction of political winds in Poland, agreed to step down because of his "concern to prevent undesirable public sentiment" and to "promote democracy."

Parliament modified the office of the presidency, setting a five-year term of office and specifying that the president was to be elected by popular vote. The election was set for November 25. Prime Minister Mazowiecki then announced that he would stand for the presidency himself.

Poland

Perhaps Mazowiecki had his falling out with Walesa because he feared that Walesa as president would repudiate his economic program. Or perhaps it was related to the fact that Mazowiecki was a university graduate and had a reputation as a learned theorist, while Walesa had only a trade-school education and a background as a shipyard electrician. Adam Michnik, editor of the Solidarity-founded newspaper *Gazeta Wyborcza* (Electoral Gazette), accused Walesa of having dictatorial tendencies. In any case, Mazowiecki's candidacy represented the end of Solidarity as the unifying umbrella organization of the noncommunist forces.

Though still the head of Solidarity, Walesa did not attempt to use it in his presidential campaign. His supporters were formed as the Center Alliance. Mazowiecki's political organization was supported by another group known under the acronym ROAD. Later in the campaign, a third candidate emerged, based on his promise to bring Western business know-how to Poland. This was Stanislaw Tyminski, a Pole who had emigrated to Canada and whose qualification was that he was a successful businessman.

The only one to attack the government's economic reform program, Tyminski edged Mazowiecki out for second place, taking 23% of the vote to Mazowiecki's 18%. Walesa came in first with about 40%. Since he did not get a majority, there had to be a second round of voting on December 9. This time, Walesa got an overwhelming 75% of the vote and was sworn in as president on December 21, 1990. Mazowiecki had submitted his resignation as prime minister after his defeat in the first round of voting. Walesa asked him to continue to serve until new parliamentary elections. He refused but remained on in a caretaker capacity. Walesa offered the position to several people, including Leszek Balcerowicz, finance minister in the Mazowiecki government. Balcerowicz declined, saying he wanted to stay on as finance minister. Walesa eventually offered the position to Jan Krzysztof Bielecki.

Before becoming prime minister, Bielecki was leader of a small free enterprise political party in the parliament, the Liberal-Democratic Congress, and head of a consulting company. From Gdansk, he had also been involved in the Solidarity underground. The Liberal-Democratic Congress was strongly committed to the development of private enterprise in Poland, and Walesa's selection of Bielecki was seen as his way of underscoring his commitment to Poland's program of economic reform.

Walesa was also anxious that new elections to the *Sejm* take place as soon as possible in order to remove the influence of the

Solidarity **Chairman Lech Walesa addresses Congress, November 1990.**

communist deputies still sitting there. Under the compact negotiated with the communists in 1989, new elections were not required until 1993. In March 1991, Walesa urged the legislature to ignore the 1989 deal. "I am convinced that Poland today needs instant elections," he told the legislature. "One has to put an end to growing disillusion and mistrust of political institutions, including Parliament." Parliament did schedule a debate on Walesa's appeal, but it ultimately decided to postpone new elections until October 1991.

Before the elections occurred, however, the *Sejm* passed a new electoral law that instituted an extreme form of proportional representation in an apparent attempt to protect as many seats as possible held by the communists and their allies. President Walesa vetoed the legislation on the basis that it would produce a too fragmented legislature. However, the communists and their allies, with control of 65% of the seats, passed it over his veto.

The election results were what Walesa predicted. Twenty-nine parties won seats in the *Sejm*, with the largest of the parties winning only 12.2% of the vote. The Democratic Left Alliance—the renamed communists—came in second with 12.1% of the vote, while their ally, the communist Peasant Party, got 8.9%. Creating a coalition government that could count on a stable majority in the *Sejm* was no easy task, and it was not accomplished until the end of December. Walesa even offered to lead a government of national unity himself,

but there was no significant support for that idea. A string of shaky, short-lived coalition governments followed.

A new electoral law in 1993 sought to reduce the number of political parties in the *Sejm*. While retaining the principle of proportional representation, the law specified that individual parties would need 5% of the vote to enter parliament; coalitions would need 8%. It was expected that the new law would reduce the number of parties represented in parliament from 29 to fewer than six. It accomplished this.

Subsequent elections were not always friendly to reformers. There was clearly a backlash against the pain of reform. As one commentator put it, "forty years of communism had ingrained expectations of social security that the new parties failed to provide." A major theme of the left during the campaign was that the post-communist governments had used all the state's resources to support capitalism and ignored the needs of workers, peasants, and pensioners.

Another factor was the matter of social policy, particularly the role of the Catholic Church. Post-communist governments had instituted religious classes in school, negotiated a Concordat with the Vatican and, after considerable arm-twisting by the Catholic hierarchy, passed a rigorous abortion law that largely reflected the Church's position on the issue. Considering that 75% of all Poles are practicing Roman Catholics, it is surprising that not a single political party with a specific religious orientation made it into the parliament in 1993. After the fall of communism there was a backlash against what was viewed as excessive involvement in politics on the part of the Roman Catholic Church.

POLITICAL SYSTEM

After nine years of effort, the *Sejm* (parliament, pronounced "same") was finally able to agree to a new constitution, and it was approved by the Polish people in a referendum in May 1997. It clearly spells out the relations between the parliament, the president, and the government, eliminating previous ambiguities. It also provides for an independent judicial review of laws. The preamble invokes God as the "source of truth, justice, goodness and beauty." The body of the constitution provides guarantees for religious instruction in public schools and grants the Catholic Church autonomy from the state. Although some right-wing politicians attacked the document, Poland's Catholic Primate, Jozef Cardinal Glemp, said, "many people accept this compromise constitution, regarding it as historically important."

Poland

Poland is a presidential-parliamentary system. The president has some powers in certain areas, but the government itself is run by the prime minister, who, in turn, is responsible to the *Sejm*. Any government must be able to receive a majority of the votes in the *Sejm* in order to assume power. Once installed, a government is difficult to unseat. It can be done only by a "constructive vote of no-confidence": First a majority must vote against the government; then it must immediately vote in favor of a new one. That is difficult in a multiparty system like Poland's.

The prime minister must have the confidence of a majority in the *Sejm*. He is the political leader of the country and is in charge of the government. He has overlapping responsibilities with the president in the area of foreign affairs and the military.

The legislature consists of two bodies, an upper house called the Senate, which was created in 1989, and a lower house, called the *Sejm*. The term of office is four years. Of the two houses, the *Sejm* is more powerful. The Senate has the right to review legislation and propose amendments, but the *Sejm* decides the final version of any legislation.

The Senate has 100 members, all elected by their regional constituents in 40 districts. The *Sejm* has 460 deputies, all of whom run in 41 electoral districts and are elected under a complex system of proportional representation. Under a 1993 law, individual parties need 5% of the vote to enter the *Sejm* while a bloc needs 8%. In 2005 only six parties and coalitions cleared these hurdles. As an exception, the German and all other ethnic minorities are exempt from the 5% rule. The reason for this rule is to limit the number of parties in parliament and thereby make coalition governments more manageable and stable. Since 2002 the governmental heads at the provincial (*wojewodztwo*), district (*powiat*) and commune (*gmina*) levels are elected through direct popular vote.

Given Poland's uncomfortable communist past, parliament passed a law in 1998 requiring all Poles seeking high office, as well as high-level civil servants and judges, to declare publicly whether they ever worked with the secret police during the communist era. If a candidate admits to such earlier activity, he or she is permitted to stand for election, and the voters can decide whether to punish the offender by not voting for him. If a candidate lies about his past, he can be banned from politics for ten years. In the 2000 presidential elections, both the winner, Aleksander Kwasniewski (kvash-nyef-skee), and the trounced Lech Walesa were cleared of charges of spying for the communist secret police because of lack of evidence. This allowed both of them to run for the presidency.

Presidential Elections

The president is directly elected every five years at a different time than parliamentary elections. If, as is usually the case, no single candidate receives a majority of votes, then a second round of elections is held two weeks later between the top two contenders. He is titular commander-in-chief of the military and also has general responsibility for the police and foreign and defense policy. Thus he can influence military deployments and relations with other countries. He can veto laws, and a three-fifths majority in parliament is required to override that veto. There is no vice president. If a president dies, as happened on April 10, 2010, then the speaker of the lower house of parliament, the *Sejm*, assumes the role of acting president and calls a new presidential election within 60 days.

The president formally appoints the prime minister and the members of the council of ministers (cabinet). He also has the right to dissolve parliament in certain limited circumstances; an example would be if a submitted budget were not approved within three months. The president is supposed to use his veto power sparingly.

In the 1995 presidential elections, Aleksander Kwasniewski, of the ex-Communist Democratic Left Alliance (SLD), defeated Walesa in a runoff election with 52% of the vote. Always more pragmatic than ideological, he publicly apologized in the early 1990s for the "injustice and misdeeds" of communism. The reasons for his victory hinged partly on Walesa's unpopularity after five years in office. Inevitably, Walesa was associated with the pain of that time, even though the powers of the presidency are quite limited.

Kwasniewski was reelected in 2000 with 54% of the votes in the first round, miles ahead of his 12 other challengers. Under the Polish system, all candidates enjoy equal and free television time, regardless of their standing in the polls or performance in prior elections. He is credited with keeping Poland united on the long road to EU entry in May 2004.

In October 2005, Lech Kaczynski of the Law and Justice (PiS) party and Donald Tusk of Civic Platform (PO) vied to be Kwasniewski's successor. Tusk was the favorite, but Kaczynski overtook him by convincing older and poorer voters that he would protect the social welfare system, which had eroded in the 16 years since the fall of communism. He also promised to preserve Catholic values, such as maintaining the ban on abortion and gay marriage. In the second round, he won 54% of the votes to Tusk's 46%.

The late President Lech Kaczynski and his twin brother, Jaroslaw, who is leader of PiS, offered social conservatism, religious nostalgia, protection of the poor and assertion of Poland's national interests.

The Late President Lech Kaczynski (right) with his twin Jaroslaw, PiS leader and ex-Prime Minister

323

Poland

Kaczynski twins as child movie stars

Born to a famous resistance fighter 56 years earlier, they won national fame in 1962 as sweet-faced 12-year-old child stars in a hit film, "The Two Who Stole the Moon." Both served as advisers to Solidarity and its leader, Walesa, and Lech Kaczynski, who had studied law, was jailed by the Communist authorities under martial law in the 1980s.

After Lech Kaszynski's untimely death on April 10, 2010, Bronislaw Komorowski assumed the role of acting president and represented the Civic Forum in the presidential campaign that followed. An aristocrat and former dissident, he had been the favorite until Jaroslaw Kaszynski, former prime minister for the PiS, entered the race upon his twin brother's tragic death.

It is not surprising that Jaroslaw enjoyed considerable sympathy in a campaign that was more about emotions than substance. While Komorowski was wooden and uncomfortable in public, Jaroslaw reminded voters that the economy had been strong during his twin's four years in office. He has a reputation of personal honesty, and he promised to veto any reforms that threatened the welfare state. Memories of his earlier pugnacious and clumsy foreign policy had faded. The Civic Forum government of Donald Tusk was thought to have reacted incompetently to the worst floods in over a decade in May and June. Komorowski came out only 5.1% ahead after the first round on June 20. He and Jaroslaw Kaszynski entered the second

round on July 4 neck-and-neck. Komorowski emerged as the victor, winning 53%.

Second Katyn Tragedy

On April 10, 2010, President Lech Kaszynski boarded a military aircraft with his wife, six out of the seven top military commanders, the deputy foreign and defense ministers, the head of the Polish Central Bank, high-ranking party leaders and many other Polish notables—96 in all. The passenger list reflected not only the country's political and military leadership. It also included personalities who had left their stamp on Polish history, such as Ryszard Kaczorowski, the last president of the London-based government in exile during the Second World War, and Anna Walentynowicz, the activist at the Gdansk shipyard whose dismissal in 1980 triggered the strike that led to the formation of Solidarity and the end of communism. President Kaszynski had a conciliatory speech in his pocket for Russian ears.

Their destination was the site of the Katyn Forest massacre on the outskirts of the Russian city Smolensk. Seventy years earlier, 21,768 of Poland's military, political and intellectual elite were murdered by order of Soviet dictator Joseph Stalin. His intention was to decapitate Polish society permanently. Kaczynski had wanted to share in the victims' memory, but he had not been invited with Prime Minister Donald Tusk to a commemoration held at the site a few days earlier. At that time,

Russian Prime Minister Vladimir Putin had spoken openly about the horror of the crimes and how both Poles and Russians had been victims of Stalin's inhuman system. He embraced the Polish prime minister and joined him in laying wreaths at the Polish officers' graves, kneeling in commemoration.

Kaczynski's plane was ninety minutes behind schedule. When it arrived over Smolensk, the airport was buried in a thick fog. Russian air traffic controllers and the onboard instruments gave the pilots 16 warnings not to try to land but to divert to another airfield. Determined that the dignitaries would not miss the ceremony, the pilots put the plane down despite frantic warnings to "pull up, pull up!" About a kilometer (two-thirds of a mile) from the runway, the plane ran into trees and broke apart. All passengers perished. There was no proof for rumors that the president had ordered the pilots to land.

The shock and pain that Poles felt were immense, and all were united in grief and disbelief. When the bodies were returned home to Warsaw, Polish flags with black ribbons of mourning were flying everywhere. Church bells rang. TV stations broadcast somber music. Thousands gathered in front of the presidential palace, lighting candles and placing flowers. Boy and girl scouts kept order. At noon, the entire country and all traffic came to a halt for two minutes as sirens sounded to remember the dead.

The impact of the calamity was magnified by the fact that it had occurred at the very spot where so many Poles had been sacrificed 70 years before. But this time no one could speak of a decapitation of the Polish state. The speaker of the *Sjem* immediately stepped into his role as acting president and set about arranging for a new presidential election. Empty posts were filled calmly. The military commanders were seamlessly succeeded by their next in command. Members of parliament were automatically replaced by the next highest vote winners from the same party in the last election. Political parties moved the next-in-line personnel up to fill newly vacant positions. Never for one moment were there any doubts about the stability of the country. Normality reigned. The political and military institutions functioned exactly as they were supposed to.

The feeling of national unity was shaken a few days later by an unexpected decision to bury the deceased president and his wife below the Wawel royal cathedral in Krakow, where Pope John Paul had once been archbishop. This is the burial site for Poland's kings, poets and national heroes, such as Tadeusz Kosciuszko, Jozef Pilsudski and Wladyslaw Sikorski. No

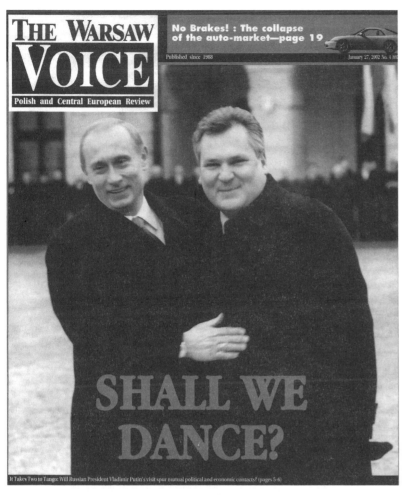

Russian Prime Minister Putin with ex-President Kwasniewski

president had been buried there, and few Poles would ever regard Lech Kaczynski as a hero. In fact, many considered him the worst president in post-communist Polish history. His approval rating was below 30% just before he died, and he was expected to lose his bid for reelection later in 2010. In the end he was buried with the heroes because in Poland any death at the site of the Katyn massacre is considered heroic.

One foreign policy byproduct of the tragedy was the display of sympathy by Russian leaders, especially Prime Minister Putin, who embraced his Polish counterpart at the site of the carnage. Polish leaders hailed the compassionate and empathetic Russian response. Putin personally oversaw the investigation. He also allowed the sobering Oscar-nominated film by Andrzej Wajda, *Katyn*, which depicts graphically the mass murder that had occurred, to be aired twice on Russian primetime television. Wajda's own father was among the victims of the wartime massacre. Russian President Dmitry Medvedev brought flowers to the Polish embassy in Moscow and told the Polish

people: "All Russians share your grief and mourning." However, a poll taken in Russia after the crash indicated that only 19% considered Stalin's secret police to have been responsible for the crime. Russia continues to refuse categorically to pay compensation for the Katyn murders.

Parliamentary Elections

Entering the September 2005 parliamentary elections, it was widely assumed that a center-right coalition of Civic Platform (PO) and Law and Justice (PiS) would take

Source: *Financial Times*

over the reins of government. PiS won 27% of the votes and 152 seats (up from 44), ahead of PO, which captured 24% and 133 seats (up from 65). They dominated the 100-member Senate, with PiS winning 45 and PO 41. Together they would have had a comfortable majority in the lower house. However, many of the two parties' leaders did not like or trust each other, and that came out in the acrimonious parliamentary elections in September and the presidential elections a month later. PiS attacked PO fiercely, caricaturing it as a party that panders to wealthy businessmen.

Beyond personality conflicts, many policy issues divided PiS and PO. This was true despite the fact that both stem from the anticommunist Solidarity movement, and both emphasize the importance of the Catholic Church. PO is economically free-market and pro-business. PiS advocates protectionism and state intervention, added welfare spending and controls on foreign investment. Both are socially conservative, but PiS has a strongly pro-Catholic stance, opposing the legalization of abortion.

PiS wishes to end the tradition of compromise between ex-communists and opposition. It talked of creating a "Fourth Republic" to get away entirely from the corrupt "Third Republic," created after 1989. In government it created a high-powered anticorruption body to investigate questionable privatization deals and crony-infested state bureaucracy. It sought to purge ex-communists from public life and to clean up the intelligence services; it dissolved the Military Intelligence Service (WSI). In April 2006 it ordered prosecutors to file charges against the last Communist leader, General Jaruzelski, for imposing martial law in 1981. In September 2008 he went on trial with six other octogenarian officers and party officials on charges of being part of a "criminal conspiracy." This was the first time Poland had sought to hold its former communist leaders responsible for imposing martial law. Because of delaying actions on the part of the infirm and aged defendants, there will probably never be a verdict.

The popular ex-Prime Minister Kazimierz Marcinkiewicz, a shy former physics teacher, spoke of a Bermuda Quadrangle of politicians, secret police agents, businessmen and criminals. Then Prime Minister and PiS leader Jaroslaw Kaczynski vowed to "destroy the system that has dominated the Third Republic for the past 17 years."

There are disagreements over foreign policy. Although both are pro-American, the PiS takes an assertive, nationalist, patriotic and populist stance, including toward the EU, Germany and Russia. As a Eurosceptic party, it was pleased that the EU's constitutional treaty failed, whereas PO is pro-EU.

Poland

POLISH POLITICS

SECULAR

LEFT

RIGHT

POLAND POWER!

PEPSI

PEPSI

GO NATO!

CONFESSIONAL

ooo ER MAYBE!

All parties support NATO membership

Credit: George Skudos

They also have very different electorates. Civic Platform's support is overwhelmingly in the dynamic, more affluent, western parts of Poland, in large cities and among younger and better-educated Poles (including 41% of students). It attracts the globalized elite that wants Poland to be respected in Europe and have one of the continent's most competitive economies. It is the party of Poles who clearly benefitted from the collapse of the old regime. Law and Justice is a populist party that does well in poorer, rural parts of society, especially in Eastern and Central Poland and among older more devoutly Catholic voters. Its success reflects the anger of those who consider themselves to be losers in the transition. The difference in the bases of the two parties is between a more modern, liberal Poland that is well integrated in Europe and the world, and a more nationalistic and fundamentalist Catholic Poland that focuses on its own interests. Jaroslaw Kaczynski assumed the prime ministership in July 2006.

Law and Justice ruled in a shaky minority government by relying on the votes of two eccentric, populist and controversial parties. The left-wing xenophobic Self-Defense (Samoobrona) had won 11.7% of

the votes and 57 seats (up from 53), and its mercurial, demagogic leader, Andrzej Lepper, landed the post as deputy speaker of parliament. The League of Polish Families (LRP) is a right-wing party linked to an ultra-Catholic radio station and has a youth wing whose rhetoric sounds anti-Semitic to some ears. These two quirky parties were questionable partners for any government.

After two years of infighting and back-biting, this unstable government collapsed, and new elections were held on October 21, 2007. It was a short, but contentious campaign. The highlight was three televised debates involving the leaders of three main parties: Donald Tusk of PO, Jaroslaw Kaczynski of PiS, and ex-President Aleksander Kwasniewski, who attempted a political comeback at the head of the Left and Democrats party (LiD). Tusk, who displayed humor, calmness and command of the issues, emerged the winner of the debates, while Kaczynski came across as bombastic and imprecise.

As has been the case in every Polish parliamentary election since the advent of democracy, the incumbents lost and the opposition won in 2007. The election was a kind of referendum on the Kaczynskis'

government, and that quality produced the largest voter turnout since 1989: 54%. Civic Platform (PO) captured 209 of the 460 seats with 41.4% of the votes. Its governing partner, the Polish Peasants' Party (PSL), led by Deputy Prime Minister Waldemar Pawlak, received 8.9% of the votes and 31 seats. This gave the ruling coalition 240 seats. Now in the opposition, Law and Justice (PiS) actually increased its vote to 32.2% and number of seats to 166. LiD won 13.2% and 53 seats, while other parties won 4.3% of the votes, but only one seat. As always, the German Minority was granted two seats.

Foreign Policy

Just as postwar Germany discarded its earlier *Schaukelpolitik* (policy of swinging back and forth) between East and West and planted its roots firmly in the West, Poland has also rejected such "to and fro." It seeks to be fixed politically where it always was culturally and emotionally: to the West. This is captured in the saying that the Poles, have "always considered that East is East and West is best, and the twain meet on Poland's eastern border."

Poland's seven neighbors represent an increase from three before the collapse of the Soviet Union in December 1991, none of which exists today: the Soviet Union, Czechoslovakia, or the GDR. For the first time in a millennium Poland is secure and at peace with all of its neighbors. For the first time in more than a century it feels safe on its eastern and western borders. With Germany, the Czech Republic, Lithuania, Slovakia and Ukraine it has developed particularly close relations. Poland enjoys its best relations among its seven neighbors with its oldest foe: Germany. The latter has proven to be a reliable partner with much to offer.

Poland's foreign policy has shown considerable continuity despite frequent changes of governments. Ties with the United States are extremely important. It has a huge American diaspora, numbering over nine million, with the largest concentrations in New York, Michigan, Pennsylvania and Illinois. Chicago is the largest concentration of Poles after Warsaw. Poland is America's most trusted ally in the area. Poland's pro-Americanism is so obvious that one European Commission official grumbled, "Poland's dream is economic integration with Europe, but political integration with the United States." When *The Economist* surveyed students at the University of Warsaw in 2001 about their political role models, the top two were Ronald Reagan and Harry Truman.

That has changed slightly. Foreign Minister Radek Sikorski, one of the most popular politicians, was a former student activist who hated the Soviet Union so much in the 1980s that he went to Afghanistan and fought with the Mujahedeen against the Russians. Later an Oxford graduate and fellow at the American Enterprise Institute in Washington, he noted that "U.S. influence and esteem have diminished in Poland." Seeing clearly that their core interests lie with the EU, Poles regard their relationship with America as less vital. The war in Afghanistan, where 18 Polish soldiers had died by mid-2010, is unpopular. Some Poles resent their government's earlier role in aiding the U.S. in its rendition policy and allegedly in hosting a secret CIA jail. The government denies these charges.

Most Central Europeans and their governments have a greater inclination toward pro-Americanism than do their Western cousins. That does not apply to President Barack Obama, who is less popular in Eastern Europe than in Western Europe. The American dream is still potent, and for generations they have gotten positive accounts of the New World from émigrés who found a better life there. Many feel that America did the most to win them their independence in 1989, and there remains a residual fear of Russia and Germany that could be countered only by

American power. Former two-time foreign minister, Wladyslaw Bartoszewski, expressed it this way: "Always at the moment when Berlin and St. Petersburg or Moscow get too close, we have been threatened."

Certainly most Poles are convinced that only the U.S. can ultimately guarantee their country's security while the EU still struggles to create a defense identity and capability. In his 2007 campaign, Prime Minister Tusk singled the U.S. out as Poland's "most important ally" while at the same time mending ties with the countries' neighbors, especially Germany but including Russia. Ambassador to the U.S., Janusz Reiter, wrote: "As long as the U.S. is a functioning reality and a united Europe is a dream, we will always choose the reality over the dream." However, current Polish policy is to support both an enlarging NATO and a common EU defense. As Bronislaw Komorowski, put it: if you live near a "forest full of bandits," it is best to have two locks on the door.

Of course, there are risks involved in Poland's and other Central European countries' steady support of the foreign policy objectives of the United States, which sees the European center of gravity shifting eastward. They can sometimes feel caught between leading Western European nations, which held the keys to the EU, and the U.S., which provides unaccustomed security. The U.S. and UK are Poland's largest sources of foreign investment, and Germany is its largest market.

The late President Kaczynski visited Washington in February 2006 and maintained that "our excellent relations with the United States make us a more desir-

able partner for the European Union." He emphasized that his country has two fundamental foreign policy priorities: "very good relations with the EU and very good relations with the U.S. We do not want a hierarchy and we also believe that the two priorities are not mutually exclusive." The Tusk government did not fundamentally change Poland's basic foreign policy, and it is not more compromising. But it adopted a more conciliatory tone, and that is good for neighborly relations.

During the Iraq crisis in the spring of 2003, French President Jacques Chirac lashed out at the Central European governments' signing of a letter supporting the U.S. in Iraq. They felt degraded to second-class status by Chirac's public statement that "these countries have been not very well behaved and rather reckless of the danger of aligning themselves too rapidly with the American position. They missed a great opportunity to remain silent." One German newspaper called Poland America's "Trojan donkey." Political scientist Andrzej Kapiszewski of Jagiellonian University in Krakow remarked: "Chirac's words were more or less like the words we heard from the Kremlin for the previous 50 years of communism." The fact that France and Germany had allied with Russia over Iraq without consulting with Poland and their other future EU partners was an unpleasant memory for Poles of great powers making deals over their heads and at their expense.

Many Poles believe that they have not fully benefited from their strong support of the U.S. Many feel hurt by American requirements that while Americans enter

Polish Peacekeeper in Bosnia Flanked by US Troops

Poland

their country visa-free, Poles must apply for expensive ($100) visas when traveling to the U.S. They must be interviewed before being granted a visa and are subjected to fingerprinting upon arrival at an American airport.

Poland seeks to keep neighboring Ukraine looking west, on the assumption that Poland cannot be safe unless Ukraine prospers. Whereas most European countries had weak and bad relations with Ukraine, Belarus, and Moldova, Poland conducts high-level meetings and an exchange of governmental officials and students on a regular basis. It moderated between the former Ukrainian government and the opposition. It sponsored roundtable talks in Warsaw and persuading ex-leader Leonid Kuchma to allow new elections in December 2004, which the "Orange Revolution" leaders won.

This role brought increased tension into Warsaw's relations with Russia, compelling Poland to build a stronger common front with its other EU partners. It also made clear to Poland that its vital interests lie close to home and that it should perhaps place less emphasis on its ties to the U.S. That is why the Tusk government, which took power in 2007, is more forthcoming toward Moscow. In return, Russia dropped its long-standing ban on meat exports from Poland.

As an EU member since May 2004, it argues quietly for an "eastern dimension" to the EU's external policy, supporting that organization's "Good Neighbor Policy" toward the East. As stable, more prosperous and accessible countries, they would be better able to resist Russian influence and keep Poland more secure. It

trades and invests in these two countries, and it formed a joint peacekeeping battalion with Ukraine, POLUKRBAT, which serves in Bosnia and Kosovo. Poland ratified a Concordat with the Vatican in 1998.

Poland's relations with Russia were satisfactory under President Walesa, but they cooled somewhat under Kwasniewski because of his support for the proposed enlargement of NATO. The fact that Poland actually received and accepted an invitation in 1997 to join NATO two years later did not help. Russia supplies almost 90% of Poland's oil and gas needs; 97% of its imported crude oil comes from that country. But Russia also needs a friendly Poland for many reasons, including the latter's crucial location for Russia's oil and gas pipelines to Germany and elsewhere in Europe. For that reason, Moscow entered an agreement with Germany in 2005 to build a pipeline under the Baltic Sea to Germany, thereby avoiding Polish territory altogether. Poles are furious, and this pipeline is opposed by all parties. In response, Poland plans its own pipeline from Norway via Denmark and hopes for German support.

Former Russian President (now Prime Minister) Vladimir Putin's visit to Poland in 2002 was the first by a Russian leader since 1993 and was hailed as a success. He gave his approval of the EU's eastward expansion and called for constructive work with NATO. Putin made symbolic gestures to try to diminish Polish distrust of Russia. He unexpectedly stopped at a monument honoring 50 victims of the 1956 revolt against Soviet rule and at one in the middle of Warsaw commemorating the main Polish underground army in World War II.

Rare Anti-War Poster during 2003 Iraq War

Putin could not bring himself to visit the monument to the 1944 Warsaw uprising, when Soviet troops stood still across the Vistula River while German units crushed the Polish fighters. Nor did he mention until several years later the massacre in the Katyn Forest in western Russia where Stalin ordered the execution of almost 22,000 Polish officers in 1940 and deported over 10,000 more to be killed in other parts of the USSR. Moscow never formally apologized for these actions. It hesitated for years to release documentation that would enable relatives of the victims to receive some justice. That changed in 2010. Russia's leaders showed compassion and support when a Polish military airplane with the president and 95 other high-level passengers crashed killing all aboard. Poland's best-known film director, Andrzej Wajda, made a much-praised film on this tragedy, *Katyn*, in 2007, and Putin allowed this to be shown on Russian television.

In 2005 the Polish government risked heating up tensions with Russia by releasing 1,700 highly secret Warsaw Pact files that included a war game during the Cold War that called for massive nuclear destruction of Poland and Western Europe. A map showed Soviet forces counterattacking NATO forces in a way that involved dropping nuclear bombs from the Dutch coast to Strasbourg, wiping out cities in Germany, France and BENELUX. There were also details of the 1968 Warsaw Pact invasion of Czechoslovakia. A further wake-up call came in August 2008, when Russia invaded Georgia. This was a

Polish and American Special Forces during Iraq War, 2003

Poland

Jagiellonian University, Cracow

reminder that Poles still live in a potentially dangerous part of the world. Deputy Defense Minister Stanislaw Komorowski referred to the year Poland joined NATO: "In 1999 everybody thought the cold war was over. But last year we had Georgia. An independent country was invaded by our partner: Russia. It changed our perception of the threat."

However, Putin signaled that he wanted good relations with Poland. In September 2009 he went to Gdansk to mark the start of the Second World War. He also invited a Polish honor guard, along with units from Britain, France and the United States, to march as representatives of the "anti-Hitler coalition" in Moscow's annual parade commemorating VE Day on May 8, 2010.

The Polish government has made it clear that it desires good relations with all of its neighbors to the east, but that its own commitment is Europe. Its economic orientation is Western, particularly since joining the EU in May 2004. This Western approach was reinforced by the slowness of economic reform in neighbors such as Belarus and Ukraine.

Its relations with Lithuania are no longer seriously affected by historic complaints concerning Lithuania's treatment of its Polish minority in the Vilnius area. Poles in Lithuania are well integrated in Lithuanian society and were given Lithuanian citizenship immediately after that country won its independence from the Soviet Union in 1991. Nor do the two countries have any border disputes. In 1997 Poland forged a "strategic alliance" with Lithuania. It created a joint battalion, LITPOLBAT, that is interoperable with

NATO and prepared to contribute to the Atlantic Alliance's security needs.

Poland was officially admitted to NATO in March 1999. Two weeks later NATO began its air attacks on Yugoslavia. Poland consistently supported the NATO actions, but the air attacks led to tenser relations with Russia and Belarus, both of which opposed the NATO actions. Poland supported the war against terrorism after the September 11 attacks in New York and Washington. It offered parts of its elite special operations forces, known as GROM, to fight alongside the Americans in Afghanistan.

Most dramatically, it was one of the few U.S. allies to lend active support in the war effort in Iraq in March–April 2003. Polish intelligence agents had sneaked CIA operatives out of Iraq before the first Gulf war in 1991, and since the end of that war a second Polish ambassador was dispatched to Iraq to represent U.S. diplomatic interests. Polish construction companies had also built many of the roads in Iraq during the 1970s, so few people knew them as well as the Poles. Opinion surveys revealed that a majority of Poles actually opposed military action in Iraq, but opposition was generally passive; only 2,000 demonstrators gathered in Warsaw to protest the war.

Opposition would perhaps have been even greater if Polish fatalities were not so low despite being subjected to waves of fierce attacks. There is a feeling that Poland derived too little benefit from its deployment: its efforts to end the visa requirement for the U.S. were rebuffed, and its military complained that it did not get as much financial assistance as it had expected.

The government accepted the call for help from Washington and sent GROM and FORMOZA (Navy Seal) special forces, anti-chemical and biological units, and a small naval contingent. Its 200 special forces entered Iraq in the first wave of the invasion in March and helped secure the oil fields in the south. This was the first military combat for Polish soldiers since the 1968 Prague Spring in neighboring Czechoslovakia, and they performed very well without suffering any casualties.

After the war, Poland assumed command of one of four occupation zones in Iraq, in the upper southern zone between Basra and Baghdad. Its own 1,700 troops are down from 2,460, the fourth-largest contingent. Two-thirds were financed by the United States. It had a total of 9,500 soldiers under its command. It also trained Iraqi security forces. Its request to Germany for a troop contribution to this unit was summarily dismissed in Berlin. By 2006, over 10,500 Polish soldiers had been deployed in Iraq. In the words of the defense minister, "They are the core of the new Polish military. They had not been in a warlike situation for half a century. They go out as civilians in uniform, but they come back as real warriors." Honoring a campaign pledge, Prime Minister Tusk ordered the country's 900 soldiers to leave Iraq the end of 2008. It had 13 trainers remaining in 2010.

Not since Poland's liberation from Communist rule in 1989 has it assumed so visible a role on the world stage. In the second half of 2007 it took over command of NATO's 9,000-strong International Security Assistance Force in Afghanistan. It maintains a battalion of about 1,100 troops in Paktika, a dangerous province that borders the Pakistani tribal areas. In 2010 its troop total in Afghanistan was 2,600, NATO's seventh-largest.

Poland maintains one of the largest armies in Europe, with 100,000 active forces as it transforms its military into a smaller, modern, mobile integrated force. It is being reshaped into a professional force that can quickly deploy to trouble spots or multilateral missions anywhere in the world. The force once included 81,000 conscripts who served for nine months. But conscription has been scrapped, and the last draftees were mustered out of the armed forces in summer 2009. It also has a reserve force of 234,000. Poland's army numbers 46,400, its navy 8,000 (who man an array of destroyers, patrol and coastal combatants, mine layers and sweepers, naval air, and four conventional submarines, all in desperate need of being upgraded), and its air forces 17,500. There are 14,100 paramilitaries, including border guards. In 2010 there were only 1,500 women soldiers, but that number is expected to rise.

Poland

Female Polish Students with Slovenian classmate at College of Europe, Warsaw

It can afford to spend 1.95% of its GDP on defense (2008). This makes it one of NATO's largest military spenders in relative terms, but it is small in absolute terms. Personnel and pension costs consume roughly half of its spending. It is putting its limited funds into developing its military projection capabilities, not its territorial defense. This is true despite the fact that Poland has become NATO's eastern frontier facing the unstable western republics of the former Soviet Union. A further problem is that its largest military bases are located in the western part of Poland, far away from Belarus and Ukraine—and Russia beyond. Nevertheless, the emphasis is on special forces, to be modernized to U.S. levels.

In 2008 the departing Bush administration beefed up the U.S.-Polish military relationship by offering security guarantees and the deployment of an American-manned Patriot missile unit with 196 missiles to defend Warsaw. For three years this battery is operated by American soldiers on temporary duty. But by the end of 2012, it will be manned by about 100 permanently stationed U.S. troops. This is the first time American soldiers have been stationed on Polish soil other than on NATO maneuvers. Poland also receives more training and equipment, such as armored Humvees. It got important help from Germany, which donated excess stocks of Leopard 2A4 tanks (128), Mig-29 fighter jets (23), and several hundred support vehicles.

It also made the largest ever purchase of American military hardware by a former Warsaw Pact country. To the consternation of the French, who had expected Poland to buy their Mirage fighters, the Poles purchased 48 American F-16 fighter jets at a cost of $3.5 billion. Washington offered a sweetheart low-interest loan to enable the Poles to pay, with no principal payments before 2011. The package includes assembly operations for F-16 engines in Poland, investments in Polish steel mills and shipyards, and high-tech ventures in Poland by Lockheed and dozens of American companies. The contract also included the training of the pilots, which will take place in both the U.S. and Poland using American and Polish instructors. Of a one-time military aid package worth $100 million to modernize the Polish forces, $40 million is earmarked for extra training of F-16 pilots in the U.S.

The U.S. already prizes Poland as a place for maneuvers. In 2001–2 it spent $60 million for such war games in Poland, which is centrally located in Europe and has far fewer restrictions than training areas in Germany. For example, maneuver damage in Germany costs the U.S. $30 million each year, compared to only $25,000 in Poland. It offers perfect military training terrain that includes vast flatlands, swamps and rugged mountains.

The Polish government was receptive to the idea of an American deployment of 10 silos for interceptor missiles to guard against attacks from the Middle East; NATO supported this. However, Russia considered this to be provocative and even threatened to deploy short-range Iskander missiles in Kaliningrad close to Poland's border. That threat was later dropped. Polish public support for the missile system rose from 27% to 41% after the August 2008 Russian invasion of Geor-

gia. Poland saw the interceptor bases as a way of permanently stationing American troops on their soil, and they believed they would have provided it with additional security against a resurgent Russia. The plan was seen as a symbol of America's credibility and commitment to regional defense.

However, newly elected President Barack Obama, who is not as focused on Eastern Europe as was his predecessor and who desires to "reset" the American-Russian relationship, was less enthusiastic about the deployment. On September 17, 2009, he dropped the original idea and ordered a less ambitious missile defense system. The Polish and Czech governments were shocked. He was unaware that September 17 was the anniversary for the Soviet Union's invasion of Poland in 1939. Obama's poor timing fueled Poland's fears of being abandoned by its most powerful ally. The headline in the Polish tabloid *Fakt* read: "Betrayal! The U.S. sold us to Russia and stabbed us in the back".

Realizing its error, the American government offered Poland, after much haggling, a battery of Patriot missiles armed with live warheads to be used in NATO exercises and to be deployed for an undetermined time at a military base in Morag, located 35 miles from the Russian enclave of Kaliningrad. The U.S. also pressed NATO to develop contingency plans to defend Poland and, by extension, to protect the vulnerable Baltic states, mainly by means of Polish troops. Poland is pushing

Willy Brandt Square where German Chancellor knelt to honor ghetto victims

330

for a stronger bilateral security commitment from America.

Poland and Germany

The Federal Republic of Germany's (FRG) first chancellor, Konrad Adenauer, said in 1956 that Germany would have to do with Poland the same as it had done with France after the Second World War. But the Cold War prevented the establishment of that kind of special relationship. This changed in 1990, when a reunified Germany could officially renounce any claims to territory Germany had lost to Poland in 1945. German Foreign Minister Hans-Dietrich Genscher argued that the reacquisition of that land would have created a "new injustice." But Germany's firm position was that only the government of a unified Germany had the democratic authority to cede formerly German territory forever.

Most Poles were uncomfortable with German unity. Germany was not the only country to have to relinquish eastern territory as a price for peace and reconciliation. Poland itself had to accept the permanent loss of its former eastern provinces in present-day Lithuania, Belarus and Ukraine. In 2004 the European Court of Human Rights ruled that about 90,000 of the 1.2 million Poles displaced from the former eastern territories still have the right to claim compensation. Like Germany, Poland accepts a role as bridge between Russia and the West as the only way to escape its traditional geographic dilemma. Its ex-foreign minister, the late Bronislaw Geremek, wrote that Poland "is a natural connecting bridge for Western Europe on its way east; and for an Eastern Europe that is opening itself to the West, Poland again is on the way."

Lech Walesa expressed grave concerns the day after the Berlin Wall fell on November 9, 1989, and his uneasiness was shared by two out of three Polish respondents in a *New York Times*/CSA survey at the time. Geremek greeted it because Poland would be a neighbor of NATO and the EU and for the first time in almost six decades would share a border with a democratic state. "Poland forever returns to where she has always belonged: the free world." As foreign minister, he took Poland into NATO. The symbol of the new mutual respect is Geremek himself. A Jew who escaped from the Warsaw ghetto at age 11 and remained in hiding until war's end and whose parents were killed by Germans in the Warsaw ghetto, he is the symbol of a new mutual respect. He accepted the Karl's Prize in Aachen and gave his acceptance speech in German although he had once vowed never to speak that language. Referring to Poland's future, he said: "The winds of history have normally blown against us Poles. Finally they are blowing in our direction."

Former German Chancellor Helmut Kohl and Genscher knew that while no European country wanted to thwart German unity, there was uneasiness about the possibility that an economically powerful Germany, 43% larger than before and more populous than any country west of Russia, would dominate Europe. Most European leaders were too polite to express these fears publicly. To minimize these fears, Germany signed landmark treaties with the USSR and Poland. On November 9 it signed a friendship treaty with the Soviet Union that amounted to the closest links the Soviets had with any major Western nation. It contains a section affirming that both nations "will refrain from any threat or use of force which is directed against the territorial integrity or political independence of the other side." Neither country would aid an aggressor against the other.

The ink was hardly dry when Germany signed a treaty with Poland on November 14, 1990, fixing their mutual border along the Oder-Neisse Line. The former German land to the East of this demarcation constituted a third of Poland's territory. This treaty inaugurated a policy of reconciliation toward Poland that would prove to be as dramatic for European peace and stability as Franco-German reconciliation since the 1950s in the West. Genscher stated bluntly, "we Germans are aware that the treaty does not surrender anything that was not lost long ago as the result of a criminal war and a criminal system." But he also admitted that settling this last major dispute of the war hurt: "For those who have lost their homelands, who suffered expulsion [after 1945], it is an especially painful one." On June 17, 1991, the two countries signed a further treaty on "good neighbors and cooperation." This treaty deliberately imitated the pioneering 1963 German-French reconciliation treaty by establishing a German-Polish foundation to promote youth contacts.

Many clichés and prejudices remain on both sides of the border, but a 2006 poll revealed that 71% of Poles consider Germans to be good neighbors and that their relations have improved since Poland joined the EU in 2004. Two-thirds of Germans have never visited their eastern neighbor and do not know the land or the people. Asked in a 2006 survey what they most associated with Poland, the top answer was "car theft and crime," closely followed by "illegal workers" and "poverty, backwardness." But the German and Polish elites have grown together to a remarkable extent.

Most Poles agree that the most important European partner they have is Germany. Not only was it Poland's most persistent and influential advocate in NATO and the EU, but it is Poland's largest trading partner (buying 26.7% of Poland's exports and providing 29.8% of its imports) and second-largest foreign investor after France. Elite Polish fears have been assuaged by the way in which Germany has become Europeanized. Geremek wrote that "Europe provides the appropriate setting for relations with Germany. . . . With

Second World War Memorial, Warsaw

Poland

this, the Polish fear of German hegemony or of political dependence on Germany has vanished."

An important link with both Germany and France is the Weimar Triangle, named after the venue of its first meeting in 1991. Traditionally Poland was politically and culturally oriented toward France. However, this primary tie was no longer feasible for Poland after 1989, given Paris's "empty chair" policy toward NATO and its obvious preference for a "deepening" of European Union integration, as opposed to "widening," which would bring in new members from the East. The best anchor for the pursuit of Polish interests became Germany. But Poland wants to widen its Western contacts in order to reduce its possible dependence on Germany. The Weimar Triangle, which brings together the three countries' heads of state and government, ministers and parliamentary representatives for informal talks on fundamental matters of mutual interest, does just that.

A symbol of the partnership at the highest level and of tension at the lower level is the bilingual Europa Universität Viadrina at Slubice (Poland) and Frankfurt an der Oder (Germany). They are separated only by the Oder River and centuries of misunderstandings. This is the first German university that is truly European. It is based on a partnership between Poznan and Frankfurt an der Oder Universities and reserves 30% of its study places for students from Central Europe. Courses are offered in both German (the predominant language of instruction) and Polish, and a few courses are given in English. Its small size (3,000 students) allows for a level of interaction, experimentation, and interdisciplinary synergism unknown in other Polish and German universities.

While the university's concept is daring and cosmopolitan, the twin-city setting reveals that there are still problems in the way the two populations deal with each other. They remain culturally and linguistically separate even though the border is completely open since December 21, 2007, when Poland joined the Schengen agreement. More and more persons in Slubice speak German, but almost no one on the German side learns Polish. About a fifth (about eight million) of Poles speak German.

Polish students find that many Eastern German students at the Frankfurt an der Oder University have little interest in mingling with them. One Western German student explained that those German students who come from the West select this university because of its multinational character and are therefore far more inclined to learn Polish and make Polish friends. Most Eastern German students attend merely because it is close to home. There have been some incidents of Poles being the victims of right-extremist attacks in Frankfurt, and they are therefore somewhat wary of moving freely at all hours of the night. Perhaps a few Polish students wonder whether all have embraced Thomas Mann's plea to the German youth in 1952 to create a European Germany, not a German Europe.

Another innovative institution located on the Polish side of the border, in Szczecin, is a Northeast Multinational Corps consisting of Polish, German and Danish troops, commanded by a Polish officer. This military cooperation, supplemented by a dramatic increase in German-Polish exercises and interaction (second only to that between the U.S. and Poland) is symptomatic of a new spirit in the Polish-German relations. Together the two countries provide the bulk of NATO forces in the East, even though Poland insists that the U.S. is and will remain its key military partner.

NATO membership gives Poland the confidence to engage its eastern neighbors, especially Russia, and it takes seriously its objective to expand the zone of stability eastward. This serves both German and American interests. Nevertheless, Poland is mindful of a possible Russian resurgence. Therefore, Poland unequivocally supported the admission of the Baltic States to NATO. It also values membership in the EU as long as it does not diminish the role of NATO in maintaining security in Europe.

Poles experience some hostility on the German side of the border because their country is a major contributor to a huge black market in labor in Germany. Many Germans (who earn more than four times as much as a Pole in Poland) fear that cheap Polish laborers will take their jobs. Many Polish workers have done this in Berlin, a city with the most construction sites in all of Europe, but with Germany's highest unemployment rate among construction workers. Foreign laborers are willing to work on weekends and accept much lower pay and benefits than are Germans. One reason the May 2005 French referendum failed was the prominence in public debate of a mythical "Polish plumber," who would come to France, work longer hours for lower wages, and drive his French counterpart out of business. These kinds of tensions highlight Germany's problems as a high-wage economy in an age of globalization and bordering on low-wage Central Europe.

To limit the effects of an influx of Polish labor, Germany negotiated within the EU a seven-year transition before there would be the free movement of labor. Poles can travel freely in EU member states and can even establish their own businesses there, offering their own often cheaper labor. About two million Poles migrated westward to find work, and half returned home. Many illegal laborers will remain in Germany, and others will join them. After entering the EU in May 2004 and the ending of controls for the two countries' citizens at the border (average time to cross is one minute), the already vibrant cross-border trade jumped. Germans not only buy cheap Polish gasoline, cigarettes and food, but even leave their cars at Polish garages for service and repairs and take advantage of cheaper fees charged by doctors, dentists and hair dressers.

Germany had been Poland's main advocate for EU membership, and until the Kaczynski twins came to power in 2005, Poles usually made a point of not mentioning the Second World War explicitly in any dealings with Germany. It has long been the rule in the EU that the war would be mentioned only in connection with the postwar miracle that European integration has brought. The twins seldom missed an opportunity to insult Germany, accusing it of "obvious anti-Polish sentiment that is often racist." They argued at the EU summit in June 2007 that Poland needed more votes in the council because it would have had a population of 66 million, not 39 million, were it not for the war. Poles are bitter about Germany's decision to join Russia in building an underwater pipeline that would avoid Poland. But the Polish defense minister went too far in comparing it with the Molotov-Ribbentrop pact in 1939. Such statements left their bilateral relations raw.

Germany opposed Poland's hard stance in 2003 on the new EU constitutional treaty. Poles feared being treated like second-class members and applauded their government's tough stance, especially on the issue of voting rights. The 2000 Nice treaty had awarded Poland almost as many votes in the EU Council of Ministers (27) as Germany (29), which has twice as many people. The Polish government also favored the inclusion of the word "God" in the preamble.

Seeing itself on the outs with much of Europe, Poland backed down in 2007 and accepted a "double-majority" voting system in the council and votes proportional to its population size, albeit with a delay until 2017. That assumed that the revised constitution, known as the "Lisbon Treaty," would unanimously be ratified, as it eventually was. Poland's parliament approved it in April 2008. Then President Lech Kaczynski delayed it to annoy Prime Minister Tusk and the Civic Platform party. Such grandstanding is risky politics in Eastern Europe, where Euroskepticism is not appealing. The EU is widely seen by

Poland

his own people and other eastern Europeans as a guarantor of stability and progress and a generous provider of funding for modernization. The president ultimately signed it.

Part of the problem was that the untraveled and monoglot twins purged the government and foreign ministry of diplomatic and EU experts. A fourth of Polish embassies were without an ambassador. All this changed after the October 2007 elections. Prime Minister Tusk restored good relations with Germany and its chancellor, Angela Merkel. He also grudgingly accepted Berlin's decision to build a memorial to the millions of Eastern Europeans, including Germans, who were expelled after the war. Warsaw had long opposed this project, arguing that it would present Germans as the victims, rather than the perpetrators of crimes during the conflict.

To defuse German criticism of lax border controls, Poland accepted the principle of "safe third state," whereby Poland would not allow its territory to be used by illegal immigrants to reach Germany and would take back those illegals who slipped through their controls. This necessitated a severe tightening of its own borders and meant that Poland serves as a kind of filter for migrants from the East heading for Germany.

The situation for the estimated 300,000–500,000 ethnic Germans still living in Poland (mainly in Opole, but also in the Mazury and Warmia areas) has greatly improved. They constitute Poland's largest ethnic minority. In 1945, following the brutal German treatment of the Polish population during the Second World War—especially of Polish Jews, who made up half of all Holocaust victims—three million Germans were expelled from Poland in accordance with the Potsdam Agreement. Many of their homes and farms were occupied by Poles deported by the Soviet Union from Poland's eastern territories, which were annexed by the USSR. This left Poland a largely (about 96%–98%) homogeneous country for the first time in its history.

Relations with Germany were inflamed again in 2004 when groups representing German deportees threatened to file damage claims against Poland. Reaction in Poland was furious even though the German government had refused to back these claims. The *Sejm* passed a nonbinding motion seeking war reparations from Germany. The controversy died down, but it revealed how many raw emotions remain on both sides. There is tension still in the air.

Until 1989 ethnic minorities in Poland faced a policy of enforced Polonization. Mainly for economic reasons, 424,000 people emigrated to the FRG from 1955 to 1974 and another 200,000 after 1975. After 1989, Poland adopted the political standards of the Organization for Security and Cooperation in Europe (OSCE) and the Council of Europe for protecting minority rights. These were written into the 1991 Treaty on Good-Neighborly Relations and Friendly Cooperation between Germany and Poland. This treaty affirms the right to use minority languages and to have non-Polish surnames.

There is a German caucus in the Polish parliament, and since 1990 the German government has provided financial support to the German community, including cultural and language assistance, as well as scholarships. From 1989 to 2000 Germany paid more than 105 million euros to Germans in Poland as an inducement to remain there. An additional seven million euros were provided by the Foundation for the Development of Silesia.

The newly elected German government of Angela Merkel claimed in 2009 that it wanted its relations with Poland to be as close as they are with France. The new foreign minister, Guido Westerwelle, sent an important signal by making Warsaw his first visit abroad.

ECONOMY

The pattern of economic development in Poland after World War II was similar in many respects to that in other countries of the area under Soviet domination. But limited natural resources and popular resistance to forced savings resulting in fewer consumer goods slowed the drive to change from a predominantly agricultural economy to one based on industry.

Centralized industrial and economic planning was adopted when the communist regime came to power. Although there were attempts between 1980 and 1989 to reduce the rigidity of central planning, they failed because of opposition from the entrenched bureaucracy. As a result, Poland continued to suffer from a severe housing shortage, high inflation and the shortage of many consumer goods.

The country faced severe economic difficulties after the collapse of communism in 1989. A major problem was with agriculture. Although about 85% of all land was privately owned under communism, government policy had always discriminated against the private peasants in an effort to persuade them to join collective farms. There was some modification of this policy over time, but the communist government did not have sufficient funds to pour into agriculture, even if it had wanted to.

The installation of a noncommunist government in 1989 led to a major change in economic policy and a firm commitment to institute a market economy. A dramatic symbol of this change is that the former ruling Communist party headquarters building was transformed into the stock exchange. Still, by the fall of 1990 a lot of Poles had mixed feelings about the reform. There were clearly some successes. Poland's currency, the zloty, had been stabilized, bringing an end to the currency black market. All over Warsaw, thousands of stalls had been set up where individuals sold a variety of products from farm produce to cassette tapes. Also, store shelves were again full, and people no longer had to stand in line or pay bribes to obtain certain products. On the other side, official statistics of the state-owned sector showed that production had plunged by 25% since communist rule. In addition, strict wage controls had cut the purchasing power of ordinary Poles. On balance, however, Poles expected to benefit eventually even if there was some pain at the moment.

Privatization

Some Poles criticized the reform because it was going too slowly. Ten months after it had been initiated, not a single large state-owned company had been privatized. Parliament debated such issues as the rights of employees in private companies and whether shares ought to be made available at a discount to employees. Many Poles were also concerned about foreigners coming in and buying everything.

In 1990 the government announced that it would issue shares in seven state-owned companies and make them available to the public for purchase. It took the government four months to prepare the shares. By that time, it had reduced the number of companies being sold to five. When the shares were offered in January 1991, the deadline for purchase had to be extended because there were not enough takers. Another approach to privatization that was discussed was to issue script or coupons to all Polish citizens, who could use them to purchase shares in companies being privatized. Since there were more than 8,000 state-owned companies, privatization would take time.

Poland got some international assistance in 1991, when Western nations agreed to forgive 50% of the $33 billion that Poland had borrowed from foreign governments. The United States was even more generous, forgiving 70% of the $3.8 billion debt it held. The government's ability to reduce the deficit in the 1994 budget to 3.9% of GDP triggered the second phase of a 50% reduction in Poland's $33 billion debt to Western governments in the Paris Club. It also led to an agreement between Poland and London Club

Poland

banks. It reduced the $13 billion debt to Western private banks by 45%.

These agreements meant that Poland has become a more attractive place for foreign investment, as evidenced by the fact that foreign investment doubled in 1995 to $2.5 billion. Another factor is that the government moved to make the zloty a hard currency in 1995. Foreign investment continued to grow after that time and reached $6.6 billion in 1997, the highest yearly amount for any Central European country since the fall of communism. By 2003 France had become the largest foreign investor in Poland, overtaking the United States and Germany. By 2000 over 50% of Poland's banks were owned by foreigners.

Nonagricultural employment accounts for about 73% of the work force in Poland. Although a significant percentage of industrial establishments remain in state hands, the rapid growth in the number of private enterprises means that the significance of state enterprises in the overall economy is decreasing. A 1996 study indicated that the private sector was by that time responsible for 60% of national output. According to Poland's privatization office, more than 2 million private companies were established between 1989 and 1997. The lack of local capital and the difficulty of getting credit have meant that the majority of private enterprises are in the areas of wholesale and retail trade, services and handicrafts. The number of private businesses by 2002 showed how vibrant the entrepreneurial spirit is in Po-

land: there were two million registered businesses, one for every 19 Poles.

The most popular form of privatization has been through "liquidation." This means that the companies have been sold or leased to their employees. At least 900 larger companies were privatized in this manner. Another method of privatization has been to transform state-owned companies into joint stock companies, then sell their shares through negotiations with investors or through a public offering. As of October 1994, 124 large-scale enterprises had been sold in this manner. In December 1994, the state drew up its Mass Privatization Program, involving the privatization of 444 of the remaining large state-owned enterprises. Under this plan, 15 National Investment Funds (NIFs) were set up as joint stock companies. The 444 enterprises were then turned into joint stock companies, with their shares distributed to the 15 NIFs. The NIFs possess all the rights of owners, including the freedom to sell off companies or assets.

There are also companies that the government did not originally expect to be able to privatize, essentially those that were either too big to close, too sick to sell, or the industries were located in single-factory towns. Included in this category were Poland's giant steel mills and coalmines. Although they were run at a loss, these mines met most of Poland's energy needs and provided an additional 20 million tons each year for export.

The Polish government was faced with the need to restructure its coal and steel

industries in order to qualify for EU membership. To meet EU requirements, the Polish cabinet adopted a plan on June 30, 1998, for reforming them. It has the EU's biggest coal reserves, and its coal industry is the second-largest in Europe after Russia's. Some 25,000 mining jobs were eliminated in 1998, and 105,000 (or 40%) were cut by 2002, leaving 142,000 jobs by 2003. The workers received either generous severance payments or a five-year preretirement leave of absence. Coal production, 137 million tons in 1997, dropped to 112 million tons by 2002. In 2002 the government approved a three-year plan for further cuts, closing seven mines and eliminating a further 35,000 jobs as a step toward privatization, but the trade unions successfully blocked these moves.

However, further reduction has its limits since Poland relies on coal for 60% of its total energy needs and, with lignite pits, 95% of its power station needs. It will continue to rely on coal because any shift to oil and gas would create an unwanted dependency on Russia. However, there is the prospect of a huge shale gas bonanza, which could transform the country's geopolitical position. If the current estimates are correct, the shale could offer centuries of gas supplies at current usage.

This fact makes it almost impossible for Poland to meet the greenhouse gas targets set by the EU. It hopes to develop a capacity to build coal-fired plants that will capture greenhouse gasses underground. It has no nuclear power plants, but it has long-range plans to build two of them on the southern shore of the Baltic Sea. An agreement to get nuclear electrical power from Lithuania was stalled, but that remains a future possibility. It worries about its overdependence on Russia's Gazprom, which supplies 40% of its gas.

The two largest labor unions are Solidarity, which has left politics after its 2001 electoral disaster, and the ex-communist All-Poland Alliance of Trade Unions (OPZZ). Both were instrumental in creating a strict labor code that is designed to protect those workers with jobs at the expense of those seeking one. One World Bank study concluded that this code is more geared towards lifetime employment in huge state enterprises than toward the 75% of jobs in the private sector. They compel many investors to sign "social packages" that commit them to maintain employment levels for a specified period of time and to pay "privatization bonuses" to employees, generous wage increases and often special contributions for a variety of causes. One result was a temporary slowdown of foreign investment, which rose sharply in 2004–5 in the wake of Poland's accession to the EU. Another is high unemployment, which in

2010 had climbed to 11.9% (twice that for those between ages 15 and 24). The average workweek had declined to 40 hours by 2001.

The Tusk government, which took power in November 2007, planned to privatize hundreds of businesses and to reduce by half the state-owned sector's contribution to the economy from 20% of GDP to 10%. The sell-off would include tourism, publishing, construction, and, most controversially, shipyards. The European Commission contended that state subsidies to the country's shipyards, amounting to 1.3 billion euros, violated competition agreements and had to end and be paid back. But in July 2009 it relented by approving a large state-aid program for the famous Gdansk shipyard. Ukraine's Donbass group agreed to purchase 83% of it. Selling such an icon to a foreign company sickened former Solidarity activists like Walesa, who called it "a crime." "No one can sell his mother." The yards at Gdynia and Szczecin were sold to a Caribbean-registered company.

Agriculture

Agriculture did not receive as much government attention as industry because it was always largely in private hands throughout the entire period of communism. Today, however, agriculture has grown in importance. Economists in 2005 estimated that out of 1.8 million Polish farms, 200,000 to 400,000 are large enough to thrive in the EU market. Poland has Europe's smallest farms, averaging only 17 acres, compared with 59 acres in Spain, France and Germany. In southern Poland, the average farmer owns just 10 acres. From 1996 to 2002 farm incomes fell more than 30%, and that continues for small farmers. EU farm subsidies are not designed for such little agrarians, who cannot afford concrete floors in their barns and special equipment for slaughtering and milking. Fewer than 20% of rural Poles live off their own farms.

EU membership alleviated the situation even though EU farm subsidies are being phased in over a ten-year period, starting at 25% of existing EU levels. Ninety percent of Polish farmers applied for the EU's direct payments. Only two-thirds of support payments come from Brussels; the Polish treasury must pay the rest. In the meantime the main sources of income for more than half of all farm workers are state benefits or jobs in the underground economy. But the EU market and subsidies are creating a rural boom for the 200,000 to 400,000 farmers with larger plots of land who are gearing up to function in a modern economy.

After joining the EU, demand for Polish produce soared, generating a three-fold increase in farm exports. Farm output has climbed 10%. The average Polish agriculture worker saw his income jump by 73% in 2004. Some are making unprecedented profits. Formerly the most skeptical of the EU, farmers are now among its most ardent supporters.

Agriculture and related industries account for only 4.3% of Poland's GDP by 2010, even though farming employs 15% of the population. By comparison, 56% of Poles work in the services sector, which produces 63.8% of GDP, and 29% are employed in industry, creating 31.8% of the nation's wealth. Poland has more than twice as many farmers than Germany and France combined. Acknowledging the significance of these statistics, the Ministry of Agriculture recommended a "massive reduction" in the rural work force. Many consolidate their land or slowly disappear from farming. The total number of farms has dropped from four million at the time communism collapsed to 2.5 million by 2009.

In an economic sense, Poland is becoming two nations. The gap in living standard between the fifth of the population living in villages or farms and their more affluent countrymen in the cities is widening. Life in the countryside is getting richer, as is the whole country: 87% of rural families now have cars, 80% washing machines and 62% computers. But their incomes are still about 30% below urban levels, and 17% live in poverty, compared with 7% in the cities.

As inequality grows, so does crime. Only a tenth of all university students are

from rural areas. A further gap is developing between Poles in the western part of the country, who are being pulled more closely to Germany, (with which Poles do far more trade than with the U.S., which is only Poland's twelfth largest trading partner accounting for 2.5% of its global turnover and 13% of its foreign investment), and those in the eastern part, who trade with economically desperate Belarus and Ukraine, with which the EU forbids visa-free travel. The income difference between Poles, on the one hand, and Belarusians and Ukrainians on the other is larger than between Poles and Germans and is growing. Poland's economic eyes are focused on the West: three-fourths of its trade is with the EU and only a tenth is with former Soviet republics. Germany alone accounts for over a fourth of its exports and imports.

Current Economic Situation

While the transition to a market economy has been largely successful, the current economic picture is mixed. Although it has not been hit as hard as others in the region by the global economic downturn of 2008–9, the Polish economy was jolted nevertheless. It was helped by the fact that its economy is not as export-dependent (40%) as many smaller countries. Also it has an admirably strong and stable government. A timely $20.5-billion credit line from the IMF in April 2009 helped stabilized Poland's banks and halt the zloty's loss of almost half its value.

The economy grew at more than 5% annually throughout the 1990s and contin-

Christmas carolling party consists of many traditional characters such as King Herod, the devil, death, and an angel
Courtesy: Embassy of Poland

Poland

**European Parliament President
Jerzy Buzek**

ued at 6.5% in 2007 after a few sluggish years; in 2009 it was still growing by 1.7% and by 3% in 2010. It was the only EU country not to fall into recession. Among the reasons is the fact that only 40% of its GDP depends upon exports while many of the smaller Central European countries are much more trade dependent. Poland's relatively large domestic market also means that it is not as vulnerable when Western European partners fall into recession. Productivity increased by 7.7% in 2005, up from 4.1% a year earlier. Labor costs are low by Western European standards. Combined with rising productivity, it is exporting well, especially its automotive industry. For example, Fiat Poland is the largest contributor to the export surge, and 90% of the Pandas produced in Poland are exported.

Inflation ran at a red-hot 35% in 1993, but had declined to 2.2% by 2010. The zloty soared in value and temporarily become one of the world's strongest currencies. It crashed during the global recession and continues to be subject to rapid swings in value. This brought much pain to Poles, who had borrowed heavily in euros and French francs to purchase property, cars and consumer goods. About 70% of mortgage holders must now pay their lenders with depreciated zlotys. The government aimed to join the euro by 2012, but that target date has been dropped. There is no firm date for its introduction.

Unemployment had risen to 11.9% in 2010. It is double that among youth. This is why so many moved west to find work, especially in Britain and Ireland. More than half returned home. To stimulate foreign investment, the government lowered the top corporate tax rate to 19%.

Since communism's fall in 1989, Poland has increased its number of students fivefold, and never before in history have Poles been so well educated and multilingual. This has made Poland an alluring place to locate servicing centers for companies' European operations. Per capita

GDP has risen from 43% of the EU-15 average to 51% in 2008. The government ran a 7% budget deficit in 2010. The public debt was 53% of GDP in 2010. By law the government must introduce spending cuts if it exceeds 55%.

In a 2005 ranking of competitive economies in the world conducted by the Swiss-based International Institute for Management Development, Poland placed 57th out of 60 countries studied because of inefficiency in government and business. The report cited inconsistency in taking political decisions, protectionism and legal barriers for business. It was singled out as having the worst telecommunication system of all countries compared, and flight connections are poor. The report concluded that in domestic enterprises employees are unmotivated, managers are unreliable, marketing is inefficient, and there appear to be no ethics in business. In 2010 the World Bank placed Poland 72th in a global ranking of places to do business. Transparency International also ranked it 70th in terms of corruption, behind its neighbors.

Increasing prosperity is visible, especially in Warsaw and other larger cities. The consumption of durable goods like home appliances and cars has grown impressively. For instance, the number of cars for each thousand people has jumped from 139 in 1990 to 351 in 2010, and the proportion of late-model automobiles has increased dramatically. Unfortunately they drive on some of Europe's worst roads; only 3% of them meet EU rules. Poland has only 186 miles (300 kilometers) of interstate highways, none near Warsaw. A quarter of its rail track is judged to be substandard to carry the debt-ridden state railway, PKP. However, the infant mortality rate, an important indicator of overall standard of living, was halved in the course of the 1990s to 9 per 1,000 live births, while life expectancy has risen to 71.3 years for men and 79.8 for women. To try to deal with the aging population, the Civic Platform government after 2007 stopped early retirements and added five years to the average retirement age. Poles were by 2010 four times wealthier on average than they had been at the end of the communist era.

European Union

Poland's economic hopes hinge on its 2004 accession to the European Union. The significance of Poland lies in its very size. It alone accounts for nearly half of the GDP of Central and Eastern Europe and for half of the GDP of all 10 EU accession states. At almost 39 million, its population is larger than all of the other accession states combined. It is the EU's sixth-largest member in terms of popula-

**Poland's National Poet:
Adam Mickiewicz**

tion and has the club's ninth-largest economy. Because of its size and sense of history, Poland was determined that it be recognized from the beginning as a "big country" whose influence will be felt in the club. Thus the negotiations between Brussels and Warsaw were detailed and hard.

Two-thirds of Polish respondents in 2001 had said they feared they would be "second-class" EU members for years after entering. They were realistic in recognizing that economic costs would outweigh benefits in the short term. Poles feel hurt by the EU's insistence that there must be a transition period of seven years before they are allowed to work freely within the EU area. They were allowed to work in Britain and Ireland, and by 2006 an estimated 300,000 worked in the former and another 100,000 in the latter. A total of 2 million had left since Poland joined the EU in 2004, but half later returned home. Sweden and Finland are also open to them.

The sale of Polish land to foreigners is a very delicate and emotional matter. Because Poland was repeatedly invaded in the past, Poles were nervous about losing their land to rich peaceful invaders from the West; that fear is strongest in western and northern Poland especially given the fact that land is about a tenth of the price in Germany. The government was able to negotiate a waiting period of seven years for the sale of land in northern and western Poland, which were once mainly German territories, and three years in the rest of the country.

On June 7–8, 2003, Poles nervously engaged in a two-day referendum on their country's entry. The constitution requires that at least 50% of registered voters participate in order for the voting to be valid.

Poland

The Wawel Cathedral of Krakow, Poland. Pope John Paul II was once Archbishop here.

Photo by Miller B. Spangler

Minister Jerzy Buzek as its president for a two-and-a-half year term. He became the first eastern European politician to occupy one of the EU's high-profile posts.

CULTURE

Ever since Poland regained its independence in 1918, successive governments have accorded respect to cultural endeavors. This tradition may have its roots in the fact that, in the 19th century when there was no independent Poland, culture, particularly literary works, provided an important bond of national unity in spite of the partition of the country among several empires. Eager to win the support of intellectuals, the communists provided lavish government subsidies for various cultural programs.

Moreover, rigid insistence on "socialist realism" was never as strong in Poland as it was in the Soviet Union, even during the time of Stalin. This permitted greater intellectual experimentation than elsewhere in the Soviet orbit. In the post-Stalin period, a cry for greater freedom and a more humane form of socialism originated in Polish literary circles, among writers who considered themselves to be loyal communists, but who insisted they had the right to describe things as they were, sordid and often heartbreaking. This was in stark contrast to the cheerful distortions of fact by party propaganda.

The *Poem for Adults* by the communist writer Adam Wazyk, published in 1955, heralded the beginning of the "thaw" in cultural as well as in political relations. The party denounced this wave of writing as "revisionist." It was eventually suppressed, as were the publications and free discussion groups created by students. The politically less controversial fields of graphic arts and music continued to flourish. At least one composer of the younger generation, Krzysztof Penderecki, achieved international fame with his "Passion According to St. Luke."

Poland has produced four Nobel Prize laureates in literature, beginning with Henryk Sienkiewicz in 1905 and Wladyslaw Reymont in 1925. In 2005 the third laureate, Czeslaw Milosz, died at age 93. He had briefly worked for the Communist government after the war, accepting plum diplomatic posts in Washington and Paris. But he defected in 1951 and became a professor at the University of California in Berkeley, where he continued to write in Polish. After the collapse of communism, he returned to Krakow. He won his Nobel Prize in 1980 for poems focusing on the complex moral problems of the 20th century, most notably *The Captive Mind*, published in 1953. This is a prose attack on writers, like himself, who collaborated

The results were an overwhelming victory for those who see Poland's future in the EU: with 59.6% turning out to vote, 78% said yes. Turnout was highest in large cities like Warsaw, where authorities offered free museum tickets to dissuade people from leaving during the weekend. The no votes came from ultraconservative Catholics worried about an erosion of traditional Polish values and from those farmers who realize that the country's two million subsistence farms would disappear when faced with EU competition.

The Catholic Church was given credit for enlarging the turnout through a pastoral letter from the pope that was read in churches across the country on the Sunday of the referendum calling on Poles to vote in favor. Pope John Paul II called membership "an act of historic justice." He added: "Poland can make a contribution with its moral and spiritual values and its religious convictions." Indeed, the government said it would insist that the EU's new constitution make reference to "Christian values," not merely to the "Greco-Roman civilization and the Enlightenment," which appeared in the preamble. It had to back down on that issue,

as well as nearly equal voting rights as twice-larger Germany. A jubilant President Kwasniewski proclaimed: "We have returned to the European family!"

Like most other new members of the EU, Poland was fearful that countries like Germany and France would be increasingly driven by national, rather than European, interests. But the Justice and Law (PiS) government that took office in October 2005, and a new president, Lech Kaczynski, introduced a significant shift in policy toward the EU by taking a strongly nationalistic and Eurosceptic turn itself.

That changed noticeably when Donald Tusk became prime minister in 2007. The tactics of the former Kaczynski government had tarnished Poland's reputation within the EU. Critics had argued that Poles were unwilling to play the delicate and intricate game of compromise and diplomacy on which the EU is based. Even ex-Foreign Minister Stefan Meller bemoaned the stereotype of "simple and quarrelsome Poles." The Tusk government has gone a long way in changing that. Partly as a reward, the European Parliament in July 2009 elected former Prime

Poland

with totalitarian rule. Fellow Nobel Prize winner, Wislawa Szymborska (1996), said of him: "After a long and fruitful life Czeslaw Milosz has joined the ranks of our greatest poets, among whom he had assured himself a place long ago."

Under communism, official statistics stressed the numerical growth of cultural institutions. Poland boasted of ten philharmonic orchestras, nine symphony orchestras, and three musical ensembles associated with the state-run radio network. No name stands out more boldly in the music world than Friedrich Chopin, whose 200th birth anniversary was celebrated in 2010. The government invested $100 million in refurbishing sites associated with his life, such as his birthplace at Zelazowa Wola, located 50 kilometers (30 miles) from Warsaw. It created a multimedia museum in a palace in central Warsaw. Chopin left for France in 1831 following the suppression of an uprising against the Russian occupiers.

Polish theater and cinema always tended to do well in terms of international recognition. They continued to enjoy official support under the Communists. The works of Slawomir Mrozek are well known in the West as well as in Poland.

Education was traditionally based on a system of eight years of compulsory primary schooling, followed by secondary general and technical schools, which about 75% cent of the elementary school graduates attended. Access to universities and specialized institutes of higher learning was controlled by entrance examinations. Although the percentage of students going to institutions of higher learning was much higher under communism than it had been in the 1930s, it was still much lower than comparable figures for Western Europe. As in the Soviet Union and other communist-governed nations, there was particular stress on the hard sciences and less on humanistic subjects, which were considered less "relevant" to the regime. About half of the students were children of white-collar workers. Only 17.7% were the sons and daughters of peasants.

By 2010 much had changed in Polish education. A third of the 500,000 students in higher education attend one of 325 private universities, all opened since 1989 to meet the pent-up demand for education. They are of widely varying quality. Business schools especially have boomed. Sixty per cent of students pay for their own studies. Annual fees for private study vary from about 2,000 zlotys ($900, more than an average month's wage of $670) to more than three times that for such subjects as medicine. Two-thirds of professors have more than one teaching job, and this fact often adversely affects their help to students.

University education is one of democratic Poland's greatest successes. More Poles are getting it than ever before: in 1988 only 6.5% of Poles had a degree, but in 2004 that had climbed to 10.2%. The premier universities remain the Jagiellonian University in Krakow and the University of Warsaw. The ministry of higher education adopted a plan to create a group of elite universities with more funding. By 2010, 25 out of 106 public universities receive 84% of the funding.

One development arising out of the declaration of martial law in December 1981 was the growth of an underground culture. Many cultural workers refused to collaborate with the regime and turned to underground publishing. Novels and short-story collections were published unofficially during this period and then hawked from door to door. Some became underground bestsellers. Art shows were held in apartment houses and churches. There were even underground cabarets. Some media, such as film, do not lend themselves to such a culture, however, and they suffered.

Educated Poles read one of two main national newspapers: *Gazeta Wyborcza* (Electoral Gazette) was created in May 1989 to help Solidarity defeat the Communists. It has always seen itself as an ideological warrior for the kind of liberal-democratic regime that Poland has developed into. Its circulation of 400,000 is declining, but it remains the largest of any serious newspaper and gets 40% of the newspaper advertizing market. *Rzeczospolita* is a daily owned by the government and Mecom of Britain. Its slant has moved to the right to capture disgruntled readers. The weekly newsmagazine, *Polityka*, was the most readable, insightful and irreverent official publication during Communist times. It is still favorite political reading for many Poles.

With the installation of Poland's first noncommunist government in 1989, all of this began to change. The old proscriptions and prohibitions were removed, and artists became free to write and publish what they liked, at least insofar as the government was concerned. Commercial considerations have since become important, however. Not everybody likes the new literature catering to popular tastes that has begun to appear. But almost no one wants to go back to the old system of state control.

Za kilka miesięcy, jeśli tak zadecydujecie, Platforma stworzy rząd, który pracuje, a nie obiecuje. Uprościmy podatki i obniżymy je do 15%. Wprowadzimy „sądy jednego dnia", skazujące chuliganów w trybie 48 godzin. Zlikwidujemy przywileje władzy.

Kiedy dostajecie kartę do głosowania, władza naprawdę jest w Waszych rękach. Użyjcie jej w dobrej sprawie.

Proszę Was o głos

Donald TUSK
Człowiek z zasadami

Religion

Religion has always played an important role in Polish life, usually as a unifying force, since about 90% of all Poles classify themselves as Roman Catholics, and half attend mass regularly. Under communism, the church actually prospered, and Poland was one of the few countries in the world where the number of persons becoming priests and nuns actually increased. As of the early 1990s, Poland had 24,678 priests, up from 20,234 in 1980. That was a ratio of one priest for every 1,280 church members, compared to one priest for every 1,650 church members in the United States. The average age of a Polish priest is 45, compared with 65 in the EU. In addition, more than 1,000 church and other religious buildings have been constructed in Poland since 1985.

Seminaries were once full, and 1,000 Polish priests served flocks in Germany. However, as secularization grows, interest in becoming a priest, monk or nun has declined noticeably. In 2004 there were 2,178 in their first year of religious studies; by 2008 that number had declined by 37% to only 1,382.

Undoubtedly the fact that Pope John Paul II was Polish plays a role in this. His photograph was to be seen almost everywhere, over shop doors, on placards hanging from rear-view mirrors in automobiles, and on key chains. After John Paul II's death in April 2005, the country was deprived of its most powerful unifying force. Ex-President Kwasniewski said: "He helped us maintain a good opinion about ourselves—sometimes maybe too good an opinion that we are important."

There was a close identity between Solidarity and the Catholic Church during the 1980s. It was therefore not surprising that one of the first things the new noncommunist government did was to reinstate religious instruction in the schools.

The church has found that the people do not share its positions in every case. The most important one is abortion, long legal in Poland under communism. In 1990, the church launched a campaign to ban all abortions, and this severely divided the country. In spite of the late Pope John Paul II's personal intervention, polls continued to show that a majority of Poles favor continuation of abortion, at least under specific circumstances.

The Polish legislature began debate on the issue of abortion in 1991. The bill it considered at that time would have barred it in all cases and set a jail term for anyone who performed or had one. That was too strong for parliament, and it refused to take any action. When Pope John Paul II visited Poland in June 1991, he brought up the issue again. Because of this continued Church pressure, the Polish Congress of Physicians adopted a new medical code in 1992 that effectively prohibited physicians from performing abortions except if the mother's life is in danger or if she was raped or if the baby has certain grave genetic defects. This was written into law in 1993 when the *Sejm* passed a bill setting restrictions on abortion.

The constitution, approved in May 1997, would have legalized abortion again. However, an appeal to the Polish Constitutional Court produced a ruling that the constitution's invoking of God as the "source of truth, justice, goodness and beauty" meant that abortions were illegal. This viewpoint was subsequently endorsed by the former center-right government that ruled from 1997 to 2001. Other potential church-state controversies are over pornography censorship, divorce, contraception and homosexuality, all areas where the Church's position is considerably more conservative and restrictive than what exists today in Polish society. Given the dramatic changes in that society, these are, in a sense, societal quarrels, rather than strictly church-and-state disputes.

Approximately 95% of all Poles are baptized Roman Catholic and identify themselves as Catholic. However, only 70% believe in heaven, according to a 2009 poll. Just 40% practice their faith regularly by attending mass most Sundays, and that figure is falling. Nevertheless, in contrast to most other European countries, Polish churches seem full. Masses are still usually standing room only.

Perhaps the most extreme Catholic views are expressed on Radio Maryja, which has a newspaper, *Nasz Dziennik*. Appealing to less educated Poles, the nuns in this operation oppose abortion and the EU. Church officials oppose this group.

FUTURE

The October 2007 elections produced a victory of the opposition center-right Civic Platform (PO), led by Prime Minister Donald Tusk. A sigh of relief was perceptible in the rest of Europe. With a solid majority in parliament, the PO-Peasants' Party government will last a full four-year term, the first to do so since the end of communism. It faces parliamentary elections in 2011, the same year that Poland will hold the rotating six-month EU presidency. It looks forward to hosting with Ukraine the 2012 European soccer championships. Its participation in the war in Afghanistan will continue to be unpopular, and Poland will probably withdraw its 2,500 troops there by 2012.

The bad blood between the two largest parties spilled over into foreign policy, a field in which the president has some say. They agreed on relations with the U.S., but they argued over relations with Russia. Tusk's party wanted to tone down the rhetoric toward Moscow. He noted: "I am one of the politicians who does not have an anti-Russian obsession." Poland under any government has demonstrated that it intends to be a leader, not a follower, among European nations. The Tusk government seeks to do this without irritating its EU partners. It is more conciliatory in tone although it remains determined to press for Poland's interests in concrete ways.

The European Commission hailed the Poles' entry into the EU in May 2004: "A great, proud nation is turning the page of a tragic century and freely takes the seat that should have belonged to it right from the start of the process of European integration." As a sign of the EU's confidence, former Prime Minister Jerzy Buzek was elected president of the European Parliament. Not only is Poland being changed by EU membership in the long run, but the reverse is also true. Poles are more patriotic, religious and family-oriented than Western Europeans.

As a consolidated, stable and sustainable democracy, Poland is successfully managing its second economic transition since 1989. It dodged the worst of the 2008–10 global recession, being the only European country whose economy actually grew in 2009. Poland has never been stronger, more secure or more prosperous. In 1989 the per capita income was $6,000; in 2008 it had grown to more than $17,000. It is a changed country. It entered the 20th century as little more than a historical or geographical concept. It entered the 21st century as a confident, thoroughly democratic nation secure within its borders and with no serious threats from its neighbors.

Poland showed its resilience and stability after April 10, 2010, when President Lech Kaczynski and 95 other Polish leaders perished in dreadful air accident at Katyn in Russia. The country calmly and correctly filled the empty posts, and its markets held steady. There was much emotion in the presidential election that followed on June 20 and July 4 between the two main contenders, Lech's twin brother Jaroslaw of the PiS and Bronislaw Komorowski of the Civic Platform. The latter emerged as the new president.

The Czech Republic

Charles Bridge over the Vltava River, Prague

Area: 78,742 sq. km. = 30,441 sq. mi.
Population: 10.2 million.
Capital City: Prague (Pop. 1,174,200).
Climate: Continental, with lower temperatures in the higher elevations of the north.
Neighboring Countries: The Federal Republic of Germany (West); Poland (North); Slovak Republic (East); Austria (South).
Official Language: Czech
Other Principal Tongues: Slovak, German
Ethnic Background: Slav
Principal Religions: Roman Catholic (39%), Protestant (4.6%), Orthodox (3%), Atheist (37%), Other (16.2%).
Chief Commercial Products: Machinery and transport equipment, semi-manufactures, chemicals, coal and other fuels, raw materials.
Chief trading customers: EU (85.3% of exports and 80.1% of imports), Germany (30.9% of exports and 31.9% of imports), Poland (8.8% of exports and 6.3% of imports), Slovakia (6% of exports and 6.3% of imports), United Kingdom (5% of exports).
Currency: Czech koruna (crown).
Former Status: part of the Austro-Hungarian Empire until 1918 (ruled from Vienna); part of Czechoslovakian Republic, 1918–1938; part of Nazi Germany, 1939–45 (incorporated into the Third Reich as Bohemia and Moravia); part of Communist-influenced Czechoslovakian Republic, 1945–48; Communist State, 1948–89; part of democratic Czech and Slovak Federal Republic, 1990–1992.
National Day: The Czech Republic has two national days, May 8 (Liberation Day) and October 28 (Foundation of the Czechoslovak Republic in 1918).
Chief of State: Vaclav Klaus, President of the Republic (February 2003).
Head of Government: Petr Necas, Prime Minister (June 2010).
National Flag: White and red horizontal stripes with a blue triangle extending from the staff to the center of the flag.

Among the countries in Central Europe undergoing the difficult transition from decades of communist misrule, this land began with a head start. Between the wars its well-educated people lived for twenty years in a successful democratic experiment and enjoyed the highest prosperity in the region. Its democratic lamp flickered for three years after the Second World War, but then the lights went out. Thanks to the courage of such free men as Vaclav Havel, who refused to live a lie, to a different kind of Soviet leader after 1985, and to the decay of the communist state at home, a "Velvet Revolution" peacefully swept away the ruins of communism, and freedom was rekindled.

The Czech Republic is in a period of self-examination in other respects as well. Before 1989 many important Czech questions could not be discussed openly; they were "on ice." Before 1939 it was a multi-cultural country, with many Germans, Jews and Hungarians, in addition to Czechs and Slovaks. Now it is smaller, more homogeneous and provincial. Czechs have just begun to question their country's policy before and during the Second World War, and a passionate controversy has erupted over the circumstances surrounding the 1948 Communist takeover.

Czech Republic

It is the modern successor state to that ancient region known as Bohemia and Moravia. Most of the countryside consists of rolling hills except for the Sudeten Mountains in the north, where individual peaks rise to over 5,000 feet. Although most of the land is suitable for cultivation, there are extensive forest areas, the largest being the Bohemian Forest, located in the west along the border with Germany.

It is today almost exclusively inhabited by ethnic Czechs, except for a tiny remnant of German-speakers in the western part of the country, left after the mass expulsions that followed World War II. In addition, the dissolution of the Czech and Slovak Federal Republic in January 1993 left approximately 300,000 Slovaks living in the Czech Republic. Most of these are individuals from rural parts of Slovakia who came west seeking employment. They are mainly found in industrial areas in the eastern part of the Czech Republic.

HISTORY

Ancient Kingdoms

In the early centuries of the Christian era, a subgroup of the Slavs, subsequently known as the West Slavs settled in the area to the south of the Carpathian and Sudeten Mountains and along the Vltava and Danube Rivers. According to the Frankish chronicle of Fredegar, a Frankish trader named Samo organized them into a unified state at the beginning of the 7th century. This collapsed at Samo's death in 658, however, and the West Slavs reverted back to their tribal organization. It was not until the 9th century that the West Slavs were again brought together under a single government with the establishment of the Moravian Empire.

It was also at about this time that Christianity was introduced into the area. The first missionaries were Roman Catholic monks, and they came mainly from Germany. The language they used for church services was Latin. Somewhat later, the Moravian king, learning of missionary efforts among the South Slavs, requested missionaries from Constantinople.

Two young monks, Cyril and Methodius, came to Moravia and, following Eastern Orthodox practices, began teaching the Slavs in their own language. In the process, they developed a script, later known as Cyrillic, to write the Slavic language. Cyrillic eventually became the basis for the written languages of the eastern and southern Slavs, though for historical reasons not of the Czechs. The reason is that, although the two brothers had great success in converting the people, they were ultimately unable to supplant the western missionaries backed by Rome. After Methodius's death in 885, the Latin form of

Bohemia and Moravia ca. 1360

Catholicism became predominant, and the area came under the sway of Rome. As a result, written Czech uses Roman rather than Cyrillic characters.

At the end of the 9th century, the Moravian Empire came under attack from groups of Magyar (Hungarian) peoples moving into the area from the east. According to Czech historians, the Magyars drove a wedge between the western and southern Slavs and also separated the Czechs from the Slovaks. In the process, the Moravian Empire disintegrated. By the beginning of the 10th century, the center of Czech development had moved westward into Bohemia, while the Slovak lands began a thousand-year period under the Hungarian crown.

The old Moravian Empire was replaced by the Kingdom of Bohemia, ruled by the princes of the Premyslid Dynasty, who became powerful in the 10th century. One of the members of this family was the legendary "Good King Wenceslas" (also known as St. Wenceslas). He was murdered by his brother, who took the throne as Boreslav I and who brought much of the former Moravian Empire under his rule. But later, under the continued harassment of the Magyars, he agreed to merge the Kingdom of Bohemia into the Holy Roman Empire. The Holy Roman Emperor recognized the right of the Bohemian nobles to elect their own ruler who would be the highest authority in Bohemia. At the same time, there was a substantial German migration into Bohemia and Moravia after this, and German influence grew steadily.

Nevertheless, a new line of Czech rulers that came to power in the mid-14th century began to reverse this trend, even managing to assert a growing influence over neighboring states. The "golden age" of Czech history occurred under Charles IV, the king of Bohemia who also became the Holy Roman Emperor. For a generation, Prague became the capital of the Holy Roman Empire. Determined to make his capital worthy of its imperial status, Charles IV supported the construction of new palaces and churches. He was also responsible for founding Prague's

341

Czech Republic

great Charles University and for the still-standing, famous Charles Bridge across the Vltava River.

The 14th century saw the beginnings of a movement for church reform in Bohemia. Though couched in religious language, the movement was primarily a reaction against the extensive landholdings of the Roman Church and the dominant role of Germans in religious and political matters. This was also the period of the Great Schism, when two separate popes, one in Rome and one in Avignon, each claimed to be the one true pope.

John Hus, the young preacher who led the reform movement, criticized the papacy and accused the clergy of being corrupt. Echoing ideas expressed earlier by John Wycliffe in England, he also maintained that the Bible was the sole authority for Christians, not the teachings of the Church.

The Council of Constance, called to heal the breach in the church and end the Great Schism, rejected Wycliffe's and Hus's teachings and ordered Hus to appear before them to answer charges of heresy. Receiving a promise of safe conduct from Holy Roman Emperor Sigismund, Hus traveled to Constance to defend his positions. Upon his arrival, the Council refused to meet with him and condemned him to death. Sigismund withdrew his safe conduct, and Hus was burned at the stake in 1415.

Hus became a martyr even to those Czechs who had not been his followers; he was a national hero who died at the hands of the Germans. Thus when Sigismund attempted to succeed to the Bohemian throne after the death of the Czech king in 1419, he set off the Hussite Wars, which lasted from 1420 to 1436. Although the wars were fought in the name of religion, they had great political and social overtones as well. They were an expression of Czech nationalism. The conflict was complicated by the fact that the Hussites were sometimes divided among themselves and in 1434 even waged war against each other. Ultimately, however, the Hussites prevailed. The Church signed a separate agreement with them, allowing them to retain Hussite rituals in return for their acknowledging the pope as head of the church.

Part of the Multinational Habsburg Empire

This agreement failed to endure, partly because the more radical Hussites were repressed and partly because the Czech Catholic nobility resisted the treaty terms during the following decades. In 1462, the pope declared the agreement invalid and requested King Mathias of Hungary to send in troops to enforce his decision. With the support of Czech Catholics, Bo-

The Austrian monarchy about 1793 (showing pre-1993 Czechoslovakia)

hemia was then incorporated into the Hungarian Kingdom.

Hungarian rule continued until 1526 when the last Hungarian king was killed at the battle of Mohacs, and the crown passed to Ferdinand of Habsburg. Since Bohemia was included among the possessions of the Hungarian crown, Ferdinand was "elected" king of Bohemia as well. In 1547, the right of the Czech nobles to elect their king was abolished, and the crown of St. Wenceslas became the hereditary property of the House of Habsburg.

Conflict between the predominantly Protestant Czechs and their Roman Catholic kings continued during the next decades. Although the Protestants were able to obtain promises from the Habsburg rulers allowing freedom of worship, they continued to fear persecution. The situation was further exacerbated when Calvinism began to spread into Bohemia.

Conflict erupted in May 1618 after two Protestant churches were closed. Angry Protestant leaders stormed Prague Castle and, in an act since known as the "Defenestration of Prague," tossed the two royal governors out of a castle window. According to tradition, they landed on a dung heap and were unhurt.

The Czech nobility then met and deposed the Habsburg ruler. Reclaiming their ancient electoral rights, they named Frederick, Elector of the Palatinate, as king of Bohemia. Frederick was both a Calvinist and the head of the Protestant Union of German Princes. This was, therefore, a direct challenge to Habsburg power and

marked the beginning of the Thirty Years' War. Frederick is known in history as the "winter king," for he retained the Bohemian crown only briefly, being defeated in 1620 by a Habsburg army at the battle of White Mountain.

After the Habsburgs reclaimed the Bohemian Crown, they decided to put an end to all dissent within the kingdom. The leaders of the revolution were executed, and other suspected opponents had their property confiscated. More than 30,000 families, including members of the Czech nobility, fled from the terror that gripped Bohemia at this time. The Czechs thus lost an important part of their national leadership. In addition, Roman Catholicism was imposed, and the German language was accorded equal status with Czech. Publications were censored, and books were burned. The Habsburgs first reasserted their hereditary claims to the Bohemian Crown, then went further and abolished the Bohemian government entirely. The Bohemian lands were governed by a separate administration located in Vienna until 1749.

The Thirty Years' War ended with the Peace of Westphalia in 1648. During the century that followed, there was a large-scale migration of German peasants into traditionally Czech lands, and this was accompanied by a gradual process of Germanization in education, in culture and in urban life.

In 1749, Maria Theresia abolished the separate Bohemian administration and merged Bohemia and Austria into a single

Czech Republic

Memorial in Bratislava to founding of Czechoslovakia

Hungarian Empire. The goal of independence was not actively pursued until the fortunes of war presented the opportunity to sever the centuries-old domination of Austria in 1918. Attainment of this goal was helped by an extensive propaganda campaign carried on by Czechs living in Paris and in the United States.

Birth of an Independent Czecho-Slovak State

The first direct contribution to independence was made by the thousands of Czech and Slovak soldiers who refused to fight with the armies of the Central Powers during World War I, choosing instead to surrender to the Russians. These prisoners of war formed a special force, the Czecho-Slovak Legion, which then fought on the side of the Russians against Germany and Austria.

When the Russian Bolsheviks (communists) signed the Treaty of Brest-Litovsk in 1918, taking Russia out of the war with Germany, the Western allies suggested the transfer of the legion to the western front by way of Siberia and Japan. They became briefly involved in the Russian Civil War after the Bolsheviks attempted to disarm them. Seizing control of the Trans-Siberian Railroad, they made their way eastward through Siberia to Japan.

Although Bohemia remained under Austrian control during World War I, a Czech National Council started to function in early 1916. Located in Paris and composed of such leading personalities as Tomas G. Masaryk, Eduard Benes (Benesh), and Milan Stefanik, it maintained

state. Although it thus lost the last shadow of a separate political existence, the tariff union between Bohemia, Moravia and Austria that followed shortly afterwards, benefited Bohemia economically, as it quickly became the most industrially developed part of the empire.

Joseph II (1765–90), who succeeded Maria Theresia, introduced a series of other changes and reforms whose chief result was to increase the number of German government officials and to create a secret police. On the other hand, Joseph II's policy of religious toleration led to a decrease in the influence of the Catholic Church. This period also marked the beginning of a period of Czech cultural revival.

The French Revolution and the Napoleonic era that followed it had a major effect on the power of the Habsburgs, but Bohemia remained largely unaffected. The period of relative tranquility that set in after the final defeat of Napoleon in 1815 was misleading, however. As the industrial revolution spread to Bohemia in the first half of the 19th century, it brought a prosperity that encouraged the growth of a new Czech nationalism. Thus while the Habsburg rulers devoted their energies to maintaining themselves and other royalty in power throughout Europe, their position was being undermined at home.

When rioting erupted in Paris in February 1848 and then spread to Berlin and Vienna, Prague also exploded in turmoil. On March 11, an assembly in Prague demanded freedom of the press, equality of languages, a legislature to represent the Czech people, and the abolition of serfdom. In June, the first Pan-Slav Congress assembled in Prague. It was dominated by Francis Palacky, a Bohemian historian who believed that Czechs could find freedom and remain within the empire at the same time.

While the congress was meeting, riots broke out against the commander of the Austrian forces in Prague. He suppressed the revolutionary movement and set up a military dictatorship. Moderate Czechs continued to press for a new constitution, but to no avail. Order was restored throughout the empire under a centralized, absolutist regime.

The creation of the "dual" monarchy in 1867 provided for a national legislature for the Austrian part of the Austro-Hungarian Empire and gave Czechs representation in Vienna for the first time. Between 1867 and World War I, Czech nationalists used this new forum to demand self-government within the Austro-

Czechoslovakia, 1918–1938, encircled by hungry neighbors

Czech Republic

contact with a resistance organization, the "Mafia," back in Bohemia.

The council's goal, which was close to being achieved by mid-1918, was to win support for the creation of an independent Czechoslovak state. Masaryk was instrumental in gaining American support for this cause. His wife was an American, Charlotte Garrigue, and this gave him connections he otherwise would not have had. Two documents signed in America would be of historic importance in laying the basis for the future Czechoslovak state.

The Pittsburgh Agreement, signed on June 30, 1918, expressed Slovak support for the union of Czech and Slovak lands in return for the promise that Slovakia would have considerable independence within the new state. The Philadelphia Agreement, signed in October by Masaryk and the leader of American Ruthenians, promised autonomy for Ruthenia, the ethnic Ukrainian part of prewar Czechoslovakia (now a part of the Ukraine).

A National Committee representing three parties, the National Democrats, Agrarians and National Socialists, was set up in Prague in July 1918. This committee, headed by Karel Kramar, proclaimed the Independent Czechoslovak State on October 28, 1918. Two days later, the Slovak National Council voted to be part of the proclaimed state. The Central National Council of the Ruthenians opted to become part of Czechoslovakia on May 8, 1919.

The First Czechoslovak Republic 1918–1939

The frontiers of the Czechoslovakian state were drawn during 1918–1919, partly as a result of military action and partly by the decisions of the postwar peace conference between the major powers. The borders between the Czechs and Poles, and between the Slovaks and Hungarians, were contested. The final settlements resulted in confusing and potentially troublesome borders. A large number of Hungarians were included in Slovak territory, and a number of Slovaks resided in Hungary. When Tomas Masaryk died in 1937, his coffin was carried by six soldiers, one for each of the country's nationalities: a Czech, a Slovak, a German, a Hungarian, a Ruthenian and a Pole.

The resulting Czechoslovakian state included minorities of Poles and Hungarians as well as about three million Germans, living mainly in northern and western Bohemia. Denied the status of one of the "state" peoples, the Germans tended to become culturally identified with Germany during the period that followed World War I. They participated fully in Czechoslovak politics, however, and were represented by several political parties.

President Tomas G. Masaryk

The Czechs, who dominated the national government, had their problems with other ethnic groups as well. Slovaks, in particular, not only felt excluded from the political process, but were concerned about their cultural integrity as well. Throughout the interwar period there were a number of differences that divided the Czechs and the Slovaks. The conflicts centered on the form and concept of the Czechoslovakian nation. The Czechs were

President Eduard Beneš

more advanced industrially than the Slovaks. Being in the majority, Czech civil servants dominated the government. The Slovaks insisted that the term "Czechoslovak nation" was no more than a coverup for Czech-dominated governmental centralization.

However, the problem was even more complex. Slovak political leaders who favored a decentralized government joined with Czechs in urging a single Czechoslovak nation. Slovaks opposed to this even asserted that they had the right to secede from Czechoslovakia.

Ruthenia presented another problem. Czechs were willing to concede that they were a separate people, but they refused to grant them the self-government that they thought they had been promised. The problem was its strategic location. Backward and inhabited by poverty-stricken peasants, Ruthenia nevertheless enabled the nation to have a border with Romania, an important ally.

In spite of these problems, the Czechoslovak Republic was an economically developed country with a democratic pattern of government. Political parties represented a wide range of outlooks. The Communist Party was legal throughout the years of the republic and claimed a substantial following. Although the government was a coalition of parties, the Agrarian Party was continuously a part of the government after 1922.

The top political leadership also provided stability. Masaryk, Czechoslovakia's first president, was reelected in 1927 and 1934. When he died in 1935, Eduard Benes, who had been foreign minister since 1918, succeeded him. Benes's policy had been directed toward encouraging strict observance of the Treaty of Versailles. He formed alliances with Romania and Yugoslavia. Later, he turned to France and then to the Soviet Union among the major powers.

Domestically, government relations with ethnic Germans deteriorated badly during the last several years before 1938. These Sudeten Germans had originally pressed for political autonomy. By 1938, however, most of them had come under Nazi influence and were demanding that territories where they were in a majority be permitted to join Germany. Hitler threw his open support to these demands in the spring of 1938. England and France had rejected the German demand in May, but were ready to give in to Hitler by September. Mussolini now proposed a four-power conference to resolve the matter. Hitler and Mussolini, plus Prime Minister Chamberlain of Great Britain and Premier Daladier of France, met at Munich, Germany, at the end of September. Czechoslovakia was not invited. Seeking a solution short of war, France and Great Britain

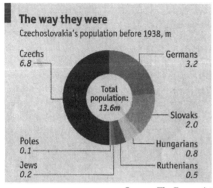

The way they were
Czechoslovakia's population before 1938, m

Czechs 6.8
Germans 3.2
Total population: 13.6m
Slovaks 2.0
Poles 0.1
Hungarians 0.8
Jews 0.2
Ruthenians 0.5

Source: *The Economist*

agreed to German annexation of the Sudeten area of Czechoslovakia.

This decision was made despite the fact that France had guaranteed Czechoslovakia's borders by a treaty of alliance in 1924. The Soviet Union also had a mutual assistance pact with Czechoslovakia that it had signed in 1935, but the Soviet Union was not represented at Munich. The Soviet agreement promised armed assistance if France also fulfilled its commitment. As a result of the Munich Pact, Germany occupied some 10,000 square miles of territory inhabited by three and one-half-million people, one-quarter of whom were Czechs.

President Benes accepted the pact under duress, partly because he was pressed by both France and Great Britain to do so. Czechoslovakia was thus dismembered so that the major powers could gain, in Prime Minister Chamberlain's words, "peace in our time."

The four great powers guaranteed the territorial integrity of the remaining parts of Czechoslovakia. But no one did anything when Hitler announced the annexation of Bohemia and Moravia on March 15, 1939, and sent in German troops to occupy the area. Slovakia became a nominally independent state, while Ruthenia was ceded to Hungary.

Czechoslovakia: "Divided and Reconstructed, 1939–1948"

During World War II, many of Czechoslovakia's leaders left the country. Eduard Benes, who had resigned on October 5, 1938, became the head of the Provisional Government organized in London in 1940. Klement Gottwald and other important Czech communists sought support in Moscow. Negotiations in March 1945 between Benes, Gottwald, and Joseph Stalin in Moscow resulted in a decision to create a "national front" government, consisting of Benes's government-in-exile plus Gottwald and his communists. Benes arrived in Kosice in March 1945 and there established his new government.

This first postwar government was drawn exclusively from parties belonging to the National Front, consisting of four Czech and two Slovak parties. Their programmatic statement, known as the Kosice program, stipulated that Czechoslovakia's future foreign policy would have an "all-Slav" foundation and would be based on an alliance with the Soviet Union. This declaration was even more meaningful because of the territorial closeness of the Soviet Union after Ruthenia was made a part of the Soviet Ukraine.

For the next three years, Czechoslovakia was governed by the National Front and functioned as a democratic nation. During this period, the Soviet Union was willing to tolerate parliamentary politics as long as the communists held the upper hand on matters of importance. Although the communists seized total power in February 1948, they could have done this at any time from 1945 onward since they were the strongest party of postwar Czechoslovakia. As it was, they dominated the National Front through their occupancy of deputy premiership, plus the ministries of Information, Interior, Agriculture and Education.

The communists received by far the largest number of votes in free elections held in 1946. By the winter of 1947–48, however, there were signs that their popular support was dropping sharply. It appeared that they were headed for defeat in elections set for May 1948.

The circumstances leading up to the communist coup began with the dismissal of eight police officers in Prague and their replacement by communists. When the minister of interior refused to reinstate the noncommunist officers, twelve noncommunist ministers resigned in the hope that this would force new elections in which the communists would be defeated.

Instead of submitting to elections, the communists threatened to use force, a threat strengthened by the arrival of Soviet Deputy Foreign Minister Valerian Zorin in Prague. Communist "action committees" took control of newspapers and occupied the headquarters of noncommunist parties. Faced with this show of strength and organization, coupled with the fear of a possible civil war, President Benes accepted a new government formed by Klement Gottwald. When Benes resigned in June 1948, Gottwald succeeded to the presidency, and Antonin Zapotocky became premier.

Jan Masaryk, son of Tomas G. Masaryk, had been foreign minister under Benes. At the time of the coup, he was reported to have committed suicide by leaping from a high window of a government building to a stone courtyard below. In 1989, after the fall of the communist regime, it was officially confirmed that he had been pushed.

Czechoslovakia Becomes a People's Republic

After the 1948 coup, Czechoslovakia was a faithful ally of the Soviet Union, imitating the Stalinist pattern of rule at home and supporting Soviet policies abroad. As in other Eastern European communist countries, a series of purges occurred between 1949 and 1954, aimed at cleansing the party of individuals who might have a greater loyalty to nationalism than to communism. Both Vladimir Clementis, foreign minister, and Rudolf Slansky, secretary general of the Czechoslovak Communist Party, were among eleven victims hanged in 1952 after having been found guilty of "Titoism" and "nationalist deviation."

The death of Joseph Stalin in the Soviet Union in 1953, followed by Gottwald's death a few days later, brought no visible change to the government. This was because the domestic scene was stable. Economic growth and an increase in the standard of living made for a relatively placid population. Because no single individual was able to assume all of Gottwald's authority within the party, there began a period of collective rule. Antonin Zapotocky, who had been premier since 1948, succeeded to the presidency, the dominant political position within the Czechoslovak system. Antonin Novotny became party leader. Reflecting a change also carried out in the Soviet Union at this time, Novotny's title was downgraded to first secretary.

The denunciation of Stalin by Soviet leader Nikita Khrushchev in 1956, plus the neighboring Hungarian revolution of the same year, failed to bring any substantial changes. The communist leadership of Czechoslovakia, rendered more monolithic by purges, remained Stalinist even after his death.

President Zapotocky died in 1957 and was succeeded by Antonin Novotny who retained his position as first secretary of the Czechoslovak Communist Party. This marked the beginning of his political ascendancy and a further period of Stalinist rule in Czechoslovakia since Novotny was no reformer.

Novotny distinguished himself by opposing nearly every proposal for political innovation and resisting any move toward de-Stalinization within Czechoslovakia. Almost alone among the members of the Communist bloc, Czechoslovakia continued to have political prisoners left over from the Stalinist purges of the early 1950s.

One symbol of the Novotny era became a huge statue of Stalin, erected in 1955 on an embankment overlooking the Vltava River in Prague. The statue survived Khrushchev's 1956 de-Stalinization campaign and even the 1961 decision of the 21st Party Congress to remove Stalin's

Czech Republic

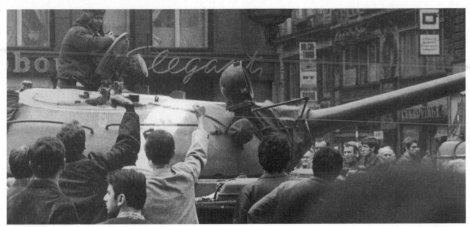

Czechs protesting 1968 invasion

Photo: Oldrich Skácha

body from the mausoleum on Red Square. It was finally taken down in October 1962.

Perhaps Novotny's proudest achievement was the new constitution he pushed through in 1960. According to the text, Czechoslovakia had become the second country—after the USSR—to make the transition to "Socialist Republic." Since the name was identical to that of the individual Soviet republics, it has even been suggested that Novotny had in mind the incorporation of Czechoslovakia into the USSR.

Novotny's troubles began after 1960. Domestically, there was a growing intellectual ferment that was pressing for greater cultural freedom. In the economic field, industry began to show the strains of the Stalinist command model. By 1962, the situation had reached crisis proportions. The government was forced to abandon its third five-year plan and to rely on makeshift annual plans for the next three years. Internationally, there was Khrushchev's continuing de-Stalinization campaign.

The events in the USSR reinforced the more liberal, reform elements in the Czech party. Rudolf Barak, minister of the interior and a member of this faction, was an obvious challenger to Novotny's leadership. Even the events in Moscow were not sufficient to boost Barak to power as long as he lacked firmer support within the party. In early 1962, Barak was removed from all positions, arrested, and sentenced to 15 years in jail for embezzlement and "conspicuous consumption." This probably meant that he had been living too luxuriously.

Barak's removal did not end Novotny's troubles. At a party congress in Prague in 1962, the Central Committee decided to conduct an inquiry into the purges of 1949–1954. The result was a declaration that Clementis and Slansky had been wrongfully convicted.

As pressure increased on Novotny, he dismissed the top officials in Slovakia. These included Karol Bacilek, first secre-

tary of the Slovak Communist Party, and Viliam Siroky, Slovak premier. Both men had aroused Slovak hatred because of their support for Prague's policies of centralization. Siroky was replaced by Josef Lenart, a more popular Slovak, and Bacilek was succeeded by Alexander Dubcek (pronounced *Doob*-chek). These changes quieted the situation and allowed Novotny to be elected to another term as president of the republic in 1964.

Long before Novotny's term of office expired, however, he fell from power. Numerous popular complaints in 1962–63 had caused Novotny to pledge economic reforms, but this remained an empty promise. It eventually became clear that political reform would have to precede economic reform. The reason was that the party disagreed over two major issues: how fast economic reforms should be implemented and how much autonomy ought to be granted to Slovakia.

Both surfaced in late 1967 when Dubcek accused Novotny of undermining the program of economic reform and of refusing to meet Slovak demands for more self-government. At the same time, there were protests from the Czechoslovak Writers' Union and demonstrations by students in Prague. This series of events, taken together, would probably have led to Novotny's dismissal, had Soviet party chief Leonid Brezhnev not thrown his support to Novotny during a visit to Prague.

Brezhnev's gesture of support only postponed the date of Novotny's fall. The internecine fighting between Novotny's and Dubcek's backers continued to sharpen. Two months later, the Central Committee separated the functions of the presidency from those of the first secretary of the Communist Party. On January 5, 1968, Alexander Dubcek took over Novotny's functions as First Party Secretary of the Czechoslovak Communist Party. A clumsy attempt at a military coup, apparently an attempt to save Novotny, was discovered, and Dub-

cek removed the participants from office. One army general committed suicide while a second fled the country, eventually making his way to the U.S.

"Socialism with a Human Face": An Experiment and its Consequences

The change in party leadership generated even greater hope that wider political, economic and social changes would follow. When Novotny finally resigned from the presidency in March 1968, it was clear that Czechoslovakia was proceeding in a new direction. A popular national military hero who had been decorated by both Tsarist and Soviet Russia, General Ludvik Svoboda (pronounced Sfo-*boh*-dah) was chosen president. Oldrich Cernik (pronounced *Chur*-nik) became premier and formed a cabinet that supported Dubcek.

The party's program for the future was adopted in April under the title of "The Czechoslovak Road to Socialism," also known as the "Action Program." The program endorsed important changes such as an end to most censorship, restrictions on the powers of the secret police, and guarantees for the expression of minority viewpoints. In light of what subsequently happened, it is also important to stress that the Action Program was concerned only with domestic matters, with nothing to suggest any change in Czechoslovakia's policies either toward the Soviet Union or the Warsaw Pact. Dubcek also repeatedly declared that the Communist Party had the leading role in the government and that his administration was committed to a continuation of socialism. In Dubcek's words, the purpose of the reform movement was to create "socialism with a human face."

These developments raised great anxiety among some of the leaders of neighboring communist countries. The great fear was that once liberalization was set in motion, it would inevitably get out of control. Moscow also began to express its worries. In May 1968, Czechoslovak visitors to the Soviet Union were advised to beware of counterrevolutionary attacks on the leading role of the party. Two months later, more than 70 writers released a document entitled "Two Thousand Words" calling for "pressure from below" for further liberalization and democratic reform. The Soviet press cited this as proof that counterrevolutionary forces existed in Czechoslovakia. In addition, the Soviet Union added some psychological pressure by delaying the departure of Soviet forces that were in Czechoslovakia for Warsaw Pact maneuvers.

At the beginning of July, neighboring communist nations suggested a joint meeting to address their concerns. The Czechoslovak government countered with a suggestion of bilateral talks. Rebuffed, Czechoslovakia's communist neighbors

Czech Republic

Czechs honoring students who died for freedom in 1968. Wenceslas Square, Prague

held their own meeting in Warsaw in mid-1968. This conference produced a document known as the "Warsaw Letter," which warned that Czechoslovakia could maintain its independence only as a "socialist" (i.e., communist) country. The letter added that reactionary forces were diverting Czechoslovakia from socialism and asked that immediate action be taken to restore censorship of the press and radio and to clamp down on anti-socialist political movements.

Prague responded by a letter of its own arguing that the party was in complete control. It could not take the suggested actions because its authority was based on responsiveness to the will of the people, who desired more freedom of expression. This exchange of letters did nothing to settle the situation, and it may even have inflamed it further. Prague's reply brought a Soviet request for a special meeting with the Czechoslovak leadership.

In the end, two meetings were held, the first in late July and the second in early August. At the second meeting, all the other Warsaw Pact nations were in attendance except Romania. Pressed to modify their program, the Czechoslovak leadership stood firm, though they did agree to a joint statement that made reference to the need to strengthen the forces of socialism against imperialist aggression.

Invasion and Its Aftermath

On the night of August 20–21, military units of the Soviet Union, Hungary, East Germany, Poland and Bulgaria invaded Czechoslovakia. Within a few hours, they had overrun the country and occupied the leading cities. TASS, the official Soviet news agency, announced that the occupa-

tion had been in response to a request for assistance against "counterrevolutionary" forces. None of the Czechoslovak leadership had made any such request, however. In fact, the entire Czechoslovak leadership—Dubcek, Cernik and Josef Smrkovsky, president of the National Assembly—had been placed under arrest at the time of the invasion.

The Soviets tried but failed to find Czech collaborators who would confirm the Soviet explanation of the invasion. Instead, the Czech Foreign Ministry publicly denounced the military move as a violation of the Warsaw Pact, and President Svoboda flatly refused to participate in the formation of a Soviet-dominated government.

The deadlock was broken when Svoboda agreed to go to Moscow for direct talks with the Soviet leaders, provided Dubcek and the other leaders traveled to Moscow with him and participated in the talks. At the meeting, it was agreed that the Dubcek administration would be allowed to remain in office, though it was made clear that Czechoslovak leaders would have to change their political outlook. In October, a treaty was signed that legalized the stationing of Soviet troops within Czechoslovakia for an unlimited time. The Czechoslovak party congress, which had met during the first week of the invasion, was also declared invalid. The liberal Central Committee selected at that time was repudiated. Finally, the Executive Committee of the Presidium was created to counteract liberals in the Presidium itself.

Retreat from Reform

One element of the reform movement survived, however. At midnight on De-

cember 31, 1968, Czechoslovakia became a federal state. With the creation of separate Czech and Slovak republics, the Slovaks had finally achieved their goal of a separate, autonomous state. Basically, the Soviet leadership had decided to try to co-opt the nationalistic, but more conservative Slovaks.

Dubcek's position soon became impossible. On the one hand, he refused to abandon his commitment to reform; on the other hand, he tried to placate conservatives by criticizing anti-Soviet attitudes, denouncing student demonstrations and re-imposing censorship.

None of this saved him. In April 1969, Dubcek was demoted from first party secretary to chairman of the Federal Assembly. Gustáv Husák, the new first party secretary, was a Slovak who earlier had been a supporter of reform. After the invasion, however, he had switched positions, arguing that the first priority for Czechoslovakia was to live in harmony with the Soviet Union. During the remainder of 1969, most of the rest of the pre-invasion reform leadership was either demoted, forced to resign or dismissed. Removed as chairman of the Federal Assembly in the fall of 1969, Dubcek was sent to Ankara as ambassador to Turkey. Eight months later, he was expelled from the communist party.

With pro-Moscow conservatives now in control of the party, the Central Committee repealed the resolution condemning the Warsaw Pact Invasion. Czechoslovakia was back in line. In May 1970, a new treaty of friendship was signed with the Soviet Union.

An extensive purge of the party was carried out between 1970 and 1975 that resulted in the dismissal of about 450,000 members—nearly one-third of the total. In general, it was the more liberal members who were purged. Having consolidated his power, Husák announced in 1976 that he was ready to begin a policy of reconciliation. Purged members were invited to apply for readmission to the party. There was one major stipulation, however: they had formally to repudiate the policies and leaders of the Prague Spring. In spite of this precondition, some ex-members were accepted back into the party, and it began to grow again.

The government was reorganized at both the federal and national levels in early 1971. Chief among the changes was that the Federal Cabinet was given the right to veto decisions of the Czech and Slovak national cabinets. In mid-1975, Husák replaced an ailing Svoboda as president of the republic, retaining his position as head of the party. The Czechoslovak power structure thus reverted to the pattern that had existed prior to Dubcek's replacement of Novotny as first secretary

Czech Republic

of the Czechoslovak Communist Party in early 1968. Husák continued to occupy both positions for 12 years, becoming a symbol and instrument of Soviet domination of Czechoslovakia (even though he had once been thrown into jail for "bourgeois nationalism").

In early 1977, a group of Czech intellectuals released a document called "Charter 77," which charged the government with a long list of human rights violations, including the exclusion of young people from institutes of higher education on the basis of their parents' political views. The document also accused the government of systematically violating the right of public expression guaranteed in the Czechoslovak constitution. A number of Western newspapers picked up the story, and news of the document soon filtered back into Czechoslovakia. The government's reaction was predictable. Charter signatories were investigated by the secret police, and several were sent to prison. The government never managed to suppress the Charter 77 movement, however, and its attempts to do so only further tarnished its international reputation. This latter charge was quickly confirmed when the domestic press refused to publish the "Charter 77" declaration.

The Beginning of the End of Communism

After Gorbachev launched his campaigns for glasnost, perestroika, and democracy in the Soviet Union, a more or less public debate began to occur within the Czechoslovak leadership. Individual Presidium members publicly argued over whether loyalty to the USSR required them to support a similar program in

General Secretary Miloš Jakeš

Czechoslovakia. It soon became clear that the top leadership was sharply divided over the issue. The hardliners, whose spokesman was Vasil Bilak, argued that events in the Soviet Union had no relevance for Czechoslovakia. On the other hand, Premier Lubomir Strougal, who emerged now as spokesman for the moderates, argued the case for Prague's own restructuring.

President Husák remained publicly neutral until just before a visit of Gorbachev to Czechoslovakia in April 1987. He then endorsed a general program of reform. But Husák was a reluctant reformer; no changes were to be implemented until the next five-year plan, scheduled to begin on January 1, 1991.

During his visit, Gorbachev used his public speeches to set forth the rationale for reform. While he did not insist that the Czechoslovak leadership implement a similar program, he had no praise for them. It was becoming clear that Husák, at 74, was no longer able to provide any clear leadership and that the issue of reform was becoming a vehicle to determine the succession.

The issue was resolved in 1987 when Husák voluntarily retired as general secretary while remaining on as president. His successor, Milos Jakes [pronounced *Ya*-kesh], a member of the ruling Presidium since 1981, was a compromise choice, a man not associated with either of the two factions within the Presidium. Although a member of the party secretariat for over 20 years, Jakes had never developed a strong political profile.

His record was rather ambivalent. Originally appointed by Dubcek to head the Party Control and Auditing Commission, he transferred his loyalty to the new leadership installed after the Soviet invasion. He subsequently presided over the post-1968 purge of the party that resulted in the expulsion of most liberals and moderates. Many of these same people, who constituted an important part of the country's cultural and technological elite, were also fired from their state jobs and forced either to take menial jobs or emigrate. Given this background, Jakes had a problem establishing credibility in his new job.

Jakes's own public statements after becoming general secretary were non-conciliatory. On at least one occasion, he characterized the Prague Spring as an attempt "to destroy the socialist system." At the same time, his speeches included references to the need for a "fundamental restructuring of all spheres of public life."

His promotion to general secretary did not put an end to the Bilak-Strougal struggle. It may even have intensified it, since they were now trying to influence a man of untried qualities. Strougal's speeches in

favor of Gorbachev-style reform apparently became embarrassing to the party, and he was forced out as premier in October 1988.

Ladislav Adamec, who succeeded Strougal was, like Jakes, a man of the middle. During a trip to Moscow in February 1989, he spoke of the need for political as well as economic reforms. At the same time, Adamec remained willing to carry out the will of the conservative majority on the Presidium.

The Velvet Revolution

All of this began to change in the late summer of 1989 as the changes sweeping across Central and Eastern Europe reached the East Germany. A human hemorrhaging commenced westward. East German vacationers began crossing the newly opened border between Hungary and Austria. Budapest informed the irate East German leaders that the human rights agreements accepted at the Helsinki Conference in 1975 superseded earlier bilateral treaties preventing the free movement of peoples.

The next avenue of escape was through Czechoslovakia. Thousands had taken refuge at the West German embassy in Prague. West German Foreign Minister Hans-Dietrich Genscher appeared on the balcony overlooking the embassy garden and told the 8,000 weary but ecstatic East German refugees who were crammed into the compound that they would be permitted to travel to West Germany. They had lived in such confined squalor that the polluted topsoil of the grounds had to be removed. Since the Czechoslovak authorities refused to allow it to be dumped within the country, it had to be transported to West Germany for disposal. Genscher described the atmosphere around the embassy at the time as being "on the knife's edge." Stasi provocateurs mingled with the refugees, and there was fear that something could go wrong at any moment, with so many persons squeezed into such a small space surrounded by a nervous and hostile Communist regime afraid for its own survival.

Czech President Vaclav Havel, then the dissident leader of the "77 Movement" that spearheaded the "Velvet Revolution" that ended communist dictatorship in Czechoslovakia, later told former German Ambassador Michael Steiner that the revolution in Germany had had an important influence on later events in Prague. Havel and some of his supporters had seen with their own eyes how women with babies had walked right through lines of machine gun-toting Czech troops surrounding the West German embassy. This convinced Havel that the people were stronger than state power and could overcome it. He

Czech Republic

**Former President Havel shares a light moment
with his private secretary**
Photo by Oldrich Skácha

saw what normal citizens could accomplish. "Freedom trains" took East Germans through the GDR into the West. The stampede grew when Czechoslovakia opened its western borders. As East Germany was forced more and more to give in to the demands of its people, disaffected Czechs intensified their own demonstrations demanding greater rights.

The culmination came on the evening of November 17, when a crowd of about 3,000 young people gathered at the entrance of Wenceslas Square (Vaclavske Namesti) and began a chant calling for free elections. They were met by a line of riot police plus an antiterrorist squad called the Red Berets, who attacked and bludgeoned them to the ground. Personally ordered by Jakes, the attack was a fatal error. It ignited the emotions of the Czech people, who responded with ten days of singing, chanting and nonstop organizing. This was Prague's so–called "velvet revolution," and at its end the communists had been elbowed from power. On November 24, with 300,000 people in the streets, Jakes called a meeting of the Central Committee and submitted resignations for himself and the rest of the Presidium.

Karel Urbanek replaced Jakes as party leader and issued an unequivocal condemnation of the violence of November 17. But it was Ladislav Adamec, the premier, who now stepped into the power vacuum and began discussions with the opposition, since November 19 organized as the Civic Forum. He continued to play that role for perhaps two weeks. During that time, the party agreed to give up its monopoly of power and to form a coalition government with the opposition. But Adamec wanted to keep a majority of the seats in the hands of the communists. When Civic Forum rejected his proposed cabinet on December 3, Adamec resigned and was replaced by Marian Calfa. The new cabinet, installed on December 10, contained a majority of non-communists. Jiri Dienstbier, a founder-member of

"Charter 77", became foreign minister while Vaclav Klaus, an economist committed to creation of a market economy, became finance minister.

As an added benefit, Gustáv Husák now submitted his resignation as president. Vaclav Havel, longtime dissident, founder of Charter 77, and prominent playwright, who never attended a university, was elected president by acclamation on December 29. Alexander Dubcek, reform communist leader of the 1968 Prague Spring, was elected leader of the national assembly.

With the new leaders all in place, the country settled in for a period of consolidation that included some dismantling of the old system. In the political and social arenas, the secret police were dissolved, and required courses in Marxism–Leninism were abolished in the universities. The government dropped its system of licensing priests and ministers. Fewer changes were made in the economic sphere. One reason for this is that everybody seemed to be waiting for new elections scheduled for June 6 in order to have a popular mandate.

One issue, the rivalry between Czechs and Slovaks, resurfaced with virulence. Upon Slovak insistence, the name of the country was changed to the Czech and Slovak Federal Republic.

The first democratic elections since 1946 finally took place in June 1990 and resulted in a victory for Civic Forum and its Slovak partner, Public Against Violence. An astonishing 96% of voters participated in the election. After the election, Vaclav Havel was reelected president, and Marian Calfa was reappointed premier.

After the June elections, there was a struggle within the leadership of the Civic Forum between free marketers and advocates for a "third way" between communism and capitalism. The spokesman for the free marketers was the finance minister, Vaclav Klaus, while Foreign Minister Jiri Dienstbier was a major spokesman for

the opposing viewpoint, which most of the 1968 communists favored. Havel tried to stay above the fray. Klaus won the first round in October 1990 when he was elected chairman of Civic Forum. In February 1991, however, the two factions decided to divide into two separate organizations. They would continue to be associated on a coordinating committee of Civic Forum chaired by President Havel.

Separation of the Republics

One other issue that demanded attention after the June 1990 elections was that of Slovak separatism. Slovaks had always been concerned about maintaining a separate identity, but now individual Slovak leaders began demanding creation of a separate, independent Slovak state. In effect, their argument was that Slovakia could not maintain its separate identity as part of a federation shared with the Czechs.

In December 1990, the Federal Assembly tried to defuse the situation by passing new legislation spelling out in greater detail the separate powers of the Czech and Slovak regional governments. The legislation also gave President Havel special powers to deal with the threat of Slovak separatism.

Although a majority of both Slovak and Czech deputies voiced support for the legislation, Slovak nationalists remained unappeased. When President Havel visited Bratislava in March 1991, he was greeted by thousands of Slovaks shouting abuse. The situation became even worse after Vladimir Meciar, the Slovak premier, took up the Slovak nationalist cause, at least partly because he feared the effect of Prague's privatization policies on Slovak industry. Meciar had gotten too far out in front of the political forces, however, and he was dismissed as premier in April 1991. Yet the issue remained alive. The new premier, Jan Carnogursky, head of Slovakia's Christian Democratic Movement, tried to straddle the issue by supporting continuation of the federation for the time being while favoring an independent Slovakia in principle.

As Slovak nationalism continued to dominate Czechoslovak politics in 1991 and 1992, President Havel was forced to spend more and more of his time on this issue. Acting as a mediator between the Czechs and Slovaks, he brought the two sides together for discussions and, at one point, called for a referendum. Public polls showed that a small majority of Slovaks supported a continuation of the federation, so the Slovak nationalists eventually rejected that suggestion. Havel also proposed some changes in the nature of the federal government, and these were presented to the Federal Assembly in De-

Czech Republic

cember 1991 in the form of three draft laws, which were never enacted.

After numerous proposals and discussions failed to produce an agreement, it was decided to hold new federal elections on June 5–6, 1992, to resolve the general issue. Slovakia held its own elections to the National Council on the same days. In the elections, the vote split along national and ideological lines. In the Czech Republic, Vaclav Klaus and his Civic Democratic Party won a convincing victory on a program of anticommunism and reform. In the Slovak Republic, Vladimir Meciar and his Movement for a Democratic Slovakia won an equally convincing victory with their blend of statism, socialism and nationalism.

When Klaus and Meciar met after the election to discuss the formation of a new federal government, the latter made it clear that he would not accept a federal state that could dictate policy to Slovakia. Among his demands were that the Slovak Republic be permitted to establish its own army and currency-issuing central bank and that it have the independent right to borrow. None of these positions was acceptable to Klaus and the talks collapsed after six and a half hours.

Because a new federal government had to be formed, Klaus suggested giving a new, temporary federal government the power to act until a referendum could be held to ask citizens whether they wanted to live in a federal state. After further talks, Czech and Slovak negotiators agreed to establish a weak interim federal government whose task would be to facilitate bringing the union to a close. The actual constitutional questions relating to the separation would be resolved in the legislatures of the two republics.

When Vaclav Havel, still trying to save the federal state, agreed to stand for reelection to the federal presidency, Slovak nationalists blocked his reelection. Havel could have stayed on in a caretaker capacity until October, since the dominant

Czech party, the Civic Democratic Party, had vowed to block any other candidate for the presidency. He was unwilling to remain under those circumstances, however, and submitted his resignation instead. Most people saw that as a further step in the dissolution of the federal government. As Havel said, had he stayed, he would have been committed by the constitution to defending a common state that no longer had much purpose.

Further negotiations produced an agreement, signed on August 26, calling for a split into two independent states by January 1. On October 1, the federal parliament rejected a bill legalizing the end of the federation, then voted itself out of existence on November 25.

Having agreed to a peaceful separation into two independent nations, the Czechs and Slovaks nevertheless recognized that their economies would be tightly bound to each other for some time and that it would be wise to retain certain elements of the former union if they could. These would include a common currency and a customs union that would allow for the free movement of goods. In addition, Czechs and Slovaks would not be required to show passports to pass from one country to another.

POLITICAL SYSTEM

The Czechs adopted a new constitution for an independent Czech Republic in December 1992. It created a presidential-parliamentary system such as had existed in the former democratic Czechoslovakia. A bicameral legislature was created. There is a 200-member Chamber of Deputies and an 81-member upper house, called the Senate.

The Presidency

The president of the Czech Republic is the titular head of state. The Chamber of Deputies and the Senate elect the president to a five-year term. The functions of

the president are largely ceremonial, unlike the powerful Czechoslovak presidency Vaclav Havel had taken over in 1990. The office nevertheless bestows a moral authority that derives partly from the expectation that the president will remain above politics and partly from the prestige of the first holder of that office: Havel. He was elected president of the Czech Republic on January 26, 1993. A courageous playwright who had refused to compromise with the repressive communist regime and who had therefore spent many years in prison, Havel embodied as nobody else the spirit of resistance to the totalitarian system.

His 1993 inaugural speech, given from a balcony of Hradcany Castle, was rather somber in tone, in contrast to his first inaugural speech. "The revolutionary times are over," he said. "This is the time of every day, common and hard work. To cultivate our best traditions today is infinitely harder than in times of great historical change and the euphoria that came with it."

Havel was reelected in January 1998. Although he had had a malignant tumor and half of the right lung removed in 1996 after he had been diagnosed with lung cancer, he nevertheless stood for reelection. The voting during the first ballot was by the lower house and the Senate each voting separately. When Havel failed to win the required majority in both houses, a second ballot then followed in which the two houses voted together. Here Havel won reelection by a single vote.

Due to his worldwide reputation, Havel could capture the attention of world leaders. No doubt this helped ensure his country's entry into NATO in 1999 and its front-rank status in negotiations to enter the European Union. All agree that he maintained his modesty, wit and sense of the absurd. No leader was less corrupted by the trappings of office than he. However, his influence at home dwindled. When his last term ended in February 2003, after three years as Czechoslovak president and a decade as Czech president, a curtain descended on the most extraordinary political figure to come out of the struggle to overthrow communism. He was the only leader in Central Europe who took control in 1989 and successfully navigated the transition from resistance to rule and then survived into the 21st century as a champion of democracy.

A Czech president is elected in the two houses of parliament. Until 2008 this was by secret ballot. After two rounds of balloting failed to produce a victor in January 2003, former Prime Minister Vaclav Klaus squeaked through with a one-vote majority in February, thanks to the votes of the Communists, whom Havel had excluded from influence during his presi-

Wenceslas Square, central Prague

dency. In February 2008 Klaus was again reelected with a bare majority after six rounds of voting. The three sessions were so stormy that three parliamentarians collapsed and had to be rushed to the hospital, while several other admitted to receiving threatening letters and obscene text messages.

Klaus is an intelligent but abrasive "political animal" with hard-hitting conservative instincts. He is the most Eurosceptic leader in the EU. In 2005 he called for a scrapping of the EU and its replacement by an "Organization of European States," which would be a free-trade block for individual states. Terms such as "State of Europe," "European nationalism" and "European citizenship" should be forgotten. He lambasted multiculturalism as a breeding ground for terrorism. In 2009 he made the entire EU nervous by threatening not to sign the revised Lisbon Treaty (constitution). In the end, he signed.

The Prime Minister and Parliament

The prime minister presides over the government and is the key political figure in the system. Appointed by the president, he must establish that he has the support of a majority of the Chamber of Deputies in order to remain in power. The president appoints members of the cabinet upon the advice of the prime minister. Their names are then submitted to the Chamber of Deputies for approval. The constitution makes it difficult to call early elections. For the first time in the 2010 elections, a voter not only has the option to vote for his preferred party, but he can instead cast votes for his favorite four candidates. This new electoral system cost some prominent politicians their seats in parliament. Turnout was 62.6%.

Since no party ever wins a majority in parliament, coalition negotiations must be held after each election. They can sometimes last a very long time: in 2007 after the government lost a vote of no-confidence in parliament, it took seven months of excruciating talks to create a functioning government. During the negotiations, a caretaker prime minister manages the basic governmental duties until a new government is in place. It is usually the prime minister of the outgoing government. But in 2007 Jan Fischer, a non-party technocrat and head of the national statistics office, took charge temporarily. His main goal was to conclude the six-month rotating EU presidency in a competent way and then serve only until a new prime minister emerged from the May 2010 elections.

President Klaus's party, the Civic Democrats (ODS), suffered embarrassing losses in the May 2010 parliamentary elections, but it was only one of three established

President Vaclav Klaus

parties to survive at all. It won 20% of the votes (down from 34.4% in 2006) and 56 seats (a loss of 28) in the 200-seat parliament. Its leader, Petr Necas, emerged as prime minister of a three-party center-right coalition with two new parties. It has a comfortable 118-seat majority. A mild-mannered father of four, who is a trained physicist, Necas is an expert in social affairs and former deputy party leader and deputy prime minister (2007–9). He became ODS party chairman only a few weeks before the election. Part of his success is his image of being untainted by corruption; he lives modestly and drives a small inexpensive car. ODS's former ally, the Christian Democrats (KDU-CSL), fell below the 5% threshold and was locked out of parliament. The same happened to the Greens.

Two new parties sprang onto the political stage, thanks to voters' disgust at corruption scandals affecting all the established parties. They formed a government with ODS. Top09, a conservative grouping headed by popular and colorful former foreign minister, Karel Schwarzenberg, snatched 16.7% of the votes and 41 seats. He is one of the few politicians not suspected of corruption because he is a wealthy aristocrat. A Habsburg prince whose parents fled Czechoslovakia in 1948 when the Communists took power, he was an independent member of the outgoing cabinet nominated by the Greens. He hosted the 2009 EU-U.S. annual summit in his noble family's spectacular Hluboka Castle. During the visit, President Barack Obama was given the red-carpet treatment and was greeted enthusiastically by crowds everywhere.

The second new party in the government is the more populist conservative Public Matters, led by the country's most popular politician, John Radek. It garnered 10.9% of the votes and 24 seats. The new three-party government quickly introduced budget-tightening policies, fol-

lowing up on measures introduced by the preceding ODS government: It had enacted a 15% flat tax and lowered corporate taxes. It also sought reductions in bureaucracy and state spending, and reform of the pension and health systems. The retirement age is being gradually raised from 62 for men and 61 for women to 65 for both by 2030. Fees of about $1.85 for a doctor's visit or a prescription and $4.00 for a day in the hospital were introduced to an outcry of protest. Czechs visit their doctors more often than any other Europeans, and many consider free health care a right, despite the fact that the system is partly financed by payroll deduction.

The left parties, which form the opposition, did poorly. The Social Democrats (CSSD) did manage to emerge as the largest party. It captured 22% of the votes (down from 35.34%) and 56 seats (a loss of 18). Its leader, Jiri Paroubek, stepped down.

The only established party that succeeded in holding its own in 2010 was the unreformed and unapologetic Communist Party of Bohemia and Moravia (KSCM). Led by Vojtech Filip, it won 11% of the votes (down from 12.8%) and 26 seats (no change). The Communists are strident opponents of NATO, which they regard as a tool of "American imperialism." Following the NATO air war in Kosovo, the party called for war crimes indictments against President Bill Clinton, British Prime Minister Tony Blair, German Chancellor Gerhard Schröder, and former NATO Secretary General Javier Solana. It is the strongest unreformed Communist party in the former Eastern bloc and has changed neither its Marxist ideology nor its name. Its 100,000 members are nostalgic for the days when they ruled by force. The main thing it altered was its logo; it is now two cherries instead of a hammer and cycle.

The Communists remain untouchables in Czech politics: no other party will work with them. But their electoral success is a warning that the rapid pace of economic reform had hurt many Czechs and that the standard of living for many had plummeted. The fact that any government must work around the Communists' one-fifth of the total seats almost ensures that any governing alliance is unsustainable. The Czech Republic must find a way out of this stalemate.

Foreign Policy

While the Communist Party controlled Czechoslovakia, it had no independent foreign policy. The Czechoslovak Ambassador to the United States once said: "The foreign policy of Czechoslovakia is the foreign policy of the Soviet Union." That all changed in December 1989. The Czechoslovak government established relations

Czech Republic

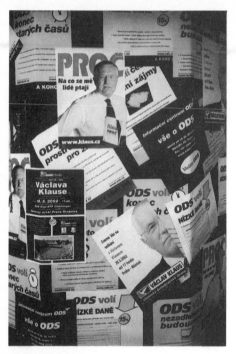

Election posters

with Israel and the Vatican, President Havel gave orders for the curtailment of worldwide arms exports, and the country carried out successful negotiations with the Soviet Union to get Soviet troops withdrawn from Czechoslovakia. The last of the troops left in June 1991.

In other signs of change during this period, both Alexander Dubcek and Vaclav Havel made trips to the United States. Havel gave a major address before a combined session of Congress. Czechoslovakia was also among those nations urging the Soviet Union to drop its insistence that a united Germany either be neutral or hold simultaneous membership in both NATO and the Warsaw Pact. Czechoslovakia wanted a united Germany to be part of NATO.

After the demise of the Soviet Union in 1991, Czechoslovakia extended diplomatic recognition to the successor republics and opened separate relations with them. It sought good relations with the newly independent Republic of Ukraine. But the Czechoslovak leadership was more attuned to the new Russian political leadership in Moscow, with whom it maintains cordial relations. Its relations with the remaining successor republics have been less extensive although ties with the Republic of Ukraine warmed after Leonid Kuchma was elected president in 1994.

American-Czech relations remain good. To facilitate travel to the U.S. the two governments agreed that Czechs can apply online for a visa waiver that allows them to avoid both the long lines outside the embassy and the odious $131 fee.

Some Czechs remain uneasy about a resurgent Russia. That fear is less of a military attack and more of Russia's economic influence, especially in the energy sector. Three-fourths of its natural gas comes from Russia. A Czech-Russian consortium led by Atomstroyexport, a Russian engineering company, is a major contender to build up to five nuclear reactors. During a visit to the Czech Republic in 2007, ex-President George W. Bush emphasized that "the Cold War is over. The people of the Czech Republic don't have to choose between being a friend to the United States or a friend with Russia. You can be both." Not all agree, especially those of the Cold War generation. They find naïve President Obama's decision in 2009 to "reset the start button" on U.S.-Russian relations and to cancel the planned antimissile system.

The Czech government would welcome greater American investment in the Czech industry, partly to offset the strong investment drive from Germany, but partly also because they would like to see a greater American economic presence. For a while the Czech Republic received the largest amount of foreign investment in Central and Eastern Europe. In the first decade of the 21st century, foreign direct investment amounted to about 10% of GDP annually.

The Czech Republic's relations with Slovakia were a little uneven as long as Vladimir Meciar remained Slovak prime minister. They have improved greatly since 1998, when a new government committed to closer cooperation with both the Czech Republic and the West replaced Meciar.

Despite a relatively low level of public support, the Czech Republic became a full member of NATO in March 1999. Czechs were divided roughly into one-third of the population in favor of NATO entry, one third against and one third undecided. Less than two weeks after joining, NATO air offensive against Serbia began in order to halt the Serbian mistreatment of Kosovo Muslims. Polls showed that Czech public opinion was against the NATO action by two-to-one. This was perhaps because of Czechs' historically good relations with Serbia and pre-1991 Yugoslavia. Nevertheless, Prague supported NATO military actions against Yugoslavia over Kosovo and granted all of NATO's operational requests for use of Czech airfields and transit across its air space and territory. It sent a military field hospital to Macedonia and pledged $30 million to help Kosovar refugees. However, it did not actively participate itself.

Havel, in particular, was an outspoken advocate of the NATO actions. The Atlantic Alliance is not only a solid cornerstone for Czech security, even though the republic faces no serious military threat.

But NATO is an important symbol of the extent to which Czechs share the West's democratic values. After the war was over, the Czech government, citing the expense of keeping a larger unit in Kosovo, proposed sending a platoon of 150 members. This would have been the smallest contingent of any NATO country except Iceland, which has no army. However, the government reversed its position after Havel criticized the plan. On June 15, the Czech Chamber of Deputies authorized an 800-member military unit for the peacekeeping duty in Kosovo. In late June 1999, he became the first NATO head of state to visit Kosovo.

Primarily because of the moral example set by Havel, the country has earned a reputation within the EU for promoting human rights at every opportunity, whether it be in Belarus, Moldova or especially Cuba. Its diplomats are among the first to raise sticky questions about democratic values in other lands. This sometimes earns them the charge that they are acting as mere messengers for the U.S. But they hasten to remind critics that the government opposes the American trade embargo against Cuba and the Guantanamo Bay prison camp.

NATO tries to persuade the country to bring its armed forces up to alliance standards. It devotes 2.1% of GDP to military spending and has a total active force of 17,932 and 3,100 paramilitary troops. Conscription was phased out by 2007. By that time planners had pared the forces, slimmed down the top-heavy command structure, reduced the number of garrisons from 140 to 50, and trained its officers and soldiers to function in the NATO language: English. The army has 12,656 troops that include a rapid-reaction brigade.

The Air force has 5,276 airmen and acquired 38 modern home-built light combat L-159 jet bombers to replace its aging fleet of Russian-made SU-22 fighters. Its supersonic fleet of MiG-21 fighters reached the end of its operational life in 2005. The government had earmarked $2 billion to replace them with new Swedish- and British-made Gripen combat aircraft by Saab, but the disastrous flooding in August 2002 required that the money be used instead for clean up. Fierce competition returned between Gripen and U.S. F-16s. In 2004 the Czechs chose to lease 14 new Gripen supersonic fighters from the Swedish government for $754 million. It also acquired transport planes. Its troops in Kuwait and Afghanistan had to be moved in commercial aircraft. Prague deployed 300 troops in Iraq, but it withdrew all of them by 2010. It sent 480 soldiers to Afghanistan and 409 to Kosovo.

Following the September 11 terrorist attacks in New York, the Czech government responded by sending a field hospital to Afghanistan to assist in the military operations. However, Czech leaders worried about becoming a terrorist target after receiving reports that the mastermind of the September 11 attacks, Mohamed Atta, had met with an Iraqi intelligence agent and discussed attacking the headquarters of U.S.-financed Radio Free Europe, which had been moved into the communist-era parliament on Wenceslas Square in Prague. Officials asked that it be moved to the edge of the city.

Although a majority of Czechs opposed the 2003 war in Iraq, their government supported the American and British allies. Even during the Cold War, the Czechs were the Warsaw Pact specialists in nuclear, biological and chemical warfare (NBC), and they maintain that specialty in NATO. Their NBC forces were deployed to Kuwait to support Operation Enduring Freedom in 2003.

The government expressed its willingness in 2007 to provide a base for an American anti-missile radar to help protect Europe and the U.S. against future nuclear weapons states in the Middle East. Then Foreign Minister Schwarzenberg argued that "a small country like the Czech Republic has to prove itself as a reliable partner and as a good ally." Despite vehement opposition from Russia, the landmark accord was signed in July 2008, the first such agreement to be reached with a Central or Eastern European country.

However, there were serious obstacles to realization. Public opinion polls consistently showed that two-thirds of Czechs oppose it. Many are unsure how exposed they want to be on the international stage, with a resurgent Russia close by. Many Czechs do not want to alienate Russia. Its ability to harass the country was demonstrated at the time of the signing when it reduced by half its oil shipments to the country for "technical reasons." There are concerns about the health effects of such a large radar, and voters in three villages near the planned base rejected it in a non-binding referendum.

Enough parliamentarians opposed the idea that the Czech government had to drop it. Parallel negotiations took place to deal with the legal status of American troops deployed on Czech soil to operate the missile site. Many Czechs do not like the idea of having foreign troops (even Americans) stationed on their soil after many decades of Soviet occupation. The stakes were high for Czech political leaders, who have invested a lot of political capital in this project. Any American withdrawal would seem like an abandonment of an ally and a diplomatic victory by Russia. That is what happened when President Obama abandoned the project in

Czechs protest U.S. anti-missile radar

2009. Czechs had earlier greeted the advent of visa-free travel to the U.S. in the fall of 2008.

Czech public opinion was tepid toward the European Union. Czechoslovakia had been admitted to associate membership in 1991, along with Hungary and Poland. The Czech and Slovak republics retained that status after separation. The Czech government began aligning its foreign policy to that of the EU. For example, when Yugoslavia broke up, the Czechs extended diplomatic recognition to the successor republics only after the EU had done so. In December 2007 the Czech Republic joined the Schengen border regime allowing free passage within EU countries.

EU entry was more complicated than NATO membership and involved more transformation and pain (e.g. in terms of the environment). A new member must incorporate 80,000 pages of EU regulations into their laws; half of them deal with agriculture. With its small agricultural sector (4% of the work force and 2.4% of GDP), the Czech Republic had fewer adjustments to make than does Poland. It has a modern economy, with 58% employed in services producing 58.7% of GDP, while 38% work in industry, creating 38.9% of the nation's wealth.

Many Czechs found the bureaucracy in Brussels to be arrogant and corrupt. President Vaclav Klaus warned that the EU could diminish Czech sovereignty and said it was like dropping a lump of sugar into a cup of coffee. The EU's public criticism of Czech preparations for membership created resentment, and the many

trade disputes with EU countries make the union appear hypocritically protectionist.

Entry was powerfully boosted by an EU report concluding that nothing in the decrees permitting the postwar expulsions was incompatible with EU laws, and Germany and Austria announced that they would not veto Czech entry because of the Sudeten issue. In the June 2003 referendum, 55% of voters turned out, and 77.33% voted in favor of entry. An exuberant ex-Prime Minister Spidla exclaimed, "for me this is the end of World War II, with all its consequences." It became a full member in May 2004.

After the EU constitution was rejected by French and Dutch voters in May and June 2005, the Czechs postponed their ratification of the constitutional treaty. In May 2007 it grudgingly supported the resurrection and revision of parts of the document, called the "Lisbon Treaty," as a basis for reforming the EU. But ratification was again a problem. Although the government was largely in favor of this Lisbon Treaty and the lower house of parliament approved it, the upper house asked the Constitutional Court to determine whether the new reform treaty was compatible with Czech law. The court ruled that it was, and in May 2009 the Senate voted to approve it.

President Vaclav Klaus is a well known Eurosceptic, and he had doubts about the reform. But a 2008 Eurobarometer poll revealed two-thirds of Czechs believed that their country had benefited from membership. Therefore Klaus eventually signed the treaty. He concluded that the country would be isolated in Europe if he denied his signature. However, he demanded and received from the EU an optout from the

Everybody loves a bride! Prague

Czech Republic

Shoppers look with skeptical amusement at relaxing skateboarders

Photo by Jon Markham Morrow

treaty's Charter of Fundamental Rights. He argued that it could have prompted a flood of property claims by Germans expelled after the war.

The Czech Republic and Germany/Austria

Germany's relations with Poland are markedly better than those with the Czech Republic. Unlike Poland, which did not diminish in size since the fall of communism, the Czech Republic became smaller (from 15 to 10 million inhabitants), while Germany (its major trading partner and foreign investor) became larger. Thus its old fears of German predominance are greater. It is small wonder that in the spring of 1990 only 37% of Czechs said they favored German unification. In a 1995 poll asking Czech respondents to decide "from which state you feel threatened," over 40% identified Russia, about 25% Germany, and only about 5% the United States. In 1996 half the Czech public regarded Germany as a danger for the Czech economy.

Also feeding fears of the Germanization of the Czech economy is the fact that four of the top 20 firms in the republic are German. This does not include Volkswagen's successful joint venture with Skoda. Some Czechs speak of a *"Kalter Anschluss"* (a "cold annexation," referring to Hitler's acquisition of Austria in 1938). Also, while Poland militarily resisted Germany at the beginning of the Second World War, Czechoslovakia did not. This fact affects national consciousness and confidence positively in Poland and negatively in the Czech Republic.

Without question, the greatest obstacle to relations between the two countries involves Sudeten Germans. Pursuant to the decree by Czech President Eduard Benes on May 19, 1945, approved in Article 13 of the Potsdam Agreement of August 2, 1945,

from two million to three million ethnic Germans were deported, and from 19,000 to 30,000 were killed or died in transit. By 2000 only 38,000 Czechs called themselves "Germans." Refugees from many parts of Eastern Europe poured into Western Germany after the war—from Silesia, Pomerania, East Prussia, and the Sudetenland. The Czech Republic entered the 21st century without ever having rescinded the Benes decrees.

Many Czechs today admit that some excesses did occur in the course of the expulsions. Witnesses reported lynchings, SS troopers being burned alive or tethered to workhorses and torn limb from limb, and innocent Germans were randomly shot, scalped, or raped. Even in late 1945, after emotions had cooled somewhat, 50,000 people turned out in Prague to watch public executions of Germans as entertainment.

Nevertheless, a majority of Czechs believes that the expulsion of these people (who before 1939 outnumbered Slovaks) was just. After all, 91% of Sudeten Germans had voted for a pro-Nazi party in the 1938 elections. In a 2002 survey only 1.4% of Czechs (7.2% in the former Sudeten area) favored a renunciation of the decrees. Most would refuse to vote for a political party that would be willing to make any concessions to the Sudeten German demands. When newly elected President Vaclav Havel offered an apology in 1990 and later used the word, "expulsion," in a 1995 speech at Prague's Charles University, he was severely criticized at home.

Recognizing that there was a minority of Sudeten Germans who had remained loyal to Czechoslovakia, then prime minister, Jiri Paroubek, recommended in June 2005 that some kind of "gesture" of recognition be made to them, some form of symbolic compensation. This was not in-

tended as an admission of guilt, but as a deepening of "the friendship between the Czechs and Germans of today." Many Czechs, including their president, angrily rejected this.

Only a month earlier tempers among expellees in Bavaria had flared up again when a statue honoring President Benes was erected in front of the Foreign Ministry in Prague, a day before the German chancellor was scheduled to visit the city. Paroubek attended the ceremony. Bavarian ex-Minister-President Edmund Stoiber called this a "provocation" and "an attack against good-neighborly relations."

Almost everywhere the Sudeten Germans integrated and over time ceased acting as effective pressure groups in German politics. The exception is the two million Sudeten Germans who moved to Bavaria, maintain their Sudeten identity, want to show solidarity with their forebears, support the conservative Christian Social Union (CSU), and are organized in such groupings as the Munich-based *Sudetendeutsche Landmannschaft*. They cannot be ignored in Bavarian politics. Czechs want the creation of conditions whereby they no longer need to worry about this issue. But in 2002 former Prime Minister Zeman raised German hackles by describing the Sudeten Germans as "traitors" and Hitler's "fifth column." The matter was so serious that ex-Chancellor Schröder cancelled a planned visit to Prague. Zeman also found himself embroiled in a dispute with the Hungarian ex-Prime Minister Viktor Orbán for demanding that the Benes decrees, which had also included Hungarians, be revoked.

The Czech Republic must deal with many claims for return of sizable amounts of property. Franz Ulrich von Kinski, the primary heir of the line of Bohemian kings, is among the more than a dozen descendants of Austro-Hungarian nobility who sued the Prague government to recover private property confiscated after World War II. Among his 157 claims is a palace on Prague's Old Town Square that houses part of the Czech national gallery. Also Prince Hans-Adam II of Liechtenstein has taken Germany to court to retrieve over 1 billion euros in real estate and art works illegally expropriated to pay German postwar debts to Czechoslovakia. Prague refuses to discuss the case, to return the properties or even to recognize Liechtenstein diplomatically.

Germany believes it is much nicer to be surrounded by countries that are "in the same club," that is, in NATO and the EU. It is therefore not surprising that it was the first ally to propose eastern enlargement of these key Western organizations. All Czech governments since 1990 regard integration into the EU as the best means of protecting national sovereignty. They like the fact that Germany, whose economic domination many Czechs fear, is itself fully integrated in the EU. Thus the Czech Republic can deal with Germany in a multilateral setting. This goes a long way to freeing the smaller republic from its 20th-century nightmare of being caught between two large and formerly aggressive powers, Germany and Russia.

Germany's policy is that negotiations over the Czech entry into the EU would not be hampered by bilateral difficulties stemming from the shadows of history. In order to elevate the "European challenge" over the memories of the past, both governments signed a "German-Czech Declaration on Mutual Relations and their Future Development" on January 21, 1997. This strengthens the foundation created by the Neighborhood Treaty (*Nachbarschaftsvertrag*) of 1992. In Havel's words, the 1997 declaration "frees us."

On February 13, 1998, the countries' leaders signed the Czech-German Fund for the Future. This paved the way for a partial compensation of Czech victims of Nazism and established a forum for a nongovernmental dialogue between Sudeten Germans and Czechs. By 1998 two-thirds of Czechs considered German-Czech relations as "rather good" or "very good." The fruits are obvious: more young Czechs are learning German than any other foreign language; 27% of Czechs claim to speak it. Also, 31% of all Czech exports are to Germany, and 30% of all direct investments are from German firms.

Austria is a major trading partner with and investor in the Czech Republic. Nevertheless, Czech-Austrian relations are also burdened by the Benes decrees and the expulsion of Sudeten Germans. Even though most resettled in Germany, some went to Austria. Many Austrians resented Prague's approval of the EU's temporary policy of ostracizing their country after the late Jörg Haider's party entered the Austrian government in February 2000. They are no doubt mystified at patriotic opposition in Prague in 2008 to erecting a copy of a horseback statue of Field Marshal Radetzky, a Czech who commanded an Austrian army in the 19th century. Like almost all reminders of the Habsburg empire, the original had been removed in 1918.

Nuclear-free Austria also vehemently protested the Czech construction of a nuclear power plant in Temelin, 30 miles from the Austrian border. It was activated in October 2000, and a second reactor was completed 15 months later. The Soviet-designed facility operates with a Western control system. After spending $3 billion to $4 billion dollars on Temelin, Czechs were extremely reluctant to close it, despite the sharpest diplomatic conflict with its Western neighbors since the end of communism.

The EU sided with the Czechs, but Vienna reminded Prague both officially and unofficially that Austria has a veto over any new country seeking membership in the exclusive club, the EU. It chose not to use that prerogative. The crisis was defused when the Czech government agreed to tighten security at the plant. State-run electricity giant, CEZ, hopes to build up to three new nuclear reactors in the Czech Republic and two elsewhere in the region. It generates three-quarters of the country's electricity, and half of that is by coal-fired plants, which are the largest source of the nation's carbon dioxide emissions. Renewable sources account for only 6% of energy it uses. The government regards nuclear power as a counter to its overdependence on Russia for oil and natural gas.

ECONOMY

Czechoslovakia was already an industrialized nation when the communists took over in 1948. The coalition government installed in 1945 had nationalized about 60% of all industry and instituted a land reform aimed at breaking up all large land holdings. Major steps had also been taken toward institutionalizing socialism and state planning. With half of their work done for them, the communists only had to complete the nationalization of industry and adapt state planning to the command model developed by the Soviet Union in the 1930s. This was accompanied by a gradual collectivization of agriculture.

Czechoslovakia's first Five-Year Plan was launched on January 1, 1949. Along with the following two subsequent Five-Year Plans, it placed a major stress on the creation of heavy industry—again a slavish following of the Soviet model. The relative neglect of consumer industries and agriculture produced a lopsided economy that began to resemble more and more an industrialized copy of the Soviet model. Food items such as meat became scarce, a severe housing shortage developed in the cities, and the quality of consumer goods declined as well. These developments obviously had an effect on morale, and as the third Five-Year Plan progressed, even heavy industry began to fall short of its targets. In 1962, with the economy in a severe recession, the third Five-Year Plan was simply abandoned.

A number of Czech economists associated with the Institute of Economics of the Czechoslovak Academy of Sciences had been critical of Stalinist concepts of command planning for a number of years. One of the most prominent and outspoken of these proposed a plan for reordering the economy that became known as the "New Economic Model." A Soviet counterpart, Yevsei Liberman, had influenced the Czech economist, and his plan, like the Liberman Plan, called for limiting the role of the central planners. Individual enterprises were to be managed on the basis of profitability; worker salaries were to be based in part on individual skills; and there was to be a major stress on upgrading technology.

President Novotny initially opposed the plan. However, as the economy continued to flounder, he gave grudging approval for its initiation in 1967 although he did specify that it leave the party's central policy-making authority intact. But it was a start in name only. As a result of contin-

Peace and quiet reign in the Krkonoše mountains AP/Wide World Photo

Czech Republic

Street musicians in front of presidential palace, Prague

ued opposition by conservatives involved in central planning, it failed to have any significant effect.

In Czechoslovakia, the reformers decided to challenge the conservative leadership and were instrumental in securing the resignation of Novotny as head of the party. Dubcek, his successor, fully supported the reform measures, and the economist who initially wrote the plan became deputy prime minister.

Even as the reformers began implementing their "New Economic Model," however, the Soviets were drawing up their own plans to invade Czechoslovakia. Afterwards, the Husák regime condemned the economic reform as a "romantic notion." The central planners again assumed control of the economy. Industry continued to be plagued by outdated technology, declining productivity and low-level products. Proposals for economic reform were never really put into effect or, if they were, had no effect.

Dismantling the Command Economy

The revolution of 1989 put a new set of leaders in power. Although there was some floundering in the first year, the government began to take the necessary steps to create a market economy. In 1991, the Federal Assembly passed a broad privatization law that committed the government to denationalize all industry. Companies nationalized after 1948 were to be returned to their original owners or their descendants, while remaining companies were to be privatized through a complex system of government-issued coupons or sold to foreign investors. The key individual responsible for the government's plans was Vaclav Klaus, then finance minister.

As the political debate between Czechs and Slovaks over the future of the common state grew in intensity in 1991, however, Klaus's plans for economic reform were thrust partially aside. In November 1991, the Czech Government announced

that it had made significant progress in its small-scale privatization program, having sold 12,333 out of 20,786 business units included in the program. Less progress had been made in large-scale privatization, but the government had held seven auctions, approved five direct sales, and prepared two public tenders.

The government began privatization of large-scale industry through its coupon program in March 1992. Czech citizens were offered books of vouchers for 1,000 crowns (approximately $35), which could then be used to bid for shares. Facilitating the process, approximately 400 investment funds were set up to manage the shareholdings. Though by law they were not permitted to hold more than 20% of the shares of any one company, they eventually ended up holding 70% of the shares on behalf of individual investors. In June 1993, with over 1,000 Czech and Slovak companies privatized, the government sponsored creation of the Prague Stock Exchange to provide a market for the shares.

As of January 1, 1993, almost 1,000 Czech companies had been privatized, and there were six million stockholders. A second round of voucher privatization in the latter part of 1994 transferred assets worth an additional $5.8 billion. All told, approximately 80% of all Czechs participated in the two sets of voucher privatizations. In addition, more than 100,000 properties worth an estimated $4 billion were returned to their former owners. By 1997, the process of privatization was essentially complete, and in 2000 an impressive 68% of GDP was generated by the private sector. In 2001 the privatization of the banking sector was completed. A year later the government sold its 51% stake in the country's largest telecommunication company, Cesky Telecom, the biggest private equity deal ever in post-communist Central Europe.

Some economists have complained that the voucher system of privatization pro-

duced a system whereby ownership was separated from oversight and the effect of this was that companies were not under strong pressure to restructure in order to become more competitive. Since ownership was widely dispersed, and the investment funds were primarily portfolio managers, there was some basis for the worry. On the other hand, companies that have not performed adequately have tended to find it difficult or impossible to raise new capital, and that has provided incentives to become more competitive. A greater worry is that the biggest Czech banks manage the biggest investment funds. That presents not only a potential conflict of interest but also opportunities for favoritism.

In February 1993 the Czech and Slovak parliaments announced that the agreement on a common currency for the two republics had been terminated. After just over a month, each republic issued its own currency. The customs union managed to survive. Trade between the two republics did fall considerably following separation, but it has since recovered. In 2010, Slovakia accounted for 6% of the Czech Republic's exports and 6.3% of its imports. The emphasis of Czech trade policy since 1993 has been to redirect its exports to Western Europe. Its growing trade with the European Union members (85.3% of exports and 80.1% of imports) far surpasses any loss of exports to Slovakia. Germany alone buys 30.9% of all Czech exports.

The Czech Republic depends on Russia's Gazprom for 80% of its gas supplies although it has been able to fend off that giant company's efforts to gain control of its transmission, distribution and retailing of gas. The Czech Republic has diversified its energy sources by purchasing Norwegian gas and transporting it across Germany. It also has a pipeline that is independent of the one that transports Russian gas to Western Europe.

The Czech Republic has been the largest recipient of foreign direct investment in Central Europe, equivalent to 10% of GDP throughout the first decade of the 21st century. This has resulted in a significant international presence, including by the U.S. For example, Hewlett-Packard, Exxon-Mobil and IBM have outsourced operations there. In 2002 the republic was the target for $9.3 billion in foreign direct investment, and it continues to grow. By 2000 over 1,200 foreign investors were manufacturing in the Czech Republic. They benefit from significant cost efficiencies, including relatively low wages. Pay is around a quarter of German levels, but social charges are near Western European levels, adding 35% to wages.

Although earnings are growing fast, they are still in line with productivity growth, which at about 4% is well above the eurozone's .4%. Productivity at foreign-owned companies is virtually at the same level as in Western Europe. Other advantages are a long Czech 39-hour workweek (1,980 hours per year vs. 1,815 in the U.S. and 1,444 in Germany), more flexibility about working practices, a central strategic location, and the ability to source locally from the republic's excellent supply base. By 2010, 97% of the banking sector was owned by foreign banks. They proved to be among the most stable in the region during the 2008–10 global economic crisis.

Perhaps the most famous company to invest in the Czech economy was Volkswagen, which invested $5.5 billion to obtain a 70% interest in the Skoda automobile plant, located in Mlada Boleslav, about 30 miles outside of Prague. In 2003 Skoda's domestic market share slipped below 50%, and around 70% of its production is exported. Car production also received a powerful boost from a Toyota-Peugeot-Citroen joint venture in Kolin (central Bohemia). At full production it will turn out 300,000 vehicles, compared with nearby Skoda Auto's 451,675 in 2004.

In 2006 Hyundai announced plans to invest one billion euros in a new auto manufacturing plant at Nosovice in eastern Czech Republic, completed in 2008. This is the country's largest foreign investment, and it will make the Czech Republic one of the EU's three largest automobile manufacturing countries. In 2008 it produced almost one million automobiles and accounted for about 10% of the entire economy. But that magnitude makes the industry very vulnerable to the kind of plunge the western European auto market experienced in 2009. Other companies included Nestlé, which took a 43% stake in the chocolate maker Cokoladovny Modrany, and Philip Morris, which obtained a 65% interest in Tabak, the cigarette maker.

Two months after the November 1989 revolution, Foreign Minister Jiri Dienstbier announced that Prague would "simply end its trade in arms" without regard to economic consequences. That turned out to be impossible, though the government did manage by 1993 to cut the output of weapons plants to 25% of 1988 levels. Political idealism no longer appears to be a controlling factor. Nevertheless, in 2002 the government decided to buy the manufacturer of the plastic explosive Semtex from the chemicals group Aliachem to reduce the possibility that the explosive would ever again be used in a terrorist action, as it was in 1988 when it brought down Pan Am Flight 103 over Lockerbie, Scotland.

Agriculture

With only 4% of its work force engaged in farming, producing 2.4% of GDP, the Czech Republic faced fewer problems than Poland in meeting the agricultural requirements for entry into the EU. The government launched a program to transform the country's agriculture. In earlier, federal legislation, collective farms had been legally transformed into cooperatives, and employees were given the right to ask for their own land. After they had taken legal title to their land, however, almost all owners arranged to lease back the land to the cooperatives. Only 1,120 of those who applied for land received more than 25 acres. Most wanted only a couple of acres to work for themselves. This was disturbing from the government's point of view because the large agricultural subsidies allotted to the cooperatives to make them competitive acted as a drain on the national budget.

The federal government sought to deal with this problem by passing a "transformation" law which reduced government oversight over the cooperatives and made their elective bodies responsible for management and decision-making. The government hoped that, given the responsibility, the cooperatives would transform themselves. To encourage them in this direction, the government cut agricultural subsidies by one-quarter in 1991. A classic example of the communist-era products making a comeback is Kofola, the Czech cola introduced in the early 1960s to try to counter the appeal of American Coke. It now produces more than in its 1970s heyday and is challenging Coke for the top spot in the Czech and Slovak soft drink market.

The Overall Economy

The Czech economy remains in transition, but it is quite strong. That is why it weathered the 2008–9 global economic recession relatively well. In 2005 the Swiss-based International Institute for Management Development ranked it 36th out of 60 states in terms of competitiveness. The government deficit had declined to 2.2% of GDP in 2008 before rising to 4.7% in 2009 and 5.5% in 2010. This public debt rose to almost 40% of GDP by 2010. Its unemployment rate had shot up to 8.7% in 2010, and inflation was down to 1.2%. In the post-communist world, its citizens' living standards are exceeded only by those in Slovenia. In the two decades since the fall of communism, per capita GDP has almost doubled to $21,000.

After three years in the doldrums, Czech prosperity was growing steadily again in 2007 and 2008, when GDP increased by 6.1% and then by 5.3%. In 2009 it contracted by 4% as a result of the global economic crisis, but it was growing again by about 1% in 2010. A real problem is the fact that 80% of GDP is generated by exports, and the bulk of those go to Western Europe. Thus Czechs are very vulnerable to the ups and downs of Western European economies.

One positive consequence of the kind of prosperity Czechs enjoy since 1989 is that

Czech Republic

they eat healthier food, have better medical care and live longer. By 2010 life expectancy for men had risen by four years to 73.4 and women by three years to 79.5. They eat fewer artery-clogging meaty foods and more chicken, fish and fresh vegetables. One habit remains constant: while the rest of the world is increasingly turning to wine, Czechs stick to beer, consuming an average of 41 gallons a year.

The birthrate is among the lowest in Europe, and the Czech population of 10.2 million is predicted to fall to 8.1 million by 2050 if immigration is restrictive. With about 230,000 legal immigrants and another 200,000 illegal ones totaling 2% of the total population, the Czech Republic has twice the percentage of other Central European nations. They take jobs most Czechs do not want, such as cleaning, construction and restaurant work.

The most convenient target for far-right groups who want to blame minority groups for the economic problems at home are the 300,000 Roma (Gypsies). The majority are unemployed and receive taxpayer-funded benefits. Xenophobic, anti-Semitic and homophobic extremists parade through towns with significant Roma populations and terrorize them and ignite or damage their homes. There are frequent clashes with the police, and in 2010 a Czech court banned the far-right Workers' Party for its involvement.

Wages, at $620 a month for the average worker in 2003, were sufficiently higher than countries to the east that a sizable black-market in labor developed. For example, it was estimated that up to 80,000 Ukrainians were working illegally in the republic. Most of the men worked in construction, while most women functioned as prostitutes. Despite its economic advance, corruption in business and politics

remains widespread. In 2003 Transparency International ranked the country 54th in the world (behind Belarus) in terms of corruption. Ex-Foreign Minister Schwarzenberg described it as a "cancer" that threatens to turn the Czech Republic into "Sicily, minus the sea and oranges."

CULTURE

Prague, the center of Czech culture, is a stunningly beautiful city full of carefully preserved ancient churches with gold-tipped spires, plus baroque, Romanesque and art nouveau buildings untouched by the bombs of World War II. On the hill above the Vltava River stands Hradcany Castle, residence of the president. St. Vitus Cathedral, Prague's great Gothic cathedral, is part of that same complex, and its spires stand out against the sky. Down the hill from Hradcany and St. Vitus, the 14th century Charles IV bridge—now a pedestrian walkway closed to traffic—leads across to the old city center. Here, in the old residence quarter of the city, one finds Wenceslas Square (Vaclavske Namesti) and Old Town (Stare Mesto) Square, with its Jan Hus Memorial.

One must give the old communist government credit: it did put a great deal of money and effort into fixing up the older buildings of Prague in their last years in power. It seemed at the time that scaffolding surrounded half of the city's architectural, historical and religious structures, but visitors to Prague have the benefit of that effort today. Czechs remain divided on plans for a new Czech National Library, designed by Jan Kaplicky. Its spotted mound has been called a "jellyfish and a mountain of slime."

Czechs enjoy a rich film tradition. Films, such as "Elementary School" and "Kolya," are post-Soviet era films that nevertheless fit well within a long-standing Czech tradition of literature and film. Their subtlety and light touch enabled good Czech films to circumvent censorship. As scholar Herb Eagle put it: "You have eccentric characters who are simply incapable of obeying the rules." "Dark Blue World," and "Divided We Fall" are accurate portrayals of wartime reality. "Dark Blue World" by director Jan Sverak, describes the more than 2,000 Czechs who fled to England in 1939 and served in the Royal Air Force. Since Nazi Germany considered them citizens of the Third Reich, their risks were doubled. If they were captured, they could be executed as traitors rather than interned as prisoners of war. "Divided We Fall" is a powerful film that focuses on the terror of Nazi occupation; it was a finalist for a 2001 Academy Award.

Prague's sprawling Barrandov Studios have produced good films since the 1930s,

thanks to its excellent facilities, skilled crews and actors. Its film industry employs 15,000 to 25,000 per year, producing such films in Prague as "The League of Extraordinary Gentlemen," "Van Helsing," and "Amadeus," which has been re-released as "Amadeus Director's Cut." The Czechs compete with the Hungarians and Romanians for the lucrative film business, but they do very well because of their considerable skills and low prices compared with London, Paris and Los Angeles. Prague also lends itself to many different kinds of scenery and can be made to look like almost anywhere. Not having been destroyed in either world war, it offers filmmakers a broad array of architecture, periods and style. Foreign film crews find inviting hotels, bars and restaurants after hours.

The fact that such films as "Bridget Jones," Hugh Grant's "Notting Hill," Matt Damon's "The Bourne Identity," and Roman Polanksi's "Oliver Twist" were filmed in Prague also lures tourists by the thousands and attracts world attention to the country. The same can be said of the world's richest top model, Karolina Kurkova. However, some tourists are no longer as welcome as they once were, especially young foreign fun-seekers, for whom the country is Central Europe's cheapest and best fleshpot.

The Czechs have contributed substantially to the world of music and literature. One needs only to recall Anton Dvorak, composer of the New World Symphony, Vilm Blodek, famous for his comic operas, Leos Janacek and Bedrich Smetana, whose music recalls the struggle for nationhood culminating in the creation in 1918 of a new state, and such figures as Smetana, Jancek and, a contemporary artist, Jaroslav Seifert, who was awarded the Nobel Prize in Literature in 1984. Seifert was one of the founders of Charter 77, the civil rights group organized to monitor the government's implementation of the Helsinki Accords. His writings were not generally available inside the country until after 1989. Seifert's poetry is not really political, however. A typical example is his "Spring in the Fisherman's Net," which follows:

In the fisherman's cork-fringed net
is spring. Young bulbs abound
on the trees and smile at us
when we look round.
In the fisherman's cork-fringed net
spaced out in three
are the stars; we are acquainted,
one always remembers me
and lights up the pathway home
in the dark at journey's end.
Not so many have the luck
to find in the stars their true girl friend.
In the fisherman's cork-fringed net

Václav Havel
Photo by Oldrich Skácha

the wind is caught. Its laughter is the
laugh all women know
when they talk about men together.
In the fisherman's cork-fringed net
the claws are caught of tender fear.
The same fear that men know
when they talk about women together.
(Tr, by ORBIS; used with permission)

The commercial aspects of culture after 1989 affect music, television and literature. The literary scene has fallen on hard times. People work and travel more and read fewer books. Internationally known writers from Communist times, such as Ivan Klima and Milan Kundera, have few equivalents in today's Czech Republic. Kundera, who is perhaps most famous for his novel, *The Unbearable Lightness of Being*, has lived as a recluse in France since 1975, where he took French citizenship. He prefers to write in French, and he is the best-known Czech fiction writer since Franz Kafka, who also did not write in Czech and was perhaps more German than Czech. Kundera's reputation was tarnished in 2008 by a well-documented accusation that as a 21-year-old student he had denounced to the Czech police a western intelligence agent working for the Americans. This resulted in a 22-year jail sentence. This sparked a national soul-searching in a nation that has always regarded him with ambivalence.

The country's best-known playwright is Vaclav Havel, whose absurdist plays were seldom seen in the outside world until the fall of communism. As a national hero and president, he did not resume his craft until 2008, when he wrote *Leaving*. This absurdist play deals with a political leader who has lost power, but refuses to admit it and refuses to vacate his official residence. Some say that he had in mind his nemesis and successor, Vaclav Klaus, but Havel denies this. The National Theatre in Prague wants to produce the play, but Havel insists that his wife, actress Dagmar Havlova, appear in the lead. "I wrote it for her."

He also published an English edition of his presidential recollections, *To the Castle and Back*, in 2008. He worries about what he calls "postcommunism," whereby former communists dominate a large part of the economy. However, his admiration for America remains intact. He noted in a 2008 interview with the *Financial Times* that "the U.S., and especially New York, is a sort of a bazaar of the entire world. . . . I find the atmosphere appealing. It's a truly free country."

The nation put its worst artistic foot forward when it selected one of its artists, David Cerny, to produce a huge 52'x52' mosaic, called Entropa, for the entrance of the European Council building in Brussels to commemorate the launching in January 2009 of the country's six-month stint as the EU presidency. Cerny was directed to hire an artist from each member state and produce a work that symbolizes the glory of a unified Europe. The result was a grotesque monstrosity.

Notorious for his rejection of establishment rules, he faked the hiring of the 27 collaborators and designed and produced it on his own, with the help of a couple of like-minded friends. The Netherlands was covered by a flood with only a few minarets peeping out of the water. Five Lithuanian soldiers are portrayed urinating on Russia. Luxembourg is depicted as a tiny lump of gold marked by a "for sale" sign. France is on strike. Britain is totally missing, which is supposed to say something. Poland has two priests hoisting the homosexual rainbow flag, while Sweden is packed in an IKEA box. Germany is presented as a series of highways that, if viewed in a certain way, resemble a swastika. Romania is a Dracula-theme amusement park.

The Bulgarian government was most enraged about its portrayal: a collection of squat toilets. Its foreign minister summoned the Czech ambassador in Sofia to lodge an official protest. The "artist" claimed that he wanted to demolish national stereotypes by mocking them. But the diplomatic outrage was such that the Czech government felt obliged to apologize for the "work."

In June 2009 the government hosted a Holocaust Era Assets Conference to discuss the tracking down of long-lost art collections that were confiscated or acquired under dubious circumstances during the Nazi time. Czech authorities are known to take extraordinary legal measures to prevent the return of looted art from their museums.

Since the 19th century, when the nationalist movement distanced itself from the Catholic Church, which it identified with the foreign domination of the Habsburgs, the country has become more and more secular. This was strengthened by four decades of communist rule. Today about 70% of Czechs profess no belief in a particular religious denomination. During the collapse of communism in 1989 the churches presented themselves as an important opposition force, but that did not last. Pope Benedikt XVI tried to reverse this and to remind Czechs of the Christian roots of their country by making a three-day pastoral visit in September 2009. In one mass in Brünn, 120,000 faithful attended.

FUTURE

The Czech Republic has largely completed the transformation from communism to capitalism, and it has done so with less pain than most other countries in Central and Eastern Europe. It joined the EU in May 2004. A poll in 2005 found Czechs to be happier than their relatively low per capita income would have predicted. Nevertheless, in politics, the idealism of the early 1990s has collapsed into cynicism, cronyism and corruption. But the revolution of November 1989 has not been forgotten. The 20th anniversary of this spectacular event was celebrated by thousands of Czechs, including Vaclav Havel, who took to the streets to re-enact the student protests that led to the overthrow of the hardline Communist regime.

The country was set back by the global recession, but thanks to its public finances and relatively stable banks, it was hurt less than most other countries in Europe. President Klaus will continue to be prickly and adversarial toward both domestic and foreign partners, including the EU and the U.S. The Czech government remains one of the most eurosceptic members of the EU, but 70% of the population admitted in a poll that they have benefited from membership. It is in no hurry to adopt the euro.

Feuding within the parties weakened and brought down four prime ministers since EU entry in 2004. The May 2010 parliamentary elections reshuffled the deck of parties and resulted in a stable 128-seat majority center-right coalition of three parties (two of them new) led by Prime Minister Petr Necas and his ODS. The new leader is known as a hard-working pragmatist, with free-market instincts and a steady commitment to the EU, NATO and the transatlantic relationship. His government pledged to focus on fiscal austerity.

Prime Minister Petr Necas

The Slovakia Republic

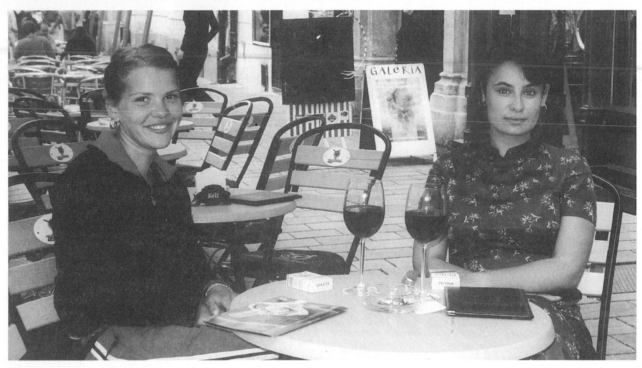

Slovak women at a street cafe in Bratislava

Area: 49,000 sq. km. = 18,819 sq. mi.
Population: 5.4 million.
Capital City: Bratislava (Pop. 427,000)
Climate: Continental, with lower temperatures in the higher elevations of the north.
Neighboring Countries: The Czech Republic (West); Poland (North); Republic of Ukraine (East); Hungary (South); Austria (West).
Official Language: Slovak
Other Principal Tongues: Magyar, Czech, Ruthenian, German
Ethnic Background: Slav
Principal Religions: Roman Catholic (60.3%), Protestant (8.4%), Orthodox (4.1%), Atheist (9.7%), Other (17.5%).
Chief Commercial Products: Machinery and transport equipment, manufactured goods, chemicals, fuels.
Chief Trading Customers: EU (86.7% of exports and 74.2% of imports), Germany (19.2% of exports and 22.8% of imports), Czech Republic (13.3% of exports and 17.8% of imports), France (6.1% of exports), Italy (5.7% of exports), Russia (9.5% of imports), Hungary (6.9% of imports).
Currency: Euro (since January 2009)
Former Status: Part of the Hungarian Kingdom of the Austro-Hungarian Empire until 1918; Part of Czechoslovakian Republic 1918–1938; Independent state under German influence, 1939–45; Part of Communist-influenced Czechoslovakian Republic, 1945–48; Part of Communist Czechoslovakia, 1948–89; Part of Czech and Slovak Federal Republic, 1990–1992.
National Day: September 1 (Constitution Day); January 1 (Creation of Independent Slovakia)
Chief of State: Ivan Gasparovic, President (June 2004).
Head of Government: Iveta Radicova, Prime Minister (June 2010).
National Flag: Three equal horizontal stripes—white, blue, red—with a shield on the left showing a two-armed white cross on a red field with a blue base.

Following Slovakia's "Velvet Divorce" with the Czech Republic in 1993, many pessimists doubted that this poorer partner would survive, let alone thrive. With its large state-owned rustbelt industries and the pollution that accompanies such economic dinosaurs, its sizable Hungarian, Gypsy (Roma) and other minorities who have not always been treated politely, and its nationalist and relatively authoritarian politics after 1989 that had tarnished its international image, it seemed to be facing a dismal future. However, its resilience after a period of stumbling inspires hope and some optimism. Slovakia is a "turnaround story."

Most of the Slovak Republic is covered by mountains or hills, but it does possess a single large plain, located to the south and east of Bratislava, the capital. It is also here that the Danube River forms the border for some distance between Slovakia and Hungary. Just north and east of Bratislava, a western spur of the Carpathian Mountains begins. They then stretch east, northeastward, widening until they cover the entire country from north to south.

The highest mountains are found in the center-north, along the border with Poland. It is here that the steep, rugged peaks of the High Tatras tower over deep valleys dotted with numerous lakes. Gerlachovsky, the tallest peak, is 8,620 feet high. It and the surrounding high terrain form the Tatra National Park. A popular place for vacationing since the 19th century, it is full of spas and holiday resorts. The Carpathian Mountains diminish in height as one moves farther eastward, but they actually run for a couple of hundred miles beyond the Slovakian border, traversing western Ukraine.

As its name implies, Slovakia is essentially a land of the Slovaks. But there are three minorities making up several percent of the population that have the status of "nationalities." These include Hungarians, mainly in the southeast, Poles in the northeast and Ukrainians and Ruthenians in the east. The latter also live on the Polish and Ukrainian sides of the border. They enjoyed one day of independence on March 15, 1918, but they show no interest in separatism today. Their most famous countryman was the Pittsburgh-born Andy Warhol. The Hungarians, who number about 560,000, are the largest minority. Carpathian Germans live in the north, the northwest and central part of Slovakia.

Slovakia has a large number of Roma (Gypsies—520,000), about 10% of the total population. They constitute the fifth largest Roma population in Europe. They are recognized as a separate nationality. During the Second World War, when Slovakia had a government that collaborated with Nazi Germany, it was official policy to sterilize Roma. Under the communists, they were offered money if they agreed to sterilization. At the same time, the government attempted to assimilate them, providing them with apartments, jobs and income although discrimination continued. Since 1989, assistance to them was reduced.

As in other Central European countries, open antipathy toward them continues to exist, and far-right hate groups, such as the Slovenska Pospolitost (Slovak Brotherhood), protest against "Roma terror" and "Roma criminality." In 2004, the government dispatched 2,000 police and soldiers to quell Roma rioting to protest welfare cuts. These were the country's worst riots since 1989, and police had to use water cannons to push the 400 Roma back into their settlement, followed by house-to-house searches.

These actions highlighted their desperate living conditions, shocking poverty and unemployment. Between 90% and 100% are jobless or dependent upon welfare. They constitute 80% of Slovakia's long-term unemployed. The poorest Roma live in clusters of wooden shacks without water mains or sewage systems. They are often segregated from "white Slovak" housing, and many children grow up without schooling.

HISTORY

In the 5th century, the forerunners of the Slovaks, then one of a group of west Slavic tribes, moved from the east into the area of modern Slovakia. Other tribes migrated farther west. Together, these various Slavic tribes settled the area to the south of the Carpathian and Sudeten Mountains and along the Vltava and Danube Rivers.

Except for a legendary, short-lived kingdom created by a Frank trader, Samo, in the 7th century, these western Slavic peoples continued to be governed by a tribal structure until the ninth century, when the Moravian Empire was established. The seat of this empire was in the western part of modern Slovakia, in the modern Slovak city of Nitra. It was also here that the first Christian church among western Slavs was built in the year 850. It is likely that the rulers of this first unified state were Slovak tribal leaders, for it was the Slovak lands that were first unified, with the remaining western Slavic lands being added later.

Although the Moravian Empire lasted less than a century, it was important because the western Slavs were converted to Christianity during this time. The first

Bohemia and Moravia ca. 1360

Christian missionaries came from Rome, but Prince Rastislav, who ruled 850–870, requested the Byzantine Emperor to send a bishop to "enlighten and instruct his people in the true faith and in their own tongue." Methodius and Cyril, the two Greek Orthodox monks sent by the emperor, introduced a Slavonic liturgy and the first written script for the Slavs, later known as Cyrillic. Because later rulers of the Moravian empire favored the priests from Western Europe, Cyrillic was replaced by Roman letters, but a written Slavic literature dates from this time.

The Moravian Empire began to disintegrate toward the end of the 9th century. First weakened from within by revolts by ambitious Czech nobles desirous of creating their own independent kingdom of Bohemia, the Moravian Empire came under attack from the south and east when Magyar peoples swept into the area, overrunning the Hungarian Plain and gradually extending their control northward to

the Carpathian Mountains. Although the Slovak rulers fought a rear-guard action against the Magyars for some time, all the Slovak lands were brought under Magyar control by about the year 1000, the date traditionally used to mark the beginning of Christianity in Hungary and the founding of the Kingdom of St. Stephen.

For nearly a thousand years—until 1918—the Slovaks remained under the Hungarian crown. Since both Magyars and Slovaks were Roman Catholics, and Latin, not Hungarian, was the language used at court and in the churches, Slovaks had no serious complaints. On the other hand, although a few Slovaks managed to rise to high position, most were peasants living on land controlled by members of the Hungarian nobility. When serfdom spread into Central Europe in the later middle ages, the majority became serfs.

When the last Hungarian king was killed at the battle of Mohacs in 1526, Hungary became a possession of the Habsburgs, whose main seat was at Vienna. This was a positive development for Slovaks because the Habsburgs, being German-speaking, had no reason to favor the Hungarians. When the Turks overran most of Hungary in the 16th and 17th centuries, it was the Slovak lands that remained unoccupied, in effect becoming the main part of the kingdom. For the next 150 years, the seat of the Hungarian government was Pressburg, better known today by its Slavic name, Bratislava, the present-day capital of Slovakia.

Joseph II of Austria abolished serfdom in the Czech part in 1781 and in Slovakia in 1785. The revolution of 1848 strengthened Hungarian nationalism and ultimately inspired a policy of Magyarization after 1867. The government prohibited the use of the Slovak language in public, decreed that all school education was to be

Slovakia

only in Hungarian, and in general did everything it could to suppress a separate Slovak identity.

Yet the revolutions affected the Slovaks as well. It was in 1848 that an assembly of Slovaks first drew up a demand for political, social and cultural equality. And even as the Hungarian government attempted to suppress Slovak nationalism, individual Slovak intellectuals worked to counteract the official policy. These included two poets, Ján Holly and Ján Kollár, and Ludovit Stúr, a writer and a political leader. Nevertheless, Slovak culture remained largely suppressed until the collapse of the Austro-Hungarian Empire in 1918.

In spite of this, a Slovak identity did begin to develop, mainly among Slovaks in emigration—in Paris and, particularly, in the United States. The first Slovak newspaper was launched in Pittsburgh in 1886. In 1907 the Slovak League in America unified various Slovak organizations and in 1914 declared the right of self-determination for the Slovak nation. A Slovak who was a general in the French army, Milan Rastislav Stefánik, opened his Paris home to Tomás Masaryk, whose wife was American, and Edvard Benes (*Ben*-esh) to discuss the creation of a Czech-Slovak state. During World War I, they threw their support behind Masaryk's vision of an independent Czechoslovak state. On October 22, 1915, Slovak and Czech representatives pledged in the Cleveland Agreement to cooperate with each other to create a future state with autonomous status for Slovaks. The Pittsburgh Agreement, signed on June 30, 1918, expressed Slovak support for the union of Czech and Slovak lands in return for Masaryk's promise that Slovakia would have considerable independence within the new state. The independent Czecho-Slovak Republic was proclaimed in Prague on October 28, 1918. Two days later, the Slovak National Council, meeting in Turciansky Svaty Martin, a town in central Slovakia, voted to be part of the proclaimed state.

The Independent Czecho-Slovak Republic

Slovakia remained a part of the independent Czecho-Slovak Republic until 1939, but that period of cohabitation was not entirely happy. The problem was that the constitution, adopted in 1920, stressed absolute majority rule and emphasized the sovereignty of the state *vis-à-vis* individual citizens.

In addition, since Czechs and Slovaks were considered to be one people, there were no separate rights for Slovaks, nor was Slovak recognized as a separate language. The lesser educated Slovaks found themselves at a disadvantage in applying for jobs in the government. Thus there were fewer than 200 Slovaks among the 8,000-odd civil servants of the central government. In Slovakia, Czechs predominantly staffed the public services. Even in the schools, half of the teachers were Czechs.

Although almost all industry was located in the Czech part of the country, no effort was made to develop Slovakia. Even some of the few factories that predated 1918 were allowed to go under. Many Slovaks believed that the Czechs were treating them as a colony. They particularly resented the presence of so many Czechs in important positions throughout Slovakia.

Individual Slovaks who spoke out on this issue often found themselves the subject of official judicial inquiry and action, charged with violating the 1923 law for the protection of the government. This prohibited "agitating . . . against the state because of its . . . constitutional unitary structure." Thus individuals who advocated federalism—as many Slovak nationalists did—were considered to be guilty of subversion. One of the more prominent cases occurred in 1928, when Professor Vojtech Tuka was arrested and sentenced to 15 years in prison for an assertion in a newspaper article that the original Slovak agreement to join the Czecho-Slovak Republic had required a referendum after ten years. In another such incident, the Slovak People's Party newspaper was closed down in 1933 and the editor arrested, after 100,000 Slovaks had demonstrated for autonomy in Nitra.

A Slovak provincial administration was actually created in 1927, but this did not satisfy Slovak leaders, who continued to press for full autonomy. The most important of these was Monsignor Andrej Hlinka, leader of the Slovak People's Party, largest of Slovakia's parties. Other parties that agitated for Slovak autonomy included the Catholic People's Party and the Slovak National Party. In addition, Slovak members of the Social Democrats and the Agrarians were often supporters of autonomy.

In 1937 Masaryk died, and Dr. Eduard Benes became a candidate for the presidency. During his campaign, Benes sought electoral support from members of the Slovak People's Party by promising autonomy for Slovakia. When Dr. Milan Hodûa, a Slovak, became Czecho-Slovak premier at this time, many Slovaks became convinced that the central government was finally ready to take their interests into consideration. After his inauguration, however, Benes supported the Slovak government that had existed since 1927 and made no attempt to accord it any greater autonomy.

When a Sudeten German crisis erupted in 1938, Slovaks were beginning to organize their own demonstrations on behalf of autonomy. At the beginning of June, the Slovak People's Party introduced a bill for Slovak autonomy. A few days later, a mass meeting in Bratislava drew 120,000 persons. When Monsignor Hlinka died in August, the situation deteriorated further, for Monsignor Jozef Tiso, his successor as head of the Slovak People's Party, was an even more outspoken advocate of Slovak autonomy.

Meanwhile, the Sudeten German crisis was coming to a head. As pressure from Nazi Germany grew, Premier Hodûa resigned on September 22, and President Benes took charge of the government. He created an all-party coalition with one seat reserved for the Slovak People's Party. Matús Cernák, the man chosen to represent the party, gave President Benes an ul-

A mountain village in Slovakia in the late 1900s

timatum in October: unless Slovak autonomy was granted within 24 hours, he would resign, and all Slovak delegates would leave the parliament. Cernák actually stepped down the next day but, in an anticlimax of sorts, President Benes submitted his own resignation on October 5. General Ján Syrovy, whom Benes had appointed as premier only days earlier, became the acting president.

The next day, representatives from all of the Slovak political parties and Slovak branches of national political parties—with the exception of the Communists and Social Democrats—met in the town of Zilina. After considerable discussion, they voted to merge their several parties to form the Slovak National Unity Party and then drew up a manifesto that announced the formation of an autonomous Slovakian government.

Acting President Syrovy accepted the Zilina manifesto and appointed Monsignor Tiso as premier of Slovakia. The autonomy of Slovakia was legalized by constitutional amendment, passed by the Prague parliament on November 19. Elections to a Slovak parliament were held on December 18. The Slovak National Unity Party, whose dominant wing was the old Slovak People's Party, ran a single unity ticket and won 97.5% of the vote. The remaining ballots were cast for small German and Hungarian ethnic parties. The Social Democrats and Communists were unrepresented because the government had deliberately delayed publication of election procedures until it was too late for these two national parties to nominate candidates. Slovakia thus had essentially a one-party government, and this situation continued throughout its existence.

Even after achieving its goal of autonomy, however, Slovak relations with Prague remained poor. The Czechs were stressing the necessity of Czecho-Slovak unity to guarantee the continued independence of the state. Czechs were also angry at the Slovaks for maintaining contacts with the Carpatho-Germans and for participating in extensive conferences with officials from Hitler's Germany. Emil Hacha, who had been elected Czecho-Slovak president on November 19, 1938, was extremely upset by these contacts, which he claimed were treasonous. On March 9, he dismissed Monsignor Tiso as premier and declared a state of emergency in Slovakia. Several ministers were arrested, but Hacha agreed to allow the deputy premier, Karol Sidor, to reconstitute the Slovak government.

"Independent" Slovakia, 1939–45

It was at this point that Hitler made his move. On March 12, a Nazi delegation arrived in Bratislava with a message from Hitler urging Premier Sidor to declare Slovakian independence. Sidor refused, but shortly thereafter Monsignor Tiso and Ferdinand Durcansky, a second Slovak nationalist, flew to Berlin to meet with Hitler. Here they were informed that Germany would recognize and support a declaration of Slovak independence. Hitler warned them, however, that he "would leave the destiny of Slovakia to the mercy of events," if they decided to remain with Prague.

There had already been reports that Hungary, which had obtained parts of southern Slovakia in November, wanted to annex the rest of Slovakia. Joachim Ribbentrop, the German foreign minister, informed Tiso and Durcansky that Hungarian troops had begun to mass along the Slovak border. Monsignor Tiso returned to Bratislava on March 14 and immediately addressed the Slovak parliament. Following his report, the parliament unanimously adopted a declaration of Slovakian independence.

Meanwhile, President Hacha, who had requested an interview with Hitler, was invited to come to Berlin on that same day. In fact, the declaration of Slovak independence had already been adopted by the time he arrived in Berlin. Hacha met with Hitler late that evening. After a long harangue, Hitler demanded that Hacha sign an agreement accepting a German protectorate over the remaining parts of the country. Hacha collapsed during the interview, but managed to recover enough to sign the capitulation. German troops entered the new Bohemia and Moravia Protectorate on March 15.

The Independent Slovakian Republic has often been referred to as a "puppet state." The political realities of the time meant that the Slovak government had generally to align its policies with those of Hitler's Germany. It is also true that the Tiso government passed anti-Jewish legislation which, among other things, required Jewish entrepreneurs to sell off 51% of their shares to Slovak partners, set a limit of 4% on the percentage of Jews in public services and the professions, and encouraged Jewish emigration to Palestine. The anti-Jewish legislation was broad and not essentially different from that in Germany itself.

These laws did not satisfy Hitler, however. In July 1940 he forced the Slovak government to agree to transfer Slovak Jews to a "resettlement" area in German-held Poland. The deportations continued until July 1942. Monsignor Tiso ordered them stopped after the Papal Nuncio informed him that Jews were being murdered in the Lublin area. This new policy remained in force over the next two years. However, when Security Minister Hassik ordered the disbanding of the labor camps and the repeal of anti-Jewish laws, the Germans assumed direct control of all matters concerning Jews in Slovakia.

The Slovak government deported and killed approximately 50,000 Jews during the war. With only *pro forma* cooperation from the Slovak government, an estimated 26,650 Jews managed to escape the net and were still in Slovakia in 1945 at the end of the war.

Meanwhile, a sort of Slovak government-in-exile came into being in December 1943 in London. A number of Slovak liberals and leftists, including communists, organized a Slovak National Council and, under the terms of a "Christmas Agreement" signed at the same time, committed themselves to "take over, at an expedient time, all political, legislative, military, and governmental executive power in Slovakia." The Christmas Agreement of 1943 was a broad democratic program that gathered diverse anti-Hitler groups under one umbrella. It contained principles of anti-fascist resistance and the future organization of liberated Slovakia. The Slovak National Council found some support for its plans in Slovakia, particularly among Protestants and some elements of the army and police. It also established some contact with partisan units in the mountains of eastern Slovakia.

In August 1944, communist-led partisans launched the so-called Slovak Nationalist Uprising. Its hand forced, the Slovak National Council endorsed the revolt on August 29, constituting itself a provisional government. The insurgents took over large parts of central Slovakia for two months, and there was widespread, but not total, popular support. Some Slovaks today compare this rebellion to the Warsaw uprising and argue that it has not been widely recognized in Western historiography because of the fact that communists led it. President Tiso, fearing the success of the revolt, requested the help of the German army. The revolt collapsed in October 1944, and German troops remained until they were forced out in 1945. Their presence destroyed any pretense that Slovakia was an independent country.

Reintegration into Czechoslovakia

The vanguard of the Soviet army entered Slovakia on October 18, 1944. Slowed by a subsequent German counteroffensive, it took until April 4, 1945, to clear the rest of Slovakia of German forces. Having reorganized his government-in-exile into a "National Front" government after consulting Stalin in Moscow, President Benes arrived in Kosice in eastern Slovakia in March 1945 and set up his government. Here the government announced its "Kosice Program," which spelled out its plans

Slovakia

Old Town Bratislava

for reconstituting the Czechoslovak state. Under its terms, "the members of the so-called Slovak governments since March 14, 1939, as well as members of the so-called Slovak Parliament" were to be arrested and charged with high treason. The program also called for the suppression of the "Slovak People's Party, and those parties which joined the latter in 1938."

Most of the members of the Slovak government fled to Bavaria at the end of the war. Taken into custody by the U.S. Army, they were extradited at the request of the Czechoslovak government and taken to Bratislava. A National Tribunal appointed to try them sat for nearly a year before rendering its verdict in April 1947. Monsignor Tiso was sentenced to death by hanging, while other members of his government received prison terms. Labor camps were set up in Slovakia, and thousands of persons deemed to "threaten the reconstruction of the state, security, the peace, public order . . . as well as those persons who profess an ideology inimical to the state" were confined in these camps without benefit of trial.

The Continuing Problem of Slovak "Particularism"

From the point of view of the Czechoslovak government, the crime for which these individuals were punished was fascism, not nationalism. At the same time, Benes and the others were well aware that Slovak "particularism" was a continuing problem that was not likely to be ended by the imprisonment or even execution of a few leaders. To defuse this issue, therefore, the central government promised

that Slovakia would be granted an autonomous status, with a parliament and a cabinet. Adopting this same approach, the communists, at this time the strongest group in the National Front government, organized a separate Slovak Communist Party. The communists did very badly in the 1946 elections in Slovakia, however, and thereafter began to place greater stress on Czechoslovak centralization.

After the communist seizure of power in Prague in early 1948, the new constitution issued three months later created a highly centralized state with nearly all power centered in the Czech capital. Yet it technically fulfilled the earlier promise of an autonomous status for Slovakia by creating a Slovak National Council with limited legislative powers relating to cultural matters, education, public health, local boundaries, encouragement of agriculture and local trade.

Two months later, however, the presidium of the Czechoslovak Communist Party negated this theoretical grant of autonomy to Slovakia by calling for a united communist party. Responding to this directive from Prague, the Slovak Communist Party voted to merge itself into the Czechoslovak Communist Party. From this time, the Communist Party organization in Slovakia was merely a branch of the Czechoslovak Communist Party, though it was allowed to keep its separate central committee and regional organization.

The significance of this change became clear in April 1950, when the national government decided to move against religious communities throughout the country. Without informing the Slovak communist lead-

ers, Prague dispatched policemen to dissolve religious orders in Bratislava and deport their members. When Slovak communists protested, they were immediately suspended from their governmental duties. A month later at the Ninth Congress of the Slovak branch of the Communist Party, charges of "deviationism" and "bourgeois nationalism" were brought against them, and a general purge followed. Among those dismissed from office were Gustáv Husák, the Slovak premier, Karol Schmidke, chairman of the Slovak National Council, and Ladislav Novomesks, commissioner of public education.

Nine months later, Husák, Schmidke and Novomesks, plus Vladimír Clementis, a Slovak who had risen to the rank of minister of foreign affairs in the central government, and several lesser known Slovak Communists, were arrested and charged with "nationalist-deviationist tendencies" as part of a general purge of "Titoist" Communists in Eastern Europe. Clementis, one of the 14 defendants in the so-called Slánsky trial, held in Prague, was found guilty of bourgeois nationalism and executed in 1952. The others remained in prison for another two years before being given a formal trial in 1954. All were found guilty. Husák was sentenced to life imprisonment, while the others got lesser sentences. After the trial, there was a widespread purge of Slovak intellectuals from party and government jobs.

Following this purge of leading Slovak Communists, leadership in Slovakia was exercised by Viliam Siroky, a Slovak of Magyar origin who headed the Slovak branch of the Communist Party, and Karel Bacílek, a Czech who had migrated to Slovakia at the end of World War I. Bacílek replaced Husák as premier. Thus there were no ethnic Slovaks in leadership roles in Slovakia. Although the Slovak Communists had never enjoyed any real popularity among the Slovak people, they were willing to make some concessions to Slovak nationalist aspirations. Their successors were viewed by ordinary Slovaks as outsiders and agents of Prague and were detested for that reason.

With the general alienation of the Slovak population, it is not surprising that the 1956 Hungarian Revolution led to an outbreak of demonstrations in a number of Slovak cities. In response, a frightened Prague government dispatched six divisions of troops to western and central Slovakia to quell the unrest, while Soviet troops were moved in to secure eastern Slovakia. Four years later, the new constitution of the Czechoslovak Socialist Republic abolished the last legal remnants of Slovak autonomy.

Yet the question of Slovak autonomy would not die. Two years later, a party

Slovaks try to reason with Warsaw Pact soldiers, 1968   Photo by Oldrich Skácha

congress in Prague voted to conduct an inquiry into the purges of 1949–1954. This reopened the Slovak issue because Vladimir Clementis was among those found to have been wrongfully convicted. The inquiry's decision on him led Slovak writers and scholars to begin agitating for the rehabilitation of those Slovak Communists who had been thrown into prison for "bourgeois nationalism." Although this produced no immediate results, one "bourgeois-nationalist" figure, Gustáv Husák, was released from prison in 1960, ostensibly as part of a general amnesty to mark the 15th anniversary of socialist Czechoslovakia.

He and the other victims of the Stalinist trials had to wait another two years for political rehabilitation. When the twelfth party congress met in 1962, one of the adopted resolutions voided the earlier convictions and made amends by stipulating that those still alive would be readmitted to the party and given better jobs, while relatives of those executed would receive financial compensation.

Karol Bacílek, the immensely unpopular first secretary of the Slovak branch of the Communist Party, and Viliam Siroky, Slovak premier, were also removed at this time. Both men had aroused Slovak hatred by a consistent policy of cooperating with the Prague government's centralization policies. Josef Lenárt replaced Siroky while Bacílek was succeeded by a Slovak, Alexander Dubcek (pronounced *Doobchek*). Czech-Slovak relations now improved and Novotny, basking in his new role as a reformer, got himself unanimously elected in 1964 for another seven-year term as president of the republic. The

apparent political calm was misleading, however. It soon became clear that there were a number of differing opinions within the party over the progress of reform.

Dubcek emerged as the leader of the anti-Novotny forces in late 1967. At a meeting of the party Central Committee, he accused Novotny of undermining the program of economic reform and of refusing to meet Slovak demands for more self-government. Although he had raised the Slovak issue, Dubcek placed greater emphasis on economic reform. It was clear that he did not want to be labeled a Slovak particularist. His position was helped by the fact that the Czechoslovak Writers' Union and student demonstrators in Prague joined in the attack against Novotny.

The reformers were not immediately successful, however. The unrest in Prague led to a visit by Soviet party chief Leonid Brezhnev as a gesture of support for Novotny. But the visit was not enough to save the falling president. When the Central Committee convened again two months later, it decided that the functions of the presidency should be separated from those of the first secretary of the Communist Party. On January 5, 1968, Alexander Dubcek became the first Slovak to assume the top post in the Communist Party of Czechoslovakia.

Defeat for Reform

The overall purpose of the entire reform movement was to create what Dubcek called "socialism with a human face." Dubcek was always careful to portray himself as a Czechoslovak leader, though his general plans for political decentralization would have also led to greater Slovak au-

tonomy. Yet the plans of the reformers were not to be. On the night of August 20–21, military units of the Soviet Union, Hungary, East Germany, Poland and Bulgaria entered Czechoslovakia, and within a few hours occupied the major cities. In the process, the entire Czechoslovak leadership—Dubcek, Cernik, and Josef Smrkovsky, president of the National Assembly—was placed under arrest. The Czech Foreign Ministry denounced the invasion as a violation of the Warsaw Pact, and President Ludvik Svoboda flatly refused to participate in the formation of a Soviet-dominated government. The deadlock was broken when he agreed to go to Moscow for direct talks with the Soviet leaders.

At Svoboda's insistence, Dubcek and the other leaders accompanied him and participated in the talks. After much discussion, it was announced that there would be no change in the political leadership, though it was clear that they would not be permitted to continue their reform political program. This became even clearer in October when the two countries signed an open-ended treaty providing for the stationing of Soviet troops within Czechoslovakia.

Compensation for Slovakia

One reform that was of great significance to Slovakia managed to survive the Soviet crushing of the Prague Spring. Since Prague was considered to be the focal point for reform communism, the Soviet leadership dropped its support for a highly centralized Czechoslovak state under Czech leadership and began to favor those conservative Slovak Communists who had earlier been removed for nationalistic tendencies. To win their support, it was decided to grant Slovakia its autonomy by turning Czechoslovakia into a federal state. This reform, put into effect at midnight on December 31, 1968, abolished the old unitary structure and created in its stead a new federal republic consisting of the two separate Czech and Slovak Socialist Republics. During 1969, there was a gradual replacement of the pre-invasion reform leadership through demotion, resignation or dismissal.

Dubcek, caught in the middle of all of this, tried to hang on by playing the centralist role. While assuring the liberals that there had been no surrender to the Soviet Union and that reform was still possible, he reassured the conservatives that there was no danger in reform. At the same time, he attempted to convince the Soviet Union that he would not be the source of additional political strife. Dubcek found it difficult to be in favor of so many conflicting political views at the same time. In April, Gustáv Husák replaced him as party secretary.

Slovakia

Husák was a complex individual himself. Although in many ways a political moderate, he was willing to preside over the end of reform for two reasons; first, because he was favorable to Slovak nationalism and liked the new federal structure; second, because he believed it was paramount for Czechoslovakia to live in harmony with the Soviet Union. Dubcek was expelled from the Communist Party in June 1970. This victory for the party's "hardliners" left Husák surrounded at the center by conservatives who also wanted to recentralize power in Prague. In early 1971, the Federal Cabinet was given the right to veto decisions of the Czech and Slovak cabinets. Slovak autonomy was once again being eroded.

Husák's own political position was not impaired by this new move toward centralization. He went along with the trend because he was, in fact, in charge of the entire country. In May 1975, he further increased his authority by replacing the ailing Svoboda as president of the republic while remaining head of the party. Husák continued to occupy both positions for the next 12 years. Thus, in a final irony, the man who had once been thrown into prison for "bourgeois nationalism" became both the symbol and instrument of Prague's domination of Slovakia.

Husák became more and more conservative in his later years, so Gorbachev's emergence as a reformer after his election as CPSU General Secretary in March 1985 presented him with a problem. After temporizing for some time, Husák announced his retirement as leader of the Czechoslovak Communist Party in 1987, though he retained his position as president of the republic. His successor was Milos Jakes (pronounced *Ya*-kesh). A Czech, Jakes kept his position as party leader for two years, until forced out in November 1989 as a result of Prague's so-called "velvet revolution."

Karel Urbanek replaced Jakes, but it was the premier, Ladislav Adamec, who opened discussions with the opposition. The party now agreed to give up its monopoly of power and to form a coalition government with the opposition. But Adamec wanted to keep a majority of the seats in the hands of the communists. When Civic Forum rejected his proposed cabinet on December 3, Adamec resigned and was replaced by Marián Calfa. The new cabinet, installed on December 10, contained a majority of non-communists.

Gustáv Husák submitted his resignation as president, thus opening the question as to who his successor should be. Alexander Dubcek, leader of the Prague Spring in 1968, and Vaclav Havel, longtime dissident, founder of Charter 77, and prominent playwright, were both contenders. But the job eventually went to Havel. On December 29, he was elected president by acclamation, while Alexander Dubcek was given the compensatory prize of becoming leader of the Federal Assembly.

Renewed Separatism

In the run-up to the June 1990 elections, the issue of democracy versus communism dominated political discussions, but the rivalry between Czechs and Slovaks began to emerge as an issue as well. Upon Slovak insistence, the name of the country was changed to the Czech and Slovak Federal Republic. As new political parties were organized to contest the elections, separate parties emerged in the two parts of the country. While the Czech reform group was organized as the Civic Forum, the Slovak partner took the name of Public Against Violence.

From the beginning Slovaks were concerned about their separate identity. But the issue that led Slovak nationalists to begin demanding the creation of a separate, independent state was economic reform. Many of the Slovak leaders feared that the swift implementation of a market system as advocated by Czech leaders such as Vá-

clav Klaus, the new Czechoslovak minister of finance, would have a disastrous effect on the Slovak economy.

The Federal Assembly attempted to defuse the situation in December 1990 by passing new legislation outlining the powers of the Czech and Slovak regional governments. The legislation also gave President Havel special powers to deal with the threat of Slovak separatism.

Although most Slovak deputies afterwards expressed their satisfaction with the legislation, the situation continued to simmer. President Havel was mobbed by thousands of Slovaks shouting abuse when he visited Bratislava in March 1991. Part of the problem was that the Slovak premier, Vladimír Meciar (*Mech*-ee-ar), had taken up the Slovak nationalist cause. Things improved somewhat after Ján Carnogursky, head of Slovakia's Christian Democratic Movement, replaced Meciar in April 1991 by. Carnogursky's position was ambiguous, however; although he supported continuation of the federation for the time being, he also said that he favored an independent Slovakia in principle.

Slovak nationalism continued to be the dominant factor in Czechoslovak politics throughout the rest of 1991 and into 1992. President Havel spent more and more of his time on this issue as he tried to act as a mediator between the Czechs and Slovaks, bringing the two sides together for discussions and, at one point, calling for a referendum on the issue. Public polls showed that a small majority of Slovaks supported a continuation of the federation. Therefore, the Slovak political leadership eventually rejected such a referendum. Havel also proposed some changes in the federal government, and the Czechoslovak government presented these to the Federal Assembly in December 1991 in the form of three draft laws.

The three draft laws were not passed, but they acted as a catalyst. An ad hoc commission of the Czech and Slovak National Councils (i.e., legislatures) announced on February 9, 1992, that its members had drawn up a draft agreement on a future common state that would be submitted to their respective legislatures. The draft agreement listed foreign policy, defense, monetary, credit, interest and currency policies and budgetary regulations as falling within the powers of the federation. Czechs and Slovaks would be equally represented in the federal bodies. It also specified that either republic could withdraw from the common state "only on the basis of the will of the majority of its citizens expressed in a referendum."

When the Presidium of the Slovak National Council met on February 12 to consider the draft, it was turned down. Two weeks later, the Slovak National Council

Relaxing in Bratislava

adopted a resolution requesting its deputies to submit their views on the draft to the Presidium and instructed the Presidium to compile a comprehensive report on the comments that the deputies submitted. The resolution further recommended that the Presidium meet with the Presidium of the Czech National Council "to jointly assess . . . the possibility of concluding the treaty."

When these maneuvers failed to produce an agreement, it was decided to hold new federal elections on June 5–6 to resolve the issue. Slovakia held its own elections to the National Council on the same days. The Christian Democratic Movement, the party of Slovak premier Jan Carnogursky, now split into two factions. The more radical faction that had been pushing for an independent Slovakia formed a new party, the Slovak Christian Democratic Movement. It announced that they would run a separate slate of candidates in the June elections. With the radicals gone, the Christian Democratic Movement reaffirmed its support for a common state.

In the June 1992 elections, the vote split along national and ideological lines. Essentially, the Czechs cast their votes for reform and anticommunist candidates, while the Slovaks supported nationalists and leftists. In the Slovak Republic, Vladimír Meciar and his Movement for a Democratic Slovakia won with their blend of statism, socialism and nationalism. In the Czech Republic, Václav Klaus and his Civic Democratic Party won an equally convincing victory on a program of anticommunism and reform.

When Meciar and Klaus met after the 1992 election to discuss the formation of a new federal government, Meciar made it clear that he would not accept a federal state that could dictate policy to Slovakia. He demanded that the Slovak Republic be authorized to establish its own army, its own currency-issuing central bank and the independent right to borrow. He also indicated that he intended to reverse some of the recent national policies as they applied to Slovakia, including restoring subsidies to state industry, increasing social benefits, and slowing privatization. None of those positions was compatible with development of a free market. Klaus and the talks collapsed after six and a half hours.

Because a new federal government had to be formed, Klaus suggested giving a new, temporary federal government the power to act until a referendum could be held asking citizens whether they wanted to live in a federal state. After further talks, Czech and Slovak negotiators agreed to establish a weak interim federal government whose task would be to bring the union to a close. The actual constitu-

tional questions relating to the separation would be resolved in the legislatures of the two republics. Further negotiations produced an agreement, signed on August 26, calling for a split into two independent states by January 1.

The process suffered a setback on October 1, when the federal parliament rejected a bill legalizing the end of the federation. After further negotiations, however, the federal parliament voted itself out of existence on November 25.

By that time, the two national legislatures had begun acting as though the federation had already disappeared; this was particularly true in the case in Slovakia. Meciar had said in June that he wanted to

Vladimir Mečiar

slow down privatization, and he began submitting bills to the Slovak legislature to accomplish that purpose. The Slovak government called for the renegotiation of several privatization agreements and stopped the sale of a number of companies. As a result, only 5.3% of Slovak industry had been privatized by the end of 1992 as compared to 25.2% for the Czech Republic.

On January 1, 1993, The Czech and Slovak Federal Republic disappeared, and in its place there emerged an independent Slovak Republic and an independent Czech Republic. The separation was peaceful, but all of the celebrations were in Bratislava, the capital of Slovakia. There was no ceremony to mark the occasion in Prague. In the speech he gave to mark the event, Prime Minister Meciar attempted a note of conciliation. "Two states have been established," he said. "Living together in one state is over. Living together in two states continues."

Slovakia since Independence

After achieving independence for Slovakia, Prime Minister Meciar reiterated

the positions he had enunciated in 1992. In his New Year's Day address, he rejected both free market economics and a ban on former communists in top government positions. He also surrounded himself with reform communists who had been active in the Prague Spring. Meciar's commitment to democracy and pluralism was not very firm. For example, the government tightened its control on the press and on television after independence, dismissing individuals suspected of oppositionist tendencies. It also began to restrict the language rights of its Hungarian minority. In 1993 the government began taking down Hungarian-language signs in border areas and formally announced that Hungarian names for Slovak towns could not be used in Hungarian-language broadcasts.

Meciar's greatest changes were in the area of economics, however. In the first months after independence, privatization came to an end for all but the smallest firms. At the same time, the government increased credits to state industry, thereby enlarging the budget deficit and contributing to the collapse of the common currency arrangement with the Czech Republic. There was a drop of almost 50% in exports to the Czech Republic, and an even greater drop in imports. Significant deposits had also been switched from Slovak to Czech banks.

Meciar undoubtedly expected that his halting of privatization and increasing of credits to state industry would have a positive effect on employment and the overall economy. In fact, they had the opposite effect. Meciar's party split in 1994 when the economic situation worsened and unemployment grew to an estimated 14.4%. Among those withdrawing from the party were Meciar's foreign minister, Jozef Moravcik (More-*av*-chick), and the deputy prime minister, Roman Kovac (*Ko*-vach). That left the Movement for a Democratic Slovakia without a parliamentary majority. Meciar was finally ousted on March 11 when he lost a parliamentary vote of confidence. Moravcik, who had led the rebellion against him, replaced him. Although a former member of the Movement for a Democratic Slovakia, Moravcik promised to revive the reform process.

New elections were scheduled to take place on September 30, 1994, so Moravcik did not have much time to make a record for himself. Nevertheless, he managed to accomplish a number of important things during the next six months, including legislation extending protection for Hungarian language rights. He opened negotiations with Hungary for a treaty to settle border questions and to improve the treatment of each other's minorities. He invited Gyula Horn, the Hungarian prime minister, to

Slovakia

Bratislava for an official visit. He restored Slovakia to international respectability.

None of that seemed to matter when the people cast their ballots on September 30 and October 1. The essential problem was that Moravcik's supporters were a disparate group of Movement for a Democratic Slovakia rebels, conservative Christian Democrats, and the Democratic Left Party (i.e., the successor to the old communist party), which had very little in common other than their opposition to Meciar. Moreover, his Movement for a Democratic Slovakia was still the best organized and financed of all the political parties. Nor did it hurt that his supporters in parliament, in attacking the new government by every means at their disposal, were viewed as heroes by most of those negatively affected by the reforms—in particular Slovakia's 15% unemployed, the peasantry and the retired.

While no party won an outright majority, Meciar's Movement for a Democratic Slovakia came in first with 35% of the vote, winning 61 of the 150 parliamentary seats. He found it extremely difficult to create a working majority coalition. Finally, Meciar announced on November 3 that he had negotiated a "voting pact" with the right-wing Slovak National Party and the left-wing Association of Slovak Workers that would allow him to form a government. Although not then a formal alliance, this voting majority pushed legislation through the parliament sacking the attorney general, dismissing the board of the National Property Fund (thus suspending privatization), blocking the sale of all state-owned companies approved by the previous government, and bringing radio, television, and the state intelligence service under the control of Meciar's party.

This trend continued and intensified. In 1995, Meciar launched a series of public attacks on President Kovác, and these continued in 1996 and 1997. Meciar also called for Kovác to step down. When this did not work, he attempted to get the parliament to dismiss the president. These moves failed because Meciar lacked the two-thirds majority in the legislature necessary to force out the president.

One of the more bizarre aspects of this struggle between Prime Minister Meciar and President Kovác occurred in August 1995 and involved the president's son, Michal Kovác Jr. Michal Jr. was mysteriously abducted in Bratislava and carried across the border into Austria, where he was later arrested on a German warrant. Most observers believe that the Slovak security service was responsible for the abduction, though no one has been able to provide any evidence that Meciar was directly involved. On the other hand, President Kovác had rejected Ivan Lexa, the head of the security service, for the post of privatization minister in 1993. It is widely believed that he may have arranged the kidnapping because he held a grudge against President Kovác. The president said later that accusations and attacks against him had begun in 1993, though he never publicly claimed that there was a political motive behind the abduction. One other thing that ties Meciar to the kidnapping is that he granted pardons to all persons involved after he took over as acting president in March 1998.

Meciar never hesitated to use appeals to Slovak nationalism to consolidate his support. In 1995, this led him to push through a new language law aimed at restricting the rights of minorities, and particularly the Hungarian minority, to use their national language. This made it illegal for radio or television broadcasts, advertising and official government information to be in anything other than Slovak. In August 1997, Meciar carried his antipathy to Hungarian-speakers even further when he officially suggested to Gyula Horn, the Hungarian prime minister, that ethnic Hungarian-speakers be repatriated to Hungary. As he put it at a party rally in Bratislava, "those people who do not want to be Slovak citizens [should] go to Hungary and live there." Subsequently, the Slovak National Party and the Slovak Workers' Party, the two junior parties in the ruling coalition, endorsed Meciar's proposal, characterizing it as a "possible and constructive solution."

POLITICAL SYSTEM

The independent Slovak Republic came into being on January 1, 1993. It is a parliamentary democracy, with the leading political office that of the prime minister. Adopted by the Slovak National Council (renamed in 1992 the National Council of the Slovak Republic) in July 1992, Slovakia's constitution formally designates the country as the Slovak Republic. It created a 150-seat assembly as the nation's legislature. The Slovak Republic is a young democracy with many parties competing for parliamentary seats. For example, in the 2010 elections 18 parties entered the race. In order to reduce the number of parties and enable a more stable coalition government to be created, the constitution requires that a party win at least 5% of the total vote in order to qualify for any seats in the assembly; in 2010 this reduced the number of parties in parliament to six. Voters choose from party lists, and seats are distributed according to proportional representation.

The parliament building itself is woefully inadequate as a modern legislative facility. It had not been built in the mid-1980s as a democratic parliament building. It is too small to contain offices for individual members of parliament and their staffs and has a very small visitors' gallery. Thus it needs to be redesigned internally, and an additional building must be constructed for office space.

The Presidency

The constitution bestows on the assembly the right to elect the head of state, to be known as the president of the republic. The legislature amended this constitutional provision on January 14, 1999, to provide for the election of the president by direct popular vote. The bill stipulated that if no presidential candidates receive more than 50% of the voters in the popular vote, a runoff between the two candidates with the most votes would take place two weeks later.

President Ivan Gasparovic

Prime Minister Iveta Radicova

While still prime minister, Vladimír Meciar wanted to be elected president. He tried to capture the presidency in 1998 and 1999. He failed both times, losing in 1999 to Rudolf Schuster, who became the first popularly elected president. Even his second defeat did not drive Meciar from the political arena as many had hoped. He recognized that about the only thing holding the government coalition together was opposition to himself and his policies.

He tried again in April 2004, winning the first round with 33% of the votes. A relative unknown came in second—Ivan Gasparovic, his one-time lieutenant and parliamentary speaker, who had broken with him in 2002. In the second round, Gasparovic surged ahead, winning 60% of the votes to Meciar's 40%, with a low turnout of 43.5%. Meciar lost his cool in a TV debate, reminding voters of what a bully and loose cannon he can be. Gasparovic had the support of leftwing populist Robert Fico. He won reelection in April 2009, winning 55.5% of the votes to Iveta Radicova's 44.5%.

Parties and Parliamentary Elections

The September 2002 elections were very important both for Slovakia and for NATO and the EU. If the favorite, Vladimír Meciar, had won, it was certain that the country would not have been admitted to these elite organizations. The United States Agency for International Development (USAID) and nongovernmental organizations from the United States poured more than $1.2 into campaigns to encourage Slovaks to vote for the moderate democratic parties that would be welcome in the Western community of nations. The results were a great relief, as 70% of eligible voters turned out to reelect the existing government.

Although Meciar's Movement for a Democratic Slovakia (HZDS), renamed in 2000 the HZDS-People's Party, did well in the 2002 elections, no party would form a coalition with it. His erratic behavior during the campaign did not help him. When a television reporter asked him, a former boxer, how he financed the $1 million in improvements to his luxurious home, he punched the man in the face. Asked the same question during a TV discussion, he stormed off the stage. Meciar had been placed under arrest in 2000 after he had refused to cooperate with investigators in connection with charges that he had paid $350,000 in bribes, called "illegal bonuses," to cabinet members when he was head of the government. Investigators also asked him about the kidnapping of the son of the Slovak president in 1995.

Meciar's voters tended to be easterners, rural folk, pensioners and low-paid workers longing for the social benefits, simple lives and guaranteed jobs communism

once offered them. They are gradually dying out. After the 2006 elections, HZDS entered Robert Fico's leftist *Smer* governing coalition. In 2010, HZDS was obliterated at the polls and failed to win its way into parliament. It is likely to die.

Also in Fico's coalition government was the radical right-wing Slovak National Party (SNS), led by firebrand Jan Slota. Slota himself was excluded from the cabinet, in part because he is widely considered a racist who cannot control his intemperate tongue. He once said that the best way of dealing with the country's 520,000 Roma (Gypsies) was with "a long whip in a small yard." His other favorite target is the Hungarian minority. He once recommended that Slovaks "get in tanks and level Budapest." It did surprisingly well in 2006. But it experienced near disaster in 2010, winning only 5% (down from 11.73%) of the votes and 9 seats (down from 20). It is in the opposition.

Emerging as the big winner in June 2006 was Róbert Fico's left-leaning *Smer* (Direction), which more than doubled its votes to 29% and 50 seats. To acquire a majority, he had to form a coalition with the two nationalist parties above. Their inclusion in the government was strongly criticized outside the country and led to his party being shunned by fellow socialists in the rest of Europe. His coalition was isolated internationally. Despite gains, he could not hold on to a majority in 2010 thanks to the collapse of his two partners. *Smer* climbed to 35% and 62 seats, but it was consigned to the opposition.

A lawyer and former Communist youth activist, who had joined the Communist party shortly before the Soviet system collapsed, he promises law and order and an

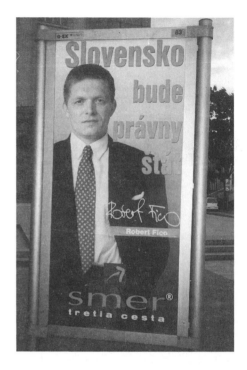

undoing of his predecessor's reforms, he had resigned in 1999 from the Party of the Democratic Left, the successor party of the Slovak Communist Party, after a disagreement on policy. He subsequently joined with several of the more pragmatic members of his former party to create a new center-left party, *Smer*. Although a committed socialist, he retains a populist and nationalist streak that bothers many people. Hoping to benefit from widespread dissatisfaction caused by the economic downturn, for which his government bore much of the blame, he tried in vain to play the nationalist card in 2010.

Parliament in Bratislava

Slovakia

Fico had a prickly relationship with the media. His populist-nationalist government enacted a "right-of-reply" law in 2008 that is Eastern Europe's most punitive and arbitrary. If anybody in a newspaper story complains, the editor must print the response without a rebuttal. He referred to some daily papers as "prostitutes."

The Slovak Democratic and Christian Union (SDKU-DS) government of Mikulás Dzurinda had won power in 2002 by promising to lead Slovakia into Europe and make it rich. Its reforms were dramatic and won praise throughout Europe, leading to full EU membership in May 2004. From 2002 to 2004 it passed more than 150 key reform laws. It introduced a 19% flat tax for profits and incomes, thereby encouraging foreign investments, which poured into the country. Local authorities can assess and collect taxes for their own budgets. It brought about a more flexible labor code and American-style welfare reforms. It reformed the pension system, introducing new personal accounts run by private companies for 9% of wages. The retirement age was raised to 62, and incentives for working longer were created. Health care was reformed, and unemployment fell.

The SDKU government's measures laid the groundwork for the country's continuing economic growth. But it failed to prepare Slovaks for the pain caused by the transition, and it lost power in June 2006. Its reforms were good for the country but hard on many individual Slovaks, especially in the eastern part of the country.

However, 4 years later, in June 2010, Slovaks were again ready for SDKU leadership. Now led by Prime Minister Iveta Radicova, it captured 15.5% (down from 18.35%) of the votes and 28 seats (a loss of three). A sociology professor nicknamed the "Tatra Tigress," she is the country's first woman prime minister and one of the rare female politicians in the region.

She was able to construct a governing coalition with three other market- and reform-friendly center-right parties: A new party led by Bela Bugar and representing the large Hungarian minority, Most-Hid (derived from the Slovak and Hungarian words for "bridge"), seeks to bridge the ethnic divide. It won 8% of the votes and 14 seats. Bugar had earlier led the now deflated Hungarian Coalition Party (SMK), which failed to clear the 5% hurdle. The Christian Democratic Movement (KDH), led by former European Commissioner for Education, Jan Figel, garnered 8.5% of the votes and 15 mandates (a gain of one). It focuses on the rule of law and fight against crime. Finally Richard Sulik led another new party, Freedom and Solidarity (SAS), into parliament, capturing 12% of the votes and 22 seats. Turnout was 58.8%. The new

Presidential Palace Bratislava

government seeks to repair the public finances through leaner government and to mend the country's relationship with Hungary, which has been rattled over questions of language and citizenship. It seeks a greater measure of ethnic harmony.

Foreign Policy

Slovakia's most important foreign relations are naturally those with the Czech Republic. Having agreed to a peaceful separation into two independent nations, the Czechs and Slovaks nevertheless recognized that their economies would be tightly bound to each other for some time and that it would be wise to retain certain elements of the former union if they could. These would include a common currency and a customs union that would allow for the free movement of goods. In addition, Czechs and Slovaks would not be required to show passports to pass from one country to another.

Although the common currency collapsed after less than two months, the customs union has survived. Trade between the two new republics fell off considerably following separation. It has since stabilized, but the decline in trade had a negative effect on both economies.

Czech-Slovak relations are on the mend. Former Prime Minister Mikulás Dzurinda worked assiduously to improve relations with all of Slovakia's neighbors and Serbia while in office from 2002–6. One reward came in October 2005, when Slovakia was overwhelmingly elected to a seat on the UN Security Council for 2006–7. This prestigious post made their country more visible in the world.

Of special importance is Slovakia's relations with Hungary, which had been es-

pecially bad under ex-prime ministers Meciar and Fico. There was disagreement over a new dam on the Danube River. Slovakia built the part it had agreed to construct, but Hungary backed out of an earlier joint agreement that it also build a part; the World Court in The Hague ruled that Hungary must finish its share of the dam, but that has yet to happen.

The more important issue was Meciar's attitude toward ethnic Hungarians. A Slovak chauvinist, he appeared to believe that allowing Slovakia's 560,000 ethnic Hungarians to use Magyar in areas where they constitute a significant percentage of the population would somehow diminish the Slovak language. His actions to limit such use prevented good relations with Hungary. In fact, it was never forbidden to use Hungarian. The question was whether to require all civil servants to speak Slovak. There are Hungarian-language schools and generally a good system of minority schools although Bratislava never granted the right to a Hungarian-language university. Unlike the older generation of ethnic Hungarians, younger ones are more likely to speak Slovak, though not well.

The Slovak parliament endorsed the Benes decrees in 2007, which had been directed against both the German and Hungarian populations in 1945–48. Plans for a joint Slovak-Hungarian history textbook were put on hold and later scrapped. Some Hungarian schoolbooks still refer to Slovakia as "Upper Hungary." The Fico government went out of its way to needle Hungary.

In September 2009 it enacted a new language law that criminalized the public use of Hungarian in areas where Hungarians do not constitute at least 80% of the local

Main Street Bratislava

with blackouts. Desperate for reliable power, it is exploring new ways to reopen its nuclear reactors, which it had to shut down as a condition for entry into the EU. Austria is a fierce critic of Slovakia's Jaslovske Bohunice nuclear-power plant.

The focus of the Slovak government since 1998 was on building relations with Western Europe that would eventually earn it invitations to join NATO and the European Union. That did not necessarily mean that Slovakia's relations with eastern countries were neglected.

In 2002 came the sought-after invitation to join the EU. Slovaks went to polls in May 2003 and overwhelmingly approved their country's entry into the EU: 92.46% voted for EU membership and only 6.2% were against. Their leaders were shocked that only 52.1% turned out to vote, but the referendum, the first ever to succeed since independence, was not binding. Parliament had the final say, and the vote there was 129 to ten. Those lawmakers opposed were the Communists, who had previously supported joining, but they argued that the terms negotiated for entry should have been more favorable.

Former Prime Minister Dzurinda was very pleased, saying that it was the "first time in the history of our country when we had decided about our path ourselves. We're entering a completely new era as a part of a united Europe." The daily newspaper *Sme* noted: "After integration Slovakia will no longer be the West of the East, but the East of the West." Formal entry occurred in May 2004. One year later it ratified the ill-fated European constitution. In July 2007 a Slovak diplomat, Miroslav Lajcak, assumed the position of Bosnia's high representative; this powerful post always goes to a representative of an EU country. However, the government opposes the majority of its fellow EU countries by not recognizing Kosovo's independence. Slovakia completed its EU integration in January 2009 by becoming the 16th member state to adopt the euro. This came just in the knick of time to help cushion its economy during its worst global economic downturn since the end of communism.

One of the obligations of membership is that it must secure its eastern border with Ukraine, where more than 40,000 illegal immigrants cross each year. This is a favorite route for smugglers because the heavily forested and mountainous border is difficult to police, and it is a short journey to the Austrian or Czech frontiers. An added problem is corruption. An estimated 10% of police are on a retainer from criminal gangs.

Eastern ties were temporarily affected by the NATO air war against Yugoslavia. Interviewed during the NATO summit in

population. Hefty fines (up to $8,000) were levied against those who use a minority language in "official business," including with police officers, teachers or doctors. Even Hungarian-language schools must conduct their administration in Slovak. It had to be the most visible language on all signs, monuments and even grave stones. All cultural events not in Slovak were required to provide simultaneous Slovak translations. Even Hungarian president, Laszlo Solyom, was prevented in August 2009 from crossing the Slovak border to unveil a statue of St. Stephen. This violated the EU's rules on freedom of movement. The latter had been the first king of Hungary and has a bad reputation in Slovakia for having been an avid promoter of Hungarian identity.

Payback time came when a populist Viktor Orban, of the Fidesz party, won the Hungarian elections in April 2010. His first piece of serious legislation was to grant Hungarian citizenship to the 2.5 million Hungarians living outside of Hungary. The then Slovak government retorted that Slovaks who fail to report such dual citizenship would be fined more than $4,000

and would probably automatically lose their Slovak passport. Fico's successor as prime minister, Iveta Radicova, announced her government's intention to scrap the law that strips Slovaks of their passports if they accept dual Hungarian citizenship. Her coalition generally seeks smoother relations with its southern neighbor. Economic relations are excellent.

Relations have improved with countries east of Slovakia, such as Russia, Belarus, and Ukraine. One factor operating here is the tendency among Slovak nationalists to stress pan-Slavic cooperation. More importantly, however, Slovakia encouraged a rebuilding of trade ties eastward.

Former Prime Minister Fico took a positive approach to Russia, stressing that Slovakia wants good relations. But he desired to keep those dealings in the "economic dimension." Slovakia gets almost all of its gas and oil from Russia. The Transpetrol pipeline (owned 51% by Slovakia and 49% by Yukos) crosses Slovakia to bring Russian crude oil to Central Europe. The government had to declare a state of emergency in January 2009 when a shortage of gas threatened the country

Slovakia

Washington in April 1999, ex-Prime Minister Dzurinda said that Slovakia was acting as a "de facto ally" of NATO. After his return to Bratislava, the government gave NATO permission to use "any Slovak means of transportation" in connection with its air campaign against Yugoslavia. Such statements infuriated the Russian and Belarussian governments, both of which had been adamant in their condemnation of NATO actions against Yugoslavia. At its Prague Summit in November 2002, NATO formally invited Slovakia to join the alliance, an invitation the government accepted without hesitation. It entered in April 2004.

In February 2005, a crowd of 4,000 Slovaks waited in the snow in Bratislava's central square for two hours to cheer President Bush's talk of freedom and praise for their country as a model for emerging democracies. During the same visit the presidents of the United States and Russia held a summit meeting. Dzurinda and Bush got along famously and have several things in common: both are joggers, and the prime minister had run the New York City marathon in 2001 and had cycled around his country in 2005. Each also has two daughters and enjoyed discussing the complications of raising girls.

Ex-Prime Minister Fico changed the tone of U.S.-Slovak relations. He favored a more accommodating approach to Russia, and he promised not to "rely on only a one-sided relationship with the USA, but to base our policy on European foreign policy." However, he was aware that most Central Europeans are convinced that the U.S. remains their ultimate security guarantor, including against Russia. That is why Slovakia's commitment to the transatlantic alliance is not questioned and why he claimed that he is pursuing a foreign policy of continuity. Fico opposed the planned U.S. missile defense shield that was to be built in Poland and the Czech Republic. "We are not happy with rockets and radars in Europe." President Obama scrapped those plans in 2009.

Slovakia maintains an active military force of 16,531, including conscripts who serve for six months. The army has 7,322 troops that include a rapid-reaction battalion. The 4,190-man air force flies old Soviet MiGs. Slovakia has cancelled all its defense contracts with Russia. It dispatched 196 peacekeepers to Cyprus, 147 to Kosovo, 34 to Bosnia and 245 to Afghanistan. It supported the American-British war effort in Iraq in 2003 and deployed to Kuwait a nuclear, biological and chemical (NBC) team that was incorporated in a Czech NBC unit; it also sent 110 de-mining engineers to Iraq itself. Polls show that three-quarters of Slovaks opposed this deployment. That made it eas-

Just married in Bratislava

ier for Fico, who called the war "unjust and wrong," to withdraw the country's tiny contingent from Iraq in 2007.

ECONOMY

Privatization was instituted as a national policy after the fall of communism, but the actual implementation was always in the hands of the Slovak government. Much of Slovakia's industry was built during the communist era. It is large-scale and has had difficulty competing during the transition to a market economy. There is, for example, an extremely large arms industry. Fears about the fate of its heavily subsidized plants helped fuel the Slovak separatist movement that resulted in the break-up of Czechoslovakia in 1993.

Privatization was always a much more controversial policy in Slovakia than in the Czech Republic, and Vladimír Meciar brought it to a halt after Slovakia achieved its independence. Yet stopping it had a negative effect on the economy. Under Meciar, GDP declined while unemployment climbed to 14.4% and inflation soared to 22%. This led to Meciar's ouster as prime minister in March 1994.

Back in power, Meciar reinstituted subsidies and raised governmental salaries and pensions. In effect, he returned Slovakia as much as he was able to the economic policies of the communist era. There were also some privatizations, but their purpose was to turn economic assets over to his supporters and allies. Slovakian economic statistics tended to look

good because Meciar kept communist-era factories running. Even when there were no customers for their goods, this eventually produced large budget and current-account deficits that threatened future growth. A study of the Slovakian economy issued by the Organization for Economic Cooperation and Development (OECD) in 1999 concluded that Slovakia was on the verge of a crisis and that it needed to implement policy changes in order to sustain growth levels.

In 1999 the new government of Mikulás Dzurinda approved a plan designed to stabilize the economy and to enhance foreign investment. The difficulty was to implement it. The Dzurinda government was a somewhat unwieldy coalition whose chief common goal had been to defeat Meciar. All parties were committed to bringing Slovakia into NATO and the EU, but they disagreed about specific policies. The government raised prices on such things as electricity in order to cut the budget deficit. Currently 90% of all electric power is produced by Slovenske Elektrarne, a state-owned company. Slovakia has nuclear power plants that generate electricity. Renewable sources account for 7% of its total energy.

Central controls kept prices for consumers artificially low, but this had to change after Slovakia joined the EU. All banks and insurance companies were state-owned. But during the two prime ministerial terms of Dzurinda from 1998, all state-owned banks, the main insurer, the gas industry, the oil pipe-line operator and Slovak Telecom were privatized.

The global economic crisis that began in the fall of 2008 and affected all advanced economies with a vengeance in 2009 was bound to hurt Slovakia, whose dependence on auto sales and exports to Germany is so great. The finance minister moaned: "We are totally dependent on exports, mainly to Germany." After all, it is the world's biggest per capita car producer. Its GDP contracted by 4.7% in 2009. The GDP of Germany, its main customer, fell at the same time. Slovakia's economy had boomed until the recession. Unemployment was at a record low of 7.3% in 2008, but it rose to 11.8% in 2009. Although joblessness was only about 3% in prosperous Bratislava, whose citizens' per capita income is about 90% of the EU average (compared with 70% in Slovakia as a whole), unemployment is closer to 20% outside the capital, the highest rate in Central Europe. In the depressed eastern part of the country, unemployment rises to a distressing 40%.

Economic growth had been 7.5% in 2008 and was Europe's fastest until it dived to minus 4.7% a year later. Inflation had fallen to 3.3% in 2008 and .6% in 2009. The

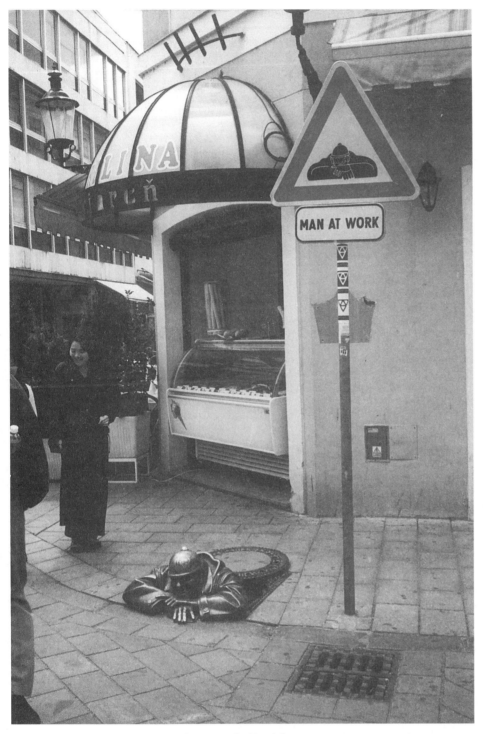

Street art in Bratislava

make Slovakia an attractive target for investment. It has the region's lowest wages. In 2007 the average monthly wage was 450 euros ($585). Slovakia's wages are about 20% of Western European and German levels. More than half of Slovaks indicate in polls that they cannot save money from their incomes because they have to spend 47% on food and a third on housing.

Induced by generous subsidies, U.S. Steel agreed to invest $480 million to revamp Slovakia's largest mill in Kocice on the southeastern edge of the country. The Zdeno Velky Steel Mill had been built in the 1950s to supply Czechoslovak weapons plants and industry throughout the Soviet bloc. After 1989 it had invested millions in up-to-date equipment from the West in order to make itself internationally competitive. Its extensive efforts to find new markets for its steel paid off initially, but its very success proved its undoing. In 1992, the EU imposed strict trade limits on steel imports from Eastern Europe, including Czechoslovakia. U.S. Steel's investment saved it. When the EU challenged in 2004 the subsidies it had received, U.S. Steel agreed to return $32 million to the Slovak state.

Foreign investment was so hot by 2005 that industrial and prime office rents in Bratislava were already higher than in nearby Vienna. Despite a fall in real estate values during the recession (up to 40% for residential housing in 2009), many Slovaks are buying housing on the Austrian side of the border because it is much cheaper than in or around the Slovak capital.

In 2003 South Korea's Samsung Electronics Slovakia (SESK) was inaugurated in Galanta, 70 kilometers from Bratislava, where 3,000 local workers will be employed. It will be the company's bridgehead to Central and Eastern European markets. The Hungarian oil and gas company (MOL) and Whirlpool have invested. Hewlett-Packard, Dell and IBM have also outsourced operations in Slovakia; Dell located its largest European headquarters in Bratislava, employing 2,100 people.

The capital is also the base for Sky-Europe, Central Europe's first low-cost airlines. When the divorce with the Czech Republic occurred in 1993, Slovakia was deprived of a national carrier. Now Sky-Europe accounts for half the air traffic at Bratislava airport and operates 79 routes in 19 countries. However, it is in trouble because of the global economic downturn. It is buffeted by high fuel prices and a probable shake-out among the excessive number of European airlines. In 2007 the final link in the Vienna-Bratislava Autobahn (freeway) was completed. This came

budget deficit had fallen to 2.1% of GDP in 2008, but it rose to 6.8% the next year. Foreign debt stood at 33% of GDP in 2007.

Slovakia got the nod from the European Commission that it could join the eurozone in January 2009. The prospect of joining was an incentive for the government to pursue sound economic policies. It is a remarkable turnaround for a country that was once a backwater to become the first

country from the old Warsaw Pact to adopt the euro.

Foreign investment is healthy. One result is that the economy is dominated by foreigners, who control most banks and important industries. This stimulates growth, which increases tax revenues and reduces the budget deficit. EU membership, relative cheap labor, and a lowering of the corporate tax rate to 19% in 2003,

Slovakia

just in time for Slovakia's joining the EU's Schengen open-border regime in December. However, city bus traffic across the border still does not exist.

Slovakia is becoming the "Detroit" of Central Europe. Volkswagen already has a major plant in Bratislava, which is the country's largest private employer. A joint venture of Toyota, Peugeot and Citroen built a new automotive plant in Trnava, western Slovakia. In 2004 Slovakia lured South Korean Hyundai affiliate, Kia Motors, as well as more investment from Peugeot and Citroen. When all these plants became fully running in 2007, they produced 850,000 cars a year, the most of any Central European country and the most per capita in the world. Slovakia hopes to be producing one car for each six citizens, most for export; 50,000 Slovaks were in the automobile industry in 2005. Some fear that this is too much dependence on the automotive sector since it already constitutes 26.5% of industrial output and 30.7% of industrial exports, rising to 50%. Indeed, the downturn in Western Europe's car market in 2009 dragged Slovakia's auto industry down with it.

To supply the assembly plants, a rapidly growing parts industry is developing. In 2005 there were 140 automotive suppliers. Ten South Korean components makers announced investments in that year. The proximity of U.S. Steel in Kocice provides a ready source of high quality steel. An American components producer, Johnson Controls, launched what the government hopes will become a trend: a $26 million technology center in the northwest city of Trencin that will ultimately employ 600. All this provides important stimuli to

the country's education system. In 2005 fees were raised at universities in an attempt to improve their quality. Students pay up to $1,000 per year, but loans and need-based scholarships are available.

Privatization in the area of agriculture was almost fully implemented prior to Slovakia's independence because the federal government had strenuously pursued agricultural transformation. Federal legislation legally transformed collective farms into cooperatives and stipulated that employees had the right to ask for their own land. Most Slovak peasants opted to remain a part of the cooperative structure, however, with only a tiny minority requesting their own land. Even those few who asked for their own acres mostly wanted only a couple of acres to work for themselves. Agriculture is an area where the government feels little need to make changes. Slovakia is gradually developing into a modern economy, with 57% of the workforce in services (producing 55.1% of GDP), 39% in industry (41.1% of GDP), and only 4% in agriculture (3.7% of GDP). There are some worries about economic competitiveness. A 2005 study by the Swiss-based Institute for Management Development ranked Slovakia 40th of 60 countries examined, behind Hungary and the Czech Republic.

The Slovak Arms Industry

In the decade from 1978 to 1988, Czechoslovakia was the world's eighth largest weapons exporter and the global leader in per capita terms. More than 100 plants produced various types of weaponry ranging from Skorpion machine pistols to L-39 jet trainers, exported to Czechoslovakia's

Warsaw Pact partners and Third World countries. Most of these plants were located in central Slovakia, which became the center of Czechoslovakia's heavy arms industry. By 1989, military production represented nearly 60% of total industrial production in Slovakia and provided employment for more than 100,000 persons.

"These plants were put up in green meadows," says Josef Fucik, head of the department for conversion of military production in the federal ministry of economics in Prague. "It was a quick fix in the '50s to give modern jobs to Slovakia. Now the bill has come due." The town of Martin, 230 km north of Bratislava, was the site of a tank plant that employed 11,000; nearby Dubnica built armored personnel carriers, while Povazská Bystríca, down the road, produced jet engines.

Two months after the 1989 revolution, Foreign Minister Jirí Dienstbier announced that Prague would "simply end its trade in arms" without regard to economic consequences. That turned out to be impossible. With so many jobs dependent on arms production, the bulk of them in a depressed region of Slovakia, the government had to modify its plans. Still, it remained pledged to cut the output of weapons plants to 25% of 1988 levels by 1993. Slovak politicians strenuously opposed the cuts, and this became a major issue in the push for Slovak independence. They did everything they could to frustrate the policy in the interim period and then reversed the policy in 1993.

While the government halted all efforts to convert arms factories to civilian production, it did not find it easy to carry out its stated policy of keeping its arms industry intact. There was, for example, no domestic demand for tanks since Slovakia is obligated by the terms of the Conventional Forces in Europe (CFE) agreement to destroy some of its current tanks. In the past, three-quarters of all arms exports went to former Warsaw Pact allies. Those sales disappeared as these countries cut their military budgets. The Soviet Union, once Czechoslovakia's largest customer, cancelled almost all purchase orders in 1991 when it would have been required to pay for such purchases in hard currency. Its subsequent collapse had a psychological effect in Czechoslovakia, but it had already ceased to be a major arms purchaser prior to that.

There have been some sales to Third World countries, but Slovakia is at a disadvantage because it produces mainly heavy battlefield weapons, not the small arms and specialized explosives most in demand in the developing world. Worse, all of Slovakia's major weapons systems are produced on license from Russia, which in many cases is competing in the

THE SLOVAK SPECTATOR

Slovak news you can trust

Vol. 14, No. 19   Monday, May 19, 2008 - Sunday, May 25, 2008   40 Sk

Top cop borrowed surveillance device

Minister says he wanted to be sure it couldn't be used for wiretapping

By Tom Nicholson
Spectator staff

SLOVAKIA'S top anti-mafia cop, Michal Kopčík, has admitted borrowing some police surveillance equipment in early April, but denied allegations by former Interior minister Vladimír Palko that he broke the law in doing so.

According to documents obtained by *The Slovak Spectator*, Daniel Tichý of the Special Police Operations branch, which is responsible for surveillance and wiretapping, noticed in early April that a surveillance device known as the 'Bulldog' had been used on six occasions from April 5-8 without authorisation. Tichý informed his superiors of the finding.

The Bulldog is a briefcase-sized device that allows the operator to locate GSM network

see BUG page 3

Prime Minister Robert Fico met part of Slovakia's ice-hockey team, which suffered some surprise defeats at the World Ice-Hockey Championship in Canada, ending up in 13th place. Fico told them that things like this happen and that he believes that next year their performance will be much better.

Ex-Prime Minister Robert Fico meets members of Slovakia's national ice-hockey team

same markets with more advanced weapons systems.

Efforts made before independence to convert parts of Slovak heavy industry to peaceful purposes were not very successful. An exception was the conversion of the ZTS Martin ("Turcanské Strojárne" factory, located in the city of Martin), a tank manufacturer. It negotiated an agreement with the German firm Hanomag to manufacture earthmoving equipment. The company also began working under license from the Italian manufacturer Lombardini to produce tractor engines and other machinery. In this instance, military production was reduced to one-quarter of overall manufactures.

CULTURE

There has always been a separate Slovak culture. Part of the Hungarian Kingdom from the 11th century, Slovaks were a peasant people heavily influenced by Hungarian culture. Slovakia is particularly known for its unique and lively folk music and dances, performed in brightly-colored traditional dress. Slovakia has changed greatly in recent years, however, and many parts of the country are now urbanized and industrialized. Bratislava became the seat of the European Music Academy and sponsors many music and theater festivals.

The works of individual Slovak artists and craftsmen compare favorably with that of other Europeans. On the other hand, because many Slovaks live in small towns or in the countryside itself, Slovak art often has more of a peasant quality about it. There is also not as large an audience for art, so artists tend to be more marginalized.

Religion

The old communist regime was extremely hostile to religion, and it went out of its way to make its practice difficult. The regime particularly restricted the Catholic Church, to which most Slovaks belong, probably because it is part of an international organization. Since the 1989 revolution, the Catholic Church has revealed that it maintained an underground church in Slovakia during those years. This involved such things as secretly providing theological training in private apartments and homes and ordaining hundreds of individuals as priests who then continued to work in their regular jobs while performing their priestly functions in secret.

As this underground church has emerged, people were surprised to learn of the double lives some of these individuals had been living. As an example, five faculty members at the communist-run Kocice University were actually Jesuit priests, including the dean of the School of Civil Engineering. It also turns out that a large percentage of the priests belong to religious orders like the Dominicans, Jesuits and Salesians, all of which were banned by the communists. There were even some married men ordained as priests, plus some women who became deacons.

The church is now attempting to sort out all of these anomalies.

FUTURE

Slovakia has made impressive economic progress since 1998, when the electorate put in power a coalition of parties committed to modernity and integration into the rest of Europe. Voters opened the way to NATO and EU membership in 2004.

The earlier Dzurinda's government until 2006 was unpopular because of painful economic restructuring and austerity. But these measures were partly responsible for the continuing impressive economic growth and adoption of the euro in 2009. Voters were not impressed by his supply-side reforms, including a 19% flat tax that provided the groundwork for strong growth and admiration abroad. The coalition fell in 2006.

Parliamentary elections in May 2010 returned a market-friendly four-party center-right coalition, led by Slovakia's first female prime minister, Iveta Radicova. Slovakia's first leftist prime minister after the end of communism, Robert Fico, and his *Smer* party returned to the opposition benches. He was accompanied by Jan Slota's shrunken xenophobic anti-Hungarian nationalists, who had strained the country's relations with its southern neighbor. The new government vows to improve those important ties. Meciar's old HZDS failed to win any parliamentary seats. Slovakia is on a new political track.

Ultra-right demonstrating in Bratislava

Hungarian Republic

Parliament on the Danube, Budapest

Area: 35,919 sq. mi. (93,030 sq. km.).
Population: 10 million
Capital City: Budapest (Pop. 1,734,000).
Climate: Continental, with long, dry summers and severe winters.
Neighboring Countries: Slovakia (North); Ukraine (East); Romania (Southeast); Serbia, Croatia (South); Slovenia, Austria (West).
Official Language: Hungarian (Magyar), a Finno-Ugrian language related to Finnish
Other Principal Tongues: Languages of small minorities, German, Serbo-Croat, Slovak, Romanian
Ethnic Background: Magyar (ca. 90%) Roma (Gypsy—6%–8%); German (2%), Jewish (0.7%) other (1%).
Principal Religions: Roman Catholic and Protestant Christianity
Chief Commercial Products: Machinery and transport equipment, agricultural and forest products, raw materials including fuels, minerals, metals.
Chief Trading Partners: EU (79% of exports and 69.5% of imports), Germany (28.2% of exports and 26.8% of imports), Italy (5.6% of exports), Austria (6.1% of imports), France (4.7% of exports), Russia (6.9% of imports), China (7.8% of imports), Slovakia (4.7% of exports).
Currency: Forint (HUF).
Former Political Status: Independent, 1918–1945; Communist State, part of Soviet Bloc, 1945–1990.
National Day: October 23
Chief of State: László Sólyom, President (June 2005)

Head of Government: Viktor Orbán, Prime Minister (April 2010).
National Flag: Horizontal red, white and green stripes.

Hungarians captured the world's attention and admiration in 1956 when they rose up against an alien unwanted master and courageously fought with stones and their bare hands against the well-armed occupation troops and their tanks. This heroic struggle failed, but it helped persuade the communist rulers to liberalize the regime and to permit reform that was daring when compared to what was allowed elsewhere in the Soviet empire. When the old European order finally crumbled in 1989, Hungary was more prepared for the new order than any other Central or Eastern European country.

The Republic of Hungary lies in the Middle Danube Basin. Two great rivers, the Danube and the Tisza, cross the rolling plains that cover most of the country. The Danube—one of Hungary's few natural frontiers—provides part of the border between Hungary and Slovakia, then turns sharply southward, passes through Budapest, and divides Hungary. Contrary to legend, its waters are not blue, but are usually brown because of the presence of silt from upstream areas.

To the east of the river lies the Hungarian Plain, a vast fertile land that explains why Hungary was called the granary of the Austro-Hungarian Empire. The northeast section along the Slovak border is covered with forested mountains, abun-

dant with wildlife. Here one can find limestone caverns and Europe's largest stalactite caves. Most importantly, the northeast contains Hungary's famous wine-producing centers, Eger and Tokaj. West of the Danube, plains turn into hills where the easternmost part of the Alps reaches into western Hungary.

Although there are several theories concerning the origins of the Hungarians, it is generally agreed that they are a Finno-Ugric people. They speak a language distantly related to Finnish and Estonian although Hungarians cannot understand those Nordic tongues. In early historic times, they were first found inhabiting a part of the Russian Plain west of the Ural Mountains. Apparently suffering attacks from even more aggressive neighbors, several Hungarian tribes migrated westward, crossed the Carpathian Mountains and settled the broad plain that spreads out from the Danube River east and south of the present-day city of Budapest.

HISTORY

Origins of the Hungarian State

Initially led by Arpad, for whom the first dynasty of Hungary was named, the Hungarians did not immediately settle down in Central Europe. They terrorized most of the surrounding people until the 10th century when the German Emperor Otto I defeated them. Although there was earlier Christian missionary work among the Hungarians, Stephen I of the Arpad Dynasty "converted" the whole nation on

St. Stephen on Heroes Square, Budapest

Christmas Day, 1000 A.D. when he accepted a cross and crown sent by Pope Sylvester II. After his death, the Church proclaimed him a saint in 1083.

The Crown of St. Stephen later became the symbol of highest authority. It represented the "unity" of all lands claimed by Hungary, including those not inhabited solely by Hungarians. During the 10th century, Slovakia was conquered; by 1003 Transylvania was under the Crown, and a century later, Croatia, Slavonia and Dalmatia were united with Hungary. By the late 14th century, the Kingdom of Hungary contained extensive areas inhabited by Saxons (Germans), Slavs, Vlachs (Romanians of Wallachia), and Székelys (Transylvanian Magyars—the Hungarian word for "Hungarians"—living in the Carpathian Mountains).

During the Middle Ages, Hungary was not isolated from the rest of Europe. At the end of the 12th century, a dynastic connection with France was established when King Béla III married the daughter of the French king; the marriage settlement showed that Hungary's national treasury equaled that of France. Hungary's early constitutional development resembled England's. The Hungarian king was forced to sign a document called the Golden Bull in 1222 which guaranteed the rights of the nobility, similar to the English *Magna Charta*.

A Mongol invasion in 1241 devastated Hungary and resulted in the loss of one-half of the population. However, the Mongols remained only for a year, so their oc-

cupation did not influence Hungary as it would Russia.

The Arpad Dynasty ended in 1301, and for two centuries foreign nobility ruled Hungary. In the 15th century, one of Hungary's greatest kings, Mathias Corvinus, ascended the throne. An enlightened Renaissance monarch, he reformed the country's administrative and judicial systems, reorganized the army, founded universities and preserved Hungary's position as an important European power.

A Part of the Multi-National Habsburg Empire

Hungary's defeat by the Ottoman Turks in 1526 was a turning point in the nation's history. After a period of civil war, the Turks incorporated the central part into their empire, while the Habsburgs claimed the western part. A third region, consisting of Transylvania and 16 neighboring counties, became a self-governing principality. This area eventually became known as Transylvania and was the center of Hungarian culture over the next two centuries. It gave Hungary such heroes as Stephen Bocskay and Gabor Bethlen. Transylvania was a model of religious tolerance among the states of Europe. Its princes, backed by armies, spread the principle throughout the rest of Hungary, forcing its adoption as the law of the land.

Transylvania was the easternmost country to participate in the great spiritual movement of the 16th century called the Protestant Reformation. By the end of that century, 90% of all Hungarians were Protestant. In 1699, however, most of Hungary, Transylvania and Croatia passed from Turkish to Austrian hands by the

Hungary c. 1350

Hungary

Peace of Karlowitz. This led to the suppression of Protestantism, which had been tolerated by the Turks as a protection against the influence of the Roman Catholic Habsburgs. Even so, enough survived that the Protestants of Hungary and Transylvania still constitute the largest such grouping in Central and Eastern Europe.

Francis Rákóczy led a rebellion in 1703 against Habsburg domination. Although it was suppressed, it was a foretaste of the nationalist movement that shook the empire a century later. In 1740 it was Hungary that threw its support behind Maria Theresia when Frederick II of Prussia challenged her claims to the traditional Habsburg territories, guaranteed by the Pragmatic Sanction. Maria Theresia was crowned queen of Hungary at Pressburg (Bratislava), and it was Hungarian support that allowed her to retain all of the Habsburg territories with the exception of Silesia. Under Maria Theresia, Hungary had its own Diet or National Assembly, composed of a House of Magnates and a House of Deputies.

Failed Revolutions

In the 1830s and 1840s, Hungary's political climate became infused with the spirit of nationalism and reform. Radicals such as Lajos Kossuth began giving speeches in the Diet advocating independence from Austria. But even more moderate leaders advocated self-government within the empire. As the revolutionary movement spread in 1848, the Diet actually passed a program known as the April Laws, which, while retaining the Habsburgs as the ruling dynasty, made Hungary internally independent.

This did not satisfy the radicals, and in 1849, under Kossuth's leadership, they declared Hungary's complete independence. The revolution was successful at first since the Hungarian army had gone over to the side of the rebels. It failed in the end, however, when Tsar Nicholas I offered a Russian army to Austria to help put down the uprising. The next several years were a period of rigid centralization as Vienna attempted to prevent any such revolutionary outbreaks in the future.

During the years of suppression, an increasing number of Magyar leaders came to realize that complete independence was impossible and that a change in Hungary's status could come only within the context of continued Habsburg rule. Their chance came in 1866 when Austria stumbled into a war with Prussia. After Prussia had defeated Austria, Francis Deak, a moderate leader, presented a plan that became the basis for the Compromise of 1867, which created the Dual Monarchy. Franz Josef became kaiser of Austria and king of Hungary. Under such a system,

Rise Hungary! Revolution in 1848

Budapest: March 22, 1919. The pouring rain does not deter the celebration of Hungary's communist revolutionaries.

Austria and Hungary each had its own constitution and parliament, but there were common ministries for Finance, Foreign Affairs and War. The Compromise of 1867 provided the basis for relations between Austria and Hungary until 1918. It also ushered in the most prosperous era of Hungary's history up to that time, despite growing nationalist tensions.

Hungary supported the Central Powers (Germany and Austria) in World War I. At the beginning of the war, Hungarian leaders signed the so-called "Truce of God,"

under which they agreed to refrain from quarreling over domestic issues during the war. By 1916, however, the truce was broken as opposition to the war increased, and extremists began a propaganda campaign against the war. Two years later, one of these leaders, Michael Karolyi, became head of the government in a war-weary defeated country. In 1918 this government proclaimed Hungary a republic, but it lasted only five months.

The Hungarian communists were made up mainly of soldiers who learned about

Hungary

Admiral Horthy

Kalvin Square in Budapest, 1930s

Composer Béla Bartók recording folk songs, 1907

Marxism while prisoners of war in Russia. They had no political experience, nor had any of them held any important post in the Hungarian labor movement during the prewar period. Released at the end of the war, they formed the main body of the Hungarian Communist Party, which was founded in November 1918. As their message of peace and prosperity began spreading among the mass of unemployed workers and soldiers, the government attempted to suppress the activities of the party by imprisoning its local leaders. Among them was Béla Kun, who had been a prisoner of war in Russia, fought in the Russian Civil War on the communist side, then organized the Hungarian section of the Soviet Communist Party and played a leading role in founding its Hungarian counterpart.

While in prison, the communists managed to come to an agreement with some prominent members of the Social Democratic Party, the strongest political group in the country at this time. This led to a merger of the two parties. When the Karolyi government resigned on March 20, 1919, because it was unwilling to accept the diminished territories proposed by the allies, the merged party under Béla Kun was able to come to power the next day without a violent revolution.

Béla Kun became the head of the new communist government, which took the name of the Hungarian Soviet Republic. It immediately nationalized all banks and all enterprises with more than 20 workers. All titles and ranks of the nobility were abolished. Private property was also abolished, and the state took over the great estates of the Hungarian nobility.

The young Soviet Republic collapsed in 1919 when Romania sent in troops to enforce the terms of the peace treaties ending World War I. Béla Kun fled the country. The Romanian army occupied Budapest until November 1919, when its Western allies persuaded it to withdraw.

Interwar Years

During the time that Béla Kun held power a number of prewar politicians who had been loyal to the old regime had set up an opposition government. Their small army, under the command of Admiral Miklós Horthy, entered Budapest in late 1919, set up an anti-Bolshevik government and asked to be recognized by the allies. However, the allies refused. Instead they demanded creation of a provisional government that would hold elections.

This led to the creation of a coalition government that included the Smallholder Party, the National Democratic Party, and the Social Democrat Party. Elections were set for January 1920. During the months before the elections, bands of terrorists roamed the country, attacking Jews, Social Democrats, members of trade unions and anyone they suspected either of having communist sympathies, or of opposing the return of the conservatives to power.

Because of the terrorism that had prevailed during the campaign, the first postwar parliament was not representative of the country. The Social Democrats decided

379

Hungary

Hungarian students at College of Europe

to boycott the elections because of the attacks on them. The new parliament first took up the question of whether Hungary was still a monarchy. King Charles had renounced all power in 1918, but had not abdicated. The parliament's decision was that Hungary would continue to be a kingdom, but without a king. A regent would be elected to act as head of state. Admiral Horthy was named Regent of Hungary in March 1920, and he retained that title and position until October 1944. King Charles died in Spain in 1922.

The Treaty of Trianon, signed on June 4, 1920, legalized the loss of territory that had taken place since 1918. Hungary thus emerged from World War I losing almost three-fourths of its prewar territory and about two-thirds of its population. Among the various losses, Slovakia and Ruthenia went to the recently-created Czechoslovakia, while Croatia, Slavonia and most of the Voivodina became part of the newly created Kingdom of Serbs, Croatians and Slovenes, which in the later 1920s became Yugoslavia. In addition, Transylvania and part of the Banat went to Romania. Since boundary lines could not follow ethnic divisions, a large Hungarian population was left in each of the lost areas.

After 1920, Hungarians used the word "dismembered" to describe Trianon Hungary. This was intended to produce the image of a broken state that for a thousand years had been held together under the legal and patriotic symbol of the Crown of St. Stephen. The treaty has had long-lasting effects. It was the underlying reason for Hungary's entry into the Second World War.

Even today some Hungarians talk about it, and the fate of Hungarians out-

side of Hungary's borders is still a major foreign policy issue. In 2005, on the 85th anniversary of the treaty, Hungarians on the street were asked their opinions of it. One pensioner said "it was shameful. It's still a current issue—the West doesn't want to give us justice." A journalist agreed that "it's absolutely a current issue. Sixty-two percent of our land was taken away, families were torn apart. They took away our railway lines." A 24-year-old librarian responded: "Wow! That's a delicate subject. . . . But for the sake of peace we have to try and forget."

Overall, the interwar period was peaceful, at least on the surface. A conservative government led by Stephen Bethlen, a Protestant aristocrat from Transylvania, held power from 1921 to 1931. Desiring a return to the "good old days," but without the Habsburgs, Bethlen ignored the need for land reform and had no understanding of worker and peasant problems. Internationally, the "Little Entente" isolated Hungary. This was an alliance consisting of Hungary's neighbors, Czechoslovakia, Romania and Yugoslavia—all of which had obtained Hungarian lands as a result of the Treaty of Trianon and intended to keep them.

The worldwide economic depression of the 1930s and Hungary's continuing desire to regain lost lands led the nation down a disastrous path to alliance with Nazi Germany. Government leadership changed five times between 1931 and 1939, but the conservatives remained in control. Anti-Jewish measures were enacted, which affected even the political leadership. The last of the five premiers, the patriotic statesman Count Paul Teleki, committed suicide as a dramatic protest

against the invasion of Yugoslavia by Germans crossing Hungarian soil.

The Second World War

Diplomatic activity preceding World War II resulted in Hungary's regaining southern Slovakia and Ruthenia; northern Transylvania was recovered in 1940. Hungary signed the Tripartite Pact of the Axis powers in November 1940, and in spite of a treaty of "eternal friendship," which lasted less than two years, between Yugoslavia and Hungary, German troops crossed Hungary to invade Yugoslavia. The next question was whether Hungary should join in the German war on Russia. On the pretext that Russian planes had bombed Kosice, Premier László Bárdossy sided with the military and published a declaration of war against Russia in mid-1941 without the consent of the parliament. War was later declared against the United States although that country had made no territorial claims whatsoever against Hungary. It is probable that the "Russian aircraft" were really German planes on which Russian markings had been painted.

Parliamentary institutions and political parties functioned until late in the war. There was no German occupation until March 1944, prompted by the advance of the Red Army. Until then Hungary's 800,000 Jews had lived in comparative safety, hoping to survive the horrors all around them. A pro-German government dissolved political parties and increased the persecution of Jews to a level not previously experienced in Hungary. With Hungarian authorities cooperating fully, over 430,000 Jews were deported to Auschwitz between May and July 1944. Others fell victim to roving bands of Hungarian Nazi Arrow Cross militia. The over half a million Hungarian Jewish victims constituted a tenth of all holocaust victims.

In the fall of 1944, Admiral Horthy and his advisers came to the conclusion that the Axis powers could not win the war. Seeking a separate armistice, Hungary sent a diplomatic team to Moscow and announced on October 15, 1944, that it had requested an armistice with the Soviet Union. Horthy's proclamation was poorly timed. The Germans were able to take control of the capital, seize him and force him to retract his proclamation. He was then compelled to abdicate.

The Hungarian Commander-in-Chief, General Béla Miklos, joined with the Soviet army when it crossed Hungary's borders. With Soviet support, Committees of National Liberation were set up in the Soviet-held areas, and a Provisional Government was formed in Debrecen. When Soviet forces besieged Budapest, the pro-German puppet government fled in Janu-

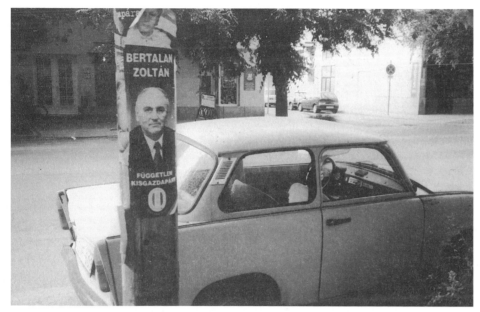

2002 election poster beside an old East German Trabant

ary 1945. The Provisional Government concluded an armistice in Moscow in January 1945.

The government of Hungary was based on a coalition of political parties that included three larger parties, the Hungarian Independence Front, the Social Democratic Party, and the Communist Party, and two smaller parties, the Smallholders' Party and the National Peasant Party. According to the terms of the armistice, Hungary was to return to its 1938 frontiers, and this provision was contained in the Peace Treaty of February 10, 1947. The agreement also provided for an Allied Control Commission with Soviet Marshal K. E. Voroshilov as its chairman.

Hungary Becomes a People's Republic

By a decree of March 1945, the Provisional Government started an extensive land reform program that was accomplished under the direction of Imre Nagy, the Communist minister of agriculture. New elections were set for late 1945. In these elections, probably the freest elections Hungarians had ever experienced, the Smallholders' Party received 57% of the vote. The Communist Party and the Social Democratic Party each received 17%. Zoltan Tildy, leader of the Smallholders, became prime minister. He was elected president after the National Assembly proclaimed Hungary a republic in early 1946. Ferenc Nagy succeeded Tildy in the office of prime minister. Although the Smallholders had won a majority of the vote in the election, the government consisted of a coalition. Imre Nagy became minister of the interior.

It is inaccurate to describe the process by which the communists came to dominate the Hungarian government as a "seizure" of power. In reality, this was achieved quite slowly and cautiously over a three-year period. The Communist Party and the Social Democratic Party were merged in mid-1948 to form the Hungarian Workers' Party (HSWP). A communist sympathizer replaced Tildy in that year, and communists dominated the cabinet. The final move was made in February 1949 with the establishment of the Hungarian Independent People's Front, a combination of all parties and mass organizations. The front presented a single list of candidates that received 96.5% of the vote in the May 1949 elections. The newly elected National Assembly proclaimed Hungary a People's Republic and adopted a constitution reflecting Hungary's official position as a member of the Soviet bloc.

The Stalinist Period

The years from 1949 to 1953 were called the "Stalinist period." Political control was wielded by Mathias Rakosi, a dedicated communist since 1918. He became Secretary General of the Communist Party in 1944, deputy prime minister until 1952, and prime minister from 1952 until 1953.

Under his supervision, a reorganized secret police, some of them former fascist Arrow Cross members, prosecuted 1.3 million persons between 1950 and 1953, opened concentration camps holding more than 40,000 inmates, purged the party and imprisoned half of the 850,000 Communist Party members. The police attacked the few remaining rich landowners, undermined the churches and kept a close watch over social life in general. The most dramatic event of this period was the trial of László Rajk, a "home communist" and one-time minister of the interior and foreign affairs. Accused on falsified evidence of conspiring with Yugoslavia's Tito, he was executed in 1949. This was followed by a purge of the party membership that eliminated all those suspected of having nationalist or anti-Rakosi sentiments. In the process, several thousand party members were also imprisoned.

By 1949, the new regime had introduced the Stalinist model of economic planning with its emphasis on central decision-making and heavy industry. All industry employing more than ten workers had been nationalized, and a program for the collectivization of agriculture had been initiated.

Lacking most raw materials, Hungary had never placed any great stress on heavy industry. It had concentrated on the development of agriculture based on the processing of its products and the manufacture of consumer goods. The new emphasis on heavy industry in the first Five-Year Plan produced spectacular growth totals in the beginning. Heavy industrial production increased fivefold, and the engineering industry showed a sevenfold increase in productivity over 1938.

By 1953, however, serious shortages had begun to appear in both raw materials and fuel supplies. A serious disproportion had begun to appear between heavy and light industry. Agriculture was beginning to stagnate under the combination of collectivization accompanied by a decline in investment. Wages and salaries had risen less rapidly than consumer prices. The result was a 20% decline in the general standard of living between 1948 and 1953.

The New Course and Revolution

There had been some muted criticism of these developments even before Stalin's death in March 1953, but the dictator's passing brought these out into the open. Imre Nagy took the lead. He challenged Rakosi's handling of the economy, accusing him of forcing the tempo of industrialization all out of proportion to the country's resources. Rakosi was forced to step down as chairman of the council of ministers although he retained his position as head of the Hungarian Workers' Party. Nagy was named in his place.

In his first speech to parliament in 1953, Nagy presented a program that later became known as the "New Course." It included an emphasis on consumer goods instead of heavy industry, abolition of collective farms when such was desired by a majority of the workers, and the release of many political prisoners, including János Kádár.

Continued disputes over these new policies, particularly in agriculture, coupled with a failure to gain support of important

Hungary

Soviet tanks guard the street intersection leading to the Danube Bridge in Budapest on November 5, 1956.   AP/Wide World Photo

party members, led to Nagy's resignation in 1955. Andras Hegedus replaced him, and Hungary returned to the old policies of heavy industrialization and collectivization. After the unkept promises of the New Course and a disappointing return to earlier policies, protests from writers and scholars began to be heard in the autumn of 1955. The following summer, the Petöfi Circle, named after a revolutionary poet killed in 1849, was formed. It provided a forum for debate among those who were critical of the government.

In an effort to appease the critics, the Soviet Union brought increased pressure on the Hungarian party to dismiss Rakosi. He resigned in mid-1956 and was replaced by Ernö Gerö. This did not quiet the discord. A number of party leaders who had been executed in the purges of 1949 were reburied with honor; the funerals turned into a mass demonstration against the government. A few weeks later, the students of Szeged University in the city of that name organized a noncommunist youth organization.

By late 1956, news of the Szeged students and of the antigovernment activities in Poland reached Budapest. This prompted students and writers to draw up a resolution and to hold a public demonstration expressing sympathy for the Polish cause. Their plan was to march to a statue of General Joseph Bem, a Polish soldier who had fought with the Hungarians against the Austrians and Russians in 1848–49. The resolution demanded the evacuation of Soviet troops from Hungary, the return of Nagy as chairman of the council of ministers, free elections and

freedom of speech and press. This was not so much in opposition to communism as it was in favor of the development of some form of socialist democracy.

Although planned only as a demonstration, the October 23 events turned swiftly into a mass revolution. This was due to poor judgment of officials and the emotions generated by the mass activity. The minister of the interior responded to news of the planned demonstration by, first, banning it, but then agreeing not to interfere. That evening, the huge crowd that had gathered in front of parliament began calling for Nagy, who addressed them briefly and then asked them to disperse.

Later in the evening, two specific events triggered an uprising. First Secretary Ernö Gerö gave a tactless and accusing speech during which he denounced the demonstrators. Then the radio station director refused to broadcast the resolution. Fighting first broke out between the demonstrators and the secret police and quickly spread into the working class districts. A gigantic statue of Stalin in the center of Budapest was toppled; because only the boots remained, the site was popularly called "Boot Square."

During the night Soviet tanks appeared, and fighting erupted between Soviet troops and revolutionaries who were by then supported by parts of the Hungarian army. The unrest spread even further into the countryside, where Workers' Councils and Revolutionary Councils were organized to replace the local communist administrations.

On October 24, Nagy replaced Hegedus as chairman of the council of ministers, and

the next day János Kádár replaced Ernö Gerö as first secretary of the Hungarian Workers' Party. Russian archives opened after the collapse of the Soviet Union in 1991 reveal that the Soviet Presidium (later called Politburo) decided unanimously on October 30 not to use military force. Anastas Mikoyan, who was in Budapest at the time as a Soviet representative of the Presidium of the Central Committee, accepted political changes and negotiated an agreement with Nagy and Kádár for the withdrawal of the Soviet army from Hungary. Mikoyan's agreement was obviously based on the premise that Nagy and Kádár, as communists, were committed to the maintenance of communist control in Hungary. However, Nagy, in announcing the Soviet troop withdrawal agreement, also promised to abolish the secret police and to bring representatives of noncommunist parties into the government.

The United States government did not help matters by talking loosely of "liberation" and "rollback" of communism, when it was not in a position to do anything about the lamentable situation. This gave Hungarians false hopes of outside rescue that were bound to be disappointed. President Eisenhower said privately during his 1956 reelection campaign: "Poor fellows, poor fellows. I wish there were some way of helping them."

The Kremlin decided that things might spin out of control in Hungary and in the rest of the Soviet empire. Reports reached Budapest on November 1 that Soviet troops had stopped their withdrawal and, reinforced by additional Soviet tanks of the latest design, were actually heading

CENTURY OF THE MILLENNIUM

Nov. 5, 1956 Russia brutally quashes the Hungarian Revolution and supports the countergovernment of Janos Kadar, a member of the former cabinet. Later, as premier, he would walk a line between supporting Soviet policies and initiating liberal reforms at home More No news Muslim students storm the U.S. embassy in Tehran in a bid to force a trial of deposed Reza Shah Pahlevi (1979). **Tomorrow Battle For Patriation Is Over (1981)**

The Globe and Mail

Cloudy, Mild High Here 65

113th Year. No. 33,354. — *Final Edition* — TORONTO, MONDAY, NOVEMBER 5, 1956. — 5 Cents Per Copy — 44 PAGES

HUNGARY CRUSHED
UN Demands Russia Withdraw, Approves Canadian Suez Plans; Paratroops Landing in Egypt

Canadian Appointed As Police Force Chief

Soviet Might Batters Budapest Rebel Force

'Hands Off,' Soviet Says—

Call Session On UN Force, PM Indicates

Assembly Condemns Russia For Its Military Intervention

Police Disperse Anti-Eden Mob

London Reports Invasion Starts Near Port Said

65 More Miners Found, Survivors May Total 101

President Asks Soviet Call Its Troops Back

---

back toward Budapest, a half of a million strong. Nagy responded by announcing Hungary's withdrawal from the Warsaw Pact (the military organization of Eastern Europe presided over by the Soviets), committing Hungary to a policy of neutrality and appealing for help from the United Nations.

Soviet troops attacked Budapest on November 4, 1956. At the same time, Kádár, now in eastern Hungary having left Budapest on the evening of November 1–2, proclaimed the establishment of a "revolutionary government of peasants and workers" to replace the "fascist" Nagy government. Although there was a great

deal of resistance by the Hungarian people, a basically unarmed people was no match for Soviet tanks, and the revolution was ruthlessly suppressed. Around 2,800 Hungarians and 700 Soviet soldiers died in the violence. Kádár was back in power with the backing of Soviet troops.

About 200,000 refugees poured into Western countries, including the U.S., making Cleveland, Ohio, the second-largest Hungarian city. Among the refugees to the U.S. was the commander-in-chief of the revolutionary forces, Bela Kiraly. He taught history at Brooklyn College and authored and published many books on Hungary and the region. He returned to Hungary in

1989 to serve in his liberated homeland's parliament. He died in 2009 at age 97. At least 225 Hungarians accused of taking part in the revolution were executed. This included Nagy, who was arrested, refused to confess to being a fascist counterrevolutionary, and was hanged in 1958.

Politics After 1956

Kádár was in a difficult position after 1956 because he lacked the support of the party and the people. Within the party, those opposed him who favored internal reform and those who accused him of selling out the revolution. Large segments of the population, including the students, writers and workers who had played such a large role in the revolution, viewed Kádár as a Soviet puppet. He was in power only because he had the support of Nikita Khrushchev, the man who had suppressed the revolution. During the first two years after the uprising, Kádár repressed the various social groups and political parties that opposed his government. Hundreds of people associated with the revolution were imprisoned.

In 1959–1960, there appeared the first indications that the government was willing to allow a relaxation of its tight control. Partial amnesty was declared, and several hundred political prisoners were released. After 1961, Kádár adopted policies intended to win popular support. The "People's Courts" that had convicted the revolutionaries were abolished, and Rákosi and Gerö were expelled from the party in 1962. This demonstrated Kádár's desire to break completely with the Stalinist policies of the past. Although he became chairman of the council of ministers in addition to first secretary of the party, there was no return to the so-called "cult of personality" of which Stalin had been accused after his death.

In 1962, Kádár reported to a party congress that collectivization had been completed the previous year, and that 90% of all farmland was now organized into cooperative and state farms. Most industrial products were from socialist enterprises. In foreign policy, Kádár expressed complete support for the Soviet policy of peaceful coexistence, for its actions in the Cuban missile crisis and its position in the disputes with China.

The congress, in turn, adopted Kádár's "one nation" policy, which declared, in effect, that the government was willing to cooperate with anyone who was not actively opposed to the Communist Party. In this respect, it was willing, he said, to recruit competent, nonparty members for government service. Further liberalization was evident by 1963, when a general amnesty was declared, freeing additional political prisoners numbering in the thou-

Hungary

sands. Travel restrictions were lowered, and tourism increased.

Kádár's popularity greatly increased as a result of these changes, and that was a considerable help when Khrushchev fell from power in November 1964. Although now "on his own," Kádár managed to hold on to power, though he did have to relinquish the office of chairman of the council of ministers in 1965. Julius Kállai got that position, while Kádár remained first secretary of the party.

Kállai was chairman of the council of ministers until 1967. He was replaced by Jenö Fock, who held the position until 1975. Fock's resignation came shortly after the Eleventh Congress of the Hungarian Socialist Workers Party (HSWP). His resignation "for reasons of health" almost certainly reflected the Soviet leadership's dissatisfaction with the relatively free-wheeling style of economic management in Hungary under the "New Mechanism." His successor as chairman of the council of ministers was György Lázár, who held the position until 1987.

The Eleventh Congress of the HSWP tightened party regulations by introducing a ban on "propagating dissent," almost certainly a gesture meant to appease their Soviet comrades. In another gesture, this time aimed at Hungarian workers, the congress endorsed the reduction of the workweek to 44 hours by 1980.

Although he held no state office after 1965, Kádár continued to be the key leader in the political system. He tended to run a rather collegial Politburo, though he did not hesitate to dismiss those members who got too far out of line. In general, he preferred technocrats rather than political types. He recognized that they were needed to carry out his economic reforms, and they were also less likely to be rivals for power. He always tried to limit the personal power of his associates.

Károly Grósz replaced the ailing György Lázár as chairman of the council of ministers. Former party boss in Budapest, Grósz had often been mentioned as a potential Kádár successor. The matter was decided in May 1988 at a special HSWP conference. It had become clear in the months leading up to the conference that Kádár intended to retire. For the first time, there was something of a campaign for the office of party leader. Grósz, who had previously had a reputation as a hard-liner, put himself forward as an aggressive and energetic pragmatist who supported further reform. He also adopted an open style reminiscent of that of Gorbachev.

Grósz succeeded Kádár as general secretary. As it turned out, however, this was not just a succession but rather something approaching a revolution in the party. Two well-known advocates of radical re-

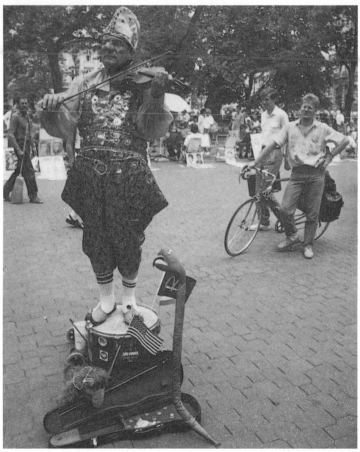

Fiddler celebrates two significant events of 1989—President Bush's visit and the opening of Budapest's McDonald's   Photo by Jon Markham Morrow

form, Rezsö Nyers and Imre Pozsgay, were added to the Politburo.

Nyers, a member of the Economic Institute of the Hungarian Academy of Sciences and a former minister of finance, had been one of the principal authors of the 1968 reform. In the early 1980s, he wrote an article for *Magyar Hírlap*, the Budapest daily, in which he advocated a larger political role for the parliament. In 1985, when the party established multiple candidacies and moved to give a larger role to parliament, it was implementing most of what Nyers had advocated in his article.

Pozsgay, chairman of the Patriotic Peoples' Front since 1982, attempted to give this umbrella organization new life and more influence. He had also argued that the party ought "to withdraw from its present relationship with the state and society and to establish a new relationship." In addition, he was on record as supporting the creation of autonomous interest groups, including independent trade unions under certain circumstances.

Speaking to the party conference following his election as general secretary, Grósz promised that he would seek "to expand democratic procedures within the party to match some of the 'practical ad-

vantages' of Western multiparty systems." Later, in a televised address to the Hungarian people, he admitted past mistakes on behalf of the party and promised a new approach "in public life, in production, in human sectors and other fields." Gorbachev was quick to put his stamp of approval on the new general secretary, calling him "a principled communist and authoritative leader" and wishing him "big successes . . . in tackling the task of improving and renovating his socialist society on Hungarian soil."

Grósz continued as chairman of the council of ministers until November 1988, when he turned the office over to Miklós Németh. A 40-year-old economist, Németh had been added to the Politburo in May 1988. Known as a strong advocate of change, he was described by János Lukács, another Politburo member, as a "young, dynamic workhorse."

His biography indicates that, after graduating from Karl Marx University in Budapest, he studied at Harvard University. He began working for the party's economic department in 1981. In 1987, he became a member of the Central Committee and, simultaneously, party secretary for economic policy. Mark Palmer, American

Ambassador to Hungary in 1988, characterized Németh as an affable man with whom the West could easily work. "He has very rich experience in the area of economic reform. He clearly has the strong backing of Grósz and a great deal of experience in the West. We believe he is committed to reform and will push ahead."

Németh's appointment was further evidence that the reformers were in charge although they still retained their alliance with the moderate Grósz. Having placed their supporters in all of the key positions, they turned their attention to institutional reform.

There was some question about where all of this was leading. The situation became even more muddled in December 1988 when Imre Pozsgay spoke out publicly in favor of a multiparty system. One week later, Grósz rejected Pozsgay's suggestion, but that actually marked the beginning of a struggle within the party over the issue. The matter was largely resolved in February 1989, when the party announced further details of proposed constitutional changes. A multiparty system was to be formally established, and additional political parties were to be permitted to operate freely. The draft also provided for the creation of a new executive presidency. Among other things, the president would be commander-in-chief of the armed forces. Free elections were scheduled for 1990.

Although the program had not formally gone into effect, independent political groups immediately began to form. In March 1989 the first of those, the Democratic Forum, had its first convention in Budapest. In addition, the Smallholders' Party and the Hungarian Social Democratic Party—both part of the first government coalition (along with the Communist Party) in 1945—were revived and began to operate as independent groups.

However, the HSWP's commitment to multiparty elections was too much for conservatives still within the party. To resolve the issue, Grósz proposed at a plenum of the Central Committee in April 1989 that the Politburo "lay down its powers and hold a new secret ballot on its composition." In the subsequent voting, four remaining conservatives were removed from the Politburo. The size of the Politburo was thus reduced from 11 to 9. In a separate move, János Kádár was dropped from the Central Committee, and his title of honorary president was abolished. He died soon afterwards.

As a sign that Hungarian leaders had had a genuine change of heart, they were prime movers in one of the most dramatic postwar developments right before the very eyes of a stunned world public: German unification. In late summer a human hemorrhaging westward commenced, as

PROFILE OF A PRESIDENT: LÁSZLÓ SÓLYOM

East German vacationers began crossing the newly opened border between Hungary and Austria. Budapest informed the irate East German leaders that the human rights agreements accepted at the Helsinki Conference in 1975 superseded earlier bilateral treaties preventing the free movement of peoples.

In June the party went through yet another leadership shake-up. The Politburo and the office of general secretary were both abolished. A four-member Presidium, with Rezso Nyers as president, replaced them. Karoly Grósz was made a member of the Presidium, but he lost most of his power. The winds of change continued to blow strongly in 1989. In October, the party dropped its old name and became the Hungarian Socialist Party.

The Post-Communist Era

In March 1990, in the first free elections since 1945 were held. Voters repudiated both the communist-reformist Hungarian Socialist Party and the resurrected communist Hungarian United Workers Party. No single party received a majority, but the conservative Democratic Forum came in first with approximately 42% of the vote. It therefore won the right to organize the new government. A coalition was formed with two smaller parties, the Independent Smallholders and the Christian Democrats, with József Antall, leader of Democratic Forum, as prime minister.

Together the three parties controlled more than 60% of the seats in the new parliament. The main opposition party was the left-liberal Alliance of Free Democrats, with Federation of Young Democrats and the Hungarian Socialist Party reduced to a tiny remnant on the left.

Antall remained prime minister for the next three and a half years, until his death in 1993. During that time, he came to dominate Hungarian politics almost completely, giving the country a political stability that distinguished Hungary from most of its Eastern European neighbors.

In the beginning, the greatest problems the new government faced were related to the economy. Its early focus was on establishing policies that would move Hungary more rapidly toward a market economy. This task appeared easier in Hungary because of all the Central and Eastern European nations the communists had already moved the country the furthest along this path. Nevertheless, state-owned enterprises still constituted 90% of the productive sector.

First of all, the government drew up a long list of laws and regulations aimed at fostering private initiative, encouraging direct foreign investment, and developing private capital markets. It also committed itself to reducing the state sector to less than 50% by 1995.

All over Central Europe, there were heated discussions about how best to

Hungary

privatize a former communist-controlled economy. In Hungary, the government opted for a company-by-company privatization, based on finding Western companies that would either take over the company entirely or come in as a partner, providing capital and technical expertise. Under this plan, foreign investment increased rapidly, and a good number of companies were able to find foreign partners or purchasers. Small and medium-sized companies were privatized locally, some to groups of employees.

In general, the process was relatively slow. Many of the newly privatized companies also found it difficult to compete, so salaries remained low, and unemployment grew significantly during this time. As a result, the government came under criticism by those who argued that it was moving too slowly and by others who feared that it was dissipating the nation's wealth. Some of this showed up in the local elections in October 1990, when the parties of the government coalition lost badly. In Budapest, the two major opposition parties won over 50% of the vote. In most places, independents won, however, possibly indicating distaste for the political partisanship that had come to dominate debate.

None of this threatened the coalition's majority in parliament, however. In fact, the government coalition had regained much of its popularity in the country by the beginning of 1992, and Antall, though still not particularly popular, was conceded to be the most effective leader in Central Europe.

POLITICAL SYSTEM

The Hungarian Republic is a multiparty parliamentary democracy. The legal system is based on the 1949 constitution substantially modified in October 1989 and adopted in 1990. It created a parliamentary form of government with guarantees for basic human rights. Supreme power is vested in parliament. The Constitutional Court, composed of judges appointed by the National Assembly for nine-year terms, can overturn parliamentary decisions and governmental decrees deemed unconstitutional. One of its most spectacular acts was that it struck out several aspects of a legislative package reducing welfare benefits for families in 1995. A committee is working on drafting a new constitution for the future.

Hungary has a ceremonial president of the republic as chief of state. The National Assembly elects the president for a term of five years. He has the power to sign or reject laws, formally appoints the prime minister and cabinet, and decides the dates of elections to the National Assembly. The

Hon. Viktor Orbán
Prime Minister

president of the republic since June 2005 is László Sólyom of the Fidesz party. He narrowly defeated the Socialist candidate, Katalin Szili, in the third round of balloting 185–182. In 1989 he had been the opposition's expert in negotiations with the Communists. He became the first president of the Constitutional Court from 1990–96, when the court rendered such groundbreaking rulings as abolishing the death penalty and restoring church properties. He is an internationally respected academic lawyer and member of the Academy of Sciences.

The National Assembly is a single-chamber parliament with a total of 386 seats. Its members are elected for a four-year term in an election that is part proportional, part constituency. Deputies can be elected in one of three ways: directly from one of 176 single-member constituencies; by being included on a county list of party candidates; or by being included on a national list; there are a total of 210 regional and party-list seats. If no candidate wins a majority in one of the 176 local districts, then a runoff election is held in that district two weeks later between the top two finishers. In order to limit the number of parties in parliament and thereby to maintain greater political stability, a party must win at least 5% of the votes in order to receive any parliamentary seats. All citizens over age 18 may vote.

The National Assembly is the fulcrum of power, with the prime minister as the country's political leader. He is the head of government and the individual responsible for government policy. He is nominated by the president and confirmed by the National Assembly. He can be removed if he loses a constructive vote of confidence in the National Assembly. This means that a government can be voted out

of office only if a replacement can immediately secure a parliamentary majority. This positive no-confidence vote, taken from Germany's Basic Law, helps ensure greater stability.

In May 2005 parliament passed a law opening communist-era secret service files. Unlike other former Warsaw Pact countries after the fall of communism, Hungary did not reveal the names of secret police collaborators and the information they had accumulated about citizens. Critics claim the law violates the protection of personal data enshrined in the constitution.

Parties and Elections

Hungary is moving ever closer to a two-party system. A sharp political polarization exists between rightist and leftist parties and between a relatively well-off western Hungary, which favors FIDESZ (Federation of Young Democrats), and a poorer and less populous east, which traditionally votes for the ex-communist Hungarian Socialist Party (MSZP). Also fishing successfully for votes is the far-right, anti-immigrant and anti-Semitic JOBBIK (Movement for a Better Hungary).

In 2004 Ferenc Gyurcsány, one of Hungary's richest men turned champion of the poor, became prime minister for the Socialist Party. With the party's popularity declining and new elections on the horizon, the party needed a more appealing prime minister. Although he was a former Communist youth league leader, his selection marked a clear break by the Socialists from a generation of leaders who came to power as reform-minded Communists in the 1980s and who created the Socialist Party out of the wreckage of the Communist Party in 1990. Later he became a polished, charismatic, Atlanticist, market-friendly and ambitious centrist reformer whose model was the "third way" of Britain's Tony Blair.

During his first term in office, Gyurcsany opened the state coffers generously and did nothing to stop the country's burgeoning budget deficit. Although this undermined the stability of the currency, worried foreign investors, and set the stage for the recession of 2008–9, it helped him in April 2006 to become the first prime minister in post-communist Hungary to be reelected. His MSZP won a comfortable majority by promising "reform without austerity."

The strident partisanship and pent-up political emotions erupted in September and October 2006. The trigger was a secret speech Gyurcsany delivered to his party members in parliament after the June 2006 general elections and the disastrous fall local elections in which the ruling Socialists lost 19 of 23 cities. He later argued that he was trying to motivate his party to accept austerity measures and public sector restructuring by saying: "No country in Europe has screwed up as much as we have.... We lied morning, noon and night." A recording of this talk, which the prime minister said was exaggerated for dramatic effect, was leaked to the main radio station and aired to a stunned public. Gyurcsany never recovered from this blunder.

Sensing a golden opportunity to topple the government, the Fidesz opposition, supported by President Solyom, demanded Gyurcsany's resignation and called on its supporters to demonstrate against the government. What followed was the worst political violence the country had experienced since 1956. An estimated 30,000 to 40,000 demonstrators, some carrying national flags and singing patriotic songs, took to the streets, burned cars, surrounded parliament, and temporarily took over the state TV station, forcing it off the air.

Similar violence accompanied the 50th anniversary of the 1956 uprising only a month later. The protesters were so aggressive that police fired rubber-coated bullets and used tear gas and water cannons to disperse them. At one point, demonstrators even commandeered two WWII-era tanks on display and drove them toward the police. The fact that the ruling Socialists grew out of the old Communist Party made this occasion particularly volatile. Fidesz refused to attend the ceremony. In fact, its parliamentarians followed Orbán out of the debating chamber every time Gyurcsany rose to speak.

Despite the fury directed against him, Gyurcsany refused to step down, and his approval rating plummeted. Fidesz succeeded in creating a political stalemate by using populist appeals to undercut anything Gyurcsany tried to do. The government could achieve almost nothing. For example, his referendum early in 2008 to raise medical and tuition fees slightly (a doctor's visit would have cost $2) was rejected by 80% of voters although there was no other money to replace the charges. This failed referendum dashed hopes of more reforms. Hungary already has the region's heaviest tax burden, and Orbán's threats to renationalize much of the economy scared away many foreign investors. This is especially serious since half of GDP is generated by foreign firms.

Orbán played on voters' anxiety and created hopes that could not be fulfilled. But his poll ratings shot up while those of Gyurcsany steadily declined. The Socialists found themselves without a majority. With social tensions rising and the global economic recession hurting Hungary badly, Gyurcsany saw no alternative to resigning in March 2009. He was replaced as prime minister by his economics minister,

Gordon Bajnai, a 41-year-old independent and former economics professor and businessman. His cabinet was composed of both Socialist politicians and unaffiliated experts. He offered an olive branch to the opposition parties to try to break the political deadlock: "The country has no money left for fighting." His government introduced economic austerity, raised the pension age from 62 to 65 beginning in 2012 (2010 average: 59.7 years), lowered benefits by about 8% and abolished the thirteenth-month pension payment.

Bajnai had only a year to turn the country around before the April 2010 elections. The Socialists were trounced. Led by Attila Mesterházy, they captured only 19.3% of the votes. They lost a devastating 131 seats, retaining only 59. They now represent less than a fifth of the electorate.

The stunning victor of the April 2010 elections was the Federation of Young Democrats (FIDESZ). Led by Viktor Orbán, who had served as prime minister from 1998 to 2002, it won 52.73% of the votes and 263 seats, a gain of 99. This gave Fidesz more than two-thirds of all parliamentary seats, enabling it to change the constitution, which it promised to do. Such reforms might involve reducing the total number of seats, trimming bloated local government, and easing dual-citizenship requirements for ethnic Hungarians. He also promised tax cuts, downsizing the bureaucracy, a crackdown on crime, a protectionist economic policy, creation of a million jobs in 10 years, and reform of the media law. In part, it owes its spectacular come-back to the severe economic recession.

Wanting to shake his reputation as an irresponsible leader, Orbán moved his Fidesz party toward the political center in the run up to the 2010 elections. In his mid-30s, Orbán had been Hungary's youngest freely elected prime minister.

His near victory in 2002 had showed how potent nationalist populism still can be. In 2006 he moderated his nationalist appeal, dropping his earlier anti-Semitic rhetoric altogether. He is still a fiery populist who spouts chauvinistic, anti-EU polemics and criticism of "unbridled capitalism." Anywhere else in Europe, his rhetoric would be intolerably nationalist. But in Hungary it sounds more moderate because of a radical right-wing party that came out of nowhere to become the nation's third-largest party in 2010 and to force Fidesz to reposition itself as a mainstream center-right party: JOBBIK.

Jobbik (Movement for a Better Hungary) won 16.67% of the votes in 2010. This enabled it for the first time to win seats in parliament: 47. Its young (31 years) leader, Gábor Vona, a former history teacher, tapped into growing nationalism to catapult his party from the fanatical fringes to the corridors of parliament. He appeals mainly to rural, unemployed disenchanted young voters who have been hit hardest by the recession. His anti-Semitic and anti-Roma rhetoric makes these groups scapegoats for the hardships the nation is suffering. It rails against "Israeli colonizers" and has Roma in mind when it says: "No work, no support." It vows to ban immigrants from diluting Hungarian purity and to revise the 1920 Trianon Treaty, which deprived Hungary of two-thirds of its prewar territory.

Its shock troops called themselves "Magyar Garda." The had uniforms reminiscent of those worn by Hungarian Nazis during the war, the Arrow Cross, which had lent a bloody hand in the Holocaust. Its Nazi rhetoric evokes Hungary's glorious past. In 2009 the Magyar Garda were outlawed, but they are still active. Their bouncers at rallies now wear slightly different outfits and call themselves "New Hungarian Garda." Orbán and Fidesz

Crown of St. Stephens

Hungary

vow not to cooperate with Jobbik and to defend Hungary from this rowdy party.

The only other party to clear the 5% hurdle and win parliamentary seats in this sixth free election since the end of communism was new: Politics Can Be Different (LMP), a green-liberal party. It captured 16 seats in 2010. An independent candidate also won a seat. The parties that had led the transition to democracy in 1990, the Liberals and Liberal-Conservatives (MDF), were wiped out, and they vanished.

Foreign Policy

During communist rule, alignment with the Soviet Union had been a basic component of foreign policy. For example, Hungary followed the lead of the USSR in breaking relations with Israel in 1967, and it joined the Soviet boycott of the 1984 Los Angeles Summer Olympics. It also supported the Soviets in quarrels with the People's Republic of China.

On the other hand, Hungary always maintained a more independent position *vis-à-vis* the Soviet Union than either Bulgaria or Czechoslovakia. Hungarians were frank about their desire for better relations with the West. Although they participated fully in the Council of Mutual Economic Assistance (CMEA, or COMECON), and the Soviet Union remained their single largest trading partner, they also pushed to increase their trade with the West and were the first to call for reform of CMEA.

The first noncommunist government since 1945 brought changes in Hungary's foreign policy. The biggest immediate one was that Budapest negotiated an agreement with the Soviet Union calling for the removal of all Soviet troops by July 1991. Hungary was also instrumental in the demise of the Warsaw Pact. When the Hungarian government announced that it intended to leave the communist alliance, Moscow, apparently fearing that other members would join the exodus, proposed that the military aspects of the organization be terminated as of April 1, 1991. The Warsaw Pact plus the CMEA, Hungary's other formal tie to Moscow, were formally dissolved on July 1, 1991. Its relations with Russia are now among equals. They are cordial, but businesslike.

West Germany's trade with Hungary grew steadily to about 30% of all Hungarian trade with the West in 1985. This made it Hungary's second largest trading partner after the Soviet Union. There was also extensive cooperation between the two countries designed to facilitate the transfer of technology. Approximately 350 cooperative agreements were signed between West German and Hungarian firms before 1989.

Ultra-right Jobbik at a protest in Budapest

Austrian entrepreneurs have also been active investors. According to the Hungarian government, approximately 1,880 joint ventures were established between foreign investors and local partners in the first 18 months of the new democratic regime. More than 60% of the investors were either Austrian or German.

American-Hungarian relations have been relatively good since 1973, when the two countries signed an agreement settling claims for damages to American property during World War ll. The U.S. government returned the St. Stephen's Crown, in American custody since World War II, to Hungary in 1978. However, not until November 2005 did the U.S. government apologize for the 1945 looting by its soldiers of a train loaded with valuable items stolen from Hungarian Jews during the war. In early 1945 the "Hungarian gold train" had pulled out of Budapest with retreating German forces, and it was abandoned near Salzburg, Austria. In May the advancing American troops found 24 of its 46 cars, and some helped themselves to many of its contents. Most of the goods, but not all, were turned over to the Intergovernmental Committee for Refugees, which auctioned the items to benefit Holocaust victims. Sued by the survivors, the U.S. government agreed to an apology and settlement of $25.5 million.

The United States granted Hungary "most-favored nation" trade status, and relations became even warmer after 1989. In general, it has been a strong supporter of multilateral economic assistance to Hungary. After coming to power in May 1990, the noncommunist government established diplomatic relations with Israel and the Vatican.

Hungary was admitted to membership in the Council of Europe in November

Line forms at the House of Terror, opened April 2002 to document Communist Repression

Hungary

1990, the first Central or Eastern European nation to seek and receive admittance. It became an associate member of the European EU in December 1991, along with Poland and Czechoslovakia. In 1997, the EU extended an invitation for Hungary to begin negotiations leading to full membership. The center-left government set up an efficient EU communications office and organized public meetings around the country. In an April 2003 referendum, 84% of voters supported entry.

The government had foreseen that participation in the voting might be a problem, so it struck the 50% turnout requirement from the law; in the end only 46% voted. The people of Budapest greeted the positive results with bursts of fireworks over the Danube and the playing of Beethoven's Ninth Symphony, the EU anthem. Officials waxed lyrical about their country's "writing its name in history," and one newspaper ran the headline, "Europe, Here We come!" Then Prime Minister Peter Medgyessy announced: "History begins again today, after an interruption of 60 years." Formal EU membership came in May 2004. Foreign Minister László Kovács rejoiced: "Finally Hungarians will be treated as equals in Europe."

EU Membership brings challenges. Hungary assumes an enormous burden in securing borders with seven countries, four of whom are not yet EU members. This became especially important after December 2007, when it joined the Schengen agreement for free movement within the EU. It has not maintained the financial discipline to adopt the euro any time soon. Its parliament had already ratified the ill-fated EU constitution before French and Dutch voters turned it down in May and June 2005. Hungary's political leaders were disappointed because the document's clause on protecting minorities, which could have helped ethnic Hungarians in neighboring countries, was lost.

Hungary was also invited in 1997 to become a member of NATO. This was approved by popular referendum in November. Hungary was formally admitted in March 1999. The beginning of NATO's air war against Yugoslavia, coming as it did only days after Hungary had become a formal member of NATO, presented the government with a particular problem. There are several hundred thousand ethnic Hungarians living in the Voivodina region of Serbia; their welfare is only one of the reasons why Hungary keeps an uneasy eye on neighboring Serbia.

Hungary did not participate in the air war, but it did grant NATO full access to its air space, gave approval for the passage of foreign peacekeeping troops through Hungary, and even their stationing in the country to support humanitarian aid missions. In addition, the Hungarian parliament approved a 350-member guard battalion to join the peacekeeping forces in Kosovo, where it helps protect the KFOR headquarters in Pristina. In January 2000 NATO closed its military base in Pecs, which had been used to supply its peacekeeping troops in Bosnia-Herzegovina, as part of its efforts to streamline its Bosnian operations.

Despite the fact that three-fourths of Hungarians opposed the American-British war in Iraq in 2003, the government defied France and Germany by signing an important open letter supporting the war effort. It provided an airbase at Taszar where the U.S. could train several hundred Iraqi exiles for use as intermediaries between an American invasion force and civilians and soldiers in Iraq. Hungary balked, however, at American suggestions that 28,000 Iraqis receive police training in Hungary. When a miffed French President Jacques Chirac condescendingly called Hungary and other Central European governments "not well brought up" and scolded them for not following his lead, then Prime Minister Medgyessy retorted in immaculate French that he was "too well brought up" to respond to Chirac's gibes and diatribes.

Budapest sent 300 mainly logistic soldiers to Iraq. A former Hungarian ambassador to Washington explained the rationale: "The Hungarian interest is not what happens in Iraq per se. It's that the trans-Atlantic relationship remains as strong and unharmed as possible, and that the United States remains a European power." Former Secretary of State Colin Powell was awarded the Grand Cross. Hungary withdrew its forces after the January 2005 Iraqi elections, largely in response to polls showing that more than 60% of Hungarians wanted their troops out. It maintains 243 peacekeepers in Kosovo, 160 in Bosnia-Herzegovina, and 360 soldiers in Afghanistan, including several companies of combat soldiers in Kandahar.

Hungary has a total active military force of 29.450. It also has 44,000 reserves, plus 12,000 paramilitaries. In 2004 it began a shift away from a conscript army to a professional force. It has 10,936 in its army, and 5,664 in its air force, which flies mainly aging upgraded Soviet-era MiGs-29s, mostly acquired from the Russian government in 1993 as part of a debt repayment deal. Fourteen of Hungary's MiG-29s had crashed by mid-2005, and the others are being phased out. In 2001 the government decided to upgrade its air capability by procuring 14 Gripen jet fighters from Sweden.

Former NATO Secretary-General Lord Robertson informed the Hungarian defense minister that his country must finally fulfill its pledges to modernize and better equip its armed forces. It has one of the lowest rates of defense spending (1.8% of GDP) and has done the least among all the new NATO allies. It has made no significant purchases of new equipment in several years, and its military is therefore technologically backward. Its reductions in manpower have rendered some units non-operational, and its troops have difficulty communicating and interoperating with NATO allies.

One Western diplomat noted: "Hungary is not a military nation. They haven't won a battle since around 1456. And there's very little support for military spending." Nevertheless, the government increased the defense budget by 16%, much of it for technical improvements and restructuring. It created uneasiness in NATO corridors when its new chief of the secret services, Sandor Laborc, was sent to fill the rotating post of chairman of NATO's intelligence committee for a year. Laborc had spent six years at the KGB's academy in Moscow in the 1980s.

Hungary and Germany

Germany was wholly supportive of Hungary's entry into the EU. Hungary is a politically stable country with only three

Hungary

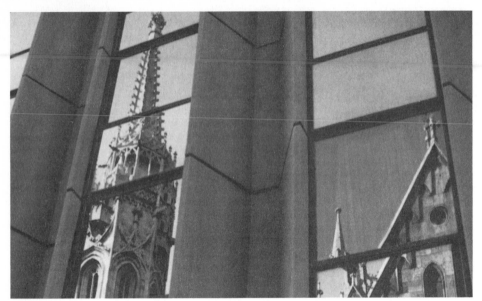

The Hilton Hotel's mirrored facade reflects the Gothic spires of Matthias Church in Old Budapest, site of the coronation of Charles II as King of Hungary in 1916.

Courtesy: Jon Markham Morrow

governments in the 1990s (compared with eight in Poland, a record in Central Europe) and a privatization program that was almost complete by the end of the 20th century. It enjoys good relations with its seven neighbors, each of which has a Magyar minority.

Unlike the Poles and Czechs, Hungarians show no dislike for Germans although they bear some animosity toward Austria, which ruled them for a half-century. There were about 370,000 Germans in Hungary at the end of the war in 1945, and most of the almost 200,000 who were driven out settled in West Germany. They integrated well and did not form the kind of influential irredentist political organizations as did the Sudeten Germans. The laws that had allowed such forced removal were repealed in the early 1990s, and the parliament's president, Katalin Szili, apologized to Germany in 2007: "Forgive us! Never again!" There are still 62,000 persons in Hungary who claim German nationality, but only 34,000 of them speak German as their mother tongue.

In May 1989 Hungary played a crucial role in German unification by opening its border with Austria to East Germans wanting to escape from the GDR. József Antall, the country's first conservative prime minister after the collapse of communism, claims that "I was always an unconditional supporter of German unification. . . . I am proud to be able to say today that German unity depended on Hungarian independence." Ex-Foreign Minister Gyula Horn played an important role in these events. A survey of elite Hungarian opinion in May 1990 confirmed the same sentiments. Germany was widely regarded as a mediator between Eastern and Western Europe and an advocate for the interest of Central Europe. There is no uneasiness about the fact that Germany is the country's most important trading partner.

Treatment of Hungarian Minorities

One problem that Hungary has with its neighbors is over minorities. Significant Magyar-speaking populations are in Romania, the Czech and Slovak republics, Carpathian Ukraine and the former Yugoslavia. Romania, with between 1.7 and 2 million ethnic Hungarians, has the most, but there are at least 600,000 in Slovakia, mainly in the area of the southern plain. There are fewer in Serbia and Montenegro, and they are chiefly in the autonomous province of Vojvodina in Serbia.

The "Yugo" Magyars became a particular problem for Hungary after Serbia terminated the autonomy status of Voivodina in 1989. This put these Magyars directly under Belgrade's rule. With the withdrawal of Croatia and Slovenia from the collapsing Yugoslavia in 1991–92, these Magyars became hostages to Hungary's actions because Serbia accused Hungary of assisting the Croatians. On a number of occasions, Yugoslav People's Army troops or military aircraft carried out incursions across the border into Hungary.

Partly because of this concern, Hungary supported the dispatch of UN peacekeeping troops, taking the position that the UN ought to be given a greater role in protecting human and minority rights. In his address to the Security Council in 1992, Geza Jeszenszky, the Hungarian foreign minister, argued that: "protecting human and minority rights is more than a legal and humanitarian issue: It is an integral part of international security. Therefore, a firm assertion of these rights by the UN Security Council is indispensable." In 2002 Voivodina's autonomy was restored. There are still occasional reports of Hungarians being mistreated.

Hungary had a running controversy with Romania concerning Romanian treatment of ethnic Magyars during the latter years of the Ceausescu regime. But the matter became more low-key after his fall. Under Ceausescu, Hungarians feared that the Romanians were attempting to "denationalize" Hungarians in Transylvania, and that feeling continued to some extent after 1989. However, the Hungarian Democratic Federation of Romania, the party that represents ethnic Hungarians in Romania, became part of the government coalition in 1997, so that fear no longer exists. In 1997, Hungary and Romania signed an agreement recognizing each other's borders and providing for the opening of a Hungarian consulate in Cluj.

Relations with Slovakia deteriorated after Vladimir Meciar became prime minister. A former communist who discovered the power of nationalism in building popular support, Meciar supported legislation requiring the use of Slovak even in areas where Hungarians were in a majority. In 1997 he suggested that ethnic Hungarians should migrate to Hungary if they were not willing to become good Slovaks.

Adding to the mutually bad relations is the quarrel over Hungary's abandonment of a 1977 agreement to construct jointly a series of dams and hydroelectric power stations on the Danube at Gabcikovo-Nagymaros. The Slovaks obtained a decision from the International Court of Justice in 1997 that Hungary had broken international law in abandoning the 1977 agreement. Meciar's defeat in the 1998 Slovak elections has changed that situation, and now the two countries are on speaking terms again. In 1998 Hungarians entered the Slovak governing coalition.

Orbán once suggested that Hungary would not support Slovakia's entry into NATO unless Bratislava gave benefits to the half million Hungarians living there. He infuriated the Czechs by implying that the Benes decrees, by which tens of thousands of Hungarians had been expelled from Czechoslovakia and had their property expropriated, were incompatible with EU membership and should be revoked. All these remarks seemed to raise some Central European ghosts of the 19th century. Nervousness rose even higher in 2007 when the Slovak parliament endorsed the Benes decrees. Then in July 2009 Slovakia enacted a new language law directed against Hungarian speakers that fined people up to $7,000 for breaking rules promoting the use of Slovak in public.

"Danube Swabians"—German-Hungarians

Minorities make up about 10% of Hungary's population. There are 200,000 to 220,000 German-Hungarians called "Danube Swabians," 100,000 to 110,000 Slovaks and 80,000 to 90,000 Croatians. Like other countries in the region, Hungary has a large Roma (Gypsy) minority numbering 600,000 to 650,000 and constituting about 8% of the total population. Roma face discrimination in Hungarian society, but the government attempts to ameliorate their lives. Like Slovakia and the Czech Republic, it has introduced pre-school programs that help Roma children learn the country's language. It also partly finances boarding schools, such as the Gandhi College in Pecs, which attempt to prepare Roma for university study. There is also a Roma station—Radio C—that serves as a vehicle for the many tribes to speak to each other. It is the first independent Roma radio station in Central Europe.

There has been some progress. In the June 2004 European Parliament elections in Hungary a woman became the first Roma ever to win a seat in that body. In 2008 the National Gallery sponsored an exhibition of contemporary Romany art. This was an especially significant gesture at a time when an outlawed small but loud-mouthed Magyar Garda (Hungarian Guard) dressing up in black paramilitary uniforms with nationalist insignias was parading around denouncing "Roma crimes" and ranting about "safeguarding national culture and traditions." Few Roma are in doubt about who the targets of such rhetoric are. Magyar Garda plays on old stereotypes of Roma as petty criminals and drains on the social welfare system at a time of economic turmoil. In 2008 alone, seven Roma were killed, and six more murders followed the next year. Over 30 Molotov cocktail attacks were launched against their homes, prompting the Roma to start protecting their neigh-

borhoods through nighttime patrols. Magyar Garda's political reward for such shameful behavior was a triumph in the 2010 parliamentary elections, in which its party, Jobbik, captured almost 17% of the votes and a stunning 47 seats.

Prime Minister Viktor Orbán denounces the Magyar Garda, but his outspoken nationalism during his earlier rule from 1998 to 2002 managed to anger almost all of Hungary's neighbors. He was a populist who tried to curry favor at home with his appeals to the sensitive subject of five million ethnic Hungarians who live outside the country's borders. He spoke of "the spiritual and cultural reunification of the Hungarian people."

Without discussing it with Hungary's neighbors, he enacted a "status law" that offered special favors in obtaining work permits to the 2.5 million Hungarians in Romania. He later had to calm Romania's government, which feared that Budapest harbored ambitions to get back Transylvania, which he called "part of Hungary's living space in the Carpathian Basin," by offering all Romanians three-month work permits. The same law irritated the Slovaks.

In September 2003 it was significantly watered down so as not to give offense to neighboring countries. Gone were the claims that Hungarians living abroad form part of a "single Hungarian nation" and the promise of special work permits with all benefits enjoyed by Hungarians. There were still "Hungarian certificates," but they could not serve as official travel or identity documents. In 2004 a Romanian-Hungarian Reconciliation Park in the Transylvanian city of Arad near the Hungarian border was opened.

In a 2004 referendum a majority of voters voted in favor (by 51.5%) of granting citizenship to the roughly 2.5 million ethnic Hungarians living abroad. However, since turnout was under 50%, it was not

adopted. The issue had divided the country and angered its neighbors.

Prime Minister Orbán proclaimed his party's 2010 election victory as a "worldwide victory for Hungary.... As of right now, the yardstick will be that which is in Hungary's interest. And Hungarians outside our borders are fully empowered to engage in the nation's work." It was not clear if that included the right to vote.

Economy

The economy that the post-communist government inherited in 1990 was one that had been moving away from an orthodox communist command economy for a good number of years, though it still retained some aspects of that original pattern. The deviation began in the 1960s under the leadership of János Kádár. For the first six years following the Soviet intervention to put down the Hungarian Revolution, Kádár enforced the old policies of heavy industrialization and collectivization that the regime had tried to get away from after the death of Stalin in 1953. The results were predictably unsatisfactory.

In 1963, with the economy in extreme stress and performing badly, Kádár took note of a reform proposal by a Professor Liberman at the University of Kiev. Intrigued, Kádár decided to try out some of Liberman's ideas. To encourage individual enterprise, the Hungarian government granted a one-year tax exemption to new artisan-type enterprises and guaranteed them access to supplies of raw materials. The result was an immediate increase in the number of working artisans in the villages, a welcome reversal of the longtime trend of migration to the cities. The reform also led to increased service facilities in the cities as tailors and repairmen and mechanics set themselves up in their own shops. Journalists dubbed the new emphasis on more plentiful consumer goods "goulash communism." The party's calculation was that citizens with full bellies would be less inclined to revolt.

In 1966, a more extensive economic reform began to be discussed. This program, which eventually became known as the "New Economic Mechanism," went into effect in 1968. The New Economic Mechanism postulated the continuation of central planning, but proposed a change in the nature of that planning. Instead of concentrating on a minute, day-to-day control over the economy, central-planning experts would concentrate on long-range goals.

Day-to-day management of the economy was delegated to the managers of individual enterprises, who were enjoined to go forward with the plan based on market demand. Although industry would remain state-owned, the state's control would be exercised indirectly by general credit and

Hungary

interest policies and, in the case of individual enterprises, by means of loans provided to finance technological innovations. Wages were to be established by individual factories, though within guidelines set by the central planners. Most important of all, the government gradually relinquished its control over prices. Before the reform began, there were over one million administered prices; by 1970, the figure had dropped to just over 1,000.

The New Economic Mechanism differed from Czech economic proposals of the same time period in envisioning a continued positive role for the central planners. It was also not accompanied by a parallel discussion of possible political reforms. It therefore managed to survive the Soviet invasion of Czechoslovakia. Kádár's condemnation of the Czech experiments and his participation in the invasion of Czechoslovakia were crucial.

The New Economic Mechanism had beneficial effects throughout the economy, but this was particularly true with regard to agriculture. The end of artificially low prices for farm products and the accompanying increase in average earnings in the countryside enhanced incentives and led to a significant growth in production. The change was spectacular. In the mid-1960s, Hungary was a net importer of agriculture products. By the end of the 1960s, it had become a net exporter. In 1990, approximately 30% of Hungary's exports were food products.

The Hungarian government instituted some further economic changes in 1984 that amounted to a strengthening of the New Economic Mechanism. In 1985, approximately three-quarters of all enterprises became eligible for a new type of

Franz Liszt

Béla Bartók

management system that gave them almost complete autonomy. In addition, a new set of financial rules was issued whereby efficient companies were permitted to pay higher wages and were actually encouraged to get rid of unnecessary employees.

The plan called for state subsidies to be eliminated, and those inefficient enterprises that could not make it on their own were to be allowed to go bankrupt. Only one major company experienced bankruptcy at this time, however, and all of its viable parts, along with employees, were taken over by other companies.

Following the change in political leadership in 1988, a further reform of the economic program was adopted. Its object was to create "a genuine commodity, monetary, capital and labor market." A long-range plan, it contemplated several years of austerity and at least 2–3 years of little or no growth before a turnaround would occur.

The most important change had to do with Hungary's small private sector. This sector, which constituted only 4%–5% of the overall economy in 1988, was to be encouraged to grow until it became approximately 30% of the overall economy.

Hungary joined the International Monetary Fund, the Bank for International Settlements, and the International Bank for Recovery and Development (The World Bank) while the communists were still in control. That same government also established a realistic exchange rate for the forint, its national currency.

Hungary deliberately reoriented itself toward world markets. In the 1970s, it began negotiating with Western companies for the opening of manufacturing facilities in Hungary. The most famous product was probably Levi's jeans, which Hungary exported throughout Eastern Europe and the Soviet Union.

In the 1980s, a number of other Western companies began operating in Hungary.

Among those was McDonald's, which opened its first store in downtown Budapest in 1987. Although fast food restaurants were still a foreign concept in Central and Eastern Europe, the government began opening its own fast food outlets in 1984 under the English name of "City Grill." They proved to be so popular that a state catering firm signed a contract with McDonald's to franchise the real thing.

On the negative side, Hungarian borrowings to finance the importation of Western technology had raised its hard-currency debt to approximately $8 billion by 1981. When the Polish economy collapsed, Western bankers began to worry about Hungary's debt as well. Arguing that it had a relatively well-managed, market-oriented economy, the government managed to retain its access to Western credit. By 1989, debt servicing consumed 38.5% of Hungary's hard-currency earnings. Its economic situation improved in the early 1990s, and for several years Hungary became the largest recipient of foreign investment in Central and Eastern Europe.

The Post-Communist Era

Hungary's greatest problem was privatizing industry. Foreign investment, particularly joint ventures, made a contribution, but it became a political issue as opposition parties asserted that the government had sold the country's patrimony to outsiders. The potency of the argument was revealed by a 1994 poll of workers indicating that only 4% strongly favored foreign investment, while 40% were opposed.

Much of this was perception since foreign investments still constituted less than 10% of GDP. In addition, the number of Hungarian-owned small firms continued to grow rapidly even as the state sector contracted. The private sector accounted for over 50% of GDP as early as 1994.

At that time, the state-owned sector still included most of the country's energy, chemical and pharmaceutical industries and nearly all banks, though there were plans to reduce state ownership to 2%. In addition, enterprises that were to remain under state control had been transferred to a new state holding agency, the State Property Company, and it was intended that even these would be partially privatized by having the State Property Company issue stock that would be sold to the public.

In the 21st century Hungary has officially completed its transition to a market economy, and 92% of its GDP is generated by the private sector. In 2005 it offered for sale a 75% minus one vote stake in the asset management of Budapest Ferihegy airport, which has increased its passenger numbers by 30% thanks to discount airlines. This would not include the airport's property and infrastructure, which would remain permanently in state hands. This would be one of the largest airport sell-offs in the world. Despite a court ruling that threatened to derail the sell-off, the government vowed to press on with the sale. It is also attempting to sell the state-owned airline Malev.

Hungarians are better off economically than they have ever been. They experienced a rude setback in 2008–9 as a result of the global downturn. Credit froze around the world in October 2008, and Hungary found itself unable to finance its budget deficit. The government was compelled to secure a $27 billion rescue package from the IMF, the World Bank and the European Union. The value of its currency, the florint, fell, and many Hungarians who had taken out loans and mortgages in foreign currencies in the boom years discovered that they had to pay back far more than they had borrowed. The economy shrank by about 6% in 2009, a far cry from the previous steady GDP growth Hungary had experienced of almost 5% per year since 1998. In 2010 that growth was .1%. Per capita GDP was 62% of the EU average in 2005 (up from 52% in 2000), compared with 47% for Poland and 72% for Slovenia. Inflation was 4.1% in 2010. Unemployment rose to 11.8% in 2010, but it may be lower since it is estimated that the black economy may account for one-fifth of GDP. Its productivity growth, at 6.3% in 2005, was one of Europe's highest. Real wages went up by more than 17% from 1999 to 2002, and the minimum wage had risen by 72%. In 2004, average gross monthly wages were 580 euros, compared with 530 in the Czech Republic and 500 in Poland.

The greatest fear is that the economic crisis might last several years while the budget deficit had gotten out of control: 4.5% in 2010. Both main parties indulged in populist spending while in power. Hungary ran a huge budget deficit of 10.1% of GDP in 2006, the highest in the EU. It must reduce that to 3% in order to adopt the euro. At 62% of GDP in 2009 and rising, its total foreign debt is over the limit of 60% to qualify for the euro. It remains burdened by an oversized public sector that consumes about half of GDP.

By 2010, 79% of Hungary's exports, most of which are advanced capital goods, went to EU countries. Its main trading partner by far is Germany, which buys over a fourth of its exports imports. It gets 6.9% of its imports from Russia. It is especially dependent upon Russia for 80% of its gas supplies. In 2006 Hungary broke with the EU's planned Nabucco pipeline project to join Gazprom's Blue Stream pipeline, which brings oil under the Black Sea from Russia to Turkey and one day on to Hungary. However, in July 2009 Hungary signed on to the plan to transport Iraqi gas through Nabucco's pipeline, circumventing Russia.

Foreign investment is slowing down. By 2005 it had attracted 48 billion euros in foreign direct investment, making it the second-leading FDI per capita country in Central and Eastern Europe after Poland. However, by 2010 foreign investors were sparking resentment among parts of the population. The ruling Fidesz party stoked this by railing against privatization and foreign investment. The right-wing press is filled with conspiracy theories about global capitalism and greedy foreign financiers. Fortunately the country's banks, most of them foreign, did not collapse during the recession.

In 2005 the Swiss-based Institute for International Management ranked Hungary 37th out of 60 countries in terms of competitiveness. It outranked EU15 members Spain, Portugal, Greece and Italy, and was one place behind the Czech Republic and three places ahead of Slovakia. It has one of the most globally integrated economies, according to the 2005 annual Globalization Index report.

During the 1990s major investors included American firms such as General Motors, General Electric, Ford, Compaq, Alcoa and Ameritech; German companies like Deutsche Telekom and in 2008 Daimler, which chose Kecskemet, Hungary, for a new 800 million euro assembly plant, its first in Central Europe; Japanese companies such as Suzuki; and Austrian firms Julius Meinl and Kleiner Bauder. General Motors invested $193 million in a joint venture project with Hungary's Raba Factory to produce 200,000 engines and assemble an estimated 15,000 Opel Astra automobiles a year. The first Opel Astra rolled off the assembly line in 1992. Suzuki, a Japanese automobile company, began manufacturing Suzuki Swifts at its plant in the town of Esztergom in 1992. Ford paid $80 million for a plant to produce electronic components for cars. General Electric purchased Tungsram, Hungary's lighting manufacturer, in 1989. Other American companies investing in Hungary include the Digital Equipment Corporation, Schwinn Bicycle Company, Cartier, Apple Computer, and US West. General Electric, Alcoa and Oracle have outsourced some of their operations to Hungary.

In addition, the Swiss have entered into joint ventures in pharmaceuticals and food. Ikea, the Swedish-based furniture group, opened a store in Budapest. Austrian and German firms were among the first large investors. In 1990, for example, nationals of these two countries sponsored more than 60% of all joint ventures although more recently most investment has come from other countries. Today the EU member countries are the source of 60% and climbing of foreign direct investment, the highest in Central and Eastern Europe. In the 1990s, the largest single investor in Hungary was the United States, which had provided a third of the $25 billion invested by foreigners in that country. But by 2003 the U.S. had fallen to the third-largest investor in Central and Eastern Europe behind Germany and the Netherlands.

Another success story is the growth in local start-up firms, particularly high tech firms. One such example is Graphhisoft, a firm started in the early 1980s, which today is one of the world's top five companies making computer-aided design software for architects, with subsidiaries in 12 countries. Another is Cygron, a firm that produces artificial-intelligence software. Cygron was having trouble marketing its Data-Scope software internationally, however, so in 1998 it sold out to MindMaker, a California-based company owned by József Kiraly, an expatriate Hungarian. Today the company is valued at between $20 million and $40 million.

Post-communist plenitude. Central market in Budapest.

Hungary

High-tech continues to be a growth industry in Hungary, largely because of the abundance of talent stemming from an education system that emphasizes mathematics and science. International companies that have built major research and development facilities in Hungary include Ericsson, Nokia, Motorola, and Siemens. By 2010, 63% of the workforce was employed in the services sector, which produces 60.8% of GDP; 32% were employed in industry, producing 37.2% of GDP. The percentage of GDP generated by the private sector has steadily risen from 18% in 1990, 55% in 1994, and 80% the end of the century to 92% today. Tourism accounts for 10% of GDP and rising. Those visitors who do not understand the difficult Hungarian language can keep informed through the English-language weeklies, *The Budapest Sun* and *The Budapest Times*.

Agriculture remains an important part of the economy although it accounts for only 5% of employment and 2% of GDP. Significant changes have taken place in this sector as well. Collective farms had already been given considerable autonomy under the communists, and numerous small businesses had also grown up in conjunction with them. Agriculture has been privatized, though legal conflicts about the ownership of land slowed the issuance of deeds in some cases. A major problem is with eastern Hungary, where a higher percentage of people subsist on small farms and where, in some areas, unemployment tops 20%. The government is addressing this problem by offering tax breaks to industry willing to relocate here. A new, major highway is also being constructed that will run from Budapest to the Romanian border.

One worrisome problem is the quality of Hungary's health care despite the fact that it spends 7% of its GDP on it. Its people are among the sickest in Europe. They go to the doctor an average of a dozen times a year, twice the Western European rate. A practice that has especially become a subject of public debate is the tipping of doctors. Without it treatment is often slow or denied. Many Hungarians think the tipping system demonstrates that doctors are not concerned with and accountable to their patients. The former Socialist government reduced the number of hospital beds by a fourth and closed three hospitals in 2006. Ultimately the health system should be changed so that the patients pay some of their costs and the culture of bribery is eliminated.

Hungarians have the lowest life expectancy in the EU (69.2 years for men and 77.4 for women) except for Latvians and Lithuanians. They also have the world's fifth-worst record (behind Latvia, Lithuania, Estonia and Russia) for suicide, with women three times more likely than men to kill themselves.

Natural Resources

Hungary is relatively short of natural resources, which means that it is heavily dependent on imports. In the past, the Soviet Union provided it with approximately 90% of its oil, iron ore and timber needs, plus a high proportion of other raw materials; Russia currently provides for 80% of Hungary's gas needs. Hungary's main domestic fuel source is a low-quality brown coal. Unfortunately, its reserves are not extensive, and coal production has started to decline. For this reason, the government made a commitment to

develop nuclear energy. There are currently three plants in operation, two of them completed in 1987. Its major power plant is in Paks, which produces 40% of Hungary's electricity. Russia is drawing up plans to modernize four Soviet-built power units at Paks, and it has a contract to provide nuclear fuel to the plants until at least 2013.

Although public sentiment turned sharply against nuclear energy as a result of the 1986 Soviet nuclear accident at Chernobyl, Hungarian plants are of a different design from the graphite-type plants found at Chernobyl. They make use of pressurized water in their design to slow down the neutrons in the fuel. Hungarian plants are also considered to be safer because the government takes many more security steps than in the former Soviet Union and has incorporated many Western design elements.

CULTURE

The Magyar language is not related to any of Europe's major languages except Finnish, and even these two languages are mutually incomprehensible. Hungarian culture is therefore distinct from that of its neighbors. There is also a strong international culture since most educated Hungarians are fluent in at least one foreign language. Hungarian plays have to be translated before they can go abroad, but one such play, "Cats Play" by Istvan Örkény, was popular when it was produced in the United States in the 1970s.

In 2002 the first Hungarian writer ever was honored with the Nobel Prize in Literature. Imre Kertesz is a Holocaust survivor whose novels concentrate on his experiences in Auschwitz and Buchenwald. His works were almost unknown in his own country since he refused to conform to the Communist rule. He led a solitary life in Hungary and eked out a living translating German-language works. Only two of his novels were translated into English: *Fateless* and *Kaddish for a Child Not Born*, both of which are semiautobiographical novels. Kertesz is a harsh critic of his native Hungary for its role in sending Jews to their deaths and for what he sees as latent anti-Semitism.

Hungarians are also noted for their films, many of which would be classified as new wave or art films. Only about 20 Hungarian films are made in a year, however, so theaters show many foreign films. One particularly successful Hungarian producer in recent years, István Szabó, made the films "Colonel Redl" and "Hanussen," both of which were released in the United States. Both deal with the cultural area of the old Austro-Hungarian Empire and were released with a German

Hungarian Patriot Lajos Kossuth cheered in New York, 1851

Hungary

Hungarian-Croatian Bilingual school in Hungary

soundtrack. His film, "Mephisto" won an Oscar. The Hungarian film "Sunshine" was an Oscar runner-up.

Composers Franz Liszt and Béla Bartok were Hungarians. Many musicians fled abroad after the failure of the 1956 revolution, and many of those were associated with the Philharmonia Hungarica. Although often mistaken for a touring orchestra from Budapest, it actually had its home base in Western Germany. But Hungary produced a new generation of musicians in time, and soloists developed a strong reputation at home and abroad. In addition, émigrés such as the pianist Peter Frankl and conductor Arpad Joo were invited back to Hungary for guest performances.

Under communism, the government supported cultural activities and spent an estimated $27 million to renovate the State Opera House in Budapest in the 1980s. The arts were heavily subsidized, with the average ticket to a full opera or first-class concert costing about $2. The government also sponsored numerous "folk festivals" throughout the country. Things have changed little in this area since 1990. Although the price for such things as a seat at

the opera has increased considerably, high culture still continues to be subsidized.

Most of Hungary's universities are public, but it has one of Europe's most successful private universities, Central European University in Budapest. It was founded and funded by George Soros, who was born in Hungary but made a fortune as a currency speculator and hedge-fund manager in the United States.

Religion

Church-and-state relations were quite bad for many years under communism. However, they began to improve at the beginning of the 1970s after Cardinal Mindszenty, who had been residing in the American Embassy from 1956 onward, agreed to go into exile; he died in Vienna in 1975. His successor, László Lékai, was named a cardinal in 1976. János Kádár summed up his position on religion at a press conference in Paris in late 1978: "We have ever considered it most important that honest religious citizens, doing a fair day's work building our country, should not be faced with irreconcilable problems of conscience by the confrontation of state and church. As the result of protracted, patient work settling the relationship between the state and the churches, a religious citizen can now, at the same time, be committed to social progress and socialism, and be a faithful son of his church."

Cardinal Lékai died in 1986. Negotiations for appointment of his successor and new bishops dragged on before the government finally gave its approval to the appointment of Cardinal László Paskai. The government had insisted that the Church take action against one of its priests, Father Gyorgy Bulanyi, who was preaching the incompatibility of Christianity and service in the military. The

Church, which had its own problems with Father Bulanyi, was nevertheless unwilling to repudiate him completely.

Church-and-state relations improved dramatically after Grösz became general secretary. For example, that the government rehabilitated József Cardinal Mindszenty and extended an invitation for the Pope to visit Hungary. One of the first acts of the new noncommunist government, installed in May 1990, was to reopen diplomatic relations with the Vatican. It followed this up by dismantling all government controls over religion. The Christian Democrats were part of the government coalition from 1990 to 1994.

By the 21st century Hungary's Jewish population was approximately 100,000, the third largest in Europe, though only a small part of the 800,000 who lived in Hungary prior to World War II. The Communist rulers blamed the Holocaust almost exclusively on the Nazis, aided by a few Hungarian "extremists." Before 1989 Jews kept a low profile although the government permitted them to run a school and the only rabbinical seminary in Eastern Europe. After the fall of communism, the local Jewish population opened two Jewish schools. Jewish publications, cultural associations, and youth groups have begun expanding, and Budapest's 4,000-seat synagogue has been renovated. Jews are represented at all levels of political life. Every Jewish child is entitled to free tuition from kindergarten to university in schools run by Jewish institutions. Jewish religious and cultural activity is reviving, especially in Budapest. As the *Washington Post* reported, "it all amounts to the revival of what was one of Europe's largest and most prolific Jewish communities." In 2004 a Holocaust Memorial Center was opened in the capital around a restored synagogue on Pava Street, which had been used in 1944 as an internment camp.

FUTURE

With a new center-right government led by Prime Minister Viktor Orbán, the government will continue to strive to overcome the deepest recession since the end of communism in 1989; 70% of respondents in May 2009 recognized the need for painful steps to get out of the crisis. The resounding victory by Orbán's Fidesz party, which captured two-thirds of the parliamentary seats, puts it in a good position to enact needed reforms. The elections took place in the context of rising social tensions. A string of attacks was directed against Roma by the thuggish and intimidating Magyar Garda and its Jobbik party, which won almost 17% of the votes in the April 2010 parliamentary elections.

Franz Liszt performs for Franz-Josef I, Emperor of Austria and King of Hungary

The Former Yugoslavia

Due to their shared histories as well as frequent geographical and cultural similarities, there is necessarily some repetition from one entry to the other.

Serb Parliament, Belgrade, with election billboard of President Boris Tadic

On April 27, 1992, after four of the six republics that had been integral parts of *The Socialist Federal Republic of Yugoslavia* had declared their independence, the remaining two, Serbia and Montenegro—the largest and smallest in the former union—proclaimed themselves the successor nation as the "new" *Federal Republic of Yugoslavia*. This rump state, renamed Serbia and Montenegro in 2002, was little more than an extension of the Republic of Serbia. Voters in Montenegro opted for independence in a May 21, 2006, referendum. Kosovo declared its independence from Serbia on February 17, 2008.

Few European regions have so concerned the world since the collapse of communism as the former Yugoslavia. It was always the most liberal and independent communist regime. Most observers were therefore optimistic about the prospects for this multiethnic and multinational federation as the last decade of the 20th century dawned. However, fate took a different course. Bloody ethnic strife seized the headlines, and the word "genocide" reappeared in the daily news for the first time since the Second World War. Events in this bleeding ex-state prompted NATO to fire its first shots in anger, and international peacekeepers are the only ones in certain parts of the area who can keep hostile ethnic groups from each other's throats.

With the demise of the Yugoslavian federal government in 1991 following the withdrawal of four of the six republics, the Federal Republic of Yugoslavia, renamed "Serbia and Montenegro" in 2003, has shrunk to a rump of its former self. It now consists only of the Republic of Serbia. On May 21, 2006, 55.5% of Montenegrin voters opted for independence, completing the disintegration of federal Yugoslavia. On February 17, 2008, Kosovo (or Kosova in Albanian) declared its independence, something that Serbia refused to accept. Serbia has only one remaining "autonomous" region, the Vojvodina. The latter is

negotiating its own independence and is largely self-ruling under UN supervision.

The Voivodina is that part of Serbia north of the Danube River. It is a rich, flat plain, divided by tributaries of the Danube flowing across it from the north. It borders on Hungary to the north, Croatia to the west, and Romania on the east. It was originally granted an autonomous status because a large minority (approximately 300,000) of the population is ethnically Hungarian.

Serbia proper is divided into three distinct regions: the lowland area of the north, an area of rolling hills in the middle and, south of that, mountain ridges cut by the Danube River flowing northward. Mountains also predominate along the western border with Montenegro and in the east along the border with Bulgaria.

The rump Yugoslavia that was left after the break-up of the country in 1992 consisted almost entirely of Serbs and the linguistically and culturally closely related Montenegrins, who split from Serbia in June 2006. The exception is the formerly autonomous region of Vojvodina, where Hungarians, other non-Slavs, and Croatians live. The Serbian government destroyed its autonomous status in 1990–91, but restored it in 2002. Today its own officials rule with some oversight from Serbia. The Hungarians there are well integrated and enjoy cultural and language rights. Vojvodina's citizens are wealthier than those living in Serbia or Kosovo.

HISTORY

The Slavic-speaking peoples of the Balkan Peninsula are classified as South Slavs. They are one of three branches of the Slavic peoples, the other two being the East Slavs (Russians, Ukrainians, Belarusians) and the West Slavs (Poles, Czechs, Slovaks). The Slavic language is a branch of the Indo-European family of languages. When the Slavic peoples first appeared in history, they were found mostly in the area of the Pripet Swamps in what are now the republics of Belarus and Ukraine.

The South Slavs began migrating into the area of the Balkans sometime in the 6th century. At first, they were dominated by two Turkic peoples also present in what became the Balkans, the Avars and Bulgars. When the Avar and Bulgar khanates crumbled in the first quarter of the 7th century, however, the Byzantine emperor signed an alliance with two of the stronger Slavic tribes, the Serbs and Croats. Supported by this alliance, the Slavic peoples either pushed the Turkic peoples out of the Balkans or submerged them in their greater numbers. By the end of the 7th century, Slavic language and culture was dominant throughout most of the northern Balkans. The exceptions were

The Former Yugoslavia

in the East where the Vlach (also called Wallachians, ancestors of modern Romanians) were in a majority and in mountainous areas of the West where the native Illyrian people (ancestors of the modern Albanians) managed to keep their culture alive.

The Serbs and Croats eventually gave their names to the areas of the Balkans they now occupy, while a third tribe, the Slovenes, who had actually been the first of the Slavic tribes to enter the Balkans, settled further west. In 748, the Slovenes were incorporated into the Carolingian Empire and converted to Roman Catholicism. They remained a part of Western culture from that time onward. The Croats were also incorporated into the Carolingian Empire for a short time at the beginning of the 9th century and converted to Roman Catholicism. At the end of the 11th century they came under the control of the Kingdom of Hungary.

The first Serb state rose about the middle of the 9th century when a number of south Serbian tribes united to oppose expansion from the Bulgar state to the southeast. Vlastimir, the ruler of this state, sought the support of the Byzantine emperor against the Bulgars. In the process, he submitted himself to the overlordship of the Byzantine emperor.

One effect of this is that Serbia became open to Byzantine cultural influences, the most important of which was Orthodox Christianity. In addition, the two missionaries from Thessalonica, Cyril and Methodius, had created a script for the Slavic language based on Greek letters. They worked in different locales: Macedonia, Bulgaria and Moravia in the present-day Czech Republic. They started a literacy movement in Ohrid, now in Macedonia. The Cyrillic alphabet was adopted by Serbia along with Orthodox Christianity. In the process a great cultural divide was created in the Balkans that ran through the middle of the Slavic settlements. Henceforth, Serbs (along with Bulgarians, Montenegrins and Macedonians) were on one side of that divide, and the Croats and Slovenes were on the other.

In spite of Byzantine assistance, Vlastimir's kingdom eventually fell under Bulgarian control. As a result, the Serb church became a part of the Bulgarian Orthodox Church. The area of Serbia next came under the control of a Macedonian kingdom created at the beginning of the 11th century. Then the Byzantine empire overthrew the Macedonian kingdom in 1018 and tried to extend its control over the area of the eastern Balkans. This led to short-lived kingdoms arising in Herzegovina and Montenegro to challenge the Byzantine control. Toward the end of the 11th century, yet another kingdom rose in the area of Novi Pazar, only to be supplanted by a revived Bulgarian kingdom after the capture of Constantinople by soldiers of the fourth crusade in 1204.

A new Serbian kingdom rose in the area of Skopje ("Skope-ye") beginning in 1282. It was called the Nemanjic Empire after the name of the dynasty. The founder of this dynasty was Stefan Nemanja. This kingdom reached its height under its ninth ruler, Stefan Dusan, who ruled from 1331 to 1355. During his reign, Serbia was an empire for the only time in its history. Although this kingdom eventually extended its control over a large part of the northern Balkans, its greatest significance was probably cultural. The Nemanjids were committed to the Orthodox Church. It was during this time that the Serbs managed to separate from the Bulgarian Orthodox Church and establish an autonomous Serbian Orthodox Church. The founder was St. Sava, one of Stefan Nemanja's sons, who helped establish the Serbians' identity and religion. The seat of the church was later moved to Pec. In 1375, it was raised to a patriarchate.

Equally important, the Nemanjics managed to create a Serbian "high culture" based on religious cohesion. They fought the influence of Roman Catholicism and worked to suppress Bogomilism, a religious heresy centered in Bosnia. They were also responsible for construction of many churches and monasteries, which have come to signify the essence of medieval Serbian Orthodoxy. Among the most renowned of these churches are the Mileseva (about 1235), Pec (1250), Moraca (1252), Sopocani (about 1260), and the Decani (1327). Many of these churches are decorated by frescoes, the most important being those of the Raska school. In addition, this period produced a number of literary works, including a biography of Stefan Nemanja. A close partnership between church and state created a culture that was both courtly and religious. This continued to define the best of what it meant to be Serbian long after the kingdom itself was no more.

This kingdom came to an end in the 14th century, when Turkish armies defeated the Serbs in the Battle of Kosovo, which took place on June 28, 1389 (June 15 by the old calendar). The leader of the Serbian forces was Prince Lazar. A Serbian assassin, Milosh Obilic, who made his way into the Turkish camp pretending to be a deserter, killed the Turkish sultan, Murad I, early in the day. He stabbed the sultan with a poisoned dagger. However, Murad's son managed to rally his forces and defeat the Serbians. Taken prisoner during the battle, Prince Lazar was beheaded.

For 70 years, Serbs were required to pay an annual tribute and to serve in the Turkish armies. However, they were allowed domestic autonomy. In 1459, the sultan placed all of Serbia under Turkish rule. All lands became his property, and all Serbs became bond slaves of the land. A new kind of elite military force was created out of conscripted Christian boys from the Balkans. Called Janissaries ("New Troops"), they almost always converted to Islam and became famous and respected warriors. They became property of the sultan and over time grew into one of the most influential power institutions in the empire. The patriarchate of Pec was suppressed for a time, but it was restored in 1557. Henceforth, Serbian culture lived on only within the Serbian Orthodox Church.

The Road to Serbian Independence

Turkish rule continued for another three and a half centuries before the Serbs raised the banner of rebellion. Under the leadership of Karageorge (Karadjordje or "Black George"), the Serbs revolted against the Turks in 1804. It was suppressed in 1813, but a more successful revolt broke out two years later under the leadership of Milosh Obrenovic.

In 1817, Serbia won the right to have its own national assembly. Milosh became Prince of Serbia and promptly had his great rival, Karageorge, murdered. This was the beginning of a feud between the Obrenovic and Karageorgevic families that continued into the 20th century, frequently disrupting the political life of the country.

After the Russo-Turkish War of 1828–29, Serbia was given the status of an autonomous principality. It was technically still under Turkish suzerainty, but it was effectively a Russian protectorate.

In 1876, Serbia became the cause of another war between Russia and Turkey after it declared war on Turkey. When it became clear that Serbia would not be able to stand against the Turks, Russia intervened in 1877. Russia defeated the Turks and forced Turkey to recognize the independence of Serbia (and Romania) in the Treaty of San Stefano. The great powers revised the Treaty at the Congress of Berlin in 1878, but the resulting Treaty of Berlin included recognition of Serbian independence.

In 1885–86, Serbia fought a war against Bulgaria after that nation and Eastern Rumelia united in 1885. The conflict began when Prince Milan demanded that Bulgaria cede some of its territory to Serbia. Prince Alexander of Bulgaria defeated Serbian forces, and it was only Austria's threat to enter the war on Serbia's side that produced an armistice. Serbia then recognized the union of Bulgaria and Eastern Rumelia.

In 1903, a palace revolution led by forces loyal to the Karageorgevic family

The Former Yugoslavia

WESTERN BALKANS 1560–1680

—— Boundary of the Holy Roman Empire   ▦ Austrian Possessions

OTTOMAN (Turkish) EMPIRE at its greatest extent.

MONTENEGRO, an area of virtually inaccessible mountains, never conquered by the Turks.

REPUBLIC OF VENICE, ruled by an elite of wealthy merchant families. Dominated the Adriatic Sea from bases in Dalmatia.

REPUBLIC OF RAGUSA (Dubrovnik), a small city-state which flourished as an important cultural center, developing distinctive local styles of architecture and sculpture, and establishing Croatian as a modern literary language.

These boundaries were essentially stable for over a century as the Austrian Habsburgs resisted further Turkish advances into Central Europe.

KINGDOM OF NAPLES, ruled by the Spanish Habsburgs as a separate kingdom.

PAPAL STATES—In these territories the Pope was the secular ruler. Other Church territories were ruled by bishops or abbots who were princes of the Holy Roman Empire.

AUSTRIAN POSSESSIONS—A collection of separate kingdoms, duchies and counties, ruled by the Austrian branch of the House of Hapsburg.

HOLY ROMAN EMPIRE—During this period all emperors were from the Austrian Habsburgs.

1680–1740

The Ottoman Empire attempted to expand into Central Europe, but the Turkish army was held at the gates of Vienna in 1683, and then forced back, liberating the entire central basin of the Danube River; the new Austro-Turkish border stabilized in 1739.

AUSTRIAN MILITARY FRONTIER—Refugee Serbian communities were settled along the border in Croatia and Slavonia (not to be confused with the present republic of SLOVENIA) by the Austrian government. A military constitution to defend the Slavonian borderland was granted in 1702 and later extended to Croatia and Transylvania.

KINGDOM OF THE TWO SICILIES—After changing hands several times, the Kingdom of Naples and the Kingdom of Sicily were combined in 1735 under a junior branch of the House of Bourbon.

The Former Yugoslavia

WESTERN BALKANS 1740–1797

Boundary of the Holy Roman Empire   Austrian Military Frontier   Austrian Possessions

The Ottoman Empire was no longer a threat, and Austria was occupied in central Europe with the rise of Prussia and the partition of Poland. Boundaries were basically stable during this period.

1797–1815

During the Napoleonic wars political boundaries and country names changed frequently.

The Venetian territories were carved up in 1797, the largest part going temporarily to Austria.

The Holy Roman Empire became extinct in 1806.

In 1809 France briefly annexed all of the eastern Adriatic coast as well as Ragusa and nearly all of present-day Slovenia.

By 1809 all territories ruled by the Roman Catholic Church had been acquired by secular states.

Meanwhile, Montenegro won a small expansion of its boundaries.

WESTERN BALKANS 1815–1860

Boundary of the German Confederation ▪ Austrian Military Frontier ▪ Austrian Possessions

In the post–Napoleonic settlements, Austria (re)gained all of the Venetian territories plus Ragusa as well as those Church territories within its borders. The Military Frontier was maintained, becoming a separate crownland in 1849 with special privileges for the Serbian settlers.

GERMAN CONFEDERATION—Created to replace the Holy Roman Empire with the same eastern and southern boundaries.

The Pope was restored as ruler of central Italy, but all other former Church territories remained secularized.

SERBIA—The Serbs had been fighting for their independence since 1804, achieving in 1817 recognition as an autonomous principality under Ottoman overlordship.

These boundaries were essentially stable during this period.

The Former Yugoslavia

THE ETHNIC/RELIGIOUS MIXTURE WITH RESULTING AGE-OLD TENSIONS

As of the 2002 census

- ☐ Slovenes
- ☰ Croats
- ⋯ Serbs
- ⧄ Bosnians (Muslims)
- ☰ Montenegrins
- ⦚ Macedonians
- ⣿ Hungarians
- ⧄ Albanians
- ▦ Ethnic mixture

Montenegro

Montenegro experienced centuries of independence while the surrounding areas seethed under Turkish control. The almost impassable mountains allowed the Montenegrins to resist repeated Turkish attempts to conquer the area. Although the Turks and later the Venetians did occupy parts of Montenegro, it was never completely controlled. The Congress of Berlin recognized its independence in 1878. During the years before World War I, the Montenegrins, like some of their neighbors, were advocates of South Slav nationalism. They lent military support to the cause in 1878 against the Turks and during the Balkan Wars of 1912–13.

World War I

A Bosnian Serb student named Gavrilo Princip assassinated Archduke Franz Ferdinand, heir to the Habsburg throne, in Sarajevo on June 28, 1914. Princip belonged to the "Black Hand" (also called "The Young Bosnia") a Serbian nationalist

The last King of Serbia, Peter I

organization formed in Serbia in 1911 with the goal of unifying all Serbs.

Austria responded to the murder with an ultimatum to Serbia, demanding in part that Austrian officials be permitted to participate in the investigation of the crime. When the Serbian government accepted only part of the terms of the ultimatum, Austria-Hungary declared war on Serbia. Because of a multitude of cross-alliances, France and Russia came into the war on the side of Serbia, while Germany entered as an ally of Austria-Hungary. Britain entered when Germany violated Belgian neutrality, and World War I began. Bulgaria and Turkey later entered on the side of Germany and Austria-Hungary, while Romania entered as an ally of

control. This brought Serbia into conflict with the Austrian Empire, since Serbia also laid claim to Austrian lands occupied by South Slavs.

Relations worsened after Austria formally annexed Bosnia-Herzegovina in 1908. Austria had obtained these lands in 1878 as part of the Treaty of Berlin, but it had not formally annexed them. Serbia, supported by Russia, threatened to go to war against Austria in 1908, but Russia was forced to back down in 1909, and Serbia was left in the lurch.

It then began putting together an alliance of Balkan countries that led to the First and Second Balkan Wars in 1912–13. Serbia obtained additional territories as a result of these conflicts. However, Austria frustrated Serbia's attempts to gain access to the Adriatic Sea coast, among other things by sponsoring creation of an independent Albania. In 1914, Serbia played an important role in the origins of World War I by sponsoring the Black Hand, the Serbian revolutionary group that carried out the assassination of Archduke Franz Ferdinand, heir to the Austrian throne, while he was paying a state visit to Sarajevo, capital city of Bosnia-Herzegovina.

led to the murder of the Obrenovic family and the ascension of the Karageorgevic dynasty to the throne. In a change of foreign policy, the new king set out in earnest to create a Greater Serbia by bringing as much of the Balkans as he could under his

The Former Yugoslavia

The last King of Montenegro, Nicholas I

France, Britain and Russia. Thus almost all of the Balkans became involved in the war.

Austrian armies reached Belgrade by December 1914, but were repelled by a counterattack. Bulgaria's entry in 1915 helped shift the equation against Serbia. The Serbian army retreated to the Adriatic coast and then to the island of Corfu. In 1918, Allied forces made their way into the Balkan Peninsula. The Serbian army joined with the Allies in defeating Bulgaria, then liberated Serbia.

A New Nation is Born

During the war, discussions were held on creating a separate state for South Slavs who had been part of the Austro-Hungarian Empire. Serb leaders hesitated at first because their longtime vision was of a single Greater Serbian Kingdom that would include all areas inhabited by Serbs. The remaining South Slavic leaders had something else in mind. They wanted a decentralized South Slavic state organized along federal lines that would allow a large amount of autonomy to the individual ethnic groups. Representatives of the two points of view signed the Corfu Pact in 1917 in which they agreed to create a South Slav state after the war under the Karageorgevic dynasty.

Although basically South Slav, what became Yugoslavia consisted literally of what was left over after France, Great Britain and the U.S. redrew a new map of Eastern Europe after World War I. On December 4, 1918, the Kingdom of the Serbs, Croats and Slovenes was proclaimed in Belgrade with Prince Alexander of Serbia as Regent. Serbia (including Macedonia and Kosovo), which had been independent before the war, formed the core of this new kingdom. The Kingdom of Montene-gro, also independent before the war, was added when the King of Montenegro resigned his throne in favor of the new South Slavic State. To this was added territories from the former Austro-Hungarian Empire—Croatia, the Voivodina, Bosnia-Herzegovina, and Slovenia—plus strategic points taken from Bulgaria along the Serbian-Bulgarian border.

Politics of the Interwar Period

The political structure of this new kingdom was supposed to be decided by the Constituent Assembly elected in 1920. In 1921 it adopted a constitution creating a centralized government. The necessary votes came from the Serbian parties and smaller ones that had "sold" their votes in return for promises of special favors. This led the Croatian Peasant Party to boycott the Assembly because of its opposition to the centralized system.

The period 1921–1928 was one of conflict between the Serbs and Croats over the question of centralism vs. federalism. The Serbs prevailed by using increasingly harsh tactics, including the arrest of the Croat opposition leader and dissolving his party. Outraged, the Croatian deputies withdrew from parliament, swearing not to return until they had been granted a federal system in which Croatia would no longer be controlled from Belgrade. The demands of the Croats were unacceptable to the Serbian leaders, and also to King Alexander.

Taking advantage of a decade of disagreement between the Serbs and Croats, the king abolished the constitution and proclaimed a royal dictatorship. He later changed the name of the country to the Kingdom of Yugoslavia, which did not alter the fact that Serbs, Croats and Slovenes lived and fought with each other within the boundaries of the kingdom. Alexander's mistake was in thinking he could create a Yugoslav nationalism by decree. He was assassinated in 1934 by Macedonian and Croatian terrorists.

From 1934 to 1941 a three-man regency ruled the country with Prince Paul as first regent. Internal affairs were left to the pre-

The combatants at the start of World War I, 1914

403

The Former Yugoslavia

mier, who governed with the support of a specially organized party, the Yugoslav Radical Union. Parties in opposition formed an alliance and demanded a new constitution that would set up a government capable of dealing with the discontented Croats. When the extent of the Serb-Croat split was revealed in 1938 elections, the government sought talks with the Croatian leadership. The result was an agreement creating an internally self-governing Croatia.

In international relations during the interwar period, Yugoslavia was most concerned about protecting its borders against the ambitions of neighboring states and the great powers who wanted to use the conflicts among the Balkan states to extend their own influence. Both the "Little Entente" and the "Balkan Entente" were supposed to serve these purposes. In 1920–21 Yugoslavia formed an alliance with Romania and Czechoslovakia, the "Little Entente," which was directed primarily against Hungarian ambitions to revise the Treaty of Trianon. France backed the "Little Entente" through treaties with Czechoslovakia (1924), Romania (1926) and Yugoslavia (1927).

After a series of conferences from 1930–1933, Greece, Turkey, Romania and Yugoslavia signed the Balkan Pact (February 1934) guaranteeing the territorial status quo against aggression by any Balkan state. In practice, this meant that the Pact was directed against Bulgaria. Several months later, the signatories adopted the Statutes of the Balkan Entente that set up a Permanent Council provided for regular meetings and extensive economic and political cooperation. Both alliance systems disintegrated by the end of the 1930s.

The rise of Germany and Italy, the inability of the League of Nations to deal with acts of aggression, and the appeasement policy of Britain and France made Yugoslavia search for new means of ensuring its security. Accordingly, it signed a pact of friendship with Bulgaria (1937) and a nonaggression and arbitration pact with Italy in the same year. This moved Yugoslavia closer to the Axis powers.

During the late 1930s, Prince Paul repeatedly appealed to the British for arms and economic assistance in order to ward off an increasingly militant Germany. His requests fell on deaf ears. Germany, Italy and Japan signed the Tripartite Pact in September 1940, which bound their nations into a military alliance. Yugoslavia was greatly alarmed, especially when Germany became insistent that Yugoslavia also sign that pact.

Prince Paul resisted and stalled for time. He wanted to transfer a whole and sovereign nation to his nephew, King Peter, then only 17 and soon to be of age. Not-

Assassination: King Alexander of Yugoslavia at Marseilles, France, October 1934

withstanding the fact that they had ignored Paul's pleas for assistance, the British were totally opposed to any action by Yugoslavia that would strengthen the hand of the Axis powers.

Feeling the noose tightening around his multiethnic nation, Prince Paul instructed his ministers to draw up three conditions for signing the pact which he felt certain Hitler would never accept: (1) that the sovereignty and territorial integrity of Yugoslavia would be respected; (2) that no

military assistance would be requested of Yugoslavia and also no passage of troops through the country in the event of war; and (3) acknowledgement of Yugoslavia's interest in a free outlet to the Aegean Sea through Salonika, Greece.

Hitler surprised Prince Paul and the Yugoslav government by readily agreeing to its terms (with no thought of respecting them), and the pact was reluctantly signed. However, Hitler omitted the second clause denying German troops access to Yugoslavia's transportation system.

The apparent alliance with the Axis powers infuriated many Yugoslavs, particularly the independent-minded Serbs. It embittered the British, with whom Prince Paul had always been close. Accordingly, Great Britain was instrumental in staging a *coup d'état* in March 1941 that resulted in the overthrow of Prince Paul's government. The new regime made the young King Peter a temporary puppet. It sent a discouraged Prince Paul into poverty-stricken exile, wrapped in the undeserved mantle of a Nazi sympathizer when, in truth, he hated Nazi Germany.

World War II

Certain Yugoslav officials and army officers bitterly opposed the government's decision to sign the Tripartite Pact and, thus, apparently to join the Axis side in 1941. Following the military coup, the army announced a policy of neutrality and continued Prince Paul's policy. The Nazis saw through this transparent plan and attacked Yugoslavia ten days later, after which Germany dissolved Yugoslavia. Germany re-

Prince Paul of Yugoslavia

tained part while other areas were distributed to friends and supporters.

Croatia was enlarged and placed in the hands of Ante Pavelic, a Nazi ally. Slovenia was divided between Germany and Italy; Macedonia was occupied by Bulgaria; parts of Bosnia and Dalmatia went to Italy; a small piece in the north was given to Hungary; and German administration was imposed on Serbia. A puppet government was established in Belgrade.

From 1941 to 1944 Yugoslavia was ravaged not only by struggles against the Nazi occupation, but also by civil war between the *Chetnik* and *Partisan* resistance forces, as well as between partisans and Ustasha forces in Croatia. The Chetniks were bands of officers and men drawn from the remnants of the Royal Yugoslav Army. Loosely organized and generally undisciplined, they were pro-Serbian and anticommunist. The Partisans, led by Josip Broz-Tito (known by his revolutionary *nom de guerre* simply as Tito) and the Yugoslav Communist Party, tried to form an organization with a broader, national following.

The Communist Party had been one of the largest parties in the Constituent Assembly elected in 1920. Its goal was the establishment of a Yugoslav Soviet Republic. In 1921, however, the government banned the party after the murder of the minister of the interior, although there was no evidence linking the party to the assassination. The party remained illegal throughout the interwar period, which meant that its members were forced to operate underground.

Tito was one of its early leaders. The son of a Croatian peasant and a Slovene mother, he had been inducted into the Austrian army during the First World War and was taken prisoner of war by a Russian detachment at the age of 23. He escaped from prison in Russia and joined the Bolsheviks, fighting with them in the Russian civil war. After he returned to Yugoslavia, he became the secretary of the Zagreb branch of the Communist Party of Yugoslavia. When the party was declared illegal in 1921, he was arrested and sentenced to five years at hard labor.

By 1937, he was the secretary general of the party, which he reorganized and purged in accordance with the latest dictates from Moscow. After the Germans occupied the country, he used his control of the party organization to create guerrilla units called "Partisans" for use against the Germans.

At first, Partisans and Chetniks attempted to fight side by side. But it soon became evident that while they were both struggling to free Yugoslavia from Axis control, their image of the country's future was totally different. The Chetniks were fighting for the return of the monarch and a Serb-dominated government. The Partisans were fighting for a federally organized, socialist republic. There was also a disagreement on general military strategy: the Partisans wanted all-out resistance while the Chetniks, afraid of German reprisals, wanted to wait for the arrival of the Allies.

Eventually the Chetniks and Partisans were fighting each other as hard as they fought the common enemy. In order to combat the Partisans and prevent the Germans from killing Serbs, the Chetniks began to collaborate with the German occupiers. Evidence of collaboration resulted in a loss of Allied support for them. The British sent a military mission to aid the Partisans several months before there was a similar move by the Soviets. The Western powers thus formally recognized the Partisans' contribution to the war effort and Tito's leadership.

Under Tito's direction, the Anti-Fascist Council for National Liberation of Yugoslavia (AVNOJ) was formed in 1942 to function as a government in liberated territories. A year later at Jajce in Bosnia, AVNOJ elected a provisional government that named Tito premier and marshal of Yugoslavia. AVNOJ thus replaced the nominal authority of the government-in-exile, located in London, and it forbade King Peter, successor to Prince Paul, to return. The British then persuaded the king to appoint Dr. Ivan Shubashich as premier of the exiled government on the assumption that Shubashich, who had been governor of Croatia until 1941, was a man who could negotiate with the Partisans.

In October 1944 Soviet and Partisan forces liberated Belgrade. It is significant that by the time Red Army forces arrived in Belgrade, the Partisans were in firm control of large parts of Yugoslavia. Tito and Shubashich signed an agreement providing for a Regency Council to act in the king's name; free elections within three months of liberation; and a legislature consisting of AVNOJ until an assembly could be convened. The "Big Three"—the U.S., the USSR and Great Britain—approved this arrangement at the Yalta Conference in February 1945, and the king was thus forced to accept it. Three regents were chosen in March 1945—a Serb, a Croat and a Slovene. None was a communist, but all had Tito's approval.

Tito formed a new government in which he was premier, and Shubashich was foreign minister. The cabinet included representatives from each of the six areas of Yugoslavia and the government-in-exile. Before the elections for a constituent assembly took place, Shubashich resigned, protesting the government's refusal to allow "collaborators" to vote. This term was loosely applied to anyone who opposed the government. The elections were boycotted by the opposition parties—the Serbian Radical Party, Agrarian Party, Democratic Party, and the Croat Peasant Party—in protest against the atmosphere of intimidation created by what had become a very active secret police. As a result, the people could vote only for the Communist People's Front list of candidates.

Yugoslavia Becomes the Socialist Federal Republic of Yugoslavia (SFRJ)

The Constituent Assembly that was elected declared Yugoslavia to be a Federal People's Republic. When a new constitution was adopted in early 1946, the Assembly changed its name to the People's Assembly. This body consisted of two houses, a Chamber of Nationalities and a Federal Chamber. The Chamber of Nationalities had 30 representatives from each of the six federal republics, plus 15 from the autonomous province of Kosovo and 20 from the autonomous region of the Voivodina. In theory, therefore, it served a function somewhat similar to that of the U.S. Senate. The Federal Chamber was the "popular body," with one representative for every 50,000 inhabitants.

The People's Assembly was not designed as a deliberative body, however. It met only twice a year, on April and October 15th, and then only to rubber-stamp government decisions. More power resided with the Presidium of the People's Assembly, since the Presidium appointed and dismissed cabinet ministers and had law-making authority when the Assembly was not in session. As with all communist regimes, however, real power rested with the Communist Party.

Marshal Josip Broz-Tito, leader of the *Partisans* in World War II

The Former Yugoslavia

Although the government remained in theory a "People's Front," the policies it instituted during this period were based on Soviet models. Larger estates were expropriated, and a beginning was made on the establishment of collective farms. In 1947, the government launched its first Five-Year Plan. In industry, emphasis was placed on electrification, chemicals and metallurgy. Foreign trade was oriented toward the Eastern Bloc nations.

The Soviet-Yugoslav Dispute of 1948

Yugoslavia had been considered such a loyal satellite that the new Communist Information Bureau, or Cominform, set up in September 1947, had established its headquarters in Belgrade. But a quarrel began over the issue of joint Yugoslav-Soviet companies. Two joint companies were actually set up, for air transport and river shipping. But the way they were operated appeared so disadvantageous to the Yugoslavs that they refused to allow any further joint companies to be formed. This led to a bitter dispute between Tito and Stalin and resulted in the curtailment of Soviet aid and a reduction of trade between Yugoslavia and the East.

The dispute marked the first time a ruling communist party had defied Moscow's authority and still remained in power. The disagreement pointed to the question of the power relations between the two countries. Tito's challenge to Moscow was possible because his political survival did not depend on Stalin's support. Unlike the communist leaders of other Eastern European countries (except Albania), Tito had not come to power by the might of the Soviet army, but because of his personal following in the Partisan movement, which had the leading role in liberating Yugoslavia at the end of the war. In fact, there were no longer any Red Army troops on Yugoslav soil in 1948.

After the war, the Yugoslav communists had thought of themselves as Moscow's most faithful followers. Tito's desire to follow the correct line was evident in the enthusiasm with which he modeled Yugoslavia's economy and constitution on those of the Soviet Union. It was in recognition of Tito's importance that Stalin set up the Cominform headquarters in Belgrade.

In light of this background, the real dispute was not Yugoslav departure from the official Moscow communist line or any other one issue. It was the refusal to be controlled by Moscow in matters that affected the interests of Yugoslavia. The question was how two communist parties and their leaders should conduct their mutual relations when each was also responsible for the interests of his own state.

Stalin's opposition to any communist power that was not under his personal control was shown by his attitude toward the plans for a Balkan federation authorized by Tito and supported by Dmitrov, the Bulgarian communist leader. The Bulgarians even agreed that after federation, Yugoslavia should annex the part of Macedonia that was within Bulgaria. By 1947, the plans included the possibility of bringing Albania, Romania and Greece into some kind of union, and there were hints of a Balkan-Danubian Federation involving Hungary.

Sensing an increase in Tito's power if there were federation, Stalin abruptly reversed his early support for the plan. When the Bulgarian leadership expressed hope for a customs union as a step towards federation, Pravda, the Moscow official newspaper, responded with an article stating that the Balkan states did not need any kind of customs union or federation. At a meeting in the Kremlin in 1948, Stalin and Foreign Minister Molotov took both Bulgaria and Yugoslavia to task: the Bulgarians for planning a customs union with Romania and the Yugoslavs for providing assistance to the Greek communists and for sending troops into Albania without Moscow's approval.

There were also other issues involved. The Yugoslavs were critical of the Soviet failure to send aid to the Partisans during the war and of Stalin's instructions to play down the role of the Communist Party in the resistance movement. They could not forget that Stalin had opposed setting up the AVNOJ as the supreme authority in 1943. The Yugoslavs were also angry at the Soviet Union for its failure to press Yugoslavia's claim to Trieste against Italy at the close of the war, presumably because Stalin did not want to antagonize the Allies by bringing up the claim.

In response, Stalin accused the Yugoslavs of directing propaganda against the Soviet Union and of having an "unduly large" peasant membership in their communist party. There were also accusations that the party was being run "undemocratically." Another charge was that the Yugoslavs treated the Soviet military advisors and civilian experts as foreigners.

The Yugoslavs requested that the dispute be settled by two-party discussions. Instead, the Soviets called a meeting of the Cominform and issued a statement in mid-1948 indicating that the member parties backed the Soviet position. The Yugoslav Communist Party was expelled from the Cominform, Stalin denounced Tito, and his name became a symbol of "nationalist deviationism" among communist leaders who courted Moscow's favor. Despite its economic and diplomatic isolation, however, Yugoslavia survived

and established a precedent for other challenges to Soviet authority that followed after Stalin's death.

Relations with the U.S. improved after Tito's expulsion from the COMINFORM, but they remained correct rather than cordial. President Harry S Truman supposedly commented privately: although Tito is a "son-of-a-bitch, at least he's our son-of-a-bitch."

Politics After 1949

Yugoslavia began to search for new trading partners, for a new foreign policy that would demonstrate its independence, and for a new statement of principles that would explain the changes introduced in the Yugoslav system after the break with Moscow. In domestic politics, the two themes that were developed were decentralization and economic democracy. The first step came in 1950 with the creation of "workers' councils" in all state-owned economic enterprises. At the same time, the former economic ministries that had directed the economy were abolished and replaced by national coordinating councils made up of representatives from each of the republics. Thus the central directive role of the state was reduced while the participatory role of the workers was enhanced at the local level.

Beginning in 1952, producers' councils were created at the local and republic levels. In 1953, the constitution was modified to incorporate the concept of workers' self-management, and a national Council of Producers was created as a second national legislative body to replace the Chamber of Nationalities. The Chamber of Nationalities was not abolished, however, but was partially amalgamated into the Federal Chamber. What was different about the national Council of Producers as well as the local and republic producers' councils was that representation was on the basis of occupation, and persons voted where they worked.

Decentralization was considered to apply primarily to economic decision-making. In the political arena, other constitutional changes were made to create a more obvious central political authority. The old executive structure of a "presidium of the National Assembly" and a Council of Ministers was abolished and replaced by a "president of the republic" with true executive powers, assisted by a Federal Executive Council. Marshal Tito became the new president. The Communist Party also changed its name at this time and became the League of Communists of Yugoslavia. However, it was not willing to give up its monopoly of political power.

Milovan Djilas, a vice premier and president of the National Assembly, published a series of articles in the communist news-

Belgrade University Library

paper *Borba*, in late 1953 in which he argued, among other things, that "no class or political movement can claim the exclusive right to represent society as a whole or to proclaim their ideas as objective truth." For this, he was expelled from the Politburo and Central Committee and forced to resign his government offices. Later he would be imprisoned for more critical things he would write. The most famous was his study of the way the new communist elite had become a privileged dominant class. It was appropriately entitled The New Class.

A new constitution was adopted in 1963 that extended the concept of worker's self-management to that of "social self-management." In a move toward greater economic democracy, more authority was given to local communes, to the governments of the republics, and to the organs of self-management in the economy. These changes compounded Yugoslavia's problems with regionalism, however, and reopened conflict between the liberals and conservatives as well as between the wealthier and poorer republics. The less-developed republics, such as Serbia and Montenegro, argued that the changes benefited only the developed republics. Croatia and Slovenia, on the other hand, argued that the changes did not go far enough and that they were still subsidizing the rest of the country.

One of the foremost opponents of the reforms was Alexander Rankovic, then vice president of Yugoslavia, strongman of the Serbian party organization, influential in the security police, and once considered a likely successor to Tito. The decision to expel him from the Central Committee in 1966 was a decisive victory for the reformists, this time backed by Tito.

Although the decision was a blow to Serb nationalists, it did not eliminate the basic anxiety of the remaining republics over Serbian domination of Yugoslavia. In order to provide the individual republics a greater stake in the general affairs of the country, a group of amendments was adopted in 1967 giving a stronger voice to the Chamber of Nationalities and in general increasing the role of the individual republics in decision-making at the center.

There was another series of amendments in 1971 that, in addition to establishing a collective presidency to handle the matter of the succession after Tito, made a number of economic changes. Worker councils were given greater authority to determine how the surplus funds of their enterprises were to be allocated. Private individuals were guaranteed the right to work with their own "means of production" and to employ workers on a contractual basis.

In 1974, a new constitution introduced a system of elections to the various legislative assemblies based on delegations drawn from occupational and interest groups. It also provided that the federal legislature—the Assembly of the Socialist Federal Republic of Yugoslavia—be made up of an equal number of delegates from each of Yugoslavia's six republics. Elections to the federal legislature were indirect. Assemblymen of the individual republics, themselves representing local occupation and interest groups, selected delegates to the federal legislature.

One purpose of the new system was to give the League of Communists of Yugoslavia (LCY) greater control over the elected representatives. Under its self-managing socialism, Yugoslavia had created a degree of economic democracy; politically, however, the LCY retained its monopoly of power.

The 1970s saw a number of purges within the party. The most prominent was the mass sacking of the Croatian wing of the LCY in 1971–72 because of alleged nationalistic deviations. Between 1972 and 1974, there were additional purges within the Serbian wing, this time because of an overly liberal attitude toward dissent within LCY ranks. Despite these mass firings, there remained a large core of veterans, both in the LCY and the government, who had remained more or less continuously in office since 1945.

The core of the problem was that the LCY attempted to withdraw from direct control of the economy while retaining an overall political ascendancy. The economic reforms devolved considerable authority to the republic level, to regional banks and to individual enterprises. The result was to create a tremendous stake in control over local economic activity. This often encouraged local decisions at variance with national political policy, in par-

The Former Yugoslavia

ticular the commitment at the national level to redistribute funds to poorer areas of the country for the purpose of financing industrialization. After Tito's death in 1980, it also acted to frustrate attempts of the new national leadership to control growing inflation through a national austerity program. What Yugoslavs discovered was that after control over the economy had been shifted to the republic and autonomous provincial level, the federal government no longer had the tools to manipulate the economy.

Foreign Policy: Communist Era

Yugoslavia was a "friend" of the West so long that it was easy to forget that its leaders remained communists and that its relations with the West were the result of Stalin having expelled it from the communist bloc. Nevertheless, this break led Yugoslavia to sign a five-year Treaty of Friendship and Assistance with Turkey and Greece in 1953 that was subsequently known as the Balkan Pact. The following year, it was converted into a defensive alliance. Yugoslavia also settled an outstanding issue with Italy that had been left over from World War II: the disposition of Trieste, by agreeing to divide the disputed land.

In addition, it built up its international prestige by actively courting the non-aligned nations of Africa and Asia. These nations accepted Yugoslavian leadership in the non-aligned movement because Tito had given Yugoslavia what they thought of as the best of all possible worlds: following a course of socialist development, though free of Soviet control, and receiving aid from the West, but without becoming an economic adjunct to capitalism.

Yugoslavia thus positioned itself between the two blocs. It was never an ally of the United States, and it welcomed the resumption of diplomatic relations with the Soviet Union in June 1953, after the death of Stalin. Thereafter, Yugoslav-Soviet relations alternated between periods of calm and storm, depending on the extent of control Moscow was attempting to exercise over Yugoslavia.

Soviet leaders Bulganin and Khrushchev visited Belgrade in 1955, and in the subsequent communiqué they acknowledged that what Yugoslavia was doing was their own business. In turn, Tito agreed to support Soviet policy on arms limitation, the division of Germany and the admission of the People's Republic of China (PRC) to the UN.

There were further improvements in Yugoslav-Soviet relations following Khrushchev's denunciations of Stalin in 1956, the dissolution of the Cominform in that same year, and the dismissal of Vyacheslav

The May 5, 1980, edition of *Politika* announces Tito's death

Molotov as Soviet foreign minister. All of these moves indicated a Soviet acceptance of the possibility of different paths toward socialism. By June 1956, the two sides announced that they had achieved a "complete normalization" of relations on party and state levels.

But this was only a brief interlude. The actions of the Soviets and the apparent willingness to deal with Yugoslavia on an independent basis created false hopes of liberalization in Poland and Hungary. Hungary embarked upon a liberal and more independent course. The result was a harsh Soviet military invasion in the fall of 1956. Subsequent Soviet attacks on "revisionism" reopened the old conflict between Tito and Moscow. It was not until 1960–61 that a new attempt to smooth relations was made, probably to counteract the effect of increasing difficulties between the Soviet Union and China.

In 1968–69, Soviet-Yugoslav relations suffered once again under the impact of an international crisis. Tito had spoken out in favor of programs of liberalization that were taking place in Czechoslovakia. When the Soviet Union and its Warsaw Pact allies intervened militarily in that country, Tito voiced his condemnation of this move in the strongest terms. He rejected the Brezhnev Doctrine, the Soviet explanation for the move, as no more than an attempt to justify a violation of the sovereignty of a communist state by invoking the higher interests of socialism.

In 1971, Leonid Brezhnev paid a visit to Yugoslavia for the first time since the invasion of Czechoslovakia. During the meeting with Tito, the Soviet leader disavowed the existence of any doctrine of limited sovereignty and, to Tito's satisfaction, endorsed the view that each country had the right to develop socialism according to its own experience. The reaffirmation of the 1955 Belgrade Declaration opened the door to better relations between the two countries.

One major issue between Yugoslavia and the Soviet Union in the 1970s was the latter's desire for a European Communist Conference. Yugoslavian participation was extremely important because without the Yugoslavs several of the Western European Communist parties would have refused to attend.

Yugoslavia's price, exacted at a 1974 preparatory meeting in Warsaw, was that the meeting was to be open to the public, that it would not become a forum for attacking parties that had declined to attend, and that all decisions were to be by consensus. Yugoslavia was supported in this stand by Romania and by the delegates representing the Italian, Spanish and French parties.

The conference finally took place in the summer of 1976 in East Berlin. Although it endorsed the main lines of Soviet foreign policy, the Soviets were not happy with other parts of the concluding document, which reiterated the Yugoslav-Romanian formula for interparty relations of "voluntary cooperation" based on the principles of equality, sovereignty, noninterference in internal affairs, and respect for different roads to socialism.

Soviet-Yugoslav relations remained at about the same level until December 1979 when the Yugoslavs condemned the Soviet invasion of Afghanistan, and relations turned cool. Yugoslavia did sign a 10-year economic agreement with the Soviet Union in 1980. As a result of the second oil crisis in 1979, Yugoslavia was finding it harder and harder to compete in Western markets. The agreement seemed to offer the promise of a long term market for Yugoslav goods. The Soviets paid in convertible rubles, however. As the Yugoslav government learned, convertible rubles were of little value if the Soviet Union was not producing the things Yugoslavia was willing to import. Belgrade eventually built up a huge credit of several billion rubles that it was unable to use.

Relations improved after Gorbachev came to power in 1985. The Yugoslavian people welcomed him enthusiastically when he visited in March 1988. He traveled and spoke around the country. In retrospect, the visit took on a greater significance because of his assertion, in the agreed joint statement at the conclusion of the stay, that every country had a right to pursue its chosen variant of communism. This statement, which was essentially a repudiation of the Brezhnev Doctrine, paved the way for the 1989 revolutions in Central and Eastern Europe.

Post-Cold War

U.S.-Yugoslav relations were always based on the premise that Yugoslavia espoused a non-expansionist communism. Therefore it was a more benign form and offered an alternate pattern of development that might influence other communist countries in Central and Eastern Europe. Because of this strategic role assigned to it, the U.S. supported a unified, federal Yugoslavia.

The 1989 collapse of communism ended this strategic role for Yugoslavia. In fact, it was exposed as a badly run communist state. Reformers in the western part of the country argued first for radical reforms, only to have their projects blocked by the Serb leadership. They then abandoned communism and carried out democratic elections. In Serbia, however, the communists changed the name of their party but managed to keep political control. Since they continued to obstruct real reform at the federal level, the democratic reformers eventually opted for independence.

The U.S. government never understood the dynamics of what was going on in Yugoslavia and continued to support a unified Yugoslavia even after it had become clear that such a Yugoslavia would be dominated by a Serbia that had not shed its communist policies. For example, even after Milosevic had destroyed the autonomy of Kosovo and the Voivodina, had instituted a boycott of goods from Slovenia, had organized Serbs in other parts to oppose their republics' policies, and undermined the economic policy of the Yugoslav government at the national level, Secretary of State James Baker announced in the summer of 1991 that the United States would not support a break-up of Yugoslavia "under any circumstances."

Thus encouraged, Milosevic, supported by the Yugoslav People's Army—the last stronghold of communism at the national level—launched his war against Croatia and threatened one against Bosnia-Herzegovina. Even in November 1991, when Serbia's aims had become clear to the world, and the EC had decided to institute economic sanctions against Serbia and Montenegro, the two aggressors, the U.S. decided to levy economic sanctions against both sides, *aggressors and victims*.

This was a classic case of a policy outliving its usefulness. The EC extended recognition to Slovenia and Croatia on January 15, 1992. The U.S. waited another three months before following suit. Ambassador Warren Zimmerman remained in Belgrade, however, and Washington continued to maintain good relations with the Serb-dominated Yugoslav government. All of this ended when, with U.S. backing, the UN voted to impose economic sanctions against Serbia and Montenegro in May 1992. The U.S. government had begun to press Serbia on its treatment of Albanians in Kosovo. On March 23, Zimmermann traveled to Prishtina to open an exhibition organized to mark the 50th anniversary of the Voice of America. While there, he held talks with representatives of Albanian parties.

Yugoslavia After Tito

Speculation about the internal and international outlook for Yugoslavia centered on the question of what would happen to the country when President Tito disappeared from the scene. The aging leader and his associates were aware of the problem. They decided to establish a system of post-Tito government designed to keep the country together in spite of deep-seated animosities among the various nationalities.

The Constitution of 1974, while making Tito president for life, provided for several collective bodies, including a rotating presidency of the supreme governing council, representative of the major national units. This body began to function when Tito, struggling for months against a terminal illness, gave up his position as chief of state. The collective leadership thus gained experience in running the state without Tito at the helm. When he finally died in May 1980, his funeral became the occasion for a glittering assembly of heads of state and other dignitaries, ranging from kings to leaders of communist states.

The new leadership functioned with modest success until 1988 although it was unable to reverse growing economic difficulties. When the government attempted to bring inflation under control, it ran up against the mandate of the 1974 constitu-

The Former Yugoslavia

tion that all significant federal decisions had to be decided by consensus. It proved to be impossible to come up with an anti-inflation policy that the leaderships of the six republics and two provinces could agree on. The result was stalemate at the center. The government was reduced to muddling through.

By 1988, the annual rate of inflation was 200% and growing. Worried about their dropping standard of living, workers launched a series of strikes. Intellectuals, losing confidence in the system, began to demand changes. In less-developed areas of the country, there was also growing dissatisfaction among individual ethnic groups who had come to believe that the system was treating them unfairly. Among the most disaffected were the ethnic Albanians of the autonomous province of Kosovo.

Greater Serbian Domination Threatens the Union

Up to that moment, one might have described the situation as serious but not threatening. What turned it into a crisis was the emergence of a new Serbian leader, Slobodan Milosevic, who launched a broad movement to reassert Serbian leadership. Arguing that the promotion of regionalism was the root cause of Yugoslavia's problems, he demanded control over the police, judiciary and economy in the two autonomous provinces of the Voivodina and Kosovo. In addition, he demanded a radical increase in Serbia's power within the Yugoslav Federation.

To achieve these goals, Milosevic began mobilizing the Serbian masses. In the Voivodina, 100,000 Serbs besieged the provincial parliament in September 1988, forcing the resignation of the entire Voivodina leadership and their replacement by Milosevic loyalists. The same tactics were also tried against Kosovo, and demonstrations and counterdemonstrations continued over the next several months.

Meanwhile, inflation continued to grow and the worsening economic situation, coupled with the growing ethnic problems, led to a collapse of the Yugoslav government on December 30, 1988. Finally, Ante Markovic, president of the Federal Executive Council, decided to take advantage of loopholes in the law and propose an economic stabilization program. Approved by the federal parliament on December 20, 1989, it went into effect on January 1, 1990. The program consisted of making the Yugoslavian dinar convertible by pegging it to the German Mark, allowing interest to rise to market levels, and removing price controls from most goods. The price of certain items, including various raw materials and energy, were frozen. The program worked. By March, inflation had sunk from over 2,000% to 8.4%.

Political developments continued to move in a direction that threatened the future of the united Yugoslav state. In January, an emergency congress of the League of Communists was held, among other things to discuss the creation of a multiparty system. There was a serious split. On one side were the hard-liners, led by Slobodan Milosevic of Serbia; on the other were those pushing for a multiparty system, led by Ciril Ribicic of Slovenia. The congress actually passed a resolution favoring creation of a multiparty system, but the Slovenian delegation walked out, thus bringing it to a halt. They were particularly incensed about an economic boycott against Slovenia that Serbia had instituted at the end of November.

Thus, while Milosevic was threatening in Serbia to colonize the province of Kosovo, Slovenia was moving toward creating a multiparty democracy and suggesting that it saw no future for itself in Yugoslavia. In the April 1990 elections, Slovenes split their votes, electing Milan Kucan, candidate of the communists, as president while giving control of the legislature to the Demos, a coalition of conservative political parties that had campaigned on a platform of independence within a year. A month later, Croatia held its own multiparty elections, which were won by the Croatian Democratic Union, which campaigned on a platform of making a confederation of sovereign states out of Yugoslavia.

Macedonia and Bosnia-Herzegovina held their own free, multiparty elections in November 1990. Montenegro and Serbia were scheduled to hold multiparty elections in December 1990. In Serbia, Milosevic decided to consolidate his control by transforming the Serbian branch of the League of Communists of Yugoslavia (LCY) into the Serbian Socialist Party. Thus the old LCY, already a minority in all of

the republics other than Montenegro and Serbia, ceased to exist as a national party except in the Yugoslav army, where the leadership remained communist. This was a strange action by someone who claimed to stand for a strong, unified country. In fact, Milosevic was a Serbian nationalist who was only interested in a united Yugoslavia if he could dominate it completely. Otherwise he would tear it apart and seize what other pieces he could.

A look at the policies he pursued bears that out. Appealing to Serbian nationalism, he demanded greater control in the two autonomous provinces of Kosovo and the Voivodina, eventually destroying their autonomy completely. In 1990, his agents began organizing Serbian nationals living in the other republics, fomenting them to demand secession of their areas from their republics and union with Serbia. He personally declared that he would rectify boundaries and reclaim Serbian lands if the federation broke up. The other republics had always reacted negatively to the idea of a Serbian-dominated Yugoslav government, which reminded them of the period after World War I when Serbs dominated the new Yugoslavia. Milosevic's Serbian chauvinism and his destruction of the autonomy of Kosovo and the Voivodina convinced many non-Serbs that he intended once again to assert Serbia's control over all of Yugoslavia. At least three separate actions he took in 1990–91 contributed to that perception.

In December 1990, in the lead-up to Serbian elections, Milosevic undermined the financial stability of the national government by illegally siphoning off $1.5 billion from the Yugoslav National Bank. The money was taken in the form of a "loan" authorized by a vote in the Serbian legislature. Both the assembly session and the removal of the money were kept secret from Yugoslavia's federal government. He then used the money to pay for pensions

Slobodan Milosevic at The Hague

and salaries, which he had raised in the run-up to Serbian elections. The increases were undoubtedly a factor in the elections, which he and his Serbian Socialist Party won handily.

The other republics were outraged when they learned of Milosevic's actions. Since the $1.5 billion was half of the new money the Yugoslav National Bank had assigned for circulation in 1991 in all six republics, his action seriously undermined the federal government's economic stabilization program.

Milosevic's second stunt was to organize a boycott of Slovenian products and to begin levying a tariff on all items brought into Serbia from that republic. This effectively negated the concept of a united Yugoslavia. His third move in his program of rule or ruin was to block election of a new federal president in May 1991. The outgoing president was Borisav Jovic, a Serb. Under Yugoslavia's system of rotating presidencies, the incoming president was the man who had held the vice presidency for the previous year, Stipe Mesic, a Croat.

To be sure, Milosevic was not the sole offender. In 1990, when the leaders of Slovenia and Croatia began pushing for a change in the structure of the Yugoslav Federation to create greater autonomy for the individual republics, they passed laws declaring their laws to be superior to federal law and also created republic militias. The sad thing is that this quarreling completely undermined the economic stabilization program of the federal government. Only the Yugoslav People's Army remained united at this point although there were clear signs that this unity was very frail and depended on the army's not getting involved in the quarrels between the individual republics.

The army also had its own problems. The most important was that there was strong sentiment within the military to preserve a united Yugoslavia, even if it meant using force against a part of the Yugoslav people. A second problem was that 70% of the officers were Serbs, and a good percentage of them were attracted to Milosevic's program. A third factor was that the army was the one remaining place where the LCY continued to exist. A final factor was that, while the officers were mainly Serbian, ordinary soldiers were conscripts who came from throughout Yugoslavia. Many feared, therefore, that the army would begin to disintegrate if it intervened against an individual republic and if it were perceived as doing so on behalf either of Serbia or the LCY.

Yugoslavia Falls Apart

On May 19, 1991, the Croatian government held a referendum on independence.

In economically torn Montenegro, a youngster holds up a sign "We wait for you, where are you, Slobo" (Serbian leader Slobodan Milosevic) during an antigovernment demonstration in Titograd (now Podgorica)

The Former Yugoslavia

After a favorable vote, the Croatian Assembly adopted a declaration of independence on June 25. The Slovene government adopted its own declaration of independence on the same day. Both governments reiterated, however, that they remained willing to join a looser Yugoslav confederation in which the central government would handle foreign policy, defense and economic matters such as a common currency.

Meanwhile, the Yugoslav People's Army (JNA) reacted to the declarations by sending an invasion force into Slovenia. That republic was selected because it had moved to take control of its international border with Italy and Austria. The JNA was not expecting much opposition, but the Slovenians fought back valiantly. Meanwhile, the rest of the world, which had encouraged the army action by asserting that they would not support a separate Slovenia or Croatia "under any circumstances," began calling for a cease-fire. At the same time, army desertions by non-Serbs were a problem.

This led to an agreement with Slovenia that it could staff the control posts if it would turn the revenues over to the central government. Other aspects of the agreement were that the JNA would return to the barracks; Slovenia and Croatia would suspend their declarations of independence for three months; and Serbia would allow Stipe Mesic to be elected president. The latter aspect of the agreement was important in a military as well as a political sense, because the president was also the JNA commander in chief.

The agreement brought peace to Slovenia, but not to Yugoslavia. One of the first actions of President Mesic was to arrange a cease-fire—the third—on July 2. That same day, in an interview that appeared on Belgrade television, General Blagoje Adzic, chief of the JNA general staff, angrily repudiated the cease-fire and thereby his own commander in chief. He then added that the army "accepted the challenge of total war that had been imposed on it" and would soon end it with a complete victory. The next day, an armored column left Belgrade for Croatia.

After Slovenia and Croatia had begun moving toward independence, Slobodan Milosevic called upon Serbs in other republics to remain loyal and not to allow the Yugoslav union to be destroyed. In Croatia, Serbs organized Serbian governments in two different parts of Croatia and declared these regions to be independent of Croatia. Hoping to conciliate the Serb leaders, the Croatian legislature passed a law guaranteeing protection for minority ethnic groups within the republic. However, the new Croat constitution described the new republic as being for

Croats. This heightened Serb fears by reawakening memories of the Second World War. Arguing that Serbs could secede from Croatia if Croatia could secede from Yugoslavia, Croatian Serbs held a referendum on July 7 affirming their intention to remain a part of the Socialist Federal Republic of Yugoslavia.

War against Croatia

President Milosevic of Serbia gave a speech on July 6, 1991, in which he told Serbs to be ready to defend themselves. He also gave Serb leaders in Croatia generous access to Serbian radio and television. The first fighting in Croatia began on July 7—the same day as the referendum—when Croatian Serbs attacked Croatian territorial defense forces near the town of Tenja.

As soon as fighting broke out, the Yugoslav People's Army (JNA) sent in its own units "to keep the peace." However, its targets were always Croatian territorial units. There were no reports whatsoever of any Serbian territorial units being in conflict with JNA forces. The fighting remained small-scale for some time, since President Franjo Tudjman had ordered Croatian units not to attack the JNA, and the JNA had its own instructions not to initiate battles, but only to intervene when new fighting occurred. Gradually, however, the JNA's control of Croatian territory spread as Serb territorial forces launched new battles in area after area.

The problem for Croatia was that Serbs insisted on living in a state controlled by Serbs. But Croatians were not entirely free of this mentality of expansion. The Republic of Bosnia-Herzegovina, which lies between Serbia and Croatia, has an extremely mixed population, with 44% Bosnjak (Muslim), 33% Serbs and about 17% Croats. President Tudjman admitted in July 1991 that members of his government had held secret talks with Serbian leaders about carving up Bosnia between Serbia and Croatia, leaving a small Muslim rump that neither wanted. Word of these talks did not help Croatia's image.

Croatia was saved by the fact that Serbia and the JNA were even more bloody-minded. In August 1991, Milosevic revealed his plans for a reconstituted Yugoslavia. They called for carving up Croatia and incorporating about a third of the territory into the new state, even though Serbs constituted only about 12% of Croatia's population at this time.

Meanwhile the JNA, which up to this time had contended that it was acting as a neutral buffer between the two sides, began bombarding Croatian cities with artillery and aircraft. In late August, much of the city of Vukovar was destroyed. By this time, perhaps 20% of the republic had

fallen under JNA or Serb militia control. On September 18, Zagreb, the capital, came under fire from aircraft and artillery.

Up to this moment, the Croatian government had been carrying out a "passive defense" and refusing to challenge the JNA directly. But it now retaliated against the JNA actions by cutting the oil lines that ran across Croatia to Serbia and laying siege to Yugoslav army barracks in Croatia. The Yugoslav navy implemented a siege around Croatia's Dalmatian ports. It later bombarded first Split, then Dubrovnik with artillery shells and missiles, damaging them considerably. Dubrovnik was rebuilt with international assistance after the war ended.

Croatia got some indirect assistance from other republics when Bosnia-Herzegovina and Macedonia publicly declared their neutrality and ordered their citizens to ignore conscription notices from the JNA. The Serbian and Montenegrin political response was to order general mobilization in both of those republics. Even in Serbia, however, many young men went into hiding rather than serve.

The European Community (EC, later the EU) had put itself forth as a peacemaker even before the war began. Subsequently it negotiated cease-fire after cease-fire, only to see each new one broken. It threatened Serbia with an economic embargo without effect. It arranged for a peace conference to begin at The Hague on September 7, 1991. The EC then appointed former British foreign minister, Lord Carrington, as chairman of the European peace conference and sent him to Yugoslavia. He met with Presidents Milosevic and Tudjman plus General Kadijevic, the Yugoslav defense minister. The three agreed that the JNA ought to return to its barracks, that the Croatian national guard should be demobilized, and that all irregular militias should be disbanded. Nothing actually happened, however, and the war went on. Kadijevic's chief of staff, the radical General Adzic, ignored him.

On October 3, the Serbs took control of the federal presidency. Branko Kostic, Montenegrin representative to the SFRJ presidency and vice president, called a meeting of the presidency and submitted a declaration of a state of emergency. With President Mesic absent and the Slovenian representative to the presidency boycotting the meeting, the proposal was passed with Kostic's own vote plus the three votes controlled by Serbia (and its two formerly autonomous regions).

By this time, it had become clear to almost everyone just what Serbia was attempting to do. After the October 3, 1991 meeting, characterized by President Gligorov of Macedonia as "illegitimate and unconstitutional," both Macedonia and

The Former Yugoslavia

Bosnia-Herzegovina withdrew their representatives to the presidency. Macedonia's representatives to the federal legislature also withdrew from that body as well.

The three-month moratorium on the independence declarations of Croatia and Slovenia—agreed to at Brioni—expired on October 7, 1991. Freed of that limitation, the Croatian and Slovenian governments severed all ties with the Socialist Federal Republic of Yugoslavia. By this time, the JNA and Serb militias occupied approximately a third of Croatia. The Yugoslav air force marked the day with an attack on the presidential palace in Zagreb at the very moment that President Tudjman was in conference with Stipe Mesic, the federal president, and Ante Markovic, the federal prime minister. As *The Economist* put it, "the attack put to rest any pretense that there is real life left in the Yugoslav federation."

Up to this time, Montenegrin troops had not been directly involved in the war. Now, however, they entered Croatia from the south, conquering the area up to Dubrovnik and establishing a land siege around that city. They were joined by JNA troops, who had pushed their way down from the north.

Serbia rejected an EU plan for a more loosely structured Yugoslavia and demilitarization of areas with minorities. It insisted that it could not abandon Serb minorities outside Serbia. It would not agree to any plan that did not permit minorities to switch the regions where they were in a majority from one republic to another. The exasperated EC instituted economic sanctions against Serbia and Montenegro. The United States, for its own reasons, instituted economic sanctions against all of Yugoslavia, including Croatia and Slovenia.

The last vestige of a united Yugoslavian government disappeared in December 1991 when Ante Markovic, the prime minister, resigned because 81% of the proposed budget for 1992 was earmarked for the army. The Yugoslav legislature, dominated by Serbia after representatives of Slovenia, Croatia and Macedonia had withdrawn, had already expressed its lack of confidence in Markovic, a Croat from Bosnia-Herzegovina.

International Recognition for Independent Republics

By this time, Germany and Austria had begun to make a public case for recognition of Slovenia and Croatia. Some other EC members, particularly France and Britain, continued to oppose recognition until Germany announced that it would proceed unilaterally if the EC took no action. British Prime Minister John Major then threw his support to Germany, and France grudgingly gave in. In December,

the EC announced that on January 15, 1992, its members would implement recognition of those Yugoslav republics that requested it and deserved it.

General Veljko Kadijevic, the Yugoslav defense minister, resigned on January 8, citing ill health. That gave Serb radicals control of the JNA. But Slobodan Milosevic, president of Serbia, had by this time switched positions, and he and the EC reached agreement on a new cease-fire and peacekeeping plan modeled on the suggestions he had put forth in November. The JNA would pull out of the three Serb enclaves in Croatia and be replaced by a peacekeeping force from the United Nations. The UN troops would disarm local militias and organize local police. Croatia would not have control over the enclaves, but neither would Serbia. The future of the enclaves would be determined at subsequent talks. The cease-fire—the 50th—went into effect on January 3. Five days later, the UN Security Council voted to send 50 UN observers to Croatia to report on the feasibility of the plan.

By January 15, 1992, four republics—Slovenia, Croatia, Macedonia and Bosnia-Herzegovina—had requested EC recognition. It recognized only the first two, largely for political considerations. EC governments were worried that recognition of Bosnia-Herzegovina would bring war to that republic. The Serbian Democratic Party, the main spokesman for Serbs in Bosnia-Herzegovina, opposed separa-

tion from Yugoslavia and threatened to lead a secession of Serb-dominated areas. Serbs formed their own "Serbian Republic of Bosnia-Herzegovina" and began arming themselves.

War in Bosnia

Because of this development, the EC advised the government of Bosnia-Herzegovina to hold a referendum on independence to establish that a majority actually wanted to break free from Yugoslavia. The referendum was held in March 1992, and produced a two-thirds majority in favor of independence. Serbs, who had boycotted the referendum, threw up barricades throughout the capital city of Sarajevo that evening, and it appeared that a major civil war was ready to break out. However, President Alija Izetbegovic defused the situation by meeting with the Bosnian Serb and Croatian leaders. The Serbs agreed to dismantle their barricades, and the other two political factions agreed to joint patrols by the Yugoslav People's Army and the Bosnian police.

On March 18, 1992, the leaders of the three communities agreed on a plan for restructuring the state, creating "three constituent units, based on national principles and taking into account economic, geographic and other criteria." The plan would have created three autonomous units within the governmental structure, one for Muslims, one for Croats and one for Serbs. Control in each municipality would have

National Library, Sarajevo, gutted by incendiary shell August 25, 1992

413

The Former Yugoslavia

been by that national group which was in an "absolute or relative majority."

Since the three communities have always lived side by side, and many families are mixed, the agreement would have been difficult to implement. In any case, it was never given a chance. The radical Serb leaders who wanted a single Greater Serbia forestalled that possibility by launching a war of conquest in April.

In essence, the Yugoslav army, overwhelmingly dominated by Serbs, split into two parts. Those with any ties to Bosnia or other non-Serb lands remaining in Bosnia joined the Muslim-Croatian army. The rest of the army removed itself to Serbia and Montenegro. Units left behind in Bosnia were provided with tanks, artillery and all the equipment of a modern army. General Ratko Mladic became the military commander of this force, while Radovan Karadzic exercised political leadership. The Yugoslav army continued to provide

support and resupply from Serbia. Thus the Yugoslav army, having learned from its involvement in Croatia that it could not afford to be seen as being present, created a proxy to continue its war for a Greater Serbia.

Within three months, this Serbian army in Bosnia had managed to capture approximately 70% of the territory. It also laid siege to the capital, Sarajevo. In the process it directed an unceasing bombardment into this once beautiful medieval city in an effort to crush resistance. With the West continuing to enforce the arms embargo it had instituted at the beginning of the fighting, the lightly armed Bosnian army was no match for the tanks and artillery of the Serbs. The siege and the shelling went on, gradually reducing large parts of the city to ruins.

Meanwhile, Serbs used their control of the Yugoslav legislature to pass new laws establishing customs zones in Serb-

inhabited areas of Croatia and parts of Bosnia-Herzegovina. In the case of Croatia, they also decreed that Yugoslav, not Croatian, law would apply in Serb areas occupied by the UN peacekeeping force. In addition, the legislature passed a law on the new Yugoslavia that required that "the new community be made up of nations and republics that want to remain in Yugoslavia." They implemented this by giving representation in the Yugoslav legislature to Serbs living outside of Serbia.

Montenegro held its own referendum in March 1993, and the people voted overwhelmingly to remain in a Yugoslav Federation. A union of two parts, one with a population of 9.98 million and the other with only 620,000, was rather odd. But that was what was left of the old Yugoslavia.

The claim that there was a "Federal Yugoslavia" that was superior to and separate from the Republic of Serbia ceased to have any validity on June 1, 1993, when

President Slobodan Milosevic of Serbia, left, shakes hands with President Franjo Tudjman of Croatia as President Alija Izetbegovic of Bosnia-Herzegovina, right, looks on following the signing of the Balkan treaty at the Elysee Palace in Paris, December 14, 1995. Behind them applauding, from left, are Spanish Premier Felipe Gonzalez (hidden), President Clinton, French President Jacques Chirac and German Chancellor Helmut Kohl.

AP/Wide World Photo

414

Waiting for the school bell in Serbia

Milosevic also stood by as a Croatian army entered Bosnia and then, in cooperation with the Bosnian army and the separate Bosnian Croat forces, gradually increased their control of Bosnian territory to just over 50%. It appears clear that the sanctions against Serbia were having their desired effect and that he concluded that his dream of a Greater Serbia could not be achieved under the then prevailing circumstances. Most of the Bosnian Serbs must have come to the same conclusion, for they now agreed to give Milosevic the power to negotiate on their behalf.

This led to the Dayton peace talks that concluded successfully with a formal signing ceremony in December 1995. It brought a suspension of the economic sanctions against Serbia and a promise that they would be permanently removed if Serbia continued to support the peace process. The Serbian economy was operating at an extremely low level by this time. Exhausted by the war, the people hoped that the peace agreement would lead to renewed growth. Outside economists suggested that Serbia should launch a major privatization program such as had already been carried out nearly everywhere else in Central and Southeastern Europe. None was pleased with the outcome. The end of the economic sanctions brought few dividends, and Milosevic actually revoked some privatization and free-market measures.

Election Unrest in Serbia

Elections to the Yugoslav legislature took place in November 1996. Because of the disarray of the opposition parties at this level, there was never any doubt that the parties of the government coalition would win a majority of the seats. Over

Milosevic ousted Dobrica Cosic as president and replaced him with Zoran Lilic, a puppet who lacked real standing either domestically or internationally. After his dismissal, Cosic said: "The federal state, if it is a state at all, is practically under the protectorate of Slobodan Milosevic and the Serbian government."

The embargo instituted against Serbia for its support of the war in Bosnia hurt the republic economically, but not to such an extent that it was willing to end its war of conquest for a Greater Serbia. Serbs actually gave President Milosevic's party an increased percentage of the vote in the 1993 elections. With the government's almost total control over the news media, it was easy to convince Serbs that they were the aggrieved party, particularly since the leadership of the Serbian Orthodox Church supported the government on this issue.

Peace Negotiations and the Dayton Accord

The change came in August 1994 when the Yugoslav government publicly withdrew support from Bosnia's Serbs after they had rejected a new UN peace plan that would have ceded them 49% of Bosnia. Serbia then announced that it had "sealed" its border with Bosnia and would not permit the export of anything except food, clothing and medicine. After much negotiation, Belgrade agreed to allow 135 civilian

observers to monitor the 370-mile frontier with Bosnia. This brought an easing of sanctions against Serbia in September.

In spite of widespread reports of violations on the part of Serbia, the UN continued to look to Milosevic as a possible negotiating partner. It attempted to win Milosevic's cooperation by offering a further relaxation of sanctions in return for his recognition of Croatia and Bosnia. He made it clear, however, that he would not recognize the independence of either republic until an overall settlement was reached. In the interim, Serbia continued to provide at least some limited support to the Bosnian and Croatian Serbs.

Milosevic's position began to change in May 1995 when the Croatian army recaptured western Slavonia, an area that had been held by Croatian Serbs since their declaration of a separate Serb state in 1991. As it became clear that the Croatian army intended to launch an invasion of the Krajina three months later, the remaining Croatian Serb enclave in the center of Croatia, the Serbian government not only did nothing, but there is some evidence that it allowed the Croatian Serbs to know that they could expect no support from Serbia. As a result, when the invasion began, the Croatian Serb government of Milan Martic collapsed, and nearly all Croatian Serbs (about 500,000) fled eastward even before the arrival of Croatian troops.

Milosevic posters in Belgrade, 2005

The Former Yugoslavia

two-thirds of the seats were indeed won by the two parties led by Milosevic and his wife, Mirjana Markovic.

Two weeks later, however, municipal elections took place throughout Serbia. In a surprise, the opposition won control over 32 municipalities, including Belgrade and industrial cities such as Kragujevac and Nis. Milosevic had always had strong support in these cities. But the dismal state of the economy, the unemployment rate of almost 50%, and the fact that even those who were employed often had to wait months for their money, had turned the workers against him.

The situation changed completely after the government moved to invalidate opposition victories in 14 of Serbia's 19 largest cities. Beginning on November 20, huge crowds of up to 100,000 demonstrators gathered daily in the middle of Bel-

grade to demand that the opposition be permitted to take their seats. Gradually, the demonstrations spread to other cities in Serbia.

Because the United States and several EU governments had made it clear that they would favor reimposing economic sanctions if Milosevic used force to suppress the opposition, the government tried to buy off the demonstrators by economic measures such as reducing the cost of electricity and promptly paying pensioners. None of this worked, however, and the demonstrations continued.

The government next tried to shut off all information about the demonstrations by closing down or seizing all private radio and television stations. Radio Free Europe countered this by picking up the broadcasts of the banned stations and re-broadcasting them over RFE frequencies.

The demonstrations continued until February, when Milosevic finally gave in and agreed to honor the opposition victories. The confrontation lasted for 78 days.

The victories temporarily introduced a small amount of political pluralism into Serbian life, but it was not destined to survive very long. Within a few months, Zejedno, the opposition political coalition, collapsed when its two main leaders began quarreling over which of them would stand for the Serbian presidency in the approaching election. Taking advantage of the disarray, Milosevic was soon able to install his own man as mayor of Belgrade and to reassert control over regional television. Seemingly politically invincible at this time, he would see less than four years later that he would have to answer for his long misrule of a disintegrating Yugoslavia.

Divided Kosovo seen at divided Mitrovica: Serb side greets visitors with a Serbian flag.

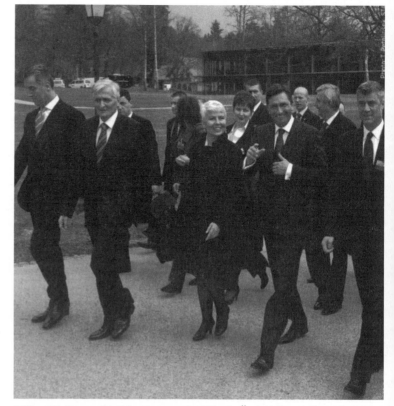

Milo Djukanović (Montenegro), Nikola Špirić (Bosnia and Herzegovina), Jadrnaka Kosor (Croatia), Borut Pahor (Slovenia), Hasim Taci (Kosovo) . . . The prime ministers of Western Balkans (minus Serbia's).

Republic of Slovenia

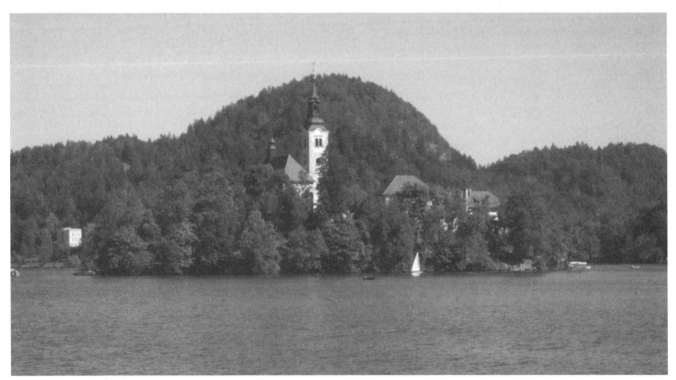

The island in Lake Bled with its ancient church

Area: 7,819 sq. mi. (20,273 sq. km., the size of New Jersey).

Population: 2 million (2004 census).

Capital City: Ljubljana (321,300, estimated). (Pronounced Lyube-lee-yanna).

Climate: Mediterranean southwest of Ljubljana; Alpine in the North; continental in the rest of the republic.

Neighboring Countries: Austria (north); Hungary (northeast); Croatia (west and south), Italy (west).

Official Languages: Slovenian. Hungarian in areas of mixed population in the northeast and Italian on the Adriatic coast. A diminishing number speak Serbian and Croatian, which are related but not identical to Slovenian; since 60% of words are different, they must be learned. English and German are widely spoken.

Ethnic Background: South Slavic with strong Germanic influences. Slovenes 88%. Croats 2%, Serbs 2%, Bosniaks 1%. Also about 8,500 Hungarians and 3,000 Italians.

Principal Religion: Roman Catholicism (58%), Orthodox Christian (2.3%), Muslim (2.4%).

Chief Commercial Products: Manufactures, machinery and transport equipment, chemicals, agricultural products and processed foods, dairy products, mineral fuels.

Chief Commercial Customers: 70% of GDP generated by exports. EU (69.3% of exports and 73.7% of imports), Germany (21.2% of exports and 19.5% of imports), Italy (14.1% of exports and 18.3% of imports), Croatia (9% of exports and 5% of imports), Austria (8.4% of exports and 12.5% of imports), France (6.6% of exports and 5.4% of imports), Russia (5% of exports), the Netherlands (3.6% of imports).

Currency: Euro (since January 1, 2007).

Recent Political Status: Part of the Austro-Hungarian Empire until 1919, part of Yugoslavia until 1991.

Independence Day: June 25, 1991. National holiday is June 25.

Chief of State: Danilo Türk, President (January 2008).

Head of Government: Barut Pahor, Prime Minister (October 2009).

National Flag: Equal horizontal stripes of white, blue, and red, with the nation's coat-of-arms on the left over the white and blue stripes. Because their flag looks so much like that of Slovakia, Slovenes are debating changing it. Parliament sponsored a competition for an alternative. The winning design has 11 horizontal blue, white and red stripes linked in the middle to form four triangles that symbolize the country's peaks and valleys. Parliament must approve it.

On the northwestern tip of former Yugoslavia and closest in geography and culture to Western Europe, the Republic of Slovenia was the first former Yugoslav republic to wrestle its independence from Belgrade. It is in the enviable position to be the first to enter both the European Union and NATO in 2004 and to adopt the euro in 2007. In the first half of 2008 it became the first ex-communist land to occupy the EU's rotating presidency.

Because of their relative prosperity, social stability and strong cultural and economic links with the West, Slovenes are inclined to consider themselves as "Central Europeans" rather than as a Balkan people. In their minds, the "Balkans" lies to the southeast. In fact, they locate themselves in the very middle of Europe. If one were to draw lines from Gibraltar to Moscow and from Scotland to Crete, they would intersect in Slovenia. The country likes to offer itself to the West as an economic and diplomatic "bridge to the Balkans."

This relatively prosperous country includes the northeastern part of the Istrian Peninsula, which gives it a coastline on

417

Slovenia

the Adriatic Sea. Koper is its major port and maritime gateway to the world. The Julian Alps run along most of the border with Italy, while the Karavanke Mountains mark the border with Austria. Somewhat farther south and southeast are the Kamnik Mountains.

The Sava River forms a wide valley between the Julian Alps and the Karavanke Mountains, then flows across the republic in a southeasterly direction. A second major river, the Drava, originates in Austria (where it is known as the Drau), then enters the republic north of the Kamnik Mountains. It flows in a southeasterly direction before crossing into Croatia. Except for the mountainous area, most of Slovenia is covered by often steep, heavily forested rolling hills, with the exception of the plateau area of gray karst limestone east of Trieste. Only half the size of Switzerland, Slovenia could be called a "one-hour country" because everything—mountains, beaches, the capital city—can be reached in about 60 minutes. Travel writer Jan Morris wrote: "When God devised Slovenia, he smiled."

About 88% of Slovenia's population belongs to the majority ethnic group. About 3,000 Italians live along the coast in the western part of the republic. At least 100,000 Slovenes live in northeastern Italy, including 17% of the population of the province of Trieste, 12% of Goriza and 5% of Udine. Approximately 8,500 Hungarians live in the northeastern part of Slovenia, but most of the minorities are people who came from other parts of former Yugoslavia in search of work: 3% Croatian, 2% Serbian and 1% Bosniak. Slovenia was Yugoslavia's most economically advanced part. Large numbers of Muslims fleeing the war in Bosnia-Herzegovina entered Slovenia between 1992 and 1995, and some remained.

HISTORY

The Slovenes migrated into the area of the western Balkans in the 6th century, the first of the Slavic peoples to enter the region. In 627 A.D., a Slavic kingdom, called Karantanija, came into existence in the Sava River Valley. It lasted about 120 years, then was incorporated into the Carolingian Empire in 748. It was at this time that the Slovenians were converted to Roman Catholicism.

In the 9th century, the Carolingian Empire was divided, and Slovenia became part of the eastern, German-dominated area. In the 10th century, it was incorporated into the Holy Roman Empire, where it remained through several changes of rulers. Eventually it passed to the Habsburgs in the 14th century after they had established their capital at Vienna. Periodic attempts at Germanization shrank

the realm of Slovenian culture. However, most of the Slovenian heartland remained intact, thanks to the efforts of native Roman Catholic priests.

Slovenian peasants were eventually made serfs, along with those in other parts of the empire. This produced a number of uprisings in the 15th and 16th centuries. But things remained very much the same until the 18th century, when Maria Theresa and her son, Joseph II, attempted to improve the lot of the people by granting them personal freedom.

After the collapse of the Austrian Empire in 1918, Slovenian leaders supported the creation of the Kingdom of Serbs, Croats and Slovenes. This became the Kingdom of Yugoslavia in 1929. Slovenia was partitioned during World War II, with Italy taking the Southwest, Hungary a small piece of land north of the Mura River called Prekomurje, and Germany the Northeast. This spawned a Slovenian resistance movement, the most significant of which was the communist-led Liberation Front. By the end of the war, the partisan army had grown to 37,000 fighters.

The war and its bloody aftermath claimed at least 100,000 Slovene lives. Thousands had been sent to labor and concentration camps, deported or held hostage. In the spring and summer of 1945, Tito's partisan forces systematically killed an estimated 100,000 alleged Axis collaborators, Chetniks and other unwanted persons in Slovenia. Many of them had attempted to surrender to British forces in southern Austria, but they were sent back. Slovenes were shocked in 2009 to see TV images of mass graves, such as Huda Jama (Bad Cave); this is only one of around 600 such postwar grave sites. During the Communist era it was impossible to talk about this issue. But the TV pictures have caused some Slovenians to question the national myth that Tito was a beneficent savior, despite the fact that his postwar victory

brought added Adriatic territories to Slovenia and Croatia.

After the defeat of Germany in 1945, Slovenia became one of the constituent republics of the People's Republic of Yugoslavia. In 1947, it received some additional territory from Italy as part of the Paris Peace Treaty. Trieste remained Italian, but its hinterland became a part of Yugoslavia. In 1954, some of the former Free Territory of Trieste (Zone B) was transferred to Slovenia. After Slovenia entered the European Union (EU) in May 2004, Trieste once again was reunited with its former hinterland.

Slovenians are a hardworking people with good leadership. They did well economically until about 1980. But Yugoslavia never recovered from the oil shock of 1979, and the wealthier parts of the country found themselves called upon to provide more assistance to badly run and ailing large-scale industry in eastern Yugoslavia. By the middle of the 1980s, political leaders in Slovenia and Croatia were pushing for a change in the economic system, but the Serbian leadership opposed them. Slovenia and Croatia proposed a loosened form of federation that would give them economic independence. This was unacceptable to Serbia.

Independence

Faced with this stalemate at the national level, Slovenia and Croatia began to push for internal changes. By the spring of 1990, Slovenia had ended the political monopoly formerly held by the Slovenian Communist Party and created a de facto pluralistic system. In April 1990, multiparty elections resulted in a legislature dominated by the six-party Democratic United Opposition, or Demos.

Demos, a coalition of conservative political parties, had campaigned on a platform of independence within a year. At the same time, Milan Kucan (Ku-*chan*), candi-

International business students in Lake Bled

418

Slovenia

date of the Communists, was elected president. Shortly thereafter, the Communists became the Party of Democratic Renewal and endorsed independence as well.

On July 2, 1990, parliament adopted a "declaration of sovereignty" by an overwhelming 187 votes to 3. In September, it took control of the "territorial defense force" (TDF), which had been first created in 1968 and which constituted an embryonic independent Slovene army. A referendum on independence was held on December 23, 1990. Of those voting, 88.5% opted for independence, "unless it proved possible to negotiate a looser Yugoslav confederation." Parliament adopted its own endorsement of the declaration on December 26. It voted in February 1991 that republic law would henceforth take precedence over laws of the Yugoslav Federation.

Slovenia began managing its own borders and customs facilities, and in May 1991 it started retaining all draftees within its own borders and incorporating them in the republic's TDF. Approximately 22,000 Yugoslav People's Army (JNA) troops were stationed on Slovene territory at the time. Even though they confiscated about 70% of the TDF's military equipment, much of it remained in Slovenian hands.

All attempts to negotiate a new union failed due to Serbian stonewalling. Serbia instituted a boycott of goods from Slovenia. Finally, Slovenia and Croatia declared their independence on June 25, 1991. The "Ten-day War" began.

On June 27, the JNA commenced military operations after the republic took charge of the border posts with Austria and Italy. Many Slovene soldiers left their JNA units and defended their own free republic, and the republic's territorial force swelled to as many as 60,000 lightly armed recruits and reservists. The Slovenes fought back, and they managed to capture some tanks and other equipment. They resisted the takeover of further border stations and blocked many roads and JNA barracks, taking about 8,000 soldiers captive and only later releasing them. The population practiced mass civil disobedience and sabotage. In ten days the fighting was over, with fewer than 100 dead and 300 wounded on both sides, compared later with 10,000 dead in Croatia and 200,000 in Bosnia.

Yugoslav leaders were clearly unprepared for a war in Slovenia. In many ways they had little appetite to fight for the breakaway republic. Serbs have no historical or ethnic claims to it, and few Serbs lived there. They were astonished that such a little people fought back so fiercely. They were also aware that a much bigger battle was about to begin in Croatia, cutting off any JNA troops left in Slovenia.

Therefore they agreed to a cease-fire and withdrew all their troops by October. Slovenia was free.

Meanwhile, the West attempted to dissuade the Slovenians and Croatians from radical actions. It refused, as U.S. Secretary of State James Baker put it, to recognize their independence "under any circumstances." It was soon appalled by the bloodshed in Croatia and began to offer mediating services.

Some of the European nations, especially Germany and Austria, even began talking about extending recognition to Slovenia and Croatia. After two cease-fires had broken down, the third held. In a compromise imposed by negotiators from the EC (now EU), Slovene agents were authorized to collect federal customs duties at the disputed customs posts, while Slovenia agreed to suspend application of its declaration of independence for three months. This brought an end to the war in Slovenia, but it actually only moved the venue of the war to Croatia. Slovenia activated its declaration of independence as of October 7.

By December, with the war in Croatia still going on, most European nations were fed up with Serbia and the JNA leadership. Germany now pressed the EC to recognize the two republics, and this was finally agreed to, effective January 15, 1992. Secretary of State Baker refused to follow suit, however, in effect continuing support for the hard-line, Serbian nationalist and ex-communist leadership of Serbia. Anything seemed better to Baker than to see one more part of Europe falling apart. This changed only after the Yugoslav army began to spread its destruction throughout most of the rest of former Yugoslavia. The United States then changed its mind and sponsored UN economic sanctions against Serbia.

POLITICAL SYSTEM

A new constitution, approved in December 1991, established a parliamentary democracy. The European Union later required some changes, such as restrictions in the original text on foreigners' right to purchase land in Slovenia. Its criminal code came into effect in 1995. Like every other democratic European country, it has no death penalty. The court system is headed by a Constitutional Court. Its members are nominated by the president and approved for nine-year, nonrenewable terms by the National Assembly.

The role of the president is largely ceremonial although ex-President Milan Kucan, a former communist leader, carved out an important role for himself in the area of foreign affairs. He won the presidency in 1992 with 52% of the vote. In

1997, he easily won reelection. One factor in his unusually good showing was that he was a strong supporter of Slovenia's entry into the European Union and NATO.

He was forbidden by the constitution to run for a third term, and in December 2002 he was succeeded by Janez Drnovsek, who resigned as prime minister to assume the presidency. Mortally ill, Drnovsek resigned in January 2008 and died one month later. In the election that had taken place in November 2007, Social Democrat Danilo Türk defeated Christian Democrat Lojze Peterle in the second round of voting by a whopping 69.2% to 30.1% margin. Türk is a former professor and diplomat, living in New York for 13 years as the country's ambassador to the UN and then, from 2000 to 2005, serving as the deputy UN Secretary General.

The president proposes a prime minister to the National Assembly after consulting with parliamentary groups. The prime minister, the official head of government, presides over the cabinet and is responsible for government policy. He must be affirmed in office by a positive vote of the National Assembly and may be removed by a negative vote of confidence. This is the most powerful office in the Slovene political system.

Slovenia has a bicameral legislature composed of two houses, the National Assembly and the National Council. The National Assembly, composed of 90 members, is the "popular" house, equivalent to the British House of Commons. It is directly elected for a four-year term. A party must win at least 4% of the total votes to qualify for seats. One seat each is reserved for the Italian and Hungarian minority groups, and these representatives can veto any legislation that specifically affects their communities.

The upper house, the National Council, is elected for five years. It has a total of 40 members, 22 of them representing local

President Danilo Türk

419

Slovenia

Oldtown Ljubljana

interests, 12 evenly divided between employers, employees and the self-employed, and six representing nonprofit activities, such as education and culture. Its powers are limited to delaying legislation.

The small country has no states or provinces. It is broken down into 193 local units called *opcine*, or municipalities or townships. Parliament or 40,000 voters can sign a petition demanding referenda, which are held frequently. For example, in November 2007 voters rejected government plans to sell off the state's 35% stake in Slovenia's largest insurer, Zavarovalnica Triglav.

Parliamentary Elections

Slovenia has been a multiparty parliamentary democracy since 1990, when a six-party Democratic United Opposition, also known as the Demos, won 55% of the vote. The Slovenian Communist Party, which had changed its name to the Party of Democratic Renewal, won 18%. The old Demos coalition has subsequently disintegrated.

In the 2000 parliamentary elections, Janez Drnovsek's Liberal Democrats were swept back into power after winning 36% of the votes and 34 seats. This was the highest share of the vote obtained by any party since 1991.

After winning the presidency in December 2002, Drnovsek relinquished the position of prime minister to his finance minister, Anton Rop. The center-left Liberal Democracy party (LDS) led a three-party coalition that controlled 58 of 90 seats in parliament. It suffered a humiliating loss in the October 2004 parliamentary elections, won for the first time since 1991 by the center-right opposition. Janez Jansa's Slovene Democratic Party almost doubled its vote, winning 29%. Its ally, the con-

servative New Slovenia party, took 9%. Together with two smaller parties—the center-right People's Party and the center-left Democratic Party of Pensioners—his coalition won a narrow majority of seats in parliament. The government promised to cut the costs of state administration and to press ahead with privatization in order to prepare for the adoption of the euro, which occurred in 2007.

Jansa had once been a freedom fighter, journalist and critic of Yugoslav defense excesses. His arrest in 1988 helped spark massive street protests in Ljubljana and pave the way for independence. He looked back: "That changed my destiny." A defense expert and former defense minister in the early 1990s, he appointed former prime minister, Andrej Bajuk, as finance minister. Rop's Liberal Democratic Party won 23% of the votes and went into opposition. After 13 years in power, it had become identified with arrogance and clientelism.

The next parliamentary elections were held in September 2008. A center-left government emerged led by Borut Pahor and his Social Democrats, which captured 30.45% of the votes and 29 of 90 seats. His coalition partners are the Liberal Democratic Party of Slovenia, which won 5.21% and five seats, and a new party: Zares—New Politics, a splinter group of breakaway Liberal Democratic dissidents, which garnered 9.37% of the votes and 9 seats.

In the opposition are the Slovenian Democratic Party, which gathered 29.26% of the votes and 28 seats; the Democratic Party of Pensioners, with 7.45% of the votes and 7 seats; the Slovenian National Party, which won 5.4% of the votes and 5 seats; and the Slovenian People's Party/Youth Party, which got 5.21% and 5 seats. Outgoing prime minister, Janez Jansa, was

accused of having taken a bribe from a Finnish company. He called this the dirtiest electoral campaign since independence in 1991.

The new prime minister, 44-year-old Borut Pahor, is a former Member of the European Parliament with a reputation for achieving compromises. He has a degree in international studies at the University of Ljubljana. During his student days he earned the money to pay for his studies by being a male model. For that he gained the nickname among his political rivals: "Barbie Doll."

Foreign Policy

The Slovenian government very much wanted to be part of the West, and it worked hard to give that orientation a physical reality. It joined NATO's "Partnership for Peace" in 1994, and full membership in NATO followed in April 2004. It had received an invitation to join at NATO's Prague summit in November 2002. The government, all political parties, and the influential Catholic Church were solidly in favor of membership, but political leaders had to make a persuasive case to the people, many of whom were skeptical of NATO's utility for the country. When voters went to the polls in March 2003 to vote on both NATO and EU entry, two-thirds supported NATO membership, but 93% gave their approval of EU membership.

Slovenia has little firepower to offer the military alliance. It maintains only 7,200 soldiers on active duty. Conscription was ended in 2004. It has a reserve strength of 3,080. It has minor air (530) and naval (47) elements with eight armed helicopters and a patrol boat. It has a paramilitary force of 4,500 police. It sends 25 peacekeepers to Bosnia and 378 to Kosovo. In

Prime Minister Borut Pahor

420

Slovenia

2010 it took over NATO command in Skopje, Macedonia. It does offer NATO valuable geography advantages, such as a land connection to Hungary, which was isolated from its NATO partners until Slovakia became a member of the alliance. Since Slovenia joined NATO Italy's air force patrols its airspace.

It signed an association agreement with the European Union in 1996 and became a full member in May 2004. Over two-thirds of its trade is with EU members, and 90% of its foreign investment comes from Germany, Italy, Austria and France.

In its campaign for dual membership, the government adopted the slogan, "At home in the EU, safe in NATO." As the results were announced, political leaders gathered to celebrate in Preseren Square in the center of Ljubljana. By joining the EU and adopting the euro in 2007, Slovenes confirmed both their independence and their alignment with Western Europe. They demonstrated that at last they were a nation free to choose for itself.

In January 2008 it becomes the smallest country except Luxembourg and the first ex-communist nation to assume the revolving six-month EU presidency. It immediately faced a practical problem: since it has very few diplomatic missions in the world, its successor to the presidency, France, agreed to provide representation in 110 countries where Slovenia has none. The year before, Slovenia had helped out its predecessor, Portugal, by representing it in Macedonia and Montenegro. Slovenia needed no help in Washington because it got the former Yugoslav embassy when the diplomatic buildings were parceled out among the parts of the former federation in December 2001. Bosnia-Herzegovina received the one in London, while Croatia got the embassy in Paris. The consulate in Paris went to Macedonia, and the ambassador's residence there was kept by Serbia.

Because of its wealth, Slovenia may end up as a net contributor to the EU budget rather than a recipient of structural funds (subsidies). By 2004 Slovenia's per capita GDP reached about 70% of the EU-15 average. But in the expanded 27-member EU, that figure climbed to over 80%, measured in purchasing power parity, and the gap is closing. That makes it ineligible for the funds.

Membership also forced it to cancel its free-trade agreements with the Balkan states, with which it had maintained trade surpluses. But Slovenian companies have become big investors in the former Yugoslavia. With their old contacts, a shared history and similar language, they are natural partners. Slovenia plays an important role in the Balkans as a bridge between them and EU and NATO.

Its top priority as holder of the EU presidency in 2008 was to keep the momentum of enlargement alive for its Balkan neighbors, including Croatia and Serbia. It skillfully coordinated the EU's response to Kosovo's declaration of independence on February 17, 2008. It supported both Kosovo's desire to secede from Serbia and Belgrade's prospects for one day entering the EU. It also helped end two years of drift in the EU's dealings with Russia by supporting the European Commission's effort to negotiate a long-term partnership accord with Moscow. In all of these matters, Slovenia's contribution was modest but useful.

Its relations with Croatia are not the best. Their rivalry is demonstrated in the clichés they have of each other: Slovenes are haughty and humorless while Croatians are lazy, lawless and too nationalistic. They have never fought a war against each other. But their disputes reflect issues that are left over from the breakup of Yugoslavia and hinder relations between all the former six republics. The two have a long-standing disagreement concerning an alleged debt of about $400 million owed by a Slovenian bank to Croatians in the earlier Yugoslav era. There are problems concerning the operation of a jointly owned nuclear power plant. They quarrel over two small stretches of land, one near the Slovenian town of Piran and the other along the southeastern border with Croatia, near Zagreb.

Most important, they disagree over territorial jurisdiction in the Adriatic Sea. Slovenia has a minuscule coastline of only 47 kilometers, compared with Croatia's 1,700 kilometers, and it has no direct access to international waters. They reached an accord in 2001, but Croatia declined to ratify it. Slovenia's hopes to negotiate a free corridor were foiled in August 2003 when Croatia announced plans to declare an exclusive economic zone within its territorial waters. This also affected fishing rights. Slovenia responded angrily by temporarily recalling its ambassador from Croatia and threatening to withhold its support for Croatian entry into the EU and NATO. When Croatia postponed its plan to declare the exclusive zone, Slovenia backed away from its threat concerning NATO, which Croatia entered in April 2009. While it seems that Croatia, with its long Dalmatian coastline, should be able to relinquish a sea lane to Slovenia, the matter is complicated by the possibility that there might be oil and gas under those waters.

In September 2004 there was a border incident in which a Slovenian group led by a member of parliament was arrested by Croatian border guards for refusing to show identity cards. The whole affair was filmed by a TV crew and aired the same night on Slovenian television. It came just before parliamentary elections. Then Prime Minister Rop was accused of overreacting, for example by threatening Croatia's admission to the EU. The daily newspaper *Delo* called the government's response "stupid, unnecessary, inadequate and irresponsible."

The disagreement flared up again on January 1, 2008, when Croatia proclaimed a 57,000 square kilometer fisheries protection zone in the Adriatic against Italy's and Slovenia's wishes. While EU officials urged Croatia not to enforce that proclamation, there was quiet frustration that Slovenia seemed to be using its role as temporary president to have the dispute moved up on the EU agenda and to slow down Croatia's accession talks in order to force Zagreb to back down.

For a long time, Slovenia refused to budge on the EU, blocking Croatia's entry until a compromise could be reached on this maritime dispute. Some critics found this a dangerous precedent in the Balkans. But in June 2010 Slovene voters in a referendum narrowly approved (51.5%) their government's November 2009 agreement (accepted by parliament in April 2010) with Croatia not to allow the 18-year dispute to stall Croatia's EU accession negotiations. Zagreb agreed not to claim disputed areas during the talks and to leave the complicated issue to be resolved later. In gratitude, Croatia's newly elected president, Ivo Josipoviç, made his first state visit to Slovenia in April 2010.

Its relations with the United States are "good" but not close. It was the first Central European country to have visa-free travel to America. Since Tito's Yugoslavia was much less isolated from the West and never dominated by the Soviet Union, Yugoslavs never felt the same warmth for the U.S. as did most other Eastern Europeans during the Cold War. However, individual members of the Slovenian government have much closer private ties. For example, former President Drnovsek traveled to the United States in 1994 to receive an honorary degree from Boston University. It was an irritant in U.S.-Slovenian relations in 1993–95 that he was a consistent critic of Western inaction in Bosnia. U.S.-Slovenian relations improved after the Dayton Accord was signed in 1995. Slovenia strongly supported NATO actions against Serbia over Kosovo in 1999.

Things were not so harmonious during the 2003 war in Iraq, which four-fifths of Slovenes opposed. Slovenes desire to stay out of armed conflicts far from home. The government was in a difficult position. It decided to sign the so-called Vilnius declaration with nine other mainly Eastern European countries and to grant an Amer-

421

Slovenia

ican request to allow airplanes with aid, refugees and wounded to use its airspace, but not those carrying troops and military supplies. It was the only signatory of the Vilnius letter not to send troops to Iraq. It publicly corrected an error made by the U.S., which had listed Slovenia as a partner in the war against Iraq. By 2007, however, it had four instructors in Iraq training Iraqi forces and 50 in Afghanistan. By dispatching more peacekeeping soldiers to Kosovo in March 2007, it has more troops abroad in NATO missions per capita than any other ally. To express his thanks in June 2008, outgoing U.S. President George W. Bush made the first stop on his last trip to Europe in Slovenia.

One of the most delicate matters the Slovene government had to deal with was the status of the 25,671 residents from other former Yugoslav republics, mainly Serbs, Croats and Bosnians, who found themselves living in Slovenia without citizenship. After independence in 1991 ethnic Slovenes were automatically granted Slovene citizenship. People from other ethnic backgrounds were required to apply for such citizenship. When 25,671 failed to do so, they were deleted from the national population register without public warning or announcement.

Referred to as "erased" people, they thereby lost their basic right to permanent residency that is a precondition for the permission to work and receive health care and pensions. In 1999 the Slovenian constitutional court ordered the government to restore their rights. A subsequent referendum on the question rejected the court decision by a vote of more than 90%, but a further court decision invalidated the referendum.

With the EU looking on approvingly, the government admitted in 2004 that it had made a mistake and proceeded to restore citizenship for the erased. This upset many ethnic Slovenes, who feared that thousands will be entitled to sue for millions of euros in back benefits and damages. A non-binding referendum in April 2004 produced a large margin of votes against the erased. Then Prime Minister Jansa pounced on the matter, angrily claiming that many of the erased were former Yugoslav military officers who had fought against Slovenia's independence. Some observers called this issue an election "gift" for Jansa without which "he never would have been elected." He halted the return of rights to the erased. But in 2010 parliament adopted (48 to 30) an amendment to the act dealing with the erased that resolved the injustices suffered by them. Those without permanent residence permits can obtain them.

Slovenia's leaders are aware of the importance of the Western Balkans for their country. It allocates 80% of its bilateral development aid to the region. It is Slovenia's second most important market, accounting for 17% of exports and 6.5% of imports. Most (67.4%) of the foreign direct investments in the area are made by Slovene companies.

Recognizing that importance, Slovenia organized and hosted a regional conference in March 2010 at Brdo pri Kranju. It was attended by all prime ministers in the area except the Serbian, who refused to go since Kosovo was participating under its independence name, The Republic of Kosovo. Also the Bosnian leader walked out when Kosovo's leader spoke, and the EU's most senior officials were disappointingly absent. The meeting was long on symbolism and short on substance. However, the picture of former adversaries sitting together, reaffirming their EU intentions, and cooperating to benefit the entire region sent a significant signal. The conclusion was: "Everyone needs everyone."

ECONOMY

When Slovenia broke away from Yugoslavia in 1991, it had a fairly modern commercial and industrial base, and it has continued performing well. It has sustained stable annual economic growth, low unemployment, and a strong trade balance. Slovenia is no longer largely agricultural. By 2010, only 2.4% of GDP was generated by agriculture although 10% are employed in that sector. The harvesting of forestry products provides an additional income for many rural inhabitants. Crops include wheat, corn, rye, oats, potatoes, rapeseed, sugar beets, and fruit. Livestock (cattle, sheep, pigs, poultry) is also raised throughout the republic. Agriculture is highly mechanized, and the standard of living in the countryside approximates that of its neighbor, Austria. Still, the government is concerned that Slovenian farmers will have difficulty competing as members of the European Union.

Slovenia has developed a modern economy, with 54% of its workforce employed

in services (producing 63.3% of GDP) and 36% in industry (34.4% of GDP). It has a significant steel industry that produces approximately three-quarters of a million tons annually. It also manufactures trucks, automobiles, furniture, domestic appliances and medicine. Other industrial products include cement, sulfuric acid, cotton and woolen fabrics, plus processed agricultural products such as sugar.

It produces its own coal, has some hydroelectric stations that yield almost a third of its electricity, and generates about a third of its electricity from atomic power. In June 2008 it had to shut down a nuclear power station because of a water leak. The government quickly apologized for initially telling its neighbors that it was only a drill, and the EU issued its first continent-wide radiation alert. All other energy must be imported, including 40% of its natural gas from Russia.

The economic dislocations associated with its declaration of independence and the resulting loss of the former Yugoslav market led to a three-year recession, but the economy began growing again in 1993 and has continued growing ever since. It launched a Privatization Act in 1992 that has been a success. Its program used a system of vouchers. This process applied only to larger firms. Most Slovenian companies were small, and they were "socially-owned," in line with Yugoslavia's system of worker self-management. Such firms were privatized through a form of internal share distribution, i.e., all shares were distributed to the employees and management. Larger firms, on the other hand, were privatized using public share offerings. In that case, 20% of the shares were transferred to the Slovene Development Fund, which sold the shares to authorized investment firms in which the public had invested their privatization vouchers.

The Slovene Development Fund also assumes outright ownership of firms in financial or organizational disorder. They are reorganized and rehabilitated, then prepared for sale to the public. This was the one group of firms where foreign direct investment was possible as a form of privatization. That was one of Slovenia's problems as it contemplated membership in the European Union. The country had to respond to EU criticism of the slow pace of economic liberalization, especially in privatizing major state-owned enterprises such as telecommunications and big banks. In 2007 it sold shares in the second-largest bank, NKBM. It had to jettison a lot of rules that once prevented foreigners from investing in the economy. By the time of EU entry, most of its largest companies remained domestically owned, and only a third of banking assets were in foreign hands. The state still has 40% of corporate capital in its possession, a high percentage for a market economy.

It had to make other changes as well. Its banking and insurance sectors were still dominated by government-owned companies that had to be merged and sold. The same was true for telephones and electricity. Telekom Slovenia remained in majority state hands, but 49% of its shares were offered for sale in January 2008. Its wireless arm, Mobitel, was the first operator to introduce advanced third-generation phone service in Eastern Europe. Mobile (91%) and Internet (over 50%) penetration rivals the most developed Western European countries.

Tourism accounts for 8% of GDP and 10% of employment. Because of the violent breakup of Yugoslavia, many tourists were frightened away for several years. The bustling modern port of Koper has become the largest and best Adriatic port in the EU and is the gateway of choice for many foreign goods entering the community. It can handle container traffic, 200,000 new cars each year, and everything from bulk minerals and agricultural produce. Its importance will increase once the government achieves its plan to build a new rail line connecting Koper and the city of Divaca. Despite protests from its national carrier, Adria Airways, which has only 10 aircraft, the no-frills easyJet airlines won permission to land in Ljubljana, thereby sharply increasing the air traffic into the country.

Slovenia's economic is very open and is 70% dependent upon exporting. Such a country is bound to be vulnerable to the kind of global downturn that affected the entire world in 2008–9. The recession presented a severe test. Slovenia's economic performance was good. Real GDP had grown 4% annually since 1994, and in 2007 it was 6.8%, the highest in the eurozone and the best for a decade. That fell to minus 6.7% in 2009 but rose to positive 1.6% in 2010. Exports had doubled. In 2008 the budget deficit was .7% of GDP. By 2010 that deficit was 5.5% of GDP. Total public debt rose from 29.3% of GDP in 2009 to 34.9% in 2010. This relatively low debt helped qualify Slovenia for the euro in 2007.

A former finance minister said this relative success was aided by the fact that "ours was a softer form of socialism than in many other places in Europe." Transparency International ranked Slovenia in 2009 as the least corrupt among ex-communist countries (27th), tied with Estonia. Inflation was 3.2% in 2008, and unemployment of 8% in 2008 was slightly above the eurozone average and continued to grow slightly as there was a serious downturn in the auto and construction industries. Property prices, which roughly doubled between 2003 and 2007, have declined. There is an under-ground economy that is estimated to be more widespread than the EU average.

Its economic problems are similar to those found in richer Western European countries: high taxes (a top rate of 41%, lowered from 50%), generous public benefits, a pay-as-you go pension system (average pension 554 euros or $720 per month) that must eventually be reformed to remain solvent. This is especially true given the country's high wages by regional standards, costly public services, rigid labor laws that provide Europe's most protected employment, large and influential trade unions and low fertility rate. The population is rapidly aging despite the fact that there were more births than deaths from 2006–9. Slovenia approaches reform cautiously. It never does anything quickly or radically.

CULTURE

Slovenian culture reflects the fact that this is an overwhelmingly Roman Catholic country even though the percentage of those identifying themselves as Catholic had fallen from 70% to 58% between 1991 and 2005. However, it differs from Croatia, which is also Roman Catholic, in that it is much more Western in orientation. Driving through the beautiful countryside, it is almost impossible to differentiate this area from Austria across the border. Towns and cities are clean and prosperous-looking, and the people dress

much as they do elsewhere in Western Europe. Only the signs in Slovenian make it clear what country you are in.

There is not a great deal of literature in Slovenian that is known outside the country. Much of what exists is religious in nature. The Freising manuscripts, dating from about the year 1000, are the earliest works available. Slovenian came into wider use during the reformation, when Protestants translated the Bible and also produced some tracts in the language. The Slovenians eventually rejected Protestantism. In the 18th century, a Roman Catholic version of the Bible appeared in Slovenian, and this was followed by grammars in the early 19th century. Slovenian came into common use only after the middle of the 19th century.

Relations between the government and the Roman Catholic Church are strained, partly based on differing interpretations of the constitution's definition of the role of the Church in public life. It has been pressing for return of all of its property nationalized during the period of communism and for the reintroduction of religious instruction in the schools. Much of its earlier property has been returned. The government has continued to emphasize the separation of church and state.

FUTURE

With its stable, democratic political system and vigorous economy, Slovenia represents one of the success stories of Central and Eastern Europe. Slovenians have good relations with all of their neighbors, and they have worked out some of their difficulties with Croatia. They achieved their chief foreign policy goal of "joining Europe" by becoming members of NATO and the European Union in 2004. In 2007 they adopted the euro. With a per capita GDP (estimated $25,640 in 2008) higher than in Greece and Portugal and twice that of neighboring Croatia, it does not face the huge income gap between old and new members that most of the other accession states must overcome. With President Danilo Türk and Prime Minister, Barut Pahor, the country faces the future in good hands.

It is hardly surprising that two international studies, in 2004 and 2005, measuring happiness in European countries gave Slovenes a 90% rating compared with 87% in the EU-15 and only 64% in the other EU accession countries. Living up to the confidence the other EU members had shown toward Slovenia, it served with success as the revolving EU presidency country the first half of 2008. This was not easy for such a small country. One western diplomat quipped: "It's a little bit like taxiing a 747 with a bicycle."

The Republic of Croatia

National Day: May 30, 1991
Head of State: Ivo Josipovic, President (elected in January 2010).
Head of Government: Jadranka Kosor, Prime Minister (July 2009).
National Flag: Three horizontal stripes from the top—red, white, blue, with a checkered crest of the country imposed on the white stripe.

Existing at the edge of great empires, Croatia has been subject to different influences throughout its history. But it has always cherished its own ancient heritage and retained its own style of life and culture. The Republic of Croatia declared its independence from Yugoslavia in June 1991. After a bitter six-month war against Serbia and the Yugoslav People's Army (JNA), it received international recognition by the members of the European Community (now EU) in January 1992.

Croatia has a long coastline on the Adriatic Sea. In the north and east, the chief topographical features are the Sava and Drava river valleys, plus the Croatian-Slavonian Mountains, a mountainous ridge that separates the two valleys. The Drava River forms the border with Hungary while the Sava forms the border with Bosnia-Herzegovina. Most of the rest of Croatia consists of either mountains or uplands.

Area: 21,829 sq. mi. (56,538 sq. km.)
Population: 4.6 million (UN 2008)
Capital City: Zagreb (779,145)
Climate: Mediterranean in the west; mild continental east of Zagreb.
Neighboring Countries: Slovenia (north); Hungary (northeast); Serbia (east); Bosnia and Herzegovina (east and south); Montenegro (southwest).
Official Language: Croatian
Other Principal Tongues: Serbian and Bosnian (both closely related)
Ethnic Background: South Slavic. Croat ca. 86%, Serb 4.5% (2001 estimate).
Principal Religions: Roman Catholicism (77%), Orthodox (11%).
Chief Commercial Products: Transport equipment, textiles, chemicals, foodstuffs, fuels, lumber, steel, plastics, cement.
Main Trading Partners: EU (55%). Italy (23.1% of exports and 16.7% of imports), Bosnia and Herzegovina (12.6% of exports and 14.8% of imports), Germany (10.4% of exports and 14.5% of imports), Austria (6% of exports and 10.1% of imports), Slovenia (8.2% of exports and 6.3% of imports), Russia (10.1% of imports).
Currency: kuna
Former Political Status: Constituent republic of Yugoslavia.

Croatian Serbs flee after Fall of Krajina, 1995.

The Great Kapela Chain traverses the northwest. Somewhat farther south, the Velebit Range begins, followed by other Dinarian Alps, which run along the border with Bosnia-Herzegovina. The long Croatian coastline consists of the Istrian Peninsula, Dalmatian Islands, and a fairly narrow strip of the mainland reaching down as far as Montenegro. This is essentially a narrow coastal plain backed by mountains. Along with the Dalmatian Islands, it became a major summer resort area for West Europeans.

This region was once the ancient Roman province of Dalmatia and includes such historic cities as Split, where the Emperor Diocletian lived after his retirement from 305 to 313. The nucleus of the town is actually the Palace of Diocletian. Another important city is Dubrovnik, founded in the 7th century and famous for its late-Renaissance buildings. Its picturesque streets, which are narrow and winding, are closed to motor vehicles. Dubrovnik was badly damaged when it was shelled by the JNA in the fall of 1991 and early 1992. But it has since been largely restored, thanks partly to a large flow of private international assistance, prompted by the horror and outrage caused by the destruction.

Prior to independence, Croats represented 78.1% of the population, and Serbs, the largest minority with about 600,000,

constituted another 12.2%. A further 2.2% listed themselves as Yugoslavs, and one percent as Muslims. The war resulted in a major shift in populations, however. Croats were pushed out of areas controlled by Croatian Serbs, and many Muslim refugees from Bosnia made their way into Croat-controlled areas of the republic in 1991–1992. Another major change occurred in the summer of 1995 when about 300,000 Serbs fled the Krajina as Croatian soldiers recaptured that area. Only about 120,000 have returned, and 85,000 were still registered in 2006 as refugees, chiefly in Serbia.

Today, Serbs number a little over 200,000 (4.5%) and are found in significant numbers only in larger cities, in the eastern part of Croatia, and in East Slavonia (the eastern-most part of Croatia, along the Danube). There are frequent bus connections from Belgrade, but transportation links remain poor. Regular air links were never restored, and travelers driving east from Zagreb see few signs guiding their way toward Belgrade. Croatia does more than twice as much trade with Slovenia as it does with Serbia, which is four times larger. Only 5% of its exports flow to Serbia, and only 1% of its imports come from there.

Visa requirements between the two countries have been suspended. Some Serbs are returning, but the young and more educated find better prospects in Serbia or elsewhere. Ethnic Croats are returning in even lower numbers. There is little work to be found. For example, in Vukovar, where some of the fiercest fighting had taken place, unemployment is officially 37%, more than twice the national average. But there is a good sign: at the town hall, Serbian and Croatian flags fly side by side.

The government is working hard to reach out to Croatian Serbs, and bilateral relations with Serbia have thawed noticeably; they are proper without being close. President Josipovic signaled his determination in 2010 to improve relations with both neighboring Serbia and Bosnia-Herzegovina. Serbia's president, Boris Tadic, had visited Zagreb in mid-2007 and apologized to Croats for war crimes committed by those "acting on behalf of my people." Much has been done to return property to those who fled, even evicting Bosnian Croats who settled in Serbs' houses. Difficult problems remain, such as the fact that both Serbia and Croatia have accused each other in the Hague war crimes tribunal of genocide during the 1991–5 Balkan War.

The governments of Croatia, Bosnia, Montenegro and Serbia have agreed to try to settle the remaining refugee issues. Montenegro became the first ex-Yugoslav entity to agree to pay war compensation, offering Croatia $460,000 for cattle its soldiers stole.

In 2006 an excellent locally produced film, *Vukovar: The Final Cut*, was made. It tells the story of the devastating siege of this eastern Croatian city in 1991. The most encouraging thing about it is that it was a joint Serbian-Croatian production.

HISTORY

During the great migrations from the area of the western Carpathian Mountains in the 7th century A.D., Croats, a Slavic people, settled in Dalmatia. Even at this time they were separate from the Serbs, constituting, along with the Slavonians, the western division of the Serbo-Croatian migration, while the Serbs formed the eastern portion.

At this time, the Croats were ruled according to tribal institutions. The first primitive form of the Croatian state started to take shape at the beginning of the 8th century. Small in numbers but militarily powerful, they conquered neighboring areas and mixed with other Slavs and the original Romanized population. While the Slovenians were being incorporated into the Carolingian Empire, the Croats fell under the domination of the Byzantine Empire beginning in 877.

Rebelling against this outside control, they formed the first united Croatian Kingdom in 910. Its ruler was Tomislav, and the kingdom he founded lasted for about two centuries. In wars waged against Bulgaria and Hungary during this time, Croatia enlarged its control over additional parts of the Dalmatian coast. Many Croatian nationalists regard this period of history as the golden age of their country. They built up a large navy and for a time at the end of the 10th century even exacted tribute from Venice.

This kingdom came to an end in 1091 when a dispute arose among rival claimants to the throne, and an appeal was made to King Ladislas I of Hungary to resolve the matter. Related to the royal house of Croatia, Ladislas took control of Croatia for himself instead. Although an insurrection broke out after Ladislas' death, it was put down by his successor, Koloman, who was crowned king of Croatia and Dalmatia in 1102. Koloman reorganized the administration of Croatia. He granted it autonomy in domestic affairs and placed it under a royal official called a "Ban." The Ban was sometimes a member of the royal house of Hungary and sometimes a Croatian nobleman.

Habsburg and Hungarian Rule

Croatia came under Habsburg rule in 1526 when the Turks killed the last Hungarian king at the battle of Mohacs. His heir and successor as king of Hungary was Ferdinand Habsburg, ruler of Austria. A year later, the Croatian Diet ratified

Croatia

the change in rulers by electing Ferdinand king of Croatia.

Not long after that, the Turks overran most of Croatia, with only the area around Zagreb remaining free. Recognizing the necessity of defending the southern border against the Turks, the Habsburgs created an area of forts and watchtowers known as the "Military Frontier." Since most of the area had been depopulated as a result of Turkish military incursions, the Habsburgs persuaded individuals to move to the area by granting them land in return for military service. Most of these settlers were Orthodox Serbs and Wallachians (also called Vlachs), who had fled from areas farther to the south and east to escape the yoke of the Turks.

The Habsburg rulers managed to free most of Croatia from the Turks by 1699. The Treaty of Carlowitz, signed in that year, acknowledged this. The newly freed areas of Croatia regained domestic autonomy, including their own Diet or legislature. However, the Habsburg rulers continued to exercise direct control over the area of the "Military Frontier" because of its strategic significance. The separate military government for the "Military Frontier" was not finally abolished until 1881. The tradition of the frontier remained long after 1881, however. It was mainly the descendants of the Orthodox Serb and Wallachian settlers of the old "Military Frontier" who refused to accept Croatian independence in 1991 and organized a separate "Serbian Republic of the Krajina" with the goal of remaining united with their fellow Serbs in Serbia and Bosnia.

The tie of Croatia to its Habsburg rulers was peculiar because it was through their title as kings of Hungary. From Croatia's point of view, their loyalty was to the "individual" who was king of Hungary, not to either Hungary or, for that matter, Austria. The Croatian nobility therefore opposed centralizing tendencies of Habsburg rulers during the 18th century. When they were no longer able to resist directly, they gradually merged themselves more and more into the Hungarian Kingdom in order to take advantage of the fact that the Habsburgs had recognized Hungary as a free and independent kingdom under its own laws. Thus, in 1790, Croatia requested that it be permitted to send three deputies to the Hungarian Diet, which would be responsible for regulating all Croatian affairs.

Having escaped the centralizing tendencies of the Habsburg rulers, Croatia found itself more and more tied to Hungary, a link that it would take a hundred years to undo. The process began in 1809 when Austria ceded a strip of territory on the Adriatic to Napoleon, who organized it into the Illyrian Provinces. They lasted only four years, and Croatia reverted back to Hungary thereafter. However, Croat nationalists trace the rise of national feeling to this short-lived government, which brought Croats, Slovenes and Serbs together for a short time.

The rise of national feeling can also be traced to the beginning of literary works in the Croatian language. It was Ljudevit Gaj (1809–72) who produced the first such works although he edited a journal, called "Illyrian News," in which he advocated the union of all south Slavs.

Another equally important development came in 1843 when Hungary attempted to establish Hungarian as the official language in Croatia. This incensed the Croats, but Hungary compounded the problem in 1848 when the parliament passed legislation that would have incorporated Croatia into the administrative system of Hungary. The Croats now allied themselves with the Habsburg monarchy and, under the command of their Ban, Baron Joseph Jelacic, a Croat force of 40,000 men helped to put down the Hungarian revolution. As a reward, Austria's 1849 constitution designated Croatia and Slavonia as an Austrian crownland separate from Hungary, assigning it also the port of Fiume.

This arrangement was reversed 18 years later when Austria signed the famous *Ausgleich* ("compromise") with Hungary, which transferred Croatia back to Hungary. Croatia remained affiliated with Hungary until 1918. In 1868, Hungary signed an agreement with Croatia giving it provincial autonomy, its own parliament, and the right to use Croatian as its official language. Many Croats were dissatisfied with this arrangement, however, so Croat national feeling continued to grow. As anti-Hungarian sentiment grew,

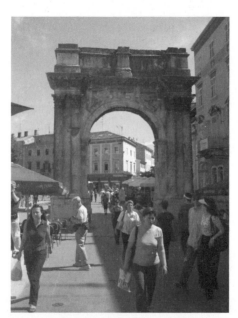

Ancient Roman Gate at Pula

so did a sense of solidarity with fellow Slavs. Croats therefore greeted enthusiastically Serbia's victories in the two Balkan Wars of 1912–13. Many still dreamed of a Croat kingdom under the Habsburgs, but the dream of a united Yugoslavia increasingly found supporters. When it became clear that Serbia was on the winning side in World War I, the stage was set for a union of south Slavs.

Croatia Joins Yugoslavia

Croatia was included in the new Kingdom of Serbs, Croats and Slovenes formed on December 1, 1918. In 1921, a constitution was adopted that created a unitary central government. Since Serbs made up about 40% of the overall population, their party, the Radical Party, tended to dominate this new kingdom. When Stjepan Radic, leader of the Croatian Peasant Party, protested this, the government responded by arresting him and banning his party. The period from 1921 to 1928 was one of constant conflict over the issue of centralism versus federalism, with Croatian nationalists advocating creation of a federal state.

When a Montenegrin assassinated Radic inside the parliament building in 1928, the Croatian deputies withdrew from the assembly, threatening not to return until a federal state had been created in which Croatians were not dominated by Serbs. King Alexander I opposed the idea of a federal state, and in 1929, he abolished the constitution and took power himself. After he had proclaimed his royal dictatorship, he changed the name of the country to Yugoslavia.

A Macedonian associated with the Croatian dissidents assassinated Alexander in 1934. Since Alexander's son, Peter, was only a child, Alexander's cousin, Prince Paul, was named regent; he ruled until 1941. In 1939, he attempted to solve the problem of nationalist dissent by creating an internally self-governing Croatia.

Paul was deposed in March 1941 after he allied Yugoslavia with Germany. The denunciation of the alliance brought a German invasion in April 1941 and German occupation of the country between 1941 and 1945. Hitler permitted an "independent" Croatia to be proclaimed in April 1941. The head of this entity was Ante Pavelic, leader of a fascist organization called *Ustasha*. The Pavelic regime was characterized by brutality and violence, much of it targeted against local Serbs. One of the problems the Croatian government has with Serbs today is that they remember the murderous actions of a previous Croatian government and are unwilling to trust the current one.

There were many Croats who opposed this *Ustasha* government. One was Josip

Broz Tito, leader of the Partisan forces against the Germans. During the war, Tito and his communist Partisans organized local committees throughout Croatia as they liberated individual areas from German or *Ustasha* control. Toward the end of the war, these committees were combined into a council of national liberation. After Zagreb was liberated, this council proclaimed itself the People's Government of Croatia. When Yugoslavia was reconstituted as the People's Republic of Yugoslavia in 1945, the People's Republic of Croatia joined as one of the six constituent republics.

The self-promoted Marshal Tito, who ruled Yugoslavia from 1945 to 1980, ruthlessly suppressed all nationalist agitation within the country. Franjo Tudjman was one of Tito's generals. In the early 1970s, he and Stipe Mesic, the last president of Yugoslavia, were among Croatian communist leaders imprisoned on charges of nationalistic deviations.

Croatian nationalist groups began to reemerge in the late 1980s. Most of these eventually joined to form the Croatian Democratic Union, which won the republic elections in April 1990. Franjo Tudjman, leader of the party, was elected president at the same time. The political program of the movement only called for increased autonomy within a more confederal Yugoslavia.

It was Yugoslavia's tragedy that a Serbian nationalist, Slobodan Milosevic, rose to power within the League of Communists of Serbia at this same time. Milosevic not only opposed all political concessions to Croatia, but also deliberately sabotaged economic reform as well. He therefore created a political stalemate that was also destroying the economy.

Croatia Wins Independence

On May 19, 1991, the Croatian government held a referendum on the question of independence. After a favorable vote, the Croatian Assembly adopted a declaration of independence on June 25. The government reiterated, however, that it was willing to continue discussions on a looser Yugoslav confederation, with the central government confined to foreign policy, defense and a common currency.

When Croatia began moving toward independence, the Serbs within the republic, egged on by Milosevic and a press dominated by Serbs, organized two autonomous regions. Despite a new law passed by the Croatian legislature guaranteeing protection for minority ethnic groups, Croatian Serbs held their own referendum on July 7 reaffirming their loyalty to the Socialist Federal Republic of Yugoslavia.

Like Slovenians, Croatians agreed to suspend their declarations of independence for three months. Serbia, in turn, agreed to allow a Croatian, Stipe Mesic, to be elected president. The latter agreement was important in a military as well as a political sense because the president was also the commander in chief of the Yugoslav People's Army (JNA).

The agreement brought peace to Slovenia, but not to Croatia. One of the first actions of President Mesic was to arrange a third cease-fire on July 2. General Blagoje Adzic, chief of the JNA General Staff, angrily repudiated it—and thereby his own commander in chief—in an interview that appeared on Belgrade television. He stated that the army "accepted the challenge of total war that had been imposed on it" and would soon end it with a complete victory. The next day, an armored column left Belgrade for Croatia.

On July 6, 1991, Milosevic gave a speech in which he told Serbs to be ready to defend themselves. He also gave Serb leaders in Croatia generous access to Serbian radio and television. The first fighting in Croatia began on July 7 when Croatian Serbs allied with Milosevic attacked Croatian territorial defense forces near the town of Tenja. Once the fighting had begun, the JNA intervened "to keep the peace," though its targets were always Croatian territorial units. Since President Tudjman ordered Croatian units not to attack the JNA, the fighting remained small scale for some time. The JNA did not initiate battles at this time and only advanced when new fighting would break out. Gradually, however, its control of Croatian territory spread as Serb territorial forces launched new battles in area after area.

Croatian Serbs insisted on living in a state controlled by Serbs. But the Croatians were not entirely free of this mentality. The Republic of Bosnia-Herzegovina, which lies between Serbia and Croatia, has an extremely mixed population, with 33% Serbs and about 17% Croats. In July, President Tudjman admitted that members of his government had held secret talks with Serbian leaders about carving up Bosnia between the two, leaving a small Muslim rump that neither wanted. Word of these talks hurt Croatia internationally.

Croatia was saved by the fact that Serbia and the JNA were even more bloody-minded. In August, Milosevic revealed his plans for a reconstituted Yugoslavia that called for carving up Croatia and incorporating about a third of the territory into the new state, although Serbs constituted only 12% of Croatia's population.

Meanwhile the JNA, which up to this time had contended that it was acting as a neutral buffer between the two sides, began bombarding Croatian cities with artillery and aircraft. In late August, much of the city of Vukovar was destroyed. By this time, perhaps 20% of the republic had fallen under JNA or Serb militia control.

On September 18, 1991, Zagreb, the capital, came under fire from aircraft and artillery. At about the same time, the Yugoslav navy instituted a blockade of Croatia's Dalmatian ports. Soon it began attacking them, beginning with the city of Split. Up to this moment, the Croatian govern-

The Opera House, Zagreb

Croatia

ment had been carrying out a "passive defense" and refusing to challenge the JNA directly. Now it cut oil lines across Croatia to Serbia and laid siege to Yugoslav army barracks in Croatia. Croatia also began getting some indirect assistance from other republics when Bosnia-Herzegovina and Macedonia adopted a position of neutrality and ordered their citizens to ignore conscription notices from the JNA. Even in Serbia, however, many young men went into hiding rather than serve.

The three-month moratorium on Croatia and Slovenia's independence declarations—agreed to at Brioni—expired on October 7. Freed of that limitation, the Croatian Assembly approved a resolution severing all ties with the Socialist Federal Republic of Yugoslavia. By this time, the JNA and the Serbs occupied approximately a third of the country. The Yugoslav air force marked the day with an attack on the presidential palace in Zagreb at the very moment that President Tudjman was in conference with Stipe Mesic, the federal president, and Ante Markovic, the federal prime minister. As the *Economist* put it, "the attack put to rest any pretense that there is real life left in the Yugoslav federation."

By this time, it had become clear to almost everyone just what Serbia was attempting to do. But it took almost three months more before Britain and France could be persuaded to abandon the ideal of a united Yugoslavia. Even then, the American government refused to abandon that ideal. But the European Community (now EU) announced in December that it would recognize Slovenia and Croatia as of January 15. The fighting continued up to that date, but tapered off afterwards. Under the terms of the eventual cease-fire, a United Nations Protection Force (UNPROFOR) was deployed in and along the boundaries of the three Serb controlled areas within Croatia, the self-declared, independent "Serbian Republic of the Krajina." The declaration of independence was only pro forma, however. The goal of the Serbians was to unite with Serbia and the Serb-occupied areas of Bosnia in a "Greater Serbia."

Croatia subsequently made three attempts to reintegrate the Serb-occupied territory into Croatia, twice in 1993 and once in March 1994. On each occasion, the Serbs launched artillery attacks on Zagreb and other Croatian towns. In addition, UNPROFOR opposed Croatian efforts to restore control over Serb-held areas.

In January 1995, with the Croatian Serbs still armed and in control of one-third of the country and continuing to act as a separate government attached to Yugoslavia, President Tudjman decided that the UNPROFOR mission had failed and that

Franjo Tudjman

it was time for it to leave. He then informed the United Nations that the UNPROFOR mandate would not be renewed when it expired in March. What worried him was that the "Contact Group" (U.S., Russia, France, Great Britain, and Germany), negotiating with the Bosnian Serbs, had accepted their demand that they be permitted to confederate with Serbia. Tudjman expected that the Croatian Serbs would make the same demand, and Krajina would be lost forever. He also recognized that, although the Croatian Serbs were heavily armed, their ministate was economically unviable on its own and was only surviving because of continuing support from Serbia by means of a thin corridor several hundred miles long across the northern part of Bosnia. Removal of the UNPROFOR troops would give Croatia the chance to cut that lifeline to Serbia.

Tudjman's decision was an enormous gamble, for it ignored the possibility that Serbia might re-intervene directly if he moved against the Croatian Serbs, and they started to lose. This was what bothered the "Contact Group," which put him under heavy pressure to reverse his decision. What finally occurred was a sort of compromise. Tudjman agreed that he would permit half of the 12,000 UNPROFOR troops to stay while the UN agreed to provide another 500 troops to police the border between Serb-held parts of Croatia and Bosnia and Serbia.

Two months later, Croatia sent its troops into the eastern section of Croatian Serb-held Krajina, known as Western Slavonia, and managed to recapture the area in just 40 hours. Although the Croatian Serbs retaliated with rocket attacks against Zagreb and other Croatian towns, Croatia held on to the pocket. Several thousand Serbs fled the area, making their way either to the remaining part of Krajina or to Serb-held Bosnia. Approximately two months later, Croatian forces overran the remaining section of Serb Krajina in just four days, between August 4 and 8. They met very lit-

tle resistance; in fact, the Croatian Serb forces just seemed to melt away. As the Croatian forces entered from the west, as many as 150,000 Serbs fled eastward into Bosnia, many making their way across Bosnia into Serbia. The refugees included the 16,000 militiamen who had made up the Serb Krajina army.

The Recovery of Eastern Slavonia

President Tudjman next set his sights on Eastern Slavonia, the remaining part of Croatia still held by Serbs. After shifting a significant part of his forces to the eastern part of the country, he made a public demand for its return.

The purpose of these actions was to ensure that Eastern Slavonia was included on the agenda of the upcoming peace talks. But he also made it clear that he would use force if diplomacy failed. "The world," Tudjman was quoted as saying, "should not deceive itself into thinking that Croatia will be prepared to postpone a settlement of this issue indefinitely."

In the end, no force was necessary. On November 12, 1995, the Croatian Serbs agreed during the Dayton peace talks to accept Croatian sovereignty over Eastern Slavonia after a transition period of one to two years. The transition period actually lasted three years. It was not turned over to Croatian control until January 1998. During that interregnum, a transitional administration set up by the UN Security Council governed the territory. Some UN peacekeeping forces were already there from the previous UN mission to Croatia, and others began arriving in January 1996. The United Nations hoped that, with a sufficiently long transition, the majority of Serbs living in the area could become reconciled to living under Croatian control and would remain.

In that sense, the operation appears to have been a failure. Although Croatia requested that UN police remain in Eastern Slavonia after Croatia took official control on January 15, this did little to convince Serbs to stay. At least 10,000 Serbs left the area in the month preceding the final transfer of authority. Most went to Serbia.

The Croatian government must bear some of the responsibility for this outflow because it made clear that Croats expelled from the area during the war would be resettled with government assistance. At the same time, the 60,000 Serbs who had lived in other parts of Croatia before the war were refused permission to return to those areas. In addition, hard-line Croatian nationalists did their best to instill fear in the Serbs by distributing pamphlets threatening to kill those Serbs who chose to remain.

The raising of the Croatian flag over the area does not mean that the area has been totally reintegrated into Croatia. About half of the Croatian population formerly resident in the area has returned, mainly due to lack of housing and job possibilities. Meanwhile, only half of the Serb refugees were resettled in other parts of Croatia, with the support of international funds. Contrary to general predictions, these transfers of population have been peaceful, with no clashes between Serbs and Croats. Moreover, Serbs are no longer fleeing across the eastern border into Serbia or applying for asylum in Western Europe.

UN War-Crimes Tribunal in The Hague

Croatia had to face up to the fact that some Croatians were involved in atrocities that occurred during the Balkan wars in the 1990s and have to answer for their deeds. This creates tensions between the pro-democratic leadership after Tudjman's death and some nationalist veterans. Under Tudjman, Croatians were portrayed exclusively as victims in the 1991 war of independence and the conflicts thereafter. Some citizens resent the democratic government's willingness to shed light on possible atrocities committed by Croatians. When ex-Prime Minister Ivica Racan decided in July 2001 to hand over two prime suspects to the UN war crimes tribunal in The Hague, several cabinet ministers resigned, and thousands of people went into the streets to protest. But Racan made the pragmatic argument that failure to hand over suspects would bring international sanctions on Croatia.

In March 2000 General Tihomir Blaskic, the former Croatian commander in Bosnia who had given himself up to the UN tribunal in 1996, was sentenced to 45 years in prison for war crimes. In March 2003 a Croatian court sentenced former General Mirko Norac to 12 years in prison for

killing Serb civilians in 1991. He had surrendered in 2001 on the condition that he not be transferred to The Hague. In June 2007 Norac again went to trial, along with another retired general, Ramim Ademi, on further charges of atrocities against ethnic Serbs.

In April 2003 Croatian police arrested a Bosnian Croat, Ivica Rajic, long sought by the international court for killing Muslims in Bosnia. At the same time a case entered a Croatian court that would have been unthinkable a few years earlier: Nevenka Tudjman, daughter of the late president, went to trial on charges of graft and abuse of power. In October 2006 a commander who had a seat in parliament, Branimir Glavas, was detained on war-crimes charges.

The government was rescued from its riskiest prosecution, that of General Janko Bobetko. Like Norac, he was a hero in the eyes of most Croats for creating and commanding an armed force that succeeded in recapturing the one-third of the country occupied by the Serbs since 1991. His failure to prosecute any subordinates who may have committed war crimes made him potentially guilty of them. As an 83-year-old diabetic with serious heart problems, his indictment in 2002 touched a raw nerve. In April 2003 he died, and his funeral became a rally for the nationalist right.

There were doubts that the Croatian Democratic Union (HDZ), the successor to Tudjman's party, which took over the government in December 2003, would continue cooperating with The Hague. It had been openly critical of the tribunal. But ex-Prime Minister Ivo Sanader moved the party from Catholic nationalism to centrist conservatism, and he pledged full cooperation. In March 2004 two retired army generals were sent to The Hague. They were

indicted for commanding forces that murdered and intimidated ethnic Serbs so they would flee Croatia. In April Zagreb transferred six Bosnian Croats to the tribunal. In July 2004 the tribunal sentenced former Croatian Prime Minister Milan Babic, who had testified against Slobodan Milosevic, to 13 years in prison for inflaming an ethnic cleansing campaign that led to the expulsion of tens of thousands of Serbs. In June 2007 a Croatian Serb, Milan Martic, was convicted of murder, torture, and the ordering of two-days of indiscriminate cluster bombing of Zagreb in May 1995.

Not until December 2005 did Spanish police apprehend the much-wanted General Ante Gotovina, while dining in a four-star hotel restaurant in the Canary Islands. Regarded by many Croatians as a hero, he was implicated in the killing of about 150 Serb civilians and in the expulsion of 150,000 Serbs during Croatia's offensive in 1995 to recapture land seized by Serbs. His passport indicated that he had globetrotted through three continents while an international manhunt took place. The EU had refused to open membership talks with Croatia until he was caught and delivered to the court. This delay quelled any illusions that Croatia would sail smoothly into the Union. It also deprived Croatians of the notion that, unlike Serbs, they had dealt effectively with the tainted moral legacy of their own "Homeland War" from 1991–95.

The trial began in March 2008 and is broadcast live in Croatia. It is expected to last over a year. The tribunal does not dispute Croatia's right to retake its land in Krajina. But it charges General Gotovina and his two co-defendants, Generals Ivan Cermak and Mladen Markac (all three heroes at home) for knowingly shelling civilian targets, allowing their forces to go on violent rampages, terrorizing civilians and looting and burning Serbian homes. The U.S. has taken a keen interest in the trial because Croatian officials argue that American military advisers helped plan the operation and directed drone aircraft over the battle zone to gain real-time intelligence used by Croatian forces. Gotovina's chief defendant is Greg Kehoe, an American who was a former prosecutor at the tribunal and head of the office that built the criminal cases against Saddam Hussein.

The tribunal had been close to indicting former leader, Franjo Tudjman, who died in December 1999. He would have been charged with leading a "joint criminal enterprise" that included expelling Serbs. The prosecution quoted from his speeches calling Krajina Serbs "a cancer on the underbelly of Croatia." He remains a Croatian hero, however, and a beautiful suspension bridge leading into Dubrovnik is named "Dr. Franjo Tudjman."

"Gotovina Hero!" Call to free a Croatian general on trial in The Hague for tolerating the murder of Serb POWs.

Croatia

In May 2009 a Croatian court convicted an opposition legislator, Branimir Glavas, of war crimes. He was the first senior politician to be held responsible for wartime atrocities against Serbs. Because of his legislative immunity, he was not incarcerated.

Croatia must deal with Serbia's January 2010 accusation at the tribunal that it had committed genocide when it expelled the Serb population in 1995. This is a belated response to a similar Croatian lawsuit against Serbia in 1999. Both countries may drop these mutual accusations in an effort to improve their bilateral relationship. Also the EU reminded Croatia in 2009 to improve its cooperation with the war crimes investigators, who have complained that the country has been slow in turning over missing documents.

President Ivo Josipović (middle) visits Slovenian President Danilo Türk (right).

POLITICAL SYSTEM

The Republic of Croatia is a parliamentary democracy with a multiparty system. The fulcrum of power had always rested with the president. With the death of former President Franjo Tudjman in December 1999, that changed, and the presidency became less powerful. Croatia has no vice president. According to the constitution, in case of the incapacity or death of the president, the speaker of the parliament assumes the president's powers temporarily. He then calls new elections 60 days after the president leaves office.

Parliament (Hrvatski Sabor) is unicameral after the Chamber of Representatives and Chamber of Counties were abolished in April 2001. It has 152 members elected directly for a term of four years. The country is divided into 10 territorial electoral units, each sending 14 members to parliament. Two additional units totaling twelve seats are reserved for non-territorial constituencies: one is for expatriate Croats, including 300,000 Croats in Bosnia-Herzegovina, and the other is for representatives of minority groups, including Serbs, living within Croatia. The leader of the coalition of parties that can maintain a majority in parliament is the prime minister, who is the most powerful figure in the political system.

At the local level are 20 county governors and assemblies.

The Presidency

Tudjman's authoritarianism and occasional abuse of human rights was a source of international concern. In 1996, his regime angered human rights activists when it sponsored two new laws whose effect was to limit basic freedoms guaranteed in the constitution. Under the first law, anyone desiring to establish an organization to monitor the actions or to supplement the work of government ministries needed the government's permission. The second law made it a crime to insult "the dignity and authority of leading officials."

Using these new laws, the government attempted in 1996 to close down two of four remaining independent newspapers, the *Feral Tribune* and the *Novi List*. Partly in response, the Council of Europe voted to postpone indefinitely Croatia's entry into that body. This led the Croatian government to pass a new press law in October that set out certain press guarantees. Croatia was admitted to the Council of Europe shortly thereafter. Pope John Paul II visited Croatia in 1998, an event exploited by Tudjman as a validation of his rule, even though the purpose of the pope's visit was religious.

Tudjman underwent emergency surgery on November 1, 1999, to repair a perforation in his large intestine. Six days later, he gave the go-ahead for parliamentary elections from his hospital bed. As it turned out, he would never leave his hospital bed alive. Complications set in, possibly a recurrence of the stomach cancer for which he had been operated on three years earlier. He eventually went into a coma and was pronounced dead on December 11.

He was succeeded by Stipe Mesic on January 24, 2000. The new president subsequently won much of the credit for dismantling the quasi-authoritarian Tudjman regime and for clearing Croatia's way back into Europe, about which he rhapsodized: "Croatia's future is a united Europe which must be a synonym for democracy, tolerance, the promotion and respect of human rights and the rule of law. Croatia, which will be based on these foundations, will have no problems in finding its rightful place in the European Union." In fact, all parties and political leaders make EU entry their top priority. Mesic was reelected in January 2005. One populist candidate whom he defeated was Boris Miksic, a Croat-American millionaire businessman, who returned to Croatia after three decades in the United States.

A prominent politician in the last years of the former Yugoslavia and its last rotating president, Mesic said that his chief goal was to speed up Croatia's integration into the European Union and NATO. The fact that he promised to abandon support for Croatian separatists in Bosnia-Herzegovina, to support the return of ethnic Serbian refugees who fled Croatia during the period of the war, and to cooperate with the war-crimes tribunal in The Hague—all three policy reversals of Tudjman positions—bolstered the chances for such integration.

The Tudjman family occupies the front pew in Zagreb Cathedral

Croatia

In October 2002 he had become the first head of state to appear as a witness at the UN tribunal in The Hague. He accused the former Serbian leader, Slobodan Milosevic, of engineering the breakup of Yugoslavia, plundering the Yugoslav treasury and National Bank to aid Serb rebels in Croatia and to finance a Serb army, using that armed force to seize Croatian territory, and generally provoking warfare that created "rivers of blood." He also confirmed that an important meeting had taken place in March 1991 between Milosevic and Tudjman. They discussed carving up Bosnia-Herzegovina and dividing it between themselves. Not surprisingly Milosevic lashed back, calling Mesic a criminal and accusing him of ordering the torching of Serb villages. In June 2003 the former U.S. ambassador in Croatia, Peter Galbraith, was also called as a witness against Milosevic. He testified that the Krajina Serb Republic had been completely dependent on Serbia and that Krajina Serb leaders had deferred to Milosevic.

In January 2010 Ivo Josipovic, a professor of international law and renowned composer, was elected president by a landslide, receiving 60% of the votes in the second round, with a turnout of almost 50%. He gathered votes from both incumbent and opposition parties. He demolished the populist mayor of Zagreb, Milan Banic. Perceived as dull and uncharismatic, Josipovic, a Social Democrat, nevertheless appealed to the voters' loss of patience with corruption, which was one of the major themes in the election. He promised to serve "without compromise in the fight against corruption and organized crime." With polls indicating that only 8% thought the country was heading in the right direction and with recession in the air, he came across as the voice of reason and moderation and offered a refreshing change, especially since he had never before held high office.

Parliamentary Elections

Former President Tudjman took advantage of the euphoria that swept Croatia following the recovery of Krajina to call for national parliamentary elections that took place in October 1995. They resulted in an absolute majority for his party, the Croatian Democratic Union (HDZ). With new parliamentary elections scheduled to take place in 2000, Western governments and institutions began to put pressure on Tudjman to modify Croatia's electoral laws. The message was that unless he did so, Croatia would not be considered for membership in any of the various Euro-Atlantic structures. In May 1999, therefore, he instructed the HDZ to hold a series of meetings with the leaders of six opposition parties to hash out a newly agreed election law.

As a result of these meetings, the HDZ agreed to relinquish exclusive control over Croatian Television and allow it to become a public broadcaster. In addition, agreement was reached on abolishing the system of separate voting lists for Croats living abroad. What this meant in practice was that such Croats would still be able to vote in Croatian elections, but it would no longer be as easy to elect a solid bloc of deputies to the Croatian parliament as voters in Herzegovina had done in the past. This change, made at the behest of the international community—which would have preferred that Bosnian Croats not be permitted to vote in Croatian elections—turned out to be meaningless in practice. The HDZ assured a strong Herzegovinian vote by placing a number of hard-line Croatians on the HDZ's parliamentary list for Croats in Bosnia-Herzegovina.

The elections, which took place on January 3, 2000, resulted in a victory for the political opposition. The new prime minister was Ivica Racan, leader of the Social Democratic Party. He had once headed the League of Communists of Croatia prior to independence, but he shifted to the center-left.

Racan tried to introduce democratic reforms and to prepare his country for EU and NATO membership. The EU and the U.S. made it clear that a crucial part of this process involves bringing war crimes suspects to court. Therefore, Croatia turned over several suspects to the war crimes tribunal in The Hague despite the political risks at home. In September 2000, Racan forced seven generals, all former Tudjman supporters, to retire when they criticized their government's crackdown on war criminals and accused Racan of betraying the country's interests and honor to the West.

The Racan coalition turned its back on Tudjman's publicly stated wish to reduce the Serb population in Croatia to 5% of the total population, compared with 12% before independence. It attempted to persuade the 200,000 ethnic Serbs who fled to Serbia and the additional 30,000 who sought refuge in Bosnia to return to their earlier homes in Croatia. Some are doing so. Property disputes and the lack of jobs remain the main obstacles. Returning refugees often find their former houses occupied by others who themselves are refugees.

Racan improved relations with Croatia's neighbors, especially Bosnia. Serbs and Croats no longer need visas to visit each other's country, and air and train service between the two has been restored and improved. However, most Croats were concerned about living standards and jobs after almost four years of difficult but necessary reforms. They were willing to turn back to the Croatian Dem-

Prime Minister Jadranka Kosor

ocratic Union (HDZ) in parliamentary elections on November 23, 2003.

Former HDZ leader Ivo Sanader had purged the party of some of the hard-line nationalists. Some were implicated in war crimes. He claimed that the party is no longer nationalist at all, but rather a center-right Christian Democratic party. A former theater director from Split, he had been head of Tudjman's office. He had studied in Austria, speaks four languages, and made it clear that foreign policy was his priority. He embraced a decidedly pro-American policy and in April 2009 led Croatia into NATO.

In July 2009 he unexpectedly resigned from politics. He gave no explanation, but he faced increasing questions about how he had gotten to be so rich while in office. He was replaced as prime minister by his deputy, Jadranka Kosor, the country's first female prime minister. She studied law at Zagreb University and was a successful journalist when she entered politics in the mid-1990s. She promised to pursue Sanader's policies, especially fighting the economic recession, resolving the border dispute with Slovenia, and overcoming the deadlock over EU membership. Sanader made a clumsy attempt at a comeback and was expelled from the HDZ in January 2010.

In the November 2007 elections, the HDZ had captured 36.6% of the votes and 66 seats (the same number as in 2003). Since that is short of a majority, Kosor rules a minority coalition that includes the Croatian Social Liberal Party (HSLS—2 seats). It relies on parliamentary support from ethnic minority representatives and the Croatian Pensioners' Party (HSU—1 seat), which entered parliament for the first time with three seats.

Zoran Milanovic led the Social Democratic Party (SDP) in the 2007 elections and won 31.2% of the votes (up from 23%)

Croatia

and 56 seats (up from 43). It generally has the support of the Croatian People's Party (HNS), which won 7 seats, and the Istrian Democratic Assembly (IDS), with 3 seats.

Other parties with seats in parliament are the Croatian Peasants' Party (HSS), with 7 seats, the Party of Rights (HSP), with one seat, the Croatian Democratic Assembly of Slavonia and Baranja (HDSSB), with 3 seats, and the Independent Democratic Serbian Party (SDSS), with 3 seats. Turnout in 2007 was 64% (down from 69% in 2003). Those 300,000 ethnic Croats living in Bosnia were also allowed to vote. Together with another 100,000 Croatian citizens living abroad and the Serb, Hungarian, Italian, Czech and Slovak minorities within Croatia, they elected a dozen members in the 152-seat parliament.

Prime Minister Koser pursued her agenda with some success, and she bolstered her country's credibility with the EU and the U.S. She unblocked accession talks with the EU by temporarily resolving a disagreement with Slovenia over the latter country's access to the sea. They agreed not to let this long-standing dispute stand in the way of Croatia's bid for EU membership. Afterwards they will submit the issue to an EU arbitration committee. With the EU's strong urging, she also embraced anti-corruption with a vigor many had thought impossible. It "is the basis for everything." "This is a fight at all levels," she proclaimed, and instituted a policy of zero tolerance. Although many Croatians want to see corruption curbed, she was not rewarded with popularity: her approval rating stood at only 35% the end of 2009, and she faces an election in 2011.

She locked horns with President Josipovic. Like many in her HDZ party, which still has high-level supporters who honor former wartime leader, Franjo Tudjman, she was furious when the president appeared in the Bosnian parliament in April 2010 and apologized for Croatia's role in the Bosnian war. He said he was "deeply sorry" that his country had "contributed to the suffering of people and divisions which still burden us today." The prime minister protested that the president should cooperate with the government in the field of foreign policy, not veer off and try to make it himself.

Foreign Policy

Croatia likes to think of itself as a Western nation, and Franjo Tudjman once argued to reporters that Croatia is not part of the Balkans. Most Croatians would agree with him. But he never managed to bring Croatia into the European mainstream, partly because many Europeans remained suspicious of his sometimes dictatorial ways and partly because of his occasional incursions into Byzantine diplomacy. During the war between 1991 and 1995, for example, he held conversations with Belgrade on at least two occasions concerning a possible division of former Yugoslav territories into a Greater Croatia and a Greater Serbia.

Tudjman feared that the West's inaction was permitting Serbia to create a Greater Serbia on its own, leaving Croats squeezed into a small part of the western Balkans. That would explain—but not justify— why he intervened in Bosnia in 1993 to support radical Bosnian Croat leaders who favored the partition of Bosnia between Croats and Serbs. Later he sent an army of up to 10,000 Croatian soldiers into Bosnia to assist the Bosnian Croats.

He negotiated an agreement with Belgrade in January 1994 that was touted as a first step toward normalizing relations. In actuality, it was a cynical agreement between Croatia and Serbia to cooperate in the division of Bosnia. But carving separate Serb and Croat territories out of Bosnia would have created a precedent for a partition of Croatia, as Western diplomats carefully pointed out to Tudjman. Thus when the West produced its own ultimatum in February 1994, demanding that the Serbs withdraw their artillery from the environs of Sarajevo, he changed his position and threw his support behind a Croat-Muslim federation in Bosnia associated with Croatia.

Tudjman's commitment to the Croat-Muslim federation was halfhearted and, at best, tactical. He always defended the right of Bosnian Croats to hold Croatian citizenship and to vote in Croatian elections. While he was alive they continued to do so. As he commented to Secretary of State Madeleine Albright when she visited Croatia in August 1998, "the main problem between the United States and Croatia is the problem of Bosnia. . . . Croatia . . . is obliged by its constitution to take care of Croats outside the Republic of Croatia."

Under Tudjman, Croatia continued to have troubled relations with its neighbors. For example, UN peacekeepers had to control Croatia's Prevlaka peninsula, a two-mile strip of land that lies on Croatia's southernmost border with Montenegro. This grants access to Boka Kotorska Bay, Montenegro's only deep-water seaport and naval base. The Yugoslav army occupied the peninsula during the war. Until December 2002 it had not been possible to return the territory to Croatian control because of Belgrade's objection. Serbia-Montenegro and Croatia signed a landmark border agreement, ceding the peninsula to Croatia. The agreement demilitarizes the area, permits Serbian and Montenegrin naval vessels to traverse the channel into the bay without stopping, and prohibits military maneuvers in the area. It calls for joint sea police patrols.

Likewise, Yugoslavia always insisted on keeping the border crossing between Croatia and Montenegro at Debeli Brijeg closed, even though the Montenegrin government had requested that it be opened. Montenegro opened the border crossing briefly in November 1998 for the Roman Catholic All Saints holiday, then attempted to open it on a regular basis in 1999. At that moment, Yugoslav army troops intervened and closed the crossing. Yugoslav soldiers and Montenegrin police began jointly manning it in April 1999. Croatia signed an agreement with the Bosnian government in September 1998 granting Bosnian nationals free access to the Croatian port of Ploce.

The U.S. government signed several accords with Croatia dealing with trade, science and technology, education and nontechnical military assistance. It engaged in intelligence cooperation with Croatia in the mid-1990s. It provided encryption gear to each of the country's regular army brigades, maintained listening posts to intercept telephone calls in Bosnia and Serbia, and flew intelligence-gathering drone aircraft from a base near Zadar along the Adriatic. Tudjman's son, Miro, claimed: "We had a *de facto* partnership," but U.S. officials confirm only that it had a "liaison relationship" with Croatia and other nations in the region. The U.S. also furnished some funds for its democratization projects. In spite of these gestures, however, Croatia's relations with the United States have been troubled.

For example, when Croatia applied to become a member of NATO's Partnership for Peace program in 1998, American Ambassador William Montgomery informed Croatian officials that Croatia would first have to make greater efforts toward democratization, allow the return of those Serbian refugees who wished to come back to Croatia, and give more support to the Dayton peace process before its membership could be considered. Washington was particularly concerned by what it perceived as Tudjman's lack of support for the Bosnian-Croat federation in Bosnia, often expressed in terms of inadequate backing for the Dayton Accords. When he expressed the desire to establish closer ties with the European Union, he received much the same reply.

Tudjman always made it clear that, although he wanted Croatia to become a member of NATO and the EU, he was unwilling to change his own policies to achieve those goals. He reiterated this stance in January 1999 during his state of the nation address. He said that foreign powers were making accession to NATO and the EU difficult with their "efforts to alter the political landscape in Croatia and force us into undesirable integrations."

Under Tudjman, the European Union refused to negotiate any major accords

432

Croatia

with Croatia. It did agree to admit Croatia to the Council of Europe in 1996. The problem for the EU was always Croatia's human rights record, in particular the numerous accusations of discrimination against Serbs living in Croatia.

A report by the Organization for Security and Cooperation in Europe, drawn up in March 1999, said of Croatia, "there has been no progress in improving respect for human rights, the rights of minorities and the rule of law." Under pressure from the United States and the European Union, the report continues, Croatia has made commitments to freedom of the press. But Croatian Television, the main source of news for most Croatians, "remains subject to political control by the ruling party."

Post-Tudjman Foreign and Defense Policy

With Tudjman's death in December 1999 and his party's repudiation at the polls in January 2000, Croatian foreign policy changed in the direction urged by the European Union and the United States. Former president, Stipe Mesic, strongly supported Croatia's membership in the EU and NATO, and he took policy positions that contributed to bringing that about. Specifically, he promised to cooperate with the war crimes tribunal at The Hague, to support the return of ethnic Serbian refugees who fled Croatia during the war, and to abandon support for Croatian separatists in Bosnia-Herzegovina.

Croatia began negotiating a "stabilization and association agreement" with the EU that placed it higher on the list of countries seeking membership in that elite European club. After Slovenia, Croatia became the strongest candidate in former Yugoslavia for accession. It applied in 2003 and became an official candidate in 2005. By continuing to hand over wanted war criminals to The Hague, the Sanader government helped the country make a giant step toward EU membership. Accession talks resumed after the indicted war criminal Ante Gotovina had been captured and handed over to the International War Crimes Tribunal in 2005.

It closed 35 chapters of reforms, more than were required for any previous applicant. It received 436 million euros in EU aid ($675 million) through 2009. In October the EU urged it to crack down harder on corruption and to tighten its "unrestricted" cooperation with the war crimes tribunal. In February 2010 the European Parliament gave the same message, but it issued a positive report of Croatia's progress. The hope is that it can join in 2012.

Croatia received some rewards for its changed foreign policy. It was admitted to NATO in April 2009. Then Prime Minister Sanader was delighted: "Croatia is going

where it belongs. Croatia is going back home [to the West]." Support at home for such membership has increased to over 60%, a welcome reversal of earlier opposition. But NATO is regarded by many Croatians as merely confirmation of Western integration and a symbolic threshold a country has to cross to get to the real prize: EU membership.

Here worrisome problems have developed. As its maritime border dispute festered, Slovenia had demonstrated that it would not approve of Croatia's entry without a compromise that respects its demands. However, the two countries agreed in 2010 not to let the dispute block Croatia's EU entry and to submit it to EU arbitration later. It has yet to reform its shipbuilding industry that employs 17,000 people but survives only with large state subsidies that Brussels does not like. "Enlargement fatigue" has set in.

Worst of all, corruption continues to show its ugly face, and Croatians and EU officials were shocked by a stunning rise in gangland-style killings. The homegrown "mafia" that profited during the wars in the 1990s had become bolder. Gangs invest in legitimate businesses and in prime real estate, but they use the old methods to get their way: murders, beatings and threats. The 26-year-old daughter of a defense lawyer involved in organized crime cases was murdered, as was a well-known investigative reporter, Ivo Pukanic, editor of the hard-hitting weekly paper, Nacional. The most unnerving realization is that the killers might be on good terms with some of the nation's political elites. All this revived doubts that Croatia is ready to be in the EU despite government efforts to crack down.

However, both Prime Minister Kosor and President Josipovic have declared war on corruption, and Kosor has booked some solid successes. Tough new laws enforced by many new police and judicial appointments have helped. Among the high-profile investigations is an indictment of a former deputy prime minister, and an ex-defense minister has been indicted. Although the chief impetus for this comes from the EU, most Croatians support these efforts, which must be taken seriously. The main problem is public procurement; the EU cannot allot funds that are siphoned off by crooked politicians and organized criminals. It has learned in the case of Romania and Bulgaria, which entered the EU in 2007, that its leverage dissipates after a country joins. If Croatia's crackdown fails, then the hopes of other Balkan countries to enter will be jeopardized.

Croatia's armed forces are subject to an arms limitation regime established under the Dayton Peace Accord. Its total active military force has been reduced to 18,600.

The military is being transformed into a small professional force that can be deployed with NATO anywhere in the world. Conscription has been abolished. The army has 11,390 soldiers, and there are 3,000 paramilitary armed police. This force is backed by 21,000 reservists. Its navy of 1,850 sailors mans one conventional submarine and seven patrol and coastal combatants, and it conducts joint exercises with the U.S. Navy. The air force has 3,500 personnel and flies 24 combat aircraft (12 of them MiGs) and 32 helicopters. It has 10,000 paramilitary forces. Alongside this transformation is a reduction of the three secret service agencies to two—one military and the other civilian under strong civilian and parliamentary oversight.

In February 2003 it was one of ten countries in Central and Eastern Europe to sign a letter supporting the American-British policy toward Iraq. It sent a 50-member military police unit to Afghanistan and supplied rifles and ammunition to the new Afghan army. By 2010 it had 290 troops fighting in Afghanistan with no "caveats" (restrictions). It offered the UN an infantry company of about 100 soldiers to perform peacekeeping in the Middle East. Its positive commitment to the work of the UN was rewarded in October 2007 when it was elected to serve a two-year term on the UN Security Council. The government generally pursues a pro-American policy.

ECONOMY

Croatia has much excellent farmland in the northeastern part of the country, but farming is carried on throughout the republic. Corn is the chief grain crop, followed by wheat. Other commercial crops include plums, used in the production of slivovitz (a dry, usually colorless brandy), grapes, which are processed into wine and other brandies, sugar beets, flax, hemp, and fruits.

The raising of livestock also plays a significant role, divided about equally between cattle and sheep. Pigs and poultry are also important farm products. Croatia still has significant forest areas, so timber products provide employment to many rural inhabitants.

Manufacturing is well developed. Most is light industry that concentrates on manufacturing goods for sale to consumers. Croatia also produces extractive products such as petroleum, coal, and bauxite. Fishing is a major industry for people along the Dalmatian coast. Its Adriatic port, Rijeka, has deep waters and is therefore capable of handling large ships. The World Bank provided the primary funding for a 215-million-euro development project of the port.

The greatest moneymaker of all is tourism, which provides a fifth of Croatia's

Croatia

GDP. But this sector languished for a while after the wars during the 1990s. Political instability in the area and the threat of renewed fighting were important deterrents. With the many justly famous resorts along the Dalmatian coast coming back to life again, tourism is booming. The country has become one of the travel industry's hottest new destinations, and tourism is becoming Croatia's chief foreign currency earner. In 2005 alone, it hosted more than 10 million visitors. Tourism struggled during the 2009–10 economic recession, but the decline was temporary. Serb tourists, who used to flock to the coast, were aggressively courted. There are still no direct flights between the two neighbors' capital cities.

The war left a stagnant economy and thousands of refugees, particularly in the area of Zagreb. The demobilization that began with the end of the war also contributed to an already massive unemployment problem. Exports covered barely half of commodity imports. In 2010 it had a relatively large foreign debt amounting to 90% of GDP. Taxes are too high. Judicial and administrative reforms are urgently needed although some successes have been achieved. With only 4.6 million people, the country has a backlog of 1.2 million cases, including issues over title deeds. The public sector spends more than half of GDP and is weighed down by inefficient state-owned industries.

Croatia was hit hard by the 2009 global recession, but it is weathering the crisis better than some of its neighbors. Its banks are relatively stable, causing one banker to rejoice: "God must be Croatian since the country is not encumbered by dangerous financial instruments and while its banks have no toxic assets." It did not have to turn to the IMF for stand-by credit.

There is other good news. Foreign investment is coming in. Inflation was down to 3% in 2010. Unemployment was 16.5% in 2010, up from 14.5% in 2009, its lowest level since the end of fighting in 1995. But it rises to 29% for youths. Strict labor laws deter employment. Real GDP growth was an admirable 5.4% in 2008, but the economy contracted by 5.7% in 2009. The budget deficit had declined to 2.6% in 2008

and 2.9% in 2009. By the standards of other EU candidates, Croatia is relatively rich. Its per capita GDP of $12,810 in 2008 was half that of Slovenia, but it was more than twice the level in Romania or Bulgaria, which were admitted to the EU in 2007.

CULTURE

The 9th century Church of St. Cross in Nin, the first Croatian capital, is often referred to as "the smallest cathedral in the world." The Plaque of Baska, dating to the year 1100, holds a Croatian inscription in the Glagolitic script. Marko Martulia (b. 1450) was particularly known for his writings in Latin, but he also wrote a poem in Croatian verses (*Judita*, 1521). Rugjer Boskovic (b. 1711) is world famous as a forerunner in the field of modern physics. Dubrovnik, renaissance cradle of artists, scientists, nobles, merchants and sailors, existed as an independent city republic for centuries. Now restored after the destruction of the recent war, it is once again a mecca for tourists.

Roman Catholicism has always been a part of Croatian tradition as well. It permeates and largely defines the culture. For example, it was Bishop Josip Juraj Strossmayer who carried out a reorganization of the University of Zagreb in 1874. This tradition became somewhat secularized in the 19th century through the writings of cultural figures such as Franjo Rachki, the Croatian historian. Even today, part of the definition of being a Croat continues to be membership in the Roman Catholic Church. Most Croats regard the pope as the highest moral authority. The Vatican was among the first to recognize Croatia's statehood in January 1992.

In June 2003 the pope made his 100th pilgrimage abroad by visiting Croatia for five days. He beatified a 20th century Croatian nun, Sister Marija Petkovic, who had founded the Daughters of Mercy and devoted her life to helping children throughout the world. He assured the people that he remembered their "sufferings caused by the war, which are still visible on your faces," but he urged Croats to move past their turbulent history. The following month the Croatian Catholic Church dem-

onstrated its power by rejecting plans to introduce yoga classes for teachers. It said that such a scheme would introduce "Hinduist religious practices dressed up as exercises into Croatian schools."

Linguistically, Croatian does not differ greatly from Serbian. Borrowed words in the vocabulary tend to come from German or Latin rather than from Greek or Turkish, as in the case of Serbia. Another difference is that Croatian uses the Roman alphabet, while Serbian uses the Cyrillic alphabet. There are differences in pronunciation as well. Croatia is notable for its efforts to define its language. Former President Tudjman introduced words to replace Serb or other foreign words.

One of Croatia's little-known gifts to men's fashion throughout the world is the necktie, or *kravata*. It came from the cravats worn by Croat soldiers in the French army during the Thirty Years War, 1618–1648.

FUTURE

The Croatian Democratic Union (HDZ), under the leadership of Prime Minister Jadranka Kosor, heads a shaky minority government. It rejuvenated itself in the nick of time for the November 2007 elections, from which it again emerged as the largest party. Her feuding with new President Ivo Josipovic of the opposition Social Democratic Party is likely to continue. Her popularity by mid-2010 had fallen to 35% while his was on the rise. Therefore she faces the 2011 parliamentary elections in a weakened condition even though she has booked some solid accomplishments in office. Her position is made worse by the public's foul mood: polls in 2010 found that only 8% of voters thought Croatia was going in the right direction; 92% considered corruption to be widespread in business, and 77% thought it was rife in government.

The delay in its EU accession talks temporarily ended in 2005 when indicted war criminal General Ante Gotovina was caught and turned over to the UN War Crimes Tribunal in The Hague. However, nagging fears of "enlargement fatigue" in the Union just will not go away. Zagreb has set a target date of 2012 for admission. More and more obstacles to entry pile up, including the resurfacing of brutal organized crime. The country's chief negotiator, Vladimir Drobnjak, still believes that joining the EU would be "the exclamation mark on our statehood and our international recognition." It did enter NATO in April 2009, but that is not the highest prize Croatians long for—EU membership. A Croatian failure to qualify for membership would be a devastating omen for the other Western Balkan countries, who are in line to join.

The tile roofs of Dubrovnik, restored after relentless shelling by Yugoslav forces in 1991–92.

Republic of Serbia

Area: 77,562 sq. km. (approximately 29,776 sq. mi.—2008 estimate after losing 15% of its land area when Kosovo became independent.)

Population: 8 million, of which 300,000 are Hungarians (2009 estimate after two million Kosovo Albanians separated from Serbia). One Serb demographer put the total population at 7.2 million in 2009.

Capital City: Belgrade (Pop. over 2 million).

Climate: Continental, with marked contrasts between summer and winter, with lowest temperatures in the high elevations. The summers are hot.

Neighboring Countries: Hungary (north); Romania, Bulgaria (east); Kosovo, Macedonia and Albania (south); Montenegro (southwest); Bosnia-Herzegovina, Croatia (west).

Official Language: Serbian

Other Principal Tongues: Albanian and Hungarian.

Ethnic Background: Slav, with Albanian ancestry in the southwest, Hungarian and Slovak in the Voivodina. Over two-thirds are Serbs.

Principal Religions: Serbian Orthodox Christianity, Islam.

Chief Commercial Products: Chemicals, farm equipment, paper, glass, textiles, sugar, flour, wheat, corn, tobacco, fruits and vegetables, lead, zinc, copper, silver, gold, chromium, coal, and consumer goods. Exports account for 28% of its economy.

Currency: Dinar

National Day: February 15 (called National Day)

Chief of State: Boris Tadic, Serbian President (since July 2004).

Head of Government: Mirko Cvetkovic, Prime Minister of Serbia (since July 2008).

National Flag: Horizontal stripes of red, blue and white. The image of Karadjordje's royal crown was added in 2004.

POLITICAL SYSTEM

The collapse of the Socialist Federal Republic of Yugoslavia in 1991–92, after four of the six republics declared their independence and withdrew, left behind a rump Federal Republic of Yugoslavia composed of Serbia and Montenegro, the largest and the smallest republics in the former union. The majority of Montenegrins also wanted out, but intense pressure from the European Union (EU) persuaded them to remain in a loose association with Serbia for at least three years until 2006. In 2002 the EU's foreign policy chief, Javier Solana, convinced Serbia's and Montenegro's leaders to accept a change in the name and the structure of their federation. The word

Belgrade. View from the Bridge of Brotherhood and Unity, also known as "Brankov Bridge"

"Yugoslavia" was consigned to history, and in 2003 the remaining federation was officially renamed the State Union of Serbia and Montenegro.

Most powers were devolved to each of the two parts, and very little authority, except foreign and defense policy and a single armed force, remained in the hands of the federal president and government. The new union had weak joint institutions. A federal parliament had limited authority, elected a weak federal president and had some say in foreign policy. Each republic retained its own economic system and currency. Montenegro officially adopted the euro in 2002, as did Kosovo (except in Serb-populated areas), while Serbia retained the dinar.

The Serbian enclaves in Croatia all collapsed, and the "Republic of Srpska" (RS) in Bosnia-Herzegovina was reintegrated into Bosnia as the Dayton Accords were implemented. That left Serbia and its two autonomous provinces of Voivodina and Kosovo, plus the Republic of Montenegro. The latter declared its independence on June 3, 2006, following a successful referendum in which 55.5% of Montenegrins voted to break the formal link with Serbia. Kosovo followed suit on February 17, 2008.

In the earlier cases of Slovene, Croat and Bosnian declarations of separation, Serbia resisted by military means. This time it accepted the inevitable and de-

clared its own independence on June 5, 2006. The last shred of the Yugoslav Federation disappeared without bloodshed. Then Serb Prime Minister Vojislav Kostunica refused to congratulate the newly independent republic. No Serb officials or Serbian members of the Montenegrin parliament attended Montenegro's independence ceremonies. But Serb President Boris Tadic saw the new development as an opportunity to demonstrate that sepa-

President Boris Tadic with ex-U.S. Secretary of State Condoleezza Rice

435

Serbia

ration in the former Yugoslavia can now be peaceful and that "we can maintain the historical good relations between us." He assured his neighbors that "Montenegro will have a reliable friend in Serbia" and that "Serbia will be the closest friend."

Montenegrin independence triggered a complicated separation and the official resignation of Svetozar Marovic, the independence-minded Montenegrin who had become federal president in 2003. The joint federal parliament was abolished. The armed forces had to be split up begin-

ment, but only narrowly by voters in a referendum.

Its preamble states that Kosovo is an "integral" part of Serbia that can never be taken away. However, that was not to be. On February 17, 2008, Kosovo declared its independence, supported by the United States and 20 EU countries. Serbia vows never to accept this, and it has largely succeeded in clinging to control over Serbs remaining in Kosovo, especially those in the north around Mitrovica. [See separate chapter on Kosovo.]

Ex-Prime Minister Vojislav Kostunica

Belgrade parliament in flames, October 5, 2000

der of his rule until October 2000 proved that it was not a constitutional state. His second term as president of Serbia ran out in 1997, and he was forbidden by the constitution to stand for a third term. He therefore decided to move to the federal level and get himself elected as president of Yugoslavia. Since the president was elected by the Yugoslav legislature, and his Socialist Party (along with the SNP, a pro-Yugoslav party from Montenegro) was in firm control there, it was not difficult for him to arrange for his election as president of Yugoslavia in July 1997.

This was a reminder of the dual nature of the post-communist regime: there was a federal structure, with a president, parliament, prime minister and government in Belgrade. There were the same institutions at the republic level in both Serbia and Montenegro. Below these two levels

ning with a reshuffling of the top ranks in the army and military intelligence service. Each side named its own top commander. Thousands of soldiers were relocated to their home countries, but each republic kept the military facilities on its own territory. Dividing dozens of embassies, diplomatic residences and other common assets may take years.

Under federation, there were common Foreign Affairs and Defense ministries. Those were now divided and each republic named separate Foreign and Defense ministers. According to an earlier agreement when the former state of Serbia and Montenegro was created, Serbia inherited membership in the United Nations and other international organizations. Montenegro had to apply as a new UN member and was quickly admitted on June 28, 2006. Both also revised their constitutions to reflect their new independent status. Serbia adopted a hastily written new 206-article constitution in October 2006. It was approved nearly unanimously in parlia-

It is not easy for many Serbs to accept their country's reduction in size. Not since the First World War has their area of influence been so small. While the Montenegrins and Kosovars were in a triumphant mood, Serbs suffered a sense of loss. It seemed like yet other defeats for their country. Serbs need time to absorb this new reality. In the long term, this development could be a blessing by freeing Serbia from the kinds of ethnic and constitutional struggles that have distracted it and weakened its efforts to become a respected and full member of the new Europe. Serbia can now focus on its own problems and its future as an ultimate member of the European Union.

Milosevic's Last Years in Power

Serbia's control until 2000 was evident in 1997 when Slobodan Milosevic, the longtime president of Serbia, had himself elected president of Yugoslavia. The fact that this suddenly became the most important political office during the remain-

Victory! Protester waving Serbian flag

Serbia

Election billboard for President Boris Tadic: "The Future Right Now"

were municipalities, which elected their own governments. Beside these three layers of government were the provinces of Voivodina in the north and Kosovo in the southwest. Both could play a part in Yugoslav government if they chose, but both had their own institutions as well. Since February 2008 Kosovo is independent, and it will never again be ruled by Serbia.

The president of Yugoslavia had always been a ceremonial position without much power. But Milosevic was not content to fill a ceremonial position. First, to maintain his control over Serbia, his political base, he got a loyal lieutenant elected as president of Serbia. This proved to be more difficult than he had anticipated. It took three elections, but he managed to have his own man, Milan Milutinovic, installed as president of Serbia in December 1997. A loyal lieutenant, Milutinovic had previously been foreign minister of Yugoslavia. His term as Serb president ran until the end of 2002. Almost immediately after leaving office he was sent to the UN War Crimes Tribunal in The Hague to face charges for alleged crimes. His trial began in July 2006, and he was acquitted in February 2009 of charges that he ordered a terror campaign in Kosovo.

A New Political System

A dramatic change in the nature of the regime came with the heady days following the October 2000 elections. All evidence pointed to a clear victory by Vojislav Kostunica and his 18-party Democratic Opposition of Serbia (DOS). Nevertheless, Milosevic, who had gained plentiful experience in manipulating elections and whose followers controlled the ballots and the polling places, claimed that Kostunica had not won a majority and that there would have to be a second round of elections.

Kostunica refused, realizing that any delay would have enabled the wily Milo-

sevic to find a way to rig the elections, as he had done in the past. A powerful human swell propelled by a populist coalition of workers, students and intellectuals took to the streets to support Kostunica. Inflamed workers took over the offices of factories, hospitals, banks and mines. Crowds stormed the parliament and state-run television station. Milosevic had had huge powers of patronage, but its beneficiaries had become hated figures in the eyes of the populace. The sheer magnitude of spontaneous "people power" forced Milosevic to concede victory, especially since the army refused to use force against the protesters, as he had ordered. The revolution was bloodless. Kostunica, who had systematically won over key leaders of the police and army, proclaimed: "For a long time, we lived in an order in which democracy never existed. It exists now!"

This model of peaceful revolution worked so well that it was studiously copied by Georgian President Mikhail Saakashvili and his followers to overthrow a corrupt and authoritarian regime in that Caucasus country in 2003. They even sent representatives to Belgrade to learn the techniques that had been so successful in October 2000, and they adopted the same slogan: "He's finished!" The Ukrainian democratic opposition also applied the model to prevent a stolen election in December 2004.

Milosevic's miscalculations were monumental. He thought the Serbian people would support him forever, but the economic devastation he had brought to Serbia had changed many minds. Under his rule the standard of living had plummeted, and Serbs could see no way out of the economic morass as long as he remained in power. Kostunica's promise of "a normal life in a normal country" was alluring. Unlike the late Croatian leader, Franjo Tudjman, Milosevic failed to recognize the post-Cold War realities and demonstrably turned his back on the West. American pro-democracy assistance amounting to tens of millions of dollars poured into Serbia to unseat Milosevic.

The newly elected Kostunica emerged from the revolutionary euphoria to face daunting problems. He could not be sure of the ultimate loyalty or limits of the army and security forces, whose leaders had been installed by Milosevic. The economic situation was depressing in the extreme. A decade of sanctions and mismanagement, intensified by the NATO air war against Serbia to end a genocidal policy against Kosovo Albanians in the spring of 1999, had left the economy in shambles, the environment severely blighted, and half of the people with no or little work. For a decade, the economy had shrunk at

the rate of 7% per year. Average wages were $38 per month.

An estimated 70% of the economy operated in illegal or semi-legal forms. Gangsterism had flourished in the 1990s, fueled by war profiteering, sanctions breaking, and a corrupt system of import permits. The underworld took full advantage of the country's isolation from law-governed states. Milosevic's cronies gained control of most of the country's businesses, an estimated 750 apartments in Belgrade, and pirated huge sums of money to enrich themselves. In 2000 the U.S. Treasury Department estimated that at least $1 billion had been spirited out of Yugoslavia through banks in Cyprus. Kostunica was one of the few prominent politicians who had no benefit from the underworld. Belgrade politicians were notorious for collecting illegal fees of up to $3,000 for licenses to open street kiosks and for skimming 40%–50% of the value of city contracts in illegal fees.

Despite this dismal outlook, Kostunica, the federal president, went into the December 23, 2000, parliamentary elections with an 80% popularity rating. His coalition won big, and his rival and nominal ally, Zoran Djindjic, became Serbia's prime minister. A philosophy professor with a razor-sharp mind, Djindjic quickly commanded more influence in Belgrade even if he was less popular than Kostunica. The son of an army officer, he had spent much of his youth in Germany studying philosophy and forging close lasting ties with that country. He was unsentimental, pragmatic and modern. For example, he wanted Kosovo's future resolved within a few years and insisted that "all options" should be open. He was also ready to see Montenegro go its own way if that was what its people wanted. His priorities were to eliminate the vestiges of Milosovic's rule in Serbia and to steer his country into the European Union, the negotiations for which began in 2002. "We must find a solution mainly by finding our place in Europe, not by seeking historical rights or national interests." Tragically, he was assassinated on March 12, 2003.

The restoration of the Serbian monarchy is highly unlikely despite a ceremony in 2001 returning Serb citizenship to Crown Prince Alexander II, a former British army officer and banker, and his wife and three sons. The ceremony took place in a suite of London's Claridge's Hotel where he had been born 55 years earlier and which Prime Minister Winston Churchill had declared to be Yugoslav soil. The son of Serbia's last reigning monarch, Petar II, who is buried in Libertyville, Illinois, Alexander was also granted the right to reclaim family properties. He moved back to the family's ancestral palace in Belgrade in July 2001.

Serbia

Drumming up votes for Kostunica

At first Alexander was emphatic that he would not reclaim the throne or challenge the country's republican constitution unless royal sentiment became stronger. But in December 2003 he said that the time was right for the restoration after he received the support of the Orthodox Church. That such a profoundly influential institution as the Church would call for the restitution of the constitutional monarch reveals the failure of yesterday's communists and today's disunited democrats to gain the public trust by presenting a cohesive plan for social reform.

Presidential Elections

Serbia elected its president in June 2004, unencumbered by the earlier 50% turnout rule, which was abolished. In the first round of voting, ultranationalist Tomislav Nikolic of the Serbian Radical Party (SRS, whose official leader, Vojislav Seselj, went on trial for war crimes in The Hague in late 2007) came out on top, with 30% of the votes. He was followed by Boris Tadic (27%) of the Democratic Party (DS). In the second round two weeks later Tadic surged ahead with 53.5% to Nikolic's 45.1%. Tadic was supported by the urban elites of Belgrade and by voters in the Western-oriented northern province of Voivodina. Nikolic found his votes in the ethnic rural heartlands in the center and south of Serbia.

This result was repeated in February 2008, when Nikolic again won the first round with 39.4% to Tadic's 35.4%. However, the incumbent president fought back in the second round, framing the election as a referendum on joining the European Union and escaping from international isolation. Although Tadic and all major Serbian politicians oppose Kosovo's independence, his then coalition partner, Vojislav Kostunica, broke with him for ap-

pearing to trade Kosovo for the lure of the EU. The then prime minister argued that Serbia should abandon its efforts to join the EU if it meant relinquishing sovereignty over Kosovo. That was not Tadic's intent, saying a year and a half later: "The EU is our central strategic priority, but not the only one."

Turnout in the runoff was an astounding 61%, the highest since Milosevic was removed from power in October 2000. In a close finish, Tadic came out on top, winning 50.5% of the votes to Nikolic's 47.8%. Although the narrow margin showed how divided Serbia remains, the majority voted for the long-term perspective of joining Europe. A majority of ethnic Serbs supported Nikolic. But responding to Tadic's call "not to return to isolation," young voters and minorities supported the president. Many Serbs say they feel isolated, alienated and closed in. Only 12% had passports, but that percentage is climbing since the EU granted Serbs visa-free travel in December 2009.

Since the overthrow of Milosevic in October 2000, the reform parties have governed Serbia. However, they have been weakened by internal divisions. The feud between Prime Minister Kostunica, who heads the Democratic Party of Serbia (DSS, renamed after the earlier DOS fell apart after 2000), and Tadic's rival Democratic Party (once led by the assassinated Djindjic) kept Tadic's party out of the governing coalition. It has severely weakened Serbia's pro-Western political forces. Kostunica, whose position as prime minister is more powerful than the presidency, grudgingly supported Tadic in the second round in order to block the ultranationalists. In return, Tadic promised to support the government. Indeed, because the presidential powers are limited, Tadic's only possibility of initiating change is by work-

ing closely with parliament and the Kostunica government.

Tadic, a former psychology professor, appealed to the international community to help ease Serbia's political isolation and to pave the way for negotiations to enter the EU. "Today we need support from the West because the citizens of Serbia voted for a pro-Western way." One week after his inauguration he traveled to Washington to deliver a simple message: "We are ready to retake our traditional place in the constellation of Western democracies." He acknowledged that the government lacks full civilian control of the security forces, which survived Milosevic's fall. Appealing to the strong Serbian nationalist sentiments, he defended the view that Kosovo remains part of Serbia. "Kosovo is not lost. If Kosovo is ever lost for the Serbs, it will also be lost for Europe."

An incident in November 2009 showed how much Serbia's political system and the power of the presidency had changed since Milosevic's time. Photos were published of Tadic and two other officials toasting the victory of Serbia over Romania in the World Cup qualifying round with full glasses of Champaign. Since drinking alcohol at and around sports venues is illegal, a judge filed misdemeanor charges against the president and other two. He ordered the three to court and levied a fine, which Tadic willingly paid even though he claimed not to have drunk from the glass.

Parliamentary Elections

Parties seeking seats in parliament must win at least 5% of the total votes. This 5% rule does not apply to those parties representing ethnic minorities. Parliamentary elections are important because the prime minister wields much more power than any president. The good news in the December 2003, January 2007 and May 2008 elections was that over half of the voters chose democratic parties over more radical and nationalist ones that seek to undo the revolution of October 2000 and block Serbia's integration with Europe.

The extreme nationalist Serbian Radical Party emerged as the strongest party in the 250-seat parliament in 2003 and 2007. Its leader was an indicted war criminal in The Hague, Vojislav Seselj, whose trial began in November 2007 and who was charged with contempt of court in 2009. Heading the ticket in 2007 and 2008 was his stand-in, Tomislav Nikolic, who lost in presidential elections in 2004 and 2008. He called for an end of Western-style reforms, an end to growing military cooperation with NATO, a questioning of the attempt to join the EU, and a return to the notion of "Greater Serbia," though as a long-term project and without going to war. Nikolic

Serbian Orthodox priests in Belgrade

almost snagged the position as parliamentary speaker in 2007, but he was removed from that post at the last moment. In the May 11 snap parliamentary elections, the Radicals fell from 81 to 77 seats and 29% of the votes.

By autumn 2008 the Radical Party was imploding as a result of an internal war between the anti-European hard-line wing of the jailed Vojislav Seselj and the allies of the more pragmatic pro-European supporters of Tomislav Nikolic. The latter was expelled with 17 of his backers and created his own party in October 2008, the Serbian Progressive Party (SNS). It has remade itself as a modern center-right party that has dropped its militant rhetoric and anti-EU stance. It attracts right-leaning voters without offending the EU or U.S. Even the Serbian Orthodox Church has started to turn its back on nationalist hardliners. The SNS has become the largest party in the opposition while the old Radicals are now a marginal rump party. Nikolic entered secret discussions with Tadic over EU agreements. The collapse left Tadic the undisputed political master in Serbia. Kostunica's smaller nationalist-leaning list captured only 30 seats in 2008. These parties, which spurned the EU's offer of membership negotiations, were consigned to the opposition.

Like the Radicals, Milosevic's old Socialist Party of Serbia (SPS) reaps votes from workers who have lost their jobs after privatization, middle-class professionals who cannot find steady employment in the new Serbia, and resentful Serbian refugees from Bosnia, Croatia and Kosovo. By the 2008 parliamentary elections, however, the party, led by Ivica Dacic, was determined to reinvent itself as a mainstream center-

left party that can share power with other democratic parties. It captured 20 seats and, after tough negotiations lasting seven weeks, entered a coalition with Tadic's pro-EU list, which captured 103 seats. Dacic became deputy prime minister and interior minister in the new government. The latter post put the Socialists in charge of the police and state security. They hold the balance of power between hard-line nationalists and pro-EU moderates. It is a paradox that they could prove to be a key party in moving the country into Europe.

A so-called "democratic bloc" consists of four main parties that basically have only one thing in common: they opposed Milosevic in 2000. They include the Democratic Party of Serbia, led by Vojislav Kostunica, who had ousted Milosevic as president in 2000 and who shows a strong nationalist streak. He complains about anti-Serb bias in the West and the war-crimes trials in The Hague. He is unbendingly opposed to Kosovo's independence. As prime minister he was responsible for calling the 2008 elections to try to undo the former province's freedom. He wanted EU membership to be postponed until European countries change their minds about supporting Kosovo's independence. Like the Radicals and Socialists, he benefits from the widespread anger and disillusionment in the country. His party fell to only 30 seats in 2008 and is consigned to the opposition.

Tadic's party, the Democratic Party, formed an alliance in 2007 that included G-17 Plus, led by Mladan Dinkic, a party of liberal Western-oriented reformers who favor letting Kosovo go, and the Liberal Democratic Party, led by Cedomir Jananovic. In May 2008 they ran under the label: For a European Serbia. They won 39% of the votes and 103 seats. Together with the Socialists, they formed a minority government that excluded Kostunica and his party. A member of Tadic's party, Mirko Cvetkovic, became prime minister. The new government declared that it would never support an independent Kosovo, but that it would focus its attention on leading Serbia into the EU, an idea supported at the time of the election by two-thirds of Serbs.

The EU sweetened the pill in a last-minute offer to Serbia of a prized Stabilization and Association Agreement (SAA). Except for Bosnia-Herzegovina, Serbia had been the only country to emerge from the wreckage of the former Yugoslavia without an EU association pact. Fearing that the EU door might close if the opportunity were lost, President Tadic signed it on April 29, 2008, despite fierce opposition from Kostunica, only two weeks before the voting. The Serb government ratified the agreement several months later, and the EU responded with an upbeat statement

and the prospect of trade concessions. In December 2009 a trade agreement with the EU demonstrated that the path to membership was open.

Tadic accepted an important pre-condition on the insistence of the Netherlands and Belgium: that the government demonstrate its full cooperation with the war crimes tribunal in The Hague. In addition, 17 European nations announced that they would no longer charge Serbs for visas. In July 2009 Serbs (except those living in Kosovo), Montenegrins and Macedonians were granted visa-free travel throughout the EU. There can be no doubt that this EU offer played a major role in the elections. The risk that Tadic ran in accepting the bid was dramatized by the fact that he received death threats for signing it.

As prime minister, Kostunica had earlier angered Western partners by stating that extraditions are not a priority and insisting that future trials of alleged Serb war criminals be held in Belgrade rather than The Hague. The international reaction was instant: NATO officials indicated that Serbia's membership in the Partnership for Peace, which had been scheduled for June 2004, would be postponed. EU leaders announced that a long-awaited "feasibility study" on future membership would be delayed. The U.S. blocked $100 million in aid. Rethinking the matter, he declared he had been misunderstood and only wanted "increased dialogue" with tribunal officials.

In 2007 Serbia's government renewed its commitment to cooperate fully with the Hague tribunal, and the latter said that Belgrade had, in fact, increased its efforts to search for suspects. Therefore the EU restarted talks leading to eventual membership. At its Riga summit in November 2006, NATO had come to the same conclusion. It reversed its long-standing prerequisite that Serbia must hand over Mladic and Karadzic before being admitted to its Partnership for Peace (PfP) program. Both organizations no doubt hoped to soften Serbia's hard-line opposition to Kosovo's independence. That did not happen. But they helped create a choice for Serbs: to cling to the illusion the Kosovo's independence could be overturned or to begin accession talks with the EU and other Western organizations. Serbs remain bitterly divided, but elections in 2008 demonstrated that the latter option is the preferred one.

Milosevic's Extradition to the War Crimes Tribunal

Milosevic, of all people, threw his hat into the ring to challenge the DOS after the 2000 elections. As the only candidate, he won reelection as leader of his Socialist Party, which was in disarray. More mod-

Serbia

erate members had already quit the party and formed two separate leftist parties. Also dreaming of a comeback was Milosevic's wife's, Mirjana Markovic's, Yugoslav Left Party. This charade ended in April 2001 when Milosevic was arrested after a gun battle with his heavily armed bodyguards and indicted on corruption charges. Western countries demanded that he be sent immediately to The Hague to be tried by the UN international war crimes tribunal.

Kostunica and Djindjic were divided on this question, the former opposed and the latter in favor. Djindjic paved the way to extraditing Milosevic by revealing evidence of mass graves of Kosovo Albanians killed by Milosevic's forces in 1999. The revelations provoked disgust in the minds of many ordinary Serbs; three-fourths of them believed by June 2001 that Milosevic should be tried for war crimes. The prime minister found the economic carrot the West held out to be essential for his impoverished country. The prospect of $1.2 billion in economic and reconstruction assistance was linked to Milosevic's extradition. Djindjic later asked: "How much would it have cost this country if this had not happened?"

Facing resistance from Kostunica and the Montenegrin faction in the governing coalition, the prime minister and the cabinet majority issued a decree that it would cooperate with the UN and hand over Milosevic. When the latter's hand-picked Constitutional Court judges ruled the decree to be unconstitutional, Djindjic resorted to one of Milosevic's own earlier measures that permitted the Serbian cabinet to ignore any federal law it did not like. Without informing Kostunica or anyone else, the cabinet simply ordered the extradition on June 28, 2001, the anniversary of the 1389 Battle of Kosovo and the 1914 assassination of Archduke Franz Ferdinand in Sarajevo. Within three hours Milosevic was in a plane bound for The Hague. There he was charged with 66 counts of war crimes and genocide in Croatia, Bosnia and Kosovo. He was the first head of state ever to be taken to court on allegations of genocide, the most serious of all war crimes.

On March 31, 2002, the cabinet issued further arrest warrants for four additional Milosevic associates who had been indicted for war crimes. Economic motives were again at play, as the U.S. froze $40 million in assistance until the Yugoslav government demonstrated its willingness to cooperate with the tribunal. A former prime minister, Zoran Zivkovic, revealed in 2005 that CIA agents took part in dozens of failed attempts by Serbian police in 2003 to capture the Bosnian Serb wartime commander, Ratko Mladic. A key

war crimes suspect shot himself outside the parliament building in protest. Dealing with Serb war crimes remains highly emotional and dangerous, as many Serbs regard themselves as victims of the wars and see The Hague tribunal as biased against them.

Many other top leaders are in custody, including the leader of the nationalist Serbian Radical Party, Vojislav Seselj. He went on a month-long hunger strike in November 2006 to win the right to conduct his own defense; he failed to have the three judges hearing his case replaced. He was charged with contempt of court in 2009. Former Bosnian Serb President Biljana Plavsic was sentenced to 11 years in a Swedish prison, but she was released early in October 2009. Top suspects, such as General Ratko Mladic and former Bosnian Serb leader Radovan Karadzic, are still in hiding and reportedly heavily guarded. In June 2007 Serbian and Bosnian Serb police worked jointly to arrest one of Mladic's top aides, Zdravko Tolimir. Further U.S. aid has been conditioned on Serbian cooperation in apprehending them.

Western demands were strengthened in June 2004 when a commission of the Republic of Srpska government finally admitted that Serbian forces had been responsible for the deaths of up to 8,000 Muslims in Srebrenica in 1995. In December 2003 a Bosnian Serb general was convicted in The Hague of commanding a two-year sniper and artillery terror campaign against the citizens of Sarajevo. Croats and Bosnian Muslims have been tried and convicted. In 2003 three Kosovo Albanians were indicted for the first time, and in 2005 the indicted Kosovo prime minister, Ramush Haradinaj, submitted himself for trial in The Hague, but he was acquitted.

Prominent witnesses were called to testify against Milosevic, such as former Slovenian President Milan Kucan, Croatian President Stipe Mesic and former NATO commander Wesley Clark. Clark testified that he has spent over 100 hours with Milosevic and was convinced that the former Serb leader was "the motivating force in most if not all" of the events in four Balkan wars in the 1990s. These were only a few of the 1,400 witnesses Milosevic said he wanted to call to the stand, including former President Bill Clinton, ex-Prime Minister Tony Blair and German ex-Chancellor Gerhard Schröder. Despite Milosevic's antics in court, including seeking to discredit every witness against him, the prosecution built a strong case against him. There was no "smoking gun" to prove that he directly ordered atrocities since he put very little on paper and often met his subordinates alone. But

Former Prime Minister Zoran Djindjic
Source: *The Economist*

there was much circumstantial evidence. His main objective in The Hague was to perform for his audience in Serbia, where the proceedings are televised, and to hammer away at his view that the Serbs were the main victims of an international plot to smash up Yugoslavia and that he was the chief peacemaker rather than the cause of the bloody wars.

As a way of fighting back, members of the country's military police arrested one of Serbia's deputy prime ministers, Momcilo Perisic, and an American diplomat at a Belgrade restaurant on charges of passing to the Americans sensitive military information. The incident, which former Prime Minister Djindjic called a "first-rate scandal" and "a blow to the country's international credibility," was a part of the army's effort to block the flow of evidence to The Hague. The government later apologized to the U.S. for holding the diplomat incommunicado for 15 hours and for roughing him up. Nevertheless, military prosecutors charged him in September 2002 for spying for the U.S. Perisic denied the allegations and correctly claimed to be the victim of a power struggle.

Facing the threat of penalties by the U.S. and the EU, the Serb government decided in 2005 to cooperate with the UN war crimes tribunal and to surrender indicted suspects. Its nervous efforts sparked controversy by treating the indictees as national heroes. For example, Kostunica called General Vladimir Lazarevic's decision to come out of hiding "patriotic, highly moral and honorable." The retired general was blessed by the leader of the Serbian Orthodox Church and was accompanied to The Hague by the justice minister. The government's sincerity was also called into question when Foreign Minister Vuk Draskovic said that Serbian security forces know the whereabouts of General Mladic and are protecting him.

The government vigorously denied reports in June 2009 that Mladic had been filmed recently engaging in a normal social life. This severely damaged the claim that Serbian officials do not know Mladic's whereabouts. In February 2010 the police raided the Belgrade home of the Mladic family and found a large cache of Swiss francs, euros and dollars that could be used to pay for his food and protection. They also found 18 of his diaries, comprising 3,500 handwritten pages, recounting in detail his activities in the war. War crimes prosecutors in The Hague asked that these diaries be admitted into evidence against his former boss, Radovan Karadzic. The government rejected the Mladic family's request that he be officially declared dead since he had not been seen in public since 2005.

After over a dozen Serbs and Bosnian Serbs had been sent for trial, the EU agreed in April 2005 to begin "stabilization and association" negotiations with both Serbia and Montenegro as a step toward eventual membership. That agreement was withdrawn in May 2006 when Serbia had failed to meet a deadline for capturing Mladic. This decision exasperated the government, which had been more aggressive in its attempts to capture the war criminal, whom some Serbs still consider a hero. It cracked down on the network of military veterans suspected of aiding the general. In December 2005 a Serbian court convicted 14 former Serb militia members of massacring 200 Croatian POWs.

Kostunica exclaimed: "Never in our history has the entire state and nation been made to suffer because of one officer." He warned that his country could break with the West if a more conciliatory international approach is not taken. He pointed to a grim development: the ultranationalist Radical Party had by 2006 become the largest party, with 40% support in the polls. Some European leaders fear that Russia may be backing the nationalist hard-liners and that EU promises of future membership may be falling victim to widespread "enlargement fatigue." This is a dangerous situation. In June 2007 the EU renewed accession talks with Serbia, and an agreement was signed on April 29, 2008. In November 2009 the Netherlands lifted its veto, and the following month Serbia formally applied to join.

In June 2005 a video was shown on Serbian television that galvanized the government's cooperation with The Hague tribunal. It had been provided by the court's prosecution and was the first graphic portrayal of what had happened in Srebrenica in 1995. It begins with a Serb Orthodox priest blessing camouflaged paramilitary troops called Scorpions. Later troops are shown taking six young men out of a truck and killing them. In the

video, shot by a Scorpion, one can clearly hear the troops insulting the scared Muslims. Only a month earlier an opinion poll had revealed that over half of Serb respondents did not believe the Srebrenica massacre had ever occurred.

The government acted quickly. Kostunica said the film showed "brutal, callous and disgraceful crime against civilians." President Tadic said in an emotional television statement that the images were proof of the "monstrous" crimes committed in Serbia's name during the Balkan wars. He added that the perpetrators had been freely walking the streets, but now they must face justice. Ten former members of the elite Scorpions were immediately arrested for the crimes, and five were arraigned on murder charges at the end of 2005.

Their trial began in February 2006. In the first trial inside Serbia that involved the Srebrenica massacres, four were convicted and jailed in April 2007. In November Serbian war crimes prosecutors indicted 14 more ex-Yugoslav soldiers and paramilitaries for torturing and killing 70 Croat civilians in late 1991. In June 2008 police arrested outside of Belgrade one of the four most wanted fugitives, Stojan Zuplijanin, a Bosnian Serb police commander accused of atrocities against Bosnian Muslims and Croats.

In February 2007 the Hague court ruled that Serbia was not responsible for genocide in Bosnia because it had not aimed to "destroy in whole or in part the Bosnian Muslim population." However, the court decided that Srebrenica was a genocidal event and that Serbia is to be blamed for failing to use its "known influence" to stop it. Bosnia had brought this charge in 1993 and was disappointed that Serbia is not required to pay it reparations. Although Serbia escaped being labeled a genocidal country and having to pay billions of euros in claims, Bosnia did obtain what it called "a recognition of Serbia's guilt."

In an effort to win favor from the EU and to improve its relationship with its neighbors, parliament in late March 2010 narrowly passed (with 127 of 250 votes) a resolution condemning the July 1995 Srebrenica massacre. The word "genocide" could not be used because it was rejected by the reformed Socialist Party (formerly Milosevic's), on whose votes the government depends. Also most Serbs do not believe the war had been one of genocide. Instead the carnage was called a "crime." It offered "condolences and apology to the families of victims because not enough was done to prevent the tragedy." It committed itself to Bosnia's territorial integrity. Following the Hague 2007 ruling, it did not accept blame for the killings.

The close vote revealed the continuing lack of consensus in Serbia on the character of the 1990s Balkan wars. Nevertheless, the resolution makes it impossible to pretend that the massacre never happened or that the number of dead had been grossly exaggerated. Also at the same time, Tadic flew to Croatia to discuss with the Croatian president the possible mutual withdrawal of charges that each had practiced genocide against the other.

Death of Milosevic in 2006

On March 11, 2006, after five years of incarceration and courtroom antics in The Hague, Milosevic was found dead in his cell at age 64. Dutch prosecutors cited his autopsy to pronounce that he had died of a heart attack. His worshipers and family cried "murder," claiming that he had been poisoned or denied proper medical treatment for his heart ailment. This fiction fitted neatly with the conspiracy theories Serb nationalists had always used to justify the ethnic cleansing ordered by a leader responsible for four disastrous Balkan wars that left a quarter of a million dead and 2.5 million homeless. There is no doubt that the tribunal would ultimately have found him guilty of war crimes.

Milosevic's Socialist Party demanded a full state funeral, but President Tadic dismissed that as "inappropriate." After much bargaining, the authorities agreed to a private funeral in Serbia and a public display in Belgrade. Tens of thousands gave him a hero's farewell. Some carried banners declaring: "Slobo is a hero and heroes never die!" and "The Tribunal kills!"

His casket was placed under a canopy in front of the parliament building, where mobs had stormed in October 2000 to end his corrupt presidency. Up to 80,000 paid their respects there. His burial took place at a family residence in his home town of Pozarevac, 35 miles southeast of Belgrade, where about 15,000 gathered. No government officials were present at either ceremony. Nor was any member of his family; all had fled abroad and are under indictment.

His vision of a "greater Serbia," which he had manipulated to propel himself to power, is dead. However, his emotional send-off reinforced the sense of victimhood in many Serbs. It also provided an unwanted boost to the Radical Party, which is more intensely nationalist than his own Socialist Party had been. His shrunken party split into Milosevic loyalists, who favor cooperation with the Radicals, and others who want to put his defeats and corruption behind them. The latter group succeeded in reinventing itself as a moderate center-left party and entered the government in July 2008.

Serbia

„zemuncima" tek krajem januara 2004.

fotke supruge i dece Pede Mijatovića

Zašto Vlada ĆUTI

NEDELJNI Telegraf

BiH 1,5 KM CG CG 0,8 €

3. 12. 2003. CENA 40 DIN. DEUTSCHLAND 2,60 € BROJ 397

IZ KONTRAOBAVEŠTAJNIH IZVORA

POVRATAK LEGIJE

● Moguće je da se vrati u Srbiju posle izbora
● Čuva ga hrvatska služba, koju kontroliše CIA
● Legija, veliki igrač u svetu špijuna, sada „uspavan"

Posle izbora ukida se Specijalni sud

Đinđić će biti optužen za svoje ubistvo!

INTERVJUI

Tomislav Nikolić Vuk Drašković

Al kaida vršlja Bosnom

Mudžahedini ISLAMIZUJU Srbe u BiH!

France 2,70 €, Austria 2,60 €, Belgium 2,70 €, Canada 4$, Czech Republic 93 CZK, Hungary 670 HUF, USA 4$, Switzerland 4,80 SFR, Greece 2,70 €, Denmark 18,50 DKK, Netherlands 2,70 €, Luxembourg 2,70 €, Sweden 30 SEK, Great Britain 1,79£, Italy 2,70 €, 210 SLT, 8 kn, 50 DEN

The return of Legije. In custody a half year later.

Assassination in Belgrade

On March 12, 2003, the reformist Prime Minister Zoran Djindjic stepped out of his armored car outside the main government building in Belgrade and was gunned down. As turbulent as Balkan politics has been, this was the first political assassination in the region since the First World War. He was mourned, as hundreds of thousands of Serbs attended his funeral and paid their respects with flowers and tears. This was the largest crowd since Tito's death in 1980.

With those shots the reality of post-Milosevic Serbia came into clear focus. It became grimly visible to what extent Serbia had been taken over by gangsters, how deeply the ex-dictator's legacy had taken root, and how close this nation was to sliding back into chaos or the status of a failed criminal state. The dictator's overthrow in 2000 had left in place much of the evil he

had fostered. To avoid bloodshed and gain the clout he needed to unseat Milosevic, Djindjic had cut a deal with certain gangland and paramilitary leaders, most notably the Red Berets' former leader, Milorad Lukovic, more commonly known as Legija, a nickname derived from his service in the French Foreign Legion in the 1980s. Djindjic would not go after some of the thugs, who were exerting influence within the army, police and security organizations and directing mafia activities such as drugs, human trafficking and prostitution, if they would help him bring down the Milosevic regime.

It was Legija's men who had rejected orders from Milosevic to crack down on the opposition and who had later agreed to arrest Milosevic and to bundle him off to The Hague. Thus the revolution that had occurred was part popular uprising and part internal power coup. Each leader, in-

cluding Djindjic, had his own ties to different sections of the security services and had to live in uneasy coexistence with unsavory elements. When the prime minister started putting pressure on the gangsters and making preparations to arrest them, they organized a plot, "Stop The Hague," and killed him.

During the Milosevic era and well into the democratic transition, this interlocking network between organized crime, corrupt security chiefs and judges, and ultranationalist politicians reigned. One TV editor described it this way: "Politics was criminalized and crime was politicized." Especially during the Milosevic era, they dominated Serbia, operating extortion rackets and drug rings, kidnapping businessmen who spoke out against them, terrorizing politicians, even murdering former President Ivan Stambolic. This ended with the assassination of Djindjic.

Nebojsa Covic, who acted as prime minister for a few days, stated unmistakably what was at stake: "We have to decide who really rules this country: the mafia and its assassins, or its elected leaders." Under a new prime minister, former Interior Minister Zoran Zivkovic, who had been an imposing and vociferous critic of Milosevic, the government cracked down with a vengeance. A state of emergency was declared until April 22, the army was ordered to swear its loyalty and take over for the police, civil liberties were temporarily suspended, and airports and train and bus stations in Belgrade were closed.

A police sweep, called Operation Sabre, resulted in over 10,000 arrests, and 4,500 were jailed while charges were filed against 3,700. One of those charged was popular singer Svetlana Raznatovic (better known as Ceca), the widow of the infamous warlord Zeljko Raznatovic (known as Arkan), who had been assassinated three years earlier. Police said she had links to the Zemun drug cartel, named after a Belgrade suburb, which had been implicated in the assassination. The authorities sent bulldozers to flatten the large shopping center that served as Zemun's criminal headquarters.

Having failed to prosecute the underworld bosses, 35 judges were forced into retirement; not a single senior official of the Milosevic era had been tried in Serbia for war crimes. The Red Berets' former leader Legija went into hiding, and he was tried in absentia. He surrendered in May 2004, and in June he joined a dozen other murder suspects being tried in Serbia's special court for organized crime and war crimes, set up in 2003. The court has made steady progress in the war on organized crime. Two weeks after his arrest assailants tried to kill Djindjic's sister, and his mother and other relatives received grade in July 2008 after 13 years on the run. The 63-year-old was disguised so thoroughly that he could move around Belgrade freely. He was sporting a huge bushy white beard, flowing grey hair with a black dyed spot on the top, and oversized horn-rimmed glasses. [See photos in Bosnia chapter] The trained psychiatrist, who did an internship at Columbia University in New York City, was living under the assumed name of Dr. Dragan Dabic, handing out business cards proclaiming himself as a "bioenergist," delivering lectures at conferences on alternative medicine, publishing articles in Serbia's *Healthy Living* magazine, counseling on Christian Orthodox spirituality and giving treatments for impotence and depression.

At The Hague he faces charges of two counts of genocide and five of crimes against humanity. Like Milosevic before him, he insists on defending himself. He bases his defense on an alleged promise by American negotiator, Richard Holbrooke, of immunity from prosecution if he agreed to step down from his presidency. Holbrooke vigorously denies this.

His arrest leaves only two key fugitives on the run: Goran Hadzic, who commanded Serb forces in Croatia, and Ratko Mladic, who led the Bosnian Serb army. Their chances of remaining free have been considerably reduced since a major political shift occurred in Serbia after the May 2008 elections. They put power into the hands of President Boris Tadic, who is determined to lead his country into the EU, and took it away from former nationalist Prime Minister Vojislav Kostunica. Karadzic was arrested within two weeks of a change of guard in the Serb intelligence services.

Tensions were high after Tadic received death threats and journalists were attacked by far-right nationalists. Thousands of Karadzic's Radical Party supporters gathered in downtown Belgrade in an attempt to prevent Karadzic's extradition to The Hague. They turned violent, smashed shops and attacked and injured more than a dozen policemen. Undaunted, Serbian authorities whisked the fugitive away several hours later before dawn and brought him to a penitentiary in Scheveningen, Netherlands. Karadzic appeared in his first public court hearing on July 31, 2008, which signaled the beginning of the legal proceedings against him. His trial resumed in March 2010 after he had exhausted his stalling tactics.

death threats to be carried out if Legija is convicted. He got 40 years in 2005 for the Stambolic murder and for attempted assassination of ex-Foreign Minister Vuk Draskovic. In February 2007 a Belgrade court convicted Milosevic's militia commander, Milorad Lukovic, and six of his men for killing four of Draskovic's associates while trying to murder him in 1999.

While on the run Legija produced a novel, *Iron Trench*, about a Serbian soldier lying critically wounded in a ditch during the war in Bosnia. Blatantly anti-Muslim in tone, it nevertheless questions what was gained by the war. Although there is some question about the book's true authorship, it quickly sold 70,000 copies. The acclaim received by *Iron Trench* and by Radovan Karadzic's novel, *The Miraculous Chronicle of the Night*, reflects the near mythic status these nationalist figures still enjoy. Two more books by Legija appeared in 2005.

Red Berets' deputy chief, Zvezdan Jovanovic, was arrested two weeks after Djindjic's murder and confessed to having been the triggerman. He had waited for three days to take his shot. He said he did it to stop suspects from being delivered to The Hague. After a three and a half-year trial in Belgrade's new special court for organized crime, Legija and Jovanovic were sentenced in May 2007 to 40 years in prison, Serbia's maximum penalty. The Supreme Court rejected their appeal in October 2009. Eleven other defendants were convicted also, five in absentia. The verdict said that the motives were to halt Djindjic's pro-Western policies, to bring Milosevic's allies back into power and to stop further extraditions to The Hague.

The crackdown also led to the discovery of former Serbian President Ivan Stambolic's body, a bitter foe of Milosevic who had been missing since August 2000, when he had been abducted while jogging in a Belgrade park. Arguing that Milosevic had given orders for the "permanent removal" of Stambolic, police charged Jovanovic and eight others with the murder; the eight were jailed in July 2005. They also issued arrest warrants for Mrs. Milosevic, Mirjana Markovic, and their son Marko, who are suspected of involvement in the killing. Both had fled the country for Russia. Some of the charges against Mirjana were dropped in July 2008 as a condition for the Socialist Party's entry into the government.

The results were breathtaking. Acting President Natasa Micic proclaimed on national television: "We have dismantled Milosevic's criminal apparatus and severed a spiral of crime that has ravaged our country for more than a decade." Only time can tell if the entire cancer has been extracted and whether Djindjic's own prediction after a previous assassination attempt will be true: "You can shoot me, you can even kill me, but this country and its democratic system will still function."

In July 2008, the biggest fish was snatched from a bus in Belgrade: Radovan Karadzic. While on the run, he had written a novel, *The Miraculous Chronicle of the Night*, a somewhat autobiographical tale set in Sarajevo in the 1980s. Born in Montenegro, Karadzic had moved to Sarajevo as a teenager. The hero is an engineer who, like Karadzic, was imprisoned when Tito died in 1980. It was a bestseller at Belgrade's international book fair and was on the short list for Serbia's top literary award, the Golden Sunflower, in 2004. It was his fourth publication after going into hiding. His other works include a children's book, a play and a selection of his poetry. The acclaim his books received reflected the near mythic status these nationalist figures still enjoy.

Under circumstances almost too bizarre to be true, Karadzic was arrested in Bel-

Foreign Policy

Even though the United States did not recognize the new Yugoslav government in 1991, it continued to staff an embassy in Belgrade over the next several years. The stated purpose was to maintain con-

Serbia

tacts with Belgrade in order to try to persuade it to agree to a negotiated peace settlement in Bosnia. After the end of the Bosnian War in 1995, American-Serbian relations improved because Washington was counting on Milosevic's continued support of the Dayton Accords to make them work. Gradually many of the sanctions against Yugoslavia were removed, and it appeared that Yugoslavia was about to shed its pariah status. That was put on hold in February 1998 after Serbia launched a series of punitive attacks on Albanian villages in Kosovo.

When those attacks did not bring satisfactory results from Serbia's point of view, Belgrade sent in additional units of paramilitary police and army units, which continued Milosevic's policy of "pacification" of the province. This resulted in the destruction of many Kosovar villages and forced several hundred ethnic Albanians to become refugees in their own country. NATO countries intervened on behalf of the Kosovars.

At the beginning of the air war against Yugoslavia in March 1999 Belgrade broke off diplomatic relations with the NATO states, and most international organizations broke ties with Belgrade. As hundreds of thousands of Albanians were pushed out of the province, they came to fill refugee camps in Macedonia and Albania, in the process threatening to destabilize those countries. All of its immediate neighbors supported NATO's demand that Serbia restore Kosovar autonomy and stop its policy of ethnic cleansing, and they favor NATO's occupation of the province. Greece voiced opposition.

Yugoslavia could not find many friends among its neighbors until Milosevic was removed from power in October 2000. Once Vojislav Kostunica had assumed the reins of power in Belgrade, he announced, "I expect support from Europe for the democratic changes in Serbia and for its return to where it has always belonged—Europe." The West responded without hesitation, quickly dropping economic sanctions and bringing Yugoslavia back into most international institutions with incredible speed, but with many conditions.

He quickly restored diplomatic relations with the U.S., Germany, France, Britain, and Yugoslavia's neighboring nations. Underscoring his promise of a new era of cooperation with Serbia's Balkan neighbors, he traveled to Macedonia for talks with other regional leaders. There he admitted that Serb soldiers and police had committed large-scale murder in Kosovo. Macedonia's late president, Boris Trajkovski, rejoiced, "we are living in truly historic times." Kostunica also became the first leader of Yugoslavia to visit non-Serb Bosnian territory since the Bosnian war

began in 1992. He met the three members of Bosnia's collective presidency at the Sarajevo airport in October 2000. As Serbian prime minister, he sent his defense minister to Albania, the first since 1947. This marked the end of the cold war between Tirana and Belgrade.

Within three weeks of Kostunica's election in 2000, Yugoslavia joined the Balkan Stability Pact, funded by the EU. On November 1, Yugoslavia was readmitted to the UN after an eight-year suspension of voting rights. Several delegates reminded him that UN membership obligates Serbia to cooperate with the UN war crimes tribunal in The Hague and to turn Milosevic over for trial, something the new president, a legal scholar and moderate Serb nationalist, had said he would not do. Immediately afterwards, his country was welcomed back into the OSCE, from which it had been suspended in 1992. In March 2003 the Council of Europe welcomed Serbia back into the organization after Serbia accepted a series of conditions concerning cooperation with the war-crimes tribunal.

Serbia will always play a crucial role in the Balkan geopolitical situation. If it is poor, turbulent and aggressive, the rest of the area will be insecure and unsettled. Like the rest of the democratic world, Washington was pleased by the change and courted Kostunica assiduously until it tired of his resistance to cooperating with the war crime trials in The Hague. It supported the Serbian government of Zoran Djindjic with financial assistance and diplomatic encouragement and continued that assistance for his successor.

The U.S. backed the lifting of the UN arms embargo on Serbia and Montenegro, which maintained united armed forces until separating in June 2006. Signaling its desire for good military ties with Serbia in May 2006, the U.S. sent two F-16 fighter jets to Batajnica Air Base near Belgrade for a courtesy visit. Arms shipments are subject to limits established under the Dayton Peace Accords and subsequent agreements with Bosnia-Herzegovina and Croatia.

Serbia armed forces have shrunken greatly since the Balkan wars. In 2010 its total active military force counted 29,125 soldiers. Of these, the army has 12,260, including 1,800 conscripts. The air force and air defense have 4,262, including 477 conscripts. They fly Soviet-era MiG aircraft. The navy has about 3,000 personnel (including 900 marines), who man four conventional submarines, three frigates, and an assortment of patrol and coastal combatants, mine sweepers and support ships. Training command has 6,212 soldiers and the department of defense 6,391. Conscripts serve nine months. Its reserve force numbers 50,151.

Major military reform is underway, and civilian service for those who do not wish to be soldiers was introduced. In 2006 Serbia and Montenegro had to sort out their military bases and personnel. Each kept the facilities on its own territory, and soldiers were free to resettle in their own countries.

Serbia signed a landmark border agreement in 2002, ceding to Croatia the Prevlaka peninsula, which controls access to Boka Kotorska Bay, Montenegro's main deep seaport. The agreement demilitarizes the area, permits Serbian and Montenegrin naval vessels to traverse the channel into the bay without stopping or conducting military maneuvers in the area, and calls for joint sea police patrols. As a result of Montenegro's declaration of independence in June 2006, Serbia lost its direct access to the sea.

In 2003 Serbia requested admission to NATO's Partnership for Peace Program as a first step toward NATO membership. This would help it reform its armed forces. But the uncertainty in 2004 about Belgrade's willingness to cooperate with The Hague caused NATO and the EU to delay cooperation, and discussions over Serbian offers in 2003 to dispatch troops and police to Afghanistan and Iraq were postponed. NATO's invitation was reissued in November 2006.

The annual March commemoration with sirens blaring honoring the victims of the 1999 NATO air war to break Serbia's hold over Kosovo reveals the continued anti-Western sentiment in Serbia over the war. Opinion polls demonstrate that only a small percentage of Serbs support their country's integration into NATO. Ex-Foreign Minister Vuk Draskovic noted: "Until NATO bombed us, most Serbs saw the West as the last great hope, the last love, the last illusion." Now reformers face a difficult challenge to convince disillusioned Serbs that the U.S., NATO and the EU have their best interests in mind.

Serbia's leaders express the wish to join the EU. In 2002 the government took first steps toward accession to the EU, and the EU convened Balkan leaders at its summit in Thessaloniki, Greece, in June 2003 to promise them membership if they keep their commitments to reform and overcome ethnic strife. This process was put on hold until Belgrade's cooperation with the war-crimes tribunal was clarified; the accession process was resumed in 2007. It culminated in the signing of a Stabilization and Accession Agreement on April 29, 2008. In November 2009 the Netherlands lifted unblocked the path to membership. The next month visa-free travel to Europe was granted, and Serbia formally applied to join. The EU informed Belgrade that it would keep the Kosovo question separate from accession talks.

No major Serbian politicians or parties accept Kosovo's declaration of independence on February 17, 2008. When it happened, some government leaders (though not President Tadic) joined the hard-line nationalist Radical Party to mobilize as many as 200,000 Serbs in the streets of Belgrade to protest. Free rail and bus tickets were given to bring in people from all over the country. Ex-Prime Minister Kostunica declared: "As long as we live, Kosovo is Serbia!" After hearing fiery speeches, mobs peeled off to loot shops and attack the American, Croatian, Bosnian, and Turkish embassies. At least 100 broke into the U.S. embassy, when it was closed, and set fire to some of the rooms. They were quickly extinguished, but not before a young demonstrator perished in the blaze.

The UN Security Council unanimously condemned the violence, which was not limited to Belgrade. In the northern Kosovo town of Mitrovica, 5,000 demonstrators confronted UN police guarding the bridge separating the Serbian and Albanian communities. Two border stations were burned when they tried to hoist Kosovo's flag. The Serb government is doing everything it can to prevent Kosovo Albanian rule from taking effect in the new country's Serb-inhabited enclaves. Its foreign minister and diplomats travel the world to dissuade countries from recognizing independent Kosovo, as 69 did in 2010, including 22 EU members.

The government will also use all legal and democratic means to prevent Kosovo from gaining membership in the UN and other international bodies, such as NATO, the World Bank or the IMF. At the UN it moved to have the International Court of Justice give an advisory opinion on whether Kosovo's declaration of independence was legal. The decision is non-binding and will undoubtedly be ambiguous. It would have to be approved by only a simple majority in the General Assembly. Regardless of the judgment, Serbia would never again be able to rule hostile Kosovo Albanians. [See separate chapter on Kosovo.]

Former Prime Minister Zoran Zivkovic announced during his August 2003 visit to Washington: "Serbia is looking for an ally in the United States, and in return Serbia can offer to be a reliable partner in the Balkans." After all, the second largest concentration of Serbs in the world is Chicago. American leaders are aware that a deeply felt Serbian nationalism inspires continuing anger over the support the U.S. provided to Kosovars. They view President Tadic as a modernizing leader, and they seek an improved relationship with Serbia. A growing number of Serbian military officers attend command staff and war colleges in the U.S., and since 2006 the Ohio National Guard helps train the Serbian army.

Vice President Joe Biden visited Serbia in May 2009 to offer it "a strong, new relationship." He said his country does not expect Serbia to recognize Kosovo's independence. But it does expect it to cooperate with the EU and others in Kosovo and to "look for pragmatic solutions that would improve the lives of all the people in Kosovo."

ECONOMY

The country still has what must be called a socialist market economy although considerable progress is being made to liberalize and privatize the economy. But it is neither a capitalist nor a totally government-directed economy. There are three basic parts. One is a small market-oriented one that generates most of the growth. There is the large, unreformed socialist system, and finally there exists an "underground" economy that generates an estimated 40% of GDP and much of the employment. Only half of working age people participate in the workforce, compared with the 66% EU average.

Economic collapse played a large role in the dissolution of Yugoslavia in the 1990s. The country had been a leader among the socialist states in economic decentralization, but it remained a socialist state. Fast economic growth in the 1970s had brought better living conditions, but a multitude of problems as well. Mounting inflation became more and more of a problem, and the foreign trade deficit began to grow. Not wishing to put an end to the economic growth, the leadership rather reluctantly responded with things like import restrictions and a ceiling on wage increases. Eventually it was also forced to begin devaluating the currency. The great increase in energy prices in 1973–74 and again in 1979 eventually proved too much for the Yugoslav economy, and it, like most of the world, slipped into recession.

While Yugoslavia's economy drifted during the 1980s, inflation grew year after year until, by the end of 1988, it had gotten out of control completely, soaring to an annual rate of 2,500%. The situation frightened the political leadership, and in desperation it turned to Ante Markovic, an exponent of the free market. He was installed as president of the Federal Executive Council in March 1989.

Even then, there was stiff opposition to his stabilization program, but he managed to get it adopted after several months. It went into effect on January 1, 1990. Within three months, the dinar had been stabilized, and inflation had been brought down to single digits. In addition, currency reserves were up and the foreign debt had been reduced to $16 billion. Foreign investment also began pouring into the country, and individual Yugoslavs started several thousand privately-owned businesses.

With the stabilization program so successful, politics reasserted itself. The second phase of Markovic's program called for beginning the privatization of state-owned industry, instituting radical changes in the federal tax structure, and making banks more independent of the government. But elections were scheduled in the various republics, so the politicians demanded that the national wage freeze be lifted instead. It was Slobodan Milosevic who most strongly opposed the privatization policy. Lacking support in the republics, the national stabilization program was put on hold.

Meanwhile, free elections in Slovenia and Croatia brought a repudiation of the old communist leadership and their replacement by nationalist leaders who began talking of the need to replace the federation by a loose confederation of sovereign nations. Domestically, these new leaders adopted free market economic policies. This contrasted with the position of Milosevic, who argued for a strong centralized Yugoslavia and against free market economic policies.

Caught between the two forces, the economic stabilization program of the Markovic government collapsed. By the beginning of 1991, inflation was again running at an annual rate of 120%, and the dinar had to be devalued by 30%. By April 1991, strikes were breaking out all over the country as thousands of enterprises were unable to meet their payrolls. Things were bad all over the country, but Serbian industry, the largest and most inefficient in the country, was worst off. Unemployment was 15% and rising as industrial production continued to plummet. Thus an economic stabilization plan that had been working was completely destroyed by national and political rivalries.

War in Bosnia and Kosovo had a terrible effect on the Serbian economy. The cost of Milosevic's financial support for the Bosnian and Croatian Serbs was an estimated 40% of Serbia's GDP. This produced a hyperinflation that effectively destroyed the Serbian currency by the end of 1993 and caused the GDP to drop by two-thirds, or to about $10 billion. This prompted a currency reform in 1993. A new dinar linked to the German mark was introduced, and this temporarily stopped the hyperinflation.

When Serbia accepted the Dayton Peace Accord, signed in December 1995, the West rewarded it by "suspending" the economic embargo and promising to remove it entirely if the peace agreement held. The Serbs now had a chance to get

Serbia

their economy back on track once again. There was, in fact, some improvement in 1996 and 1997. A major effect of the air war in 1999 was that a great deal of Yugoslavia's infrastructure was destroyed.

Under former Prime Minister Djindjic's and his successor's stewardship from October 2000 to the end of 2003, Serbia made impressive economic progress. It reduced public spending, sold state assets and regularized taxation. Its privatization law of 2001 won international praise, and privatization is advancing quickly. In 2006 the mobile phone network was privatized, and the oil sector is to follow. Although much industry is still publicly owned, there is a significant private sector. In agriculture, 84% of the land is in private hands. The purchase and sale of land is permitted, and there exists a free market in agricultural products.

A major problem is that investors have fear because the rule of law is weak. Nevertheless, the U.S. government removed the remaining barriers to economic cooperation and trade with Serbia, and America has become the country's largest investor. In 2003 U.S. Steel bought the ailing Smederevo steel works. At first, U.S. Steel Serbia suffered heavy losses, but the cash investment eventually paid off; it is now Serbia's largest exporter. The American tobacco giant Philip Morris purchased a Serbian cigarette factory and became the largest foreign investor in the country.

Serbia survived massive layoffs in a major car factory in Kragujevac, the hub of ex-Yugoslavia's motor industry. In 2009 Fiat announced it would begin making 200,000 cars every year in Kragujevac as part of a joint venture that is creating 4,700 jobs. It purchased a 67% share in the country's main automaker, Zastava, which had once produced what one author called "the worst car in history," the Yugo. It took over the management, is bringing technology, and introducing stricter quality control. In the same year, Yura, a South Korean auto parts maker, set up a plant in Kragujevac, which employs 1,000.

Serbia closed insolvent banks. This strengthened those that remained so that when the global economic downturn hit Serbia in 2008, prompting a run on its banks and the withdrawal of 20% of their deposits, all 33 banks were able to meet their obligations, with the help of the central bank and EU. In 2005 Microsoft opened a software center in Belgrade, a year in which 7,000 new firms were registered.

In 2008 the Russian state-owned gas monopoly, Gazprom, purchased a controlling share (51%) of the Serbian state oil monopoly, NIS. It thereby incorporated Serbia into the South Stream gas pipeline that will run under the Black Sea, through Bulgaria and into Western Europe. This was a blow to the EU's plans to build its own Nabucco pipeline that would be outside Russian control. Serbia thereby becomes a hub for Russian energy supplies and strengthens Russia's dominance of the European energy market. In return, Russia will not only build a pipeline through Serbia, but also a huge gas storage facility. Gazprom will invest about $725 million toward modernizing Serbia's energy infrastructure. Russia will also take three metric tons of spent fuel from the closed Vinca nuclear reactor and thereby keep this nuclear material out of terrorists' hands. To diminish reliance on Russian gas slightly, Serbia's state-owned gas supplier, Srbijagas, signed a contract with HEAT, an Austrian company, to build a stopgap gas supply line.

Serbs are poorer than they were before the recent wars, and their country is one of Europe's poorest. With a per capita GDP of only about $7,400, living standards remain low. Average monthly income in 2009 is about 430 euros ($560). But thanks to foreign investment, real economic growth reached 7.5% in 2004 and 6% for the three following years, bringing the country's GDP to half of its level in 1990. Its economy contracted by 3.5% in the recession year 2009 and grew only about 1% the following year. The IMF helped in the economic crisis with a loan. Earlier runaway inflation fell to an annual rate of 17.2% in 2005, but prices are still at a level that many Serbs find uncomfortably high. A major burden for Serbia is the presence of 94,000 refugees, a huge number for a country of 8 million people.

Foreign debt in 2005 was almost $13 billion, compared to a GDP of $24.3 billion. In 2008 that debt amounted to 60% of GDP. Serbia reached a deal in 2004 to write off 62% of its debt to the London Club of creditors. This cleared its way back into the international financial mainstream. Unemployment was officially 17% in 2010, but because of the thriving underground economy, the actual figure is probably under 15%.

The country's main challenge is to survive the ongoing global economic crisis, which hit the country just when it had barely recovered to prewar levels. It is managing rather well despite lower growth rates and rising unemployment. One banker noted: "Serbia's had 20 years of crisis . . . so the worst is already behind us." In the longer term it must establish a truly free-market economy and get the economy out of the hands of organized criminals.

American drug enforcement officials praised Serbia in 2010 for seizing a 2.7 ton shipment of cocaine from South America and arresting 11 Serb and Montenegrin suspects. Many Balkan gangs operate in Latin America. More action can be expected as Serbia and Croatia have intensified their collaboration. In May 2010 they announced plans for a regional center to combat organized crime, and the following month they signed a defense cooperation agreement.

CULTURE

The withdrawal of Croatia, Slovenia, Bosnia-Herzegovina and Macedonia from Yugoslavia has not eliminated all of the cultural differences that fascinate foreign visitors, but it has reduced them considerably. What is left is essentially Serbian culture, characterized by the Serbian language, written in a 30-character Cyrillic alphabet, and the Serbian Orthodox religion. This "federation" still includes 620,000 Montenegrins, but they speak a language that is almost identical to Serbian, use the Cyrillic alphabet, and are Orthodox Christians.

Serbia also includes more than 300,000 ethnic Hungarians, who are concentrated in the Voivodina, where they constitute the largest minority with 14% of the residents. Voivodina has a total population of two million. It is the wealthiest part of Serbia and home to 60,000 Slovaks. The province has six official languages, including Ruthenian, Slovak and Hungarian, and schooling is in their own language. Latin letters are widely used. It has its own provincial government with a prime minister. The beginning of 2010 a new autonomy statute went into effect for Voivodina. Although some nationalists said this could ultimately lead to independence, about two-thirds of its population are Serbs, who have no interest in independence.

Approximately 70,000 Albanians constitute the majority in the Presevo Valley within Serbia. The Sandzak area in Serbia has a predominantly Muslim, but non-Albanian, population. A little over half of the approximately 236,000 Sandzak Muslims are Bosniaks. Most Albanians are Muslim although there is a small minority that is Roman Catholic and even a few who are Orthodox. They show little solidarity with Kosovo Albanians, and they argue among themselves whether their spiritual center should be Sarajevo or Belgrade. Hungarians are usually Roman Catholic or Protestant.

There are many clichés about the country's diverse peoples. Words that have been used to describe Serbs include "emotional," "hot-tempered," and "proud." Their enemies tend to use words like "hegemonic" and "bullying." Montenegrins are usually described as "proudly independent" by admirers, "rural rustics" by detractors. Both Serbs and Montenegrins are also described as "fierce fight-

Ivo Andric

ers." Such adjectives should not be taken too seriously because they are more a reflection of Serbia's and Montenegro's relations with their neighbors than any underlying reality.

In the drowsy farm village of Medju, near the Romanian border, the American Olympic swimmer and later popular Tarzan actor, Johnny Weissmuller, was born in 1904. Although his family emigrated to the U.S. when he was a baby, his birthplace honors him with a bronze Tarzan statue. About 20 kilometers (12 miles) away is another village, Zitiste, where a bronze statue of Rocky Balboa, made famous in the many Sylvester Stallone "Rocky" boxing films, also was erected. In 2008 another village unveiled what it claims is Europe's first statue to the late Jamaican reggae star, Bob Marley. Such monuments to Hollywood icons and pop culture are springing up all over the Balkans.

Serbs can be justly proud of the beautiful Serbian Orthodox churches and monasteries that date from a great blossoming of culture during the Middle Ages. In January 2010 hundreds of thousands marched in a somber funeral procession in Belgrade to mourn the death of popular Patriarch Pavle. Known for his modesty and humility, he had since 1990 led the seven million-member church through the country's post-communist adjustment and ethnic conflicts. Irinej Gavrilovic was elected to replace him.

The nation also has an admirable literary tradition. In 1961 Ivo Andric, a former Yugoslav diplomat, was awarded the Nobel Prize in Literature. His epic novel, *The Bridge over the Drina*, describes the long and troubled relationship between Muslims, Catholics, Orthodox Christians and occupiers in his native city of Visegrad in Bosnia. Modern Belgrade is a stately and beautiful city.

FUTURE

Organized crime remains the greatest threat to stability in Serbia and the Balkans. The government's determined crackdown in 2003 weakened but did not eliminate such criminals. The major obstacle to reform can be found in the former pillars of Milosevic's regime, including the police, army and state security services.

Enthusiasm in Western Europe for enlarging the EU to include the Balkans has waned. It insists on "debalkanizing" the Balkans, meaning establishing fixed borders and more stability. It may take almost a decade for Serbia to achieve their desired membership in the organization. In December 2009 Serbia formally applied to join.

The government had announced in 2008 that it would restore full relations with the EU and return their ambassadors to those countries that had recognized Kosovo's independence. By 2010, 69 countries had recognized Kosovo, of which 22 are EU members. The government is determined to mend ties with Europe and Washington.

While moderating its tone, it made clear that its opposition to Kosovo's independence has not changed. It was a bitter pill, and all major parties and politicians oppose it. No Serbian politician is willing to take responsibility for the loss of Kosovo. It has successfully sealed off the Serbs who live in the northern part of Kosovo around Mitrovica and continues to rule them and provide services. However, Serbia will not be able to reverse Kosovo's independence. The whole issue of Kosovo will continue to grate on Serbs although many admit privately that Kosovo is gone forever.

There will be no constructive relations between the two countries for years. Nevertheless, in May 2010 Serbian war crimes prosecutors uncovered the third mass grave containing the bodies of hundreds of ethnic Albanian civilians killed during the 1999 war then transported to Serbia to hide the atrocities. Three other such graves were discovered in Kosovo itself. Hundreds have been exhumed and returned home for burial.

Serbia's leaders are working to repair ties with Serbia's Balkan neighbors, who had been intimidated or hurt by Milosevic's aggressive regime. A dramatic parliamentary apology to Bosnia in 2010 for the 1995 massacre in Srebrenica is a step in this direction. The best hope for Serbia is an alliance of democrats, which is now in power. It is an excellent sign that in 2008 Boris Tadic's Democratic Party hung on to the presidency and won the subsequent parliamentary elections. Serbs were twice given a choice between integrating with today's Europe or returning to the past. They chose Europe.

President Tadic celebrates his reelection in 2008.

The Republic of Bosnia-Herzegovina

Sarajevo lives again!

Area: 19,696 sq. mi. (51,129 sq. km.)

Population: 3.84 million (UN estimate 2009 although no one knows exactly)

Capital City: Sarajevo (526,000)

Ethnic Background: South Slavic. Three subdivisions—Bosnjak (Muslim 44%), Serb (33%), and Croat (17%)—are recognized although they are cultural and religious rather than ethnic.

Climate: Continental in the north; Mediterranean in the southwest.

Neighboring Countries: Serbia, (east); Montenegro, (southeast); Croatia (west and north).

Official Languages: Bosnian, Serbian, Croatian. All are easily mutually comprehensible.

Other Principal Tongue: Albanian

Principal Religions: Islam, Serbian Orthodox, Roman Catholicism

Chief Commercial Products: Steel, coal, iron ore, lead, zinc, manganese, bauxite, vehicle assembly, textiles, tobacco products, furniture, domestic appliances, oil refining, grains, potatoes, plums, livestock, timber, cement.

Main Trading Partners: Croatia (20.7% of exports and 24.6% of imports), Slovenia (16.7% of exports and 12.7% of imports), Italy (16.7% of exports and 10.5% of imports), Germany (13% of exports and 12.3% of imports).

Currency: marka (June 1998, pegged to the euro, 2:1). The Croatian kuna still circulates in the area of the Croatian Republic of Herzeg-Bosnia, while the Serbian dinar still tends to be the currency used in the area of the Bosnian Serb Republic.

Former Political Status: Constituent republic of Yugoslavia.

Chief of State: Three-member presidency. The position of chair of the presidency is rotated every eight months among the Serb, Croat and Moslem members. As of 2010 they were: Haris Silajdzic (Bosnjak), Zeliko Komsic (Croatian), Nebojsa Radmanovic (Serb).

Head of Government: Nikola Spiric, Prime Minister (since January 2007). The prime minister serves four years. The position no longer rotates on an eight-month basis. Each of the two entities—Republika Srpska (Serb Republic—RS) and the Federation of Bosnia and Herzegovina (referred to simply as "The Federation)—has its own president and prime minister.

National Flag: A yellow right-angled triangle with its base at the top is superimposed against a blue background. A row of 9 white stars runs along the side of the triangle opposite the right angle.

Shortly before his death in 1897 Bismarck had predicted, "one day the great European War will come out of some damned foolish thing in the Balkans." That happened on July 28, 1914, when Gabriel Princip, a Bosnian Serb nationalist, assassinated the Austrian archduke

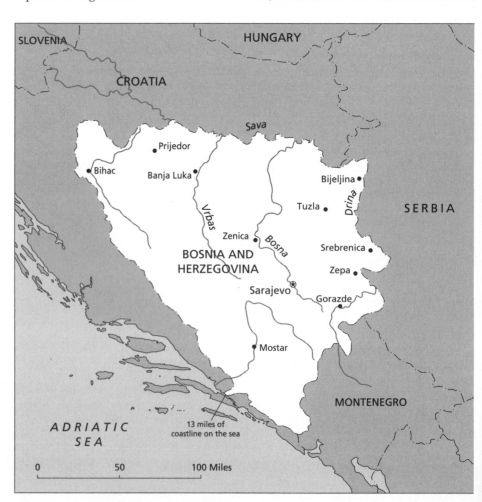

and his wife in Sarajevo. The shots of Sarajevo sounded the end of an almost 50-year absence of major wars among European great powers. Group rivalry and bloodshed are not new to Bosnia, the most ethnically diverse part of the entire volatile Balkans. In the last decade of the 20th century, this precarious republic offered Europeans the grisly spectacle of the worst human barbarity since the Second World War. Blood and belonging outweigh all other values.

The Republic of Bosnia-Herzegovina is the independent successor state to the Socialist Republic of Bosnia-Herzegovina that was part of the Socialist Federal Republic of Yugoslavia until 1991. It is roughly triangular. It also has a tiny, 13-mile section of coastline on the Adriatic Sea, but no harbor. It has an area of 19,696 square miles (51,129 sq. km.), almost all of which is mountainous. Herzegovina, the name that applies to the southern part of the republic, is derived from *Herzog*, a Germanic title for "duke," taken by a local ruler in the 15th century. Today Croats dominate it. The name Bosnia is derived from the Bosna River, a tributary of the Sava River. Its 168-mile course is almost entirely within the republic. It begins in Herzegovina in the south, flows northeastward through Bosnia and enters the Sava River at the border. The Sava River, in turn, forms the western border with Croatia.

A second river, the Drina, forms a large part of the border with Serbia. It is also a tributary of the Sava. Two further rivers flow from south to north across the republic, the Vrbas to the west of the Bosna and the Una in the extreme northwest. The source of all of these rivers is the mountain chain known as the Dinarian Alps, which runs in a northwest-southeastern direction across the western part of the republic.

Individual peaks soar to over 7,500 feet, though wide valleys running in the same direction separate the ridges. The center of the republic is a piedmont region with an average height of 1,500 feet, while the Sava and Drina River valleys produce lowlands in the east. About half of the land is arable. Most of the remainder is covered by forests of pine, beech and oak.

The exception is the area of Herzegovina in the south. A native proverb says, "Bosnia begins with the forest, Herzegovina with the rock." The mountains of Herzegovina are of gray Karst limestone, filled with crevices, sinkholes and pits, and they overwhelm the viewer with their barren desolation. Most of this area has very little population. It is only possible to live in the fertile river valleys that cut through the mountains and in some upland hollows where there is arable soil. Bosnia's weather is generally mild with cold winters. In Herzegovina, on the other hand, summers are often oppressively hot.

The population of the Republic of Bosnia-Herzegovina is an estimated 3.84 million as a result of 100,000 war dead and even more lost to emigration. The prewar figure was 4.3 million. No one knows exactly how many Bosnians are inside the country. The last census was taken in 1991. Since the prime minister of the Republika Srpska will accept a new census only if people are asked about their ethnicity, Bosnjaks and Croats in 2009 voted against it. This is the most diverse of the republics of the old Yugoslav Federation. No single group is in a majority, but Bosnjaks have been the largest grouping with 44%. Serbs account for 33% of the population, while Croats constitute a further 17%. The term "Bosnjak" has replaced "Muslim" as an ethnic term. This avoids confusion with the religious term "Muslim," a believer in Islam.

The differentiation on which the concept of the three "nations" of Bosnia-Herzegovina is based is religion and culture, not ethnicity. The Muslims there are a Slavic people who converted to Islam during Turkish rule. The language they speak is now referred to as Bosnian. No one now refers to "Serbo-Croatian" as a language. Bosnian, Serbian and Croatian are essentially dialects of the same language. Serbs are mainly adherents of the Serbian Orthodox Church, while Croats are almost all Roman Catholics.

HISTORY

Slavic-speaking peoples settled the present-day area of Bosnia-Herzegovina as early as the 7th century A.D. It first emerged as a separate political entity toward the end of the 12th century when a nobleman named Kulin managed to gain control of most of the lands along the Bosna River, which became known as the Ban of Bosnia. Kulin's principality did not last long, but one of the things he did was to convert to Bogomilism and make it the state religion.

Bogomilism had originated two centuries earlier, farther to the east in Bulgaria. By the 12th century it had become well established in Bosnia. It shared many common characteristics with Catharism or Albigensianism, in particular a belief in a Manichaean dualism. Its distinguishing belief was that the world is governed by two principles, good and evil, the first spiritual and the second material. The physical world, being material, was viewed as the realm of the devil. Both the Roman Catholic and Greek Orthodox churches condemned this dualism as heretical, so Bogomils found themselves rejected by both West and East.

Early in the 13th century, the Roman Catholic Church dispatched a papal legate to the area to institute a purge of the local clergy. Somewhat later, Dominican missionaries were sent in to fight the heresy. They came with military might provided by the Hungarian monarchy. These forces brought Bosnia under Hungarian control. In 1299, the Hungarian king granted Bosnia as a fief to a Croatian aristocrat named Paul Subic. The latter brought in Franciscan missionaries to help stamp out the Bogomils.

Subic passed the principality on to his son, Mladen, but the local nobility overthrew the latter in 1322. Stephen Kotromanic, a native Bosnian replaced him as *Ban*. Kotromanic was succeeded by his nephew, Stephen Tvrtko, who expanded the principality greatly during his lifetime, annexing part of Dalmatia to the west and part of modern-day Montenegro to the south. Tvrtko eventually took the title "Stephen I, King of Serbia, Bosnia, Dalmatia, Croatia, and the Primorje."

His younger brother succeeded Tvrtko and was crowned as Stephen II in 1391. By the time of his death seven years later, the Turks had launched an invasion of Bosnia, and the kingdom began to disintegrate. It soon broke down into several principalities, most of them paying a yearly tribute to the Turks. The ruler of one of these principalities opted to become a vassal of the Holy Roman Emperor instead. For this the title of *Herzog* (duke) of St. Sava was bestowed on him. Over time, this title became attached to the land instead of the ruler, and in its modern form is Herzegovina.

After the Ottoman Turks conquered Constantinople in 1453, the Turks decided to take control of the Balkan Peninsula directly. The new invasion of Bosnia began in 1460. Some parts tried to hold out against the Turks. However, many of the Bogomil leaders saw the Muslim Turks as being preferable to the Hungarian Roman Catholics, still trying to stamp out Bogomilism, and allied themselves with the Turks. Afterwards, most of these Bogomils converted to Islam.

These new converts adopted the dress, titles, and etiquette of the Turkish court, while retaining their lands, their language, and most of their old customs. They also became the local military caste, which gave them a rank just below that of the Turkish governor. They remained loyal to the Ottoman Empire, and some of them even rose to the highest offices in the empire. One such was Ali Pasha, who became grand vizier in 1570. His successor, Mahomet Beg Sokolovic, also came from Bosnia. Meanwhile, most of the peasants remained Orthodox Christians.

Little changed until the 17th century, when the Austrian Empire, then still known

Bosnia-Herzegovina

as the Holy Roman Empire, began to push down into the Balkans. Prince Eugene of Savoy burned Sarajevo in 1697. A portion of the seacoast area of Herzegovina plus a part of Bosnia that bordered on the Sava River passed to Austria in 1718. Turkey took the Bosnian territory back in 1739, but it reverted to Austrian control in 1791.

In the first half of the 19th century, an estrangement began to develop between the Muslim aristocrats of Bosnia and the Ottoman government, primarily over the issue of traditional privileges. There were several revolts between 1820 and 1850 that led the regime to strip the aristocracy of most of its privileges. The peasantry was also growing dissatisfied as a result of increasing tax obligations and this led to other rebellions.

Things came to a head in July 1875 when a revolt among Christian peasants soon spread throughout the country and turned into a war specifically against Turks. The revolt next spread to Herzegovina, then to Bulgaria. Serbia and Montenegro declared war against the Ottoman Empire in July 1876.

Austro-Hungarian Rule

Russia and the Austro-Hungarian Empire had been rivals in the Balkans throughout the 19th century. Alexander II, the Russian tsar, opened negotiations with the Austro-Hungarian government immediately after Serbia entered the war against Turkey. The agreement the two sides signed at Reichstadt stipulated, among other things, that Austro-Hungary would receive territorial concessions in case of a change in the *status quo* in the Balkans. When Serbia subsequently began losing its war against Turkey, Russia entered the conflict as Serbia's ally in July 1877.

Having won against Turkey, Russia negotiated a treaty under which Turkey recognized the independence of Serbia and Romania and agreed to the establishment of a large Bulgarian state. However, when the Austro-Hungarian government heard about the terms of the treaty of Stefano, it was outraged. The creation of a large Bulgarian state clearly constituted a change in the status quo, but the treaty made no mention of corresponding territorial concessions to Austro-Hungary. Vienna then threatened Russia with war and German Chancellor Otto von Bismarck, had to step in to preserve the peace. His solution was a congress of European nations that he would host in Berlin.

The Congress of Berlin awarded Austro-Hungary administrative control of Bosnia-Herzegovina. The territory was not formally annexed at this time because the prime minister in Vienna, a Hungarian, did not want any more Slavs in the empire. This was a technicality, however. From this mo-

ment onward, Bosnia-Herzegovina became a part of the Austro-Hungarian Empire. In 1908, after a successful revolt of the Young Turks against the Ottoman Empire, Vienna formally annexed Bosnia-Herzegovina.

The "damned foolish thing in the Balkans" that Bismarck had predicted occurred on July 28, 1914, with the assassination of the Austrian archduke in Sarajevo. Austria held Serbia responsible for this act and, ultimately backed by Germany, made unacceptable demands on Serbia. By the first week of August Europe was locked into a war. Four devastating years later, the Austro-Hungarian Empire was in collapse following its defeat in World War I. The Serbs, with Allied blessing, claimed all of the South Slavic lands for a new Kingdom of Serbs, Croats and Slovenes, which was proclaimed on December 4, 1918. In 1929, this new state changed its name to Yugoslavia.

Incorporation into Yugoslavia

The area of Bosnia-Herzegovina was submerged within this centralized state of South Slavs. Bosnia-Herzegovina was at this time both poor and rural, with no strong local political leaders. Serbs tended to look to Serbia, while Croats looked to Croatian leaders outside of Bosnia. The people of the republic were satisfied to be part of Yugoslavia, even though Bosnia remained primarily rural. When things began falling apart in the late 1980s, its political leadership had its own ideas about what should be done.

Political discussions remained within the League of Communists of Bosnia-Herzegovina, the monopoly party, until 1990, when new elections were scheduled. After it authorized the formation of additional political parties, the old system collapsed. Three new parties won the November 1990 elections: the Muslim Party of Democratic Action, which gained 86 assembly seats; the Serbian Democratic Party, which won 70 seats; and the Croat Democratic Union, which got 45 seats. These three political parties subsequently formed a coalition and they elected Alija Izetbegovic, leader of the Party of Democratic Action, as president of the republic. During the communist era he had been imprisoned for his Islamic convictions, and he died in October 2003, a hero among his Bosnjak people.

Bloody Road to Independence

The political leadership of Bosnia-Herzegovina mainly stood aside in 1990–91 as the quarrel between the Serbs on one side and the Croats and Slovenes on the other grew more heated. It favored continuation of a united Yugoslavia, but it also wanted economic reforms, repudiation of the communist leaders, and a more

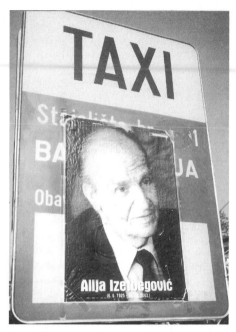

Bosniaks mourn death of Alija Izetbegovic

decentralized political structure. When Croatia and Slovenia declared their independence on June 25, 1991, Bosnian leaders once again urged calm on both sides. After the Serbs and the Yugoslav People's Army began their war against Croatia, however, the Bosnian leadership began to prepare for the breakup of the country. It was unwilling to remain in a truncated Yugoslavia dominated by Serbia.

Bosnian representatives stopped participating in the institutions of the Yugoslav federal government on October 3, 1991, after Serbian and Montenegrin leaders engineered a coup and took control of the Yugoslav presidency. On December 20, the Bosnian government voted to ask the European Community (EC, now EU) for recognition as an independent state. The government was divided on the issue, with the Muslims and Croats voting for independence and the Serbs insisting that Bosnia-Herzegovina remain part of the larger Yugoslav federal state. The Serbs then threatened to form their own "Serbian Republic of Bosnia-Herzegovina" encompassing those territories where they were in a majority.

On March 18, 1992, the leaders of the three communities agreed in principle to restructure the state, creating "three constituent units, based on national principles and taking into account economic, geographic and other criteria." The effect would have been to create three autonomous units within the governmental structure, one for Muslims, one for Croats and one for Serbs. Control in each municipality would have been exercised by that national group which was in an "absolute

Bosnia-Herzegovina

Sarajevo market 10 years after 1994 atrocity

or relative majority." The agreement would have been extremely difficult to implement since the three communities had always lived side by side, and many families were mixed. Its main value, therefore, was more as a way to forestall a civil war rather than as a practical blueprint.

In April, the EU and the United States recognized the independence of Bosnia-Herzegovina. Although gratifying in the abstract, it had a negative side: the Serbian Democratic Party withdrew from the coalition, its two Serbian members of the presidency resigned, and Serb leaders announced the formation of a "Serbian Republic of Bosnia-Herzegovina" which intended to remain part of Yugoslavia.

The Yugoslav Army was still stationed in Bosnia at that time. It announced that it would move its forces to Serbia and Montenegro. In fact, it divided its forces, leaving in Bosnia all those who had any connection with Bosnia or other non-Serb states. These forces, provided with tanks, artillery and all the equipment needed to fight a modern war, became the army of the Bosnian Serbs.

With a UN arms embargo making it impossible for the Bosnian government to obtain any significant weaponry, Bosnia found itself completely outgunned. Within three months, the Bosnian Serbs controlled 70% of the Bosnian territory. The Bosnian Croats, who were receiving military assistance from Croatia, dominated most of the rest. Serbs surrounded the capital, Sarajevo, with heavy weapons and snipers and besieged the city for three years. While periodically engaging in diplomatic discussions in Geneva, they continued their shelling. By the time it was

over, about 10,500 Sarajevans, including 1,500 children, were dead. Meanwhile, the West continued its arms embargo against Bosnia.

Convinced that Bosnia had lost the war, UN negotiators tried to get the leadership to agree to a partition that would have left the Serbs in control of half of the territory. But the Bosnian government refused to sign, and the siege went on. Convinced that the West intended to allow Serbia to succeed in creating a "Greater Serbia," the Bosnian Croats, encouraged by the Croatian government, switched sides and attempted to enlarge the area they controlled at the expense of the Bosnian government.

A change came in February 1994 when Western public opinion, appalled by a particularly atrocious shelling of Sarajevo that killed 66 people and injured 200 others, caused Western governments to take action. This produced a NATO ultimatum that the Serbs remove their heavy artillery pieces from a 12.5-mile zone around Sarajevo. The Serbs refused, whereupon the UN proposed a compromise: the Serb guns could remain where they were, and the UN Protection Force (UNPROFOR) would dispatch peacekeepers to these locations, in theory to assure that the Serbs did not resume their bombardment of Sarajevo.

The Serbs agreed to accept UN peacekeepers at their artillery sites. This was a mistake because the compromise placed the UN forces in a situation where they could become hostages, should a new war of wills erupt between the UN and the Serbs. The compromise temporarily ended the shelling, however, and an overland route to Sarajevo, closed for two years, was also reopened. Sarajevo

began to return to something approaching normality.

The NATO ultimatum to the Serbs paid yet another dividend. In this new atmosphere, the Bosnian Croats were persuaded that they could hold more of Bosnia by joining a U.S.-sponsored Bosnian-Croat federation than by continuing on their own. A separate federation government was subsequently set up and has continued to exist.

These two successes did not bring an end to the war. Forced to stop their artillery barrages of Sarajevo, the Serbs merely intensified their attacks against other besieged Bosnian government enclaves, including the towns of Tuzla and Gorazde. The UN protested these new attacks, but the Serbs continued with the artillery barrages until NATO once again used force, shooting down four Serbian jets over Bosnia. Bosnian Serbs still controlled 70% of Bosnia and continued their pressure on the rest.

Diplomatic Activity to Achieve Peace

The United Nations released a new peace plan in July 1994 that again proposed a division of the country giving the Bosnian Serbs 49% of Bosnia. Reversing his earlier stance, President Milosevic of Serbia endorsed the new peace plan, then broke publicly with Bosnian Serb leaders and "sealed" the border between Serbia and Bosnia when they rejected it. He also agreed to allow the placement of 135 civilian monitors along the 370-mile border to verify that aid to the Bosnian Serbs had stopped. Although almost no one believes that Serbia really ended all support for the Bosnian Serbs at this time, the amount of assistance did diminish.

Reacting to this additional pressure, the Bosnian Serbs attempted to sabotage the peace plan by launching attacks on the UNPROFOR peacekeepers. By firing on planes attempting to land at Sarajevo airport, they managed to shut down the UN food airlift and end all commercial flights into the capital. The first UN reaction was to do nothing, presumably because of a fear that any action against the Bosnian Serbs would bring Serbia formally back into the war. In fact, Sir Michael Rose, commander of UNPROFOR in Bosnia, threatened to call in air strikes against Bosnian government forces at the beginning of August after the Bosnian army tried to drive back Bosnian Serb forces just north of the Sarajevo.

A disagreement between the U.S. and other members of the "Contact Group" also broke out in August 1994 when Washington began urging an end to the military embargo against the Bosnian government. The U.S. government stopped enforcing the embargo in November after the UN

Bosnia-Herzegovina

General Assembly adopted a resolution urging the Security Council to lift the arms embargo on Bosnia. This was the second such General Assembly resolution, an earlier one having been passed in 1993. Since France and Great Britain, both permanent members of the Security Council with the power of veto, opposed lifting the embargo, however, no action was taken.

At the end of December 1994, ex-President Jimmy Carter mediated a 4-month "cessation of hostilities" between the Bosnian Serbs and the Bosnian government. The truce held for a while, but both sides used it mainly to strengthen their forces. It came to an end at the beginning of April 1995 when the Bosnian government struck preemptively in an attempt to disrupt Bosnian Serb communications facilities.

The Bosnian Serb response was to seize their heavy artillery pieces from UN-supervised storage areas and begin a new artillery barrage on Sarajevo. They also renewed their siege of the city, cutting it off from the outside world. General Rupert Smith, UNPROFOR commander in Bosnia, demanded a stop to the artillery barrage and a lifting of the siege. When the Bosnian Serbs did not respond, he called for a NATO air strike on an ammunition dump near Pale, the Bosnian Serb "capital." The Bosnian Serbs then launched a mortar barrage on the city of Tuzla that resulted in 70 civilian deaths. When General Smith ordered a second NATO air strike, the Bosnian Serbs took 350 UNPROFOR peacekeepers hostage. It was now the UN that blinked.

General Bernard Janvier, the overall UN military commander in former Yugoslavia, and Yasushi Akashi, the UN's special representative in former Yugoslavia, overruled General Smith's recommendation to continue the NATO bombing, they took away his authority to call in air strikes. UNPROFOR, they announced, would not take sides.

Anxious to win release of the UNPROFOR hostages, the UN agreed to hand back several hundred tanks, howitzers and mortars to the Bosnian Serbs in June 1995. The so-called weapons collection points ceased to exist. This eliminated the UN hostage situation, but the Serbs, with their heavy weapons back, began shelling Sarajevo again, killing nine civilians lining up for water on June 24. Meanwhile, the UN "safe-haven" cities of Zepa, Srebrenica and Gorazde were once more cut off by surrounding Serb forces and were being slowly starved out. Even UN peacekeeper forces stationed in these cities could not be re-supplied.

Considering the situation on the ground in Bosnia to be unacceptable, the governments of France and Great Britain now decided to up the ante. Recognizing that the

SOURCE: U.S. government
June 1992

452

Calendar of Radovan Karadzic (m) with Serbian heroes on sale in Bosnia Serb sector

lightly armed UN peacekeeper force was incapable of defending itself, they decided to create a heavily armed 12,500-man rapid reaction force separate from the UNPROFOR. These troops began arriving in Bosnia in July, but the new force came too late to prevent the fall of Srebrenica on July 11, then Zepa on July 22.

Women, children, and older men subsequently made their way from the fallen enclaves to Bosnian government-controlled areas, but more than 8,000 Bosnian men remained missing. Later, it became clear that most had been shot, their bodies dumped into mass graves, shortly after being taken prisoner by General Mladic's forces. He bears a major responsibility for these deaths since he was in charge of the sieges of both Srebrenica and Zepa and personally toured Zepa on July 27, 1995. He gave an interview at the time to the weekly newspaper *Svet* in which he boasted: "By autumn we'll take Gorazde, Bihac and in the end Sarajevo, and we'll finish the war in Bosnia." On the eve of the Srebrenica massacre he defiantly asserted on Bosnian Serb TV that the time had come to avenge centuries of conquest by the Ottoman Muslims.

The Tide Turns: Dayton

This turned out to be the high water mark for the Bosnian Serbs, however. The events associated with Srebenica and Zepa plus the continued shelling of Sarajevo appalled the international community, which now began calling for some decisive action. On August 30, NATO demanded that the Bosnian Serbs pull back their artillery from around Sarajevo.

When General Mladic refused, NATO launched air strikes against Bosnian Serb command posts, ammunition dumps and radar sites. NATO continued its bombing

until September 2, then gave the Bosnian Serbs until September 4 to begin removing their artillery. Mladic again refused, whereupon the air strikes were resumed on September 6. The bombing continued for another two weeks before the Bosnia Serbs relented and began removing their heavy weapons from the vicinity of Sarajevo.

At least three brigades of Croatian army troops entered Bosnia in early September. Operating in conjunction with Bosnian Croat and Muslim forces, they launched

an offensive that gradually reduced the amount of land held by Bosnian Serbs from 70% to about 50%.

Meanwhile, things were beginning to happen on the diplomatic front. The first breakthrough occurred on August 29, 1995, when Karadzic agreed that President Milosevic was empowered to negotiate on behalf of the Bosnian Serbs. Next, the U.S. government invited the foreign ministers of Serbia, Bosnia and Croatia to a meeting in Geneva. On September 8, the three foreign ministers agreed to a statement of principles for peace in Bosnia. This, in turn, paved the way for the Dayton peace talks, which resulted in an accord signed by the presidents of the three republics on November 21, 1995. Estimates of the toll of the devastating three and one-half-year war vary from about 100,000 (according to the Sarajevo-based Research and Documentation Center) to a quarter million killed; of those, about 66% were Bosnjaks, 26% ethnic Serbs and 8% ethnic Croats; 1.8 million were uprooted.

The agreement provided for the division of Bosnia between a Bosnian Serb entity and a Bosnian-Croat federation. The two sub-entities were to have their own presidents and their own legislatures. But there would still be a central government with a group presidency, a two-house legislature, a court and a central bank.

The agreement also called for a NATO force of 60,000 members to keep the peace;

A Bosnian Serb soldier holds a refugee child   AP/Wide World Photo

453

Bosnia-Herzegovina

A chat in a Mostar cemetery

it began arriving at the end of the year. The various opposing forces then withdrew to agreed positions and the situation began to stabilize. However, it was only a truce, not reconciliation. When the Serb-occupied suburbs of Sarajevo were turned over to Bosnian government control in March 1996, almost all Serbs fled, but not before dismantling and taking whatever was transportable and burning or dynamiting anything that remained, including houses, public buildings and factories.

This attitude persisted during the run up to internationally monitored elections that took place on September 14, 1996. The Dayton Accords had specified that individuals were to be permitted to return to their previous place of residence to vote. Those—mostly Muslims—who tried to do this were turned back from both the Serb and Croat controlled areas. The elections also reflected this division, with people in each area permitted to vote only for candidates representing the dominant national grouping.

The same men whose followers had fought a bitter four-year war won the open positions on the three-person collective presidency. Thus the new collective presidency consisted of Alija Izetbegovic, leader of the Muslim Party of Democratic Action; Kresimir Zubak (later replaced by Ante Jelavic), leader of the Croat Democratic Community; and Momcilo Krajisnik, head of the Serbian Democratic Party.

The three-member presidency formally took office in October but Krajisnik boycotted the ceremony because he was un-

willing to take an oath of allegiance to Bosnia. The two-chamber legislature, also scheduled to meet in October, did not finally become organized until January 1997, again because of Serb objections to taking an oath of allegiance to Bosnia and to meeting in Sarajevo.

The inaugural session finally took place in the Serb-controlled town of Lukavica. Here a new council of ministers was named, with Muslim and Serb co-chairs: Haris Silajdzic, representing the Muslim-Croat Federation, and Boro Bosic, representing the Republic of Serbia. Silajdzic characterized the creation of the joint institutions for Bosnia as being "the victory of democracy over dictatorship" and spoke optimistically of "the reintegration of Bosnia-Herzegovina with Europe." Others at the ceremonies were not nearly as optimistic.

Bosnia as an International "Protectorate"

The collective presidency for all of Bosnia held its first meeting on September 30, 1996. The session had to be held in a hotel at the edge of Sarajevo because Krajisnik, the Serb member, refused to meet in a government building downtown, citing security concerns. He then did not show up to take a formal oath of office in October because he was unwilling to swear allegiance to a united Bosnia. The newly elected national legislature, scheduled to meet for its first session in October, was postponed for the same reason. It finally met in January 1997 after it was agreed to dispense with the oath. As these

events made clear, the international community could create joint institutions, but it could not force cooperation among the still quarreling factions, even with the offer of large amounts of foreign assistance.

As a result, the six nations that oversaw the Bosnian peace effort—the United States, France, Germany, Italy, Great Britain, and Russia—decided in December 1997 to authorize a high representative to make decisions on behalf of Bosnia whenever the divided Bosnian government was unable to do so. He stepped in to resolve issues such as media licensing, housing and tariff laws. When the joint legislature found itself deadlocked on issues such as a common license plate, passport, currency, flag, and national emblem, the high representative made the selections for the Bosnians.

It was also his office that was responsible for the creation of a new currency. As a preliminary step, the German mark was accepted in 1997. On June 22, 1998, the Bosnian government began issuing a new currency, the marka, whose value was equal to one German mark. The marka began circulating almost immediately in the area of the Croat and Muslim Federation, but it was ignored in the Bosnian Serb area. Its value is now pegged to the euro. Bosnia-Herzegovina received the former Yugoslav embassy in London when the diplomatic buildings were parceled out among the parts of the former federation in December 2001.

Whenever Bosnian elected officials attempted to obstruct the Dayton Accords, the high representative did not hesitate to dismiss them. There thus exists a sort of international protectorate over Bosnia whose goal is to create a situation where separatism and particularism will be harder and harder to maintain. This has proved to be an extremely difficult task.

The goal of the high representative's office is to create the circumstances whereby as many as possible of the 2.2 million displaced persons and refugees could return to their former homes, as stipulated in the Dayton Accords. About 1.2 million fled abroad while 1.2 million were displaced within Bosnia. A start was made in 1997 when top officials in the Muslim and Croat federation agreed to allow 120,000 refugees to return to 156 villages in central Bosnia under the control of the other nationality. This was surprisingly successful.

In 2004 the one-millionth Bosnian refugee had returned home. A year later half of them had returned to their prewar homes where they are a minority. Some of them have sold their reclaimed properties. Over 90% of claims by lawful owners to get their property back have been settled. Not all returnees go back to where they originally came from. Only 400,000 are known to be still waiting to go home, and

Bosnia-Herzegovina

A column of Bosnian policemen, Sarajevo   AP/Wide World Photo

the number of returnees is tailing off. Some will never return. Many former Serb residents of Sarajevo are wary of returning. Elderly Bosnians are particularly inclined to go back to their earlier homes to finish out their years where they had always lived. Because of the lack of jobs, younger Bosnians go either to Sarajevo or abroad if they can. A 2004 survey by the UN Development Program revealed that more than half of young people would leave Bosnia if given a chance. Legal changes across Bosnia provide more protection for minorities and more input into local government.

There has been much rebuilding in formerly ethnically cleansed areas, and most infrastructure has been rebuilt. Some of it was financed by foreign sources including the Arab world. Saudi Arabia spent over $500,000 on religious and humanitarian projects, in part in order to spread its rigid interpretation of Islam in a country where most Muslims are not conspicuously pious. Some Western efforts to rebuild mosques in Serb cities, such as Banja Luka, in order to reintegrate Bosnian Muslims driven out during the war and reestablish Islamic religious life led to riots sparked by Serb nationalists. In September 2002 saboteurs blew up a mosque there only three months after it was reopened. Four years later a

beautiful new mosque was serving the needs of Muslims in Banja Luka.

Such violence, which is much diminished, merely underscored how hard it is to diminish the extreme nationalism that separates Bosnia's ethnic groups. But there have been signs of progress. The main Bosnian Serb party, the Serb Democratic Party (SDS), says it has abandoned its dreams of a "Greater Serbia," and the leading Croat party, the Croatian Democratic Union (HDZ) has also given up its earlier hopes for union with Croatia.

Military Forces

Neither Croatia nor Serbia poses a military threat to Bosnia. Bosnia's armies have therefore been reduced to small numbers, as have the foreign peacekeepers in the country. In 2005 the U.S. maintained only 150 troops in Bosnia to help local authorities adopt defense reforms and hunt down war crime suspects. Even such a symbolic presence was important because the local populations regard the United States as the ultimate key to maintaining stability and order in the country. By 2007 all 150 had been withdrawn. In 2003 Bosnia became the first country in the Balkans to ratify a deal with the U.S. exempting Americans on its soil from prosecution in the newly created International Criminal Court.

About a thousand Russian peacekeepers served under American command and, because of the historically close ties between Serbs and Russians, were able to achieve some compromises from Bosnian Serbs that other nationalities could not. In addition to soldiers from most NATO countries, there were peacekeepers from such far-flung countries as Morocco, the Baltic states and Albania. The result of the peacekeepers' presence was enforced peace for the local population and for the foreign troops. In the four years of warfare before the Dayton Accords, more than a thousand UN peacekeepers had been killed or wounded in Bosnia; after Dayton there was not a single U.S. or NATO casualty from hostile action.

On December 2, 2004, in "Operation Althea," the EU took over the NATO-led mission, renaming it EUFOR. SFOR ceased to exist. It already commanded the 300-strong peacekeeping force in Macedonia, as well as the police mission in Bosnia once run by the UN. But NATO continues to work with the EU in Bosnia. It provides planning and assets, as well as reserve forces, if there should be an upsurge of ethnic violence, which by 2005 was no longer expected. Both have the authority to arrest alleged war criminals. NATO maintains a small mission in Sarajevo led by an American general to assist with defense reforms, counterterrorism and war criminals. It shares a headquarters building and facilities with EUFOR.

In the transfer of command to the EU, the American troops were replaced by Finns. Nevertheless, about 80% of EUFOR's 7,000 troops previously served in the NATO force. They simply switched their badges. They are a lighter-weight force. The deployment of EUFOR was merely one part of an overall strategy to stabilize the Balkans. NATO's departure signified the end of Bosnia's "postwar" era and the beginning of a more conventional "political and economic transition." It underscores European and American confidence that peace is irreversibly secured. By 2010, only a couple of hundred EU troops and 11 American soldiers remained, down from 2,500 the year before.

A defense committee attached to the central government provides some coordination for funding to the two separate armies that exist. Since 2002 the United States refuses to provide military assistance to the armies in Bosnia unless such help goes through the defense committee and therefore funds projects in which all three groups participate and cooperate with each other.

When the Dayton Accords were signed in 1995, the two political entities kept the armed forces they had at the time and had to accept an arms-limitation regime. Some

Bosnia-Herzegovina

Party activists drumming up votes in Sarajevo, 2006

people referred to "two and one-half armies" since Bosnian Croats maintained most forces separate from their joint army with the Bosnjaks.

The defense law calls for joint institutions at the level of Defense Ministry and general staff. In order to satisfy the conditions for joining NATO's Partnership for Peace (PfP), Bosnian Serb, Croat and Bosnjak leaders agreed in 2003 to a joint command of their armed forces. Bosnia now has a state defense minister and general staff to command the two armies. They also agreed in 2004 to reduce their combined number of active soldiers from 19,800 to 11,100 in 2010. In addition to a unified military command that is now in place, they are facing the daunting task of unifying the complex networks of their intelligence services. Separate armies have been abolished, and the process of integration is well underway. Bosnia deployed 36 soldiers to Iraq, 10 to Afghanistan and 7 to Kosovo. At the end of its Riga summit in 2006, NATO formally invited Bosnia to join its PfP program.

POLITICAL SYSTEM

The government of the state of Bosnia-Herzegovina (BiH) was remade as a part of the Dayton Accords. It called for the creation of a Bosnian government composed of two entities: the Federation of Bosnia and Herzegovina (which includes both Bosnjaks and Croats and is usually referred to simply as "the Federation") and the Republika Srpska (RS—Republic of the Serbs). These two entities divided the territory of Bosnia on a 51%–49% basis. Each has a high degree of autonomy,

its own rules, its own complete administration, its own army, and its own customs and tax regimes. In 2004 the central state began collecting customs duties. In 2005 it began collecting a value-added tax of 17% in an attempt to bring a lot of the underground economy into the open.

Together, they elect a Bosnian government with its own three-person presidency, composed of a Bosnian Serb, a Bosnian Croat and a Bosnjak. After the October 2006 elections, they were Haris Silajdzic (Bosnjak), Zeliko Komsic (Croat) and Nebojsa Radmanovic (Serb). Since 2002 each serves a four-year term and can be re-elected. The chair of the presidency rotates every eight months. This is mostly a ceremonial role except for control of the small armed forces. They have proven that they can sometimes cooperate constructively.

There is a two-chamber legislature. The lower house is the House of Representatives. The upper is the House of the Peoples; two-thirds of its members are elected from the Federation and one-third from the RS. A valid majority must include the support of at least one-third of the members representing each entity. The national government is the Council of Ministers. One of the 10 ministers is chosen as prime minister. Since January 2007 he is Nikola Spiric, a Serb. The prime minister serves four years, and the position no longer rotates on an eight-month basis. His powers are limited. For example, the earlier prime minister, Adnam Terzik, fired Bosnia's Foreign Minister Mladen Ivanic in June 2005, but the latter simply refused to go.

There is a self-governing district, Brcko, under the sovereignty of the central state government and under international su-

pervision. It belongs to neither of Bosnia's two entities. This city controls the narrow passage between the eastern and western parts of Bosnia and had been run by the Serbs. It became a neutral district jointly administered by Serbs, Croats and Muslims. It had a majority Muslim population prior to the beginning of the Bosnian war. It is Bosnia's only truly multiethnic city and one of the few cities in Bosnia where the three main ethnic groups work and attend school together. In March 2009 all three sides endorsed a deal over its future.

The center has its own court and central bank. In addition to these central institutions, the federation and RS have their own elected parliaments, presidents and prime ministers. Each of 10 cantons has its own powerful assembly and local government. International authorities supervise elections at all levels. There is considerable frustration in dealing with the many levels of administration and overlapping jurisdictions.

In an attempt to create a more efficient and stronger state, the U.S. and its European partners convened a meeting in Washington of the nine top Serbian, Muslim and Croatian leaders from Bosnia. Under intense American and European pressure, the nine signed a Commitment to Pursue Constitutional Reform aiming at a constitution that would have only one president. The package failed to win the necessary two-thirds support in parliament. This disappointing failure left both the EU and U.S. without a clear plan for strengthening the political system to ensure that Bosnians are ready for self-rule. The reform agenda is in bad shape.

The Bosnjak-Croat Federation, which is supposed to control 51% of Bosnia, is still in some ways a fiction. Power is concentrated in the two separate Croat and Bosnjak entities. In particular, Herzog-Bosna, the Croatian half of the federation—which according to the terms of the Dayton Accords was supposed to have been disbanded in January 1996—continued to exist. For a while it operated in some manner as an integral part of the Republic of Croatia. Croatian currency, stamps, uniforms, telephone area code rates, and even customs levies were used throughout Herzog-Bosna. Bosnian Croats were permitted to vote in parliamentary elections in the Republic of Croatia.

They now receive less support and encouragement from the more democratic Croatian governments that took office after Franjo Tudjman died in 1999. They can have automatic citizenship in the more prosperous Croatia, and many, especially the young, take it and move there, leaving only about half of Bosnia's prewar Croat population of about 830,000 behind. Croatia's leaders made a strategic decision that

Bosnia-Herzegovina

Reconstructed bridge at Mostar. Muslim side on left and Croat side on right

accession to the EU is more important than Greater Croatia. Croatia's president, Ivo Jasipovic, appeared in the Bosnian parliament in April 2010 and apologized for Croatia's role in the Bosnian war. He said he was "deeply sorry" that his country had "contributed to the suffering of people and divisions which still burden us today." Serbian leaders have made a similar decision by renouncing Greater Serbia. Bosnia's borders are no longer contested.

Bosnian-Croat connections with the Bosnjak half of the federation are improving, but they remain limited. One symbol intended to heal the rupture is the bridge at Mostar, destroyed in the fighting in November 1993. It was renamed "New-Old Bridge" and reopened with much fanfare in July 2004. It was carefully reconstructed with funds from the World Bank and other donors in the identical style using the same methods and materials employed by Turkish architects five centuries ago. It remains to be seen whether this historical treasure will ultimately bring together Croats, who make up about 60% of the population, and Bosnjaks (approximately 40%) in the city of 100,000 that is the only truly mixed Bosnian city. In the meantime they live on separate sides of the bridge and do not interact much. The schools are divided on strictly ethnic lines.

The tense October 2006 elections for the central parliament and the three-man presidency demonstrated once again the deep ethnic divisions that persist. Bosnjak and Croat voters elected leaders who want to unify the country and take it into the EU. Nevertheless, some Bosnian Croat leaders have said that if the division in two states continues, they would request a third state for Croats.

Bosnian Serbs overwhelmingly backed Milorad Dodik, their prime minister, who harvested many votes by suggesting that he might organize a referendum to demand independence; he often repeats this threat. He has argued that if Montenegro and Kosovo can break away from Serbia, then his state can sever from Bosnia. Bosnian Serbs seem as resolved as ever that they should preserve their separate identity and withhold their loyalty from the unified state even though the constitution does not permit secession. They refuse to let go of their own police force, and that was the chief obstacle to beginning accession talks with the EU. Finally the intransigent leaders accepted a watered-down version of police reform in June 2008.

In return, the EU's stabilization and association agreement with Bosnia, which began the process toward membership, went into effect. The EU is about the only thing all sides agree upon. Sarajevo publisher, Damir Uzunovic, remarked: "We will be the last country in the region to join the EU because they can't do anything else with us." But Carl Bildt, foreign minister of the EU presidency country, Sweden, said in July 2009 that Bosnia's politicians must recognized that their interminable disputes are causing them to fall behind their neighbors on the path to the EU. For example, they were excluded from a decision to offer some Balkan countries visa-free travel to most EU states.

To enact the reforms the people and the EU need, the Muslim leader in the three-headed presidency, Haris Silajdzic, argues for a more centralized state. For example, such a strong government could complete the country's part of a 210-mile super-highway linking Budapest to the Adriatic Sea. As it is, local bickering has prevented all but a 12-mile stretch from being completed inside Bosnia. Milorad Dodik absolutely rejects such a powerful center and threatens to secede unless the RS is left free to be run as a quasi-sovereign state. He emphasizes: "Bosnia is divided, not just on the surface, but essentially." To underscore such autonomy, his government announced plans to open offices in European capitals and Washington. Silajdzic counters by condemning the Dodik's RS as a "genocidal" creation that must be scrapped.

Ethnic tensions continue in all aspects of life, and a maze of rival ethnically controlled bureaucracies are rife with corruption. Real power is often exercised behind closed doors far from the democratic process and public scrutiny. As long as administrative structures are weak, elections can do little to foster responsible government. Political stalemate will probably leave the country underdeveloped. The only good news is that few experts believe there will be large-scale violence.

Office of the High Representative
The entire political system has since Dayton been overseen by the UN high representative, who is always a European. Paddy Ashdown of the UK was a powerful activist in this post. In 2004, he fired six Serb police officers and three other officials for failing to arrest war crimes suspects. This was backed by the U.S. government, which froze the assets of the Serb Democratic Party and forbade its leaders from entering the United States. Subsequent to that crackdown, the Bosnian Serb government rendered seven Bosnian Serb indictees to The Hague. In 2005 he sacked the Croat in the tripartite presidency, Dragan Covic, for refusing to resign in the face of serious corruption charges.

Ashdown was again at loggerheads with the RS government in June 2005 when it rejected plans to reform the police, a key EU demand before it can open accession talks. The divided country has 15 police forces that cooperate with each other only voluntarily. Reform is essential because each is under the control of old

Bosnia-Herzegovina

U.S. soldiers would stay in Bosnia-Herzegovina (until 2008)

ity for military and civilian administration. This could leave civilian authorities powerless in the face of violence, but the possibility of such violence has diminished considerably. Few people expect a renewal of international or ethnic hostilities.

Both Europeans and Americans had hoped that this position could be phased out and that the European Commission could open a mission in the country and oversee its transformation in a less imperial way. Ashdown was criticized for his assertive style. A 2005 report on the Balkans spearheaded by former Italian Prime Minister Giuliano Amato concluded that "the powers and activities of the high representative. . . have blocked the development of self-government," adding that the post had "outlived its usefulness." "There is a danger that it . . . takes up so much oxygen that elements of civil society could be stunted." Most expert observers agree.

Ashdown's replacement, Christian Schwarz-Schilling, a German politician with deep experience in Bosnia, announced in 2006 that he would be the last high representative and that the UN-mandated post would be abolished in June 2007. He promised in the meantime to use its powers only if there is a threat to peace or in dealing with war-crimes suspects. He offered to apply kinder and gentler forms of persuasion.

However, real authority was not transferred to elected authorities. After a year of no progress toward state restructuring and inter-ethnic integration, the sixth High Representative was sent to Bosnia in July 2007: Slovak diplomat, Miroslav Lajcak. His mandate to overrule national authorities was to last only until June 2008. But he displayed determination to keep the government functioning. When the Bosnian Serb president hindered the central government from making necessary decisions by refusing to have his ministers attend sessions, Lajcak allowed the government to make decisions even when some ministers are absent. Dodik was furious. Not surprisingly, Lajcak was vilified by the Serb and Bosnian Serb news media.

When Lajcak became Slovak foreign minister in January 2009, he was replaced by Valentine Inzko, an Austrian diplomat with Slovene origins. He is the fourth man sent to be the last in his job. His office stayed open until the end of 2009. After that, Inzko was instructed to remain only in his much weaker capacity as the EU's special representative, with no legal powers. With only about 200 EU troops and 11 U.S. soldiers remaining, there is little muscle behind him.

The High Representative has been so demeaned that none of the parties, especially the Bosnian Serbs, pay any attention to his efforts. To find a way out of this

political cliques, and it will take a long time to change that. Ashdown called this the "nexus of politics, crime and the police." The Bosnian Serb government objects to any reform that would strip it of control of its own police.

In this lamentable situation the UN high representative became the central legislative power. He could unseat elected officials and impose legislation directly if the fractious parliamentarians could not act. This is a role the UN had never wanted to play. Originally the high representative was supposed only to promote compliance with the Dayton Accords. But he exercised near dictatorial power. Polls indicated that Ashdown was twice as popular with voters as even the favorite Bosnian politicians.

If Bosnian officials did not make changes he thought necessary, then he made them himself. If the Bosnians did it, the EU regarded it as a plus for the country. If Ashdown had to do it, it was a minus. For instance, he threatened to fire Bosnian Serb leaders in 2004 if they failed to recognize the evidence and admit to responsibility for the Srebrenica massacre in 1995. They did it. Now they try harder to find and apprehend indicted war criminals.

The high representative has no formal authority over the many international agencies involved in the transition; 55 of them are organized in the Peace Implementation Council (PIC), which oversees international strategy in Bosnia. NATO, the EU, and the UN have separate responsibil-

Bosnia-Herzegovina

Bosnjak student (right) with her French classmate at the College of Europe.

mess, the EU and U.S. launched a diplomatic effort in October 2009, part of what is called the "Butmir process," to discuss the future of the office. The EU wants to shut it down, but American diplomats worry that Bosnia could fall apart without foreign supervision. The effort failed. No consensus was reached, and the office of the High Representative was not closed.

The UN Tribunal for War Crimes

"Ethnic cleansing" was a Serb policy practiced from the beginning of the war. In areas under their control, the Serbs systematically destroyed mosques and, less systematically, Roman Catholic churches. They also either destroyed or seized the homes of Muslims and Catholics, forcing them to flee these areas. Some 750,000 Muslims plus a smaller number of Catholic Croats were forced out of these areas. Large numbers of non-Serbs were also arrested and put in concentration camps. Muslim women were systematically raped, either in their homes or after they had been detained. Such atrocities occurred particularly during the first year of the war while the Serbs were consolidating control over the 70% of the country they controlled until the Dayton Accords.

The reports of such atrocities were so widespread and well documented that the United Nations decided to set up a war crimes tribunal. The International Criminal Tribunal for the former Yugoslavia, established at The Hague, began operating in 1994.

Of all the evidence it collected, some of the most important came from a Serb defector, Cedomirt Mihailovic, a former member of the Serb secret police. The documents include a directive from Serbian state security services in Belgrade concerning the running of concentration camps in Bosnia. This refuted Serbian government assertions that it was not directly involved in the war.

Another document, also from Serbian state security services, gave explicit instructions to the Serbian paramilitary commander known as Arkan (later assassinated in Belgrade). It concerned the eviction and killing of Muslims in the Bosnian town of Bijeljina, which was cleansed of Muslims at the beginning of the war. In 1995, Richard Goldstone, chief prosecutor for The Hague tribunal, named Radovan Karadzic, leader of the Bosnian Serbs, and Ratko Mladic, commander of the Bosnian Serb army, as suspected war criminals. Indictments were returned against them in July 1995. A number of other indictments were issued.

In 2002 NATO troops tried and failed to capture Karadzic. They missed catching him in Pale by only two hours in January 2004. The intensification of NATO's efforts to apprehend war criminals reportedly drove Karadzic, Mladic and others into hiding in Serbia. A disguised Karadzic was finally caught in Belgrade in July 2008 and sent to The Hague for trial.

The search for alleged war criminals was also seen as necessary to bring "balance" after U.S. troops seized six Arabs in Sarajevo in January 2002 on charges of plotting to attack the U.S. embassy and other American facilities in Bosnia; all six had close ties with al Qaeda. Two Bosnian court orders had forbidden that the men be turned over to the Americans, but the government, pressured by the U.S. embassy, permitted it anyway.

In 2002 U.S. troops arrested a Bosnian Muslim suspected of having links to al Qaeda for spying on an American base. During the war from 1992–95, Bosnia had been a magnet for foreign Muslims wanting to fight for Islam. In July 2007 the former wartime army chief of staff, Rasim Delic, went on trial in The Hague for failing to prevent beheadings, rapes and other war crimes by "El Mujahid," a unit of mostly Arab Islamic volunteers. Many mujaheddin, or holy warriors, were expelled, but some remained, married Bosnian women, and received citizenship and passports as an expression of gratitude. In 2007 the citizenship of hundreds of them was revoked in response to a request by the U.S.

Foreign intelligence agencies have long warned that Islamic militants were organizing themselves in the area between the cities of Zenica, Tuzla, Sarajevo and Travnik in order to use Bosnia as a launching pad for terrorist attacks in Europe. Police say that they hide explosives in lemons and tennis balls and seek to establish training camps in the hills near Sarajevo. A joint US-Croatian intelligence report in 2006 claimed that so-called "white Muslim" terrorists are being recruited in Bosnia. These fighters with European features would be able to infiltrate Western European cities and targets more easily than Middle Eastern Muslims.

In 2007 and 2008 the Bosnian government conducted a broad review of foreign-born residents who had come during the 1992–95 war, married local women and remained despite repeated calls by the U.S. and international organizations for their deportation. About 70% of them are of Arab or South Asian origin. The Dayton peace accord requires all combatants "not of local origin" to withdraw, but hundreds ignored that. In 2007 the government "denationalized" at least 500 people, and deportations began while others left on their own. In February 2010 about 600 police raided Gornja Moaca, a village of Muslim hardliners in the northeast of the country. It sheltered foreign-born Mujahideen war veterans who the authorities suspected of spreading religious hatred.

Bosnia's war left a spiritual legacy. There is a resurgence of Muslim piety, and more women cover themselves in a Muslim way of dress. Mosques are full. Sarajevo presents a more pronounced Muslim face to the world.

By 1999, four cases had been completed and three more were under way. In addition, there were 26 prisoners awaiting trial in the tribunal's detention center near The Hague. They included two generals, Radoslav Kristic, a Bosnian Serb army commander, and Tihomir Blaskic, commander of the Croat forces in southern Bosnia between 1992 and 1994. In July 1999, Radislav Brdanin, a member of the Bosnian

Bosnia-Herzegovina

Convertible Mark, Bosnia's currency

Serb parliament, was arrested, while Talic, another Serb general, was arrested in August while on a visit to Vienna.

The case against the Croat general, Tihomir Blaskic, was concluded in March 2000. At first found guilty of ordering a series of attacks on Muslim villagers in Bosnia while his forces were attempting to secure the area for Croatia, Blaskic was sentenced to 45 years in prison. Four years later his sentence was radically reduced on appeal to nine years after most of the convictions against him were dropped. Even more significant, the decision indirectly indicted the government of Croatia. "The Republic of Croatia did not content itself with merely remaining a spectator on the sidelines or even seek simply to protect its borders," the court ruled. "It intervened in the conflict, pitting Muslims and Croats of central Bosnia against each other."

A steady stream of indictments and convictions followed in 2001. Krstic was convicted of genocide at the "safe haven" of Srebrenica and sentenced to 46 years in prison. This was the tribunal's first conviction of genocide. In 2004 the tribunal confirmed its judgment that what happened during the war in Bosnia was genocide. The judge told five more Bosnian Serbs who were convicted of war crimes, "you participated in this hellish orgy of persecution." In July 2009 two Bosnian Serb cousins, Milan and Sredoje Lukic, were sentenced for war crimes including locking Muslims in two houses and burning them alive, killing at least 119.

Indictments were also brought against high-ranking Muslims for war crimes. Minister for Refugees Sefer Halilovic gave himself up to the tribunal to face charges of having commanded Muslim soldiers who murdered villagers and dumped their bodies in the Neretva River. He was acquitted. In 2006 two Muslim army commanders—Enver Hadzihasanovic and Amir Kubura—were convicted at The Hague for failing to restrain foreign Mus-

lim volunteers who murdered Bosnian Croats and Serbs. In 2008 former commander Rasim Delic was sentenced to three years for failing to prevent atrocities committed by foreign Islamist fighters against captured Serb soldiers.

In February 2003 Biljana Plavsic, known earlier as the "Iron Lady" for her ruthless leadership and virulent nationalism and anti-Muslim utterances, was sentenced to 11 years despite her expression of remorse and the fact that former U.S. Secretary of State Madeleine Albright had testified that Plavsic had been instrumental in carrying out a peace plan. The only woman indicted

for war crimes, she said she had been driven by "blinding fear" that Serbs would be victims, but instead had become "victimizers" in their defensive zeal. After the war she had undergone a pragmatic conversion. While serving a war crimes sentence in a Swedish prison, she published a book about the Bosnian war. She was released early in October 2009.

In April a Muslim commander who had tried to defend Srebrenica and who is therefore a hero among many Bosnian Muslims, Nasser Oric, was delivered to the war crimes tribunal on charges of atrocities against Bosnian Serbs. In July 2006 he was found guilty of failing to prevent the murder and torture of Serb captives and sentenced to two years time served. He was immediately released and got a hero's welcome when he returned to Sarajevo.

He was one of seven Muslims indicted. Even former Bosnjak leader Alija Izetbegovic was being investigated for war crimes by the tribunal when he died in October 2003, a hero in his land. A Bosnian Serb commander, Momir Nikolic, pled guilty to the massacre of up to 8,000 Muslim men and boys at Srebrenica and became the first former Bosnian Serb officer to agree to provide testimony. Mass graves continue to be found in Bosnia. In 2004 Bosnian Serb government officials admitted their people's culpability for the

Srebrenica lives on, 2006

460

massacre. Nevertheless, in June 2004 High Representative Ashdown dismissed 60 leading Bosnian Serb politicians, including the parliamentary speaker, interior minister, police, mayors and members of parliament, for failing to arrest Radovan Karadzic. He also froze the bank accounts of the main Bosnian Serb party.

In 2003 Bosnian Serb General Stanislav Galic was sentenced to 20 years for ordering his troops to fire on civilians going about their daily lives during the 44-month siege in Sarajevo. His forces dug into the surrounding hills and rained sniper and artillery fire down on pedestrians, buses, streetcars, funerals, market places and soccer fields killing 10,500 people (including 1,800 children) and wounding 50,000 more. In June 2007 a major catch was made: Zdravko Tolimir, one of the main suspects in the Srebrenica massacre.

A special court was created in Sarajevo in March 2005 that took over cases from the UN war crimes tribunal and is monitored by that body. It was initially staffed mainly by international prosecutors and judges, and their Bosnian counterparts gradually took over. Bosnia was the first country in the region entrusted with trying such cases independently.

Not until June 2004 did a Bosnian Serb government commission admit that Bosnian Serb forces were responsible for the Srebrenica massacre. This was followed in November by an official Bosnian Serb government apology after reviewing the commission's findings. It added a commitment to arrest those responsible for the atrocities. In March 2005 the Bosnian Serb government launched a publicity campaign urging citizens to help it track down war crimes fugitives. It brought the blunt message: "Either they go to The Hague or we go to hell." A month later Bosnian Serb authorities announced that they were investigating nearly 900 officials of their own government to determine whether they might have had a role in the massacre.

For those who still had doubts about the Srebrenica massacre, a video was shown on Serbian television in June 2005 that had been provided by the War Crimes Tribunal prosecution in The Hague. It was the first graphic portrayal of what happened in Srebrenica in 1995. It begins with a Serb Orthodox priest blessing camouflaged paramilitary troops called Scorpions. Later troops are shown taking six young men out of a truck and killing them at close range. In the video, shot by a Scorpion, one can clearly hear the troops insulting the scared Muslims. Nine faces of suspects could be recognized. Only a month earlier an opinion poll in Serbia had revealed that over half of Serb respondents did not believe the Srebrenica massacre had ever occurred.

The video revived bitter wartime memories of Serbs executing Muslims. Ten former members of the elite Scorpions were immediately arrested for the crimes, and five were arraigned on murder charges at the end of 2005. Their trial began in February 2006. In the first trial inside Serbia that involved the Srebrenica massacres, four were convicted and jailed in April 2007.

In February 2007 the Hague court ruled that Serbia was not responsible for genocide in Bosnia because it had not aimed to "destroy in whole or in part the Bosnian Muslim population." However, the court decided that Srebrenica was a genocidal event and that Serbia is to be blamed for failing to use its "known influence" to stop it. Bosnia had brought this charge in 1993 and was disappointed that Serbia is not required to pay it reparations. Although Serbia escaped being labeled a genocidal country and having to pay billions of euros in claims, Bosnia did obtain what it called "a recognition of Serbia's guilt."

Some Bosnjaks responded to the ruling by demanding special status that would separate Srebrenica from the Bosnian Serb area. Bosnian Serb Prime Minister Milorad Dodik rejected this. But he designated the town of 10,000, in which Muslims are now a minority, a "region of economic and social concern" and ordered enhanced infrastructure investment that might lure some former residents back.

Dodik had already signaled sensitivity to this massacre by attending the 2003 memorial service for the approximately 8,000 victims of the Srebrenica massacre in 1995. He spoke of "respect for the dead" and reconciliation and peace. Local Bosnian Serb police provided security for the commemoration, attended also by former President Bill Clinton. Shortly thereafter the federal president of Serbia and Montenegro, Svetozar Marovic (a Montenegrin) offered a landmark apology to Bosnia for the 1992–95 war, followed in 2004 by Bosnian Serb government apologies. Such utterances would have been inconceivable only a few years earlier.

After the Hague ruling, survivors of the Srebrenica crime filed a lawsuit against the UN and the Dutch government. The latter had already accepted "political responsibility" for the UN mission's failure to protect Muslims and donates about $20 million in aid to Bosnia each year. One third of that sum is reserved for projects related to rebuilding Srebrenica.

In an effort to win favor from the EU and to improve its relationship with its neighbors, the Serbian parliament in March 2010 narrowly passed (with 127 of 250 votes) a resolution condemning the July 1995 Srebrenica massacre. The word "genocide" could not be used because it was rejected by the reformed Socialist Party (formerly Milosevic's), on whose votes the Serbian government depends. Also most Serbs do not believe the war had been one of genocide. Instead the carnage was called a "crime." It offered "condolences and apology to the families of victims because not enough was done to prevent the tragedy." It committed Serbia to Bosnia's territorial integrity. Following the 2007 Hague ruling, it did not accept blame for the killings. However, the resolution makes it impossible for Serbs to pretend that the massacre never happened or that the number of dead had been grossly exaggerated.

Street scene in Sarajevo, 2003

Bosnia-Herzegovina

Karadzic, in disguise and as Bosnian Serb President

Source: *The Economist*

While on the run, Radovan Karadzic wrote a novel, *The Miraculous Chronicle of the Night*, a somewhat autobiographical tale set in Sarajevo in the 1980s. Born in Montenegro, Karadzic had moved to Sarajevo as a teenager. The hero is an engineer who, like Karadzic, was imprisoned when Tito died in 1980. It was a bestseller at Belgrade's international book fair and was on the short list for Serbia's top literary award, the Golden Sunflower, in 2004. It was his fourth publication after going into hiding. His other works include a children's book, a play and a selection of his poetry. The acclaim his books received reflected the near mythic status these nationalist figures still enjoy.

Under circumstances almost too bizarre to be true, Karadzic was arrested in Belgrade in July 2008 after 13 years on the run. The 63-year-old was disguised so thoroughly that he could move around Belgrade freely. He was sporting a huge bushy white beard, flowing grey hair with a black dyed spot on the top, and oversized horn-rimmed glasses. The trained psychiatrist, who did an internship at Columbia University in New York City, was living under the assumed name of Dr. Dragan Dabic, handing out business cards proclaiming himself as a "bioenergist," delivering lectures at conferences on alternative medicine, publishing articles in Serbia's *Healthy Living* magazine, counseling on Christian Orthodox spirituality and giving treatments for impotence and depression.

At The Hague he faces charges of 11 counts of genocide and crimes against humanity. Like Milosevic before him, he insisted on defending himself. He tried to rest his case on a fictitious promise of im-munity by U.S. negotiator Richard Holbrooke in 1996 if he would disappear from public life. Holbrooke vigorously denied the allegation, and the court rejected the motion.

After he had run out of stalling tactics, he launched his rambling defense in March 2010 by brushing aside the accusations against him as "myths." His was a "holy cause" that aimed to prevent Bosnian Muslims from establishing an Iran-type Islamic state and expelling all Christians. What happened at Sarajevo was not a siege at all, just a case of combatants fighting each other. He dismissed the massacre at Srebrenica as merely a case of people dying during four years of fighting. The notorious concentration camps were normal "investigation centers." The true victims were the Serbs.

Karadzic's arrest leaves only two key fugitives on the run: Goran Hadzic, who commanded Serb forces in Croatia, and Ratko Mladic, who led the Bosnian Serb army. In February 2010 Serb police raided the Belgrade home of the Mladic family and found a large cache of Swiss francs, euros and dollars that could be used to pay for his food and protection. They also found 18 of his diaries, comprising 3,500 handwritten pages, recounting in detail his activities in the war. War crimes prosecutors in The Hague asked that these diaries be admitted into evidence against Karadzic. The Serb government rejected the Mladic family's request that he be officially declared dead since he had not been seen in public since 2005.

Their chances of remaining free have been considerably reduced since a major political shift occurred in Serbia after the May 2008 elections. They put power into the hands of President Boris Tadic, who is determined to lead his country into the EU. Karadzic was arrested within two weeks of a change of guard in the Serb intelligence services.

ECONOMY

Prior to 1992, industry contributed just over half of the GDP. Bosnia-Herzegovina is still mainly agricultural. Herzegovina, with its warmer climate has traditionally specialized in semitropical crops like pomegranates, lemons, olives, rice and tobacco. Farther north, the chief crops are cereal grains and soybeans, supplemented by potatoes, melons, grapes, plums, mulberries and figs. Cattle, sheep, pigs, and poultry are raised throughout the republic.

Before the war, Bosnia-Herzegovina was a major manufacturer of military equipment. It also manufactured Volkswagen automobiles, and there was some textile manufacturing in the larger cities. The majority of its industry was extractive.

It produces coal, iron, copper, manganese, lead, mercury, bauxite and silver, as well as marble and building stone. Asphalt and lignite are found in the southern part of Herzegovina. Timber is another major industry.

Three and a half years of war left most of Bosnia-Herzegovina in ruins, particularly most of its cities. At the same time, much of the countryside was rendered unusable because of the millions of land mines scattered by the various factions. The economy has begun to revive somewhat, but much of this is associated more with money coming into the economy because of the presence of foreign troops plus international aid efforts rather than a domestic economic revival.

Bosnia received more than $14 billion in aid from 1996 and 2007. It came from 17 foreign governments, 18 UN agencies, 27 IGOs and 200 NGOs. The magnitude of aid it received can be seen in the fact that from 1995 to 2002, its per capita development aid was 246 euros ($320), compared with 23 euros for the south and east Mediterranean, 9 for Belarus, Ukraine and Moldova combined, and 4 for the former Soviet republics in Central Asia. This inpouring of funds helps explain the construction boom, but they have diminished drastically in recent years. The IMF granted it a standby credit of $1.5 billion in 2009.

Except for the expenses associated with the SFOR (replaced by EUFOR) and the cost of relief efforts, much of this aid has been funneled through the Bosnian government and its two "national" entities. A considerable portion of this was reportedly siphoned off to individuals through massive corruption. In 1999, for example, the antifraud unit of the Office of the High Representative publicly charged that up to $1 billion had disappeared from public funds or had been stolen from international aid projects and that this malfeasance had occurred as a result of fraud carried out by the various entities of the Bosnian government.

No one denies that corruption and cronyism are rampant in Bosnia. Another effect of all the foreign aid money pouring into the country has been to distort salary schedules throughout the economy. As an example, a driver for the United Nations earns $600 a month; a doctor at Sarajevo's Kosovo hospital is paid $300. The average monthly take-home wage in 2009 was 400 euros ($520). As a result, many professionals have abandoned their positions to take unrelated jobs that pay more money.

Official unemployment in 2009 stood at 44%, higher in the RS than in the Federation. However, the World Bank estimates that only 16%–20% have no work at all. The reason is that the thriving underground economy is probably worth more than 40% of GDP. Because of this "grey economy," which functions behind the backs of the tax authorities, Bosnia is a land of considerable hidden wealth. This provides grounds for greater confidence in the country's economic potential.

To try to bring some of that out into the open, it levied a uniform 17% VAT in July 2005. Bosnia is poorer than it was before the war. Until the global economic downturn in 2009, which has hurt Bosnia, GDP growth was healthy (5.4% in 2008); it

shrank by 4% in 2009 but rose by about .5% in 2010. Inflation fell from over 6% in 2000 to 1% in 2009; it remains low under a currency board system that pegs the convertible mark to the euro at rate of about 2:1.

About 20% live below the poverty line and another 30% just above it. Those figures would be even worse except for the fact that an estimated 250,000 Bosnians left the country for permanent settlement elsewhere, 170,000 through official resettlement programs. Remittances from Bosnians working abroad amounted to 23% of GDP, but they dipped during the recession, as did foreign direct investment. Unable to find work at home, thousands of young Bosnians continue to leave every year in search of a better life. Over half of the young want to emigrate, and three-fourths believe the economy is going downhill. It is the professionals who are most likely to leave. They seek their fortune abroad. Between 1998 and 2000 an estimated 30,000 university-age youths emigrated because of the dismal economic prospects; there are eight universities in the country. Politicians are widely considered to be corrupt, and organized crime is chronic.

The largest problem is that Bosnia has barely begun the transition from a centralized economy to a market-oriented one. In the Muslim-Croat Federation, only 1.4% of state-owned property has been privatized. The U.S. government was so frustrated at the lack of progress that it ended a major aid program aimed at easing the transition to a market economy. All over

Call to prayer. Muslim worshipers in Sarajevo

Bosnia, larger industry technically remains in state hands although nearly all of it is closed and has been that way since the beginning of the war.

Few international donors and investors see a future in reviving rusting industrial works. Foreign investment is discouraged by corruption, excessive red tape and the facts that ownership rights are unclear, contract law is difficult to enforce, and the courts are slow and inefficient. Although Western European investors see few tempting opportunities, Daimler-Chrysler announced in 2003 that in the following 10 years it will invest in the reconstruction of Bosnian industries, especially aluminum, electrical and mining operations. Retailers from neighboring Croatia and Slovenia have moved into the Bosnian market. But without more foreign capital, alternative sources of employment will be difficult to find outside the underground or illegal sector.

Another unresolved problem is that most industry was integrated before the war on a Yugoslavia-wide basis, with raw materials coming from other republics and finished products shipped to customers throughout the country. Not only have most of those links disappeared, but economic ties between the Muslim, Croatian and Serb parts of Bosnia have largely disappeared. They have been replaced by an integration of the Croatian and Serbian sectors into the economies of Croatia and Serbia.

Bosnia remains the poorest country in the region with the exception of Albania. Its GDP has still not reached its pre-war size. It carries a heavy debt load and has

Sarajevo City Hall, 1912

Bosnia-Herzegovina

a large trade deficit. This makes it difficult for the government to become creditworthy. Most Bosnians' everyday lives have not improved since the war. Sarajevo's wartime scars have largely disappeared, but one sees more war damage outside the city center.

Bosnians of all ethnic groups have been hurt by the world recession that struck in 2008–9. To try to cope with the economic turndown, the Muslim-Croat Federation has reined in state spending (which constitutes almost half of GDP) by cutting public salaries and veterans benefits by 10%. The latter cuts unleashed street clashes between police and veterans, who received $200 to $665 per month for their earlier military service. But today's crisis presents far less of a threat to the average citizen than did the bloody war in the 1990s. Few people speak today about a renewed outbreak of violence, and few diplomats expect it. For most Bosnians, it is economic worries and jobs that are most pressing. This is a good sign of progress.

CULTURE

One of the most important cultural elements in Bosnia-Herzegovina is that approximately 44% of the population is Muslim. Now called Bosnjak, they are a Slavic people who converted to Islam and speak Serbo-Croatian.

In the 10th century, a new religious sect arose in Bulgaria under the leadership of an Orthodox monk called Bogomil. Bogomilism, as it came to be called, spread through various parts of the Balkans and by the 12th century was well established in Bosnia. Kulin, the Bosnian leader, converted to Bogomilism and established it firmly throughout Bosnia, where it came to be known as the "Bosnian Church." Both the Roman Catholic and Orthodox churches eventually condemned it as a heresy.

Various attempts were made to stamp out this heresy beginning in the 13th century. However, the church still existed in the late 15th century when this area was overrun and incorporated into the Ottoman Empire. Most of the Bogomil aristocracy allied themselves with the Turks and assisted them in their conquest of the area. They converted to Islam, impelled by opportunistic motives and their hatred of the Roman Catholic Hungarians, who had waged religious war against them for the previous two centuries. Their descendants are the modern Bosnian Muslims who fought for their existence against efforts by Serbs in Bosnia and Serbia to wipe them out through a process of ethnic cleansing.

Bosnian Serbs are predominantly Orthodox Christian, while Bosnian Croats are largely Roman Catholic. In June 2003

The daily Sarajevo newspaper *Ljiljan* announces the withdrawal of British UN troops from the country via Tuzla airport, 1995

the pope made his second trip to Bosnia and celebrated mass for 45,000 pilgrims at the Petricevac monastery, which had been destroyed by Serb saboteurs in 1995. During the Second World War a Catholic priest from Petricevac, near Banja Luka, had led Croat fascists armed with knives and hatchets to a nearby village where they butchered 2,300 Serbs, including 500 women and children. The pontiff asked for God's forgiveness for "so much suffering and bloodshed" inflicted by Roman Catholics and others. He beatified Ivan Merz, a theologian in the early 1900s who would be Bosnia's first saint.

In 2006 an internationally acclaimed Bosnian film, *Grbavica*, won the Golden Bear Award (the top honor) at the Berlin International Film Festival. Directed by young Bosnian documentary filmmaker Jasmila Zbanic, it is an extraordinary movie about a Muslim medical student raped by a Serb during the Bosnian war. She gives birth to a girl. After it opened in Sarajevo, the Bosnian parliament voted to recognize raped women as war victims and give them financial assistance.

It is remarkable that the starring role of the mother was played by Mirjana Karanovic, Serbia's best-known film actress.

Until very recently it would have been unthinkable for a Serb to play the victim of Serbs in Bosnia. The film was shot in Sarajevo, a city that remains largely segregated. Serbs live outside the town in an area called "new Sarajevo," while Muslims dominate the city proper. Before the film opened in Belgrade, Karanovic predicted that it would be received peacefully. "We Serbs are in a crisis of spirit. We don't know who our heroes are and who are the villains."

FUTURE

Although the Dayton Accords brought an end to the fighting, they did not reunite the country. The follow-through the West had hoped would lead to sustainable peace, cooperation and economic recovery has not yet succeeded although some progress has been made. Most Serbs in Serbia and within Bosnia do not want to divide Bosnia and attach its Serb half with Serbia. However, the Bosnian Serb government and its leader, Milorad Dodik, often threaten to hold a referendum on independence, especially after Kosovo declared its independence from Serbia in February 2008.

Bosnia-Herzegovina

Poisonous ethnic tensions continue to pervade every sphere of life. Few anticipate a renewal of violence. But the Dayton structure is unwieldy and increasingly unworkable. It has resulted in a Byzantine system of government that produces endless blocking and gridlock among the community leaders. Progress is almost impossible.

Elections confirm that the leaders of the parties responsible for the war are still very much in charge in their respective enclaves. This includes the elections to be held in October 2010. Ethnic nationalism remains strong although the leaders on the top are sometimes able to cooperate with each other. Three nationalist political parties remain in power in separate ethnic enclaves. A top UN official lamented that creating normal government and life in Bosnia is "like trying to build a house where ashes are still burning."

The maintenance of a functioning government has depended to a considerable extent on a UN high representative who once wielded near dictatorial powers, but who is now often ignored. This office is to be replaced someday by a gentler EU representative in Sarajevo. In 2009 the seventh High Representative was appointed: Austrian diplomat Valentin Inzko. In the near future he should relinquish most of his power. American diplomats worry, and nobody knows what would follow.

In May 2009 Vice President Joe Biden stopped in Bosnia to warn against "the sharp and dangerous rise in nationalist rhetoric" and to assure the Bosnians that "we are back, we will stand with you." It is difficult to judge how much influence the U.S. will have; it has only 11 troops there, and the EU's military contingent has declined to about 200. Although it is not yet a "failed state," Bosnia is a center for the trafficking of narcotics and women. Organized crime is chronic and deeply rooted. Bosnia is a persistent drain on Western aid and defense budgets.

There is good news. Bosnia is an increasingly uncongenial hideout for war criminals. A University of Lausanne study showed that crimes against individuals are no more common in Bosnia today than in Switzerland. Thus it is relatively safe. There is no threat from outside the country. With dramatic political changes in Serbia and impressive economic reform in Croatia, there is more competition for Western aid monies. Western aid to Bosnia will continue to be reduced, but the country remains entirely reliant on international assistance. There is also far too little foreign investment, and it is declining.

The bloody ethnic fighting has not been renewed. Bosnia's borders are no longer challenged, and there is a single customs and border-police service. Over a million refugees and victims of ethnic cleansing have returned to their homes or reclaimed their property. All Bosnians now carry the same passport and can move around the country freely and safely although they were denied visa-free travel to EU states. Free and peaceful democratic elections have been held repeatedly at all levels of government even though the outcome has not always been welcome.

More and more decisions are being made by the country's own elected leaders. Separate armies have been abolished. A stabilization and association agreement (SAA), which begins the process toward EU membership, was signed. But the EU withheld its signature until the Bosnians agreed on police reform. Finally in June 2008 the intransigent leaders accepted a watered-down version of such a reform. In return the EU's SAA went into effect. But it lags behind its neighbors in advancing toward entry.

Bosnia accepted a two-year seat on the UN Security Council for 2010–11. NATO presented it with a Membership Action Plan (MAP) and invited it to join its Partnership for Peace program. The goal remains to integrate the region into Europe, and the EU is key to that aspiration. But it is hard to foresee any real economic recovery as long as the politics of ethnic animosity continues to divide the people and prevent necessary reforms.

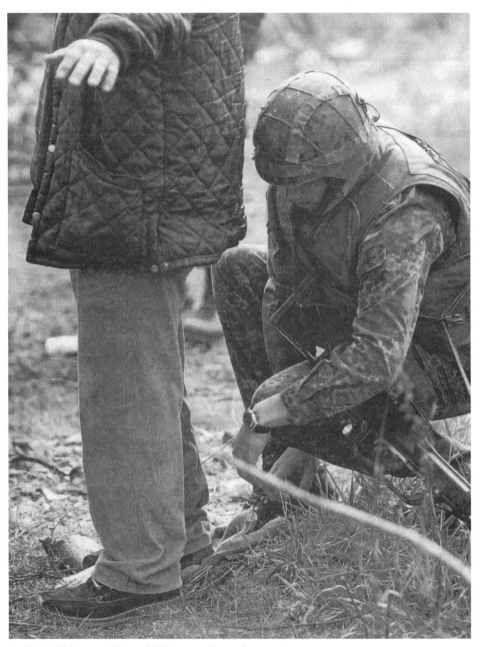

A diminishing number of EU troops keep the peace

The Republic of Montenegro

National Flag: Montenegro adopted its pre-1918 flag in July 2004—a red flag emblazoned with a double-headed eagle.

Montenegro, whose name means "Black Mountain," has a landscape of forested mountains and a sparkling Adriatic coast ideal for tourism. The Dinarian Alps extend into the republic from the north. In the south, the Albanian Alps run west–east along the border with Albania. Montenegro also has a coastline on the Adriatic Sea that includes one good, deep-water port. Skadar (Shkodër) Lake forms part of the border with Albania. The northern half of the lake belongs to Montenegro. The rugged interior is largely uninhabited and is an ideal habitat for wolves and bears. The Tara canyon and the walled city of Kotor are World Heritage Sites.

The country experienced centuries of independence while the surrounding areas seethed under Turkish control. The almost impassable mountains allowed the Montenegrins to resist repeated Turkish attempts to conquer the area. Although the Turks and later the Venetians did occupy parts of Montenegro, it was never completely controlled. The Congress of Berlin recognized its independence in 1878. During the years before World War I, the Montenegrins, like some of their neighbors, were advocates of South Slav nationalism. They lent military support to the cause in 1878 against the Turks and during the Balkan Wars of 1912–13.

After World War I it became a part of Yugoslavia, and in 2002 it remained in a loose link with Serbia. On May 21, 2006, 55.5% of its voters opted for independence from Serbia, and its parliament approved of complete independence on June 3, 2006. Serbia recognized that two days later. The modern state is much larger than historic Montenegro.

INDEPENDENCE

The Republic of Montenegro declared its independence on June 3, 2006, following a successful referendum in which 55.5% of Montenegrins voted to break the formal link with Serbia; voter turnout was 88%. In the earlier cases of Slovene, Croat and Bosnian declarations of separation, Serbia resisted by military means. This time it accepted the inevitable and declared its own independence on June 5, 2006. The last shred of the Yugoslav Federation disappeared without bloodshed.

Montenegro's prime minister, Milo Djukanovic, a resourceful politician who was the only Balkan leader to cling to power throughout Yugoslavia's breakup, argued that the move toward separate statehood is "a river so strong that it can-

Area: 4,378 sq. mi. (13,812 sq. km., roughly the size of Connecticut)

Population: 598,000 (UN 2008)

Capital City: Podgorica (Pop. 170,000).

Climate: Continental, with marked contrasts between summer and winter. The lowest temperatures are in the high elevations. The summers are hot.

Neighboring Countries: Bosnia-Herzegovina (northwest); Croatia (west), Serbia (northeast); Albania (south).

Official Languages: Serbian, Montenegrin (which has two more letters than Serbian), Albanian.

Ethnic Background: South Slavic. Montenegrin 41%, Serbian 30%, Bosnian 9%, Albanian 7% (approximately 50,000), other 13%. About 140,000 Montenegrins live in Serbia.

Principal Religions: Orthodox Christian (70%), Islam (21%), Roman Catholic (4%), Protestant (2%), other 3%. Orthodox Christians are divided into a Montenegrin Orthodox Church and a Serbian Orthodox Church.

Chief Commercial Customers: Serbia is the main trading partner. Also Italy (41.9% of exports and 14.4% of imports), Greece (15.7% of exports), Switzerland (9.6% of exports), Slovenia (12.6% of imports, Bosnia-Herzegovina (9.1% of imports).

Currency: Euro

Recent Political Status: Part of Yugoslavia until 2006.

Independence Day: June 3, 2006 (following a referendum on May 21, 2006, in which 55.5% of the voters opted for independence from Serbia).

Chief of State: Filip Vujanovic, President of Montenegro (since May 2003).

Head of Government: Milo Djukanovic, Prime Minister of Montenegro (since February 2008).

466

President Filip Vujanovic

not dry up." He presented his country's choice as "between Montenegro joining the EU as an independent, modern state with a clear sense of identity, or joining as a junior partner in an unbalanced, dysfunctional union with big brother Serbia, constantly fearful of losing our identity. The truth is that the imposed union between our two states does not work properly, and its continued existence would delay the integration of both states into the EU."

There can be no doubt that the two countries' political cultures had diverged significantly in the preceding eight years since Djukanovic had split from Serbia. He had kept his country out of the Kosovo war, as well as he could, and tried to make amends to the international community for what federal Yugoslavia had done. For example, Montenegro became the first former Yugoslav entity to agree to pay war compensation by offering Croatia $460,000 for cattle its soldiers had rustled in June 1991.

His statement reveals how important the EU is in both Montenegro's and Serbia's hopes for the future. A key argument in favor of independence was that Montenegro might be able to join more quickly than its former partner, which is burdened by the requirement to capture war criminals and deliver them to The Hague. It was the EU that insisted that the threshold for victory be 55%, not a mere 50%, and after the referendum it appealed to the two countries to arrange a Czechoslovak-style "velvet" divorce. But it also warned both sides that EU membership is not inevitable and that there would be no shortcut to joining. Nevertheless, the prospect of EU membership is an essential part of the independence package. It initialed an agreement with the EU in 2007 and has begun the process of accession.

Serbian Prime Minister Vojislav Kostunica refused to congratulate the newly in-dependent republic. No Serb officials or Serbian members of the Montenegrin parliament attended Montenegro's independence ceremonies. But Serbian President Boris Tadic saw the new development as an opportunity to demonstrate that separation in the former Yugoslavia can now be peaceful and that "we can maintain the historical good relations between us." He assured his neighbors that "Montenegro will have a reliable friend in Serbia" and that "Serbia will be the closest friend."

Although there is diminishing tension in the air, the issue of Montenegrin sovereignty never stirred the same kind of deep passion in Serbia as does Kosovo. Both Serbs and Montenegrins share a Slavic background and a language although Montenegrins debate whether they speak "Serbian," "Montenegrin," or "Serbian-Montenegrin." Montenegrin has two more letters than does Serbian and is filled with unique proverbs, metaphors and figurative speech. Both the Latin and Cyrillic alphabets have equal status, and one sees both in public use. However, the former is increasingly popular. They share the Orthodox faith although the place of the Serbian and Montenegrin Orthodox churches is not settled in the constitution. The loss of Montenegro does not engender the same sense of loss as does Kosovo. In fact, at the time of the referendum, 60% of Serbs favored independence from the much poorer Montenegro, only one-eighth its size with a tenth of its population.

The Process of Separation

Montenegrin independence triggered a complicated separation and the official resignation of Svetozar Marovic, the independence-minded Montenegrin who had become federal president in 2003. The joint federal parliament was abolished. The armed forces had to be split up beginning with a reshuffling of the top ranks in the army and military intelligence service. Each side named its own top commander. Thousands of soldiers were relocated to their home countries, but each republic kept the military facilities on its own territory. Dividing dozens of embassies, diplomatic residences and other common assets may take years.

Under federation, there were common Foreign and Defense ministries. Those were now divided and each republic named separate Foreign and Defense ministers. Under an earlier agreement when the former state of Serbia and Montenegro was created, Serbia inherits membership in the United Nations and other international organizations. Montenegro had to apply as a new member and was admitted on June 28, 2006. By its first anniversary as a sovereign state, it had joined the United Nations, the World Bank, the IMF and NATO's Partnership for Peace (PfP).

Both also revised their constitutions to reflect their new independent status; Montenegro requires a two-thirds majority in parliament to change its constitution. In the wording of its declaration of independence, Montenegro sees itself as a "multiethnic, multicultural and multireligious society . . . based on the rule of law and market economy." Its national strategic goal is integration in the European Union and NATO. In November 2006 NATO invited both Montenegro and Serbia to join its Partnership in Peace program, which is an initial step toward full membership. Montenegro retained its ancient national anthem, aptly named "Oh, The Bright May Dawn."

The Road to Independence

President Slobodan Milosevic, a Serb who came from Montenegro, appointed Bulatovic as prime minister of Yugoslavia in 1998, apparently hoping that the appointment would help Bulatovic defeat Djukanovic. What he got instead was a statement from Djukanovic that Bulatovic's new government was "illegitimate, illegal and un-Yugoslav" and that he would recognize neither Bulatovic nor his cabinet.

Djukanovic appointed 20 of his supporters to represent Montenegro in the 40-member federal Yugoslav upper house. The effect of these appointments was to deny Milosevic the necessary two–thirds majority he needed to change the 1992 constitution to increase his powers.

Djukanovic also publicly condemned Milosevic's policy toward Kosovo and expressed his support for the restoration of Kosovar autonomy. In June 1998, the Montenegrin parliament passed a resolution demanding that Milosevic immediately end the violence in Kosovo. After endorsing the demands of the international Contact Group, the resolution also stated that all Montenegrin troops were to be removed from Kosovo and returned to barracks in Serbia or Montenegro if Milosevic chose not to accept the Contact Group demands. Separately, Djukanovic reiter-

Djukanovic wins 2006 elections

Montenegro

ated that Montenegro wanted no part of the war in Kosovo. Such policies won much international approval and helped Montenegro gain a reputation as a kind of democracy under Serbian dictatorship. Thus it received international assistance while Serbia was subjected to sanctions.

The Montenegrin government was particularly concerned about the large numbers of Kosovar refugees who had made their way across the border into Montenegro to escape Serb military actions. By July 1998, there were already 18,000 of them in Montenegro, and more arrived every day. Unlike Serbia, Montenegro was attempting to help the refugees as much as possible. It also permitted the UN High Commission for Refugees to operate in the republic. As large numbers continued to come, however, the Montenegrin government began deporting some of them to Albania. In September 1998, for example, it transported some 3,200 Kosovars. By that time, the refugees already in Montenegro constituted 11% of the population, and the government concluded that it simply could not handle more. But by April 1999, the number had grown to 55,000. Montenegrins were also still caring for 25,000 refugees from the wars in Croatia and Bosnia. Refugees thus constituted 15% of its population in 1999.

The Montenegrin government consistently condemned Serbia's policies in Kosovo and was friendly to the West. But once NATO began its air war against Yugoslavia, its targets included airports and military targets in Montenegro as well as in Serbia. Podgorica's civilian airport became one such target because the Yugoslavian military had a wing of its airplanes located there.

Because of Montenegro's opposition to Milosevic's goals, it became the target of Yugoslav government actions. When NATO's air war over Kosovo began in the spring of 1999, Milosevic removed the military commander in Montenegro because he was considered to be friendly to President Djukanovic. His successor was a Milosevic loyalist. In April, Milosevic also attempted to take over control of the Montenegrin paramilitary police on the pretext that they should come under national control during wartime. Djukanovic resisted that action, but the NATO bombing of targets in Montenegro aroused the instinctive patriotism of many Montenegrins and created some supporters for Milosevic's cause.

NATO's air war ended in June 1999 after Milosevic's capitulation, but the hostilities between Belgrade and Podgorica continued. Anti-Milosevic demonstrations throughout Serbia, which followed the end of the war, put him on the defensive. However, he temporarily survived these

**Prime Minister
Milo Djukanovic**

efforts to force him out of power, and he renewed his attempts to regain control over Montenegro. On his part, Djukanovic moved to reestablish friendly relations with Albania and Croatia and to reopen the border with those countries. In April 2000, Albania and Montenegro signed an agreement on economic, trade, and cultural cooperation during a visit by the Albanian foreign minister to Podgorica. One border crossing was opened with another to follow.

The Montenegrin government set up its own customs and trade regime in September 1999. Two months later, the German mark (followed later by the euro) was made the official currency as the government attempted to shield the Montenegrin economy from the inflation raging next door. Milosevic's response was to declare an embargo on all trade with Montenegro. Political relations remained tense. Djukanovic announced that Montenegro would not participate in the 2000 federal elections because "the federal state does not exist."

This did not yet mean a final breakup of Yugoslavia. The advice Djukanovic got

Study break at Podgorica University

from abroad—both from the United States and most Western European countries—was that he should take no precipitous actions, lest they lead to war with Serbia. At the same time, polls in Montenegro indicated that Montenegrins were split on the question of independence: 41% favored it in 2004, and 39% opposed it, and 20% were undecided. Most Montenegrins have relatives in Serbia and want to maintain close and friendly ties with it. Such polling figures argued for caution on Djukanovic's part.

In October 2000 the situation changed dramatically in Serbia when voters threw Milosevic out of the Yugoslav president's office and elected a democratically oriented opposition politician, Vojslav Kostunica. The Montenegrin government had boycotted the election and had asked its people to do the same. Kostunica's election raised expectations that the two republics could reconcile their differences. Kostunica insisted that Montenegro must remain linked to Serbia, which would lose its access to the Adriatic and Mediterranean Seas without it. But he stated that he favored drawing up a new constitution that would make Montenegro feel more equal with Serbia. He was willing to allow the Montenegrin people to decide in a referendum if they wanted to become independent. In 2002 he supported dropping the term "Yugoslavia" altogether and renaming the state "Serbia and Montenegro." Within two weeks of his election he traveled to Podgorica to reassure President Milo Djukanovic and to offer him the prime ministership in his new government. The latter declined.

The U.S. and European countries made public their opposition to Montenegrin independence. Even though Montenegro already enjoyed what many observers would call independence, Western leaders worried that even a referendum on the subject could set off another round of secession and violence in the Balkans. Djukanovic called early parliamentary elections in October 2002 and won a clear parliamentary majority with 39 of 75 seats; he took over the post of prime minister. His close political ally and deputy leader of his pro-independence Democratic Party of Socialists, Filip Vujanovic, won a landslide victory for the presidency in May 2003, capturing 63.3% of the votes. He promised to move his land toward mainstream Europe and to organize a referendum on Montenegro's independence in three years.

After the government announced a referendum in 2006 to decide the question of independence, the Serb prime minister rejected Podgorica's proposal that the two entities retain close links but be recognized as independent. Montenegro aspired to both NATO and EU membership as an independent state. The EU decided to take a "twin-track approach" allowing both republics to negotiate with it separately but in tandem. It issued a feasibility study in April 2005 concluding that accession talks could begin.

Montenegro faced an image problem. Prime Minister Djukanovic and his allies were suspected of sex trafficking, cigarette smuggling and other mafia activities. It did not look good when a journalist investigating these charges joined a long list of assassination victims when he was gunned down in May 2004. Djukanovic also faced an ethics problem in 2009 when his government bailed out a troubled bank that belonged largely to his brother and to a lesser extent to himself and his sister.

The country also has historic affection for Russia. Russians responded by purchasing hotels, land and holiday homes; 11% of tourists in 2004–5 came from Russia. During the 2008–9 global economic crisis, Russian tourism declined drastically, and despite a fall in property prices by 50% or more, Russian investment money dried up at least temporarily. The IMF estimated that the economy would grow by only 2% in 2009, a rapid decline.

Russian oligarch, Oleg Deripaska, bought (for the Rusal company) the aluminum plant known as KAP (Kombinat Aluminijuma Podgorca) at the edge of Podgornica, which provides more than half of Montenegro's industrial production, accounts for 80% of its exports and constitutes as much as 40% of its GDP. The government had tried hard and unsuccessfully to sell the conglomerate to Alcoa of the US and Alcan of Canada. It belches out toxic fumes, consumes huge amounts of subsidized electricity, and loses lots of money since the collapse of aluminum prices on the world market. Deripaska threatened to close it unless the government provided it with subsidies. Because of its importance within such a small national economy, the government caved in and granted it the money in 2009 for another 4 years.

The March 2002 agreement brokered by the EU to rename Yugoslavia and to restructure its federal institutions prevented a referendum for three years. It was finalized a year later and included EU promises of economic and political assistance. But this agreement could be reconsidered after the three years had elapsed. In 2004 the Montenegrin government already started talks with Serb officials about possibly dissolving the union. It worried about suffering economically and being dragged down with Serbia, which faced international criticism over its lack of cooperation with the war-crimes tribunal in

Caution, "school," in Cyrillic

The Hague. It was also hesitant to share possible oil and gas wealth with Serbia if Ramco Energy, a Scottish oil company, succeeded in its prospecting off the coast of Montenegro.

Serb Prime Minister Kostunica had noted pessimistically: "This looks like a marriage doomed to divorce." He was right. The deal officially sanctioned the existence of separate economies with different currencies (the dinar for Serbia and the euro for Montenegro) and conflicting legal systems. Montenegrin linguists are striving to purify their language of Serbian influences although their language is still indistinguishable from that spoken in Serbia.

In July 2004 the Montenegrin parliament adopted a new flag, national anthem and a statehood day, as part of the drive for independence. The flag is the one it had when Montenegro was a sovereign state from 1878 to 1918; it is red emblazoned with a double-headed eagle. Both Serbia and Montenegro raced to approve new anthems before the Athens Olympics because fans in both republics had developed the embarrassing habit of drowning out the Yugoslav anthem with jeers and boos whenever it was played at national sports events. Serbia and Montenegro's last joint international appearance was an athletic event: it fielded a combined team in the world soccer championship in Germany in June 2006 and was quickly eliminated.

The referendum was memorable for several reasons. There was a complete absence of violence in this highly divided society, in which at least a third of its residents are Serb, with another 50,000 Albanians. International observers certified that the voting was fair. The result was

clear, with 55.5% voting yes and 45.5% no. That did not stop the Serb members of parliament from boycotting the session on June 3, 2006, when independence was formally proclaimed. This made Montenegro the world's 192nd sovereign state and completed the process of federal Yugoslavia's disintegration.

Djukanovic dominated the news media, but a televised debate was held before the polling that gave voters one last change to compare the arguments for and against. In that debate, the leader of the opposition to separation, Predrag Bulatovic, accused Djukanovic of trying to establish a "private state." The latter helped finance the return of thousands of the 16,000 Montenegrin expatriates (equal to 3% of the total voter turnout), including several hundred New Yorkers, to vote for independence. Serbian railways also provided free tickets to mostly anti-independence Montenegrins in Serbia to return home and vote no. The Albanian minority solidly supported severance from Serbia. When the preliminary results were announced, Podgorica was alive with the thunder of fireworks and celebratory gunfire. Crowds rushed into the main streets, honking horns and waving the national flag.

Montenegro has a small military force of 3,127 active duty soldiers, of which 2,500 are army, 401 are navy, and 226 are air force. There are 10,100 paramilitary forces, of which 6,000 are Ministry of Interior Personnel and 4,100 special police.

POLITICAL SYSTEM

The president is directly elected by universal suffrage for a five-year term. It is a parliamentary democracy, and the most powerful political position is that of the prime minister, whose party or coalition must command a majority in parliament for its most important legislation. A party must win at least 3% of the total votes in order to qualify for any parliamentary seats.

Two leaders emerged in the lead-up to independence after a half-decade of struggle. Under the leadership of President Momir Bulatovic, Montenegro had been a loyal supporter of Milosevic's policies until 1997. But Bulatovic was challenged for the presidency by his prime minister, Milo Djukanovic, who accused him of being a puppet of Milosevic. Djukanovic won and subsequently began to take an independent line *vis-à-vis* Milosevic.

The 1998 parliamentary elections were essentially a rerun of the battle between Djukanovic and Bulatovic for the presidency, with the additional factor that Milosevic did everything in his power to help Bulatovic defeat Djukanovic and take control of the legislature. When all of the

Montenegro

results were in, however, the coalition led by Djukanovic had won 49.5% of the vote, while Bulatovic's Socialist Party had captured only 36%.

Montenegrins gradually distanced themselves from Serbia's war policies, and in 1997 the ruling party of reformed Communists split in two. Ultimately the separate groups developed into two political blocs: one pro-independence and the other pro-union with Serbia.

Filip Vujanovic was elected president of Montenegro in May 2003. He was re-elected in April 2008, winning 51.4% of the votes while the pro-Serbia candidate, Andrija Mandic, got 20.4%. His reelection helped cement the country's westward political and economic course since independence.

Vujanovic's predecessor in office and Montenegro's most influential politician, Milo Djukanovic, had assumed the more powerful post of prime minister of Montenegro in November 2002. The prime minister is responsible to the 81-seat parliament, the Skupstina.

The majority was composed of the Democratic Party of Socialists (DPS) and the Social Democratic Party (SDP). In independent Montenegro's first election in September 2006, this ruling coalition won 41 of the 81 seats. In the opposition were the Serbian People's Party (SNS—a radical faction of the pro-Serbian camp), the Socialist People's Party (SNP), the People's Party (NS), the Liberal Alliance of Montenegro (LSCG), the Democratic Union of Albanians (DUA), and the Democratic Alliance of Montenegro (DSCG). The two pro-Serbian opposition blocs won 23 seats. A newly created Movement for Change, a social-democratic party, captured 11 seats in its first outing.

In November 2006 Djukanovic stepped down as prime minister to make way for a less centralized, less autocratic rule. He stayed on as leader of his DPS party and remained extremely influential in the country. He was replaced by his own party companion, former justice minister Zeliko Sturanovic, who was favored because he was free of some of the murky maneuverings in which his party had been involved as Yugoslavia came unraveled and Serbia was subject to international sanctions. Although diagnosed for lung cancer, he remained in power until February 2008, when he handed the keys to the prime minister's office back to the 46-year-old Djukanovic, who remains very close to President Vujanovic.

Djukanovic decided to have the next elections 18 months early, in March 2009, in order to strengthen his position in the midst of the global recession that was bound to hurt Montenegro and his government. Turnout was a respectable 66.2%.

For the sixth time, he emerged as prime minister; in 1991 he had won the post at age 29. His four-party pro-western coalition, led by his DPS and called European Montenegro, captured almost 52% of the votes and 47 seats, an increase of five. This gives the government a solid parliamentary majority.

Much of his power stems from the fact that the opposition is divided. Only three other parties cleared the 3% hurdle to win seats: The newly named Socialist Party of Montenegro (SNP) won 16.8% of the votes and 16 seats, a gain of 8. New Serb Democracy got 9.2% and 8 seats (up from zero), and the Movement for Change—We Can won 6% of the votes and 5 seats, a lost of 6.

Voters clearly showed their preference for familiar leadership in time of economic distress. He enlarged the size of his cabinet from four to 18 members. The 47-year-old Djukanovic also announced that he would serve as prime minister only until 2011, when he will pass the reins to Svetozar Marovic and retire from politics.

ECONOMY

Montenegro hopes to attract foreign investors to utilize the country as a regional base for the entire Balkans. In addition to the privatization of the large aluminum works, KAP (aluminum being the country's main export), Hungary's Magyar Telecom purchased a 51.1% share of the fixed line telecommunications company, Telekom Crne Gore. Among the other large investors are Belgium's Interbrew, Greece's Hellenic Petroleum and Japan's Daido Metal. Exiled former Thai prime minister, Thaksin Shinawatra, acquired Montenegrin citizenship. Many hope he will invest some of his billions in the country.

Net foreign direct investment in 2005 was $490 million, four times as much as in 2004. It hopes that its lowest corporate tax in Europe, at 9%, will lure more. Personal income tax rates are between 15.5% and 23.5%, and the VAT is 17%. It takes only four days and three documents to register a limited liability company.

With its appealing Adriatic coastline, it is no surprise that tourism offers so much promise. One million tourists visited the country in 2006, up 17% over the previous year. It accounts for almost 15% of GDP and provides more than 22,000 jobs, many of them seasonal. Of course, this industry is vulnerable to the ups and downs of the world economy, as Macedonians saw in 2009. Tourism could triple within the next decade making Montenegro one of the world's fastest growing tourist destinations.

The country already uses the euro although the EU made it known in October 2007 that its use is technically incompatible with EU law. But Montenegro was not asked to abandon the common currency. The government defended itself by arguing that its adoption in 2002 was a necessary step toward independence and future EU membership.

On October 15, 2007, it signed a stabilization and association agreement with the EU, and in April 2009 its application to become a candidate for membership was approved. In its report, the European Commission praised "important progress" in bringing its legal framework and state institutions up to EU standards. But it said that "the fight against corruption and organized crime remains a major challenge." From December 19, 2009, Montenegrins enjoy visa-free travel to most EU states. EU and NATO membership remains the gov-

Prime Minister Milo Djukanovic addresses a rally

ernment's top foreign policy priority. A February 2009 poll confirmed that EU membership is desired by 72% of Montenegrins, whereas support for NATO is much weaker: 39% for and 39% against.

A new tunnel for cars through the mountains between Podgorica and the coast cuts travel time to as little as 40 minutes. This tunnel changes the dynamics of coastal tourism. In addition to tourist income, the country receives remittances from its expatriates totaling 1.3% of GDP; if unrecorded transfers are included, one could add 50%–100%. In addition to the tourists, thousands of Bosnians, Serbs, Kosovars and Albanians pour into the country to work in construction, agriculture and the tourist industry.

The main challenge is to emerge from the global recession and from one of Europe's worst economies. Average salaries are only about 375 euros ($500) per month. By 2006 the economy was growing by 6.5% per capita annually, and the boom continued until the onset of the global crisis in 2009, which saw growth fall to minus 5.3% and remain close to zero in 2010. Per capita GDP climbed since 2006 from $4,200 to $7,000. Unemployment was officially 14.6% in 2007 and 11% in 2008, but it is inching upward again. Inflation was a low 1.8%. Its foreign trade was in deficit. Its main partners are Serbia, Italy (41.9% of exports and 14.4% of imports), Greece (15.7% of exports), Switzerland (9.6% of exports), Slovenia (12.6% of imports) and Bosnia-Herzegovina (9.1% of imports).

Other challenges include the small elite that profited from privatization and became rich, powerful and very influential in the government. Along with an influx of Russian, British and Irish investors, they doubled the price of houses in only a year, but by 2009 property prices plunged more than 50%. Nepotism is rampant; without connections it is difficult to get ahead.

Corruption and organized crime are also deeply rooted problems. In 2010 a Montenegrin gangster, Darko Saric, was indicted in Serbia for organizing a 2.7 ton cocaine shipment from South America that was seized by Serbian drug authorities. Montenegro freed three of his alleged accomplices when Serbia failed to provide evidence against them, thereby damaging relations between the two countries. Saric vanished. Montenegrin Deputy Prime Minister Igor Luksic protested that his country is battling corruption with some success. Freedom House in New York cited improvement, and Transparency International gave Montenegro a better rating than any other Western Balkan country except Croatia.

FUTURE

Europe's second-newest country faces serious challenges. The referendum campaign and the results revealed deep divisions within its society. Citizens identifying themselves as Montenegrins, Albanians, or Muslims overwhelmingly voted for independence. The third or more who claim to be Serbs voted against it. Montenegro must work very hard to heal the wounds of the campaign and create a setting in which the Serb population can play a constructive role in the country's political life. The tension even spilled over into the Orthodox Churches, with the Montenegrin and Serbian communities denying each other canonical legality.

Over time the intensity of the internal identity debate has declined although foreign relations with Serbia remain frosty or worse. When in October 2008 Montenegro officially recognized Kosovo's independence, thousands of pro-Serb Montenegrins protested in the streets of Podgorica, storming the parliament and chanting "Kosovo is Serbia!" In violent clashes, over 34 persons were injured. Serbia expelled the country's ambassador, but it soon accepted him back when it realized how little such a move had accomplished.

Montenegrins see the ultimate solution in membership in the EU. The process has begun. All parties and 72% of the people support this effort. But they must be patient. Western European members have grown wary of rapid EU enlargement.

Source: *International Herald Tribune*

The Republic of Kosovo

Map of Kosovo

Area: 10,887 sq. km.

Population: 2.2 million, (2008 estimate). A census is scheduled for May 2011.

Capital City: Prishtina (Pop. 550,000 estimate 2008).

Climate: Continental, with marked contrasts between summer and winter, with lowest temperatures in the high elevations. The summers are hot and the winters cold and snowy.

Neighboring Countries: Serbia (north); Montenegro (northwest); Albania (southwest); Macedonia (south).

Official Languages: Albanian, Serbian and other minority languages, including Turkish. Because so many languages are spoken, the national anthem, adopted in June 2008, has no words.

Ethnic Background: Albanian approximately 90%, Serbian 5%, Other 5% (Bosniak [1.9%], Roma [1.7%], Turkish [1%], Ashkali, Egyptian, Gorani)

Principal Religions: Muslim, Serbian Orthodox Christianity, Roman Catholicism

Chief Commercial Products: Scrap metal, minerals

Currency: Euro. Serbian dinar in Serb enclaves.

National Day: February 17 (Independence Day). Before 2008 it was November 28, the Albanian national holiday.

Chief of State: Fatmir Sejdiu, President (since February 2006).

Head of Government: Hashim Thaçi, Prime Minister (since January 2008).

National Flag: Gold outline of Kosovo on a field of blue with six white stars at the top representing the six major ethnic groups.

The youngest country in Europe, Kosovo is located to the southwest of Serbia. Over 90% of its people are ethnically Albanian. This is a mountainous region. The highest mountains, the Albanian Alps (in Serbian the *Mokra Mountains*), are located in the northeastern part of the country. A second mountain, the Sar, arises in the southwest along the Macedonian border. It contains the Sharr Mountain National Park, established in 1986 and Kosovo's only national park. There is a plateau region in the center, with lower mountains rising again to the east.

Kosovo has two plain regions: the Metohija/Dukagjin basin is located in the west, and the Plain of Kosovo is in the east. The chief rivers are the White Drin, running toward the Adriatic Sea with tributaries like the Erenik, the Sitnica, the South Morava in the Goljak area and the Ibar in the north. Its largest lakes are Badovac, Batlava, Radonjic and Gazivoda. About 39% of the country is forested, and 52% is considered agricultural of which 31% is covered by pastures and 69% is arable.

Kosovo is a young country in several respects. It did not declare its independence until February 17, 2008, and its first constitution came into effect the following June 15th. It is the seventh state to emerge from the Yugoslavia that dissolved in the 1990s. Unlike most European nations, Kosovo had a booming birthrate, and half of its population is under age 25. However, fertility is falling. In 1950, the rate was 7.8 children per woman, but by 1990 it had fallen to 3.6. Now it is 2.2, just over the level needed for a stable population. Ethnic Albanians boycotted the 1991 census, so estimates of Kosovo's total population vary from 2.1 million to 2.5 million. Over 90% are Albanians. There will be a new census in May 2011. But in order to be accurate, it will require cooperation between Albanians and Serbs living in the country.

The prime minister at the time of independence and again in 2008, Hashim Thaçi, noted that "a Kosovo identity does not exist." Very few Serbs would call themselves "Kosovar." Most Kosovars are secular Muslims who consider themselves to be "Albanian." For them, religion has always been secondary to being Albanian. They are proud that language and nationality, not religion, are the defining societal elements.

Orthodox Serbs constitute the largest Christian minority, but their church is riven by political and doctrinal divisions. Dozens of their churches were destroyed after the 1999 war, and an empty hulk of the unfinished, abandoned cathedral looms in Prishtina. However, there are many intact beautiful monasteries, such as those in Gracanica, Decani and Peja (Pec).

Conversions to Christianity have become common, and there are an estimated 65,000 Catholics. Downtown Prishtina is the location for the first cathedral in the world named after Mother Teresa. The world-famous nun had been born into an Albanian family in Skopje, Macedonia. It was ready for services in 2010. Of the 15,000 or so Protestants, one pastor estimates that only 2,000 attend church regularly.

Kosovo

A contest was held to design the new flag, and the only ground rules were that it reflect the multi-ethnic population. However, many entries ignored that and submitted variations of the red and black Albanian flag that had served as the nation's colors until independence. The banner that was ultimately adopted had the colors of the European Union (blue and gold) with six white stars to represent the two largest ethnic groups—Albanians (about 90%) and Serbs (5%)—and four additional tiny communities.

The Long Road to Independence

The interest of earlier political leaders in the individual Yugoslav republics to retain the maximum amount of scarce investment funds for local use led to grievances upon which local nationalism then fed. The autonomous region of Kosovo in the Republic of Serbia became particularly disaffected. It is the homeland of ethnic Albanians, who in the 21st century constitute over 90% of the province's population (after half the Serbs who had lived there fled following the 1999 war). Half of the 100,000 Serbs living in Kosovo are in the north, bordering on Serbia proper, with the part of Mitrovica north of the Ibar River as their main city. A good number of its residents are Serbs displaced from other parts of Kosovo. The other half are in enclaves scattered across the land and bordering on Macedonia. All together, the Serbian minority is predominant in about 15% of the country's territory.

Kosovo has little industry but considerable mining potential. It was always one of the poorest parts of Yugoslavia. Its unemployment rate was perennially the highest (around 50%), but many Kosovars find work in the underground "black" economy, behind the backs of the tax collectors.

At the beginning of the 1980s, dissatisfaction with the local situation produced a wave of nationalist agitation. Riots began in Kosovo in March–April 1981, led by youths from the University of Prishtina (in mid-1981 renamed "Kosovo University"). Eventually, thousands of demonstrators joined in clashes with police and openly propounded nationalistic slogans. Originally limited to the capital city of Prishtina, the demonstrations spread to other parts of Kosovo and then to the neighboring Republic of Macedonia (where another 374,000 ethnic Albanians live).

The university was closed on April 2, 1981, and the Yugoslav regime began a policy of "rooting out Albanian nationalism" and purging local organizations of Albanian nationalist elements. The university had undoubtedly become a hotbed of Albanian nationalist sentiment, but the underlying cause of the agitation was almost certainly economic. While there were demands for creation of a separate Albanian Republic of Kosovo, there was no strong sentiment to merge the province with Albania. It is generally conceded that the standard of living of the people of Kosovo was higher than that of Albanians in Albania. They also had more freedom and, unlike the Albanians, were permitted to practice their religion. For these reasons, only a tiny minority supported union with Albania in the early 1980s.

The abolition of Kosovo's autonomous status in early 1989 was followed by Serb attempts to stamp out all manifestations of Albanian nationalism. Among other things, the Serbs fired all Albanian teachers and issued new regulations requiring that all instruction be given only in the Serbian language. This policy extended also to Kosovo University.

Serbia's reestablishment of control over Kosovo left a sullen populace, but it also forced the main Albanian political party, the Democratic League of Kosovo, to respond in a more radical manner than it might otherwise have done. It declared the Republic of Kosova [the Albanian spelling] to be independent in 1991; this was confirmed by a popular referendum. It elected its first government in 2002.

The Serbian government's reaction was to carry out a massive purge throughout the province, dismissing Albanians from all important posts in the province. It also ordered arbitrary arrests, seized property, and tolerated (possibly even encouraged) widespread police brutality. Although Serbs were only ten percent of the population, they now filled all governmental offices and all significant positions in hospitals, universities, businesses, and schools.

The Republic of Kosova never received any international recognition, and the large number of Yugoslav army units stationed throughout the province until mid-1999 acted as a guarantee of continued Serbian control. Yet, in a real sense, it is possible to trace the slow birth of the Republic of Kosova from 1991 onward. The Albanians slowly constructed a parallel government and society over the next couple years.

Ibrahim Rugova (1944–2006)

473

Kosovo

Damage by precision bombing in Belgrade, still visible in 2005

the ferocity with which the retaliatory actions were carried out.

In late 1997 the KLA began launching guerrilla attacks against Serb military targets in Kosovo. In January 1998, KLA rebels killed two Serbian soldiers. Responding to these attacks, the Serb government dispatched combined police and paramilitary units from the Ministry of Interior "to restore order." The Serbs rounded up thousands of Albanians and questioned them, often under torture. On March 6, they launched a series of "punitive raids" against Albanian villages. Armed with mortars, helicopter gunships, armored vehicles and heavy artillery, they shelled individual villages that had been identified as centers of rebel support. One such target was the Drenica region, where two days of heavy Serb assault resulted in the deaths of more than 80 villagers, including many women and children.

The killings led the United States, United Kingdom, Germany, France and Italy to agree to place an embargo on sales of arms to Yugoslavia. But Belgrade rejected demands that Serbia pull its special paramilitary forces out of Kosovo and open talks with the Kosovar Albanian political leadership. Continued pressure did elicit a suggestion from the Serbian government that it was willing to open talks with Kosovo and that the issue of "self-rule" could be on the agenda. Since the Serbian government had branded the KLA as a terrorist organization, however, Milosevic made it clear that no discussions could be carried on with representatives of this organization.

Unarmed and isolated, the Albanian political leadership opted for a program of passive resistance and noncooperation. Perhaps they were lucky. Ibrahim Rugova, the man they elected as president of their "Republic" in 1991, was firmly committed to a policy of nonviolence. He persuaded his people to go along with him. Rugova and his "government" collected their own taxes and used the monies to set up schools where the children could be educated in their own language and clinics where the people could receive medical assistance. Withdrawing into their own Albanian world, their only contact with Serbs was when they were stopped, and often harassed, by heavily armed Serbian police. Meanwhile, ordinary Serbs lived in their own villages, guarded by Serbian soldiers. Thus, even while a war went on for nearly three years in neighboring Bosnia, Kosovo remained quiet.

Milosevic's War against the Ethnic Albanians in Kosovo

After remaining quiet throughout the Bosnian War, Kosovo finally exploded in 1998. The reasons can be traced to the actions of younger, more radical Albanians who had grown more and more frustrated by the failure of Ibrahim Rugova's passive resistance program to bring about any easing of the Serb repression.

In 1997, a new, more violent leadership arose to challenge the very idea of nonviolence. This organization, calling itself the Kosovo Liberation Army (KLA, also known by its Albanian initials, UCK), had actually been in existence since 1992. But it played no significant role until it managed to obtain weapons from Albania during the collapse and civil war that raged there in 1997.

This collapse of Albanian governmental authority led to a flood of all kinds of mil-

itary equipment as troop units dissolved, and military warehouses were ransacked. It was mostly guns and other small weaponry that made their way across the mountains into Kosovo. However, when they arrived, some KLA leaders began to dream about driving the Serbs out of the province and creating an independent Kosovo.

Some recognized that they were still too lightly armed and too badly trained to achieve that on their own. But they hoped that a series of attacks on the Serbs might help stir up world opinion and publicize the plight of the Kosovar Albanians. They clearly expected President Milosevic to order retaliatory actions against them although it is not certain that they expected

Wagon train, June 1999: A long line of ethnic Albanians traverse a mountain road in northern Albania on the way back to Kosovo.

Don't kill my freedom. Surrender the weapons

In a curious coincidence, the Kosovar Albanians had presidential and parliamentary elections scheduled for March 22, 1998. Amazingly, they managed to carry them out in the midst of the Serb occupation. Moreover, more than 80% of Albanian voters participated, even though the Serbs condemned and tried to stop them. In fact, voting could not be carried out in several villages that were under tight Serb police control.

Since Ibrahim Rugova was overwhelmingly reelected as president, Serbia had its "negotiating partner" whenever it desired to settle the dispute peacefully. Moreover Rugova was an individual firmly committed to a policy of non-violence. But the Serbs did not really want to talk.

In April 1998 Milosevic sent paratroop units to Kosovo to seal the frontier with Albania. In May, the units' mission was enlarged to include the Kosovar Albanian villages in the vicinity of the Albanian border. Since the inhabitants of these villages were considered to be supporters of the KLA, Yugoslav soldiers began clearing the area by burning the villages and forcing the inhabitants to flee. Initially the number of dead remained small although the refugees figure had grown to perhaps 20,000 by the end of May.

The KLA was also active during this time, organizing attacks on Serbian soldiers and attempting to establish control over parts of Kosovo. For a time, they claimed to dominate one-third of Kosovo, but this was misleading. Lightly armed and badly trained, they usually were forced to flee when they came into direct contact with units of the Yugoslav army.

NATO Gets Involved

Still, their occasional successes and their claim that they would not accept anything less than independence for Kosovo made it difficult for the various NATO members who wanted to see an end to the fighting and killing there. NATO made it clear again and again that it would go no fur-

ther than to put pressure on Serbia to restore Kosovar autonomy. On the other hand, as long as the KLA continued to demand independence, NATO would stand aside and do nothing. That is what happened for another two months.

Meanwhile, the number of Kosovar refugees continued to grow until it reached an estimated 300,000 by September. This finally produced a UN Security Council resolution demanding that Serbia withdraw part of its forces from Kosovo. Following up on this, U.S. envoy Richard Holbrooke negotiated a deal in mid-October 1998 that led to a cease-fire. Shortly thereafter, the first of 2,000 unarmed civilians began arriving in Kosovo under a mandate from the Organization for Security and Cooperation in Europe (OSCE) to monitor the truce.

The cease-fire lasted for approximately three months, but it began to break down in January. In many cases, it was KLA guerrillas who began the process by ambushing one or two Serb policemen. Either the Serb paramilitary forces or units of the Yugoslav army would then retaliate, usually destroying one or more villages and often killing many of the inhabitants.

A particularly atrocious killing in January 1999 threatened to disrupt the entire peace process: 45 ethnic Albanians were found dead in the village of Recak. William Walker, head of the OSCE's verification team, blamed the killings on the Serbs after he had visited the site. Milosevic's reaction was to order Walker expelled from Kosovo. He later backed down, but attitudes hardened all around from this moment.

Western officials now proposed a new round of talks, to be held at Rambouillet, in France. Germany, Great Britain, France, the United States and Russia hosted the talks. Representatives of Milosevic and three factions from Kosovo were presented with a draft settlement plan. Basically it would have guaranteed Kosovo autonomy under a sort of NATO protec-

Three people, One heart, One Kosovo. Support the return of refugees

Zahir Pajaziti, one of KLA's first founders. Statue in Prishtina

torate for three years, after which the final status of the province would be decided. Neither side accepted the plan during the first round of negotiations although the Kosovar delegation did offer a pledge to sign the Rambouillet Accord after it had held consultations in Kosovo.

Milosevic, on the other hand, said that he could accept Kosovo autonomy, but could not agree to the stationing of NATO forces there. Meanwhile, fighting was on the increase even as the negotiations went on. By mid-March 1999 an estimated 80,000 ethnic Albanian Kosovars had been forced to flee their homes as more Serb troops were moved into Kosovo.

In the end, Milosevic refused to sign the Rambouillet Accords, but the Kosovars did. Accordingly, NATO began an air war against Yugoslavia on the night of March 24, 1999, with raids on airfields and arms factories in and around Belgrade and on other targets in Kosovo and Montenegro. President Bill Clinton announced that the purpose of the bombing was to protect unarmed ethnic Albanian citizens from Serb attacks by getting Milosevic to agree to the Rambouillet Accords.

Meanwhile, Milosevic launched what was obviously a long-planned program of ethnic cleansing in Kosovo. By the end of April there were an estimated 917,000 refugees. Approximately 357,000 fled to Albania, while a further 130,000 were admitted to Macedonia. Montenegro, which opposed Milosevic's policy toward Ko-

Kosovo

Map of Kosovo with Serbian town names and arrows showing escape exits for Albanian Kosovars before and after the 1999 war

However, most refugees took longer to return. When they did, they found destroyed houses and villages with little of value left. Some international assistance was available for rebuilding, but they faced a hard task rebuilding their lives. Meanwhile Serb families streamed northward with their goods, either to Serbia proper, to Montenegro, or to Serbian enclaves in northern Kosovo or elsewhere in the province protected by NATO peacekeepers.

Milosevic was indicted as a war criminal in May 1999, and that became another complication. One effect was to increase public support for NATO's actions. Another was to make it even less thinkable that the Kosovars should in any way be put back under Serb rule as long as Milosevic remained in control in Yugoslavia. Many feared that Milosevic would cling to power even more tenaciously since its loss might mean an international trial followed by prison.

In Serbia Milosevic moved quickly to repair most of the war damage resulting from the NATO bombing although the visitor to Belgrade can still see evidence of the damage done by NATO's precision bombing attacks. Not until June 2003 was the last debris from the bombed bridges over the Danube cleared away so that large ships could pass.

Since the war Bill Clinton is a hero in Kosovo, with a street and businesses named after him and an honorary degree from Kosovo University in Prishtina. In 2009 an 11-foot gold-colored statue of him was unveiled in gratitude on one of Prishtina's main streets. In general, the U.S. is still glorified in Kosovo, as a replica of the Statue of Liberty on top of the Victory Hotel in Prishtina demonstrates.

One was reminded of this again in October 2008 and May 2009 when Secretary of Defense Robert Gates and Vice President Joe Biden visited the country. Gates pledged to maintain U.S. military presence and train and equip Kosovo soldiers until a united Kosovo state was stable. Thousands of Kosovars lined the road from the airport into Prishtina cheering and waving the Stars and Stripes and signs reading "Kosovo loves you" and "Thank you, U.S.A." to give Biden a hero's welcome. Biden proclaimed: "We are back. We will stand with you." He called Kosovo's independence "irreversible." But he stressed the importance of continuing to reach out to the Serb minority, and he visited the Serb monastery of Decani to pay his respects.

Milosevic faced opposition from the leadership of the Serbian Orthodox Church, which urged him to step down. He did not hesitate to use all the apparatus of the state to repress the opposition, including to intimidate or to close down all opposition-

sovo, had taken in another 72,000. Some of the remaining refugees had already been moved to countries such as Germany, Austria, Norway, Greece, Romania, Turkey and the United States. As the refugees continued pouring out of Kosovo, the camps and the rescue workers were overwhelmed.

Yugoslav forces continued to expel ethnic Albanians from their villages, which were then destroyed. Estimates of those killed by Serbian forces ran from a low of 10,000 to a high of 100,000, but no one really knows. It appeared, however, that Milosevic had decided to create facts on the ground by expelling all or nearly all ethnic Albanians. In May 2010 Serb war crimes prosecutors uncovered the third mass grave containing the bodies of hundreds of ethnic Albanian civilians killed during the 1999 war then transported to Serbia to hide the atrocities. Three other such graves were discovered in Kosova it-

self. Hundreds have been exhumed and returned home for burial.

As NATO continued its bombing, additional voices were raised about the need for ground troops to put a stop to the ethnic cleansing. Several NATO members did begin moving troops into the area on a contingency basis. But everyone recognized that it would take weeks for any nation to have troops ready to go in, even if a political decision to that effect were made.

That decision was rendered unnecessary when Milosevic accepted NATO's terms on June 3. It took another six days before a firm agreement was reached and another several days before NATO forces began entering Kosovo. Kosovar Albanian refugees began trickling back in even before all Serbian forces had left the province and before NATO could certify that it was safe to do so. Many were villagers intent on planting their crops before it was too late.

controlled media. In October 2000 Serbian voters unceremoniously threw him out of power, and courageous demonstrators prevented him from remaining at the helm even after he lost the election.

Kosovo after the Fall of Milosevic

The breaking of Milosevic's hold on power in Serbia brought rejoicing throughout Serbia and the West. But it created difficulties for Kosovar Albanians. For most of the world, NATO's bombing in 1999 was a humanitarian rescue mission, but for most ethnic Albanians it was the culmination of a national liberation struggle. Milosevic's authoritarianism and status as an indicted war criminal were their strongest arguments that independence was both inevitable and morally necessary. With him gone and with the Serbian government's continuing insistence that Kosovo is a province of Yugoslavia, Kosovars found what little international support they had for independence to have evaporated. Western governments had always opposed independence on the grounds that it might destabilize Macedonia. UN Resolution 1244 declared at the end of the war that Kosovo belonged to Yugoslavia. At most, the international community supported substantial autonomy, but that was not what most Kosovars wanted. One diplomat explained: "The Albanians never really believed us when we said independence was out."

One of the reasons Western leaders and the EU tried so hard to keep Serbia and Montenegro together was that the total collapse of the former Yugoslav federation would have made it impossible to contain Kosovars' separatist demands. The new Serbian constitution still classifies Kosovo as part of Serbia. This infuriated many Kosovo Albanians. Their tense relations with UN officials in Kosovo encouraged Serbs there to organize in 2003 a union of Serb municipalities and to assert that if Kosovo becomes independent, the 40,000 Serbs in the northern area would secede and join Serbia proper. This was an outcome international officials wanted to prevent. But it became harder and harder to avoid dealing with Kosovo's final status.

Revenge killings of Serbs also weakened international sympathy, as did deadly raids in 2000 by a new Liberation Army of Presevo Medvedja and Bujanovac (known by its Albanian initials, UCPMB) across the eastern border into Serbia's Presevo Valley, where 70,000 ethnic Albanians live and constitute the majority. UCPMB wanted to unite them with Kosovo. Its guerrillas, well-armed from hidden KLA caches, operated across a three-mile buffer zone between Serbia and NATO troops (primarily the 1,700 American soldiers deployed in Kosovo) to ambush Serb policemen. Former Serbian President and Prime Minister Vojislav Kostunica, who had publicly and sharply opposed the NATO air war against Serbia in 1999, needed to court Western support and therefore avoided the kind of brutal response that Milosevic would have ordered. He did complain that NATO did not adequately guard the border to Serbia and had done too little to disarm the KLA fighters completely.

Indeed, out of fear of casualties, the 31 Western countries sending protection forces to Kosovo hesitated aggressively to root out the KLA, which maintained a shadow presence in the province. Nevertheless, what was different is that NATO and Serbia were now cooperating to prevent another Balkan conflict. Belgrade restrained its response to the Presevo raids, and NATO tried to cut off the flow of weapons to the guerrillas. In spring 2001 NATO permitted Serbian soldiers to move into the 5-kilometer buffer zone along the border to interdict KLA infiltration. KLA activists redirected their raids across the Macedonian border where that nation's Albanian population is concentrated. The intruders were beaten back by Macedonian military forces.

Local elections in Kosovo in October 2000 revealed just how badly the KLA had squandered the popularity it once enjoyed. Its officials had seized property and businesses and often behaved arrogantly toward people that only a year ago had viewed them as liberators. The party it had formed, the Democratic Party of Kosovo (PDK), led by Hashim Thaçi, who in February 2008 became the prime minister who declared Kosovo's independence, was humiliated at the polls. The PDK lost in most of the 27 municipalities it had controlled since July 1999. The big winner in

Kosovo President Fatmir Seidiu

Kosovo

the election, which tested the mood in the province, was the nonviolent Democratic League of Kosovo (LDK), led by the reclusive scholar, Ibrahim Rugova. It captured more than 60% of the votes, with almost 60% participating. Whereas the West had forced the KLA to disband and disarm, voters forced it to abandon its political role temporarily.

The predominance of Rugova's LDK was again confirmed in the 2001 and October 2004 elections to create a provincial government. The UN, represented from June 2004 to June 2006 by no-nonsense Danish diplomat Soren Jessen-Petersen, could hand over to it many of the political powers the UN had wielded since 1999 while retaining the right to veto any decision by local institutions. In the 2004 voting for seats in the 120-seat provincial assembly, 33 parties participated, and turnout was 53%. Rugova's party won 45% of the votes, while Ramush Haradinaj's Alliance for the Future of Kosova (AAK) came in third with 8% of the votes and nine seats. Together they formed a governing coalition, with Haradinaj as prime minister. Kosovo Serbs boycotted the election, but they are guaranteed a quota of at least ten seats.

The Kosovo government's challenges are great. It remains a deeply impoverished land with extensive war damage, strong tensions among the various ethnic groups, and a high level of corruption and organized crime. Criminal gangs, operating under the guise of Albanian nationalist militias, traffic in drugs, weapons, and women for the European sex industry. In 2008, Transparency International, a Berlin-based anticorruption watchdog, ranked Kosovo as the world's fourth most corrupt economy, after Cameroon, Cambodia and Albania. Bribery is commonplace.

An indigenous police force of 7,000, created and trained by 2,000 UN police officers from around the world and by EU specialists in EULEX, have helped to decrease serious crime. Official unemployment hovers at 50%, and it is even higher among Kosovars under age 30, who constitute 70% of the total population. But the underground economy provides work for some of these. Stylish new cafes and shopping malls in Prishtina partly disguise the fact that the average month's pay is only 250 euros ($325). One sees building, especially of private housing, going on everywhere in Kosovo. However, corruption and the pressing need to improve the rule of law discouraged foreign investors from putting their money into the moribund economy.

That the 14,000 remaining foreign peacekeepers (declining over time to 10,000), including 1,600 Americans, were still needed to maintain order was demonstrated in

Former Prime Minister Ramush Haradinaj returns from The Hague

March 2004 when the worst outburst of violence occurred since the 1999 war. It began after a Serbian youth from a village near Prishtina was allegedly injured in a drive-by shooting. According to an Albanian youth who escaped, a gang of Serbs then chased three Albanian boys into the fast-flowing Ibar River, which divides the two communities of Mitrovica, where they drowned. In revenge Albanian mobs drove some 4,100 Serbs in scattered enclaves from their homes and killed 19 and injured more than 900. Orthodox clergy claim that around 25 churches and monasteries were destroyed, triggering revenge attacks against mosques inside of Serbia.

NATO troops were unprepared and took two days to quell the violence and evacuate besieged Serbs. They rushed in 2,000 reinforcements to bring their total troop level to about 20,000. EU, NATO, U.S. and Serbian government officials were furious. Ex-Prime Minister Rexhepi called it a "disaster" and promised to rebuild the houses and churches. Then Serb Prime Minister Kostunica called the events a "pogrom." After the violence, Serbs boycotted Kosovo's institutions, including the government. It was followed by a 35% drop in the rate of refugees returning to Kosovo after fleeing in 1999.

The September 11, 2001, terrorist attacks in the U.S. significantly reduced Kosovo's claim to the world's, especially America's, attention and funding. Nevertheless, a start had been made on training a national army, and 60 countries dispatched civilian or military personnel; more than $2 billion have

Kosovo Serbs in Mitrovica like Russian Prime Minister Putin and rock music, 2008

Сепак
ДЕМОКРАТСКА РЕПУБЛИКА МАКЕДОНИЈА

Година IV број 126 22.2.2008. цена 50 денари

Форум

www.forum.com.mk

КОСОВО
Држава со хипотека

Орце Камчев: ОЛИГАРСИТЕ ЗЕДОА Сѐ
Sинго ни ја украде водата

Macedonian magazine, *Forum*, notes Kosovar Albanians' gratitude to America

Kosovo

been spent since 1999 to help the province. The sustained investment of money and soldiers has paid off. The country now has 105 banks with ATMs available. About 6,000 Serbs have returned to their homes in Kosovo, and their language can be heard in the principal cities.

Finally Albanian extremists are being taken to court. This is a sensitive issue because many Kosovo Albanians regard all former guerrillas as heroes. In 2002 an international court in Kosovo sentenced five former guerrillas to prison for abducting and beating four fellow ethnic Albanians. This was the first time any former KLA members were convicted of such crimes. In 2003 the UN war-crimes tribunal in The Hague for the first time indicted four ex-KLA guerrillas for acts committed during the 1998–9 war; four had been delivered to The Hague by 2004. One, Fatmir Limaj, was a member of the Kosovo parliament and later transport minister.

In April 2003 the UN administrator took the unprecedented step of branding an Albanian rebel group as terrorist—the Albanian National Army (ANA)—which unlike previous Albanian groups had a cell structure. In 2005 the tribunal in The Hague completed the first trial of a Kosovo Albanian by convicting Haradin Bala of murder and torture. A major problem with trying Kosovo Albanians was the difficulty of finding witnesses willing to risk their lives by testifying.

In March 2005 even Kosovo's prime minister, Ramush Haradinaj, surrendered to UN authorities. A former refugee in Switzerland, where he was a nightclub bouncer, he returned to Kosovo where he rose to be the most visible KLA commander, losing two brothers and sustaining three wounds himself in the conflict. Unlike Rugova, a pacifist, Haradinaj is a war hero. After the war, he founded the AAK, and following the October 2004 elections he became Europe's youngest prime minister at age 36. He was the most charismatic and effective leader Kosovo had had in its five years of quasi-independence under UN administration. He displayed a mixture of energy, discipline and attention to detail, and he knew how to get results.

The Serbian government was furious about his appointment, and investigators from the war-crimes tribunal soon appeared to question him about allegations of abuse toward Serbs. His decision to go to The Hague came as a surprise. In order to prevent the kind of disastrous unrest that had happened a year earlier, NATO temporarily increased its troop strength by 1,000. Haradinaj was permitted to return to Kosovo immediately to await the beginning of his trial in 2007. In the autumn of that year he was freed of all charges and returned to Kosovo as a national hero.

Haradinaj was first replaced as prime minister by Bajram Kosumi. Then in March 2006 the Kosovar assembly elected by a vote of 65 to 33 the popular former KLA commander and subsequently head of the Kosovo police force, Agim Çeku. He made it clear that there was no other possible solution to Kosovo's status than independence. But he reached out to Serbs by switching into Serbian during his acceptance speech and called on all minorities to participate in the region's political life and consider it their home.

Serbians strongly opposed his appointment and consider him a war criminal. When he accepted an invitation from the Bulgarian parliament in June 2009 to discuss Kosovo's integration into international organizations, Serbia demanded that he be arrested on an Interpol arrest warrant and extradited to Serbia on charges that he had allegedly ordered the murder of 669 Serbs during the Kosovo War. Çeku vigorously denies the charges and emphasizes that he had never been indicted by the International Criminal Tribunal in The Hague. But he was detained and interrogated for 72 hours before being released. It was an embarrassment for Sofia, which recognizes Kosovo's independence, albeit with reservations.

Negotiations on Kosovo's Status

The violence of March 2004 created a renewed sense of urgency over Kosovo. The UN had avoided starting final status talks for fear of inflaming Kosovo's political atmosphere and that of its neighbors. But the population is losing patience. In July 2004 the Kosovo parliament adopted constitutional changes that include the right to call a referendum on independence from Serbia and to transfer control for international relations and public security from the UN mission to the Kosovo government. UN officials denied that Kosovo has the authority to do this.

A tentative first step toward an agreement had already been taken in Vienna in October 2003 with second-echelon government officials from Kosovo and Serbia reading prepared statements to each other in the presence of UN, EU and NATO dignitaries. The Serb government suspended these "Vienna talks" in December 2004 when Haradinaj was appointed prime minister of Kosovo. Although talks between government officials were discontinued after the March 2004 violence, communications continued between leading figures on both sides outside of Kosovo. The Greek government played a particularly useful role in facilitating these contacts.

On May 27, 2005, the UN Security Council set a diplomatic process in motion. A UN envoy assessed the situation in advance of a "status envoy" in the fall to arrange negotiations between Kosovo's Albanians and Serbia. The Kosovo government showed that it was implementing reforms ranging from financial transparency to security guarantees for the Serb minority. The U.S., Britain, France,

Former Kosovo Prime Minister Agim Çeku   Source: *European Voice*

480

Prime Minister Hashim Thaçi

Germany and Russia agreed that Kosovo should have "conditional independence." Serbs would have to make the best of it. The conditions were that the rights of the Serb and other minorities must be protected, that there would be no return to the pre-1999 situation, and that there would be no "Greater Albania" linking all ethnic Albanians in one state. The goal was "final status" talks on independence.

Negotiations under the chairmanship of UN special envoy, Martti Ahtisaari, were to open in the Kinsky Palace in Vienna in January 2006. But they had to be postponed for a month because of the death of Kosovo's key negotiator, President Ibrahim Rugova. He died at age 61 of lung cancer days before the scheduled negotiations were to begin. His people gave him a lavish state funeral. Thousands honored his flag-draped coffin that was transported through the streets of Prishtina. Four presidents and representatives of over 40 countries attended the ceremony, including U.S. Secretary of State Condoleezza Rice.

Rugova was replaced as chief negotiator and largely ceremonial president by law professor and close colleague Fatmir Seidiu, who was elected by the Kosovo assembly. He is a political moderate, and he pledged both to achieve independence, to guarantee minority rights, and to make Kosovo "at peace with itself and its neighbors."

The Serbian government responded in anger. Then Prime Minister Kostunica said Belgrade would not accept an imposed solution in Kosovo. He attended the June 28, 2006, anniversary of the famous 14th century Battle of Kosovo in Gracanica, where he declared: "No one is

on firmer, truer ground in the talks on Kosovo's final status than Serbia." Moderate Serbian President Boris Tadic, who became the first Serbian leader to visit Kosovo since the end of the 1999 war, asserted that "independence for Kosovo is unacceptable for me. I will never endorse it." However, other Serbs hint that they could accept "more than autonomy but less than independence."

Nobody underestimated the difficulties involved. No Serbian leader wants to go down in history as the one who gave away Kosovo, which many Serbs regard as their historical birthright. Yet many Serbs were aware that they would not be able to prevent independence.

The hard problems remain: the divided city of Mitrovica, the return of all refugees, the security of Serbian enclaves, and the serious social and economic crisis. There developed a widespread conviction that the Kosovo issue must finally be solved in order to avoid "prolonging the pain and increasing the risks for the region," in former UN envoy Jessen-Petersen's words. The International Crisis Group had reported in 2005 that Kosovo stood on the edge of renewed conflict.

After lengthy negotiations between the Kosovo and Serbian governments, EU envoy Martti Ahtisaari drew up a plan in 2007 that envisioned a decentralized Kosovo government with the authority to sign international treaties and the responsibility to protect minorities and Serb religious sites and to prepare the return of Serb refugees. This would be conditional independence under temporary international guidance. The governmental system and its checks and balances are highly complex, with a "double majority" in par-

liament where minority interests are concerned and with Albanians having to submit to Serb local rule in some communities. For his skillful mediation and negotiation, Ahtisaari was awarded the Nobel Peace Prize in 2008. Receiving his prize, he asserted that "Kosovo is independent, and it will remain independent. The progress there is irreversible."

Conditions are not ideal for democracy in Kosovo: the economy is in terrible shape, unemployment is high, and organized crime and corruption are too prevalent, as in the rest of the Balkans. But Kosovars have elected their leaders for many years, their legislative assembly has acted responsibly, and on the whole they have shown respect for the rights of minorities. They were ready to take control of their own governance on February 17, 2008.

Russia threatened to use its veto in the UN Security Council to prevent independence unless it was approved by Serbia. The U.S. and most EU countries supported the Ahtisaari plan, but they tried to avoid a clash with Putin's Russia. If he used his UN veto, the UN representative in Kosovo would legally be obligated to annul any declaration of independence. Therefore the matter was postponed until later in 2007. Then Prime Minister Agim Çeku proposed November 28, 2007, the Albanian national holiday, as a good day to proclaim independence, but he stated that his government did not want to act without the backing of Washington and Brussels.

What did take place on November 7, 2007, was a final parliamentary election to legitimize the government that would declare independence soon thereafter. After Rugova had died almost two years earlier, his center-right League of Democratic Kosovo (LDK), to which President Sejdui belongs, had been gripped by a leadership struggle and lost its traditional position as largest party. It fell to 22% of the votes and 25 of 120 seats.

The winner was the center-left Democratic Party of Kosovo (PDK), led by a 39-year-old former KLA leader, Hashim Thaçi, with 34% of the votes and 37 seats. The PDK is one of two parties that have their roots in the Kosovo Liberation Army (KLA). The other is the center-right Alliance for the Future of Kosovo (AAK), led by former KLA commander and prime minister, Ramush Haradinaj, who was cleared of war crimes shortly before the election. Thaçi had often clashed with the pacifist Rugova, and there were rivalry and tensions with Sejdui. But both of these two large parties favored independence and cooperated to make that happen on February 17, 2008. Thaçi said soon after taking office: "We can't wait until all states

E hëne • 18 shkurt, 2008

Express

www.gazetaexpress.com N° 1068, Viti III, Çmimi: 0.20 € • E perditshme e pavarur kosovare

KOSOVA REPUBLIKE

Kjo nuk është më vetëm një parullë e shkruar fshehurazi nëpër mure dhe askush më kurrë nuk do të dënohet më 60 ditë burg për të. Tash, Kosova është Republikë përnjëmend. Sot, fillon njohja.

Kosovo investigative reporter Alban Bokshi

sovo's future status in a careful and coordinated manner.

Independence and Political System

Kosovars yearned for independence, and they maintained a positive attitude. Several annual surveys by Gallup International from 2006 on revealed that they are among the five most optimistic nations of the world; another Gallup poll in 2009 found that Kosovars were the most satisfied among seven western Balkan countries. That optimism paid off on February 17, 2008, when Kosovo declared its independence from Serbia. The outcome was freedom for the entire province with certain conditions, including protections for Serbs and other minorities, supervision by the EU and protection by NATO and other foreign troops for years. Gratitude for America's support was strong and visible, with demonstrators unfurling giant American flags and chanting "Thank you, USA," and "God bless America."

As a gesture of conciliation, Prime Minister Thaçi addressed the parliament on February 17, 2008, in both Albanian and Serbian, and he pledged to protect Serbs' rights. But the Serbs would have none of it. With the support of the government in Belgrade, Kosovo Serbs set fire to two border posts between northern Kosovo and Serbia and completely destroyed them. NATO troops were forced to intervene. The Serb minister for Kosovo stated that these attacks were "in accordance with the general government policies." In Belgrade, the news was received with despair and anger. About 2,000 furious Serbs converged on the U.S. embassy and set it on fire. One protester perished in the flames. The Serbian government formally proposed that Kosovo be divided along ethnic lines, but the chief EU envoy, Pieter Feith, was clear: "This country . . . should not end up even with soft partition."

The violence continued in March, when UN police officers raided a UN courthouse in Mitrovica that had been seized by Serbs. The latter responded by shooting guns and throwing rocks and grenades. One Ukrainian officer was killed and dozens were hurt. This was part of a Serb campaign to make Prishtina's rule over northern Kosovo impossible. This area already had parallel institutional structures linked to Serbia, and pensions and pay come from Serbia.

Kosovo's new constitution went into effect on June 15, 2008. It is a pro-EU docu-

are ready to recognize us." They formed a grand coalition in which the PDK got seven cabinet seats and the LDK five. Three ministries were offered to minorities, two of them Serbs. Neither of the large governing parties is happy with this coalition. The government's and prime minister's popularity plunged in 2010.

A third party that had been created only a year earlier, the Alliance for New Kosovo, got 12% of the votes. It is led by Swiss entrepreneur and major investor in Kosovo, Behgjet Pacolli. The only Islamic party to compete in this largely secular country won a mere 2% of the votes. Widespread disillusionment among voters was demonstrated by the low 43% turnout. Serbs shunned the polling altogether. A Serbian List for Kosovo and Metohija (SLKM) had been formed in 2004 and won several seats. But they have boycotted Kosovo's institutions and have never taken their seats in the Kosovo Assembly.

A UN-sponsored troika process, consisting of representatives of the EU, U.S. and Russia, made one last effort, but it failed to reach a compromise. The process ended in December 2007. A joint EU-U.S. statement declared that the UN Security Council was not in a position to agree on the way ahead. It endorsed the view that the potential for a negotiated solution had been exhausted and that the EU stood ready to play a leading role in implementing a settlement defining Ko-

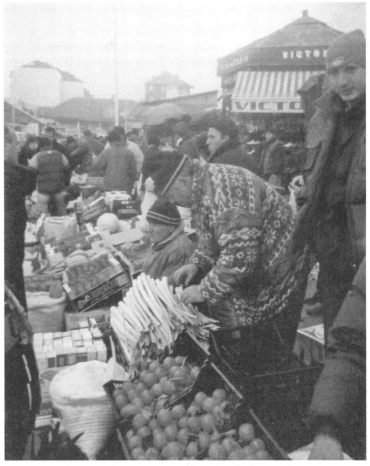

Kosovo farmers on market day in Mitrovica

Kosovo

A graffiti-covered monument—24 meters wide and three meters high to celebrate Kosovo—a newly free nation

ment built around the Western-backed "settlement package." It cedes final authority to an EU-led "civilian office," led by the International Civilian Representative (ICR). The post involves sweeping powers, and the first appointee is Pieter Feith from the Netherlands. The EU fully supports Kosovo's progress under its Stabilisation and Association Process, meaning ultimate EU membership for both it and Serbia. The constitution gave no role to the UN.

The main thrust of the new constitution is decentralization of power and the maximum feasible autonomy at the local level. Kosovo is composed of 30 municipalities, which form the basic territorial units of local self-government. In communities with Serbian majorities, the Albanian minority must be governed in local matters by Serbs. Serb majority municipalities have the authority to provide secondary health care, offer higher education, oversee cultural affairs, including the protection and promotion of the religious and cultural heritage, be involved in the selection of local station police commanders, and receive funds from institutions in Serbia.

In the first elections held after the independence of the newest country in the world, voters elected their local governments in November 2009. The big news was the turnout: 45% in all of Kosovo and 20% in the Serb enclaves. Fearing a Serb boycott, the government and diplomatic community were delighted that so many Serbs voted and ran for office even though they largely ignore the state centered in

Prishtina. In the other Serb enclaves outside the north, Serbs have grudgingly accepted the new state even though they reject independence from Serbia.

To protect the rights of minorities in the single-chamber Assembly of Kosovo, a "double majority" is required on all issues that affect minorities. This means that two-thirds of the whole assembly and two-thirds of the representatives of the minorities (especially Serbs), who are guaranteed at least 20 of 120 seats (100 of which are directly elected by the people for four-year terms), must approve. Depending on the size of the government, two or three of the ministers are required to be from the minorities. The judiciary is independent. The assembly elects the president for five years and approves the government.

Because Russia, which has a veto in the UN Security Council, supports Serbia's rejection of Kosovo freedom as "illegal" (on the grounds that it has not been approved by the Security Council), the UN was unable to withdraw completely, as it had planned to do. UN resolution 1244, adopted in 1999 after the Kosovo War, requires the UN mission to stay until a new resolution decides the status of the territory; Russia blocks such a new resolution. A perplexed UN Secretary-General Ban Ki-moon said that a "UN umbrella" would remain. Nobody knew exactly what this meant. Its future role in the new state was unclear as it shrank to 10% of its former size but did not disappear. UNMIK remains an indispensable intermedi-

ary in Kosovo's international dealings, and it directly administers Serb-claimed Mitrovica, which has come to symbolize the ethnic divide.

In December 2008 the UN handed over responsibility for civilian law enforcement, customs and judiciary to the EU and local authorities in Prishtina. Handing off the supervisory role to the EU was problematic. The EU's 2,220-strong police and justice (EULEX) presence was delayed, but by 2009 it was in place all across Kosovo.

NATO's KFOR remains to maintain the fragile peace. But it decided in June 2009 to reduce its numbers from the roughly 14,000 troops from more than 30 countries (including about 1,600 Americans) to around 10,000, calling this a "purely deterrent presence." They are backed by a new lightly armed Kosovo Security Force under NATO guidance. It is to develop into what Prime Minister Thaçi called "a multi-ethnic force in the service of the country and all of its citizens," including Serbs.

To make things worse, the defiant Serb minority greeted the new constitution by announcing that it had set up its own elected 43-seat parliament in Mitrovica within Kosovo. Serbs had done the same thing in Croatia and Bosnia in the early 1990s. Of the 43 assembly members, 35 come from the north of Kosovo even though more than half of Kosovar Serbs live in enclaves elsewhere in the country. Serb municipal elections had been in May, an act that the UN and EU had branded as illegal. The new assembly convened on a highly symbolic day: June 28, the anniversary of the epic Kosovo battle in 1389. Its first act was to declare that Kosovo remains "an inseparable part of Serbia" and that its secession was "illegal."

Serbia pretends that Kosovo is not independent. For example, in March 2010 its president, Boris Tadic, refused to participate in a Balkan summit meeting in Slovenia unless Kosovo's representatives attending under the name, "Kosovo-UNMIK." This would have implied that Kosovo was not independent, so Kosovo's leaders refused to back down. Tadic stayed home. One other participating state, Bosnia-Herzegovina, does not recognize Kosovo's independence, but its leader attended anyway (albeit leaving the room when the Kosovar prime minister gave his speech).

The Kosovo government pretends to be sovereign all over the country. But the area north of the Ibar River is still ruled de facto by Serbia and uses its currency, the dinar. Serbia has consolidated its grip over Serbian-settled areas, especially in the north. To the Kosovo Albanians' chagrin, their future is still tied to Serbia.

All this amounts to a depressing mess for Kosovars. The international reaction was mixed. While 69 countries, including the United States, 22 of 27 EU members, neighbors Montenegro and Macedonia and large Muslim countries starting with Saudi Arabia, had recognized independent Kosovo by 2010, such major EU countries as Spain, Greece, Romania, Slovakia and Cyprus, as well as Russia, China, India, Egypt and Brazil had not. Two-thirds of the UN's 192 members had not yet recognized it in 2010. Until it is a UN member or is supported by two-thirds of its members, a country cannot belong to the Universal Postal Union, required for international postal service. It cannot have a phone prefix or its own Internet domain name. Kosovo rents dialing codes from Slovenia and Monaco.

Russia and China veto in the Security Council Kosovo's joining the UN. Serbia persuaded the General Assembly to submit the question of Kosovo's independence to the International Court of Justice for a non-binding advisory ruling on its legality. Any rendered opinion is bound to be ambiguous giving both sides the latitude to interpret it as they want. Serbia would follow up with requesting a UN General Assembly resolution calling for new talks on Kosovo's status. This infuriates European and American diplomats. Only eight countries maintain embassies to the Republic of Kosovo: Albania, Austria, Germany, the United Kingdom, the United States, Switzerland (also representing Liechtenstein) and Italy. But over time, more will be opened.

There is, however, lots of good news. The violence and ethnic cleansing that many observers had predicted have not taken place. A mass exodus of Serbs has been averted. Kosovo today is largely peaceful. Tensions between ethnic Albanians and Serbs are low. Most of Kosovo's Serb police officers, who were exhorted by Serbia to resign, have returned to work. Kosovo Albanian ministers and top Serbian officials are talking directly. Serbia's most pro-EU government ever, led by President Boris Tadic, assigned new people to deal with Kosovo. Supported by the U.S., Germany, France and the UK, Kosovo was admitted to the IMF and World Bank in May 2009, despite a Serbian letter of warning sent to all 185 members.

ECONOMY

A key for improving the economy and attracting investment, in addition to solving the "status question," has been the strengthening of a rule of law and the gradual diminution of violence, organized crime and corruption. The latter exist at a high level. For example, in April 2010 the offices of Transport Minister Fatmir Limaj, a former KLA fighter and close political ally of Prime Minister Thaçi, were raided by EULEX police and prosecutors for evidence relating to fraud in road construction contracts. Members of his family were caught at Prishtina's airport trying to leave the country with suitcases containing millions in cash. Large public companies, such as the Kosovo Energy Corporation (KIK), are routinely looted by their executives, most of them political appointees. The government is under growing pressure from European and American diplomats to crack down on such corruption.

Criminal relationships permeate even political parties and institutions. Criminal gangs, operating under the guise of Albanian nationalist militias, traffic in drugs, weapons, and women for the European sex industry. Its economic weakness has produced a thriving black economy in smuggled gasoline, cigarettes and cement, among other commodities. In 2008, Transparency International, a Berlin-based anti-corruption watchdog, ranked Kosovo as the world's fourth most corrupt economy, after Cameroon, Cambodia and Albania. Bribery is commonplace.

This has tarnished the country's image abroad and discourages foreign investment. It has inspired a new kind of business school, the American University in Kosovo (AUK), founded in 2003 in the hilly eastern outskirts of Prishtina, to produce graduates imbued with the university's honor code: each student publicly vows not to "cheat, steal or plagiarize" and to "show respect to all." Most do not seek their fortunes abroad. They remain in Kosovo to serve their young country despite official unemployment of 40%. Prishtina was ranked 12th overall out of 23 southeastern European cities in a 2009 World Bank study in terms of ease of doing business; Prizren was 8th.

Because of the many weapons in the hands of civilians, law enforcement inefficiencies, and widespread devastation following the Kosovo War, both revenge killings and ethnic violence surged significantly. The number of reported murders rose 80% in 2001. Reported arsons rose 140%. The number of reported serious crimes increased between 1999 and 2000, but since then it resembles more the patterns of other European cities.

Police action has improved greatly. By 2008, recorded murder rates had declined steadily, falling by 75% since 2003 to under three per 100,000 people. This is a figure comparable to that of Switzerland, Ireland, or Finland. Landmines laid by both the Serbs and KLA during the Kosovo War, as well as unexploded NATO ordnance, remain a problem.

Kosovo has one of the most underdeveloped economies in Europe, with an annual per capita income estimated at 3,000 euros ($3,900) in 2010. That is roughly a tenth that of Slovenia. It was the poorest province of Yugoslavia and received substantial development subsidies from the Yugoslav federation. Additionally, in the 1990s a combination of bad economic policies, international sanctions, inadequate external trade and ethnic conflict and war severely damaged the economy. Its imports exceed its exports ten-fold, and this drives up the country's relatively huge current account deficit, which in 2008 amounted to 23% of GDP. It imports most of its food, including such staples as meat and milk. The country is again producing its own wine, especially in the Rahovic area, where it was made as early as 28 BC.

However, there are pockets of apparent prosperity in Prishtina. Kosovo looks more like a poor part of the rich European continent than a developing country. Many families have members abroad who send money home, and they rely on it. Such remittances account for an estimated 15–20% of GDP, but they declined during the recession. In 2008 they outweighed foreign direct investment by 550 million euros to 350 million euros. In addition, generations of Kosovars worked as guest workers in Europe, and their pensions constitute a huge infusion into the economy. The service sector constitutes 60% of the economy. The best paying jobs are with international organizations.

About 40% are still officially counted as unemployed (two-thirds of the youth).

Kosovo

With 25,000 young people entering the work force annually, the economy would have to grow by 7% in each of 15 years in order to bring joblessness under control. The underground economy is large and provides unreported and untaxed work for many. To lure foreign investment, the country has the lowest tax burden in Europe: 10% for both the highest personal income and for corporate profits.

International assistance is crucial and accounts for around 34% of GDP. By 2008 the EU had pledged two billion euros and the U.S. $350 million. Serbia pledged 120 million euros to the Serb enclaves in Kosovo. In July 2008 a donor's conference in Switzerland raised one billion euros ($1.3 billion). Kosovo is a newborn nation with the expected economic uncertainties. In many ways it has to start from scratch.

Its one big economic advantage is that Kosovo is rich in all kinds of minerals. It took 70% of former Serbia's mineral deposits (and 90% of its coal) with it when it broke free in 2008. Despite irritating daily power cuts lasting for hours, there are 14 billion tons of lignite coal reserves (the world's fifth-largest proven reserves of this low-grade coal). Some of it will be used in a new power plant by 2012. There are already two large coal-fired electrical power plants, named "Kosovo A" and "Kosovo B." Electricity demand is increasing by 7% each year, and a staggering 44% of electricity entering the distribution network is either stolen or not paid for.

There are also vast deposits of nickel, lead, zinc, cadmium, bauxite and even some gold. Halloysite, an aluminosilicate clay mineral used as a raw material for porcelain and bone china, has been discovered. It is only one of five known exploitable deposits of this very high-value clay; one of the other four is in Utah. The problem is that its extraction infrastructure is old and in need of large investments. That is why mining has been stalled since 1999.

Its most important mining complex is Trepca. However, it is politically explosive because it is run jointly by ethnic Serbs and Albanians, and its mines and processing factories are spread between the Serb-dominated north and the Albanian-dominated south. Geological surveys show that 88% of Kosovo's mineral wealth is the southern part of the land.

Kosovo's economy remains weak. The private sector that has emerged since 1999 is mainly small-scale. The industrial sector is weak, and the electric power supply remains unreliable. This is a critical constraint on the economy. Free-trade agreements have been signed with Croatia, Bosnia and Herzegovina, Albania and Macedonia. UNMIK introduced an external trade regime and customs administration in September 1999 when it established customs border controls in Kosovo. All goods imported into Kosovo faced a flat 10% customs duty fee. In 2009 Kosovo replaced its UN-issued customs stamps with its own. However, Serbia, which is one of its most important trading partners, refused to accept the new stamps. Neither country backed down, so that crucial trading relationship has suffered.

Kosovo's biggest export is scrap metal from old cars. The euro is the official currency although the Serb enclaves still use the dinar. The chief means of entry to this landlocked country, apart from the main highway leading northward from Skopje, Macedonia, and the new super highway leading from northern Albania to Prishtina, is Prishtina International Airport. The latter, along with the Postal and Telecommunication Company of Kosovo (PTK) and the KED energy company, are slated to be privatized.

Macedonia is Kosovo's largest import and export market (constituting 20% of total Kosovo trade), followed by Serbia (12%), Germany (10%), China (5%–9%) and Turkey (6% of total imports). As a whole, the EU is its biggest trade partners and is responsible for a third of its imports and over half of its exports. Kosovo faces the threat of an economic embargo by Serbia. However, given the magnitude of Serbian exports to Kosovo, such a tactic would probably hurt Serbia more than Kosovo.

FUTURE

Kosovo's future looks brighter than it has in decades. Having declared its independence and adopted a new constitution in 2008, both with the support of 22 EU member states and the United States, it is prepared to make up for two decades of stagnation caused by discrimination, resistance and warfare. It faces determined opposition from Serbia, supported by an assertive Russia, which will not accept the new reality of Kosovo's freedom any time soon. This makes UN membership a distant dream.

A bad omen for the desired harmony between Kosovars and Serbs occurred in Mitrovica in July 2010. Petar Miletic, a Serb member of parliament and leader of the Independent Liberal party, was shot in his home and wounded in the knee.

It will take years of hard work to qualify for EU membership. But it has entered the stabilization and association process and intends to pursue this important goal to completion.

Change of command, KFOR

The Republic of Macedonia

View of Skopje. Church of St. Kliment

Area: 9,928 sq. mi. (25,713 sq. km.)

Population: 2,022,547 (2003 census)

Capital City: Skopje, pronounced *Scope-yeh* (467,800).

Climate: Mediterranean in the south; mild, temperate elsewhere.

Neighboring Countries: Albania (west); Greece (south); Bulgaria (east); Kosovo (north); Serbia (north).

Official Language: Macedonian

Other Principal Tongues: Albanian, Turkic, Serbian.

Ethnic Background: South Slavic Macedonian (64.18%) and Albanian (25.17%).

Principal Religions: Orthodox Christianity; Islam.

Chief Commercial Products: Agricultural products, chemicals, steel, textiles.

Main Trading Partners: Serbia and Montenegro (23% of exports and 7.5% of imports), Germany (15.5% of exports and 9.5% of imports), Greece (15% of exports and 8% of imports), Russia (15% of imports).

Currency: denar

Former Political Status: Constituent Republic of Yugoslavia.

National Day: August 2

Chief of State: Gjorgje Ivanov, President (April 2009).

Head of Government: Nikola Gruevski, President of the Government (Prime Minister; August 2006).

National Flag: A golden eight-ray sun is centered on a red field. The flag was slightly revised in 1995 so it no longer looks like the sixteen-pointed Star of Vergina associated with Alexander the Great.

When one first hears the word, Macedonia, one's imagination flies back to the 4th century B.C., when Alexander the Great ruled the world from this starkly beautiful mountainous region. Modern Macedonia has little, if anything, to do with that particular past, however. The only re-Hellenized part of Alexander's home kingdom is to be found across the border in Greece, whose northernmost province also bears the name Macedonia. Macedonians in the Republic of Macedonia formed the southern tier of unified Yugoslavia.

In September 1991 they became the only citizens of that collapsed state who were able to gain their independence peacefully. The Macedonians overwhelmingly voted "yes" in a referendum on independence. They were also the first people in the world to establish "preventive peacekeeping," whereby they persuaded the United Nations to establish a stabilizing presence before the outbreak of ethnic violence. This is a small, multiethnic country that is determined to maintain its

self-rule without the bloodshed that has stained the former Yugoslav republics to the north.

Located in the southwestern Balkans, Macedonia borders on Greece to the south, Albania to the west, Kosovo to the northwest, Serbia to the northeast and Bulgaria to the east. The valley of the Vardar River, commonly referred to as the Vardar Plain, dominates the center of the republic. This lowland area is the only place in the Balkans where the mountains can be traversed both north-south and east-west.

The Vardar River begins in the northwestern part of the republic and flows north and east until it reaches Skopje, the capital. It continues southeastward down through Macedonia, hemmed in by mountains to the west and east, then crosses into Greece. At the Greek border, it becomes the Axios River. Flowing through Greek Macedonia, it empties into the Gulf of Salonica. This provides Macedonia with a natural outlet toward the south although this is dependent on the status of relations with Greece. This passage was closed between February 1994 and October 1995 as a result of a Greece embargo instituted against Macedonia in an attempt to force it to change its name.

The east-west route connects the Albanian port of Durres with Bulgaria in the east. Albania's long isolation means that the western route has been little used in recent times.

A chain of mountains (really a series of ridges) running in a southwest-northeast direction dominates the western part of Macedonia. Fairly wide valleys are located between the ridges. A second chain of mountains, the Sar, runs west-east along the border with Serbia. In the center, the Crna Gora (Black Mountains) reach down into Macedonia from Serbia, stopping just north of Skopje. Another mountain, the Osogovske Planini (Osogovo Chain), marks most of the border with Bulgaria.

487

Macedonia

Ethnic Macedonian speakers represent 64.18% of the total population. Macedonian belongs to the family of South Slavic languages. Ethnic Albanians, the largest minority, make up 25.17% of the total. Ethnic Albanians live mainly in the western part of the republic. Other minorities include Turks (4%), Romi (Gypsies, 2.3%), Serbs (2%), and Vlachs (1%), who are related to Romanians and have their own language. Almost all Serbs live in the northeastern part, near the city of Kumanovo and villages on Mount Skopska Crna Gora near the capital of Skopje.

HISTORY

The name Macedonia is an ancient one, going back to the 4th century B.C. and earlier. There was also a larger Macedonia that was part of the Ottoman Empire from 1371 to 1912. It was an area of mixed populations. The Turks ruled non-Islamic peoples through their religious structures, and most Macedonians are Orthodox Christians. Thus the Turks made no differentiation between Greek and Slavic-speaking individuals.

In 1913, this historic Macedonia was divided up by Greece, Bulgaria and Serbia after they had wrested it from the Ottoman Empire in the First Balkan War. Greece carried out a Hellenization of the territories it obtained. Therefore, Macedonian speakers are almost exclusively found inside the Republic of Macedonia. There are Macedonian-speaking minorities in western Bulgaria, which always treated Macedonians as Bulgarians, in Greece, where an estimated 50,000 are not officially recognized, and in Albania and Serbia. Macedonians tended to become amalgamated in the larger Bulgarian population. Serbia treated the Macedonians as Serbs until World War II. During the war, Macedonians fought with the Partisan Movement of the communist leader, Marshal Tito. After the war, he turned Yugoslavia into a federal republic, and the Socialist Republic of Macedonia became one of the six constituent republics.

Independence

The failure of unified Yugoslavia to solve its economic problems led to a slow disintegration. Macedonians never took the lead in this process, but like the Slovenians and Croatians they supported abandonment of communist economic policies. In 1990, the legislature asserted Macedonia's sovereignty, and elections resulted in the first noncommunist government.

By the beginning of 1991, Macedonians supported a major reformation of Yugoslavia although they continued to favor some form of union. When Serbia and Montenegro reelected their communist leaders, the stage was set for a confrontation. It was the new Slovenian and Croatian leaders who made the strongest case for change. But it was the Serbian stonewalling that eventually convinced Macedonians that they could not remain part of a Yugoslavia dominated by Serbia. In September 1991, therefore, Macedonians followed the lead of Slovenia and Croatia and voted in a referendum for a "sovereign and independent" republic.

On October 3, 1991, Branko Kostic, Montenegrin representative to the Yugoslav collective presidency, called a meeting in his role as vice president and proposed declaring a state of emergency. Since the president, Stipe Mesic, was not present, and the Slovenian delegate was boycotting the meeting, Kostic got his resolution passed with the support of the three votes controlled by Serbia (Serbia plus its two formerly autonomous regions of Voivodina and Kosovo). As a result, the Macedonian delegate to the presidency withdrew from subsequent meetings, and the Macedonian Assembly condemned Kostic's actions as unconstitutional and invalid. The Macedonian government then condemned the war against Croatia, declared its neutrality, called upon Macedonian soldiers to return to Macedonia, and requested the Yugoslavia People's Army to withdraw its local forces. Not wanting to drive Macedonia into an alliance with Croatia, Belgrade agreed to have all of its troops out of Macedonia by April 15, 1991. The Macedonian delegates to the Yugoslav legislature also stopped attending parliamentary sessions in November.

In January 1992, the Macedonian Assembly passed two amendments to the constitution demanded by the EC (now EU) as a price for recognition. The first stated that Macedonia does not have any territorial claims against its neighbors. The second stated that Macedonia will not interfere in the internal affairs of the neighboring sovereign countries. Other related actions included repealing the two sections of the constitution that provided for participation in federal organs, including the presidency, and recalling all Macedonians in the diplomatic staff. In addition, the assembly approved the formation of a Macedonian national army of 25,000–30,000 troops. International diplomatic recognition was slow in coming. That, too, is now an accomplished fact although it required some concessions on the part of the Macedonian government.

There have always been serious concerns about a possible political destabilization caused by one or more of Macedonia's neighbors trying to interfere in domestic politics. Those fears were brought once more to the fore in October 1995 when there was an attempt on ex-President Gligorov's life. A car bomb was set off at the side of the road just as his official limousine passed enroute to his office. The driver was killed, and several bystanders were injured. Gligorov himself was hit in the head by a piece of shrapnel and had to be hospitalized. No group took credit for the attempt on the president's life. Speculation as to who was responsible includes Bulgarian extremists or Macedonian nationalists who objected to concessions that he made to Greece relating to the flag and constitution.

POLITICAL SYSTEM

Macedonia is a multiparty parliamentary democracy with a presidential-parliamentary system of government. The most important political figure is the president of the government, referred to in most democracies as "prime minister." He must command a majority in parliament. The first free parliamentary elections took place in 1990.

The Presidency

The president is elected directly for a term of five years. If a candidate fails to win a majority of votes in the first round of elections, a runoff is held two weeks later between the top two candidates. To be valid, the turnout for this second round must be at least 50%. The position is largely, though not entirely, ceremonial. He has the right to veto legislation although parliament can re-pass the legislation over his veto. Perhaps his chief power is that, because he is elected by the entire nation, he can exercise a sort of national leadership.

Boris Trajkovski was president from December 1999 until February 2004, when he was killed in a tragic small-plane crash while flying in thick fog to an international investment conference in Mostar, Bosnia. He is widely credited with easing tensions and finding a compromise between the Macedonian majority and Albanian minority, thereby preventing a serious outbreak of violence in 2001 from degenerating into a civil war. He fought off calls within his own party to take a tough line toward the Albanian rebels. The election of his successor was refreshingly free of nationalist rhetoric.

Under the constitution, a deceased president is replaced by the parliamentary speaker, who must hold new elections within 40 days. Elected president in April 2004 was Prime Minister Branko Crvenkovski of the Social Democratic Union of Macedonia (SDSM). As prime minister, he had advocated reconciliation, saying "a man who cannot forgive is not a man." In the second round, with a turnout of 53.7%,

Crvenkovski captured 62.7% of the votes to 37.3% for Sasko Kedev of the Internal Macedonian Revolutionary Organization-Democratic Party for Macedonian Unity. Kedev claimed fraud, but the OSCE judged the elections to have been "generally consistent with international standards." In his swearing-in ceremony, Crvenkovski vowed to press on with efforts to achieve reconciliation with Macedonia's ethnic Albanian minority and to prevent any resumption of violence.

In April 2009 a man was chosen as president who had never before run for public office: Gjorgje Ivanov of the conservative governing party, VMRO-DPMNE. In the second round, he received twice as many votes as his Social Democratic opponent, Ljubomir Frchoski. The election did not spark the chaos and violence that was witnessed in the preceding year. Ivanov was a law professor at the University of Skopje. He pledged in his campaign not to bend to Greek pressure over the country's name: "I go to bed with Macedonia in the evening and wake up with Macedonia in the morning." He is known in the public as a sharp-tongued political commentator who had made a name by opposing the Ohrid agreement and who is unpopular with ethnic Albanians.

Parliament

Parliamentary elections occur every four years. Macedonia has a 120-seat parliament (*Sobranie*), 85 of which are elected in single constituencies on the basis of the majority principle. The remaining 35 are selected by proportional representation. This latter system was instituted in 1994 as a concession to the smaller political parties.

Early parliamentary elections took place in June 2008 after Greece had prevented its entry into NATO because of the 17-year dispute over the country's name. In addition, the Democratic Party of Albanians had pulled out of the governing coalition when its demand was not met that the newly independent Kosovo be recognized. Prime Minister Nikola Gruevski gambled on a snap election and won a parliamentary majority in a landslide victory. The results were a reminder that Macedonia remains a multiethnic country despite the power-sharing compromise that had prevented a civil war only a few years earlier. There was little voting across ethnic lines. The polling was marred by violence in the Albanian areas, where one man was killed and nine wounded in gun battles. OSCE monitors also commented that the poll did not fully meet international standards.

Emerging again as the winner of the June 2008 elections was the VMRO-DPMNE, which along with its smaller al-

lies in an umbrella "For a Better Macedonia," won 48.8% of the votes and 63 of 120 seats. Nikola Gruevski, a former World Bank economist, amateur boxer and stage actor, remained prime minister.

Despite the fact that Gruevski has a parliamentary majority and cannot be "held hostage" by an Albanian party, his VMRO-DPMNE chose as its governing coalition partner the Union for Democratic Integration (DUI), led by Ali Ahmeti and the strongest party among ethnic Albanians. A former factory worker, who lived in Swiss exile, Ahmeti enjoys hero status among Albanians for playing a crucial role in the peace process and keeping a lid on tensions in conflict areas. It received 12.8% of the votes and 18 seats in 2008.

DUI's participation in the previous government had shown just how much Macedonian politics had changed. More than half of the DUI legislators are former members of the Albanian National Liberation Army. However, unlike Kosovo Albanians, who declared outright independence and their own state, Ahmeti's followers fought for their Albanian rights within the Macedonian state to be recognized and respected.

The other major Albanian party, the Democratic Party of Albanians (DPA), again did poorly, winning only 8.5% of the votes and 11 seats. It is in the opposition.

The main opposition party is the center-left SDSM, the largest grouping under an umbrella called "Sun-Coalition for Europe." It won 23.7% of the votes and 27 seats. It is the successor party to the League of Communists of Macedonia and was the ruling party for the first six years after independence.

One reason for parties' desire to be included in the government is that being out of power means to be without patronage. For example, within days of Gruevski's taking office in July 2006, 544 managers and top officials in state companies were sacked or sidelined, and hundreds of civil servants were replaced by VMRO or DPA loyalists.

One of the government's priorities is the prosecution of ex-government ministers for corruption. "Nobody will be protected," President Crvenkovski assured. Usually acts of corruption are prosecuted only when the opposition wins an election. It promptly charged or arrested the former economics minister, the head of the state health care fund, and the directors of a state-owned printing company. Others were put under investigation. For the first time in Macedonia's history, a member of the government structure was charged by his own party. State Secretary for Defense Ljupco Popovski was accused of accepting bribes worth more than 20,000 euros. The fact that only the Min-

President Gjorgje Ivanov

istry of Economy can issue trade licenses and permits keeps the door to bribery open.

The Berlin-based Transparency International estimated that corruption scares off many foreign investors. A 2004 report by the European Commission concluded: "The high level of corruption and the mistrust towards institutions it generates remain major deterrent facts to growth and investment, and beyond this, to the success of many reforms which have been initiated to accelerate the transition of the country towards a modern democracy and economy."

Ohrid Peace Accord

The DUI had achieved recognition in the Western-brokered Ohrid peace accord signed in 2001. It made Albanian an official language in areas where Albanians represent more than 20% of the population. Street signs in Skopje are in Albanian as well as Macedonian. Albanians

Prime Minister Nikola Gruevski

Macedonia

were granted the status of full partners in the country, hitherto denied. Proportional employment of the ethnic Albanians in the administration was a key provision. All of these steps have meant that there is less interethnic hatred than in neighboring Kosovo. Albanians in Macedonia want to prevent, not rekindle, violence.

Nevertheless, at the time of the 2002 elections the U.S. had his name on a black-list of extremists, and the Macedonian state prosecutor had an arrest warrant against him for alleged war crimes. Many Macedonian Slavs regard him as a terror-ist who sparked a conflict that cost hun-dreds of lives, and the supporters and leaders of both partners in the governing coalition remain intensely suspicious of each other.

The Ohrid agreement was put to a test in November 2004 when hard-liners among the Slav majority managed to have a referendum scheduled that would have prevented the granting of autonomy to the Albanian minority. It was in response to a government law redrawing munici-pal districts to make ethnic Albanians a dominant force in 16 out of 83 (reduced in number from 123) municipal districts. Es-pecially controversial were provisions that widened Skopje's city limits to in-clude several Albanian-dominated dis-tricts. This pushed the city's population to over 20% Albanian, thereby qualifying the capital as a bi-communal, bilingual city.

Envoys from the U.S. and EU went to Macedonia to campaign against the refer-endum, making it clear that rejecting the Ohrid agreement would be a step back into the dangerous politics of ethnic con-flict. The government pled with voters to boycott the polling. If 50% of eligible vot-ers do not vote in a referendum, then any result is invalid. That is exactly what hap-pened. Only 26% voted, so the constitu-tional changes to devolve power were back on track. On November 10, 2004, three days after the failed referendum, politicians from all sides reassembled at Lake Ohrid to recommit themselves to the reconciliation process.

Ethnic Politics

Macedonian nationhood has been con-tested throughout history. National iden-tity is therefore weak and insecure. Re-gional identity tends to be stronger, and many Macedonians identify with their neighbors, such as Serbs to the north, Al-banians to the north and west and Bulgar-ians to the east. There is no effective na-tional strategy to strengthen a sense of Macedonian identity.

A major issue faced by any government is the ethnically mixed nature of Macedon-ian society. As Macedonia moved to open up its political system following the col-lapse of communism, nationalist-minded Albanians began making increased de-mands for greater political and cultural autonomy. One aspect is the question whether it should be possible to display the Albanian flag on government build-ings where ethnic Albanians constitute the majority of the population and have taken control of the municipal government. The previous administration had made display of the Albanian flag illegal in 1997 by pass-ing a law regulating the public display of national symbols. When the mayor of Gos-tivar installed an Albanian flag over the city hall in July 1997, the national govern-ment responded by dispatching police forces to the city with orders to remove the flag. The resulting clashes between ethnic Albanians and police left three dead and at least 50 persons injured. Approximately 320 persons were arrested. Today one sees only Albanian flags in predominantly Al-banian areas.

Former Prime Minister Georgievski's government, which supported improved interethnic relations, pushed through an amnesty law in 1999. Ex-President Gli-gorov vetoed the law, but it was then passed over his veto one month later. This ended the jail terms of some 900 persons who had been convicted for violating the 1997 law on the public display of national symbols. Among those freed were the mayors of Gostivar and Tetovo.

Another pressing issue for ethnic Alba-nians is the protection of their language and the lack of possibilities for higher ed-ucation in Albanian. They regard their ability to use their language in official dealings and in education as an important part of their identity as a nation. However, given the diversity of the country's popu-lation, Macedonians believe there has to be one official language—Macedonian—to prevent the country from splitting apart. The government established Albanian-language classes at the pedagogic faculty of Skopje University, but for several years it rejected demands by ethnic Albani-ans for their own university. In response, Albanians set up their own Albanian-language university at Tetovo, a major-ity ethnic Albanian city of a quarter of a million inhabitants. Although the only available facility was a cluster of shabby, reinforced-concrete apartment buildings, this new university quickly grew until it had 300 faculty and 6,000 students.

The government refused to give the uni-versity official accreditation, arguing that an Albanian-language university would stoke nationalist sentiments among ethnic Albanians. But under intense international pressure, ex-Prime Minister Georgievski's government grudgingly endorsed creation of an Albanian-language university. The war in Kosovo and disagreements within the government coalition put this matter on further hold until 2000, when the right to such a university was granted. Tetovo's Albanian-language university officially opened in 2001 although in 2002 it was still not completely legal. There is another pri-vate university in Tetovo, Southeastern European University, which offers instruc-tion in Macedonian, Albanian and English. The University of Skopje gives Albanian-language courses in the education school. Instruction in Macedonian is offered at two universities: the University St. Cyril and Methodius (named after the founders of the Cyrillic alphabet, who once resided in Macedonia) in Skopje and the Univer-sity St. Climent Ohridski in Bitola.

In February 2001 ethnic violence broke out for a half-year that was so serious that only NATO intervention and important constitutional changes could save the country from civil war. An Albanian rebel group calling itself the National Libera-tion Army (NLA) attacked police stations and other government facilities controlled by Slavs. They subsequently seized vil-lages in the mountains and expanded their military action to the outskirts of the capital. They demanded more rights for Albanian-speakers, but the Macedonian government (which contained members of the Albanian minority) regarded the ac-tions as a scarcely disguised attempt to separate Albanian areas and unite them with neighboring Kosovo, from where most of the rebels' weapons came. NATO and EU countries feared that the warfare could get out of control, draw peacekeep-ers out of Kosovo, and perhaps even spill over Macedonian borders and destabilize the entire region. Therefore they became intensely involved with the settlement of the crisis by bringing both sides to the ne-gotiation table. The result was the 2001 "Framework Agreement," known as the Ohrid accord.

In "Operation Essential Harvest" a NATO force of 4,500 collected more than 4,000 rebel weapons while the Macedon-ian parliament approved of constitutional changes designed to meet the Albanian demands for greater civil rights, protec-tion of their language, and greater repre-sentation in Macedonia's government ser-vice, including the police. They agreed on a law for local self-government by devolv-ing powers to municipalities. Very im-portant was the promise of amnesty for rebels taken captive. It was hoped that this would sufficiently defuse the tensions so that Macedonian police and refugees could return to the rebel heartland in the north and persuade fighters in the hills to come down and resume their civilian lives without fear of arrest. Not until March 2002 did that amnesty take place. To re-ward the country, the World Bank and EU organized a one-day pledge conference that produced 515 million euros in assistance to Macedonia.

About 700 NATO troops remained in the country to supervise the peace plan. Many Macedonians found the settlement too generous to the minority and tended to blame the troubles on NATO's gentle treatment of armed ethnic Albanians in Kosovo. The settlement did prevent a larger war, but it did not put an end to the tensions that had led to the conflict in the first place. Many ethnic Albanian villages and neighborhoods still remained off-limits to the police, and violent incidents were a daily occurrence and went unchallenged by the local police.

The August 2001 Ohrid agreement did not bring complete stability to an insecure country. In September 2003 ethnic Albanian gunmen kidnapped a policeman. A police operation was launched to track down the perpetrators, resulting in the death of two ethnic Albanian guerrillas and the temporary exodus from some villages near the Kosovo border. The fighters were part of the Albanian National Army (AKSH), which talks of "Greater Serbia" encompassing all ethnic Albanians. They spend most of their time, however, smuggling cigarettes. The end of 2003 the government offered lottery prizes to persons who surrender guns to the authorities. An estimated 170,000 illegal weapons remain in private hands, but only 900 were turned in.

In May 2004 the government charged a former interior minister, Ljube Boskovski, with staging the killing of seven South Asian migrants two years earlier in a bizarre attempt to win for the government a free hand to deal harshly with the country's ethnic Albanian minority. He allegedly arranged for the seven to be smuggled from Bulgaria into Macedonia and murdered. The crime scene was changed to make it seem as if they were armed Islamic militants heading for Western Europe. In March 2005 he was indicted by the war crimes tribunal in The Hague, and he surrendered to the court. This was the first such indictment in Macedonia.

Foreign Relations

Macedonia opted for independence because it believed that Serbia would dominate any federation with Croatia and Slovenia gone. Nevertheless, it wants to maintain good economic relations with Serbia and all other neighboring countries. It also favors a common market among the former republics. Macedonia has good relations with Bulgaria and Turkey, fairly good relations with Albania, and increasingly good relations with Greece.

The European Union did not extend recognition to Macedonia at the time it recognized Slovenia and Bosnia-Herzegovina. Greece, an EU member and Macedonia's most important neighbor from an economic standpoint, objected to its use of the name Macedonia and to the 16-pointed star it had on its flag. Athens insisted that Macedonia had to change its name before it could be recognized. It feared that an independent Macedonia could exert some influence on its own citizens in Greek Macedonia and make territorial claims even though Macedonia had signed an agreement with Greece disavowing any such claims.

Greece finally dropped its objections to Macedonia's admission to the United Nations in April 1993, provided it would agree to use the clumsy name "Former Yugoslav Republic of Macedonia," or FYROM for short. On that basis, Macedonia received general recognition and UN membership. It was also understood that Macedonia's flag would not be flown at the United Nations. Macedonians dislike the name FYROM.

When ex-President Trajkovski visited Washington in February 2002, he requested that his country be called Macedonia: "We are only struggling for our name." In his first foreign policy act in his second term, November 2004, President Bush officially recognized the republic as "Macedonia." The timing was not accidental: it was announced at the time of a referendum on the Ohrid agreement and was intended to induce moderate Slav Macedonians not to undo the reforms. The State Department called it a reward for the ethnic progress that has taken place. Macedonians were delighted, and Greece's protests were more restrained than earlier. By 2007 more than half the UN members recognize the country by its name, "Macedonia."

Greece managed to keep the European Union, which still uses FYROM, from extending diplomatic recognition to Macedonia until December 1993. The United States, which had sent 500 American troops to Macedonia in July 1993 as part of a 1,000-troop United Nations presence, had refrained from recognizing Macedonia for the same reason. The EU move allowed the United States to reverse itself and extend diplomatic recognition to Macedonia in February 1994.

Greece's reaction was to announce an embargo on all imports and exports to Macedonia, other than food and medicine. The EU attempted to get the trade blockade removed. When Athens refused, the EU brought Greece before the European Court of Justice. The embargo continued until October 1995. Greece agreed to lift the embargo after the Macedonian parliament gave in to Greek demands and voted to change the flag and constitution. The new flag consists of an eight-ray golden sun on a red background.

Athens continues to assert that the name Macedonia applies only to its own northern region and that the former Yugoslav republic must find another name for itself. It makes this issue a condition for Macedonia's future EU membership. The UN mediates talks between the two states to resolve the disagreement. Greece proposed the name, "Makedonija-Skopje," but the Macedonians said no.

They even waved a red flag by naming Skopje's international airport after Alexander the Great. This act prompted Greece to postpone the country's entry into NATO in April 2009 even though more than 120 countries, including the U.S. and Russia, had already accepted the name, "Macedonia." The government was angered by being locked out from the Atlantic Alliance, but it took further steps, dubbed "antiquization" by the opposition, that risk sacrificing the support the country has in the world. It named the main highway to Greece after Alexander and the national sports stadium after Alexander's father, Philip. It is also planning to erect a huge 36-meter (40-yard) high statue of Alexander in the center of Skopje.

Athens proposes adding words like "upper" or "new" to the name, and it rejected a last-minute compromise of "Republic of Macedonia (Skopje)." Prime Minister Gruevski did not make things easier in July 2008 when he demanded Greek recognition of a Slavic Macedonian ethnic minority in the officially homogeneous Greece.

Despite these name problems, Greek-Macedonian relations improved after 1995, and their economic relations flourish. In particular, normal transportation and economic and diplomatic communication have been established. In a further sign of the change, ex-Foreign Minister Theodoros Pangalos visited Skopje in 1998 and had praise for the new Macedonian government.

Greece has sought to expand its economic presence in Macedonia since 1995. By 1998 it had become Macedonia's third-largest trading partner. In August 2001 it sent 150 troops to Macedonia as part of a NATO commitment to disarm ethnic Albanian rebels. It has become the biggest investor in Macedonia. It owns the oil refinery there and has built a pipeline from Thessaloniki to Skopje. The country's largest bank, a leading supermarket chain, and a mobile-phone operator are all controlled by Greek interests.

Macedonia signed a trade and cooperation treaty with the EU in 1996. In its June 2003 summit in Greece, the EU agreed that Macedonia would be among the Balkan countries that should join. It already signed a Stabilization and Association Agreement (SAA) with the EU. Entry into

Macedonia

the EU is an issue on which there is a consensus; 87% supported it in a 2004 poll. The official application for membership was the very last document President Trajkovski signed before his fatal flight in 2004. Finally in December 2005 the EU granted it the official status as a candidate for entry. This news was greeted by other Balkan countries that hope to join. The EU provides 210 million euros ($300 million) in assistance from 2007–9, but says Macedonia must do more to control corruption. Although Macedonia has EU candidate status, it still has no date for the start of accession negotiations. However, it is making some progress in the reforms the EU requires. From December 19, 2009, its citizens have visa-free travel to most EU states.

It is a member of the Council of Europe and the OSCE. It is actively taking part in the Partnership for Peace program. It wishes to become a full member of NATO, and this is supported by more than 90% of its citizens. This did not happen in 2009, but it remains important. Full membership would guarantee the country's borders in a region where others might be tempted to change them. Although it does not yet belong to the alliance, it has sent 4% of its forces on NATO missions, almost 10 times the proportion Greece has provided.

Its active military force numbers 8,000 soldiers, including conscripts who serve six months. All but 1,200 are in the land forces. There are 800 in the Army Air Force with four combat aircraft and 12 armed helicopters and 400 in a Marine Wing that operates five river patrol craft. There are a total of 4,850 in the reserves and 7,600 paramilitary police (7,600 of whom are armed). Macedonia deployed 40 support soldiers to Iraq under U.S. command and has 165 troops in Afghanistan, including special forces and medical personnel. It provided a helicopter transport unit for EU peacekeepers in Bosnia-Herzegovina. It hopes to raise its foreign deployments from 200 in 2007 to 1,000 by 2013.

Macedonia found itself drawn more and more deeply into the problems caused by continuing Serbian repression in the neighboring Serbian province of Kosovo. Macedonia's involvement actually began as early as July 1993 when the United Nations authorized a 1,000-troop UN force for Macedonia in an attempt to keep Macedonia from being drawn into the fighting and then consuming much of the rest of ex-Yugoslavia. When the military campaign against the Kosovar Liberation Army, which Serb forces launched in early 1998, began to create large quantities of ethnic Albanian refugees and reports of Serb atrocities against ethnic Albanians,

NATO countries intervened diplomatically and eventually got Serbia to agree to a cease-fire. It went into effect in October 1998. It was to be monitored by 2,000 civilian "verifiers" stationed throughout the province of Kosovo.

Concerned about the need to rescue the civilian monitors should renewed fighting break out in the province, NATO opened discussions with the Macedonian government about the placement of a NATO rapid reaction force in Macedonia. A French-led coalition of 1,800 European soldiers began arriving in Macedonia in December 1998. Three months later, the mission of the rapid reaction force had changed, and its numbers had grown to 12,000 soldiers.

When in 1999 Serbia launched a systematic campaign in Kosovo aimed at driving a significant portion of the ethnic Albanians out, Macedonia became one of two primary destinations for these refugees. Belgrade added to the flood by arranging to have trainloads of refugees transported to the Macedonian border. By 1999, approximately 400,000 Kosovar Albanians had found refuge in Macedonia. Some were able to stay with relatives.

Macedonia, a poor country, was ill equipped to take care of such numbers of refugees. The UN and NATO forces originally sent there for other purposes were reassigned to help with this task. Macedonia also began receiving assistance from various international aid organizations. The next couple of months proved to be an unusually difficult time for the country as it grappled with the large number of refugees. Slobodan Milosevic's capitulation in June and the NATO takeover of Kosovo solved that problem. Most of the Kosovar refugees left the camps in Macedonia and made their way back home.

The United Nations, NATO and EU continued to maintain a significant presence in the country. Macedonia got the former Yugoslav consulate in Paris when the diplomatic buildings were parceled out among the parts of the former federation in December 2001.

On March 31, 2003, the EU launched its first military mission, named Concordia, when it assumed from NATO the command over about 320 peacekeeping troops and 80 civilians in Macedonia. They are drawn from 27 current or pending member states of the EU. A German admiral is in overall command, and a French general directs operations on the ground. The force uses NATO plans and equipment. In an operation called "Promixa," the EU provided about 200 police officers to work alongside the local police in areas affected by the 2001 conflict.

Despite its support for the UN's and NATO's Kosovo policy, Macedonian Slavs

were nervous about the negative impact an independent Kosovo could have on Macedonia's own assertive Albanian minority. Although no prominent Kosovo or Albanian officials talk about a "Greater Albania" nation-state combining all 6 million Albanians, Kosovo's independence in February 2008 could have an effect on the dreams of some Macedonian Albanians. Armed Kosovars who crossed Macedonia's borders in an unsuccessful attempt to "liberate" the Albanian minority had strengthened these concerns in April 2001 although Macedonian troops drove them out.

When Macedonia officially recognized Kosovo in October 2008, Serbia expelled the Macedonian ambassador in an attempt to punish it and 50 other countries for not supporting Serbia's position. Realizing several months later that it had painted itself into a disastrous diplomatic corner, Belgrade dropped its punitive measures.

ECONOMY

Macedonia is overwhelmingly agricultural, with most people living in the Vardar River Valley or the valleys interspersed between ridges in the west. Because of the limited farmland available, many young workers live and work in other Western countries. The chief crops are wheat, barley, corn, tobacco, cotton, rice, sunflowers and sugar beets. Cattle raising is also important. The per capita income of Macedonia trails that of Serbia.

Almost all industry is concentrated in the Skopje area. Heavy industry consists of steel and chemicals. Light industry includes textiles, furniture, porcelain, and chinaware.

By 1996, 750 companies, accounting for 40% of GDP, had been privatized. Another 250 were privatized during 1996, while an additional 200 companies were privatized between 1997 and 1999. Macedonia began privatizing its banks in 2000.

The economy declined by approximately 23% between 1990 and 1996. It bottomed out in 1996, but then it began growing in 1997 and has continued. In 2006 growth was 3.2%, and it rose to 4% in 2007. Inflation at 3.2% in 2006 and 2.8% in 2007 was negligible. On the negative side, the trade deficit widened. There was a corresponding increase in Macedonia's current account deficit, which may be somewhat smaller than official statistics show. Not all remittances, estimated to be almost 5% of GDP, from Macedonians working abroad get counted in the statistics. Total foreign debt was 36.1% of GDP in 2007.

The official unemployment rate stood at a stunning 36% in 2007. Wages and prices in Macedonia are relatively high. This reduces the country's competitiveness. In part because of the high level of corruption, there is not enough foreign investment to create jobs. However, more Macedonians are working than the statistics would indicate. The "grey economy" is estimated to account for half of GDP. Also many workers take jobs secretly in order to be classified officially as unemployed. That way they qualify for free state insurance.

Average wages, at 400 euros ($520) per month, are tempting for investors. Greece is currently the largest source of foreign investment in the Macedonian economy. Approximately 300 Greek companies employ about 20,000 Macedonians. In 1999 the government allowed the Greek company Hellenic Petroleum to purchase Okta, Macedonia's only state oil refinery. The country relies on the Greek port of Thessalonica for its oil, and a pipeline connects the port with the Okta refinery.

Energy is in critically short supply since Bulgaria shut down two reactors at its Kozluduy nuclear power plant. Macedonia produces only about three-fourths of its electricity needs and is compelled to purchase expensive imports from Germany, Austria and the Czech Republic. Macedonia has been the recipient of significant amounts of international aid as a result of the war in Kosovo and the ensuing refugee crisis.

The country's economy is sputtering as a result of the global economic downturn in 2008–2009, and it will take some time for Macedonia to work itself out of it. Exports of metals, textiles and agricultural produce have slumped, unemployment has risen and remittances have shrunk. Unable to borrow money abroad for a stimulus policy, the government is forced to cut public spending.

CULTURE

There is a separate Macedonian culture. Although some Macedonians deny it vehemently, aspects of it are similar to that of Bulgaria. There is a more middle class and cosmopolitan culture associated with the city of Skopje. Macedonia must guard its rich archaeological sites more carefully after illicit plundering and selling. Poverty has inclined thieves to loot ancient Greek and Roman tombs, especially in search of jewelry.

Religion is the second defining influence. The majority of Macedonians are Orthodox Christians. The Church was part of the Serbian Orthodox Church until 1967, when it broke away and formed the Macedonian Orthodox Church. The Serbian Orthodox Church has never accepted the split, however, and does not recognize the Macedonian Church. Approximately a quarter of the population is Muslim. Most of these speak Albanian as their first language.

FUTURE

Macedonia survived its greatest fear in 1999 when the situation in Kosovo blew up, and the country coped surprisingly well. The unity Macedonians showed in doing as much as they could to help the refugees was impressive. Nevertheless, the Kosovo situation has been and continues to be slightly destabilizing in some ways, even though all refugees have returned to Kosovo, which declared its independence on February 17, 2008. Macedonia's official recognition of that independence in October 2008 will continue to irritate Serbia.

Many Macedonians worried about would happen when NATO left, but the EU-led peacekeeping forces succeeded in maintaining order. There is no appetite for a return to armed conflict. The country was not admitted to NATO at the 2009 summit, and full membership awaits the resolution of the tiresome dispute with Greece on the country's official name. Membership in the Atlantic Alliance is supported by over 90% of the people. Ex-President Bush said: "America's position is clear: Macedonia should take its place in NATO as soon as possible." EU membership is being held up for the same reason.

It is fortunate that Macedonia has not relapsed into all-out civil war, as many had predicted, and that fighting has not spilled over into neighboring countries. But the ethnic Albanian rebel attacks in 2001, which forced the government to adopt constitutional changes granting greater civil and language rights to the Albanian minority, as well as the renewed violence on a smaller scale in 2002, 2003 and at election time in 2006 and 2008, were reminders that Macedonia still lacks complete stability, police control, and confidence between the two ethnic communities. It continues to need Western intervention to keep them in check.

The ethnic divide remains as entrenched as ever although Macedonians elected governments that try hard to reduce tensions. Lawlessness in the former conflict areas remains a serious problem, and Macedonia is still subject to private vendettas, politically motivated murders, and the illegal activities of rebel armies and smuggling rings.

President Gjorgje Ivanov and Prime Minister Nikola Gruevski vow to continue the policy of ethnic reconciliation. In July 2004 the government adopted a long-delayed plan to grant more powers to local councils. This was the most difficult step in implementing the 2001 Ohrid agreement. The move to give Albanians more control over municipalities in which they form majorities sparked violent clashes in Struga, where dozens were injured. Macedonian mobs stoned Albanian-owned shops and torched government vehicles. The failure of the November 2004 referendum that would have undone the Ohrid agreement was a positive sign for the future. Nevertheless, much work remains to be done by the Gruevski government.

Born in Skopje, Mother Teresa moves closer to sainthood

The Republic of Albania

Muslims at noon prayers in front of Et'hem Bey Mosque, central Tirana

Area: 28,749 sq. km. = 11,000 sq. mi.
Population: 3,200,000 (2005 estimate)
Capital City: Tirane (or Tirana) (Pop. 850,000; 2004 estimate).
Climate: Mediterranean, with wet winters and hot, dry summers on the coast. The interior is colder in the winter.
Neighboring Countries: Montenegro, (north); Kosovo, (northeast); Macedonia (east); Greece (south).
Official Language: Albanian
Other Principal Tongues: Greek
Ethnic Background: Illyrian, an ancient Indo-European group, mixed with Slav, Greek and Turkish ancestry.
Principal Religions: Islam (70%); Eastern-rite Orthodox Christianity (20%); Roman Catholic Christianity (10%). Most people refer to themselves now as non-practicing, though interest in religion is growing.
Chief Commercial Products: Tobacco, cigarettes, timber, wood, dairy products.
Main Trading Partners: Italy (68% of exports and 28% of imports), Greece (8% of exports and 14% of imports), Turkey (6.5% of imports), Germany (2% of exports and 8% of imports), China (2% of exports and 7.5% of imports).
Currency: lek
Former Political Status: Part of the Roman and Byzantine empires; conquered by the Ottoman Turks in the 15th century and under Turkish control until 1912, following which there were six years of conflicts and change associated with the Balkan Wars and World War I.

Incorporated into Italy by Mussolini in 1939. Communist state from 1945 to 1991.
National Day: November 28, Independence Day
Chief of State: Bamir Topi, President (since July 2007).
Head of Government: Sali Berisha, Prime Minister (since September 2005).
National Flag: Red, with a black, two-headed eagle.

Albania is a small, largely mountainous land located along the eastern shores of the Adriatic Sea. Its forbidding mountains, combined with a language of mysterious origins totally different from any other in Europe, have served to isolate this small nation throughout much of its history. During the communist era, this isolation was strengthened by an eccentric and self-absorbed regime that had major difficulties getting along with other communist countries, let alone with the rest of the outside world. Its transition to democracy has been especially rough. In 1997 it fell into chaos closely resembling a Hobbsian state of nature, according to the country's justice minister. The future will reveal whether this starkly beautiful land with generous people will enjoy stability, democracy, prosperity, and community with the rest of Europe.

In spite of its small size, Albania has a widely varied climate, the major factor being the mountains. About one-seventh of its land area consists of a series of small

plains running north to south down along the coastline. Here the climate is hot and humid in the summer and relatively warm in most winters. Semitropical crops such as citrus can be produced, but other crops include figs, wine grapes and olives. Farther inland, the plains are at increasing elevations and are correspondingly cooler—the average temperature in July is 63°F in these regions. Here the chief crop grown is grain. As the elevation rises even more, the green foliage of rolling pastures gives way to sparse evergreens and scattered brush. Gray and brown craggy peaks rise steeply to the sky. The air is thin, cold and clear. This is the home of the eagle, where few sounds interrupt the stillness.

In this setting, the people continue the isolated life they have experienced for centuries. There are some settlements that have little or no contact with the rest of Albania because of their inaccessibility. The few towns that exist are usually the result of a need for a place to trade agricultural goods. Fishermen ply the cool waters of Lake Shkoder in flat-bottomed boats. Although there is mineral wealth, it is almost impossible to extract it profitably because of the lack of transportation.

Most of the Albanians of today are remote descendants of the Illyrians, an ancient people of the Indo-European group. At one time, they were to be found throughout most of the Balkan Peninsula, but they were either gradually absorbed or driven out as successive waves of Slavs moved into the area. They are now found only in the western part of the Balkans. Even so, they spill across borders and are in the Serbian province of Kosovo, Montenegro, Macedonia, and Greece. There are also colonies of Albanians in Italy, but that is the result of past migrations and recent illegal immigration. In addition, there are about 600,000 persons of Albanian descent living in the United States.

Southern Albania (in Greece, known as North Epirus) has a significant Greek minority, estimated by Albania to be 3% of the total population or 90,000 and by Greece to be 200,000. There are also some Macedonians who live on the Albanian side of the border. Because of the poor economic conditions in Albania, however, most of the men of this area actually live and work in Greece, with only the women and children left behind.

HISTORY

Early Albanian Governments

The Kingdom of Illyria came into being in the 3rd century B.C., centered around an ancient city on the site of present-day Shkoder. Conquered by the Romans in 167 B.C., the area remained a part of the Roman Empire for the next five centuries. When the Empire dissolved in the fourth century A.D., Illyria became a part of the Eastern Roman—later Byzantine Empire.

As the Slavs arrived in the Adriatic region in the 6th and 7th centuries, most of the Illyrians were absorbed; the rest settled along the southern Adriatic coast where Albania is now located. During the centuries that followed, Albania was conquered and re-conquered by various Eastern and Western armies. The most lasting influence was that of the Serbs and the Venetians (Italians).

The Albanians were conquered by the Ottoman Turks in the 15th century and incorporated into their empire. Although

the Albanians had put up stiff resistance to the Ottoman conquest, once they had been absorbed politically, they allowed themselves to be absorbed culturally as well. Albania was the only part of the Balkan Peninsula where the majority of the population converted to Islam.

Albanian nationalism was awakened by the decisions of the major powers at the Congress of Berlin, which was held after the Russian-Turkish war of 1877–1878. The great powers awarded to Montenegro (now a part of Yugoslavia) and Greece territories the Albanians claimed as their own.

They formed the League of Prizren to protest the division of lands they felt should not be given to neighboring countries, but this effort was not successful. They also demanded local control within a reformed Turkish Empire rather than independence that would have put them at the mercy of other foreign powers. Both Italy and Austria-Hungary had been showing interest in the area. Although the Turks supported the League in its protest against the expansion of neighboring states, they rejected the demand for local control. The Turks suppressed the League in 1881 and banned use of the Albanian language in 1886.

The League was a means of expressing the first national feelings of the Albanians in their native land. When it and Albanian liberty were crushed, Albanian communities living in Italy and the United States took up the national movement. Turkish oppression continued, and there was a series of rebellions from 1909 to 1912 that resulted in Albanian control of almost all of what is now that country.

The remaining Turkish power was eliminated in the First Balkan War of 1912. On November 28 of that year, a national assembly met at Vlore and proclaimed Albania's independence. Ismail Qemal headed the first provisional government.

The Birth of a Modern Albania

The Treaty of London ending the First Balkan War (1912) left the question of Albania to an ambassadorial conference of the major powers. They agreed with the demand for independence, but as might have been expected, they redrew the map of the region. Shkoder, demanded by Montenegro, was left to Albania; Kosovo, inhabited by a large number of Albanians, was given to Serbia, creating a problem that lingers to this day. In the south, the powers gave part of northern Greece to Albania, but with Greek support, the people revolted.

The great powers also provided a hand-picked ruler for Albania—William of Wied, a German Prince. Italian-supported Essad Pasha, successor of Ismail Qemal,

was actually the most important man in the country. The years 1912–1914 were turbulent. There were rebellions in the north and south where borders were disputed. General dissatisfaction reigned throughout the country. Prince William fled at the outbreak of World War I.

Four years of utter anarchy followed, with the armies of Serbia, Montenegro (now republics of Yugoslavia), Greece, Italy, France, Austria and Bulgaria occupying parts of Albania. At the end of the war, Italy occupied Albania, with Serbia holding the northeastern region and Korc in the possession of the French.

On December 25, 1918, delegates from all parts of Albania met at Durres to elect a provisional government and to send a delegation to the Paris Peace Conference to present a demand that Albania's 1913 borders be restored. Greece, Italy and Yugoslavia had made a secret deal to divide Albania among them. This was firmly rejected by U.S. President Woodrow Wilson. His action, combined with the determination of the Albanian leaders, saved the tiny nation.

In order to understand events that followed World War I, it is necessary to remember that Albania was still a primitive country. Although unique and interesting culturally, it was backward. There was no written Albanian language and no educa-

Albanians under the Turks (1910), and as an independent kingdom (1912)

Albania

tion system. There were only a few miles of road and one bridge. There was no industry in the whole country. Albania was divided into many localities along social, religious and geographic lines, and the basic unit of power was the clan. Government control was at best scanty.

A parliamentary and cabinet system of government emerged in 1920. Italy, preoccupied with its own problems, reluctantly recognized Albania's government. The major powers finally resolved the border questions in 1926. Two political parties were organized, the Progressive Party, dominated by Moslem leaders, and the Popular Party, headed by a liberal Greek Orthodox Bishop, Fan S. Noli, who had a U.S. college degree.

Ahmed Bey Zogu, one of the leaders of the Popular Party, became Albania's premier in 1922 when he stayed to defend the capital against a revolt after the rest of the government had fled. Two years later, he resigned and fled to Yugoslavia when an angry band of demonstrators marched on the capital. Noli, his successor, hoped to introduce a reform program that would drag Albania into the 20th century. This could not be done without massive outside aid or internal unity. Noli could muster neither. Zogu returned with the support of Yugoslav troops; the National Assembly proclaimed Albania a republic and elected him president for seven years.

Ruthless and determined, Zogu had a constituent assembly proclaim Albania a "democratic, parliamentary and hereditary kingdom" in 1928 with himself as King Zog I. He sought financial assistance from Italy. By the mid 1930s, this ripened into Italian control of Albania's economy. Complaining that Zog was misusing Italian money, the fascist dictator, Benito Mussolini, sent an invasion force that swept Albania on April 7, 1939. Zog fled to Greece and then to London with his queen of only 354 days, Hungarian countess Geraldine Apponyi de Nagi-Appony, and their 11-day-old son Leka. Victor Emmanuel, figurehead king of Italy became king of Albania. Italy mounted an invasion of Greece through Albania. It was repulsed by Greek and Yugoslav armies that were able to occupy much of Albania until a German attack in 1941.

Albania Reborn as a People's Republic

Resistance groups were organized in 1941–42 by communists and noncommunists. The Albanian Communist Party was founded in 1941 with Yugoslav help. Among its leaders was Enver Hoxha (pronounced HOE-djah), a young man educated in France and Belgium and considered one of the "intellectuals" in the party. It set up the National Liberation Movement (LNC), which for a time included

King Zog I

the clan chief Abbas Kupi and his guerrilla fighters.

Another resistance group, the Balli Kombetär National Front, had an antiroyalist and strongly nationalistic outlook. The two groups came close to joining in 1943, but the LNC, on the advice of the Yugoslav communist leader Tito, backed out. Soon the two groups were fighting each other. A provisional government headed by Enver Hoxha was formed in October 1944, moving to Tirana as the government of Albania upon withdrawal of the German forces.

Albania was proclaimed a People's Republic in 1946. The absence of competing political parties and assistance from Yugoslavia's communists enabled Hoxha to assume power with relative ease. After World War II, the Yugoslavs desired to assume the role the Italians had before the war. An economic treaty was forged in 1946 providing for a customs union, coordination of economic planning, currency equalization and the formation of "joint companies." Yugoslav advisers appeared in greater numbers, and there was even talk of union between the two nations.

Enver Hoxha

The Yugoslavian embrace was apparently too stifling for Hoxha, but there was little he could do about it at the time. In the meantime, the Yugoslavs threw their support to Koci Xoxe, who as minister of the interior controlled the police and security forces. What saved Hoxha was the Soviet-Yugoslav split that occurred at this time. Accusing Xoxe of being a supporter of Tito, Hoxha had him and his followers purged at the First Congress of the Albanian Party of Labor (APL) in November 1948; Xoxe was later executed.

Hoxha clearly dominated the APL, but he was not without his critics. The next major challenge came in the early 1950s, this time from moderates who objected to dislocations caused by a policy of industrialization and collectivization. After 1953, they also began calling for de-Stalinization as was occurring in Russia. The spokesmen for this point of view were two members of the Politburo, Bedri Spahiu and Tuk Jakova. With Stalin dead and the Soviet leadership moving cautiously toward de-Stalinization, Hoxha could not simply purge these critics.

He actually made a gesture toward the moderate wing of the party in 1954 when he gave up the position of chairman of the council of ministers, though he turned it over to one of his own supporters, Mehmet Shehu. A year later, he managed to get both Spahiu and Jakova expelled from the Politburo. Yet another challenge came in 1956 at the Third Party Congress, but this came from middle-ranking bureaucrats and military officers. Hoxha crushed it easily.

The last contest occurred in 1974–75. It appears not to have been a direct challenge to Hoxha, but rather to some of his policies. Now wielding absolute power, Hoxha purged the dissenters. Between July and December 1974, he removed the entire top level of the military establishment, including the defense minister, Beqir Balluku, who was also a member of the Politburo. His dispute with the military was apparently over the extent of party control in such areas as military training and discipline. He followed this ouster with a purge of the nation's top economic and managerial elite when they challenged the role of the party in their areas.

An ailing and tired Hoxha died in early April 1985 at the age of 77. Ramiz Alia, whom Hoxha had groomed as successor, took his place. Alia, born in 1925, had been a longtime associate of Hoxha, though it was only in 1982 that he became the designated successor.

Alia belonged to the first generation of Albanian communist leaders although he was 17 years younger than his mentor. He became a member of the party in 1943 when it was still only an aspirant to power

Enver Hoxha makes a point to elderly villagers, while Ramiz Alia (left) listens attentively.

and became a full Politburo member and a member of the powerful Secretariat in 1961. When he was appointed president of the presidium of the People's Assembly (titular head of state) in 1982, he retained all of his party posts. Thus, he was already a member of the Secretariat at the time of Hoxha's death and only had to assume the additional duty of first secretary.

Although no one challenged Alia for the office of first secretary, it soon became clear that the other members of the Politburo considered him to be not more than a first among equals. Since the Politburo was dominated by hard-liners, he was extremely cautious in initiating changes for the first few years. No additions were made to the Politburo, even though that body had three fewer members than in 1982. Alia did make two lesser appointments—the addition of one person to the Secretariat and the replacement of the chairman of the state planning commission.

At the Ninth Congress of the Albanian Party of Labor in 1986, Alia had fulsome praise for Hoxha, to whom, he said, Albania owed boundless gratitude. At the same time, the new Five Year Plan adopted at the congress put much more stress on foreign trade than in the past.

The Collapse of Communism

A slow, and extremely cautious, movement away from the old Hoxha system in general accompanied the new emphasis on trade. But it remained glacial until March 1990 when Alia, responding to the recent extraordinary changes elsewhere in Central and Eastern Europe, launched his own campaign of "democratic" change. Among other things, Alia promised contested elections by secret ballot, including within the Albanian Labor Party; limits on terms of office; a decentralization of decision-making authority to district officials and individual enterprises; some price decontrol; and the introduction of economic incentives in industry and agriculture.

Subsequent changes were, in some ways, even more significant. In April 1990, the assembly approved a law lifting criminal penalties for attempts to escape across the frontier. This was followed in May by a new law explicitly granting citizens the right to travel abroad. The assembly also lifted the old laws outlawing the practice of religion and declared religious belief to be a matter of individual conscience. Finally, it created the office of justice minister and gave it the task of creating a new system of courts and defense attorneys. None of this represented a basic reform of the system, however, for there was no change in the monopoly role of the party.

The May 1990 law granting citizens the right to travel abroad raised expectations among the Albanian populace, which were subsequently frustrated by Albanian officialdom. Toward the end of June, some 5,000 Albanians took refuge in a dozen foreign embassies in Tirana and demanded to be allowed to leave the country. After several days, the Albanian authorities gave in to the demands, and the refugees were allowed to leave. Over the next four months, an additional 25,000 persons were issued passports and left the country legally.

In the cities, demonstrations began occurring periodically, and some people took to wearing crosses and shouting anticommunist slogans in the streets. Occasionally, violence erupted when officials of the secret police ripped the crosses off people's chests.

Meanwhile the government continued its program of liberalization. Collective farmers were told that they could have private plots and that they would be permitted to sell excess produce in local open-air markets. Cultural controls were also relaxed. At Enver Hoxha University in Tirana, a disco began playing rock music every Saturday night. The prohibition against individuals owning private automobiles was also lifted, though that change had little practical significance since almost no private individual could afford to own one.

These gestures on the part of the party leadership only emboldened people to demand more. Nearly all of the protests were in the cities and overwhelmingly made up of young people, particularly young men. In December 1990, about 2,000 students at Enver Hoxha University organized a protest demonstration demanding greater democracy. After three days, the ruling Party of Labor, meeting in emergency session, gave in and endorsed "the creation of independent political organizations" and scheduled new elections for February 1991. Albanian communists, like their fellow party members in Eastern Europe and the Soviet Union, had been persuaded to give up their monopoly of political power. The next day, the first oppositional political party, the Democratic Party, was organized. Approximately 80,000 people attended the rally for the new party.

By January 1991, three additional oppositional parties, the Republicans, the Forum for Human Rights, and the Ecological Party, had come into being. Charging that an election date of February 10 would not give them adequate time to prepare, they demanded that the elections be postponed until a later date. The government gave in and rescheduled them for March 31.

The period January–March 1991 was filled with demonstrations, political rallies, additional student strikes, and some violence. Oppositional newspapers also began appearing. At Enver Hoxha University, students decided that Hoxha's name should be stricken from the university's official title and organized a strike that later was turned into a hunger strike. The authorities allowed it to continue for 12 days and then surrounded the university with special troops. Demonstrations in support of the students erupted in urban areas across Albania. In two cities, Tirana and the port city of Durres, statues of Hoxha were toppled.

Albania

The government again backed down and agreed to remove Hoxha's name from Tirana University.

Ramiz Alia, under attack from hard-line party members, decided to dismiss Adil Carcani, the hard-line chairman of the council of ministers, and assume personal control of the government apparatus by creating a "temporary presidential council." Named head of the new government was Fatos Nano, an economist who had been made deputy chairman of the council of ministers in January. Alia's actions made clear what up to that time had been only suspected: the communist Party of Labor had split into two factions, orthodox Marxist-Leninists who wanted to stamp out dissent and reformers who supported Ramiz Alia.

Meanwhile, thousands of Albanians again began fleeing the country, first to Greece, and then, at the beginning of March, in commandeered ships to Italy. Many appeared to be fleeing the violence and bloodshed that were accompanying the street demonstrations. The government declared martial law in the port city of Durres in an attempt to stop the exodus, but about 12,000 Albanians eventually made it out of the country anyway. They were not well-received in Italy, however, and many later returned home.

The March 31, 1991, elections were something of an anticlimax. The political opposition won in the cities, but the Party of Labor, managing to retain its hold over the countryside, won two-thirds of the seats in the People's Assembly. Ramiz Alia lost his own race in the city of Tirana, but was reelected chairman of the presidium of the People's Assembly on April 30. Fatos Nano was reappointed as chairman of the council of ministers.

As the Party of Labor very quickly learned, electoral majorities do not necessarily create a mandate to rule, particularly if, as in this case, that majority might have been the result of intimidation and

fraud. At least, those were the sort of charges the political opposition hurled against the party although no evidence was ever produced to substantiate the claims. But no evidence was really necessary. The party's almost total repudiation in the cities meant that it had lost the support of the workers, the very class it claimed to represent, and therefore its political credibility.

As it turned out, the new mandate lasted just over one month. After two weeks of verbal sparring between the government and the political opposition, a group of newly formed, independent trade unions called for a general strike. With almost total worker support, it made clear, as nothing else could, that the party's claim to be the party of the workers was a fraud. During the three and a half weeks it continued, the general strike brought industrial production to a complete halt and established conclusively that the party had lost control of the cities. On Skanderberg Square in central Tirana, where demonstrators had torn down a huge statue of Enver Hoxha in February, 50,000 demonstrators battled police with rocks, bottles and fire bombs on May 29, leaving the front steps of the Palace of Culture on the Square shattered and fire-blackened.

The opposition demanded the resignation of the communist government and the formation of a new interim government that would include representatives of the opposition parties. Workers demanded that their wages be doubled and the 48-hour workweek be reduced. The party acceded to all demands in the first week of June. Fatos Nano, in submitting his resignation as chairman of the council of ministers to the legislature, warned of food shortages and the threat of famine. "You have no idea how bad the situation is," he told the legislators.

The new cabinet was sworn in on June 12, 1991. Its head was Ylli Bufi, a member of the Party of Labor but whose training was as an engineer, not a party apparatchik. His reputation was that of an open-minded reformer. Half of the 24-member cabinet was selected by the communists, while another 12 members came from the opposition. In theory, this government of national unity was supposed to be a government of technicians, with members selected as individuals, without reference to party. In fact, seven of the 12 opposition cabinet seats went to members of the main opposition party, the Democratic Party. The other five seats were allotted to the smaller Republican, Social-Democratic, and Agrarian parties. Sali Berisha, head of the Democratic Party, was one of the opposition leaders entering the cabinet.

The Tenth National Congress of the Party of Labor was scheduled to take place

on June 10–12. Prior to the beginning of the congress, President Ramiz Alia submitted his resignation as head of the party, and Xhelil Gjoni, the new party secretary, delivered the keynote address. The speech probably shocked some of the delegates with its attacks on Enver Hoxha's collectivization of agriculture and his "brutal pursuit of 'class struggle,' under which intellectuals and churchgoers were persecuted and jailed, some merely for listening to foreign radio broadcasts or reading the Bible." The congress had its surreal moments, such as when Hoxha's widow, Nexhmije, asserted that, if her husband were still alive, he would be a supporter of democracy and Albanian membership in the European Community. At the conclusion of the congress, the party voted to become the Socialist Party of Albania, hoping apparently that a change in name might help to stem a further decline in popular support.

Tumult in the Post-Communist Era

The task of the new government was not an enviable one. Shops were empty and the people were angry. Industrial production was down drastically, and exports were down by 50% over the previous year. In the countryside, communists and anticommunists quarreled about whether to break up the collective farms, while peasants held off on planting.

The government tried to solve the land problem first. In July 1991, the legislature passed a law authorizing peasants to obtain small parcels of land from the collective farms. That helped although communists in the legislature insisted on a clause to forbid peasants from selling any of their newly acquired land. In addition, because the legislation was passed so late in the crop year, a good percentage of the land never did get planted. The fall harvest would be much smaller.

The new government did get some good news, however. The aid already being provided from Italy, the United States and Turkey would continue and be expanded. The EU offered a trade and cooperation agreement that would allow additional sales to the EU of such Albanian products as chromium and make Albania eligible for technical assistance. In addition, the EU promised Albania 50,000 tons of wheat.

None of this was enough, however. The food situation grew worse over the summer, and unemployment continued to grow, reaching over 35% by August. As a result, an estimated 10,000 Albanians commandeered a freighter, the Vlora, and sailed for Italy. Five months earlier, the Italian government, faced with 24,000 refugees on its hands, had tried to persuade them to return to Albania. About half went willingly.

Albania

This once isolated nation had built bunker fortifications (which are still in place)

Most of the rest remained in Italy, unemployable because they were unskilled. This time, the government decided it would use different tactics. When the Vlora arrived, its passengers were taken in hand by riot squads and locked up in a sports stadium. Five days later, most were given $40 in cash, a T-shirt and a pair of jeans, and flown back to Albania. If the treatment was rather brisk and perhaps a little harsh, the Italian government accompanied this with an offer of $85 million in food aid and another $50 million to purchase imported materials to keep the factories running.

Grateful for the aid, Tirana agreed to try to stop future mass departures by placing its ports under military control and instituting joint coastal patrols with Italian warships. Barbed wire was later strung around the port of Durres to keep would-be stowaways out of the port area.

The government announced a privatization program in September that called for 25,000 state businesses to be sold. But this brought protests from the unions that up to 100,000 jobs would be lost as a result. They demanded that the government guarantee unemployed workers 80% of their usual salary, and this was actually written into law in November 1991. The average worker's salary was less than $30 a month. Even so, there was a question where the government would get the money to pay the unemployed workers. The budget deficit was already over 20% of GDP, and climbing.

Meanwhile, in the countryside, the people had gotten tired of waiting for the government to make up its mind about the collective farms, and they had begun sharing out land and livestock on their own. These "spontaneous privatizations" produced a sort of anarchy in the countryside as looters stripped farm buildings of floors, window frames, roof tiles and even bricks. There were also reports of embittered ex-farm directors dynamiting greenhouses and farm buildings on their way out and farmers burning fields they claimed as their own rather than let a rival family have them.

Ylli Bufi visited the United States in November and thus became the first Albanian prime minister to visit Washington. Shortly after his return, however, the Democratic Party pulled out of the government coalition and it fell. Its head, Sali Berisha, accused the Socialists of hindering economic and political reforms. The charges were true. The Socialists were wary of market economy solutions to problems and did force the Democrats to compromise with them. But the real reason for the pull-out was that new elections were supposed to take place in May 1992, and the Democrats wanted them to occur as early as February. When the People's Assembly refused to agree to move up the elections, the Democrats withdrew from the cabinet. The Democrats wanted to fight the elections from outside the government. This coincided with new food riots that broke out in December 1991, apparently triggered by a comment by Bufi that food reserves would last only a week.

Bufi submitted his resignation as chairman of the council of ministers and was replaced by Vilson Ahmeti. Ahmeti was to preside over a caretaker government that would prepare for new elections. On December 23, President Alia announced that the elections would be moved up after all and would take place on March 22, 1992.

The period between December and March was a trying time for Albania. With the population barely surviving on foreign humanitarian assistance, there were once again attempts to flee the country, followed by food riots as thousands of people stormed warehouses and seized what goods they found there. With anarchy spreading, it became unsafe to go out at night as armed groups of young men roamed the streets attacking people.

During the election campaign, there were also disturbing signs that Albanians were being given an exaggerated idea of what the world could do for them. For example, one journalist quoted "ragged peasants in the countryside" as saying that Albania's Democratic Party leaders and U.S. Secretary of State Baker "will be bringing them shoes and food." A common shout at election rallies was "America will save us."

The Democratic Party won 62% of the vote in the March 22 elections, giving them an absolute majority in the People's Assembly. Including the votes of the Republican and Social Democratic parties, the opposition actually got three-quarters of all votes cast. The big losers were the Socialists with 25% of the vote, down from 67% a year earlier. Since the Democrats had made it clear that they would remove Ramiz Alia as president if they and their allies won a two-thirds majority in the People's Assembly, Alia saved them the trouble and submitted his resignation on April 3. The People's Assembly then elected Sali Berisha, leader of the Democratic Party, as the new president of the republic.

Sali Berisha, a French-trained cardiologist and Hoxha's erstwhile personal physician, had very little political experience when he became president. Similarly Aleksander Meksi, his chairman of the council of ministers, had graduated from Tirana University with a degree in engineering. Most of his subsequent experience was with the institute for cultural monuments and the institute of archaeological excavations as a "restorer and student of monuments of medieval architecture." These two men took control of a country that was, and still is, the poorest in Europe, that was suffering from a breakdown in political and economic life and that had an unemployment rate approaching 50%. The electoral campaign also raised exaggerated hopes among the populace.

Political Trials

The economy did begin to grow again in 1993, but most people saw no improvement in their own situation. As a result, support for the government began to wane. Under extreme pressure to turn matters around, President Berisha adopted an authoritarian approach, thereby antagonizing some of the members of his own Democratic Party. This led to the expulsion of five MPs, including Gramoz Pashko, a for-

Albania

Chicken salesman at Tirana market

mer deputy prime minister, while two other party members resigned. Meanwhile, the Social Democratic Party, completely reorganized by Fatos Nano, a young economist who had served as chairman of the council of ministers for a short time in 1991, began gaining in popularity and appeared to have a good opportunity to win new parliamentary elections scheduled for 1996.

Perhaps for that reason, the government brought charges against Fatos Nano for misappropriating state funds in early 1994 and put him on trial. The charges related to the administration of Italian aid money provided during the time that Fatos was chairman of the council of ministers. It was easy to show that the program had been administered incompetently, but the government was unable to provide any evidence that Nanos benefited financially. Nevertheless, the court found him guilty and sentenced to 12 years in prison.

In June 1994, Ramiz Alia, Albania's last communist leader, was also brought to trial and was found guilty of abuse of power and other charges. He was sentenced to nine years in prison. Nine other former top communists were found guilty at the same time and given sentences ranging from three to nine years. Enver Hoxha's widow was imprisoned. Some of these individuals were undoubtedly guilty of the crimes with which they were charged. There is some irony in Alia's conviction, however, since it was he who permitted Albania's first multiparty elections

that swept him from power in March 1992.

These various trials had a chilling effect politically. They also led to growing fears that Berisha was becoming just another in a long line of authoritarian Albanian rulers. That latter perception may help explain the severe defeat Berisha suffered in 1994 over approval of a new constitution. The draft constitution, drawn up by a parliamentary committee with advice from Western experts, lost in parliament when it failed to win the two-thirds majority necessary to pass it. This was mainly because of opposition by defectors from Berisha's own party. Rather than working for a compromise in parliament, Berisha decided to submit the draft constitution to the people in a popular referendum. Campaigning throughout the country for its adoption, Berisha turned the referendum into a vote of confidence in himself. The result was that the constitution was rejected by a 54% vote. Ismail Kadare, an Albanian writer, commented afterwards, "Albanians were not against the constitution but against the style of the propaganda. The television propaganda was frantic. It annoyed everybody and recalled the days of Communism."

Unlike most Central and Eastern European nations, Albania as of 2008 had not opened up the secret files that were kept on citizens during the communist era. In any case, since the secret service burned many files during the transition year to democracy, there are large gaps in them. It is

estimated that more than 100,000 people are still serving long jail sentences, performing forced labor in chrome and copper mines, or suffering banishment with their families to remote mountain regions.

Anarchy

Parliamentary elections took place on May 26, 1996, but there were such crude irregularities in the run-up to the election, including clubbing of opposition supporters by the police, polling stations packed with Berisha people, plus charges of ballot-stuffing, that independent observers found them rife with fraud. The opposition, which won only a handful of seats, refused to take their seats in parliament, and they maintained their boycott over the next nine months.

Things came to a head in January 1997 when an "investment" scheme that had promised savers interest rates of 50% a month collapsed. This was, it developed, only one of at least nine such pyramid schemes that had been operating in the country and which, collectively, had managed to skim off at least $1 billion in Albanian savings. The government moved to close down the schemes, but it was too late. Six weeks of rioting and unrest led to the collapse of nearly all authority. The whole southern part of the country passed out of government control and even parts of the army went over to the opposition. Almost 1,500 people were killed.

Berisha tried everything—the threat of force, a promise partially to reimburse what people had lost—but it was to no avail. Finally, Berisha dismissed Aleksander Meksi, chairman of the council of ministers, on March 1, 1997 and, after consultations with the various opposition parties, replaced him with Bashkim Fino, a 35-year-old Socialist from the southern town of Gjirokaster. Fino headed a caretaker cabinet, made up of representatives of all major political parties, charged with holding new parliamentary elections by June.

These concessions had no immediate effect on the revolt in the south. Although the Socialists appeared to be well-poised to benefit from the political unrest, they, in fact, had little or no control over the insurgents in the south. The rebels' two nonnegotiable demands were Berisha's resignation and reimbursement for money lost in the collapsed pyramid schemes. In early March, Berisha arranged for his reelection as president by the parliament, but that act turned out to be irrelevant. By March 13, when the new government was sworn in, the country had disintegrated into anarchy, and the government had lost control even in Tirana, the capital.

All over the country, the people had armed themselves by breaking into or tak-

500

ing over military depots, and a civil war appeared to be eminent. As the government lost control, about 300 prisoners were released from the Central Jail in Tirana, including Fatos Nano, the leader of the Socialist Party, and Ramiz Alia, the last communist ruler of Albania. On March 16, President Berisha granted an amnesty to both men plus 49 others who had been released.

By early April, Fino had begun to assert some authority in most parts of Albania, and an armed force of 6,000, assembled under the auspices of the Organization for Security and Cooperation in Europe (OSCE), was arriving at major ports. The OSCE force was led by Italy, which also provided 2,500 of the troops. The force quickly moved to ensure, first, the distribution of aid, then, the establishment of stability to allow new elections in June 1997, won by the Socialist Party.

A New Constitution, a Rejected Monarchy

The Socialists and their allies immediately announced that they would use their two-thirds majority to amend the constitution to create a parliamentary republic. The new parliament convened on July 23, 1997, although the Democrats boycotted the session in a protest against plans to change the constitution. Sali Berisha submitted his resignation as president on the same day.

Albanians had the opportunity in 1997 to choose another kind of chief of state: a monarch. In 1993 Leka, the son of the last king, had returned to Albania, but he was quickly thrown out. Four years later, he returned, accompanied by his mother, former Queen Geraldine, and they were received courteously. In a referendum on the restoration of the monarchy, Leka lost, but a surprising 30% of Albanians voted in favor. A few months before her death in November 2002, Geraldine resettled in Albania with her son, who still calls himself "king," and his family.

Fatos Nano immediately took charge of the country. This took the form of a purge of the judiciary, security forces, and the military of those the Socialists labeled "incompetent political appointees." In fact, these were, in the main, persons who had some connection with the Democratic Party, and they were replaced by persons associated with one of the parties of the government coalition. The Democrats accused the government of appointing its loyalists to all government jobs, and there was undoubtedly a great deal of that. On the other hand, a number of persons appointed to positions in the media were persons of professional ability with no particular ties to the Socialist Party. In addition, most mayors retained their posi-

tions, even though many were members of the Democratic Party.

The Democratic Party boycotted the parliament and the parliamentary commission drawing up the new constitution because it did not want to give the process any legitimacy by participating. Parliament approved the document on October 21, 1998. When the constitution was submitted to a popular referendum in November 22, 1998, the Democratic Party boycotted this vote as well. This may have had some effect, since only 50.57% of the electorate turned out to vote on the constitution. However, 93.5% of those who did turn out to vote cast their ballots in favor of the new constitution. It went into effect November 28, 1998.

Kosovo War

In March 1999 thousands of ethnic Albanians began streaming across the border from Kosovo, particularly after NATO began an air war against Yugoslavia in late March. Serbian President Slobodan Milosevic's response to the bombing was to launch what was obviously a long-planned program of ethnic cleansing in Kosovo province that resulted in an estimated 357,000 refugees fleeing across the border into Albania during the month of April. When the Kosovars began coming in, Albanians provided what assistance they could, freely sharing what they had and often taking them into their own homes.

But this is, after all, the poorest country in Europe, and there was no way Albania could have handled the situation alone. Thus it soon found itself playing host to thousands of NATO troops (who had come in to help the refugees and also offer protection against possible Serb invasion), plus international aid groups who arrived to help the refugees. Fortunately, Milosevic's acceptance of NATO's terms

in early June brought an end to the bombing. Soon afterwards most of the refugees began making their way back to Kosovo.

Albania's assistance to the Kosovar refugees was rewarded by a wave of international economic assistance that began to flow into Albania in the summer of 1999. Thus in May, a group of international aid donors meeting in Brussels pledged Albania $200 million to help it cope with the refugees and to continue economic reform. In June, the World Bank approved two loans, the first a structural adjustment credit of $45 million to help the government complete privatization efforts and strengthen the judiciary and the second a $24 million loan designed to improve irrigation.

That same month, Germany pledged $20 million while the IMF granted a new loan for $12.9 million and increased credits also available under a 1998 agreement by $13.1 million. In December, the World Bank extended yet another $13.65 million loan. This helped finance the reconstruction of two roads damaged by NATO vehicles and refugee convoys during the Balkan campaign earlier in the year. The first connects Durres with Kosovo and the second links Berat with Corovode. The Albanian government remained nervous about violence in Kosovo spilling over into Albania.

POLITICAL SYSTEM

Albania's constitution, approved in November 1998, establishes a parliamentary democracy. The "supreme organ of state power" is a 140-member People's Assembly, which is elected for a four-year term. Beginning with the June 2009 elections, proportional representation from party lists is the electoral system used. Using their two-thirds majority in the People's

Girls march in central Tirana carrying signs declaring "I respect the other's opinion"

Albania

President Bamir Topi

Prime Minister Sali Berisha

Assembly, the Socialists and their allies changed the way government operates even before this was incorporated in the new constitution. The office of the presidency has become a ceremonial position without political authority. The president is elected by parliament for a five-year term and is expected to remain above political partisanship.

The president after 1997 was Rexhep Meidani, a former professor of physics. In July 2002 he was replaced by Alfred Moisiu. In July 2007 Bamir Topi assumed the title. He won the three-fifths majority required only after four rounds of voting. A 50-year-old biologist, he is Albania's first head of state never to have belonged to the Communist Party. He is also one of the few senior politicians not to have been seriously tainted by scandal.

The office of prime minister, which replaced the position of chairman of the council of ministers, is the fulcrum of authority. The Democratic Party helped quiet the domestic situation when it ended its ten-month boycott of the parliament in July 1999. The youthful former weight lifter, Ilir Meta, who had served earlier as deputy prime minister, became prime minister in October 1999. He promised to bring Albania closer to the European Union and to continue his effort to set reforms in motion and to improve the economy.

Meta was forced to resign in January 2001 because of serious feuding within his Socialist Party. It started when party leader Fatos Nano accused Meta's government of corruption and incompetence and challenged his right to rule. The left won the June 2001 elections. This was the Socialists' second straight win, a rarity in the Balkans.

The next prime minister in 2002 was Pandeli Majko, who had occupied that post earlier. In July 2002 he was replaced by Fatos Nano, and Ilir Meta became for-

eign minister. Much of Nano's and Meta's time and energy was devoted to feuding with each other. A rebellious group in the Socialists' parliamentary party refused to support the government thereby paralyzing the legislature.

Nano and Berisha faced off again in the July 2005 elections in which Nano, who suffered from a mounting "fed up factor" in the minds of voters, sought a third straight election win. Berisha came out on top. Both supported full integration with Western Europe through NATO and EU membership. Albania is the only Balkan country that has failed to conduct an election accepted by the international community. This time it agreed to work closely with the OSCE mission in Tirana to revise its electoral law, redraw constituency boundaries and update the voter registers.

The OSCE declared the 2005 elections to have been only partly in compliance with international standards. There was little fraud, but allegedly considerable intimidation and vote-buying. The appearance of fairness is important. In 2004 the EU had postponed talks over membership because of failure to deal with organized crime and corruption in the police and judiciary. Nano challenged the results for 60 days before conceding victory on September 1, 2005.

Even the June 2009 parliamentary elections, in which a deputy and two activists were killed in campaign scuffles, were declared by the OSCE to have failed to meet the highest international standards, despite "tangible progress." It determined that in 22 out of 66 polling centers, vote counting

was "bad or very bad." An investigation of one ballot box found that most of the votes had been cast by persons who were either out of the country or did not have a valid identity document. Also civil servants at 30% of the polling places were allegedly threatened with dismissal if they did not vote for the Democratic Party (DP).

In 2009 the electoral alliance around the right-of-center DP captured 75 of 140 seats; 68 of them are held by the DP and seven by a leftwing splinter group and two smaller parties. It is led by Sali Berisha, former president and personal physician of Enver Hoxha and the man who has dominated Albanian politics since 1991. The opposition Socialists and their electoral partners, led by Tirana's colorful mayor Edi Rama, won 70 seats; 64

Election for mayor in Tirana: "Come with us"

502

of them are held by Socialists. In his campaign Rama drew heavily on quotations from a book of Barack Obama's speeches. Ilir Meta's Socialist Movement for Integration (LSI) played the kingmaker. He allied his party's four seats to Berisha, who therefore remains prime minister. As his reward, Meta became president of the parliament, and two of his party comrades got cabinet posts.

Claiming that their victory would be proven if the ballot boxes were opened to inspectors, the Socialist opposition vowed to boycott parliament until a partial recount could take place. They maintained that they did not want to change the result, but rather to ensure that future elections are free of fraud. The resulting prolonged paralysis prevented parliament from passing laws that require a three-fifths majority. These include many reforms needed to meet EU standards. This lamentable situation reveals the country's divisive politics and weak judiciary, which did not intervene.

In February 2010 the Council of Europe urged Albania's leaders to end their stand-off. In May the European Parliament summoned the party leaders to Strasbourg to issue an even sterner warning: the EU accepts only well-functioning democracies as members. Either resolve the issue, or Albania's bid could be suspended. Its hope to be granted visa-free travel within the 25-nation EU Schengen area was also in danger.

Foreign Policy

Because of Albania's small size, foreign affairs have always played an extremely important role. Between 1945 and 1948, it was Yugoslavia that played "Big Brother" and attempted to dominate Albania. When Enver Hoxha rebelled, he had no choice but to throw Albania into the arms of the Soviet Union. This marriage lasted as long as Stalin was alive. Hoxha had no difficulty switching his loyalty to the new Soviet leadership in 1953, at least for a while. The country entered the Council for Mutual Economic Assistance (CMEA), the Soviet-dominated economic organization for Eastern Europe, in 1949 and the Warsaw Pact in 1955. Almost all foreign trade was with the USSR and other members of the CMEA.

Signs of a Soviet-Yugoslav reconciliation in 1955 made Hoxha apprehensive. He feared that the Soviets might accept his removal as the price for Yugoslavia's renewed friendship. But the situation was saved for Albania by an international crisis—Soviet intervention in Hungary in 1956, which led to a decided cooling in Russian-Yugoslav relations.

The Soviet leader Nikita Khrushchev continued to push "de-Stalinization" after 1956, which was at cross-purposes with Hoxha's desire to retain absolute, one-man power. He was also disturbed by Moscow's proposal in the CMEA for an "international socialist division of labor." It appeared that Albania's role would be to furnish the CMEA with foodstuffs and raw materials. That would mean the death of Hoxha's cherished industrialization program. It became evident that China was also becoming disgruntled with the Soviets' leadership. Hoxha decided to become a Chinese protégé. By late 1959, Albanian speeches were already assuming a Chinese slant on political issues. The Chinese were delighted to have at least vocal support in their disputes with the Russians.

The new direction of Albanian policy became clear at a meeting in Bucharest, Romania, in 1960 when the Albanian delegation backed the Chinese. The next occasion for a confrontation came in November 1960 at a Moscow conference of 81 communist parties. In spite of, or perhaps because of, Soviet pressure in the intervening months—including a denial of wheat deliveries at a time when famine threatened Albania—Hoxha attacked Soviet leader Khrushchev in language that outdid even the Chinese criticism.

The dispute was brought into the open in 1961 when Khrushchev attacked the Albanian party, which in turn denounced him. Diplomatic relations between Moscow and Tirana were broken in 1961. After the break Albania also ceased to participate in CMEA or the Warsaw Pact. When the Chinese countered with an attack on Yugoslavia, the style of the dispute was set until the later open rupture between Moscow and Beijing in 1963.

Albania accepted Chinese "guidance" in party and state affairs after its break with the Soviet Union in 1961 and between 1960 and 1975 received approximately half a billion dollars in interest-free credits from China. With almost 2,000 Chinese technical experts, Albania was able to set up some 30 new industrial projects, chiefly for the production of energy, irrigation and processing of raw materials. Albania was even exporting modest amounts of oil to Greece, with which it had concluded a trade agreement for the first time since World War II.

When the Soviet Union and its allies invaded Czechoslovakia in 1968, Albania officially announced its formal withdrawal from the Warsaw Pact. Concerned about its security, it also launched an effort to improve relations with neighboring countries. For the first time since 1948, Albania began to cultivate better relations with Yugoslavia. This policy began to bear fruit in 1970. Trade between the two countries increased; Yugoslav tourists were permitted to enter Albania, and cultural exchanges between the University of Tirana and the Albanian-language University of Prishtina in Kosovo Province were approved. The two countries raised their diplomatic staffs to embassy level shortly thereafter.

The presence of 1.6 million ethnic Albanians living in Yugoslavia, so often in the past a basis for disagreements between the two countries, for a time helped contribute to a healing as cultural contacts between the ethnic Albanians on both sides

Old part of the medieval city of Gjirokastër in southern Albania
Photo by Martha Grenon

Albania

of the border increased in frequency. Relations worsened again in 1976, however, as a new wave of unrest and Albanian "unity" activity began in Kosovo.

A number of violent demonstrations occurred among the students at Prishtina University in 1981, accompanied by demands to exclude Kosovo from Yugoslavia's program of cultural cooperation with Albania when the program came up for renewal in 1984. In retaliation, Tirana accused Yugoslavia of practicing a policy of "cultural genocide" against ethnic Albanians living within its borders and broke off talks on a new cultural exchange agreement in 1984. Yugoslavia continued to be Albania's chief trading partner, but the level of trade dropped after 1984 and then stagnated.

Economic factors probably played a role in this development, but political factors were clearly dominant. The Serbian government's subsequent actions against ethnic Albanians in Kosovo, in particular the termination of that province's autonomy in 1989, diminished the possibility of improved relations between the two countries. The situation was further compounded in 1991, when Albania extended diplomatic recognition to the self-proclaimed independent "Republic of Kosovo."

Albania's relations with the People's Republic of China soured in the late 1970s because of a change that occurred in China's foreign policy at this time. Hoxha disapproved of the warming trend in Chinese-American relations that had begun in the early 1970s. But he was particularly angered when the People's Republic extended an invitation to Marshal Tito to visit China. Albania launched an anti-China campaign in 1977, and this led to a break in Chinese-Albanian relations in 1978. China discontinued all economic and military assistance to Albania and withdrew all of its technical experts.

Diplomatic relations were resumed in 1979, but they did not regain their earlier warmth, largely for ideological reasons. This time the reason was the economic reform that Deng Xiaoping launched when he came to power in 1978. Hoxha disliked Deng's move and considered him to be a revisionist. Relations began to improve after Hoxha's death in 1985, however. Today, Albania's relations with the People's Republic of China are good. In 2009 a Chinese delegation made its first high-level visit to Albania since ties had been severed in the mid-1980s. Its main interest is in securing raw materials, including chrome and copper.

Albania continued to reject diplomatic relations with either the United States or the Soviet Union as long as Hoxha was alive. However, it did come out of its self-imposed isolation to a limited extent in the early 1980s. There was an improvement in relations with Greece, Italy and France, and Albania opened talks with Great Britain and West Germany in an attempt to resolve bilateral differences that prevented the establishment of diplomatic relations.

British-Albanian differences were over an Albanian gold reserve placed in London prior to World War II and British demands that Albania pay compensation for sinking a British ship off the Albanian coast in 1946. The sticking point in Albanian-West German relations was Albania's demand for $2 billion in reparations from Bonn for damage done in Albania during World War II. Germany was unwilling to concede the principle of reparations, but it did suggest the possibility of a loan or credits to finance a major industrial plant in Albania.

This process speeded up after Enver Hoxha died in April 1985. His successor, Ramiz Alia, though committed to a general continuation of Hoxha's policies, supported a policy of opening up more to the rest of the world. An agreement on border demarcation was signed with Greece. In general, diplomatic contacts increased with Western European and Third World countries.

At the same time, the Albanian Party of Labor continued to reject party-to-party relations with other communist countries during this period and the only ones represented by an ambassador in Tirana were Romania, North Korea, and the People's Republic of China. Albania did sign a major trade agreement with East Germany, which agreed to provide Albania with industrial technology, including agricultural machinery, in return for Albanian chrome ore. A further cautious breakthrough occurred in 1987 when Albania reestablished diplomatic relations with Canada and West Germany.

In 1988 Albania and Bulgaria agreed to elevate their diplomatic relations to the ambassadorial level. Albania also agreed to attend a foreign ministers conference on the Balkans hosted by Yugoslavia. The foreign ministers of Albania, Yugoslavia, Romania, Bulgaria, Greece and Turkey met in Belgrade in February 1988. Their talks covered a number of issues, including trade, regional economic interests, communications, and creation of a nuclear-free and chemical weapons-free Balkans. Not much of a concrete nature was accomplished, but they did agree to meet again. For Albania, the very fact of its participation represented a breakthrough.

Post-Communist Foreign Policy

The wave of political change sweeping across Central and Eastern Europe in the last months of 1989 did not affect Albania directly, but it did change the world in which it operated. Prefacing his remarks with a specific reference to recent international developments, Alia told the Central Committee in April 1990 that "the problem of the reestablishment of diplomatic relations with the United States of America and the Soviet Union is on the agenda." Albania resumed diplomatic relations with Moscow soon afterwards. The first contacts between American and Albanian diplomats occurred in May 1990, but diplomatic relations were not officially renewed until March 1991.

After a government of national unity including members of the political opposition was installed in early June, Albania found additional doors opening to it. It was admitted to the European Bank for Reconstruction and Development in September and the IMF and World Bank in October. Membership in these organizations made Albania eligible for technical assistance and also loans.

Albania's relations with the United States also improved after the change in government in June 1991. Washington supported Albania's applications for membership in international organizations and promised it humanitarian economic assistance. Ylli Bufi, chairman of the council of ministers, traveled to the United States in November, the first Albanian leader to come to Washington. Although the visit was technically private, Bufi did meet with Arnold Kanter, U.S. undersecretary of state for political affairs.

The main purpose of the visit was economic, however. In addition to an agreement that he signed with the Overseas Private Investment Corporation to guarantee American investments in Albania, Bufi met with officials of the departments of the Treasury, Commerce, and Agriculture and with members of the House Foreign Affairs and Senate Foreign Relations committees. He also met with officials of the World Bank.

Relations with the United States underwent a major change after Sali Berisha was elected president in 1992. Journalist Flora Lewis, who visited Albania in 1993, reported that there is "a constant flow of American military personnel coming and going to give advice and check the situation." Since Albanians feared that the Yugoslav war might spread first to Kosovo and then to Albania, they saw America as a protector. The United States made no commitments to Albania at this time, though the Clinton Administration, worried about the war spreading to Kosovo, did express its disquiet to the Serbian government.

Albania said that it would resist any attack from across the border, but its weapons, almost entirely Soviet or Chinese-made versions of Soviet weapons from the 1950s and early 1960s, would be almost

504

useless against well-armed Serbian forces. This is one reason why President Berisha, visiting NATO headquarters in Brussels in 1992, said that Albania would like to join the Western alliance. That would come 17 years later, in April 2009, when it formally joined NATO. This was a moment of enormous symbolic and psychological importance; Albania belongs to the West.

Albania's relations with the Vatican expanded when, in 1993, John Paul II became the first pope to visit Albania since the Middle Ages. Only about ten percent of the population is Roman Catholic, but the pope got a warm welcome. President Berisha greeted the pontiff. Their two speeches made an interesting dialogue about the Balkans. John Paul II, addressing a rally in Tirana, advised: "Do not let the sense of nation that you feel strongly at this moment degenerate into the kind of intolerant and aggressive nationalism that claims its victims still today and fuels ferocious hatreds in several parts of the world, some not far from here."

President Berisha's speech touched on the same theme. "The Holy Father," he said, "has come to the Balkans today at a time when not far from us, in Bosnia-Herzegovina, criminal demons are committing massacres and ethnic cleansing, are exterminating an entire people. We can never permit the ethnic cleansing of Albanians from their territory, and we insist that the region's crisis will never be resolved without a solution of the question of Albanians in Kosovo." Berisha asserted in 2009: "That is the greatest accomplishment of my country after independence."

Tirana became even more outspoken in its support for Albanians outside its borders. This prompted Macedonian accusations of meddling. There were, in fact, two separate issues involved here. The first was the dream of a "Greater Albania" uniting all six million Albanians in a single government. A few nationalists espouse this viewpoint, but they represent only a small fraction of the population. The second, and more significant, issue was Kosovo, where Albanians make up 95% of the population. President Berisha's fear was that the Bosnian War could spread to Kosovo. He was convinced that if that happened, Albania and probably Macedonia could be drawn in as well.

President Berisha was influenced by Albanian nationalists, who acknowledged that their dream of a Greater Albania depended on a major upheaval in the Balkans. Worried by the war in Bosnia, Berisha increased his government's contacts with more radical ethnic Albanians in Macedonia—those who favored joining Albania—presumably to be ready to act should the war spread. When in 1995 it became clear that this was undermining

the main party of ethnic Albanians who were part of the governmental coalition in Macedonia, however, Berisha reversed the policy. He reduced ties with the radicals and reiterated his support for Macedonia's current borders.

Albanian relations with Greece are primarily governed by the fact that there are significant numbers of ethnic Greeks living in southern Albania. The Greek government, which refers to southern Albania as Northern Epirus, claims the right to speak on behalf of ethnic Greeks living in Albania. In recent years, the situation was exacerbated by the Orthodox Bishop of the Greek Province of Epirus, who put pressure on Athens to use force to protect the rights of ethnic Greek minorities in Albania. The Greek government was never willing to go that far, but it did threaten in 1995 to expel the 150,000 Albanian citizens living and working in Greece.

Greece and Albania signed an agreement in April 2009 delineating their continental shelf and maritime borders in the Ionian Sea. Another factor affecting Albanian-Greek relations was that Greece was one of Serbia's strongest supporters during the Bosnian War. But Greece is also a strong proponent of Albanian membership in the EU. Tirana formally applied in 2009, and the accession process has begun.

Albania's relations with both the United States and Western Europe cooled considerably. The United States was particularly critical of irregularities in the parliamentary elections in 1996 and several times called for new elections. By 1997, Washington had taken the position that Berisha's resignation was essential. When, therefore, Berisha appealed for the European Union and NATO to send peacekeeping troops to restore order after his government had lost control, the word he received was that the first step toward restoring order had to be his own resignation.

After Fatos Nano became prime minister in 1997, Washington officially promised to provide financial support for the reconstruction and democratization of Albania. Other countries extended offers of economic assistance, including Germany, which pledged $18 million in 1997. Albania's relations with Greece also improved at this time.

Rexhep Meidani, who replaced Berisha as president, did not differ greatly in his position on Kosovo. In August 1998, for example, he gave an interview in which he endorsed an interim policy of autonomy but added, "for me the final solution is quite clear; . . . the Albanians can no longer live under the Serbian regime." But Meidani went on to make clear that he favored an independent Kosovo, not a "Greater Albania." As prime minister, Ilir Meta also dismissed such dreams:

Born in Skopje of Albanian parents, Mother Teresa is honored in Tirana

"Greater Albania is a project that doesn't exist even in our minds." However, not all politicians are willing to ignore such an idea. President Meidani endorsed the Rambouillet agreement in March, then the NATO bombing campaign that followed Yugoslavia's rejection of the agreement.

Kosovo's declaration of independence on February 17, 2008, was cause for jubilation there and in Albania proper. The old idea of a "greater Albania" binding all 6 million Albanians in one nation-state was seldom mentioned. Only one out of ten Kosovo Albanians said in polls that they wanted to belong to Albania, but that possibility is being increasingly discussed. Of course, there are cultural links, fostered by the electronic media. Language binds them although southern Albanians speak a Tosk dialect, which predominates in books and newspapers, while Kosovars speak the Geg dialect.

The two countries, along with the Albanian enclaves in Macedonia and Montenegro, will become natural trading partners when the transportation links between

Albania

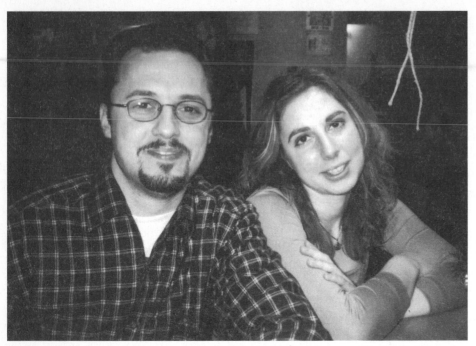

Good neighbor policy. Albanian student with his Greek classmate at the College of Europe.

them are improved. There is no cross-border rail connection. On the old roads, a drive from the two capitals of Tirana and Prishtina via the old capital city of Prizren takes ten hours. That is why a $1.4 billion-dollar project to improve the road from the northern Albanian port of Durres to Prishtina, completed the end of 2009, is so important: the trip now takes less than three hours. A donor conference sponsored by the World Bank and the EU raised more than one billion euros for Kosovo in June 2008. Part of this sum is devoted to improving the connecting roads. The Central European Free Trade Agreement (CEFTA), as well as a bilateral trade accord, is in place to facilitate regional trade.

Military

The number of American and other NATO troops in Albania began to increase greatly in March 1999, particularly after Serbian forces began driving ethnic Albanians out of Kosovo more or less simultaneously with the beginning of the NATO bombing campaign. With large numbers of refugees pouring over the border, numerous international aid missions also moved in to provide assistance. While offering whatever help it could to refugees from Kosovo, Albania welcomed both the NATO troops and the international aid missions. After the war, Albania consistently advocated an independent Kosovo without which there could be no long-term stability. Despite the distrust that exists in the relationship with Serbia, Tirana tries to maintain discourse and a constructive tie with it.

It hoped that such timely assistance to NATO allies could pave the way for Albania's membership in the alliance, which seemed unlikely for many years. The reasons were that its democracy was not yet sufficiently stable, and its armed forces were not ready. But the restructuring of its military was completed in 2010. Conscription was 12 months before it was abolished. A fully professional army is taking shape. There is stiff competition among young Albanians to join the new force. Albania has reduced its active duty soldiers to 14,295 under one command: the separate navy and air force are being combined with the army, and there are 500 paramilitary forces. Bases in Durrës and Vlorë operate mainly patrol and coastal combatants and mine warfare vessels. All fixed-wing aircraft, including the 26 aged

MiG aircraft, were grounded. When one of them crashed in September 2004, killing the pilot, critics demanded that the entire MiG fleet stop flying out of Tirana's international airport and be sent to a museum. That has happened. Instead it is building a helicopter-based force for transporting ground forces, conducting medical evacuations, and engaging in combat; it possesses 16 helicopters and 10 reconnaissance and utility planes. It is developing a niche capability in de-mining.

In 2010, it had deployed about 350 soldiers with NATO forces in Afghanistan and with the Americans in Iraq. In Afghanistan, its 140 soldiers participate in a medical team with Macedonia and Croatia and take part in training the Afghan army. All of its 250 troops in Iraq have been withdrawn, but it helped guard the airport at Mosul with the 101st Airborne Division. It has 13 peacekeepers in Bosnia-Herzegovina and 63 in Chad.

Albania was one of 10 former communist countries to sign the so-called Vilnius Letter expressing support for the Iraq war at an "important" time. It opened its airspace, land routes and territorial waters to allied nations during the war. It also offered access to its military bases, which the U.S. did not need. Albania signed an agreement with the U.S. to shield American soldiers serving in Albania from prosecution by the International Criminal Court.

After the war, American leaders expressed their gratitude by promising to help Albania gain full membership in NATO, which occurred in April 2009. They offered high-level training and exercises designed to help improve its military capabilities and sent a number of military experts to work in Albania's Defense Ministry. While taking part in an Albanian-American military exercise in April 2005, an American transport plane crashed in central Albania, killing all nine on board. They helped promote an Adriatic Charter to improve relations between Albania,

Macedonia, Croatia and the rest of Europe. In September 2003 Albania, Macedonia and Croatia agreed to a Common Declaration on defense.

Ex-Secretary of Defense Donald Rumsfeld said, "I value the relationship that the United States has with Albania. It's important to us." The U.S. supported Albania's successful bid to join NATO, along with Croatia, in April 2009. Partly in gratitude, Albania agreed in December 2008 to accept five Uighur detainees (Muslims from western China) from Guantanamo prison. It was the first country to accept detainees who were not its former residents. They became celebrities in Tirana, appearing on TV chat shows and giving interviews.

In the fall of 2004 Albania discovered to its own amazement that it possessed several hundred canisters of lethal military chemicals, the same kind of sulfur mustard Saddam Hussein had used against Iranians and his own Kurdish population in the 1980s. At a time in 1979 when Albanian dictator Hoxha had alienated himself from all patron countries, he tried to control his own population by stirring up hysteria over an imagined attack by a combination of enemies including Yugoslavia, the Soviet Union, the U.S. and China. He ordered the country's biggest public works project ever—the construction of 750,000 concrete bunkers, one for every four Albanians at the time. Most are still there. He also purchased large quantities of weapons, and he ordered the poison gas from China and had it stored in a remote bunker in the mountains. When he died in 1985, the cache was forgotten until it was discovered in 2004.

Albania garnered international praise for immediately disclosing the stockpile's existence. The U.S. assumed responsibility for constructing a custom-made mobile incinerator to be towed along steep mountain roads to the very door of the bunker and to destroy the chemicals there. It helped install fences and surveillance gear to protect the stocks. It also offered $20 million to finance the project. This was the first time the U.S. offered to do this outside the former Soviet Union. Aware that this gave Albania the opportunity to strengthen its ties with the West and to demonstrate that it is a partner in the struggle against terrorism, Defense Minister Pandeli Majko called its actions a "psychological" break with the past. "After the Cold War, we have passed from a phase of irresponsibility and entered a phase of responsibility and transparency."

However, a disastrous explosion at a military depot near Tirana airport on March 15, 2008, highlighted a problem that sets Albania apart from its new Atlantic allies. The country is still sitting on about 100,000 tons of excess outdated ammunition in unstable condition of Chinese and Soviet origin stored in various depots throughout the country. The blast could be heard as far away as the Macedonian capital of Skopje, 100 miles distant, and the tremors were felt far beyond Tirana. A massive ball of fire shot up from the site, and shrapnel and shell fragments rained down on homes, businesses and vehicles. The fire raged for 14 hours, and 26 persons died, 10 more disappeared, and more than 250 were injured; more than 2,300 homes and businesses were destroyed. The defense minister was sacked, and damaged homes are being rebuilt with government subsidies.

ECONOMY

Before Enver Hoxha's death in 1985, Albania billed itself as the world's first "true socialist economy." One reason for this claim was that 100% of the "means of production" had been nationalized under Hoxha. Until 1990, this extended even to motor vehicles, which could be owned only by the state. Citizens were permitted to own bicycles, however. That proud boast lost all of its glitter long before the defeat of the Socialist Party of Albania in the 1992 elections. But the truth behind that boast continues to give government ministers headaches as they work to privatize the economy and move Albania toward a market economy.

Albania launched its first Five-Year Plan in 1951 with a goal of a rapid development of industry and national self-sufficiency, including agriculture. Growth during the first two Five-Year Plans was fairly rapid since Albania was starting from almost nothing. It slowed thereafter, but this can largely be blamed on the halt in Soviet economic aid after the break in relations in 1961. There was fairly rapid growth between 1966 and 1970—reflecting the assis-

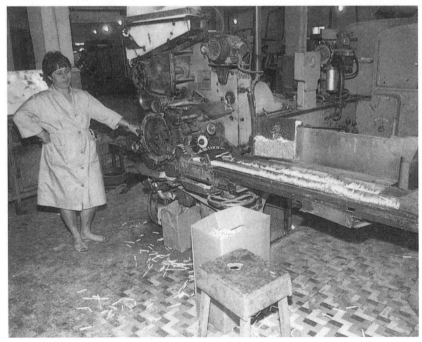

A cigarette factory in Durres   Photo by Martha Grenon

Albania

tance that the country got from China—but there was a slowdown after 1970.

Albania achieved full collectivization of agriculture in 1967 and followed this up by a reduction in the size of peasants' private plots. Albanian agriculture regularly achieved only about 50% of its assigned production targets in the late 1960s and early 1970s. This sector also suffered from the loss of Chinese assistance after the Albanian-Chinese diplomatic break. As a result, the government abandoned its long-term goal of self-sufficiency and began to develop foreign trade.

Albania is still the least developed country in Europe, but the regime's policy of industrialization did produce substantial changes in a number of areas. For example, Albania has significant resources of chrome, iron, coal, copper and petroleum, and there was significant development in these areas during the years of communism.

By the late 1980s, Albania had the capacity to produce over 800,000 tons of chrome a year, making it the world's third-largest producer of that vital metal at the time. In the 1970s, Albania constructed an oil refinery with an annual capacity of one million tons and began exporting crude oil and refined petroleum products to Italy, Greece, Germany, Switzerland and Romania. Other exports included electric power, copper, coal, textiles and food products.

Red tape and too much control from Tirana had created a situation of slow growth that the bureaucrats were unable to reverse. Severe shortages developed, particularly of raw materials, modern machinery and consumer goods. Food items such as meat and cheese had to be rationed, though staples such as bread, sugar and milk remained adequate until 1990. Fruits and vegetables were also still freely available at that time.

In 1990, however, Ramiz Alia promised to institute a number of economic reforms aimed at decentralizing decision-making and creating some economic incentives in industry and agriculture. Though developments elsewhere in Eastern Europe were an important influencing factor, the state of the Albanian economy played the more important role in the political developments in 1990–91. A common complaint, both of people demonstrating in the cities and of others who fled the country, was the lack of any hope for their own future. Part, but not all, of that pessimism was caused by the failure of the communist system itself.

The other serious, long-term problem was for years Albania's rate of population growth, which was higher than its rate of economic growth. That has changed. A birthrate of 2.1 children per woman is the replacement rate. Albania, along with

Eating well in a Tirana Restaurant

Kosovo and the Albanian minority in Macedonia, is among the few European countries that not only maintain but exceed that rate. Steady 6% growth in the economy now sustains that continued increase in population. Over 50% of its population is under 30. However, this does create pressure on farmland, since many Albanians are still farmers.

Post-Communist Era

Since 1992, all Albanian governments have been committed to the privatization of state-owned industry and the creation of a market economy. However, they have not been able to make much progress in the area of privatization because of the dire state of the economy. When the government removed subsidies on state industry in 1991, about half of industry closed down or laid-off workers and went on short hours.

With social discipline breaking down, Albania entered a period of anarchy. The Berisha government managed to reverse that trend and to restore order in the cities, though roving bands of robbers continued to operate in parts of the countryside. Meanwhile, industrial production continued to drop, with many plants working at 5% capacity by 1993. The situation then stabilized, and the economy began growing again in 1993. For the next couple of years, Albania had one of the fastest growing economies in Europe, though it started from a very low baseline.

In 1994, the government launched a major program of privatization, selling off all (1,800 in total) small state-owned enterprises with fewer than 300 employees and less than $500,000 in assets. Many new small and medium-sized private companies were also started, creating an estimated 100,000 jobs. By 2005, the private sector accounted for almost 80% of output, much of it in the underground economy. Privatization continues. Germany's Hochtief won a concession to manage Tirana's Mother Teresa Airport.

An estimated 850,000 or more Albanians (approximately one-fourth to one-third of the population) work abroad, at least 600,000 in Greece and 200,000 in Italy. More would like to leave the country if they could. Those abroad include more than 10,000 professionals, including university professors and researchers. Their absence raises fears that Albania will lack the skilled professionals it needs to complete the transition to a market economy and handle the administrative demands made by EU integration.

On the plus side, Albanians living abroad remit a billion euros (about $1.45 billion) a year, equivalent to about 11% of GDP. That declined by 6.2% in the first half of 2009, but few came home. Remittances made it possible for the government to stabilize the value of the lek, and it contributed heavily to the success of privatizations. Remittances also helped maintain the country's high growth rate (6% annually for six years leading up to 2008, one of the highest in the Balkans) until the global economic downturn in 2009, when economic growth was an estimated 2.5%. It was one of the few European economies that did not shrink in that recession year, and it needed no bailout. Along with the proceeds of organized crime, they also reduce poverty, contain social tensions, fuel a building boom (until the world recession temporarily turned the boom into a bust), support many families and offset a large trade deficit. Tourism adds another 750 million euros to the economy.

Albania taps an unusual source of assistance. Because of past migrations from this poor land, about 600,000 persons of Albanian descent live in America. They were heavy contributors to Albania's Democratic Party in the run-up to the 1992 elections, and for a while they invested in their old homeland. Some even returned to offer their foreign skills. Most of this consisted of Albanian-Americans providing capital to Albanian relatives to set up or buy businesses. Much was invested in pyramid schemes that began to collapse in early 1997.

For a while, the news from the countryside was a little better. The old collective form of farming basically disappeared as a result of the legislature's 1991 decision to allow peasants to obtain their own parcels of land. The peasants themselves carried out most of the implementation of that decision, and they did so in a haphazard manner. The peasants were unable to agree among themselves about who owned what lands. As a result, only about half of the agricultural land was planted in 1991.

Most of the quarrels over land ownership were resolved by 1992, and about 80% of the land was in private hands although the distribution of land deeds was a much slower process. This had a negative economic effect, for peasants without land deeds are unable to use their land as collateral for borrowing. There has been a mass migration from desperately poor rural areas into the cities. Albania now imports most of its food, including fresh produce from Greece and Macedonia. However, it is the world's largest exporter of sage (grown wild) and one of Europe's major exporters of medicinal herbs.

The collapse of several pyramid "investment" schemes in January 1997 led to a complete loss of confidence in the government and banks in general. By March the government had lost control of almost all of the country. It was estimated that a third of Albania's capital reserves evaporated in the collapse, and the resulting anarchy set the country back even further. Since Albania was already receiving one third of its annual budget of $960 million from the European Union, Italy organized a rescue operation that involved moving Italian and other troops into Albania to restore order.

The Value Added Tax was raised from 12% to 20% in 1998. The tax rate on corporate profits and personal income was

Happier faces for long-isolated Albania: music students in the city of Korce

made a flat 10% to lure foreign investors and make businesses more willing to pay their taxes. In general, taxes remain a problem because as much as 30% of the economy is underground, meaning that economic activity occurs behind the backs of the tax collectors. Tax evasion also stems from many citizens' conviction that government officials are corrupt and would only pocket their tax money.

They have a point. Bribes are paid to register companies, obtain permits and licenses, and avoid harassment by tax authorities. According to the World Bank, 77% of companies bribe officials. In 2008 Transparency International ranked Albania 105th out of 180 countries in terms of corruption perception. This was lower than all other former communist countries in the Balkans. This is one reason why foreign direct investment lags behind the rest of Southeastern Europe. The judiciary has a bad reputation as corrupt, poorly trained, and heavily politicized. The EU has particularly focused on judicial reform as a condition for completing a stabilization and association agreement. The central government made a start toward making earnings visible to the tax officials by paying its own employees through banks. Until recently, officials all the way up to the prime minister were paid in cash.

Some economic progress has been made. In 2005 Albania was the only country in Southeast Europe where economic output exceeded 1989 levels. Inflation by 2007 was 2.9%. GDP per capita income doubled between 1999 and 2005, but it was

still only $3,670 in 2008, a tenth that in Greece. Albania remains Europe's poorest country after Moldova. Amnesty International estimates that about one in five lives below the poverty line of $2 per day. In mountainous districts, the figure rises to 45%. One must often bribe to receive adequate health care. Unemployment was officially 12% in 2010, higher for women and in the countryside, where much of the population is employed in subsistence farming. There is a wide gap between a minority of well-off and the struggling underclass. Half of the wealth is controlled by a fifth of the population. That is why so many live and work outside the country.

The efforts to privatize large state-owned companies, to build better roads, to collect more taxes, and to overcome the chronic power and water shortages continue. By 2007 only one-sixth had running water, and less than a fifth had uninterrupted electricity. City dwellers suffered power cuts of at least 6 hours a day, rising to about 12 hours in the countryside. However, those shortages have eased as generating capacity has increased. As more and more Albanians move into the cities and furnish their homes with modern appliances, demand for electricity is growing at three times the European average. Hydropower units produce 90% of its electricity, but droughts reduce water levels in dams that feed the antiquated hydropower plants. An estimated 30% of power supply is lost in transmission. The problem is aggravated by the shutdown of two nuclear reactors in Bulgaria, which

Albania

cut electricity exports by two-thirds and drove up energy prices all over the Balkans, including Albania. That reflects itself in slower economic growth and fewer foreign investments.

Problems remain that make it very difficult to attract foreign investment. The budget deficit had fallen by almost half, but it rose from 3.7% in 2008 to 6.8% in 2009 and back to 3.9% in 2010. Political polarization and widespread corruption continue to be problems. A report by the International Crisis Group estimated in 2003 that almost half of the GDP was accounted for by criminal activity. However, there is widespread tolerance for it. Many see criminal wealth as "progress."

The country has become a transit route and warehouse for international traffickers of drugs, cigarettes, immigrants, and women and children for prostitution or begging in the rest of Europe. The Albanian and Italian navies cooperate in trying to stop them from crossing the Adriatic, but few were caught. In 2005 the government forbade the use of speedboats, the favored transportation used by traffickers to get people out of the country. Through stricter border controls and revenge killings of traffickers by the victims' families, trafficking of women has been significantly reduced. The country's role as a major transit point for human trafficking from the East to western Europe has practically ended.

CULTURE

The two elements that defined traditional Albanian culture were religion—primarily Islam—and the way of life associated with the peasantry of the Balkans. After 1945, the Albanian Party of Labor introduced its own double agenda, an economic goal of industrialization and a social goal of creating the "new socialist person." Industrialization raised the urban population and led to increased mechanization of the countryside. In addition, because of its need for trained technicians, the regime set up many new technical schools that eventually produced an educated urban elite. Albania is still basically a rural and peasant society, however, with over half of the people living in villages where clan or feudal relationships persist.

Albania remains heavily clan-oriented. A negative aspect of this is the ancient rite of Kanun ("blood must be paid with blood") to settle feuds between families. This odious practice, practiced in the northern part of Albania, had been outlawed during the 40-year communist reign of Enver Hoxha and almost completely disappeared. But it erupted again after the collapse of communism ushered in a new atmosphere of lawlessness. It is estimated that 20,000 people have been trapped by such feuds since 1991, with 9,500 killed and about 1,000 children deprived of schooling. The only safe place for a man marked for death is within the confines of his home, which is off limits. Women and children are spared, but even those men who escape abroad are sometimes hunted down and murdered.

In an attempt to reduce the negative aspects of this, the chiefs of the best-known families in the north met in 2005 and adopted a new "code of honor" for vendettas to replace the one in effect for more than six centuries. The main improvement is that families have the right to exact vengeance only on the perpetrator of a wrong, not on every male family member bearing the same last name as the wrongdoer. The innocent should be spared.

If this works, it would be an enormous relief for more than 800 families with more than 2,000 children who live cloistered lives in Albania out of fear of being killed in a private vendetta. This change comes as Albanian authorities are intensely working on resolving the problem. They are drafting laws with severe sanctions, including the seizure of property, for those who commit such murders. Changes in the penal code include sentences of 25 years to life in prison for those who kill in a blood feud. That has helped diminish the practice. According to the minister for corruption and humanitarian problems, "vengeance is also a crime."

In 1964, Hoxha launched an ideological and cultural revolution aimed at eliminating religion, the influence of family and sectional loyalties, and prejudices toward women. Albania became the only country in the world to prohibit all religious practice. All churches and mosques were closed and most religious leaders were imprisoned. In addition, a major effort was made to end the traditional Islamic seclusion of women and to bring them into the workplace. Three years later, Albania became the world's first officially atheist country.

The party relaxed some of its controls beginning in 1970, but the cultural revolution resumed in 1973. Now the targets were young people, the military and the technicians. The party reorganized the education system to make it stricter. Party officials who had advocated a moderate line were purged. Intellectuals were sent to factories and collective farms to do manual labor. This did not succeed in changing the basic culture of the country, but it enforced a surface conformity. It is not even clear that closing all of the mosques and churches reduced the number of believers although it did succeed in driving religion underground.

The prohibition against all public religious rituals left a void, and the regime attempted to fill this by creating a new calendar of secular festivals. National holidays such as Albanian Independence Day (November 28) formed the core of the new calendar, but days were also set aside for honoring the worker and a number of agricultural festivals.

In April 1990, the regime rescinded laws prohibiting the practice of religion. In November, the party voted to return all houses of worship to their respective religious communities. Most churches and mosques had been converted into things like gymnasiums, movie theaters and warehouses, and others had been allowed to fall into disrepair. Therefore, implementation was slow. About 40 churches had been turned over to religious authorities by April 1991, and this process continues into the 21st century.

Class outing

510

A much more serious problem in re-building the church is the shortage of priests. There were fewer than 10 Greek Orthodox priests in the country in April 1991 and only 32 Catholic priests. All were elderly and most had spent long years in prison. The head of Albanian Catholics, the Apostolic Administrator of Durres, was a 76-year-old man who lived in total retirement in a small village in the north of the country.

On March 21, 1991, a symbolic mass was said in Shkoder Cathedral, though the building was not really in a condition to be used. Its two towers had been demolished in 1967, its portal was boarded up, and inside the yellow plaster was peeling everywhere. In another symbolic act, Mother Teresa, an ethnic Albanian born into a prosperous family in nearby Skopje, Macedonia, came to Shkoder in March 1991. She attended the first mass at Shkoder Cathedral and founded a convent nearby. The three nuns in residence opened an orphanage for unwanted Albanian children. Mother Teresa had founded her own order in India and adopted Indian citizenship. Her adopted country rejected Tirana's request in 2009 to send her remains from Calcutta to Albania for reburial.

The Islamic community has taken back its remaining mosques, but they are also in a dilapidated condition. One mosque, the Xhamia e Plumbit, an 18th century mosque that stands before the gates of Shkoder, had been rehabilitated somewhat and is currently in use. Moslem clerics suffered a treatment similar to Chris-

tians, and they are also elderly men who have served long terms in prison. Muslim and Catholic leaders condemned the proposed 2009 law to make Albania the first Balkan country to legalize gay marriage.

Perhaps the only Albanian writer with an international reputation is Ismail Kadare, who lives in both Albania and France. He graduated from Tirana University and went to Moscow to study at the Maxim Gorky Literature Institute. Since he mastered the technique of writing his 30 books in a manner that could be read in two different ways, he was not sent to labor camps or executed during the communist era, as were other critical authors. In fact, his career flourished in Hoxha's regime, and he belonged both to parliament and the regime-sponsored Writers Union. He was one of the few Albanians allowed to travel abroad. His fiction offers rare insights into life under tyranny. His best novels are said to be *The Three-Arched Bridge* and *Broken April* (1978) and *The Palace of Dreams* (1981); *Chronicle in Stone* (1971) is autobiographical.

FUTURE

Anno 2008 was the "year of Albanians," with Kosovo winning its independence on February 17, and NATO membership offered to Albania in April. Albania has progressed from failed state to an imperfect but functioning democracy.

The EU's summit in Greece in June 2003 gave it and other Balkan nations the assurance that they can also join some day. The Stabilization and Association Agreement (SAA) talks had stalled because of lack of progress in the critical area of justice and home affairs. But in June 2006 it signed an SAA with the EU, and it formally applied for admission in 2009. However, it will take at least a decade to secure full membership. Many members doubt that Albania is ready, given unsolved problems of corruption and inadequate legal institutions.

The EU told the country's leaders that if they are interested in membership, they must push through key reforms rather than feuding with each other and boycotting parliament. It must tackle corruption head on. In 2008 Transparency International ranked it among Europe's 10 most corrupt countries. The next year the World Bank placed it 173d out of 186 countries in the handling of construction permits. It was told to reform its electoral practices (not a single set of elections since 1991 have been judged entirely free and fair), improve the standards of state administration, and upgrade electrical generation and the transportation system.

There has been progress in the economic area. The government has made

notable advances in privatization. Road improvement has been impressive although there is still much work to be done. Tirana, one of the least appealing examples of communist taste and neglect, got a facelift under dynamic Mayor Edi Rama. Bulldozers cleared away hundreds of illegally constructed buildings and kiosks to make way for parks and flower beds. The old politburo quarter, off-limits earlier to the common people, underwent a radical transformation becoming the hottest spot for night life, with cafes, restaurants and a nightclub. Even Enver Hoxha's former residence now houses a coffee bar. Rama admitted: "Of course, Tirana will never become Paris or Rome, but that doesn't mean we shouldn't make the effort." The United Nations awarded him a prize for environmental development. Remittances from about a million Albanians working abroad are important economic stimuli, and some foreign investors have returned.

Albania's desire to join NATO was fulfilled in April 2009. Prime Minister Berisha had asserted in 2007: "We are determined to take any decision, adopt any law, undertake any reform that would make Albania suitable to receive the invitation to join the Western military alliance." Its dispatch of soldiers to Afghanistan, Iraq and Bosnia gained it powerful advocates for membership. But Albania is full of antiquated weapons and ammunition left over from the communist era that must be destroyed in a safe way.

The warmth of American-Albanian relations was demonstrated by the hero's welcome President George W. Bush received in June 2007 when he became the first sitting American president ever to visit the country. Albanians lined the road leading into Tirana wearing cardboard Uncle Sam hats and cheering him. He was awarded the nation's highest honor, the Order of the Flag medal, was put on a new line of commemorative postage stamps, and had the street in front of the parliament building named after him. The prime minister declared him to be "the greatest and most distinguished guest we have ever had in all times." The good feelings toward America have been strengthened by President Woodrow Wilson's support of Albanian independence and opposition to carving up Albania 95 years earlier and by U.S. willingness to defend Albanians in Kovovo and that country's independence.

Albania is Europe's poorest country after Moldova. Corruption is rife, and organized crime and trafficking plague the land. These are heady challenges. But it is more politically stable today than at any time since the communist regime crumbled in 1991.

Memorial to National Hero Skenderbeu on main square, Tirana

Romania

Sinaia Monastery

Area: 91,699 sq. mi. (237,500 sq. km.). The size of North Carolina and Virginia combined.

Population: 21.6 million (2007 estimate)

Capital City: Bucharest (Pop. 1,928,000)

Climate: Continental, with moderate rainfall.

Neighboring Countries: Moldova, Ukraine (Northeast); Bulgaria (South) Serbia (West); Hungary (Northwest).

Official Language: Romanian

Other Principal Tongues: Hungarian, German

Ethnic Background: Ancestry rooted in Dacian and Roman heritage, with some Slav intermixture.

Principal Religions: Romanian Orthodox Christianity (87%), Protestant (6.8%), Catholic (5.6%).

Chief Commercial Products: Textiles, basic metals and products, machinery and equipment, minerals and fuels, chemicals, agricultural products.

Chief Commercial Customers: EU (72% of exports and 71.3% of imports), Italy (17.2% of exports and 12.8% of imports),

Germany (17% of exports and 17.2% of imports), France (7.7% of exports), Hungary (7% of imports).

Currency: leu (plural: lei; reformed in July 2005 by dropping four zeros from the denominations).

Former Political Status: Independent states in the east and south from the 13th century; Turkish control from the 15th and 16th centuries in the south and east; increasing Russian influence in the 19th century; independent in 1878 after Russian-Turkish conflict. The western sector was under the Hungarian Crown in the Middle Ages under independent princes in the 16th century, and under Habsburg control and later part of Austria-Hungary until 1918, when it became a part of Romania. Communist state, part of Soviet Bloc, 1945–1989.

National Day: December 1 (Date in 1918 when Transylvania became part of Romania).

Chief of State: Traian Basescu, President (elected December 2004).

Head of Government: Emil Boc, Prime Minister (December 2008).

Type of Government: Multiparty democracy.

National Flag: Vertical stripes of blue, yellow and red.

In the first half of the 20th century Romania's capital city of Bucharest earned a reputation as the "Little Paris of the East" because of its wide boulevards and stylish villas. Communism and a self-serving ruling communist dynasty under Nicolae Ceausescu from 1965 to 1989 changed that and much else. Under his regime the increasingly impoverished Romanian people were forced to make every sacrifice in order to secure the country's independence from Moscow and to fulfill the megalomaniac dreams of its repressive leader. It is now a country with much work to do to catch up with the rest of democratic Europe. Balkan in geography, Orthodox in religion, Latin in language and temperament, and European in ambition, Romania is the Balkans' largest nation.

Romania

Dacia c. 110 A.D.

Wallachia, Moldavia, Transylvania, c. 1555

The dominant feature of Romania's geography is the chain of mountains that separate Moldova and Muntenia (formerly Wallachia) from Transylvania in the west. This has been most commonly described as a giant reverse "S" composed of the Eastern and Southern Carpathians. They extend westward as far as the magnificent cliffs of the Iron Gate, located on the banks of the Danube River, where it flows through the Alps. This mountain range continues through Bulgaria, where the bottom of the "S" forms the massive Balkan Range. About one-fourth of Romania is covered by forests, which are an important source of wood and timber products.

The Danube flows eastward for more than 200 miles from the Iron Gates, forming the border between Romania and Bulgaria. One hundred miles from the Black Sea, the river turns north and eventually east again, flowing through Romania to the Black Sea. The area between the river and the sea in this region is known as Dobruja and has been the object of many disputes in the past. Romania's seaports, Constanta and Mangalia, lie on the Black Sea. Recently canals have been completed through Dobruja and Bulgaria, making transit along the Danube to the Black Sea shorter by more than 100 miles.

The other geographical feature is a plain that begins in the southwest, just south of the Iron Gate, and broadens as one travels eastward. By the time one gets to Bucharest, the "valley"—for it is actually the northern side of the Danube River Valley—has widened to about 80 miles. East of Bucharest, it widens out into a broad plain, which becomes the delta of the Danube River. This plain is the chief grain-growing region of Romania. Although mountains dominate the center and north of the country, much of this area actually consists of mountain valleys or plateaus. It is thus agriculturally productive.

Although most of the population is ethnic Romanian, minorities constitute approximately 12%. The two historic prov-

inces of Moldova and Wallachia are overwhelmingly ethnic Romanian, but Transylvania has significant Hungarian and German minorities. Estimates of minorities vary considerably, but Hungarians are about 6.6% of the population, Germans .3%, Ukrainians .3%, Russian .2%, and Turkish .2%. Roma (Gypsies) officially are 2.5%, but that percentage may be as high as 10%. The census allows citizens to say what they are, and some Roma categorize themselves as "Romanian." Other minorities include Jews, Armenians, Gypsies, Serbs, Turks, Bulgarians and Greeks.

HISTORY

Origins of the Romanian State

The Romanians trace their earliest history back to an unknown time when their ancestors, the Dacians, formed a state in the Danube area. Conquered by the Roman Emperor Trajan (Marcus Ulpius Traianus) in 106 A.D., Dacia became a province of Rome, remaining under its rule until the Emperor Aurelian (Lucius Domitius Aurelianus) withdrew Roman forces in 271. Although the Latin heritage of the present-day Romanians is reflected in their name and language, they are not completely distinct from their Slavic neighbors. This is because the Dacians were subjected to Slavic influence during the centuries that followed the Roman withdrawal. Some Romans remained and with the Dacians formed the modern Romanian nation.

Not much is known about the life of the Dacians until the 13th century. Possibly they found safety from the invasions of the barbarians from Central Asia by mov-

513

Romania

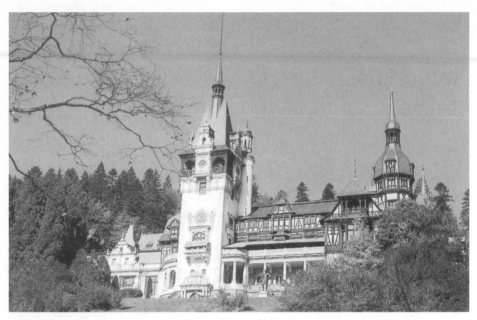

Peles Castle, Sinaia, built by Carol I

ing high into the Carpathian Mountains, living in pastoral isolation.

There are three major areas that constitute Romania today: Muntenia (former Wallachia), Moldova and Transylvania. The first became an independent state in the 13th century and Moldova did the same in 1359. Transylvania, which had been inhabited by the ancient Dacians, was under the Hungarian Crown during the Middle Ages, under independent princes (but still responsible to the Hungarian monarch) during the time the surrounding area was part of the Turkish Ottoman Empire in the 16th and 17th centuries, under the Habsburgs after 1687, and under Hungarian (Magyar) control after 1867. It finally became part of Romania after World War I.

The Turkish Ottoman Empire gained control of Wallachia and later Moldova in the 15th and 16th centuries. They were not incorporated into the empire, but were allowed a measure of independence in choosing their princes, called *Hospodars*.

At the beginning of the 18th century, the Turkish rulers started to select puppet Greek princes. Until the 19th century, Wallachia and Moldova were nominally under Ottoman rule, which was not always rigid and was often shared with other powers. In addition to Turkish control of their internal affairs, the Romanians were also subjected to the cultural influence of the French, economic domination by the Greeks and political intervention of the Russians.

The Treaty of Adrianople, signed in 1829, recognized Russian interest in the two principalities. In it the Turkish sultan agreed that rulers elected by the two states could not be removed without Rus-

sian consent. It further provided that Russia could briefly occupy the area. During this occupation, which lasted from 1829 to 1834, the principalities were governed by a Russian commander, Count Paul Kisselev, who helped prepare the "Organic Statutes," which became the basic law of Moldova and Wallachia.

According to the statutes, the two principalities would be separate, each with its own assembly of wealthy landowners who would in turn elect a prince. The forces of nationalism and revolution soon undermined this system of separation. As the revolutions of 1848 spread across Europe, some echoes were felt in Romania as well. In Wallachia, revolutionaries forced the ruler to abdicate and set up a provisional government, which proclaimed as its goal the unification of all Romanians into a single state. Russia then intervened to suppress the revolution, but the goal was finally accomplished 13 years later.

Russian occupation of Moldova and Wallachia in 1853 was one of the causes of the Crimean War, which followed in 1854–1856. Under the terms of the Treaty of Paris, which ended the conflict, Moldova and Wallachia were placed under the joint protection of France, Great Britain, and Austria. After the Paris Peace Conference, these powers decided that each Romanian principality was to have a separate assembly and prince. On matters of common concern, the parliaments could meet together.

This attempt to keep the two principalities separate was reversed in 1859 when both chose Alexandru Ioan Cuza to be their prince. Two years later, he proclaimed the unified Romanian state, with Bucharest as the capital. He made efforts

toward land reform, freeing the peasants from their feudal obligations. But the peasants were not given enough land to live on, and they remained indebted to the landlords. Cuza was ousted in a military coup staged in 1866 by both conservatives and liberals, who favored installation of a member of European royalty as ruler in Romania.

They selected Karl of Hohenzollern-Sigmaringen (a distant relative of the king of Prussia) as prince of Romania. Romania subsequently became an independent state as a result of the Russo-Turkish War of 1877–78, and was then declared to be a kingdom. He took the title of King Karol I (Carol I) of Romania in 1881, the title he used until the end of his reign in 1914. Shortly after Carol was installed as prince, a new, democratic constitution was adopted, which led to the creation of two political parties—the Liberal Party representing the middle class and the Conservative Party representing the landowners. These two political parties essentially alternated in power throughout Carol's reign. The large peasant class had no voice in government.

Under the terms of the Treaty of Berlin, signed after the Russian-Turkish War of 1877–78, the province of Bessarabia (returned to Romania by the Treaty of Paris in 1856 and called "Basarabia" in Romanian), reverted to Russia. Romania was compensated by receiving the region of Northern Dobruja from Turkey.

The Balkans were relatively quiet during the rest of the 19th century, but that changed soon after 1900. A revolution in Serbia in 1903 brought a new dynasty to the throne, while Bulgaria declared its independence from the Ottoman Empire in 1908. That was partly a reaction to the "Young Turk" revolution carried out in the

Carol I

Ottoman Empire in 1908. Although people in the Balkans feared that the "Young Turk" revolution would strengthen the Ottoman Empire in the long run, the short-term effect was to weaken the Ottoman Empire and make it vulnerable to attack from without.

This is essentially what happened in 1912, when the First Balkan War erupted. In that war, Serbia, Bulgaria and Greece attacked and defeated the Ottoman forces, then they seized almost all of the Ottoman Empire's remaining territories in the Balkans. Then the three victors fell to quarreling over the spoils, which led Bulgaria to go to war against Serbia in the Second Balkan War in 1913. Romania, which had avoided involvement in the First Balkan War, now allied itself with Serbia against Bulgaria. For its efforts it obtained the Southern Dobruja from Bulgaria.

Romania remained neutral during the first two years of the First World War, but British and French promises of Bukovina, Transylvania and other Hungarian lands lured it into the war on the allied side. The war did not go well for Romania. When its troops invaded Transylvania, German forces counterattacked and then pushed on to Bucharest, which they occupied on December 6, 1916. Romania sued for peace in early 1918, but as the tide turned against Germany it reentered the war. Romania was thus on the winning side at the peace conference. It was in a particularly good position to press territorial demands, since its troops had occupied Transylvania and Bessarabia near the end of the war.

Romania after World War I

At the conclusion of the war, Romania took Bessarabia back from Russia by the simple expedient of sending in troops af-

Ferdinand I

ter the Bessarabian parliament declared the Moldovan Democratic Republic and voted in 1918 to unite with Romania. This lasted until 1939 when Russia repossessed Bessarabia. The peace settlement then gave Romania Bukovina (formerly part of Austria), plus Transylvania and part of the Banat (both formerly Hungarian territory). It also kept Southern Dobruja, which it had taken from Bulgaria in the Second Balkan War.

Romania had thus doubled in size. Now its chief task was assimilating all of the people living in these new territories. The areas that created the most trouble were Transylvania and Bessarabia. Transylvania had a large Szekler population related to the Magyars of Hungary that rejected assimilation. In addition, the Hungarian government rejected Romania's claim to the area and encouraged the Szekelys to retain their Hungarian identity. In spite of vigorous opposition from Transylvania, Romania adopted a new constitution that gave the country a highly centralized government.

Bessarabia had been a subject of dispute with Russia since the beginning of the 19th century. In 1812, Russia acquired the territory from the Ottoman Empire. The Treaty of Paris transferred southern Bessarabia to Moldova in 1856. Russia took it back in 1878 at the conclusion of the Russo-Turkish War. After 1918 Romania had Bessarabia back, though it could hope to keep it only as long as the new revolutionary Soviet government in Russia remained weak. Moreover, although Bessarabians spoke Romanian, the province also included numerous other minority groups who had no reason to want to be part of Romania.

Romania had internal problems as well. Perhaps its greatest was the need for land reform. Eventually, the government broke up many of the larger estates in areas such as Transylvania and distributed smaller parcels of land to the peasants. This allowed more peasants to support themselves. But most peasants, then almost 80% of the population, continued to live in poverty. Romania embarked on a program of industrialization financed by taxes levied on the peasantry.

King Ferdinand, who had succeeded his uncle to the throne in 1914, reigned until 1927. His son, Carol II, did not take the throne immediately because he preferred to live in Paris with the attractive Madame Lupescu. As a result, Michael, Carol's young son, was nominal ruler from 1927 to 1930, with Nicholas, Carol's brother, as regent. Carol finally returned to Bucharest in 1930 and persuaded parliament to revoke the law excluding him from the throne. Well known for his many romantic escapades, he renounced his throne twice to pursue his amorous ad-

ventures. He earned his nickname, "the playboy king."

From 1930 to 1940, King Carol actively promoted the disintegration of the traditional political parties by playing off party leaders against each other and, in the process, strengthening his own power. By 1938 Romania was a royal dictatorship.

During the late 1920s, a group called The League of the Archangel Michael was organized. In accordance with its Biblical name, it was supposed to do battle with the devil. In Romania, the devil turned out to be anyone who opposed the League, which was fascist and anti-Jewish in outlook. Its name was later changed to the Iron Guard, by which it was better known outside Romania. After his return, King Carol subsidized the group, and it became the largest fascist party in the Balkans.

In the 1937 elections, the National Peasants Party received the largest vote, but the King refused to ask its leader, Maniu, to form a government. Instead, the leader of the fascist National Christian Party was named premier. His dismissal in 1938 marked the beginning of Carol's dictatorship. A new constitution was drafted, the Iron Guard was outlawed, and the Front of National Rebirth, Romania's fascist party, replaced political parties.

In the 1920s and early 1930s, succeeding governments had supported the League of Nations and "Little Entente" as ways to preserve the balance of power in the Balkans. From 1936 onward, however, Romania cultivated closer ties with Hitler's Germany. In spite of this, Romania lost in the first year of the Second World War the territories acquired after the First World War. Russia took Bessarabia back, as well as Northern Bukovina. Hungary got Northern Transylvania, while Bulgaria took back Southern Dobruja.

An Ally of Nazi Germany

Carol II abdicated in September 1940 and fled Romania. He ultimately settled in Portugal, died in 1953, and a half-century later in 2003 his remains were returned to Romania where they were interred in the town of Curtea de Arges with national honors. General Ion Antonescu formed a government backed by the Iron Guard. Two months later, on November 23, 1940, Romania joined the Axis powers. The cooperation between General Antonescu and the Iron Guard did not last long. With Hitler's blessing, he suppressed an attempted revolt by the Guard in January 1941. Hitler's concern for stability in Romania was greater than his support for "like-minded" parties whose activities disrupted the country of an ally.

From early 1941 until mid-1944, the country was governed by Antonescu's military dictatorship, with the backing of

Romania

Carol II with son Michael in 1936

German troops. Romania participated in military operations against the Soviet Union after Germany invaded that country, and it made heavy contributions to the Axis war effort, including liquidating Jews. There were several pogroms, including one in Iasi in 1941, where as many as 12,000 Jews were murdered. Before the war Romania (including Bessarabia) had one million Jews; only about 6,000 remain. In October 2009 a monument was unveiled in Bucharest honoring the 300,000 Jews and Roma who perished in the Holocaust. Nevertheless, some Romanians still admire Marshal Ion Anonescu because he had fought against the Soviet Union to recover Romanian territory.

Although there was only a very weak anti-Nazi movement in Romania, it was the first Axis satellite to defect at the close of the war. On August 23, 1944, King Michael (Carol's son), backed by the National Peasants Party, the Liberal Party, the Socialist Party, and the Communist Party, ousted the Antonescu government. Romania then declared war on Germany. Negotiations that had started in Cairo were ended in September in Moscow with the signing of an armistice.

The Romanian People's Republic is Born

Prior to World War II, the Romanian Communist Party had been weak and unpopular. Outlawed in 1924, its pro-Russian attitude and advocacy of self-determination for Bessarabia and Transylvania were contrary to prevailing opinion. The government quickly suppressed a communist-sponsored railroad strike in 1933 and arrested dozens of party members.

During the 1930s and 1940s, there were two groups of Romanian communists: the "home" communists who were behind bars in Romania and the "Muscovites" who had fled to the Soviet Union to avoid being jailed and persecuted. In the early postwar period, the power struggle between the two groups became the most significant feature in domestic politics. The "Muscovite" communists—Ana Pauker ("Red Ana"), Vasile Luca, Teohari Georgescu, and Emil Bodnaras—returned to Romania in 1944.

In October, the communists joined with the Social Democratic Party, the Union of Patriots, and the Ploughmen's Front to form the National Democratic Front. The first objective of this union of parties was to launch an attack on the National Peasants Party, headed by General Constantin Sanatescu, which controlled important posts in the government. Nicolae Radescu replaced Sanatescu.

Early in 1945, the communists started a campaign to publicize a program that they hoped would bring them to power: agrarian reform, a new government and the return to Romanian administration of that part of Transylvania transferred to Hungary during World War II. There was a communist-supported demonstration in early 1945 in which several people were killed. A few days later, Andrei Vyshinsky, one of Molotov's deputies in the Soviet Foreign Ministry, demanded the resignation of the Radescu government. He further specified that a National Democratic Front government, led by Petru Groza, should be put in power. Radescu could offer no resistance since Romanian troops had been ordered out of Bucharest.

The new government included noncommunists as well as communists, but the important Ministry of the Interior, which controlled the police, was given to Teohari Georgescu, one of the "Muscovite" communists. Northern Transylvania was returned, and a land reform program was started. General Ion Antonescu was executed in mid-1945.

The Soviet Union recognized the new government headed by Groza. The United States and Britain did not, however. In a compromise, a special commission was created to advise King Michael, titular head of state, which included representatives of the National Peasants' Party and the Liberal Party. This new, "broadened" government then set the time for new elections.

The enlarged government took office in early 1946 and was recognized by the Western powers the following month. Elections, in which women could vote for the first time, were held in November 1946. In the months before the elections, the communists pressured some of the other parties into running a common list of "government" candidates. The result was a victory at the polls for this bloc.

A peace treaty signed on February 10, 1947, formally returned Transylvania to Romania. It specified that other frontiers were to follow the line of January 1, 1941. This meant that Bessarabia and Northern Bukovina remained part of the Soviet Union, and Southern Dobruja stayed with Bulgaria.

The communists eliminated opposition from other political parties outside the Na-

516

tional Democratic Front in 1947. Ion Mihalache, Iuliu Maniu, and other leaders of the National Peasants Party were arrested and sentenced to life imprisonment on charges of conspiring with American intelligence officers. The National Peasants' Party was outlawed, and government officials from the Liberal Party who had agreed to a common list of candidates in the elections were dismissed in late 1947. The left-wing Social Democrats, who had also joined in the common list of candidates, were absorbed into the Communist Party, which now became the United Workers Party. It retained this name until 1965, when it again became the Communist Party of Romania. Having neutralized all opposition, the communists removed the last remnant of the old system by forcing King Michael to abdicate at the end of 1947.

A new constitution was adopted in 1948, and the Romanian People's Republic was officially born. The story of internal politics in the following years involved a struggle for power between the "home" and "Muscovite" communists. Initially the "Muscovite" group controlled the government; Ana Pauker was foreign minister, Vasile Luca was minister of finance, and General Emil Bodnaras was minister of war.

A "home" communist, Gheorghe Gheorghiu-Dej, had helped organize the railroad strike in 1933 and was arrested and sentenced to 12 years in prison. He escaped in August 1944 and in October 1945 became secretary general of the Communist Party. This meant that he was titular head of the party while Ana Pauker and her associates were in control of the government. During the postwar years, he consolidated his power and gained sufficient support from within party ranks to remove Pauker, Luca, and Georgescu from their party and government posts in 1952.

The subsequent official Romanian explanation of this purge is an example of rewritten history. The move was described as the beginning of Romania's independence from foreign domination. The fact is that there was no real change in Romanian foreign policy or in Romania's relations with Russia until the late 1950s and early 1960s. Also of significance was the execution in 1954 of Lucretiu Patrascanu, a moderate national communist who had been removed from office in 1948. This event took place two years after the supposed beginning of Romania's new national course.

A more probable explanation of the 1952 purge was that the victory of the "home" communists resulted from an internal power struggle in which Gheorghiu-Dej had the support of General Bodnaras and probably Moscow. The reason for dismissing Pauker and her followers was their supposed responsibility for economic failures.

Nicolae Ceausescu

In addition to his party post, Gheorghiu-Dej became chairman of the Council of Ministers in 1952. Holding the highest party and government offices, he had become the real ruler of Romania. The death of Stalin in 1953 brought upheavals in the communist world, and Gheorghiu-Dej adapted to these changes. He continued to exercise the primary power in Romania until his death in 1965.

Following Stalin's passing, the Soviet leadership adopted the principle of collective leadership. Gheorghiu-Dej obediently resigned his party post, retaining for himself the position of chairman of the Council of Ministers. Gheorghe Apostol, the trade union chief, became first secretary of the Communist Party. However, Gheorghiu-Dej soon realized that the party post was more important than the government position, so he took it back in 1955, giving up his government position instead. Chivu Stoica became the new chairman of the Council of Ministers. Two further changes occurred in 1961. Gheorghiu-Dej decided

that it would be convenient for him to have a government post, so he added the title of president of the Council of State (ceremonial head of state). He also concluded that Stoica was becoming too ambitious, so he replaced him with Ion Gheorghe Maurer.

The Ceausescu Era Begins

In 1965 Gheorghiu-Dej died unexpectedly at the age of 63. There was no designated successor, so his offices were divided among his subordinates. Nicolae Ceausescu (Cha-oo-SHES-koo) was Gheorghiu-Dej's deputy in the party secretariat, and he managed to obtain the top party post, that of Secretary General.

Ceausescu had joined the Romanian Communist Party in the 1930s through its youth organization. A protégé of Gheorghiu-Dej, he became a full member of the party Politburo in 1955 at the age of 37. Over the next 10 years, he occupied himself as a member of the Central Committee Secretariat. His special area of responsibility was party organization and cadres, a position that allowed him to exercise extensive control over party appointments. In 1965, however, he was only one of three individuals who wielded power in a collective leadership.

It was under these circumstances that the Ninth Congress of the Romanian Communist Party met in July 1965. The congress approved a new constitution—the one in force until the revolution of 1989—and a new set of party laws. Its adoption was largely symbolic. It did not change the system in any important respect, though it did announce that Romania was no longer a "People's Republic" and that it would be known as the "Socialist Republic of Romania." It made explicit that it was the Romanian Communist Party that exercised all leadership within the state. It placed a general emphasis on national independence. At the same time, it abolished the Szekler autonomous region, which had

TV picture shows the Ceausescus upon their capture

Romania

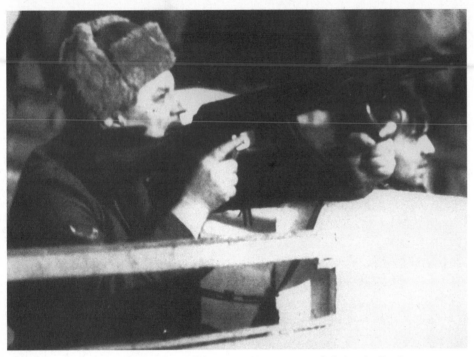

A soldier points his rifle at enemy positions during street fighting in Bucharest.

originally been set up in Transylvania to give the Hungarian-speaking minority a modicum of self-government.

The National Assembly elected Ceausescu to succeed Chivu Stoica as president of the Council of State. He was on his way toward establishing his preeminent authority within the country. Over the next several years, Ceausescu also became chairman of the National Defense Council, supreme commander of the armed forces, and chairman or honorary chairman of a number of party and state commissions and committees. The culmination of all this came in 1974 when the constitution was amended to create the position of president of the republic. Of course, it was filled by Ceausescu. This accumulation of offices was accompanied by the development of a full-blown "cult of personality" around Ceausescu. In speeches and in the press, he began to be referred to as the "hero of heroes" and the years of his rule as "the years of light." In later years, he was given credit for everything that happened in the country.

More ominously, he also placed his family in important positions of power in the government and party. Three of his brothers held senior posts in the government, one on the Council of Ministers, while his wife, Elena, was first deputy chairman of the Council of Ministers, member of the Permanent Bureau of the Political Executive Committee (Romania's equivalent of a Politburo), and chairman of the National Council for Science and Technology. She became the regime's chief censor. Finally, his son, Nicu, was First Secretary of the Union of Communist Youth and a candidate member of the Political Executive Committee. Nicu's wife was also a member of the Central Committee.

Ceausescu trained an oversized omnipresent secret police organization, called Securitate, composed of handpicked privileged agents who were fanatically loyal to him. They kept the general populace in a constant state of terror. He used public funds to finance such grandiose schemes as his creation of a grand avenue and presidential palace, which he had been building in the middle of Bucharest.

The construction of this extravagant structure nearly bankrupted the country, consuming an estimated third of GDP at one point. It employed 20,000 construction workers, and it required so many megawatts of power that Bucharest suffered electrical shortages for years. Today it houses both parliamentary chambers it is the second largest office building in the world, after the Pentagon. Ceausescu would turn over in his grave if he could see the country's flag flanked by those of NATO and the EU in front of his palace.

His many homes had golden bathroom fixtures and other objects of splendor. Ceausescu also continued the grand program, launched in 1988, of transforming the countryside by razing half of Romania's villages by the year 2000 and moving the inhabitants into new high-rise buildings in "agro-industrial" centers.

Ceausescu's Fall

All of this was swept away at the end of 1989 in a violent uprising that ended in Ceausescu's and his wife's deaths by firing squad on December 25. Proud of his independence from Moscow, Ceausescu had rejected Gorbachev's policy of reform and made every effort to isolate his countrymen from events going on elsewhere in Central and Eastern Europe. In November 1989, he had reaffirmed his policies at a party congress and had been reelected head of the party for a further five-year term. It was probably this act of reaffirmation that was responsible for his downfall. His policies had caused a significant decline in Romanians' standard of living over the previous decade.

The revolt actually began as an ethnic dispute in the city of Timisoara, in the western part of Romania when a Hungarian Reformist priest was arrested. Grossly exaggerated reports in the West spoke of up to 60,000 deaths. In the end it was only 100 deaths, but still a tragic massacre. It spread to Bucharest, the capital, when Ceausescu called a mass meeting for December 21 to denounce the events in Timisoara. Instead, the people began shouting "freedom" and "democracy," and Ceausescu stalked off. That afternoon, the streets were full of people demonstrating against him. In the evening, his wife ordered the secret police to begin firing on the people and had the Securitate burn the victims. General Milea, the defense minister, refused to obey a similar order to the army. He committed suicide the next morning after Ceausescu called him a traitor. But the army now joined the revolution. Ceausescu and his wife fled the capital, but they were captured, driven around the countryside in a tank for two days, taken to a remote military base, tried in a hastily prepared military court, and summarily executed.

The Securitate fought on for a few days more, often resorting to underground tunnels and weapons caches. But the army gradually managed to restore order. In the meantime, a group calling itself the National Salvation Front emerged as the new political leadership in the country. In March 2005 the Securitate files began to be opened in an effort to heal the wounds of communism. Historians estimate that there were a half-million Securitate officers and millions of informers who spied on their fellow countrymen. In 2006 the Institute for the Investigation of the Crimes of Communism was established to look into the activities of the secret services. No senior Communist or Securitate official had ever been put on trial. Securitate agents have proved to be pervasive and resilient, with extensive political and business connections.

In general, many of the "new democrats" who rushed forward to promote capitalism had actually been from the

Romania

Palace on Revolutionary Square, where Ceausescu gave his last speech. The monument reads: "The Glory of our Martyrs." In 2004 the Senate moved from this building to the Palace of the Parliament.

privileged Communist party elite (called *nomenclatura*) that had promoted communism before the revolution. Many of these former Communists control much of Romania's wealth today. The Romanian edition of *Forbes'* Rich List in December 2009, the 20th anniversary of Ceausescu's fall, provided details of how 85% of the richest 100 people in Romania are from the former *nomenclatura*.

The New Regime

The Front, at first made up almost exclusively of former establishment figures who had fallen out with Ceausescu, was enlarged within a few days to take in various noncommunist elements. It then began referring to itself as the Council of National Salvation. In the third week of January, it announced that multiparty elections would take place in May and that it intended to run its own candidates. This brought condemnation from the leaders of the three largest opposition parties. After a series of negotiations, the Council agreed to make room for representatives of other parties. On February 1, it brought the representatives of 29 other political parties into the government coalition. By this time, it had grown to approximately 180 members. It also underwent a name change and became the Provisional Council for National Unity. A new ten-member Executive Committee, headed by Acting President Ion Iliescu, came into existence at this time.

Meanwhile, having reorganized itself as a political party, the original National Sal-

vation Front announced that it, not the Council, would field candidates in the upcoming May 20 elections. As its candidate for president, it nominated Ion Iliescu. Most of the leadership of the Front had been members of the old Romanian Communist Party, and the local branches of the National Salvation Front set up at the time of the revolution were largely made up of ex-officials. Thus, while the old Communist Party structure had collapsed, a large percentage of its membership transferred their loyalties to the National Salvation Front.

Eventually, some 80 political parties came into existence, though only three of them had any significant political support in the country. Two of these, both parties that were outlawed when the communists took over, were the Liberals and the Peasant Party. The third, the Hungarian Democratic Union, represents the interests of ethnic Hungarians. Although the opposition attacked the National Salvation Front because of its high component of ex-communists, there was, in fact, little to differentiate between them as far as programs were concerned. All said that they were committed to the creation of a multiparty democracy and a market economy.

In the May 1990 elections, Ion Iliescu was elected president with approximately 83% of the vote while the National Salvation Front took 66% of the seats in the National Assembly. Election observers announced that there had been some irregularities in the voting, but overall the election had been free.

For approximately six months, the policies of the new government remained unclear as factions within the Front debated whether Romania would move toward a free market or attempt to develop some sort of mixed economy with the government continuing to play an important role. Petre Roman, the new chairman of the Council of Ministers (prime minister), called for a transformation to a market economy within two years. Others talked about a gradual transition that would safeguard jobs and wages. The Peasants Party and the National Liberal Party, the two main opposition parties, had argued for a rapid transition to a market economy and privatization of land and industry. Their showing in the May 1990 elections strengthened the hand of those who argued for a mixed economy.

Still some progress was made. Over the summer, legislation was passed encouraging the creation of small businesses and authorizing the government to turn state enterprises into privately owned companies. Other legislation authorized the government to sell apartment houses built after 1948. Longtime bureaucrats found it easy to frustrate the intent of these laws.

A larger issue was that the democratic credentials of the government came into question after it encouraged miners to attack a group of antigovernment demonstrators on University Square in Bucharest in June 1990. Six individuals were killed in the resulting violence, and the headquarters of some of the opposition political parties were ransacked. Antigovernment rallies continued over the summer. As a result, the Romanian government found itself boycotted by potential donor countries, in spite of its desperate need for economic assistance.

In October, Petre Roman submitted to parliament another package of land, banking and tax proposals, which he said were intended to speed Romania's transition to a market economy. Among the proposals was that prices of nonessential goods and services would be freed, though the government would continue to subsidize the price of energy, fuel and rent for another year and control the price of basic foods and services. Although Romanians were talking about these proposals as radical and likely to contribute further to the spiral of inflation that had hit the country, they were actually yet another example of gradualism that would leave the underlying problems unsolved.

The government did take one set of actions of a positive nature. It redistributed almost a third of the country's arable land to private farmers. The result was an unusually good grain harvest and an increase in meat and fresh products in the unregulated farmers' areas.

Romania

It began converting the National Bank into a Western-style central bank in December 1990. The bank was to give up all of its retail operations and confine itself to issuing currency and controlling monetary policy. The Foreign Trade Bank, which formerly performed certain central bank functions, gave up its monopoly over foreign exchange. Private banks were also authorized at this same time. Eight private banks came into existence within the next six months, the first being the Banca Comerciala Ion Tiriac SA (renamed Tiriac Bank), founded by a Romanian expatriate, the ex-tennis player Ion Tiriac.

Although Roman's economic reforms had the support of international economists, their implementation led to a drop in the standard of living of most Romanians as inflation outpaced wage increases. The matter became serious in September 1991 when 52,000 coal miners in western Romania went on strike over pay and prices. Several thousand made their way to Bucharest, where they demanded the resignation of Petre Roman. The demonstrations soon turned violent. Before they were over three persons had been killed, and hundreds had been wounded. President Iliescu, whose relations with his prime minister had been bad for some time, fired Roman and promised the miners that he would form a new "government of national openness." With so much violence and disappointment, many Romanians now refer to this time as the "stolen revolution."

Roman afterwards charged that Iliescu and his allies had called on the miners to demonstrate and that it was all a communist plot to remove him and reverse his economic reform. There is no evidence of that. It appears, rather, that he took advantage of the miners' protest to get rid of Roman. It does not seem to have been a policy matter either, for the man Iliescu named as Roman's replacement, Theodor Stolojan, had at one point been minister of finance in Roman's government and later was his minister for privatization. A strong believer in reform, he pledged his new government to a continuation of Roman's economic policies. His was a government of national unity.

In the lead up to the September 1992 elections, the National Salvation Front split over whether to support Iliescu. The pro-Iliescu faction became the Democratic National Salvation Front, while Roman's wing organized itself as the Front for National Salvation. Iliescu won in the second round, taking 61.4% of the votes.

POLITICAL SYSTEM

The Revolution of 1989 overthrew the old Communist regime and installed a revolutionary regime whose stated goals were the creation of a multiparty democracy and a market economy. Free elections occurred in May 1990. The new government gave itself 18 months to draw up a constitution, and it accomplished that when the new constitution was approved in a popular referendum on December 8, 1991. It lacked specific guarantees of rights for minorities that ethnic Hungarians had demanded. This was rectified in September 1996 when Romania signed a new treaty with Hungary that included a section wherein each side promised to treat its minorities according to high "European standards." Minorities are guaranteed seats in parliament.

In 2003 ninety percent of Romanian voters supported amending the constitution to promote market and democratic reforms necessary for entry into the European Union (EU). The government was so afraid that the required minimum of 50% of eligible voters would not turn out to vote, thereby invalidating the referendum, that government officials, doctors, party members and even priests were enlisted to go door to door in some regions to encourage people to vote. In areas with snow, voting officials carried ballot boxes directly to people's houses and asked them to vote on the spot. They set up special voting booths at railway stations and made loud-speaker announcements that travelers could vote there, even if their identity cards had expired. The final participation was 55%.

Romania has a bicameral parliament. Since both chambers are elected in the same way by the people, both have the same legitimacy. The method was changed for the November 30, 2008, elections and is now a "mixed member proportional representation system." Some members are elected through party lists and others are elected individually. New multimember constituencies called "electoral colleges" (*colegii electorale*) were drawn up. If a candidate wins more than 50% of the votes in the constituency on the first round, he/she gets a seat. In those constituencies left over in which no candidate wins 50% the first round, the seats are distributed according to proportional representation. This means that a party wins a percentage of seats based on the percentage of votes it wins. A party must win at least 5% of the votes nationwide to win any seats although special rules apply to parties representing national minorities.

The Senate has 137 members. The Chamber of Deputies, or lower house, has a differing number of seats from election to election. From 2000 to 2004, it had 344 seats, thereafter 332. In the Chamber of Deputies there is one representative for every 70,000 inhabitants; in the Senate one

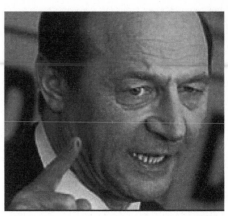

President Traian Basescu

for every 160,000. In a November 2009 nonbinding referendum, an overwhelming majority of voters favored abolishing one of the two parliamentary chambers and reducing the number of members.

Many sets of presidential and parliamentary elections have taken place in an orderly fashion. Most observers now concede that Romania has completed the transition to a multiparty democracy. No single party or coalition commands a majority.

The Presidency

The president, who is popularly elected, exercises overall executive power. He is expected to set general policy and act as spokesman for the nation. In addition, he has specific responsibilities in the areas of foreign affairs and defense. He nominates the prime minister, who must be confirmed by the Grand National Assembly. He has some supervision over the judicial system and controls the security services. Laura Stefan of the Romanian Academic Society think-tank described his powers in this way: "The president deals with big issues, deciding how things should move forward, but he doesn't actually do anything directly." Presidential and parliamentary elections are normally held at the same time although that was not the case in November-December 2009. Among the democratic-era presidents were Emil Constantinescu of the Democratic Convention Alliance (1996 to 2000) and Ion Iliescu of the Party of Social Democracy (1990–1996 and 2000–2004).

In December 2004 Traian Basescu, a former oil tanker captain, transport minister and mayor of Bucharest, unexpectedly and narrowly defeated the sitting prime minister, Adrian Nastase, in the second round to win the presidency. A no-nonsense politician with an unpolished brand of charisma, Basescu benefited from a strong showing in a TV debate, public anger at the alleged rigging of ballots by

Palace of the Parliament, housing both the Chamber of Deputies and Senate

the Social Democrats, and perhaps the simultaneous "orange revolution" in neighboring Ukraine, which brought reformers into office. He championed a government anticorruption drive, a successful Romanian entry into the EU in 2007, and, in his words, "making Romania a democratic country in real terms." His two-party Justice and Truth Alliance (which split in 2007) experienced soaring popularity after his election.

Nevertheless, most politicians came to loath him as confrontational, devious and threatening. He bullies and manipulates opponents and allies alike. Due to his rough governing style, he has made very few friends in the political establishment. After the government fell and was reconstituted as a minority coalition in March 2007, the first thing the new parliament did was to vote 322 to 108 to impeach Basescu. He was accused of using the secret services, which he controls, to discredit his many political enemies (for which no proof was found) and of creating political deadlock. This was the culmination of months of recriminations, mudslinging and feuding that included a live call-in TV show on which the president and prime minister called each other a liar.

In the May 19, 2007, referendum, 74% of voters voted for the president to remain in office; turnout was only 44%. This result did not end the bickering that has been an obstacle to reforms. His triumph was marred by a scandal that continues to tarnish his image. On the day of the voting, he was accosted by a female journalist who tried to film an impromptu interview with him on her cell phone. He lost his temper, insulted her and grabbed her phone, telling her she could have it back later. Unaware that it was still recording, he complained to his wife about the "aggressive, stinking gypsy." He later apologized for that indiscretion.

Nevertheless, he won reelection in December 2009 against ex-Foreign Minister Mircea Geoana of the leftist Social Democratic Party by the thinnest of margins: 50.33% to 49.66%. Geoana's greatest drawback was his cozy ties with the tycoons who dominate big business and media. Although international concluded that the vote largely met their standards, Ceoana alleged fraud and filed a complaint with the Constitutional Court, which can invalidate election results. The court unanimously rejected the complaint. However, such a small margin of victory will plague Basescu's presidency.

Parliament and Prime Minister

The prime minister chooses his cabinet, which must also be confirmed by the Grand National Assembly. The prime minister articulates specific policies, maintains liaison with the legislature, and oversees the day-to-day operations of government. Many parties compete for seats, and they change their names frequently.

The corruption watchdog Transparency International ranks Romania as the most corrupt EU country after Bulgaria (and 70th in the world). Bribery is endemic, including for securing medical treatment or favors from teachers or professors. The government appointed a respected nonparty justice minister, Monica Macovei, to take corruption by the horns. Bribery and kickbacks have long greased Romanian hands, but the EU made it clear that its timely entry into the club would depend on how well it dealt with this endemic problem. Legitimately worried about backsliding, it also implemented a post-accession monitoring program.

Macovei introduced the biggest judicial shake-up in the country's history. New law requires that officials and their families must publish their assets and incomes on the Internet. This includes villas, cars, gifts and other perks. Not desiring to do this, a third of all judges and prosecutors quit in the first year. Forty border police, nine members of parliament, four members of the Tariceanu government and the deputy prime minister were charged.

As a result of making such a disclosure on a form required by the EU, former Prime Minister Adrian Nastase was charged with graft in a landmark case. He tried to explain his acquisition of three apartments, jewelry and cash worth more than $1 million as gifts from his wife's dead aunt. His nickname, "Four House Nastase," and his well-heeled lifestyle visibly above his official salary had long raised questions about his commitment to bring corruption under control. His Social Democratic Party (PSD) is both a party and an economic elite. Its leading supporters sold the best state assets, mostly to themselves at discounted prices, and then proclaimed a free-market revolution. Although the PSD is back in power, Nastase was again indicted on corruption charges along with four accomplices in January 2009. A Romanian anti-corruption specialist noted: Romania "is becoming a country where the powerful have to account for what they've done."

Trials are now to be randomly assigned to judges by a computer so that those charged cannot steer their case into the court of a friendly judge. Millions of dollars have been invested in computerized databases for police and courts, and the hiring of prosecutors and judges is done on the basis of open competition rather than cronyism. A secret police unit, which was suspected of blackmailing prosecutors and judges, has been closed down. These new laws enabled the soft-spoken female judicial chief to face down tycoons and politicians accustomed to justice ministers who take orders rather than give them. Unhappy with the effect a public sector pay cut could have on their 600-euro salaries (equivalent to an emergency doctor and university professor), the judges went on strike in September 2009, saying that the conditions under which they have to work are a "humiliation" that

Romania

would be made worse by the cuts. They vowed only to hear "urgent cases." Given the independence they have been granted from politicians, there was little the government could do about this. The EU, which has pressured Romania to improve its judicial system to fight corruption, had watched with concern this rare strike.

As expected, the fragile government fell in March 2007, and a minority government, composed of Calin Tariceanu's Liberals and the Hungarian ethnic party, was formed. In April Monica Macovei was dropped from the new cabinet for not being "a team player." Her activities had come too close to too many politicians. She had suffered a vote of no-confidence in the Senate, and her reforms were incomplete. Romania was already under fire from the EU for not fighting corruption sufficiently. But in May 2007 the government finally created the Agency for Integrity, which the EU required of it. Its head until August 2008, Daniel Morar, quickly became intensely disliked by most politicians and the media.

Nevertheless, now that Romania is a full member, the EU has lost its most powerful leverage against it, and the elites feel like they are off the hook. In its July 2008 report on corruption, the EU wrote of regression on all fronts, of all high-level corruption trials having been rebuffed by courts, and of the absence of a single verdict on a prominent corruption case. An advisor to President Basescu concluded that "the fight against corruption is the key to everything that is going on now in Romania," and it is a cause of the political paralysis that prevails. However, he has been selective in his anti-corruption efforts.

The next parliamentary elections in November 2008 came none too soon. The successful parties' percentages were almost identical in the Grand National Assembly and Senate elections. The prior governing center-left alliance around the Social Democratic Party (PSD) captured the most votes in the lower house (33.1%) but fewer seats than the Democratic Liberal Party (PD-L), led by now Prime Minister Emil Boc, which won 32.4% of the votes and 115 seats. The PD-L is President Basescu's party after his former Justice and Truth Alliance split in 2007 into the two Liberal parties. The National Liberal Party (PNL) got 18.6% of the votes. The Democratic Union of Hungarians from Romania (UDMR), which advocates Magyar interests, received 6.4% of the votes.

Corneliu Vadim Tudor's rowdy nationalist Greater Romania Party, which does especially well in rural areas, failed to win the required 5% of votes nationwide, so it got no seats. Tudor is a vituperative nationalist who was once Nicolae Ceausescu's court poet. He denies that the Holocaust ever happened, but he does not deny his earlier ties to the Securitate secret police. In subsequent elections for the European Parliament in June 2009, Tudor led his party to win 8.7% of the votes and two seats. Such elections tend to be protest elections against national governments, and his party's relative good showing was a response to the painful global economic recession with which Romania was having to cope. His party comrade, George "Gigi" Becali, was banned from leaving the country pending a criminal trial for kidnapping.

Boc, a young (born 1966) former mayor of Transylvania's largest city, Cluj-Napoca,

Prime Minister Emil Boc

did not enter politics until 2003. His PD-L formed a grand coalition government with the PSD. However, in October 2009, after only ten months in office, that coalition split in the run-up to the presidential elections. Boc lost the first successful no-confidence vote since the end of communism. He led a caretaker government until December 23, 2009, when parliament approved a new centrist government under his leadership composed of his PD-L, the Hungarian UDMR, and a few independents. The formation of this majority government and the passage of the 2010 budget persuaded the IMF and EU to resume their agreed payments to Romania.

Foreign Policy in the Communist Era

Romania first obtained the freedom to develop its own independent foreign policy in 1958, when Soviet troops were withdrawn from the country. From then on Romania prohibited the permanent stationing of foreign troops on its soil. But the issue over which it split with the Soviet Union, its desire to industrialize, first became an issue in 1961–62. It was at this time that the Soviet Union proposed the creation of a supranational planning group within the Moscow-dominated Council for Mutual Economic Assistance (CMEA, also known as COMECON) to decide which country should produce how much of what. The Soviets wanted an international division of labor that would allow some countries to emphasize industrial production while others (notably Romania and Bulgaria) were intended to be a source of raw materials and agricultural products. The Soviet-Chinese dispute gave Romania the chance to defy Moscow. The first sign of opposition came in 1963 when Romania refused to support the creation of the CMEA group.

Building opposite Bucharest University with banner for Social Democrat party

Author with young Romanian diplomats in Bucharest

In 1964, the Romanian Central Committee issued a statement that has been described as a "Declaration of Independence" in economic as well as in political matters. In the economic area, it asserted the right to develop its own natural resources. In political affairs, it rejected the idea that any communist party was superior to another, claiming the right of each party to develop its own policies. Its attitude toward the Warsaw Pact military alliance was similar to its view of CMEA.

Romanian leaders successfully resisted Soviet attempts in 1966 to strengthen the Warsaw Pact by creating a permanent Eastern European political authority and by increasing the integration of the various military units from each country. When the Soviet Union and other Warsaw Pact allies intervened in Czechoslovakia in 1968, Ceausescu criticized the invasion and pledged to resist any Soviet incursion into Romanian territory. Romania maintained this critical attitude toward the Soviet Union from that time onward. It always rejected Warsaw Pact maneuvers on Romanian soil and refused even to attend the annual meeting of Warsaw Pact nations in 1971.

Relations improved somewhat in the middle of the 1970s. But in 1979 Ceausescu publicly aired his differences with the Soviet Union over Soviet Middle Eastern policy (especially the diplomatic isolation of Israel) and Soviet demands that Warsaw Pact allies increase their military expenditures.

In 1980, Romania openly, if indirectly, criticized the Soviet invasion of Afghanistan. Ceausescu attacked countries that "gravely threaten the cause of people's independence." The Romanian position became even clearer in 1981 when it abstained on a United Nations vote demanding the withdrawal of foreign troops from Afghanistan. All of the Soviet Union's Eastern European client states voted against the resolution.

He also took an independent position with regard to Soviet SS-20 missiles and Theater Nuclear Force (TNF) negotiations. In 1983, after the Soviets withdrew from the TNF talks in Geneva, Ceausescu issued a public call for both the Soviet Union and the United States to stop deploying nuclear missiles and to resume arms control negotiations. Another example of Romania's independence was the Soviet decision to boycott the 1984 Summer Olympics. Every other Soviet "ally" joined in the move, but Romania sent its athletes to Los Angeles and brought back 32 medals, including 20 golds, to place third in the total number of medals won.

Romania's relations with the Soviet Union became more complex after the Soviet Communist Party's 27th Congress in 1986. Ceausescu forthrightly condemned Gorbachev's programs for economic reform, but at the same time Romania's economic ties to the Soviet Union actually increased. Gorbachev finally paid a visit to Romania in 1987. The Soviet press gave the visit low-key treatment, but the Romanian press was far more enthusiastic. Several economic agreements were signed, but it was clear that political differences remained.

Under Ceausescu, relations with other countries were basically determined by those countries' ties with the Soviet Union. Thus the primary thrust of Romanian foreign policy in those years was to establish close links with those countries opposed to an expansion of Soviet power. A second, related interest was Romania's desire to expand its trade with the West. Neither of these principles involved a turning away from communism. Domestically, Romania remained among the most orthodox of communist nations.

During those years, it maintained its closest relations with the People's Republic of China. The reasons for this are clear. In addition to a common ideology, the two nations strongly opposed Soviet domination of the communist world. Romania consistently supported the Chinese arguments in the Sino-Soviet quarrels. In addition, there was a regular exchange of high-level diplomatic missions between the two countries and an extensive promotion of cultural contacts and trade.

Relations with Western Europe and the United States developed on another basis during those years, with trade perhaps being the most important factor. Romania never made the mistake of thinking it could ignore its geopolitical position entirely, or that it could depend on any country other than itself in case of extreme Soviet displeasure. It was nevertheless the first Central or Eastern European nation to establish diplomatic relations with the Federal Republic of Germany.

Ceausescu and Relations with the United States

Until about 1985 it went out of its way to encourage better relations with the United States. The breakthrough dated from 1967 when Richard Nixon, visiting various European capitals, stopped in Bucharest and was personally received by Ceausescu. Two years later, then President Nixon decided to pay a state visit to Romania as part of a round-the-world trip. He thus became the first American president to make a state visit to a communist country. Nixon suggested the visit to "needle our Moscow friends," but he wanted to show his appreciation for the way he had been treated in 1967. The visit took on a symbolic importance beyond that, however.

First of all, a Romanian Communist Party conference, to which the Soviet leadership had been invited, had to be rescheduled in order to make the visit possible. Originally scheduled to attend the conference, Brezhnev and Kosygin canceled out of the rescheduled conference. Secondly, as reported by a New York newspaper, Nixon received "a warm reception from hundreds of thousands of flag-waving Romanians in the largest and most genuinely friendly welcome of his global tour." President Nixon asked Ceausescu to act as a channel of communication to the Chinese. The subsequent breakthrough in American-Chinese rela-

Romania

tions therefore owed something to the Ceausescu connection.

The Nixon trip to Romania was followed by a Ceausescu visit to the United States the following year. Lasting two weeks, it had an obvious political component, but its major emphasis was economic. He met with a number of American businessmen, signed a contract for a $10 million aluminum sheet-rolling mill and an agreement for an exchange of researchers and university teachers. Ceausescu visited the United States twice after that time, in 1973 and again in 1978.

On the American side, President Gerald Ford stopped in Bucharest in 1975. The U.S. accorded Romania "most favored nation" trade status, meaning that the U.S. conducted normal trading relations with it. The United States also sponsored Romanian applications for membership in international organizations such as the International Bank for Reconstruction and Development (World Bank) and the International Monetary Fund (IMF).

Beginning in the 1980s, the United States became increasingly critical of Romanian internal developments. This was accompanied by occasional threats to withdraw "most favored nation" status unless the Romanian government made certain internal changes. One instance was a tax on Jewish emigration that Romania had instituted. Under the Reagan administration, the American government focused increasingly on Romanian treatment of Christian evangelicals.

The matter came to a head in 1987 when the U.S. Senate voted to suspend Romania's "most favored nation" status for six months to signal that it disapproved of Romania's human rights record. To put an end to such recriminations, Ceausescu responded by voluntarily renouncing all such trade concessions.

Romania's actions did not put an end to American criticism of Romania's human rights record, however. Several times in the last two years of Ceausescu's rule, Washington criticized his program to transform the countryside by razing villages and replacing them with high-rise "agro industrial" complexes. The basis for the criticism was that the program, although billed as an economic measure, was being implemented almost exclusively in areas where there were Hungarian and German ethnic minorities. A major goal of the program appeared to be the destruction of those centers of non-Romanian culture so that their inhabitants could be assimilated into the majority Romanian culture.

Post-Cold War

Romania's foreign policy changed after the overthrow of Ceausescu in December 1989 and the creation of a new government committed to democracy and a market economy. But it shifted less than one might have thought. The new leadership attempted to establish a friendly relationship with all nations, and in general it succeeded. Even the Soviet Union welcomed the overthrow of Ceausescu and followed this up with friendly gestures, such as opening the border between Moldova and Romania for a day so that relatives could visit back and forth.

The repudiation of communism after the failure of the August 1991 *coup* against Gorbachev, followed by the subsequent collapse of the Soviet Union, obviously changed that relationship with Moscow. Romania quickly moved to establish diplomatic relations with the successor republics, but the changes were more in form than in substance. With the notable exception of the newly independent Republic of Moldova, Romania's main interest in the successor republics was economic as it struggled to hold on to export markets.

Romania's relations with Moldova are complicated. Except for that part east of the Dniester (Nistru) River (always inhabited largely by Russians and Ukrainians and still hosting Russian troops), Moldova had been part of Romania prior to 1940. A majority of the people living there speak Romanian although the Cyrillic alphabet was used until 1989. In the wake of the Soviet Union's collapse, the clocks were changed from Moscow to Bucharest time, and a new flag identical to Romania's was introduced. In Transdniester today the population mix is approximately 60% Russian and Ukrainian and 30% Moldovan. In general they get along well. Most Russians and Ukrainians speak only Russian, but unlike in Estonia and Latvia, that does not cause major problems.

In August 2004 Romania promised to supply Moldova with electricity in the event that Transdniester cut its power supplies. To show his support for the Romanian-speaking neighbor, newly elected President Basescu chose Moldova for his first foreign trip. In theory, Bucharest supports the reincorporation of Moldova, though on a purely voluntary basis. Reunification is no longer a central political issue, and a 2009 poll revealed that only 15% of Moldovans would support it if a referendum were now held. It is mainly intellectuals and the young who feel the most Romanian and would accept a union with Romania. Many see Romania as a promising symbol of European integration. This is an emotional issue in Moldova.

Moldovans who can prove that their forebears were Romanian before 1940 can acquire Romanian citizenship and passports, and thousands do so. Out of a population of four million, about a million have applied for Romanian citizenship, but Romanian officials can process only about 20,000 applications each year. One of the main complaints among discontented Moldovan youth in the tumultuous month of April 2009 was their government's restrictions on citizenship and travel to Romania. In response, the Romanian government offered fast-track citizenship for up to one million Moldovans who have at least one grandparent who was once a Romanian citizen. Because Romania offers so many passports to Moldovans, it could not complain in 2010 when the Hungarian government passed a law permitting the many Hungarians in Romania to have dual citizenship. EU membership complicates the relationship

Central Square, Brasov, one of seven former Austrian cities

He was particularly irked by the French foreign minister's insult that he lacked "a European reflex." This crack was made only a month before French voters rejected Europe's new constitution.

The European Union and NATO

All Romanian governments supported the country's efforts to join the European Union. In 2003 Minister of European Integration Hildegard Puwak stated unmistakably: "We have always shared the same values as the European people. We feel as part of the European family. Acting on this European dream, we have focused all our national resources toward preparing for EU accession." That dream came true on January 1, 2007.

The EU and the U.S. government warned it frequently about its widespread corruption, which endangers development. The newspapers are full of stories about scandals of all kinds. Ordinary Romanians, whose per capita income in purchasing power terms is only 28% of the EU15 average (compared with a 45% average in Central Europe), complain about having to pay off bureaucrats and about large companies that pay few taxes. Transparency International's corruption perception index in 2009 ranked Romania among the bottom three among EU members. Both Romania and Bulgaria must still account to the EU on how they are fighting corruption, but the Union has lost its most powerful leverage: membership.

Nobody denies the country's problems. It has the lowest per capita income and highest infant mortality rate in Central Europe and is the poorest country ever to enter the EU, except Bulgaria. Its environmental standards are low, its education spending too low, and corruption is pervasive. It must reform its antiquated agriculture (which employs a third of the workforce and produces a tenth of GDP), continue to tackle corruption, and raise the living standards for the 20% of their population under the minimum existence level in 2005.

Romania recognizes that its enthusiastic support for U.S. policy can cause tension with the EU. It was outraged when Romania defied the EU by being the first country to sign an agreement promising not to surrender American citizens to the newly created International Criminal Court (ICC). That accord was never ratified. In 2003 it raised eyebrows in Brussels when it gave a $2.5 billion contract without a tender to the American company, Bechtel, to build an interstate highway across Transylvania.

Romania obviously enjoys the EU's largess; among Central European countries, Romania is the largest recipient of EU funds after Poland. There are signs

Timisoara Opera Square

with Moldovans. The Romanian government promised a special regime for Moldovans living within 30 kilometers (19 miles) of the border. However, Romania's entry into the Schengen agreement in 2011 creates even further hassle and expense for Moldovans.

It was predominantly young Moldovans who rioted in April 2009 when the Communist Party claimed victory in the first round of parliamentary elections, allegedly through fraud. Several government buildings, including the parliament, were burned, and three persons died. The Communist government accused "certain forces" from Romania of having masterminded the outburst, expelled the Romanian ambassador, and imposed a visa requirement on Romanian visitors. Bucharest made a rare public rebuke of the EU by demanding a tougher line toward Moldova. The tension seemed to have quieted down by the time the Communists lost power in July 2009. That could signal a Moldovan shift away from Moscow and toward the EU.

The United States welcomed the overthrow of the Ceausescu regime, and its early attitude toward the new government was extremely favorable. Among other things, Secretary of State James Baker arranged a short visit to Bucharest in the spring of 1990. But the United States was also critical of some of the actions of the new government. It decided after the death of six demonstrators in June 1990 that all assistance to Romania would be put on hold.

Washington went along with inclusion of Romania in the aid consortium for Eastern Europe. But it was not until Petre Ro-

man visited Washington in 1991 that one could speak of a noticeable thawing of relations. Relations warmed further in 1992 as the administration began to give the Romanian government good marks for such things as allowing greater press freedom, holding democratic elections, and bringing the intelligence services under legislative control. This trend culminated in the granting of "most favored nation" trading status to Romania in 1993. On the occasion of his October 2003 visit to the U.S. and meeting with the American president, ex-President Iliescu stated that "the United States today is an exceptional partner and a friend of Romania."

President Basescu agrees. He aspires that Romania become a regional power, like Poland, which requires close ties with the United States and Britain. He has even spoken of a "Bucharest-London-Washington axis." This is especially important given the Black Sea's geostrategic significance. Half of the oil that flows into Western European markets comes via that waterway, as does much of the illegal traffic in drugs, people and arms. His slogan is: securitize the Black Sea basin and democratize the states around its shores, three of which—Ukraine, Moldova and Georgia—are trying to wriggle free of Russian tutelage.

He is aware that France is Romania's second-largest investor (after the Netherlands) and third-largest customer and that France has been an important supporter of Romania's entry into the EU. However, he became irritated by France's criticism of such close Anglo-Saxon ties and warned Paris to stop lecturing his country about what foreign policy it should pursue. "We have no lessons to receive."

Romania

everywhere that the road on which one is driving was financed by the EU. An EU project lasting until 2007 involved the construction of a major highway linking Nadlac and Sibiu, which will ultimately be incorporated into the Budapest-Sofia-Athens highway. The unfinished Transylvania Highway would require only an 8-hour drive from Bucharest to Vienna. Romania still has only two interstate highways. The European Investment Bank lent Romania 131 million euros to rehabilitate and furnish about 1,400 pre-university schools all over the country.

Romanian leaders regard NATO membership as the key to solving many of the country's economic and diplomatic problems. Ex-President Iliescu viewed it as allowing his country "to be integrated into the civilized world." Romania enjoyed strong French support when it first applied for membership in NATO, but it was turned down in 1999 chiefly because of American refusal. The alliance had long-standing worries about democratic reform, corruption, and military readiness. It also singled out Romania's treatment of minorities, particularly of the Roma. Romania was the first country to join NATO's Partnership for Peace in the hope of enhancing its prospects for full membership later. It supported NATO actions over Kosovo and agreed to allow NATO planes limited access to the country's air space. It also accepted 6,000 refugees from Kosovo. However, fearing destabilization of Serbia and the wider Balkans, it did not recognize Kosovo's independence after its February 2008 declaration.

Romania's and neighboring Bulgaria's value in NATO eyes skyrocketed in the wake of the September 11 terrorist attacks in the U.S. Indeed the strategic significance of the entire Black Sea region grew because it became a staging area for the war effort in Afghanistan. In the words of ex-Foreign Minister Mircea Geoana, "September 11 transformed the Black Sea into a natural springboard." His country regarded itself as a "de facto NATO Ally" in the struggle against terrorism. For this reason both Turkey and Greece supported the candidacies of Romania and Bulgaria on the grounds that NATO's southern flank has become strategically crucial for combating traditional threats, as well as "new threats," such as terrorism, transborder crime and trafficking in weapons, drugs, and human beings, including illegal immigrants and women often destined to involuntary prostitution. The government denies any knowledge of rumors that the U.S. maintained a secret CIA prison on its territory.

Romania and Bulgaria joined NATO in April 2004. Romania already hosts such NATO maneuvers as the information and communications "Combined Endeavor 05" in May 2005 with 1,200 soldiers and 43 partner nations involved. Their admittance provides a geographic bridge between northern and central Europe and Greece and Turkey. It provides the U.S. and its NATO partners a foothold much closer to the current areas of danger to Europe and North America: the unstable Caucasus and the troubled Transcaucasian region of the former Soviet Union, including Chechnya, the Middle East and Central Asia, all located across the Black Sea. In April 2008 it hosted the largest ever NATO summit, which extended membership to Croatia and Albania. Of the 5,000 officials who attended, 1,500 were from the U.S.

Romania cooperated closely with the U.S. to demonstrate what it can contribute as military partners. It unconditionally offered its air space and use of all port and land facilities, and it refurbished airstrips for allied use. It sent its "Carpathian Hawks" battalion to perform peacekeeping duties in Kabul and guard duty at the U.S. base at Kandahar. Its specialized mountain unit serves in the mountainous area helping the U.S.-led force hunt down the remnants of the Taliban and al Qaeda. In 2003 it used its own C-130 transport aircraft to carry its troops to Afghanistan; in 2010 it had 990 soldiers in the ISAF command in that country. It also has tripled its soldiers assigned to peacekeeping missions. It has made available to American troops a military base in Constanta that serves as staging ground for troop rotation in the Balkans. It sent 57 peacekeepers to Bosnia and 151 to Kosovo.

It joined the ten new democracies in Eastern and Central Europe in signing the Vilnius letter supporting the U.S.-British war effort in Iraq in 2003. It rejected an intemperate outburst from French President Jacques Chirac criticizing all ten for missing a good opportunity to remain silent and warning of consequences for joining the EU. Romanians were very disappointed since they had long regarded France as its closest European friend. But they were reassured by Defense Secretary Donald Rumsfeld: "Let me be clear: those countries have not been invited as junior partners, allowed to join the grownups' table so long as they sit quietly. No, they have been invited to lead."

Romania opened its airspace to allied aircraft heading to the war in Iraq and permitted 1,000 American soldiers to use the Mihael Kogalniceaunu (widely known as MK) airbase and the nearby Black Sea port of Constanta as a bridge for troops and equipment from the U.S. and Germany to the Middle East. Negotiations were completed in 2006 to make these bases permanent, and the first American troops came in 2007; there is a permanent party of ca. 100 at MK, with 2,000 soldiers rotating through at any given time. It sent a chemical and biological warfare unit to Kuwait. Its intelligence service also foiled Iraqi attempts to use Romania as a staging ground to organize terrorist attacks on Israel and Western Europe. It declared 10 Iraqi diplomats and 31 others as *persona non grata* and expelled them. It deployed a mechanized infantry battalion with 800 soldiers to Iraq. Fearing for its credibility as a NATO and EU member, it refused to withdraw them in 2005 when several U.S. allies did so. This is despite polls in 2005 showing that 55% of Romanians want their troops to come home. It was among the last three of 38 allies to withdraw its remaining troops from Iraq in July 2009. However, it left 13 trainers in the country.

As the U.S. contemplates moving its European bases farther east, it views both Romania and Bulgaria as its anchors in the southeast, much as Poland is in the north. Romania also has the advantage of being one of the few countries in the region that has no outstanding disputes with any of its Black Sea neighbors and partners. It is in the process of improving its relations with Russia after an icy decade following the collapse of communism. But for the first time since its birth in 1859, Romania has no great regional or global power as its immediate neighbor. But Romanians view the Black Sea as the frontier between an ordered West and a chaotic and potentially dangerous East. Close ties with Washington make good sense, and there is little domestic resistance to this.

It boosted its military budget to 2.4% of GDP, a higher percentage than most western European countries, to speed up the restructuring process. In 2010 the country had 73,350 active-duty forces (down from ca. 300,000 in 1989), including conscripts who serve 12 months. Of those, 43,000

Romanians critiquing the book you are reading

serve in the land forces, 7,150 in the navy that man seven principal surface combatants, as well as patrol and mine warfare vessels, and 9,700 in the air force. The latter fly Soviet-era Lancer aircraft and MiG-21s. The latter's airworthiness expires in 2011, and the government is torn between replacing them with 48 Eurofighter or Swedish Grippen planes or American F-16s. It must also purchase modern helicopters that can be used in NATO deployments like Afghanistan. By law, military contractors must perform 80% of the production in Romania. In 2010 the Supreme Defense Council approved a U.S. proposal to base missile interceptors in the country, to be operational by 2015. Moscow was extremely upset despite assurances from the Romanian president that none would be directed against Russia.

It has a reserve force of 45,000, as well as 79,900 paramilitary that include 22,900 border guards and 57,000 gendarmerie. Romania embarked on a policy to modernize its equipment, reduce the ranks of its top-heavy armed forces, and build a non-conscript professional force by 2010. It offered to provide one of the 13 EU "battle groups," each with 1,500 troops intended to act on very short notice ahead of forces from other bodies such as the UN.

ECONOMY

At the end of World War II, Romania was still an overwhelmingly agricultural economy with over three-quarters of the

Prosperous farmers in Bran

work force employed in farming. Bucharest, center of what industry there was, was large and relatively modern. There were only three other cities in the country with populations of over 100,000 persons. The political elites who had dominated the government during the interwar period had been committed to a policy of industrialization but, except for the petroleum industry, they were not notably successful.

Immediately following World War II, a land reform act set an upper limit of 123 acres (50 hectares) on all individuals. This also provided for the expropriation of all real property of individuals alleged to have been fascist collaborators. The collectivization of agriculture was begun in 1949. In theory it was voluntary, but peasants who refused to join a collective found themselves required to deliver a set amount of produce to the state at an artificially low price.

Collectivization was completed in 1962 although subsequently there was further amalgamation of collective farms that brought together single villages into new multi-village cooperatives. Under the communist regime, the state purchased, processed, and distributed most agricultural products. It ran town and city markets where individuals and state and collective farms could market some of their produce. Agricultural output increased considerably during the period 1970–1977 but largely stagnated after that. This was particularly true for animal production. From 1979 onward, Romanians had trouble finding beef and pork in the markets. One reason for this was the government's decision to place a greater emphasis on exporting agricultural products as part of its program to pay off the foreign debt.

All but 9.4% of the land was controlled by the state. The privately held land (nearly all located in mountainous areas deemed unsuitable for extensive cultivation) plus the private plots of individual collective farmers provided over half of the country's potatoes, fruit, meat, milk and eggs. In fact, the small private sector produced an estimated one-third of Romania's total agricultural production.

In spite of its shortcomings, collectivization, with its emphasis on mechanization, did bring about major changes in the countryside. The old, traditional farming methods were largely supplanted, and productivity accordingly increased. Excess agricultural workers were drawn into the industrial work force.

Starting from a relatively low base in 1948, Romania introduced an industrialization program using the Stalinist command model. This resulted in one of the fastest growth rates in the world. The driving force behind the Stalinist command

model was the very high investment level. Up to 35% of gross national product was determined by the state. This results in a rapid growth rate if one is dealing with a situation in which there is a surplus of labor and adequate raw materials, as was the situation in Romania in the 1950s and 1960s. On the other hand, a high investment level means that there is less left over for consumption, and living standards will necessarily remain low. This was the case for postwar Romania.

Under communism, Romania's industrialization program concentrated on the creation of heavy industry rather than consumer goods. The major industries built or expanded during this period include oil refineries, chemical plants and various sorts of metal-working and machine-building enterprises. In later years, a major area of emphasis was electric power generation.

Two huge hydroelectric stations, the Iron Gate II project with Yugoslavia and the Turnu-Magurele project with Bulgaria, were constructed during the 1980s. Romania's first nuclear power plant was completed in the second half of the 1980s. These new sources of energy were designed to promote a continued growth in industry in general and the metallurgical sector in particular. Two other projects the government pursued in the 1980s were an expansion of the Galati steel complex and construction of a new steel complex at Calarasi.

In the final years under Ceausescu, Romania had largely exhausted the possibilities of the Stalinist demand model and had reached the point where both labor and raw materials were scarce. In fact many of the raw materials had to be imported. Instead of moving toward decentralized decision-making and placing greater emphasis on quality as opposed to quantity, he stubbornly clung to the command model.

The situation was exacerbated by Ceausescu's determination to pay back the foreign debt of approximately $13 billion that he had run up during his industrialization spree in the 1970s. To accomplish that, he instituted a harsh austerity program and cut Romania's hard currency imports by more than two-thirds. Romania also began to reorient its trade toward the CMEA countries, in particular with the Soviet Union. Between 1980 and 1989, the proportion of Romania's trade with other members of the CMEA grew from a third to just over a half. The government was also able to pay off its hard currency debt by the beginning of 1989, but only by dropping Romania's standard of living to perhaps the lowest in Europe. During his last years, food was rationed, cities were unlighted at night, and gas and electricity were available only on a limited basis.

Romania

The first sign that the Romanian people were losing their patience came in 1987 when riots broke out among workers in Brasov. They were triggered by a new government decree announcing additional penalties for workers who failed to fulfill production quotas. They were met by tanks, police dogs and tear gas. For several days, Brasov was off-limits to all foreigners.

The government did not have difficulty putting down the riots, but the blows to Ceausescu's credibility and to the regime's legitimacy were more severe. Once again, workers had risen up in protest against a so-called workers' state. One indication of this loss of credibility was that, for the first time in memory, a number of prominent Romanians dared to criticize the regime publicly. One such was Silviu Brucan, former ambassador to the United States and the United Nations, who urged the government to recognize the legitimacy of the workers' grievances. Several government ministers also dared to defend themselves against charges that they were responsible for the widespread shortages.

In spite of these signs of growing domestic opposition, Ceausescu held to his policy of austerity and used the funds thus accumulated to pay off Romania's foreign debt. In April 1989 it had paid off the last of its foreign loans and was debt-free.

Post-Communist Era

The answer of the Romanian people came in December 1989, when they rose up and brought down the entire regime. Romania installed a noncommunist government committed to multiparty democracy and a market economy since the beginning of 1990. But the individuals making up the new government in 1990 were badly divided among themselves as to the proper path to follow. They had been in power for about a year before taking any action to begin transforming the economy. They also made decisions during that first year that temporarily eased the lot of the Romanian people, but they had negative longer-term consequences.

One of those decisions was to use part of Romania's foreign currency reserves, then about $1.8 billion, to import food for domestic consumption. The government continued the policy in 1991. However, by that time, it had used up most of its foreign currency reserves and turned to financing consumption through an enlarged budget deficit. In effect, Romania was living beyond its means after 1989 and could not afford to do it any longer. International aid helped to close the gap, but the standard of living declined further after 1992.

Economic statistics for this period look awful. For example, industrial production

Bran Castle in Transylvania. Despite the legend, Dracula was never here.

decreased by over 40% after 1989 and then remained at that lower level. Part of this drop resulted from the disruptions of the revolution itself, but there were larger causes as well. Domestically, shortages of energy and raw materials played an important role. Internationally, Romania lost a significant part of its export market when the Soviet Union collapsed. It also lost a major source of raw material imports.

Romanian workers were unhappy about the economic situation, but they were also extremely fearful about change. Freeing prices had produced a virulent inflation that had eroded wages, while talk of privatization of state firms raised the specter of future unemployment. Surprisingly, polls taken during this period indicated that a majority of the Romanian people continued to favor both privatization and the development of a market economy.

The news from the countryside was also negative. The breakup of the collective and state farms gave land to the peasants, but they had no farm machinery to work the land. In the early 1990s it was common to see peasants using milk cows for plowing. They have since replaced the milk cows with oxen. Much of the land was fragmented. Many of the former collective farm bosses ended up with large holdings and enjoy annual subsidies from the EU's Common Agricultural Program (CAP). Romanian agriculture is likely to remain at a relatively primitive level for a number of years. In 2009 it imported 70% of its agricultural products. The extent to which

Romania has not yet developed a modern economy is shown by the fact that 30% of the workforce in 2010 was still employed in the agricultural sector (producing 10% of GDP), compared with 39% in services (55.9% of GDP) and 31% in industry (36.7% of GDP).

Under the EU policy of concentrating rural holdings millions of Romanians will have to leave the land within the next decade. Romanian law encourages larger plots and cooperation among land owners, who are required to sell their holdings if they do not cultivate their land within three years. Foreign companies are also purchasing Romanian agricultural assets. The giant American enterprise, Cargill, bought Olpo Podari, the largest Romanian sunflower oil maker. Cargill already owned about 10% of the country's silo capacity after acquiring Comcereal in 2005. A bright spot is the wine industry, which ranks sixth in Europe in production. However, Romanians prefer plum brandy and beer, and they consume an average of only 20 liters of wine every year, compared with the European average of 37.

Because of the severe deterioration in the infrastructure that occurred during the last several Ceausescu years, a great deal of money had to go into rebuilding rather than into new growth. The government did launch a voucher privatization program in 1995 that began the process. Citizens received vouchers valued at $325 that they were able to use to purchase shares in 3,905 companies to be privatized. Very little information was made available on the companies, however, so the public had scant ability to choose intelligently. In addition, since very few companies were considered to be profitable, few citizens bothered to turn in their vouchers. Finally, the state retained 40% of the shares, which meant that it retained effective control of the privatized companies.

In 1997 the government proclaimed what it described as the "test of fire" for reforms. Responding to IMF criticism of the slow pace of liquidation or privatization of money-losing enterprises owned by the state, it announced the closure of 17 enterprises, including three refineries that had originally been built for export markets that never materialized. The decision was a necessary one, but it meant that 30,000 people lost their jobs. Similar actions with regard to money-losing coalmines produced layoffs for 32,000 miners. These various reforms produced the desired result; by 1998, the private sector had grown from 52% of GDP in 1996 to 62% of GDP. However, in 2008, more than 40% of the workforce was still on the state payroll.

Privatization continues. Many large companies were liquidated, including the Minvest mining company, the hard coal pits in the Jiu Valley, and the lignite mines in Ploiesti. Some were reopened after reorganization, and others were offered for privatization. In 2005 the state sold 50% plus one share of the Banca Comerciala Romana (BCR) and the Romanian Savings Bank (CEC). The state-owned oil company, Petrom, whose sales are equal to about 4% of GDP, was privatized in 2004. It had been a vast off-budget reserve of cash, cheap credit and patronage.

In 1999 Renault took over the Dacia car plant in Mioveni with the intention of pro-

Romania dropped four zeros from its money, 2005.

ducing the modern-day equivalent of the Yugo, a 5,000-euro car that people in the region could afford. This put Romania on the region's auto industry's map. The last Dacia sedan rolled off the assembly line in July 2004, and the carmaker began making the Logan, which Renault also makes and sells in other countries. The company exports 85% of its production, but the home market has great potential: there are just 167 cars per 1,000 population, compared with 351 in Poland and 566 in Poland. The Renault connection saved Dacia and the whole Romanian auto industry during the great recession of 2008–10. In September 2009 Ford announced that it had bought a state-owned plant in Craiova to build its new Transit van.

Its labor costs are low (1.76 euros per hour in 2004 vs. 5.29 euros in Poland and the EU average of 25.30 euros), and GDP per capita is only 15% of the EU average. But by 2008 wages and income were growing by 25% every year. With business-

friendly incentives, and a good training system in a country-wide network of technical colleges and universities left over from the Communist era, it hopes to attract even more foreign investment. American multinationals like Hewlett-Packard and Oracle have already entered. In 2008 Nokia, the world's largest cell phone manufacturer, closed its German plant and relocated in Cluj, Romania, where wages are one-tenth of those in Germany.

By 2000, the portion of Romania's GDP generated by the private sector was 60%. Foreign investors are taking a greater interest although Romania continues to attract far less foreign investment per capita than the Central and Eastern European average. One reason is corruption. In 2005 the *World Yearbook of Competitiveness* ranked Romania 55th among 60 states in terms of economic competitiveness.

Inflation continues to come down from its 2001 rate of 40% to 6.4% in 2008. The energy sector contributes 20% to the nation's GDP. Faced with depleting local oil fields, expected to run out by about 2012, the newly privatized oil and gas concern, Petrom, Romania's largest company, is active in Central Asia, particularly Kazakhstan, while a smaller company, Rompetrol, is extracting crude oil in Ecuador. There are prospects for oil and gas drilling offshore. That is why Romania took Ukraine to the International Court of Justice in 2004 to try to end a long-running dispute over Black Sea exploration rights.

Despite its deep suspicion of Russian domination of energy supply routes through Gazprom, it gets half its gas imports from Russia. In July 2009 it also signed on to the Nabucco pipeline that will bring gas from Iraq and elsewhere into Europe without crossing Russia. A pipeline is being constructed in Romania that will carry Caspian and Russian crude oil from Constanta to refineries in Western Europe and also via deep-sea tankers to the U.S. Constanta is the entry point for

La mulți ani și la mai mare!

Îmi place
să vin aici,
în zilele senine.
Dacă văd 1 avion,
înseamnă
că o să mă întâlnesc
cu cineva cunoscut
în ziua aceea.
Dacă văd 2,
o să-mi meargă bine
toată săptămâna.
Iar dacă nu văd
nici unul...
mă duc
la McDonald's™.
i'm lovin'it.

i'm lovin' it

Romania

60% of Romania's imports. It is also the locale for the country's only nuclear power plant. Using Canada's Candu technology, it will have five units; two units function already. When completed, the complex will provide 10% of the country's energy (compared with 30% hydropower) and will export electricity.

The fall in 2000 of Slobodan Milosevic in neighboring Serbia provided some hope for Romania. The government estimated that the West's economic sanctions against Serbia (now lifted) and the bombing of the Danube bridges that blocked water traffic to western Europe until 2003 cost Romania at least $7 billion.

By 2000 the overall economy was still only three-quarters as large as it had been in 1989. But it became the EU's fastest-growing economy in 2008 after an eight-year boom averaging over 6% annually. The average monthly wage was climbing 25% per year, higher in towns, but in the countryside people struggled to subsist. The information technology sector was booming, and the use of mobile phones and the Internet was rising fast. The banking system was functioning normally, and credit card use was growing quickly. Mass media were thriving, and a lively free press and 68 TV stations now exist.

The budget deficit in 2008 was 2.7% of GDP. Total foreign debt was 47.3% of GDP, both within the range to qualify for the euro. As a step toward the euro, Romania reformed its currency, the leu (plural: lei), in July 2005 by dropping four zeros from the eye-popping numbers on its money. However, as much as half of its economy is still underground, unreported and untaxed. To encourage citizens to pay their taxes and to lure foreign investment, the government introduced a 16% flat tax on corporate profits and personal income in 2005.

Thanks to robust growth and to the employment abroad of an estimated 2.5 million Romanians (one-fifth of the workforce), unemployment was down to a post-communist low of 3.8% in 2008. It was below 2% in Bucharest and Transylvanian boom towns, creating a tight labor market, especially for skilled labor. Italy and Spain are the favorite foreign countries for Romanians because of similarities in climate, culture and language. Until the 2009 downturn, they sent home about 3 billion euros in remittances each year. In spite of their EU membership, Romanians did not enjoy the unrestricted right to work in all the partner countries until 2011. Since the downturn was felt all over Europe, the migrant workers were not only able to send fewer remittances home, but many of them returned to join the tight job market.

Growth came to a halt in 2009, as Romania was severely hurt by the global recession. Its GDP contracted by about 7%, as exports fell sharply, foreign investment declined, and unemployment rose from 3.8% in 2008 to 5.3% in 2009.

To deal with the crisis, the government borrowed $27 billion from the IMF, the EU, the World Bank and the European Bank for Reconstruction and Development. It also introduced a painful austerity policy that aims to cut the budget deficit from 7.2% of GDP to 5.9% by the end of 2010. Public wages are to decline by one-fourth and pensions by 15%. Thousands of "privileged pensions" are to be scrapped, and up to 100,000 public sector jobs are to be slashed. The unions rejected this medicine and sent their members out into the streets to make this unmistakably clear.

CULTURE

The Romanians take great pride in their Latin origin although over the centuries they have also been subject to Hungarian, Slavic and Turkish cultural influences. Romania's Hungarian minority constitutes almost 7% of the total population and is located primarily in the Tisa Plain and in Transylvania. Although they speak a Magyar dialect, the Szeklers are distinguishable from the Hungarians on historic grounds. They have been in Transylvania since the Middle Ages when they were frontier guards for the Magyar settlements. The Hungarian Magyars recognized them as a free people of noble birth and as one of the privileged nations of Transylvania, along with the Saxons (Germans) and the Magyars. Roma and other minorities make up 3.6% of the population.

Most Romanians (87%) belong to the Romanian Orthodox Church, but Roman Catholicism and Calvinism are strong among the Hungarian population. The old communist constitution guaranteed freedom of religion with qualifications. For instance, the organization of "religious cults" was regulated by law. The Church could not operate schools other than seminaries. The Church budget was under state control, and its officials had to be acceptable to the state. The secret service (Securitate) also thoroughly infiltrated the clergy. For example, Metropolitan Daniel, who was elected on September 12, 2007, had been permitted to travel abroad. This would have been impossible for anyone who did not cooperate with the Ceausescu regime.

The Iliescu government adopted a "hands-off" attitude toward religion, neither supporting nor interfering. The subsequent Constantinescu government took a more specifically pro-religion stance, although it was primarily symbolic. For instance, icons of the Romanian Ortho-

Romanians counted the days until EU entry

dox Church lined Constantinescu's office shelves, and he made a point of having an Orthodox priest say a prayer at political meetings. A 2005 opinion poll found that the Church is the public institution most trusted by Romanians—87% placed it on the top of their list. Of the other institutions, 72% mentioned the army, 59% the mass-media, and 48% the presidency, while 63% distrust the trade unions, 67% the judiciary, and 73% the parliament.

There has been considerable movement from rural to urban areas since World War II. The population is now about 55% urban and 45% rural. The more recent exodus of as many as 2.5 million Romanians from villages in the poorest regions in the south and east to find work abroad has led to immense social dislocation in those areas. Bucharest is still by far the largest city, containing more than one-fifth of Romania's city dwellers. It is modern and a center of cultural expression. In the countryside, folk music, art and colorful costumes are noticeable.

Moviegoers can admire the Romanian countryside in the many films that are now shot there. Its two major studios Castel and Media Pro Pictures, are reporting dramatic growth in their business. The biggest undertaking by 2003 is the American Civil War epic, "Cold Mountain," starring Nicole Kidman and Jude Law. Director Anthony Minghella had entire farms built, complete with planted tobacco and corn. One battle scene required 1,000 Romanian extras. With its low labor costs, Romania is ideally suited for such movie-making.

Free primary education is compulsory for eight years, and there are universities in Bucharest and in 20 other cities. As a sign of close historic ties with France, a section of the University of Bucharest offers entire curricula and degree programs in French; it does the same in English. Romania is the only country where more secondary-school pupils study French than English. A major change since communism is that almost a third of university students attend more than 40 private universities.

Romania has made a cultural mark on the world through its composers, such as George Enescu and Ciprian Porumbescu, sculptors like Constantin Brancusi, and painters, including Nicolae Grigorescu and Nicolae Tonitza. In a new "Park of Totalitarianism" in Bucharest, other works are displayed that not everybody would consider to be "art," but as parts of Romanian history. It contains statues and busts from the Communist era of leaders such as Ceausescu, his predecessor Gheorghe-Gherorghiu Dey and even Vladimir Lenin himself.

In 2009 Herta Müller won the Nobel Prize in Literature. Her award coincided with the 20th anniversary of the fall of communism in Romania. She became the 12th woman to receive the prize. She was largely unknown both abroad and outside of literary circles in Romania and Germany. Born in 1953, she grew up in the German-speaking city of Nitzkydorf in the Banat region of Romania. Only the mayor and the policeman spoke Romanian. Her ancestors were Banat Swabians from southern Germany.

Thanks to Romania's minority rights even during communism, she was schooled in German and wrote in German from the very beginning of her literary career. As a university student, her thoughts and ideals collided with the rigid communist regime, and she joined an organization calling itself the Action Group Banat to seek freedom of speech. Hounded by the Securitate, which spied on them and planted bugs in their home, she emigrated to Berlin in 1987 with her then husband, Richard Wagner, also a German language writer.

Her 20 books deal with the challenges of living in a dictatorship. Among her four novels translated into English are *The Land of Green Plums* and *The Appointment*. Her last book in 2009 published just before she received the prize is a masterpiece about life in Soviet labor camps: *Everything I Own I Carry With Me*.

One questionable form of commercial activity has been cleaned up: adoptions by foreign parents. The Ceausescu dictatorship had encouraged procreation and prohibited birth control, so 100,000 abandoned children lived terrible lives in crammed, understaffed and ill-equipped orphanages. Since the dictator's fall, 50,000 babies have been sent abroad for $20,000 to $50,000 each.

After the EU demanded a change of this corrupt adoption system, Romania declared a moratorium on foreign adoptions in 2001 and adopted new laws in 2004 making the moratorium permanent. Adoption is considered as a "last resort," and Romanian couples would be given priority. Only foreign couples able to prove their direct kinship with a child would be eligible. There were still about 30,000 children in orphanages in 2006, some of them living in appalling conditions. But the numbers declined after the moratorium went into effect because the financial incentives for offering children for adoption had disappeared. The EU funds day-care centers and foster care within Romania as an alternative to adoption.

One woman who would never put her child up for adoption is 67-year-old Adriana Iliescu, a university professor and author of children's books. After years of fertility treatments, she became the world's oldest new mother in 2005 by giving birth to a baby girl.

In 2003 Romanian authorities acted decisively in another social situation. They ordered that a 12-year-old Gypsy girl, the daughter of the head of Romania's Roma (Gypsies), be separated from a 15-year-old boy she had been forced to marry and that all intimate relations between them cease until they are old enough to be legally married. The wedding sparked a national debate about forced marriages among Roma adolescents. They were both ordered to attend school.

No one knows the size of the Roma population in Romania—perhaps one to two million out of four to twelve million in Europe. They cannot always communicate with each other since their language, originally related to Sanskrit, has splintered into dozens of mutually incomprehensible dialects. Communism largely put an end to their traditional nomadism. Many have no birth certificates, and some never set foot in a school, which shuts them out of the modern job market. Only 17.2% attend preschool, compared with 67% of other children, and only about a fifth receives secondary education.

Many engage in organized begging using their children to soften up passersby. Many Romanians blame them for much of the crime that occurs. More than half of them live in extreme poverty, compared with a rate of 9.3% among the rest of the population; 88% are below the poverty line. They lag far behind the general population in life expectancy, infant mortality, employment and literacy. Polls in 2008 showed how much discrimination they face: four out of five Romanians would not want Roma neighbors.

FUTURE

At Christmas-time 2009 Romanians celebrated the 20th anniversary of their successful revolution against communist dictatorship. Despite many difficult problems, their lives are freer and more prosperous today than ever before. Romanians kept up their faith in the future by glancing at a huge digital electronic clock in the middle of a busy Bucharest traffic island called "Europe Square." It ticked off the days until Romania joined the EU on January 1, 2007.

Romania has considerable potential if it can stay the course in modernizing and reforming its economy after the current recession is over. Privatization has been largely completed, and economic growth has returned. Wages and income are on the rise. It receives support from the European Union and the IMF, and it can look forward to ever increasing economic integration with the rest of Europe. However, the EU will continue to monitor Romania's poor record in reducing corruption. A bright light is NATO. The September 11 terrorist attacks in the U.S. greatly enhanced the strategic value of the Black Sea area, and Romania skillfully demonstrated that it would be a useful ally.

Democracy has been strengthened as old communist habits become weaker. The November 2008 parliamentary elections produced a new prime minister, Emil Boc, and a grand coalition of the two largest parties. That collapsed ten months later when Boc lost the first ever vote of no-confidence. Boc worked for two months to create a different ruling majority that finally brought together his and President Basescu's Democratic Liberal Party (PD-L), the Democratic Union of Hungarians from Romania (UDMR), which advocates Magyar interests, and several independents. Basescu won a second 5-year presidential term by the skin on his teeth in December 2009.

The new Boc government and President Basescu will gradually guide the country out of the recession that affected all of Europe in 2008–10. The tough austerity measures the Boc government introduced in 2010 not only unleashed a storm of protest in the streets. His government barely survived a vote of no-confidence in June. It is doubtful that the president and prime minister will be able to overcome the slowdown in reforms, the pervasive corruption and the persistent bickering and feuding.

Republic of Bulgaria

Rila Monastery

Area: 42,729 sq. mi. (110,993 sq. km.). The size of Virginia.

Population: 7.7 million (2007)

Capital City: Sofia (Pop. 1.24 million; 2007 estimate)

Climate: Mediterranean in the South, cooler in the North.

Neighboring Countries: Romania (North); Turkey, Greece (South); Serbia, Macedonia (West).

Official Language: Bulgarian

Other Principal Tongue: Turkish

Ethnic Background: Ethnic Bulgarian (Slav) 83.6%; Turkish 9.5%; Roma 4.6%; other 2.3%.

Principal Religions: Bulgarian Orthodox 83.8%; Muslim 12.1%; other 4.1%.

Chief Commercial Products: Clothing and textiles, base metals, iron and steel, chemicals, minerals and fuels, machinery and transport equipment, agricultural and forest products.

Chief Trading Partners: EU (60.8% of exports and 58.5% of imports), Turkey (11.5% of exports), Germany (10.2% of exports and 14.8% of imports), Italy (10.1% of exports and 7.5% of imports), Greece (9% of exports), Russia (10.6% of imports), Ukraine (5.1% of imports).

Currency: lev/leva (singular/plural).

Former Political Status: Bulgarian state 681–1018; Byzantine rule 1018–1185; Second Bulgarian state 1185–1396; Part of Ottoman Empire, 1396–1878; Autonomous Principality, 1878–1908; Independent, 1908–1944; Communist State, part of Soviet Empire, 1945–1990.

National Day: March 3 (Liberation from the Ottoman Empire in 1878).

Chief of State: Georgi Parvanov, President (January 2002).

Head of Government: Boijko Borissov, Prime Minister (July 2009).

National Flag: Three horizontal stripes, white, green, red.

One of the last countries to win its independence from the Ottoman Empire in 1878, Bulgaria has stood on its own two feet longer than most of its neighbors. Since Russia had played a key role in helping the country win its freedom, this was one of the few countries in Eastern and Central Europe in which the population harbored genuinely positive sentiments toward Russia and Russians during the 20th century. One of Sofia's main avenues is still called Boulevard of the Tsar Liberator on which one can sip coffee in a Viennese café. Its Western ambiance points to that part of Europe on which Bulgarians' sights and yearnings are fixed.

Sitting in that café in Sofia, Croatian author Slavenka Drakulič reflected on the concept of "Europe." She wrote in her book, *Café Europa. Life After Communism*: "What does Europe mean in the Eastern European imagination? It is certainly not a question of geography. . . . It is something distant, something to be attained, to be deserved. It is also something expensive and fine: good clothes, the certain look and smell of its people. Europe is plenitude: food, cars, light, everything—a kind of festival of colors, diversity, opulence, beauty. It offers choice: from shampoo to political parties. It represents freedom of expression. It is a promised land, a new Utopia, a lollipop. And through television, that Europe is right there, in your apartment, often in colors much too bright to be real."

The Republic of Bulgaria is a relatively small, square-shaped country bordering on the Black Sea to the east and bounded by the Danube River to the north. The Black Sea coast has not only beautiful sandy beaches that are now being developed, but it is also the site of the major tourist center of Varna. Stretching from west to east is the Balkan Range (*Stara Planina*) separating the fertile Danubian Plain in the north from the Thracian Plain in the south.

In the exact center of the country there is the Kazanlik "Valley of Roses" where fragrance and beauty combine with commercial value in the production of rose oil. The southwest is dominated by the rugged Rila Mountains—which include Mount Musala, the highest peak in the Balkans—and by the snow-capped Pirin Mountains. South of Plovdiv, Bulgaria's second largest city along the Maritsa River, lie the Rhodope Mountains, where hundreds of mineral springs can be found.

In the 7th century an Asiatic people called the Bulgars crossed the Danube River and settled in the area known today as the Republic of Bulgaria. Within two centuries after their conquest of the region, the Bulgars had become completely absorbed into the native Slav population, adopting their language and culture.

Cyril and Methodius, two brothers who were missionaries, devised an alphabet in order to translate the Bible and religious writings into the Slavic language of the people. They had been born in Thessalonica, sons of a noble Byzantine family of Slav-Bulgarian lineage. All Slavs at the time ultimately adopted their alphabet. Their Bible contributed to the conversion of the Bulgarians to Christianity, which became the official state religion in 863. The conversion of all non-Christians began. The invention and dissemination of books and literacy in the Bulgarian language spoken at the time was of prime importance for the cultural history of Bulgaria and Eastern Europe in general. The Bulgarians' conversion thus brought them their first literary language and early contact with the Byzantine Empire.

HISTORY

The beginning of the Bulgarian state dates from 681 when Bulgaria was united under the leadership of Asparukh, its first khan (leader). His successors as khans embarked on a policy of elevating Bulgaria to a status equal in territory, population, and economic and military strength to the great European political giants of the day, such as the empire of the Franks. By 852 Bulgaria's borders had been extended to include what is now Hungary, Romania, Moldova, Macedonia and northern Greece. It was a European superpower.

Khan Boris converted to Christianity in 863 under the auspices of the Greek Church. Tsar Simeon, who died in 927, was responsible for the establishment of an independent Bulgarian patriarchate. This is called the "Golden Age of the Slav culture" in the Slavonic language. Now religiously separate from Constantinople, subsequent tsars fought constant wars against Constantinople, particularly as they expanded the territory under their control until they governed most of what are now large parts of Albania, Serbia, Macedonia and Greece. In time, an individual tsar might even challenge the political authority of the Byzantine Empire.

It was in response to just such a challenge that the Byzantine Emperor Basil II (976–1025) destroyed a Bulgarian army and, indirectly, the Bulgarian state. According to tradition, Samuel, the Bulgarian tsar sent a large army toward Constantinople, intending to lay siege to the city. Basil II's forces met the Bulgarian soldiers before they could reach Constantinople.

In the succeeding battle, Basil II defeated the Bulgarians, also taking many prisoners. To teach Samuel a lesson, he ordered 14,000 of the Bulgarian prisoners to be blinded, then sent them back to Samuel. It is said that Samuel died of shock on seeing what had happened to his men. Basil II then converted Bulgaria into a province of the Byzantine Empire.

Between the 12th and 14th centuries (1185–1393) a second Bulgarian kingdom existed. Its most famous tsar was Ivan Assen II (1216–1241), who dominated the whole region. The Bulgarian liberation insurrection in 1185 had been sparked by

heavy special taxes imposed on the Bulgarian lands to meet exorbitant expenses for the wedding of the Byzantine emperor with a juvenile Hungarian princess. The initial economic motives of the rebellion were quickly forgotten, however, as the restoration of the Bulgarian state became the primary objective. After incessant warfare and a brilliant victory in 1230, Bulgaria had achieved the situation in which it had found itself in the 10th century: its territory encompassed almost the entire Balkan Peninsula.

The Bulgarians went on to defeat hordes of Tatars, which until then had been invincible. These Asians had engulfed all states west of the Ural Mountains, including Russia, and had conquered Hungary. They attacked Bulgaria in order to secure their flank before invading Western Europe.

Their humiliating defeat in 1241 ended once and for all their hopes of conquering Western Europe. Bulgaria's territorial expansion fostered successful economic and cultural development. The Bulgarian patriarchate was fully restored in 1235 and became the only Eastern Orthodox religious institution that enjoyed the backing of a well-established political power. It thus achieved great authority in the entire East.

The expanding Ottoman Turks, under the leadership of Sultan Murad I, first occupied Bulgaria, Macedonia and Albania. Along with the Serbian kingdom, Bulgaria was the first land to be conquered by the Ottomans. This was devastating for the Bulgarians because of the especially long Turkish occupation. Its domination was especially heavy because Bulgaria, then called by its three historical provinces—Moesia, Thrace and Macedonia—was geographically so close. The Turks then defeated the Serbs at Kosovo in 1389. Four years later, Bulgaria was formally incorporated into the Ottoman Empire, where it remained until 1878. The empire's inhabitants were organized into administrative units on the basis of their faith, with a religious leader as head of each unit. The Turks thereby used the Orthodox Church to administer the Bulgarians.

The Birth of Modern Bulgaria

The liberation of Bulgaria from Turkish control was the product of a war between Russia and Turkey that ended in Turkish defeat. The Russians had arguably envisioned a single, large Bulgarian state. This was stipulated in the resulting Treaty of San Stefano on March 3, 1878, the date still celebrated as national liberation day.

Bulgaria

Russian Orthodox church in Sofia

The Austrians and British objected, however, and Russia was forced to permit a rewriting of the treaty at the Congress of Berlin. The result, signed in 1878, was that the western portion of Bulgaria was returned to Turkey while the remaining area was divided into two parts, separated by the Balkan Mountains. This is why Bulgarians call the Congress of Berlin "the catastrophe." The northern part became Bulgaria and was established as a self-governing territory with the right to select its own prince. The portion south of the mountains became the autonomous Turkish territory of East Rumelia. The division did not last, however; in 1885, the East Rumelians merged with the rest of Bulgaria without a shot being fired. The nation as a whole remained a self-governing autonomous principality until it declared its complete independence from the Ottoman Empire in 1908.

There were three main problems that Bulgaria faced in the period following Ottoman rule. The first concerned territory. The Great Bulgaria envisioned in the Treaty of San Stefano had included much of the territory the Bulgarians had lived in at the time of their greatness in the 10th century. The Treaty of Berlin had reduced those territories by nearly two-thirds. The Union of East Rumelia and Bulgaria in 1885 partially solved the problem, but still left Bulgaria with claims to additional territory. It was this question that led to Bulgarian participation in the two Balkan Wars of 1912–13, to an alliance with Germany and Austria in World War I and to an alliance with Germany in World War II.

The second problem was the status of neighboring Macedonia. In the 19th century, was still part of the Ottoman Empire. Most outsiders assumed that they must be either Serbians or Bulgarians and the Bulgarian and Serbian governments took this same position, each claiming the Macedonians as separated brethren. To complicate the situation more, Greece also claimed the area, arguing that Macedonia was historically Greek. As a result of this Greek-Serbian-Bulgarian rivalry, until the First World War each state waged a constant battle to increase its influence through a variety of means, including political propaganda, school subsidies, Orthodox Church authority and, worst of all, terrorism.

The third problem was the nature of Bulgaria's relationship with Russia. On one hand, there had been a great deal of popular affection for Russia as the liberator of Bulgaria from Turkish rule. On the other hand, this affection had been mingled with a fear that the price of Russian friendship might be Bulgarian servitude.

Bulgaria was the only nation in the Balkans to join the Central Powers (Germany and Austro-Hungary) in World War I. It had done so in order to win back territory lost in the Treaty of San Stefano in 1878, and Germany promised what Bulgaria wanted. But this not only resulted in defeat in 1918, but a loss of even more territory. During the interwar period Bulgaria denounced as excessively harsh the terms of the treaty settling the war and the boundaries of the southern Balkans.

From 1919 to 1939, Bulgarian history was troubled. There were political plots from left- and right-wing groups, assassinations, mass murders and constant acts of individual terrorism. One of the most important groups in the country, especially in the years between 1923 and 1934, was the Internal Macedonian Revolutionary Organization (*VMRO*). This was a terrorist group fighting for Macedonian self-government and undermining any political leaders who pursued policies inconsistent with this goal.

The early post-World War I period years were dominated by Alexander Stamboliiski, a colorful, strong-willed leader of the Agrarian Party. During the period he was prime minister, which lasted until 1923, reforms in the tax structure, legal system and land ownership were carried out. The land reforms were not as drastic as they were elsewhere in the Balkans since Bulgaria was basically a peasant society with few large landholdings. While Stamboliiski was in office, the Communist Party of Bulgaria was the second-largest party in the country. After a right-wing military regime came to power in 1923, the party was banned, and its leaders, one of which was Georgi Dimitrov, had to go into exile.

After ten years of IMRO terrorism and government inefficiency, a military coup was launched in 1934. Colonel Kimon Georgiev, the leader of the Zveno group—an organization of reform-minded intellectuals and politicians—became prime minister. In less than a year, he was out of office. His powers went to King Boris III, who ruled Bulgaria as a royal authoritarian from 1935 until his death in 1943.

Bulgaria joined the Axis in 1941, but it refused to declare war on the Soviet Union when that nation was invaded by Germany. During 1941, as a by-product of a German attack on Yugoslavia, Bulgaria occupied almost all of Macedonia, part of Serbia and also took over Western Thrace, a part of Greece.

Bulgaria was the only state in the region in which not a single Jew was deported or killed. In agreement with its German ally, the Bulgarian government adopted anti-Jewish laws in March 1943. But the speaker of the parliament used his influence to prevent the second step: the deportation of Bulgarian Jews. His supporters and the general population launched mass protests against the deportation order issued by the government. Thus the entire 50,000-strong Jewish community was saved. This inspiring action shows what an individual could do to prevent terrible evil.

But the story is more complicated and troubling, as Bulgarian-American film maker Jacky Comforty shows in his award-winning documentary, "The Optimists." Bulgarian Jews suffered terrible abuse. They were prevented from studying in universities, removed from teaching and government jobs, banished to deserted places within the country, and denied diplomatic protection abroad. In

VMRO active in Bulgaria today

their occupation areas, Bulgarian soldiers rounded up 7,500 Macedonian Jews and 4,000 Jews from Thrace and delivered them to the Germans for deportation.

It is rumored that because he opposed Bulgarian military participation on the eastern front, King Boris III was poisoned by the Germans and died in 1943, three days after visiting Hitler in Germany. His six-year-old son, Simeon, succeeded him. A three-man regency exercised state power. Under the administration of Prime Minister Ivan Bagrianov, a less pro-Axis policy was adopted. Thousands of political prisoners were released. In 2001 Simeon II was to become prime minister in a radically different Bulgaria.

Bulgaria announced in 1944 that it was ready to seek a separate peace with the Allies. However, the Soviet Union declared war on Bulgaria a few days later, and the Soviet army entered the country.

Bulgaria Becomes a People's Republic

Technically, a native resistance group calling itself the Fatherland Front overthrew the government at this time. This was a "popular front" grouping that had come into existence during World War II with the assistance and under the sponsorship of the Communist International (Comintern). An undoubted factor in this sponsorship was that Georgi Dimitrov, the Bulgarian communist who had fled the country in 1923, was now secretary general of the Comintern.

The communist role in the Fatherland Front was very strong, but it was a genuine "popular front," encompassing the Agrarian Union, one wing of the Social Democrats, and Zveno. The prime minister of the new government was Colonel Kimon Georgiev, a member of Zveno. The communists were a minority in the cabinet, but they controlled the key ministries of Justice and Interior. This gave them control over both the police and the courts, and they used this to institute a systematic purge of opposition figures.

Since all of the parties of the Fatherland Front were pro-Russian and united in their hatred of the "German collaborators" who had frozen them out of power in the past, there was strong support among the other parties for these actions. Those executed included the three regents, former prime ministers Bagrianov and Bozhilov, 26 former cabinet ministers and 68 deputies from the wartime Assemblies. In addition, special "People's Courts" were set up throughout the country, and thousands of additional individuals were sentenced to death and executed.

Having eliminated the "German collaborators," the communists next turned to their partners in the Fatherland Front. Under the terms of the "Declaration of Eu-

Sofia, looking toward Sveta Nedelja Square around "Holy Sunday Church"
Photo: Miller B. Spangler

rope," signed by the "Big Three" at Yalta in February 1945, free elections were to be held throughout Eastern Europe. Determined to establish their own political dominance, the communists demanded a common Fatherland Front list of candidates with a prearranged ratio giving them half of the seats in the new assembly.

Zveno, more a military faction than a political party, accepted these terms. The Agrarian Union and the Social Democrats did not. The communists thereupon produced their own Agrarian collaborator, Alexander Obhov, and managed to get him elected head of the party by packing the congress of the Agrarian Union. Similar tactics were used against the Social Democrats. The elections, which took place in November 1945, produced an 86% majority for the Fatherland Front.

Georgi Dimitrov, who had been elected president of the Central Committee of the Bulgarian Communist Party at a party congress in March 1945, returned to Sofia in the midst of the election campaign. Although clearly the preeminent leader of the party that dominated the government, he did not enter the government at this time. One reason may have been that the American and British governments challenged the validity of the November elections and demanded that the true leaders of the Agrarian Front and Social Democrats be brought back into the government. This became the subject of the Moscow Conference of December 1945, but American and British pressure was of no effect.

By the summer of 1946, the communists felt strong enough to campaign against Zveno, the remaining independent element in the Fatherland Front. An attack

was launched in the communist press against the founder of Zveno, General Velchev, who held the position of minister of war. Velchev eventually was forced to resign from the cabinet. Colonel Georgiev remained as prime minister until the autumn when he, too, was forced out.

Bulgaria was still technically a monarchy up to this point. However, a plebiscite, held in September 1946, resulted in a vote in favor of a republic. A month later, new elections were held for a Grand National Assembly, which was charged with preparing a new constitution.

The Fatherland Front won those elections and Georgi Dimitrov took the office of premier (subsequently renamed "chairman of the council of ministers") in the new government. Some legal opposition continued for a while, however, since the independent factions of the Agrarian Union and the Social Democrats had both run candidates in the elections and had managed to get a few of their candidates elected. They were permitted to make speeches in the assembly, but this was soon replaced by a campaign of intimidation. Things came to a head in June 1947 when Nikola Petkov, leader of the independent faction of the Agrarian Union, was arrested on the floor of the assembly—even though his parliamentary immunity should have protected him. Charged with preparing for a *coup d'état*, he was found guilty and sentenced to death.

Somewhat later, Georgi Dimitrov addressed a specific warning to the few Social Democrats remaining in the assembly. "As you remember," Dimitrov informed them, "from this rostrum I many times warned your political allies from Nikola Petkov's group. They did not listen to me.

Bulgaria

Dinner with the Tomovi family in Varna

They took no notice of all my warnings. They broke their heads, and their leader is now under the ground. You should now think it over, lest you share their fate." The following July, Kosta Lulchev, head of the Social Democrats, was arrested, along with six of the nine remaining deputies from that party, and he was subsequently sentenced to 15 years imprisonment.

The Dimitrov government presented Bulgaria with a new constitution in December 1947. As might have been expected, it was modeled closely after the 1936 "Stalin Constitution" of the USSR. Bulgaria now became a "people's republic" while its government became almost a carbon copy of the Soviet model, except that the legislature consisted of one house only. Bulgaria had no need for a separate house representing different nationalities such as existed in Russia and Yugoslavia. Like the Soviet Union, theoretical sovereignty rested with the legislature, but the actual decision-making was carried out by a presidium and a separate council of ministers. Reflecting the fulcrum of power, Georgi Dimitrov took the position of chairman of the council of ministers for himself.

Internecine Struggles

Having eliminated the opposition, the communists turned against each other. The charge was "nationalist deviation," and the ostensive cause was Yugoslav leader Tito's break with the Soviet Union in 1948. It turned into a struggle between communists who had served an apprenticeship in the Soviet Union and those who had remained behind. It was largely directed from Moscow. Stalin apparently became convinced that he could not trust any of the "native" communists.

The most significant of that group was Traicho Kostov, who had risen to the position of vice-chairman of the council of ministers in charge of economic affairs and who was widely considered to be Dimitrov's probable successor. The list of charges eventually filed against him was rather extensive, but the most serious was that he had kept secret information on Bulgarian economic matters from Soviet representatives, not realizing, as *Rabotnichesko Delo*, the communist party newspaper phrased it, that "secrets and commercialism do not exist in our dealings with the Soviet Union." Kostov was sentenced to death and executed in late 1949. Several of his associates, including the finance minister, the foreign trade minister, the director of the national bank and the commercial attaché in Moscow, were sentenced to long terms in prison. Other leading native communists were tried, sentenced and eliminated. In addition, a purge of the party ranks resulted in about 20% of the membership being expelled from the party.

In the midst of the purge, Georgi Dimitrov died while on a trip to the Soviet Union. His immediate successor was Vasil Kolarov, but he died six months later in 1950 and was in turn replaced by Vulko Chervenkov. The latter was Dimitrov's brother-in-law and had spent many years in the Soviet Union. Known as an arch-Stalinist, he was almost certainly responsible for the severity of the purge of the "native" communists. By using the weapon of "nationalist deviation," he eliminated all possible rivals and consolidated his own power position.

The purges had one final result. At the Kostov trial, an attempt was made to portray the defendant as an American agent

who had been encouraged in his actions by Donald Heath, the head of the U.S. Legation in Sofia. This was followed by the arrest of five Bulgarians employed by the U.S. Legation and a subsequent "spy trial" of other alleged American agents. Finally, the U.S. government had enough. In 1950, it broke off diplomatic relations with Bulgaria.

Chervenkov was the most ruthless of Bulgaria's postwar rulers, but he did not get to enjoy his power for very long. After Stalin's death in 1953, his old patron was dead. Nikita Khrushchev's rise to power threatened Chervenkov's position. Khrushchev was determined to heal the breach with Tito of Yugoslavia, and Chervenkov had distinguished himself as an enemy of Tito. In 1954, he gave up the position of general secretary of the central committee—the top party position—although he managed to retain the leading state position, that of premier. Chervenkov actually managed to hold on to most of his power for another two years, but he was never able to overcome his Stalinist past. When Khrushchev launched his attack against Stalin in 1956, Chervenkov found himself accused of Stalin's chief crime—promoting a "cult of personality"—and was again forced to accept a demotion, this time to deputy chairman of the council of ministers.

The Beginning of the Zhivkov Era

The man who got Chervenkov's party position in 1954—changed at this time from general secretary to first secretary—was Todor Zhivkov. His first membership in the Bulgarian Communist Party dates back to 1932, and he had been one of the organizers of the partisan underground in the Sofia area during World War II; he commanded the partisan regiments in and around Sofia at the time of the 1944 Fatherland Front seizure of power. Lacking close ties to the "Moscow" communists, who had returned to Bulgaria to take charge of the party, Zhivkov spent the next four years in various subordinate positions.

His breakthrough came in 1948 when he became first secretary of the Sofia City Committee and, simultaneously, a member of the party Central Committee. From this time, his rise was more rapid. He became an alternate member of the Politburo in 1950 and a member of the Secretariat. A year later, he was admitted to full Politburo membership. Thus, when Chervenkov came under attack in 1954 as a Stalinist, Zhivkov was able to move into the position of first secretary of the Central Committee, a position he held until November 1989.

Zhivkov's rapid rise after 1948 would indicate that he got his start as Cherven-

Bulgaria

kov's protégé, and his actions after 1954 would bear that out. It was not until Chervenkov had been further demoted in 1956 that Zhivkov made his own bid for greater power. In 1957, he increased his control by removing some of his opponents, but it was not until 1962 that he consolidated his position by taking the additional title of chairman of the council of ministers (now renamed premier). At the same time, he severed his last connection with Chervenkov and had him dismissed from the government. The break was over foreign policy. Zhivkov favored closer relations with Yugoslavia and, in general, wanted to bring Bulgarian foreign policy closer into alignment with Soviet foreign policy under Khrushchev. After Chervenkov's dismissal, Zhivkov publicly endorsed Soviet policies in the Cuban missile crisis of 1961, made moves toward establishment of better relations with Yugoslavia and totally supported the Soviet Union in its disputes with China.

One of the problems Zhivkov had to face was the trend toward a more relaxed and liberal leadership that had started prior to the time he became premier. Detention camps had been closed, and limits were placed on the secret police. Writers and scholars were given more freedom to express their views. In some cases this new freedom was used to criticize the government. Zhivkov's position was not secure enough to tolerate such criticism. He had eliminated his rivals from the top level of the party, but he still faced the opposition of lesser members who had been supporters of Chervenkov.

Other problems were created by popular discontent with a shortage of food, consumer goods and housing. Economic reform was needed to stifle criticism, but it would have met with opposition from the "dogmatists" and those who profited from the present setup. Zhivkov's only alternative was to end the brief period of liberalization and to reimpose restrictions. Even though this was a step backwards, it was not a return to the repressive atmosphere of the Stalinist days. Meanwhile, Zhivkov tried to shore up his own position by tying himself closely to his Soviet benefactor, Khrushchev. When the latter lost power in November 1964, Zhivkov's position became precarious and his gestures of loyalty toward the new Soviet leadership could not disguise the loss of support that he experienced at this time.

A few months later, the inner turmoil of Bulgaria was underlined by the most unusual event in its postwar history. In April 1965, a plot to overthrow the government was discovered in Sofia. The coup had been planned for the April 14 meeting of the Politburo, at which time the plotters intended to arrest leading party members

and to occupy important areas to prevent Soviet military action within Bulgaria.

Soviet military spies discovered the plot, and the coup was quickly prevented. It was not until mid-May, however, that the Bulgarians received their first official explanation of the plot. It was declared to be an unimportant event caused by a small group of pro-Chinese plotters. This was not the case. The conspirators were not insignificant people but, rather, were former World War II freedom fighters, Bulgarian communists, high-ranking army officers and top-level party members. It is probable that they wanted to remove Zhivkov in the hope that a new leadership would bring a new course of independence for Bulgaria in its relations with the Soviet Union.

After the attempt failed, one Central Committee member committed suicide, others were tried secretly, and there was the usual purge of anyone with questionable loyalty. A renewed pledge of allegiance to the Soviet Union was required. Shaken by the events of 1965, Zhivkov initiated a series of reforms, particularly in the economy. They were designed to allow some decentralization of decision-making. But the entrenched bureaucracy and conservatives opposed them so strenuously that they were phased out in 1968. Although he had initiated them, Zhivkov's support was never more than half-hearted, so it did not reflect adversely on him when they were discontinued.

Zhivkov continued as premier until 1971 when a new constitution created the position of president of the State Council. When he gave up his previous position, it went to Stanko Todorov. Zhivkov was named president of the State Council. This relieved him of many day-to-day duties connected with running the government, but still gave him a government post as titular head of state. Todorov was subsequently replaced as premier by Grisha Filipov, who continued to hold that position until 1986.

By this time, Zhivkov was 75, and the Politburo had gotten old along with the secretary general. The example of Gorbachev's significant personnel changes since coming to power a year earlier began to create strong pressure on Zhivkov to step down and allow a new generation of leadership to take over. As a result, a significant reshuffle occurred among Bulgaria's senior government and party leaders, though Zhivkov managed to retain his own hold on power. Filipov retired as premier and was replaced by Georgi Atanasov, still in his forties.

At the Party Congress in 1986, Zhivkov was reelected to another five-year term. There were no changes made in either the Politburo or Secretariat, though there was

a fairly significant turnover in membership on the Central Committee. About 80 out of 250 members were retired and replaced by younger individuals from the city and regional party organizations.

Perestroika Comes to Bulgaria

In January 1988, the Bulgarian Communist Party held a special party conference whose purpose was to discuss the progress of perestroika in Bulgaria. What was outlined was a relatively cautious approach to reform modeled closely on developments in the Soviet Union. Enterprises were to operate under a form of self-management with the right to set prices, salaries and production goals, but all of this would be within general guidelines set in Sofia. There was also a suggestion that terms of office of higher party officials might be limited, though implementation was not to begin until the next party congress in 1991.

A new political shake-up of sorts occurred in July 1988 when Zhivkov ousted three men from the Politburo who had been strong supporters of reform. It appears that Zhivkov might also have been concerned about his own political survival. One of those removed, Chudomir Alexandrov, a young technocrat in the mold of Gorbachev, had been tipped by many as the next leader of the party. In any case, the result, according to Stephen Ashley, head of Bulgarian research at Radio Free Europe, was "to reduce the Politburo to a tight clique of former partisans and Zhivkov's long-standing protégés."

In spite of Zhivkov's purge, pressure for change continued to build within the country. Domestically, Bulgarian industrialization had brought into existence a significant and growing "middle" class of technicians, engineers, teachers, doctors, and other better-educated individuals. They wanted a larger role in decision-making and resented the interference of political operatives in their areas of expertise. Internationally, the Bulgarians had always looked to the Soviet Union for leadership and so were inevitably affected by the wave of changes occurring there. Zhivkov's own first reaction was to go along with Moscow's reforms, and for a while glasnost and perestroika became the new watchwords in Bulgaria. Local newspapers were suddenly filled with unprecedented debates, and "independent associations" were authorized by law.

But when a human-rights group was formed to monitor rights abuses, Zhivkov considered this to be too great a challenge. Moving to isolate the group, he expelled those who happened also to be members of the Bulgarian Communist Party. Another leading communist, Svetlin Rusev, lost his seat on the Central Committee

Bulgaria

when he organized an independent environmental committee to protest pollution in the city of Ruse.

Perhaps the greatest challenge came in November 1988 when a group of 100 leading intellectuals formed the "Club for the Support of Perestroika and Glasnost." Once again, Zhivkov reacted by arresting the leaders and expelling them from the party. In effect, he had rejected glasnost and perestroika and opted for repression and the status quo. While pleasing some people, such actions alienated intellectuals and set the stage for Zhivkov's own eventual departure.

That came in November 1989 in a palace *coup* organized by Zhivkov's foreign and defense ministers, in a sort of counterpoint to the revolutionary ferment then sweeping across Eastern Europe. Petar Mladenov, the man who engineered the *coup*, had been Zhivkov's foreign minister for the previous 19 years. During that time, he had kept his mouth shut and was awarded by promotions that eventually put him in the politburo. After Gorbachev launched his policy of perestroika, however, Mladenov became attracted to the new ideas, in particular as they applied in the international arena.

Increasingly, however, he found his efforts frustrated by actions Zhivkov was taking for domestic reasons. Thus, in May 1989, only four months after Mladenov had signed a new international human rights accord in Vienna, Zhivkov launched a new campaign encouraging the emigration of ethnic Turks. When Mladenov organized a 35-nation environmental conference in Sofia in October and invited an independent Bulgarian group, Eco-Glasnost, to participate, Zhivkov had his secret police rough up Eco-Glasnost members in a Sofia park. Mladenov was embarrassed and his attempt to polish up Bulgaria's image was largely negated.

Mladenov first submitted his resignation and, when it was not accepted, he decided that Zhivkov had to go. Cautiously, he began sounding out other politburo members. This brought a promise of support from Dobri Dzhurov, the defense minister. Dzhurov, a World War II partisan colleague of Zhivkov and longtime politburo member, had been revolted for years by Zhivkov's behavior and incessant efforts to advance the career of his son, Vladimir. His support was particularly important because he could guarantee the loyalty of the army. Mladenov also got promises of support from Georgi Atanasov, the premier, and Andrei Lukanov, the minister for foreign economic relations.

Meanwhile, a wave of change was beginning to sweep across Eastern Europe and this strengthened Mladenov's case further. Even Zhivkov realized by this

time that some concessions were necessary. In a statement published in the party newspaper on October 29, Zhivkov conceded the failure of earlier Bulgarian reform efforts and promised to introduce changes along Soviet lines. He had very little credibility left by that time, however.

The Communist Regime Crumbles

The pivotal Politburo meeting took place on November 9. Mladenov made a motion calling for Zhivkov's resignation and proposing himself as general secretary. He won on a vote of five to four. The next day, Gorbachev put his stamp of approval on the change by sending Mladenov a highly complimentary, congratulatory message.

One of Mladenov's first actions as General Secretary was to reinstate 11 former party members who had been purged because of their membership in a dissident organization called the Independent Discussion Club for the Support of Glasnost and Perestroika. He followed this up with a statement pledging support for greater diversity and promising that, in the future, street rallies by antigovernment groups would be allowed. That same week, Eco-Glasnost was granted official recognition, making it a legal organization.

Mladenov next called a meeting of the Central Committee for November 16. Here, Zhivkov and three of his supporters were removed from the Politburo, while a fourth was dropped as a Central Committee secretary. Half a dozen other men were also dismissed, including two nonvoting members of the politburo. In addition, the Central Committee recommended that Mladenov take over Zhivkov's other post as head of state.

The next day, the National Assembly met to implement the recommendation of the Central Committee. At the same time, it also repealed a law making it a crime to say anything likely "to create dissatisfaction with the government and its under-

The Bulgarian National Theater

takings" and declared an amnesty for persons convicted under the old legislation. Speaking afterwards, Mladenov told the legislature that he favored political and economic restructuring and that the National Assembly "should play a democratic alternative to the administrative command system that reigned before." Later, he told journalists "personally, I am for free elections." Another interesting aspect of the proceedings was that a number of the members of the Assembly rose to give anti-Zhivkov speeches. All of this was broadcast to the nation via live television.

Mladenov clearly wanted controlled change. But news of the events happening elsewhere in Eastern Europe reverberated through Bulgaria, and popular demands began to mount. Mladenov visited Moscow at the beginning of December 1989. Asked there by journalists what his reaction was to the decisions of the Czechoslovak and East German communist parties to give up their constitutional monopoly of power, he first suggested that he would leave that up to to the Bulgarian people to decide. He then added that although he could not predict how the issue would be resolved, "I foresee changes in the Constitution."

Back in Bulgaria, popular demonstrations, which had begun occurring on an almost daily basis, grew larger in size, and their demands became more far-reaching. A new, umbrella organization, the Union for Democratic Reform, was also formed to coordinate the actions of the opposition. Responding to these pressures, Mladenov called another meeting of the Central Committee on December 8. Six more members of the Politburo were ousted, plus 27 members of the Central Committee.

This second purge in a month only seemed to whet the appetite of the opposition. Two days later, 50,000 of them gathered for another pro-democracy rally in the middle of Sofia. All of this was fully covered by the controlled press and state television. The next day, Mladenov went on television to promise that the monopoly on power of the Bulgarian Communist Party would be abolished, and there would be free elections in the spring. "We need to adopt the principle of a multiparty system," he said.

Mladenov's promises did not placate the opposition. On December 14, when the National Assembly took up a bill to scrap Article I of the Constitution, which guaranteed the party's leading role, 20,000 demonstrators surrounded the legislature and began shouting for an immediate end to the party's monopoly on power. When Stanko Todorov, the Assembly's chairman, told them that Article I had already been suspended, but that it could not be repealed for a month because of another constitutional provision, he was met by

Bulgaria

The Saint Kliment Ohridski University, Sofia

cries of "we do not believe you," "resign," and "Berlin, Prague, Sofia." The next day, the Assembly unanimously passed a declaration affirming that Article I would be stricken from the constitution at its next session in January. Mladenov also announced that round-table discussions with opposition leaders would begin the following week.

In a new development, ethnic minorities organized a mass rally against government persecution at the end of December. That same day, the Central Committee met and voted to reverse Zhivkov's policy of assimilation, calling it "a grave political error." Under the new policy, ethnic Turks could take back their old names and speak Turkish in public. The government subsequently adopted this policy. For the first time, this led to a demonstration of another sort, as thousands of anti-Turkish Bulgarian nationalists gathered outside the National Assembly chanting "Bulgaria for the Bulgarians" and demanding that the government's action be rescinded. In a curious reversal of past developments, the communists and the democratic opposition now came together to reaffirm the new policy.

When the National Assembly met on January 15, 1990, and voted to delete Article I from the constitution, the action came as a sort of anticlimax. Round table discussions between the communists and the opposition, a coalition of 13 new parties, movements and groups collectively referred to as the Union of Democratic

Forces (UDF), began in January. At the beginning of February, Mladenov offered to form a coalition government with the opposition. When this offer was refused, Andrei Lukanov replaced Georgi Atanasov as premier.

At a hastily called party congress, the party voted to change its name to the Bulgarian Socialist Party. This was accompanied by a general restructuring of the party. The old power position of general secretary was abolished and replaced by a chairman. In another change, the congress also endorsed the creation of an executive presidency. The National Assembly voted these changes into law at the beginning of April. Mladenov was elected president, and Alexander Lilov became the new chairman of the Bulgarian Socialist Party.

Multiparty elections took place in June 1990, and the Bulgarian Socialist Party won with almost 53% of the vote. The UDF got only about a third of the seats in the Assembly, with the rest going to a third party, the Movement for Rights and Freedoms, which represented approximately a half-million Turkish-speakers, plus independents. Although the Socialists won in the overall vote, their main support came from the countryside. The UDF actually won in the urban areas. For this reason, the UDF thought of itself as having won the election, and it refused to cooperate with the Socialists.

Before the Socialists could get their new government installed, President Petar

Mladenov came under attack for remarks he had made in December 1989 ordering tanks to be used against the Bulgarian people. He resigned on July 6. After almost a month of stalemate, the Bulgarian Assembly named Zhelyu Zhelev president. He had led the democratic opposition in the June elections and had spent 17 years under house arrest under the former regime. He was a compromise candidate backed by all the parties.

Meanwhile the Socialists, divided between conservatives and reformers, were having difficulty getting a government organized. They first offered to form a coalition government with the UDF. When the opposition refused, it took the Socialists three months to get their new government chosen and approved. Andrei Lukanov was reappointed premier in September, but his tenure turned out to be short. By November, thousands of Bulgarians were demanding his resignation. He won a vote of confidence in the Assembly, but the demonstrations continued. One issue was an unpopular austerity plan put into effect by the government and widespread shortages of food, gasoline and consumer goods. But a greater issue was a lack of confidence in a government led by an ex-communist.

The Post-Communist Era Begins

Lukanov finally stepped down on November 29, 1990, after the Confederation of Independent Trade Unions began a general strike aimed at forcing him out of

Bulgaria

Let's finish what we've started (Simeon Movement), 2005

One for all, all for one. Bulgarian Coalition (Socialists)

office. His successor, Dimitar Popov, was chosen on December 7. Popov, a non-politician who had been head of Sofia's municipal court before becoming prime minister (the term replacing premier), was apparently selected to stand above the parties and lead a coalition government that could be supported by all factions.

Although originally considered to be a caretaker government, Popov submitted a far-reaching program in January 1991 that began moving Bulgaria toward a free market. Price controls were loosened, interest rates were increased, a new land ownership law was passed, and proposals were submitted to reform the banking and tax laws and begin the privatization of state-owned enterprises. Prices rose tenfold, interest rates soared to about 50% and unemployment began edging up. On the positive side, shop windows and market stands began filling up, and food became plentiful, though things like medicines, fertilizers, toilet paper, sugar, petroleum products and pesticides remained scarce. Polls indicated that Bulgarians had become more optimistic, apparently convinced that their present sacrifices would pay dividends later.

Parliamentary elections were set for October 1991. In the lead-up to the elections, the Union of Democratic Forces broke into four factions and numerous new political parties came into being. Only three parties had crossed the 4% threshold, the UDF with 34% of the vote, the Bulgarian Socialist Party with 33%, and the Movement for Rights and Freedoms with 7.5%. This gave the UDF 111 seats, the BSP 106 seats, and the MRF 23 seats.

President Zhelev designated Filip Dimitrov, head of the UDF, to form a cabinet on November 5. Since it lacked a parliamentary majority, Dimitrov offered to form a coalition with the MRF. The MDR, an ethnic Turkish party that mainly represents Bulgaria's Moslem population and is reputedly led by a number of ex-security officials from the Communist era, refused to enter the cabinet. But it agreed to support the government in the National Assembly. In the end, the 14-member cabinet contained a number of "technicians" chosen for their expertise and belonging to no party. Only 8 of the 14 were members of the parliament.

In his opening policy statement, Prime Minister Dimitrov set forth long- and short-term goals. His long-term goal would be to replace the previous system; his short-term goal would be to stabilize the country's economy and curb inflation. His specific policies included amending the Foreign Investment Act passed by the previous government, privatization, the reform of banking, tax reform, and amending the Land Act.

This was the last significant victory for the Union of Democratic Forces, however. Although Prime Minister Dimitrov managed to make an important start on most of his short-term goals, the economic pain they engendered produced a split in the Union of Democratic Forces, which in turn led to the fall of his ministry later in the year. He subsequently served as Bulgaria's ambassador to the United States and United Nations. He now teaches political science at the American University in Bulgaria.

POLITICAL SYSTEM

Bulgaria has a parliamentary type of government. A popularly elected president is a figurehead who represents the nation. The president is considered to be the spokesman for the nation, but he has little power. He is commander in chief of the armed forces. The prime minister is the fulcrum of political power. He is formally nominated by the president and confirmed by the 240-member National Assembly. He presides over the cabinet and oversees day-to-day affairs of government. He thus is responsible for implementation of policy.

The Presidency

Presidential elections take place every five years. In November 1996 Petar Stoyanov, then a little-known lawyer, defeated the incumbent, Zhelyu Zhelev, winning 60% of the vote. His landslide victory was seen as a vote of no-confidence in the ruling Socialists. He accused the Socialists of isolating Bulgaria from the rest of Europe, and he argued that Bulgaria had to imple-

Entrance to presidential palace, Sofia

President Georgi Parvanov

ment sweeping reforms such as had been so successful in Central Europe. He favored bringing Bulgaria into the European Union and NATO.

In November 2001 Stoyanov was voted out of office, receiving only 46.5% of the votes in an election with 55% turnout. The new president was Georgi Parvanov, former history professor and member of the Socialist Party, who captured 53.5% of the votes. He pledged to strive for membership in the EU and NATO. He earned respect for his ability to keep fractious coalition governments focused on the reforms required for EU entry. He was decisively reelected in October 2006, winning 76% of the votes in the second round against the leader of the nationalist and racist Ataka (Attack) party, Volen Siderov, who campaigned against the large Muslim and Roma minorities.

Parliamentary Elections

A hybrid proportional voting is used. In order to keep fringe parties out of 240-seat parliament and thereby maximizing the likelihood that stable governments can be created and maintained, a threshold of 4% was established. This means that a party must win at least 4% of the votes nationwide to become eligible for a parliamentary seat. In a new system adopted for the July 2009 elections, 209 of the 240 seats are distributed according to proportional representation. This means that a party gets a percentage of those 209 seats in accordance with the percentage of votes it wins nationwide. The other 31 seats are awarded to the winner in each of 31 voting constituencies. Whoever gets the most votes, wins the seat. Thus every Bulgarian has a representative from his/her constituency.

In June 2001 elections were held following a bizarre political development: the astonishing rise of former King Simeon II, who had become tsar in 1943 and was only six years old when he was forced to leave after a rigged plebiscite that abol-

ished the monarchy. He never abdicated. He thus represents a link to a more prosperous past when Bulgaria was known as the Switzerland of the Balkans. He spent nearly 55 years in exile, becoming a businessman in Spain, learning eight languages and cultivating a refined courteous manner. He has friends and relatives in royal houses all over Europe and the Middle East.

He spent Christmas 1998 in Sofia, when he also met with Prime Minister Kostov, although the conversation apparently had no political overtones. According to the Bulgarian press, he briefed Simeon on the costs of maintaining the two palaces, three hunting lodges and two country houses that the government had decided to turn back to Simeon, in line with a decision of the Constitutional Court in June 1998. Simeon thus became one of the richest men in Bulgaria. He subsequently donated a small castle and surrounding park, located on the outskirts of Sofia, to the city's municipality. Of perhaps greater political interest, in December 1998 the Bulgarian government requested the Constitutional Court to invalidate the 1946 referendum that abolished the monarchy.

He moved back to Bulgaria in April and created his party, The National Movement of Tsar Simeon II, only 11 weeks before the elections. He was greeted with enthusiasm. One diplomat said, "It's as if he landed from another planet like some kind of messiah." He generated a wave of sentiment for the pre-communist past that fueled expectations that he could create a prosperous future. His real name is Simeon Saxe-Coburg-Gotha, but he Bulgarized it to Simeon Saks Koburgotski. His aides address him as "Your Majesty," but most Bulgarians simply call him "Simeon." He himself did not run for a parliamentary seat.

He promised to transform Bulgaria within 800 days by attracting foreign investment, cutting taxes and rooting out corruption. Because so many voters identified him with the Bulgarian nation, his opponents could not easily attack him. His party took about 40% of the votes, but it failed to win a parliamentary majority. He formed a coalition government with the center-right Union of Democratic Forces, the Socialist Party, and the Turkish Movement for Rights and Freedoms (MRF). Simeon, who became prime minister, was the first monarch to regain power in Europe in an election since Louis Napoleon a century and a half earlier. Within months his popularity had declined markedly as doubts grew about his ability to solve Bulgaria's problems. After his 800 days had ticked off, he and his government had yet to fix many of the problems they promised to solve. He lost power in 2005.

Prime Minister Boyko Borissov

Despite some impressive economic and diplomatic gains, some Bulgarians had not yet seen the benefits from economic reforms by the time new elections took place on July 5, 2009. This was especially true since Bulgaria had been hard hit by the global economic crisis. Citizens had been embarrassed by the EU's unrelenting criticism of the failure to stem corruption. The results contained a pointed protest message.

The favorite won decisively: GERB (Citizens for the European Development of Bulgaria). It is a new populist center-right party committed to fighting crime and corruption and led by Sofia's charismatic and rough talking ex-mayor, Boyko Borissov, who became prime minister. He is a former black-belt karate champion and national karate team coach, ex-police general, and bodyguard to both ex-Communist leader Zhivkov and later to King Simeon.

With a turnout of 60%, GERB received more than twice as many votes as the now opposition Socialist Party of Bulgaria (BSP), 39.7% and 116 seats to 17.7% and only 40 seats (a loss of 42). GERB entered parliament for the first time. The Movement for Rights and Freedoms (MRF), the ethnic Turkish party led by Ahmed Dogan that has held the balance of power in most post-communist governments, got 14.45% of the votes and 43 seats (a gain of 4). It is often criticized by anti-corruption campaigners, especially since Dogan boasts publicly of his ability to channel state funds and wield political power.

The nationalist and far-right party, National Union Attack (Ataka), led by Volen Siderov, grabbed 9.36% of the votes and 21 seats, after having won 12% of the votes in the European Parliament elections a month earlier. Because it campaigns on a racist platform by targeting the Turkish and Roma minorities, other parties are hesitant to deal or coalesce with it, as GERB ultimately did. Ataka de-

Bulgaria

Parliament

mands the scrapping of Turkish-language news bulletins on public TV and radio, which are guaranteed by law. The 750,000 Turkish speakers, 10% of the total population, face some residual resentment in the wider Bulgarian society because of what many regard as the unwelcome consequences of earlier Turkish colonial oppression and deportations carried out in 1913. Turkish speakers, by contrast, are inclined to remember most vividly the deportations of Turks in the late 1980s by Bulgarian Communist authorities.

The conservative Blue Coalition garnered 6.76% of the votes and 15 seats (a loss of 22). The new conservative Order, Law and Justice Party, led by Yane Yanev, barely cleared the 4% hurdle, winning

Simeon's 800 days run out!

Source: *The Sofia Echo*

4.13% and 10 seats. Yanev produces classified information to support his claims so often that many accuse him of being a front man for the secret services, a charge he denies. The National Movement for Simeon II (NDSV) was shut out of parliament, and Simeon promptly resigned his leadership of the party.

Borissov, who as Sofia's mayor had made his reputation as a fighter against corruption and crime, borrowed a page from Barack Obama's book, campaigning under the slogan: "Bulgaria, yes we can!" He is committed to improving Bulgaria's tarnished image in the EU, speed up judicial reform, stamp out corruption and slash public spending. This will not be easy, as prior governments promised many of the same things. Borissov's government was ratified in parliament by three parties: Blue Coalition, Ataka, and the new Justice, Law and Order party, whose leaders said they would not join his cabinet, but support his government as long as it pursues anti-corruption and economic reforms.

Foreign Policy

Some Bulgarians admired the Russian people and looked to Russia for assistance and leadership. The Bulgarian government banned a domestic communist party in 1923, and it established diplomatic relations with the Soviet Union in 1934. When Bulgaria became a communist state after 1945, the first principle of Bulgarian foreign policy became loyalty to the Soviet Union. Georgi Dimitrov, the new Bulgarian leader, had been a loyal servant of Stalin since the 1920s.

After 1948, Bulgaria's traditional rivalry with Yugoslavia reinforced this orientation. Following Tito's quarrel with Stalin, Bulgaria replaced Yugoslavia as the principal country through which Soviet influence was projected in the area of the southern Balkans.

This relationship with the Soviet Union was reflected not only in Bulgaria's relations with its neighbors, but in its relations with the United States as well. As the Cold War began, Bulgaria joined the Soviet Union in making extravagant attacks on the United States. As a result, diplomatic relations, broken by the U.S. in 1950, were not renewed until 1959. Formal, but cool, relations continued until the 1970s, when Bulgaria became interested in exporting to the United States.

The government agreed to end jamming of Voice of America radio broadcasts and also signed a consular convention which accorded greater protection for Americans in Bulgaria. Deputy Prime Minister Ivan Popov paid a visit to the United States in 1974, and it appeared that American-Bulgarian relations would continue to improve. But the Soviet Union renounced its trade agreement with the United States in 1975 over the issue of Jewish emigration, and the Bulgarians followed suit, abandoning their efforts to expand trade. Thereafter, American-Bulgarian relations simply mirrored the state of American-Soviet relations. For example, when the Soviets announced a boycott of the 1984 Olympic contests in Los Angeles, Bulgaria was the very first country to indicate that it would not participate either.

There was an evolution toward greater independence in Bulgaria's relations with the Soviet Union in the 1980s. The first signs came in 1984–85 when the Soviet Union instituted a political-economic boycott of Western Europe after arms negotiation talks had failed to resolve the issue of intermediate range ballistic missiles in Europe. Interested in obtaining new technology from Western Europe to reverse several years of declining growth rates, the Bulgarian government was unwilling to go along at first. After some pressure from Moscow, it went along with a political freeze, but it did everything it could to maintain its economic ties to Western Europe. Gorbachev's rise to power was welcomed in Bulgaria, and his foreign policy of cooperation with the West found particular support.

Bulgaria instituted a political opening to the West in 1987, when Zhivkov paid an official visit to West Germany. Bulgaria, he told his hosts, wanted to expand its economic relations with Bonn and the European Community (now EU). Even then, West Germany was Bulgaria's largest trading partner outside of the Moscow-dominated Council for Mutual Economic Assistance (CMEA, also known as COMECON). Since that time, Germany has been unified, CMEA and the Soviet Union have collapsed, and Bulgaria has lost most of its markets in Eastern Europe and the former Soviet Union.

Bulgaria and Greece had no diplomatic relations whatsoever until 1964. Relations remained cool for another ten years, becoming cordial only after 1974. They were particularly good during the years of the left-wing Greek government of Andreas Papandreou. In the late 1990s, Greece announced that it supported Bulgaria's application for membership in NATO. In the 21st century Greece has been a key supporter of Bulgaria's efforts to enter NATO and the EU.

Post-Cold War

Relations with Yugoslavia followed the pattern of Soviet-Yugoslav affairs. There was one additional complication: the traditional rivalry over Macedonia. Sofia never recognized Macedonian as a separate language, and on occasion it felt called upon to speak out on behalf of "Bulgarians" living in the Yugoslav republic of Macedonia. The death of Tito in 1980 brought no change, for better or worse. The collapse of Yugoslavia in 1991 when Croatia and Slovenia seceded, coupled with the subsequent decision of the Republic of Macedonia to seek recognition as an independent country, changed that situation.

Bulgaria was the first state that extended diplomatic recognition to the Republic of Macedonia in 1991. The Bulgarian government still did not recognize that there is such a thing as a Macedonian "language" at this time, but it did recognize the existence of a Macedonian "state." It never officially conceded that Macedonian is a separate language. However, the two countries' prime ministers declared in 1998 that they would sign documents in both official languages.

Romania is the one nation with which Bulgaria has maintained consistently friendly relations over the years. Romania was the only one of Bulgaria's neighbors that was also a member of the Soviet bloc. The two nations have continued to cooperate since 1989. Ex-communists continued to play important political roles in both societies, and both were at first denied economic assistance by the EU and the United States. Thanks to an EU mediating role, Romania pledged to build a second bridge to connect the two countries at Vidin in western Bulgaria and Calafat in Romania. Traffic over the existing bridge between Ruse in Bulgaria and Georeiu in Romania doubled from 2000–4. Bulgaria has distanced itself from Russia,

once its patron, but it continues to cultivate economic relations with the successor states to the old Soviet Union, in particular Russia and Ukraine.

Bulgaria became a member of the Central Europe Free Trade Agreement (CEFTA) in 1998. This links Bulgaria economically with the Czech Republic, Hungary, Poland, Romania, Slovakia, and Slovenia. By 2002 the members of the CEFTA had entirely phased out tariffs among themselves. CEFTA is also seen as a steppingstone to the European Union. At its December 2002 Copenhagen summit the EU granted Bulgaria a "roadmap" that led to full membership January 1, 2007.

The EU also earmarked 1.5 billion euros in pre-accession assistance, but most of it was frozen as punishment for not having reduced corruption. Now that Bulgaria has officially joined, that aid could rise to the equivalent of 3.7% of GDP, 1.7% of that for agricultural subsidies, if only the country could meet the EU's anti-corruption standards. In 2009 the EU agreed to release $27 million in farm subsidies and $129 million to help modernize Bulgaria's agriculture once it was convinced that the government had adopted financial controls to protect against corruption and fraud.

European integration and infrastructure development are closely linked. One sees signs everywhere that the roads on which one is driving were built or improved with EU funding. The EU is helping fund an interstate highway linking Sofia to the Greek border and ultimately to Athens in the south and Budapest in the north. A rail line connecting Athens via Sofia to Vienna, Prague and Nuremberg is also in the works, as is one that would connect Sofia and Macedonia's capital of Skopje.

The EU demands that combating corruption be the first priority. In a 2008 report of 180 countries, the Berlin-based Transparency International ranked Bulgaria 57th (down from 64th in 2007) in terms of overall corruption. In 2009 it was still ranked among the three worst offend-

Former Czar and Prime Minister Simeon dumped in 2005

Bulgaria

President Parvanov honors 100 years of diplomatic relations with the U.S.

ers in the EU. Bulgaria's geographical location on the Black Sea and along the Turkish border makes it easy prey for all kinds of smugglers and organized criminals; many in the EU see it as a hub between the Middle East and Europe for trafficking in people, weapons and drugs.

Bulgarians generally regard customs officials, the police, judges, prosecutors, health care administrators, politicians and businessmen as persons who respond to bribes. A 2006 poll revealed that three-fourths regard customs officials as the worst. The problem is systemic and has deep roots. The first business groups to emerge from the country's transition from communism specialized in trading, mixed with smuggling and organized crime. They recruited former secret service agents to help them. After two decades, it is extremely difficult to untangle all these elements.

Suspicions were strengthened by the killings in 2003 of a series of high-profile business leaders, including Bulgaria's richest man, Ilya Pavlov, a day after he had testified in the murder trial of five men charged with assassinating former Prime Minister Andrei Lukanov. Two years later the country's most prominent banker, Emil Kyulev, was gunned down in broad daylight in the middle of Sofia. In April 2008 Georgi Stoev, an investigative writer of books on mafia activities, was murdered in the capital.

In January 2010 another prominent investigative journalist and radio presenter

who wrote about organized crime groups was shot dead in the light of day in downtown Sofia. A murky figure who dealt with both the police and the crime groups (known as *mutri*, or "mugs" and often led by former security service officers), Boris "Bobi" Tsankov was a colorful and controversial figure who was always short of cash to support his flamboyant lifestyle and fancy cars. The fact that this was the first gangland killing since Prime Minister Borisov had come to power in 2009 indicates that the gangsters still hold sway over the country and how little progress has been made to crack down on their activity and bring their bosses to justice.

Over the past decade there have been more than 200 contract killings in Sofia and Black Sea resorts. This extends even to soccer: in the dozen years to mid-2007, no fewer than 15 club owners or backers have died violently. Three presidents of the Lokomotiv Plovdiv team were gunned down within two years from 2005–7. While this is on a level with Western European countries, what stands out is that courts have been unable to issue convictions in these or other corruption cases. No murderer or high-level official has been found guilty, and there have been few arrests.

It is the climate of impunity and the fact that all ministries leak information and EU funds to mobsters that worry the EU and others. One consultant called the promised $15 billion in EU aid the "motherlode" for the corrupt. With the EU breathing

down its neck, Bulgaria started to improve the situation in 2006 by dismissing 40 police officers for corruption and making trafficking in humans a crime. But the problems continue. In 2008 the economy minister, the head of the highways agency, and the interior minister (who admitted to meeting personally with crime bosses) resigned. In July 2008 the parliament was even deliberating impeaching President Parvanov over alleged links with a suspected criminal group.

The EU admitted Bulgaria on January 1, 2007. But the European Commission sent both Bulgaria and Romania early-warning letters informing them that they are lagging in such fields as judicial reform and the fight against corruption. Bulgaria was chided for "insufficient progress in tackling organized crime." The country is being subjected to an unprecedented EU monitoring regime. Sensing that this criticism was coming, the Bulgarian government made an unusual request in May for legal expertise from the Commission to help deal with the country's biggest corruption scandal at that time: the economy and energy minister and an investigator were accused of obstructing a high-level investigation in order to protect friends.

Suspecting that some former secret police agents in the dismantled Durzhavna Sigurnost are involved with organized crime, parliament approved a law in December 2006 to open up Cold War files in order to unmask such persons and to determine who once collaborated with the intelligence service. It is the last Central European country to do this. At a lower level, investors complain often of administrative obstacles, demands for kickbacks and inefficiency in the judicial system.

The EU does not fully trust the Bulgarian government with information and funds. The sad truth is that many Bulgarians also have little trust. In one 2009 Eurobarometer poll, over 80% said they did not trust their government, parliament and courts, but almost 75% said they trust the EU. Its problem at this point is that it no longer has as much leverage against Bulgaria as it once had before the country joined. Many EU officials point to the Bulgarian case as evidence why the enlargement process should be slowed down. The most it can do is to admonish and to reduce or withhold financial assistance, but this can hit Bulgaria hard.

The EU also casts a wary eye on Bulgarians nominated by Sofia for top posts. In 2010 the government nominated former Foreign Minister Rumiana Jeleva to be the new EU commissioner for humanitarian aid and crisis response. After reading press accounts of her and her husband's business activities, she was questioned pointedly in the European Parliament hearings about her financial interests and competence for the job. It was decided that she did not have a firm enough grasp of her portfolio to serve. Her nomination was withdrawn, and World Bank Vice-President Kristalina Georgieva was put forward instead. In the previous year, another ex-foreign minister and later ambassador to France and UN-ESCO, Irina Bokova, was chosen without controversy as director general of the UN Educational, Scientific and Cultural Organization in Paris. Bokova was the daughter of a top newspaper editor in the Communist era, when she entered the foreign service. She is a popular member of the Socialist Party, the successor party of the Bulgarian Communists.

Defense Policy

When fighting erupted in Kosovo in March 1999, the Bulgarian government endorsed NATO policy on Kosovo and gave limited permission for NATO forces to transit the country en route to Kosovo, even promising logistical support in such a case. Bulgaria's aspiration to become a full member of NATO was fulfilled in April 2004. The alliance had long-standing worries about democratic reform, corruption, and military readiness. It also singled out Bulgaria's treatment of minorities, particularly of the Roma.

The chances that Bulgaria would be admitted to NATO skyrocketed in the wake of the September 11 terrorist attacks in the U.S. Indeed the strategic significance of the entire Black Sea region grew because it is a staging area for the war effort in Afghanistan. In the words of Romanian ex-Foreign Minister Mircea Geoana, "September 11 transformed the Black Sea into a natural springboard."

The Bulgarian government considers itself an ally against terrorism. For this reason both Turkey and Greece supported the candidacies of Romania and Bulgaria on the grounds that NATO's southern flank has become strategically crucial for combating traditional threats, as well as "new threats," such as terrorism, transborder crime and trafficking in weapons, drugs, and human beings, including illegal immigrants and women destined to often involuntary prostitution.

The government was so desirous of NATO and EU entry that when a UN investigation revealed the extent of Bulgaria's arms sales to unsavory regimes, the government closed many of its arms industries. This was a serious financial blow to cities that depend on weapons production. By 2001 foreign arms sales had dropped by 90% from the peak years under communism. In 2002 it uncovered and halted illegal exports of weapons parts to Syria, thereby improving its image as a country that does not sell arms to

The Bulgarian and Romanian flags flying with the EU colors

blacklisted states. However, in 2008 the American military was caught off guard and alarmed by the shipment of three planeloads of small arms and ammunition to Iraqi Kurds.

Bulgaria cooperated closely with the U.S. to demonstrate what it can contribute as military partners. It unconditionally offered its air space and use of all port and land facilities, and it refurbished airstrips for allied use. It sent peacekeepers to Kabul. Ex-Foreign Minister Solomon Passy stated that his country had from the beginning acted on the proposition that "if you want to become a member of NATO,

Mountain Hike

behave as if you are one." He said the bases would be "an invaluable investment in the security of the region and in Bulgaria's future prosperity."

In 2006 the U.S. and Bulgaria signed a 10-year agreement permitting the use of three bases near the Black Sea for transport and training activities. They are Novo Selo training area, Bezmer air base in the southeast, and Graf Ignatievo airfield in central Bulgaria. Up to 3,000 American soldiers are stationed there at any one time. Fearing that the U.S. could use these bases to attack other countries, such as Iran, a majority of Bulgarians registered their opposition in a 2006 poll.

Bulgaria joined NATO in April 2004. This was received with rejoicing. An official at the Foreign Affairs Ministry, Angel Bandjov, exclaimed: "Finally we are back where we belong, and there is no way back to criminality, totalitarian dictatorship and Russian claims. We still have many things to reform and many efforts to make, but the watershed is passed."

Its admittance provides a geographic bridge between Northern and Central Europe and Greece and Turkey. It provides the U.S. and its NATO partners a foothold much closer to the current areas of danger to Europe and North America: the unstable Caucasus and the troubled Transcaucasian region of the former Soviet Union, includ-

Bulgaria

ing Chechnya, the Middle East and Central Asia, all located across the Black Sea.

It joined the 10 new democracies in Eastern and Central Europe in signing the Vilnius letter supporting the American-British war effort in Iraq in 2003. It rejected an intemperate outburst from French President Jacques Chirac criticizing all 10 for missing a good opportunity to remain silent and warning of consequences for joining the EU. President Parvanov stated: "Bulgaria insists on mutual respect." Some Bulgarians were reassured by Defense Secretary Donald Rumsfeld: "Let me be clear: those countries have not been invited as junior partners, allowed to join the grown-ups' table so long as they sit quietly. No, they have been invited to lead." Many analysts in and out of Bulgaria say that Chirac's remarks were a serious miscalculation and had the effect of uniting Eastern and Central European countries against France and the French position toward Iraq.

Bulgaria opened its airspace to allied aircraft heading to the war in Iraq and permitted American soldiers to use the previously closed Sarafovo military base near the Black Sea port of Burgas as a bridge for troops and equipment from the U.S. and Germany to the Middle East. This airport had operated since September 11 as a *de facto* American base with approximately 200 American soldiers stationed there. The U.S. plans to shut down many of its remaining bases in Germany and establish smaller bases farther east filled with rotating troops without their families and posed to strike quickly. It views both Romania and Bulgaria as its anchors in the southeast, much as Poland is in the north.

Bulgaria deployed an infantry battalion of 460 troops to Iraq under Polish command. By March 2005, eight soldiers had been killed, one of them by American troops in a friendly fire incident. In July

2004 militants beheaded two captured Bulgarian truck drivers. Most of its troops, the 334-light infantry battalion, were withdrawn from Iraq at the end of 2005; by 2009 all remaining 155 had been pulled out. Opinion polls revealed that more than 60% opposed their country's military commitment to Iraq. Bulgarian soldiers remain part of the peacekeeping forces in Kosovo, Bosnia and Afghanistan. It was among the first countries to recognize Kosovo's independence in February 2008.

Bulgaria boosted its military budget above 2% of GDP to speed up the restructuring process. In 2005 the country began a restructuring its military forces. By 2010 it had 34,975 active-duty troops. Conscripts serve nine months. There are also 302,500 reservists plus 34,000 paramilitaries. The army numbers 16,278, the navy 3,471 who man one conventional submarine, four frigates, and an assortment of patrol and coastal combatants and mine warfare vessels, and 6,706 in the air force flying Soviet-era MiGs and combat helicopters. In 2008 it auctioned off some of its Second World War-era tanks, including German Panzers and 140 Soviet T-34s. In 2006–7 it had smelted down 2,500 Soviet-era models.

NATO's Membership Action Plan (MAP) for Bulgaria required it to reduce its military from 250,000 to below 100,000 by 2004. Hundreds of senior officers were retired, and a corps of younger leaders has been trained to move into command roles; 2,175 of them are certified as competent in English.

Like Romania, Bulgaria cheered the fall of Slobodan Milosevic in Serbia in 2000. A democratic Yugoslavia benefits Bulgaria. Both countries were seriously hurt by the economic sanctions levied against that pariah state (now lifted), as well as by the destruction of the Danube bridges in Serbia, which until 2003 cut off their river connection with western Europe. The For-

eign Affairs Ministry calculated that the sanctions and bridge destruction had cost the country $6 billion. It lost a third of its tourist income in the wake of the 1999 bombing campaign against Serbia and is working to recoup that and more. It reached an agreement with Serbia to build a highway between Sofia and Nish.

Bulgarians experienced a serious foreign policy blow in May 2004 when a Libyan court tortured and sentenced five Bulgarian nurses to death by firing squad after convicting them of deliberately infecting hundreds of Libyan children in 1999 with blood products contaminated with HIV in order to conduct experiments. The Bulgarian government called the verdicts "unfair and absurd." Independent medical studies concluded that the infections at the hospital had predated the nurses' arrival by several years. Its western partners, the EU and the U.S., supported the Bulgarian position. The verdict was later overturned, but a retrial resulted again in death sentences.

In an effort to show solidarity to the nurses in May 2005, President Georgi Parvanov toured the hospital that had seen the HIV outbreak and visited the nurses in prison. The president refused to pay "blood money" to the victims' families, arguing that it would amount to an admission of guilt. As the retrial of the nurses was about to begin in May 2006, a Bulgarian newspaper published cartoons satirizing Libya's leader, Col. Qaddafi, and its judicial system. They were sent to 100 newspapers worldwide and drew a sharp protest from the Libyan government.

Finally in July 2007, after more than eight years in prison, the five returned home to an emotional welcome. More than anything, their freeing was the result of patient EU negotiations. Although the parties claim that no direct payments were made to Libya, up to $400 million was donated from various sources, including the U.S., to a fund to be given to the families of the infected. There were also promises of improved aid and trade ties between the EU and Libya. The nurses' release demonstrated that a powerful and influential EU can accomplish more than smaller and poorer member states on their own.

ECONOMY

Bulgaria was still predominantly an agricultural society at the end of World War II. Using the Stalinist model, the government started the first of its Five-Year Plans in 1949. The emphasis was always on the industrial sector, and this resulted in a transformation of the Bulgarian economy. Today, 93.8% of the GDP is attributable either to industry, construction or services.

Agriculture

In spite of this significant shift, agriculture continues to play an important role in the Bulgarian economy. Although the population has become predominantly (70%) urban, 9% are farmers and 26% are still employed in agriculture-related jobs. In 2010 they produced only 6.2% of GDP.

Bulgaria placed a heavier emphasis on the development of agriculture than did the other Central and Eastern European countries. Collectivization, begun in 1948, was carried out more quickly than elsewhere. By 1950, 43% of the land had been collectivized; by 1960 this figure reached 100%. This is even more surprising when one considers that Bulgaria is a mountainous country, and much of the land is not suitable for intensive cultivation. Extensive wineries have been established in the hills, and they produce good wines that are reasonably priced by Western standards.

Originally some 3,200 collective farms were set up, roughly corresponding to the number of villages in the country. These were then merged into 930 economic units beginning in 1960. A further consolidation began in 1969 when Bulgaria launched what it termed agro-industrial complexes (AICs). The AICs became the model for subsequent Soviet experiments of this nature. There were 281 such AICs in the country, and they had their own factories for the processing of the harvests.

After the victory in the 1991 elections of parties committed to creation of a market economy, the government launched a new economic program that included liquidation of the AICs. In a two-step process, peasants were granted immediate ownership of the private plots they cultivated under communism, while the remainder of the land was made available for their use on a temporary basis. A complicated land reform law enacted by the Socialists resulted in over 1.7 million conflicting claims, so that by 1997 less than 10% of the remaining land had been privatized. As a result, the average size of a private plot had grown to just less than three acres, while the remaining land being worked by the peasants, which had been transferred on a temporary basis only, could neither be used for collateral nor be sold.

The process of the privatization of agriculture is still incomplete. The consumer faces severe shortages and very high prices. The National Statistical Office determined in 2000 that the average Bulgarian family has to devote 43% of its income for food. Its food and drink industries faced major challenges to meet EU quality norms. Only 3.5% did so in 2003.

Industry and Trade

In the 1990s, the situation in industry has been, if anything, worse than that of agri-

culture. The reason is that almost all of Bulgaria's industry was created after World War II, and it was composed mainly of large monopoly units that operated on the basis of orders from Sofia. Moreover, many factories were specifically set up to produce goods for export to the Soviet Union or other members of the CMEA. By 2010 the services sector employs 57% of the population and produces 61.5% of GDP, while the industrial sector employs 34% and creates 32.3% of GDP. The largest foreign exchange earner and one of the country's biggest employers is the tourist industry, which accounts for 13% of GDP. It is Bulgaria's fast growing industry. By 2005 the number of visitors had risen from 3.2 million in 2001 to 4.8 million.

In 1989, over 80% of Bulgaria's foreign trade was carried on with other communist states. Most of those markets evaporated with the collapse of communism. The disarray in the Soviet economy was particularly painful for Bulgaria since over 50% of Bulgaria's foreign trade was with the Soviet Union alone. Short of hard currency, the Soviet Union canceled 70% of its Bulgarian orders at this time.

The Bulgarian governments in power up to 1997, though verbally committed to creating a market economy, basically managed to do so only in the area of retail trade. By 1995, only 34 enterprises classified as either medium and large had been privatized.

Privatization and Investment

Under plans drawn up by the government of Prime Minister Lyuben Berov, profitable state enterprises were to be

turned into joint stock companies, with stock then sold to the public. Unprofitable state enterprises were to be broken up and absorbed as part of other groups. The Bulgarian Socialist Party, which won the 1994 elections, partially implemented these plans, but they so were marred by wide-scale corruption that most privatized enterprises ended up in the hands of the old communist elite. When the new owners proceeded to strip the privatized enterprises of their remaining assets, a near collapse of the economy resulted, causing such a revulsion against the Socialists that they were driven from power in 1997.

The caretaker government of Stefan Sofiyansky, installed in 1997, reversed the policies of the previous government and put an end to the downward plunge of the economy. In particular, he closed down most of the major state-owned money-losing enterprises and cut out all energy subsidies, thus forcing prices up to world market levels. That restored some of the confidence in the Bulgarian lev and caused inflation to drop drastically, from 243% in February to 12% in March.

The government of Ivan Kostov, installed in May 1997, built on this beginning. Most importantly, he got the Bulgarian parliament to pass a law creating a currency board within the Bulgarian National Bank to keep its money stable. It made it impossible for the National Bank to continue to fuel inflation. In particular, the value of the lev was pegged to the German Mark (now to the euro), overseen by an independent "currency board." Further, the National Bank was required to maintain 100% foreign reserves backing for all

Bulgaria

currency in circulation. It is forbidden to finance government budget deficits. The effect of these measures was to restore confidence in the domestic currency and to reduce inflation to negligible amounts.

These moves restored international confidence in the Bulgarian economy and this, in turn, led to increased foreign investment. The international financial institutions also resumed lending to Bulgaria. The IMF, World Bank and EU provided crucial loans during the 2008–9 global recession. Foreign investment surged in 2004 to the equivalent of 10% of its GDP. To help keep the money coming, the personal and corporate tax was cut to 10% in 2008, the lowest tax rate for business in southeastern Europe.

The government also began a policy of privatization aimed at completing Bulgaria's transition to a market economy. Bulgaria's banks were the first to be privatized, with international bankers playing a leading role. Next came several large privatization deals negotiated with foreign investors. Then, in 1998, the Bulgarian parliament passed a new privatization plan that provided for the sale of more than a thousand state companies. This list was later extended so that 71.1% of state-owned assets had been sold by 2004, earning the country more than $2 billion. One of the most courageous and difficult decisions was to sell a controlling 59% stake in the Neftochim refinery complex at Burgas, on the Black Sea, to Russia's Lukoil in 2001.

By 2004 the economy was largely in private hands, with the state's share at only 21.1%. Housing has been successfully privatized. In Sofia, 95% own their own homes, while the rest pay horrendously high rents by the standards of the local population.

The country's privatization agency concentrates on the sale of infrastructure sectors excluded from previous privatizations, such as hydroelectric power stations, thermoelectric power stations, regional companies for electric power distribution, coal-mining enterprises, enterprises for the maintenance of power equipment, and even companies running water supply and sewage systems.

In 2008 a dispute flared over what responsibility the state should assume for the failing Soviet-era Kremikovtzi steel company near Sofia, which employs 8,000 workers. It is a huge source of pollution and urgently needs refurbishing, which the owners (the state 25% and Global Steel of India 75%) claim they cannot pay. Thousands of angry workers staged protests, clashed with police and blocked roads in central Sofia in October 2008 and again for an entire week in April 2009 demanding that the government find an investor for the sprawling plant.

Energy and Performance

Coal supplies 38% of its electricity, with another 7%–9% derived from hydroelectric power. Bulgaria has become a key link in the transit of Russian gas to western Turkey, Greece and the rest of the Balkans. Burgas is home to the region's largest oil refinery.

Bulgaria has long been the leading electricity exporter in southeast Europe and was the fourth-largest in Europe. Its Kozloduy nuclear complex on the Danube provided more than 40% of its own electrical needs, and it covered about 80% of the electricity deficits in the region, especially Greece (40%) and Serbia (30%).

In 2002 the EU strong-armed it to close the two oldest and smallest of the units at Kozloduy that used Chernobyl-era technology. Two additional Soviet-era reactors were decommissioned the end of 2006 as a result of an EU threat to delay accession talks. Two other more modern units not considered a risk remain in operation. These shutdowns cut electricity exports by two-thirds and led to severe power shortages and soaring energy prices all over the Balkans, but especially in Albania, Montenegro, Greece and Serbia.

The country plans to restore its role as the biggest electrical power exporter with two large projects. It will construct a second nuclear complex at Belene on the Danube, 30 miles (50 kilometers) from Kozloduy. It will also build a coal-fired power plant at Maritsa East One, in the southeast. These plans are supported by 80% of the population, according to opinion polls. In a January 2009 resolution, parliament required the government to re-open talks with the European Commission on restarting the two Soviet-era reactors. They are unlikely to meet with success since the EU had concluded that they could not meet its safety standards.

Bulgaria cooperated with an international team of nuclear specialists in 2003 to recover 37 pounds of highly enriched uranium (enough for a small bomb) from a nuclear research facility and transport it to Russia for conversion into less dangerous atomic fuel. The operation was funded by the U.S., and special Bulgarian police secured the facility and transported the uranium to the airport for shipment to Russia.

In January 2009 Bulgarians got an ice-cold eye opener about their close ties with Russia when the latter shut off the flow of natural gas through pipelines in Ukraine in a dispute over pricing. This left many Bulgarians, who get all their gas from Russia, without heat in the midst of a bitter cold snap. The incident revealed how vulnerable Bulgaria is to Russia, which can use its energy dominance to get its way. It sparked renewed anti-government riots in the freezing streets, led by protesters carrying signs reading, "We are tired of living in the EU's poorest and most corrupt country."

In an attempt to limit its dependence on one source of energy supplies, Bulgaria has entered a variety of agreements. One was with Greece, signed in 2007, to build a 175-mile (280-km) oil pipeline to carry

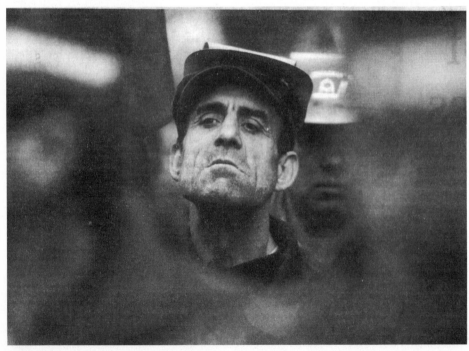

Steel worker protesting in Sofia, 2009

Russian and Caspian oil from the Bulgarian Black Sea port of Burgas to Alexandroupolis, Greece, on the Mediterranean. This would have enabled tankers to offload their oil in Bulgaria rather than navigating the narrow Bosporus fully loaded. However, residents of Burgas successfully resisted it because of environmental concerns, and the government pulled out of the deal in June 2010.

In 2008 it signed on to Russia's 900-kilometer (600-mile) South Stream pipeline project, which will make Burgas a European gateway for Russia's natural gas deliveries. It signed up to the consortium building the ITGI pipeline that seeks to circumvent Russia and deliver gas from Azerbaijan to the EU. It also joined the Nabucco pipeline project pushed by the EU and U.S., signing an agreement in July 2009 to bring Iraqi gas around Russia into Europe.

To a window shopper in Sofia things are going well, with the stores full of Western consumer goods and restaurants and cafés doing a brisk business. Many people are well dressed. But per capita GDP has risen from 33% to only 38% of the EU average since joining the EU. This is the lowest in the EU and below that of neighboring Romania. According to projections, it will take more than two decades for Bulgarians to achieve incomes of two-thirds of the EU average.

Bulgaria was hit hard by the global economic downturn of 2008–10. Inflation was down from 600% per month to under 6% in 2006, but rising food and fuel costs and wage increases of almost 25% annually in 2007 and 2008 drove it back to over 14% in 2008; in the 2009 recession, it declined again to 1.5%. The economy grew annually by about 5% from 2000–2007 and by 5.5% in 2008. After the economy had contracted by almost 18% from 1995–7, it was impressive to have successive years of healthy growth. In 2009, however, growth plummeted to minus 5%.

Unemployment had declined from 20% in 2001 to below 6% in 2008 as foreign investment has picked up and the tourism and IT sectors have expanded. The rate in formerly booming Sofia and Varna was below 3%. However, it rose to 7% nationwide in 2009, more if one added in the large Roma community and long-term elderly unemployed. Real estate values fell sharply, and the construction boom is temporarily over. This added to the jobless rolls. Average salaries had increased from $168 per month in 2003 to over 300 euros ($390) in 2009. Remittances from the 1.2 million Bulgarians who work outside the country exceeded a billion euros ($1.30 billion) in 2008, worth around 5% of GDP. Many of them lost their jobs abroad because of the global economic crisis, and some returned home and push up the jobless rate.

Thanks to five straight budget surpluses (3.3% of GDP in 2008), its national debt was halved to below 30% of GDP between 2001 and 2006, and by 2008 it stood at only 15%. They also gave the government some maneuvering room in dealing with the economic crisis in 2009. Its economic performance outstripped many of the new Central and Eastern European member states that joined the EU in 2004. In 2003 the World Economic Forum ranked Bulgaria 64th out of 102 states in terms of competitiveness. It also moved up from 62nd to 52th place out of 175 countries in the UN human development rating.

While the country slowly adjusts to a free market economy, a lively underground economy thrives behind the backs of the tax collectors. Estimates are that two-thirds of imports enter the country by dubious means, that a half million Bulgars live from this flourishing "shadow economy" and that one-fifth of the GDP is derived from it. Adoption of the euro has been postponed indefinitely.

CULTURE

Bulgaria was still mainly a peasant society when the communists came to power in 1945 and began to transform it. They got rid of the private farms and herded the peasants into either collective or state farms. Some of the traditional peasant culture died as a result, but much of it survived. The Bulgarian Communist Party had greater success in the cities, though not in the way it had hoped. The workers who came to the cities to work in the new industry abandoned most of their traditional peasant ways.

The party's attempts to create communist intellectuals through its emphasis on education actually produced the new elite that overthrew the communists. Many students are enrolled at state institutions, and 27,900 students are studying in nine private universities. Perhaps the most famous is the American University of Bulgaria at Blagoevgrad. Much of its funding comes from the USAID. After Bulgaria entered the EU in 2007, that funding ended. The U.S. also has a debt to Bulgaria: John Atanasoff, who was born in Bulgaria in 1903, emigrated to America and invented the computer.

The problem for Bulgaria will continue to be to keep its well-educated and enterprising young at home. By some estimates, the country has lost a quarter of its population since the fall of communism in 1989, falling from about 10.5 million then to 7.7 million now. The dismantling of the Bulgarian bureaucracy, which had employed 60% of the citizens and majority of educated people during the communist era, created youth unemployment of over one-third and stoked such emigration. A brain drain hampers the country's efforts to catch up economically. This problem is

Students from all over the Balkans enjoying a good laugh at the American University

Bulgaria

compounded by a "baby bust," which means that the population is declining by .7% annually, Europe's fastest rate.

To deal with the consequences of these demographic problems, the country successfully persuaded about 500,000 Bulgarians living in Moldova and Ukraine to return home. They were offered a fast-track process to acquire Bulgarian citizenship after five years.

There was disappointing news after entering the EU in 2007 that Bulgarians would not be free to move around within the community for a period of up to 7 years. In the past, Bulgarians working abroad have preferred Spain, Germany, Italy and Greece. Not all EU15 countries have opened their doors to them.

Religion is being accorded a greater role, and the government has become officially neutral. Anti-Turkish legislation was quickly withdrawn when democracy came, and the Turkish-speaking minority may now use Turkish in public. They are also permitted to take back their former Turkish names. There are about a half million ethnic Turks in the country, most of whom are Muslim. The party that represents Turks, the MRF, has held the balance of power in most post-communist governments.

The poorest minority is that of the Roma (Gypsies), estimated to number four to twelve million in all of Europe and about 800,000 in Bulgaria, or approximately 11% of the population. The official figure is 350,000. They were forced to stop their nomadic ways in the 1950s, and 84% live below the poverty line. Fewer than a fifth are believed to attend primary school, and a quarter are illiterate. In some places their unemployment rate is over 90%. In 2005 they demonstrated in Sofia, where the leaders of eight Central European nations were meeting to launch a 10-year program to end prejudice and discrimination. Bulgaria's government has a daunting task to overcome centuries of discrimination against them and to integrate them into the nation's life.

The Bulgarian Orthodox Church was accorded a special position even under the old regime. It has begun to speak out and take a more active role. Its membership is estimated at three million. There are up to 60,000 Roman Catholics in the country, plus an even larger and growing number of Protestants, divided into Pentecostals, Congregationalists, Seventh-Day Adventists, Methodists and Baptists. They no longer suffer persecution. There are also several other identifiable minority groups, including Armenians.

FUTURE

The economic situation is gradually improving. But it will be a decade or more before ordinary Bulgarians begin to experience a modicum of prosperity and have euros in their pockets.

Bulgaria entered NATO in April 2004 and will continue to be a cooperative supporter of American policy. It entered the EU in January 2007, but it finds itself under close scrutiny. If it fails to take energetic and effective measures against corruption and organized crime, it will continue to lose important EU subsidies and respect.

A majority of Bulgarians back efforts to defeat corruption. They elected a new government in July 2009 under popular but unpredictable former Sofia mayor, Boyko Borissov, with a mandate to clean up the country. His job is not easy, but he and his hard-line interior minister, Tsvantan Tsvetanov, are the most popular politicians in Bulgaria because of the efforts they are making. The culture of impunity is gone although convictions are still far off. A former prime minister, Sergei Stanishev, is undergoing two investigations, and former defense minister, Nicolay Tsonev, has been arrested. Law-enforcement agencies now screen any candidates for high public office. Critics contend that the crackdown has brought paralysis in public administration. One expert said: "Before, the administration did nothing without a bribe. Now they simply do nothing."

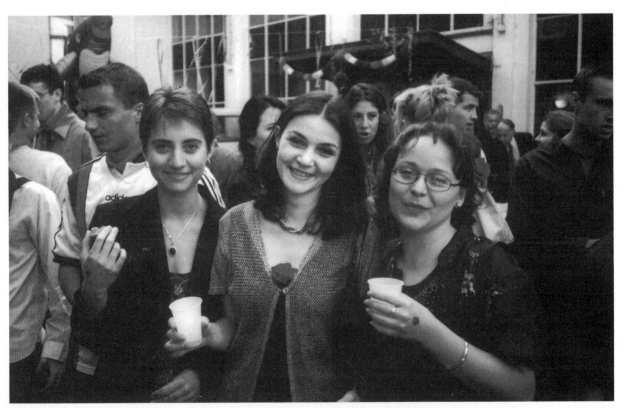

Bulgarian student (center) with other European classmates at College of Europe, Bruges. She is now a diplomat.

WEB SITES AND BIBLIOGRAPHY OF
KEY ENGLISH LANGUAGE BOOKS

WEB SITES
Useful Web Sites on the UN, EU, OECD, NATO and other:

www.un.org (Web site for United Nations. Many links.)

www.unsystem.or (Official UN website)

http://europa.eu.int (EU server site)

http://ue.eu.int (The Council of European Union site)

http://europa.eu.int/comm (European Commission site)

http://www.euobserver.com (EU news)

http://www.euractiv.com (European news)

www.EU-Values.org (Site maintained by students and staff of the College of Europe, Bruges)

http://www.europarl.eu.int (European Parliament)

http://european-convention.EU.int/ (Site for EU constitutional convention)

www.euractiv.com (Diverse news on EU and Europe)

www.aktion-euro.de (Site for the euro currency)

www.europeanaccess.co.uk (Links to various subjects)

www.psr.keele.ac.uk\official.htm (Collective site for many governments and international organizations)

www.eurunion.org (EU delegation of the European Commission to the U.S.)

www.oecd.org/daf/cmis/fdi/statist.htm (OECD site)

www.osce.org (Site of OSCE)

www.nato.int/structur/nids/nids.htm (NATO documentation, NATO Review)

www.nato.org and www.NATO.int (Web sites for NATO. Many links.)

www.wto.org (World Trade Organization site)

www.worldbank.org/html/Welcome.html (World Bank news, publications with links to other financial institutions)

www.ceip.org (Carnegie Endowment for International Peace, using a fully integrated Web-database system)

www.cia.gov/index.html (Central Intelligence Agency)

www.odci.gov/cia (Includes useful CIA publications, such as *The World Factbook* and maps)

www.state.gov/www/ind.html (U.S. Department of State, including country reports)

lcweb2.loc.gov/frd/cs/cshome.html (Library of Congress with coverage of over 100 countries)

www.euobserver.com (EU information)

www.xe.com/ucc/ (Site with most up-to-date foreign currency values)

http://www.linktoyourroots.hamburg.de (an internet database to help Americans trace their European roots)

Newspapers, Journals and Television with good coverage on European affairs:

www.chicagotribune.com (Named best overall US newspaper online service for newspapers with circulation over 100,000.)

www.csmonitor.com (Respected U.S. newspaper, *Christian Science Monitor*. Named best overall US newspaper online service for newspapers with circulation under 100,000.)

www.economist.com (British weekly news magazine)

www.neweurope.info (Weekly newspaper focusing on EU affairs)

www.nytimes.com (Respected U.S. newspaper, *The New York Times*)

www.washingtonpost.com (Respected U.S. newspaper, *The Washington Post*)

www.IHT.com (*International Herald Tribune*, published and distributed in Europe)

www.Europeanvoice.com (Weekly news on EU and European Affairs)

www.ft.com (authoritative British newspaper, *Financial Times*)

www.foreignaffairs.org (One of best-known international affairs journal)

www.cnn.com (Latest news with external links)

www.news.BBC.co.uk (British Broadcasting Corporation site)

www.c-span.org (Includes C-SPAN International)

http://www.setimes.com/html2/english/default.htm (Online political magazine on Balkan affairs)

Central and Eastern Europe:

www.embassy.org/embassies (A site with links to all embassy web sites in Washington D.C.)

http://www.eurasianet.org (News for Eurasia)

www.centraleurope.com (Contains updated information and news)

www.ucis.pitt.edu/reesweb (Full index on Central Europe and former USSR) http://php.indiana.edu/~amgrose/ceepg.html (Political science resources on the region)

www.fas.harvard.edu/~aaass/(Provides links to Slavic resources)

www.cco.caltech.edu (Bosnia home page)

www.esiweb.org (site of Berlin-Based European Stability Initiative working to restore stability to southeastern Europe)

www.osa.ceu.hu (Extensive site of Open Society Archives of Central European University)

www.zzz.ee/tbr/ (comprehensive Baltic links provided by the Baltic Review)

www.balticsww.com/cityp/citypape.htm (Site of *City Paper* published in Tallinn, Estonia, but with coverage of all Baltic States)

www.baltinfo.org (Baltic information)

http://www.setimes.com/html2/english/default.htm (*South Eastern European Times*, political magazine)

Country Sites:

www.sweden.nw.dc.us/sweden/ (Sweden embassy)

www.swedentrade.com/ (Swedish trade)

http://www.sweden.se (Swedish news site)

http://www.riksdagen.se (Swedish parliament site)

www.regjeringen.no/en (Norwegian Government)

www.norway.com (English-language site to inform foreigners on life in Norway)

www.norway.org (Norwegian embassy)

www.Norwaypost.com (Norwegian newspaper in English)

www.norseman.no (cultural ties with Norway)

www.norway.org/News_and_events/Norway-in-the-US/caucus (Congressional Caucus promoting Norwegian-American heritage and culture)

www.sofn.com (Norwegian heritage and culture, especially in U.S.)

www.denmarkemb.org (Danish embassy)

http://www.berlingske.dk (respected Danish newspaper)

http://virtual.finland.fi (Government institutions, current events, culture)

http://epin.org (Finnish Institute of International Affairs site)

www.projectfinland.org (colorful, interactive site introducing American children to their Finnish counterparts)

www.virtual.Finland.Fi (site sponsored by Finnish foreign ministry)

www.iceland.org/ (Icelandic site)

www.baltictimes.com (English-language weekly covering news in all three Baltic republics)

www.BalticsWorldwide.com (general information on the Baltics)

www.estemb.org (Estonian embassy Washington)

www.lichr.ee (Estonian legal information; Center for Human Rights)

www.riik.ee (Estonian government links)

www.mfa.gov.lv (Latvian foreign ministry)

www.lem.gov.lv (Latvian economics ministry)

www.mod.gov.lv (Latvian ministry of defense)

www.elta.lt (Lithuanian News Agency)

www.urm.lt (Lithuanian Ministry of Foreign Affairs)

www.std.lt (Lithuanian statistical data including census figures)

www.NewKaliningrad.ru (opposition website)

www.germany-info.org (German subjects of all kinds with copious links)

www.bundestag.de (German parliament online)

http://www.weltpolitik.net (Research Institute of the German Council on Foreign Relations site)

www.AICGS.org (Site of American Institute for Contemporary German Studies, Washington D.C.)

www.berlin.de/partner (News of Berlin)

www.sozialisten.de (German PDS site)

www.magazine-deutschland.de (Site of the monthly magazine, *Deutschland*, with general news)

http://g-s-a.org (Site for the German Studies Association in the United States)

www.germanoriginality.com (Site to discover America's German heritage)

www.statistik-bund.de/wahlen/index.htm (German election news site)

www.austria.org (Austrian embassy site)

www.austriantradeus.org (U.S.-Austrian trade site)

www.Keele.AC.UK/Kepru (Site of Austria specialist, Prof. Kurt Richard Luther, on diverse political topics relating to Austria)

www.pnb.pl (Polish news bulletin)

www.prezydent.pl (Polish president)

www.kprm.gov.pl (Polish government)

www.sejm.gov.pl (Polish parliament)

www.senat.gov.pl (Polish senate)
www.mzn.gov.pol (Polish ministry of foreign affairs)
www.wp.mil.pl (Polish ministry of national defense)
www.bbn.gov.pol (Polish National Security Committee)
www.pnb.com (Polish News Bulletin)
www.pkw.gov.pl (State Election Commission, official election results in Poland)
http://www.mzv.cz (Czech Ministry of Foreign Affairs)
www.praguepost.com (Prague English-language newspaper)
http://www.government.gov.sk (Slovakian government site with photo gallery)
www.nrsr.sk (Slovakia)
www.ekormanyzat.hu/english (General Hungarian site with excellent links)
http://www.hungaryemb.org (Hungarian embassy site)
http://www.budapestsun.com/dailynews/bpsundailynews71.htm   (Hungarian
   English-language newspaper)
www.hungarytourism.com (Hungarian tourism)
www.mfa.gov.hu (Hungarian foreign affairs)
http://www.serbia.sr.gov.yu (Serbian government site)
http://www.gov.yu (Serbia government site)
http://www.mfa.gov.yu (Serbia foreign ministry)
www.titoville.com/ (a site with all kinds of information about Tito)
www.b92.net (Serbian site in English with news, photos, analyses)
http://www.visit-montenegro.org/ (Montenegrin tourism)
http://ec.europa.eu/enlargement/montenegro/index_en.htm (EU site)
http://www.wto.org/english/thewto_e/acc_e/a1_montenegro_e.htm (WTO site)
http://www.einnews.com/montenegro/ (Montenegro news site)
http://www.uvi.si/eng/slovenia/ (a central site for Slovenia)
http://www.uvi.si/eng/service (Slovenian Public Relations and Media Office)
www.gov.si (Slovenian government site)
www.uvi.si (Slovenian information office)
http://www.vlada.hr/english/about-government.html (Croatian government)
http://www.mvp.hr/mvprh-www-eng/index.html (Croatian Ministry of Foreign
   Affairs)
http://www.fbihvlada.gov.ba/engleski/index.html (Government of Bosnia and
   Herzegovina)
http://www.mvp.gov.ba/Index_eng.htm (Bosnian Ministry of Foreign Affairs)
http://www.vladars.net/en/ (Government of Serbian Republic in Bosnia)
http://www.ohr.int (Office of High Representative in Kosovo)
http://www.gov.mk/English/index.htm (Macedonian government site)
http://www.president.gov.mk/index_eng.htm (Macedonian president and cabinet)
www.macedonia.org (Many Macedonian sites)
http://directory.macedonia.org/ (Site with wide variety of links on Macedonia)
http://www.press.org.mk/ (Macedonian news agencies)
http://www.newbalkanpolitics.org.mk/ (Online political magazine on Macedonian
   affairs)
www.mchamber.org.mk (Macedonian economic, political, cultural, historical
   information)
www.vmacedonia.com/welcome.asp (Macedonian tourism)
www.AlbanianNews (English-language newspaper)
www.Albanian.com (General news and information)
www.Albania.co.uk (General news and information)
www.romania.org (news and culture in Romania)
www.rol.ro (Romania online, includes photos)
www.guv.ro (Romanian government site)
www.ministerulturismului.ro (Romanian tourism, including photos)
www.bulgaria.com/history/bulgaria/(Bulgarian history)
www.novinite.com (Site for subscribing to English-language *Sofia Morning News*,
   Bulgaria)

NORDIC EUROPE GENERAL

Archer, Claire, and Maxwell, Stephen, eds. *The Nordic Model*. Vermont: Gower, 1980.
Arter, David. *Scandinavian Politics Today*. New York: St. Martin's, 1999.
Connery, Donald S. *The Scandinavians*. New York: Simon Schuster, 1966.
Derry, T. K. *History of Scandinavia: Norway, Sweden, Denmark, Finland and Iceland*. Min-
   neapolis: Univ. of Minnesota Press, 1980.
Einhorn, Eric S. and Logue, John. *Modern Welfare States. Politics and Policies in Social
   Democratic Scandinavia*. Westport, CT: Greenwood Press, 1990.
Erikson, Robert, et al, eds. *The Scandinavian Model. Welfare States and Welfare Research*.
   New York: M.E. Sharpe, 1987.
Griffiths, Tony. *Scandinavia. A History from the Napoleonic Era to the Third Millennium*.
   London: Hurst, 2004.

Gstöhl, Sieglinde. *Reluctant Europeans: Norway, Sweden, and Switzerland in the Process of Integration*. Boulder, CO: Lynn Rienner, 2002.

Helle, Knut, ed. *The Cambridge History of Scandinavia. Volume I: Prehistory to 1520*. Cambridge, Cambridge University, 2003.

Ingelbritsen, Christine. *The Nordic States and European Unity*. Ithaca, NY: Cornell University Press, 1998.

Lansen, Lene and Ole Waever. *European Integration and National Identity. The Challenge of the Nordic States*. New York: Routledge, 2001.

Logue, John and Einhorn, Eric S. *Modern Welfare States: Scandinavian Politics and Policy in the Global Age*. New York: Praeger, 2003. (A new edition of their 1989 study).

Oberg, Jan, ed. *Nordic Security in the 1990s*. New York: St. Martin's, 1992.

Turner, Barry, and Nordquist, Gunilla. *The Other European Community: Integration and Cooperation in Nordic Europe*. New York: Martin Robertson, 1982.

Wendt, Franz. *Cooperation in the Nordic Countries: Achievements and Obstacles*. Atlantic Highlands, NJ: Humanities, 1981.

SWEDEN

Bucken-Knapp, Gregg. *Defending the Swedish Model. Social Democrats, Trade Unions, and Labor Migration Policy Reform*. Lanham, MD: Lexington Books, 2009.

Esping–Andersen, Gösta. *Politics Against Markets: The Social Democratic Road to Power*. Princeton: Princeton University Press, 1985.

Hadenius, Stig. *Swedish Politics During the 20th Century*. Stockholm: Swedish Institute, 1985.

Heclo, Hugh, and Madsen, Henrik. *Policy and Politics in Sweden*. Principled Pragmatism. Philadelphia: Temple University Press, 1987.

Koblick, Steven, ed. *Sweden's Development from Poverty to Affluence, 1750–1970*. Minneapolis: Univ. of Minnesota Press, 1975.

Lorenzen, Lilly. *Of Swedish Ways*. New York: Barnes and Noble, 1978.

Lundqvist, Lennart J. *Sweden and ecological governance. Straddling the fence*. Manchester: Manchester University Press, 2004.

Metcalf, Michael. *The Riksdag: A History of the Swedish Parliament*. New York: St. Martin's, 1988.

Misgeld, Klaus, et al, eds. *Creating Social Democracy. A Century of the Social Democratic Labor Party in Sweden*. University Park: Penn State Press, 1994.

Miles, Lee. *Sweden and European Integration*. Brookfield, VT: Ashgate, 1997.

Milner, Henry. *Sweden. Social Democracy in Practice*. Oxford: Oxford University Press, 1989.

Oakley, Stewart. *The Story of Sweden*. London: Faber Faber, 1976.

Persson, Inga, ed. *Generating Equality in the Welfare State. The Swedish Experience*. Oxford: Oxford University Press, 1991.

Ruin, Olof. Tage Erlander. *Serving the Welfare State, 1946–1969*. Pittsburgh: University of Pittsburgh Press, 1990.

Samuelsson, Kurt. *From Great Power to Welfare State: 300 Years of Swedish Social Development*. London: George Allen and Unwin, 1968.

Scott, Franklin D. *Sweden: The Nation's History*. Minneapolis: University of Minnesota Press, 1977.

Sundelius, Bengt, ed. *The Committed Neutral: Sweden's Foreign Policy*. Boulder, CO: Westview Press, 1989.

Tilton, Tim. *The Political Theory of Swedish Social Democracy. Through the Welfare State to Socialism*. Oxford: Oxford University Press, 1990.

NORWAY

Archer, Clive. *Norway Outside the European Union. Norway and European Integration from 1994 to 2004*. New York: Routledge, 2004.

_____ and Ingrid Sogner. *Norway, European Integration, and Atlantic Security*. Thousand Oaks, CA: Sage, 1998.

Derry, T. K. *A History of Modern Norway: 1814–1972*. New York: Oxford University Press, 1973.

Heidar, Knut. *Norway. Center and Periphery*. Boulder, CO: Westview Press, 2000.

Hoidal, Oddvar K. *Quisling. A Study in Treason*. Oxford: Oxford University Press, 1989.

Holst, Johan Jorgen. *Norwegian Foreign Policy in the 1980's*. Oxford: Oxford University Press, 1988.

Jonassen, Christen J. *Value Systems and Personality in a Western Civilization: Norwegians in Europe and America*. Columbus: Ohio State University Press, 1983.

Lovoll, Odd S. *Norwegian—American Studies*. Northfield, MN: St. Olaf College, 1989.

Østerud, Øyvind, ed. *Norway: The Transformation of a Political System*. Special issue of *West European Politics*, Vol. 28, Nr. 4, September 2005.

Popperwell, Ronald G. *Norway*. New York: Praeger, 1973.

Princess Märtha Louise, *Princess Märtha Louise's Wonderful World*, 2007.

Ramsøy, Natalie R., ed. *Norwegian Society*. Oslo/N.Y.: Universitatsvorlaget, 1977.

Selbyg, Arne. *Norway Today*. New York: Oxford University Press, 1986.

Skard, Sigmund. *The United States in Norwegian History*. Westport, CT: Greenwood Press, 1976.

Strom, Kaare and Svasand, Lars, eds. *Challenges to Political Parties: the Case of Norway*. Ann Arbor: University of Michigan, 1997.

Su-Dale, Elizabeth. *Culture Shock! Norway. A Guide to Customs and Etiquette*. Minneapolis: Scandisc, 1995.

DENMARK

Arenson, Theo. *The Family of Kings*. London: Castles, 1976.

Fitzmaurice, John. *Politics in Denmark*. New York: St. Martin's Press, 1981.

Holbraad, Carsten. *Danish Neutrality. A Study in the Foreign Policy of a Small State*. Oxford: Oxford University Press, 1991.

Johansen, Hans Christian. *The Danish Economy in the Twentieth Century*. New York: St. Martin's Press, 1987.

Lundbak, Henrik. *Danish Unity. A Political Party Between Fascism and Resistance*. Museum Tusculanum Press, 2003.

Miller, Kenneth E. *Denmark. A Troubled Welfare State*. Boulder, CO: Westview Press, 1991.

Oakley, Stewart. *A Short History of Denmark*. New York: Praeger, 1972.

Petrow, Richard. *Better Years: The Invasion and Occupation of Denmark and Norway, April 1940–May 1945*. New York: Morrow, 1975.

_____. *The Story of Denmark*. New York: Praeger, 1972.

ICELAND

Anonymous. *The Saga of King Hrolf Kraki*. New York: Penguin, nd.

Baring-Gould, Sabine. *Iceland: Its Scenes and Sagas*. London: Hurst, 2005.

Durrenburger, E. Paul and Pálsson, Gísli. *The Anthropology of Iceland*. Iowa City: University of Iowa Press, 1989.

Gislason, Gylfi. *The Problem of Being an Icelander. Past, Present and Future*. Reykjavik: Almenna Bokofelagio, 1973.

Karlsson, Gunnar. *Iceland's 1100 Years. The History of a Marginal Society*. London: Hurst, 2001.

Laxness, Halldor. *Independent People. An Epic*. New York: Vintage, 1996.

Magnusson, Sigurdur Gylfi. *Wasteland With Words: A Social History of Iceland*. Reaction Books, 2010.

Smiley, Jane. *The Sagas of Icelanders*. New York: Viking, 2000.

Thorhallsson, Baldur, ed. *Iceland and European Integration*. New York: Routledge, 2004.

Tomasson, Richard F. *Iceland. The First New Society*. Minneapolis: University of Minnesota, 1980.

FINLAND

Arter, David. *Politics and Policy–Making in Finland*. New York: St. Martin's, 1987.

Austin, Daniel F. C. *Finland as a Gateway to Russia*. Brookfield, VT: Ashgate, 1996.

Engman, Max and Kirby, David, eds. *Finland. People, Nation, State*. Bloomington: Indiana University Press, 1989.

Jakobson, Max. *Finland in the New Europe*. Westport, CT: Praeger, 1998.

Jutikkala, Eino, and Kauko, Pirinen. *A History of Finland*. New York: Praeger, 1974.

Koivisto, Mauno. *Landmarks. Finland in the World*. Helsinki: Kirjayhtymä, 1985.

Maude, George. *The Finnish Dilemma*. London: Oxford University Press, 1976.

Nickels, Silvie, ed. *Finland: An Introduction*. London: George Allen Unwin, 1973.

Paasi, Anssi. *Territories, Boundaries and Consciousness: the Changing Geographies of the Finnish-Russian Border*. New York: Wiley, 1997.

Pentila, Risto E.J. *Finland's Search for Security Through Defence, 1944–89*. New York: St. Martin's, 1990.

Puntila, L.A. *The Political History of Finland 1809–1966*. London: Heinemann, 1975.

Rinehart, Robert, ed. *Finland and the United States*. Washington, DC: Institute for the Study of Diplomacy, 1993.

Singleton, Fred and Upton, Anthony F. *A Short History of Finland*. Cambridge: Cambridge University, 1995.

Tiilikainen, Teija H. *Europe and Finland*. Brookfield, VT: Ashgate, 1998.

Wuorinen, John H. *A History of Finland*. New York: Columbia University Press, 1965.

BALTIC REPUBLICS

Clemens, Walter C., Jr. *Baltic Independence and Russian Empire*. New York, NY: St. Martin's Press, 1991.

_____. *The Baltic Miracle: Complexity Theory and European Security*. Lanham, MD: Rowland & Littlefield, 2000.

_____. *The Baltic Transformed*. Boulder, CO: Rowman & Littlefield, 2001.

Gerner, Kristian, and Hedlund, Stefan. *The Baltic States and the End of the Soviet Empire*. New York: Routledge, 1993.

Hansen, Birthe, and Heurlin, Bertel, eds. *The Baltic States in World Politics*. New York: St. Martin's, 1998.

Hiden, John, and Salmon, Patrick. *The Baltic Nations and Europe: Estonia, Latvia and Lithuania in the Twentieth Century*. New York: Longman, 1991.

Krickus, Richard J. *The Kaliningrad Question*. NY: Rowman & Littlefield, 2002.

Landgren, Signe Maria. *The Baltic States. New Participants in the European Security Debate*. Stockholm: SIPRI, 2000.

Lieven, Anatol. *The Baltic Revolution: Estonia, Latvia, Lithuania and the Path to Independence*. New Haven, CT: Yale University Press, 1993.

Manning, Clarence. *The Forgotten Republics*. New York, NY: Philosophical Library, 1952.

Misiunas, Romuald J. and Taagepera, Rein. *The Baltic States: Years of Dependence, 1940–1990*. Berkeley: University of California, 1993.

Palmer, Alan. *Northern Shores: A History of the Baltic Sea and its Peoples*. John Murray, 2005.

Rubulis, Aleksis. *Baltic Literature*. Notre–Dame, IN: University of Notre Dame Press, 1970.

Smith, Graham, et al., eds. *The Baltic States: Estonia, Latvia and Lithuania*. New York: Routledge, 2002.

Thomson, Claire. *The Singing Revolution: A Political Journey Through the Baltic States*. London: Michael, 1992.

Trapans, Jan Arveds (ed.). *Toward Independence: The Baltic Popular Movements*. Boulder, CO: Westview Press, 1991.

ESTONIA

Howell, Margie, ed. *Estonia and Russia, Estonians and Russians: A Dialogue*. Stockholm: Olof Palme International Center, 1996.

Laar, Mart. *War in the Woods: Estonia's Struggle for Survival 1944–1956*. Washington, DC: Compass, 1992.

Poom, Ritva et al. *Estonian Short Stories*. Chicago: Northwestern University, 1995.

Raun, Toivo U. *Estonia and the Estonians*. Updated 2d ed. Stanford: Hoover, 2001.

Smith, David J. *Estonia. Independence and European Integration*. New York: Routledge, 2002.

Taagepera, Rein. *Estonia: Return to Independence*. Boulder, CO: Westview Press, 1993.

Thomson, Claire. *Estonia—Culture Smart!* (A quick guide to customs and etiquette), 2007.

LATVIA

Dreifelds, Juris. *Latvia in Transition*. New York: Cambridge University, 1997.

Ezergailis, Inta Miske. *Nostalgia and Beyond. Eleven Latvian Women Writers*. Lanham, MD: University Press of America, 1997.

Pabriks, Artis and Aldis Purs. *Latvia: the Challenges of Change*. New York: Routledge, 2001.

Plakans, Andrejs. *The Latvians. A Short History*. Stanford: Hoover, 1995.

Purs, Aldis and Artis Pabriks. *Latvia. State and Society*. New York: Routledge, 2002.

LITHUANIA

Ashbourne, Alexandra. *Lithuania: The Rebirth of a Nation, 1991–1994*. Lanham, MD: Rowman & Littlefield, 1999.

Briedis, Laimonas. *Vilnius. City of Strangers*. Baltos Lankos/CEU Press, 2009.

Daumantas, Juozas. *Fighters for Freedom: Lithuanian Partisans versus the USSR*. New York, NY: Manyland Books, 1975.

Lane, Thomas. *Lithuania. Stepping Westward*. New York: Routledge, 2002.

Vardys, V. Stanley, and Sedaitis, Judith B. *Lithuania: The Rebel Nation*. Boulder, CO: Westview Press, 1996.

CENTRAL AND EASTERN EUROPE HISTORY GENERAL

Frucht, Richard, ed. *Encyclopedia of Eastern Europe. From the Congress of Vienna to the Fall of Communism*. NY: Garland, 2000.

Held, Joseph, ed. *The Columbia History of Eastern Europe in the Twentieth Century*. New York: Columbia University, 1992.

Judson, Pieter M., ed. *Constructing Nationalities in East Central Europe*. 6th Edition. New York: Berghahn, 2004.

Palmer, Alan. *The Lands Between: A History of East–Central Europe Since the Congress of Vienna*. New York, NY: Macmillan, 1970.

Pridham, Geoffrey and Attila Agh, eds. *Prospects for democratic consolidation in East-Central Europe*. Manchester: University of Manchester Press, 2001.

Ramet, Sabrina P., ed. *Eastern Europe. Politics, Culture, and Society Since 1939.* Bloomington, IN: Indiana University, 1998.

Roberts, Andrew. *The Storm of War: A New History of the Second World War.* New York: HarperCollins, 2011.

White, Steve, Batt, Judy and Lewis, Paul G., eds. *Developments in Central and East European Politics.* Durham: Duke University, 2003.

Wolchik, Sharon L. and Jane L. Curry. *Central and East European Politics: From Communism to Democracy.* Lanham, MD: Rowman & Littlefield, 2008.

THE COMMUNIST ERA

Ash, Timothy Garton. The Magic Lantern. *The Revolution of '89 Witnessed in Warsaw, Budapest, Berlin and Prague.* New York: Vintage, 1993.

d'Encausse, Helen Careere. *Decline of an Empire: The Soviet Socialist Republics in Revolt.* trans. Martin Sokolinsky and Henry A. La Farge. New York, NY: Newsweek Books, 1978.

Gaddis, John Lewis. *The Cold War: A New History.* New York: Penguin, 2006.

Fischer–Galati, Stephen, ed. *Eastern Europe in the 1980s.* Boulder, CO: Westview Press, 1981.

Naimark, Norman, and Gibianskii, Leonid. *The Establishment of Communist Regimes in Eastern Europe, 1944–1949.* Boulder, CO: Westview, 1997.

Rupnik, Jacques. *The Other Europe. The Rise and Fall of Communism in East-Central Europe.* New York: Pantheon, 1989.

Schnitzer, Martin. *U.S. Business Involvement in Eastern Europe: Case Studies of Hungary, Poland and Romania.* New York, NY: Praeger, 1981.

Triska, Jan F. and Charles Gati, eds. *Blue Collar Workers in Eastern Europe.* Winchester, MA: Allen and Unwin, 1981.

Volgyes, Ivan. *Politics in Eastern Europe.* Chicago, IL: The Dorsey Press, 1986.

POST–COMMUNIST CENTRAL AND EASTERN EUROPE

Attila and Gabriella Ilonszki. *Parliaments and Organized Interests: The Second Steps.* Budapest, Hungary: Hungarian Centre for Democracy Studies, 1996.

Barany, Zoltan, and Volgyes, Ivan, eds. *Legacies of Communism in Eastern Europe.* Baltimore, MD: Johns Hopkins University, 1995.

Biscop, Swen and Johan Lembke, eds. *EU Enlargement and the Transatlantic Alliance: A Security Relationship in Flux.* Boulder, CO: Lynne Rienner, 2007.

Bremmer, Ian and Ray Taras, eds. *Nations and Politics in the Soviet Successor States.* New York, NY: Cambridge University Press, 1993.

Brown, J. F. *Surge to Freedom: The End of Communist Rule in Eastern Europe.* Durham, NC: Duke University Press, 1991.

Bugajski, Janusz. *Nations in Turmoil: Conflict and Cooperation in Eastern Europe.* 2nd ed. Boulder, CO: Westview Press, 1995.

Buckley, Mary, *Post–Soviet Women: From the Baltic to Central Asia.* New York, NY: Cambridge University Press, 1997.

Cottey, A. and D. Averre, eds. *New Security Challenges in Post-Communist Europe. Securing Europe's East.* Manchester, UK: Manchester University Press, 2002.

Crawford, Keith. *East Central European Politics Today.* New York: Manchester University, 1996.

Dawisha, Karen, and Parrott, Bruce, eds. *The Consolidation of Democracy in East-Central Europe.* New York: Cambridge University, 1997.

DeBardeleben, Joan, and Hannigan, John, eds. *Environmental Security and Quality After Communism.* Boulder, CO: Westview Press, 1994.

Derleth, J. William. *The Transition in Central and Eastern European Politics.* Upper Saddle River, NJ: Prentice Hall, 2000.

Dimitrova, Antoaneta L., ed. *Driven to change. The European Union's enlargement viewed from the East.* Manchester: Manchester University Press, 2004.

Einhorn, Barbara. *Cinderella Goes to Market: Citizenship, Gender, and Women's Movements in East Central Europe.* London, England: Verso, 1993.

Ekiert, Grzegorz and Hanson, Stephen E., eds. *Capitalism and Democracy in Central and Eastern Europe.* Cambridge: Cambridge University, 2003.

Gardner, Hall, ed. *Central and Southeastern Europe in Transition.* Westport, CT: Praeger, 2000.

Gärtner, Heinz et al, eds. *Europe's New Security Challenges.* Boulder, CO: Lynne Rienner, 2001.

Graubard, Stephen R., ed. *Eastern Europe . . . Central Europe . . . Europe.* Boulder, CO: Westview Press, 1991.

Hamilton, F.E. Ian, et al. *Transformation of Cities in Central and Eastern Europe. Towards Globalization.* Washington: Brookings, 2005.

Heller, Agnes, and Feher, Ferenc. *From Yalta to Glasnost: The Dismantling of Stalin's Empire.* Cambridge, England: Basil Blackwell, 1990.

Heenan, Patrick, and Lamontagne, Monique, eds. *The Central and Eastern Europe Handbook*. London: Fitzroy Dearborn, 1999.

Higley, John, and Lengyel, Gyrgy, eds. *Elites After State Socialism*. Lanham, MD: Rowman & Littlefield, 2000.

Hitchcock, William I. *The Struggle for Europe: The Turbulent History of a Divided Continent 1945–2002*. New York: Doubleday, 2003.

Holman, Otto. *Integrating Central Europe. EU Expansion and the Double Transformation in Poland, the Czech Republic and Hungary*. New York: Routledge, 2002.

Hupchick, Dennis P. and Cox. Harold E. *A Concise Historical Atlas of Eastern Europe*. New York: St. Martin's, 1996.

Hupchick, Dennis P. *The Balkans. From Constantinople to Communism*. NY: Palgrave, 2002.

Katzenstein, Peter J. ed. *Mitteleuropa. Between Europe and Germany*. Providence, RI: Berghahn, 1997.

Kotkin, Stephen. *Uncivil Society: 1989 and the Implosion of the Communist Establishment*. New York: Modern Library, 2009.

Jansky, Libor et al. *The Danube. Environmental Monitoring of an International River*. New York: UN Publications, 2004.

Jeffries, Ian. *Eastern Europe at the Turn of the Twenty-First Century. A Guide to the Economies in Transition*. New York: Routledge, 2002.

Johnson, Lonnie R. *Central Europe. Enemies, Neighbors, Friends*. New York: Oxford University, 1996.

Kovrig, Bennett. *Of Walls and Bridges: The United States and Eastern Europe*. New York, NY: New York University Press, 1991.

Lampe, John R., ed. *Creating Capital Markets in Eastern Europe*. Baltimore, MD: Johns Hopkins University, 1992.

Larrabee, F. Stephen. *NATO's Eastern Agenda in a New Strategic Era*. Santa Monica, CA: Rand, 2004.

Lewis, Paul G. *Political Parties in Post-Communist Eastern Europe*. NewYork: Routledge, 2001.

Mahncke, Dieter and Wayne C. Thompson and Wyn Rees. *Redefining Transatlantic Relations: The Challenge of Change*. Manchester, UK: Manchester University Press, 2004.

Marer, Paul, and Kves, Andras, eds. *Foreign Economic Liberalization: Transformations in Socialist and Market Economies*. Boulder, CO: Westview Press, 1991.

Mason, David S. *Revolution in East–Central Europe: The Rise and Fall of Communism*. 2d ed. Boulder, CO: Westview Press, 1996.

Mazower, Mark. *The Balkans*. NY: Modern Library, 2000.

Meyer, Michael. *The Year that Changed the World. The Untold Story Behind the Fall of the Berlin Wall*. New York: Scribner, 2009.

Michta, Andrew A. *America's New Allies. Poland, Hungary, and the Czech Republic in NATO*. Seattle: University of Washington, 1999.

Millard, Frances. *Elections, Parties, and Representation in Post-Communist Europe*. New York: Palgrave, 2004.

Ramet, Sabrina Petra. *Nihil obstat: Religion, Politics, and Social Change in East–Central Europe and Russia*. Durham, NC: Duke University Press, 1998.

Ramet, Sabrina Petra (ed.). *Rocking the State: Rock Music and Politics in Eastern Europe and Russia*. Boulder, CO: Westview Press, 1994.

Remington, Thomas F., ed. *Parliaments in Transition: The New Legislative Politics in the Former USSR and Eastern Europe*. Boulder, CO: Westview Press, 1994.

Rose, Richard and Neil Munro. *Elections and Parties in New European Democracies*. Washington D.C.: CQ Press, 2003.

Roskin, Michael G. *The Rebirth of East Europe*. 4th ed. Upper Saddle River, NJ: Prentice Hall, 2002.

Rothschild, Joseph. *Return to Diversity: A Political History of East Central Europe Since World War II*. Rev. ed. NY: Oxford University, 1999.

Rueschemeyer, Marlyn, ed. *Women in the Politics of Postcommunist Eastern Europe*. Armonk, NY: M. E. Sharpe, 1998.

Rywkin, Michael. *Moscow's Lost Empire*. Armonk, NY: M.E. Sharpe, 1994.

Sarotte, Mary Elise. *The Struggle to Create Post-Cold War Europe*. Princeton: Princeton University, 2009.

Sebestyen, Victor. *Revolution 1989: The Fall of the Soviet Empire*. New York: Pantheon, 2009.

Shlapentokh, Vladimir, and Sendich, Munir, eds. *The New Russian Diaspora: Russian Minorities in the Former Soviet Republics*. Armonk, NY: M. E. Sharpe, 1994.

Smith, Graham et al. *Nation–Building in the Post–Soviet Borderlands: The Politics of National Identities*. NY: Cambridge University Press, 1998.

Stark, David and Lszl Bruszt. *Postsocialist Pathways: Transforming Politics and Property in East Central Europe*. New York: Cambridge University Press, 1998.

Stokes, Gale. *The Walls Came Tumbling Down: The Collapse of Communism in Eastern Europe*. New York: Oxford University Press, 1993.

_____. *Three Eras of Political Change in Eastern Europe.* New York: Oxford University, 1997.

Toman, Michael A., ed. *Pollution Abatement Strategies in Central and Eastern Europe.* Baltimore, MD: Johns Hopkins University, 1994.

Tongeren, Paul van, et al, eds. *Searching for Peace in Europe and Eurasia: An Overview of Conflict Prevention and Peacebuilding Activities.* Boulder, CO: Lynne Reinner, 2002.

Turnock, David, ed. *Eastern Europe and the Former Soviet Union.* New York: Oxford University, 2000.

Weigel, George. *The Final Revolution: The Resistance Church and the Collapse of Communism.* NY: Oxford University Press, 1992.

GERMANY

Adenauer, Konrad. *Memoirs, 1945–1953.* Chicago, Regnery, 1966.

Alba, Richard et al, eds. *Germans or Foreigners? Attitudes Toward Ethnic Minorities in Post-Reunification Germany.* NY: Palgrave, 2003.

Anonymous. *A Woman in Berlin. Eight Weeks in a Conquered City.* Translated by Philip Boehm. New York: Metropolitan Books, 2005.

Ardagh, John. *Germany and the Germans: After Unification.* rev. ed. New York, Penguin Books, 1991.

Ash, Timothy Garton. *In Europe's Name. Germany and the Divided Continent.* New York: Random House, 1994.

_____. *The File. A Personal History.* (Stasi). New York: Random House, 1997.

Aust, Stefan. *Baader-Meinhof. The Inside Story of the R.A.F.* NY: Oxford University, 2009.

Balfour, Michael. Germany. *The Tides of Power.* New York: Routledge, 1992.

Barbieri, William A. Jr. *Ethics of Citizenship. Immigration and Group Rights in Germany.* Durham, NC: Duke University, 1998.

Bark, Dennis L. and Gress, David R. *A History of West Germany.* Cambridge, MA: Basil Blackwell, 1989.

Beevor, Antony. *Berlin: The Downfall 1945.* New York: Penguin, 2002.

Bracher, Karl D. *The German Dictatorship: The Origins, Structure, and Effects of National Socialism.* New York: Praeger, 1970.

Brandt, Willy. *My Life in Politics.* New York: Penguin, 1992.

Buse, Dieter K. and Doerr, Juergen C., eds. *Encyclopedic History of Modern Germany.* 2 vols. Hamden, CT: Garland, 1997.

Cecil, Lamar. *Wilhelm II.* 2 vols. Chapel Hill: University of North Carolina, 1996.

Childs, David. *The Fall of the GDR: Germany's Road to Unity.* London: Pearson Longman, 2001.

Clay, Lucius. *Decision in Germany.* Garden City, N.Y.: Doubleday, 1950.

Craig, Gordon A. *From Bismarck to Adenauer: Aspects of German Statecraft.* New York: Harper and Row, 1965.

_____. *Germany 1866–1945.* New York: Oxford University Press, 1978.

_____. *The Germans.* rev. ed. New York: Penguin, 1992.

Conradt, David P. *The German Polity.* 7th ed. New York: Longman, 2000.

_____. et al, eds. *Power Shift in Germany. The 1998 Election and the End of the Kohl Era.* New York: Berghahn, 2000.

_____, et al, eds. *A Precarious Victory. Schroeder and the German Elections of 2002.* New York: Berghahn, 2004.

Dalton, Russell J. *Politics in Germany.* 2d ed. New York: Harper Collins, 1993.

Darmstaedter, Friedrich. *Bismarck and the Creation of the Second Reich.* Sumerset, NJ: Transaction, 2008.

Edinger, Lewis and Brigitte Nacos. *From Bonn to Berlin.* New York: Columbia University Press, 1998.

Elias, Norbert. *The Germans.* New York: Columbia University, 1996.

Erb, Scott. *German Foreign Policy: Navigating a New Era.* Boulder, CO: Lynne Rienner, 2003.

Fisher, Marc. *After the Wall: Germany, the Germans, and the Burdens of History.* New York: Simon Schuster, 1995.

Friedrich, Jörg. *The Fire: The Bombing of Germany, 1940-1945.* New York: Columbia University Press, 2006.

Fulbrook, Mary. *A Concise History of Germany.* Cambridge: Cambridge University Press, 2004.

_____. *History of Germany 1918–1990: The Divided Nation.* London: Blackwell, 2003.

_____. *Anatomy of a Dictatorship. Inside the GDR, 1949–1989.* New York: Oxford University Press, 1999.

Fest, Joachim. *Hitler.* New York: Random House, 1975.

Gedmin, Jeffrey. *The Germans. Portrait of a New Nation.* Washington D.C.: AEI Press, 1995.

Genscher, Hans-Dietrich. *Rebuilding a House Divided. A Memoir by the Architect of Germany's Reunification.* New York: Broadway Books, 1998.

Giersch, Herbert, et al. *The Fading Miracle. Four Decades of Market Economy*. Cambridge: Cambridge University Press, 1992.

Glaessner, Gert–Joachim and Wallace, Ian, eds. *The German Revolution of 1989: Causes and Consequences*. Oxford: Berg, 1992.

Green, Simon. *The politics of exclusion. Institutions and immigration policy in contemporary Germany*. Manchester: Manchester University Press, 2004.

Griffith, William E. *The Ostpolitik of the Federal Republic of Germany*. Cambridge, MA: MIT Press, 1978.

Grosser, Dieter, ed. *German Unification: The Unexpected Challenge*. Oxford: Berg, 1992.

Gunlicks, Arthur. *The Länder and German Federalism*. Manchester: Manchester University Press, 2003.

Hamilton, Daniel S. Beyond Bonn. *Crafting U.S. Policy Toward the Berlin Republic*. Washington, DC: Brookings, 1994.

Hamilton, Richard. *Who Voted for Hitler?* Princeton: Princeton University Press, 1982.

Hampton, Mary and Christian Soe, eds. *Between Bonn and Berlin. German Politics Adrift*. Lanham, MD: Rowman & Littlefield, 1998.

Hancock, M. Donald and Welsh, Helga, eds. *German Unification. Process and Outcomes*. Boulder, CO: Westview Press, 1992.

Hancock, M. Donald and Henry Krisch. *Politics in Germany*. Washington, DC: CQ Press, 2008.

Herspring, Dale R. *Requiem for an Army. The Demise of the East German Military*. New York: Roman & Littlefield, 1998.

Hockenos, Paul. *Joschka Fischer and the Making of the Berlin Republic*. New York: Oxford University Press, 2008.

Holborn, Hajo. *The History of Modern Germany*. 3rd ed. Princeton: Princeton Univ. Press, 1982.

Jarausch, Konrad and Gransow, Volker, eds. *Uniting Germany. Documents and Debates*. Providence, RI: Berghahn, 1995.

Keithly, David M. *The Collapse of East German Communism. The Year the Wall Came Down, 1989*. Westport, CT: Praeger, 1992.

Koehler, John O. Stasi. *The Untold Story of East Germany's Secret Police*. Boulder, CO: Westview Press, 2000.

Lange, Thomas and Goeffrey Pugh. *The Economics of German Unification*. Williston, VT: Edger Elgar, 1998.

Langenbacher, Eric, ed. *Launching the Grand Coalition. The 2005 Bundestag Election and the Future of German Politics*. New York: Berghahn, 2007.

Lankowski, Carl. *Germany and the European Community*. New York: St. Martin's, 1992.

Leithner, Anika. *Shaping German Foreign Policy: History, Memory, and National Interest*. Boulder, CO: First Forum, 2009.

Lieven, Anatol and Dmitri Trenin, eds. *Ambivalent Neighbors. The EU, NATO, and the Price of Membership*. Washington, D.C.: Brookings, 2003.

Livingston, Robert Gerald and Sanders, Volkmar. *The Future of German Democracy*. New York: Continuum, 1994.

Longhurst, Kerry. *Germany and the Use of Force. The Evolution of German Security Policy, 1990–2003*. Manchester: Manchester University, 2005.

Maier, Charles S. *Dissolution. The Crisis of Communism and the End of East Germany*. Princeton: Princeton University, 1997.

Mann, Golo. *The History of Germany Since 1789*. New York: Praeger, 1968.

Markovits, Andrei S., and Rich, Simon. *The German Predicament. Memory and Power in the New Europe*. Ithaca: Cornell University, 1997.

Marsh, David. *The Germans: The Pivotal Nation. A People at the Crossroads*. New York: St. Martin's, 1990.

McAdams, A. James. *Judging the Past in Unified Germany*. Cambridge: Cambridge University Press, 2001.

Merkl, Peter H. *The Origin of the West German Republic*. New York: Oxford University Press, 1965.

Millar, Peter. *1989: The Berlin Wall: My Part in its Downfall*. New York: Acadia, 2010.

Müller, Jan-Werner. *Another Country. German Intellectuals, Unification, and National Identity*. New Haven: Yale University, 2000.

Newnham, Randall E. *German Foreign Policy. Navigating a New Era*. Boulder, CO: Lynne Rienner, 2003.

Niven, Bill. *Facing the Nazi Past. United Germany and the Legacy of the Third Reich*. New York: Routledge, 2001.

Opp, Karl Dieter, et al. *Origins of Spontaneous Revolution. East Germany 1989*. Ann Arbor: University of Michigan Press, 1995.

Padgett, Stephen, ed. *Adenauer to Kohl. The Development of the German Chancellorship*. Georgetown University Press, 1994.

Phillips, Ann L. *Power and Influence after the Cold War. Germany in East-Central Europe*. Lanham, MD: Rowman & Littlefield, 2000.

Pommerin, Reiner. *The American Impact on Postwar Germany*. Providence, RI: Berghahn, 1995.

Pond, Elizabeth. *Beyond the Wall. Germany's Road to Unification*. Washington, DC: Brookings, 1993.

Pulzer, Peter. *German Politics, 1945–1995*. New York: Oxford University Press, 1995.

Reeves, Richard. *Daring Young Men: The Heroism and Triumph of the Berlin Airlift, June 1948-May 1949*. New York: Simon & Schuster, 2009.

Schoenbaum, David. *Hitler's Social Revolution: Class and Status in Nazi Germany 1933–1939*. Garden City, N.Y.: Anchor Books, 1967.

Schulze, Hagen. *Germany. A New History*. Cambridge, MA: Harvard University Press, 2001.

Schweitzer, C.C., et al, eds. *Politics and Government in Germany, 1944–1994. Basic Documents*. 2d rev. ed. Providence, RI: Berghahn, 1995.

Sinn, Hans-Werner. *Can Germany Be Saved?: The Malaise of the World's First Welfare State*. Cambridge, MA: MIT Press, 2007.

Smyser, W.R. *How Germans Negotiate. Logical Goals, Practical Solutions*. Herndon, VA: United States Institute of Peace Press, 2003.

Sperling, James, ed. *Germany at fifty-five. Berlin ist nicht Bonn?* Manchester: Manchester University Press, 2004.

Stent, Angela E. *Russia and Germany Reborn. Unification, the Soviet Collapse, and the New Europe*. Princeton: Princeton University, 1999.

Stephan, Alexander. *Americanization and Anti-Americanism. The German Encounter with American Culture after 1945*. New York: Berghahn, 2007.

Stern, Fritz. *Five Germanys I Have Known*. New York: Farrar, Straus & Giroux, 2007.

Stürmer, Michael. *The German Empire: 1871–1919*. NY: Weidenfeld & Nicolson, 2000.

Szabo, Stephen F. *The Diplomacy of German Unification*. New York: St. Martin's, 1992.

_____. *Parting Ways. The Crisis in German-American Relations*. Washington: Brookings, 2004.

Taylor, Frederick. *The Berlin Wall. A World Divided, 1961-1989*. New York: HarperCollins, 2007.

Thompson, Wayne C. *In the Eye of the Storm. Kurt Riezler and the Crises of Modern Germany*. Iowa City: University of Iowa Press, 1980.

_____. *The Political Odyssey of Herbert Wehner*. Boulder, CO: Westview Press, 1993.

_____. and Thompson, Susan L. and Juliet S. *Historical Dictionary of Germany*. (Contains many entries and lengthy chronology and bibliography). Metuchen, NJ: Scarecrow Press, 1994.

Timmins, Graham. *Politics of New Germany*. New York: Routledge, 2006.

Turner, Henry A. *Germany from Partition to Reunification*. New Haven, CT: Yale University Press, 1992.

Turner, Lowell. *Fighting for Partnership. Labor and Politics in Unified Germany*. Ithaca, NY: Cornell University Press, 1998.

Uris, Leon. *Armaggedon*. London: Corgi, 1963.

Wallander, Celeste A. *Mortal Friends, Best Enemies. German-Russian Cooperation after the Cold War*. Ithaca: Cornell University, 1999.

Wawro, Geoffrey. *The Franco-Prussian War. The German Conquest of France in 1870–1871*. Cambridge, Cambridge University, 2003.

Weitz, Eric D. *Weimar Germany: Promise and Tragedy*. Princeton: Princeton University Press, 2007.

Wolf, Markus. *Man without a Face. The Autobiography of Communism's Greatest Spymaster*. New York: Times Books Random House, 1997.

Yoder, Jennifer A. *From East Germans to Germans? The New Postcommunist Elites*. Durham, NC: Duke University, 1999.

AUSTRIA

Bader, William B. *Austria Between East and West 1945–1955*. Stanford: Stanford University Press, 1966.

Beller, Steven. *A Concise History of Austria*. New York: Cambridge University Press, 2007.

Berg, Matthew Paul. *The Struggle for a Democratic Austria. Bruno Kreisky on Peace and Social Justice*. New York: Berghahn, 2000.

Bischof, Günter, et al, eds. *The Kreisky Era in Austria*. New Brunswick, NJ: Transaction, 1993.

_____, et al, eds. *Austria in the European Union*. Summerset, NJ: Transaction, 2002.

_____ and Fritz Plasser, eds. *The Changing Austrian Voter*. Sumerset, NJ: Transaction, 2008.

Bluhm, William T. *Building an Austrian Nation. The Political Integration of a Western State*. New Haven: Yale University Press, 1973.

Fitzmaurice, John. *Austrian Politics and Society Today*. New York: St. Martin's, 1991.

Gruber, Helmut. *Red Vienna. Experiment in Working–Class Culture, 1919–1934*. Oxford: Oxford University Press, 1991.

561

Hamann, Brigitte. *Hitler's Vienna: Dictator's Apprenticeship*. New York: Oxford University Press, 1999.

Herzstein, Robert E. *Waldheim. The Missing Years*. New York: Arbor House W. Morrow, 1988.

Johnson, Lonnie. *Introducing Austria. A Short History*. Riverside, CA: Ariadne, 1992.

Johnson, William M. *The Austrian Mind. An Intellectual and Social History*. Berkeley: University of California Press, 2000.

Krzyzanowski, Michal and Ruth Wodak. *The Politics of Exclusion. Debating Migration in Austria*. Sumerset, NJ: Transaction, 2008.

Luther, Richard, and Muller, Wolfgang C., eds. *Politics in Austria. Still a Case of Consociationalism?* Portland, OR: Frank Cass, 1992.

Luther, Kurt Richard. *Austria 1945–1995*. Brookfield, VT: Ashgate, 1998.

Mitten, Richard. *The Politics of Antisemitic Prejudice. The Waldheim Phenomenon in Austria*. Boulder, CO: Westview, 1992.

Pelinka, Anton and Plasser, Fritz, eds. *The Austrian Party System*. Boulder, CO: Westview, 1989.

Pelinka, Anton. *Austria: Out of the Shadow of the Past*. Boulder, CO: Westview, 1999.

Schorske, Carl F. *Fin–De Siècle Vienna. Politics and Culture*. New York: Vintage Books, 1981.

Segar, Kenneth and Warren, John, eds. *Austria in the Thirties: Culture and Politics*. Riverside, CA: Ariadne, 1992.

Spaulding, E. Wilder. *The Quiet Invaders: The Story of the Austrian Impact Upon America*. Vienna, 1968.

Steininger, Günter Bischof and Michael Gehler, eds. Austria in the Twentieth Century. Sumerset, NJ: Transaction, 2008.

Sully, Melanie A. *The Haider Phenomenon*. New York: Columbia University Press, 1997.

Wodak, Ruth and Anton Pelinka, eds. *The Haider Phenomenon*. Sumerset, NJ: Transaction, 2001.

POLAND

Bethell, Nicholas. *Gomulka, His Poland and His Communism*. Harmondsworth, England: Penguin Books, 1972.

Brumberg, Abraham (ed). *Poland, Genesis of a Revolution*. New York, NY: Random House, 1983.

Bukowczyk, John J. *Polish Americans and Their History. Community, Culture, and Politics*. Pittsburgh: University of Pittsburgh Press, 1996.

Davies, Norman. *Heart of Europe, The Past in Poland's Present*. New ed. NY: Oxford: Oxford University, 2001.

_____. *God's Playground. A History of Poland*. Vol. II: 1795 to the Present. NY: Oxford, 2005.

_____. *Rising '44. The Battle for Warsaw*. London: Pan Books, 2004.

Garton Ash, Timothy. *The Polish Revolution. Solidarity*. Third Edition. New Haven: Yale University, 2002.

Glazyca, George and Ryszard Rapacki. *Poland into the 1990s: Economy and Society in Transition*. New York, NY: St. Martin's, 1991.

Gross, Jan T. *Neighbors. The Destruction of the Jewish Community in Jedwabne, Poland*. Princeton: Princeton University Press, 2001.

Halecki, O. *A History of Poland*. New York, NY: Dorset Press, 1992.

Haltof, Marek. *Polish National Cinema*. New York: Berghahn, 2002.

Jasiewicz, Krzysztof. *Polish Politics after the 1997 parliamentary elections: Back to a polarized polity?* The National Council for Eurasian and East European Research, 1998.

Karpinski, Jakub. *Countdown: The Polish Upheavals of 1956, 1970, 1976, 1980*. trans. by Olaga Amsterdamska and Gene M. Moore. New York, NY: Karz–Cohl, 1982.

Kurski, Jaroslaw. *Lech Walesa: Democrat or Dictator?* Boulder, CO: Westview Press, 1993.

Lukowski, Jerzy and Zawadzki, Hubert. *A Concise History of Poland*. Cambridge: Cambridge University, 2001.

Nagengast, Carole. *Reluctant Socialists, Rural Entrepreneurs: Class, Culture, and the Polish State*. Boulder, CO: Westview Press, 1993.

Michta, Andrew A. *The Soldier-Citizen: The Politics of the Polish Army after Communism*. London: Macmillan, 1997.

Olson, Lynne. *For your Freedom and Ours. The Kosciuszko Squadron. Forgotten Heroes of World War II*. London: Arrow Books, 2003.

Pisarska, Katarzyna. *The Polish American Community's lobbying for Poland's Inclusion into NATO*. Lodz, Poland: Mediton, 2003.

Sanford, George. *Poland. The Conquest of History*. Amsterdam: Harwood Academic publishers, 1999.

Sutherlin, John W. *The Greening of Central Europe. Sustainable Development and Environmental Policy in Poland and the Czech Republic*. Lanham, MD: University Press of America, 2000.

Taras, Ray and Marjorie Castle. *Democracy in Poland*, 2d ed. Boulder, CO: Westview Press, 2003.

Thompson, Kenneth W. *The Presidency and Governance in Poland*. Lanham, MD: University Press of America, 1997.

Walesa, Lech. *The Struggle and the Triumph, An Autobiography*. Arcade Publishing, 1994.

Wolczuk, Kasia and Wolczuk, Roman. *Poland and Ukraine. Maintaining a Strategic Partnership through a New Iron Curtain?* Washington D.C.: Brookings, 2003.

Zaborowski, Marcin. *Germany, Poland and Europe*. Manchester: Manchester University, 2005.

Zamoyski, Adam. *The Polish Way, A Thousand Year History of Poles and Their Culture*. Hippocrene Books, 1994.

THE CZECH AND SLOVAK REPUBLICS

Agnew, Hugh. *The Czechs and the Lands of the Bohemian Crown*. Stanford: Hoover, 2004.

Benes, Edward. *Memoirs of Dr. Edward Benes*. London, England: Allen Unwin, 1954.

El Mallakh, Dorothea H. *The Slovak Autonomy Movement, 1935–1939: A Study in Unrelenting Nationalism*. Boulder, CO: East European Quarterly, 1979.

Fawn, Rick. *The Czech Republic. A nation of velvet*. New York: Routledge, 2005.

Fogel, Daniel S. *Managing in Emerging Market Economies: Cases from the Czech and Slovak Republics*. Boulder, CO: Westview Press, 1994.

Golan, Galia. *Reform Rule in Czechoslovakia: The Dubcek Era, 1968–1969*. Cambridge, England: Cambridge University Press, 1975.

Havel, Vaclav. *The Art of the Impossible. Politics as Morality in Practice*. New York: Alfred A. Knopf, 1997.

_____. *To the Castle and Back*. New York: Knopf, 2007.

Heimann, Mary. *Czechoslovakia: The State That Failed*. New Haven: Yale University, 2009.

Henderson, Karen. *The Politics of Slovakia. Voters, Parties and Democracy 1989–2004*. New York: Routledge, 2006.

Innes, Abby. *Czechoslovakia. The Short Goodbye*. New Haven: Yale University Press, 2001.

Journalist M. *A Year is Eight Months*. Garden City, NY: Doubleday Co., 1971.

Kaplan, Karel. *The Short March: The Communist Takeover in Czechoslovakia 1945–1948*. New York: St. Martin's, 1987.

Keane, John. *Vaclav Havel: A Political Tragedy in Six Acts*. New York: Basic Books, 2000.

King, Jeremy. *Budweisers into Czechs and Germans. A Local History of Bohemian Politics, 1848–1948*. Princeton: Princeton University, 2005.

Kirschbaum, Stanislav J. *A History of Slovakia*. New York: St. Martin's, 1995.

Kraus, Michael, and Stanger, Allison, eds. *Irreconcilable Diofferences? Explaining Czechoslovakia's Dissolution*. Lanham, MD: Rowland & Littlefield Publishers, Inc., 2000.

Kusin, Vladimir V. *From Dubcek to Charter 77*. New York, NY: St. Martin's Press, 1978.

Leff, Carol Skalnik. *The Czech and Slovak Republics*. Boulder, CO: Westview Press, 1996.

Littell, Robert, ed. *The Czech Black Book*. New York, NY: Praeger, 1969.

Mamatey, Victor S., and Luza, Radomir. *A History of the Czechoslovak Republic, 1918–1948*. Princeton: Princeton University, 1973.

Mikus, Joseph A, J.D. *Slovakia, A Political History: 1918–1950*. Milwaukee, WI: The Marquette University Press, 1963.

Musil, Jií, ed. *The End of Czechoslovakia*. Budapest: Central European University, 1995.

Paul, David W. *Czechoslovakia: Profile of a Socialist Republic at the Crossroads of Europe*. Boulder, CO: Westview Press, 1981.

Scherpereel, John A. *Governing the Czech Republic and Slovakia: Between State Socialism and the European Union*. Boulder, CO: First Forum, 2009.

Skilling, H. Gordon. *Czechoslovakia's Interrupted Revolution*. Princeton: Princeton University, 1976.

Steiner, Eugen. *The Slovak Dilemma*. Cambridge, England: Cambridge University Press, 1973.

Tampke, Jürgen. *Czech-German Relations and the Politics of Central Europe*. NY: Palgrave, 2003.

Wheaton, Bernard and Zdenek Kavan. *The Velvet Revolution: Czechoslovakia, 1988–1991*. Boulder, CO: Westview Press, 1992.

HUNGARY

Batonyi, Gabor. *Hungary*. New York: Routledge, 2006.

Braun, Aurel, and Barany, Zoltan, eds. *Dilemmas of Transition: The Hungarian Experience*. Lanham, MD: Rowman & Littlefield Publishers, 1999.

Benzinger, Karl P. *Imre Nagy, Martyr of the Nation*. Lanham, MD: Rowman & Littlefield, 2008.

Cartledge, Bryan. *The Will to Survive: A History of Hungary*. London: Timewell Press, 2006.

Ferge, Zsursa. *A Society in the Making: Hungarian Social and Societal Polities, 1945–75*. White Plains, NY: E.M. Sharpe, 1980.

Gati, Charles. *Failed Illusions: Moscow, Washington, Budapest, and the 1956 Hungarian Revolt*. Stanford: Stanford University Press, 2006.

Gough, Roger. *A Good Comrade: Janos Kadar, Communism and Hungary*. London: I.B. Tauris, 2006.

Halpern, L, and Wyplosz, Charles, eds. *Hungary: Towards a Market Economy*. New York, NY: Cambridge University Press, 1998.

Hare, Paul et al., eds. *Hungary: A Decade of Economic Reform*. Winchester, MA: Allen Unwin, 1981.

Held, Joseph, ed. *The Modernization of Agriculture: Rural Transformation in Hungary*. New York, NY: Columbia University Press, 1980.

Kerly, Bla K., ed. *Lawful Revolution in Hungary, 1989–1994*. New York, NY: Columbia University Press, 1996.

Korda, Michael. *Journey to a Revolution: A Personal Memoir and History of the Hungarian Revolution of 1956*. New York, HarperCollins, 2006.

Kourig, Bennett. *Communism in Hungary: From Kun to Kadar*. Stanford, CA: Hoover Institution Press, 1979.

Kun, Joseph C. *Hungarian Foreign Policy: The Experience of a New Democracy*. New York, NY: Praeger, 1993.

Lendvai, Paul. *The Hungarians. A Thousand Years of Victory in Defeat*. Princeton: Princeton University, 2004.

Lessing, Erich. *Revolution in Hungary: The 1956 Budapest Uprising*. London: Thames & Hudson, 2006.

Marton, Kati. *Enemies of the People: My Family's Journey to America*. New York: Simon & Schuster, 2009.

Molnár, Miklós. *A Concise History of Hungary*. Cambridge: Cambridge University, 2001.

Sebestyen, Victor. *Twelve Days: The Story of the 1956 Hungarian Revolution*. New York: Pantheon, 2006.

Slyon, Lzszl, and Brunner, Georg, eds. *Constitutional Judiciary in a New Democracy: The Hungarian Constitutional Court*. Ann Arbor, MI: The University of Michigan Press, 1999.

Sugar, Peter F., ed. *A History of Hungary*. Bloomington, IN: Indiana University Press, 1994.

Swain, Nigel. *Hungary: the Rise and Fall of Feasible Socialism*. New York: Verso, 1992.

Thorpe, Nick. *'89: The Unfinished Revolution: Power and Powerlessness in Eastern Europe*. London: Reportage Press, 2009.

THE BALKANS AND EX–YUGOSLAVIA

Barnett, Neil. *Tito*. London: Haus, 2006.

Bennett, Christopher. *Yugoslavia's Bloody Collapse: Causes, Course and Consequences*. New York: NYU Press, 2000.

Borowiec, Andrew. *Yugoslavia After Tito*. New York, NY: Praeger, 1977.

Cviiç, Christopher. *Remaking the Balkans*. London: Pinter, 1995.

Cohen, Lenard J. *Broken Bonds: The Disintegration of Yugoslavia*. (2nd ed); Boulder, CO: Westview Press, 1995.

_____. *Serpent in the Bosom. The Rise and Fall of Slobadan Milosevic*. Boulder, CO: Westview, 2002.

Djilas, Milovan. *Wartime*. New York: Routledge, 1990.

Dragnich, Alex N. *Yugoslavia's Disintegration and the Struggle for Truth*. New York: Columbia University Press, 1996.

Dunn, William N., and Obradovic, Josip. *Workers' Self–Management and Organizational Power in Yugoslavia*. Pittsburgh, PA: University of Pittsburgh Press, 1978.

Fischer, Bernd J., ed. *Balkan Dictators. The 'Strongmen" of South-Eastern Europe*. London: Hurst, 2005.

Gallagher, Tom. *The Balkans after the Cold War. From Tyranny to Tragedy*. New York: Routledge, 2005.

_____. *The Balkans in the New Millennium. In the Shadow of War and Peace*. New York: Routledge, 2005

Gerolymatos, Andre. *The Balkan Wars*. NY: Basic Books, 2003.

Glenny, Misha. *The Fall of Yugoslavia: The Third Balkan War*. 3d rev. ed. New York, NY: Penguin Books USA, Inc., 1996.

_____. *The Balkans. Nationalism, War and the Great Powers, 1804–1999*. New York: Viking, 2000.

Jelavich, Barbara. *History of the Balkans: Twentieth Century*. Vol. 2. New York: Cambridge University, 1983.

Jeffries, Ian. *Former Yugoslavia at the Turn of the Twenty-First Century. A Guide to the Economies in Transition*. New York: Routledge, 2002.

Kaplan, Robert D. *Balkan Ghosts. A Journey Through History*. New York: Vintage Books, 1996.

Kurspahic, Kemal. *Prime Time Crime. Balkan Media in War and Peace*. Herndon, VA: United States Institute of Peace Press, 2003.

Lampe, John. *Yugoslavia as History: Twice There Was a Country*. 2d ed. New York: Cambridge University, 2000.

Lydall, Harold. *Yugoslavia in Crisis*. New York: Oxford University, 1989.

Mazower, Mark. T*he Balkans: A Short History*. London: Weidenfeld & Nicolson, 2000.

Meier, Viktor, and Ramet, Sabrina. *Yugoslavia: A History of its Demise*. New York: Routledge, 1999.

Merrill, Christopher. *Only the Nails Remain. Scenes From the Balkan Wars*. Lanham, MD: Rowman & Littlefield, 1999.

Meyer, Edward C. *Balkans 2010*. Washington, D.C.: Brookings, 2002.

Morton, Jeffrey S., et al. *Reflections on the Balkan Wars. Ten Years after the Break-up of Yugoslavia*. NY: Palgrave, 2004.

Naimark, Norman M. *Fires of Hatred. Ethnic Cleansing in Twentieth-Century Europe*. Cambridge, MA: Harvard University Press, 2000.

Pond, Elizabeth. *Endgame in the Balkans. Regime Change, European Style*. Washington: Brookings, 2008.

Ramet, Sabrina P. *Nationalism and Federalism in Yugoslavia, 1962–1991*. Bloomington, IN: Indiana University Press, 1992.

_____. Balkan Babel. *The Disintegration of Yugoslavia from the Death of Tito to the Fall of Milosevic*, 4th ed. Boulder, CO: Westview, 2002.

Resic, Sanimir and Tournquist-Plewa, Barbara, eds. *Balkans in Focus. Cultural Boundaries in Europe*. Nordic Academic Press, 2002.

Sell, Louis. *Slobodan Milosevic and the Destruction of Yugoslavia*. Durham, NC: Duke University Press, 2002.

Shay, Shaul. *Islamic Terror and the Balkans*. Sumerset, NJ: Transaction, 2008.

Shrenk, Martin et al. *Yugoslavia: Self Management Socialism and the Challenges of Development*. Baltimore, MD: Johns Hopkins University, 1979.

Sher, Gerson S. *Praxis: Marxism Criticism and Dissent in Socialist Yugoslavia*. Bloomington, IN: Indiana Univ. Press, 1977.

Silber, Loura, and Little, Allan. *Yugoslavia: Death of a Nation*. New York: Penguin, 2000.

Sirc, Ljubo. *The Yugoslav Economy Under Self–Management*. New York, NY: St. Martin's Press, 1979.

Stankovic, Slobodan. *The End of the Tito Era*. Stanford, CA: Hoover Institution Press, 1981.

Stavrianos, L.S. *The Balkans since 1453*. New York: New York University, 2000.

Ullman, Richard H., ed. *The World and Yugoslavia's Wars*. New York: Council on Foreign Relations, 1996.

Vuic, Jason. *The Yugo: The Rise and Fall of the Worst Car in History*. Hill and Wang, 2010.

Wingfield, William Frederic. *A Tour in Dalmatia, Albania, and Montenegro*. Cosimo Classics, 2007 (written in 1853).

SLOVENIA

Benderly, Jill and Evan Kraft, eds. *Indpendent Slovenia*. London: Macmillan, 1994.

Burgher, Bob. *Culture Smart! Slovenia: A Quick Guide to Customs and Etiquette*. 2006.

Cox, John K. *Slovenia. Evolving Loyalties*. New York: Routledge, 2005.

Ferfila, Bogomil, and Phillips, Paul. *Slovenia*. Lanham, MD: University Press of America, 2000.

Gow, James and Cathie Carmichael. *Slovenia and the Slovenes. A Small State and the New Europe*. London: Hurst, 2000.

Sabic, Zlatko and Bukowski, Charles, eds. *Small states in the post-Cold War world: Slovenia and NATO enlargement*. NY: Praeger, 2002.

CROATIA

Bartlett, Will. *Croatia. A Crossroads Between East and West*. New York: Routledge, 2002.

Drakuliç, Slavenka. *Café Europa. Life after Communism*. New York: Penguin, 1996.

_____. S. *A Novel About the Balkans*. New York: Viking, 2000.

Goldstein, Ivo. *Croatia: a History*. London: Hurst, 1999.

Irvine, Jill A. *The Croate Question. Partisan Politics in the Formation of the Yugoslav Socialist State*. Boulder, CO: Westview, 1993.

Tanner, Marcus. *Croatia: A Nation Forged in War*. New Haven, CT: Yale University Press, 2001.

Ugresiç, Dubravka. *The Culture of Lies*. University Park: Pennsylvania State University, 1998.

SERBIA

Anzulovic, Branimir. *Heavenly Serbia: From Myth to Genocide*. New York: NYU Press, 2000.

Bujosevic, Dragan and Radovanovic, Ivan. *The Fall of Milosevic. The October 5th Revolution.* NY: Palgrave, 2003.

Djukiç, Slavoljub. *Milosevic and Markovic. A Lust for Power.* Montreal: McGill-Queen's University Press, 2001.

Gordy, Eric D. *The Culture of Power in Serbia. Nationalism and the Destruction of Alternatives.* State College: Penn State University Press, 1999.

Gow, James. *The Serbian project and its adversaries. A Strategy of War Crimes.* London: Hurst, 2003.

Judah, Timothy. *The Serbs: History, Myth, and the Destruction of Yugoslavia.* New Haven, CT: Yale University Press, 1997.

LeBor, Adam. *Milosevic. A Biography.* New Haven: Yale University, 2004.

Macdonald, David Bruce, ed. *Balkan Holocausts? Serbian and Croatian Victim Centered Propaganda and the War in Yugoslavia.* Manchester: Manchester University Press, 2003.

Pavolwitch, Stevan K. *Serbia: the History behind the Name.* London: Hurst, 2002.

Thomas, Robert. *The Politics of Serbia in the 1990s.* New York, NY: Columbia University Press, 1999.

_____. *Serbia under Milosevic. Politics in the 1990s.* London: Hurst, 1999.

BOSNIA

Andric, Iva. *The Bridge on the Drina.* Chicago: University of Chicago Press, 1977, reprinted in 1995 by Harvill, London.

Bose, Sumantra. *Bosnia After Dayton. Nationalist Partition and International Intervention.* London: Hurst, 2002.

Chandler, David. *Bosnia. Faking Democracy after Dayton.* 2d. ed. Sterling, VA: Pluto, 2000.

Cousens, Elizabeth M. and Charles K. Cater. *Toward Peace in Bosnia. Implementing the Dayton Accords.* Boulder, CO: Lynn Rienner, 2001.

Donia, Robert J. and John V.A. Fine. *Bosnia & Herzegovina: A Tradition Betrayed.* Yonkers, NY: Labyrinth, 1994.

Friedman, Francine. *The Bosnian Muslims.* Boulder, CO: Westview Press, 1995.

_____. *Bosnia. A Polity on the Brink.* New York: Routledge, 2002.

Mahmutcehajic, Rusmir. *Bosnia the Good. Toleration and Tradition.* Budapest: Central European University Press, 1997.

Malcolm, Noel. *Bosnia: A Short History.* New York: NYU Press, 2000.

Rohde, David. *Endgame: The Betrayal & Fall of Srebrenica, Europe's Worst Massacre Since World War II.* Yonkers, NY: Labyrinth, 1997.

Sacco, Joe. *Safe Area Gorazde.* London: Jonathon Cape, 2007. (A graphic non-fiction account of the Bosnian war. Text with comic-like illustrations, but good first-hand reporting.)

Sells, Michael A. *The Bridge Betrayed. Religion and Genocide in Bosnia.* Berkeley: University of California, 1996.

Smith, David James. *One Morning in Sarajevo: 28 June 1914.* London: Weidenfeld & Nicolson, 2008.

Stover, Eric and Gilles Peress. *The Graves.* Yonkers, NY: Labyrinth, 1998.

MONTENEGRO

Roberts, Elizabeth. *Realm of the Black Mountain: A History of Montenegro.* Ithaca, NY: Cornell University Press, 2007.

KOSOVO

Campbell, Greg. *The Road to Kosovo. A Balkan Diary.* Boulder, CO: Westview, 2000.

Clark, Howard. *Civil Resistance in Kosovo.* Herndon, VA: Pluto, 2000.

Daalder, Ivo H. and O'Hanlon, Michael E. *Winning Ugly. NATO's War to Save Kosovo.* Washington: Brookings, 2001.

Duijzings, Ger. *Religion and the Politics of Identity in Kosovo.* NY: Columbia University Press, 2003.

Hammond, Philip, and Herman, Edward S. *Degraded Capability: The Media and the Kosovo Crisis.* Herndon, VA: Pluto, 2000.

Judah, Tim. *Kosovo. War and Revenge.* New Haven: Yale University, 2000.

Kostovicova, Denisa. *Kosovo. The Politics of Identity and Space.* New York: Routledge, 2005

Latawski, Paul and Smith, Martin A. *The Kosovo crisis and the evolution of post-Cold War European security.* Manchester: Manchester University Press, 2003.

Malcolm, Noel. *Kosovo: A Short History.* New York: HarperPerennial, 2000.

Maliqi, Shkëlzen. *Kosovo. Separate Worlds. Reflections and Analyses.* Pristina: MM, 1998.

Mertus, Julie A. *Kosovo. How Myths and Truths Started a War.* Berkeley: University of California, 1999.

O'Neill, William G. *Kosovo: An Unfinished Peace.* Boulder, CO: Lynn Rienner, 2002.

Rezun, Miron. *Europe's Nightmare. The Struggle for Kosovo.* Westport, CT: Praeger, 2001.

Schnabel, Albrecht and Ramesh Thakur, eds. *Kosovo and the Challenge of Humanitarian Intervention.* New York: United Nations University Press, 2000.

Shkëlzen, Maliqi. *Kosovo. Separate Worlds. Reflections and Analyses*. Pristina: MM, 1998.

Smith, Martin A. and Latowski, Paul. *The Kosovo Crisis*. Manchester: Manchester University Press, 2003.

Vickers, Miranda. *Between Serb and Albanian: A History of Kosovo*. New York, NY: Columbia University Press, 1998.

MACEDONIA

Brown, Keith. *The Past in Question: Modern Macedonia and the Uncertainties of Nation*. Princeton: Princeton University, 2003.

Cowan, Jane K., ed. *Macedonia. The Politics of Identity and Difference*. Herndon, VA: Pluto, 2001.

Peltifer, James, ed. *The New Macedonian Question*. New York: Palgrave, 2001.

Phillips, John. *Macedonia. Warlords and Rebels in the Balkans*. New Haven: Yale University, 2004.

Poulton, Hugh. *Who are the Macedonians?* Bloomington, IN: Indiana University Press, 1994.

Sokalski, Henryk J. *An Ounce of Prevention. Macedonia and the UN Experience in Preventive Diplomacy*. Herndon, VA: U.S. Institute for Peace, 2003.

Szajkowski, Bogdan. *Macedonia*. New York: Routledge, 2006.

ALBANIA

Biberaj, Elez. *Albania: A Socialist Maverick*. Boulder, CO: Westview Press, 1990.

Costa, Nicholas J. *Albania: A European Enigma*. Boulder, CO: East European Monographs, 1995, distributed by Columbia University Press.

Fischer, Bernd J. *Albania at War. 1939–1945*. London: Hurst, 2003.

Hall, Derek. *Albania and the Albanians*. New York: Pinter, 1994.

Hamm, Harry. *Albania: China's Beachhead in Europe*. London, England: Victor Gollancz, 1977.

Hoxha, Enver. Ed. By Jon Halliday. *The Artful Albanians: The Memoirs of Enver Hoxha*.

Kola, Paulin. *The Search for Greater Albania*. London: Hurst, 2003.

London: Chatto and Windus, 1986.

Lemel, Harold W., ed. *Rural Property and Economy in Post-Communist Albania*. New York: Berghahn, 2000.

Marmullaku, Ramadan. *Albania and the Albanians*. London, England: Hurst, 1975.

Pano, Nicholas C. *Albania*. New York: Routledge, 2006.

Prifti, Peter R. *Land of the Albanians. A Crossroads of Pain and Pride*. Tirana: Horizont, 2002.

_____. *Albania Since 1944*. Cambridge, MA: MIT Press, 1978.

Vickers, Miranda, and Pettifer, James. *Albania: From Anarchy to Balkan Identity*. New York: NYU Press, 2000.

Vickers, Miranda. *The Albanians. A Modern History*. NY: I.B. Touris, 2001.

Winnifrith, Tom, ed. *Perspectives on Albania*. New York: St. Martin's, 1992.

ROMANIA

Braun, Aurel. *Romanian Foreign Policy Since 1965*. New York, NY: Praeger, 1978.

Graham, Lawrence S. *Romania: A Developing Socialist State*. Boulder, Colo.: Westview Press, 1982.

King, Robert R. *History of the Romanian Communist Party*. Stanford, CA.: Hoover Institution Press, 1980.

Nelson, Daniel N., ed. *Romania in the 1980s*. Boulder, Colo.: Westview Press, 1981.

_____, ed. *Romania after Tyranny*. Boulder, CO: Westview, 1992.

Papadimitriou, Dimitris and David Phinnemore. *Romania and the European Union. From Marginalization to Membership?* New York: Routledge, 2006.

Rady, Martyn. *Romania in Turmoil. A Contemporary History*. NY: IB Touris, 1992.

Radulescu, Domnica. *Gypsies in European Literature and Culture*. Boone Bridge Books, 2008.

_____. *Train to Trieste*. NY: Alfred A. Knopf, 2008. (Novel translated into nine languages about the author's escape from Romania.)

_____. *Black Sea Twilight*. (A second novel based on the author's life in and escape from Romania). London: Transworld Publishers/Doubleday, 2010.

Roper, Steven D. *Romania. The unfinished revolution*. New York, Routledge, 2005.

Shen, Raphael. *The Restructuring of Romania's Economy: A Paradigm of Flexibility and Adaptability*. Westport, CT: Praeger, 1997.

BULGARIA

Bell, John D., ed. *Bulgaria in Transition*. Boulder, CO: Westview Press, 1998.

Bristow, John A. *The Bulgarian Economy in Transition*. Brookfield, VT: Edward Elgar, 1996.

Crampton, Richard J. *A Short History of Modern Bulgaria*. New York: Cambridge University, 1987.

Dellin, L.A.D., ed. *Bulgaria*. New York, NY: Praeger, 1957.

Dimitrov, Vesselin. *Bulgaria. The Uneven Transition*. New York: Routledge, 2002.

Giatzidis, Emil. *An introduction to post-communist Bulgaria. Political, economic and social transformation*. Manchester: Manchester University Press, 2002.

Jones, Derek C., and Miller, Jeffrey, eds. *The Bulgarian Economy: Lessons from Early Transition*. Brookfield, VT: Ashgate, 1997.

Todorov, Tzvetan. *The Fragility of Goodness. Why Bulgaria's Jews Survived the Holocaust*. Princeton: Princeton University Press, 2001.

Zhivkov, Todor. *Modern Bulgaria: Problems and Tasks in Building an Advanced Socialist Society*. New York, NY: International Publishers, 1974.

Zloch-Christy, Iliana, ed. *Bulgaria in a Time of Change: Economic and Political Dimensions*. Brookfield, VT: Avebury, 1996.

Roma musicians in Belgrade